INDEX TO

LITERARY BIOGRAPHY

First Supplement

by

Patricia Pate Havlice

Volume I: A-K

The Scarecrow Press, Inc.
Metuchen, N.J., & London   1983

Library of Congress Cataloging in Publication Data

Havlice, Patricia Pate.
   Index to literary biography.

   Bibliography: p.
   1. Authors--Biography--Indexes. I. Havlice,
Patricia Pate. Index to literary biography.
I. Title.
Z6511.H38 Suppl. [PN451] 016.809   82-25051
ISBN 0-8108-1613-X

PREFACE

This first supplement to <u>Index to Literary Biography</u> covers approximately 53,000 authors found in 57 reference books published between 1969 and 1981. More non-Western writers are included than in the main volume, reflecting increased attention given to these authors in the last few years.

The supplement follows the format of the original work. Each entry includes the author's real name, pseudonyms, dates of birth and death, nationality, type of writing engaged in, and a letter code referring the user to a volume of the bibliography containing that author's biography. Some information here does not agree with that in the base volume due to variations in the sources on which this suplement is based.

In compiling this supplement I used the University of Houston Clear Lake Campus Library, the Pasadena (Texas) Public Library, Freeman Memorial Library (Houston, Texas) and the Galveston (Texas) Public Library. I would like to thank the staffs of these institutions for their help. Special thanks to Edward J. Havlice for being my sunshine and support.

P. P. H.

BIBLIOGRAPHY

AM   American Writers: A Collection of Literary Biographies. New York: Scribner, 1974.

AMP   American Poets Since World War II. Detroit: Gale, 1980.

AS   Ash, Brian. Who's Who in Science Fiction. New York: Taplinger, 1976.

BA   Bain, Robert, Joseph M. Flora, and Louis D. Rubin, Jr. Southern Writers: A Biographical Dictionary. Baton Rouge: Louisiana State University, 1979.

BO   Bondanella, Peter and Julia Conway Bondanella. Dictionary of Italian Literature. Westport, Conn.: Greenwood, 1979.

BOR   Borklund, Elmer. Contemporary Literary Critics. New York: St. Martin's, 1977.

BR   Bradbury, Malcolm, Eric Mottram, and Jean Franco. The Penguin Companion to American Literature. New York: McGraw-Hill, 1971.

BRI   British Writers. New York: Scribner, 1979. Vols. 1-3, indexed.

BU   Buchan-Brown, John, ed. Cassell's Encyclopedia of World Literature. New York: Morrow, 1973.

CL   Columbia Dictionary of Modern European Literature. 2nd rev. and enlarged ed. New York: Columbia University, 1980.

CO   Commire, Anne. Something About the Author. Detroit: Gale Research Book Tower, 1972- . Vols. 3-25, indexed.

COM   Commire, Anne. Yesterday's Authors of Books for Children ... Early Times to 1960. Detroit: Gale, 1977. Vols. 1 and 2, indexed.

CON   Contemporary Authors: A Bio-Bibliographical Guide to Current Authors and Their Works. Detroit: Gale, 1974- . Vols. 41-103, indexed.

COW   Cowart, David and Thomas L. Wymer, eds. Twentieth-Century American Science-Fiction Writers. Detroit: Gale, 1981.

CR   Creative Canada: A Biographical Dictionary of Twentieth-Century Creative and Performing Artists. Toronto: University of Toronto, 1971. Vol. 1, indexed.

DA Daiches, David. The Penguin Companion to English Literature. New York: McGraw-Hill, 1971.

DE De Montreville, Doris, ed. Third Book of Junior Authors. New York: Wilson, 1972.

DEM De Montreville, Doris and Elizabeth D. Crawford, eds. Fourth Book of Junior Authors and Illustrators. New York: Wilson, 1978.

ENG Engelbarts, Rudolf. Librarian Authors: A Bibliography. Jefferson, N.C.: McFarland, 1981.

GR Grant, Michael. Greek and Latin Authors 800 B.C.-A.D. 1000. New York: Wilson, 1980.

HE Helterman, Jeffrey and Richard Layman, eds. American Novelists Since World War II. Detroit: Gale, 1978.

HER Herdeck, Donald E. African Authors: A Companion to Black African Writing, Vol. 1 1300-1973. Washington, D.C.: Inscape Corp., 1974.

HI Hisamtsu Sen-ichi. Biographical Dictionary of Japanese Literature. Tokyo: Kodansha International, 1977.

HIL Hill, Marnesba D. and Harold B. Schleifer. Puerto Rican Authors: A Biobibliographic Handbook. Metuchen, N.J.: Scarecrow, 1974.

HO Hogan, Robert, editor-in-chief. Dictionary of Irish Literature. Westport, Conn.: Greenwood, 1979.

JA Jahn, Janheinz, ed. Who's Who in African Literature: Biographies, Works, Commentaries. Tübingen: Horst Erdmann Verlag, 1972.

KI Kirkpatrick, D. L., ed. Twentieth-Century Children's Writers. New York: St. Martin's, 1978.

KIB Kibler, James E., Jr., ed. American Novelists Since World War II: Second Series. Detroit: Gale, 1980.

LA Lang, D. M. and D. R. Dudley. The Penguin Companion to Classical, Oriental and African Literature. New York: McGraw-Hill, 1969.

MAG Magill, Frank N., ed. Cyclopedia of World Authors. Rev. ed. Englewood Cliffs, N.J.: Salem, 1974.

MAL Malkoff, Karl. Crowell's Handbook of Contemporary American Poetry. New York: Crowell, 1973.

MAR Martinez, Julio A. Chicano Scholars and Writers: A Bio-Bibliographical Directory. Metuchen, N.J.: Scarecrow, 1979.

MCC McCormick, Donald. Who's Who in Spy Fiction. New York: Taplinger, 1977.

MCG McGraw-Hill Encyclopedia of World Drama. New York: McGraw-Hill, 1972.

MCN MacNicholas, John. Twentieth-Century American Dramatists. Detroit: Gale, 1981.

MY   Myerson, Joel, ed. The American Renaissance in New England. Detroit: Gale, 1978.

MYE   Myerson, Joel, ed. Antebellum Writers in New York and the South. Detroit: Gale, 1979.

NI   Nicholls, Peter, ed. The Science Fiction Encyclopedia. New York: Dolphin Books, 1979.

PAL   Paluka, Fran. Iowa Authors: A Bio-bibliography of Sixty Native Writers. Iowa City, Iowa: Friends of the University of Iowa Libraries, 1967.

PO   Pollard, Arthur, ed. Webster's New World Companion to English and American Literature. New York: World, 1973.

PRU   Prusek, Jaroslav. Dictionary of Oriental Literature. New York: Basic Books, 1974.

REI   Reilly, John M., ed. Twentieth Century Crime and Mystery Writers. New York: St. Martin's, 1980.

RO   Rood, Karen Lane. American Writers in Paris, 1920-1939. Detroit: Gale, 1980.

RU   Ruoff, James E. Crowell's Handbook of Elizabethan and Stuart Literature. New York: Crowell, 1975.

SEY   Seymour-Smith, Martin. Who's Who in 20th Century Literature. New York: Holt, Rinehart and Winston, 1976.

SH   Shockley, Ann A. and Sue P. Chandler. Living Black American Authors: A Biographical Directory. New York: Bowker, 1973.

ST   Steinbrunner, Chris and Otto Penzler, eds. Encyclopedia of Mystery and Detection. New York: McGraw-Hill, 1976.

TH   Thorlby, Anthony. Penguin Companion to European Literature. New York: McGraw-Hill, 1969.

VCD   Vinson, James, ed. Contemporary Dramatists. 2nd ed. New York: St. Martin's, 1974.

VCN   Vinson, James, ed. Contemporary Novelists. 2nd ed. New York: St. Martin's, 1976.

VCP   Vinson, James, ed. Contemporary Poets. 2nd ed. New York: St. Martin's, 1975.

VD   Vinson, James and D. L. Kirkpatrick. Dramatists. New York: St. Martin's, 1979.

VN   Vinson, James and D. L. Kirkpatrick. Novelists and Prose Writers. New York: St. Martin's, 1979.

VP   Vinson, James and D. L. Kirkpatrick. Poets. New York: St. Martin's, 1979.

WA   Wakeman, John. World Authors 1950-1970. New York: Wilson, 1975.

WAK   Wakeman, John, ed. <u>World Authors 1970-1975.</u> New York: Wilson, 1980.

WAR   Ward, Martha E. and Dorothy A. Marquardt. <u>Authors of Books for Young People.</u> 2nd ed. suppl. Metuchen, N.J.: Scarecrow, 1979.

'A., Dr.' see SILVERSTEIN, Alvin
à BECKETT, Gilbert Abbott, 1811-56, English; plays, journalism BU
A YING (Ch'ien Hsing-ts'un), 20th century, Chinese; fiction PRU
'A.A.' see WILLIS, George A.A.
'AE' see WILLIS, George A. A.
'A. M.' see MEGGED, Aharon
AAKER, David Allen, 1938- , American; nonfiction CON
AAKJAER, Jeppe, 1866-1930, Danish; poetry, fiction BU CL TH
'AALBEN, Patrick' see JONES, Noel
AALTO, Alvar, 1898-1976, Finnish; nonfiction CON
A-AMANG, Boé, 1938- , Cameroonian; play JA
AANDAHL, Vance, 1944- , American; fiction NI
AANRUD, Hans, 1863-1953, Norwegian; fiction, plays CL
AARDEMA, Verna Norberg, 1911- , American; juveniles CO WAR
AARESTRUP, Carl Ludvig Emil, 1800-56, Danish; poetry BU TH
AARON, Chester, 1923- , American; plays, juveniles CO WAR
AARONS, Edward Sidney ('Paul Ayers'; 'Edward Ronns'), 1916-75, American; fiction, journalism CON REI ST
AASEN, Ivar Andreas, 1813-96, Norwegian; nonfiction, poetry BU TH
AASENG, Rolf Edward, 1923- , American; nonfiction CON
'ABAG' see GOTTLOBER, Abraham B.

ABAJIAN, James De Tar, 1914- , American; nonfiction CON
ABARBANEL, Isaac see ABRAVANEL, Isaac
ABARBANEL, Judah (Leone Ebreo; Leo Judaeus; Abravanel), 1460-1535?, Italian; nonfiction, poetry BO BU TH
ABARBANEL, Karin, 1950- , American; nonfiction CON
ABASHELI, Aleksandre, 1884-1954, Georgian; poetry PRU
ABASHIDZE, Grigol, 1913- , Georgian; poetry, fiction, plays, juveniles PRU
ABASIYANIK, Sait Faik, 1906-54, Turkish; fiction PRU
ABBA, Giuseppe Cesare, 1838-1910, Italian; nonfiction, poetry BU
ABBAD y LASIERRA, Iñigo, 1745-1813, Spanish; nonfiction HIL
ABBAS, Khvaja Ahmad, 1914- , Urdu; journalism, fiction CON PRU VCN
ABBATTUTIS, Gian A. see BASILE, Giambattista
ABBAZIA, Patrick, 1937- , American; nonfiction CON
ABBEY, Edward, 1927- , American; nonfiction, fiction CON
'ABBEY, Kieran' see REILLY, Helen K.
'ABBEY, Margaret' see YORK, Margaret E.
'ABBOT, Anthony' (Charles Fulton Oursler), 1893-1952, American; plays, journalism, fiction REI ST
ABBOT, Charles Greeley, 1872-1973, American; nonfiction CON
'ABBOTT, Alice' see BORLAND, Kathryn K.; SPEICHER, Helen R.

1

ABBOTT, Carl John, 1944- ,
American; nonfiction CON
ABBOTT, Claude Colleer, 1889-
1971, British; poetry, non-
fiction CON
ABBOTT, Edwin A., 1838-1926,
English; fiction NI
ABBOTT, George Francis, 1887- ,
American; plays CON MCG
VCD
ABBOTT, Horace Porter, 1940- ,
American; nonfiction CON
ABBOTT, Jacob, 1803-79, Amer-
ican; juveniles CO MY
ABBOTT, James Hamilton, 1924- ,
American; translations, non-
fiction CON
ABBOTT, Jerry Lynn, 1938- ,
American; nonfiction CON
ABBOTT, Raymond Herbert,
1942- , American; fiction
CON
ABBOTT, Robert Tucker, 1919- ,
American; juveniles WAR
ABBOTT, Rowland Aubrey,
1909- , English; nonfiction
CON
ABBOTT, Sarah, American; juven-
iles WAR
ABBOTT, Sidney, 1937- , Amer-
ican; nonfiction CON
ABBOTTS, John, 1947- , Amer-
ican; nonfiction CON
ABBS, Peter, 1942- British; non-
fiction CON
ABBT, Thomas, 1738-66, German;
nonfiction BU
ABD UL-KARIM, Master, 1908-61,
Pashtun; fiction PRU
ABD-al-BAHA, Abbas Effendi, 1844-
1921, Persian; nonfiction, po-
etry BU
ABD-al-HAMID al Katif, -749,
Arab; nonfiction BU
'ABDALLAH, Omar' see HUMBAR-
ACE, Demir A.
ABDALLAH ANSARI, Khwaja, 1006-
88, Persian; poetry BU
ABDALMU'TI HIJAZI, 1935- ,
Egyptian; poetry PRU
ABDASSABUR SALAH, 1931- ,
Egyptian; plays, nonfiction,
poetry PRU
ABDELSAMAD, Moustafa Hassan,
1941- , Egyptian; nonfiction
CON
ABDILLAAHI, Muwse, 1880- ,
Somalian; poetry HER LA

ABDÜLHAH HAMID TARHAN, 1852-
1937, Turkish; poetry, plays
ẞU
ABDULHAK SINASI HISAR, 1888-
1963, Turkish; fiction, non-
fiction BU
ABDUH, Muhammad (Abdo), 1849- ,
1905, Egyptian; nonfiction PRU
ABDUL, Raoul, 1929- , American;
juveniles CO
ABDUL RAUF SINGKEL, 1615?-93,
Sumatran; nonfiction LA
ABDULHAMID MOHMAND, -1732?,
Pashtun; poetry PRU
ABDU'L-KARIM of BULRRI, Shah,
1536-1642, Sindhi; poetry PRU
ABDULLA, Muhammed Said, 1940?- ,
Kenyan; fiction HER
'ABDULLAH, Achmed' (Alexander
Nicholayevitch Romanoff), 1881-
1945, Russian-English; fiction,
film ST
ABDULLAH bin ABDUL KADIR, 1796-
1854, Malayan; nonfiction, trans-
lations LA PRU
ABDULLAHI, Guda, 1946- , Niger-
ian; nonfiction CON
ABDULLAHI dan MUHAMMADU,
1766-1829, Arab; nonfiction,
poetry BU
ABDU'l-LATIF BHITA 'i, Shah,
1689-1752, Sindhi; poetry PRU
ABDULQADIR KHAN KHATAK, 1650-
1720, Pashtun; poetry, transla-
tions PRU
ABDUL-RAUF, Muhammad, 1917-
Egyptian-American; nonfiction
CON
ABDURRAHMAN MOHMAND, 1659?-
1720?, Pashtun; poetry PRU
ABE KOBO (Abe Kimifusa), 1924- ,
Japanese; plays, nonfiction, po-
etry, fiction AS BU CON NI
PRU WA
ABEDI, Sheikh Kalute bin Amri,
1924- , Swahili; poetry BU
HER
ABEL, Bob, 1931- , American;
nonfiction CON
ABEL, Caspar, 1676-1763, German;
poetry BU
ABEL, Elie, 1920- , Canadian-
American; nonfiction CON
ABEL, Ernest Lawrence, 1943- ,
Canadian-American; nonfiction
CON
ABEL, Lionel, 1910- , American;
plays, nonfiction, translations

CON WA
ABEL, Raymond, 1911- , American; juveniles CO
ABEL, Richard Cox, British; journalism, fiction NI
ABEL, Robert Halsall, 1941- , American; nonfiction, fiction CON
ABEL, Theodora Mead, 1899- , American; nonfiction CON
ABELARD, Peter, 1079-1142, French; nonfiction BU MAG TH
ABELE SPELEN, 14th century, Dutch; plays BU
ABELL, Kathleen, 1938- , Canadian; juveniles CO CON
ABELL, Kjeld, 1901-61, Danish; plays BU CL MCG TH WAK
ABELLA, Alexander, 1950- , American; nonfiction CON
ABELLA, Irving Martin, 1940- , Canadian; nonfiction CON
ABELS, Jules, 1913- , American; nonfiction CON
ABELSON, Robert Paul, 1928- , American; nonfiction CON
ABER, William McKee, 1929- , American; nonfiction CON
ABERCROMBIE, Barbara Mattes, 1939- , American; juveniles, poetry, fiction CO CON
ABERCROMBIE, Lascelles, 1881-1938, English; poetry, nonfiction DA PO VP
ABERCROMBIE, Nigel James, 1908- , British; nonfiction CON
ABERCROMBY, Patrick, 1656-1716, Scots; nonfiction BU
ABERNATHY, David Myles, 1933- , American; nonfiction CON
ABERNATHY, Robert, 1924- , American; fiction NI
ABERNATHY, William Jackson, 1933- , American; nonfiction CON
ABERNETHY, Peter Link, 1935- , American; nonfiction CON
ABERNETHY, Robert Gordon, 1927- , Swiss-American; juveniles CO
ABERNETHY, Virginia, 1934- , American; nonfiction CON
ABHINAVAGUPTA, 10th century, Indian; nonfiction PRU
ABILDGAARD, Ove, 1916- ,

Danish; poetry BU
ABISCH, Roslyn Kroop ('Mr. Sniff'; 'A. K. Roche'), 1927- , American; juveniles CO WAR
ABISH, Walter, 1931- , Austrian-American; poetry CON
'ABISODU' see MADDY, Pat
ABLE, James Augustus, Jr., 1928- , American; fiction CON
ABLEMAN, Paul, 1927- , British; fiction, plays, poetry CON NI VCD VCN
ABLER, Ronald, 1939- , American; nonfiction CON
ABLER, Thomas Struthers, 1941- , American; nonfiction CON
ABLESIMOV, Alexander Onisimovich, 1742-83, Russian; fiction, plays BU
ABOAB, Isaac, fl. 1300, Spanish; nonfiction BU TH
ABODAHER, David J., 1919- , American; juveniles CO WAR
ABOUT, Edmond, 1828-85, French; fiction BU MAG NI TH
ABOVIAN, Khatchatur, 1809-48, Armenian; poetry, fiction, nonfiction PRU
ABRAHALL, Clare H. see HOSKYNS-ABRAHALL, Clare C.
ABRAHAM, Gerald Ernest Heal, 1904- , British; journalism, nonfiction CON
ABRAHAM a SANCTA CLARA (Johann Ulrich Megerle), 1644-1709, German; nonfiction BU TH
ABRAHAM BEDERSI, 1240-1300, French; poetry, nonfiction BU
ABRAHAM IBN HASDAI, -1240, Spanish; poetry BU
ABRAHAMS, Doris Caroline see 'BRAHMS, Caryl'
ABRAHAMS, Gerald, 1907-80, British; nonfiction CON
ABRAHAMS, Howard Phineas, 1904- , American; nonfiction CON
ABRAHAMS, Peter Henry Lee ('Peter Graham'), 1919- , South African; fiction, poetry, journalism, nonfiction BU CON DA HER JA VCN VN WA
ABRAHAMS, Robert David, 1905- , American; juveniles CO
ABRAHAMS, William Miller, 1919- , American; fiction, nonfiction CON

ABRAHAMSEN, Christine Eliza-
beth ('Cristabel'; 'Kathleen
Westcott'), 1916- , Amer-
ican; fiction CON NI
ABRAHAMSEN, David, 1903- ,
Norwegian-American; nonfic-
tion CON
ABRAHAMSON, Mark J., 1939- ,
American; nonfiction CON
ABRAHAMSSON, Bengt, 1937- ,
Swedish; nonfiction CON
ABRAMOV, Alexander, Russian;
fiction NI
'ABRAMOV, Emil' see DRAITSER,
Emil
ABRAMOV, Fyodor Aleksandro-
vich, 1920- , Russian; fic-
tion CL
ABRAMOV, Sergei, Russian; fic-
tion NI
ABRAMOVITCH, Sholem J. see
'MENDELE, Moicher S.'
ABRAMOVITZ, Anita Zeltner
('Anita Brooks'), 1914- ,
American; nonfiction, juven-
iles CO CON
ABRAMS, Alan Edwin, 1941- ,
American; nonfiction CON
ABRAMS, George Joseph ('George
Hipp'), 1918- , American;
nonfiction, fiction CON
ABRAMS, Harry Nathan, 1904-
79, American; nonfiction
CON
ABRAMS, Joy, 1941- , Amer-
ican; juveniles CO CON
ABRAMS, Linsey, 1951- , Amer-
ican; fiction CON
ABRAMS, Meyer Howard, 1912- ,
American; nonfiction BOR
CON
ABRAMSON, Harold Alexander,
1889-1980, American; journal-
ism, nonfiction CON
ABRAMSON, Harold Julian, 1934- ,
American; nonfiction CON
ABRAMSON, Jesse P., 1904-79,
American; nonfiction CON
ABRAMSON, Martin, 1921- ,
American; nonfiction CON
ABRAMSON, Michael, 1944- ,
American; nonfiction CON
ABRAMSON, Paul Robert, 1937- ,
American; nonfiction CON
ABRASHKIN, Raymond, 1911- ,
American; juveniles WAR
ABRAVANEL, Isaac (Abarbanel),
1437-1508, Hebrew; nonfic-

tion BU TH
ABRAVANEL, Judah see ABAR-
BANEL, Judah
ABRECHT, Mary Ellen Benson,
1945- , American; nonfiction
CON
ABREU, Casimiro José Marques
de, 1839-60, Brazilian; poetry
BR
ABREU, Maria Isabel, 1919- ,
Brazilian-American; nonfiction
CON
ABRIL, Mariano ('Florete'), 1861-
1935, Puerto Rican; poetry,
journalism HIL
ABRO, Jamaluddin, 1924- , Sindhi;
fiction PRU
ABRUQUAH, Joseph Wilfred, 1921- ,
Ghanaian; fiction HER JA
ABSE, Dannie, 1923- , British;
fiction, plays, poetry CON
VCD VCN VCP WA
ABSE, David Wilfred, 1915- ,
Welsh; nonfiction CON
ABT, Clark Claus, 1929- , Ger-
man-American; nonfiction CON
ABU DULAMA IBN al-DJAUN, 720-
77/87, Arab; poetry HER
ABU MADI, Iliya, 1889/90-1957,
Syrian-American; poetry BU
PRU
ABU NUWAS, 747/62-813/15, Arab;
poetry BU LA PRU
ABU RISHA, Umar, 1910- , Syrian;
poetry BU
ABU SA'ID, Fazl Allah, 967/68-
1049, Persian; poetry BU PRU
ABU SHABAKA, Ilyas, 1903-47,
Lebanese; poetry BU
ABU SHADI, Ahmad Zaki, 1892-
1955, Egyptian; poetry PRU
ABU TAMMAM, early 9th century,
Arab; poetry BU PRU
ABUBAKAR, Alhaji Sir Tafawa
Balewa, 1912-66, Hausa; fic-
tion BU HER JA
ABUBAKAR IMAM, Alhaji, 1911-
66, Nigerian; fiction, nonfiction
BU HER JA
ABULAFIA, Todros, 1247-1303?,
Hebrew; poetry BU TH
ABU'L-ALA, Ahmad ibn Abdullah
al-Ma'arri, 973-1058, Arab;
poetry BU LA
ABU'l-ALAHIYA, 748-825/26, Arab;
poetry BU PRU
ABU'L-FARAJ, Gregory see BAR
HEBRAEUS

ABU'L-FARAJI, Ali ibn Husain,
al-Isfahani, 879-967, Arab;
nonfiction LA
ABU'L-FIDA, Isma'il, 1273-1331,
Arab; nonfiction PRU
ABU'L-HASAN see ZIRYAB
ABU'L-HASAN, ¯-1711, Sindhi;
poetry PRU
ABU-LUGHOD, Janet Louise,
1928- , American; nonfiction
CON
ABUN-NASR, Jamil Miri,
1932- , ?; nonfiction CON
ABUSHADY, Ahmad Zaki, 1892-
1955, Egyptian; poetry BU
ABTSU, 1233-83, Japanese; po-
etry BU HI
ACART de HESDIN, 14th century,
French; poetry BU
ACARYA, Bhanubhakta, 1814-69,
Nepali; poetry PRU
ACCIUS, Lucius, 170-86 B.C.,
Latin; poetry, plays BU
GR LA
ACCOLTI, Bernardo (Unico Are-
tino), 1458-1535, Italian; po-
etry, plays BU
ACCOLTI, Francesco (Francesco
Griffolini; Francesco Aretino),
1416-84/88, Italian; poetry BU
ACCORNERO, Mark, 1945- ,
American; nonfiction MAR
ACE, Goodman, 1899-1982, Amer-
ican; tv, nonfiction CON
ACEVEDO, Baltazar A., Jr.,
1945- , American; nonfiction
MAR
ACEVEDO DIAZ, Eduardo, 1851-
1921, Uruguayan; fiction BR
BU
'ACHARD, Marcel' (Marcel Auguste
Ferréol), 1899-1974, French;
plays, film BU CL CO MCG
TH WAK
'ACHCHYGYYA, Amma' (Nyukulay
Jögyörebís Muordinap), 1906- ,
Yakut; plays, poetry PRU
ACHEBE, Chinua, 1930- , Niger-
ian; fiction, poetry, juveniles,
nonfiction BU DA HER JA LA
SEY VCN VCP VN WA
ACHENBAUM, Wilbert Andrew, 1947- ,
American; nonfiction CON
'ACHILLES' see LAMB, Charles B.
ACHILLES TATIUS, 2/3rd cen-
turies, Greek; fiction BU GR
ACHILLINI, Claudio, 1574-1640,
Italian; poetry TH

ACHTERBERG, Gerrit, 1905-62,
Dutch; poetry BU CL SEY
TH WAK
ACILIUS, Gaius, fl. 155 B.C.,
Roman; nonfiction LA
ACKER, Helen, American; juven-
iles CON
ACKER, Robert Flint, 1920- ,
American; nonfiction CON
ACKERLEY, Joe Randolph, 1896-
1967, English; nonfiction, plays,
fiction, poetry CON WA
ACKERMAN, Bruce A., 1943- ,
American; nonfiction CON
ACKERMAN, Diane, 1948- , Amer-
ican; nonfiction CON
ACKERMAN, Edward A., 1911-73,
American; nonfiction CON
ACKERMAN, Eugene Francis, 1888-
1974, American; juveniles CO
ACKERMAN, Forrest J. ('Dr. Acu-
la'; 'Jacques De Forest Erman';
'Alden Lorraine'; 'Hubert George
Wells'; 'Weaver Wright'), 1916- ,
American; fiction AS CON NI
ACKERMAN, Gerald Martin, 1928- ,
American; nonfiction CON
ACKERMAN, J. Mark, 1939- ,
American; nonfiction CON
ACKERMAN, Robert Edwin, 1928- ,
American; nonfiction CON
ACKLAND, Rodney, 1908- , Brit-
ish; plays, film, nonfiction,
fiction CON VCD
ACKLEY, Charles Walton, 1913- ,
American; nonfiction CON
ACKLEY, Hugh Gardner, 1915- ,
American; nonfiction CON
ACKLEY, Randall William, 1931- ,
American; poetry CON
ACKOFF, Russell Lincoln, 1919- ,
American; nonfiction CON
'ACLAND, Alice' see WIGNALL,
Anne
ACLAND, James H., 1917- ,
Canadian; nonfiction CON
ACOMB-WALKER, Evelyn, 1910- ,
American; nonfiction CON
ACOMINATUS, Michael see CHO-
NIATES, Michael
ACOMINATUS, Nicetas see CHO-
NIATES, Nicetas
ACORN, Milton, 1923- , Canadian;
poetry, translations CON VCP
ACOSTA, Adalberto Joel, 1909- ,
American; nonfiction, fiction
MAR
ACOSTA, Frank X., 1945- ,

American; nonfiction MAR
ACOSTA, José de, 1539-1600,
Spanish; nonfiction BR BU
ACOSTA, José Julian, 1825-91,
Puerto Rican; journalism,
nonfiction HIL
ACOSTA, Oscar Zeta, American;
fiction MAR
ACOSTA, Robert T., 1934- ,
American; nonfiction MAR
ACQUAH, Gaddiel Robert (Ac-
quaah), 1884-1954, Ghanaian;
fiction, poetry HER
ACQUAVIVA, Sabino Samele,
1927- , Italian; nonfiction
CON
'ACRE, Stephen' see GRUBER,
Frank
ACROPOLITES, George, 1217-
82, Byzantine; nonfiction LA
ACTON, Harold, 1904- , English;
nonfiction WA
ACTON, Jay, 1949- , American;
nonfiction CON
ACTON, Sir John Emerich Ed-
ward Dalberg, 1834-1902,
English; nonfiction DA
ACTON, Thomas Alan, 1948- ,
English; nonfiction CON
'ACULA, Dr.' see ACKERMAN,
Forrest J.
ACUÑA, Hernando de, 1520?-80?,
Spanish; poetry BU TH
ACUÑA, Manuel, 1849-73, Mex-
ican; poetry, plays BR BU
ACUÑA, Rodolfo F., 1932- ,
American; nonfiction MAR
ACZEL, Tamas, 1921- , Hun-
garian-American; nonfiction,
poetry, fiction CON
ADACHI, Barbara Curtis ('Cath-
erine Anthony'), 1924- ,
American; nonfiction CON
ADAIR, Ian, 1942- , Scots; non-
fiction CON
ADAIR, John Glenn, 1933- ,
American; nonfiction CON
ADAIR, Margaret Weeks, -1971,
American; juveniles CO
ADALI-MORTTY, Geormbeeyi,
1916/20- , Ghanaian; poetry
HER JA
'ADAM' see LEBENSON, Abra-
ham D.
'ADAM, Ben' see DRACHMAN,
Julian M.
ADAM, Michael, 1919- , Eng-
lish; nonfiction CON

'ADAM, Onkel' see WETTERBERGH,
Carl A.
ADAM, Paul, 1862-1920, French;
fiction BU
ADAM, R. J. see 'MacTYRE, Paul'
ADAM de la BASSEE, -1286,
French; poetry BU
ADAM de la HALLE (Adam Le
Bossu; Adam d'Arras), 1240?-
88?, French; poetry, plays
BU MCG TH
ADAM of BREMEN, 1045-81/85,
German; nonfiction BU
ADAM of ST. VICTOR, 1110-80,
Latin; poetry BU TH
ADAMA van SCHELTEMA, Carel
Steven, 1877-1924, Dutch; po-
etry CL
ADAME, Leonard, 1947- , Amer-
ican; poetry MAR
ADAMNAN, St. 624?-704, Irish;
nonfiction BU DA
ADAMOV, Arthur, 1908-70, Rus-
sian-French; plays, transla-
tions, nonfiction BU CL MAG
MCG TH WA
ADAMOVICH, Georgy Viktorovich,
1894-1972, Russian; poetry,
nonfiction CL
ADAMS, Adrienne, 1906- , Amer-
ican; juveniles CO CON DE
ADAMS, Alice Boyde, 1926- ,
American; fiction CON
ADAMS, Andy, 1859-1935, Amer-
ican; nonfiction COM
ADAMS, Anne Hutchinson, 1935- ,
American; nonfiction CON
ADAMS, Arthur Merrihew, 1908- ,
American; nonfiction CON
ADAMS, Arthur Stanton, 1896-1980,
American; nonfiction CON
ADAMS, Brooks, 1848-1927, Amer-
ican; nonfiction BR
ADAMS, Cedric M., 1902-61,
American; journalism, nonfic-
tion CON
ADAMS, Charlotte, American;
juveniles WA
'ADAMS, Chuck' see TUBB, Edwin
C.
ADAMS, Cleve Franklin ('Franklin
Charles'; 'John Spain'), 1895-
1949, American; fiction REI
ST
'ADAMS, Dale' see QUINN, Elisa-
beth
ADAMS, Elsie Bontia, 1932- ,
American; nonfiction CON

ADAMS, Florence, 1932- ,
American; juveniles CON
ADAMS, Francis Alexandre,
1874-1975, American; non-
fiction, fiction CON
ADAMS, Frank Clyde, 1916- ,
American; nonfiction CON
ADAMS, Franklin Pierce, 1881-
1960, American; poetry CON
ADAMS, George Matthew, 1878-
1962, American; journalism,
nonfiction CON
ADAMS, George Worthington,
1905- , American; nonfiction,
CON
ADAMS, Harriet ('Victor Appleton'),
-1982, American; fiction NI
ADAMS, Hazard, 1926- , Amer-
ican; juveniles CO
ADAMS, Henry Brooks, 1838-
1918, American; nonfiction,
fiction AM BR BU MAG PO
SEY VN
ADAMS, Herbert, 1874-1952, Eng-
lish; fiction, poetry ST
ADAMS, Howard Joseph, 1928- ,
Canadian; nonfiction CON
ADAMS, James Edward, 1941- ,
American; nonfiction CON
ADAMS, James Luther, 1901- ,
American; nonfiction, trans-
lations CON
ADAMS, James Mack, 1933- ,
American; nonfiction CON
ADAMS, James Rowe, 1934- ,
American; nonfiction CON
ADAMS, Joey, 1911- , Amer-
ican; nonfiction CON
ADAMS, John, English; fiction NI
ADAMS, John, 1735-1826, Amer-
ican; nonfiction MAG
'ADAMS, John Paul', see KINNI-
ARD, Clark
ADAMS, Kenneth Menzies, 1922- ,
Australian; nonfiction CON
ADAMS, Laura, 1943- , Amer-
ican; nonfiction CON
ADAMS, Laurie (Schneider),
1941- , American; nonfic-
tion CON
ADAMS, Leon David, 1905- ,
American; nonfiction CON
ADAMS, Les, 1934- , American;
nonfiction CON
ADAMS, Louis Jerold, 1939- ,
American; nonfiction CON
ADAMS, Marion, 1932- , Aus-
tralian; nonfiction CON

ADAMS, Michael Charles Corring-
ham, 1945- , British; non-
fiction CON
ADAMS, Nathan Miller, 1934- ,
American; nonfiction CON
ADAMS, Paul Lieber, 1924- ,
American; nonfiction CON
ADAMS, Philip R., 1908- , Amer-
ican; nonfiction CON
ADAMS, Rachel Leona White, 1905?-
79, American; nonfiction CON
ADAMS, Ramon Frederick, 1889-
1976, American; nonfiction
CON
ADAMS, Randolph Greenfield, 1892-
1951, American; nonfiction
ENG
ADAMS, Richard George, 1920- ,
English; fiction, juveniles CO
CON KI WAK WAR
ADAMS, Richard Perrill, 1917-77,
American; fiction, poetry, non-
fiction CON
ADAMS, Robert Franklin ('Frank
Adamson'; 'Peter Eberhardt'),
1932- , American; fiction
CON
ADAMS, Robert McCormick, 1926- ,
American; nonfiction CON
ADAMS, Robert Martin, 1915- ,
American; nonfiction BOR
ADAMS, Rolland Leroy, 1905?-79,
American; journalism CON
ADAMS, Russell Baird, Jr., 1937- ,
American; nonfiction CON
ADAMS, Russell L., 1930- ,
American; nonfiction CON SH
ADAMS, Ruth Joyce, American;
juveniles CO
ADAMS, Sally Pepper, American;
nonfiction CON
ADAMS, Sam, 1934- , Welsh;
poetry, fiction CON
ADAMS, Samuel Hopkins, 1871-
1958, American; fiction, film
NI ST
ADAMS, Theodore Floyd, 1898-
1980, American; nonfiction
CON
ADAMS ESQUIVEL, Henry, 1940- ,
American; nonfiction MAR
ADAMSKI, George, 1891- , Polish-
American; fiction AS
ADAMSON, Alan Herbert, 1919- ,
Canadian; nonfiction CON
ADAMSON, Donald, 1939- , Eng-
lish; nonfiction, translations
CON

'ADAMSON, Frank' see ADAMS,
Robert F.
ADAMSON, Joseph III ('Warren
Wintergreen'), 1945- , Amer-
ican; nonfiction CON
ADAMSON, Joy, 1910-80, Eng-
lish; juveniles, nonfiction
CO CON DEM
ADAMSON, Wendy Wriston,
1942- , American; juveniles,
nonfiction CO CON
ADAS, Michael, 1943- , Amer-
ican; nonfiction CON
ADCOCK, Almey St. John ('Hil-
ary March'), 1894- , Eng-
lish; fiction, radio CON
ADCOCK, Elizabeth Sharp ('Betty
Adcock'), 1938- , American;
poetry, fiction CON
ADCOCK, Kareen Fleur, 1934- ,
New Zealander; poetry VCP
WAK
ADDAMS, Charles Samuel, 1912- ,
American; nonfiction CON
ADDAMS, Jane, 1860-1935, Amer-
ican; nonfiction AM
ADDARIAN, Garnik, 1925- , Ar-
menian; poetry PRU
ADDE, Leo, 1927?-75, American;
journalism, nonfiction CON
ADDEO, Edmond G., American;
fiction NI
ADDEO, Jovita A. 1939- , Amer-
ican; nonfiction CON
ADDIE, Pauline Betz, American;
juveniles WAR
'ADDISON, Gwen' see HARRIS, Al-
fred
'ADDISON, Hugh' (Harry Collinson
Owen), 1882-1956, English;
journalism, fiction NI
ADDISON, Joseph ('Isaac Bicker-
staffe'), 1672-1719, English;
poetry, nonfiction BRI BU
DA MAG MCG PO VN
ADDISON, Lloyd, 1937- , Amer-
ican; poetry, nonfiction CON
SH
ADDONA, Angelo F., 1925- ,
American; juveniles CO
ADDY, John, 1915- , British;
nonfiction CON
'ADDY, Ted' see WINTERBOTHAM,
Russell R.
ADE, George, 1866-1944, Amer-
ican; fiction, plays, journal-
ism BR BU MCG VN
ADE, Walter Frank Charles,

1910- , Canadian-American;
nonfiction, translations CON
'ADELBERG, Doris' see ORGEL,
Doris
ADELMAN, Bob, 1930- , Amer-
ican; nonfiction CON
ADELMAN, Clifford, 1942- ,
American; nonfiction CON
ADELMAN, Janet Ann, 1941- ,
American; nonfiction CON
ADELMANN, Frederick Joseph,
1915- , American; nonfiction
CON
ADELSON, Daniel, 1918- , Amer-
ican; nonfiction CON
ADELSON, Leone, 1908- , Amer-
ican; juveniles CO CON
ADEMOLA, Frances Quashie-Idun,
1930?- , Ghanaian; journal-
ism, nonfiction HER
ADEN, John Michael, 1918- ,
American; nonfiction CON
ADENET le ROI, 1240-1300, French;
poetry BU
ADENEY, David Howard, 1911- ,
English; nonfiction CON
ADER, Paul Fassett ('James Allen'),
1919- , American; fiction
CON
ADERBACH, Joel David, 1940- ,
American; nonfiction CON
ADES, Dawn, 1943- , British;
nonfiction CON
ADIGA, Sopalakrishna, 1918- ,
Indian; poetry PRU
ADISESHIAH, Malcolm Sathianathan,
1910- , Indian; nonfiction
CON
ADIVAR, Halide Edib, 1883-1964,
Turkish; fiction LA PRU
ADKINS, Jan, 1944- , American;
juveniles CO WA
ADKINS, Nelson Frederick, 1897-
1976, American; nonfiction
CON
ADLARD, John, 1929- , English;
nonfiction CON
'ADLARD, Mark' (Peter Marcus
Adlard), 1932- , English; fic-
tion AS CON NI
ADLER, Allen A., 1916- , Amer-
ican; film NI
ADLER, Carol, 1938- , American;
poetry CON
ADLER, Carole Schwerdtfeger,
1932- , American; juveniles
CON
ADLER, David A., 1947- , Amer-

ican; juveniles, fiction CO
CON
ADLER, Denise Rinker, 1908- ,
American; nonfiction CON
ADLER, Elmer, 1884-1962, Amer-
ican; journalism, nonfiction
CON
ADLER, Freda, 1934- , Amer-
ican; nonfiction CON
ADLER, Hans Arnold, 1921- ,
German-American; nonfiction
CON
'ADLER, Irene' see PENZLER,
Otto; STORR, Catherine C.
ADLER, Irving ('Robert Irving'),
1913- , American; juveniles
DE
ADLER, Jack, American; plays,
nonfiction CON
ADLER, Jacob ('B. Kovner'),
1873?-1974, American; fic-
tion CON
ADLER, John Hans, 1912-80,
Czech-American; nonfiction
CON
'ADLER, Kathleen'' see JONES,
Kathleen E.
'ADLER, Lula' see ROSENFELD,
Lulla
ADLER, Manfred, 1936- , Amer-
ican; nonfiction CON
ADLER, Mortimer Jerome,
1902- , American; nonfic-
tion CON
ADLER, Norman Tenner, 1941- ,
American; nonfiction CON
ADLER, Peggy, American; juven-
iles CO
ADLER, Renata, 1938- , Amer-
ican; nonfiction CON
ADLER, Ruth, 1915-68, American;
juveniles DE
ADLER, Warren, 1927- , Amer-
ican; fiction, nonfiction CON
ADLERBETH, Baron Gudmund
Jöran, 1751-1818, Swedish;
poetry BU
ADLERBLUM, Nina II., 1802-
1974, American; nonfiction
CON
ADNEW, Seth Marshall, 1921?-67,
American; juveniles WA
ADOFF, Arnold, 1935- , Amer-
ican; juveniles, poetry, nonfic-
tion CO CON DEM
ADOKI, G. E. 1910?- , Niger-
ian; fiction HER
'ADOLFO NONES' see VALLE,

Rafael del
ADONIAS FILLHO, Adonias Aguiar,
1915- , Brazilian; fiction BR
ADONIS, 1930- , Syrian; poetry
PRU
ADORJAN, Carol Madden, 1934- ,
American; juveniles, fiction,
nonfiction CO CON
'ADORNO' (Theodor Wiesengrund),
1903-69, German; nonfiction
BU CON WAK
ADOTEVI, Stanislas Spéro, 1934- ,
Dahoman; nonfiction JA
ADRET, Solomon ('Rashba'), Span-
ish; nonfiction BU
ADRIAN, Edgar Douglas, 1889-
1977, British; nonfiction CON
ADSHEAD, Gladys Lucy, 1896- ,
English; juveniles CO
ADSUAR, Jorge, 1883-1926, Puerto
Rican; journalism HIL
ADUAMAH, Enos Yao, 1940- ,
Ghanaian; fiction HER
'ADWAITA' (Johan Andreas der
Mouw), 1863-1919, Dutch; po-
etry, nonfiction BU
ADWANI, Sir Bheeromal Mehrchand,
1876-1953, Sindhi; nonfiction,
translations, plays PRU
ADY, Endre, 1877-1919, Hungarian;
poetry, fiction, nonfiction BU
CL SEY TH
ADZIGIAN, Denise Allard, 1952- ,
German-American; nonfiction
CON
AEBI, Ormond, 1916- , American;
nonfiction CON
AELFRIC, 955-1020? English; non-
fiction BU DA
AELIAN (Claudius Aelianus), 170-
235, Greek; nonfiction BU GR
AELIUS TUBERO, Quintus, fl. 50
B.C., Roman; nonfiction LA
AENEAS SILVIUS, 1405-64, Latin;
nonfiction TH
AENEAS TACTICUS, 4-3rd centuries
B.C., Greek; nonfiction BU
GR
AERS, David, 1946- , American;
nonfiction CON
AESCHINES, 397/89-30/22 B.C.,
Greek; nonfiction BU GR LA
AESCHINES of SPHETTUS, early
4th century B.C., Greek; non-
fiction BU LA
AESCHYLUS, 525-456 B.C., Greek;
poetry, plays BU GR LA MAG
MCG

AESOP, 6th century B.C.,
Greek; fiction BU GR MAG
'AESOP, Abraham' see NEW-
BERY, John
AETHERIA see EGERIA
ÄEUZOV, Muktar, 1897-1961,
Kazak; plays PRU
AFANSYEV, Alexander Niko-
layevich, 1826-71, Russian;
nonfiction BU
AFAWARK, Gabra Iyasus, 1868-
1947, Ethiopian; fiction, po-
etry HER
AFFLIGHEM, William van, 1210-
97, Dutch; poetry BU
AFGHANI, Ali-Muhannad, 1925- ,
Persian; fiction BU PRU
AFINOGENOV, Aleksandr, 1904-
41, Russian; plays BU CL
MCG TH
AFRANIUS, Lucius, 150 B.C.- ,
Roman; plays BU GR
AFREM, 315-73, Syrian; poetry,
nonfiction PRU
AFRICANO, Lillian ('Lillian Atal-
lan'), 1935- , American; non-
fiction CON
'AFRICANUS' see SANCHO, Igan-
tius
AFTERMAN, Allen, 1941- , Amer-
ican; nonfiction CON
AFZAL KHAN KHATAK, 1661-
1747?, Pashtun; nonfiction,
translations PRU
AFZELIUS, Arvid August, 1785-
1871, Swedish; poetry BU
AGAN, Patrick, 1943- , Amer-
ican; nonfiction CON
AGANOOR-POMPILI, Vittoria,
1853-1910, Italian; poetry
BU
AGAPETUS the DEACON, fl. 527,
Byzantine; nonfiction BU
'AGAPIDA, Fray Antonio' see
IRVING, Washington
AGAR, Herbert Sebastian, 1897-
1980, American; nonfiction,
journalism; CON
AGAR, Michael Henry, 1945- ,
American; nonfiction CON
AGARBICEANU, Ion (Agirbiceanu),
1882-1963, Rumanian; fiction,
nonfiction BU CL
AGARD, Nadema, 1948- , Amer-
ican; juveniles CO
AGARKAR, Gopal Ganés, 1856-
95, Marathi; nonfiction, journal-
ism PRU

AGAROSSI, Elena ('Aga Rossi'),
1940- , Italian; nonfiction
CON
AGASSI, Joseph, 1927- , Israeli;
nonfiction CON
AGASSIZ, Jean Louis Rodolphe,
1807-73, Swiss-American; nonfiction BR MY
'AGATAMON SANSAIJO' (Yuya Shi-
zuko, 1733-52; Udono Yonoko,
1729-88; Shindo Tsukubako, 18th
century), Japanese; poetry HI
AGATE, James, 1877-1947, English;
nonfiction DA
AGATHANGEGHOS, 5th century,
Armenian; nonfiction PRU
AGATHIAS SCHOLASTICUS, 531/36-
80/82, Byzantine; nonfiction,
poetry BU GR LA
AGATHON, 447-401 B.C., Greek;
poetry BU GR LA
AGAY, Denes, 1911- , Hungarian-
American; nonfiction CON
AGBODEKA, Francis, Ghanaian;
nonfiction CON
AGEE, James, 1909-55, American;
poetry, fiction, nonfiction AM
BA BR BU HE MAG PO SEY
VN
AGER, Cecelia, 1902-81, American;
journalism CON
AGGELER, Geoffrey Donovan,
1939- , American; nonfiction
CON
AGGESEN, Svend, 1130- , Danish;
nonfiction BU
AGGREY, James Emmanuel Kwegyir,
1875-1927, Ghanaian; nonfiction
HER JA
'AGHILL, Gordon' see SILVER-
BERG, Robert; GARRETT,
Randall
AGINSKY, Bernard Willard, 1905- ,
American; nonfiction CON
AGINSKY, Ethel Goldberg, 1910- ,
American; nonfiction CON
AGIRBICEANU, Ion see AGARBI-
CEANU, Ion
AGLE, Nan Hayden, 1905- , Amer-
ican; juveniles CO DEM
AGMON, Nathan, 1896- , Israeli;
fiction, plays BU
AGNEW, Edith Josephine ('Marce-
lino'), 1897- , American; ju-
veniles CO
AGNEW, James Barron, 1930- ,
American; nonfiction CON
AGNEW, Patience McCormick-

Goodhart, 1913?-76, Anglo-
American; nonfiction CON
AGNON, Shmuel Yoseph, 1888-
1970, Israeli; fiction BU
CL LA TH WA
AGOR, Weston Harris, 1939- ,
American; nonfiction CON
AGOSTINI de del RIO, Amelia,
1896-. , Puerto Rican; po-
etry, fiction HIL
AGRAIT, Gustavo, 1909- ,
Puerto Rican; fiction HIL
AGREDA, Sor María Coronel de
Jesús de, 1602-65, Spanish;
nonfiction BU
AGRELL, Alfhild Teresia Martin,
1849-1923, Swedish; fiction,
plays BU
AGRESS, Hyman, 1931- , Amer-
ican; nonfiction CON
'AGRICOLA, Johannes' (J. Schnit-
ter), 1494-1566, German; non-
fiction TH
AGRICOLA, Rudolf (Roelof Huysman),
1442-85, Dutch; nonfiction,
translations BU
AGRIPPA, Marcus Vipsanius, 63-
12 B.C., Roman; nonfiction
LA
'AGUENORA' see ROQUE de Du-
PREY, Ana
AGUERO, Kathleen, 1949- ,
American; poetry, nonfiction
CON
AGUILAR, Gaspar Honorat de,
1561-1623, Spanish; plays
BU TH
AGUILAR, J. V., American;
nonfiction MAR
AGUILAR, Ricardo D., 1947- ,
American; nonfiction MAR
AGUILAR, Rodolfo Jesus, 1936- ,
Costa Rican-American; non-
fiction CON
AGUILERA MALTA, Demetrio,
1909- , Ecuadorian; journal-
ism BR
AGUILO i FUSTER, Maria, 1825-
97, Catalan; poetry, nonfiction
BU
AGUIRRE, Adalberto, Jr., 1950- ,
American; nonfiction MAR
AGUIRRE, Nataniel, 1843-88, Bo-
livian; fiction BR BU
AGUNWA, Clement, 1936/40- ,
Nigerian; fiction HER JA
AGUOLU, Christian Chukwunedu,
1940- , Nigerian; nonfic-

tion CON
AGUSTI, Ignacio, 1913-74, Spanish;
fiction, journalism, poetry,
nonfiction CL
AGUSTINI, Delmira, 1886-1914,
Uruguayan; poetry BR BU
AGUZZI-BARBAGLI, Danilo,
1924- , Italian-Canadian; non-
fiction CON
AGYEY, Saccidananda H. see
AJÑEYA, Saccidananda
'AHAD HA-AM' (Asher Ginzberg),
1856-1927, Jewish; nonfiction
BU TH
AHERN, James see 'HERNE, James
A.'
AHERN, Emily M., 1944- , Amer-
ican; nonfiction CON
AHERN, James F., 1932- , Amer-
ican; nonfiction CON
AHERN, John Francis, 1936- ,
American; nonfiction CON
AHERN, Margaret McCrohan ('Peg
O'Connell'), 1921- , American;
juveniles CO
AHERN, Mary Eileen, 1860-1938,
American; nonfiction ENG
AHERN, Thomas Francis, 1947- ,
American; nonfiction CON
AHKNATON (Amenhotep), fl. 1367-
50 B.C., Egyptian; poetry
PRU
'AHLGREN, Ernst' (Victoria Bene-
dictsson), 1850-88, Swedish;
fiction BU TH
AHLIN, Lars Gustaf, 1915- ,
Swedish; fiction BU CL TH
AHLSEN, Leopold, 1927- , Ger-
man; plays MCG
AHLSTROEM, Goesta Werner,
1918- , Swedish-American;
nonfiction CON
AHMAD, Aziz, 1914- , Urdu;
fiction, nonfiction, translations
PRU
AHMAD, Ishtiaq, 1937- , Indian;
nonfiction CON
AHMAD, Mawlavi, late 19th cen-
tury, Pashtun; fiction, poetry
PRU
AHMAD, Nazir, 1836-1912, Urdu;
fiction, journalism, transla-
tions PRU
AHMAD FARIS al-SHIDYAQ, 1801-
87, Lebanese; nonfiction BU
AHMAD KHAN, Sir Sayyid, 1817-
98, Urdu; nonfiction BU PRU
AHMADJAN KHAN BAHADUR,

Munshi, 1882-1951, Pashtun;
translations, fiction PRU
AHMADU, Malam Ingawa, 20th
century, Hausa; fiction BU
AHMED HAMDI TANPINAR, 1901-
62, Turkish; fiction BU
AHMED HASIM, 1884-1933, Turk-
ish; poetry BU CL
AHMEDI, Taceddin Ibrahim, 1335-
1413, Turkish; poetry PRU
'AHO, Juhani' (Johannes Brofeldt),
1861-1921, Finnish; fiction,
plays BU TH
AHOKAS, Jaakko Alfred, 1923- ,
Finnish; nonfiction, translations
CON
AHSEN, Akhter, 1931- , Pakis-
tani; nonfiction CON
AHWAS al-ANSARI, 655?-723/28,
Arab; poetry PRU
'AI' (Florence Anthony), 1947- ,
American; poetry CON
'AI CH'ING' (Chiang Hai-Ch'êng),
1910- , Chinese; poetry, non-
fiction BU PRU
'AI WU' (T'ang Tao-Kêng), 1904- ,
Chinese; fiction BU PRU
AICHINGER, Helga, 1937- ,
Austrian; juveniles CO DEM
AICHINGER, Ilse, 1921- , Aus-
trian; fiction, radio, poetry
BU CL CON THE
AICHINGER, Peter, 1933- , Ca-
nadian; nonfiction CON
AIDENOFF, Abraham, 1913-76,
American; nonfiction CON
AIDOO, Christian Ama Ata,
1942- , Ghanaian; plays,
fiction CON HER JA VCD
AIG-IMOUKHUEDE, Frank, 1935- ,
Nigerian; poetry, plays, jour-
nalism HER JA
AIKEN, Clarissa Lorenz, 1899- ,
American; juveniles CO
AIKEN, Conrad Potter ('Samuel
Leake, Jr.'), 1889-1973,
American; poetry, fiction,
plays AM BR BU CO CON
MAG PO SEY VN VP
AIKEN, George, 1830-76, Amer-
ican; plays MCG
AIKEN, Irene Nixon, American;
juveniles CON
AIKEN, Joan Delano, 1924- ,
British; juveniles, fiction
DE KI REI
AIKEN, John Kempton ('John Pa-
get'), 1913- , American;

fiction CON
AIKIN, John, 1747-1822, English;
nonfiction, translations BU
AIKIN, Lucy, 1781-1864, English;
nonfiction BU
AIKMAN, David B. T., 1944- ,
Anglo-American; nonfiction
CON
AILLY, Pierre d', 1350-1420,
French; nonfiction BU
AILRED, 1110-67, English; non-
fiction BU
AIMERIC de BELENOI, fl. 1217-42,
Provençal; poetry BU
AIMERIC de PEGUILHAN, 1195-
1230, Provençal; poetry BU
AIMES, Angelica, 1943- , Amer-
ican; fiction CON
'AINSLIE, Tom' see CARTER,
Richard
AINSWORTH, Charles Harold,
1935- , American; nonfiction
CON
AINSWORTH, Dorothy Sears, 1894-
1976, American; nonfiction
CON
AINSWORTH, Geoffrey Clough,
1905- , British; nonfiction
CON
'AINSWORTH, Harriet' see CADELL,
Violet E.
AINSWORTH, Norma (Norma Paul
Ruedi), American; juveniles
CO
'AINSWORTH, Patricia' see BEGG,
Patricia N.
AINSWORTH, Ruth Gallard, 1908- ,
English; juveniles; CO KI
AINSWORTH, William Harrison
('Will Brown'; 'Cheviot Tiche-
burn'), 1805-82, English; fic-
tion, poetry BU CO DA MAG
PO VN
AIRAS de SANTIAGO, Joan, fl.
1250, Galician; poetry BU
'AIRD, Catherine' (Kinn Hamilton
McIntosh), 1930- , English;
fiction, plays, nonfiction REI
ST
AIRD, Eileen Margaret, 1945- ,
English; nonfiction CON
AIROLA, Paavo Olavi, 1915- ,
Finnish-American; nonfiction
CON
'AISLIN' see MOSHER, Terry
'AISTIS', Jonas' (Jonas Aleksandra-
vicius), 1908?-73, Lithuanian-
American; poetry, nonfiction

CL CON
AISTROP, Jack, 1916- , Amer-
ican; juveniles CO
AITCHISON, Janet, 1962- ,
English; juveniles CON
AITKEN, Dorothy, 1916- ,
American; juveniles CO
AITKEN, William Russell ('Stu-
art Scott'), 1913- , Scots;
nonfiction CON
AITKIN, Donald Alexander, 1937- ,
Australian; nonfiction CON
AITMATOV, Chingiz, 1928- ,
Russian; fiction CON
AJAO, Motolami Aderogba, 1930- ,
Nigerian; fiction JA
AJAO, S., Nigerian; plays JA
AJAY, Betty, 1918- , American;
nonfiction CON
AJAYI, Jacob Festus Adeniyi,
1929- , Nigerian; nonfiction
CON
AJÑEYA, Saccidananda Hirananda
(Agyey), 1911- , Hindi; po-
etry PRU
AKAR, John Joseph, 1927- ,
Sierra Leonean; plays, fic-
tion, journalism HER JA
AKAZOME EMON, 11th century,
Japanese; poetry HI
AKBAR ILAHABADI, 1846-1921,
Urdu; poetry PRU
AKEN, Hein van, -1330?, Dutch;
poetry BU
AKEN, Piet van, 1920- , Flemish;
fiction BU CL
'AKENS, Floyd' see BAUM, Ly-
man F.
AKENSIDE, Mark, 1721-70, Eng-
lish; poetry BU DA PO VP
AKENSON, Donald Harman, 1941- ,
American; nonfiction CON
AKER, George Frederick, 1927- ,
American; nonfiction CON
AKERET, Robert Ulrich, 1928- ,
American; nonfiction CON
'AKERS, Alan Burt' (Kenneth Bul-
mer), American; fiction NI
AKERS, Ronald Louis, 1939- ,
American; nonfiction CON
AKHA, 1615-74, Gujarati; poetry
BU
AKHMADULINA, Bella Akhatovna,
1937- , Russian; poetry CL
CON SEY TH WA
'AKHMATOVA, Anna' (Anna Andre-
yevna Gorenko), 1889-1966,

Russian; poetry BU CL SEY
TH WA
AKHNATON see AHKNATON
AKHNATON, Askia see ECKELS,
Jon
AKHTAL, -710, Arab; poetry BU
PRU
AKHTOY (Khety), fl. 1971-1828
B.C., Egyptian; nonfiction PRU
AKHUND DARWEZ, 1540?-1639,
Pashtun; nonfiction PRU
AKHUNDZADÄ, Mirzä Fäthali (Ak-
hundov), 1812-78, Azerbaijani;
poetry, plays PRU
AKHURST, Bertram A., 1928- ,
American; nonfiction CON
AKIF, Mehmed Ersoy see ERSOY,
Mehmet A.
AKIGA, Benjamin (B. Akiga Sai),
1898- , Nigerian; nonfiction,
journalism HER JA
AKINS, Zoë, 1886-1958, American;
poetry, film, plays MCG
AKINSEMOYIN, Kunle, 1930?- ,
Nigerian; poetry, fiction HER
AKMAKJAIN, Hiag, 1926- , Amer-
ican; nonfiction CON
AKPABOT, Samuel, E., 1930/32- ,
Nigerian; poetry, nonfiction
CON JA
AKPAN, Ntieyong Udo, 1924/40- ,
Nigerian; fiction HER JA
AKSAKOV, Ivan Sergeyevich, 1823-
86, Russian; journalism, po-
etry BU
AKSAKOV, Konstantin Sergeyevich,
1817-60, Russian; nonfiction BU
AKSAKOV, Sergey Timofeyevich,
1791-1859, Russian; fiction
BU TH
AKSENOV, Vasily Pavlovich (Aksyo-
nov), 1932- , Russian; fiction,
plays CL CON TH WA
AKUTAGAWA, Ryunosuke, 1892-
1927, Japanese; fiction, non-
fiction BU HI LA PRU WA
ALABASTER, William, 1567-1640,
English; poetry, plays, DA PO
RU VP
AL-ADAWIYAH, Rabi'ah, 714-801,
Arab; poetry BU
ALAGEYAVANNA, fl. 1590-1620,
Sinhalese; poetry LA PRU
'ALAIN' (Emile Auguste Chartier),
1868-1951, French; nonfiction
BU CL TH WAK
ALAIN-FOURNIER (Henri Alain
Fournier), 1886-1914, French;

fiction BU CL MAG SEY TH
ALAMANNI, Luigi, 1495-1556,
Italian; poetry BO BU TH
'ALAN, Jack' see GREEN, Alan B.
ALAN of LILLE (Alanus de Insu-
lis), 1128?-1203, French; po-
etry BU TH
ALAOL, 1597?-1673?, Bengali;
poetry PRU
ALAPINI, Julien, 1906- , Da-
homan; nonfiction JA
ALARCON, Juste S., 1930- ,
American; nonfiction MAR
ALARCON, Pedro Antonio de,
1833-91, Spanish; fiction
BU MAG TH
ALAS y UREÑA, Leopoldo
('Clarín'), 1852-1901, Span-
ish; fiction, nonfiction BU
CL TH
ALATORRE, Richard, 1944- ,
American; nonfiction MAR
ALAVI, Aqa Buzurg (Bozorg),
1904/08- , Persian; fiction
BU PRU
ALBA of GAMEZ, Cielo Cayetana
('Tana de Gamez'), 1920- ,
Spanish-American; nonfiction,
translations CON
'ALBAN, Antony' (Anthony A.
Thompson) American?; fiction
NI
ALBANESE, Catherine Louise,
1940- , American; nonfiction
CON
ALBARET, Celeste Gineste,
1891- , French; nonfiction
CON
ALBASINI, Joāo, 1890?-1925, Mo-
zambican; fiction, journalism
HER
ALBAUGH, Edwin Doll, Jr.,
1935- , American; journal-
ism, nonfiction CON
ALBAUM, Melvin, 1936- , Amer-
ican; nonfiction CON
ALBEE, Edward, 1928- , Amer-
ican; plays AM BR BU MAG
MCG MCN PO SEY VCD VD
WA
ALBERDINGK THIJM, Josephus
Albertus ('Pauwels Forees-
tier'), 1820-89, Dutch; poetry,
fiction, journalism BU
ALBERIC von BISINZO, fl. 1120,
French; poetry BU
ALBERS, Josef, 1888-1976, Ger-
man-American; poetry, non-

fiction CON
ALBERT, Burton, Jr. ('Brooks
Healey'), 1936- , American;
juveniles, nonfiction CO CON
ALBERT, Heinrich, 1604-51, Ger-
man; poetry BU
ALBERT, Louise, 1928- , Amer-
ican; fiction CON
ALBERT, Marvin H. ('Anthony
Rome'), American; fiction,
film CON
ALBERT, Mimi Abriel, 1940- ,
American; fiction, poetry CON
ALBERT i PARADIS, Catarina ('Vic-
tor Català'), 1873-1966, Span-
ish; fiction BU CL
ALBERT of AIX, fl. 1121, French;
nonfiction TH
ALBERT of STADE, 1200-61, Ger-
man; nonfiction, poetry BU
ALBERTAZZI, Adolfo, 1865-1924,
Italian; fiction BU
ALBERTAZZIE, Ralph, 1923- ,
American; nonfiction CON
ALBERT-Birot, Pierre, 1876-1967,
French; poetry BU CL
ALBERTI, Leon Battista, 1404-72,
Italian; nonfiction BO BU TH
ALBERTI, Rafael, 1902- , Span-
ish; poetry, plays BU CL CON
MCG TH
ALBERTI, Robert Edward, 1938- ,
American; nonfiction CON
ALBERTINUS, Agidius, 1560-1620,
German; translations, nonfiction
BU TH
ALBERTS, Frances Jacobs, 1907- ,
American; juveniles CO
ALBERTSON, Chris, 1931- , Ice-
landic-American; nonfiction
CON
ALBERTUS MAGNUS, 1206-80, Ger-
man; nonfiction BU TH
ALBERUS, Erasmus, 1500-53, Ger-
man; nonfiction BU
ALBERY, Nobuko (Nobuko Morris),
Japanese; nonfiction, fiction
CON
ALBI, Frank Emanuel, 1930- ,
American; nonfiction MAR
ALBIN, Peter Steigman, 1934- ,
American; nonfiction CON
ALBINI, Joseph Louis, 1930- ,
American; nonfiction CON
ALBINOVANUS PEDO, early 1st
century, Roman; poetry LA
ALBINSON, James P. ('Jack Al-
binson'), 1932- , American;

nonfiction CON
ALBO, Joseph, 1380-1444, Spanish, nonfiction BU TH
ALBORNOZ, Aurora de, Spanish; poetry HIL
AL'BOV, Mikhail Nilovich, 1851-1911, Russian; fiction BU
'ALBRAN, Kehlog' see SHACKET, Sheldon R.
'ALBRAND, Martha' (Heidi Huberta Freybe; 'Katrin Holland'; "Christine Lambert'), 1912- , German-American; fiction, plays; MCC REI ST
ALBRECHT, Friedrich Wilhelm, 1774-1840, German; poetry BU
ALBRECHT, Lillie Vanderveer, 1894- , American; juveniles CO
ALBRECHT, William Price, 1907- , American; nonfiction CON
ALBRECHT von EYB, 1420-75, German; translations, nonfiction BU
ALBRECHT von HALBERSTADT, early 13th century, German; poetry, translations BU TH
ALBRECHT von JOHANNSDORF, fl. 1185-1209, Bavarian; poetry BU
ALBRECHT von SCHARFENBERG, fl. 1280, German; translations, poetry BU TH
ALBRIGHT, John Brannon, 1930- , American; nonfiction CON
ALBRIGHT, Joseph Medill, 1937- , American; journalism, nonfiction CON
ALBUQUERQUE, Afonso de, 1461-1515, Portuguese; nonfiction BU
ALCAEUS, 620 B.C.- , Greek; poetry BU GR LA
ALCALA GALIANO, Antonio, 1789-1865, Spanish; nonfiction BU
ALCALA YAÑEZ de RIBERA, Jerónimo de, 1563-1632, Spanish; fiction BU
'ALCANTARA, Osvaldo' see LOPES, Baltasar
ALCÂNTARA MACHADO, António Castilho de, 1901-35, Brazilian; fiction BR
ALCAZAR, Baltasar del, 1530-1606, Spanish; poetry BU TH

ALCEU AMOROSO LIMA, 1893- , Brazilian; nonfiction BR
ALCIATO, Andrea (Alciati), 1492-1550, Italian; nonfiction, poetry BO BU
'ALCIBIADE' see PRAZ, Mario
ALCIDAMAS of ELAEA, 4th century B.C., Greek; nonfiction BU
'ALCIDES, Gerardo' see DOMINGUEZ, José de J.
ALCIPHRON, 2-3rd centuries, Greek; nonfiction BU
ALCMAER, Heinric van, late 15th century, Dutch; poetry BU
ALCMAN, 7th century B.C., Greek; poetry BR GR LA
ALCOFORADO, Mariana, 1640-1723, Portuguese; letters BU
ALCORN, John, 1935- , American; juveniles DE
ALCOTT, Amos Bronson, 1799-1888, American; nonfiction, poetry BR BU MY
ALCOTT, Louisa May, 1832-88, American; juveniles, poetry, fiction AM BR BU COM KI MAG MY VN
ALCOTT, William Andrus, 1798-1859, American; nonfiction MY
ALCOVER, Joan, 1854-1926, Catalan; poetry BU CL
ALCUIN (Ealhwine), 735-804, English; poetry, nonfiction BU DA TH
'ALCYONE' see KRISHNAMURTI, Jiddu
ALD, Roy A., American; nonfiction CON
ALDA, Alan, 1936- , American; tv, film CON
ALDANA, Francisco de, 1537-78, Spanish; poetry BU TH
'ALDANOV, Mark Alexandrovich' (M.A. Landau), 1886-1957, Russian; fiction BU CL TH
ALDECOA, Ignacio, 1925-69, Spanish; fiction CL
'ALDEN, Carella' see REMINGTON, Ella-Carrie
ALDEN, Douglas William, 1912- , American; nonfiction CON
ALDEN, Isabella Macdonald, 1841-1930, American; juveniles COM
ALDEN, John Richard, 1908- , American; nonfiction CON

ALDEN, Robert Leslie, 1937- ,
American; nonfiction CON
ALDER, Francis Anthony, 1937- ,
American; juveniles; CON
ALDER, Henry Ludwig, 1922- ,
German-American; nonfiction
CON
ALDERMAN, Barbara Joy,
1931- , American; nonfic-
tion CON
ALDERMAN, Clifford Lindsey,
1902- , American; juven-
iles CO
ALDERMAN, Edwin Anderson,
1861-1931, American; non-
fiction BA
ALDERMAN, Geoffrey, 1944- ,
British; nonfiction CON
ALDERSON, Joanne Bartels,
1930- , American; nonfic-
tion, plays CON
ALDHELM, 650-709, Anglo-
Saxon; nonfiction BU
'ALDING, Peter' see JEFFRIES,
Roderic
ALDINGTON, Richard, 1892-1962,
English; poetry, fiction, non-
fiction BR CON DA MAG
PO VN
ALDISS, Brian Wilson, 1925- ,
English; fiction, nonfiction
AS NI VCN WAK
'ALDON, Adair' see MEIGS, Cor-
nelia L.
ALDOUS, Anthony Michael, 1935- ,
British; nonfiction CON
ALDRED, Cyril, 1914- , English;
nonfiction CON
'ALDRICH, Ann' see MEAKER,
Marijane
ALDRICH, Bess Streeter, 1881-
1954, American; fiction PAL
ALDRICH, Thomas Bailey, 1836-
1907, American; poetry, fic-
tion, juveniles, plays BR BU
CO KI MAG ST WAR
ALDRIDGE, Adele, 1934- , Amer-
ican; poetry CON
ALDRIDGE, James, 1918- , Au-
stralian; fiction, plays, non-
fiction, juveniles CON VCN
ALDRIDGE, John Watson, 1922- ,
American; nonfiction, fiction
BOR WA
ALDRIDGE, Josephine Haskell,
American; juveniles CO
CON
ALDRIN, Edwin Eugene, Jr.,

1930- , American; nonfiction
CON
ALDWINCKLE, Russell Foster,
1911- , British; nonfiction
CON
'ALDYNE, Nathan', see Mc-DOW-
ELL, Michael
AL-E AHMAD, Jalal, 1920/23-
69/71, Persian; nonfiction,
fiction BU PRU
ALEANDRO, Girolamo, 1480-1542,
Italian; nonfiction BU
ALEARDI, Aleardo, 1812-78, Italian;
poetry BO BU TH
ALECIS, Guillaume (Alexis), 1425?-
86?, French; poetry BU
ALECSANDRI, Vasile, 1821-90,
Rumanian; poetry, plays BU
MCG TH
ALEGRE, Caetano da Costa, 1864-
90, Portuguese; poetry HER
JA
ALEGRIA, Ciro, 1909-67, Peruvian;
fiction BR BU MAG
ALEGRIA, Jose S., 1887-1965,
Puerto Rican; journalism, po-
etry HIL
ALEGRIA, Ricardo E., 1921- ,
Puerto Rican; nonfiction, jour-
nalism CO HIL
ALEIXANDRE, Vicente, 1898- ,
Spanish; poetry, journalism
BU CL CON TH WA
ALEKSANDRAVICIUS, Jonas see
'AISTIS, Jonas'
'ALEKSANDROV' see MURN, Josip
ALEMAN, Mateo, 1547-1613?,
Spanish; fiction BU MAG TH
ALEMBERT, Jean Le Rond, 1717-
83, French; nonfiction BU TH
ALENCAR, José Martiniano de,
1829-77, Brazilian; fiction BR
BU
ALEPOUDELIS, Odysseus see 'ELY-
TIS, Odysseus'
'ALERAMO, Sibilla' (Rina Faccio),
1876-1960, Italian; fiction po-
etry BO BU CL
ALESSANDRA, Anthony Joseph,
1947- , American; nonfiction
CON
ALEWIJN, Abraham Martijnsz, 1664-
1721, Dutch; poetry, plays BU
ALEXANDER, Anna Barbara ('Anne
Alexander'; 'Barbara Cooke'),
1913- , American; juveniles
CON
ALEXANDER, Boyd ('John Lacey'),

1913-80, English; nonfiction,
translations CON
ALEXANDER, Charles Khalil
('Basheer Qadar'; 'Mario
Quimber'), 1923-1980,
Egyptian-American; plays
CON
ALEXANDER, Christine, 1893-
1975, American; nonfiction
CON
ALEXANDER, Conel Hugh O'Don-
el, 1909-74, Irish; nonfiction
CON
ALEXANDER, David, 1907-73,
American; juveniles, fiction
CON ST WAR
ALEXANDER, David Michael,
1945- , American; fiction
CON
ALEXANDER, Denis, 1945- ,
English; nonfiction CON
ALEXANDER, Eben Roy, 1899?-
1978, American; journalism
CON
ALEXANDER, Ernest Robert,
1933- , American; nonfiction
CON
ALEXANDER, Frances Laura,
1888- , American; juven-
iles CO
ALEXANDER, Frank, 1943- ,
American; nonfiction, poetry
CON
ALEXANDER, George Jonathan,
1931- , German-American;
nonfiction CON
'ALEXANDER, Gil' see RALSTON,
Gilbert A.
ALEXANDER, Harold Lee ('Zane
Alexander'), 1934- , Amer-
ican; nonfiction CON
ALEXANDER, Herbert Ephraim,
1927- , American; nonfiction
CON
ALEXANDER, Holmes Moss,
1906- , American; nonfic-
tion, fiction CON
ALEXANDER, I. J., 1905?-74,
American; nonfiction CON
ALEXANDER, James Eckert,
1913- , American; journal-
ism; CON
'ALEXANDER, Jan' see BANIS,
Victor J.
ALEXANDER, Jean, 1926- ,
American; nonfiction CON
ALEXANDER, Jocelyn Anne (Arun-
del), 1930- , American; juven-

iles CO
ALEXANDER, John Kurt, 1941- ,
American; nonfiction CON
ALEXANDER, John N. , 1941- ,
American; nonfiction CON
'ALEXANDER, Kathryn' see CALD-
WELL, Kathryn S.
ALEXANDER, Kenneth John Wilson,
1922- , Scots; nonfiction CON
ALEXANDER, Lloyd Chudley, 1924- ,
American; juveniles, transla-
tions, nonfiction CO DE KI
ALEXANDER, Louis George, 1932-
British; nonfiction, juveniles
CON
ALEXANDER, Martha, 1920- ,
American; juveniles CO CON
DEM
ALEXANDER, Marthann, 1907- ,
American; nonfiction CON
ALEXANDER, Martin, 1930- ,
American; nonfiction CON
ALEXANDER, Michael Joseph,
1941- , English; nonfiction,
translations CON
ALEXANDER, Michael Van Cleave,
1937- , American; nonfiction
CON
ALEXANDER, Raymond Pace, 1898-
1974, American; juveniles, non-
fiction CO CON
'ALEXANDER, Robert' see GROSS
Michael R.
ALEXANDER, Robert, British;
fiction NI
ALEXANDER, Robert William ('Joan
Butler'), 1906?-80, American;
nonfiction CON NI
ALEXANDER, Shana, 1925- ,
American; nonfiction CON
ALEXANDER, Stanley Walter ('Han-
nibal'), 1895-1980, British;
nonfiction CON
ALEXANDER, Sue, 1933- , Amer-
ican; juveniles CO CON
ALEXANDER, Thomas Glen, 1935- ,
American; nonfiction CON
ALEXANDER, Vincent, 1925-80,
American; nonfiction CON
ALEXANDER, Sir William, 1577?-
1640, Scots; poetry, plays DA
RU
ALEXANDER, William, 1826-94,
Scots; fiction DA
ALEXANDER, William Mortimer,
1928- , American; nonfiction
CON
ALEXANDER, Yonah, 1931- ,

American; nonfiction CON
'ALEXANDER, Zane' see ALEX-
ANDER, Harold L.
ALEXANDER de VILLA DEI
(Alexandre de Ville-Dieu),
1160?-1203?, French; non-
fiction TH
ALEXANDER NECKHAM, 1157-
1217, English; poetry BU
ALEXANDER of APHRODISIAS,
early 3rd century, Greek;
nonfiction BU GR
ALEXANDER the GREAT, 356-
23 B.C., Greek; nonfiction
LA
ALEXANDRE, Philippe, 1923- ,
French; nonfiction CON
ALEXANDRE du PONT, 13th
century, French; poetry BU
ALEXANDRE of BERNARI (de
Paris), fl. 1190, French;
poetry BU
ALEXANDRESCU, Grigore M.
(Alecsandrescu), 1812-85,
Rumanian; poetry BU
ALEXEEV, Wassilij, 1906- ,
Russian-American; nonfiction
CON
ALEXEIEFF, Alexandre A.,
1901- , Russian-American;
juveniles CO
ALEXEYEV, Sergey A. see
'NAVDÉNOV, S.'
ALEXIOU, Margaret, 1939- ,
British; nonfiction CON
ALEXIS, 390/80-280/70 B.C.,
Greek; plays, poetry BU GR
ALEXIS, Jacques-Stéphen, 1922-61?,
Haitian; fiction BU
'ALEXIS, Willibald' (George Wil-
helm Häring), 1798-1871,
German; fiction BU
ALFANI, Gianni, 1260/70-1320,
Italian; poetry BU
al-FARUQI, Ismai'il Raji, 1921- ,
American; nonfiction CON
ALFASI, Isaac Ben Jacob, 1013-
1103, Jewish; poetry BU
ALFEREZ, La Monja see ERAUSO,
Catalina de
ALFIERI, Vittorio, 1749-1803,
Italian; poetry, plays, nonfiction
BO BU MCG
ALFONSO X 'El Sabio', 1221-84,
Spanish; poetry BU
ALFORD, Bernard William Ernest,
1937- , British; nonfiction
CON

ALFORD, Henry, 1910-71, English;
nonficiton BU
ALFORD, Robert Ross, 1928- ,
American; nonfiction CON
ALFRED, 849-99, Saxon; nonfiction
BU DA
'ALFRED, Richard' see HAVER-
STOCK, Nathan A.
ALFRED, William, 1922- , Amer-
ican; plays; MCG VCD WA
ALFVEN, Hannes see 'JOHANNES-
SON, Olof'
ALGARIN, Miguel, 1941- , Puerto
Rican; tv, plays, nonfiction
CON
ALGAROTTI, Francesco, 1712-64,
Italian; poetry BU
ALGER, Horatio ('Arthur Lee
Putnam'), 1834-99, American;
juveniles, fiction BR BU CO
PO VN
ALGER, Leclaire Gowans (Sorchi
Nic Leodhas), 1898-1969, Amer-
ican; juveniles CO CON DE
'ALGERY, Andre' see COULET du
GARD, Rene
ALGREN, Nelson, 1909-81, Amer-
ican; fiction BR BU CON PO
SEY VCN VN
AL-HADI, Sayyid Shaykh bin, 1867-
1934, Malayan; journalism,
fiction PRU
ALHAMISI, Ahmed Akinwole, Amer-
ican; nonfiction SH
AL-HARIZI, Judal Ben Shlomoh,
1165?-1235, Hebrew; poetry
TH
ALI, Abdullah Gureh, 1940?- ,
Somalian; poetry HER
ALI, Ahmed, 1906/12- , Pakis-
tani; fiction, plays, transla-
tions, nonfiction BU LA PRU
VCN
ALI, Sabahattin, 1906-48, Turkish;
fiction PRU
ALI DUUH, 19-20th centuries, Somal-
ian; poetry LA
ALI HAJI, Raja, 1808-68?, Malay-
an; nonfiction LA
ALI SIR NEVAÎ, 1441-1501, Turk-
ish; poetry BU
ALIANO, Richard Anthony, 1946- ,
American; nonfiction CON
ALIBERT, François Paul, 1873-
1953, French; poetry BU
ALIBRANDI, Tom, 1941- , Amer-
ican; nonfiction CON
ALICE, Princess (Countess of

Athlone), 1883-1981, British;
nonfiction CON
ALIESEN, Jody, 1943- , Amer-
ican; poetry CON
ALIGER, Margarita Iosifovna,
1915- , Russian; poetry BU
CL TH
ALIGHIERI, Jacopo, -1348,
Italian; poetry BU
ALIGHIERI, Pietro, -1364,
Italian; poetry BU
'ALIKI' (Aliki Liacouras Bran-
denberg), 1929- , American;
juveniles DE
'ALIMAYO, CHIKUYO' see FRANK-
LIN, Harold L.
ALIMJAN, Hamid see OLIMJON,
Hamid
ALIOTO, Robert Franklyn, 1933- ,
American; nonfiction CON
ALISHAN, Ghevond, 1820-1901,
Armenian; poetry, nonfiction
PRU
ALISJAHBANA, Sutan Takdir,
1908- , Indonesian; fiction,
nonfiction PRU
ALISON, Sir Archibald, 1792-
1867, Scots; nonfiction BU
ALITTO, Guy Salvatore, 1942- ,
American; nonfiction CON
ALIYU dan SIDI, fl. 1902-20,
Hausa; poetry BU
ALKEMA, Chester Jay, 1932- ,
American; juveniles, nonfic-
tion CO CON
ALKIRE, Leland George, Jr.,
1937- , American; nonfiction
CON
ALLABACK, Steven Lee, 1939- ,
American; nonfiction CON
ALLABY, John Michael, 1933- ,
English; nonfiction CON
ALLAIRE, Joseph Leo, 1929- ,
American; nonfiction CON
ALLAMAND, Pascale, 1942- ,
Swiss; juveniles CO CON
ALLAN, Andrew Edward Fair-
bairn, 1907- , Canadian;
plays CR
'ALLAN, Dennis' see DENNIS-
TON, Elinore
ALLAN, Elkan, 1922- , British;
nonfiction CON
ALLAN, John David, 1945- ,
Canadian-American; nonfiction
CON
ALLAN, Mabel Esther ('Jean Es-
toril'; 'Priscilla Hagon'; 'Anne

Pilgrim'), 1915- , Anglo-
American; juveniles, fiction
CO KI
ALLAN, Ted ('Edward Maxwell'),
1916/18- , Canadian; fiction
plays, film CON NI VCD
ALLAND, GUY, 1944- , American;
nonfiction CON
ALLARD, Dean Conrad, 1933- ,
American; nonfiction CON
ALLARD, Harry, American; juven-
iles WAR
ALLARD, Michel Andrien, 1924-76,
French; nonfiction CON
ALLARDT, Erik, 1925- , Finnish;
nonfiction CON
'ALLARDYCE, Paula' see TORDAY,
Ursula
ALLAUN, Frank Julian, 1913- ,
British; nonfiction CON
ALLBEURY, Ted ('Richard Butler'),
1917- , English; fiction CON
MAC REI
ALLEE, Marjorie Hill, 1890-1945,
American; juveniles CO
ALLEN, Agnes Banister, 1898-
1959, English; juveniles DEM
'ALLEN, Alex B.' see HEIDE,
Florence P.
ALLEN, Alexander Richard, 1929- ,
Canadian; nonfiction CON
ALLEN, Alfred, 1925- , Irish;
poetry HO
'ALLEN, Allyn' see EBERLE, Ir-
mengarde
ALLEN, Anita see SCHENCK, Anita
'ALLEN, Betsy' see CAVANNA,
Betty
ALLEN, Carl, 1961- , American;
juveniles CON
ALLEN, Charles Grant, 1848-99,
British; fiction NI ST
ALLEN, Charlotte Vale, 1941- ,
Canadian; fiction CON
'ALLEN, Clay' see PAINE, Lauran
B.
ALLEN, David Franklyn, 1943- ,
British; nonfiction CON
ALLEN, Donald Emerson, 1917- ,
American; nonfiction CON
ALLEN, Donald R., 1930- , Amer-
ican; nonfiction CON
ALLEN, Durward Leon, 1910- ,
American; nonfiction CON
'ALLEN, E. C.' see WARD, Eliza-
beth C.
ALLEN, Edward David, 1923- ,
American; nonfiction CON

ALLEN, Elisabeth Offutt, 1895- ,
American; poetry, fiction
CON
ALLEN, Francis Robbins, 1908- ,
American; nonfiction CON
ALLEN, Frederick Garfield ('Gary
Allen'), 1936- , American;
nonfiction CON
ALLEN, Garland Edward, 1936- ,
American; nonfiction CON
ALLEN, Gerald, 1942- , Amer-
ican; nonfiction CON
ALLEN, Gertrude Elizabeth,
1888- , American; juveniles,
nonfiction CO CON
'ALLEN, Grace' see HOGARTH,
Grace
ALLEN, Gwenfread Elaine,
1904- , American; nonfic-
tion CON
ALLEN, Harold Joseph, 1925- ,
American; nonfiction CON
ALLEN, Henry Wilson ('Clay
Fisher'; 'Will Henry'),
1912- , American; fiction
CON NI
ALLEN, Herman R., 1913?-79,
American; nonfiction CON
ALLEN, Hervey, 1889-1949,
American; fiction, poetry,
nonfiction BR MAG
ALLEN, Ira R., 1948- , Amer-
ican; nonfiction CON
ALLEN, Irwin, 1916- , Amer-
ican; film NI
ALLEN, Jack, 1899- , English;
juveniles DEM
'ALLEN, James' see ADER, Paul
F.
ALLEN, James Egert, 1896-1980,
American; nonfiction CON
SH
ALLEN, James Lane, 1849-1925,
American; fiction BA BU VN
ALLEN, Jay Presson, 1922- ,
American; plays, fiction,
film CON MCG
'ALLEN, John' see PERRY,
Ritchie J. A.
ALLEN, John Logan, 1941- ,
American; nonfiction CON
ALLEN, Jon Lewis, 1931- ,
Anglo-American; nonfiction
CON
ALLEN, Judson Boyce, 1932- ,
American; nonfiction CON
ALLEN, Kenneth S., 1913- ,
British; nonfiction, juven-

iles CON
ALLEN, Kenneth William, 1941- ,
American; nonfiction CON
ALLEN, L. David, 1940- , Amer-
ican; fiction NI
ALLEN, Lawrence A., 1926- ,
American; nonfiction CON
ALLEN, Leonard, 1915?-81, Amer-
ican; journalism; CON
ALLEN, Leroy, 1912- , American;
juveniles, nonfiction CO CON
ALLEN, Leslie Christopher, 1935- ,
British; nonfiction CON
ALLEN, Leslie H., 1887?-1973,
American; nonfiction CON
ALLEN, Linda, 1925- , British;
juveniles, nonfiction, poetry;
CON
ALLEN, Louis, 1922- , English;
nonfiction CON
'ALLEN, Marcus' see DONICHT,
Mark A.
ALLEN, Marjorie, 1931- , Amer-
ican; juveniles CO CON
'ALLEN, Mark' see DONICHT,
Mark A.
ALLEN, Merrill James, 1918- ,
American; nonfiction CON
ALLEN, Merritt Parmelee, 1892-
1954, American; juveniles CO
ALLEN, Michael Derek, 1939- ,
British; fiction CON
ALLEN, Michael John Bridgman,
1941- , British; nonfiction
CON
ALLEN, Minerva Crantz, 1935- ,
American; poetry CON
ALLEN, Nina Strömgren, 1935- ,
Danish-American; juveniles CO
ALLEN, Paul, 1948- , American;
fiction CON
ALLEN, Phyllis Greig, English;
nonfiction CON
ALLEN, Phyllis Sloan, 1908- ,
Canadian-American; nonfiction
CON
ALLEN, Ralph, 1913-66, Canadian;
journalism, fiction BU CR
ALLEN, Robert, 1946- , British;
poetry CON
ALLEN, Robert Lee, 1942- ,
American; nonfiction CON SH
ALLEN, Robert Sharon, 1900-81,
American; nonfiction CON
ALLEN, Robert Thomas, 1911- ,
Canadian; nonfiction, fiction
CR
ALLEN, Rodney F., 1938- ,

American; nonfiction CON
ALLEN, Rupert Clyde, 1927- ,
American; nonfiction CON
ALLEN, Ruth Finney, 1898-1979,
American; journalism CON
ALLEN, Samuel Washington ('Paul
Vesey'), 1917- , American;
juveniles, nonfiction, transla-
tions, poetry CO CON SH
ALLEN, Sarah Sawyer, 1920- ,
American; fiction CON
ALLEN, Shirley Seifreid, 1921- ,
American; nonfiction CON
ALLEN, Steve, 1921- , Amer-
ican; juveniles WAR
ALLEN, Tony, 1945- , British;
nonfiction, plays CON
ALLEN, Walter Ernest, 1911- ,
English; fiction, nonfiction
BOR CON DA SEY VCN WA
ALLEN, William, 1940- , Amer-
ican; nonfiction, fiction CON
ALLEN, William Sidney, 1918- ,
English; nonfiction CON
ALLEN, William Stannard,
1913- , British; nonfiction
CON
'ALLERTON, Mary' see GOVAN,
Christine N.
ALLEY, Rewi, 1897- , New
Zealander; poetry, nonfiction,
translations CON VCP
'ALLEYN, Ellen' see ROSSETTI,
Christina
ALLIGHAM, Garry, 1898- ,
South African; fiction NI
ALLILUYEVA, Svetlana, 1926- ,
Russian; nonfiction CON
ALLINGHAM, Margery, 1904-66,
British; fiction, plays MCC
NI REI ST
ALLINGHAM, Michael, 1943- ,
British; nonfiction CON
ALLINGHAM, William, 1824-89,
Irish; poetry, plays, juveniles
BU DA HO PO VP
ALLINSMITH, Wesley, 1923- ,
American; nonfiction CON
ALLINSON, Beverley, 1936- ,
Canadian; juveniles CON
ALLINSON, Gary Dean, 1942- ,
American; nonfiction CON
ALLISON, Bob, American; juven-
iles CO
ALLISON, Graham Tillett, Jr.,
1940- , American; nonfiction
CON
ALLISON, Harrison Clarke,

1917- , American; nonfiction
CON
ALLISON, John Murray, 1889- ,
American; nonfiction CON
ALLISON, Michael Frederick,
1936- , English; nonfiction
CON
ALLISON, Ralph Brewster, 1931- ,
American; nonfiction CON
ALLISON, Richard Bruce, 1949- ,
American; nonfiction CON
ALLISON, Rosemary, 1953- ,
American; juveniles CON
ALLMAN, John, 1935- , American;
poetry, nonfiction CON
ALLMAN, T. D., 1944- , Amer-
ican; nonfiction CON
ALLMENDINGER, David Fredericks,
Jr., 1938- , American; non-
fiction; CON
ALLON, Yigal, 1918-80, Israeli;
nonfiction CON
ALLOTT, Kenneth, 1912-73, Brit-
ish; poetry, plays, fiction, non-
fiction CON
ALLOTT, Robert, fl. 1600, English;
poetry BU
ALLOWAY, Lawrence, 1926- ,
Anglo-American; nonfiction
CON
ALLRED, Dorald Mervin, 1923- ,
American; nonfiction CON
ALLRED, G. Hugh, 1932- , Ca-
nadian-American; nonfiction
CON
ALLRED, Gordon T., 1930- ,
American; juveniles CO
ALLSEN, Philip Edmond, 1932- ,
American; nonfiction CON
ALLSOP, Kenneth, 1920-73, English;
fiction, nonfiction, journalism
CO WA
ALLSTON, Washington, 1779-1843,
American; poetry, fiction BA
BR BU MY
ALLSWANG, John Myers, 1937- ,
American; nonfiction CON
ALLVINE, Fred C., 1936- ,
American; nonfiction CON
ALLVINE, Glendon, 1893?-1977,
American; nonfiction CON
ALLWORTH, Edward Alfred, 1920- ,
American; nonfiction CON
'ALLYSON, Kym' see KIMBRO,
John M.
ALMADA-NEGREIROS, José de,
1893-1970, Portuguese; poetry,
fiction, plays, nonfiction CL

'ALMAFUERTE' (Pedro Bonifacio
Palacios), 1854-1917, Argen-
tinian; poetry BR
ALMAGUER, Tomas, 1948- ,
American; nonfiction MAR
ALMARAZ, Felix D., Jr.,
1933- , American; nonfic-
tion MAR
ALMAZ, Michael, 1921- , Is-
raeli; plays CON
ALMEDINGEN, E. M. (Martha
Edith), 1898-1971, Russian-
English; juveniles, fiction,
poetry, nonfiction CO DE
KI WA WAR
ALMEIDA, Guilherme de, 1890- ,
Brazilian; poetry BR
ALMEIDA, José Américo de,
1887- , Brazilian; fiction
BR BU
ALMEIDA, José Valentim Fialho
de, 1857-1911, Portuguese;
fiction BU
ALMEIDA, Manuel Antonio de,
1831-61, Brazilian; fiction
BR BU
ALMEIDA, Nicolau Tolentino de,
1740-1811, Portuguese; po-
etry BU
ALMOND, Gabriel Abraham,
1911- , American; nonfic-
tion CON
ALMOND, Paul, 1931- , Cana-
dian; film CON
ALMOND, Richard, 1938- ,
American; nonfiction CON
'ALMONTE, Rosa' see PAINE,
Lauran B.
ALMQUIST, Don, 1929- , Amer-
ican; juveniles CO
ALMQVIST, Carl Jonas Love,
1793-1866, Swedish; fiction,
poetry, plays BU TH
ALMY, Millie, 1915- , Amer-
ican; nonfiction CON
ALOMAR, Gabriel, 1873-1941,
Catalan; poetry BU CL
'ALONE' see DIAZ ARRIETA,
Hernán
ALONSO, Dámaso, 1898- ,
Spanish; poetry, nonfiction
BU CL TH
ALONSO, Juan Manuel, 1936- ,
Argentinian-American; fiction,
nonfiction CON
ALONSO, Manuel A., 1822-89,
Puerto Rican; journalism
HIL

ALORNA, Leonor de Almeida, 1750-
1839, Portuguese; poetry BU
ALOTTO, Robert Ignatius, 1937- ,
American; nonfiction CON
ALPER, Benedict Solomon, 1905- ,
American; nonfiction CON
ALPER, Gerald A., American;
fiction NI
ALPER, Max Victor, 1944- ,
American; nonfiction CON
ALPERN, Andrew, 1938- , Amer-
ican; nonfiction CON
ALPERN, David Mark, 1942- ,
American; journalism CON
ALPERN, Gerald David, 1932- ,
American; nonfiction CON
ALPEROVITZ, Gar, 1936- ,
American; nonfiction CON
ALPERS, Paul Joel, 1932- ,
American; nonfiction CON
ALPERT, Mark Ira, 1942- ,
American; nonfiction CON
ALPERT, Paul, 1907- , Russian-
American; nonfiction CON
ALPERT, Richard ('Ram Dass'),
1931- , American; nonfiction,
fiction CON
ALPHANUS of SALERNO, -1085,
Italian; poetry BU
ALPHEN, Hieronymus van, 1746-
1803, Dutch; poetry BU
'ALPLAUS, N. Y.' see RUBIN,
Cynthia E.
ALROY, Gil Carl, 1924- , Ruman-
ian-American; nonfiction CON
ALSCHULER, Rose Haas, 1887-
1979, American; juveniles CON
ALSOP, George, 1636?-73?, Amer-
ican; nonfiction BA
ALSOP, Guleilma Fell, 1881-1978,
American; nonfiction CON
ALSOP, Joseph Wright, Jr.,
1910- , American; journalism,
nonfiction WA
ALSOP, Mary (O'Hara), 1885-1980,
American; juveniles CO CON
KI
ALSOP, Stewart, 1914-74, Amer-
ican; journalism, nonfiction
CON
'ALSTERLUND, Betty' see PILKING-
TON, Betty
'ALSTERN, Fred,' see STERN, Al-
fred
ALSWANG, Betty, 1920?-78, Amer-
ican; nonfiction CON
ALT, Arthur Tilo, 1931- , Amer-
ican; nonfiction CON

ALT, David, 1933- , American;
nonfiction CON
ALTA, 1942- , American; po-
etry, nonfiction CON
ALTABE, Joan B., 1935- ,
American; nonfiction CON
ALTAMIRANO, Ignacio Manuel,
1834-93, Mexican; fiction
BR BU MAG
ALTAMIRA y CREVEA, Rafael,
1866-1951, Spanish; nonfic-
tion BU
ALTBACH, Edith Hoskino, 1941- ,
American; nonfiction CON
ALTENBERND, August Lynn,
1918- , American; nonfic-
tion CON
ALTER, Moshe J. see 'ROSEN-
FELD, Morris'
ALTER, Jean Victor, 1925- ,
Polish-American; nonfiction
CON
ALTER, Judith MacBain, 1938- ,
American; fiction, juveniles
CON
ALTER, Robert Bernard, 1935- ,
American; nonfiction CON
ALTER, Robert Edmond ('Robert
Raymond'; 'Robert Retla'),
1925-65, American; juveniles
CO
ALTERMAN, Nathan, 1910-70,
Israeli; poetry BU WA
ALTH, Max Octavious ('Harry C.
Collins'), 1927- , American;
fiction, nonfiction CON
ALTHAUSER, Robert Pierce,
1939- , American; nonfiction
CON
'ALTHEA' see BRAITHWAITE,
Althea
ALTHER, Lisa, 1944- , Amer-
ican; nonfiction, fiction CON
ALTHOUSE, Lawrence Wilson,
1930- , American; nonfiction
CON
ALTHUSSER, Louis, 1918- ,
French; nonfiction CL
ALTMAN, Edward Ira, 1941- ,
American; nonfiction CON
ALTMAN, Frances, 1937- ,
American; juveniles CON
ALTMAN, Irwin ('Larry Altman'),
1928/30- , American; fiction,
nonfiction CON
ALTMAN, Nathaniel, 1948- ,
American; nonfiction CON
ALTMAN, Richard Charles,

1932- , American; nonfiction
CON
ALTMAN, Robert, 1925- , Amer-
ican; film CON
'ALTMAN, Thomas' see BLACK,
Campbell
ALTMANN, Alexander, 1906- ,
Hungarian-British; nonfiction
CON
ALTMANN, Berthold, 1902?-77,
German-American; nonfiction
CON
ALTOLAGUIRRE, Manuel, 1905-59,
Spanish; poetry BU CL TH
ALTOMA, Salih Jawad, 1929- ,
Iraqi; poetry, nonfiction CON
ALTSHELER, Joseph Alexander,
1862-1919, American; juveniles
COM
ALUKO, Timothy Mofolorunso,
1918/20- , Nigerian; fiction
BU CON HER JA LA VCN
'ALUN' (John Blackwell), 1797-
1840, Welsh; poetry BU
'ALURISTA' (Alberto Baltazar
Urista), 1947- , American;
nonfiction, poetry CON MAR
ALVAR, fl. 600-900?, Tamil; po-
etry LA
ALVARENGA, Manuel Inácio da
Silva, 1749-1814, Brazilian;
poetry BR
ALVARENGA PEIXOTO, Ignácio
José de, 1744-93, Brazilian;
poetry BR
ALVARES de AZEVEDO, Manuel
Antónes, 1831-52, Brazilian;
poetry BR
ALVARES de ORIENTE, Fernão,
1540-95, Portuguese; fiction,
poetry BU
ALVAREZ, Alejandro Rodriquez
see 'CASONA, Alejandro'
ALVAREZ, Alfred, 1929- , Brit-
ish; nonfiction, poetry, fiction,
play BOR VCP WA
ALVAREZ, Eugene, 1932- , Amer-
ican; nonfiction CON
ALVAREZ, Francisco, 1847-81,
Puerto Rican; poetry HIL
ALVAREZ, Hector A. see 'MURENA,
H. A.'
'ALVAREZ, John' see del RAY,
Lester
ALVAREZ, José Sixto ('Fray
Mochó'), 1858-1903, Argentin-
ian; nonfiction BU
ALVAREZ, Joseph A., 1930- ,

ALVAREZ 24

American; juveniles CO
ALVAREZ, Rodolfo, 1936- ,
American; nonfiction MAR
ALVAREZ, Salvador, 1924- ,
American; nonfiction MAR
ALVAREZ, Walter Clement, 1884-
1974, American; nonfiction
CON
ALVAREZ de CIENFUEGOS,
Nicasio, 1764-1809, Spanish;
poetry, plays BU
ALVAREZ de TOLEDO PELEICER
y TOVAR, Gabriel, 1662-1714,
Spanish; poetry, plays BU TH
ALVAREZ del VAYO, Julio, 1891-
1975, Spanish; nonfiction,
journalism CON
ALVAREZ GATO, Juan, 1440/50-
1510, Spanish; poetry BU
ALVAREZ NAZARIO, Manuel,
Puerto Rican; nonfiction
HIL
ALVAREZ QUINTERO, Joaquin,
1873-1944, Spanish; plays
BU CL MCG TH
ALVAREZ QUINTERO, Serafín,
1871-1938, Spanish; plays
BU CL MCG TH
ALVARO, Corrado, 1895-1956,
Italian; fiction, plays, journal-
ism BO BU CL TH WA
ALVERSON, Donna, 1933- ,
American; fiction CON
ALVES, Marcio Moreira, 1936- ,
Brazilian; fiction CON
ALVEY, Edward, Jr., 1902- ,
American; nonfiction CON
ALVIN, Juliette, British; nonfic-
tion CON
ALVIREZ, David, 1936- , Amer-
ican; nonfiction MAR
'ALYN, Marc', 1937- , French;
journalism, poetry, nonfiction
CON
ALZAGA, Florinda, 1930- ,
Cuban-American; nonfiction
CON
'ALZEY, Konrad von' see NIES,
Konrad
AMADI, Elechi, 1934- , Niger-
ian; fiction BU HER JA
AMADO, Jorge, 1912- , Brazil-
ian; fiction BR BU CON MAG
WA
AMADON, Dean, 1912- , Amer-
ican; nonfiction CON
'AMADOR, Americo, see ELZA-
BURU, Manuel

'AMADOU' see MADDY, Pat
AMALI, Samson O. O., 1947- ,
Nigerian; fiction, poetry, plays
JA
AMALRIK, Andrey Alekseyevich,
1938-80, Russian; plays, jour-
nalism CL CON
AMAN, Mohammed M., 1940- ,
Egyptian-American; nonfiction
CON SH
AMANAT, Sayyid Agha Hasan,
1816-59, Urdu; poetry, plays
PRU
AMANN, Peter H., 1927- , Austri-
an; nonfiction CON
AMANN, Victor Francis, 1927- ,
American; nonfiction CON
AMANUDDIN, Syed, 1934- ,
Indian-American; nonfiction,
poetry CON
AMAR, Andrew Richard, 1934- ,
Ugandan; nonfiction JA
AMARCIUS, fl. 1040, German?;
poetry BU
'AMARE, Rothayne' see BYRNE,
Stuart J.
AMARU, pre-9th century, Sanskrit;
poetry PRU
AMARY, Issam Bahjat, 1942- ,
Israeli; nonfiction CON
AMATO, Joseph Anthony, 1938- ,
American; nonfiction CON
AMAYA, Mario Anthony, 1933- ,
American; nonfiction CON
AMBASZ, Emilio, 1943- , Ar-
gentinian-American; nonfiction
CON
AMBERG, Martin Hans, 1912- ,
German-American; journalism
CON
AMBERG, Richard Hiller, Jr.,
1942- , American; journalism
CON
AMBHANWONG, Suthilak ('Suthinee'),
1924- , Thai; nonfiction CON
AMBLER, Effie, 1936- , Amer-
ican; nonfiction CON
AMBLER, Eric ('Eliot Reed'),
1909- , English; fiction,
film, plays MCC REI ST VCN
AMBLER, John Steward, 1932- ,
American; nonfiction CON
AMBROGINI, Angelo see POLIZ-
IANO, Angelo
AMBROISE, fl. 1200, French;
poetry BU
AMBROSE, Alice, 1906- , Amer-
ican; nonfiction CON

AMBROSE, John William, Jr.,
1931-   , American; nonfic-
tion CON
AMBROSE, St. (Aurelius Ambro-
sius), 339?-97, Latin; non-
fiction BU GR LA
AMBROSI, Hans Georg, 1925-   ,
Rumanian; nonfiction CON
AMBROZ, Oton, 1905-   , Amer-
ican; journalism, nonfiction
CON
AMBRUS, Victor G., 1935-   ,
Hungarian-British; juveniles
DE
AMBRUS, Zoltán, 1861-1932,
Hungarian; fiction TH
AMEIPSIAS, fl. 424-04 B.C.,
Greek; plays, poetry BU
AMENEMOPE, 11th century
B.C., Egyptian; nonfiction
PRU
AMENHOTEP see AHKNATON
AMENT, Pat, 1946-   , Amer-
ican; nonfiction CON
'AMERICANO, Leon' see DIEGO,
José de
AMERINE, Maynard Andrew,
1911-   , American; nonfic-
tion CON
AMERINGER, Charles D., 1926-   ,
American; nonfiction CON
AMERMAN, Lockhart, 1911-69,
American; journalism, po-
etry CO
AMERY, Harold Julian, 1919-   ,
English; nonfiction CON
AMES, Evelyn, 1908-   , Amer-
ican; fiction, poetry, juven-
iles CO CON
AMES, Gerald, 1906-   , Amer-
ican; juveniles CO CON DE
WAR
'AMES, Jennifer' see GREIG,
Maysie
AMES, Lee Judah ('Jonathan Da-
vid'), 1921-   , American; ju-
veniles CO
'AMES, Leslie' see ROSS, William
E. D.
AMES, Lois Winslow, 1931-   ,
American; nonfiction CON
AMES, Mildred, 1919-   , Amer-
ican; juveniles, fiction CO
CON
AMES, Polly Scribner, 1908-   ,
American; nonfiction CON
AMES, Rachel see 'GAINHAM,
Sarah'

AMES, Rose (Wyler; 'Peter Thay-
er'), 1909-   , American; ju-
veniles CO CON DE
AMEY, Lloyd Ronald, 1922-   ,
Australian-Canadian; nonfiction
CON
AMFITEATROV, Alexander Valin-
tinovich, 1862-1923, Russian;
fiction BU
AMFITHEATROF, Erik, 1931-   ,
Italian; nonfiction CON
'AMI, Ben' see ELIAV, Arie L.
AMICHAI, Yehuda, 1924-   , Hebrew;
poetry, fiction, plays CON
WAK
AMICIS, Edmondo de, 1846-1908,
Italian; fiction, nonfiction
MAG
'AMICUS CURIAE' see FULLER,
Edmund M.
AMIDON, Bill Vincent ('Jesse Tay-
lor'), 1933-79, American; non-
fiction, plays, fiction CON
AMIEL, Barbara, 1940-   , British;
journalism, nonfiction CON
'AMIEL, Denys' (Guillaume Roche),
1884-   , French; plays CL
MCG TH
AMIEL, Henri Frédéric, 1821-81,
Swiss; nonfiction, poetry BU
TH
AMIEL, Joseph, 1937-   , American;
fiction CON
AMIHAI, Jehuda, 1924-   , Israeli;
poetry, fiction BU
AMIN, Ali, 1913?-76, Egyptian;
journalism CON
AMIN, Samir, 1931-   , American;
nonfiction CON
'AMINI, Johari M.' see KUNJUFU,
Johari M.
AMIR, Aharon, 1923-   , Israeli;
poetry BU
AMIR, Menachem, 1930-   , Is-
raeli; nonfiction CON
AMIR HAMZAH, 1911-46, Indo-
nesian; poetry LA
AMIR KHOSROE, 1253-1325, Per-
sian; poetry PRU
AMIR MAHMUD see 'EBNE YAMIN'
AMIR MINA'I, Munshi Ahmad,
1828?-1900, Urdu; poetry PRU
AMIRI, Merza Sadeq Khan, 1860/61-
1917, Persian; poetry, journalism PRU
AMIS, Kingsley ('Robert Markham'),
1922-   , English; fiction, poetry, nonfiction AS BU DA

MAG MCC NI PO REI SEY
VCN VCP VN WA
AMIS, Lola Elizabeth Jones,
1930- , American; plays
SH
AMIS, Martin, 1949- , English;
fiction CON
AMISHAI-MAISELS, Ziva see
MAISELS, Maxine S.
AMMAN DIHLAVI, Mir, 1745?-
1806, Urdu; fiction PRU
AMMAR, Abbas, 1907?-74, Egyp-
tian; nonfiction CON
AMMERMAN, David Leon, 1938- ,
American; nonfiction CON
AMMERS-KÜLLER, Johanna van,
1884- , Dutch; fiction MAG
AMMIANUS MARCELLINUS,
325/30-95?, Greek; nonfiction
BU GR LA
AMMIRATO, Scipione, 1531-1601,
Italian; nonfiction, poetry
BO BU
AMMON, Harry, 1917- , Amer-
ican; nonfiction CON
AMMONS, Archie Randolph,
1926- , American; poetry
BA MAL VCP VP WA
AMO, Anton Wilhelm (Antonius
Guilielmus), 1703-57?, Ghan-
aian; nonfiction HER JA
AMOAKU, J. K. , 1936- , Ghan-
aian; juveniles CON
AMOERS, Jan, early 15th century,
Dutch; poetry BU
AMON, Aline, 1928- , French-
American; juveniles, nonfiction
CO CON WAR
AMON d'ABY, François Joseph,
1913- , Ivory Coast; plays,
nonfiction JA
AMORIE van der HOEVEN, Abra-
ham des, Sr. , 1798-1855,
Dutch; poetry BU
AMORIE van der HOEVEN, Arab-
ham des, Jr. , 1821-48, Dutch;
poetry BU
AMORIM, Enrique, 1900-60, Uru-
guayan; fiction BR BU
AMOROS, Juan Bautista ('Silverio
Lanza'), 1856-1912, Spanish;
fiction BU
AMORY, Cleveland, 1917- , Amer-
ican; nonfiction CON
AMOS, Winsom, 1921- , American;
poetry CON
AMOSOV, Nikolai Mikailovitch,
1913- , Russian; fiction NI

AMOSS, Berthe, 1925- , American;
juveniles CO
AMPZING, Samuel, 1590-1632,
Dutch; poetry BU
AMRINE, Michael, 1919?-74, Amer-
ican; nonfiction CON
AMSTER, Linda, 1938- , American;
nonfiction CON
AMUZEGAR, Jahangir, 1920- ,
Iranian; nonfiction CON
AMY, Francisco J. , 1837-1912,
Puerto Rican; poetry, journal-
ism, translations HIL
AMYOT, Jacques, 1513-93, French;
translations BU TH
ANACREON, 570?-485 B.C. , Greek;
poetry BU GR LA
ANAHORY, Terêncio, 1934- , Cape
Verde Islander; poetry HER
JA
ANAND, Mulk Raj, 1905- , Indian;
fiction, nonfiction, juveniles
BU CON DA PRU VCN VN WA
ANAND, Valerie ('Fiona Buckley'),
1937- , British; fiction, non-
fiction CON
ANANIA, Michael, 1939- , Amer-
ican; poetry VCP
ANANOU, David, 1917- , Togolese;
fiction HER JA
ANANTA THURIYA, 1112?-73, Bur-
mese; poetry PRU
ANASTAS, Peter, 1937- , Amer-
ican; translation, nonfiction
CON
ANASTASIOU, Clifford John; 1929- ,
Canadian; nonfiction CON
ANASTASIUS of SINAI, fl. 640-700,
Byzantine; nonfiction BU
'ANATOLI, A.' see KUZNETSOV,
Anatoly V.
ANAU, Benjamin (Anavi; degli Man-
si), 13th century, Italian; po-
etry BU
ANAXAGORAS, 500-428 B.C.,
Greek; nonfiction BU GR LA
ANAXANDRIDES, 380-340 B.C.,
Greek; plays BU
ANAXIMANDER, 610-546 B.C.,
Greek; nonfiction BU GR LA
ANAXIMENES, -528/25 B.C.,
Greek; nonfiction BU GR LA
ANAYA, Rudolfo Alfonso, 1937- ,
American; fiction CON MAR
ANCEL, Marc, 1902- , French;
nonfiction CON
ANCHIETA, Padre José de, 1534-97,
Spanish; poetry, nonfiction BR

27

ANCHOR, Robert, 1937- , American; nonfiction CON
ANCKARSVARD, Karin Inez, 1915-69, Swedish; juveniles, fiction CO CON DE
ANCONA, George, 1929- , American; juveniles, nonfiction CO CON WAR
ANDAY, Mehih Cevdet, 1915- , Turkish; poetry, journalism, fiction CL PRU
ANDELIN, Helen B., 1920- , American; nonfiction CON
ANDELMAN, Eddie, 1936- , American; nonfiction CON
ANDERSCH, Alfred, 1914-80, German; fiction, nonfiction BU CL CON TH
ANDERSEN, Barbara, 1948- , American; nonfiction CON
ANDERSEN, Benny, 1929- , Danish; poetry, fiction, nonfiction CL CON
ANDERSEN, Christopher Peter, 1949- , American; journalism, nonfiction CON
ANDERSEN, Doris, 1909- , Canadian; juveniles KI
ANDERSEN, Hans Christian ('Villiam Christian Walter'), 1805-75, Danish; juveniles, plays, fiction, poetry, nonfiction BU COM MAG TH
ANDERSEN, Jefferson, 1955?-79, American; nonfiction CON
ANDERSEN, Marianne Singer, 1934- , Austrian-American; nonfiction CON
ANDERSEN, Richard, 1931- , American; nonfiction CON
ANDERSEN, Richard, 1946- , American; nonfiction, fiction CON
'ANDERSEN, Ted' see BOYD, Waldo T.
ANDERSEN, Tryggve, 1866-1920, Norwegian; fiction CL
ANDERSEN, Yvonne, 1932- , American; juveniles WAR
ANDERSON, Alan H., Jr., 1943- , American; nonfiction CON
ANDERSON, Alan Ross, 1925-73, American; nonfiction CON
ANDERSON, Allan, 1915- , Canadian; nonfiction CON
ANDERSON, Arthur James Outram, 1907- , American; translation, nonfiction CON

ANDERSON, Bernard Eric, 1936- , American; nonfiction CON
ANDERSON, Bernhard Word, 1916- , American; nonfiction CON
ANDERSON, Bernice Goudy, 1894- , American; juveniles CON
ANDERSON, Bob, 1947- , American; nonfiction CON
ANDERSON, C. W., 1891-1971, American; juveniles DE
ANDERSON, Carl Lennart, 1919- , American; nonfiction, translations CON
ANDERSON, Carolyn, 1941- , American; nonfiction CON
ANDERSON, Charles Burroughs, 1905- , American; nonfiction CON
ANDERSON, Charlotte Maria, 1923- , Austrian-American; nonfiction CON
ANDERSON, Chester, 1923- , American; fiction, poetry NI
ANDERSON, Chuck, 1933- , American; nonfiction CON
ANDERSON, Clarence William, 1891-1971, American; juveniles, nonfiction CO CON
'ANDERSON, Clifford' see GARDNER, Richard
ANDERSON, Colin, English; fiction NI
ANDERSON, David Poole, 1929- , American; journalism, juveniles, nonfiction CON
ANDERSON, Dillon, 1906-73, American; nonfiction CON
ANDERSON, Donald Francis, 1938- , Canadian-American; nonfiction CON
ANDERSON, Doris Hilda, 1925- , Canadian; journalism, fiction CON
ANDERSON, E. Ruth, 1907- , American; nonfiction CON
ANDERSON, Edwin Hartfield, 1861-1947, American; nonfiction ENG
ANDERSON, Elbridge Gerry, 1907- , American; poetry, plays CON
'ANDERSON, Ella' see MacLEOD, Ellen J. A.
ANDERSON, Elliott, 1944- , American; translations, nonfiction CON
ANDERSON, Eloise Adell, 1927- , American; fiction, poetry, juveniles CO CON

ANDERSON, Erica, 1914- ,
Austrian-American; nonfic-
tion CON
ANDERSON, Frederick Irving,
1877-1947, American; fiction,
journalism REI ST
ANDERSON, Freeman Burket,
1922- , American; nonfiction
CON
ANDERSON, George Christian,
1907-76, American; nonfic-
tion CON
ANDERSON, Godfrey Tryggve,
1909- , American; nonfiction
CON
ANDERSON, Helen Jean, 1930- ,
American; juveniles WAR
ANDERSON, Hobson Dewey, 1897-
1975, American; nonfiction
CON
ANDERSON, Howard Peter, 1932- ,
American; nonfiction CON
ANDERSON, Ian Gibson, 1933- ,
Scots; nonfiction CON
ANDERSON, Irvine Henry, 1928- ,
American; nonfiction CON
ANDERSON, Jackson Northman,
1922- , American; nonfiction
CON
ANDERSON, James, British; fic-
tion REI
ANDERSON, James Desmond,
1933- , American; nonfiction
CON
ANDERSON, James Francis, 1910- ,
American; nonfiction, transla-
tions CON
ANDERSON, Jean, 1930- , Amer-
ican; nonfiction CON
ANDERSON, Jeanne, 1934?-79,
American; nonfiction CON
ANDERSON, Jennifer, 1942- ,
Australian; nonfiction CON
ANDERSON, Jerry Maynard,
1933- , American; nonfic-
tion CON
ANDERSON, Joan Wester, 1938- ,
American; nonfiction CON
ANDERSON, John Freeman, 1945- ,
American; nonfiction CON
ANDERSON, John Kerby, 1951- ,
American; nonfiction CON
ANDERSON, John Lonzo, 1905- ,
American; juveniles DE WAR
ANDERSON, John Richard Lane,
1911-81, British; juveniles
CO
ANDERSON, Kenneth Norman,

1921- , American; nonfiction
CON
ANDERSON, LaVere Francis Sho-
enfelt, 1907- , American; ju-
veniles CON
ANDERSON, Lee Stratton, 1925- ,
American; journalism CON
ANDERSON, Lester William, 1918-
73, American; nonfiction CON
ANDERSON, Lucia (Lewis), 1922- ,
American; juveniles, nonfiction
CO CON
ANDERSON, Luther Adolph, Amer-
ican; nonfiction CON
ANDERSON, Madelyn Klein, Amer-
ican; nonfiction CON
ANDERSON, Maggie, 1948- , Amer-
ican; poetry CON
ANDERSON, Margaret, 1891-1973,
American; journalism CON
ANDERSON, Margaret Jean, 1931- ,
Scots-American; juveniles CON
ANDERSON, Marvin Walter, 1933- ,
American; nonfiction CON
ANDERSON, Mary Quirk, 1939- ,
American; juveniles CO CON
WAR
ANDERSON, Maxwell, 1888-1959,
American; plays BR BU MAG
MCG MCN PO VD
ANDERSON, Mona, 1910- , Amer-
ican; nonfiction CON
ANDERSON, Norman Dean, 1928- ,
American; juveniles CO
ANDERSON, Odie, 1943- , Amer-
ican; fiction SH
ANDERSON, Olive Mary, 1915- ,
American; nonfiction CON
ANDERSON, Olof W., American;
fiction NI
ANDERSON, Patrick John, 1915-
79, British; poetry, nonfiction
CON VCP
ANDERSON, Paul Howard, 1947- ,
English; nonfiction CON
ANDERSON, Peggy, 1938- , Amer-
ican; nonfiction CON
ANDERSON, Poul William ('Wins-
ton P. Sanders'), 1926- ,
American; fiction, juveniles
AS COW NI WA WAR
ANDERSON, Quentin, 1912- ,
American; nonfiction BOR
ANDERSON, R. C., 1883?-1976,
British; nonfiction CON
ANDERSON, Randall C., 1934- ,
American; nonfiction CON
ANDERSON, Ray Sherman,

1925- , American; nonfiction
CON
ANDERSON, Robert, 1917- ,
American; plays BR MCG
MCN VCD WA
ANDERSON, Robert Charles
('Charles Cottle'), 1930- ,
American; journalism, non-
fiction CON
ANDERSON, Robert David,
1942- , Welsh; nonfiction
CON
ANDERSON, Robert Henry, 1918- ,
American; nonfiction CON
ANDERSON, Robert Newton,
1929- , Canadian; nonfic-
tion CON
ANDERSON, Ruth Nathan, 1934- ,
American; nonfiction, jour-
nalism CON
ANDERSON, Sherwood, 1876-
1941, American; fiction, po-
etry, plays, nonfiction AM
BR BU MAG PO SEY VN
ANDERSON, Shirley (Lord),
1934- , English; nonfiction
CON
'ANDERSON, Sonia' see DANIEL,
William R.
ANDERSON, Teresa ('Teresa M.
McCarthy'), 1944- , Amer-
ican; nonfiction, poetry, plays
CON
ANDERSON, Theodore Robert,
1927- , American; nonfiction
CON
ANDERSON, Theodore Wilbur, Jr.,
1918- , American; nonfiction
CON
ANDERSON, Tom, 1910- , Amer-
ican; journalism CON
ANDERSON, Tommy Nolan,
1918- , American; nonfiction
CON
ANDERSON, Walter, 1944- ,
American; journalism CON
ANDERSON, Wayne Jeremy,
1908- , American; nonfiction
CON
ANDERSON, William A., 1927- ,
American; nonfiction SH
ANDERSON, William Charles,
1920- , American; fiction
NI
ANDERSON, William Harry, 1905-
72, American; nonfiction CON
ANDERSON, William Scovil, 1927- ,
American; nonfiction CON

ANDERSON SCARVIA, Bateman,
1926- , American; nonfiction
CON
ANDERSSON, Dan, 1888-1920,
Swedish; poetry, fiction BU
CL TH
ANDERSSON, Ingvar, 1899?-1974,
Swedish; nonfiction CON
ANDERSSON, Theodore, 1903- ,
American; nonfiction CON
ANDERTON, David Albin, 1919- ,
American; nonfiction CON
ANDERTON, Joanne Marie Gast,
1930- , American; nonfiction
CON
ANDERVONT, Howard Bancroft,
1898-1981, American; nonfic-
tion CON
ANDINO AMEZQUITA, José, 1751-
1835, Puerto Rican; journalism
HIL
'ANDO JISHO' (Ando Hachizaemon),
1658-1745, Japanese; fiction
BU
ANDOCIDES, 440-390 B.C., Greek;
nonfiction BU LA
ANDONIAN, Jeanne (Beghian; 'Jan-
ine May'), 1891?-1976, Amer-
ican; fiction, nonfiction CON
ANDRADA, Andrés Fernández de,
early 17th century, Spanish;
poetry TH
ANDRADE, Costa ('Fernando Costa
Andrade'; 'Flávio Silvestre'),
1936- , Angolan; poetry, fic-
tion HER JA
ANDRADE, Eugenio de, 1923- ,
Portuguese; poetry, translations
CL
ANDRADE, Joaquim de S. see
'SOUSÂNDRADE'
ANDRADE, José Oswald de Sousa,
1890-1954, Brazilian; poetry,
fiction, plays BU WAK
ANDRADE, Mario Pinto de, 1928- ,
Angolan; poetry, nonfiction JA
LA
ANDRADE, Mário Raul de Morais,
1893-1945, Brazilian; poetry,
fiction BR BU
ANDRADE, Olegario Victor, 1841-
82, Argentinian; poetry, jour-
nalism BR BU
ANDRADE, Oswald de, 1890-1954,
Brazilian; poetry, fiction BR
ANDRADE, Victory Manuel, 1905- ,
Bolivian; nonfiction CON
ANDRADE e SILVA, José Bonifacio

de, 1765-1838, Brazilian; po-
etry BU
ANDRAIN, Charles Franklin,
1937- , American; nonfiction
CON
ANDRE, Evelyn Marie, 1924- ,
American; juveniles, nonfic-
tion CON
ANDREA, Monte, fl. 1260-80,
Florentine; poetry BU
ANDREAE, Johann Valentin,
1586-1654, German; poetry
BU
ANDREAS, Burton Gould, 1921- ,
American; nonfiction CON
'ANDREAS, Thomas' see WIL-
LIAMS, Thomas A.
ANDREAS CAPELLANUS, f.
1175-80, French; poetry, non-
fiction BU TH
ANDREASEN, Alan Robert, 1934- ,
Canadian-American; nonfiction
CON
ANDREAS-SALOME, Lou, 1861-
1937, German; fiction, non-
fiction CL
ANDREE, Richard Vernon, 1919- ,
American; nonfiction CON
ANDREINI, Giovan Battista, 1576-
1654, Italian; plays BO
ANDRELINI, Publio Fausto, 1462-
1518, Italian; poetry BU
ANDREOPOULOS, Spyros George,
1929- , Greek-American;
nonfiction CON
ANDRES, Glenn Merle, 1941- ,
American; nonfiction CON
ANDRES, Juan, 1740-1817, Span-
ish; nonfiction BU
ANDRES, Stefan, 1906-70, Ger-
man; fiction, poetry, plays,
BU TH WA
ANDRESEN, Heinrich, 1875-1958,
German; poetry BU
ANDRESEN, Ingeborg, 1878-1955,
German; plays BU
ANDRESEN, John Henry, Jr.,
1917- , American; nonfiction
CON
ANDRESEN, Sophia de Melho Brey-
ner, 1919- , Portuguese; po-
etry, fiction, juveniles CL
'ANDRESKI, Iris' see GILLESPIE,
Iris S.
ANDRESKI, Stanislav Leonard,
1919- , Polish-American; non-
fiction CON
ANDREU IGLESIAS, Cesar, 1915- ,

Puerto Rican; journalism,
fiction HIL
ANDREVON, Jean Pierre, 1937- ,
French; fiction NI
ANDREW, James Dudley, 1945- ,
American; nonfiction CON
ANDREW, John Alfred, III, 1943- ,
American; nonfiction CON
ANDREW, Prudence Hastings,
1924- , British; juveniles,
fiction KI
ANDREW of CAESAREA, 6th cen-
tury, Byzantine; nonfiction BU
ANDREW of CRETE, 660-740?,
Byzantine; poetry BU
ANDREWES, Lancelot, 1555-1626,
English; nonfiction BU DA PO
RU
'ANDREWS, A. A.' see PAINE,
Lauran B.
ANDREWS, Allen, 1913- , English;
nonfiction CON
ANDREWS, Arthur Douglas, Jr.
('Ana Ort'), 1923- , American;
poetry, nonfiction CON
ANDREWS, Barry Geoffrey, 1943- ,
Australian; nonfiction CON
ANDREWS, Bart, 1945- , Amer-
ican; nonfiction CON
ANDREWS, Bruce, 1948- , Amer-
ican; nonfiction, poetry, fiction
CON
ANDREWS, Clement Walker, 1858-
1930, American; nonfiction
ENG
ANDREWS, Daniel Marshall, 1899?-
1973, American; nonfiction,
journalism CON
ANDREWS, Dorothea Harris, 1916-
76, American; journalism, non-
fiction CON
ANDREWS, Earl Frank, 1937- ,
American; nonfiction CON
ANDREWS, Eric Montgomery,
1933- , British; nonfiction
CON
ANDREWS, Ernest Eugene, 1932- ,
American; nonfiction CON
ANDREWS, Frank Emerson, 1902-
78, American; juveniles, fic-
tion, nonfiction CO CON
ANDREWS, Frank Meredith, 1935- ,
American; nonfiction CON
ANDREWS, George Fredrick,
1918- , American; nonfiction
CON
ANDREWS, Henry Nathaniel, Jr.,
1910- , American; nonfiction

CON
ANDREWS, James David, 1924- ,
American; nonfiction, po-
etry CON
ANDREWS, James P., 1936?-80,
American; journalism, CON
ANDREWS, James Sydney, 1934- ,
Irish; juveniles CO WAR
ANDREWS, John William, 1898-
1975, American; nonfiction,
poetry CON
ANDREWS, Julie (Julie Edwards),
1935- , English; juveniles
CO WAR
ANDREWS, Lewis M., 1946- ,
American; nonfiction CON
ANDREWS, Lyman, 1938- ,
American; poetry CON
ANDREWS, Michael Frank,
1916- , American; nonfic-
tion CON
ANDREWS, Raymond, 1934- ,
American; fiction CON
ANDREWS, Roy Chapman,
1884-1960, American; ju-
veniles CO
ANDREWS, Stanley, 1894- ,
American; nonfiction CON
ANDREWS, Virginia Cleo, Amer-
ican; fiction CON
ANDREWS, William Robert,
1937- , American; nonfic-
tion CON
'ANDREYÈVICH' see SOLOU-
YÈV, Evgeny A.
ANDREYEV, Leonid Nikolayevich,
1871-1919, Russian; fiction,
plays BU CL MAG MCG TH
ANDREYEVSKY, Sergey Arkadye-
vich, 1847-1918, Russian;
nonfiction, poetry BU
'ANDREZEL, Pierre' see BLIX-
EN, Karen
ANDRIANANJASON, Victor
Georges, 1940- , Madagas-
can; nonfiction JA
ANDRIĆ, Ivo, 1892-1974/5, Yu-
goslav; fiction, poetry BU
CL CON MAG SEY TH WA
ANDRIEU CONTREDIT, -1248,
French; poetry BU
ANDRIST, Ralph K., 1914- ,
American; juveniles WAR
ANDROS, Dee Gus, 1924- ,
American; nonfiction CON
ANDROTION, 4th century B.C.,
Greek; nonfiction LA
ANDRUS, Paul, 1931- , Amer-

ican; nonfiction CON
ANDRUS, Vincent, 1942- , Amer-
ican; journalism, nonfiction
CON
ANDRZEJEWSKI, Jerzy (George),
1909- , Polish; fiction BU
CL SEY TH WA
ANDUJAR, Manuel, 1913- , Span-
ish; fiction, plays CL
ANDUZE-DUFY, Raphael see COU-
LET du GARD, Rene
ANEAU, Barthélemy, 1500-61,
French; plays BU
ANEIRIN, fl. 600, Welsh; poetry
BU DA
'ANET, Claude' (Jean Schopfer),
1868-1931, Swiss; fiction NI
'ANGEBERT, Jean Michel' see
BERTRAND, Michel
ANGEL, Frank, Jr., 1916- ,
American; nonfiction MAR
ANGEL, Heather, 1941- , Brit-
ish; nonfiction CON
ANGEL, John Lawrence, 1915- ,
American; nonfiction CON
ANGEL, Marc Dwight, 1945- ,
American; nonfiction CON
ANGELELLA, Michael, 1953- ,
American; nonfiction CON
ANGELES, Carlos A. 1921- ,
Filipino; poetry VCP
ANGELES, Fray Juan de los, 1536?-
1609, Spanish; nonfiction BU
ANGELI, Pietro Angelo, 1517-96,
Italian; poetry BU
'ANGELIQUE, Pierre' see BA-
TAILLE, Georges
ANGELL, George, 1945- , Amer-
ican; nonfiction CON
ANGELL, Judie, 1937- , Amer-
ican; juveniles CO CON
ANGELL, Madeline, 1919- ,
American; juveniles CO CON
ANGELL, Robert Cooley, 1899- ,
American; nonfiction CON
ANGELL, Roger, 1920- , Amer-
ican; fiction CON
ANGELL, Tony, 1940- , Amer-
ican; nonfiction CON
ANGELO, Frank, 1914- , Amer-
ican; nonfiction CON
ANGELO, Valenti, 1897- , Italian-
American; juveniles CO KI
ANGELOU, Maya, 1928- , Amer-
ican; fiction, plays, nonfiction
CON SH
'ANGELUS SILESIUS' (Johann Schef-
fler), 1624-77, German; poetry

BU TH
ANGERMANN, Gerhard Otto,
1904- , German-American;
plays, nonfiction CON
ANGHEL, Dimitrie, 1872-1914,
Rumanian; poetry, plays BU
ANGIER, Bradford, American;
juveniles CO WAR
ANGIER, Roswell P., 1940- ,
American; nonfiction CON
ANGILBERT, Abbot, fl. 814,
French?; poetry TH
ANGIOLETTI, Giovanni Battista,
1896-1961, Italian; fiction,
nonfiction, journalism BU
ANGIOLIERI, Cecco, 1260-1312/13,
Sienese; poetry BO BU
ANGLADE, Jean, 1915- ,
French; fiction, poetry,
nonfiction CON
ANGLE, Paul McClelland, 1900-
75, American; juveniles, non-
fiction CO CON
ANGLO, Sydney, 1934- , British;
nonfiction CON
ANGLUND, Joan Walsh, 1926- ,
American; juveniles, poetry
DE KI
'ANGO, Fan D.' see LONGYEAR,
Barry B.
ANGOFF, Allan, 1910- , Amer-
ican; nonfiction CON
ANGOFF, Charles ('Richard W.
Hinton'), 1902-79, American;
nonfiction CON
ANGRIST, Stanley Wolff, 1933- ,
American; juveniles CO
ANGUS, Fay, 1929- , Australian-
American; nonfiction CON
'ANGUS, Ian' see MACKAN,
James A.
ANGUS, Marion, 1866-1946, Scots;
poetry BU DA
ANGUS, Sylvia, 1921- , Amer-
ican; fiction CON
'ANGUS, Tom' see POWELL,
Geoffrey S.
ANGUS-BUTTERWORTH, Lionel
Milner, 1900- , English;
nonfiction CON
ANHALT, Edward ('Andrew Holt'),
American; film CON
ANHAVA, Tuomas, 1927- , Fin-
nish; poetry, nonfiction TH
'ANICAR, Tom' see RACINA, Tom
ANICHKOV, Evgeny Vasilyevich,
1866-1937, Russian; nonfic-
tion BU

ANIS, Mir Babar Ali, 1802-74,
Urdu; poetry PRU
ANJOS, Augusto dos, 1884-1914,
Brazilian; poetry BR
ANKER, Charlotte, 1934- , Amer-
ican; juveniles, plays CON
ANKER LARSEN, Johannes, 1874-
1957, Danish; fiction, plays
BU TH
ANNA, Commena, 1083-1148, By-
zantine; nonfiction BU LA
ANNA, Timothy E., 1944- ,
American; nonfiction CON
ANNAN, Noel Gilroy, 1916- ,
English; nonfiction CON WA
ANNAND, James King, 1908- ,
Scots; poetry, juveniles, non-
fiction CON
ANNAS, George J., 1945- , Amer-
ican; nonfiction CON
ANNATURAI, C. N. ('Anna'), 1909-
69, Indian; journalism, fiction,
plays PRU
'ANNE-MARIEL' see GOUD, Anne
ANNENKOV, Pavel Vasilyevich,
1812-87, Russian; nonfiction
BU
ANNENSKY, Innokenty Fydorovich,
1856-1909, Russian; poetry,
translations, plays BU CL
MCG TH
ANNETT, Cora see SCOTT, Cora
A.
ANNIS, Linda Ferrill, 1943- ,
American; nonfiction CON
ANNO, Mitsumasa, 1920/26- ,
Japanese; juveniles CO CON
DEM
ANOBILE, Richard Joseph, 1947- ,
American; fiction CON
ANOCIDES, 440-390 B.C., Greek;
nonfiction GR
ANOFF, Isador Samuel, 1892- ,
American; nonfiction CON
ANOUILH, Jean, 1910- , French;
plays BU CL MAG MCG SEY
TH
ANOZIE, Sunday Ogbonna, 1942- ,
Nigerian; nonfiction HER JA
ANSARI, Sheykh ol-Eslam Abu
Esma'il, 1006-89, Persian;
poetry PRU
ANSBACHER, Max G. 1935- ,
American; nonfiction CON
ANSCHEL, Eugene ('Egon Polcher'),
1907- , German-American;
nonfiction CON
ANSCHEL, Kurt R., 1936- ,

American; nonfiction CON
ANSEL, Walter, 1897- , American; nonfiction CON
ANSELL, Jack, 1925-76, American; fiction CON
ANSELM, St., 1033-1109, French; nonfiction BU DA
'ANSKI, S.' (Shloyme Zanul Rappoport), 1863-1920, Russian; fiction, plays BU MCG TH
ANSLIJN, Nicolaas Nzn., 1777-1838, Dutch; juveniles BU
ANSLINGER, Harry Jacob, 1892-1975, American; nonfiction CON
ANSLO, Reyer, 1626-69, Dutch; poetry, plays BU
ANSON, Cyril Joseph, 1923- , English; nonfiction CON
ANSON, Jay, 1921-80, American; journalism, tv, film, nonfiction CON
ANSPACH, Donald F., 1942- , American, nonfiction CON
ANSTER, John, 1789-1867, Irish; poetry BU
ANSTEY, Christopher, 1724-1805, English; poetry BU DA PO VP
'ANSTEY, Edgar' see SLUSSER, George E.
'ANSTEY, F.' (Thomas Anstey Guthrie), 1856-1934, British; fiction NI
'ANSTRUTHER, James' see MAXTONE GRAHAM, James A.
ANTAL, Adèle S. C. O. von see 'WALLIS, A. S. C.'
ANTAR, (Antarah Ibn Shaddan el'Absi), 550?-615, Arab; poetry BU HER
ANTARA b. SHADDAD, 6th century, Arab; poetry PRU
ANTELL, Gerson, 1926- , American; nonfiction CON
ANTHONY, Barbara ('Antonia Barber'), 1932- , British; juveniles CON
'ANTHONY, C. L.' see SMITH Dodie
'ANTHONY, Catherine' see ADACHI, Barbara C.
'ANTHONY, David' see SMITH, William D.
ANTHONY, Earl, American; nonfiction SH
ANTHONY, Edward, 1895-1971, American; juveniles CO

'ANTHONY, Evelyn' (Evelyn Bridget Patricia Ward-Thomas), 1928- , British; fiction MCC REI
ANTHONY, Florence see 'Ai'
ANTHONY, Geraldine Cecilia, 1919- , American; nonfiction CON
'ANTHONY, Gordon' see STANNUS, James G. D.
ANTHONY, James R., 1922- , American; nonfiction CON
ANTHONY, Joseph Garner, 1899- , American; nonfiction CON
ANTHONY, Michael, 1932- , West Indian; fiction BU VCN
'ANTHONY, Piers' (Piers Anthony Dillingham Jacob), 1934- , Anglo-American; fiction AS COW NI
ANTHONY, Susan Brownell, 1916- , American; nonfiction CON
ANTHONY, William Philip, 1943- , American; nonfiction CON
ANTICAGLIA, Elizabeth, 1939- , American; juveniles, nonfiction CO CON
'EL ANTILLANO' see BETANCES, Ramon E.
ANTIMACHUS of COLOPHON, 5-4th centuries B.C., Greek; poetry BU
ANTIPATER of SIDON, 2nd century B.C., Greek; nonfiction, poetry BU
ANTIPHANES, 408/05-334/31 B.C., Greek; plays, poetry BU
ANTIPHON, 480-11 B.C., Greek; nonfiction BU LA
ANTIPHON of ATHENS, 5th century B.C., Greek; nonfiction BU
ANTIPHON of RHAMNUS, 480-411 B.C., Greek; nonfiction GR
ANTISTHENES of ATHENS, 455-360 B.C., Greek; nonfiction BU GR LA
ANTOINE, André, 1858-1943, French; nonfiction CL
ANTOINE-DARIAUX, Genevieve, 1914- , French; nonfiction, fiction CON
ANTOKOLSKY, Pavel Grigoryevich, 1896-1978, Russian; poetry BU CL TH WAK
ANTON, Frank Robert, 1920- , Canadian; nonfiction CON
ANTON, Ludwig, 1872- , German; fiction NI

ANTON, Michael James, 1940- ,
American; nonfiction, juven-
iles CO CON
ANTON ULRICH, Duke of Bruns-
wick, 1633-1714, German; po-
etry, fiction BU
ANTONA-TRAVERSI, Camillo,
1857-1934, Italian; plays, non-
fiction MCG
ANTONA-TRAVERSI GRISMONDI,
Giannino, 1860-1939, Italian;
plays MCG
ANTONELLI, Luigi, 1882-1942,
Italian; plays BO MCG
'ANTONI' see IRANEK-OSMECKI,
Kazimierz
ANTONICK, Robert J. see 'KAMIN,
Nick'
ANTONIN, Josef J. see 'KARA-
SEKZE LVOVIC, Jiří'
'ANTONINUS, Brother' (William
Everson), 1912- , American;
poetry BR VCP WA
'ANTONIO, Mário' (Mário Antonio
de Oliveira), 1934- , Angolan;
poetry, fiction HER JA
ANTONIO, Nicolás, 1617-84, Span-
ish; nonfiction BU
ANTONIOU, Demétrios Ioánnis,
1906- , Greek; poetry WAK
ANTONIUS, John A. see 'ENGEL-
MAN, Jan'
ANTONIUS, Marcus, 143-87 B.C.,
Roman; nonfiction LA
'ANTONY, Peter' (Anthony Joshua
SHAFFER, 1926- , British;
fiction, plays; Peter Levin
SHAFFER, 1926- , British;
fiction, plays) DA MCG REI
ST VCD VD WA
ANTONYCH, Bohdan Ihor, 1909-
37, Ukrainian; poetry CL
ANTOUN, Richard Taft, 1932- ,
American; nonfiction CON
ANTREASIAN, Garo Zareh,
1922- , American; nonfic-
tion CON
ANTRIM, William H., 1928- ,
American; nonfiction CON
ANTROBUS, John, 1933- , Brit-
ish; plays CON VCD
ANTSCHEL, Paul, see 'CELAN,
Paul'
ANVARI, Ouhadoddin Ali (Auchad-
al-Din), 1126-89/90, Persian;
poetry BU PRU
'ANVIC, Frank' see SHERMAN,
Jory T.

'ANVIL, Christopher' (Harry C.
Crosby, Jr.), American; fic-
tion AS NI
'ANWAR' see ISHAK bin HAJI MU-
HAMMAD
ANWAR, Chairil, 1922-49, Indo-
nesian; poetry, translations
PRU WAK
ANWEILER, Oskar, 1925- , Polish-
German; nonfiction CON
ANZENGRUBER, Ludwig (Ludwig
Gruber), 1839-89, Austrian;
plays, fiction BU MCG TH
AOKI, Haruo, 1930- , Korean-
American; nonfiction CON
APELFELD, Aharon, 1932- ,
Israeli; fiction BU
APHTHONIUS, fl. 400, Greek;
nonfiction BU
APICIUS, Marcus Gavius, 1st cen-
tury, Latin; nonfiction BU
APIN, Rivai, 1927- , Indonesian;
poetry, nonfiction, journalism
PRU
APITZ, Bruno, 1900-79, American-
German; journalism, fiction
BU CON
APOLINAR, Danny, 1934- , Amer-
ican; nonfiction CON
'APOLLINAIRE, Guillaume' (Wil-
helm Apollinaris de Kostro-
witski), 1880-1918, French;
poetry, fiction, nonfiction BU
CL MAG MCG SEY TH
APOLLODORUS, 2nd century B.C.,
Greek; poetry BU
APOLLODORUS of ATHENS, 180-
120/10 B.C., Greek; nonfiction
GR
APOLLODORUS of CARYSTUS, fl.
285 B.C., Greek; poetry LA
APOLLODORUS of GELA, fl. 315
B.C., Greek; poetry LA
APOLLONIUS DYSCOLUS, fl. 150,
Greek; nonfiction BU
APOLLONIUS of TYANA, 1st cen-
tury, Greek; nonfiction LA
APOLLONIUS RHODIUS, 295-30/15
B.C., Greek; poetry BU GR
LA
APOSTOLIDES, Alexander, fl.
1950's, American; fiction NI
APOSTOLON, Billy Michael, 1930- ,
American; nonfiction CON
APP, Austin Joseph, 1902- ,
American; nonfiction CON
APPADORAI, Angadipruam, 1902- ,
Indian; nonfiction CON

APPAR, 7th century, Tamil; po-
etry PRU
APPARAW, Gurajtada Wendkata,
1862-1915, Telugu; poetry
PRU
APPEL, Allan, 1946- , Amer-
ican; poetry CON
APPEL, Benjamin, 1907-77,
American; juveniles, fiction,
nonfiction CO CON NI
APPEL, Kenneth Ellmaker, 1896-
1979, American; nonfiction
CON
APPEL, Martin Eliot, 1948- ,
American; nonfiction CON
APPELBAUM, Judith; 1939- ,
American; nonfiction CON
APPELBAUM, Stephen Arthur,
1926- , American; nonfic-
tion CON
APPELMANS, Gheraert, fl. 1300,
Dutch; nonfiction BU
APPIAH, Peggy, 1921- , English;
fiction, juveniles CO CON KI
APPIAN (Appianos), 95-160, Greek;
nonfiction BU GR LA
APPIGNANESI, Lisa, 1946- ,
Polish-English; nonfiction CON
APPLBAUM, Ronald L., 1943- ,
American; nonfiction CON
APPLE, Max Isaac, 1941- ,
American; nonfiction, fiction
CON
APPLE, Raymond Walter, Jr.,
1934- , American; journal-
ism, nonfiction CON
APPLEBAUM, Samuel, 1904- ,
American; nonfiction CON
APPLEBAUM, Stan ('Robert
Keith'), 1929- , American;
juveniles, plays CON
APPLEBEE, Arthur Nobel, 1946- ,
American; nonfiction CON
APPLEBY, John T., 1909?-74,
American; nonfiction CON
APPLEBY, Joyce Oldham, 1929- ,
American; nonfiction CON
APPLEGARTH, Margaret Tyson,
1886-1976, American; non-
fiction CON
APPLEGATE, Richard, 1913-79,
American; journalism CON
APPLETON, Arthur, 1913- ,
British; nonfiction CON
APPLETON, Jane Frances,
1934- , American; nonfic-
tion CON
'APPLETON, Victor' see ADAMS,

Harriet
APPLETON, William S., 1934- ,
American; nonfiction CON
APPLEWHITE, Cynthia, American;
fiction CON
APPLEWHITE, Edgar Jarratt, Jr.,
1919- , American; nonfiction
CON
APPLEWHITE, James William,
1935- , American; poetry
CON
APPS, Jerold Willard, 1934- ,
American; nonfiction CON
'APRIL, Steve' see 'LACY, Ed'
APRILOV, Vassil, 1789-1847, Bul-
garian; nonfiction BU
APRILY, Lajos, 1887-1967, Hun-
garian; poetry TH
APRONTI, Jawa, 1940- , Ghana-
ian; poetry, nonfiction HER
APSLER, Alfred, 1907- , Austrian-
American; juveniles CO WAR
APT, Jerome Leon, 1929- , Amer-
ican; nonfiction CON
APTALIAN see 'VAHYAN, Vahe'
APTE, Hari Narayan, 1864-1919,
Marathi; fiction BU PRU
APTEKAR, Jane, 1935- , Scots-
American; nonfiction CON
APUKHTIN, Alexey Nikolayevich,
1841-93, Russian; poetry BU
APULEIUS, Lucius, 125-75, Roman;
fiction, nonfiction BU GR LA
MAG
AQL, Sa'id, 1912- , Lebanese;
poetry, plays, fiction PRU
AQQAD, Abbas Mahmud, 1889-
1964, Egyptian; poetry, non-
fiction BU PRU
AQUILANO, Serafino see 'CIMIN-
ELLI, Serafino de'
'AQUILLO, Don' see PRINCE,
Jack H.
AQUIN, Hubert, 1929- , Canadian;
fiction BU CR
AQUINAS, St. Thomas, 1225-74,
Italian; nonfiction MAG TH
AQUINO, Rinaldo d', 13th century,
Italian; poetry TH
ARAFAT, Ibtihaj Said, 1934- ,
American; nonfiction CON
ARAGON, Louis ('Saint Roman
Arnaud'; 'Francois La Colere'),
1897- , French; poetry, fic-
tion, nonfiction, plays BU CL
CON SEY TH
ARAGON de SHEPRO, Theresa,
1943- , American; nonfic-

tion MAR
ARAGONA, Tullia d', 1508-56,
Italian; poetry BU
ARAGVISPIRELI, Shio, 1867-
1926, Georgian; nonfiction
PRU
ARAI HAKUSEKI, 1657-1725,
Japanese; nonfiction HI
ARAKIDA HISAOI, 1746-1804,
Japanese; nonfiction HI
ARAKIDA MORITAKE, 1473-1549,
Japanese; poetry BU
ARAKIDA REIJO, 1732-1806, Ja-
panese; fiction HI
'ARAMIS' see BONAFOUX y
QUINTERO, Luis
ARANA, Felipe N., 1902-63,
Puerto Rican; poetry HIL
ARANA SOTO, Salvador, 1908- ,
Puerto Rican; nonfiction HIL
ARANGO, Jorge Sanin, 1916- ,
Colombian-American; nonfic-
tion CON
ARANGUREN, José Luis L.,
1909- , Spanish; nonfiction
CL
ARANHA, José Pereira da Graça,
1868-1931, Brazilian; fiction
BR
ARANOW, Edward Ross, 1909- ,
American; nonfiction CON
ARANY, János, 1817-82, Hungar-
ian; poetry, nonfiction BU
TH
ARASON, Jón, 1484-1550, Ice-
lander; poetry BU
ARATA, Esther Spring, 1918- ,
American; nonfiction CON
ARATOR, fl. 540, Roman; poetry
BU TH
ARATUS of SOLI, 315?-240?, B.C.,
Greek; poetry, nonfiction BU
GR LA
ARBASINO, Alberto, 1930- ,
Italian; nonfiction, journalism,
fiction CL WA
ARBAUD, Joseph d', 1871-1950,
French; poetry, fiction CL
ARBEITER, Jean S., American;
juveniles WAR
ARBES, Jakub, 1840-1914, Czech;
fiction, nonfiction BU
ARBLAY, Frances d' see BURNEY,
Fanny
ARBO, Sebastian Juan, 1902- ,
Catalan; fiction, nonfiction CL
ARBOGAST, William F., 1908-79,
American; nonfiction CON

ARBOLEDA, Julio, 1817-62, Co-
lombian; poetry BU
ARBUCKLE, Robert Dean, 1940- ,
American; nonfiction CON
ARBUCKLE, Wanda Rector, 1910- ,
American; nonfiction CON
ARBUTHNOT, John, 1667-1735,
Scots; nonfiction BU DA PO
ARBUZOV, Alexey Nikolayevich,
1908- , Russian; plays BU
CL CON MCG TH
ARCANA, Judith, 1943- , Amer-
ican; nonfiction CON
ARCE, Hector, 1935-80, American;
nonfiction CON
ARCE de VAZQUEZ, Margot,
1904- , Puerto Rican; non-
fiction HIL
ARCELLANA, Francisco, 1916- ,
Filipino; fiction, nonfiction
PRU
'ARCH, E. L.' see PAYES, Rachel
C.
ARCHAMBAULT, Paul, 1937- ,
American; nonfiction CON
ARCHDEACON, Thomas John,
1942- , American; nonfiction
CON
'ARCHER, Frank' see O'CONNOR,
Richard
ARCHER, Fred C., 1916?-74,
American; nonfiction CON
ARCHER, Gleason Leonard, Jr.,
1916- , American; nonfiction
CON
ARCHER, Horace Richard,
1911-78, American; nonfic-
tion CON
ARCHER, Jeffrey Howard, 1940- ,
British; nonfiction CON
ARCHER, John Hal, 1914- , Ca-
nadian; juveniles, nonfiction
CON
ARCHER, Jules, 1915- , Amer-
ican; juveniles CO
'ARCHER, Lee' (Ziff-Davis house
name) NI
ARCHER, Marion Fuller, 1917- ,
American; juveniles WA
ARCHER, Myrtle Lilly, 1926- ,
American; fiction, nonfiction
CON
ARCHER, William, 1856-1924,
Scots; journalism, plays, non-
fiction BU DA PO
ARCHER, William George,
1907- , English; poetry,
nonfiction CON

ARCHIBALD, Joseph Stopford,
1898- , American; juveniles
CO
ARCHIBALD, Rupert Douglas,
1919- , Trinidadian; plays
CON VCD
ARCHIBALD, William, 1924-70,
American; plays MCG
ARCHIL, 1647-1713, Georgian;
poetry PRU
ARCHILOCHUS, 710-648? B.C.,
Greek; poetry BU GR LA
ARCHIMEDES, 287-12 B.C.,
Greek; nonfiction BU GR LA
ARCHPOET, fl. 1160, German;
poetry BU TH
ARCHYTUS, early 4th century
B.C., Greek; nonfiction GR
ARCINIEGA, Tomas A. 1937- ,
American; nonfiction MAR
ARCINIEGAS, Germán, 1900- ,
Colombian; nonfiction, jour-
nalism BR CON
ARCONE, Sonya ('Sonya Goodman'),
1925-78, American; fiction
CON
ARCTINUS of MILETUS, 7-6th
centuries B.C., Greek; po-
etry GR
ARDALAN, Nader, 1939- ,
Iranian; nonfiction CON
'ARDEN, Barbie' see STOUTEN-
BERG, Adrien
ARDEN, Jane, British; plays
CON VCD
ARDEN, John, 1930- , English;
plays BU DA MCG PO SEY
VCD VD WA
'ARDEN, William' see 'COLLINS,
Michael'
ARDIES, Tom, 1931- , Canadian;
fiction REI
ARDIZZONE, Edward Jeffrey,
1900-79, English; juveniles
CO CON KI
ARDIZZONE, Tony, 1949- ,
American; nonfiction, fiction
CON
ARDOIN, John Louis, 1935- ,
American; nonfiction CON
ARDREY, Robert, 1908-80, Amer-
ican; plays, fiction, journalism
CON NI VCD
AREF, Mirza Abolqasem Qazvini,
1882-1934, Iranian; poetry
PRU
AREHART-TREICHEL, Joan,
1942- , American; juveniles,

nonfiction CO CON
ARELLANO, Juan Estevan, 1947- ,
American; fiction MAR
AREM, Joel Edward, 1943- ,
American; nonfiction CON
ARENA, John I., 1929- , Amer-
ican; nonfiction CON
'ARENALES, Ricardo ' see 'BARBA
JACOB, Porfirio'
ARENDT, Hannah, 1906-75, German-
American; nonfiction BR CON
WA
ARENE, Paul, 1843-93, French;
journalism, poetry, fiction
BU
ARENELLA, Roy, 1939- , Amer-
ican; juveniles CO
ARENS, William, 1940- , Amer-
ican; nonfiction CON
ARENSBERG, Conrad Maynadier,
1910- , American; nonfiction
CON
ARENT, Arthur, 1904- , American;
plays MCG
ARETHAS, Archbishop of Caesarea,
850-932, Byzantine; nonfiction
BU LA
'ARETINO' see BRUNI, Leonardo
ARETINO, Francesco see ACCOLTI,
Francesco
ARETINO, Pietro, 1492-1556, Ital-
ian; nonfiction, plays BO BU
MAG MCG TH
ARETINO, Unico see ACCOLTI,
Bernardo
AREVALO MARTINEZ, Rafael,
1884- , Guatemalan; poetry,
fiction BR BU
AREY, James A., 1936- , Amer-
ican; nonfiction CON
ARGAN, Giulio Carlo, 1909- ,
Italian; nonfiction CON
ARGENSOLA, Bartolomé Leonardo
de, 1561-1631, Spanish; poetry,
nonfiction BU TH
ARGENSOLA, Lupercio Leonardo
de, 1559-1613, Spanish; poetry,
plays, nonfiction BU TH
ARGENTI, Philip, 1891?-1974,
British; nonfiction CON
ARGENZIO, Victor, 1902- , Amer-
ican; nonfiction CON
'ARGHEZI, Tudor' (Ion Theodorescu),
1880-1967, Rumanian; poetry,
fiction, nonfiction BU CL SEY
TH WAK
ARGOTE de MOLINA, Gonzalo,
1548-98, Spanish; nonfiction BU

American; nonfiction CON
ARLEY, Catherine, 1935- ,
French; nonfiction CON
ARLOW, Jacob A.', 1912- ,
American; nonfiction CON
ARLT, Roberto, 1900-42, Argen-
tinian; fiction, plays BR BU
SEY
ARMACOST, Michael Hayden,
1937- , American; nonfiction
CON
ARMAH, Ayi Kwei, 1938/39- ,
Ghanaian; fiction, translations,
poetry BU CON HER JA VCN
ARMAS, Jose, 1944- , American;
nonfiction MAR
ARMATAS, James P., 1931- ,
American; nonfiction CON
ARMATTOE, Raphael Ernest
Grail, 1913- , Ghanaian; non-
fiction, poetry HER JA LA
ARMBRISTER, Trevor, 1933- ,
American; nonfiction CON
ARMBRUSTER, Franz Owen,
1929- , American; nonfic-
tion CON
ARMER, Alberta Roller, 1904- ,
American; juveniles CO
ARMER, Laura Adams, 1874-
1963, American; juveniles,
fiction CO DA CON
ARMERDIN, George D., 1899- ,
American; nonfiction CON
ARMIN, Robert, 1568-1615, Eng-
lish; poetry, plays BU
ARMINGTON, John Calvin,
1923- , American; nonfic-
tion CON
ARMISTEAD, Samuel Gordon,
1927- , American; nonfic-
tion CON
ARMITAGE, Merle, 1893-1975,
American; nonfiction CON
PAL
'ARMOUR, John' see PAINE,
Lauran B.
ARMOUR, Richard Willard,
1906- , American; poetry,
juveniles, plays CO KI
'ARMS, Johnson' see HALLI-
WELL, David W.
ARMS, Suzanne, 1944- , Amer-
ican; nonfiction CON
'ARMSTRONG, Anthony' see
WILLIS, George A. A.
'ARMSTRONG, Anthony C.' see
ARMSTRONG, Christopher
J. R.

ARMSTRONG, April Oursler, 1926- ,
American; nonfiction CON
ARMSTRONG, Arthur Hilary, 1909- ,
British; nonfiction CON
ARMSTRONG, Benjamin Leighton,
1923- , American; nonfiction
CON
ARMSTRONG, Brian Gary, 1936- ,
American; nonfiction CON
ARMSTRONG, Charlotte ('Jo Valen-
tine'), 1905-69, American; po-
etry, plays, fiction REI ST
WA
ARMSTRONG, Christopher J. R.
('Anthony C. Armstrong'),
1935- , British; translations,
nonfiction CON
ARMSTRONG, David Michael,
1944- , American; nonfiction
CON
ARMSTRONG, George D., 1927- ,
American; juveniles CO
ARMSTRONG, Gerry Breen, 1929- ,
American; juveniles; CO
ARMSTRONG, Hamilton Fish, 1893-
1973, American; journalism,
nonfiction CON
'ARMSTRONG, Henry H.' see AR-
VAY, Harry
ARMSTRONG, John, 1709-79, Scots;
poetry BU DA VP
ARMSTRONG, John Byron ('John
Byron'; 'Charles Willard'),
1917-76, American; journalism,
nonfiction CON
ARMSTRONG, Jon Scott, 1937- ,
American; nonfiction CON
ARMSTRONG, Joseph Gravitt,
1943- , American; journal-
ism CON
ARMSTRONG, Judith Mary, 1935- ,
Australian; nonfiction CON
ARMSTRONG, Louise, American;
juveniles WAR
ARMSTRONG, Marjorie Moore,
1912- , American; nonfiction
CON
ARMSTRONG, Martin, 1882-1974,
British; poetry, fiction CON
ARMSTRONG, Orland Kay, 1893- ,
American; nonfiction CON
'ARMSTRONG, Raymond' see 'COR-
RIGAN, Mark'
ARMSTRONG, Richard ('Cam Ren-
ton'), 1903- , English; juven-
iles, fiction CO CON DE KI
ARMSTRONG, Robert Plant, 1919- ,
American; nonfiction CON

ARMSTRONG, Thomas, 1899-
1978, British; nonfiction CON
ARMSTRONG, Wallace Edwin,
1896-1980, British; nonfiction
CON
ARMSTRONG, William H.,
, 1914- ,
American; juveniles, nonfic-
tion CO DE KI
ARMSTRONG, William Martin,
1919- , American; nonfiction
CON
ARMYTAGE, Walter Harry Green,
1915- , British; fiction NI
ARNASON, Hjorvardur Harvart,
1909- , Canadian-American;
nonfiction CON
ARNASON, Jón, 1819-88, Icelander;
fiction BU
'ARNAUD, Georges' (Henri Girard),
1917- , French; fiction, plays
MCG
'ARNAUD, Saint Romain' see ARA-
GON, Louis
ARNAUDOV, Mihail, 1878- , Bul-
garian; nonfiction BU
ARNAULD, Antoine, 1612-94,
French; nonfiction BU
ARNAUT, Daniel, fl. 1180-1210,
Provençal; poetry BU TH
ARNAUT de MAREUIL, fl. 1180,
Provençal; poetry BU
ARNDT, Ernst Moritz, 1769-1860,
German; poetry BU
ARNER, Sivar, 1909- , Swedish;
fiction, plays BU TH
'ARNETT, Caroline' see COLE,
Lois D.
ARNETT, Ross Harold, Jr.,
1919- , American; nonfic-
tion CON
'ARNETTE, Robert' (Ziff-Davis
house name) NI
ARNEZ, Nancy L., American; fic-
tion SH
ARNICHES y BARRERA, Carlos,
1866-1943, Spanish; plays
BU CL MCG
ARNIM, Bettina von Brentano,
1785-1859, German; nonfic-
tion BU TH
ARNIM, Ludwig Joachim von,
1781-1831, German; poetry,
plays, fiction BU TH
ARNO, Enrico, 1913- , German;
juveniles DEM
ARNOBIUS, 235- , Latin; nonfiction BU GR LA
ARNOLD, Alvin Lincoln, 1929- ,

American; nonfiction CON
ARNOLD, Bruce, 1936- , British;
fiction CON
ARNOLD, Charles Harvey, 1920- ,
American; nonfiction CON
ARNOLD, Charlotte Elizabeth Cram-
er, American; nonfiction CON
ARNOLD, Corliss Richard, 1926- ,
American; nonfiction CON
ARNOLD, Edwin Lester, 1857-1935,
British; fiction AS NI
ARNOLD, Elliott, 1912-80, Amer-
ican; juveniles, fiction CO CON
ARNOLD, Frank Edward, 1914- ,
British; fiction NI
'ARNOLD, G. L.' see LICHTHEIM,
George
ARNOLD, Gottfried, 1666-1714,
German; poetry, nonfiction BU
ARNOLD, Janet, 1932- , British;
nonfiction CON
'ARNOLD, Joseph H.' see HAYES,
Joseph A.
'ARNOLD, Margot' see COOK, Pe-
tronelle M. M.
ARNOLD, Mary Ann, 1918- ,
American; nonfiction CON
ARNOLD, Matthew, 1822-88, Eng-
lish; poetry, nonfiction, plays
BU DA MAG PO VP
ARNOLD, Milo Lawrence, 1903- ,
American; nonfiction CON
ARNOLD, Olga Moore, 1900-81,
American; journalism, fiction
CON
ARNOLD, Oren, 1900- , American;
juveniles CO
ARNOLD, Peter, 1943- , Amer-
ican; nonfiction CON
ARNOLD, R. Douglas, 1950- ,
American; nonfiction CON
ARNOLD, Richard Klein, 1923- ,
American; plays, fiction CON
ARNOLD, Robert Evans, 1932- ,
American; nonfiction CON
ARNOLD, Thomas, 1795-1842,
English; nonfiction BU DA
ARNOLD-FORSTER, Mark, 1920- ,
English; nonfiction CON
ARNOLD von IMMESSEN, late 15th
century, German; plays BU
ARNOLDUS GEILHOVEN (Gheylho-
ven), -1442, Dutch; nonfiction
BU
'ARNOLDY, Julie' see BISCHOFF,
Julia B.
ARNOSKY, Jim, 1946- , American;
juveniles CO CON

ARNOTHY, Christine, 1930- ,
Hungarian-American; nonfic-
tion CON
ARNOTT, Kathleen, 1914- , Eng-
lish; juveniles CO CON
ARNOUX, Alexandre, 1884- ,
French; poetry, plays, fiction
MCG
ARNOV, Boris, Jr., 1926- ,
American; juveniles CO
ARNOW, Harriette Simpson,
1908- , American; fiction,
nonfiction BA KIB VCN WA
ARNOW, Leslie Earle, 1909- ,
American; nonfiction CON
ARNSTEIN, Helene Solomon,
1915- , American; juveniles,
nonfiction CO CON
ARNTSON, Herbert Edward,
1911- , American; juveniles
CO
ARNULF of LOUVAIN, fl. 1240-
48, Latin; poetry TH
ARNY, Mary Travis, 1909- ,
American; nonfiction CON
ARNY, Thomas Travis, 1940- ,
American; nonfiction CON
AROLAS, Juan, 1805-49, Spanish;
poetry BU TH
AROMIRE, Abayomi, 1944- , Ni-
gerian; plays JA
ARON, Raymond Claude Ferdinand,
1905- , French; nonfiction,
journalism BU CL CON WA
ARON, Robert, 1898-1975, French;
nonfiction CON
ARONIN, Ben 1904-80, American;
tv, juveniles CO CON
ARONSON, Alexander, 1912- ,
German-Israeli; nonfiction
CON
ARONSON, Harvey, 1929- ,
American; fiction, nonfiction
CON
ARONSON, Jay Richard, 1937- ,
American; nonfiction CON
ARONSON, Marvin L., 1925- ,
American; nonfiction CON
ARONSON, Stina Bergqvist, 1892-
1956, Swedish; fiction, poetry,
plays BU
AROS, Andrew Alexandre, 1944- ,
American; nonfiction CON
ARP, Hans ('Michel Seuphor'),
1887-1966, Alsatian; poetry,
nonfiction, fiction BU CON
SEY TH
ARPAD, Joseph John, 1937- ,

American; nonfiction CON
'ARPEL, Adrien' see NEWMAN,
Adrien A.
ARPINO, Giovanni, 1927- , Ital-
ian; fiction CL
ARRABAL, Fernando, 1932- ,
Spanish; plays, fiction BU CL
MCG TH WA
ARRAS, Adam d' see ADAM de la
HALLE
'ARRE, Helen' see ROSS, Zola H.
ARREBO, Anders, 1587-1637, Dan-
ish; poetry BU TH
ARREOLA, Juan José, 1918- ,
Mexican; fiction, plays BR
ARRIAN (Flavius Arrianus), 95-175,
Greek; nonfiction BU GR LA
ARRIAS, Amador, 1530-1600, Por-
tuguese; nonfiction BU
ARRIAZA y SUPERVIELA, Juan
Bautista, 1770-1837, Spanish;
poetry BU TH
ARRIGHI, Mel, 1933- , American;
fiction, plays CON
ARRIVI, Francisco, 1915- , Puerto
Rican; poetry, plays HIL
ARROWOOD, McKendrick Lee Clin-
ton, 1939- , American; juven-
iles CO
ARROWSMITH, Pat, 1930- , Brit-
ish; fiction, poetry CON
ARROWSMITH, William Ayres,
1924- , American; translations,
nonfiction WA
ARROYO, Luis Leobardo, American;
nonfiction MAR
ARROYO, Stephen Joseph, 1946- ,
American; nonfiction CON
ART, Robert Jeffrey, 1942- ,
American; nonfiction CON
ARTAUD, Antonin, 1896-1948,
French; plays, poetry, nonfic-
tion BU CL MCG SEY TH WA
ARTEAGA, Esteban de, 1747-98,
Spanish; nonfiction BU
ARTEAGA, Lucio, 1924- , Spanish-
American; nonfiction CON
ARTEMIDORUS, 2nd century, Greek;
nonfiction GR
ARTES, Dorothy Beecher, 1919- ,
American; nonfiction, juveniles
CON
'ARTHUR, Alan' see EDMONDS,
Arthur D.
'ARTHUR, Burt' see SHAPPIRO,
Herbert A.
'ARTHUR, Frank' (Arthur Frank
Ebert), 1902- , British; fic-

tion, plays, juveniles REI
'ARTHUR, Herbert' see SHAP-
PIRO, Herbert A.
'ARTHUR, Hugh' see CHRISTIE-
MURRAY, David H. A.
ARTHUR, Robert, American;
juveniles WAR
ARTHUR, Ruth Mabel, 1905-79,
Scots; juveniles CO CON KI
WAR
ARTHUR, Timothy Shay, 1809-85,
American; fiction BR BU
MYE VN
ARTIS, Vicki Kimmel, 1945- ,
American; juveniles CO CON
ARTMANN, Hans Carl, 1921- ,
Austrian; poetry, fiction,
plays, translations BU CL
CON
ARTSYBASHEV, Mikhail Petrovich,
1878-1927, Russian; fiction BU
CL MAG
ARTZ, Max, 1897-1975, Polish-
American; nonfiction CON
ARTZYBASHEFF, Boris Mikhailo-
vich; 1899-1965, Russian-
American; juveniles CO
ARUEGO, Ariane see DEWEY,
Ariane
ARUEGO, Jose, 1932- , Filipino;
juveniles CO DEM
ARUMUKAM, Nallur Kantappillai
('Arumka Navalar'), 1822-79,
Tamil; nonfiction PRU
ARUNACALAKAVI, late 18th century,
Tamil; poetry PRU
ARUNAKIRINATAR, 15th century,
Tamil; poetry PRU
ARUNDEL, Honor Morfydd, 1919-
73, Welsh; poetry, juveniles
plays CO CON DEM KI WAR
ARUNDEL, Jocelyn A. see ALEX-
ANDER, Jocelyn A.
ARUNDEL, Russell M., 1903-78,
American; nonfiction CON
ARVAY, Harry ('Henry H. Arm-
strong'), 1925- , Austrian-
Israeli; nonfiction CON
ARVERS, Alexis Félix, 1806-50,
French; poetry, plays BU
'ARVILL, Robert' see BOOTE,
Robert E.
ARVIN, Frederick Newton, 1900- ,
American; nonfiction BOR
ARVIN, Kay Krehbiel, 1922- ,
American; nonfiction CON
ARVIO, Raymond Paavo, 1930- ,
American; nonfiction CON

ARVIZU, Steven F., 1942- , Amer-
ican; nonfiction MAR
ARY, Donald Eugene, 1930- ,
American; nonfiction CON
ARYA SURA, 4th century, Indian;
fiction BU PRU
ARZOLA, Marina, 1939- , Puerto
Rican; poetry HIL
ASACHI, Gheorghe, 1788-1869, Ru-
manian; nonfiction, journalism,
poetry BU
ASADI, Abu Mansur Ali, 1010-80,
Persian; poetry PRU
ASADI, Ali Ibn Ahmad Tusi, 11th
century, Persian; poetry, non-
fiction BU
ASALACHE, Khadambi, 1934/35- ,
Kenyan; fiction, poetry HER
JA
ASAMANI, Joseph Owusu, 1934- ,
Ghanaian; nonfiction CON
ASARE, Bediako, 1930?- , Ghana-
ian; fiction, journalism HER
'ASARE, Kwabena' see KONADU,
Samuel A.
ASARE, Meshack Yaw, 1945- ,
Ghanaian; juveniles, nonfiction,
plays CON
ASAYAMA BONTO, 1349?-1427,
Japanese; poetry HI
ASBELL, Bernard ('Nicholas Max'),
1923- , American; nonfiction
CON
ASBJORNSEN, Peter Christen,
1812-85, Norwegian; fiction,
juveniles BU CO
ASCASUBI, Hilario ('Paulino Lucero
Anceto el Gallo'), 1807-75,
Argentinian; poetry BR BU
'ASCENSIUS' see BADE, Josse
ASCH, Frank, 1946- , American;
juveniles CO CON DEM WAR
ASCH, Sholem, 1880-1957, Yiddish;
fiction, plays BR BU CL MAG
MCG TH
ASCHAM, Roger, 1515-68, English;
nonfiction, letters BU DA PO
RU
ASCHEIM, Skip, 1943- , American;
poetry, nonfiction CON
ASCHER, Abraham, 1928- , Ger-
man-American; nonfiction CON
ASCLEPIADES of SAMOS (Sicelidas),
fl. 320-290 B.C., Greek; non-
fiction BU GR LA
'ASCOLI, Cecco d' see STABILI,
Francesco
ASCOLI, Max, 1898-1978, Italian-

American; journalism, nonfic-
tion CON
ASCONIUS PEDIANUS, 9 B.C.-
76 A.D., Roman; nonfiction
BU
ASELLIO, Sempronius, fl. 100
B.C., Roman; nonfiction LA
ASENJO, Conrado, 1881- ,
Puerto Rican; nonfiction HIL
ASENJO, Federico ('Claro Os-
curo'), 1831-93, Puerto Rican;
journalism HIL
ASEYEV, Nikolay Nikolayevich,
1889-1963, Russian; poetry
BU CL TH
ASGRIMSSON, Eysteinn, -1361,
Icelander; poetry BU
ASH, Alan, British; fiction
NI
ASH, Anthony Lee, 1931- ,
American; nonfiction CON
ASH, Brian, 1936- , English;
journalism NI
ASH, Maurice Anthony, 1917- ,
American; nonfiction CON
ASH, Rene Lee ('A. R. Lee'),
1939- , American; nonfiction
CON
'ASH, Roberta' see GARNER,
Roberta
A'SHA MAYMUN, 6-7th centuries,
Arab; poetry BU PRU
ASH'ARI, Abu'l-Hasan, 873/74-
935/36, Arab; nonfiction PRU
ASHBEE, Paul, 1918- , British;
nonfiction CON
ASHBERY, John Lawrence, 1927- ,
American; poetry, plays, fic-
tion BR MAL PO VCP VP
WA
ASHBY, Eric, 1904- , English;
nonfiction CON
ASHBY, Lloyd W., 1905- , Amer-
ican; nonfiction CON
ASHBY, Neal, 1924- , American;
nonfiction CON
ASHBY, Rubie Constance ('Ruby
Freugon'), 1899- , English;
fiction ST
ASHCRAFT, Morris, 1922- ,
American; nonfiction CON
'ASHDOWN, Clifford' (R. Austin
FREEMAN; John James PIT-
CAIRN, 1860-1936, English;
fiction ST
ASHE, Arthur, 1943- , American;
nonfiction CON
'ASHE, Douglas' see BARDIN,

John F.
ASHE, Geoffrey Thomas, 1923- ,
English; juveniles CO
'ASHE, Gordon' see CREASEY,
John
'ASHE, Mary Anne' see BRAND,
Christianna M.
'ASHE, Penelope' see KARMAN,
Mal; YOUNG, Billie
ASHENAFI, Kebede, 1937- , Ethi-
opian; fiction HER
ASHENFELTER, Orley Clark,
1942- , American; nonfiction
CON
ASHER, Robert Eller, 1910- ,
American; nonfiction CON
ASHER BEN YECHIEL (Asheri),
1250-1327, Spanish; nonfiction
BU
'ASHEY, Bella' see BREINBURG,
Petronella
'ASHFORD, Daisy' see ASHFORD,
Margaret Mary
ASHFORD, Gerald, 1907- , Amer-
ican; journalism, nonfiction,
plays CON
ASHFORD, H. Ray, 1926- , Ca-
nadian; nonfiction CON
'ASHFORD, Jeffrey' see JEFFRIES,
Roderic
ASHFORD, Margaret Mary ('Daisy
Ashford'), 1881-1972, English;
juveniles, fiction CO DA
ASHI, 352-427, Iraqi; nonfiction
BU
ASHLEY, Bernard, 1935- , Brit-
ish; juveniles CON KI
'ASHLEY, Elizabeth' see SALMON,
Annie E.
ASHLEY, Franklin, 1942- , Amer-
ican; nonfiction CON
ASHLEY, Maurice Percy, 1907- ,
English; nonfiction CON
ASHLEY, Michael Raymond, 1948- ,
British; nonfiction CON NI
ASHLEY, Nova Trimble, 1911- ,
American; nonfiction, poetry
CON
ASHLEY, Paul Pritchard, 1896-
1979, American; nonfiction
CON
ASHLEY, Rosalind Minor, 1923- ,
American; nonfiction CON
ASHLOCK, Patrick Robert, 1937- ,
American; nonfiction CON
'ASHMORE, Lewis' see RABORG,
Frederick A., Jr.
ASHNER, Sonie Shapiro, 1938- ,

American; nonfiction CON
ASHRAF KHAN KHATAK, 1635-
93, Pashtun; poetry PRU
ASHTON, Francis Leslie, 1904- ,
English; fiction NI
ASHTON, Winifred see 'DANE,
Clemence'
ASHTON-WARNER, Sylvia ('Sylvia';
'Sylvia Henderson'), 1908- ,
New Zealander; fiction, non-
fiction CON DA VCN WA
ASHWORTH, Kenneth Hayden,
1932- , American; nonfiction
CON
ASIMOV, Isaac ('Paul French'),
1920- , American; nonfiction,
fiction AS BR BU COW DE
NI REI VCN WA
ASIN PALACIOS, Miguel, 1871-
1944, Spanish; nonfiction BU
ASINOF, Eliot, 1919- , Amer-
ican; juveniles CO
ASIU, César Q. see 'MORO,
César'
ASK, Upendranath, 1910- , Hindi;
journalism, fiction PRU
ASKELÖF, Johan Christoffer, 1787-
1848, Swedish; journalism BU
ASKENASY, Hans George, 1930- ,
German-American; nonfiction
CON
AŠKERC, Anton, 1856-1912, Slov-
ene; poetry BU
'ASKEW, Jack' see HIVNOR,
Robert
ASKEW, Sarah Byrd, 1863/77-
1942, American; nonfiction
ENG
ASKEW, William Clarence, 1910- ,
American; nonfiction CON
ASKIN, Alma, 1911- , American;
nonfiction CON
ASKWITH, Betty Ellen, 1909- ,
English; fiction, nonfiction,
poetry CON
ASMA bint USUMAN, 1800-60, Ni-
gerian; poetry BU
ASNYK, Adam Prot, 1838-97,
Polish; poetry, plays, fiction
BU CL TH
'ASPAZIJA' (Elza Rozenberga),
1868-1943, Latvian; poetry,
plays BU
ASPENSTRÖM, Karl Werner,
1918- , Swedish; poetry,
fiction, plays BU CL MCG
ASPINWALL, Dorothy Brown,
1910- , Canadian-American;

translations, nonfiction CON
ASPLUND, Karl, 1890- , Swedish;
poetry, nonfiction BU
ASPRIN, Robert Lynn, 1946- ,
American; fiction CON
ASPY, David Nathaniel, 1930- ,
American; nonfiction CON
ASSAEL, Henry, 1935- , Amer-
ican; nonfiction CON
ASSAGIOLI, Roberto, 1893?-1974,
Italian; nonfiction CON
ASSEBERGS, Willem J. see 'DUIN-
KERKEN, Anton van'
ASSELBROKE, Archibald Algernon,
1923- , British; journalism
CON
ASSELIJN, Thomas, 1620-1701,
Dutch; plays BU
ASSELINEAU, Roger Maurice ('Rog-
er Maurice'), 1915- , French;
translations, nonfiction CON
ASSENEDE, Diederic van, 13th cen-
tury, Dutch; poetry BU
ASSER, 850-909, Welsh; nonfiction
BU DA
ASSIS, Antonio de, Jr., 1870?-
1960?, Angolan; fiction, jour-
nalism HER
ASSIS, Joaquim Maria Machado de,
1839-1908, Brazilian; fiction
BR
ASSOUCY, Charles Couppeau d',
1605-77, French; poetry BU
ASTER, Sidney, 1942- , Canadian;
nonfiction CON
ASTEROPHERUS, Magnus Olai,
-1647, Swedish; plays BU
ASTIER, Pierre Arthur Georges,
1927- , Franco-American;
nonfiction CON
ASTIER de la VIGERIE, Emmanuel
d', 1900-69, French; nonfiction
DU
ASTILL, Kenneth N., 1923- ,
American; nonfiction CON
'ASTLEY, Juliet' see LOFTS, Norah R.
ASTLEY, Thea Beatrice, 1925- ,
Australian; fiction, nonfiction
CON VCN
ASTLEY, William see 'WARUNG,
Price'
ASTOL, Eugenio, 1868-1948, Puerto
Rican; journalism, poetry HIL
'ASTON, James' see WHITE, Ter-
ence H.
ASTON, Michael Anthony, 1946- ,
English; nonfiction CON
ASTOR, John Jacob, 1864-1912,

American; fiction NI
ASTOR, Michael Langhorne, 1916-80, English; nonfiction CON
ASTRACHAN, Samuel, 1934- ,
American; fiction CON
ASTURIAS, Miguel Angel, 1899-1974, Guatemalan; poetry,
fiction BR BU CON MAG
SEY WA
ASTYDAMAS, Greek; poetry
BU
ASUKAI MASATSUNE, 1170-1221,
Japanese; poetry HI
ASVAGHOSA, 2nd century, Sanskrit;
poetry, plays BU LA PRU
ATA MALIK JUVAINI, Ala-al-Din,
1226-83, Persian; nonfiction
BU
ATAC, Nurullah, 1898-1957, Turkish; nonfiction BU
'ATALLAH, Lillian' see AFRICANO, Lillian
ATAMIAN, David, 1892?-1978,
Turkish-American; poetry,
diary, journalism; CON
ATANACKOVIĆ, Bogoboj, 1826-58, Serbian; fiction BU
ATCHEMIAN, see MAHARI, Gurgen
ATCHITY, Kenneth John, 1944- ,
American; nonfiction CON
ATCHLEY, Dana Winslow, 1941- ,
American; nonfiction CON
ATCHLEY, Robert C., 1939- ,
American; nonfiction CON
ATENE, Rita Anna, 1922- ,
American; juveniles CO
ATHANASIUS, St., 295/300-73,
Greek; nonfiction BU GR LA
ATHENAEUS, 2nd century, Greek;
nonfiction BU GR LA
ATHERTON, Gertrude Franklyn,
1857-1948, American; fiction,
nonfiction, plays BR BU NI
VN
ATHERTON, James Christian,
1915- , American; nonfiction
CON
ATHERTON, Pauline, 1929- ,
American; nonfiction CON
ATHERTON, Sarah see BRIDGMAN, Sarah
ATHERTON, Wallace Newman,
1927- , American; nonfiction
CON
ATHEY, Irene Jowett, 1919- ,
Anglo-American; nonfiction
CON

ATILES GARCIA, Guillermo, 1882-1955, Puerto Rican; poetry,
journalism HIL
ATISH, Khvaja Haidar, 1767-1846,
Urdu; poetry PRU
ATIYEH, George Nicholas, 1923- ,
Lebanese-American; nonfiction
CON
ATKESON, Ray A., 1907- , American; nonfiction CON
ATKEY, Bertram, 1880-1952, English; fiction ST
'ATKEY, Philip' see 'PEROWNE,
Barry'
ATKIN, Flora Blumenthal, 1919- ,
American; plays, juveniles
CON KI
ATKIN, J. Myron, 1927- , American; nonfiction CON
ATKIN, Mary Gage, 1929- , American; fiction CON
ATKINS, Chester Greenough, 1948- ,
Swiss-American; nonfiction
CON
ATKINS, Frank see 'AUBREY,
Frank'
ATKINS, John Alfred, 1916- ,
English; fiction NI
ATKINS, Meg Elizabeth ('Elizabeth
Moore'), British; fiction CON
ATKINS, Paul Moody, 1892-1977,
American; nonfiction CON
ATKINS, Russell, 1926- , American; poetry, nonfiction CON
SH
ATKINS, Thomas Radcliffe, 1939- ,
American; nonfiction CON
ATKINSON, Anthony Barnes, 1944- ,
British; nonfiction CON
ATKINSON, Hugh Craig, 1933- ,
American; nonfiction CON
ATKINSON, Justin Brooks, 1894- ,
American; nonfiction CON
'ATKINSON, M.E.' see FRANKAU,
Mary E.A.
Atkinson, Margaret Fleming, American; juveniles CO
'ATKINSON, Mary' see HARDWICK,
Mollie
ATKINSON, Mary Evelyn, 1899-1974, British; juveniles, plays
KI
ATKINSON, Ron, 1932- , American; nonfiction, poetry CON
ATKINSON, Sara, 1823-93, Irish;
nonfiction HO
ATKISSON, Arthur Albert, Jr.,
1930- , American; nonfic-

tion CON
ATKYNS, Glenn Chadwick, 1921- ,
American; nonfiction CON
ATLAS, Helen Vincent, 1931- ,
American; translations, non-
fiction CON
'ATLEE, Philip' (James Atlee
Phillips), 1915- , ?; fiction
REI
ATRE, Prahlad Kesáv, 1898-1970,
Marathi; plays, journalism,
fiction PRU
ATTA KOFFI, Raphaël, 1942- ,
Ivory Coast; fiction JA
ATTALIATES, Michael, late 11th
century, Byzantine; nonfiction
LA
ATTAR, Farid Al-Din Abu Hamid
(Faridoddin), 1193/1220-35,
Persian; poetry BU LA
ATTAWAY, Robert Joseph,
1942- , American; fiction
CON
ATTAWAY, William, American;
nonfiction SH
ATTEA, Mary, 1929- , Amer-
ican; nonfiction, poetry CON
ATTEBERRY, William Louis,
1939- , American; nonfiction
CON
ATTENBOROUGH, Bernard George
('James S. Rand'), English;
fiction CON
ATTENBOROUGH, John, 1908- ,
British; fiction, nonfiction
CON
ATTERBOM, Per Daniel Amadeus,
1790-1855, Swedish; poetry,
nonfiction BU TH
'ATTERLEY, Joseph' see TUCK-
ER, George
ATTHILL, Robin, 1912- , Brit-
ish; poetry, nonfiction CON
'ATTICUS' see FLEMING, Ian L.
ATTICUS, Titus Pomponius, 109-
32 B.C., Roman; nonfiction
BU LA
ATTNEAVE, Carolyn Lewis,
1920- , American; nonfiction
CON
ATTWELL, Arthur Albert, 1917- ,
American; nonfiction CON
ATWATER, Florence Hasseltine,
American; juveniles CO
ATWATER, James David, 1928- ,
American; journalism, fiction,
nonfiction CON
ATWATER, Montgomery Meigs,

1904- , American; juveniles
CO
ATWATER, Richard Tupper, 1892-
1938, American; juveniles, po-
etry KI
ATWOOD, Ann Margaret, 1913- ,
American; juveniles CO CON
DEM WAR
ATWOOD, Margaret Eleanor, 1939- ,
Canadian; fiction, poetry, non-
fiction CON VCN VCP VP
WAK
ATYEO, Don, 1950- , Australian;
nonfiction CON
AUB, Max, 1903-72, Spanish; fic-
tion, plays, nonfiction CL
AUBANEL, Théodore, 1829-86,
French; poetry BU CL TH
AUBERJONOIS, Fernand, 1910- ,
Swiss; fiction, poetry, nonfic-
tion CON
AUBERT, Alvin Bernard, 1930- ,
American; poetry, nonfiction
CON VCP
AUBIGNAC, Francois Hédelin, Abbé
d', 1604-76, French; nonfiction,
plays BU TH
AUBIGNE, Théodore Agrippa d',
1551-1630, French; poetry BU
AUBIN, Henry Trocme, 1942- ,
American; nonfiction CON
'AUBREY, Frank' (Frank Atkins),
British; fiction NI
AUBREY, John, 1626-97, English;
nonfiction BU DA MAG PO
REI
AUBURN, Mark Stuart, 1945- ,
American; nonfiction CON
'AUCH, Lord' see BATAILLE,
Georges
AUCHINCLOSS, Louis Stanton,
1917- , American; fiction,
plays, nonfiction BOR BR HE
PO VCN VN WA
AUCHMUTY, James Johnston,
1909- , Irish; nonfiction CON
AUDEFROI le BASTART, 13th cen-
tury, French; poetry BU
AUDELAY, John (Awdelay), 15th
century, English; poetry BU
AUDEMARS, Pierre ('Peter Hode-
mart'), 1909- , British; fic-
tion REI
'AUDEN, Renee' see WEST, Uta
AUDEN, Wystan Hugh, 1907-73,
American; nonfiction, poetry,
plays, translations BOR BU
CON DA MAG MCG PO SEY

VCP VD VP
AUDIBERTI, Jacques, 1899-1965,
French; poetry, fiction, plays
BU CL MCG TH WA
AUDISIO, Gabriel, 1900- ,
French; poetry, fiction BU
AUDUBON, John James, 1785-
1851, American; nonfiction
BR
AUEL, Jean Marie, 1936- ,
American; fiction CON
AUERBACH, Berthold, 1812-82,
German; fiction BU
AUERBACH, Erich, 1892-1957,
German-American; nonfiction
WA
AUERBACH, Erna, -1975,
German-British; nonfiction
CON
AUERBACH, George, 1905?-73,
American; plays CON
AUERBACH, Marjorie Hoffberg,
1932- , American; juveniles
WAR
AUERBACH, Nina, 1943- ,
American; nonfiction CON
AUERBACH, Stevanne (Fink),
1938- , American; nonfiction
CON
AUERBACH, Stuart Charles,
1935- , American; journal-
ism; CON
AUERBACH, Sylvia, 1921- ,
American; nonfiction CON
AUERSPERG, Anton A. G. von
see 'GRÜN, Anastasius'
AUFI, Muhammad, 13th century,
Persian; nonfiction BU
AUFIDIUS BASSUS, -54/68
A.D., Roman; nonfiction
GR LA
AUFRICHT, Hans, 1902- ,
Austrian-American; nonfic-
tion CON
AUGARDE, Steve, 1950- , Brit-
ish; juveniles CO
AUGIER, Emile, 1820-89, French;
plays BU MCG TH
AUGUST, Eugene Robert, 1935- ,
American; nonfiction CON
AUGUSTIJNKEN van DORDT,
14th century, Dutch; poetry
BU
AUGUSTIN, Ann Sutherland,
1934- , American; nonfic-
tion CON
'AUGUSTINE, Erich' see STOIL,
Michael J.

AUGUSTINE, St. 354-430, Latin;
nonfiction BU GR LA MAG
'AUGUSTSON, Ernest' see RYDEN,
Ernest E.
AUGUSTUS, 63 B.C.-14 A.D.,
Roman; nonfiction GR LA
AUHADI, Taqi, 1565-1630, Indo-
Persian; poetry, nonfiction
PRU
AUKOFER, Frank Alexander, 1935- ,
American; nonfiction CON
AUKRUST, Olav, 1883-1929, Nor-
wegian; poetry BU CL TH
AULETTA, Ken, 1942- , Amer-
ican; journalist CON
AULETTA, Richard Paul, 1942- ,
American; nonfiction CON
AULNOY, Marie Catherine, 1650/51-
1705, French; fiction BU
AULT, Donald Duane, 1942- ,
American; nonfiction CON
AULT, Phillip H., 1914- , Amer-
ican; juveniles, journalism,
nonfiction CO CON WAR
AULTMAN, Richard Eugene,
1933- , American; nonfiction
CON
AUMANN, Francis Robert, 1901- ,
American; nonfiction CON
AUMONIER, Stacy, 1887-1928,
English; fiction ST
AUNG, Maung Htin ('The Fourth
Brother'; U. Htin Aung),
1910- , Burmese; juveniles
CO
AURAND, Harold Wilson, 1940- ,
American; nonfiction CON
AURAND, Leonard William, 1920- ,
American; nonfiction CON
AURANDT, Paul Harvey ('Paul
Harvey'), 1918- , American;
nonfiction CON
AURELIUS, Marcus (Marcus Aurel-
ius Antoninus), 121-180, Latin;
nonfiction BU GR LA MAG
AURELIUS VICTOR, Sextus, fl.
389, Roman; nonfiction BU LA
AURELL, Tage, 1895- , Swedish;
plays BU
'AURISPA, Giovanni' (G. Pichu-
merio), 1375?-1459, Italian;
nonfiction BU
AURTHUR, Robert Alan, 1922-78,
American; plays, fiction, film
CON
AUSLAENDER, Rose Scherzer,
1907- , German-American;
poetry BU

AUSLAND, John Campbell, 1920- ,
American; nonfiction CON
AUSONIUS, Decimus Magnus, 310-
95, Latin; nonfiction, poetry
BU GR LA
'AUSTEN, George' see BANNER-
MAN, James
AUSTEN, Jane, 1775-1817, Eng-
lish; fiction BU DA MAG
PO VN
AUSTER, Nancy Eileen Rose,
1926- , American; nonfiction
CON
AUSTER, Paul, 1947- , Amer-
ican; poetry, translations,
nonfiction, plays CON
AUSTIN, Alfred, 1835-1913, Eng-
lish; journalism, poetry,
plays, nonfiction DA VP
AUSTIN, Charles Marshall,
1941- , American; nonfic-
tion CON
AUSTIN, Elizabeth Schling,
1907- , American; juveniles
CO WAR
'AUSTIN, Frank' see 'BRAND,
Max'
AUSTIN, Frederick Britten, 1885-
1941, English; fiction NI
AUSTIN, Henry Wilfred, 1906- ,
British; journalism, nonfic-
tion CON
AUSTIN, James Henry, 1925- ,
American; nonfiction CON
AUSTIN, John, 1790-1859, English;
nonfiction BU
AUSTIN, John, 1922- , English;
nonfiction CON
AUSTIN, John Langshaw, 1911-60,
English; nonfiction WAK
AUSTIN, Kenneth Ashurst, 1911- ,
Australian; nonfiction CON
AUSTIN, Lettie Jane, 1925- ,
American; nonfiction CON
SH
AUSTIN, Margot, American;
juveniles CO
AUSTIN, Michel Mervyn, 1943- ,
Australian; nonfiction CON
AUSTIN, Mildred Aurelia, Amer-
ican; poetry CON
AUSTIN, Norman, 1937- , Amer-
ican; nonfiction CON
AUSTIN, Oliver Luther, Jr.,
1903- , American; juveniles,
nonfiction CO CON WAR
AUSTIN, Reid, 1931- , Amer-
ican; nonfiction CON

'AUSTIN, Tom' see JACOBS, Linda
C.
'AUSTWICK, John' (Austin Lee;
'Julian Callender'), 1904-65,
British; fiction REI
AUSUBEL, Herman, 1920-77, Amer-
ican; nonfiction CON
AUSUBEL, Marynn H., 1931?-80,
American; nonfiction CON
AUTEN, James Hudson, 1938- ,
American; nonfiction CON
AUTOBEE, George, 1949- , Amer-
ican; nonfiction MAR
AUTON, Jean d', 1465-1528, French;
nonfiction BU
'AUTRA, Ray' see TRAORE, Mama-
dou
AUTTON, Norman William James,
1920- , American; nonfiction
CON
AUVERGNE, Martial d', 1430?-
1508, French; poetry BU
AVA, fl. 1130, German; poetry
BU
AVAKIAN, Arra Steve, 1912- ,
American; nonfiction CON
AVAKUMORIC, Ivan, 1926- ,
Yugoslav-Canadian; nonfiction
CON
AVALLONE, Michael Angelo, Jr.
('Nick Carter'; 'Troy Conway';
'Priscilla Dalton'; 'Mark Dane';
'Jean-Anne de Pre'; 'Dora High-
land'; 'Steve Michaels'; 'Doro-
thea Nile'; 'Edwina Noone';
'Vance Stanton'; 'Sidney Stuart';
'Max Walker'), 1924- , Amer-
ican; fiction NI REI ST
AVANCINI, Nicolaus von, 1612-86,
Austrian; plays BU
AVELINE, Claude, 1901- , French;
fiction, nonfiction BU
AVELLANEDA, Alonso Fernández
de, Spanish; fiction BU
AVENDAÑO, Fausto, 1941- , Amer-
ican; nonfiction, fiction MAR
AVENI, Anthony Francis, 1938- ,
American; nonfiction CON
AVENTINUS, Johannes, 1477-1534,
German; nonfiction BU
AVERBAKH, Leopold Leonidovich,
1903- , Russian; nonfiction
BU
AVERCHENKO, Arkady Timofeye-
vich, 1881-1925, Russian; fic-
tion BU CL
AVERILL, Edgar Waite, 1906- ,
American; nonfiction CON

AVERILL, Esther Holden, 1902- ,
American; juveniles, nonfic-
tion KI
'AVERY, Al' see MONTGOMERY,
Rutherford G.
AVERY, Catherine Barber, 1909- ,
American; nonfiction CON
AVERY, Gillian Elise, 1926- ,
British; juveniles, nonfiction
CO DEM
AVERY, Ira ('Mavis Hathaway'),
1914- , American; nonfiction,
fiction, plays, journalism
CON
AVERY, Kay, 1908- , American;
juveniles CO
'AVERY, Lynn' see COLE, Lois
D.
AVEY, Ruby ('Vicki Page'),
1927- , British; fiction CON
'AVI' see WORTIS, Avi
AVIANUS, fl. 400, Latin; fiction
BU
AVICE, Claude ('Pierre Barbet';
'David Maine'; 'Olivier Sprig-
el'), 1925- , French; fiction
CON NI
AVICENNA see IBN-SINA
AVIDAN, David, 1934- , Israeli;
poetry, journalism BU
AVIEN(I)US, Rufius Festus, 4th
century, Latin; poetry BU LA
AVILA, Blessed Juan de, 1500-69,
Spanish; nonfiction BU
AVILA, Lilian Estelle, Amer-
ican; nonfiction CON
AVILA, Vernon L., 1941- ,
American; nonfiction MAR
AVISON, Margaret Kirkland,
1918- , Canadian; poetry
CR SEY VCP VP
AVITUS, 450-525, Latin; poetry
TH
AVRAMOVIC, Dragoslav, 1919- ,
Yugoslav-American; nonfiction
CON
'AVRELIN, M.' see STEINBERG,
Aaron Z.
AVRICH, Paul Henry, 1931- ,
American; nonfiction CON
AVRIEL, Ehud, 1917- , Austrian-
Israeli; nonfiction CON
AVRUTIS, Raymond, 1948- ,
American; nonfiction CON
AVSEYENKO, Vasily Grigoreye-
vich, 1842-1913, Russian;
nonfiction BU
AVVAKUM, Protopop, 1620-82,

Russian; nonfiction BU
AWANO SEIHO, 1899- , Japanese;
poetry HI
AWBHATHA, U., 1758-98?, Burm-
ese; translations PRU
AWDELAY, John see AUDELAY,
John
AWDELEY, John, fl. 1559-77, Eng-
lish; nonfiction BU
AWDRY, Wilbert Vere, 1911- ,
British; juveniles, nonfiction
CON
AWOLOWO, Obafemi, 1909- ,
Nigerian; nonfiction CON HER
JA
AWOONOR, Kofi (George Awoonor-
Williams), 1935- , Ghanaian;
poetry, fiction, translations,
plays BU HER JA VCP WAK
AXELL, Herbert Ernest, 1915- ,
British; nonfiction CON
AXELRAD, Jacob, 1899- , Amer-
ican; nonfiction CON
AXELROD, David Bruce, 1943- ,
American; poetry, nonfiction,
plays CON
AXELROD, George, 1922- , Amer-
ican; plays, fiction CON MCG
VCD WA
AXELROD, Herbert Richard, 1927- ,
American; nonfiction CON
AXELROD, Steven Gould, 1944- ,
American; nonfiction CON
AXINN, June, 1923- , American;
nonfiction CON
'AXTON, David' see KOONTZ, Dean
R.
AYALA, Francesco, 1906- , Span-
ish; translations, fiction BU
CL
AYALA, Francisco, 1934- , Span-
ish-American; nonfiction CON
AYALA, John Louis, 1943- , Amer-
ican; nonfiction MAR
AYALA, Reynaldo, 1934- , Amer-
ican; nonfiction MAR
AYARS, James Sterling, 1898- ,
American; juveniles CO
AYAZ SHAIKH MUBARAK, 1922- ,
Sindhi; poetry PRU
AYCKBOURN, Alan, 1939- , Eng-
lish; plays VCD WAK
AYCOCK, Roger D. see 'DEE,
Roger'
AYDELOTTE, William Osgood,
1910- , American; nonfiction
CON
'AYDY, Catherine' see TENNANT,

Emma
AYER, Sir Alfred Jules, 1910- ,
English; nonfiction WA
'AYER, Brian' see PETROCELLI,
Orlando R.
AYER, Frederick, 1917?-74, Amer-
ican; nonfiction CON
AYER, Jacqueline Brandford,
1930/32- , American; juven-
iles, nonfiction CO CON DE
KI
AYER, Margaret, American;
juveniles CO CON
AYERRA y SANTA MARIA, Fran-
cisco de, 1630-1780, Puerto
Rican; poetry HIL
AYERS, Bradley Earl, 1935- ,
American; nonfiction CON
AYERS, Robert Hyman, 1918- ,
American; nonfiction CON
AYERS, Ronald, 1948- , Amer-
ican; fiction CON
AYGI, Gennady, 1934- , Chuvash;
poetry CL
AYGUESPARSE, Albert, 1900- ,
Belgian; poetry, fiction, non-
fiction CL
AYLEN, Leon William, 1935- ,
South African; nonfiction, tv
CON
AYLESWORTH, John B., 1938- ,
Canadian-American; fiction NI
AYLESWORTH, Thomas Gibbons,
1927- , American; juveniles
CO WAR
AYLING, Harold Keith O., 1898-
1976, Anglo-American; jour-
nalism, nonfiction, fiction
CON
AYLING, Stanley Edward, 1909- ,
English; nonfiction CON
AYMAR, Brandt, 1911- , Amer-
ican; juveniles CO
AYME, Marcel, 1902-67, French;
fiction, plays BU CL CON
MCG NI TH
AYNES, Edith Annette (Pat),
1909- , American; nonfiction,
fiction CON
AYNI, Sadriddin, 1878-1954, Tajik;
poetry, nonfiction PRU
AYRAUD, Pierre see 'NARCEJAC,
Thomas'
AYRENHOFF, Kornelius Her-
mann von, 1733-1819, Austri-
an; plays BU
AYRER, Jakob, 1543?-1605, Ger-
man; plays BU TH

AYRES, James Eyvind, 1939- ,
British; nonfiction CON
AYRES, Paul see AARONS, Edward
S.
AYRES, Philip, 1638-1712, English;
translations, nonfiction BU
AYRES, Robert Underwood, 1932- ,
American; nonfiction CON
AYRTON, Michael ('Michael Gould'),
1921-75, British; nonfiction CON
AYTMANOV, Chingiz, 1928- ,
Kirghiz; translations, fiction
CL PRU
AYTON, Sir Robert (Aytoun), 1570-
1637/38, English; poetry BU
DA VP
AYTOUN, William Edmonstoune,
1813-65, Scots; nonfiction,
translations, poetry BU DA
AYVAZIAN, L. Fred ('Kenneth
Flagg'; 'Fred Levon'), 1919- ,
Turkish-American; fiction, non-
fiction CON
AYYUB, Dhu'n-Nun, 1908- , Iraqi;
fiction PRU
AZA, Vital, 1851-1912, Spanish;
poetry, plays BU
AZAD, Muhammad, 1830-1910, Urdu;
nonfiction, poetry PRU
AZAÑA, Manuel, 1880-1940, Span-
ish; nonfiction, fiction BU CL
AZAR, Edward E., 1938- , Amer-
ican; nonfiction CON
AZAT JAMALDINI, Abdu'l-vahid,
1918- , Baluchi; poetry, fic-
tion PRU
AZCARATE, Gumersindo de, 1840-
1917, Spanish; nonfiction BU
AZEGLIO, Massimo d', 1798-1866,
Italian; fiction BU TH
AZEVEDO, Aluízio Tancredo Belo,
1857-1913, Brazilian; fiction,
journalism BR BU
AZEVEDO, Guilherme, 1839-82,
Portuguese; poetry TH
AZEVEDO, Pedro Corsino de, 1905-
42, Cape Verde Islander; po-
etry HER
AZIKIWE, Benjamin Nnamde, 1904- ,
Nigerian; nonfiction, journal-
ism HER JA
AZIZ NESIN, 1915- , Turkish;
plays BU
'AZORIN' (José Martinéz Ruíz),
1894-1967, Spanish; nonfiction,
fiction BU CL CON TH
AZRIN, Nathan Harold, 1930- ,
American; nonfiction CON

AZUELA, Mariano, 1873-1952,
Mexican; fiction BR BU
MAG WA
AZUMA TSUNEYOII, 1401-94,
Japanese; poetry HI
AZUMI, Atsushi, 1907- , Ja-
panese; nonfiction, poetry
CON
AZUONYE, Chukwuma, 1945- ,
Nigerian; nonfiction, fiction
JA

B

'B. B.' see NAIRNE, Carolina O.
'BB' see WATKINS-PITCHFORD,
Denys J.
'B. V.' see THOMSON, James
BA, Mallam Amadou Hampaté,
1899/1920- , Malian; fiction,
nonfiction HER JA
BA, Oumar, 1900?- , Mau-
ritanian; poetry, nonfiction
HER
BA'AL SHEM TOV, Israel,
1700-60, Russian; nonfic-
tion BU
BA'ALBAKKI, Layle, 1937- ,
Lebanese; fiction, nonfiction
PRU
BAAR, James A., 1929- , Amer-
ican; nonfiction CON
BAAR, Jindřich Šimon, 1869-
1925, Czech; fiction BU
BAARS, Conrad Walterius, 1919- ,
Dutch-American; nonfiction
CON
BAASTAD, Babbis E. see FRIIS-
BAASTAD, Babbis E.
BAATH, Albert Ulrik, 1853-1912,
Swedish; poetry BU
BAB, The, Siyyid Ali Muhammad,
1819-50, Persian; nonfiction
BU
BABA, Ahmad al-Tinbukhti, 1556-
1627, Arab; nonfiction HER
BABA TAHER ORYAN HAMADANI,
1000-55/56, Persian; poetry
BU PRU
BABALOLA, Abeboye see BADA-
LOLA, Adeboye
BABRIUS, 1st century A.D.,
Greek; fiction GR
BABUR, Muhammad Zahiruddin,
1483-1530, ?; poetry, trans-
lations PRU
BABAYEVSKY, Semën Petrovich,

1909- , Russian; fiction BU
BABBIDGE, Homer Daniels, Jr.,
1925- , American; nonfiction
CON
BABBIE, Earl Robert, 1938- ,
American; nonfiction CON
'BABBIS, Eleanor' see FRIIS-
BAASTAD, Babbis E.
BABBITT, Bruce Edward, 1938- ,
American; nonfiction CON
BABBITT, Irving, 1865-1933, Amer-
ican; nonfiction BR BU PO
SEY
BABBITT, Natalie, 1932- , Amer-
ican; juveniles, poetry CO
CON DEM KI WAR
BABCOCK, Dennis Arthur, 1948- ,
American; juveniles CO CON
BABCOCK, Dorothy Ellen, 1931- ,
American; nonfiction CON
BABE, Thomas, 1941- , American;
plays CON
BABEL, Isaak Emanuilovich, 1894-
1941?, Russian; fiction, poetry,
plays BU CL MCG SEY TH
BABIN, Maria Teresa, 1910- ,
Puerto Rican; nonfiction HIL
BABINGTON, Anthony Patrick,
1920- , Irish; nonfiction CON
BABITS, Mihály, 1883-1941, Hungar-
ian; poetry, fiction, translations
BU CL NI SEY TH
BABITZ, Eve, 1943- , American;
fiction CON
BABITZ, Sol, 1911- , American;
nonfiction CON
'BABLI, Hillel' (Hillel Rashcgolsk),
1893-1961, American; poetry
BU
BABRIUS, 1st century, Greek; fic-
tion BU
BABRIUS (Valerius?), 2nd century,
Greek; poetry LA
BABSON, Marian, American; fic-
tion CON REI
BABSON, Roger Ward, 1875-1967,
American; nonfiction CON
BABST, Diederich Georg, 1741-
1800, German; poetry BU
BABULUS the STAMMERER see
NOTKER
BABUR, Zahiruddin Muhammed,
1483-1530, Turkish; poetry
BU LA
BACA, Albert Roy, 1930- , Amer-
ican; nonfiction MAR
BACA, Gilberto Matias, 1947- ,
American; nonfiction MAR

BACALL, Lauren, 1924- ,
American; nonfiction CON
BACARISSE, Mauricio, 1895-1931,
Spanish; poetry BU
BACCAN, 1907- , Hindi; poetry,
translations PRU
BACCHELLI, Riccardo, 1891- ,
Italian; poetry, fiction, plays,
nonfiction BO BU CL MAG
TH WA
BACCHYLIDES, 524/21-452 B.C.,
Greek; poetry BU GR LA
BACCIOCCO, Edward Joseph, Jr.,
1935- , American; nonfiction
CON
BACH, Alice Hendricks, 1942- ,
American; juveniles CON
WAR
BACH, Kent, 1943- , American;
nonfiction CON
'BACH, P. D. Q.' see SCHICKELE,
Peter
BACH, Richard David, 1936- ,
American; juveniles CO
BACH, Wilfrid, 1936- , German;
nonfiction CON
BACHELARD, Gaston, 1884-1962,
French; nonfiction BU CL
CON SEY WA
BACHEM ALENT, Rose Marie,
German-American; nonfiction
CON
BACHI, Amurath E. H. see
WOENSEL, Pieter van
BACHMAN, Fred, 1949- ,
American; juveniles CO
BACHMAN, Jerald Graybill,
1936- , American; nonfic-
tion CON
BACHMANN, Ingeborg, 1926-73,
Austrian; poetry, fiction,
translations, plays BU CL
CON TH WA
BACHMURA, Frank Thomas,
1922- , American; nonfiction
CON
BACHOFEN, Johann Jacob, 1815-
87, German; nonfiction BU
BACHUR, Elijah (Levita; Tishbi;
Germanus), 1468-1549, Heb-
rew; nonfiction BU TH
BACHYA IBN PAKUDA (Bachya
Ben Joseph), -1080, Span-
ish; poetry, nonfiction BU
BAČINSKAITE, Salomeja see
'NERIS, Salomeja'
BACKER, Dorothy, 1925- ,

American; nonfiction, fiction
CON
'BACKGAMMON, Daisy' see MUR-
RAY, John F.
BACMEISTER, Rhoda Warner,
1893- , American; juveniles
CO
BACON, Delia, 1811-59, American;
nonfiction MY
BACON, Edmund Norwood, 1910- ,
American; nonfiction CON
BACON, Edward ('Francis Boon'),
1906-81, British; nonfiction,
fiction CON
BACON, Elizabeth ('Betty Morrow'),
1914- , American; juveniles CO
BACON, Francis, 1561-1626, Eng-
lish; nonfiction BRI BU DA
MAG NI PO RU VN
'BACON, Joan Chase' see BOWDEN,
Joan C.
BACON, John, 1940- , American;
translations, nonfiction CON
BACON, Josephine Dodge (Daskam;
'Ingraham Lovell'), 1876-1961,
American; fiction, juveniles,
poetry CON
BACON, Lenice Ingram, 1895- ,
American; nonfiction CON
BACON, Margaret Hope, 1921- ,
American; juveniles CO
BACON, Marion, 1901?-75, Amer-
ican; nonfiction CON
BACON, Martha Sherman, 1917-81,
American; juveniles, fiction,
poetry CO CON KI WAR
BACON, Nancy, 1940- , American;
nonfiction, fiction, journalism,
film CON
BACON, Phillip, 1922- , Amer-
ican; nonfiction CON
BACON, Roger, 1214/20-92?, Eng-
lish; nonfiction BU DA
BACON, Ronald Leonard, 1924- ,
New Zealander; juveniles, fic-
tion, nonfiction KI
BACON, Thomas, 1700?-68, Amer-
ican; nonfiction BA
BACOVIA, George (George Vasilius),
1881-1957, Rumanian; poetry
BU CL SEY TH
BACQUE, James, 1929- , Canadian;
fiction CON
BACULARD d'ARNAUD, Francois
Thomas de, 1718-1805, French;
poetry, fiction BU
BACZYNSKI, Krzysztof Kamil (Jan
Bugaj), 1921-44, Polish; poetry

BU CL
BADALOLA, Adeboye (Babalola),
1926/30- , Nigerian; nonfic-
tion HER JA
BADAWI, Mohamed Mustafa,
1925- , Egyptian; nonfiction,
translations CON
BADCOCK, Christopher Robert,
1946- , British; nonfiction
CON
BADDELEY, Alan David, 1934- ,
British; nonfiction CON
BADE, Jane Ruth; 1932- , Amer-
ican; juveniles, nonfiction,
fiction CON
BADE, Josse ('Ascensius'), 1461/
62-1535, French; printer BU
BADE, Patrick, 1951- , British;
nonfiction CON
BADE, William Lemoine, 1928- ,
American; fiction NI
BADEN-POWELL, Dorothy, 1920- ,
British; nonfiction CON
BADEN-POWELL, Robert Stephen-
son, 1857-1941, English; ju-
veniles CO
BADER, Barbara, American;
juveniles WAR
BADER, Douglas Robert, 1910- ,
British; nonfiction CON
BADER, Julia, 1944- , Amer-
ican; nonfiction CON
BADGER, John d'Arcy, 1917- ,
Anglo-Canadian; nonfiction
CON
BADGER, Reid, 1942- , Amer-
ican; nonfiction CON
BADGLEY, Robin Francis, 1931- ,
Canadian; nonfiction CON
BADIAN, Seydou Kouyaté (Seydu
Kouyaté), 1928- , Malian; fic-
tion, poetry, plays HER JA
BADILLO, Herman, 1929- ,
Puerto Rican; nonfiction CON
BADRUDDIN CHACHI, 1346- ,
 Indo-Persian; poetry PRU
BÄCKSTRÖM, Per Johan Edvard,
1841-86, Swedish; poetry,
plays BU
BAEDA see BEDE
BAEHR, Consuelo, 1938- , Amer-
ican; nonfiction, fiction CON
BAEHR, Patricia Goehner, 1952- ,
American; juveniles CON
BAEKELMANS, Lode, 1879-1965,
Flemish; fiction, plays BU
BAENA, Juan Alfonso de, early
15th century, Spanish; poetry

BU TH
BAENZIGER, Hans, 1917- ,
Swiss-American; nonfiction
CON
BAER, Adela Swenson, 1931- ,
American; nonfiction CON
BAER, Curtis O., 1898- , Franco-
American; nonfiction CON
BAER, Donald Merle, 1931- ,
American; nonfiction CON
BAER, Earl E., 1928- , American;
nonfiction CON
BAER, Judith Abbott, 1945- ,
American; nonfiction CON
BAER, Marianne, 1932- , Amer-
ican; fiction CON
BAER, Rosemary, 1913- , Amer-
ican; nonfiction CON
BAER, Walter, S., III, 1937- ,
American; nonfiction CON
BAERG, Harry John, 1909- ,
American; juveniles CO
BAERLE, Caspar van, 1584-1648,
Dutch; poetry BU
BAERMANN, Jürgen Niklas, 1785-
1850, German; plays BU
'BAERTMAEKER, Jan de' see
SMEKEN, Jan
BAERWALD, Sara, 1948- , Amer-
ican; nonfiction CON
'BAETTICHER, Hans' see 'RINGEL-
NATZ, Joachim'
BAEUML, Franz Heinrich, 1926- ,
Austrian-American; nonfiction
CON
BAEZ, Joan, 1941- , American;
nonfiction MAR
BAFFICO, Giuseppe, 1852-1927,
Italian; journalism, fiction,
plays MCG
'BAGBY, George' see STEIN,
Aaron M.
BAGBY, George William, 1828-83,
American; journalism, nonfic-
tion BA
BAGE, Robert, 1728-1801, English;
fiction BU VN
BAGEHOT, Walter, 1826-77, Eng-
lish; nonfiction BU DA PO
BAGG, Graham William, 1917- ,
English; nonfiction CON
BAGG, Robert Ely, 1935- , Amer-
ican; poetry CON
BAGGER, Carl Christian, 1807-46,
Danish; poetry, fiction BU
BAGGESEN, Jens, 1764-1826,
Danish; poetry BU TH
BAGHDADI, Shawqi, 1928- ,

Syrian; fiction PRU
BAGIN, Donald Richard, 1938- ,
American; nonfiction CON
BAGINSKI, Frank, 1938- , Amer-
ican; cartoons CON
BAGLEY, Desmond, 1923- , Brit-
ish; fiction REI
BAGLEY, Edward Rosecrans,
1926- , American; nonfiction
CON
BAGNALL, R. D., 1945- ,
English; fiction NI
BAGNEL, Joan (Cipolla), 1933- ,
American; fiction, nonfiction
CON
BAGNI, Gwen see DUBOV, Gwen
BAGNOLD, Enid, 1889-1981, Eng-
lish; fiction, plays, poetry,
nonfiction, journalism, trans-
lations CO CON DEM VCD
VCN VD
'BAGRITSKY, Eduard Georgievich'
(E. Dzyubin), 1897-1934, Rus-
sian; poetry BU CL TH
'BAGRYANA, Elisaveta' (E. Bel-
cheva), 1893- , Bulgarian;
poetry BU TH
'BAGRYNOWSKI, K.' see SIERO-
SZEWSKI, Waclaw
BAHADUR, Krishna Prakash,
1924- , Indian; nonfiction,
translations CON
BAHAR, Muhammad Taqi ('Malik'),
1886-1951, Persian; poetry
BU PRU
BAHAT, Dan, 1938- , Polish-
Israeli; nonfiction CON
BAHA-U'LLAH, Mirza Husain-ali,
1817-92, Persian; nonfiction
BU
BAHELELE, Jacques N., 1911- ,
Zairian; fiction, poetry HER
BAHLKE, Valerie (Worth), 1933- ,
American; poetry, juveniles
CO CON
BAHLMAN, Dudley Ward Rhodes,
1923- , American; nonfiction
CON
BAHNSON, Agnew H., Jr., 1915-
64?, American; fiction NI
BAHR, Edith Jane, 1926- , Amer-
ican; nonfiction, fiction CON
BAHR, Hermann, 1863-1934, Austri-
an; plays, fiction BU CL MCG
TH
BAHR, Robert, 1940- , American;
nonfiction CON
BAHRAM GUR, fl. 420-38, Persian;

poetry PRU
BAIER, Kurt Erich, 1917- ,
Austrian-American; nonfiction
CON
BAÏF, Jean Antoine de, 1532-89,
French; nonfiction, poetry BU
TH
BAÏF, Lazare de, 1496-1547, French;
nonfiction, translations BU
BAIHAQI, Muhammad Abu'l-Fazl,
995-1077, Persian; nonfiction
BU
BAILEY, Alfred Goldsworthy,
1905- , Canadian; poetry,
nonfiction CR
BAILEY, Alfred Marshall, 1894- ,
American; nonfiction CON
BAILEY, Alice Cooper, 1890- ,
American; juveniles CO
BAILEY, Bernadine Freeman,
American; juveniles CO
BAILEY, Beryl Loftman, 1920?-
77, Jamaican; nonfiction CON
BAILEY, Carolyn Sherwin, 1875-
1961, American; juveniles,
play, poetry CO KI
BAILEY, Charles Waldo, 1929- ,
American; journalism, fiction
NI
BAILEY, Chris Harvey, 1946- ,
American; nonfiction CON
BAILEY, Corinne Jane, 1943- ,
American; poetry CON
BAILEY, David Charles, 1930- ,
American; nonfiction CON
BAILEY, Don, 1942- , Canadian;
poetry, fiction CON
BAILEY, Francis Lee, 1933- ,
American; nonfiction CON
BAILEY, Henry Christopher, 1878-
1961, British; fiction, plays,
nonfiction, juveniles REI ST
BAILEY, Hilary, 1936- , English;
fiction AS NI
BAILEY, Hillary Goodsell, 1894- ,
American; nonfiction CON
BAILEY, Jackson Holbrook, 1925- ,
American; nonfiction CON
BAILEY, James Martin, 1929- ,
American; nonfiction CON
BAILEY, James Osler, 1903- ,
American; fiction, nonfiction
NI
BAILEY, James Richard, 1919- ,
English; nonfiction CON
BAILEY, Jane Horton, 1916- ,
American; juveniles fiction
CO CON

BAILEY, Kenneth P., 1912- ,
American; nonfiction CON
BAILEY, Lloyd Richard, 1936- ,
American; nonfiction CON
BAILEY, Maralyn Collins Harrison, 1941- , English; juveniles, nonfiction CO CON
'BAILEY, Matilda' see RADFORD, Ruby L.
BAILEY, Maurice Charles, 1932- ,
English; juveniles, nonfiction CO CON
BAILEY, Minnie Elizabeth Thomas,
American; nonfiction CON
BAILEY, Patrick, 1925- , English; nonfiction CON
BAILEY, Paul, 1937- , English; fiction, plays SEY VCN WAK
BAILEY, Paul Dayton, 1906- ,
American; fiction NI
BAILEY, Pearl Mae, 1918- ,
American; nonfiction CON SH
BAILEY, Philip James, 1816-1902, English; poetry BU DA VP
BAILEY, Ralph Edgar, 1893- ,
American; juveniles CO
BAILEY, Raymond Hamby, 1938- ,
American; nonfiction CON
BAILEY, Robert, Jr., 1945- ,
American; nonfiction CON
BAILEY, Robert Wilson, 1943- ,
American; nonfiction CON
BAILEY, Ronald W., American; nonfiction SH
BAILEY, Sydney Dawson, 1916- ,
British; nonfiction CON
BAILLARGEON, Pierre, 1916-67, Canadian; fiction, nonfiction, plays, poetry CR
'BAILLEN, Claude' see DELAY-BAILLEN, Claude
BAILLIE, Hugh, 1890-1966, American; journalism CON
BAILLIE, Joanna, 1762-1851, Scots; poetry, plays BU DA VD
BAILLIE, Lady Grizel Hume, 1665-1746, Scots; songs, poetry BU DA
BAILLON, André, 1875-1932, Belgian; fiction CL
BAILON, Abelino Mendoza, 1923- , American; nonfiction MAR
BAILYN, Bernard, 1922- , American; nonfiction CON

BAIN, Alexander, 1818-1903, Scots; nonfiction BU
BAIN, Carl E., 1930- , American; nonfiction CON
BAIN, Chester Ward, 1919- ,
American; nonfiction CON
BAIN, Kenneth Bruce ('Richard Findlater'), 1921- , British; nonfiction CON
BAIN, Robert, 1932- , American; nonfiction CON
BAINBRIDGE, Beryl Margaret, 1934- , English; fiction, plays VCN WAK
BAINE, Rodney Montgomery, 1913- ,
American; nonfiction CON
BAINES, John M., 1935- , American; nonfiction CON
BAINVILLE, Jacques, 1879-1936, French; nonfiction BU
BAIR, Deirdre, 1935- , American; nonfiction CON
BAIR, Frank E., 1927- , American; nonfiction CON
BAIRD, Duncan H., 1917- , American; nonfiction CON
BAIRD, Eva Lee, American; juveniles WAR
BAIRD, Irene Todd, 1901- , Canadian; fiction, poetry, nonfiction CR
BAIRD, Jay William, 1936- ,
American; nonfiction CON
BAIRD, Joseph L., 1933- , American; nonfiction CON
BAIRD, Marie-Terese, 1918- ,
Belgian-English; fiction CON
BAIRD, Martha Joanna, 1921- ,
American; poetry, nonfiction CON
BAIRD, Nancy Disher, 1935- ,
American; nonfiction CON
BAIRD, Robert Dahlen, 1933- ,
American; nonfiction CON
BAIRD, Ronald James, 1929- ,
American; nonfiction CON
BAIRD, Thomas P., 1923- ,
American; juveniles, fiction CON WAR
BAIRD, William David, 1939- ,
American; nonfiction CON
BAIRSTOW, Jeffrey Noel, 1939- ,
English; nonfiction CON
BAJZA, Jozef Ignác, 1755-1836, Slovak; poetry, fiction BU
BAK, Wojciech, 1907-61, Polish; poetry TH
BAKALAR, James B., 1943- ,

American; nonfiction CON
BAKALIS, Michael J., 1938- ,
American; nonfiction CON
BAKALOV, T. see TSERKOVSKI,
Tsanko
BAKELESS, John Edwin, 1894- ,
American; juveniles CO
BAKELESS, Katherine Little,
1895- , American; juveniles
CO
BAKELY, Donald Carlisle, 1928- ,
American; nonfiction CON
BAKER, Adelaide Nichols, 1894- ,
American; plays CON
BAKER, Adolph, 1917- , Amer-
ican; nonfiction CON
BAKER, Alan, 1951- , English;
juveniles CO CON
'BAKER, Allison' see CRUMBAK-
ER, Alice
'BAKER, Asa' see DRESSER,
Davis
BAKER, Augusta, 1911- , Amer-
ican; nonfiction, juveniles CO
SH
BAKER, Betty Lou, 1928- , Amer-
ican; juveniles CO DE KI
'BAKER, Bill' see BAKER, Charles
W.
BAKER, Bill, 1936- , American;
journalism CON
BAKER, Bill Russell, 1933- ,
American; nonfiction CON
BAKER, Carlos Heard, 1909- ,
American; nonfiction, fiction,
poetry BOR WA
BAKER, Charles William ('Bill
Baker'), 1919- , Austrian-
American; nonfiction CON
BAKER, Dorothy, 1907-68, Amer-
ican; fiction BR SEY
BAKER, Eleanor Zuckerman, 1932- ,
American; nonfiction CON
BAKER, Elizabeth Faulkner, 1886?-
1973, American; nonfiction
CON
BAKER, Elliott, 1922- , Amer-
ican; fiction, plays CON
VCN
BAKER, Elsie ('Meg Woodson'),
1929- , American; nonfiction
CON
BAKER, Frank, 1936- , Amer-
ican; nonfiction CON
BAKER, Frederick Sherman,
1902-76, American; nonfic-
tion CON
BAKER, George, 1915-75, Amer-

ican; fiction CON
BAKER, George Pierce, 1866-1935,
American; nonfiction, plays
BR MCG SEY
BAKER, Gladys Lucille, 1910- ,
American; nonfiction CON
BAKER, Herbert George, 1920- ,
Anglo-American; nonfiction
CON
BAKER, Herschel Clay, 1914- ,
American; nonfiction CON
BAKER, Houston A., 1943- ,
American; nonfiction CON SH
BAKER, Howard Wilson, 1905- ,
American; poetry, fiction, non-
fiction, plays BR VCP
BAKER, James Lawrence, 1941- ,
American; nonfiction CON
BAKER, James T., 1940- , Amer-
ican; nonfiction CON
BAKER, James Volant, 1903- ,
English; nonfiction CON
BAKER, James W., 1924- , Amer-
ican; journalism, cartoons, non-
fiction, juveniles CO CON
BAKER, Janice Edla, 1941- ,
American; juveniles CO CON
BAKER, Jean Hogarth Harvey,
1933- , American; nonfiction
CON
BAKER, Jeannie, 1950- , British;
juveniles CO CON
BAKER, Jeffrey John Wheeler,
1931- , American; juveniles
CO CON
BAKER, John F., 1931- , British;
journalism CON
BAKER, John Randal, 1900- , Eng-
lish; nonfiction CON
BAKER, John Wesley, 1920- ,
American; nonfiction CON
BAKER, Keith Michael, 1938- ,
English; nonfiction CON
BAKER, Kenneth Frank, 1908- ,
American; nonfiction CON
BAKER, Laura Nelson, 1911- ,
American; juveniles CO
BAKER, Liva, 1930- , American;
juveniles WAR
BAKER, Lucinda, 1916- , Amer-
ican; fiction CON
BAKER, Margaret, 1890- , Eng-
lish; juveniles CO
BAKER, Margaret Joyce, 1918- ,
English; juveniles CO KI
BAKER, Mary Elizabeth Gillette,
1923- , American; juveniles
CO WAR

BAKER, Mary Ellen Penny, American; nonfiction CON
BAKER, Mary Gladys Steel ('Sheila Stuart'), 1892-1974, American; juveniles CO
BAKER, Michael Henry Chadwick, 1937- , English; nonfiction CON
BAKER, Miriam see NYE, Miriam
BAKER, Nancy Carolyn Moll, 1944- , American; journalism, nonfiction CON
BAKER, Nina Brown, 1888-1957, American; juveniles CO
BAKER, Oleda, 1934 , American; nonfiction CON
BAKER, Rachel, 1904-78, American; nonfiction CON
BAKER, Sir Richard, 1568-1644/45, English; nonfiction, translations BU
BAKER, Robert Bernard, 1937- , American; nonfiction CON
BAKER, Robert G., 1928- , American; nonfiction CON
BAKER, Robert Michael Graham, 1938- , English; juveniles CO
BAKER, Russell Wayne, 1925- , American; journalism, nonfiction CON WAK
BAKER, Samm Sinclair, 1909- , American; juveniles CO
BAKER, Scott MacMartin, 1947- , American; fiction CON
BAKER, William Joseph, 1938- , American; nonfiction CON
BAKER, William Wallace, 1921- , American; nonfiction CON
BAKER-CARR, Janet, 1934- , British; nonfiction CON
BAKER-WHITE, John, 1902- , British; nonfiction CON
BAKEWELL, Kenneth Graham Bartlett, 1931- , British; nonfiction CON
BAKHTIAR, Laleh Mehree, 1938- , Iranian; nonfiction CON
BAKHUIZEN van de BRINK, Reinier Cornelis, 1810-65, Dutch; nonfiction BU
BAKI, Mahmud Abdulbakî, 1526/27-1600, Turkish; poetry BU PRU
'BAKIN' (Takizawa Okikuni; Takizawa Tokuru), 1767-1848, Japanese; fiction BU HI PRU

BAKISH, David Joseph, 1937- , American; nonfiction CON
BAKJIAN, Andy, 1915- , American; nonfiction CON
BAKKEN, Henry Harrison, 1896- , American; nonfiction CON
BAKKER, Cornelius Bernardus, 1929- , Dutch-American; nonfiction CON
BAKKER, Elna Sundquist, 1921- , American; nonfiction CON
'BAKLANOV, Grigory Yakovlevich' (Grigory Yakolevich Fridman), 1923- , Russian; fiction CL
BAKSHIAN, Aram, 1944- , American; nonfiction CON
BAKULA, William John, Jr., 1936- , American; nonfiction CON
BAKUNIN, Mikhail Alexandrovich, 1814-76, Russian; nonfiction BU
'BAKUNTS, Aksel' (Aleksandr Tevosian), 1899-1937, Armenian; fiction PRU
BAKWIN, Harry, 1894-1973, American; nonfiction CON
'BALAAM' see LAMB, Geoffrey F.
BALABAN, John, 1943- , American; poetry, translations CON
BALACHANDRAN, Madhavarao, 1938- , Indian-American; nonfiction CON
BALACHANDRAN, Sarojini, 1934- , Indian-American; nonfiction CON
'BALAGTAS' see BATAZAR, Francisco
BALAGURA, Saul, 1943- , American; nonfiction CON
BALAKIAN, Nona, 1919- , Turkish-American; nonfiction CON
BALAKIAN, Peter, 1951- , American; poetry CON
BAL'AMI, Muhammad Abu Ali, -974?, Persian; nonfiction BU PRU
BALANCY, Pierre Guy, 1924-79, Mauritanian; journalism, nonfiction CON
BALANDIER, Georges Leon, 1920- , French; nonfiction CON
BALASKAS, Arthur, 1940- , South African; nonfiction CON
BALASSI, Baron Bálint (Balassa), 1554-94, Hungarian; poetry BU TH
BALAWYDER, Aloysius, 1924- ,

Canadian; nonfiction CON
BALBI, Gerolamo, -1530?,
Italian; nonfiction BU
BALBIN, Bohuslav, 1621-88,
Czech; nonfiction, poetry
BU
BALBO, Cesare, 1789-1853,
Italian; nonfiction BU TH
BALBUENA, Bernardo de, 1568-
1627, Spanish; poetry BR
BU HIL
'BALBUS' see HUXLEY, Sir
Julian
BALCH, Glenn, 1902- , Amer-
ican; juveniles, fiction CO
BALCHEN, Bernt, 1899-1973,
Norwegian-American; nonfic-
tion CON
BALCHIN, Nigel Marlin ('Mark
Spade'), 1908-70, English;
fiction CON DA NI
BALCHIN, William George Victor,
1916- , British; nonfiction
CON
BALCON, Michael, 1896-1977,
British; nonfiction CON
BALDE, Jakob, 1604-68, German;
poetry BU TH
BALDELLI, Giovanni, 1914- ,
Italian-English; poetry CON
BALDERSON, Margaret, 1935- ,
Australian; juveniles DEM
KI
BALDERSTON, John Lloyd, 1889-
1954, American; plays MCG
BALDERSTON, Katharine Canby,
1895-1979, American; nonfic-
tion CON
BALDICK, Robert, 1927-72, Brit-
ish; nonfiction CON
BALDINI, Antonio, 1889-1962,
Italian; nonfiction BU CL TH
BALDREE, Jasper Martin, Jr.,
1927- , American; nonfiction
CON
BALDUCCI, Carolyn Feleppa,
1946- , American; juveniles
CO WAR
BALDWIN, Anne Norris, 1938- ,
American; juveniles CO WAR
BALDWIN, Arthur W., 1904?-76,
British; nonfiction CON
'BALDWIN, Bates' see JENNINGS,
John E.
BALDWIN, Bee, New Zealander;
fiction NI
BALDWIN, Christina, 1946- ,
American; nonfiction CON

BALDWIN, Clara, American; juven-
iles CO CON
'BALDWIN, Dick' see RABORG,
Frederick A., Jr.
BALDWIN, Edward Robinson (Ned),
1935- , American; nonfiction
CON
BALDWIN, Faith, 1893-1978, Amer-
ican; fiction, nonfiction, poetry
CON
BALDWIN, Gordon C. ('Lew Gor-
don'), 1908- , American; ju-
veniles CO WAR
BALDWIN, Hanson Weightman,
1903- , American; nonfiction
CON
BALDWIN, James ('Robert Dudley'),
1841-1925, American; juveniles
CO
BALDWIN, James Arthur, 1924- ,
American; fiction, plays, non-
fiction AM BR BU CO HE
MAG MCG MCN PO SEY SH
VCD VCN VN WA
BALDWIN, John D., 1930- ,
American; nonfiction CON
BALDWIN, Joseph Glover, 1815-
64, American; fiction BA BU
MYE VN
BALDWIN, Joyce Gertrude, 1921- ,
English; nonfiction CON
BALDWIN, Leland Dewitt, 1897-
1981, American; nonfiction
CON
BALDWIN, Marshall Whithed, 1903-
75, American; nonfiction CON
BALDWIN, Robert Edward, 1924- ,
American; nonfiction CON
BALDWIN, Roger Edwin, 1929- ,
American; nonfiction CON
BALDWIN, Stanley C., 1929- ,
American; nonfiction CON
BALDWIN, William, fl. 1547-60,
English; poetry, nonfiction
BU RU
BALE, John, 1495-1563, English;
plays, nonfiction BU DA MAG
MCG RU VD
BALES, Carol Ann, 1940- , Amer-
ican; juveniles CON
BALES, Robert Freed, 1916- ,
American; nonfiction CON
BALESCU, Nicolae, 1819-52, Ru-
manian; nonfiction BU
BALET, Jan Bernard, 1913- ,
German; juveniles CO CON
DE
'BALFORT, Neil' see FANTHORPE,

Robert L.
BALFOUR, Conrad George, 1928- , American; nonfiction CON
'BALFOUR, John' see MOORE, James
'BALFOUR, Patrick' see KINROSS, Patrick
BALIAN, Lorna Kohl, 1929- , American; juveniles CO CON WAR
BALINSKI, Stanislaw, 1899- , Polish; poetry, fiction, nonfiction, translations CL
BALINT, György, 1906-43, Hungarian; journalism, nonfiction TH
BALJEU, Joost, 1925- , Dutch; nonfiction CON
'BALKAVI' (Tryambak Bapuji Thombare), 1890-1918, Marathi; poetry PRU
BALKIN, Richard, 1938- , American; nonfiction CON
BALL, Brian Neville, 1932- , English; fiction NI
BALL, David, 1937- , American; nonfiction, poetry CON
BALL, Doris B. C. see 'BELL, Josephine'
BALL, Edith L., 1905- , American; nonfiction CON
BALL, Hugo, 1886-1927, Swiss; nonfiction, poetry BU CL SEY TH
BALL, John Dudley, Jr., 1911- , American; fiction, juveniles NI REI ST
BALL, Marion Jokl, 1940- , South African-American; nonfiction CON
BALL, Robert Myers, 1914- , American; nonfiction CON
BALL, Sylvia Patricia ('E. Squires England'; 'Eric Squires'; 'Patricia Squires'), 1936- , English; fiction CON
'BALL, Zachary' see MASTERS, Kelly R.
BALLANTINE, John Winthrop, 1920- , American; nonfiction CON
BALLANTINE, Joseph W., 1890?-1973, American; nonfiction CON
BALLANTINE, Richard, 1940- , American; nonfiction, fiction CON

BALLANTRAE, Bernard Edward Fergusson, 1911-80, British; nonfiction, poetry CON
BALLANTYNE, David Watt, 1924- , New Zealander; fiction, plays, juveniles CON VCN
BALLANTYNE, Robert Michael ('Comus'), 1825-94, Scots; juveniles, nonfiction BU CO DA KI VN
BALLANTYNE, Sheila, 1936- , American; fiction CON
BALLARD, Allen Butler, Jr., 1930- , American; nonfiction CON
BALLARD, James Graham, 1930- , British; fiction, plays AS NI VCN WA
'BALLARD, K. G.' see ROTH, Holly
BALLARD, Lowell Clyne, 1904- , American; juveniles CO
BALLARD, Martin, 1929- , British; juveniles KI
BALLARD, Willis Todhunter ('P. D. Ballard'; 'Parker Bonner'; 'Nick Carter'; 'Harrison Hunt'; 'John Hunter'; 'Neil MacNeil'; 'John Shepherd'), 1903- , American; fiction REI
BALLEM, John, 1925- , American; fiction, nonfiction CON
BALLEN, Roger, 1950- , American; nonfiction CON
BALLER, Warren Robert, 1900- , American; nonfiction CON
BALLESTER i MORAGUES, Alexandre, 1934- , Catalan; plays CL
BALLESTEROS, David, 1933- , American; nonfiction MAR
BALLESTEROS, Octavio A., 1936- , American; nonfiction MAR
BALLINGER, Bill Sanborn ('B. X. Sanborn'; 'Frederic Freyer'), 1912-80, American; tv, fiction, plays CON REI ST
BALLINGER, Violet Margaret (Margaret Hodgson), 1894- , Scots-South African; nonfiction CON
BALLON, Robert Jean, 1919- , Belgian; nonfiction CON
BALLONOFF, Paul Alan, 1943- , American; nonfiction CON
BALLOW, Tom, 1931- , American; juveniles CON
BALME, Maurice George, 1925- ,

English; nonfiction CON
BALMER, Edwin, 1883-1959,
American; fiction NI REI ST
BALMES URPIA, Jaime, 1810-48,
Spanish; nonfiction BU
BAL'MONT, Konstantin Dmitriye-
vich, 1867-1943, Russian;
poetry BU CL TH
BALMORI, Jesus, 1886-1948,
Filipino; poetry PRU
BALOGH, Thomas, 1905- ,
Hungarian-English; nonfiction
CON
BALOGUN, Ola, 1945- , Niger-
ian; fiction, plays HER JA
BALOW, Tom, 1931- , Ameri-
can; juveniles CO
'BALSAMO, José' see MORALES
CABRERA, Pablo
BALSDON, Dacre, 1901-77, Brit-
ish; fiction NI
BALSEIRO, José A., 1900- ,
Puerto Rican; nonfiction, po-
etry, fiction CON HIL
BALSIGER, David Wayne ('David
Wayne'), 1945- , American;
nonfiction CON
BALTAZAR, Francisco ('Bala-
gatas'), 1788-1862, Filipino,
poetry LA PRU
BALTAZZI, Evan Serge, 1919- ,
American; nonfiction CON
BALTES, Paul B., 1939- ,
German-American; nonfiction
CON
BALTHAZAR, Earl Edward,
1918- , American; nonfic-
tion CON
BAL'TRUSHAITIS, Jurgis, 1873-
1944, Russian; poetry BU
BALUCKI, Michal ('Elpidon'; 'Za-
lega'), 1837-1901, Polish;
plays CL
BALY, Monica Eileen, 1914- ,
British; nonfiction CON
BALZAC, Honoré de, 1799-1850,
French; fiction, plays BU
MAG MCG NI ST TH
BALZAC, Jean Louis Guez de,
1597-1654, French; nonfiction
BU TH
BALZER, Richard Jay, 1944- ,
American; nonfiction CON
BALZER, Robert Lawrence,
1912- , American; nonfic-
tion CON
BAMBER, George, American;
fiction NI

BAMBERGER, Bernard Jacob,
1904-80, American; nonfiction
CON
BAMBOTE, Pierre Makambo,
1932- , Central African; po-
etry HER JA
BAMBROUGH, John Renford,
1926- , American; nonfiction
CON
BAMDAD, Ahmad, 1925- , Per-
sian; poetry BU
BAMFORD, Paul Walden, 1921- ,
American; nonfiction CON
'BAMFYLDE, Walter' see BEVAN,
Tom
'BAMM, Peter' (Kurt Emmrich),
1897- , German; fiction, non-
fiction BU TH
BAMMAN, Henry A., 1918- ,
American; juveniles CO
BANA, 7th century, Sanskrit; non-
fiction, poetry BU LA PRU
BANAPHUL, 1899- , Bengali; po-
etry, fiction PRU
'BAÑAS, L. K.' American; non-
fiction MAR
BANBURY, Philip, 1914- , British;
nonfiction CON
BANCES y LOPEZ-CANDAMO,
Francisco Antonio, 1662-1704,
Spanish; plays BU MCG TH
BANCHS, Enrique, 1888-1968, Ar-
gentinian; poetry BR BU
BANCROFT, Anne, 1923- , Eng-
lish; nonfiction CON
BANCROFT, George, 1800-91,
American; nonfiction BR MY
PO
BANCROFT, Griffing, 1907- ,
American; juveniles CO
BANCROFT, Iris Nelson ('Andrea
Layto'; 'Ingrid Nielson'),
1922- , American; fiction
CON
'BANCROFT, Laura' see BAUM,
Lyman F.
BANCROFT, Peter, 1916- , Amer-
ican; nonfiction CON
'BANCROFT, Robert' see KIRSCH,
Robert R.
BANDEIRA FILHO, Manuel Car-
neiro de Sousa, 1885/86-1968,
Brazilian; poetry BR BU WA
BANDELLO, Mateo, 1480/85-
1561/62, Italian; poetry BO
BU RU TH
BANDY, Leland A., 1935- , Amer-
ican; journalism CON

BANDYOPADHYAY, Bibhutibhusan, 1894-1950, Bengali; fiction, nonfiction PRU
BANDYOPADHYAY, Manik, 1908-56, Bengali; fiction PRU
BANDYOPADHYAY, Tarasankar, 1898-1971, Bengali; fiction PRU
BANEL, Joseph, 1943- , Canadian; juveniles CON
BANER, Skulda Vanadis, 1897-1964, American; juveniles CO
BANERJE, Bibhuti Bhusan, 1894-1950, Bengali; fiction BU
BANERJE, Tarasankar, 1898- , Bengali; fiction BU
BANFIELD, Alexander William Francis, 1918- , Canadian; nonfiction CON
BANFIELD, Edward Christie, 1916- , American; nonfiction CON
BANG, Betsy, 1912- , American; nonfiction CON
BANG, Herman, 1857-1912, Danish; fiction BU CL TH
BANG, Molly Garret ('Garrett Bang'), 1943- , American; juveniles CO CON
BANGERT, Ethel Elizabeth, 1912- , American; fiction CON
BANGERT, William Valentine, 1911- , American; nonfiction CON
BANGERTER, Lowell Allen, 1941- , American; nonfiction CON
BANGHART, Charles Kenneth, 1910?-80, American; journalism CON
BANGS, John Kendrick, 1862-1922, American; fiction, journalism NI ST
BANIM, John, 1798-1842/44, Irish; fiction, plays, poetry BU HO VN
BANIM, Michael, 1796-1874, Irish; fiction BU HO
BANIS, Victor Jerome ('Jan Alexander'), 1937- , American; nonfiction, fiction CON
BANISTER, Gary L., 1948- , American; nonfiction CON
BANISTER, Manly Miles, 1914- , American; fiction, translations CON NI
BANK, Mirra, 1945- , American;

nonfiction, fiction CON
BANK, Theodore Paul II ('Ted Bank'; 'Ted Kirk'), 1923- , American; nonfiction CON
BANKI, Hans-Georg, 1920- , Swiss; nonfiction CON
BANKOLE, Timothy, 1920- , Sierra Leonese; poetry, journalism HER
BANKS, Hal Norman, 1921- , American; nonfiction CON
BANKS, Harlan Parker, 1913- , American; nonfiction CON
BANKS, James Houston, 1925- , American; journalism, nonfiction CON
BANKS, Jane ('Taylor Banks'), 1913- , American; nonfiction CON
BANKS, John, fl. 1677-96, English; plays VD
BANKS, Laura Stockton Voorhees, 1908?-80, American; journalism, juveniles CO CON
BANKS, Raymond E., 1918?- , American; fiction AS NI
BANKS, Russell, 1940- , American; nonfiction CON
'BANKS, Taylor' see BANKS, Jane
BANKSON, Douglas Henneck, 1920- , American; plays CON
BANNA'I see BENA'I
'BANNER, Angela' see MADDISON, Angela M.
BANNER, James Morrill, Jr., 1935- , American; nonfiction CON
BANNER, Lois Wendland, 1939- , American; nonfiction CON
BANNER, Melvin Edward, 1914- , American; nonfiction CON
BANNER, William Augustus, 1915- , American; nonfiction CON
BANNERMAN, Helen Brodie, 1863-1946, British; juveniles CO KI
BANNERMAN, James ('John Charles Kirkpatrick McNaught'; 'George Austen'; 'Mark Carter'; 'Peter Davidson'; 'Robert Elliott'; 'Lajos Dohanyi Lajos'), 1902- , Canadian; radio CR
'BANNERMAN, Mark' see LEWING, Anthony C.
BANNICK, Nancy Meredith, 1926- , American; nonfiction CON
BANNING, Lance Gilbert, 1942- , American; nonfiction CON

BANNISTER, Donald, 1928- ,
English; nonfiction CON
'BANNISTER, Pat' see DAVIS,
Lou Ellen
BANNON, Barbara Anne, 1928- ,
American; journalism CON
BANNON, Laura, -1963, Amer-
ican; juveniles CO
BANTA, Martha, 1928- , Amer-
ican; nonfiction CON
'BANTI, Anna' (Lucia Longhi
Lopresti), 1895- , Italian;
fiction, nonfiction BO CL
WA
BANTOCK, Gavin Marcus, 1939- ,
British; poetry, plays VCP
BANVILLE, John, 1945- , Irish;
fiction HO
BANVILLE, Théodore de, 1823-
91, French; poetry, nonfiction,
plays BU MCG TH
BANVILLE, Thomas George,
1924- , American; nonfiction
CON
'BAPTIST, R. Hernekin' see
LEWIS, Ethelreda
BAPTISTE, Victor N., 1930- ,
American; nonfiction MAR
BAR HEBRAEUS (Abu'l-Faraj,
Gregory), 1226-86, Syrian;
nonfiction LA
BARAC, Antun, 1894-1955, Croa-
tian; nonfiction CL
BARACH, Arnold B., 1913- ,
American; nonfiction CON
BARADA, William Richard,
1913- , American; nonfiction
CON
BARAHENI, Reza, 1935- ,
Iranian-American; poetry,
translations, plays BU CON
BARAHONA de SOTO, Luis,
1547-95, Spanish; poetry BU
BARAKA, Imamu Amiri see
JONES, Leroi
BARAM, Phillip Jason, 1938- ,
American; nonfiction CON
BARANAUSKAS, Antanas (Baronas),
1835-1902, Lithuanian; po-
etry BU
BARANET, Nancy Neiman, 1933- ,
American; nonfiction CON
BARANGA, Aurel, 1913- , Ru-
manian; plays BU
BARANOVICH, Lazar, 1620-93,
Russian; nonfiction BU
BARANTSEVICH, Kazimir Stan-
islavovich, 1851-1927, Rus-

sian; fiction BU
BARASCH, Moshe, 1920- , Ru-
manian-Israeli; nonfiction CON
BARASH, Asher, 1889-1952, Israeli;
poetry, fiction BU LA TH
BARATASHVILI, Nikoloz, 1817-45,
Georgian; poetry PRU
BARATYNSKY, Evgeny Abramovich
(Boratynsky), 1800-44, Russian;
poetry BU TH
BARBA, Alma Maria Acevedo,
1928- , American; nonfiction,
juveniles MAR
'BARBA JACOB, Porfirio' (Miguel
Angel Osorio Benítez; 'Maín
Ximénez'; 'Ricardo Arenales'),
1883-1942, Colombian; poetry
BR BU
BARBACH, Lonnie Garfield, 1946- ,
American; nonfiction CON
'BARBARE, Rholf' see VOLKOFF,
Vladimir
'BARBARY, James' see BAUMANN,
Amy B.; BEECHING, Jack
BARBAULD, Anna Letitia Aikin,
1743-1825, English; poetry BU
DA VP
BARBEAU, Arthur Edward, 1936- ,
American; nonfiction CON
BARBEAU, Charles Marius, 1883- ,
Canadian; nonfiction BU
BARBEE, David Edwin, 1936- ,
American; nonfiction CON
'BARBER, Antonia' see ANTHONY,
Barbara
BARBER, Bernard, 1918- , Amer-
ican; nonfiction CON
BARBER, Cyril John, 1934- ,
South African-American; non-
fiction CON
BARBER, Dulan F. ('David Fletch-
er'), 1940- , English; fiction,
juveniles CON
BARBER, Jesse, 1893-1979, Amer-
ican; nonfiction CON
BARBER, Lucy Lombardi, 1882?-
1974, American; nonfiction CON
BARBER, Lynn, 1944- , British;
journalism, nonfiction CON
BARBER, Philip W., 1903-81,
American; plays CON
BARBER, Samuel, 1910-81, Amer-
ican; composer CON
BARBER, Stephen Guy ('Guy Ber-
nard'), 1921-80, American;
nonfiction CON
BARBER, Theodore Xenophon, 1927- ,
American; nonfiction CON

BARBER, William Joseph, 1925- ,
American; nonfiction CON
BARBERA, Mario, 1939- , Amer-
ican; nonfiction CON
BARBERINO, Andrea da, 1370-
1432, Italian; fiction BU
BARBERO, Yves Regis Francois,
1943- , Franco-American;
fiction CON
'BARBET, Pierre' see AVICE,
Claude
'BARBETTE, Jay' see SPICER,
Bart
BARBEY d'AUREVILLY, Jules
Amédée, 1808-89, French;
fiction, nonfiction BU TH
BARBI, Michele, 1867-1941,
Italian; nonfiction BU
BARBIER, Henri Auguste,
1805-82, French; poetry
BU TH
BARBIERI, Francisco, 1823-94,
Spanish; nonfiction .BU
BARBIERI, Giovanni Maria, 1519-
74, Italian; poetry BU
BARBILIAN, Dan see 'BARBU,
Ion'
BARBLAN, Gudench, 1860-1916,
Raeto-Romansch; poetry BU
BARBOSA, Domingos Caldas,
1738?-1800, Angolan; poetry
HER
BARBOSA, Jorge (Vera Cruz),
1902-71, Cape Verde Island-
er; poetry, fiction CL HER
JA
BARBOSA de OLIVEIRA, Antonio
Rui, 1849-1923, Brazilian;
nonfiction BR
BARBOTIN, Edmond, 1920- ,
French; nonfiction CON
BARBOUR, Arthur Joseph, 1926- ,
American; nonfiction CON
BARBOUR, Brian Michael, 1943- ,
American; nonfiction CON
BARBOUR, Douglas Fleming,
1940- , Canadian; poetry,
nonfiction CON VCP
BARBOUR, Floyd, American;
anthologies SH
BARBOUR, John, 1316/20-95,
Scots; poetry BU DA PO VP
BARBOUR, Michael George,
1942- , American; nonfiction,
poetry, fiction CON
BARBOUR, Nevill, 1895-1972,
British; journalism, nonfiction
CON

BARBOUR, Ralph Henry ('Richard
Stillman Powell'), 1870-1944,
American; juveniles CO
BARBOUR, Roger William, 1919- ,
American; nonfiction CON
BARBOUR, Ruth Peeling, 1924- ,
American; plays, journalism
CON
'BARBOUR, Thomas L.' see LE-
SURE, Thomas B.
BARBROOK, Alexander Thomas,
1927- , English; nonfiction
CON
BARBU, Eugen, 1924- , Rumanian;
fiction, journalism BU
'BARBU, Ion' (Dan Barbilian), 1895-
1961, Rumanian; poetry BU
CL TH
BARBUD, fl. 600, Persian; poetry
PRU
BARBUSSE, Henri, 1873-1935,
French; fiction BU CL MAG
NI TH
'BARCA, Amilcar' see MELENDEZ
MUNOZ, Miguel
BARCHEK, James Robert, 1935- ,
American; nonfiction CON
BARCHUS, Agnes Josephine, 1893- ,
American; nonfiction CON
BARCLAY, Alan, English; fiction
NI
BARCLAY, Alexander, 1475?-1552,
Scots; poetry, translations,
nonfiction BU DA RU VP
'BARCLAY, Ann' see GREIG, Maysie
'BARCLAY, Gabriel,' House Name
NI
BARCLAY, Glen St. John, 1930- ,
New Zealander; nonfiction CON
BARCLAY, Hartley Wade, 1903-
78, American; nonfiction CON
BARCLAY, Isabel see DOBELL,
Isabel M. B.
BARCLAY, John, 1582-1621, Scots;
poetry, nonfiction, fiction BU
DA MAG
BARCLAY, Oliver Rainsford ('A. N.
Triton'), 1919- , English; non-
fiction CON
BARCLAY, William, 1907-78, Scots;
nonfiction CON
BARCYNSKI, Leon Roger ('Osborne
Phillips'), 1949- , British;
nonfiction CON
BARD, James Alan, 1925- ,
American; nonfiction CON
BARD, Morton, 1924- , Austrian-
American; nonfiction CON

BARDACH, John Eugene, 1915- ,
Austrian-American; nonfiction
CON
BARDARSON, Hjalmar Roegnvaldur,
1918- , Icelander; nonfiction
CON
'BARDE, Sined der' see DEVIS,
Johan N. C.
BARDECHE, Maurice, 1909- ,
French; nonfiction CL
BARDENS, Amey E., 1894?-
1974, American; nonfiction
CON
BARDI, Pietro Maria, 1900- ,
Italian-Brazilian; nonfiction
CON
BARDIN, John Franklin ('Douglas
Ashe'; 'Gregory Tree'),
1916-81, American; fiction
CON REI
BARDOLPH, Richard, 1915- ,
American; nonfiction CON
BARDON, Edward John, 1933- ,
American; nonfiction CON
BARDON, Jack Irving, 1925- ,
American; nonfiction CON
BARDOT, Louis ('Pilou'), 1896-
1975, French; poetry CON
BARDWELL, Leland, 1930?- ,
Irish; poetry, fiction HO
BARDWICK, Judith Marcia,
1933- , American; nonfic-
tion CON
BARE, Arnold Edwin, 1920- ,
American; juveniles CO
BARE, Colleen Stanley, Amer-
ican; juveniles CON
BAREA, Arturo, 1897-1957, Span-
ish; fiction BU CL
BARETSKI, Charles Allan, 1918- ,
American; nonfiction CON
BARETTI, Giuseppe, 1719-89,
Italian; nonfiction, poetry,
translations, journalism BO
BU TH
BARFIELD, Arthur Owen, 1898- ,
English; fiction BOR NI
BARFORD, Carol, 1931- , Amer-
ican; juveniles CON
BARFORD, Philip Trevelyan,
1925- , British; nonfiction
CON
BARGAGLI, Girolamo, 1537-86,
Italian; poetry, plays MCG
BARGATE, Verity, 1941?-81,
British; fiction CON
BARGELLINI, Piero, 1897-1980?,
Italian; nonfiction CON

BARGER, James David, 1947- ,
American; nonfiction CON
BARGONNE, Charles see 'FARRE-
RE, Claude'
BARHAM, Richard Harris ('Thomas
Ingoldsby'), 1788-1845, English;
poetry BU MAG VP
BARHEBRAEUS, Grigor Abu'l Faraj
bar, 1225/26-86, Syrian; non-
fiction, poetry PRU
BARILLET, Pierre, 1923- , French;
film, plays MCG
BARING, Arnulf Martin, 1932- ,
German; nonfiction CON
BARING, Maurice, 1874-1945, Eng-
lish; poetry, fiction, nonfiction,
plays BU PO VN
BARING-GOULD, Sabine, 1834-
1924, English; songs, fiction
DA VN
BARISH, Matthew, 1907- , Amer-
ican; juveniles, nonfiction CO
CON WAR
BARJAVEL, René, 1911- , French;
fiction, journalism, film AS
NI
BARKALOW, Frederick Schenck,
Jr., 1914- , American; non-
fiction CON
BARKAS, Janet, 1948- , Amer-
ican; nonfiction CON
'BARKEE, Asouff' see STRUNG,
Norman
BARKER, Albert W. ('Reefe King';
'Hawk Macrae'), 1900- ,
American; juveniles, fiction
CO CON
BARKER, Audrey Lillian, 1918- ,
British; fiction, tv VCN
BARKER, Carol M., 1942- ,
American; nonfiction CON
BARKER, Charles Albro, 1904- ,
American; nonfiction CON
BARKER, Dudley ('Lionel Black';
'Anthony Matthews'), 1910-80?,
British; journalism, nonfiction,
fiction CON REI
BARKER, Elliott Speer, 1886- ,
American; nonfiction CON
BARKER, Eric, 1905-73, American;
poetry CON
BARKER, Sir Ernest, 1874-1960,
English; nonfiction CON DA
BARKER, Esther Temperley,
1910- , American; plays,
journalism CON
BARKER, George Granville, 1913- ,
English; poetry, fiction, plays

BU DA MAG PO SEY VCP
VP
BARKER, Gerard Arthur, 1930- ,
German-American; nonfiction
CON
BARKER, Harley Granville see
GRANVILLE-BARKER, Harley
BARKER, Howard, 1946- , Brit-
ish; plays CON VCD
BARKER, James Nelson, 1784-
1858, American; plays BR
BU MCG VD
BARKER, Jane Valentine, 1930- ,
American; nonfiction CON
BARKER, Joseph, 1929- , Brit-
ish; fiction CON
BARKER, Larry Lee, 1941- ,
American; nonfiction CON
BARKER, Mary Anne, 1831-1911,
New Zealander; fiction BU
BARKER, Melvern, 1907- ,
American; juveniles CO
BARKER, Nicolas John, 1932- ,
British; nonfiction CON
BARKER, Rodney Steven, 1942- ,
English; nonfiction CON
BARKER, Ronald ('E. B. Ron-
ald'), 1921?-76, British; fic-
tion CON
BARKER, S. Omar ('Jose Canusi';
'Phil Squires'; 'Dan Scott'),
1894- , American; juveniles
CO
BARKER, Terence S., 1941- ,
English; nonfiction CON
BARKER, Will ('Doug Demarest'),
1908- , American; juveniles CO
BARKER, William John, Amer-
ican; nonfiction CON
BARKHOUSE, Joyce, 1913- ,
Canadian; nonfiction, juven-
iles, journalism CON
BARKIN, Kenneth David, 1939- ,
American; nonfiction CON
BARKLEY, James Edward,
1941- , American; journal-
ism CO
BARKLEY, Vada Lee, 1919- ,
American; nonfiction CON
BARKOW, Al, 1932- , American;
nonfiction CON
BARKSDALE, Ethelbert Courtland,
1944- , American; nonfiction
CON
BARKSDALE, Richard Kenneth,
1915- , American; nonfiction,
fiction CON SH
BARKSTED, William, fl. 1611,

English; poetry BU
BARLACH, Ernst, 1870-1938, Ger-
man; plays, poetry BU CL
MCG TH
'BARLAY, Bennet' see CROSSEN,
Kendell F.
BARLIN, Anne Lief, 1916- ,
Franco-American; nonfiction
CON
BARLOUGH, Jeffrey Ernest, 1953- ,
American; nonfiction CON
BARLOW, Genevieve, 1910- ,
American; juveniles WAR
BARLOW, James, 1921-73, British;
fiction CON NI
BARLOW, James Stanley, Jr.,
1924- , American; nonfiction
CON
BARLOW, Jane, 1857-1917, Irish;
poetry, fiction HO
BARLOW, Joel, 1754-1812, Amer-
ican; poetry, nonfiction BR
BU PO VP
'BARLOW, Robert O.' see MEYER,
Heinrich
BARLOW, Sanna M. see ROSSI,
Sanna M.
BARLOW, Thomas Edward, 1931- ,
American; nonfiction CON
BARLOW, Wilfred, 1915- , British;
nonfiction CON
BARLTROP, Robert ('Robert Cost-
er'), 1922- , British; non-
fiction CON
BARMAN, Alicerose, 1919- ,
American; nonfiction CON
BARMASH, Isadore, 1921- ,
American; nonfiction CON
BARNA, Yon, 1927- , Rumanian-
American; nonfiction CON
'BARNABAS' see WEST, Charles C.
BARNABY, Ralph Stanton, 1839- ,
American; juveniles, nonfiction
CO CON WAR
BARNARD, Lady Anne Lindsay,
1750-1825, Scots; poetry, songs
BU DA
BARNARD, Charles Nelson III,
1924- , American; nonfiction
CON
BARNARD, Christiaan Neethling,
1922- , South African; non-
fiction CON
BARNARD, Howard Clive, 1884- ,
British; nonfiction CON
BARNARD, John Lawrence, 1912?-
77, American; fiction, nonfic-
tion CON

BARNARD, Leslie Gordon, 1890-
1961, Canadian; fiction,
plays CR
BARNARD, Robert, 1936- ,
British; nonfiction CON
BARNARD, William Dean, 1942- ,
American; nonfiction CON
'BAR-NATAN, Moshe' see LOU-
VISH, Misha
BARNE, Kitty Marion, 1883-
1957, British; juveniles, plays,
fiction KI WAR
BARNER, Bob, 1947- , Amer-
ican; juveniles CON
BARNES, Arthur Kelvin ('Kelvin
Kent'), 1911-69, American;
fiction AS NI
BARNES, Barnabe, 1570-1609,
English; poetry, plays BU
DA VP
BARNES, Barry, 1943- , Brit-
ish; nonfiction CON
BARNES, Clive Alexander,
1927- , Anglo-American;
nonfiction CON
BARNES, Djuna Chappell, 1892-
1982, American; plays, fiction
BR BU SEY VCD VCN VN
BARNES, Douglas, 1927- , Brit-
ish; nonfiction CON
BARNES, Frank Eric Wollencott,
1907-62, American; juveniles
CO
BARNES, Harry Elmer, 1889-
1968, American; nonfiction
CON
BARNES, J., 1944- , British;
nonfiction CON
BARNES, Jack, 1920- , Amer-
ican; journalism CON
BARNES, Jack, 1940- , Amer-
ican; nonfiction CON
BARNES, Joanna, 1934- , Amer-
ican; nonfiction, fiction CON
BARNES, John, 1908- , Amer-
ican; nonfiction CON
BARNES, John Arundel, 1918- ,
British; nonfiction CON
BARNES, Julian, 1946- , Brit-
ish; fiction, nonfiction CON
BARNES, Juliana, see BERNERS,
Juliana
BARNES, Mary, 1923- , British;
nonfiction CON
BARNES, Myra Edwards, 1933- ,
American; nonfiction NI
BARNES, Peter, 1931- , English;
plays, film CON VCD

BARNES, Robert Morson, 1940- ,
American; nonfiction CON
BARNES, William, 1801-86, Eng-
lish; poetry, nonfiction BU DA
PO VP
BARNESS, Richard, 1917- , Amer-
ican; fiction CON
BARNETSON, William Denholm,
1917-81, Scots; journalism
CON
BARNETT, Franklin, 1903- ,
American; nonfiction, fiction
CON
BARNETT, Homer Garner, 1906- ,
American; nonfiction CON
BARNETT, Leo, 1925- , Amer-
ican; juveniles WAR
BARNETT, Lincoln, 1909-79, Amer-
ican; journalism, nonfiction
CON WA
BARNETT, Malcolm Joel, 1941- ,
American; nonfiction CON
BARNETT, Marva Tuttle, 1913- ,
American; nonfiction CON
BARNETT, Maurice, 1917-80,
British; nonfiction CON
BARNETT, Michael, 1930- , Eng-
lish; nonfiction CON
BARNETTE, Henlee Hulix, 1911- ,
American; nonfiction CON
BARNEY, John Stewart, 1868?-
1925, American; fiction NI
BARNEY, Kenneth D., 1921- ,
American; nonfiction CON
BARNEY, Natalie, 1876-1972,
American; fiction RO
BARNEY, Stephen Allen, 1942- ,
American; nonfiction CON
BARNEY, William Lesko, 1943- ,
American; nonfiction CON
BARNFIELD, Richard, 1574-1627,
English; poetry BU DA PO
RU VP
BARNHART, Joe Edward, 1931- ,
American; nonfiction CON
BARNHOUSE, Donald, American;
nonfiction CON
BARNHOUSE, Ruth Tiffany, 1923- ,
Franco-American; nonfiction
CON
BARNIE, John, 1941- , Welsh;
nonfiction, poetry CON
BARNOON, Shlomo, 1940- , Amer-
ican; nonfiction CON
BARNOUW, Victor, 1915- , Dutch-
American; nonfiction CON
BARNS, John Wintour Baldwin,
1912-74, British; nonfiction CON

BARNSLEY, Alan Gabriel see
'FIELDING, Gabriel'
BARNSTONE, Willis, 1927- ,
American; juveniles CO
BARNUM, Jay Hyde, 1888?-1962,
American; juveniles CO
BARNWELL, D. Robinson, 1915- ,
American; juveniles WAR
BARNWELL, William Curtis,
1943- , American; fiction
CON
BARO, Gene, 1924- , American;
poetry VCP
BAROFF, George Stanley, 1924- ,
American; nonfiction CON
BAROJA y NESSI, Pío, 1872-1956,
Spanish; fiction BU CL SEY
TH
BAROLINI, Antonio, 1910-71,
Italian; poetry, fiction, jour-
nalism CL
BAROLINI, Helen, 1925- , Amer-
ican; translation, poetry, radio
CON
'BAROLL, Grady' see BOGRAD,
Larry
BAROLSKY, Paul, 1941- , Amer-
ican; nonfiction CON
BARON, Devorah, 1887-1956, Is-
raeli; fiction BU
BARON, Herman, 1941- , Amer-
ican; nonfiction CON
BARON, Mary Kelley, 1944- ,
American; poetry CON
BARON, Ora Wendy ('Wendy Dim-
son'), 1937- , English; non-
fiction CON
BARON, Oscar ('Orson T. Borden'),
1908?-76, American; nonfiction
CON
'BARON, Othello' see FANTHORPE,
Robert L.
BARON, Robert Alex, 1920- ,
American; nonfiction CON
BARON, Salo Wittmayer, 1895- ,
Austrian-American; nonfiction
CON
BARON, Virginia Olsen, 1931- ,
American; juveniles WAR
BARONDESS, Sue (Kaufman), 1926-
77, American; fiction CON
BARONE, Michael, 1944- , Amer-
ican; nonfiction CON
BARONIAN, Hagop, 1842-91, Ar-
menian; fiction BU
BARONIO, Cesare, 1538-1607,
Italian; nonfiction BU TH
BAROODY, Jamil Murad, 1905-79,

Lebanese-American; nonfiction
CON
BAROOSHIAN, Dickran Vahan,
1932- , American; nonfiction
CON
BARR, Alfred Hamilton, Jr.,
1902-81, American; nonfiction
CON
BARR, Betty ('Betty Skipper'),
1932- , British; juveniles
CON
BARR, Beverly, American; nonfic-
tion CON
'BARR, Densil Neve' (Douglas Nor-
ton Buttrey), fl. 1940's-50's,
American?; fiction CON NI
BARR, Donald, 1921- , American;
fiction, juveniles CO NI WAR
BARR, Donald Roy, 1938- , Amer-
ican; nonfiction CON
BARR, Jeff, 1941- , American;
nonfiction CON
BARR, Jene, 1900- , Russian-
American; juveniles CO
BARR, Jennifer, 1945- , Amer-
ican; nonfiction CON
BARR, John Jay, 1942- , Amer-
ican; nonfiction CON
BARR, Robert, 1850-1912, Scots;
fiction, journalism NI ST
BARR, Tyrone C., fl. 1959, Brit-
ish; fiction NI
BARRACLOUGH, Geoffrey, 1908- ,
English; nonfiction CON WA
BARRACLOUGH, Solon Lovett,
1922- , American; nonfiction
CON
BARRAGA, Natalie Carter, 1915- ,
American; nonfiction CON
BARRATT-BROWN, Michael,
1918- , British; nonfiction
CON
BARRAULT, Jean Louis, 1910- ,
French; nonfiction CL
BARRAX, Gerald William, 1933- ,
American; poetry CON SH
BARRELL, Sarah Webb, 1946?-79,
American; journalism CON
BARREN, Charles, 1913- , Eng-
lish; fiction NI
BARRERA, Mario, 1939- , Amer-
ican; nonfiction MAR
BARRES, Augustin Maurice, 1862-
1923, French; fiction, nonfiction
BU CL TH
BARRETO, Affonso Henriques de
Lima, 1881-1922, Brazilian;
fiction BR

BARRETO, Rui Moniz see 'NO-
GARI, Rui'
BARRETO de MENESES, Tobias,
1839-89, Brazilian; nonfiction
BR
BARRETT, Anne Mainwaring,
1911- , British; juveniles,
plays KI
BARRETT, Bob, 1925- , Amer-
ican; fiction CON
BARRETT, Clifton Waller, 1901- ,
American; nonfiction CON
BARRETT, Dean ('Yum Char'),
1942- , American; nonfiction
CON
BARRETT, Eugene Francis,
1921- , American; nonfiction
CON
BARRETT, Geoffrey John ('Cole
Rickard'; 'Bill Wade'), Eng-
lish; fiction NI
BARRETT, Harold, 1925- , Amer-
ican; nonfiction CON
BARRETT, Harry Bemister, ('Hen-
ry Bemister'), 1922- , Ca-
nadian; nonfiction CON
BARRETT, Henry Charles, 1923- ,
American; nonfiction CON
BARRETT, Ivan J., 1910- ,
American; nonfiction CON
BARRETT, James Lee, 1929- ,
American; film CON
BARRETT, John Henry, 1913- ,
British; nonfiction CON
BARRETT, Judith, 1941- , Amer-
ican; juveniles CON WAR
BARRETT, Laurence Irwin, 1935- ,
American; nonfiction, journal-
ism fiction CON
BARRETT, Leonard Emanuel,
1920- , West Indian-American;
nonfiction CON
BARRETT, Marvin, 1920- ,
American; nonfiction CON
BARRETT, Max ('Maye Barrett'),
Australian; fiction CON
BARRETT, Michael Dennis, 1947- ,
American; nonfiction CON
BARRETT, Neal, Jr., Amer-
ican; fiction NI
'BARRETT, Raina' see KELLY,
Pauline A.
BARRETT, Ron, 1937- , Amer-
ican; juveniles CO
BARRETT, Rona, 1936- , Amer-
ican; fiction CON
BARRETT, William Edmund, 1900- ,
American; fiction NI

BARRETT, William R., 1922?-77,
American; journalism CON
BARRIAULT, Arthur, 1915?-76,
American; journalism, nonfic-
tion CON
BARRIE, Sir James Matthew, 1860-
1937, English; plays, fiction
BU COM DA KI MAG MCG PO
SEY VD
BARRIENTOS, Guido Alan, 1931- ,
American; nonfiction MAR
BARRIER, Norman Gerald, 1940- ,
American; nonfiction CON
BARRIERE, Théodore, 1823-77,
French; plays TH
BARRIGER, John Walker, 1899-
1976, American; nonfiction
CON
BARRILI, Anton Giulio, 1836-1908,
Italian; fiction, journalism BU
BARRINGER, Daniel Moreau, 1900- ,
American; juveniles WAR
BARRINGTON, Sir Jonah, 1760?-
1834, Irish; nonfiction HO
BARRINGTON, Margaret, 1895?- ,
Irish; fiction HO
'BARRINGTON, Maurice' see BRO-
GAN, Denis W.
'BARRINGTON, Michael' (Michael
Moorcock; Barrington J. Bayley)
fiction NI
BARRIO, Raymond, 1921- , Amer-
ican; fiction MAR
BARRIO-GARAY, Jose Luis, 1932- ,
Spanish; nonfiction CON
BARRIOS, Eduardo, 1884-1963,
Chilean; fiction, plays BR BU
MAG
BARRIOS, Miguel de (Daniel Leví
de Barrios), 1625?-1701?,
Spanish; poetry BU
BARRIS, Alexander, 1922- , Amer-
ican; nonfiction, tv CON
BARRIS, George, American; juven-
iles WAR
BARRO, Robert Joseph, 1944- ,
American; nonfiction CON
BARROLL, John Leeds III, 1928- ,
American; nonfiction CON
BARRON, Ann Forman ('Annabel
Erwin'), American; fiction,
nonfiction CON
BARRON, Charlie Nelms, 1922-77,
American; nonfiction CON
BARRON, Donald Gabriel, 1922- ,
British; fiction NI
BARRON, Gloria Joan, 1934- ,
American; nonfiction CON

BARRON, Jerome Avre, 1933- ,
American; nonfiction CON
BARRON, Richard Neil, 1934- ,
American; nonfiction CON
NI
BARROS, João de, 1496-1570,
Portuguese; nonfiction BU TH
BARROW, Andrew, 1945- , Brit-
ish; nonfiction CON
BARROW, Isaac, 1630-77, English;
nonfiction BU
BARROW, Joseph Louis ('Joe
Louis'), 1914-81, American;
nonfiction CON
'BARROW, Pamela' see HOWARTH,
Pamela
BARROW, Robin, 1944- , English;
nonfiction CON
BARROW, Terence, 1923- , New
Zealander-American; nonfiction
CON
'BARROW, William' see FULLER,
Hoyt W.
BARROWS, Anita, 1947- , Amer-
ican; poetry, translations
CON
BARRY, Anne, 1940- , American;
nonfiction CON
BARRY, Clive, 1922- , Austral-
ian; fiction VCN
BARRY, Jack, 1939- , American;
poetry, nonfiction CON
BARRY, James Potvin, 1918- ,
American; juveniles CO
BARRY, Jerome Benedict, 1894-
1975, American; poetry, fic-
tion CON
'BARRY, Jocelyn' see BOWDEN,
Jean
BARRY, John Vincent William,
1903-69, Australian; nonfic-
tion CON
BARRY, Joseph Amber, 1917- ,
American; nonfiction CON
BARRY, Katharina Watjen, 1936- ,
German-American; juveniles
CO
BARRY, Mary Jane, 1928- ,
American; nonfiction CON
BARRY, Philip, 1896-1949, Amer-
ican; plays BR BU MCG
MCN PO VD
BARRY, Robert Everett, 1931- ,
American; juveniles CO
BARRY, Roger Graham, 1935- ,
Anglo-American; nonfiction
CON
BARRY, Scott, 1952- , Amer-

ican; nonfiction CON
BARSACQ, Andre, 1909-73, Russian-
French; plays DA
BARSIS, Max, 1894-1973, Austrian-
American; ? CON
BARSON, John, 1936- , American;
nonfiction CON
BARSOTTI, Charles, 1933- , Amer-
ican; nonfiction CON
BARSTOW, Stanley, 1928- , Brit-
ish; fiction, plays VCN
BART, Lionel, 1930- , English;
plays CON
BART, Pauline Bernice, 1930- ,
American; nonfiction CON
BART, Peter, 1932- , American;
journalism, nonfiction, fiction
CON
BARTEL, Pauline Christine, 1952- ,
American; nonfiction CON
BARTELS, Susan Ludvigson, 1942- ,
American; poetry CON
BARTER, Alice Knar, 1918- ,
Turkish-American; nonfiction
CON
BART-WILLIAMS, Gaston, 1938- ,
Sierra Leonean; poetry, plays
HER JA
BARTH, Edna Smith ('Edna Weiss'),
1914-80, American; juveniles
CO CON WAR
BARTH, Fredrik, 1928- , German;
nonfiction CON
BARTH, Gunther, 1925- , German-
American; nonfiction CON
BARTH, John Simmons, 1930- ,
American; fiction; AM BA BU
HE MAG PO SEY VCN VN WA
BARTH, Richard, 1943- , Amer-
ican; fiction CON
BARTH, Roland Sawyer, 1937- ,
American; nonfiction CON
BARTHEL, Ludwig Friedrich, 1898-
1962, German; nonfiction BU
BARTHELEMY, Nicolas, 1478-1540,
French; nonfiction BU
BARTHELME, Donald, 1931- ,
American; fiction, juveniles
BR CO HE NI VCN VN WA
WAR
BARTHELMES, Albert Wesley,
Jr. ('Sisyphus'), 1922-76,
American; journalism, nonfic-
tion CON
BARTHES, Roland, 1915-80, French;
nonfiction BU CL CON SEY WA
BARTHOLOMAEUS ANGLICUS (Bar-
tholomew de Glanville), fl.

1230-50, English; nonfiction
BU
BARTHOLOMAY, Julia A., 1923- ,
American; nonfiction CON
BARTLETT, Bruce Reeves, 1951- ,
American; nonfiction CON
BARTLETT, Jean Anne, 1927- ,
American; fiction CON
BARTLETT, John, 1820-1905,
American; nonfiction MY
BARTLETT, Jonathan, 1931- ,
American; nonfiction CON
'BARTLETT, Kathleen' see PAINE,
Lauran B.
BARTLETT, Kim, 1941- , Amer-
ican; fiction CON
BARTLETT, Nancy White, 1913-
72, American; fiction CON
BARTLETT, Phyllis, 1908?-73,
American; nonfiction CON
BARTLETT, Robert Merrill,
1899- , American; juveniles
CO
BARTLETT, Vernon ('Peter Old-
feld'), 1894- , English; po-
etry, nonfiction, fiction CON
BARTLEY, Diana E. Pelaez-
Rivera, 1940- , American;
nonfiction CON
BARTLEY, Numan Vache, 1934- ,
American; nonfiction CON
BARTLEY, Robert LeRoy, 1937- ,
American; journalism CON
BARTOL, Cyrus Augustus, 1813-
1900, American; nonfiction
MY
BARTOLE, Genevieve, 1927- ,
Canadian; poetry CON
BARTOLI, Daniello, 1608-85,
Italian; nonfiction BU
BARTON, Bernard, 1784-1849,
English; poetry BU
BARTON, Bruce Walter, 1935- ,
American; nonfiction CON
BARTON, Byron, 1930- , Amer-
ican; juveniles CO CON WAR
BARTON, Del, 1925-71, Amer-
ican; fiction CON
'BARTON, Erie' see FANTHORPE,
Robert L.
BARTON, Eustace R. see 'EUSTACE,
Robert'
BARTON, H. Arnold, 1929- ,
American; nonfiction CON
BARTON, John Bernard Adie,
1928- , British; nonfiction
CON
'BARTON, Lee' see FANTHORPE,

Robert L.
BARTON, Lewis Randolph, 1918- ,
American; nonfiction CON
BARTON, Richard Fleming, 1924- ,
American; nonfiction CON
BARTON, Roger Avery, 1903-76,
American; nonfiction CON
'BARTON, S. W.' see WHALEY,
Barton S.
BARTON, Samuel ('A. B. Roker'),
American; fiction NI
BARTON, Thomas Frank, 1905- ,
American; nonfiction CON
BARTON, William, 1950- , Amer-
ican; fiction NI
BARTON, William Renald III,
1950- , American; fiction
CON
BARTOS-HÖPPNER, Barbara,
1923- , German; juveniles
CO DEM
BARTRAM, William, 1739-1823,
American; nonfiction BR BU
BARTRINA, Joaquin María, 1850-
80, Spanish; poetry BU
BARTSCHT, Waltraud, 1924- ,
American; translations, non-
fiction CON
BARTUSIS, Mary Ann, 1930- ,
American; nonfiction CON
BARTZ, Patricia (McBride), 1921- ,
Australian; nonfiction CON
BARUCH, Dorothy Walter, 1899-
1962, American; juveniles CO
BARUCH, Löb, see BÖRNE, Lud-
wig
BARUDI, Mahmud Sami, 1839-1904,
Egyptian; poetry BU PRU
BARUK, Henri Marc, 1897- ,
French; nonfiction CON
BAR-YOSEF, Yehoshua, 1912- ,
Israeli; fiction, plays BU
BARZINI, Luigi, 1908- , Italian;
journalism, nonfiction WA
BARZMAN, Ben, Canadian-
American; fiction, film NI
BARZUN, Jacques Martin, 1907- ,
Franco-American; nonfiction,
translations CON ST
BAS, Joe, 1932- , American;
nonfiction CON
'BAS, Rutger' see RUTGERS van
der LOEFF, Anna B.
BASA, Eniko Molnar, 1939- ,
Hungarian-American; nonfiction
CON
BASANAVICIUS, Jonas, 1851-1927,
Lithuanian; nonfiction BU

BASCO, David ('Milford Polroon'),
1912- , American; nonfiction
CON
BASELEY, Godfrey, 1904- ,
American; nonfiction CON
BASH, Harry, 1926- , German-
American; nonfiction CON
BASHAM, Don Wilson, 1926- ,
American; nonfiction CON
BASHEIKH HUSEIN, Ahmad, 1909-
61, Swahili; poetry BU
BASHIRA, Damali, 1951- , Amer-
ican; poetry CON
BASHIROV, Gomar, 1901- ,
Tatar; journalism, fiction
PRU
BASHKIRTSEFF, Maria Konstan-
tinovna (Bashkirtseva), 1860-
94, Russian; nonfiction BU
'BASHO' (Matsuo Munefusa), 1644-
94, Japanese; poetry BU HI
LA MAG PRU
BASHSHUR, Rashid L., 1933- ,
Syrian-American; nonfiction
CON
BASHSHAR ibn BURD, -783,
Arab; poetry BU PRU
BASICHIS, Gordon Allen, 1947- ,
American; nonfiction CON
BASIL, St. (Basil the Great),
329/30-79, Greek; nonfiction
BU GR LA
BASIL, Douglas C., 1923- ,
Canadian-American; nonfiction
CON
BASIL, Otto, 1901- , Austrian;
nonfiction, poetry CON
BASILE, Giambattista (Gian Alesio
Abbattutis), 1575-1632, Italian;
poetry, fiction BO BU TH
BASILE, Gloria Vitanza ('McKayla
Morgan'; 'Michaela Morgan'),
1929- , American; fiction
BASILE, Jean, 1932- , Canadian;
fiction, poetry CR
BASILE, Robert Manlius, 1916- ,
American; nonfiction CON
BASIUK, Victor, 1932- , Amer-
ican; nonfiction CON
BASKERVILL, William Malone,
1850-99, American; nonfiction
BA
BASKETT, John, 1930- , British;
nonfiction CON
BASKIN, Barbara Holland, 1929- ,
American; nonfiction CON
BASLER, Thomas Gordon, 1940- ,

American; nonfiction CON
BASON, Frederick Thomas ('The
Gallerite'), 1907-73, British;
nonfiction CON
BASON, Lillian, 1913- , American;
juveniles CO CON WAR
'BASS, Eduard' (Eduard Schmidt),
1888-1946, Czech; fiction, non-
fiction BU
BASS, Ellen, 1947- , American;
nonfiction, poetry CON
BASS, Henry Benjamin, 1897-1975,
American; nonfiction CON
BASS, Howard Larry, 1942- ,
American; nonfiction, poetry
CON
BASS, Jack Alexander, 1946- ,
Canadian; nonfiction CON
BASS, Lawrence Wade, 1898- ,
American; nonfiction CON
BASS, Robert Duncan, 1904- ,
American; nonfiction CON
'BASS, T. J.' (Thomas J. Bassler),
American; fiction NI
BASS, Virginia Wauchope, 1905- ,
American; nonfiction CON
BASS, William Marvin III, 1928- ,
American; nonfiction CON
BASSANI, Giorgio ('Giacomo Marcho'),
1916- , Italian; poetry, fiction,
nonfiction BO BU CL CON
SEY WA
BASSANO, Enrico, 1899- , Italian;
plays MCG
BASSARABESCU, Ion Alexandru,
1870-1952, Rumanian; fiction
BU
BASSE, Eli, 1904-79, British; tv,
radio CON
BASSE, William, 1580-1654, Eng-
lish; poetry BU
BASSETT, Flora Marjorie ('Marnie
wbassett'), 1890?-1980, Aus-
tralian; nonfiction CON
BASSETT, George William, 1910- ,
Australian; nonfiction CON
BASSETT, James Elias, 1912-78,
American; fiction, journalism
CON
'BASSETT, John K.' see KEATING,
Lawrence A.
BASSETT, John Spencer, 1867-
1928, American; nonfiction
BA
BASSETT, Mary Grace, 1927- ,
American; journalism CON
BASSETT, Ronald ('William Clive'),
1924- , British; nonfiction,

film CON
BASSLER, Thomas J. see 'BASS,
  T.J.'
BASSO, Aldo Peter, 1922- ,
  American; nonfiction CON
BASSO, Hamilton, 1904-64, Amer-
  ican; fiction, journalism BA
  BR CON
BASSO, Teresita, 1944- , Amer-
  ican; nonfiction MAR
BASSOFF, Bruce, 1941- , Amer-
  ican; nonfiction CON
BASTARD, Lucien see 'ESTANG,
  Luc'
BASTEN, Fred Ernest, American;
  nonfiction CON
BASTERRA, Ramón de, 1888-
  1928, Spanish; poetry, non-
  fiction BU CL
BASU, Arindam, 1948- , Indian;
  fiction CON
BASU, Buddhadeb, 1908- , Ben-
  gali; plays, fiction, poetry,
  nonfiction PRU
BASU, Romen, 1923- , American;
  fiction CON
BASU, Samarés ('Kalkut'), 1923- ,
  Bengali; fiction PRU
BATAILLE, Georges ('Lord Auch';
  'Pierre Angelique'), 1897-1962,
  French; fiction, nonfiction, po-
  etry BU CL CON WA
BATAILLE, Gretchen M., 1944- ,
  American; nonfiction CON
BATAILLE, Henri, 1872-1922,
  French; plays, poetry BU
  CL MCG TH
BATCHELLER, John M., 1918- ,
  American; nonfiction CON
BATCHELOR, Clarence Daniel,
  1888-1977, American; car-
  toons CON
BATCHELOR, David, 1943- ,
  British; fiction CON
BATCHELOR, John, 1942- ,
  British; fiction, nonfiction
  CON
'BATCHELOR, Reg' see PAINE,
  Lauran B.
BATE, Lucy, 1939- , American;
  juveniles, plays CO CON
BATE, Norman Arthur, 1916- ,
  American; juveniles CO
BATE, Sam, 1907- , American;
  plays CON
BATE, Walter Jackson, 1918- ,
  American; nonfiction BOR
  WA

BATEMAN, Barbara Dee, 1933- ,
  American; nonfiction CON
BATEMAN, Robert Moyes, 1922- ,
  English; tv, radio, fiction NI
BATES, Arthemia J., 1920- ,
  American; fiction CON
BATES, Barbara Snedeker ('Stephen
  Cuyler'; 'Jim Roberts'), 1919- ,
  American; juveniles CO
BATES, Betty, 1921- , American;
  juveniles CO
BATES, Caroline Philbrick, 1932- ,
  American; journalism, nonfic-
  tion CON
BATES, Daisey, American; non-
  fiction SH
BATES, Elizabeth, 1921- , Amer-
  ican; juveniles CON
BATES, Harry ('Anthony Gilmore'),
  1900- , American; fiction AS
  NI
BATES, Herbert Ernest ('Flying
  Officer X'; 'John Gawsworth'),
  1905-74, English; fiction, po-
  etry, plays, nonfiction BU
  CON DA SEY VN
BATES, Jefferson Davis, 1920- ,
  American; journalism, nonfic-
  tion CON
BATES, Lucius Christopher, 1901?-
  80, American; nonfiction CON
BATES, Marston, 1906-74, Amer-
  ican; nonfiction CON
BATES, Peter Watson, 1920- ,
  New Zealander; nonfiction CON
BATES, Ralph, 1899- , English;
  fiction DA
BATES, Robert Hinrichs, 1942- ,
  American; nonfiction CON
BATES, Ronald Gordon Nudell,
  1924- , Canadian; poetry CR
BATES, Scott, 1923- , American;
  nonfiction, poetry CON
BATES, Timothy Mason, 1946- ,
  American; nonfiction CON
BATESON, Charles Henry, 1903- ,
  New Zealander; nonfiction CON
BATESON, Frederick Wilse, 1901- ,
  English; nonfiction BOR WA
BATESON, Gregory, 1904-80, Anglo-
  American; nonfiction CON
BATHERMAN, Muriel, see SHEL-
  DON, Muriel
BATHKE, Edwin Albert, 1936- ,
  American; nonfiction CON
BATHKE, Nancy Edna, 1938- ,
  American; nonfiction CON
'BATHURST, Sheila' see SULLI-

VAN, Sheila
BATIRAY, 1832-1910, Darg; poetry
PRU
BATIUK, Thomas Martin, 1947- ,
American; cartoons CON
BATKI, John, 1942- , American;
translations, poetry CON
BAT-MIRIAM, Yocheved, 1901- ,
Israeli; poetry BU
BATRA, Raveendra Nath, 1943- ,
Indian-American; nonfiction
CON
BATSON, George Donald, 1918-77,
American; plays CON
BATSON, Larry, 1930- , Amer-
ican; juveniles CON
BATTALIA, O. William, 1928- ,
American; nonfiction CON
BATTELLE, Phyllis Marie,
1922- , American; journalism,
nonfiction CON
BATTEN, Charles Linwood, Jr.,
1942- , American; nonfiction
CON
BATTEN, Harry Mortimer, 1888-
1958, British; juveniles CO
BATTEN, Jack, 1932- , Canadi-
an; fiction CON
BATTEN, James Knox, 1936- ,
American; nonfiction CON
BATTEN, Mary, 1937- , Amer-
ican; juveniles, nonfiction,
film CO CON WAR
BATTEN, Peter, 1916- , British;
nonfiction CON
BATTERBERRY, Ariane Ruskin,
1935- , American; juveniles,
nonfiction CO CON
BATTERBERRY, Michael Carver,
1932- , British; nonfiction,
juveniles CON WAR
BATTERSBY, James Lyons,
1936- , American; nonfic-
tion CON
BATTISTA, Miriam, 1912?-80,
American; plays CON
BATTLE, Allen Overton, 1927- ,
American; nonfiction CON
BATTLE, Gerald Nichols, 1914- ,
American; juveniles, poetry
CON
BATTLES, Roxy Edith Baker,
1921- , American; juveniles,
fiction CO CON WAR
BATTO, Bernard Frank, 1941- ,
American; nonfiction CON
BATTS, Michael S., 1929- ,
Anglo-Canadian; nonfiction CON

BATTY, Linda Schmidt, 1940- ,
American; nonfiction CON
BATY, Gaston, 1885-1952, French;
play director CL
BATY, Gordon Bruce, 1938- ,
American; nonfiction CON
BATY, Roger Mendenhall, 1937- ,
American; nonfiction CON
BATYUSHKOV, Konstantin Nikolaye-
vich, 1787-1855, Russian; po-
etry BU
BAUBY, Cathrina, 1927- , Amer-
ican; nonfiction CON
'BAUCHART' see CAMUS, Albert
BAUDART, Willem, 1565-1640,
Dutch; translations, nonfiction
BU
BAUDE, Henri, 1430?-96, French;
poetry BU
BAUDELAIRE, Charles Pierre,
1821-67, French; poetry, non-
fiction BU CL MAG TH
BAUDOUY, Michel Aimé, 1909- ,
French; juveniles CO DE
BAUDRI of BOURGUEIL, 1046-1130,
Latin; nonfiction, poetry BU
TH
BAUER, Caroline Feller, 1935- ,
American; nonfiction CON
BAUER, George C., 1942- ,
American; nonfiction CON
BAUER, Harry Charles, 1902-79,
American; journalism CON
BAUER, Jo Hanna Ruth, 1918- ,
Austrian-American; nonfiction,
poetry CON
BAUER, Malcolm Clair, 1914- ,
American; journalism CON
BAUER, Marion Dane, 1938- ,
American; juveniles CO CON
BAUER, Peter Thomas, 1915- ,
Hungarian-British; nonfiction
CON
BAUER, Raymond Augustine, 1916-
77, American; nonfiction CON
BAUER, Robert Albert, 1910- ,
Austrian-American; nonfiction
CON
BAUER, Walter, 1904- , German-
Canadian; poetry, fiction, non-
fiction, juveniles CON
BAUER, Wolfgang, 1941- , Austri-
an; plays CL
BAUERNFELD, Eduard von, 1802-
90, Austrian; plays BU
BAUERNSCHMIDT, Marjorie, 1926- ,
American; juveniles CO
BAUGH, Albert Croll, 1891-1981,

American; nonfiction CON
BAUGH, Daniel Albert, 1931- ,
American; nonfiction CON
BAUGHAN, Blanche Edith, 1870-
1958, New Zealander; poetry,
nonfiction VP
BAUGHMAN, Dorothy, 1940- ,
American; juveniles, fiction,
nonfiction CON
BAUGHMAN, John Lee, 1913- ,
American; nonfiction CON
BAUGHMAN, Millard Dale, 1919- ,
American; nonfiction CON
BAUGHMAN, Urbanus E., Jr.,
1905?-78, American; nonfic-
tion CON
BAUKHAGE, Hilmar Robert, 1889-
1976, American; nonfiction
CON
BAULCH, Jerry T., 1913- ,
American; journalism CON
BAUM, Allyn Zelton, 1924- ,
American; juveniles CO
BAUM, David William, 1940- ,
American; nonfiction CON
BAUM, Kurt, 1876-1962, German-
American; poetry BU
BAUM, Lyman Frank ('Laura Ban-
croft'; 'Floyd Akens'; 'Edith
Van Dyne'; 'John Estes Cook';
'Suzanne Metcalf'; 'Schuyler
Stanton'; 'Captain Hugh Fitz-
gerald'), 1856-1919, Amer-
ican; fiction, juveniles BR
CO DE KI NI VN
BAUM, Patricia, American; juven-
iles WAR
BAUM, Paull Franklin, 1886-1964,
American; nonfiction CON
BAUM, Richard Dennis, 1940- ,
American; nonfiction CON
BAUM, Robert James, 1941- ,
American; nonfiction CON
BAUM, Thomas, 1940- , Amer-
ican; nonfiction CON
BAUM, Vicki, 1888-1960, Austri-
an; fiction BU CON MAG
BAUM, Willi, 1931- , Swiss-
American; juveniles CO
BAUMAN, Clarence, 1928- ,
Canadian-American; nonfiction
CON
BAUMANN, Amy Brown ('Alexis
Brown'; 'James Barbary'),
1922- , English; juveniles,
translations CO
BAUMANN, Charles Henry, 1926- ,
American; nonfiction CON

BAUMANN, Charly, 1928- , Ger-
man; nonfiction CON
BAUMANN, Elwood D., Canadian;
juveniles WAR
BAUMANN, Hans, 1914- , Ger-
man; juveniles DE
BAUMANN, Kurt, 1935- , Swiss;
juveniles CO CON
BAUMBACK, Clifford Mason,
1915- , American; nonfiction
CON
BAUMGAERTEL, Max Walter,
1902- , German; nonfiction
CON
BAUMGARDT, David, 1890-1963,
German; nonfiction CON
BAUMGART, Reinhard, 1929- ,
German; fiction BU
BAUSANI, Alessandro, 1921- ,
Italian; nonfiction, translations
CON
BAUSCH, Richard Carl, 1945- ,
American; fiction CON
BAUZA, Guillermo, 1916- ,
Puerto Rican; poetry, plays,
fiction HIL
BAUZA, Obdulio, 1907- , Puerto
Rican; poetry HIL
BAVIN, Bill, 1919- , British;
nonfiction, fiction CON
'BAWDEN, Nina' (Nina M. M.
Kark), 1925- , British; fiction,
juveniles CO DEM KI REI
VCN WAR
'BAX' see BAXTER, Gordon F.,
Jr.
BAX, Clifford, 1886-1962, English;
plays, fiction, poetry, nonfic-
tion MCG VD
BAX, Martin Charles Owen, 1933- ,
English; nonfiction, fiction
CON NI
'BAX, Roger' see 'GARVE, Andrew'
BAXANDALL, Rosalyn Fraad,
1939- , American; nonfiction
CON
BAXT, George, 1923- , American;
fiction, plays REI
BAXTER, Charles, 1947- , Amer-
ican; poetry CON
BAXTER, Douglas Clark, 1942- ,
American; nonfiction CON
'BAXTER, George, Owen' see
'BRAND, Max'
BAXTER, Gordon Francis, Jr.
('Bax'), 1923- , American;
fiction, nonfiction CON
BAXTER, James Keir, 1926-72,

New Zealander; poetry, plays, nonfiction BU CON DA VCP VD VP WA

BAXTER, James Phinney (Finney) III, 1893-1975, American; nonfiction CON

BAXTER, James Sidlow, 1903- , Australian; nonfiction CON

'BAXTER, John' see HUNT, Everette H.

BAXTER, John, 1939- , Australian; fiction, journalism AS NI

BAXTER, Michael John, 1944- , American; journalism CON

'BAXTER, Phylis' see WALLMANN, Jeffrey M.

BAXTER, Richard, 1615-91, English; nonfiction BU DA PO RU

'BAXTER, Valerie' see MEYNELL, Laurence W.

BAXTER, William Francis, 1929- , American; nonfiction CON

BAXTER, Zenobia L., 1907- , American; nonfiction SH

BAY, Howard, 1912- , American; nonfiction CON

BAY, Jens Christian Bay, 1871-1962, American; nonfiction ENG

BAY LAUREL, Alicia, 1949- , American; juveniles, poetry CON

BAYALINOV, Kasymaly, 1902- , Kirghiz; fiction PRU

BAYATI, Abdalwahhab, 1926- , Iraqi; poetry PRU

BAYAZID ANSARI, Pir Roshan, 1524-80?, Pashtun; nonfiction PRU

BAYBARS, Taner ('Timothy Bayliss'), 1936- , English; nonfiction, poetry, translations, fiction CON VCP

'BAYER, Oliver W.' see PERRY, Eleanor

BAYERLE, Gustav, 1931- , Hungarian-American; nonfiction CON

BAYH, Birch Evan, Jr., 1928- , American; nonfiction CON

BAYH, Marvella Hern, 1933-79, American; nonfiction CON

BAYKURT, Fakir, 1929- , Turkish; fiction BU

BAYLE, Pierre, 1647-1706, French; nonfiction BU TH

'BAYLEBRIDGE, William' (Charles

William Blocksidge), 1883-1942, Australian; poetry DA

BAYLES, Ernest Edward, 1897- , American; nonfiction CON

BAYLES, Michael Dale, 1941- , American; nonfiction CON

BAYLESS, Raymond, 1920- , American; nonfiction CON

BAYLEY, Barrington J. ('P. F. Woods'; 'Michael Barrington'), 1937- , English; fiction, juveniles AS NI

BAYLEY, John Oliver, 1925- , British; nonfiction, poetry, fiction BOR CON

BAYLEY, Peter Charles, 1921- , British; nonfiction CON

BAYLIS, John, 1946- , American; nonfiction CON

'BAYLISS, Timothy' see BAYBARS, Taner

BAYLOR, Byrd ('Byrd Baylor Schweitzer'), 1924- , American; juveniles CO CON DEM WAR

BAYLOR, Frances Courtenay, 1848-1920, American; fiction BA

BAYM, Max I., 1895- , American; nonfiction CON

BAYNE, David Cowan, 1918- , American; nonfiction CON

BAYNE, Stephen Fielding, Jr., 1908-74, American; nonfiction CON

BAYNES, Pauline Diana, 1922- , English; juveniles CO DE

BAYRD, Edwin, 1944- , American; nonfiction CON

BAYTON, James A., 1912- , American; nonfiction SH

'BAZAN, Cesar de' see VIZCARRONDO, Julio L. de

BAZARRABUSA, Timothy B., 1912- , Ugandan; fiction JA

BAZELON, Irwin, 1922- , American; nonfiction CON

BAZHAN, Mykola, 1904- , Ukrainian; poetry CL TH

BAZHOV, Pavel Petrovich, 1879-1950, Russian; fiction BU

BAZIN, André, 1918-58, French; nonfiction WAK

'BAZIN, Hervé' (Jean Pierre Hervé-Bazin), 1911- , French; fiction BU CL CON WA

BAZIN, Nancy Topping, 1934- , American; nonfiction CON

BAZIN, René, 1853-1932, French;
fiction CL TH
BEACH, Bert Beverly, 1928- ,
Swiss-American; nonfiction
CON
'BEACH, Charles' see REID,
Mayne
BEACH, Edward Latimer, 1918- ,
American; juveniles CO
BEACH, Mark B., 1937- , Amer-
ican; nonfiction CON
BEACH, Rex, 1877-1949, Amer-
ican; fiction, plays, nonfiction
MAG
BEACH, Stewart Taft, 1899-1979,
American; nonfiction, fiction
CO CON
BEACH, Sylvia, 1887-1962, Amer-
ican; publisher BR BU RO
'BEACH, Webb' see BUTTER-
WORTH, William E.
BEACH, William Waldo, 1916- ,
American; nonfiction CON
'BEACHCOMBER' see MORTON,
John B.
BEACHCROFT, Nina, 1931- ,
British; juveniles CO CON
KI
BEACHY, Lucille, 1935- , Amer-
ican; nonfiction CON
BEADELL, Len, 1923- , Austral-
ian; nonfiction CON
BEADLE, Leigh Patric, 1941- ,
English; nonfiction CON
BEAGLE, Peter Soyer, 1939- ,
American; fiction AS NI
BEAGLEHOLE, John Cawte, 1901-
71, New Zealander; nonfiction,
poetry BU
BEAKLEY, George Carroll, Jr.,
1922- , American; nonfiction
CON
BEAL, Gwyneth (Gwyneth Morgan),
1943- , British; juveniles
CON
BEAL, M. F., 1937- , American;
fiction, nonfiction CON
BEALE, Betty, American;
journalism CON
BEALE, Charles Willing, 1845- ?,
American; fiction NI
BEALER, Alexander Winkler III,
1921-80, American; juveniles,
nonfiction CO CON WAR
BEALES, Derek Edward, 1931- ,
British; nonfiction CON
BEALL, James Lee, 1924- ,
American; nonfiction CON

BEALS, Carleton, 1893- , Amer-
ican; juveniles CO
BEALS, Frank Lee, 1881-1972,
American; nonfiction CON
BEAM, C. Richard, American;
nonfiction CON
BEAM, George Dahl, 1934- ,
American; nonfiction CON
BEAM, Philip Conway, 1910- ,
American; nonfiction CON
BEAME, Rona, 1934- , American;
juveniles CO CON
'BEAMISH, Tufton Victor' see
CHELWOOD, Tufton V.
BEAN, Constance Austin, Amer-
ican; nonfiction CON
BEAN, Lowell John, 1931- ,
American; nonfiction CON
BEAN, Mabel (Greene), 1898?-
1977, American; journalism
CON
BEAN, Orson, 1928- , American;
nonfiction CON
BEANEY, Jan see UDALL, Jan
BEAR, Joan ('Elizabeth Mayhew'),
1918- , English; fiction CON
BEAR, John, 1938- , American;
nonfiction CON
BEARCHELL, Charles, 1925- ,
American; nonfiction CON
BEARD, Charles Austin, 1874-
1948, American; nonfiction
BR CO MAG PO
BEARD, Daniel Carter, 1850-1941,
American; juveniles CO WAR
BEARD, James Andrews, 1903- ,
American; nonfiction CON
BEARD, Mary, 1876-1958, Amer-
ican; nonfiction MAG
BEARDEN, Romare Howard, 1914- ,
American; juveniles, nonfiction
CO CON
BEARDMORE, George ('Cedric
Beardmore'; 'Cedric Stokes';
'George Wolfenden'), 1908-79,
English; juveniles, nonfiction,
fiction CO CON
BEARDSLEY, Aubrey, 1872-98,
English; nonfiction PO
BEARDSLEY, Richard King, 1918-
78, American; nonfiction CON
BEARDSWORTH, Millicent Monica,
1915- , British; fiction CON
BEARDWOOD, Roger, 1932- ,
Anglo-American; journalism,
nonfiction CON
BEARNE, Colin Gerald, 1939- ,
British; nonfiction CON

BEASER, Herbert W., 1913?-79, American; nonfiction CON
BEASLEY, Edward, Jr., 1932- , American; tv, nonfiction SH
BEASLEY, William Conger, Jr., 1940- , American; fiction, poetry CON
BEASLEY, William Gerald, 1919- , English; nonfiction CON
BEASLEY-MURRAY, George Raymond, 1916- , American; nonfiction, translations CON
BEATON, Cecil, 1904-80, British; nonfiction, plays CON
BEATRICE, Countess of Die, fl. 1160, French; poetry BU
BEATTIE, Ann, 1947- , American; fiction CON
BEATTIE, James, 1735-1803, Scots; poetry, nonfiction BU DA PO VP
BEATTS, Anne Patricia, 1947- , American; nonfiction, tv CON
BEATTY, Hetty Burlingame, 1907-71, American; juveniles CO CON
BEATTY, Jerome, Jr., 1918- , American; juveniles CO
BEATTY, John Louis, 1922-75, American; juveniles, fiction, nonfiction CO CON DE KI
BEATTY, Morgan, 1902-75, American; journalism, nonfiction CON
BEATTY, Patricia ('Jean Bartholomew'), 1922- , American; juveniles, fiction DE KI
BEATTY, Richmond Croom, 1905-61, American; nonfiction BA
BEATTY, Rita Gray, 1930- , American; nonfiction CON
BEATTY, Robert Owen, 1924-76, American; nonfiction CON
BEATTY, William Kaye, 1926- , Canadian-American; nonfiction CON
BEATUS RHENANUS (Bild aus Rheinau), 1485-1547, Alsatian; nonfiction BU
BEATY, Arthur David, 1919- , British; fiction, nonfiction VCN
BEATY, Betty ('Karen Campbell'; 'Catherine Ross'), British; fiction CON
BEATY, Jerome, 1924- , American; nonfiction CON
BEAUCHAMP, Edward Robert,

1933- , American; nonfiction CON
BEAUCHAMP, Kathleen M. see MANSFIELD, Katherine
BEAUCHAMP, Tom L., 1939- , American; nonfiction CON
BEAUFRE, Andre, 1920-75, French; nonfiction, fiction CON
'BEAUFRITZ, William' see CRITCHLEY, Julian M.
BEAULIEU, Maurice, 1924- , Canadian; poetry CR
BEAUMAN, Katharine Bentley, 1902- , American; nonfiction CON
BEAUMARCHAIS, Pierre Augustin Caron de, 1732-99, French; plays BU MAG MCG TH
'BEAUMONT, Beverly' see von BLOCK, Sylvia
'BEAUMONT, Charles' (Charles Nutt), 1929-67, American; fiction AS CON NI
BEAUMONT, Cyril William, 1891-1976, English; nonfiction CON
BEAUMONT, Francis, 1584/85-1616/25, English; plays, poetry BRI BU DA MAG MCG PO RU VD
BEAUMONT, George Ernest, 1888-1974, British; nonfiction CON
BEAUMONT, Sir John, 1583/84-1627, English; poetry, plays BU VP
BEAUMONT, Joseph, 1616-99, English; poetry BU VP
BEAUMONT, Roger Alban, 1935- , American; nonfiction CON
BEAUMONT, Simon van, 1574-1654, Dutch; poetry BU
BEAUSANG, Michael Francis, Jr., 1936- , American; nonfiction CON
BEAUSOBRE, Julian M. de see NAMIER, Julia
BEAUSOLEIL, Beau, 1941- , American; poetry CON
BEAUVOIR, Simone de, 1908- , French; nonfiction, fiction, plays BU CL SEY TH
BEAVER, Victor, 1928- , Australian; poetry CON VCP
BEAVERBROOK, William Maxwell, 1879-1964, Canadian; journalism, nonfiction CON
BEBEL, Heinrich, 1472-1518, German; nonfiction, fiction BU
BEBEY, Francis, 1929- , Cam-

eroonian; fiction, nonfiction
CON HER JA
BEBLER, Alex Anton, 1937- ,
American; nonfiction CON
BECCADELLI, Antonio (Panormi-
ta), 1394-1471, Italian; non-
fiction, poetry BU
BECCARI, Agostino de, -1590,
Italian; poetry BU
BECCARI, Antonio (Antonio da
Ferrara), 1315-70?, Italian;
poetry BU
BECCARIA, Cesare, 1738-94,
Italian; nonfiction BO BU TH
BECHDOLT, John Ernest, 1884-
1954, American; fiction NI
BECHER, Johannes Robert, 1891-
1958, German; fiction, poetry,
nonfiction BU CL TH
BECHER, Ulrich, 1910- , Ger-
man; fiction, plays, poetry
BU CON MCG
BECHKO, Peggy Anne, 1950- ,
American; fiction CON
BECHSTEIN, Ludwig, 1801-60,
American; juveniles WAR
BECHTEL, Louise Seaman, 1894- ,
American; juveniles CO
BECHTOL, William Milton, 1931- ,
American; nonfiction CON
BECK, Alan Marshall, 1942- ,
American; nonfiction CON
BECK, Barbara L., 1927- ,
American; juveniles CO
BECK, Beatrix, 1914- , Belgian;
fiction BU CL
BECK, Calvin Thomas, 1937- ,
American; nonfiction CON
BECK, Clive, 1939- , Canadian;
nonfiction CON
'BECK, Harry' see PAINE, Lauran
B.
BECK, Helen Louise, 1908- ,
Austrian-American; nonfiction
CON
BECK, Horace Palmer, 1920- ,
American; nonfiction CON
BECK, James H., 1930- , Amer-
ican; nonfiction CON
BECK, James Murray, 1914- ,
Canadian; nonfiction CON
BECK, John Jacob, Jr., 1941- ,
American; nonfiction CON
BECK, Julian, 1925- , Amer-
ican; nonfiction, poetry CON
BECK, Marilyn Mohr, 1928- ,
American; nonfiction CON
'BECK, Phineas' see CHAMBER-

LAIN, Samuel
BECK, Robert, American; fiction
SH
BECK, Thomas Davis, 1943- ,
American; nonfiction CON
BECK, Toni, 1925- , American;
nonfiction CON
BECK, Warren, 1921- , Amer-
ican; fiction, nonfiction VCN
BECKER, Adolph Carl, Jr., 1924- ,
American; nonfiction CON
BECKER, B. Jay, 1904- , Amer-
ican; nonfiction CON
BECKER, Beril, 1901- , Amer-
ican; juveniles CO WAR
BECKER, Bruce, American; non-
fiction CON
BECKER, Carl L., 1873-1945,
American; nonfiction PAL
BECKER, Ernest, 1925-74, Amer-
ican; nonfiction CON
BECKER, Gary Stanley, 1930- ,
American; nonfiction CON
BECKER, Jillian Ruth, 1932- ,
South African; fiction, nonfiction
CON
BECKER, John Edward, 1930- ,
American; nonfiction CON
BECKER, John Leonard, 1901- ,
American; juveniles CO
BECKER, Jürgen, 1932- , German;
radio, fiction, plays, poetry
BU CL
BECKER, Jurek, 1937- , German;
fiction CL CON
BECKER, Knuth, 1891/93-1974,
Danish; poetry, fiction BU CL
TH
BECKER, Lawrence Carlyle,
1939- , American; nonfiction
CON
BECKER, Marion Rombauer, 1903-
76, American; journalism, non-
fiction CON
BECKER, Peter, 1921- , South
African; nonfiction CON
BECKER, Stephen David, 1927- ,
American; fiction, nonfiction,
translations VCN
BECKETT, Kenneth Albert ('Keith
Bower'), 1929- , English;
nonfiction CON
BECKETT, Lucy, 1942- , Eng-
lish; nonfiction, poetry CON
BECKETT, Samuel, 1906- , Irish;
fiction, plays, poetry BU CL
DA HO MAG MCG PO SEY TH
VCD VCN VCP VD VN

BECKFORD, George Leslie,
1934- , Jamaican; nonfiction
CON
BECKFORD, William, 1760-1844,
English; fiction BU DA MAG
PO VN
BECKHAM, Barry Earl, 1944- ,
American; fiction, nonfiction
SH VCN
BECKHAM, Stephen Dow, 1941- ,
American; nonfiction CON
BECKHART, Benjamin Haggott,
1897-1975, American; nonfic-
tion CON
BECKINGHAM, Charles Fraser,
1914- , English; nonfiction,
translations CON
BECKINSALE, Monica, 1914- ,
British; nonfiction CON
BECKMAN, Aldo Bruce, 1934- ,
American, nonfiction CON
BECKMAN, Gail McKnight,
1938- , American; nonfic-
tion CON
BECKMAN, Gunnel, 1910- ,
Swedish; juveniles CO DEM
BECKMANN, David Milton, 1948- ,
American; nonfiction CON
BECKMANN, Petr, 1924- , Czech-
American; nonfiction, transla-
tions CON
BEČKOVIČ, Matija, 1939- , Ser-
bian; poetry, nonfiction BU
BECKWITH, Brainerd Kellogg,
1902- , American; journal-
ism, fiction, nonfiction CON
BECQUE, Henry François, 1837-
99, French; plays, journalism
BU MCG TH
BECQUER, Gustavo Adolfo, 1836-
70, Spanish; poetry BU CL
TH
BEDDOES, Thomas Lovell, 1803-
49, English; poetry, plays BU
DA MAG PO VP
BEDE (Baeda), 674-735, English;
nonfiction BU DA
'BEDE, Cuthbert' see BRADLEY,
Edward
BEDE, Jean-Albert, 1903-77,
Franco-American; nonfiction
CON
BEDELL, George Chester, 1928- ,
American; nonfiction CON
'BEDFORD, A. N.' see WATSON,
Jane W.
'BEDFORD, Annie North' see
WATSON, Jane W.

BEDFORD, Charles Harold, 1929- ,
Canadian; nonfiction CON
'BEDFORD, Donald F.' see FEAR-
ING, Kenneth
BEDFORD, Emmett Gruner, 1922- ,
American; nonfiction CON
'BEDFORD, Kenneth' see PAINE,
Lauran B.
BEDFORD, Sybille, 1911- , Brit-
ish; fiction, nonfiction VCN
WA
BEDFORD-JONES, Henry James,
1887-1949, Canadian-American;
fiction NI
BEDI, Rajindar, 1915- , Urdu;
fiction, plays PRU
'BEDIAKO' see KONADU, Samuel
A.
BEDIKIAN, Antriganik A., 1886?-
1980, Turkish; nonfiction CON
BEDIL, Abdulqadir (Bidel), 1644-
1721, Persian; poetry PRU
BEDIL, Qadir Bakhsh of Rohri,
1814-72, Sindhi; poetry PRU
BEDINGER, Margery, 1891- ,
American; nonfiction CON
BEDINGER, Singleton Berry,
1907- , American; nonfiction
CON
BEDNAR, Alfonz, 1914- , Slovak;
fiction BU
BEDNARIK, Charles Philip, 1925- ,
American; nonfiction CON
'BEDNY, Demyan' (Efim Alexey-
wich Predvorov), 1883-1945,
Russian; poetry BU
BEDRIJ, Orest John, 1933- ,
American; nonfiction CON
BEE, Helen L. (Douglas), 1939- ,
American; nonfiction CON
'BEE, Jay' see BRAINERD, John
W.
BEEBE, Burdetta Faye, 1920- ,
American; juveniles WAR
BEEBE, Charles William, 1877-
1962, American; juveniles, non-
fiction CO CON
BEEBE, Frank Lyman, 1914- ,
Canadian; nonfiction CON
BEEBE, Frederick Sessions, 1914-
73, American; nonfiction CON
BEEBE, Ida Ann, 1919- , Amer-
ican; nonfiction CON
BEEBY, Betty, 1923- , American;
juveniles CO
BEECH, Linda, American; juven-
iles WAR
'BEECHAM, Justin' see WINTLE,

Justin B.
BEECHER, Catherine Esther;
1800-78, American; nonfiction
MY
BEECHER, Henry Ward, 1813-
87/95, American; nonfiction,
fiction BR BU MYE
BEECHER, John, 1904-80, Amer-
ican; poetry VCP
BEECHER, William M., 1933- ,
American; nonfiction, journal-
ism CON
BEECHING, Jack ('James Barbary'),
1922- , English; poetry, ju-
veniles, fiction CO NI
BEEDELL, Suzanne Mollie, 1921- ,
British; nonfiction CON
'BEEDING, Francis' (John Leslie
Palmer, 1885-1944; Hilary
Aidan St. George Saunders,
1898-1951), English; fiction
MCC NI REI ST
BEEKMAN, John, 1918- , Amer-
ican; nonfiction, translations
CON
BEEKS, Graydon, 1919- , Amer-
ican; juveniles CON
BEELER, Nelson Frederick, 1910- ,
American; juveniles, nonfiction
CO CON
BEELO, Adrianus, 1798-1878,
Dutch; poetry, plays BU
BEEMAN, Richard Roy, 1942- ,
American; nonfiction CON
BEER, Barrett Lynn, 1936- ,
American; nonfiction CON
BEER, Ethel S., 1897-1975, Amer-
ican; nonfiction CON
BEER, Johann, 1655-1700, Ger-
man; fiction BU TH
BEER, Patricia, 1924- , British;
fiction, nonfiction, poetry
CON VCP
BEER, Samuel Hutchison, 1911- ,
American; nonfiction CON
BEER, Thomas, 1889-1940, Amer-
ican; nonfiction, fiction PAL
BEERBOHM, Sir Max, 1872-1956,
English; nonfiction, fiction
BU DA MAG PO VN
BEER-HOFMANN, Richard, 1866-
1945, Austrian; plays, poetry,
fiction BU CL MCG TH
BEERS, Dorothy Sands, 1917- ,
American; juveniles, poetry,
nonfiction CO CON
BEERS, Jan van, 1821-88, Flem-
ish; poetry BU

BEERS, Lorna, 1897- , American;
fiction, nonfiction, juveniles
CO CON
BEERS, Paul Benjamin, 1931- ,
American; nonfiction CON
BEERS, Victor Gilbert, 1928- ,
American; nonfiction, juveniles
CO CON
BEESLY, Patrick, 1913- , British;
nonfiction CON
BEESON, Trevor Randall, 1926- ,
British; nonfiction CON
BEETON, Ridley, 1929- , South
African; nonfiction, fiction
CON
BEETS, Nicolaas ('Hildebrand'),
1814-1903, Dutch; poetry, fic-
tion BU TH
BEEVERS, John Leonard ('John
Clayton'), 1911-75, English;
nonfiction, poetry CON
BEEZLEY, William Howard Taft,
1942- , American; nonfiction
CON
BEFU, Harumi, 1930- , American;
nonfiction CON
BEGBIE, Edward Harold, 1871-
1929, English; fiction, journal-
ism NI
BEGG, Alexander Charles, 1912- ,
New Zealander; nonfiction CON
BEGG, Neil Colquhoun, 1915- ,
New Zealander; nonfiction CON
BEGGS, Edward Larry, 1933- ,
American; nonfiction CON
BEGHIAN, Jeanne see ANDONIAN,
Jeanne
BEGLEY, Kathleen Anne, 1948- ,
American; juveniles, nonfiction
CO CON
BEGNAL, Michael Henry, 1929- ,
American; nonfiction CON
BEGOUEN, Max, French; fiction
NI
BEGOVIC, Milan, 1876-1948, Cro-
atian; plays, poetry BU CL
BEGUIN, Albert, 1901-57, Swiss;
translations, nonfiction CL
BEHAIM, Michael, 1416-74, Ger-
man; poetry TH
'BEHAINE, René' (René Béhanne),
1880-1966, French; fiction BU
BEHAN, Brendan, 1923-64, Irish;
plays BU CON DA HO MCG
PO SEY VD WA
BEHARA, Devendra Nath, 1940- ,
Indian; nonfiction CON
BEHAZIN, Mohammad E'temadzade,

1915- , Iranian; fiction,
translations BU PRU
BEHEIM, Michael, 1416-72, Ger-
man; nonfiction BU
BEHENNE, René see 'BEHAINE,
René'
BEHLER, Ernst, 1928- , Ger-
man; nonfiction CON
BEHLMER, Rudy, 1926- , Amer-
ican; nonfiction CON
BEHM, Marc, 1925- , American;
fiction, film CON
BEHME, Robert Lee, 1924- ,
American; nonfiction CON
BEHN, Aphra Johnson (?), 1640?-
89, English; plays, poetry,
fiction BU DA MAG MCG
PO VD
BEHN, Harry, 1898-1973, Amer-
ican; journalism, poetry,
translations CON KI
BEHN, Noel, 1928- , American;
fiction REI
BEHNEY, John Bruce, 1905- ,
American; nonfiction CON
BEHNKE, Frances L., Amer-
ican; juveniles CO
BEHNKE, John, 1945- , Amer-
ican; juveniles CON
BEHNKEN, Heinrich, 1880-1960,
German; plays, fiction BU
BEHR, Joyce, 1929- , American;
juveniles CO
BEHRAMOGLU, Ataol, 1942- ,
Turkish; poetry PRU
BEHRENS, Ernst, 1878-1970, Ger-
man; poetry, plays BU
BEHRENS, Helen Kindler, 1922- ,
English; nonfiction CON
BEHRENS, June York, 1925- ,
American; juveniles CO
BEHRMAN, Carol Helen, 1925- ,
American; juveniles CO CON
BEHRMAN, Daniel, 1923- ,
American; nonfiction CON
BEHRMAN, Samuel Nathaniel,
1893-1973, American; plays
BR BU CON MCG MCN PO
VD
BEICHMAN, Arnold, 1913- ,
American; nonfiction CON
BEIER, Ulli see 'IJIMERE, Obo-
tunde'
BEIGEL, Allan, 1940- , Amer-
ican; nonfiction CON
BEIGEL, Herbert, 1944- , Amer-
ican; nonfiction CON
BEILENSON, Edna ('Elisabeth

Deane'), 1909-81, American;
nonfiction CON
BEIM, Norman, 1923- , American;
plays CON
BEIMILLER, Carl, 1913?-79, Amer-
ican; journalism, nonfiction,
juveniles, fiction CON
BEINE, George, Holmes, 1893- ,
American; nonfiction CON
BEIRNE, Joseph Anthony, 1911- ,
American; nonfiction CON
BEISER, Arthur, 1931- , Amer-
ican; juveniles, nonfiction
CO CON
BEISER, Germaine, 1931- , Amer-
ican; juveniles CO
BEISSEL, Henry Eric, 1929- ,
German-Canadian; poetry, plays,
translations, fiction CON VCP
BEISSEL, Johann Conrad, 1690-
1768, German-American; non-
fiction BU
BEITZ, Charles Richard, 1949- ,
American; nonfiction CON
BEITZINGER, Alfons Joseph,
1918- , American; nonfiction
CON
BEK, Alexander Alfredovich,
1903- , Russian; fiction BU
BEKESSY, Jean see 'HABE, Hans'
BEKKER, Balthasar, 1634-98,
Dutch; nonfiction BU
BEKKER, Hugo, 1925- , Dutch-
American; nonfiction CON
BEKLENNISHOV, Yuriy see 'KRY-
MOV, Yuriy S.'
BEKOUKIAN, Kerop, 1907- ,
Turkish-Canadian; nonfiction
CON
BELAIR, Felix, Jr., 1907-78,
American; journalism CON
BELANEY, Archibald Stansfeld
see 'GREY OWL'
BELANGER, Jerome David, 1938- ,
American; nonfiction CON
BELASCO, David, 1853-1931, Amer-
ican; plays BU MCG MCN VD
BELAVAL, Emilio, 1903- , Puerto
Rican; plays, nonfiction, fic-
tion HIL
BELCARI, Feo, 1410-84, Italian;
poetry, plays BU MCG
BELCH, Caroline Jean, 1916- ,
American; nonfiction CON
BELCHEVA, E. see 'BAGRYANA,
Elisaveta'
BELEHRADEK, Jan, 1896-1980,
British; nonfiction CON

BELEV

BELEV, Gyoncho, 1889-1962, Bul-
garian; fiction BU
BELFER, Nancy, 1930- , Amer-
ican; nonfiction, film CON
BELEFIGLIO, Valentine John,
1934- , American; nonfiction
CON
BELIN, David W., 1928- , Amer-
ican; nonfiction CON
BELING, Willard Adolf, 1919- ,
American; nonfiction CON
BELINSKY, Vissarion Grigorye-
vich, 1811-48, Russian; plays,
nonfiction BU TH
BELITT, Ben, 1911- , American;
poetry, translations BR VCP
BELKIN, Samuel, 1911-76, Polish-
American; nonfiction CON
'BELKNAP, B. H.' see ELLIS,
Edward S.
BELKNAP, Robert Harlan, 1917- ,
American; nonfiction CON
BELL, Adrian Hanbury, 1901-80,
British; fiction, nonfiction
CON
BELL, Arthur, 1939- , Amer-
ican; nonfiction CON
BELL, Carol, see FLAVELL,
Carol W.
BELL, Charles Greenleaf, 1916- ,
American; poetry, fiction
VCP
BELL, Clive, 1881-1964, English;
nonfiction CON DA
BELL, Corydon Whitten, 1894- ,
American; juveniles CO DE
BELL, Daniel, 1919- , American;
journalism, nonfiction WAK
BELL, David Robert, 1932- ,
British; nonfiction CON
BELL, David Sheffield, 1945- ,
American; nonfiction CON
BELL, David Victor John, 1944- ,
Canadian; nonfiction CON
'BELL, Emily Mary' see CASON,
Mabel E.
BELL, Eric T. see 'TAINE, John'
BELL, Frederic, 1928- , Amer-
ican; juveniles WAR
BELL, Gail Winther, 1936- ,
American; nonfiction, fiction
CON
BELL, Gerald Dean, 1937- ,
American; nonfiction CON
BELL, Gertrude (Margaret Low-
thian), 1868-1926, English; non-
fiction DA
BELL, Gertrude Wood, 1911- ,

American; juveniles CO WAR
'BELL, Gina' see IANNONE, Jeanne
K.
BELL, Irene Wood, 1944- , Amer-
ican; nonfiction CON
BELL, Jack L., 1904-75, American;
journalism, nonfiction CON
BELL, James Adrian, 1917- ,
American; journalism CON
BELL, James B., 1932- , Amer-
ican; nonfiction CON
'BELL, Janet' see CLYMER, Eleanor
BELL, John C., 1902-81, American;
journalism CON
BELL, John Donnelly, 1944- ,
American; journalism, nonfic-
tion CON
BELL, John Elderkin, 1913- ,
Canadian-American; nonfiction
CON
BELL, John Jay, 1871-1934, Scots;
fiction, nonfiction DA
BELL, John Patrick, 1935- ,
American; nonfiction CON
'BELL, Josephine' (Doris Bell
Collier Ball), 1897- , Eng-
lish; fiction REI ST
BELL, Joyce ('Jean Colin'), 1920- ,
English; fiction, nonfiction,
journalism CON
BELL, Julian, 1908-37, English;
poetry, nonfiction DA
BELL, L. Nelson, 1894-1973,
American; nonfiction CON
BELL, Leland Virgil, 1934- ,
American; nonfiction CON
BELL, Martin, 1918- , British;
poetry VCP
BELL, Marvin Hartley, 1937- ,
American; poetry MAL VCP
WAK
BELL, Michael Davitt, 1941- ,
American; nonfiction CON
'BELL, Neil' (Stephen Southwold),
1887-1964, English; fiction NI
BELL, Norman Edward, 1899- ,
American; juveniles CO CON
BELL, Oliver Sydney, 1913- ,
Anglo-American; nonfiction
CON
BELL, Quentin, 1910- , English;
nonfiction CON WAK
BELL, Raymond Martin, 1907- ,
American; juveniles CO
BELL, Robert Ivan, 1942- ,
American; nonfiction CON
BELL, Rudolph Mark, 1942- ,
American; nonfiction CON

BELL, Sam Hanna, 1909- ,
Irish; fiction HO
BELL, Sarah Fore, 1920- ,
American; nonfiction CON
BELL, Sidney, 1929- , Amer-
ican; nonfiction CON
BELL, Stephen Scott, 1935- ,
American; nonfiction CON
BELL, Thelma Harrington,
1896- , American; juveniles
CO DE
'BELL, Thornton' see FANTHORPE,
Robert L.
BELLAH, James Warner, 1899-
1976, American; fiction, jour-
nalism, film CON
'BELLAIRS, George' (Harold Blun-
dell), 1902- , English; fic-
tion CON REI ST
BELLAK, Leopold, 1916- ,
Austrian-American; nonfic-
tion CON
BELLAMANN, Henry, 1882-1945,
American; fiction, poetry
MAG
BELLAMANN, Katherine, 1877-
1956, American; fiction, po-
etry BA
BELLAMY, Edward, 1850-98,
American; fiction BR BU
MAG NI PO VN
BELLAMY, Francis Rufus, 1886-
1972, American; fiction NI
BELLAMY, Guy, 1935- , Eng-
lish; fiction CON
'BELLAMY, Harmon' see BLOOM,
Herman I.
BELLAMY, Jacobus, 1757-86,
Dutch; poetry BU
BELLAMY, James Andrew,
1925- , American; nonfic-
tion CON
BELLAMY, Joe David, 1941- ,
American; nonfiction, fiction
CON
BELLAMY, Ralph, 1904- , Amer-
ican; nonfiction CON
BELLAY, Joachim du, 1522-60,
French; poetry MAG
BELLEAU, Rémy, 1528-77,
French; poetry BU TH
BELLEFOREST, François de,
1530-83, French; transla-
tions RU
BELLEM, Robert Leslie ('Frank-
lin Charles'; 'John A. Sax-
on'), 1902-68, American;
fiction, plays REI

BELLEMANS, Daniel, 1642-74,
Flemish; poetry BU
BELLEMERE, Jean see 'SARMENT,
Jean'
BELLENDEN, John, 1492?-1587,
Scots; nonfiction, translations
BU DA
BELLER, Anne Scott, American;
nonfiction CON
BELLER, Elmer Adolph, 1894-
1980, American; nonfiction
CON
BELLERBY, Frances Parker,
1899-1975, British; poetry,
fiction CON VCP
BELLI, Carlos Germán, 1927- ,
Peruvian; poetry BR BU
BELLI, Giuseppe Gioacchino, 1791-
1863, Italian; poetry BO BU
BELLIDO, José María, 1922- ,
Spanish; plays CL
BELLINCIONI, Bernardo, 1452-
92, Italian; poetry BU
BELLMAN, Carl Michael, 1740-
95, Swedish; poetry BU TH
BELLMAN, Richard Ernest, 1920- ,
American; nonfiction CON
BELLO, Alhaji Sir Ahmadu, 1909- ,
Nigerian; nonfiction BU JA
BELLO, Andrés, 1781-1865, Chil-
ean; poetry BR BU
BELLO, Francesco (Il Cieco di
Ferrara), -1505, Italian; po-
etry BU
BELLOC, Hilaire, 1870-1953, Eng-
lish; nonfiction, poetry, fiction,
journalism BU COM DA KI
MAG PO VP
BELLOW, Saul, 1915- , American;
fiction, plays AM BR BU HE
MAG NI PO SEY VCD VCN VN
BELLOWS, James Gilbert, 1922- ,
American; journalism, nonfic-
tion CON
BELLOWS, Thomas John, 1935- ,
American; nonfiction CON
'BELLOY, Dormont de' (Pierre
Laurent Buirette), 1727-75,
French; plays BU
'BELL-ZANO, Gina' see IANNONE,
Jeanne K.
BELMONT, Eleanor Robson, 1879-
1979; nonfiction CON
BELMONT, Herman S., 1920- ,
American; nonfiction CON
BELMONTE, Thomas, 1946- ,
American; nonfiction CON
BELMONTE BERMUDEZ, Luis de,

1587?-1650?, Spanish; plays
BU
BELOTE, Julainne, 1929- ,
American; nonfiction CON
BELOTE, William Milton, 1922- ,
American; nonfiction CON
BELOV, Vasily Ivanovich, 1932- ,
Russian; fiction CL
BELPRE, Pura, 1899- , Puerto
Rican; juveniles, translations,
fiction CO CON DEM
BELSER, Lee, 1925- , Amer-
ican; journalism CON
BELSER, Raymond de see 'RUY-
SLINCK, Ward'
BELTING, Natalia Maree, 1915- ,
American; juveniles CO DE
BELTON, John Raynor, 1931- ,
American; juveniles CO CON
BELTRAN, Pedro Gerardo, 1897-
1979, Peruvian; journalism
CON
'BELVAIN, Michel' see 'MALINDA,
Martial'
'BELVEDERE, Lee' see GRAY-
LAND, Valerie M.
'BELY, Andrey' (Boris Nikolaye-
vich Bugaev), 1880-1924,
Russian; poetry, fiction, non-
fiction BU CL SEY TH WA
BELYAEV, Alexander, 1884-1942,
Russian; fiction NI
BELYAYEV, Yury Dmitrievich,
1876-1917, Russian; fiction
BU
BELZ, Herman Julius, 1937- ,
American; nonfiction CON
BEMBA, Sylvain see 'MALINDA,
Martial'
BEMBO, Pietro, 1470-1547, Ital-
ian; nonfiction, poetry BO
BU TH
BEMELMANS, Ludwig, 1898-1962,
American; fiction, nonfiction,
poetry, juveniles BR CO CON
KI VN
BEMIS, Samuel Flagg, 1891-1973,
American; nonfiction CON
'BEMISTER, Henry' see BARRETT,
Harry B.
'BEN, Ilke' see HARPER, Carol E.
BEN AVIGDOR (Arieh Leib Shalko-
vits), 1866-1921, Hebrew; non-
fiction BU TH
BEN no NAISHI, 13th century,
Japanese; poetry HI
BEN YEHUDA (Eliezer Perelmann),
1858-1922, Israeli; nonfiction

BU LA TH
BENAGH, Jim, 1937- , American;
juveniles, nonfiction CON WAR
BENA'I (Banna'i; Binoi), 1453-
1512, Persian; poetry PRU
'BEN-AMI' (M. Rabinovitch), 1858-
1932, Russian-Israeli; nonfic-
tion TH
BEN-AMOS, Dan, 1934- , Israeli;
nonfiction CON
BENARDETE, Jane Johnson,
1930- , American; nonfiction
CON
BENARY-ISBERT, Margot, 1889-
1979, German-American; ju-
veniles, translations CO
BENASUTTI, Marion, 1908- ,
American; juveniles CO
BENAVENTE, Fray Toribio de
('Motilinía'), -1565, Spanish;
nonfiction BR
BENAVENTE y MARTINEZ, Jacinto,
1866-1954, Spanish; plays BU
CL MAG MCG TH
'ben-AVRAHAM, Chofetz C.' see
PICKERING, Stephen
BENAWA, Abdurrauf, 1913- ,
Afghan; poetry, plays, non-
fiction PRU
BENCHLEY, Nathaniel Goddard,
1915-81, American; juveniles,
fiction, journalism CO DEM
KI WA WAR
BENCHLEY, Peter Bradford,
1940- , American; juveniles
fiction CO
BENCHLEY, Robert Charles,
1889-1945, American; nonfic-
tion, fiction BR VN
BENCUR, Matej see 'KUKUCIN,
Martin'
BENDA, Julien, 1867-1956, French;
fiction BU CL TH
BENDAVID, Avrom, 1942- ,
Dutch; nonfiction CON
BENDER, David Ray, 1942- ,
American; nonfiction CON
BENDER, Frederic Lawrence,
1943- , American; nonfiction
CON
BENDER, Hans, 1919- , German;
poetry, fiction, nonfiction CL
BENDER, John Bryant, 1940- ,
American; nonfiction CON
BENDER, Lucy Ellen, 1942- ,
American; juveniles CO
BENDER, Richard, 1930- ,
American; nonfiction CON

BENDER, Ross Thomas, 1929- ,
Canadian-American; nonfiction
CON
BENDER, Stephen Joseph, 1942- ,
American; nonfiction CON
BENDER, Thomas, 1944- ,
American; nonfiction CON
BENDICK, Robert Louis, 1917- ,
American; juveniles, nonfiction CO CON
BENDINER, Elmer, 1916- ,
American; nonfiction CON
BENDIXSON, Terence, 1934- ,
British; nonfiction CON
BENDRE, Dattatreya Ramacandra,
1896- , Indian; poetry PRU
BENEDEIZ, fl. 1125, Anglo-
Norman; fiction BU
BENEDEK, Therese, 1892- ,
Hungarian-American; nonfic-
tion CON
BENEDETTI, Mario, 1920- ,
Uruguayan; fiction, nonfiction
BR BU
BENEDICT, St. of Nursia, 480-
543, Latin; nonfiction GR
BENEDICT, Bertram, 1892?-
1978, American; nonfiction
CON
BENEDICT, Dorothy Potter, 1889-
1979, American; juveniles,
translations CO CON
BENEDICT, Lois Trimble, 1902-
67, American; juveniles CO
BENEDICT, Michael Les, 1945- ,
American; nonfiction CON
BENEDICT, Rex Arthur, 1920- ,
American; juveniles, poetry,
translations CO KI WAR
BENEDICT, Robert Philip, 1924- ,
American; nonfiction CON
BENEDICTSSON, Victoria Maria
Bruzelius see 'AHLGREN,
Ernst'
BENEDICTUS, David, 1938- ,
British; fiction, plays CON
VCN
BENEDIKT, Michael, 1937- ,
American; poetry, plays,
translations MAL VCP
BENEDIKTOV, Vladimir Grigorye-
vich; 1807-73, Russian; po-
etry BU
BENEDIKTSSON, Einar, 1864-
1940, Icelander; poetry BU
CL
BENEFIELD, June, 1921- ,
American; nonfiction CON

BENELLI, Sem, 1877-1949, Italian;
plays, poetry BO BU CL MCG
BENESOVA, Božena Zapletalová,
1873-1936, Czech; fiction BU
BENET, James, 1914- , American;
nonfiction CON
BENET, Juan, 1927- , Spanish;
plays CL
BENET, Laura, 1884-1979, Amer-
ican; juveniles, poetry CO
CON
BENET, Mary Kathleen, 1943- ,
English; nonfiction CON
BENET, Stephen Vincent, 1898-
1943, American; poetry, fic-
tion, juveniles, plays BR BU
COM MAG NI PO RO SEY VP
WAR
BENET, Sula, 1903/06- , Polish-
American; juveniles, transla-
tions, nonfiction CO CON
BENET, William Rose, 1886-1950,
American; poetry, nonfiction
BR VP
BENETAR, Judith, 1941- , Amer-
ican; nonfiction CON
BENEVOLO, Leonardo, 1923- ,
Italian; nonfiction CON
BEN-EZER, Ehud, 1936- , Is-
raeli; fiction CON
BENEZRA, Barbara Beardsley,
1921- , American; juveniles
CO
BENFIELD, Richard E., 1940- ,
American; journalism CON
BENFORD, Gregory, 1941- ,
American; fiction, nonfiction
AS CON NI
BENFORD, Harry Bell, 1917- ,
American; journalism, nonfic-
tion CON
BENFORD, Timothy Bartholomew,
1941- , American; nonfiction
CON
BENGANI, Redvus Robert, 1899?- ,
Zulu; fiction HER
BENGE, Eugene Jackson, 1896- ,
American; nonfiction CON
BENGELSDORF, Irving S., 1922- ,
American; nonfiction CON
BENGONO, Jacques, 1938- ,
Cameroonian; fiction, poetry
JA
BENGTSON, Vern L., 1941- ,
American; nonfiction CON
BENGTSSON, Frans Gunnar, 1894-
1954, Swedish; poetry, fiction,
nonfiction BU TH

BENGUEREL i LLOBET, P.,
1905- , Catalan; fiction CL
BEN-GURION, David, 1886-1973,
Israeli; nonfiction CON
BENHAM, Mary Lile, 1914- ,
Canadian; nonfiction CON
'BEN-HORAV, Naphthali' see
KRAVITZ, Nathaniel
BENIAK, Valentín, 1894- , Slo-
vak; poetry BU
BENICHOU, Paul, 1908- , Amer-
ican; nonfiction CON
BENITEZ, Jaime, 1908- , Puerto
Rican; nonfiction HIL
BENITEZ, Maria Bibiana, 1783-
1873, Puerto Rican; poetry
HIL
BENITEZ, Miguel A. O. see 'BAR-
BA JACOB, Porfirio'
BENITSKY, Alexander Petrovich,
1780-1809, Russian; poetry,
fiction BU
BENIUC, Mihai, 1907- , Ru-
manian; poetry BU
BENIUSEVICUITE-ZYMANTIENE,
Julija see 'ZEMAITE'
BENIVIENI, Girolamo, 1453-1542,
Italian; poetry BO
'BENJAMIN, Alice' see BROOKE,
Avery R.
BENJAMIN, Anna Shaw, 1925- ,
American; translations, non-
fiction CON
BENJAMIN, Burton Richard,
1917- , American; journal-
ism CON
BENJAMIN, Edward Bernard,
1897- , American; nonfiction
CON
BENJAMIN, Gerald, 1945- ,
American; nonfiction CON
BENJAMIN, Joseph, 1921- , Eng-
lish; nonfiction CON
BENJAMIN, Park, 1809-64, Amer-
ican; poetry, nonfiction MYE
BENJAMIN, Walter ('Detlev Holz';
'C. Conrad'), 1892-1940, Ger-
man; nonfiction BU CL TH
WAK
BENJAMIN of Tudela (ben Jonah),
fl. 1160-73, Spanish; nonfic-
tion BU TH
BENJAMINSON, Peter, 1945- ,
American; journalism CON
'BENJI, Thomas' see ROBINSON,
Frank M.
ben-JOCHANNAN, Yosef, 1918- ,
American; nonfiction CON

BENLOWES, Edward, 1602-76,
English; poetry BU PO VP
BENN, Gottfried, 1886-1956, Ger-
man; poetry BU CL SEY TH
WA
BENNANI, Ben Mohammed, 1946- ,
American; nonfiction, transla-
tions, poetry CON
BENNETT, Abram Elting, 1898- ,
American; nonfiction CON
BENNETT, Adrian Arthur, 1941- ,
American; nonfiction CON
BENNETT, Alan, 1934- , British;
plays, tv CON VCD
BENNETT, Alfred Gordon, 1901- ,
British; film, fiction AS NI
'BENNETT, Daniel' see GILMORE,
Joseph L.
BENNETT, Daphne Nicholson,
Anglo-American; nonfiction
CON
BENNETT, Dennis J., 1917- ,
English; nonfiction CON
BENNETT, Enoch Arnold, 1867-
1931, English; fiction, plays,
journalism BU DA MAG MCG
PO SEY ST VN
BENNETT, Geoffrey M. see 'SEA-
LION'
BENNETT, George Harold, 1930- ,
American; poetry, plays, fic-
tion CON SH
'BENNETT, Gertrude B. see
'STEVENS, Francis'
BENNETT, Gertrude Ryder, Amer-
ican; poetry CON
BENNETT, Gwendolyn B., 1902- ,
American; poetry SH
BENNETT, Hal Zina, 1936- ,
American; juveniles, nonfiction
CON
BENNETT, Isadora ('Wesley Mor-
gan'), 1900-80, American;
plays, journalism CON
BENNETT, Jack Arthur Walter,
1911-81, New Zealander; non-
fiction CON
BENNETT, James David, 1926- ,
American; nonfiction CON
BENNETT, Jay, 1912- , American;
fiction, juveniles, plays, radio,
tv CON WAR
BENNETT, John, 1865-1956, Amer-
ican; journalism, poetry, fic-
tion, juveniles COM
BENNETT, John Michael, 1942- ,
American; poetry, nonfiction
CON

BENNETT, John W., 1918- ,
American; nonfiction CON
BENNETT, Jonathan Francis,
1930- , New Zealander;
nonfiction CON
BENNETT, Josephine Waters,
1899-1975, American; nonfic-
tion CON
BENNETT, Judith, -1979, Amer-
ican; journalism CON
BENNETT, Lerone, Jr., 1928- ,
American; journalism, non-
fiction BA CON SH
BENNETT, Louise, Jamaican;
poetry VCP VP
BENNETT, Margot, 1912-80,
English; fiction, plays NI
REI
BENNETT, Michael, 1943- ,
American; plays, CON
BENNETT, Neville, 1937- ,
British; nonfiction CON
BENNETT, Noel, 1939- , Amer-
ican; nonfiction CON
BENNETT, Rainey, 1907- ,
American; juveniles CO DEM
BENNETT, Richard, 1899- ,
Irish-American; juveniles CO
BENNETT, Rita Maria, 1934- ,
American; nonfiction CON
BENNETT, Robert L., 1931- ,
American; nonfiction CON
BENNETT, Russell Horadley,
1896- , American; juveniles
CO
BENNETT, Thomas Leroy, 1942- ,
American; nonfiction CON
BENNETT-COVERLY, Louise Si-
mone ('Miss Lou'), 1919- ,
West Indian; poetry BU CON
BENNETT-ENGLAND, Rodney
Charles, 1936- , English;
nonfiction CON
BENNIE, William Andrew, 1921- ,
American; nonfiction CON
BENNING, Barbara Lee Edwards,
1934- , American; nonfic-
tion CON
BENNIS, Warren G., 1925- ,
American; nonfiction CON
BENOIS, Alexander Nikolayevich,
1870-1960, Russian; nonfiction
BU
BENOÎT, fl. 1175, French; poetry
BU
BENOIT, Emile, 1910-78, Amer-
ican; nonfiction CON
BENOIT, Pierre, 1886-1962,

French; fiction BU CL CON
BENOIT, Pierre Maurice, 1906- ,
French-Canadian; nonfiction,
fiction CON CR
BENOÎT de SAINTE MAURE, fl.
1150, French; poetry BU TH
BENOLIEL, Jeanne (Quint), 1919- ,
American; nonfiction CON
BENONI, Marc see 'BLANCPAIN,
Marc'
BENSE, Walter Frederick, 1932- ,
American; nonfiction CON
BENSEN, Alice R., 1911- ,
American; nonfiction CON
BENSEN, Donald R., 1927- ,
American; anthologist NI
BENSERADE, Isaac de, 1613-91,
French; plays, poetry BU
'BENSOL, Oscar' see GILBERT,
Willie
BENSON, A. George, 1924- ,
American; nonfiction CON
BENSON, Arthur Christopher,
1862-1925, English; poetry,
fiction, nonfiction DA NI
'BENSON, B. A.' see BEYEA,
Basil
BENSON, Ben, 1920?-59, American;
fiction ST
BENSON, Benjamin, 1915- , Amer-
ican; fiction REI
BENSON, Carmen, 1921- , Amer-
ican; nonfiction CON
'BENSON, Daniel' see COOPER,
Colin Symons
BENSON, Edward Frederick, 1867-
1940, English; fiction, plays,
nonfiction DA NI REI VN
BENSON, Elizabeth Polk, 1924- ,
American; nonfiction CON
BENSON, Eugene, 1928- , Irish-
Canadian; plays CON
BENSON, Frederick William ('Ted
Benson'), 1948- , American;
journalism, nonfiction CON
'BENSON, Ginny' see BENSON,
Virginia
BENSON, Godfrey Rathbone, 1864-
1945, English; nonfiction, fic-
tion ST
BENSON, Herbert, 1935- , Amer-
ican; nonfiction CON
BENSON, Kathleen, 1947- , Amer-
ican; nonfiction, juveniles CON
BENSON, Lyman David, 1909- ,
American; nonfiction CON
BENSON, Mary, 1919- , South
African-American; nonfiction

CON
BENSON, Maxine Frances, 1939- ,
American; nonfiction CON
'BENSON, Rachel' see JOWITT,
Deborah
BENSON, Robert Hugh, 1871-1914,
English; fiction NI
BENSON, Rolf Eric, 1951- ,
American; nonfiction CON
BENSON, Ruth Crego, 1937- ,
American; nonfiction CON
BENSON, Stella, 1892-1933, Eng-
lish; fiction, nonfiction, diary
DA SEY VN
'BENSON, Ted' see BENSON,
Frederick W.
BENSON, Virginia (Ginny), 1923- ,
American; nonfiction, fiction
CON
BENSTOCK, Shari, 1944- , Amer-
ican; nonfiction CON
BENT, Alan Edward, 1939- ,
American; nonfiction CON
'BENTEEN, John' see HAAS, Ben-
jamin L.
BENTHALL, Jonathan, 1941- ,
English; nonfiction CON
BENTHAM, Jeremy, 1748-1832,
English; nonfiction BU DA
PO
'BENTHIC, Arch E.' see STEWART,
Harris, B., Jr.
BENTIVOGLIO, Ercole, 1507-73,
Italian; poetry, plays BU
BENTIVOGLIO, Guido, 1579-1644,
Italian; nonfiction BU
BENTLEY, Beth Rita, 1928- ,
American; nonfiction, poetry
CON
BENTLEY, Edmund Clerihew,
1875-1956, English; journal-
ism, fiction, poetry REI ST
BENTLEY, Eric Russell, 1916- ,
American; plays, nonfiction,
translations BOR VCD
BENTLEY, Gerald Eades, 1901- ,
American; nonfiction CON
BENTLEY, Nicolas Clerihew,
1907-78, English; fiction, non-
fiction, poetry CO CON REI
BENTLEY, Phyllis Eleanor, 1894-
1977, English; juveniles, fic-
tion, nonfiction CO DA REI
ST
BENTLEY, Richard, 1662-1742,
English; nonfiction BU DA
BENTLEY, Virginia Williams,
1908- , American; nonfic-

tion CON
BENTLEY-TAYLOR, David, 1915- ,
British; nonfiction CON
BENTO, Texeira, 1556?-1600,
Brazilian; poetry BR
BENTON, Dorothy Gilchrist, 1919- ,
American; poetry CON
BENTON, John Frederic, 1931- ,
American; nonfiction CON
BENTON, Kenneth Carter, 1909- ,
English; fiction CON MCC
REI
BENTON, Peggie ('Shifty Burke'),
1906- , English; translations,
nonfiction CON
BENTON, Richard Glasscock,
1938- , American; nonfiction
CON
'BENTON, Robert' see BUSE, Renee
BENTON, Thomas Hart, 1889-1975,
American; cartoons, nonfiction
CON
'BENTON, Will' see PAINE, Lauran
B.
BENTON, William, 1900-73, Amer-
ican; nonfiction CON
BENTOV, Itzhak, 1923?-79, Czech;
nonfiction CON
BENTZ, William Frederick, 1940- ,
American; nonfiction CON
BENVENISTE, Asa, 1925- , Brit-
ish; poetry, plays CON VCP
BENVENISTE, Guy, 1927- ,
Franco-American; nonfiction
CON
BENVENISTI, Meron Shmuel,
1934- , Israeli; nonfiction
CON
BEN-YITZHAK, Abraham, 1883-
1950, Hebrew; poetry BU
BENYO, Richard, 1946- , Amer-
ican; nonfiction CON
BENZ, Frank Leonard, 1930- ,
American; nonfiction CON
'BEN-ZION, Sh.' (Simcha Alter
Gutmann), 1870-1932, Hebrew;
fiction BU TH
BENZON, Carl Otto Valdemar,
1856-1927, Danish; plays BU
BENZONI, Juliette, 1920- , French;
fiction CON
BEOLCO, Angelo see RUZZANTE,
Il
BEORSE, Bryn ('Brynjolf Bjorset'),
1896- , Norwegian-American;
nonfiction, fiction CON
BEOWULF POET, 8th century?,
?; poetry VP

BEQUAERT, Lucia Humes, American; nonfiction CON

BERANGER, Pierre Jean de, 1780-1857, French; poetry BU TH

BERARDO, Felix Mario, 1934- , American; nonfiction CON

BERCEO, Gonzalo de, 1195-1252, Spanish; poetry BU TH

BERCHEN, Ursula, 1919- , American; nonfiction CON

BERCHEN, William, 1920- , German-American; nonfiction CON

BERCHET, Giovanni, 1783-1851, Italian; poetry, translations BO BU TH

BERCK, Martin Gans, 1928- , American; nonfiction CON

BERCKMAN, Evelyn Domenica, 1900-78, American; fiction, nonfiction REI ST

BERCOVICI, Rion, 1903?-76, American; journalism, nonfiction CON

BERCOVITCH, Sacvan, 1933- , Canadian-American; nonfiction CON

BERDICHEWSKI, Micah Joseph (Micha Yoseph Bin Gorion), 1865-1921, Hebrew; nonfiction, fiction BU TH

BERDIE, Douglas Ralph, 1946- , American; nonfiction CON

BERDYAYEV, Nikolay Alexandrovich, 1874-1948, Russian; nonfiction BU CL MAG

BERE, Rennie Montague, 1907- , English; nonfiction CON

BERELSON, Bernard, 1912-79, American; nonfiction CON

BERELSON, Howard, 1940- , American; juveniles CO

BERENDT, Joachim Ernst, 1922- , German; nonfiction CON

BERENDZEN, Richard Earl, 1938- , American; nonfiction CON

BERENG, David Cranmer Theko, 1900- , Lesothon; poetry JA

BERENSON, Bernard, 1865-1959, American; nonfiction BR BU

BERENSTAIN, Janice, American; juveniles CO

BERENSTAIN, Michael, 1951- , American; juveniles CON

BERENSTAIN, Stanley, 1923- , American; juveniles CO

BERENT, Waclaw ('Wl. Rawicz'), 1873-1940, Polish; fiction BU CL TH

BERENY, Gail Rubin, 1942- , American; nonfiction CON

BERESFORD, Anne, 1929- , British; poetry, plays CON VCP

BERESFORD, Elisabeth, British; juveniles, plays, fiction, tv CO CON KI

BERESFORD, John Davys, 1873-1947, British; fiction NI

BERESFORD, Leslie, British; fiction NI

BERESFORD-HOWE, Constance, 1922- , Canadian; fiction CON

BERESINER, Yasha, 1940- , Turkish-British; nonfiction CON

BERG, Alan David, 1932- , American; nonfiction CON

BERG, Björn, 1923- , German-American; juveniles DEM

BERG, Frederick Sven, 1928- , American; nonfiction CON

BERG, Goesta, 1903- , Swedish; nonfiction CON

BERG, Jean Horton, 1913- , American; juveniles CO CON WAR

BERG, Larry Lee, 1939- , American; nonfiction CON

BERG, Lasse, 1943- , Swedish; nonfiction CON

BERG, Leila, 1917- , British; juveniles, translations, plays, nonfiction CON KI

BERG, Rick, 1951- , American; nonfiction CON

BERG, Stephen, 1934- , American; poetry VCP

BERG, Thomas LeRoy, 1930- , American; nonfiction CON

BERG, Viola Jacobson, 1918- , American; nonfiction CON

BERG, William, 1938- , American; nonfiction CON

BERGAMIN, José, 1894/97- , Spanish; nonfiction BU CL

BERGAUST, Erik, 1925-78, Norwegian-American; juveniles, nonfiction, poetry CO CON

BERGE, Carol, 1928- , American;

BERGE   90

poetry, fiction BR VCP
BERGE, Hans Cornelis ten,
1938- , Dutch; poetry BU
BERGELSON, David, 1884-1952,
Yiddish; fiction, plays BU
TH
BERGEN, Polly, 1930- , Amer-
ican; nonfiction CON
BERGENGRUEN, Werner, 1892-
1964, German; fiction, po-
etry, translations BU CL
TH WA
'BERGER, Col.' see MALRAUX,
André
BERGER, Andrew John, 1915- ,
American; nonfiction CON
BERGER, Elmer, 1908- , Amer-
ican; nonfiction CON
BERGER, Harold L., 1923- ,
American; nonfiction NI
BERGER, Hilbert J., 1920- ,
American; nonfiction CON
BERGER, Ivan Bennett ('Bennett
Evans'; 'Martin Leynard'),
1939- , American; nonfiction,
journalism CON
BERGER, John Joseph, 1945- ,
American; nonfiction CON
BERGER, John Peter, 1926- ,
English; fiction, translations,
film, nonfiction CON VCN
WAK
BERGER, Joseph, 1924- , Amer-
ican; nonfiction CON
BERGER, Marilyn, 1935- , Amer-
ican; journalism CON
BERGER, Melvin H., 1927- ,
American; juveniles CO
BERGER, Michael Louis, 1943- ,
American; nonfiction CON
BERGER, Morroe, 1917-81, Amer-
ican; nonfiction CON
BERGER, Phil, 1942- , American;
nonfiction, juveniles CON WAR
BERGER, Raoul, 1901- , Russian-
American; nonfiction CON
BERGER, Robert William, 1936- ,
American; nonfiction CON
BERGER, Terry, 1933- , Amer-
ican; juveniles CO
BERGER, Thomas Louis, 1924- ,
American; fiction, plays BR
HE NI PO VCN WA
BERGER, Yves, 1934/36- ,
French; fiction, journalism,
nonfiction CON NI
'BERGERET, Hugues' see DES-
MARCHAIS, Rex

BERGERET, Ida (Treat), 1889?-
1978, American; journalism,
nonfiction CON
BERGERON, David Moore, 1938- ,
American; nonfiction CON
BERGERON, Paul H., 1938- ,
American; nonfiction CON
BERGERON, Victor Jules ('Trader
Vic'), 1902- , American; ju-
veniles, nonfiction CON WAR
BERGESON, John Brian, 1935- ,
American; nonfiction CON
BERGEY, Earle, -1952, American;
illustrations AS
BERGGOL'TS, Ol'ga, 1910-75, Rus-
sian; poetry CL TH
BERGH, Herman van den, 1897-
1967, Dutch; poetry, nonfiction
BU CL
BERGH, Pieter Theodoor Helvetius
van den, 1799-1873, Dutch;
plays, poetry BU
BERGH, Samuel Joahnnes van den,
1814-68, Dutch; poetry, trans-
lations BU
BERGHAHN, Volker Rolf, 1938- ,
German-British; nonfiction
CON
BERGHE, Jan van den ('Jan van
Diest'), -1559, Dutch; poetry
BU
BERGIER, Jacques, 1912-78,
French; nonfiction CON
BERGIN, Allen E., 1934- , Amer-
ican; nonfiction CON
BERGIN, Kenneth Glenny, 1911-81,
British; nonfiction CON
BERGMAN, Andrew, American;
fiction, nonfiction REI
BERGMAN, Arleen Eisen, 1942- ,
American; nonfiction CON
BERGMAN, Bernard Aaron, 1894-
1980, American; journalism
CON
BERGMAN, Bo Hjalmar, 1869-1967,
Swedish; poetry, fiction BU TH
BERGMAN, Ernst Ingmar ('Buntel
Eriksson'; 'Ernest Riffe'),
1918- , Swedish; film, plays
CL CON
BERGMAN, Floyd Lawrence, 1927- ,
American; nonfiction CON
BERGMAN, Hannah Estermann,
1925- , German-American;
nonfiction CON
BERGMAN, Hjalmar Elgerus, 1883-
1931, Swedish; plays, fiction,
poetry BU CL MCG TH WA

BERGMAN, Shmuel Hugo, 1883-
1975, Czech-Israeli; nonfic-
tion CON
BERGMANN, Anton, 1835-74,
Flemish; fiction BU
BERGMANN, Ernst W., 1896?-
1977, American; journalism,
nonfiction, tv CON
BERGMANN, Fred Louis, 1916- ,
American; nonfiction CON
BERGMANN, Frithjof H., 1930- ,
German-American; nonfiction
CON
BERGOLTS, Olga Fëdorovna,
1910- , Russian; poetry BU
BERGROTH, Kersti Solveig,
1886- , Finnish; plays, fic-
tion, nonfiction TH
BERGSOE, Jorgen Vilhelm, 1835-
1911, Danish; fiction BU
BERGSON, Henri, 1859-1941/42,
French; nonfiction BU CL
MAG SEY TH
BERGSTEDT, Harald Alfred, 1877-
1965, Danish; poetry, fiction
BU
BERGSTEIN, Eleanor, 1938- ,
American; nonfiction CON
BERGSTEN, Staffan, 1932- ,
Swedish; nonfiction CON
BERINGER, Richard E., 1933- ,
American; nonfiction CON
BERK, Fred, 1911?-80, Austrian;
nonfiction CON
BERK, Howard, 1926- , Amer-
ican; fiction NI
BERK, Ilhan, 1916- , Turkish;
poetry PRU
BERKE, Joseph Herman, 1939- ,
English; nonfiction CON
BERKEBILE, Donald Herbert,
1926- , American; nonfiction
CON
BERKEBILE, Fred Donovan ('Wil-
liam Donovan'; 'William Ern-
est'; 'Don Stauffer'), 1900-78,
American; nonfiction, fiction
CON
'BERKELEY, Anthony' (Anthony
Berkeley Cox; 'Francis Iles'),
1893-1971, British; fiction,
plays, nonfiction CON REI
ST
BERKELEY, David Shelley, 1917- ,
American; nonfiction CON
BERKELEY, George, 1685-1753,
Irish; nonfiction BU DA HO
MAG PO

BERKEY, Barry Robert, 1935- ,
American; nonfiction, juveniles
CO CON
BERKHEY, Johannes Le Franq van,
1729-1812; poetry BU
BERKIN, Carol Ruth, 1942- ,
American; nonfiction CON
BERKLEY, Constance, 1931- ,
American; poetry SH
BERKMAN, Edward Oscar (Ted),
1914- , American; nonfiction,
film, tv CON
BERKMAN, Harold William, 1926- ,
American; nonfiction CON
BERKMAN, Richard Lyle, 1946- ,
American; nonfiction CON
BERKMAN, Sue, 1936- , Amer-
ican; nonfiction CON
BERKOVITZ, Irving Herbert,
1924- , American; nonfiction
CON
BERKOVITZ, Yitzchak Dov (Berko-
witz), 1885-1967, Israeli; fic-
tion, plays BU TH
BERKOW, Ira, 1940- , American;
journalism, nonfiction CON
BERKOWITZ, Freda Pastor, 1910- ,
American; juveniles CO
BERKOWITZ, Morris Ira, 1931- ,
American; nonfiction CON
BERKOWITZ, Sol, 1922- , Amer-
ican; nonfiction CON
BERKOWITZ, Yitzhak D. see BERK-
OVITZ, Yitzchak D.
BERKSON, Bill, 1939- , American;
poetry VCP
BERKSON, William Kollar, 1944- ,
American; nonfiction CON
BERL, Emmanuel, 1892-1976,
French; nonfiction, journalism,
fiction CL
BERLANSTEIN, Lenard Russell,
1947- , American; nonfiction
CON
BERLE, Milton, 1908- , American;
nonfiction, fiction CON
BERLIN, Ellin Mackay, 1904- ,
American; fiction, nonfiction
CON
BERLIN, Ia, 1941- , American;
nonfiction CON
BERLIN, Irving, 1888- , Amer-
ican; songs MCG
BERLIN, Sir Isaish, 1909- ,
British; nonfiction CON WA
BERLIN, Michael Joseph, 1938- ,
American; journalism, nonfic-
tion CON

BERLIN, Normand, 1931- , American; nonfiction CON
BERLIN, Sven, 1911- , British; nonfiction, fiction, tv CON
BERLINER, Franz, 1930- , Danish; juveniles CO
BERLINER, Herman Albert, 1944- , American; nonfiction CON
BERLINER, Joseph Scholom, 1921- , American; nonfiction CON
BERLONI, William, 1956- , American; nonfiction CON
BERLYE, Milton K., 1915- , American; nonfiction CON
BERMAN, Arthur Irwin, 1925- , American; nonfiction CON
BERMAN, Bruce David, 1944- , American; nonfiction CON
BERMAN, Connie, 1949- , American; nonfiction CON
BERMAN, Edgar Frank, 1924- , American; nonfiction CON
BERMAN, Eleanor, 1934- , American; nonfiction CON
BERMAN, Harold Joseph, 1918- , American; nonfiction CON
BERMAN, Larry, 1951- , American; nonfiction CON
BERMAN, Simeon Moses, 1935- , American; nonfiction CON
BERMAN, Susan, 1945- , American; nonfiction, fiction CON
BERMAN, William Carl, 1932- , American; nonfiction CON
BERMANGE, Barry, 1933- , British; plays CON VCD
BERMANT, Chaim Icyk, 1929- , British; fiction, nonfiction CON VCN
BERMEL, Albert Cyril, 1927- , Anglo-American; nonfiction, plays, translations CON
BERMUDEZ, Jerónimo ('Antonio de Silva'), 1530?-90?, Spanish; plays BU
BERMUDEZ de CASTRO, Salvador, 1817-83, Spanish; poetry BU
BERN, Maria (Rasputin), 1900?-77, Russian; nonfiction CON
BERNA, Paul, 1910- , French; juveniles CO CON DE
BERNABEI, Alfio, 1941- , Italian-British; plays CON
'BERNADETTE' see WATTS, Bernadette
BERNAGIE, Pieter, 1656-99, Dutch; plays BU
BERNAL, Ernest M., Jr., 1938- , American; nonfiction MAR
BERNAL, Ignacio, 1910- , Mexican; nonfiction CON
BERNAL, John Desmond, 1901-71, Irish; nonfiction CON WA
BERNAL, Judith F. ('Judith F. Dunn'), 1939- , American; nonfiction CON
BERNAL, Martha E., 1931- , American; nonfiction MAR
BERNANOS, Georges, 1888-1948, French; fiction, nonfiction BU CL MAG SEY TH
BERNAOLA, Pedro, 1916-72, Puerto Rican; poetry HIL
BERNARD, Carlo see 'BERNARI, Carlo'
BERNARD, George, 1939- , American; film, nonfiction CON
'BERNARD, Guy' see BARBER, Stephen G.
BERNARD, Harvey Russell, 1940- , American; nonfiction CON
BERNARD, Jacqueline de Sieyes, 1921- , Franco-American; juveniles CO WAR
'BERNARD, Jay' see SAWKINS, Raymond H.
BERNARD, Jean Jacques, 1888-1972, French; plays BU CL MCG TH
BERNARD, Jean Marc, 1881-1915, French; poetry, nonfiction CL
BERNARD, Kenneth, 1930- , American; plays, fiction, poetry CON VCD
'BERNARD, Marley' see GRAVES, Susan B.
BERNARD, Paul see 'BERNARD, Tristan'
BERNARD, Paul Peter, 1929- , Belgian-American; nonfiction CON
BERNARD, Rafe, English; fiction NI
BERNARD, Thelma Rene, 1940- , American; fiction CON
'BERNARD, Tristan' (Paul Bernard), 1866-1947, French; fiction, plays, journalism BU MCG
BERNARD, Will, 1915- , American; nonfiction CON
BERNARD-LUC, Jean, 1909- , French; film, plays MCG
BERNARD of CLAIRVAUX, 1090-1153, French; nonfiction BU TH

BERNARD of MORLAS (of Cluny),
fl. 1140, French; poetry
BU TH
BERNARD SILVESTER (Silvestris;
Bernard of Tours), fl. 1150,
French; poetry BU
BERNARDES, Diogo, 1532?-
96/1605, Portuguese; poetry
BU TH
BERNARDES, Padre Manuel,
1644-1710, Portuguese; non-
fiction BU TH
BERNARDEZ, Francisco Luis,
1900- , Argentinian; poetry
BR
BERNARDIN de SAINT-PIERRE,
Jacques Henri, 1737-1814,
French; fiction BU TH
BERNARDINO da SIENA, 1380-
1444, Italian; nonfiction BU
'BERNARI, Carlo' (Carlo Ber-
nard), 1909- , Italian; fic-
tion BO CL
BERNART de VENTADORN (Ven-
tadour), fl. 1150-95, Proven-
çal; poetry BU TH
BERNART MARTI ('Le Pintor'),
late 12th century, Provençal;
poetry BU
BERNASEK, Antonin see 'TOMAN,
Karel'
BERNDT, Walter, 1900?-79, Amer-
ican; cartoons, journalism
CON
'BERNE, Arlene' see ZEKOWSKI,
Arlene
BERNE, Stanley, 1923- , Amer-
ican; nonfiction CON
BERNER, Carl Walter, 1902- ,
American; nonfiction CON
BERNER, Jeff, 1940- , Amer-
ican; nonfiction CON
BERNER, Robert Barry, 1940- ,
American; poetry, transla-
tions CON
BERNERS, John Bourchier, 1467-
1533, English; translations
RU
BERNERS, Juliana (Bernes;
Barnes), early 15th century,
English?; nonfiction BU
BERNERT, Eleanor see SHELDON,
Eleanor
BERNHARD, Thomas, 1931- ,
Austrian; poetry, fiction,
plays, journalism BU CL
CON
BERNHARDSEN, Christian Rosen-

vinge, 1923- , Norwegian;
juveniles WAR
BERNHARDT, Frances Simonsen,
1932- , American; nonfiction
CON
BERNHEIMER, Martin, 1936- ,
German-American; journalism
CON
BERNI, Francesco, 1497/98-1535,
Italian; poetry BO BU TH
BERNOLAK, Anton, 1762-1813,
Slovak; nonfiction BU TH
BERNS, Walter Fred, 1919- ,
American; nonfiction CON
BERNSTEIN, Alvin Howell, 1939- ,
American; nonfiction CON
BERNSTEIN, Carl, 1944- , Amer-
ican; nonfiction CON
BERNSTEIN, David, 1915?-74,
American; journalism, nonfic-
tion CON
BERNSTEIN, Douglas A., 1942- ,
American; nonfiction CON
BERNSTEIN, Henry Léon Gustave
Charles, 1876-1953, French;
plays BU CL MCG TH
BERNSTEIN, Hillel, 1892?-1977,
Russian-American; journalism,
fiction CON
BERNSTEIN, Joanne Eckstein,
1943- , American; juveniles,
nonfiction CO CON
BERNSTEIN, Joseph Milton, 1908?-
75, American; translations
CON
BERNSTEIN, Leonard, 1918- ,
American; songs MCG
BERNSTEIN, Margery, 1933- ,
American; juveniles CON
BERNSTEIN, Marvin David, 1923- ,
American; nonfiction CON
BERNSTEIN, Philip Sidney, 1901- ,
American; nonfiction CON
BERNSTEIN, Theodore Menline,
1904- , American; juveniles
CO
'BEROALDE de VERVILLE, Fran-
cois Vatable' (Brouart), 1556-
1629?, French; fiction, poetry
BU
BEROALDO, Filippo, 1453-1505,
Italian; nonfiction BU
BEROFSKY, Bernard, 1935- ,
American; nonfiction CON
BEROSSUS, fl. 290 B.C. Baby-
lonian; nonfiction LA
BEROUL, fl. 1180-1200, French;
poetry BU

BERQUE, Jacques Augustin,
1910-   , French; nonfiction
CON
BERR, Georges, 1867-1942,
French; plays MCG
BERRETT, LaMar Cecil, 1926-   ,
American; nonfiction CON
BERRIAULT, Gina, 1926-   ,
American; fiction WA
BERRIDGE, Elizabeth, 1921-   ,
English; fiction CON
BERRIEN, Edith Heal see HEAL,
Edith
BERRIGAN, Daniel J., S.J.,
1921-   , American; poetry,
plays, nonfiction VCP
BERRIGAN, Ted, 1934-   , Amer-
ican; poetry, plays BR CON
VCP
BERRILL, Jacquelyn Batsel,
1905-   , American; juveniles
CO
BERRINGTON, Hugh Bayard,
1928-   , English; nonfiction
CON
'BERRINGTON, John ' see BROWN-
JOHN, Alan C.
'BERRISFORD, Judith M. see
LEWIS, Judith M.
BERRY, Adrian Michael, 1937-   ,
English; nonfiction CON
BERRY, Barbara J. (B. J. Berry),
1937-   , American; juveniles
CO
BERRY, Boyd McCulloch, 1939-   ,
American; nonfiction CON
BERRY, Bryan, 1930-55, British;
fiction AS NI
BERRY, Burton Yost, 1901-   ,
American; nonfiction CON
BERRY, Charles H., 1930-   ,
· Canadian; nonfiction CON
BERRY, Cicely, 1926-   , Brit-
ish; nonfiction CON
BERRY, D. C., 1942-   , Amer-
ican; poetry CON
BERRY, Edward I., 1940-   ,
American; nonfiction CON
'BERRY, Erick' see BEST, Allena
C.
BERRY, Francis, 1915-   , British;
poetry, plays, nonfiction VCP
BERRY, Frederic Aroyce, Jr.,
1906-78, American; nonfiction
CON
BERRY, Henry, 1926-   , Amer-
ican; nonfiction CON
BERRY, James, 1932-   , Amer-

ican; juveniles, film WAR
BERRY, James Gomer, Viscount
Kemsley, 1883-1968, Welsh;
journalism CON
BERRY, Jane (Cobb), 1915?-79,
American; juveniles, journal-
ism CO CON
BERRY, Jason, 1949-   , American;
nonfiction CON
BERRY, Jocelyn, 1933-   , Amer-
ican; nonfiction CON
BERRY, Le Héraut see LE BOU-
VIER, Gilles
BERRY, Lynn, 1948-   , American;
poetry CON
BERRY, Nicholas Orlando, 1936-   ,
American; nonfiction CON
BERRY, Paul, 1919-   , British;
nonfiction CON
BERRY, Roland Brian, 1951-   ,
British; nonfiction CON
BERRY, Thomas Edwin, 1930-   ,
American; nonfiction CON
BERRY, Wendell Erdman, 1934-   ,
American; poetry, fiction, non-
fiction BA BR CON KIB VCP
BERRY, William David, 1926-   ,
American; juveniles CO CON
BERRYMAN, James Thomas, 1902-
71, American; cartoons, jour-
nalism CON
BERRYMAN, John, 1914-72, Amer-
ican; poetry, nonfiction, fiction
AM BR BU MAG MAL PO SEY
VCP VP
BERSANI, Leo, 1931-   , American;
nonfiction CON
BERSEZIO, Vittorio, 1828-1900,
Italian; plays, fiction BU
'BERSHADSKY, Isaiah' (Isaiah
Domachevitsky), 1872-1910,
Hebrew; nonfiction BU TH
BERSON, Harold, 1926-   , Amer-
ican; juveniles CO DEM
BERSON, Lenora E., 1926-   ,
American; nonfiction CON
BERST, Charles Ashton, 1932-   ,
American; nonfiction CON
BERSUIRE, Pierre, 1290?-1362,
French; translations, nonfiction
BU
BERTAUT, Jean, 1552-1611, French;
poetry BU
BERTCHER, Harvey Joseph, 1929-   ,
American; nonfiction CON
BERTHOLD, Margot, 1922-   ,
German; nonfiction CON
BERTHOLD, Mary Paddock, 1909-   ,

American; fiction CON
BERTHOLD von HOLLE, fl. 1250-
60, German; poetry BU
BERTHOLD von REGENSBURG,
1210-72, German; nonfiction
BU
BERTHRONG, Donald John, 1922- ,
American; nonfiction CON
BERTIN, Charles, 1919- , Bel-
gian; poetry, fiction, plays
CL
BERTINORO, Obadiah di, 1450-
1500, Italian; poetry BU
BERTKEN, Suster, 1427-1514,
Dutch; poetry BU
BERTMAN, Stephen Samuel,
1937- , American; nonfiction
CON
BERTO, Giuseppe, 1914-78, Italian;
fiction, plays BO BU CL
BERTOL, Roland, American;
juveniles WAR
BERTOLA de' GIORGI, Aurelio,
1753-98, Italian; poetry,
nonfiction BU
BERTOLAZZI, Carlo, 1870-1916,
Italian; plays, journalism
MCG
BERTOLINO, James, 1942- ,
American; poetry CON VCP
BERTOLOME ZORZI, fl. 1230-
90, Provençal; poetry BU
BERTON, Peter Alexander, 1922- ,
Polish-American; nonfiction
CON
BERTON, Pierre Francis de
Marigny, 1920- , Canadian;
nonfiction, juveniles CR
BERTON, Ralph, 1910- , Amer-
ican; plays, nonfiction CON
BERTONASCO, Marc Francis,
1934- , Italian-American;
nonfiction CON
BERTRAM, James Munro, 1910- ,
New Zealander; nonfiction
CON
BERTRAM, Jean de Sales,
American; plays CON
'BERTRAM, Noel' see FAN-
THORPE, Robert L.
BERTRAN de BORN, fl. 1170-
1200, Provençal; poetry BU
TH
BERTRANA, Prudenci, 1867-1942,
Catalan; fiction CL
'BERTRAND, Aloysius', (Jacques-
Louis Napoleón), 1807-41,
French; poetry BU TH

BERTRAND, Alvin Lee, 1918- ,
American; nonfiction CON
'BERTRAND, Charles' see CARTER,
David C.
BERTRAND, Lewis, 1897?-1974,
American; translations CON
BERTRAND, Michel ('Jean Angebert';
'Jean-Michel Angebert'; 'Michel
Angebert'), 1944- , French;
nonfiction CON
BERTRAND de BAR-sur-AUBE,
fl. 1200, French; poetry BU
BERTSCH, Hugo, 1851-1935, German-
American; fiction BU
'BERWICK, Jean' see MEYER,
Jean S.
BERWINSKI, Ryszard Wincenty,
1819-79, Polish; poetry BU
BERZSENYI, Dániel, 1776-1836,
Hungarian; poetry, nonfiction
BU TH
BESANCENEY, Paul H., 1924- ,
American; nonfiction CON
BESANT, Sir Walter, 1836-1901,
English; fiction, journalism
BU DA NI PO VN
BESAS, Peter, 1933- , German;
nonfiction CON
BESCHI, Constanzo Giuseppe, 1680-
1746, Tamil; poetry, nonfiction
PRU
BESCHLOSS, Michael Richard,
1955- , American; nonfiction
CON
BESCI, Kurt, 1920- , Austrian;
plays MCG
BESHOAR, Barron Benedict, 1907- ,
American; nonfiction CON
BESIER, Rudolph, 1878-1942,
Dutch-English; translations,
plays MCG
'BESIKI' (Busarion Gabashvili),
1750-91, Georgian; poetry
PRU
BESKOW, Bernard von, 1796-1868,
Swedish; poetry, plays BU
BESKOW, Bo, 1906- , Swedish;
nonfiction CON
BESKOW, Elsa Maartman, 1874-
1953, Swedish; juveniles CO
WAR
BESNARD, Lucien, 1872- , French;
plays MCG
BESOLOW, Thomas E., 1867- ,
Liberian; nonfiction JA
BESSA-LUIS, Agustina, 1922- ,
Portuguese; fiction CL
BESSARION, John, 1395/1403-72,

Byzantine; nonfiction BU LA
BESSA-VICTOR, Geraldo (Geraldo Bessa Vítor), 1917- ,
Angolan; poetry, fiction, nonfiction HER JA
BESSENYEI, György, 1747-1811,
Hungarian; nonfiction BU
BESSER, Gretchen Rous, 1928- ,
American; translations, nonfiction CON
BESSER, Johann von, 1654-1729,
German; poetry BU
BESSER, Milton, 1911-76, American; journalism, nonfiction
CON
BESSETTE, Gerard, 1920- ,
Canadian; fiction, poetry BU
CR
BESSOM, Malcolm Eugene, 1940- ,
American; nonfiction CON
BESSY, Maurice, 1910- , French;
nonfiction, fiction, translations, film CON
BEST, Allena Champlin ('Erick Berry'; 'Anne Maxon'), 1892-1974, American; juveniles CO
BEST, Charles Herbert, 1899-1978, Canadian; nonfiction
CON
BEST, Herbert, 1894- , American; fiction NI
BEST, Judith A., 1938- , American; nonfiction CON
'BEST, Marc' see LEMIEUX, Marc
BEST, Oswald Herbert, 1894- ,
British; juveniles, fiction, nonfiction KI
BEST, Otto Ferdinand, 1929- ,
German-American; translations, nonfiction CON
BESTE, Konrad, 1890-1958, German; fiction BU
BESTER, Alfred, 1913- , American; fiction AS COW NI
BESTUL, Thomas Howard, 1942- ,
American; nonfiction CON
BESTUZHEV-MARLINSKY, Alexander Alexandrovich, 1797-1837, Russian; fiction BU
BESUS, Roger, 1915- , French;
fiction TH
BETAB, Sufi Abduhaqq Khan, 1888-1969, Afghan; poetry PRU
BETANCES, Ramon Emeterio
('El Antillano'; 'Bin Tah'),
1827-98, Puerto Rican; nonfiction HIL
BETANCOURT, Sr. Jeanne, 1941- ,

American; nonfiction CON
BETENSON, Lula Parker, 1884- ,
American; nonfiction CON
'BETH, Mary' see MILLER, Mary B.
BETHANCOURT, T. Ernesto ('Tom Paisley'), 1932- , American; juveniles CO CON
BETHELL, Jean Frankenberry, 1922- , American; juveniles CO
BETHELL, Mary Ursula, 1874-1945, Anglo-New Zealander; poetry DA SEY VP
BETHELL, Nicholas William, 1938- , English; nonfiction, translations CON
BETHELL, Tom, 1940- , Anglo-American; nonfiction CON
BETHERS, Roy, 1902- , American; juveniles CO
BETHGE, Eberhard, 1909- , German; nonfiction CON
'BETHUNE, J. G.' see ELLIS, Edward S.
'BETI, Mongo' ('Ega Toto'; Alexandre Biyidi), 1932- , Cameroonian; fiction BU HER JA LA
BETJEMAN, Sir John, 1906- ,
English; poetry, plays, nonfiction BU DA PO SEY VCP
VP
BETOCCHI, Carlo, 1899- , Italian; poetry BO BU CL WA
BETSCHLA, Andrea see BEZZOLA, Andrea
BETSCHLA, Eduard see BEZZOLA, Eduard
BETTELHEIM, Bruno, 1903- ,
American; nonfiction CON WAK
BETTELHEIM, Charles, 1913- ,
French; nonfiction CON
BETTELHEIM, Frederick Abraham, 1923- , Hungarian-American; nonfiction CON
BETTELONI, Vittorio, 1840-1910,
Italian; poetry BU
'BETTERIDGE, Anne' see POTTER, Margaret N.
'BETTERIDGE, Don' see NEWMAN, Bernard
BETTERTON, Thomas, 1635?-1710,
English; plays BU
BETTI, Liliana, 1939- , Italian;
nonfiction, tv CON
BETTI, Ugo, 1892-1953, Italian;
plays, poetry, fiction, journal-

ism BO BU CL MCG TH
WA
BETTINELLI, Saverio, 1718-1808,
Italian; poetry BU
BETTS, Charles Lancaster, Jr.,
1908- , American; nonfiction
CON
BETTS, Doni, 1948- , American;
nonfiction CON
BETTS, Doris, 1932- , Amer-
ican; journalism, fiction BA
BETTS, George, 1944- , Amer-
ican; nonfiction, poetry CON
BETTS, Richard Keven, 1947- ,
American; nonfiction CON
BETZ, Eva Kelly ('Caroline
Peters'), 1897-1968, Amer-
ican; juveniles CO
BETZ, Hans Dieter, 1931- ,
German-American; nonfiction
CON
BEUF, Ann Hill, 1939- , Amer-
ican; nonfiction CON
BEURDELEY, Michel, 1911- ,
French; nonfiction CON
BEUTEL, William Charles,
1930- , American; journal-
ism CON
BEUTHIEN, Angelius Erich Wil-
helm, 1834-1926, German;
poetry, plays BU
BEUTTLER, Edward Ivan ('Ivan
Butler'), British; fiction CON
BEVAN, Tom ('Walter Bam-
fylde'), 1868-1930's, British;
juveniles COM
BEVERIDGE, Andrew Alan, 1945- ,
American; nonfiction CON
BEVERIDGE, George, David, Jr.,
1922- , American; journal-
ism CON
BEVERIDGE, Meryle (Secrest;
'June Doman'), 1930- ,
British; nonfiction CON
BEVERLEY, Robert, 1673?-1722,
American; nonfiction BA BR
BEVIER, Michael, American; non-
fiction CON
BEVINGTON, Helen, 1906- ,
American; poetry, nonfiction
WA
BEVIS, Em Olivia, 1932- ,
American; nonfiction CON
BEVK, France, 1890-1970, Slo-
vene; nonfiction, juveniles,
fiction BU
BEWES, Richard, 1934- , Brit-
ish; nonfiction CON

BEWICK, Thomas, 1753-1828,
English; juveniles CO
BEWLEY, Marius, 1918-73, Amer-
ican; nonfiction BOR CON
'BEY, Isabell,' see BOSTICCO,
Mary
BEYATH, Yahya Kemal, 1884-1958,
Turkish; poetry CL PRU
BEYE, Charles Rowan, 1930- ,
American; nonfiction CON
BEYEA, Basil ('B. A. Benson'),
1910- , American; nonfiction,
plays, fiction CON
BEYER, Andrew, 1943- , Amer-
ican; journalism, nonfiction
CON
BEYER, Audrey White, 1916- ,
American; juveniles CO
BEYER, Robert, 1913?-78, Amer-
ican; nonfiction CON
BEYER, William Gray, American;
fiction NI
BEYERCHEN, Alan, 1945- , Amer-
ican; nonfiction CON
BEYERHAUS, Peter Paul, 1929- ,
German; nonfiction CON
BEYERS, Charlotte Kempner,
1931- , American; journal-
ism, nonfiction CON
BEYHAQI ABU'L-FAZL Mohammad,
996-1077, Persian; nonfiction
PRU
BEYLE, Marie H. see 'STENDHAL'
'BEYNON, John' see HARRIS, John
BEZBARUA, Laksminath, 1868-
1938, Assamese; poetry, jour-
nalism PRU
BEZE, Théodore de, 1519-1605,
French; nonfiction, plays BU
TH
BEZIO, May Rowland, -1977,
American; nonfiction CON
'BEZRUC, Petr' (Vladimír Vašek),
1867-1958, Czech; poetry BU
CL TH
BEZYMENSKY, Alexander Ilytich,
1898- , Russian; poetry BU
BEZZOLA, Andrea (Betschla),
1840-97, Raeto-Romansch; po-
etry BU
BEZZOLA, Eduard (Betschla;
'N. U. Spigna'), 1875-1948,
Raeto-Romansch; poetry BU
'BHAKTIVEDANTA, A. C.' see
PRABHUPADA, Bhaktivedanta
BHAMAHA, 6th century, Indian;
nonfiction PRU
BHAN, Chandar see 'BRAHMAN'

BHANA, Surendra, 1939- , Indian; nonfiction CON
BHANJ, Upendra, Oriyan; poetry PRU
BHARATA, 4th century, Sanskrit; plays BU
'BHARATHITHASAN' see CUPPUR-ATTINAM, Kanaka
BHARATI see PARATI, Cupperamaniyam
BHARAVI, 6th century, Sanskrit; poetry BU PRU
BHARDWAJ, Surinder Mohan, 1934- , Indian-American; nonfiction CON
BHARTI, Satya ('Jill Jacobs'; 'Jill Safian'), 1942- , American; fiction, nonfiction CON
BHARTRHARI, fl. 500, Sanskrit; nonfiction PRU
BHARTRHARI, 7th century, Sanskrit; poetry, nonfiction BU LA PRU
BHASA, 4th century, Sanskrit; plays BU PRU
BHATIA, Hans Raj, 1904- , Pakistani; nonfiction CON
BHATIA, Jamunadevi ('June Bhatia'; 'June Edwards'; 'Helen Forrester'; 'J. Rana'), 1919- , British; fiction CON
BHATIA, Krishan, 1926?-74, Indian; journalism, nonfiction
BHATNAGAR, Joti, 1935- , Indian; nonfiction CON
BHATT, Jagdish Jeyshanker, 1939- , Indian-American; nonfiction CON
BHATT, Udaysankar, 1898- , Hindi; plays PRU
BHATTA, Motiram, 1865-96, Nepali; poetry, fiction PRU
BHATTA NARAYANA, fl. 800, Sanskrit; plays BU PRU
BHATTACHARYA, Bhabani, 1906- , Indian; fiction, nonfiction, translations BU VCN
BHATTI, fl. 650, Sanskrit; poetry BU PRU
BHAVABHUTI, early 8th century, Sanskrit; plays BU LA PRU
BHÉLY-QUÉNUM, 1928- , Dahoman; juveniles, fiction HER JA LA
BHOJA, 11th century, Paramaran;

nonfiction PRU
BHUTTO, Zulfikar Ali, 1928- , Pakistani; nonfiction CON
BIAGI, Shirley, 1944- , American; journalism CON
BIAL, Morrison David, 1917- , American; nonfiction, juveniles, poetry CON
BIALIK, Chaim Nachman, 1873-1934, Hebrew; poetry, translations, nonfiction BU LA TH WA
BIALK, Elisa Krautter, 1912- , American; journalism, juveniles WAR
BIALOSZEWSKI, Miron, 1922- , Polish; poetry BU CL
BIANCHI, Hombert, 1912?-80, American; journalism, nonfiction CON
BIANCIARDI, Luciano, 1922-71, Italian; fiction, translation, journalism, nonfiction CL
BIANCO, Andre, 1930- , French; nonfiction CON
BIANCO, Margery Williams, 1881-1944, British; juveniles, fiction, plays, translations CO KI
BIANCO, Pamela, 1906- , Anglo-American; juveniles CON
BIANCO da SIENA (di Santi), 1350-1412?, Italian; poetry BU
BIANCOLLI, Louis Leopold, 1907- , American; translations, nonfiction CON
BIBACULUS, Marcus Furius, 103 B.C.-?, Roman; poetry LA
BIBB, David Porter, III, 1937- , American; nonfiction CON
BIBBY, John Franklin, 1934- , American; nonfiction CON
BIBBY, Violet, 1908- , British; juveniles CO CON KI WAR
BIBERMAN, Edward, 1904- , American; nonfiction CON
BIBESCO, Marthe Lucia ('Lucile Decaux'), 1887-1973, Rumanian-French; nonfiction CON
BIBIENA, Il see DOVIZI, Bernardo
BIBLE, Charles 1937- , American; juveniles, nonfiction, poetry, journalism CO CON
BICANIC, Rudolf, 1905-68, Croatian; nonfiction CON
BICE, Clare, 1908-76, Canadian; juveniles CO KI

BICHSEL, Peter, 1935- , Swiss;
journalism, nonfiction CL
CON
BICK, Edgar Milton, 1902-78,
American; nonfiction CON
BICKEL, Alexander Mordecai,
1924-74, Rumanian-American;
nonfiction CON
BICKELHAUPT, David Lynn,
1929- , American; nonfic-
tion CON
BICKERS, Richard Leslie Towns-
hend ('Mark Charles'; 'Ri-
cardo Cittafino'; 'Philip Dukes';
'Paul Kapusta'; 'Burt Keene';
'Fritz Kirschner'; 'Gui Le-
fevre'; 'Gerhardt Mueller';
'David Richards'; 'Richard
Townshend'), 1917- , Amer-
ican; fiction, nonfiction CON
'BICKERSTAFFE, Isaac see
SWIFT, Jonathan; ADDISON,
Joseph
BICKERSTAFFE, Isaac, 1735-
1802/08, Irish; plays BR BU
VD
BICKERSTETH, Geoffrey Langdole,
1884-1974, British; nonfiction
CON
BICKERTON, Derek, 1926- ,
Anglo-American; fiction, non-
fiction CON
BICKFORD, Elwood Dale, 1927- ,
American; nonfiction CON
BICKLEY, Robert Bruce, Jr.,
1942- , American; nonfic-
tion CON
BIDA, Constantine, 1916- ,
Canadian; nonfiction CON
BIDDISS, Michael Denis, 1942- ,
English; nonfiction CON
BIDDLE, Arthur William, 1936- ,
American; nonfiction CON
BIDDLE, Francis Beverley, 1886-
1968, French; nonfiction CON
BIDDLE, Katherine Garrison
(Chapin), 1890-1977, Amer-
ican; plays, nonfiction CON
WA
BIDDLE, Perry Harvey, Jr.,
1932- , American; nonfic-
tion CON
BIDEL, Abdulqadir see BEDIL,
Abdulqadir
BIDERMANN, Jakob, 1578-1639,
German; plays, fiction, non-
fiction BU TH
BIDLOO, Govert, 1649-1713,

Dutch; poetry, plays BU
BIDWELL, Dafne Mary, 1929- ,
British; fiction CON
BIDWELL, Marjory Elizabeth Sarah
('Elizabeth Ford'; 'Mary Ann
Gibbs'), British; fiction, non-
fiction CON
BIDYALANKARANA, Prince, 1876-
1945, Thai; nonfiction LA
BIDYASGAR, Isvarcandra, 1820-91,
Bengali; translations, journal-
ism, nonfiction PRU
BIE, Cornelis de, 1627-1715, Flem-
ish; poetry, plays BU
BIEBER, Margarete, 1879-1978,
German-American; nonfiction
CON
BIEBL, Konstantin, 1898-1951,
Czech; poetry BU
BIEGEL, John Edward, 1925- ,
American; nonfiction CON
BIEGEL, Paul, 1925- , Dutch;
juveniles, nonfiction CO CON
BIELER, Ludwig, 1906-81, Aus-
traian; nonfiction CON
BIELER, Manfred, 1934- , Ger-
man; fiction, radio BU CL
BIELSKI, Marcin, 1495?-1575,
Polish; nonfiction, poetry BU
BIEMILLER, Carl Ludwig, 1912-
79, American; juveniles CO
WAR
BIEN, Joseph Julius, 1936- ,
American; translations, non-
fiction CON
BIENEKY, Horst, 1930- , Ger-
man; fiction, poetry, nonfic-
tion CL CON
BIENEN, Henry Samuel, 1939- ,
American; nonfiction CON
BIENKOWSKI, Zbigniew, 1913- ,
Polish; poetry BU
BIENVENU, Bernard Jefferson,
1925- , American; nonfiction
CON
BIENVENU, Richard Thomas,
1936- , American; nonfiction,
translations CON
BIER, William Christian; 1911-80,
American; nonfiction CON
BIERBAUM, Otto Julius, 1865-1910,
German; poetry, fiction BU
TH
BIERBOWER, Austin, 1844-1913,
American; fiction NI
BIERCE, Ambrose, 1842-1914?,
American; fiction, nonfiction,
journalism AM AS BR BU

MAG NI PO ST VN
BIERHORST, John William, 1936- ,
American; juveniles CO WAR
BIERI, Arthur Peter, 1931- ,
American; nonfiction CON
BIERLEY, Paul Edmund, 1926- ,
American; nonfiction CON
BIERMAN, Arthur Kalmer, 1923- ,
American; nonfiction CON
BIERMANN, Lillian M. see WEH-
MEYER, Lillian
BIERMANN, Wolf, 1936- , Ger-
man; poetry, plays, BU CL
CON
BIERNATZKI, William Eugene,
1931- , American; nonfiction
CON
BIERT, Cla, 1920- , Raeto-
Romansch; poetry BU
BIERY, William Richard, 1933- ,
American; fiction CON
BIETENHOLZ, Peter Gerard,
1933- , Swiss-Canadian; non-
fiction CON
BIFRUN, Jàcham U. Tuetschét,
1506-72, Raeto-Romansch;
translations BU
BIGELOW, Donald Nevius, 1918- ,
American; nonfiction CON
BIGELOW, Karl Worth, 1898-1980,
American; nonfiction CON
BIGELOW, Robert Sydney, 1918- ,
Canadian; nonfiction CON
BIGG, Patricia Nina ('Patricia
Ainsworth'), 1932- , Aus-
tralian; fiction CON
BIGGERS, Earl Derr, 1884-1933,
American; fiction, plays BR
REI ST
BIGGLE, Lloyd, Jr., 1923- ,
American; fiction AS COW
NI
BIGGS, John, Jr., 1895-1979,
American; fiction, nonfiction
CON
BIGGS, John Burville, 1934- ,
Australian; nonfiction CON
BIGNE, Gace de la, 14th cen-
tury, French; poetry BU
BIGNELL, Alan, 1928- , Brit-
ish; nonfiction, plays, jour-
nalism CON
BIGONGIARI, Piero, 1914- ,
Italian; nonfiction, poetry,
translations CL
BIHALJI-MERIN, Oto ('Peter
Merin'; 'Peter Thoene'),
1904- , Yugoslav; nonfic-

tion CON
BIHARI LAL (Biharlal), 1595/1603-
63/64, Hindi; poetry BU PRU
BIHLER, Penny, 1940- , Amer-
ican; poetry, fiction CON
BIJLA, J. see 'RZEWUSKI, Henryk'
BIJNS, Anna, 1493-1575, Dutch;
poetry BU TH
'BIJSCHRIFTEN, Een B. in' see
KATE, Jan J. L. ten
BIKKIE, James Andrew, 1929- ,
American; nonfiction CON
BIKLEN, Douglas Paul, 1945- ,
American; nonfiction CON
BIKOUTA-MENGA, Gaston G. see
'MENGA, Guy'
BILAC, Olavo Brás Martins dos
Guimarães, 1865-1918, Bra-
zilian; poetry BR
BILAS, Richard Allen, 1935- ,
American; nonfiction CON
BILBASAR, Kemal, 1910- , Turk-
ish; fiction PRU
BILD aus RHEINAU see BEATUS
RHENANUS
BILDERBACK, Dean Loy, 1932- ,
American; nonfiction CON
BILDERDIJK, Willem, 1756-1831,
Dutch; poetry, plays BU TH
BILENCHI, Romano, 1909- ,
Italian; journalism, fiction BO
BILHANA, fl. 1100, Kashmiri; po-
etry BU PRU
BILL'-BELOTSERKOVSKY, Vladimir
Naumovich, 1885- , Russian;
plays BU TH
BILLECK, Marvin, 1920- , Amer-
ican; juveniles DEM
BILLETDOUX, Francois Paul,
1927- , French; journalism,
fiction, plays BU CL MCG
TH WA
BILLINGER, Richard, 1893-1965,
Austrian; poetry, fiction,
plays MCG
'BILLINGS, Ezra' see HALLA,
Robert C.
BILLINGS, John Shaw, 1838-1913,
American; nonfiction ENG
'BILLINGS, Josh' (Henry Wheeler
Shaw), 1818-85, American;
fiction BR BU VN
BILLINGS, Richard N., 1930- ,
American; nonfiction CON
BILLINGS, Warren Martin, 1940- ,
American; nonfiction CON
BILLINGSLEY, Andrew, 1926- ,
American; nonfiction CON SH

BILLINGTON, Elizabeth Thain, American; nonfiction CON
BILLINGTON, Joy, 1931- , Anglo-American; journalism CON
BILLINGTON, Michael, 1939- , American; nonfiction CON
BILLINGTON, Ray Allen, 1903-81, American; nonfiction CON
BILLMEYER, Fred Wallace, Jr. , 1919- , American; nonfiction CON
BILLOUT, Guy René, 1941- , French; juveniles, nonfiction CO CON
BILLY, André, 1882-1971, French; fiction, nonfiction BU TH
BILSLAND, Ernest Charles ('Bilko Bilsland'), 1931- , American; cartoons CON
BIMLER, Richard William, 1940- , American; nonfiction CON
'BIN TAH' see BETANCES, Ramon E.
BINDER, Aaron, 1927- , American; fiction CON
BINDER, David, 1931- , English; nonfiction CON
'BINDER, Eando' (Earl Andrew BINDER, 1904- ; Otto Oscar BINDER, 1911-75), American; fiction AS CON NI
BINDER, Frederick Moore ('Andrew Moore'), 1920- , American; fiction CON
BINDER, Leonard, 1927- , American; nonfiction CON
BINDER, Otto O. , see 'BINDER, Eando'
BINDING, Rudolf Georg, 1867-1938, German; fiction, poetry CL
BINDMAN, Arthur Joseph, 1925- , American; nonfiction CON
BINDOFF, Stanley Thomas, 1908-80, British; nonfiction CON
BING, Elisabeth D. , 1914- , German-American; nonfiction CON
BING, Jon, 1944- , Norwegian; fiction, translations NI
BING, Rudolf, 1902- , American; nonfiction CON
BINGAMAN, Ron, 1936- , American; nonfiction CON
BINGER, Carl Alfred L. , 1889-1976, American; nonfiction CON

BINGER, Walter, 1888?-1979, American; nonfiction CON
BINGHAM, Caroline, 1938- , English; nonfiction CON
BINGHAM, David Andrew, 1926- , American; nonfiction CON
BINGHAM, Evangeline Marguerite ('Geraldine Elliot'), 1899- , English; fiction CON
BINGHAM, John (Lord Clanmoris), 1908- , British; fiction, plays MCC REI
BINGHAM, Morley Paul, 1918- , American; nonfiction CON
BINGLEY, David Ernest ('Dave Carver'; 'Henry Chesham'; 'Will Coltman'; 'George Fallon'; 'David Horsely'; 'John Roberts'; 'Christopher Wigan'), 1920- , English; fiction CON
BINH-NGUYEN-LOC, 1914- , Vietnamese; fiction, poetry, nonfiction PRU
BINKLEY, Olin Trivette, 1908- , American; nonfiction CON
BINNS, Archie Fred, 1899- , American; fiction, nonfiction CON
BINNS, James Wallace, 1940- , English; nonfiction CON
BINOI see BENA'I
BINYON, Claude, 1905-78, American; film, nonfiction CON
BINYON, Laurence, 1869-1943, English; poetry, nonfiction, translations BU DA PO VP
BINZEN, William, 1889-1979, German; translations, juveniles CO CON WAR
BION 2nd century B.C. , Greek; poetry BU
BION of SMYRNA, fl. 100 B.C. , Greek; poetry LA
BION the BORYSTHENITE, 325-255 B.C. , Greek; nonfiction, poetry GR LA
BIONDO, Flavio, 1392-1463, Italian; nonfiction BO BU
BIOW, Milton H. , 1882?-1976, American; nonfiction CON
BIOY CASARES, Adolfo, 1914- , Argentinian; fiction, plays BR NI
BIRABEAU, André, 1890- , French; plays MCG
BIRCH, Alison Wyrley, 1922- , American; journalism, poetry

CON
BIRCH, Bruce Charles, 1941- ,
American; nonfiction CON
BIRCH, Cyril, 1925- , British;
fiction, nonfiction CON
BIRCH, Daniel Richard, 1937- ,
American; juveniles CON
BIRCH, Herbert G., 1918-73,
American; nonfiction CON
BIRCH, Reginald Bathurst, 1856-
1943, Anglo-American; juven-
iles CO
BIRCH, William Garry, 1909- ,
American; nonfiction CON
BIRCHALL, Ian Harry ('Curtis
McNally'), 1939- , British;
nonfiction CON
BIRCHAM, Deric Neale, 1934- ,
New Zealander; nonfiction
CON
BIRCK, Sixt see BIRK, Sixt
BIRD, Florence Bayard ('Anne
Francis'), 1908- , American;
nonfiction, juveniles CON
BIRD, Harrison K., 1910- ,
American; nonfiction CON
BIRD, James Harold, 1923- ,
British; nonfiction CON
BIRD, Lewis Penhall, 1933- ,
American; nonfiction CON
BIRD, Patricia Amy, 1941- ,
American; nonfiction CON
BIRD, Robert Montgomery, 1806-
54, American; plays, fiction
BR BU MAG MCG VD
BIRD, Traveller, American;
juveniles WAR
BIRD, Vivian ('Vic Beer'), 1910- ,
British; journalism, nonfic-
tion CON
BIRD, William, 1888-1963, Amer-
ican; journalism RO
BIRDSALL, Steve, 1944- , Aus-
tralian; nonfiction CON
BIRDWHISTELL, Ray L., 1912- ,
American; nonfiction CON
BIRENBAUM, Halina, 1929- ,
Polish; fiction, nonfiction
CON
BIRIMISA, George, 1924- ,
Croatian-American; plays
CON VCD
BIRK, Sixt (Birck), 1501-54,
German; plays BU
BIRKEN, Sigmund von, 1626-81,
German; poetry, plays BU
BIRKIN, Andrew Timothy, 1945- ,
British; film CON

BIRKIN, Charles, Lloyd ('Charles
Lloyd'), 1907- , British; fic-
tion CON
'BIRKLEY, Dolan' see 'OLSEN,
D. B."
BIRKLEY, Marilyn, 1916- , Amer-
ican; nonfiction CON
BIRKS, Tony, 1937- , British;
nonfiction CON
BIRKSTED-BREEN, Dana (Breen),
1946- , American; nonfiction
CON
BIRMINGHAM, George A. ('Canon
James Owen Hannay'), 1865-
1950, Irish; fiction, plays HO
BIRMINGHAM, John, 1951- , Amer-
ican; nonfiction CON
BIRMINGHAM, Lloyd, 1924- ,
American; juveniles CO
BIRMINGHAM, Maisie, 1914- ,
British; fiction CON
BIRMINGHAM, Stephen, 1932- ,
American; fiction, nonfiction
CON
BIRN, Randi Marie, 1935- ,
Norwegian-American; nonfic-
tion CON
BIRN, Raymond Francis, 1935- ,
American; nonfiction CON
BIRNBAUM, Norman, 1926- ,
American; nonfiction CON
BIRNBAUM, Philip, 1904- ,
Polish-American; nonfiction,
translations CON
BIRNBAUM, Phyllis, 1945- ,
American; fiction, nonfiction,
translations CON
BIRNEY, Alfred Earle, 1904- ,
Canadian; poetry, fiction, plays,
poetry BU CR DA VCN VCP
VP WAK
BIRNIE, Whittlesey, 1945- , Amer-
ican; nonfiction CON
BIRO, Charlotte Slovak, 1904- ,
Hungarian-American; nonfiction
CON
BIRO, Val Balint, 1921- , British;
juveniles KI
BIRRELL, Augustine, 1850-1933,
English; nonfiction DA
BIRT, David, 1936- , British;
juveniles CON
BIRUNI, Abu al Rayhan M. I. A.,
973-1048/51, Muslim; nonfic-
tion BU LA PRU
BIRYUKOV, Pavel Ivanovich, 1860-
1931, Russian; nonfiction BU
BISCHOFF, David Frederick,

1951- , American; juveniles,
fiction CON
BISCHOFF, Frederick Alexander,
1928- , Austrian-American;
nonfiction CON
BISCHOFF, Julia Bristol ('Julie
Arnoldy'), 1909-70, American;
juveniles CO
BISH, Robert Lee, 1942- , Amer-
ican; nonfiction CON
BISHIN, William Robert, 1939- ,
American; nonfiction CON
BISHIR, John William, 1933- ,
American; nonfiction CON
BISHOP, Bonnie, 1943- , Amer-
ican; journalism, juveniles
CON
BISHOP, Claire Huchet, Amer-
ican; juveniles, nonfiction CO
CON KI
BISHOP, Curtis Kent ('Curt
Brandon'; 'Curt Carroll'),
1912-67, American; juven-
iles CO
BISHOP, Elizabeth, 1911-79, Amer-
ican; poetry, juveniles AM
BR CO CON DEM MAL PO
VCP VP WAR
BISHOP, George Victor, 1924- ,
Canadian-American; nonfiction
CON
'BISHOP, Jack' see DORMAN,
Michael
BISHOP, James, 1929- , British;
nonfiction CON
BISHOP, John, 1908- , English;
nonfiction CON
BISHOP, John Melville, 1946- ,
American; nonfiction CON
BISHOP, John Peale, 1892-1944,
American; poetry, nonfiction
BA BR BU RO VP
BISHOP, Michael, 1945- , Amer-
ican; fiction CON NI
BISHOP, Morris, -1973, Amer-
ican; nonfiction, translations
CON
BISHOP, Robert, 1938- , Amer-
ican; nonfiction CON
BISHOP, William Warner, 1871-
1955, American; nonfiction
ENG
BISSELL, Claude Thomas, 1916- ,
Canadian; nonfiction CON
BISSELL, Elaine, American;
fiction, tv CON
BISSELL, Richard Pike, 1913-77,
American; fiction, plays, non-

fiction CON PAL WA
BISSET, Donald, 1910- , British;
juveniles CO KI
BISSET, Ronald, 1950- , Scots;
nonfiction CON
BISSETT, Bill, 1939- , Canadian;
poetry, plays CON VCP
BISSETT, Donald John, 1930- ,
American; poetry, juveniles,
nonfiction CON
BISTICCI, Vespasiano da, 1421-98,
Italian; nonfiction TH
BITA, Lili, Greek-American;
plays CON
BITKER, Marjorie M., 1901- ,
American; fiction CON
BITOV, Andrey Georgiyevich,
1937- , Russian; fiction CL
BITTER, Gary Glen, 1940- ,
American; juveniles, nonfiction
CO CON
BITTLE, William Elmer, 1926- ,
American; nonfiction CON
BITTLINGER, Arnold, 1928- ,
German; nonfiction CON
BITTNER, Vernon John, 1932- ,
American; nonfiction CON
BITZIUS, Albert see 'GOTTHELF,
Jeremias'
BIVINS, John, 1940- , American;
nonfiction CON
BIXBY, Jerome Lewis ('Jay B.
Drexel'; 'Harry Neal'; 'Alger
Rome'), 1923- , American;
fiction AS NI
BIXBY, William Courtnay, 1920- ,
American; juveniles CO
BIXLER, Norma, 1905- , Amer-
ican; nonfiction CON
BIXLER, Paul Howard, 1899- ,
American; nonfiction CON
BIXLER, Roy Russell, Jr., 1927- ,
American; nonfiction CON
BIYIDI, Alexandre see 'BETI,
Mongo'
BIZARDEL, Yvon ('Yvon Lapa-
quellerie'), 1891- , French;
nonfiction, fiction CON
BIZZARRO, Salvatore, 1939- ,
American; nonfiction CON
BJERKE, Robert Alan, 1939- ,
American; nonfiction CON
BJERREGAARD, Henrik Anker,
1792-1842, Norwegian; plays,
poetry BU
BJORKLUND, Karna L., Amer-
ican; juveniles WAR
BJÖRLING, Gunnar, 1887-1960,

Finnish-Swedish; poetry, non-
fiction CL TH
BJOERNEBOE, Jens, 1920-76,
Norwegian; fiction CON
BJORN, Thyra Ferre, 1905-75,
Swedish-American; nonfiction,
fiction CON
BJORNEBOE, Jens Ingvald, 1920-
76, Norwegian; fiction, po-
etry, plays BU CL CON
BJORNSON, Bjornstjerne Marti-
nus, 1832-1910, Norwegian;
fiction, poetry, plays BU
CL MAG MCG TH
BJORNSON, Richard, 1938- ,
American; nonfiction CON
BJORNVIG, Thorkild Strange,
1918- , Danish; poetry,
nonfiction BU CL TH
'BJORSET, Brynjolf' see BE-
ORSE, Bryn
BLACHLY, Frederick, 1881?-
1975, American; nonfiction
CON
BLACK, Albert George, 1928- ,
American; nonfiction CON
BLACK, Algernon David, 1900- ,
American; juveniles CO
'BLACK, Betty.' see SCHWARTZ,
Betty
BLACK, Brady Forrest, 1908- ,
American; nonfiction CON
BLACK, Campbell ('Thomas Alt-
man'; 'Jeffrey Campbell'),
1944- , Scots-American;
fiction CON
BLACK, Clinton Van De Brosse,
1918- , Jamaican; nonfiction
CON
BLACK, Creed Carter, 1925- ,
American; journalism CON
'BLACK, David' see WAY, Robert
E.
BLACK, David Macleod, 1941- ,
Scots; poetry VCP
'BLACK, Dianne', 1940- , Ca-
nadian; fiction CON
BLACK, Earl, 1942- , American;
nonfiction CON
'BLACK, Gavin' (Oswald Morris
Wynd), 1913- , Scots; fic-
tion, plays REI
BLACK, Harry George, 1933- ,
American; nonfiction CON
BLACK, Irma Simonton, 1906-
72, American; juveniles CO
'BLACK, Ishi' see GIBSON, Wal-
ter B.

BLACK, Ivan, 1904?-79, American;
poetry CON
BLACK, Ladbroke, 1877- , Eng-
lish; fiction NI
'BLACK, Lionel' see BARKER,
Dudley
BLACK, Malcolm Charles Lamont,
1928- , British; nonfiction
CON
'BLACK, Mansell' see TREVOR,
Elleston
BLACK, Max, 1909- , Russian-
American; nonfiction CON
BLACK, Robert Clifford III, 1914- ,
American; nonfiction CON
BLACK, Roe Coddington, 1926- ,
American; nonfiction CON
BLACK, Stanley Warren III, 1939- ,
American; nonfiction CON
BLACK, Stephen William, 1881-
1932, South African; fiction,
journalism, plays BU
BLACK, William, 1841-98, Scots;
fiction, journalism BU
BLACK, William Joseph, 1934?-77,
American; nonfiction CON
BLACKALL, Eric Albert, 1914- ,
Anglo-American; nonfiction
CON
BLACKAMORE, Arthur, 1679?-
1723?, American; poetry, fic-
tion BA
BLACKBEARD, Bill, 1926- ,
American; nonfiction CON
BLACKBURN, Alexander Lambert,
1929- , American; nonfiction,
fiction CON
BLACKBURN, Barbara see LEADER,
Evelyn B.
'BLACKBURN, Claire' see JACOBS,
Linda C.
BLACKBURN, Douglas, 1857-1926,
South African; fiction, journal-
ism BU
BLACKBURN, Graham John,
1940- , Anglo-American;
nonfiction CON
BLACKBURN, John Brewton,
1952- , American; juveniles
CO
BLACKBURN, John Fenwick,
1923- , English; fiction AS
MCC NI REI
BLACKBURN, Laurence Henry,
1897- , American; nonfiction
CON
BLACKBURN, Norma Davis,
1914- , American; nonfiction

CON
BLACKBURN, Paul, 1926-71,
American; poetry, transla-
tions BR CON MAL WAK
BLACKBURN, Simon, 1944- ,
American; nonfiction CON
BLACKBURN, Thomas Carl,
1936- , American; nonfiction
CON
BLACKBURN, Thomas Eliel,
1916- , British; poetry,
plays, nonfiction CON VCP
WA
BLACKBURNE, Neville Alfred,
1913- , English; nonfiction
CON
BLACKER, Carlos Paton, 1895-
1975, English; nonfiction CON
BLACKETT, Veronica (Heath),
1927- , English; juveniles
CO CON
BLACKEY, Robert, 1941- ,
American; nonfiction CON
BLACKFORD, Charles Minor III,
1898- , American; nonfiction
CON
BLACKFORD, Staige Davis, 1931- ,
American; journalism CON
BLACKIE, Bruce Lothian, 1936- ,
American; nonfiction CON
BLACKIE, John Ernest, 1904- ,
British; nonfiction CON
BLACKIE, John Stuart, 1809-95,
Scots; translations, poetry
BU
BLACKIE, Pamela, 1917- , Brit-
ish; nonfiction CON
BLACKLOCK, Thomas, 1721-91,
Scots; poetry DA
BLACKMAN, Victor, 1922- ,
British; nonfiction CON
BLACK-MICHAUD, Jacob, 1938- ,
English; nonfiction CON
BLACKMORE, Dorothy S. , Amer-
ican; nonfiction CON
BLACKMORE, John Thomas,
1931- , American; nonfiction
CON
BLACKMORE, Sir Richard,
1650/55-1729, English; po-
etry, nonfiction BU DA VP
BLACKMORE, Richard Doddridge,
1825-1900, English; fiction,
poetry, nonfiction DA MAG
PO VN
BLACKMUR, Richard Palmer,
1904-65, American; poetry,
nonfiction BOR BR BU PO

'BLACKSTOCK, Charity' see TOR-
DAY, Ursula
'BLACKSTOCK, Lee' see TORDAY,
Ursula
BLACKSTOCK, Nelson, 1944- ,
American; nonfiction CON
BLACKSTONE, Bernard, 1911- ,
British; nonfiction CON
BLACKSTONE, Tessa Ann Vosper,
1942- , British; nonfiction
CON
BLACKSTONE, Sir William, 1723-
80, English; nonfiction BU
BLACKWELL, David, 1919- ,
American; nonfiction SH
BLACKWELL, John see 'ALUN'
BLACKWELL, Lois S., 1943- ,
American; nonfiction CON
BLACKWELL, Roger Dale, 1940- ,
American; journalism, nonfic-
tion CON
BLACKWELL, Samuel Earl, Jr.,
1913- , American; fiction,
plays CON
BLACKWOOD, Algernon, 1869-1951,
English; fiction, juveniles,
plays DA NI REI ST
BLACKWOOD, Andrew Watterson,
1882-1966, American; nonfiction
CON
BLACKWOOD, Caroline, 1931- ,
Irish-American; fiction, non-
fiction CON HO
BLACKWOOD, Paul Everett, 1913- ,
American; nonfiction CON
'BLADE, Alexander', Ziff Davis
house name NI
BLADEL, Roderick LeRoy, Amer-
ican; nonfiction CON
BLADEN, Vincent Wheeler, 1900- ,
English; nonfiction CON
BLADES, Ann Sager, 1947- ,
Canadian; juveniles CO CON
KI
BLADES, Brian Brewer, 1906-77,
American; nonfiction CON
BLADES, James, 1901- , English;
nonfiction CON
BLADOW, Suzanne Wilson, 1937- ,
American; juveniles CO CON
BLAFFER, Sarah Campbell, 1946- ,
American; nonfiction CON
BLAGA, Lucian, 1895-1961, Ru-
manian; poetry, plays, non-
fiction BU CL TH
BLAGDEN, David, 1944- , Amer-
ican; nonfiction CON
BLAGOWIDOW, George, 1923- ,

Polish-American; nonfiction
CON
BLAHOSLAV, Jan, 1523-71, Czech;
nonfiction, translations BU
'BLAINE, John' see GOODWIN,
Harold L.; HARKINS, Philip
BLAINE, Margery Kay ('Marge
Blaine'), 1937- , American;
juveniles CO CON WAR
BLAINE, William Lee, 1931- ,
American; nonfiction CON
BLAIR, Carvel Hall, 1924- ,
American; nonfiction CON
BLAIR, Clay Drewry, Jr., 1925- ,
American; nonfiction CON
BLAIR, Don, 1933- , American;
nonfiction CON
BLAIR, Eric H. see 'ORWELL,
George'
BLAIR, Frank, 1915- , Amer-
ican; journalism, nonfiction
CON
'BLAIR, Hamish' (J. F. Andrew
Blair), 1872-1935, Scots; fic-
tion, journalism NI
BLAIR, Hugh, 1718-1800, English;
nonfiction BU DA PO
BLAIR, James, 1655/56-1743,
American; nonfiction BA
BLAIR, Jane Nemec, 1911- ,
American; nonfiction CON
BLAIR, John Malcolm, 1914-76,
American; nonfiction CON
BLAIR, Joseph Allen, 1913- ,
American; nonfiction CON
BLAIR, Philip Mark, 1928- ,
American; nonfiction CON
BLAIR, Robert, 1699-1746, Scots;
poetry BU DA PO VP
BLAIR, Ruth Van Ness, 1912- ,
American; poetry, juveniles
CO WAR
BLAIR, Sam, 1932- , American;
nonfiction CON
BLAIR, Walter, 1900- , Amer-
ican; juveniles CO
BLAIS, Marie Claire, 1939- ,
Canadian-American; fiction,
poetry, plays BU CR WA
'BLAISDELL, Anne' see LINING-
TON, Elizabeth
BLAISDELL, Foster Warren,
1927- , American; nonfiction
CON
BLAISDELL, Harold F., 1914- ,
American; nonfiction CON
BLAISDELL, Paul Henry, 1908- ,
American; nonfiction CON

BLAISE, Clark, 1940- , Amer-
ican; nonfiction CON
'BLAKE, Bud' see BLAKE, Julian
W.
BLAKE, David Haven, 1940- ,
American; nonfiction CON
BLAKE, Fay Montaug, 1920- ,
American; nonfiction CON
BLAKE, Gary, 1944- , American;
plays, nonfiction, journalism
CON
BLAKE, George, 1893-1961, Scots;
fiction BU DA
BLAKE, James, 1922-79, Scots-
American; nonfiction, fiction
CON
'BLAKE, Jonas' see HARDY, C.
Colburn
BLAKE, Julian Watson ('Bud
Blake'), 1918- , American;
fiction CON
'BLAKE, Justin' see BOWEN, John
G.
BLAKE, Kathleen, 1944- , Amer-
ican; nonfiction CON
BLAKE, Minden Vaughan (Mindy),
1913- , New Zealander; non-
fiction CON
'BLAKE, Nicholas' see LEWIS,
Cecil Day
BLAKE, Norman Francis, 1934- ,
British; nonfiction, translations
CON
'BLAKE, Olive' see SUPRANER,
Robyn
BLAKE, Patricia; 1933- , Amer-
ican; nonfiction CON
'BLAKE, Patrick' see EGLETON,
Clive F.
BLAKE, Peter Jost, 1920- ,
German-American; nonfiction
CON
BLAKE, Quentin, 1932- , English;
juveniles CO
BLAKE, Reed Harris, 1933- ,
American; nonfiction CON
BLAKE, Richard Aloysius, 1939- ,
American; nonfiction CON
BLAKE, Robert, 1916- , English;
nonfiction WA
'BLAKE, Sally' see SAUNDERS,
Jean
BLAKE, Thomas, American?;
fiction NI
'BLAKE, Walker E.' see BUTTER-
WORTH, William E.
BLAKE, William, 1757-1827, Brit-
ish; poetry, nonfiction BRI

BU DA MAG PO VP WAR
BLAKELEY, Phyllis Ruth, 1922- ,
Canadian; nonfiction CON
BLAKEMORE, Colin Brian;
1944- , British; nonfiction
CON
BLAKER, Alfred Arthur, 1928- ,
American; nonfiction CON
BLAKESLEE, Thomas Robert,
1937- , American; nonfiction
CON
BLAKEY, Scott, 1936- , Amer-
ican; journalism, nonfiction
CON
BLAKEY, Walker Jameson, 1940- ,
American; nonfiction CON
BLAKISTON, Georgiana, 1903- ,
British; nonfiction CON
'BLAMAN, Anna' (Johanna Petro-
nella Vrugt), 1905-60, Dutch;
fiction BU CL
BLAMIRE, Susanna, 1747-94, Eng-
lish; poetry BU
BLAMIRES, David Malcolm, 1936- ,
English; poetry, nonfiction
CON
BLANC, Suzanne, American; fic-
tion REI
BLANCE, Ellen, 1931- , English;
juveniles CON
BLANCH, Lesley, 1907- , Brit-
ish; nonfiction, fiction CON
BLANCHARD, Allan Edward,
1929- , American; journal-
ism CON
BLANCHARD, Birdsall Everard,
1909- , American; nonfiction
CON
BLANCHARD, J. Richard, 1912- ,
American; nonfiction CON
BLANCHARD, Kendall Allan,
1942- , American; nonfic-
tion CON
BLANCHARD, Nina, American;
nonfiction CON
BLANCHARD, Paula Barber,
1936- , American; nonfiction
CON
BLANCHE, August, 1811-68,
Swedish; fiction, plays BU
BLANCHET, Eileen, 1924- ,
Canadian; nonfiction CON
BLANCHETTE, Oliva, 1929- ,
American; nonfiction CON
BLANCHOT, Maurice, 1907- ,
French; fiction, nonfiction
BU CL WA
BLANCK, Gertrude, 1914- ,

American; nonfiction CON
BLANCK, Jacob Nathaniel, 1906-74,
American; nonfiction CON
BLANCO, Antonio Nicolas, 1887-
1945, Puerto Rican; poetry,
plays HIL
BLANCO, George M., 1937- ,
American; nonfiction MAR
BLANCO, Richard Lidio, 1926- ,
American; nonfiction CON
BLANCO, Tomas, 1900- , Puerto
Rican; fiction, nonfiction HIL
BLANCO FOMBONA, Rufino, 1874-
1944, Venezuelan; fiction BR
BU
BLANCO WHITE, Jose Maria
(Blanco Crispo), 1775-1841,
Spanish; poetry BU TH
'BLANCPAIN, Marc' (Marc Benoni),
1909- , French; fiction BU
BLAND, Hester Beth, 1906- ,
American; nonfiction CON
'BLAND, Jennifer' see BOWDEN,
Jean
BLAND, Randall Walton, 1942- ,
American; nonfiction CON
BLAND, Richard, 1710-76, Amer-
ican; nonfiction BA
BLANDFORD, Percy William,
1912- , English; juveniles
WAR
BLANK, Blanche Davis, American;
nonfiction CON
BLANK, Joseph P., 1919- , Amer-
ican; nonfiction CON
BLANKENSHIP, Edward Gary,
1943- , American; nonfiction
CON
BLANPIED, Pamela Wharton,
1937- , American; nonfiction
CON
BLANSHARD, Paul, 1892-1980,
American; journalism, nonfic-
tion CON
BLASCO IBANEZ, Vicente, 1867-
1928, Spanish; fiction BU CL
MAG TH
BLASER, Robin Francis, 1925- ,
American-Canadian; poetry
CON VCP
BLASHFORD-SNELL, John Nicholas,
1936- , British; nonfiction
CON
BLASING, Mutlu Konuk, 1944- ,
American; translations, nonfic-
tion CON
BLASSINGAME, John Wesley, 1940- ,
American; nonfiction CON

BLATCHFORD, Christie, 1951- ,
Canadian; journalism CON
BLATT, Burton, 1927- , Amer-
ican; nonfiction CON
BLAU, Abram, 1907-79, Canadian;
nonfiction CON
BLAU, Eric ('Milton Blau'),
1921- , American; poetry,
plays CON
BLAU, Sheldon Paul, 1935- ,
American; nonfiction CON
BLAU, Zena Smith, 1922- ,
American; nonfiction CON
BLAUFARB, Douglas Samuel,
1918- , American; nonfic-
tion CON
BLAUMANIS, Rudolfs, 1863-1908,
Latvian; fiction, plays BU
BLAUSTEIN, Albert P. see 'DE
GRAEF, Allen'
BLAUSTEIN, Elliott Harold,
1915- , American; nonfic-
tion CON
BLAUSTEIN, Esther, 1935- ,
American; fiction CON
BLAY, J. Benibengor, 1900/15- ,
Ghanaian; poetry, fiction,
plays HER JA LA
BLAYNEY, Margaret Statler,
1926- , American; nonfiction
CON
'BLAYRE, Christopher' (Edward
Heron-Allen), 1861-1943, Eng-
lish; fiction NI
BLAZE, Wayne, 1951- , Amer-
ican; nonfiction CON
BLAZIER, Kenneth Dean, 1933- ,
American; nonfiction CON
BLEAKLEY, David Wylie, 1925- ,
Irish; nonfiction CON
BLECHMAN, Barry M., 1943- ,
American; nonfiction CON
BLECHMAN, Burt, 1927- , Amer-
ican; fiction BR VCN
BLEDSOE, Albert Taylor, 1809-
77, American; journalism,
nonfiction BA MYE
BLEDSOE, Jerry, 1941- , Amer-
ican; journalism, nonfiction
CON
'BLEECK, Oliver' see THOMAS,
Ross
'BLEEKER, Mordecai' see MOR-
GAN, Fred F.
BLEGVAD, Erik, 1923- , Danish-
English; juveniles CO CON
DE
BLEGVAD, Lenore, 1926- ,

Danish; juveniles CO CON DE
BLEHERIS (Breri; Bledhericus),
English?; fiction BU
BLEIBERG, Germán, 1915- ,
Spanish; poetry BU CL
BLEIBERG, Robert Marvin, 1924- ,
American; journalism, nonfic-
tion CON
BLEICH, Harold, 1930?-80, Amer-
ican; nonfiction CON
BLEIER, Robert Patrick (Rocky),
1946- , American; nonfiction
CON
BLEILER, Everett F., 1910- ,
American; nonfiction AS NI
BLEMMYDES, Nicephorus, 1197?-
1272?, Byzantine; nonfiction
LA
BLENERHASSET, Thomas, 1550-
1625, English; poetry BU
BLESSING, Richard Allen, 1929- ,
American; nonfiction CON
BLESSINGTON, Marguerite Power,
Countess of, 1789-1849, Eng-
lish; fiction BU
BLEST GANA, Alberto, 1830-1920,
Chilean; fiction BR BU
BLETTER Robert, 1933?-76, Amer-
ican; nonfiction CON
BLETTER, Rosemarie Haag, 1939- ,
German-American; nonfiction
CON
BLEVINS, Leon Wilford, 1937- ,
American; nonfiction CON
BLEVINS, Winfred Ernest, Jr.,
American; nonfiction, poetry,
fiction, translations CON
BLEYTHING, Dennis Hugh, 1946- ,
American; nonfiction CON
BLICHER, Steen Steensen, 1782-
1848, Danish; poetry, fiction
BU TH
BLICKER, Seymour, 1940- , Ca-
nadian; juveniles CON
BLIGGER von STEINACH, fl. 1190-
1200, German; poetry BU
BLIGHT, John, 1913- , Australian;
poetry CON VCP
BLIND HARRY see HARY
BLINDERMAN, Abraham, 1916- ,
American; nonfiction CON
BLINN, Walter Craig, 1930- ,
American; nonfiction CON
BLISH, James Benjamin ('Donald
Laverty'; 'John MacDougal'),
1921-75, American; fiction,
nonfiction, plays AS CON COW
NI VCN WA

BLISHEN, Edward, 1920- , English; juveniles CO
BLISS, Carey Stillman, 1914- , American; nonfiction CON
BLISS, Edward, Jr., 1912- , American; nonfiction CON
BLISS, George William, 1918-78, American; journalism CON
BLISS, John Michael, 1941- , Canadian; nonfiction CON
'BLISS, Reginald' see WELLS, Herbert G.
BLISS, Ronald Gene, 1942- , American; juveniles CO CON
BLISSETT, Marlan, 1938- , American; nonfiction CON
BLITZSTEIN, Marc, 1905-64, American; composer MCG
BLIVIN, Bruce, 1889-1977, American; journalism, nonfiction CON
BLIXEN, Karen ('Osceola'; 'Pierre Andrezel'; Dinesen), 1885-1962, Danish; fiction BU CL DA MAG SEY TH
BLIZZARD, Samuel Wilson, Jr., 1914?-76, American; nonfiction CON
BLOCH, Ariel Alfred, 1933- , German-American; nonfiction CON
BLOCH, Blanche, 1890-1980, American; nonfiction, fiction, plays CON
BLOCH, Dorothy, 1912- , American; nonfiction CON
BLOCH, Ernst, 1885-1977, German; nonfiction BU CON
BLOCH, Jean Ricard, 1884-1947, French; fiction BU CL
BLOCH, Lucienne, 1909- , Swiss-American; juveniles CO
BLOCH, Lucienne Schupf, 1937- , Belgian-American; fiction
BLOCH, Marie Halun, 1923- , American; juveniles CO DEM KI
BLOCH, Robert ('Collier Young'), 1917- , American; fiction, plays, nonfiction AS CO NI REI ST
BLOCHER, Henri Arthur, 1937- , French; nonfiction CON
BLOCH-MICHEL, Jean, 1912- , French; fiction, nonfiction WA
BLOCHMAN, Lawrence Goldtree, 1900-75, American; journalism, fiction, juveniles CO CON REI ST
BLOCK, Allan Forrest, 1923- , American; poetry CON
BLOCK, Irvin, 1917- , American; juveniles CO
BLOCK, Jack, 1931- , American; nonfiction CON
BLOCK, Joel David, 1943- , American; nonfiction CON
BLOCK, Lawrence ('Chip Harrison'; 'Paul Kavanagh'), 1938- , American; fiction, nonfiction REI
BLOCK, Michael, 1942- , American; journalism, nonfiction CON
BLOCK, Ralph, 1889-1974, American; nonfiction CON
BLOCK, Seymour Stanton, 1918- , American; nonfiction CON
BLOCK, Stanley Byron, 1939- , American; nonfiction CON
BLOCK, Thomas Harris, 1945- , American; fiction CON
BLOCK, Walter Edward, 1941- , American; nonfiction CON
BLOCKSIDGE, Charles W. see 'BAYLEBRIDGE, William'
BLODGETT, Beverley, 1926- , American; nonfiction CON
BLODGETT, Richard, 1940- , American; nonfiction CON
BLOEM, Diane Brummel, 1935- , American; nonfiction CON
BLOEM, Jakobus Cornelis, 1887-1966, Dutch; poetry BU CL TH
BLOFELD, John Eaton ('Chu Ch'an'), 1913- , English; nonfiction, translations CON
BLOK, Aleksandr Aleksandrovich, 1880-1921, Russian; poetry, plays BU CL MAG MCG SEY TH
BLOK, Anton, 1935- , Dutch; nonfiction CON
'BLOKE' see MODISANE, William
BLOM, Karl Arne ('Bo Lagevi'), 1946- , Swedish; fiction, translations CON
BLOMBERG, Erik Axel, 1894-1965, Swedish; poetry, nonfiction BU
BLONDAL, Patricia Anne Jenkins, 1927-59, Canadian; fiction CR
BLONDEL, Jean Fernand Pierre, 1929- , French; nonfiction CON

BLONDEL, Joan, 1906-79, American; fiction CON
BLONDEL, Maurice, 1861-1949, French; nonfiction CL
BLONDEL, Roger, see 'BRUSS, B. R.'
BLONDEL de NESLE, early 13th century, French; poetry BU
BLOOD, Charles Lewis, 1929- , American; juveniles, nonfiction CON
BLOOD, Marje ('Paige McKenzie'), American; fiction CON
'BLOOD, Matthew' see DRESSER, Davis
'BLOODSTONE, John' see BYRNE, Stuart J.
BLOOM, Erick Franklin, 1944- , American; nonfiction, poetry CON
BLOOM, Freddy, 1914- , American; juveniles CON
BLOOM, Harold, 1930- , American; nonfiction BOR WAK
BLOOM, Herman Irving ('Harmon Bellamy'; 'Barry Hart'), 1908- , American; journalism CON
BLOOM, John Porter, 1924- , American; nonfiction CON
BLOOM, Melvyn Harold, 1938- , American; nonfiction CON
BLOOM, Pauline, American; nonfiction, fiction CON
BLOOMBERG, Edward Michael, 1937- , American; nonfiction CON
BLOOMBERG, Max Arthur (Marty), 1938- , American; nonfiction CON
BLOOMBERG, Morton, 1936- , American; nonfiction CON
BLOOME, Enid P., 1925- , American; juveniles CON WAR
BLOOMFIELD, Anthony, 1922- , British; fiction WA
BLOOMFIELD, Arthur Irving, 1914- , Canadian-American; nonfiction CON
BLOOMFIELD, Arthur John, 1931- , American; nonfiction CON
BLOOMFIELD, Harold H., 1944- , American; nonfiction CON
BLOOMFIELD, Masse, 1923- ,

American; nonfiction CON
BLOOMFIELD, Robert, 1766-1823, English; poetry, plays BU PO VP
BLOOMGARTEN, Shloime, see 'YEHOASH'
BLOS, Joan Winsor, 1928- , American; juveniles CON WAR
BLOS, Peter, 1904- , German-American; nonfiction CON
BLOSS, Fred Donald, 1920- , American; nonfiction CON
BLOSSOM, Frederick A., 1878?-1974, American; nonfiction CON
'BLOT, Thomas' (William Simpson), American; fiction NI
BLOUET, Brian Walter, 1936- , Anglo-American; nonfiction CON
BLOUNT, Charles, 1654-93, English; nonfiction BU
BLOUNT, Margaret, 1924- , British; fiction CON
BLOUNT, Roy ('Noah Sanders'; 'C. R. Ways'), 1941- , American; nonfiction, fiction, poetry CON
BLOUSTEIN, Edward J., 1925- , American; nonfiction CON
BLOW, Ernest J., South African; fiction NI
BLOW, Michael, American; juveniles WAR
BLOW, Suzanne Katherine, 1932- , American; nonfiction CON
BLOY, Léon Marie, 1846-1917, French; fiction BU CL TH
BLUE, Betty Anne, 1922- , American; nonfiction CON
BLUE, Frederick Judd, 1937- , American; nonfiction CON
BLUE, Rose, 1931- , American; juveniles CO CON WAR
BLUEBOND-LANGNER, Myra, 1948- , American; nonfiction CON
BLUESTEIN, Daniel Thomas ('Daniel B. Thomas'), 1943- , American; poetry CON
BLUESTEIN, Gene, 1928- , American; nonfiction CON
BLUH, Bonnie, 1926- , American; nonfiction, fiction CON
BLUM, Carol Kathlyn, 1934- , American; nonfiction CON
BLUM, Harold P., 1929- , American; nonfiction CON
BLUM, Leon, 1872-1950, French;

nonfiction CL
BLUM, Lucille Hollander, 1904- ,
American; nonfiction CON
BLUM, Ralph, 1932- , American;
fiction NI
BLUM, Stella, 1916- , Amer-
ican; nonfiction CON
BLUMAUER, Johannes Aloys, 1755-
98, Austrian; plays, poetry
BU
BLUMBERG, Gary ('Michael Brad-
ley'), 1938- , American; non-
fiction, fiction CON
BLUMBERG, Harry, 1903- ,
American; nonfiction CON
BLUMBERG, Leonard U., 1920- ,
American; nonfiction CON
BLUMBERG, Nathan Bernard,
1922- , American; nonfiction
CON
BLUMBERG, Phillip Irvin, 1919- ,
American; nonfiction CON
BLUMBERG, Rhoda, 1917- ,
American; nonfiction CON
BLUMBERG, Robert Stephen,
1945- , American; nonfiction
CON
BLUME, Friedrich, 1893-1975,
German; nonfiction CON
BLUME, Judy Sussman, 1938- ,
American; juveniles, fiction
DEM KI WAR
BLUMENFELD, Harold, 1905- ,
American; nonfiction CON
BLUMENFELD, Meyer, 1905-80,
American; nonfiction CON
BLUMENFIELD, Samuel Leon,
1926- , American; nonfiction
CON
BLUMENTHAL, L. Roy, 1908-75,
American; nonfiction CON
BLUMENTHAL, Monica David,
1930-81, German-American;
nonfiction CON
BLUMENTHAL, Norm, American;
nonfiction CON
BLUMENTHAL, Walter Hart,
1883- , American; poetry,
nonfiction PAL
BLUMIN, Stuart Mack, 1940- ,
American; nonfiction CON
BLUMRICH, Josef Franz, 1913- ,
Austrian-American; nonfiction
CON
BLUMROSEN, Alfred William,
1928- , American; nonfiction
CON
BLUNDELL, Harold see 'BELL-

AIRS, George'
BLUNDEN, Edmund Charles, 1896-
1974, English; poetry, nonfic-
tion, plays BU CON DA MAG
PO SEY VCP VP
BLUNK, Frank M., 1897?-1976,
American; journalism CON
BLUNSDEN, John Beresford, 1930- ,
English; nonfiction CON
BLUNT, Wilfrid Scawen, 1840-1922,
English; poetry, nonfiction DA
PO VP
BLUSKOV, Iliya, 1839-1913, Bul-
garian; fiction BU
BLUVSTEIN, Rahel, 1890-1931,
Hebrew; poetry LA TH
BLY, Robert Elwood, 1926- ,
American; poetry, translations
BR MAL PO SEY VCP VP WA
BLY, Thomas J., 1918?-79, Amer-
ican; journalism CON
BLYTH, Alan, 1929- , English;
nonfiction CON
BLYTH, Jeffrey, 1926- , Amer-
ican; nonfiction CON
'BLYTH, John' see HIBBS, John
BLYTH, Myrna, 1948- , Amer-
ican; fiction, nonfiction CON
BLYTON, Carey, 1932- , English;
juveniles, nonfiction CO CON
BLYTON, Enid Mary ('Mary Pol-
lock'), 1897-1968, British; po-
etry, nonfiction, juveniles CO
CON KI
BOA, Kenneth, 1945- , American;
nonfiction CON
BOADELLA, David, 1931- , Eng-
lish; nonfiction CON
BOALT, Hans Gunnar, 1910- ,
Swedish; nonfiction CON
BOARD, Chester Stephen, 1942- ,
American; nonfiction CON
BOARDMAN, Arthur, 1927- ,
American; fiction CON
BOARDMAN, Fon Wyman, Jr.,
1911- , American; juveniles
CO
BOARDMAN, Francis, 1915-76,
American; nonfiction CON
BOARDMAN, Gwenn R., 1924- ,
Anglo-American; fiction CO
CON
BOARDMAN, John 1927- , British;
nonfiction CON
BOARDMAN, Peter David, 1950- ,
British; nonfiction CON
BOARDMAN, Thomas Volney, 1930- ,
British; nonfiction AS NI

BOARDWELL, Robert Lee, 1926- ,
American; nonfiction CON
BOAS, Franz, 1858-1942, German-
American; nonfiction MAG
'BOATENG, Yaw Maurice see
BRUNNER, Maurice Y.
BOATRIGHT, Mody Coggin, 1896-
1970, American; nonfiction
CON
BOATWRIGHT, Howard Leake, Jr.,
1918- , American; nonfiction
CON
BOBA, Imre, 1919- , Hungarian-
American; nonfiction CON
BOBBE, Dorothie de Bear, 1905-
75, American; journalism, non-
fiction, juveniles CO CON
'BOBETTE' see SIMENON, Georges
BOBKER, Lee R., 1925- , Amer-
ican; nonfiction CON
BOBORYKIN, Peter Dmitrievich,
1836-1922, Russian; fiction
BU
BOBROV, Semen Sergeyevich, 1767-
1810, Russian; poetry BU
BOBROW, Davis Bernard, 1936- ,
American; nonfiction CON
BOBROWSKI, Johannes, 1917-65,
German; poetry, fiction BU
CL CON TH WAK
BOCAGE, Louis C.-B. du see
'VERNEUIL, Louis'
BOCAGE, Manuel Maria Barbosa
du, 1765-1805, Portuguese;
poetry BU TH
BOCANGEL y UNZUETA, Gabriel,
1608-58, Spanish; poetry BU
TH
BOCCACCIO, Giovanni, 1313-75,
Italian; poetry, nonfiction, fic-
tion BO BU MAG TH
BOCCALINI, Traiano, 1556-1613,
Italian; nonfiction BO BU TH
BOCHNER, Salomon, 1899- , Amer-
ican; nonfiction CON
BOCK, Alan William, 1943- ,
American; nonfiction CON
BOCK, Harold I., 1939- , Amer-
ican; juveniles CO
BOCK, Joanne, 1940- , Amer-
ican; nonfiction CON
BOCK, Paul John, 1922- , Amer-
ican; nonfiction CON
BOCK, William Sauts, 1939- ,
American; juveniles CO
BOCKL, George, 1909- , Amer-
ican; nonfiction CON
BOCKUS, Herman William, 1915- ,

American; nonfiction CON
BOCOCK, Robert James, 1940- ,
British; nonfiction CON
'BOD, Peter' see VESENYI, Paul E.
BODANSKY, Oscar, 1901-77, Russian-
American; nonfiction CON
BODDIE, Charles Emerson, 1911- ,
American; nonfiction CON SH
BODDY, Frederick Arthur, 1914- ,
English; nonfiction CON
BODDY, William Charles, 1913- ,
British; nonfiction CON
BODE, Janet, 1943- , American;
nonfiction CON
BODE, Roy E., 1908- , Amer-
ican; journalism CON
BODECKER, Niels Mogens, 1922- ,
Danish; juveniles, poetry CO
CON KI
BODEL, Jean, -1209/10, French;
plays, poetry BU MCG
BODELSEN, Anders, 1937- ,
Danish; fiction, journalism
CL NI
BODEN, Margaret A., 1936- ,
British; nonfiction CON
BODENHAM, Hilda Morris ('Hilda
Boden'; 'Pauline Welch'),
1901- , English; juveniles
CO WAR
BODENHAM, John, 1558-1600?,
English; nonfiction BU
BODENHEIM, Maxwell, 1893-1954,
American; poetry, plays, fic-
tion, nonfiction BA BR VN
BODEY, Hugh Arthur, 1939- ,
English; nonfiction CON
BODGER, Joan see MERCER, Joan
BODIAN, Nat G., 1921- , Amer-
ican; nonfiction CON
BODIE, Idella Fallaw, 1925- ,
American; juveniles, fiction
CO CON
BODIN, Jean, 1530-96, French;
nonfiction BU
BODIN, Paul, 1909- , French;
journalism, fiction, nonfiction
CON
BODINGTON, Nancy Hermione see
'SMITH, Shelly'
BODKER, Cecil Skaar Jacobsen,
1927- , Danish; poetry, plays,
juveniles, fiction BU CO CON
BODKIN, Amy Maud, 1875-1967,
British; nonfiction BOR
BODKIN, Cora, 1944- , American;
nonfiction CON
BODKIN, Matthais McDonnell, 1850-

1933, Irish; fiction, plays, nonfiction REI ST
BODLEY, Sir Thomas, 1544/45- 1613, English; nonfiction BU ENG
BODMER, Johann Jakob, 1698- 1783, Swiss; poetry, plays, nonfiction BU TH
BODMER, Walter Fred, 1936- , German-British; nonfiction CON
BODO, Murray, 1937- , American; nonfiction, poetry CON
BODO, Peter T., 1949- , Austrian-American; journalism, nonfiction CON
BODOH, John James, 1931- , American; nonfiction CON
BODSWORTH, Charles Frederick, 1918- , Canadian; fiction, nonfiction VCN
BODTCHER, Ludvig Adolph, 1793- 1874, Danish; poetry BU TH
'BODWELL, Richard' see SPRING, Gerald M.
BOECE, Hector (Boethius), 1465- 1536, Scots; nonfiction BU DA
BOECKLE, Franz, 1921- , Swiss; nonfiction CON
BOECKMAN, Charles, 1920- , American; juveniles CO WAR
BOËX, Joseph H. see 'ROSNY, J. H.'
BOËX, Justin see 'ROSNY, J. H.'
BOEGE, Ulrich Gustav, 1940- , German-American; nonfiction CON
BOEGEHOLD, Betty Doyle ('Donovan Doyle'), 1913- , American; juveniles CON
BOEHLOW, Robert Henry, 1925- , American; nonfiction CON
'BOEHM, Herb' see VARLEY, John
BOEHM, William Dryden, 1946- , American; nonfiction CON
BÖHME, Jakob, 1575-1624, German; nonfiction BU TH
BOEHRINGER, Robert, 1885?- 1974, German; poetry, nonfiction CON
BOELEN, Bernard Jacques, 1916- , Dutch-American; nonfiction CON
BÖLL, Heinrich, 1917- , German; fiction, plays, translations, poetry BU CL SEY TH WA
BOENDALE, Jan van, 1280-1352,

..Dutch; poetry BU
BOOK, Martin Fredrik, 1883-1961, ..Swedish; nonfiction BU
BOOVARSSON, Guðmundur, 1904- 74, Icelander; fiction, nonfiction, poetry CL
BOER, Charles, 1939- , American; poetry, translations, nonfiction CON VCP
BORJESSON, Johan, 1790-1866, .. Swedish; poetry, plays BU
BÖRNE, Ludwig (Löb Baruch), 1786-1837, German; nonfiction BU
BOESCH, Mark Joseph, 1917- , American; juveniles CO
BOESEL, David, 1938- , American; nonfiction CON
BOESEN, Victor ('Jesse Hall'; 'Eric Harald'), 1908- , American; juveniles CO WAR
BOESIGER, Willi, 1904- , Swiss; nonfiction CON
BOETHIUS, Anicius Manlius Severinus, 480-524, Roman; nonfiction BU GR LA MAG TH
BOETIE, Dugmore, 1920-66, South African; fiction HER
BOETIUS à BOLSWERT, 1580-1633, .. Dutch; nonfiction BU
BÖTTIGER, Carl Vilhelm, 1807-78, Swedish; poetry, nonfiction BU
BOETTINGER, Henry Maurice, 1924- , American; nonfiction CON
BOFF, Vic, 1915- , American; nonfiction CON
BOFILL i MATES, Jaume see 'GUERAU de LIOST'
BOGAERS, Adrianus, 1795-1870, Dutch; poetry, nonfiction BU
'BOGAN, Mrs. Bogan of' see NAIRNE, Carolina O.
BOGAN, James, 1945- , American; poetry, nonfiction CON
BOGAN, Louise, 1897-1970, American; poetry, nonfiction CON
BOGARD, Travis Miller, 1918- , American; nonfiction CON
'BOGARDE, Dirk' see VAN DEN BOGARDE, Derek J.
BOGART, Carlotta, 1929- , American; nonfiction CON
BOGART, Leo, 1921- , American; nonfiction CON
BOGATYRYOV, Konstantin, 1924?- 76, Russian; poetry, translations CON

BOGDANOR, Vernon, 1943- ,
British; nonfiction CON
'BOGDANOV, A.' (Alexander
Alexandrovich Malinovsky),
1873-1928, Russian; nonfic-
tion BU
BOGDANOVICH, Ippolit Fëdoro-
vich, 1743-1802, Russian; po-
etry BU
BOGEN, Constance, American; ju-
veniles WAR
BOGEN, James Benjamin, 1935- ,
American; nonfiction CON
BOGEN, Nancy Ruth, 1932- ,
American; nonfiction CON
BOGGAN, Elton Carrington,
1943- , American; nonfiction
CON
BOGGS, James, 1919- , Amer-
ican; nonfiction CON SH
BOGGS, Ralph Steele, 1901- ,
American; juveniles CO
BOGGS, William III, 1942- ,
American; fiction, tv CON
BOGLE, Sarah Comly Norris,
1870-1932, American; nonfic-
tion ENG
BOGNINI, Joseph Miezan, 1936- ,
Ivory Coast; poetry HER JA
BOGORAZ, Vladimir Germano-
vitch, 1865-1936, Russian;
fiction NI
BOGOROV, Ivan, 1818-92, Bul-
garian; nonfiction BU
BOGRAD, Larry ('Grady Baroll'),
1953- , American; juveniles,
fiction CON
BOGUSLAWSKI, Dorothy Beers,
1911?-78, American; nonfic-
tion CON
BOGUSLAWSKI, Wojciech, 1757-
1829, Polish; plays BU
BOGUSZEWSKA, Helena, 1886- ,
Polish; fiction BU
BOGZA, George, 1908- , Ruman-
ian; nonfiction BU
BOHANA, Aileen Stein, 1951- ,
American; journalism CON
BOHDAL, Susi, 1951- , Austrian;
juveniles CO CON
BOHN, Frank, 1878-1975, Amer-
ican; journalism, nonfiction
CON
BOHN, Joyce Illig, 1940?-76,
American; journalism CON
BOHNET, Michael, 1937- , Ger-
man; nonfiction CON
BOHOMOLEC, Franciszek, 1720-

84, Polish; plays, poetry BU
'BOHR, Theophilus' see THISTLE,
Melville W.
BOIARDO, Matteo Maria, 1441-94,
Italian; poetry BO BU MAG
TH
BOIE, Heinrich Christian, 1744-
1806, German; poetry BU
BOIKO, Claire Taylor, 1925- ,
American; plays CON
BOILEAU, Nicolas (Déspreaux),
1636-1711, French; poetry,
nonfiction BU MAG TH
BOILEAU, Pierre, 1906- , French;
fiction WA
BOILES, Charles Lafayette, Jr.
('Carlos Lafayette'), 1932- ,
Canadian; translations, nonfic-
tion CON
BOISROBERT, Francois Le Metel
de, 1589-1662, French; nonfic-
tion, fiction, plays BU TH
BOISSEVAIN, Jeremy, 1928- ,
English; nonfiction CON
BOISSONNEAU, Alice, Canadian;
fiction CON
BOITO, Arrigo ('Tobia Gorri'),
1842-1918, Italian; poetry,
fiction, nonfiction BO BU TH
BOITO, Camillo, 1836-1944, Italian;
fiction BO
BOJER, Johan, 1872-1959, Nor-
wegian; fiction, plays BU CL
MAG TH
BOK, Bart Jan, 1906- , Dutch-
American; nonfiction CON
BOK, Hannes, 1914-64, American;
fiction AS NI
BOK, Priscilla Fairfield, 1896- ,
American; nonfiction CON
BOKENHAM, Osbern (Bokenam),
1392?-1447?, English; transla-
tions BU
BOKENKOTTER, Thomas, 1924- ,
American; nonfiction CON
BOKER, George Henry, 1823-90,
American; plays, poetry BR
BU MCG VD
BOKSER, Ben Zion, 1907- , Polish;
nonfiction CON
BOKUN, Branko, 1920- , Yugoslav-
English; fiction, nonfiction CON
BOKWE, John Knox, 1855-1922,
Xhosan; poetry HER JA
BOLAMBA, Antoine Roger, 1913- ,
Zairian; poetry, journalism
HER JA LA
BOLAND, Bertram John, 1913-76,

English; journalism, fiction, plays AS NI REI
BOLAND, Bridget, 1913- , British; plays, fiction CON VCD
BOLAND, Eavan Aisleing, 1944- , Irish; poetry HO
BOLCH, Ben Wilsman, 1938- , American; nonfiction CON
BOLCOM, William Elden, 1938- , American; nonfiction CON
BOLD, Alan Norman, 1943- , Scots; poetry, fiction, nonfiction VCP
BOLDING, Amy, 1910- , American; nonfiction CON
'BOLDREWOOD, Rolf' (Thomas Alexander Browne), 1826-1915, Australian; fiction, nonfiction BU DA VN
BOLES, Paul Darcy, 1919- , American; juveniles CO
BOLES, Robert, American; fiction SH
'BOLESLAWITA' see KRASZEWSKI, Józef I.
BOLGAN, Anne Catherine, 1923- , American; nonfiction CON
BOLGAR, Boyan, 1910- , Bulgarian; fiction, nonfiction BU
BOLGER, Philip Cunningham ('Corporal Trim'), 1927- , American; nonfiction CON
BOLIAC, Cezar (Bolliac), 1813-81, Rumanian; poetry, journalism BU
BOLIAN, Polly, 1925- , American; juveniles CO
BOLING, Katharine Singleton, 1933- , American; plays, fiction CON
BOLINGBROKE, Henry St. John, Viscount, 1678-1751, English; nonfiction BU DA PO
BOLINTINEAU, Dimitrie, 1819-72, Rumanian; poetry BU
BOLITHO, Harold, 1939- , Australian; nonfiction CON
BOLITHO, Henry Hector ('Patrick Ney'), 1897-1974, New Zealander; nonfiction CON DA
BOLIVAR, Simón, 1783-1830, Venezuelan; nonfiction BR BU
BOLKHOVITINOV, Nikolai Nikolaevich, 1930- , Russian; nonfiction CON
BOLKOSKY, Sidney Marvin, 1944- , American; non-

fiction CON
BOLLAND, Jean, 1596-1665, Dutch; nonfiction BU
BOLLES, Donald F., 1928-76, American; journalism, nonfiction CON
BOLLES, Richard Nelson, 1927- , American; nonfiction CON
BOLLIGER, Max, 1929- , Swiss; juveniles CO DEM
'BOLLING, Hal' see SCHWALBERG, Carolyn E.
BOLLING, Robert, 1738-75, American; nonfiction BA
BOLLOTEN, Burnett, 1909- , Welsh-American; nonfiction CON
BOLNER, James Jerome, 1936- , American; nonfiction CON
BOLOGNA, Joseph, American; film, plays, tv CON
BOLOGNESE, Donald Alan, 1934- , American; juveniles CO CON DEM
BOLOGNESE, Elaine see RAPHAEL, Elaine
BOLOMBO, G., Zairian; fiction HER
BOLSHAKOFF, Serge, 1901- , Russian; nonfiction CON
BOLT, Bruce Alan, 1930- , Australian-American; nonfiction CON
BOLT, Carol, 1941- , Canadian; plays CON VCD
BOLT, Ernest Collier, Jr., 1936- , American; nonfiction CON
BOLT, Robert Oxton, 1924- , English; plays, film BU DA PO VCD WA
BOLTHO, Andrea, 1939- , German; nonfiction CON
BOLTON, Carole Roberts, 1926- , American; juveniles, fiction CO CON WAR
BOLTON, Charles E., 1841-1901, American; fiction NI
BOLTON, Edmund, 1575-1633, English; poetry, translations, nonfiction BU
'BOLTON, Evelyn see BUNTING, Anne E.
BOLTON, Guy Reginald, 1884-1979, British; film, plays CON
'BOLTON, Isabel' see MILLER, Mary B.

BOLTON, James, 1917-81, Amer-
ican; nonfiction CON
BOLTON, Theodore, 1889-1973,
American; nonfiction CON
BOMAR, Cora Paul, 1913- ,
American; nonfiction CON
BOMBAL, María Luisa, 1910- ,
Chilean; fiction BR
BOMELA, Bertrand M., 1928- ,
Xhosan; fiction HER
'BOMKAUF' see KAUFMAN, Bob G.
BOMPIANI, Valentino, 1898- ,
Italian; plays MCG
BON, Francesco Augusto, 1788-
1858, Italian; plays MCG
BONACHEA, Enrique Rolando,
1943- , Cuban-American;
nonfiction CON
BONACICH, Edna, 1940- , Amer-
ican; nonfiction CON
BONAFOUX y QUINTERO, Luis
('Aramis'; 'Juan de Madrid'),
1855-1918, Puerto Rican;
journalism, fiction HIL
BONAGIUNTA, Orbicciana de Luc-
ca, 13th century, Italian; po-
etry BO BU
BONANNO, Margaret Wander,
1950- , American; fiction CON
BONANSEA, Bernardino Maria,
1908- , Italian-American;
nonfiction CON
BONAPARTE, Felicia, 1937- ,
Rumanian-American; nonfiction
CON
BONAR, Horatius, 1808-89, Scots;
hymns BU
BONARDI, Luigi see 'MALERBA,
Luigi'
BONARELLI, Guidobaldo della
Rovere, 1563-1608, Italian;
poetry, plays BU
'BONAVENTURA' (Friedrich Gott-
lob Wetzel), 1779-1819, Ger-
man; fiction BU
BONAVENTURA, St. (Giovanni da
Fidanza), 1221-74, Italian; non-
fiction BU TH
BONCHO, -1714, Japanese; po-
etry HI
BONCOURT, Louis C. C. de see
'CHAMISSO, Adalbert von'
BOND, Brian, 1936- , English;
nonfiction CON
BOND, Christopher Godfrey,
1945- , British; plays, fic-
tion CON VCD
BOND, Douglas Danford, 1911-76,

American; nonfiction CON
BOND, Edward, 1934/35-69, Eng-
lish; plays, poetry PO SEY
VCD VD
'BOND, Evelyn' see HERSHMAN,
Morris
BOND, Gladys Baker ('Jo Mendel';
'Hall Beth Walker'), 1912- ,
American; juveniles CO
BOND, Harold, 1939- , American;
poetry CON
'BOND, J. Harvey' see WINTER-
BOTHAM, Russell R.
BOND, Jean Carey, American;
juveniles WAR
BOND, Julian, 1940- , American;
nonfiction, poetry CON SH
BOND, Michael, 1926- , English;
juveniles DE
BOND, Nancy Barbara, 1945- ,
American; juveniles, fiction
CO CON WAR
BOND, Nelson Slade, 1908- ,
American; fiction AS NI
'BOND, Ray' see SMITH, Richard R.
BOND, Ruskin, 1934- , American;
juveniles CO
BOND, Thomas Edward, 1934- ,
English; plays, WAK
BOND, Thomas Michael, 1926- ,
English; juveniles, tv, radio,
plays CO KI WAR
BONDANELLA, Peter Eugene,
1943- , American; nonfiction
CON
BONDAREV, Yury Vasilyevich,
1924- , Russian; nonfiction
CL
BONDEROFF, Jason Dennis, 1946- ,
American; juveniles CON
BONDIE, Dietaiuti, late 13th cen-
tury, Florentine; poetry BU
BONDURANT, Joan Valerie, 1918- ,
American; nonfiction CON
BONE, Edith, 1889?-1975, Amer-
ican; nonfiction, translations
CON
BONE, Jesse Franklin, 1916- ,
American; fiction, nonfiction
AS CON NI
BONE, Quentin, 1918- , American;
nonfiction CON
BONE, Robert Adamson, 1924- ,
American; nonfiction CON
BONELLIA, Helen Janet, 1937- ,
Canadian-American; nonfiction
CON
BONER, John Henry, 1845-1903,

American; poetry BA
BONER, Ulrich, fl. 1324-49, German; fiction BU
BONET, Honoré, 1345?-1406?, French; nonfiction BU
'BONETT, John and Emery' (John Hubert A. COULSON, 1906- ; Felicity Winifred CARTER, 1906- ,), English; fiction REI ST
BONETTI, Edward, 1928- , American; poetry, fiction CON
BONEWITS, Philip Emons Isaac, 1949- , American; journalism, nonfiction CON
BONEY, Francis Nash, 1929- , American; nonfiction CON
BONFANTE, Larissa, Italian-American; translations, nonfiction CON
BONFIGLIOLI, Kyril, English; fiction AS
BONFINI, Antonio, 1427-1502/05, Italian; nonfiction BU
'BONGARTZ, Heinz' see THORWALD, Juergen
BONGHI, Ruggero, 1826-95, Italian; journalism BU
BONGIE, Laurence Louis, 1929- , Canadian; nonfiction CON
BONHAM, Barbara Thomas, 1926- , American; juveniles CO
BONHAM, Frank, 1914- , American; juveniles, tv, fiction DE KI
BONHOEFFER, Dietrich, 1906-45, German; nonfiction WA
BONI, Albert, 1892-1981, American; nonfiction CON
BONI, Margaret Bradford, 1893?-1974, American; juveniles, nonfiction CON WAR
BONI, Nazi, 1910-69, Upper Voltan; fiction, nonfiction HER JA
BONIFACE (Wynfrith), 675-754, English; nonfiction BU
BONIFACI CALVO, fl. 1250-70, Provençal; poetry BU
BONIFACIO de ANDRADA e SILVA, José, 1765-1838, Brazilian; poetry BR
BONIME, Florence ('Florence Cummings'), 1907- , American; fiction CON
BONINGTON, Christian Storey,

1934- , English; nonfiction CON
BONJEAN, Charles M., 1935- , American; nonfiction CON
BONNE, Nii Kwabena III, 1888-1960?, Ghanaian; nonfiction HER
BONNEFOY, Yves, 1923- , French; poetry, nonfiction, translations BU CL CON SEY TH WA
BONNELL, Dorothy Haworth, 1914- , American; juveniles WAR
BONNELYCKE, Emil Christian Theodor, 1893-1953, Danish; poetry, fiction BU
BONNER, John Tyler, 1920- , American; nonfiction CON
BONNER, Mary Graham, 1890-1974, American; juveniles CO CON
'BONNER, Parker' see BALLARD, Willis T.
BONNER, Paul Hyde, 1893-1968, American; fiction CON
BONNER, Sherwood, 1849-83, American; fiction BA
BONNER, William Homer, 1924- , American; nonfiction CON
BONNETTE, Jeanne ('Jeanne De Lamarter'), 1907- , American; fiction, poetry CON
BONNEY, Hanning Orrin, 1903-79, American; nonfiction CON
BONNEY, Lorraine Gagnon, 1922- , Canadian-American; nonfiction CON
BONNEY, Mabel Therese, 1897-1978, American; journalism CON
BONNICE, Joseph Gregory, 1930- , American; nonfiction CON
BONNIE, Richard Jeffrey, 1945- , American; nonfiction CON
BONNY, Helen Lindquist, 1921- , American; nonfiction CON
BONO, Philip, 1921- , American; nonfiction CON
BONOMA, Thomas Vincent, 1946- , American; nonfiction CON
BONOMI, Patricia Updegraff, 1928- , American; nonfiction CON
BONSAL, Philip Wilson, 1903- , American; nonfiction CON
BONSALL, Crosby Newell ('Crosby Newell'), 1921- , American;

juveniles CO CON DE KI
BONSELS, Waldemar, 1881-1952,
German; fiction, poetry,
plays CL
BONTECOU, Eleanor, 1890?-1976,
American; nonfiction CON
BONTEKOE, Willem Ysbrandsz
(Decker), 1587-1630, Dutch;
nonfiction BU
BONTEMPELLI, Massimo, 1878-
1960, Italian; fiction, poetry,
plays, journalism BO BU
MCG TH
BONTEMPO, Charles Joseph,
1931- , American; nonfiction
CON
BONTEMPS, Arna Wendell, 1902-
73, American; fiction, poetry,
juveniles, plays, nonfiction
BA CO CON PO WAK
BONTLY, Thomas John, 1939- ,
American; nonfiction CON
BONTRAGER, John Kenneth,
1923- , American; nonfic-
tion CON
BONVESIN de la RIVA, 1240-
1315?, Italian; translations,
poetry BU
BONY, Jean Victor, 1908- ,
French; nonfiction CON
BONZON, Paul Jacques, 1908-78,
French; juveniles, nonfiction
CO CON DEM
BOODY, Shirley Bright, 1919- ,
Canadian; nonfiction CON
BOOHER, Dianna Daniels,
1948- , American; juveniles,
fiction, nonfiction CON
BOOKBINDER, David Joel, 1951- ,
American; nonfiction CON
BOOKER, Simeon Saunders,
1918- , American; nonfiction
SH
BOOK-SENNINGER, Claude, 1928- ,
Franco-American; nonfiction
CON
BOOKSPAN, Martin, 1926- ,
American; nonfiction CON
BOOKSTEIN, Abraham, 1940- ,
American; nonfiction CON
'BOON, Francis' see BACON, Ed-
ward
BOON, Louis Paul ('Boonje'), 1912-
79, Flemish; fiction, poetry,
nonfiction, journalism BU
CL CON SEY
BOONE, Gray Davis, 1938- ,
American; journalism CON

BOONE, Louis Eugene, 1941- ,
American; nonfiction CON
BOONE, Muriel, 1893- , Amer-
ican; nonfiction CON
BOONE, Pat, 1934- , American;
journalism CO
BOORER, Wendy, 1931- , English;
nonfiction CON
BOORMAN, Howard Lyon, 1920- ,
American; nonfiction CON
BOORMAN, John, 1933- , English;
film NI
BOORSTEIN, Edward, 1915- ,
American; nonfiction CON
BOORSTIN, Daniel Joseph, 1914- ,
American; nonfiction WA
BOOTE, Robert Edward ('Robert
Arvill'), 1920- , English; non-
fiction CON
BOOTH, Ernest Sheldon, 1915- ,
American; nonfiction CON
'BOOTH, Geoffrey' see TANN,
Jennifer
'BOOTH, Irwin' see HOCH, Ed-
ward D.
BOOTH, Ken, 1943- , British;
nonfiction CON
BOOTH, Martin, 1944- , British;
poetry, juveniles, nonfiction
CON VCP
BOOTH, Philip, 1925- , American;
poetry BR MAG VCP WA
BOOTH, Rosemary Frances ('Fran-
ces Murray'), 1928- , Scots;
juveniles, fiction CON
BOOTH, Stephen, 1933- , Amer-
ican; nonfiction CON
BOOTH, Taylor Lockwood, 1933- ,
American; nonfiction CON
BOOTH, Wayne Clayson, 1921- ,
American; nonfiction BOR
BOOTHBY, Guy Newell, 1867-1905,
Australian; fiction ST
BOOTHE, Clare (Luce), 1903- ,
American; journalism, plays,
fiction CON MCG
BOOTON, Catherine Kage, 1919- ,
American; fiction CON
BOOTY, John Everitt, 1925- ,
American; nonfiction CON
BOPP, Raul, 1898- , Brazilian;
poetry BR
'BOR, Matej' (Vladimir Pavšič),
1913- , Slovene; poetry,
plays, fiction, translations
BU
BOR, Pieter, 1559-1635, Dutch;
nonfiction BU

'BORAH, Timm' see ZECH, Paul
BORAISCHA, Menahem, 1888-
1949, Yiddish; poetry TH
BORATYNSKY, Yevgeny see BAR-
ATYNSKY, Evgeny A.
BORBERG, Svend, 1888-1947,
Danish; plays, nonfiction BU
BORCHARDT, Rudolf, 1877-1945,
German; poetry, nonfiction,
translations BU CL TH
BORCHERT, Wolfgang, 1921-47,
German; fiction, poetry,
plays BU CL MCG TH WA
BORCK, Caspar Wilhelm von,
1704-47, German; transla-
tions BU
BORDEAUX, Henri, 1870-1963/64,
French; fiction BU CL
BORDEN, Henry, 1901- , Ca-
nadian; nonfiction CON
'BORDEN, Orson T.' see BARON,
Oscar
BORDES, Francois ('Francis Car-
sac'), 1919-81, American; non-
fiction, fiction CON NI
BORDEWIJK, Ferdinand ('Ton
Ven'), 1884-1965, Dutch; fic-
tion, poetry, plays BU CL
TH WAK
BORDIER, Georgette, 1924- ,
French; juveniles CO
BORDIN, Edward S., 1913- ,
American; nonfiction CON
BORDING, Anders Christensen,
1619-77, Danish; poetry BU
BORDLEY, James, III, 1900- ,
American; nonfiction CON
BORDOW, Joan (Wiener), 1944- ,
American; nonfiction CON
BOREHAM, Gordon F., 1928- ,
Canadian; nonfiction CON
'BOREL, Petrus' (Joseph Pierre
Borel), 1809-59, French;
poetry BU TH
BOREL, Raymond C., 1927- ,
French; fiction, film CON
BOREMAN, Yokuteil, 1825-90,
Hebrew; fiction TH
BOREN, James Harlan, 1925- ,
American; nonfiction CON
BORENSTEIN, Audrey Farrell,
1930- , American; transla-
tions, nonfiction CON
BORETZ, Benjamin Aaron,
1934- , American; nonfic-
tion CON
BORGEN, Johan Collett Müller,
1920-79, Norwegian; fiction,

plays, nonfiction BU CL TH
BORGENICHT, Miriam, 1915- ,
American; fiction REI
BORGER, Elias Anne, 1784-1820,
Dutch; poetry BU
BORGES, Jorge Luis, 1899- ,
Argentinian; poetry, nonfiction
BR BU MAG NI REI SEY WA
BORGESE, Elisabeth Mann, 1918- ,
German; fiction, nonfiction
CON
BORGESE, Giuseppe Antonio, 1882-
1952, Italian; plays, fiction,
poetry BO BU CL TH
BORGHI, Giuseppe, 1790-1847,
Italian; poetry BU
BORGHINI, Raffaello, 1541-88?,
Italian; poetry, plays BU
BORGHINI, Vincenzo, 1515-80,
Italian; nonfiction BU
BORGO, Ludovico, 1930- , Italian-
American; nonfiction CON
BORGZINNER, Jon A., 1938-80,
American; journalism CON
BORING, Phyllis Zatlin, 1938- ,
American; nonfiction CON
BORIS, Martin, 1930- , American;
fiction CON
BORJA, Corinne, 1929- , Amer-
ican; juveniles, nonfiction CO
CON
BORJA, Robert, 1923- , Amer-
ican; juveniles CO CON
BORKIN, Joseph, 1911-79, Amer-
ican; nonfiction CON
BORKOVEC, Thomas D., 1944- ,
American; nonfiction CON
BORLAND, Hal ('Ward West'),
1900-78, American; juveniles,
nonfiction CO CON WA
BORLAND, Kathryn Kilby ('Alice
Abbott'; 'Jane Land'; 'Ross
Land'), 1916- , American;
juveniles CO CON
BORMEESTER, Abraham, 1618-45?,
Dutch; plays BU
BORN, Ernest Alexander, 1898- ,
American; nonfiction CON
BORN, Nicholas, 1937-79, German;
poetry, fiction CL
BORNEMAN, Wilhelm, 1766-1851,
German; poetry BU
BORNHEIMER, Deane Gordon,
1935- , American; nonfiction
CON
BORNSTEIN, Diane Dorothy, 1942- ,
American; nonfiction CON
BORNSTEIN, Ruth, 1927- ,

American; juveniles CO CON
WAR
BORNTRAGER, Karl A., 1892- ,
American; nonfiction CON
'BORODIN, George' see SAVA,
George
'BORODIN, Sergey Petrovich
(Amir Sargidzhan), 1902- ,
Russian; fiction BU
BOROWITZ, Albert Ira, 1930- ,
American; nonfiction CON
BOROWITZ, Eugene Bernard,
1924- , American; nonfiction
CON
BOROWSKI, Tadeusz, 1922-51,
Polish; poetry, fiction BU
CL
BOROWY, Waclaw, 1890-1950,
Polish; nonfiction BU
BORRAS, Frank Marshall, -1980,
British; nonfiction CON
BORRETT, William Coates,
1894- , Canadian; fiction
CR
BORRIE, John, 1915- , New
Zealander; nonfiction CON
BORROFF, Edith, 1925- , Amer-
ican; nonfiction CON
BORROW, George Henry, 1803-81,
English; nonfiction, transla-
tions BU DA MAG PO VN
BORSI, Giosuè, 1888-1915, Italian;
poetry, journalism, juveniles
BU
BORSIERI, Pietro, 1786-1852,
Italian; poetry BO
BORSKI, Lucia Merecka, Polish-
American; juveniles CO CON
BORSODI, Ralph, 1888-1977, Amer-
ican; nonfiction CON
BORSSELEN, Philibert van, 1575-
1627, Dutch; poetry BU
BORSTEN, Orin, 1912- , Amer-
ican; plays, nonfiction CON
BORSTIN, Paul Terry, 1944- ,
American; fiction, nonfiction,
film CON
BORTEN, Helen Jacobson, 1930- ,
American; juveniles CO
BORTH, Christian C., 1895?-1966,
American; nonfiction, journal-
ism CON
BORTOLI, Georges, 1923- ,
French; nonfiction CON
BORTSTEIN, Larry, 1942- ,
American; juveniles CO
BORUCH, Robert Francis, 1942- ,
American; nonfiction CON

BORUP, Morten, 1446-1526, Danish;
poetry BU
BOS, Charles du, 1882-1939, French;
nonfiction BU
BOS, Lambert van den (Sylvius),
1620-98, Dutch; poetry, plays,
translations BU
BOSBOOM-TOUSSAINT, Anna Louisa
Geertruida, 1812-86, Dutch;
fiction BU TH
BOSCAN, Almugáver, 1490-1542,
Spanish; poetry BU TH
BOSCH, Andrés, 1926- , Spanish;
fiction CL
BOSCH, Bernardus, 1746-1803,
Dutch; poetry BU
BOSCH, Jeronimo de, 1740-1811,
Dutch; poetry BU
BOSCO, Henri, 1888-1976, French;
fiction, poetry BU CL CON
TH WA
'BOSCO, Jack' see HOLLIDAY,
Joseph
BOSE, Buddhadeva, 1908- , In-
dian; poetry, fiction LA WAK
BOSE, Tarun Chandra, 1931- ,
Indian; nonfiction CON
BOSERUP, Ester, 1910- , Danish;
nonfiction CON
BOSHAQ, Ahmad Abu Eshaq, fl.
1424-27, Persian; poetry PRU
BOSHELL, Gordon, 1908- , Eng-
lish; juveniles, poetry, fiction
CO CON
BOSHER, Kate Langley ('Kate
Cairns'), 1865-1932, American;
fiction BA
BOSHINSKI, Blanche, 1922- ,
American; juveniles CO
BOSLEY, Harold Augustus, 1907-75,
American; nonfiction CON
BOSLEY, Keith, 1937- , English;
fiction, poetry, translations,
juveniles CON VCP
BOSLOOPER, Thomas, 1923- ,
American; nonfiction CON
BOSMAN, Herman Charles, 1905-
51, South African; poetry, fic-
tion BU WA
BOSS, Judy, 1935- , American;
nonfiction CON
BOSS, Richard Woodruff, 1937- ,
Dutch-American; nonfiction
CON
BOSSDORF, Hermann, 1877-1921,
German; plays BU
BOSSERMAN, Charles Phillip,
1931- , American; nonfiction,

translations CON
BOSSHART, Jakob, 1862-1924,
Swiss; fiction BU CL
BOSSOM, Naomi, 1933- , American; nonfiction, juveniles CON
BOSSUET, Jacques-Bénigne, 1627-1704, French; nonfiction BU TH
BOSTICCO, Mary ('Isabelle Bey'), British; nonfiction CON
BOSTICK, William Allison, 1913- , American; nonfiction CON
'BOSTON, Charles K.' see GRUBER, Frank
BOSTON, Lucy Maria, 1892- , British; juveniles, plays, fiction CO CON DE KI
BOSTON, Robert, 1940- , American; fiction CON
BOSTON, Thomas, 1676-1732, Scots; nonfiction BU
BOSTROM, Christopher Jacob, 1797-1866, Swedish; nonfiction BU
BOSTWICK, Arthur Elmore, 1860-1942, American; nonfiction ENG
'BOSWELL' see GORDON, Giles A.
BOSWELL, Sir Alexander, 1775-1822, Scots; poetry BU
BOSWELL, Jackson Campbell, 1934- , American; nonfiction CON
BOSWELL, James, 1740-95, Scots; nonfiction, fiction, poetry BRI BU DA MAG PO VN
'BOSWORTH, Frank' see PAINE, Lauran B.
BOSWORTH, J. Allan, 1925- , American; juveniles CO
BOSWORTH, Patricia, 1933- , American; nonfiction CON
BOTE, Hermann, -1520?, German; nonfiction, poetry BU
BOTELHO, Abel Acácio de Almeida, 1856-1917, Portuguese; fiction BU
BOTELHO de OLIVEIRA, Manuel, 1636-1711, Brazilian; poetry BR BU
BOTELHO GOSALVEZ, Raúl, 1917- , Bolivian; fiction, nonfiction BR
BOTERO, Giovanni, 1543/44-1617, Italian; nonfiction BO BU

BOTEV, Hristo, 1847-76, Bulgarian; nonfiction, journalism BU TH
BOTEZ, Demostene, 1893- , Rumanian; poetry BU
BOTJER, George Francis, 1937- , American; nonfiction CON
BOTKIN, Benjamin Albert, 1901-75, American; nonfiction CON
BOTO, Eza see 'BETI, Mongo'
BOTTA, Anne Charlotte Lynch, 1815-91, American; poetry MYE
BOTTA, Carlo, 1766-1837, Italian; nonfiction BU
BOTTERILL, Calvin Bruce, 1947- , Canadian; nonfiction CON
BOTTING, Douglas Scott, 1934- , Anglo-American; juveniles, nonfiction CON
BOTTNER, Barbara, 1943- , American; juveniles CO CON WAR
BOTTO, Antonio Tomás, 1900-59, Portuguese; poetry CL
BOTTO, Jan see 'KRASKO, Ivan'
BOTTO, Ján, 1829-81, Slovak; poetry BU TH
'BOTTOME, Phyllis' (Phyllis Forbes-Dennis), 1884-1963, English; fiction CON DA MCC
BOTTOMLEY, Gordon, 1874-1948, English; poetry, plays BU DA PO VD
BOTTOMS, Anthony Edward, 1939- , British; nonfiction CON
BOTTOMS, Lawrence Wendell, 1908- , American; nonfiction CON
BOTTRALL, Ronald, 1906- , British; poetry, nonfiction CON DA SEY VCP WAK
BOTWINICK, Jack, 1923- , American; nonfiction CON
BOUCE, Paul Gabriel, 1936- , French; nonfiction CON
BOUCHARD, Lois Kalb, 1938- , American; juveniles WAR
'BOUCHER, Anthony' (William Anthony P. White; 'H. H. Holmes'), 1911-68, American; fiction, nonfiction, plays AS COW NI REI ST
BOUCHER, Jonathan, 1738-1804, American; poetry, nonfiction BA
BOUCHER, Wayne Irving, 1934- , American; nonfiction CON
BOUCHET, Guillaume, 1514-94,

French; nonfiction BU
BOUCHET, Jean, 1476-1557,
French; nonfiction BU
BOUCICAULT, Dion, 1820/22-90,
Irish; plays BR BU DA HO
MCG VD
BOUDEWIJNS, Katharina, 1520-
1603?, Dutch; poetry BU
BOUDON, Raymond, 1934- ,
French; nonfiction CON
BOUDREAU, Eugene Howard,
1934- , American; nonfic-
tion CON
BOUGHNER, Daniel Cliness, 1909-
74, American; nonfiction CON
BOUGHTON, James Murray,
1940- , American; nonfiction
CON
BOUGHTON, Willis Arnold, 1885-
1977, American; nonfiction,
fiction, poetry, juveniles
CON
BOUHELIER, Saint Georges de,
1876-1947, French; poetry,
plays TH
BOUILHET, Louis, 1829-69,
French; nonfiction, plays BU
TH
BOUISSAC, Paul Antoine, 1934- ,
French-Canadian; fiction, non-
fiction CON
BOULARAN, Jacques see 'DEVAL,
Jacques'
BOULETTE, Maria Teresa Ra-
mirez, 1939- , American;
nonfiction MAR
BOULLE, Pierre Francois, 1912- ,
French; fiction, juveniles AS
BU CO NI REI WA
BOULOGNE, Jean, 1942- , Ca-
nadian; nonfiction CON
'BOULT, S. Kye' see COCHRANE,
William E.
BOULTON, Jane, 1921- , Amer-
ican; fiction CON
BOULTON, Marjorie, 1924- ,
English; poetry, nonfiction,
fiction, plays CON
BOULWARE, Marcus Hanna,
1907- , American; nonfiction
CON SH
BOUMA, Donald Herbert, 1918- ,
American; nonfiction CON
BOUMA, Mary La Grand,
American; nonfiction CON
BOUNDS, Sydney J., 1920- ,
British; fiction NI
BOURAOUI, Hedi Andre, 1932- ,

Canadian; poetry, nonfiction,
fiction CON
BOURASSA, Joseph Napoléon Henri,
1868-1952, Canadian; journalism
BU
BOURBON, Nicolas the Elder,
1503-48?, French; poetry BU
BOURCHIER, John, Lord Berners,
1467-1532/33, English; transla-
tions, nonfiction BU DA
BOURDALOUE, Louis, 1632-1704,
French; nonfiction TH
BOURDET, Edouard, 1887-1945,
French; plays CL MCG TH
BOURDON, Sylvia Diane Eve,
1949- , German; nonfiction
CON
BOURET, Jean, 1914- , French;
nonfiction CON
BOURGES, Elémir, 1852-1925,
French; fiction BU CL TH
BOURGET, Paul, 1852-1935,
French; fiction, nonfiction,
plays, poetry BU CL MAG
TH
BOURGUIGNON, Erika Eichhorn,
1924- , Austrian-American;
nonfiction CON
BOURILLON, Henri see 'HAMP,
Pierre'
BOURJAILY, Monte Ferris, 1894-
1979, Lebanese-American;
journalism, nonfiction CON
BOURJAILY, Vance Nye, 1922- ,
American; fiction BR HE VCN
WA
BOURLIAGUET, Léonce, 1895-1965,
French; juveniles, nonfiction
CON DEM
BOURNE, Aleck William, 1886-
1974, British; nonfiction CON
BOURNE, Eulalia, American; non-
fiction CON
'BOURNE, George' see STURT,
George
'BOURNE, Lesley' see MARSHALL,
Evelyn
BOURNE, Lyle Eugene, Jr.,
1932- , American; nonfiction
CON
BOURNE, Miriam Anne Young,
1931- , American; juveniles
CO WAR
'BOURNE, Peter' see 'GRAEME,
Bruce'
BOURNE, Peter Geoffrey, 1939- ,
Anglo-American; nonfiction
CON

BOURNE, Randolph Silliman, 1886-
1918, American; nonfiction
AM BR BU PO
BOURNE, Vincent, 1695-1747, Eng-
lish; poetry DA
BOURNEUF, Alice E., , 1912-80,
American; nonfiction CON
BOURSAULT, Edme, 1638-1701,
French; plays, fiction BU
MCG TH
BOUSOÑO, Carlos, 1923- , Span-
ish; poetry, nonfiction BU
CL TH WA
BOUSQUET, Joë, 1897-1950,
French; poetry, nonfiction
CL
BOUSSENARD, Louis, 1847-1910,
French; fiction NI
BOUSTEAD, John Edmund, 1895-
1980, British; nonfiction CON
BOUTELLEAU, Jacques see 'CHAR-
DONNE, Jacques'
BOUTENS, Peter Cornelis, 1870-
1943, Dutch; poetry, plays
BU CL TH WAK
BOUTIER, Pierre, 15th century,
French; nonfiction BU
BOUTON, James Alan; 1939- ,
American; nonfiction CON
BOUVE, Edward Tracy, Amer-
ican; fiction NI
BOVA, Benjamin William, 1932- ,
American; fiction, juveniles
AS CO NI WAR
BOVASSO, Julie, 1930- , Amer-
ican; plays VCD
BOVEE, Courtland Lowell, 1944- ,
American; nonfiction CON
'BOVEE, Ruth' see PAINE, Lau-
ran B.
BOWDEN, Elbert Victor, 1924- ,
American; nonfiction CON
BOWDEN, Etta, American; fic-
tion NI
BOWDEN, Gregory Houston, 1948- ,
English; nonfiction CON
BOWDEN, Henry Warner, 1939- ,
American; nonfiction CON
BOWDEN, Jean ('Jocelyn Barry';
'Jennifer Bland'; 'Avon Cur-
ry'; 'Belinda Dell'), 1925- ,
Scots; nonfiction, fiction CON
'BOWDEN, Jim' see SPENCE,
William J. D.
BOWDEN, Joan Chase ('Joan
Chase Bacon'; 'Jane Godfrey';
'Charlotte Graham'; 'Kathryn
Kenny'), 1925- , British;

juveniles CON
BOWDEN, Phil, American; fic-
tion NI
BOWDITCH, James Lowell, 1939- ,
American; nonfiction CON
BOWDLE, Donald Nelson, 1935- ,
American; nonfiction CON
BOWDLER, Roger, 1934- , Brit-
ish; fiction CON
BOWDLER, Thomas, 1754-1825,
English; nonfiction BU
'BOWE, Kate' see TAYLOR, Mary A.
'BOWEN, Betty M.' see WEST,
Betty
BOWEN, Catherine Drinker, 1897-
1973, American; juveniles,
nonfiction CO CON
BOWEN, Elizabeth, 1899-1973,
Irish; fiction, nonfiction BU
CON DA HO MAG PO SEY VN
BOWEN, Ezra, 1927- , American;
nonfiction CON
BOWEN, Francis, 1811-90, Amer-
ican; nonfiction MY
BOWEN, Haskell L., 1929- ,
American; nonfiction CON
BOWEN, John, 1916- , British;
nonfiction CON
BOWEN, John Griffith ('Justin
Blake'), 1924- , British; fic-
tion, plays, juveniles NI VCD
VCN WA
BOWEN, Joshua David, 1930- ,
American; juveniles CO
'BOWEN, Marjorie' see 'SHEARING,
Joseph'
BOWEN, Peter, 1939- , Canadian;
nonfiction CON
BOWEN, Ralph Henry, 1919- ,
American; nonfiction CON
BOWEN, Robert O., 1920- , Amer-
ican; fiction, nonfiction VCN
BOWEN, Robert Sydney ('James
Robert Richard'), 1900-77,
American; journalism, juveniles
CO CON
BOWEN-JUDD, Sara see WOODS,
Sara H.
'BOWER, Barbara' see TODD, Bar-
bara E.
BOWER, Donald Edward ('Don Tow-
er'), 1920- , American; non-
fiction CON
BOWER, Eli Michael, 1917- ,
American; nonfiction CON
BOWER, Fay Louise, 1929- ,
American; nonfiction CON
BOWER, Julia Wells, 1903- ,

American; nonfiction CON
'BOWER, Keith' see BECKETT, Kenneth A.
BOWER, Muriel, 1921- , American; nonfiction CON
BOWER, Robert Turrell, 1919- , American; nonfiction CON
BOWER, Sharon Anthony, 1932- , American; nonfiction CON
BOWERING, George Harry, 1935- , Canadian; poetry, nonfiction, fiction, plays CR VCP
BOWERING, Marilyn Ruthe, 1949- , Canadian; poetry CON
BOWERS, Claude G., 1878-1958, American; nonfiction MAG
BOWERS, Edgar, 1924- , American; poetry BR VCP WA
BOWERS, John Waite, 1935- , American; nonfiction CON
BOWERS, Kenneth S., 1937- , American; nonfiction CON
BOWERS, Quentin David, 1938- , American; nonfiction CON
BOWERS, Ronald Lee, 1941- , American; nonfiction CON
BOWERS, Warner Fremont ('W. B. Fremont'; 'B. F. Warner'), 1906- , American; nonfiction CON
BOWERS, William, 1916- , American; film, plays CON
BOWERS, William Joseph, 1935- , American; nonfiction CON
BOWERSOCK, Glen Warren, 1936- , American; nonfiction CON
BOWES, Anne see La Bastille
'BOWIE, David' see JONES, David R.
BOWIE, Janetta Hamilton, 1907- , Scots; nonfiction, juveniles CON
BOWKER, Francis E., 1917- , American; nonfiction CON
BOWKER, Robin Marsland, 1920- , English; nonfiction CON
BOWKER, Rogers, 1848-1933, American; nonfiction ENG
BOWLBY, John, 1907- , English; nonfiction CON
BOWLER, Reginald Arthur, 1930- , Canadian; nonfiction CON
BOWLES, Chester Bliss, 1901- , American; nonfiction CON
BOWLES, Ella Shannon, 1886-1975, American; nonfiction CON

BOWLES, Frank Hamilton, 1907-75, American; nonfiction CON
BOWLES, Jane Sydney, 1918-73, American; fiction, plays BR CON SEY WA
BOWLES, Norma Louise, American; nonfiction CON
BOWLES, Paul Frederick, 1910- , American; fiction, translations BR KIB SEY VCN VN
BOWLES, William Lisle, 1762-1850, English; poetry, nonfiction BU DA PO VP
BOWLEY, Rex Lyon, 1925- , British; nonfiction CON
BOWMAN, Albert Hall, 1921- , American; nonfiction CON
BOWMAN, Bruce, 1938- , American; nonfiction CON
BOWMAN, Derek, 1931- , British; nonfiction, translations CON
BOWMAN, Herbert Eugene, 1917- , American; nonfiction CON
BOWMAN, James Cloyd, 1880-1961, American; fiction, nonfiction, juveniles CO CON
BOWMAN, John Stewart, 1931- , American; juveniles CO WAR
BOWMAN, Karl M., 1888-1973, American; nonfiction CON
BOWMAN, Kathleen Gill, 1942- , American; nonfiction CON
BOWMAN, Ned Alan, 1932- , American; translations, nonfiction CON
BOWMAN, Raymond Albert, 1903-79, American; nonfiction CON
BOWMAN, Robert T., 1910- , Canadian; nonfiction CON
BOWMAN, Ward Simon, Jr., 1911- , American; nonfiction CON
BOWMER, Angus Livingston, 1904-79, American; nonfiction CON
BOWRING, Sir John, 1792-1872, English; nonfiction, translations BU
BOWSER, Eileen, 1928- , American; nonfiction CON
BOWSER, Frederick Park, 1937- , American; nonfiction CON
BOWSKILL, Derek, 1928- , British; nonfiction, plays CON
BOWYER, Charles, 1926- , British; nonfiction CON
'BOX, Edgar' see VIDAL, Gore
BOXER, Charles Ralph, 1904- , American; nonfiction, trans-

lations CON
BOXERMAN, David Samuel,
1945- , American; nonfic-
tion CON
'BOY' see ZELENSKI, Tadeusz
BOY, Angelo Victor, 1929- ,
American; nonfiction CON
BOYAJIAN, Cecile see STARR,
Cecile
BOYCE, Chris, 1943- , Scots;
fiction NI
BOYCE, David George, 1942- ,
Irish; nonfiction CON
BOYCE, George Arthur, 1898- ,
American; juveniles, nonfic-
tion CO CON
BOYCE, Joseph Christopher,
1943- , Scots; fiction CON
BOYCE, Joseph Nelson, 1937- ,
American; journalism CON
BOYCE, Richard Fyfe, 1896- ,
American; nonfiction CON
BOYD, Andrew Kennedy Hutch-
ison, 1825-99, Scots; nonfic-
tion BU
'BOYD, Ann S.' see SCHOON-
MAKER, Ann
BOYD, Beverly Mary, 1925- ,
American; nonfiction, poetry
CON
BOYD, Elizabeth, 1904?-74,
American; nonfiction CON
'BOYD, Frank' see KANE, Frank
BOYD, Jack, 1932- , American;
nonfiction CON
BOYD, James, 1888-1944, Amer-
ican; fiction, poetry, plays
BA BR MAG VN
BOYD, James Sterling, 1917- ,
American; nonfiction CON
'BOYD, John' (Boyd B. Up-
church), 1912/19- , Irish-
American; plays, fiction AS
COW HO NI
BOYD, Julian Parks, 1903-80,
American; nonfiction CON
BOYD, Lorenz, American; ju-
veniles WAR
BOYD, Mark Alexander, 1563-
1601, Scots; poetry DA
BOYD, Martin à Beckett ('Martin
Mills'), 1893-1972, Aus-
tralian; fiction, poetry, non-
fiction, juveniles BU DA VN
BOYD, Mildred Worthy, 1921- ,
American; juveniles WAR
BOYD, Myron Fenton, 1909- ,
American; nonfiction CON

BOYD, Robert H., 1912- , Amer-
ican; nonfiction CON
BOYD, Robert Louis Fullarton,
1922- , Scots; nonfiction
CON
BOYD, Shylah ('Frances Whyatt'),
1945- , American; poetry,
fiction CON
BOYD, Sue Abbott, American;
poetry CON
BOYD, Waldo T. ('Robert Parker';
'Ted Andersen'), 1918- , Amer-
ican; juveniles CO WAR
BOYD, William, 1885- , Scots-
Canadian; nonfiction CON
BOYD, William Harland, 1912- ,
American; nonfiction CON
BOYD, Zachary, 1585-1653, Scots;
nonfiction, poetry BU DA
BOYE, Karin Maria, 1900-41,
Swedish; poetry, fiction BU
CL SEY TH WAK
BOYER, Brian D., 1939- , Amer-
ican; nonfiction CON
BOYER, Bruce Hatton ('B. H.
Tate'), 1946- , American;
fiction CON
BOYER, Carl Benjamin, 1906-76,
American; nonfiction CON
BOYER, L'Abbé Claude, 1618?-98,
French; plays BU
BOYER, Dwight, 1912- , Amer-
ican; nonfiction CON
BOYER, Elizabeth Mary, 1913- ,
American; fiction CON
BOYER, John William, 1946- ,
American; nonfiction CON
BOYER, Paul Samuel, 1935- ,
American; nonfiction CON
BOYER, Richard Lewis, 1943- ,
American; fiction CON
BOYER, Richard O., 1903-73,
American; nonfiction CON
BOYER, Robert Ernst, 1929- ,
American; nonfiction, juveniles
CO CON
BOYERS, Robert, 1942- , Amer-
ican; nonfiction CON
BOYESEN, Hjalmar Hjorth, 1848-
95, American; fiction, plays,
poetry, nonfiction, juveniles
VN
BOYL VIVES de CANESMA, Carlos,
1577-1618, Spanish; plays BU
BOYLAN, Brian Richard, 1936- ,
American; nonfiction, plays,
film CON
BOYLAN, Leona Davis, 1910- ,

American; nonfiction CON
BOYLE, Andrew Philip More,
1919- , Scots; nonfiction
CON
BOYLE, Ann Peters, 1916- ,
American; juveniles CO
BOYLE, Hal, 1911-74, American;
journalism CON
BOYLE, Jack, American; fic-
tion, plays REI
BOYLE, John Andrew, 1916-79,
English; nonfiction, transla-
tions CON
BOYLE, John Hunter, 1930- ,
American; nonfiction CON
BOYLE, Kay, 1903- , American;
fiction, poetry, juveniles BR
BU RO SEY VCN VCP VN
'BOYLE, Mark' see KIENZLE,
William X.
BOYLE, Mary, 1882?-1975, Amer-
ican; nonfiction CON
BOYLE, Patrick, 1905- , Irish;
fiction HO
BOYLE, Hon. Robert, 1627-91,
Anglo-Irish; nonfiction BU
BOYLE, Roger, 1621-79, Anglo-
Irish; plays, fiction BU VN
BOYLE, Stanley Eugene, 1927- ,
American; nonfiction CON
BOYLE, William, 1853-1923,
Irish; plays, poetry HO MCG
BOYLEN, Margaret Currier, 1921-
67, American; fiction CON
'BOYLESVE, René' (René Tardi-
veau), 1867-1926, French; fic-
tion BU CL
BOYLSTON, Helen Dore, 1895- ,
American; fiction, juveniles
CO CON KI
BOYNTON, Searles Roland, 1926- ,
American; nonfiction CON
BOYSEN, Johann Wilhelm ('Boysen
van Nienkarken'), 1834-70,
German; poetry BU
BOYSON, Emil, 1897- , Nor-
wegian; poetry, fiction CL
BOYUM, Keith Orel, 1945- ,
American; nonfiction CON
BOZE, Arthur Phillip, 1945- ,
American; poetry CON
'BOZEMAN, Beverley' see FUL-
LER, Beverley
BOZEMAN, Theodore Dwight,
1942- , American; nonfiction
CON
BOZIC, Mirko, 1919- , Croatian;
fiction, plays, BU TH

BOZVELI, Neofit, 1785-1848, Bul-
garian; nonfiction BU
BRAAK, Ivo, 1906- , German;
plays BU
BRAAK, Menno Ter, 1902-40,
Dutch; nonfiction, fiction BU
CL TH
BRAATEN, Oskar Alexander, 1881-
1939, Norwegian; fiction, plays
BU CL
BRABANT, Jan, Duke of, 1254?-
94, German; poetry BU
BRABB, George Jacob, 1925- ,
American; nonfiction CON
BRABEC, Barbara, 1937- , Amer-
ican; nonfiction CON
BRACCIOLINI, Francesco, 1566-
1645, Italian; poetry, plays
BU
BRACCIOLINI-POGGIO, Gian Fran-
cesco 1380-1459, Italian; non-
fiction BO BU
BRACCO, Roberto, 1862-1943,
Italian; fiction, plays, poetry,
journalism BO BU CL MCG
BRACE, Edward Roy, 1936- ,
American; nonfiction CON
BRACE, Geoffrey Arthur, 1930- ,
British; nonfiction CON
BRACE, Gerald Warner, 1901-78,
American; nonfiction, fiction
CON
BRACE, Richard Munthe, 1915-77,
American; nonfiction CON
BRACEGIRDLE, Brian, 1933- ,
British; nonfiction CON
BRACEGIRDLE, Cyril, 1920- ,
English; nonfiction CON
BRACEWELL, Ronald Newbold,
1921- , Australian; nonfiction
CON
BRACEY, John H., 1941- , Amer-
ican; nonfiction SH
BRACHER, Karl Dietrich, 1922- ,
German; nonfiction CON
BRACK, O. M., Jr., 1938- ,
American; nonfiction CON
BRACKENRIDGE, Hugh Henry,
1748-1816, American; poetry,
plays, journalism BR BU
MAG PO VN
BRACKENRIDGE, Robert Douglas,
1932- , American; nonfiction
CON
BRACKETT, Leigh D., 1915-78,
American; fiction, film AS
CON COW NI
BRACY, William, 1915- , Amer-

ican; nonfiction CON
BRADBURY, Bianca, 1908- ,
American; poetry, juveniles,
fiction CO DEM
'BRADBURY, E. P.' see MOOR-
COCK, Michael
BRADBURY, Malcolm, 1932- ,
English; fiction, plays, po-
etry BOR VCN WAK
BRADBURY, Peggy, 1930- ,
American; nonfiction, juven-
iles CON
BRADBURY, Ray Douglas, 1920- ,
American; fiction, plays, ju-
veniles, nonfiction AS BR
BU CO COW HE NI REI VCN
BRADDOCK, Richard Reed, 1920-
74, American; nonfiction CON
BRADDON, Mary Elizabeth ('Bab-
bington White'), 1837-1915,
English; fiction, plays BU
REI ST VN
BRADDON, Russell, 1921- , Aus-
tralian; fiction, nonfiction NI
BRADDY, Haldeen, 1908-80, Amer-
ican; nonfiction CON
BRADFIELD, Roger, 1924- ,
American; juveniles WAR
BRADFORD, Barbara Taylor,
1933- , British; journalism,
nonfiction CON
BRADFORD, Benjamin, 1925- ,
American; plays CON
BRADFORD, Ernie Dusgate,
1922- , British; nonfiction
CON
BRADFORD, Ernle, 1922- ,
English; nonfiction WA
BRADFORD, Gamaliel, 1863-1932,
American; nonfiction BU MAG
BRADFORD, J. S., English;
fiction NI
BRADFORD, Melvin Eustace,
1934- , American; nonfiction
CON
BRADFORD, Peter Amory, 1942- ,
American; nonfiction CON
BRADFORD, Reed Howard, 1912- ,
American; nonfiction CON
BRADFORD, Richard Headlee,
1938- , American; nonfiction
CON
BRADFORD, Richard Roark,
1932- , American; fiction
CON
BRADFORD, Roark Whitney Wick-
liffe, 1896-1948, American;
fiction, plays BA VN

BRADFORD, Robert Whitmore,
1918- , American; nonfiction
CON
BRADFORD, Walter, American;
nonfiction SH
'BRADFORD, Will', see PAINE,
Lauran B.
BRADFORD, William, 1590?-1657,
American; nonfiction BR BU
MAG PO
BRADLEE, Benjamin Crowninshield,
1921- , American; nonfiction
CON
BRADLEY, Andrew Cecil, 1851-
1935, English; nonfiction DA
BRADLEY, Bert Edward, 1926- ,
American; nonfiction CON
'BRADLEY, Concho' see PAINE,
Lauran B.
BRADLEY, Edward ('Cuthbert Bede'),
1827-89, English; fiction BU
BRADLEY, Francis Herbert, 1846-
1924, English; nonfiction BU
BRADLEY, Hassell, 1930- , Amer-
ican; nonfiction CON
BRADLEY, Ian Campbell, 1950- ,
British; nonfiction CON
BRADLEY, Katherine H. see
'FIELD, Michael'
BRADLEY, Marion Zimmer, 1930- ,
American; fiction, nonfiction,
translations AS CON COW NI
'BRADLEY, Michael' see BLUM-
BERG, Gary
BRADLEY, Omar Nelson, 1893-
1981, American; nonfiction
CON
BRADLEY, Ritamary, 1916- ,
American; nonfiction CON
BRADLEY, Sculley, 1897- , Amer-
ican; nonfiction CON
BRADLEY, Virginia, 1912- , Amer-
ican; nonfiction, juveniles CO
CON
BRADLEY, William, 1934- , Amer-
ican; poetry, nonfiction CON
BRADLEY, William Aspenwall,
1878-1939, American; nonfic-
tion, fiction RO
BRADLEY, William Warren, 1943- ,
American; nonfiction CON
BRADNER, Enos, 1892- , Amer-
ican; nonfiction CON
BRADSHAW, Brendan, 1937- ,
Irish; nonfiction CON
BRADSHAW, George, 1909?-73,
American; nonfiction CON
BRADSHAW, Gillian Marucha,

1956- , American; fiction CON
BRADSHAW, William R.., 1851- ,
American; fiction NI
BRADSTREET, Anne Dudley, 1612-
72, American; poetry AM BR
BU PO VP
BRADT, Acken Gordon, 1896- ,
American; nonfiction CON
BRADWARDINE, Thomas, 1290-
1349, English; nonfiction BU
'BRADWELL, James' see KENT,
Arthur W. C.
BRADY, Darlene Ann, 1951- ,
American; nonfiction CON
BRADY, Esther (Wood), 1905- ,
American; juveniles CON
BRADY, Frank, 1934- , Amer-
ican; nonfiction CON
BRADY, George Stuart, 1887-1977,
American; nonfiction, fiction
CON
BRADY, Irene, 1943- , American;
juveniles CO
BRADY, James Winston, 1928- ,
American; nonfiction CON
BRADY, John, 1942- , American;
nonfiction CON
BRADY, Leo, 1917- , American;
plays CON
BRADY, Maxine L., 1941- ,
American; nonfiction, juven-
iles CON WAR
BRADY, Michael, 1928- , Amer-
ican; fiction CON
'BRADY, Nicholas' see 'JORDAN,
Leonard'
'BRADY, Peter' see DANIELS,
Norman
BRADY, Sally Ryder, 1939- ,
American; fiction CON
BRÄKER, Ulrich, 1735-98, Swiss;
nonfiction BU TH
BRAESCU, Gheorghe, 1871-1949,
Rumanian; fiction BU
BRAESTRUP, Peter, 1929- ,
American; nonfiction CON
BRAGA, Rubem, 1913- , Brazil-
ian; nonfiction BR
BRAGA, Téofilo, 1843-1924, Por-
tuguese; poetry BU
BRAGDON, Clifford Richardson,
1940- , American; nonfic-
tion CON
BRAGDON, Elspeth MacDuffie
('Elspeth'), 1897- , Amer-
ican; juveniles CO
BRAGDON, Henry Wilkinson, 1906-
80, American; nonfiction CON

BRAGDON, Lillian Jacot, American;
juveniles, nonfiction CO CON
BRAGG, Mabel Caroline ('Watty
Piper'), 1870-1945, American;
juveniles CO DEM
BRAGG, Melvyn, 1939- , British;
fiction, plays CON VCN WAK
'BRAHMAN' (Chandar Bhan), 1574-
1662, Indo-Persian; poetry,
translations PRU
'BRAHMS, Caryl' (Doris Caroline
Abrahams), 1901- , English;
fiction, plays, radio, film,
tv, nonfiction REI
BRAHS, Stuart John, 1940- ,
American; nonfiction CON
BRAHTZ, John Frederick Peet,
1918- , American; nonfiction
CON
BRAIDER, Donald, 1923-76, Amer-
ican; fiction, nonfiction CON
BRAIMAH, Joseph Adam, 1916- ,
American; nonfiction CON
BRAIMAN, Susan ('Susan Gettle-
man'), 1943- , American;
nonfiction CON
BRAIN, George Bernard, 1920- ,
American; nonfiction CON
BRAIN, Robert, 1933- , Austrian;
nonfiction CON
BRAINARD, Joe, 1942- , Amer-
ican; nonfiction CON
BRAINE, John, 1922- , English;
fiction, nonfiction BU DA
MAG MCC PO VCN VN WA
BRAINERD, Charles Jon, 1944- ,
American; nonfiction CON
BRAINERD, John Whiting ('Jay
Bee'), 1918- , American;
nonfiction, poetry CON
BRAININ, Reuben, 1862-1939/40,
Hebrew; nonfiction, fiction BU
TH
BRAITHWAITE, Althea ('Althea'),
1940- , British; juveniles
CO CON
BRAITHWAITE, Max, 1911- ,
Canadian; nonfiction, juveniles
CON
BRAITHWAITE, Richard see BRATH-
WAITE, Richard
BRAKE, Mike, 1936- , British;
nonfiction CON
BRAKHAGE, Stan, 1933- , Amer-
ican; nonfiction CON
'BRALLEPUT, Karel' see CAR-
MIGGELT, Simon J.
BRALVER, Eleanor, 1913- ,

American; nonfiction CON
BRALY, Malcolm, 1925-80, American; film, nonfiction CON
BRAM, Elizabeth, 1948- , American; juveniles CON
'BRAMAH, Ernest' (Ernest Bramah Smith), 1868-1942, English; fiction, nonfiction NI REI ST
'BRAMBEUS, Baron' see SENKOVSKY, Osip I.
BRAMBLE, Forbes, 1939- , British; plays, fiction CON
BRAMMELL, Paris Roy, 1900- , American; nonfiction CON
BRAMMER, William, 1930?-78, American; nonfiction CON
BRAMS, Steven John, 1940- , American; nonfiction CON
BRAMSTON, James, 1694?-1744, English; poetry BU
'BRAMWELL, Charlotte' see KIMBRO, John M.
BRAMWELL, Dana G. 1948- , American; plays CON
BRANCATI, Vitaliano, 1907-54, Italian; fiction, plays BO BU CL MCG TH WA
BRANCATO, Robin Fidler, 1936- , American; fiction CO CON
BRANCH, Melville Campbell, 1913- , American; nonfiction CON
BRANCH, Pamela Jean, 1920-67, English; fiction ST
BRANCH, William Blackwell, 1927/29- , American; plays, film, tv CON SH
BRAND, Christianna Milne ('Mary Anne Ashe'; 'Annabel Jones'; 'Mary Roland'; 'China Thompson'; Mary Christianna Lewis), 1909- , British; fiction, plays, juveniles, nonfiction CON KI REI ST
BRAND, Dollar, 1935?- , South African; poetry HER
BRAND, Eugene Louis, 1931- , American; nonfiction CON
BRAND, Mary Christianna see BRAND, Christianna M.
'BRAND, Max' (Frederick Faust; 'Frank Austin'; 'George Owen Baxter'; 'Walter C. Butler'; 'George Challis'; 'Evan Evans'; 'John Frederick'; 'Frederick Frost'; 'David Manning'; 'Peter Henry Morland'; 'Nicholas Sil-

ver'), 1892-1944, American; fiction, plays, poetry, nonfiction REI ST
BRAND, Millen, 1906-80, American; fiction, poetry, film CON
BRAND, Sandra, 1918- , Austrian-American; nonfiction CON
BRAND, Stewart, 1938- , American; nonfiction CON
'BRAND, Susan' see ROPER, Susan B.
BRANDABUR, Edward, 1930- , American; nonfiction CON
BRANDÃO, Antonio, 1584-1637, Portuguese; nonfiction BU
BRANDÃO, Raúl Germano, 1867-1930, Portuguese, fiction, plays BU CL TH
BRANDEL, Arthur Meyer, 1913?-80, American; nonfiction CON
BRANDELL, Erik Gunnar, 1916- , Swedish; nonfiction CON
BRANDEN, Victoria Fremlin ('Joanne Stylla'), Canadian; fiction, nonfiction, plays, juveniles CON
BRANDENBERG, Aliki L. see 'ALIKI'
BRANDENBERG, Franz, 1932- , Swiss-American; juveniles CO
BRANDER, Michael, 1924- , American; nonfiction CON
BRANDES, Carl Edvard Cohen, 1847-1931, Danish; plays, fiction, nonfiction BU TH
BRANDES, Georg Morris Cohen, 1842-1927, Danish; nonfiction BU CL TH
BRANDES, Norman Scott, 1923- , American; nonfiction CON
BRANDES, Paul Dickerson, 1919- , American; nonfiction CON
BRANDES, Raymond S., 1924- , American; nonfiction MAR
BRANDHORST, Carl Theodore, 1898- , American; juveniles CO
BRANDI, John, 1943- , American; poetry, fiction, nonfiction CON VCP
BRANDNER, Gary, 1933- , American; fiction, nonfiction CON
BRANDON, Brumsic, Jr. 1927- , American; juveniles CO CON
'BRANDON, Curt' see BISHOP, Curtis K.
BRANDON, Donald Wayne, 1926- ,

American; nonfiction CON
BRANDON, Dorothy, 1899?-1977,
American; journalism, non-
fiction CON
'BRANDON, Frank' see BULMER,
Kenneth
BRANDON, James Rodger, 1927- ,
American; nonfiction, trans-
lations CON
BRANDON, John Gordon, 1879-
1941, Australian; fiction,
plays REI
BRANDON, Oscar Henry, 1916- ,
American; nonfiction CON
BRANDON, Samuel George Fred-
erick, 1907-71, British; non-
fiction CON
BRANDON, William, 1914- ,
American; nonfiction, trans-
lations CON
BRANDON-COX, Hugh, 1917- ,
British; nonfiction CON
BRANDRETH, Gyles, 1948- ,
English; juveniles, nonfiction
CON
BRANDT, Adolf see 'STILLFRIED,
Felix'
BRANDT, Anthony, 1936- , Amer-
ican; nonfiction, poetry CON
BRANDT, Geeraerdt, 1626-85,
Dutch; nonfiction, poetry,
plays BU
BRANDT, Jane Lewis ('Lange Lew-
is'), 1915- , American; fic-
tion CON
BRANDT, Jorgen Gustava, 1929- ,
Danish; poetry, nonfiction, fic-
tion BU CL
BRANDT, Lucile (Long), 1900- ,
American; nonfiction, poetry
CON
BRANDT, Nathan Henry Jr.,
1929- , American; nonfic-
tion CON
'BRANDT, Tom' see DEWEY,
Thomas B.
BRANDT, Willy, 1913- , German;
nonfiction CON
BRANDTS, Robert Percival,
1930- , American; poetry,
nonfiction CON
BRANDYS, Kazimierz, 1916- ,
Polish; fiction, plays, non-
fiction BU CL
BRANDYS, Marian, 1912- , Ger-
man; nonfiction, juveniles
CON
BRANFIELD, John Charles,

1931- , English; nonfiction,
juveniles CO CON WAR
BRANIN, Manlif Lelyn, 1901- ,
American; nonfiction CON
BRANLEY, Franlyn Mansfield,
1915- , American; juveniles
CO
BRANN, Eva Toni Helene, 1929- ,
German-American; nonfiction
CON
BRANNER, Hans Christian, 1903-
66, Danish; fiction, plays BU
CL CON TH WA
BRANNER, Robert, 1927-73, Amer-
ican; nonfiction CON
BRANNIGAN, William, 1936- ,
American; nonfiction CON
BRANSCUM, Robbie, 1937- ,
American; juveniles CO CON
BRANSFORD, Kent Jackson, 1953- ,
American; nonfiction CON
BRANSON, David, 1909- , Eng-
lish; nonfiction CON
BRANSON, Henry Clay, 1924- ,
American; fiction REI ST
BRANSON, Margaret Stimmann,
1922- , American; nonfiction
CON
BRANSTON, Ronald Victor Brian,
1914- , English; nonfiction
CON
BRANT, Irving Newton, 1885-1976,
American; journalism, nonfic-
tion CON PAL
BRANT, Sebastian, 1457/58-1521,
German; fiction, poetry BU
TH
BRANTÔME, Pierre de Bourdeilles
de, 1540?-1614, French; non-
fiction BU TH
BRANZBURG, Paul Marshal, 1941- ,
American; journalism CON
BRASCH, Charles Orwell, 1909-73,
New Zealander; poetry BU
DA WAK
BRASCH, Ila Wales, 1945- , Amer-
ican; nonfiction CON
BRASCH, Walter Milton, 1945- ,
American; plays CON
BRASCHI, Wilfredo, 1918- ,
Puerto Rican; journalism, fic-
tion HIL
BRASH, Margaret M. see 'KEN-
DALL, John'
BRASHER, Nell, 1912- , Amer-
ican; nonfiction, fiction CON
BRASHER, Thomas Lowber, 1912- ,
American; nonfiction CON

BRASHLER, William, 1947- ,
American; nonfiction CON
BRASIER, Virginia, 1910- ,
American; poetry CON
BRASILLACH, Robert, 1909-45,
French; fiction, nonfiction
CL TH
BRATESCU-VOINESTI, Ion Alex-
andru, 1868-1946, Rumanian;
fiction BU
BRATHWAITE, Errol Freeman,
1924- , New Zealander; fic-
tion, plays CON VCN
BRATHWAITE, L. Edward, 1930- ,
Barbadian; poetry, plays, non-
fiction BU VCP VP WAK
BRATHWAITE, Richard (Braith-
waite), 1588?-1673, English;
nonfiction, poetry BU
BRATNY, Roman, 1921- , Polish;
fiction CL
BRATT, Elmer Clark, 1901-70,
American; nonfiction CON
BRATTER, Herbert Max, 1900-
76, American; nonfiction
CON
BRATTON, Helen, 1899- , Amer-
ican; juveniles CO
BRATTSTROM, Bayard Holmes,
1929- , American; poetry,
nonfiction CON
BRAU, Salvador, 1842-1912,
Puerto Rican; poetry, jour-
nalism, fiction, plays HIL
BRAUDE, Michael, 1936- , Amer-
ican; juveniles CO
BRAUDEL, Fernand Paul, 1902- ,
French; nonfiction CON WAK
BRAUDES, Avraham, 1907- ,
Polish; poetry BU
BRAUDES, Reuben Asher, 1851-
1902, Hebrew; fiction BU
BRAUDY, Susan Orr, 1941- ,
American; nonfiction CON
BRAUER, Carl Malcolm, 1946- ,
American; nonfiction CON
BRAULT, Jacques, 1933- ,
Canadian; poetry, fiction BU
BRAUN, Arthur, 1876-1976, Amer-
ican; journalism CON
BRAUN, Eric, 1921- , British;
nonfiction CON
BRAUN, Lev, 1913- , Czech-
American; nonfiction CON
BRAUN, Lillian Jackson, Amer-
ican; fiction REI
BRAUN, Sidney David, 1912- ,
American; nonfiction CON

BRAUND, Harold (Hal), 1913- ,
Australian; nonfiction CON
BRAUNTHAL, Alfred, 1898?-1980,
Austrian-American; journalism
CON
BRAUTIGAN, Richard Gary, 1935- ,
American; fiction, poetry BR
CON HE NI VCN VCP WAK
BRAVERMAN, Harry, 1920-76,
American; nonfiction CON
BRAVERMAN, Kate, 1950- ,
American; poetry, fiction
CON
BRAVMANN, Rene A., 1939- ,
Franco-American; nonfiction
CON
BRAVO-ELIZONDO, Pedro, 1931- ,
American; nonfiction MAR
BRAWLEY, Benjamin Griffith,
1882-1939, American; poetry,
fiction, nonfiction BA
BRAWLEY, Ernest, 1937- , Amer-
ican; fiction CON
BRAWLEY, Paul Leroy, 1942- ,
American; nonfiction CON
BRAWNE, Michael, 1925- , Amer-
ican; nonfiction CON
BRAXATORIS, Ondrej see 'SLAD-
KOVIC, Andrej
BRAY, Anna Eliza Kempe, 1790-
1883, English; fiction, juven-
iles BU
BRAY, John Francis, 19th century,
English; fiction NI
BRAY, John Jefferson, 1912- ,
Australian; nonfiction CON
BRAY, Thomas, 1656-1730, Eng-
lish; nonfiction ENG
BRAY, Virginia Elizabeth Nuckolls,
1895?-1979, American; non-
fiction CON
BRAYMAN, Harold, 1900- , Amer-
ican; nonfiction CON
BRAYMER, Marjorie Elizabeth,
1911- , American; juveniles
CO
BRAZELL, Karen, 1938- , Amer-
ican; translations, nonfiction
CON
BRAZELTON, Thomas Berry,
1918- , American; nonfiction
CON
BRAZIER, Arthur M., American;
nonfiction SH
BRAZIL, Angelo, 1869-1947, Brit-
ish; juveniles, plays KI
BRAZILL, William J. Jr., 1935- ,
American; nonfiction CON

'BRAZOS, Waco' see JENNINGS,
Michael
BREALEY, Richard A., 1936- ,
English; nonfiction CON
BREAN, Herbert, 1907/08-73,
American; fiction, journalism
CON REI ST WA
BREARS, Peter Charles David,
1944- , American; nonfiction
CON
BREASTED, Charles, 1898?-1980,
American; journalism, nonfic-
tion CON
BREAULT, William, 1926- ,
American; nonfiction CON
BREBEUF, Georges de, 1616?-
61, French; poetry BU
BREBNER, Winston, 1924?- ,
American; fiction NI
BRECHER, Charles Martin, 1945- ,
American; nonfiction CON
BRECHER, Jeremy, 1946- ,
American; nonfiction CON
BRECHT, Arnold, 1884-1977,
German-American; nonfiction
CON
BRECHT, Bertolt, 1898-1956, Ger-
man; plays, poetry, fiction
BU CL MAG MCG SEY TH
BRECHT, Edith, 1895-1975, Amer-
ican; juveniles CO
BRECKLER, Rosemary ('Rosemary
Winters'), 1920- , American;
nonfiction, plays CON
'BREDA, Tjalmar' see DE JONG,
David Cornel
BREDAHL, Christian Hviid, 1784-
1860, Danish; poetry BU
BREDEL, Willi, 1901-64, German;
fiction BU
BREDEMEIER, Mary Elizabeth,
1924- , American; nonfiction
CON
BREDERO, Gerbrand Adriaensz,
1585-1618, Dutch; poetry,
plays BU TH
BREDVOLD, Louis Igantius 1888-
1977, American; nonfiction
CON
BREE, Germaine, 1907- , Amer-
ican; nonfiction WA
BREEN, Dana see BIRKSTED-
BREEN, Dana
BREEN, Jon L., 1943- , Amer-
ican; fiction ST
BREEN, Joseph John, 1942- ,
American; nonfiction CON
BREEN, Timothy Hall, 1942- ,

American; nonfiction CON
BREESE, Gerald Williams, 1912- ,
American; nonfiction CON
BREGENDAHL, Marie, 1867-1940,
Danish; fiction BU TH
BREGER, Louis, 1935- , Amer-
ican; nonfiction CON
BREGGIN, Peter Roger, 1936- ,
American; fiction, nonfiction
CON NI
BREGMAN, Jacob Israel, 1923- ,
American; nonfiction CON
BREHM, Bruno, 1892- , Austrian;
fiction BU
BREHM, Shirley Alice, 1926- ,
American; nonfiction CON
BREINBURG, Petronella ('Bella
Ashey'; 'Mary Totham'), 1927- ,
English; juveniles, plays CO
CON
BREINES, Paul, 1941- , Amer-
ican; nonfiction CON
BREIOFJORO, Sigurdur Eiríksson,
1798-1846, Icelander; poetry
BU
BREISKY, William John, 1928- ,
American; juveniles, nonfiction
CO CON
BREIT, Harvey, 1909-68, Amer-
ican; poetry, plays, fiction,
journalism WA
BREIT, Marquita Elaine, 1942- ,
American; nonfiction CON
BREITBART, Vicki, 1942- ,
American; nonfiction CON
BREITINGER, Johann Jakob, 1701-
76, Swiss; nonfiction BU TH
BREITMAN, George, 1916- ,
American; nonfiction CON
BREITNER, I. Emery, 1929- ,
Hungarian-American; nonfiction
CON
BREKKE, Paal, 1923- , Nor-
wegian; poetry, fiction, non-
fiction CL
BREMER, Claus, 1924- , German;
poetry, translations BU
BREMER, Francis John, 1947- ,
American; nonfiction CON
BREMER, Frederika, 1801-65,
Swedish; fiction BU TH
BREMOND, Henri, 1865-1933,
French; nonfiction BU CL TH
BREMSER, Ray, 1934- , Amer-
ican; poetry VCP
BREMYER, Jayne Dickey ('Lee
Dickey'), 1924- , American;
nonfiction CON

BRENDEL, Otto Johannes, 1901-
73, German-American; non-
fiction CON
BRENDER à BRANDIS, Gerrit,
1751-1802, Dutch; poetry,
plays BU
BRENDON, Piers George, 1940- ,
American; nonfiction CON
'BRENNAN, Christopher' see
KININMOUTH, Christopher
BRENNAN, Christopher John,
1870-1932, Australian; poetry
BU DA VP WA
BRENNAN, Dennis, American;
juveniles WAR
BRENNAN, Donald George, 1926-
80, American; nonfiction
CON
BRENNAN, James, 1944- , Irish;
fiction HO
BRENNAN, John N. H. see 'WEL-
COME, John'
BRENNAN, Joseph Lomas ('Steve
Lomas'), 1903- , American;
juveniles CO
BRENNAN, Joseph Payne, 1918- ,
American; poetry, fiction ST
BRENNAN, Maeve, 1917- , Irish-
American; fiction CON
BRENNAN, Nicholas, English;
juveniles WAR
BRENNAN, Richard Oliver, 1916- ,
American; nonfiction CON
'BRENNAN, Tim' see CONROY,
Jack W.
'BRENNAN, Will' see PAINE,
Lauran B.
BRENNER, Anita, 1905-74, Amer-
ican; journalism, translations,
juveniles CON
BRENNER, Barbara Johnes, 1925- ,
American; juveniles CO DEM
BRENNER, Erma, 1911- , Amer-
ican; nonfiction CON
BRENNER, Fred, 1920- , Amer-
ican; juveniles DEM
'BRENNER, Isabel' see SCHUCH-
MAN, Joan
BRENNER, Joseph (Yoseph) Hay-
yim, 1881-1921, Hebrew; fic-
tion BU LA TH
BRENNER, Marie, 1949- , Amer-
ican; nonfiction CON
BRENNER, Sofia Elisabet Weber,
1659-1730, Swedish; poetry
BU
BRENNER, Summer, 1945- ,
American; poetry CON

BRENNER, Yoseph Chaim see
BRENNER, Joseph H.
BRENNI, Vito Joseph 1923- ,
American; nonfiction CON
BRENT, Peter Ludwig see 'PETERS,
Ludovic'
BRENT, Stuart, American; juveniles,
nonfiction CO CON
'BRENT of BIN BIN' (Miles Frank-
lin), Australian; fiction BU
BRENTANO, Clemens, 1778-1842,
German; poetry, fiction, plays
BU TH
BRENT-DYER, Elinor M., 1895-
1969, British; juveniles, fic-
tion CON KI
BRENTON, Howard, 1942- , Brit-
ish; poetry, plays, tv CON VCD
BRERI see BLEHERIS
BRESKY, Dushan, Canadian; non-
fiction CON
BRESLAU, Alan Jeffry, 1926- ,
American; nonfiction CON
BRESLAUER, Samuel Daniel,
1942- , American; nonfiction
CON
BRESLIN, Catherine, 1936- ,
American; nonfiction, fiction
CON
BRESLIN, Herbert H., 1924- ,
American; nonfiction CON
BRESLIN, James, 1930- , Amer-
ican; journalism, fiction, non-
fiction CON
BRESSETT, Kenneth Edward,
1928- , American; nonfiction
CON
BRESSLER, Leo Albert, 1911- ,
American; nonfiction CON
BRESSLER, Marion Ann, 1921- ,
American; nonfiction CON
BRETEL, Jacques, fl. 1285,
French; poetry BU
BRETEL, Jean, -1272, French;
poetry BU
BRETNOR, Reginald C. ('Grendel
Briarton'), 1911- , Russian-
American; nonfiction, transla-
tions AS CON NI
BRETON, Albert, 1929- , Ca-
nadian; nonfiction CON
BRETON, André, 1896-1966,
French; poetry, fiction BU
CL MAG SEY TH
BRETON, Nicholas, 1551?-1623/26,
English; poetry, nonfiction,
fiction BU DA MAG PO RU VP
BRETON de los HERREROS, Manuel,

1796-1873, Spanish; plays,
poetry BU MCG TH
BRETT, Bernard, 1925- , English; juveniles CO CON
BRETT, Dorothy, 1883-1977,
American; juveniles, nonfiction CON
BRETT, Grace Neff, 1900-75,
American; juveniles CO
'BRETT, Leo' see FANTHORPE,
Robert L.
'BRETT, Michael' see TRIPP,
Miles B.
BRETT, Peter David, 1943- ,
American; poetry, fiction
CON
BRETT, Simon Anthony, 1945- ,
British; fiction, plays CON
REI
BRETT, William H., 1846-1918,
American; nonfiction ENG
BREUER, Bessie, 1893-1975,
American; fiction, plays
CON
BREUER, Miles John, 1889-1947,
American; fiction AS NI
BREUGELMANS, Rene, 1925- ,
Belgian-Canadian; nonfiction
CON
BREUGHEL, Gerrit Hendricksz
van, 1573-1635, Dutch; poetry
BU
BREUNIG, LeRoy Clinton, 1915- ,
American; nonfiction CON
BREW, John Otis, 1906- , American; nonfiction CON
BREW, Osborne Henry Kwesi,
1928- , Ghanaian; poetry,
fiction HER JA LA VCP
BREWER, Gil, American; fiction
REI
BREWER, Jeutonne, 1939- ,
American; nonfiction CON
BREWER, John Mason, 1896- ,
American; nonfiction SH
BREWER, Sam Pope, 1909?-76,
American; journalism, nonfiction CON
BREWER, Thomas, fl. 1624, English; fiction BU
BREWER, William C., 1897?-1974,
American; nonfiction CON
BREWINGTON, Marion Vernon,
1902-74, American; nonfiction
CON
'BREWSTER, Benjamin' see FOL-
SOM, Franklin B.
BREWSTER, Sir David, 1781-1868,

Scots; nonfiction BU
BREWSTER, Dorothy, 1883-1979,
American; nonfiction CON
BREWSTER, Elizabeth Winifred,
1922- , Canadian; poetry,
fiction CR VCP
BREWTON, John Edmund, 1898- ,
American; juveniles CO
BREYER, Norman Lane, 1942- ,
American; nonfiction CON
BREYTENBACH, Breyten, 1939- ,
Afrikaans; poetry BU
BREZA, Tadeusz, 1905-70, Polish;
fiction BU CL
BREZINA, Ján, 1917- , Slovak;
poetry, nonfiction BU
'BREZINA, Otokar' (Václav Ignác
Jebavý), 1868-1929, Czech;
poetry BU CL TH WA
BREZOVACKI, Tito, 1757-1805,
Croatian; plays BU TH
'BRIAN, Alan B.' see PARULSKI,
George R., Jr.
'BRIARTON, Grendel' see BRET-
NOR, Reginald C.
BRICE, Germain (Brixius), 1500?-
38, French; poetry BU
BRICK, John, 1922-73, American;
fiction, nonfiction, juveniles
CO CON
BRICKER, Victoria Reifler, 1940- ,
American; nonfiction CON
BRICKMAN, Marshall, 1941- ,
American; film CON
'BRICUTH, John' see IRWIN, John
T.
BRIDEL, Bedřich, 1619-80, Czech;
poetry BU
BRIDEL, Philippe, 1757-1845,
Swiss; poetry BU
'BRIDGE, Ann' (Lady Mary Dolling
O'Malley'), 1889-1974, British;
fiction, nonfiction CON REI
BRIDGE, Raymond, 1943- , American; nonfiction CON
'BRIDGECROSS, Peter' see CAR-
DINAL, Roger T.
BRIDGEMAN, Harriet, 1942- ,
British; journalism, nonfiction
CON
BRIDGER, Gordon Frederick,
1932- , English; nonfiction
CON
BRIDGERS, Sue Ellen, 1942- ,
American; juveniles CO CON
'BRIDGES, Howard' see STAPLES,
Reginald T.
BRIDGES, Robert, 1844-1930,

English; poetry, nonfiction BU
DA PO SEY VP
BRIDGES, Victor George, 1878-
1972, British; fiction, plays,
poetry REI
BRIDGES, William Andrew, 1901- ,
American; juveniles CO
BRIDGET, St. , 1302/03-73, Swed-
ish; nonfiction BU
BRIDGMAN, Elizabeth, 1921- ,
American; juveniles CON
BRIDGMAN, Sarah (Atherton),
1889?-1975, American; fiction
CON
'BRIDIE, James' (Osborne Henry
Mavor), 1888-1951, Scots;
plays BU DA MCG PO SEY
VD WA
BRIDWELL, Norman, 1928- ,
American; juveniles CO
BRIEFS, Goetz Antony, 1889-
1974, German-American; non-
fiction CON
BRIEN, Roger, 1910- , Canadian;
poetry CR
BRIER, Bob, 1943- , American;
nonfiction CON
BRIER, Howard Maxwell, 1903-69,
American; juveniles CO
BRIER, Royce, 1894-1975, Amer-
ican; journalism, nonfiction
CON
BRIEUX, Eugène, 1858-1932,
French; plays, journalism
BU CL MCG TH
BRIGADERE, Anna, 1861-1933,
Latvian; plays, fiction, poetry
BU
BRIGGS, Berta N. , 1884?-1976,
American; nonfiction CON
BRIGGS, Charles Frederick, 1804-
77, American; fiction MYE
BRIGGS, Charlie, 1927- , Amer-
ican; nonfiction, fiction CON
BRIGGS, Ellis Ormsbee, 1879-
1976, American; nonfiction
CON
BRIGGS, Fred, 1932- , Amer-
ican; journalism CON
BRIGGS, Jean, 1925- , British;
nonfiction CON
BRIGGS, Katharine Mary, 1898-
1980, British; nonfiction CO
CON
BRIGGS, Kenneth Arthur, 1941- ,
American; nonfiction CON
BRIGGS, Lloyd Cabot, 1909-75,
American; nonfiction CON

BRIGGS, Peter, 1921-75, American;
nonfiction CON
BRIGGS, Raymond R. , 1934- ,
English; juveniles CO CON
DE
BRIGGS, Vernon M. , Jr. , 1937- ,
American; nonfiction CON
MAR
BRIGGS, Walter Ladd, 1919- ,
American; journalism, nonfic-
tion CON
BRIGHAM, John Carl, 1942- ,
American; nonfiction CON
BRIGHOUSE, Harold ('Olive Con-
way'), 1882-1958, English;
plays, fiction MCG PO VD
BRIGHT, Deobrah Sue, 1949- ,
American; nonfiction CON
BRIGHT, Greg, 1951- , British;
nonfiction CON
BRIGHT, Richard Eugene, 1931- ,
American; nonfiction CON
BRIGHT, Robert ('Michael Douglas'),
1902- , American; juveniles,
fiction, poetry CO CON KI
BRIGHTBILL, Charles Kestner,
1910-66, American; nonfiction
CON
BRIGHTON, Howard, 1925- ,
American; nonfiction CON
'BRIGHTON, Wesley, Jr.' see
LOVIN, Roger R.
BRIGNANO, Russell Carl, 1935- ,
American; nonfiction CON
BRIGOLA, Alfredo Luigi, 1923- ,
American; nonfiction CON
BRIK, Elsa see 'TRIOLET, Elsa'
BRIK, Osip Maximovich, 1888- ,
Russian; fiction BU
BRILEY, John Richard, 1925- ,
American; fiction, film, plays,
nonfiction CON
BRILL, Steven, American; non-
fiction CON
BRILLAT-SAVERIN, Anthelme,
1755-1826, French; nonfiction
BU
BRILLIANT, Alan, 1936- , Amer-
ican; poetry, translations VCP
BRILLIANT, Ashleigh, 1933- ,
Anglo-American; nonfiction,
poetry CON
BRILOFF, Abraham Jacob, 1917- ,
American; nonfiction CON
BRIMBERG, Stanlee, 1947- ,
American; juveniles CO CON
BRIN, David, 1950- , American;
fiction CON

BRIN, Herbert Henry, 1915- ,
American; poetry, fiction
CON
BRIN, Ruth Firestone, 1921- ,
American; juveniles CO
BRINCKERINCK, Johannes, 1359-
1419, Dutch; nonfiction BU
BRINCKLOE, Julie Lorraine,
1950- , American; juveniles
CO CON
BRINCKMAN, John, 1814-70, Ger-
man; poetry BU
BRINDEL, June Rachuy, 1919- ,
American; juveniles, plays,
nonfiction, poetry, fiction
CO CON WAR
BRINDZE, Ruth, 1903- , Amer-
ican; nonfiction CO CON
BRINEGAR, David Franklin,
1910- , American; journalism
CON
BRINES, Francisco, 1932- , Span-
ish; poetry CL
BRINES, Russell Dean, 1911- ,
American; nonfiction CON
BRINEY, Robert Edward, 1933- ,
American; fiction, nonfiction
CON
BRINGHURST, Robert, 1946- ,
American; nonfiction, trans-
lations, poetry CON
BRINGSVAERD, Tor Age, 1939- ,
Norwegian; fiction, transla-
tions NI
BRINITZER, Carl ('Usikota'),
1907-74, German-British;
nonfiction, translations CON
BRINK, André, 1935- , Afri-
kaans; fiction, plays, trans-
lations BU LA
BRINK, Carol Ryrie, 1895-1981,
American; juveniles, plays,
fiction KI
BRINK, Jan ten, 1834-1901, Dutch;
nonfiction BU
BRINK, Terry Lee, 1949- ,
American; plays CON
BRINK, Wellington, 1895-1979,
American; journalism, non-
fiction CON
BRINKERHOFF, Dericksen Mor-
gan, 1921- , American; non-
fiction CON
BRINKLEY, David, 1920- ,
American; journalism CON
BRINKLEY, Joel, 1952- ,
American; journalism CON
BRINKMAN, George Loris,

1942- , American; nonfiction
CON
BRINKMAN, Grover, 1903- ,
American; nonfiction CON
BRINKMANN, Rolf Dieter, 1940-
75, German; poetry CL
BRINNIN, John Malcolm, 1916- ,
American; poetry, nonfiction
BR SEY VCP
BRINSMEAD, Hesba Fay ('Pixie
Hungerford'), 1922- , Aus-
tralian; juveniles CO DEM
KI
BRINTON, Henry, 1901- , British;
fiction NI
BRION, Marcel, 1895- , French;
nonfiction, fiction CL
BRISBANE, Albert, 1809-90, Amer-
ican; nonfiction MYE
BRISBANE, Robert Hughes, 1913- ,
American; nonfiction CON SH
'BRISCO, Patty' see MATTHEWS,
Clayton; MATTHEWS, Patricia
BRISCOE, Jill, 1935- , English;
nonfiction CON
BRISLEY, Joyce Lankester, 1896- ,
British; juveniles, poetry,
plays CO CON KI
BRISMAN, Leslie, 1944- , Amer-
ican; nonfiction CON
'BRISSAC, Malcolm de' see DICK-
SINSON, Peter
BRISSENDEN, Paul Frederick,
1885-1974, American; nonfic-
tion CON
BRISTOL, Lee Hastings, Jr.,
1923-79, American; nonfiction
CON
BRISTOW, Gwen, 1903-80, Amer-
ican; fiction, journalism CON
ST
BRISTOW, Joan, American; juven-
iles WAR
'BRITAIN, Dan' see PENDLETON,
Donald E.
BRITCHKY, Seymour, 1930- ,
American; nonfiction CON
'BRITINDIAN' see SOLOMON, Sam-
uel
BRITO, Aristeo, American; poetry
MAR
BRITO, Bernardo de, 1568-1617,
Portuguese; nonfiction BU
BRITSCH, Ralph Adam, 1912- ,
American; nonfiction CON
BRITSCH, Todd Adam, 1937- ,
American; nonfiction CON
BRITT, Albert, 1874-1969, Amer-

ican; nonfiction CON
BRITT, Steuart Henderson, 1907-
79, American; journalism,
nonfiction CON
BRITTAIN, Vera Mary, 1896-1970,
English; fiction DA
BRITTAIN, William ('James Knox'),
1930- , American; fiction,
juveniles CON REI
BRITTAINS, John Ashleigh,
1923- , American; nonfic-
tion CON
BRITTAN, Gordon Goodhue, Jr.,
1939- , American; nonfiction
CON
BRITTER, Eric Valentine, 1906-
77, British; nonfiction CON
BRITTING, Georg, 1891-1964, Ger-
man; poetry, fiction TH
BRITTON, Dorothea Sprague,
1922- , American; nonfiction
CON
BRITTON, Peter Ewart ('Peter
Lemesurier'), 1936- , British;
nonfiction, translations CON
BRKIC, Jovan, 1927- , Yugoslav-
American; nonfiction CON
BRO, Bernard Gerard Marie,
1925- , French; nonfiction
CON
BRO, Marguerite Harmon, 1894-
1977, American; juveniles CO
CON
BROAD, Charlie Dunbar, 1887-
1971, English; nonfiction CON
WA
BROAD, Jay, 1930- , American;
plays CON
BROADBENT, Edward, 1936- ,
Canadian; nonfiction CON
BROADBENT, W. W., 1919- ,
American; nonfiction CON
BROADFOOT, Barry, 1926- ,
Canadian; nonfiction CON
BROADHEAD, Helen (Cross),
1913- , American; juveniles
CO CON
BROADLEY, Margaret Ericson,
1904- , American; nonfic-
tion CON
BROADRIBB, Violet, American;
nonfiction CON
BROADUS, Robert Newton,
1922- , American; nonfic-
tion CON
BROADWELL, Martin M.,
1927- , American; nonfic-
tion CON

BROAT, Isidore Gerald, 1927- ,
British; fiction CON
BROBECK, Florence, 1895-1979,
American; nonfiction CON
BROCE, Thomas Edward, 1935- ,
American; nonfiction CON
'EL BROCENSE' see SANCHEZ de
las BROZAS, Francisco
BROCH, Hermann, 1886-1951,
Austrian-American; fiction,
plays BU CL MAG SEY TH
BROCK, Alice May, 1941- , Amer-
ican; nonfiction CON
BROCK, Betty Carter, 1923- ,
American; juveniles CO WAR
BROCK, Dewey Heyward, 1941- ,
American; nonfiction CON
BROCK, Edwin, 1927- , British;
poetry, plays, fiction VCP
WAK
BROCK, Emma Lillian, 1886-1974,
American; juveniles CO CON
BROCK, Gerald Wayne, 1948- ,
American; nonfiction CON
'BROCK, Lynn' (Alister McAllister;
'Anthony Wharton'), 1877-1943,
Irish; fiction, plays HO REI
ST
BROCK, Michael George, 1920- ,
British; nonfiction CON
'BROCK, Rose' see HANSEN, Jo-
seph
BROCK, Stanley Edmunde, 1936- ,
Anglo-American; nonfiction
CON
BROCK, Vandall Kline, 1932- ,
American; poetry, nonfiction
CON
BROCK, Virginia, American; ju-
veniles WAR
BROCKES, Barthold Hinrich, 1680-
1747, German; poetry BU TH
BROCKETT, Eleanor Hall, 1913-67,
English; juveniles CO
BROCKMAN, Harold, 1902-80,
American; nonfiction CON
BROCKMAN, Norbert, 1934- ,
American; nonfiction CON
BROCKWAY, Archibald Fenner,
1888- , English; fiction NI
BROD, Max, 1884-1968, Austrian;
fiction, plays BU TH
BROD, Ruth (Hagy), 1911-80, Amer-
ican; journalism, nonfiction
CON
BRODATZ, Philip, 1915- , Amer-
ican; nonfiction CON
BRODE, Douglas, 1943- , Amer-

ican; nonfiction CON
BRODE, Wallace R., 1900?-74,
American; nonfiction CON
BRODER, David Salzer, 1929- ,
American; journalism, non-
fiction CON
BRODER, Patricia Janis, 1935- ,
American; nonfiction CON
BRODERICK, Dorothy M., 1929- ,
American; juveniles CO
BRODERICK, Francis Lyons,
1922- , American; nonfic-
tion CON
BRODERICK, John, 1927- ,
Irish; fiction HO
BRODERICK, Richard Lawrence
('Kenny Richards'), 1927- ,
American; nonfiction CON
BRODEUR, Paul Adrian, Jr.,
1931- , American; fiction,
nonfiction VCN
BRODIE, Bernard, 1910-78, Amer-
ican; nonfiction CON
BRODIE, Fawn McKay, 1915-81,
American; nonfiction CON
BRODIE, Harlowe Keith Ham-
mond, 1939- , American;
nonfiction CON
BRODIN, Pierre Eugene, 1909- ,
French; nonfiction, juveniles
CON WAR
BRODINE, Virginia Dare, 1915- ,
American; nonfiction CON
BRODSKY, Archie, 1945- , Amer-
ican; nonfiction, fiction CON
BRODSKY, Joseph Alexandrovich,
1940- , Russian-American;
poetry CL CON WA
BRODSKY, Michael Mark, 1948- ,
American; fiction, plays CON
BRODWIN, Leonora Leet, 1929- ,
American; nonfiction CON
BRODY, Jane Ellen, 1941- ,
American; journalism, non-
fiction CON
BRODY, Polly, 1919- , Amer-
ican; nonfiction CON
BRODY, Sándor, 1863-1924, Hun-
garian; fiction, journalism
CL TH
BRODY, Saul Nathaniel, 1938- ,
American; nonfiction CON
BRODZINSKI, Kazimierz Maciej
Josef, 1791-1835, Polish;
poetry, translations, non-
fiction BU
BROECKAERT, Karl, 1767-1826,
Flemish; fiction BU

BROEKER, Galen, 1920- , Amer-
ican; nonfiction CON
BROEKHUIZEN, Joan van, 1649-
1707, Dutch; poetry BU
BROEKMAN, Marcel, 1922- ,
Dutch-American; nonfiction
CON
BROER, Lawrence Richard, 1938- ,
American; plays, nonfiction
CON
BROESAMLE, John Joseph, 1941- ,
American; nonfiction CON
BROFELDT, Johannes see 'AHO,
Juhani'
BROFFERIO, Angelo, 1802-66,
Italian; poetry, plays BU
BROGAN, Denis William ('Maurice
Barrington'), 1900-74, Scots;
nonfiction CON
'BROGAN, Elise' see URCH, Eliza-
beth
BROGAN, James Edmund, 1941- ,
American; nonfiction CON
BROH, Charles Anthony, 1945- ,
American; nonfiction CON
BROH-KAHN, Eleanor, 1924- ,
American; nonfiction CON
'BROIDO, Vera' see COHN, Vera
BROKAMP, Marilyn ('Mary Lynn'),
1920- , American; juveniles
CO CON
BROKE, Arthur (Brooke), -1563,
English; translations CON
BROKHIN, Yuri, 1934- , Russian-
American; nonfiction CON
BROKHOFF, John Rudolph, 1913- ,
American; nonfiction CON
BROLIN, Brent Cruse, 1940- ,
American; nonfiction CON
BROMBERG, Walter, 1900- ,
American; nonfiction CON
BROME, Alexander, 1620-66, Eng-
lish; poetry, translations BU
BROME, Herbert Vincent, 1910- ,
British; fiction, nonfiction
CON
BROME, Richard, 1590?-1652/53,
English; plays BU DA MAG
MCG PO RU VD
BROMELL, Henry, 1947- , Amer-
ican; fiction CON
BROMFIELD, Louis, 1896-1956,
American; fiction, plays, jour-
nalism BR MAG RO VN
BROMHEAD, Peter Alexander,
1919- , English; nonfiction
CON
BROMIGE, David Mansfield, 1935- ,

Canadian; poetry, plays, fiction VCP
BROMLEY, David Grover, 1941- ,
American; nonfiction CON
BROMLEY, Dudley, 1948- ,
American; nonfiction CON
BROMYARDE, John de, fl. 1390,
English; nonfiction BU
BRONDFIELD, Jerome, 1913- ,
American; juveniles, nonfiction, tv, fiction CO CON
BRONFENBRENNER, Urie,
1917- , Russian-American;
nonfiction CON
BRONIEWSKI, Wladyslaw, 1898-
1962, Polish; poetry BU CL
BRONIN, Andrew, 1947- , American; nonfiction CON
BRONK, William, 1918- , American; poetry, nonfiction CON
BRONNE, Carlo, 1901- , Belgian; poetry, nonfiction CL
BRONNEN, Arnolt, 1895-1959,
Austrian; plays CL MCG
BRONOWSKI, Jacob, 1908-74,
English; plays, nonfiction
CON WA WAR
BRONSON, Bertrand Harris,
1902- , American; nonfiction
CON
'BRONSON, Lynn' see LAMPMAN,
Evelyn S.
BRONSON, Wilfrid Swancourt,
1894- , American; juveniles
CON
BRONSON, William Knox, 1926-
76, American; nonfiction CON
'BRONSON, Wolfe' see RABORG,
Frederick A., Jr.
BRONSON-HOWARD, George Fitzalan, 1884-1922, American;
journalism, plays, fiction
ST
BRONSTEIN, Leo, 1903?-76,
Polish-American; nonfiction
CON
BRONSTEIN, Lynn, 1950- ,
American; poetry, nonfiction
CON
BRONTË, Anne, 1820-49, English;
fiction BU DA MAG PO VN
BRONTË, Charlotte, 1816-55,
English; fiction BU DA MAG
PO VN
BRONTË, Emily Jane, 1818-48,
English; poetry, fiction BU
DA MAG PO VN VP
'BRONTE, Louisa' see ROB-

ERTS, Janet L.
BROOK, Victor John Knight, 1887-
1974, British; nonfiction CON
BROOKE, Arthur see BROKE,
Arthur
BROOKE, Avery Rogers ('Alice
Benjamin'), 1923- , American;
nonfiction CON
BROOKE, Brian, 1911- , South
African; nonfiction CON
BROOKE, Bryan Nicholas, 1915- ,
English; nonfiction CON
BROOKE, Charlotte, 1740-93, Irish;
translations BU
BROOKE, Dinah, 1936- , English;
translations, plays CON
BROOKE, Henry, 1703-83, Irish;
fiction, plays, translations
BU DA MAG VD
BROOKE, Jocelyn, 1908-66, English; fiction NI
BROOKE, Leonard Leslie, 1862-
1940, British; juveniles CO
KI
BROOKE, Robert Taliaferro, 1945- ,
American; fiction CON
BROOKE, Rupert, 1887-1915, English; poetry, nonfiction BU DA
MAG PO SEY VP
BROOKE, Stopford Augustus, 1832-
1916, English; nonfiction DA
'BROOKE-HAVEN, P.' see WODEHOUSE, P. G.
BROOKER, Bertram Richard ('Huxley Herne'; 'Richard Surrey'),
1888-1955, Canadian; nonfiction,
fiction CR
BROOKE-ROSE, Christine, 1923/26- ,
English; nonfiction, fiction,
translations NI VCN WA
BROOKES, Stella Brewer, American;
nonfiction SH
BROOKHOUSER, Frank, 1912?-75,
American; fiction, journalism
CON
BROOKINS, Dana, 1931- , American; juveniles CON
BROOKINS, Dewey C., 1904- ,
American; journalism NI
BROOKMAN, Rosina Francesca
('Rosina Francesca'), 1932- ,
Hungarian-American; nonfiction
CON
'BROOKS, Anita' see ABRAMOVITZ,
Anita Z.
BROOKS, Anne, American; juveniles WAR
BROOKS, Charles Edward, 1921- ,

American; nonfiction CON
BROOKS, Charles Timothy, 1813-
83, American; poetry, trans-
lations MY
BROOKS, Charles V. W., 1912- ,
American; nonfiction CON
BROOKS, Charles William Shirley
('Epicurus Rotundus'), 1816-
74, English; fiction, plays
BU
BROOKS, Charlotte K., American;
nonfiction, juveniles CO CON
SH
BROOKS, Cleanth, 1906- , Amer-
ican; nonfiction BA BOR BR
BU SEY
BROOKS, David Hopkinson, 1929- ,
American; fiction CON
BROOKS, Deems Markham, 1934- ,
American; nonfiction CON
BROOKS, Edwy Searles see
'GRAY, Berkeley'
BROOKS, Gary Donald, 1942- ,
American; nonfiction CON
BROOKS, Gregory, 1961- ,
American; juveniles CON
BROOKS, Gwendolyn, 1917- ,
American; poetry, fiction BU
CO DEM MAG MAL SH VCP
VP
BROOKS, Harold Allen, 1925- ,
American; nonfiction CON
BROOKS, Hunter Otis, 1929- ,
American; nonfiction CON
BROOKS, James L., 1940- ,
American; journalism, tv
CON
BROOKS, Janice Young ('Amanda
Singer'), 1943- , American;
nonfiction, fiction CON
BROOKS, Jeremy, 1926- , Brit-
ish; fiction, plays, juveniles
VCN
BROOKS, Jerome, 1931- , Amer-
ican; fiction CO CON
'BROOKS, John' see SUGAR,
Bert R.
BROOKS, Karen, 1949- , Amer-
ican; nonfiction CON
BROOKS, Lester, 1924- , Amer-
ican; juveniles CO WAR
BROOKS, Maria Zagorska,
1933- , Polish-American;
nonfiction CON
BROOKS, Mel, 1926- , Amer-
ican; film CON
BROOKS, Nelson Herbert, 1902-
78, American; nonfiction CON

BROOKS, Pat, 1931- , American;
nonfiction CON
BROOKS, Peter, 1938- , Amer-
ican; nonfiction CON
BROOKS, Polly Schoyer, 1912- ,
American; juveniles CO
BROOKS, Richard, 1912- , Amer-
ican; fiction, film CON
BROOKS, Robert Angus, 1920-76,
American; nonfiction CON
BROOKS, Robert Emanuel, 1941- ,
American; nonfiction CON
BROOKS, Terry, 1944- , Amer-
ican; fiction CON
BROOKS, Thomas Reed, 1925- ,
American; journalism, juveniles,
nonfiction CON WAR
BROOKS, Timothy Haley, 1942- ,
American; nonfiction CON
BROOKS, Van Wyck, 1886-1963,
American; nonfiction, poetry,
translations AM BOR BR BU
MAG PO
BROOKS, W. Hal, 1933- , Amer-
ican; nonfiction CON
BROOKS, Walter Rollin, 1886-1958,
American; juveniles, fiction
CO KI
BROOKS-DAVIES, Douglas, 1942- ,
British; nonfiction CON
BROOKSHIER, Frank, American;
nonfiction CON
BROOME, Charles Larue, 1925- ,
American; nonfiction CON
BROOME, William, 1689-1745,
English; poetry, translations
BU
BROOMFIELD, Gerald Webb, 1895-
1976, British; nonfiction CON
BROPHY, Brigid, 1929- , Irish;
fiction, journalism, nonfiction,
plays BU SEY VCD VCN WA
BROPHY, Elizabeth Bergen, 1929- ,
American; nonfiction CON
BROPHY, James Joseph, 1912- ,
American; nonfiction CON
BROPHY, Jere Edward, 1940- ,
American; nonfiction CON
BROPHY, Robert see RAY, R. J.
BROPHY, Robert Joseph, 1928- ,
American; nonfiction CON
BRORSON, Hans Adolph, 1694-1764,
Danish; poetry BU TH
BROSBOLL, Johan Carl Christian
('Carit Etlar'), 1816-1900,
Danish; fiction BU
BROSE, Olive Johnson, 1919- ,
American; nonfiction CON

BROSMAN, Catharine (Savage),
1934- , American; nonfiction,
poetry CON
BROSNAHAN, Leonard Francis,
1922- , New Zealander; non-
fiction CON
BROSNAN, James Patrick, 1929- ,
American; juveniles CO
WAR
BROSNAN, John, 1947- , Aus-
tralian; fiction, journalism
NI
BROSSARD, Chandler ('Daniel
Harper'), 1922- , American;
fiction, nonfiction, plays BR
CON VCN
BROSTER, Dorothy Kathleen, 1877-
1950, English; fiction NI
BROSTERHUYSEN, Johan van,
1596-1650, Dutch; nonfiction
BU
BROTHERS, M. Jay, 1931- ,
American; fiction, film CON
BROTHERTON, Manfred, 1900?-
81, American; journalism,
nonfiction CON
BROUE, Pierre, 1926- , French;
nonfiction CON
BROUGH, Robert Clayton, 1950- ,
American; nonfiction CON
BROUGHAM, Henry Peter, 1778-
1868, English; nonfiction BU
DA
BROUGHTON, Diane, 1943- ,
American; nonfiction CON
BROUGHTON, Geoffrey, 1927- ,
British; nonfiction CON
BROUGHTON, Jacksel Markham,
1925- , American; nonfiction
CON
BROUGHTON, James Richard,
1913- , American; poetry,
plays BR CON VCP
BROUGHTON, John Cam Hobhouse,
Baron, 1786-1869, English;
nonfiction BU DA
BROUGHTON, Panthea Reid,
1941- , American; nonfic-
tion CON
BROUGHTON, Thomas Alan,
1936- , American; poetry
CON
BROUILLARD, André L. see
'NORD, Pierre'
BROUMAS, Olga, 1949- , Amer-
ican; poetry CON
'BROUN, Emily' see STERNE,
Emma G.

BROUN, Heywood Campbell, 1888-
1939, American; journalism,
nonfiction WAR
'BROUSSARD, Vivian L.' see MAR-
TINETZ, Vivian L.
'BROUWER, A.' see LOOY, Jacobus
van
BROWDER, Lesley Hughes, Jr.,
1935- , American; nonfiction
CON
BROWDER, Olin Lorraine, Jr.,
1913- , American; nonfiction
CON
BROWDER, Sue, 1946- , Amer-
ican; nonfiction CON
BROWDER, Walter Everett, 1939- ,
American; fiction CON
BROWER, Charles Hendrickson,
1901- , American; nonfiction
CON
BROWER, Daniel Roberts, 1936- ,
American; nonfiction CON
BROWER, David Ross, 1912- ,
American; nonfiction CON
BROWER, Millicent, American;
fiction, poetry, nonfiction,
juveniles CO CON
BROWER, Pauline York, 1929- ,
American; juveniles CO CON
BROWER, Reuben Arthur, 1908-75,
American; nonfiction CON
BROWIN, Frances Williams ('Fran-
ces B. Williams), 1898- ,
American; juveniles CO
'BROWN, Alec', English?; fiction
NI
'BROWN, Alexis' see BAUMANN,
Amy B.
BROWN, Anne Ensign, 1937- ,
American; nonfiction, juveniles
CON
BROWN, Annice Harris, 1897- ,
American; poetry CON
BROWN, Anthony Eugene, 1937- ,
American; nonfiction CON
BROWN, Archibald Haworth, 1938- ,
Scots; nonfiction CON
BROWN, Arthur Allen, 1900- ,
American; fiction, nonfiction
CON
BROWN, Barbara Banker, 1917- ,
American; nonfiction CON
BROWN, Benjamin F., 1930- ,
American; nonfiction CON
BROWN, Bert Robert, 1936- ,
American; nonfiction CON
BROWN, Betty see JONES, Eliza-
beth B.

'BROWN, Billye W.' see CUTCHEN, Billye W.

BROWN, Bob, 1886-1959, American; nonfiction, poetry, fiction, journalism RO

BROWN, Calvin Smith, 1909- , American; nonfiction CON

BROWN, Carl Fraser, 1910- , American; nonfiction CON

'BROWN, Carter' (Alan Geoffrey Yates), 1923- , British; fiction REI

BROWN, Cassie, 1919- , Canadian; plays CON

BROWN, Cecil M., 1943- , American; fiction, plays CON SH

'BROWN, Charles' see CADET, John

BROWN, Charles Brockden, 1771-1810, American; fiction, nonfiction AM BR BU MAG PO ST VN

BROWN, Charles Nikki, 1937- , American; nonfiction CON

BROWN, Charles Thomas, 1912- , American; nonfiction CON

BROWN, Christopher Paterson, 1939- , American; nonfiction CON

BROWN, Christy, 1932-81, Irish; fiction, poetry HO

BROWN, Claude, 1937- , American; nonfiction CON SH

BROWN, Clifford Waters, Jr., 1942- , American; nonfiction CON

BROWN, Courtney Conrades, 1904- , American; nonfiction CON

BROWN, Curtis Franklin, 1925- , American; nonfiction CON

BROWN, Daniel Gilbert, 1924- , American; nonfiction CON

'BROWN, Daniel R.' see CURZON, Daniel

BROWN, David Clifford, 1929- , English; nonfiction CON

BROWN, Deaver David, 1943- , American; nonfiction CON

BROWN, Dee Alexander, 1908- , American; juveniles CO WAR

BROWN, Denise Scott (Denise Scott Brown Venturi), 1931- , American; nonfiction CON

BROWN, Dennis Albert, 1926- , English; nonfiction CON

BROWN, Diana, 1928- , British;

fiction CON

BROWN, Donald Fowler, 1909- , American; translations, nonfiction CON

BROWN, Donald Robert, 1925- , American; nonfiction CON

BROWN, Doris E., 1910?-75, American; juveniles, nonfiction CON

'BROWN, Douglas' see GIBSON, Walter B.

BROWN, Edward Killoran, 1905-51, Canadian; nonfiction BU

BROWN, Eleanor Frances, 1908- , American; juveniles CO

BROWN, Elizabeth Louise, 1924- , American; nonfiction, fiction CON

BROWN, Emily Clara, 1911- , American; nonfiction CON

BROWN, Ernest Francis, 1903- , American; nonfiction CON

BROWN, Eugene Richard, 1942- , American; nonfiction CON

BROWN, F. Keith, 1913?-76, American; nonfiction CON

BROWN, Fern G., 1918- , American; juveniles CON

BROWN, Forrest ('Ford Browne'; 'Rae Brown'), American; fiction CON

BROWN, Francis Andrew, 1915- , American; nonfiction CON

BROWN, Francis Robert, 1914- , American; nonfiction CON

BROWN, Frank Arthur, Jr., 1908- , American; nonfiction CON

BROWN, Frank Edward, 1908- , American; nonfiction CON

BROWN, Fredric, 1906-72, American; fiction, plays, juveniles, nonfiction AS COW NI REI ST WA

BROWN, Geoff, 1932- , English; fiction CON

'BROWN, George' see WERTMULLER, Lina

BROWN, George Douglas see 'DOUGLAS, George'

BROWN, George Earl, 1883-1964, American; juveniles CO

BROWN, George Isaac, 1923- , American; nonfiction CON

BROWN, George Mackay, 1921- , British; poetry, plays, fiction, juveniles BU VCN VCP WAK

BROWN, Gwilym Slater, 1928-74, American; nonfiction, journal-

ism CON
BROWN, H. Rap, American; non-
fiction SH
BROWN, Harcourt, 1900- , Ca-
nadian; nonfiction CON
BROWN, Harrison Scott, 1917- ,
American; fiction, nonfiction
CON NI
BROWN, Harry Gunnison, 1880-
1975, American; nonfiction
CON
BROWN, Harry Peter McNab
('Artie Greengroin'), 1917- ,
American; poetry, film CON
BROWN, Hazel Elizabeth, 1893- ,
American; nonfiction CON
BROWN, Hugh Auchincloss, 1879-
1975, American; nonfiction
CON
BROWN, Irene Bennett, 1932- ,
American; juveniles CO
BROWN, Ivor John, 1891-1974,
English; juveniles, journalism,
nonfiction CO CON DA
BROWN, James, 1934- , Amer-
ican; nonfiction CON
BROWN, James Cooke, 1921- ,
American; fiction NI
BROWN, James Duff, 1862-1914,
English; nonfiction ENG
BROWN, James Goldie, 1901- ,
New Zealander; fiction NI
BROWN, James Wiley, 1909- ,
American; nonfiction CON
BROWN, James Wilson, 1913- ,
American; nonfiction CON
BROWN, Jamie, 1945- , Cana-
dian; nonfiction, fiction, film
CON
BROWN, Janet, 1947- , Amer-
ican; nonfiction CON
BROWN, Jim M., 1940- , Amer-
ican; nonfiction CON
BROWN, Joe David, 1915-76,
American; journalism, fiction,
nonfiction CON
BROWN, Joh, 1810-82, Scots;
nonfiction BU DA
BROWN, John Lackey, 1914- ,
American; nonfiction, poetry
CON
BROWN, John M. see 'SWEVEN,
Godfrey'
BROWN, John Mason, 1900- ,
American; nonfiction BR
BROWN, Joseph Edward, 1929- ,
American; juveniles, nonfic-
tion CON

BROWN, Joseph Paul Summers,
1930- , American; fiction
CON
BROWN, Judith Gwyn, 1933- ,
American; juveniles CO CON
BROWN, Judith Margaret, 1944- ,
English; nonfiction CON
BROWN, Julia Prewitt, 1948- ,
American; nonfiction CON
BROWN, Kenneth H., 1936- ,
American; plays, fiction VCD
BROWN, Kevin V., 1922- , Amer-
ican; journalism, nonfiction
CON
BROWN, Laurence Binet, 1927- ,
New Zealander; nonfiction CON
BROWN, Leigh, American; fiction
CON
BROWN, Lennox John, 1934- ,
American; plays, poetry CON
BROWN, Letitia Woods, 1915-76,
American; nonfiction CON
BROWN, Louis Morris, 1909- ,
American; nonfiction CON
BROWN, Lyle Clarence, 1926- ,
American; nonfiction CON
BROWN, Mac Alister, 1924- ,
American; nonfiction CON
BROWN, Marc Tolon, 1946- ,
American; juveniles CO CON
BROWN, Marcia, 1918- , Amer-
ican; juveniles, translations
CO CON
BROWN, Marel, 1899- , American;
poetry, juveniles, nonfiction
CON
BROWN, Margaret Wise ('Golden
MacDonald'; 'Timothy Hay';
'Juniper Sage'), 1910-52, Amer-
ican; poetry, juveniles COM
KI
BROWN, Margery, American; ju-
veniles CO
BROWN, Marian A., 1911- , Amer-
ican; nonfiction CON
BROWN, Marion Marsh, 1908- ,
American; juveniles CO
BROWN, Marvin L., Jr., 1920- ,
American; nonfiction CON
BROWN, Maurice F., 1928- ,
American; nonfiction CON
BROWN, Morna D. see 'FERRARS,
Elizabeth X.'
BROWN, Myra Berry, 1918- ,
American; juveniles CO
BROWN, Nathaniel Hapgood, 1929- ,
American; nonfiction CON
BROWN, Ned, 1882?-1976, Amer-

ican; journalism CON
BROWN, Newell, 1917- , American; nonfiction CON
BROWN, Norman Donald, 1935- , American; nonfiction CON
BROWN, Norman O., 1913- , American; nonfiction BR WA
BROWN, Pamela, 1924- , English; juveniles CO
BROWN, Parker Boyd, 1928- , American; nonfiction CON
BROWN, Patricia L., American; nonfiction SH
BROWN, Peter Currell, English; fiction NI
BROWN, Peter Lancaster, 1927- , English; fiction, nonfiction CON
'BROWN, Rae' see BROWN, Forrest
BROWN, Raymond Edward, 1928- , American; nonfiction CON
BROWN, Raymond Kay, 1936- , American; nonfiction CON
BROWN, Raymond Lamont, 1939- , British; nonfiction CON
BROWN, Re Mona, 1917- , American; nonfiction CON
BROWN, Rex Vandesteene, 1933- , English; nonfiction CON
BROWN, Richard David, 1939- , American; nonfiction CON
BROWN, Richard Eugene, 1937- , American; nonfiction CON
BROWN, Richard Howard, 1929- , American; nonfiction CON
BROWN, Rita Mae, 1944- , American; translations, fiction CON
BROWN, Robert Craig, 1935- , American; nonfiction CON
BROWN, Robert Edward, 1945- , American; poetry CON
BROWN, Robert Joseph, 1907- , American; juveniles CO
BROWN, Robin, 1937- , British; fiction, tv CON
BROWN, Roger Glenn, 1931- , American; nonfiction CON
BROWN, Ronald, 1900- , American; nonfiction CON
BROWN, Rosalie (Moore), 1910- , American; juveniles CO
BROWN, Rosel George, 1926-67, American; fiction AS CON NI
BROWN, Rosellen, 1939- , American; poetry, fiction CON
BROWN, Roy Frederick, 1921- , British; juveniles, plays CON

DEM KI
BROWN, Seyom, 1933- , American; nonfiction CON
BROWN, Sheldon S., 1937- , American; nonfiction CON
BROWN, Stanley Branson, 1914- , English; nonfiction CON
BROWN, Stanley Coleman, 1928- , American; nonfiction CON
BROWN, Stanley Harold, 1927- , American; nonfiction CON
BROWN, Sterling Allen, 1901- , American; poetry, nonfiction CON SH VP WAK
BROWN, Steven Randall, 1939- , American; nonfiction CON
BROWN, Susan Jenkins, 1896- , American; translations, nonfiction CON
BROWN, Terence, 1944- , Irish; nonfiction CON
BROWN, Theo Watts, 1934- , Australian; nonfiction CON
BROWN, Thomas ('Dudley Tomkinson'), 1663-1704, English; fiction, plays, poetry, translations BU VN
BROWN, Thomas H., 1930- , American; nonfiction CON
BROWN, Tillman Merritt, 1913- , Canadian; nonfiction CON
BROWN, Velma Darbo ('Lynn'), 1921- , American; nonfiction CON
BROWN, Vinson, 1912- , American; juveniles CO
BROWN, Virginia Suggs, 1924- , American; juveniles CON SH
BROWN, Walter Reed, 1929- , American; nonfiction, juveniles CO CON
BROWN, Warren William, 1894-1978, American; journalism, nonfiction CON
BROWN, Wayne, 1944- , Trinidadian; poetry CON VCP
BROWN, Weldon Amzy, 1911- , American; nonfiction CON
'BROWN, Will' see AINSWORTH, William H.
BROWN, William Campbell, 1928- , American; nonfiction CON
BROWN, William Garrott, 1868-1913, American; nonfiction, fiction BA
BROWN, William J., American; nonfiction CON
BROWN, William Louis (Bill),

1910-64, American; juveniles
CO
BROWN, William Norman, 1892-
1975, American; nonfiction
CON
BROWN, William Wells, 1815?-
84, American; nonfiction,
plays, fiction BA MYE VN
BROWN, Zenith J. see 'FORD,
Leslie'
BROWNE, Anthony Edward, 1946- ,
British; juveniles CON
BROWNE, Charles F., see
'WARD, Artemus'
BROWNE, Elliott Martin, 1900-80,
British; nonfiction CON
'BROWNE, Ford' see BROWN,
Forrest
BROWNE, Frances, 1816-79, Irish;
poetry, fiction, juveniles HO
BROWNE, Gary Lawson, 1939- ,
American; nonfiction CON
BROWNE, George Sheldon, Brit-
ish; fiction NI
BROWNE, Hablot Knight ('Phiz'),
1815-82, English; illustrations
CO
BROWNE, Harry, 1933- , Amer-
ican; nonfiction CON
BROWNE, Henry (Harry), 1918- ,
British; nonfiction CON
BROWNE, Howard ('John Evans'),
1908- , American; fiction,
film, nonfiction CON NI ST
BROWNE, Joy, 1944- , Amer-
ican; nonfiction CON
'BROWNE, Matthew' see RANDS,
William B.
BROWNE, Michael Dennis, 1940- ,
British; poetry, plays VCP
BROWNE, Raymond, 1897- ,
American; nonfiction CON
BROWNE, Roland A., 1910- ,
Canadian; nonfiction CON
BROWNE, Theodore R., 1911?-79,
American; plays CON
BROWNE, Sir Thomas, 1605-82,
English; nonfiction BRI BU
DA MAG PO RU VN
BROWNE, Thomas A. see 'BOL-
DREWOOD, Rolf'
BROWNE, William, 1590/91-
1643/45, English; poetry BU
PO RU VP
BROWNE, William Hand, 1828-
1912, American; nonfiction BA
BROWNELL, Blaine Allison,
1942- , American; nonfiction

CON
BROWNELL, William Crary, 1851-
1928, American; nonfiction
BR
BROWNING, Don Spencer, 1934- ,
American; nonfiction CON
BROWNING, Elizabeth, 1924- ,
English; fiction CON
BROWNING, Elizabeth Barrett,
1806-61, English; poetry,
translations BU DA MAG
PO VP
'BROWNING, John S.' see WIL-
LIAMS, Robert M.
BROWNING, Norma Lee, 1914- ,
American; fiction, nonfiction
CON
BROWNING, Preston Mercer, Jr.,
1929- , American; nonfiction
CON
BROWNING, Reed, 1938- , Amer-
ican; nonfiction CON
BROWNING, Robert, 1812-89, Eng-
lish; poetry, plays BU COM
DA MAG MCG PO VP
BROWNING, Robert Lynn, 1924- ,
American; nonfiction CON
'BROWNING, Sterry' see GRIBBLE,
Leonard R.
BROWNJOHN, Alan Charles ('John
Berrington'), 1931- , British;
poetry, juveniles CO VCP
WAK
BROWNLEE, Frank, 1875-1950,
South African; fiction BU
BROWNLEE, Oswald Harvey,
1917- , American; nonfiction
CON
BROWNLEE, Walter, 1930- ,
English; fiction, nonfiction
CON
BROWNLEE, Wilson Elliot, Jr.,
1941- , American; nonfiction
CON
BROWNMILLER, Susan, 1935- ,
American; juveniles, nonfiction
CON
BROWNSON, Orestes Augustus,
1803-76, American; journalism,
fiction, nonfiction BR BU MY
PO
BROWNSON, William Clarence,
Jr., 1928- , American; non-
fiction CON
BROWNSTEIN, Michael, 1943- ,
American; poetry, fiction VCP
BROXHOLME, John Franklin ('Dun-
can Kyle'), 1930- , English;

nonfiction CON
BROY, Anthony, 1916- , Amer-
ican; nonfiction CON
BROYLES, William Dodson, Jr.,
1944- , American; journal-
ism CON
BROZEK, Josef Maria, 1913- ,
Czech-American; nonfiction,
translations CON
'BRU, Hedin' (Hans Jacob Jacob-
sen), 1901- , Faroese; fic-
tion BU
BRUBAKER, Dale Lee, 1937- ,
American; nonfiction CON
BRUCE, Charles Tory, 1906- ,
Canadian; poetry, fiction, non-
fiction CR
BRUCE, Curt, 1946- , Amer-
ican; nonfiction CON
BRUCE, Dickson, D., Jr.,
1946- , American; nonfic-
tion CON
BRUCE, Dorita Fairlie, 1885-
1970, British; juveniles KI
BRUCE, George, 1909- , British;
poetry, plays, nonfiction BU
CON VCP
BRUCE, James, 1730-94, Scots;
nonfiction BU
'BRUCE, Lenny' see SCHNEIDER,
Leonard A.
'BRUCE, Leo' see CROFT-COOKE,
Rupert
BRUCE, Mary Grant, -1958,
Australian; juveniles KI
BRUCE, Mary McCullough,
1927- , American; juven-
iles WAR
BRUCE, Michael, 1746-67, Scots;
poetry BU DA
BRUCE, Raymon Rene, 1934- ,
American; nonfiction, plays
CON
BRUCE, Robert Vance, 1923- ,
American; nonfiction CON
BRUCE-NOVOA, Juan, 1944- ,
American; fiction, poetry,
nonfiction MAR
BRUCH, Hilde, German-American;
nonfiction CON
BRUCHESI, Jean, 1901- , Ca-
nadian; poetry, nonfiction BU
CR
BRUCKER, Clara Hantel, 1892?-
1980, American; nonfiction
CON
BRUCKER, Herbert, 1898-1977,
American; journalism, non-

fiction CON
BRUCKER, Roger Warren ('Warren
Rogers'), 1929- , American;
nonfiction CON
'BRUCKNER, Ferdinand' (Theodor
Tagger), 1891-1958, Austrian;
plays MCG
BRUCKNER, Karl, 1906- , Aus-
trian; juveniles DEM
BRUDER, Judith, American; non-
fiction CON
BRUEGEL, Johann Wolfgang (John),
1905- , Austrian-British;
translations, nonfiction CON
BRUEGMANN, Robert, 1948- ,
American; nonfiction CON
'BRÜHL, Gustav' see 'KARA
GIORG'
BRÜLOW, Caspar, 1585-1627,
German; plays BU
BRUEMMER, Fred, 1929- ,
Latvian-Canadian; nonfiction
CON
BRUENING, William Harry, 1943- ,
American; nonfiction CON
BRUEYS, David Augustin de, 1640-
1723, French; plays MCG
BRUFF, Nancy, American; poetry
fiction CON
BRUGGEN, Carry van de Haan,
1881-1932, Dutch; fiction, non-
fiction BU
BRUGGER, Robert J., 1943- ,
American; nonfiction CON
BRUGGER, William, 1941- ,
British; nonfiction CON
BRUGMAN, Johannes, 1400-73,
Dutch; poetry BU
BRUHEIM, Jan Magnus, 1914- ,
Norwegian; poetry CL
BRUHN, John Glyndon, 1934- ,
American; nonfiction CON
BRUIN, Claas, 1671-1732, Dutch;
poetry, plays BU
'BRUIN, John' see BRUTUS, Den-
nis V.
BRUINS, Elton John, 1927- ,
American; nonfiction CON
BRULEZ, Raymond, 1895- ,
Flemish; fiction, plays BU
BRULLER, Jean Marcel see 'VER-
CORS'
'BRULLS, Christian' see SIMENON,
Georges
BRUMBAUGH, Thomas Brendle,
1921- , American; nonfiction
CON
BRUMGARDT, John Raymond,

1946- , American; nonfic-
tion CON
BRUMMEL, Mark Joseph, 1933- ,
American; nonfiction CON
BRUN, Ellen, 1933- , Danish;
nonfiction CON
BRUN, Henri, 1939- , Canadian;
nonfiction CON
BRUN, Johan Nordal, 1745-1816,
Norwegian; plays, poetry BU
BRUN von SCHÖNEBECK, late
13th century, German; poetry
BU
BRUNDAGE, Burr Cartwright,
1912- , American; nonfiction
CON
BRUNDAGE, John Herbert see
'HERBERT, John'
BRUNDAGE, Percival Flack,
1892-1979, American; nonfic-
tion CON
BRUNE, Joan de the Elder, 1588-
1658, Dutch; poetry BU
BRUNE, Joan de the Younger,
1618-49, Dutch; poetry BU
'BRUNEAU, Jean' see SYLVES-
TRE, Guy
BRUNEAU, Thomas C., 1939- ,
American; nonfiction CON
BRUNER, Herbert B., 1894-1974,
American; nonfiction CON
BRUNER, Jerome Seymour,
1915- , American; nonfiction
CON
BRUNER, Richard Wallace,
1926- , American; juveniles,
nonfiction CON WAR
BRUNER, Wally, 1931- , Amer-
ican; nonfiction CON
BRUNET, Marta, 1901-66, Chilean;
fiction BR
BRUNET, Michel, 1917- , Ca-
nadian; nonfiction CON
BRUNETIERE, Ferdinand, 1849-
1906, French; nonfiction CL
BRUNETTI, Mendor Thomas, 1894-
1979, American; nonfiction
CON
BRUNETTO LATINI, 1220?-95?,
Italian; poetry BO
BRUNHOFF, Jean de, 1899-1937,
French; juveniles CO
BRUNHOFF, Laurent de, 1925- ,
French; juveniles CO CON
BRUNHOUSE, Robert Levere,
1908- , American; nonfic-
tion CON
BRUNI, Leonardo ('Aretino'),

1370/73-1444, Italian; nonfic-
tion BO BU TH
BRUNIUS, Bernardus, 18th century,
Dutch; translations BU
BRUNNER, Edmund de Schweinitz,
1889-1973, American; nonfic-
tion CON
BRUNNER, John, 1934- , English;
fiction AS NI
BRUNNER, Maurice Yaw ('Yaw
Maurice Boateng'), 1950- ,
Ghanaian; juveniles, tv CON
BRUNNGRABER, Rudolf, 1901- ,
German; fiction NI
BRUNO, Giordano, 1548-1600,
Italian; poetry, nonfiction BO
BU MCG TH
BRUNO, Harold R., Jr., 1928- ,
American; journalism CON
BRUNO, James Edward ('Eldon
Summer'), 1940- , American;
nonfiction CON
BRUNO, Vincent J., 1926- , Amer-
ican; nonfiction CON
BRUNS, Frederick R., Jr., 1913?-
79, American; journalism, non-
fiction CON
BRUNSKILL, Ronald William,
1929- , British; nonfiction
CON
BRUNSTEIN, Karl Avrum, 1933- ,
American; nonfiction CON
BRUNT, Peter Astbury, 1917- ,
British; nonfiction CON
BRUNTON, David Walter, 1929- ,
American; nonfiction CON
BRUS, Wlodzimierz, 1921- ,
Polish-British; nonfiction CON
BRUSH, Douglas Peirce, 1930- ,
American; nonfiction CON
BRUSH, Judith Marie, 1938- ,
American; nonfiction CON
BRUSH, Stephen George, American;
nonfiction CON
BRUSILOFF, Phyllis, 1935- ,
American; nonfiction CON
'BRUSS, B. R.' (Roger Blondel),
1895- , French; fiction NI
BRUSTEIN, Robert Sanford, 1927- ,
American; nonfiction WA
BRUTEAU, Beatrice, 1930- ,
American; nonfiction CON
BRUTON, Eric Moore, 1915- ,
British; fiction, juveniles, non-
fiction REI
BRUTTEN, Milton, 1922- , Amer-
ican; nonfiction CON
BRUTUS, Dennis Vincent ('John

Bruin'), 1924- , South Af-
rican; poetry BU CON HER
JA LA VCP
BRUUN, Bertel, 1937- , Danish-
American; nonfiction CON
BRUUN, Malthe Conrad, 1775-
1826, Danish; poetry BU
BRY, Gerhard, 1911- , German-
American; nonfiction CON
BRYAN, Courtland Dixon Barnes,
1936- , American; fiction,
nonfiction CON
BRYAN, Jack Yeaman, 1907- ,
American; fiction CON
BRYAN, John E., 1931- ,
Anglo-American; nonfiction
CON
BRYAN, Joseph III, 1904- ,
American; nonfiction CON
BRYAN, Marion Knighton, 1900-
74, American; nonfiction CON
'BRYAN, Mavis' see O'BRIEN,
Marian P.
BRYAN, Merwyn Leonard, 1937- ,
American; nonfiction CON
BRYAN, William Wright, 1905- ,
American; nonfiction CON
'BRYANT, Anita J.' see GREEN,
Anita J.
BRYANT, Bernice Morgan, 1908- ,
American; juveniles CO
BRYANT, Cyril Eric, Jr., 1917- .
American; nonfiction CON
BRYANT, Dorothy, 1930- , Amer-
ican; fiction CON
BRYANT, Edward Winslow, Jr.
('Lawrence Talbot'), 1945- ,
American; fiction CON NI
BRYANT, Gay, 1945- , British;
nonfiction CON
BRYANT, Henry Allen, Jr.,
1943- , American; nonfiction
CON
BRYANT, James Cecil, Jr.,
1931- , American; nonfiction
CON
BRYANT, Keith Lynn, Jr.,
1937- , American; nonfiction
CON
BRYANT, L. A., 1927- , Amer-
ican; nonfiction SH
'BRYANT, Peter' see GEORGE,
Peter
BRYANT, Shasta Monroe, 1924- ,
American; nonfiction CON
BRYANT, Traphes Lemon, 1914- ,
American; nonfiction CON
BRYANT, William Cullen, 1794-

1878, American; poetry AM
BR BU MAG MYE PO VP
BRYANT, Willis Rooks, 1892-1965,
American; nonfiction CON
BRYCE, James (John?), 1838-1922,
American; nonfiction BR MAG
BRYCHTA, Alex, 1956- , Czech-
English; juveniles CO CON
BRYDEN, John Marshall, 1941- ,
American; nonfiction CON
BRYDGES, Sir Samuel Egerton,
1762-1837, English; nonfiction,
fiction BU DA
BRYENNIUS, Nicephorus, 1062-
1138, Byzantine, nonfiction
LA
BRYERS, Paul, 1945- , British;
journalism, fiction CON
BRYFONSKI, Dedria Anne, 1947- ,
American; nonfiction CON
'BRYHER' (Annie Winifred Eller-
man), 1894- , British; fiction,
nonfiction VCN
BRYKS, Rachmil, 1912-74, Polish-
American; poetry, fiction CON
BRYLL, Ernest, 1935- , Polish;
poetry, fiction, plays CL
BRYNOLF, Algotsson, 1250-1317,
Swedish; hymns BU
BRYSON, Bernarda (Shahn),
1903/05- , American; juven-
iles, nonfiction CO CON DE
BRYSON, Conrey, 1905- , Amer-
ican; nonfiction CON
BRYSON, Phillip James, 1939- ,
American; nonfiction CON
BRYSON, Reid Allen, 1920- ,
American; nonfiction CON
BRYUSOV, Valeriy Yakovlevich,
1873-1924, Russian; poetry,
nonfiction, fiction BU CL TH
BRZEKOWSKI, Jan, 1903- , Polish;
poetry, fiction BU CL
BRZOZOWSKI, Leopold Stanislaw
Leon ('Adam Czepiel'), 1878-
1911, Polish; nonfiction, fic-
tion BU CL
BUARQUE de HOLANDA, Sérgio,
1902- , Brazilian; nonfiction
BR
BUBAR, Margaret Weber, 1920-78,
American; nonfiction CON
'BUBB, Mel' see WHITCOMB, Ian
BUBECK, Mark Irving, 1928- ,
American; nonfiction CON
BUBER, Martin, 1878-1965, Aus-
trian; nonfiction SEY
BUCCELLATI, Giorgio, 1937- ,

Italian-American; nonfiction
CON
BUCCHIERI, Theresa F., 1908- ,
American; nonfiction CON
BUCHAN, Alastair Francis, 1918-
76, British; journalism, non-
fiction CON
'BUCHAN, David' see WOMACK,
David A.
BUCHAN, John, 1875-1940, Scots;
fiction, nonfiction, juveniles
BU COM DA MAG MCC PO
REI ST VN
BUCHAN, Stuart, 1942- , Aus-
tralian; nonfiction CON
BUCHAN, Thomas Buchanan,
1931- , Scots; poetry, plays,
fiction VCP
BUCHANAN, Betty Joan ('Joan
Shepherd'), 1923- , Amer-
ican; fiction CON
BUCHANAN, Cynthia, 1942- ,
American; fiction CON
BUCHANAN, Eric David, 1933- ,
Scots; nonfiction CON
BUCHANAN, George, 1506-82,
Scots; nonfiction, poetry
BU DA RU
BUCHANAN, George Henry,
1904- , British; poetry,
plays, fiction, nonfiction HO
VCN VCP
BUCHANAN, Jarie see 'PETRIE,
Rhona'
BUCHANAN, Robert Williams,
1841-1901, English; poetry,
fiction, plays BU DA
BUCHANAN, William Jesse,
1926- , American; nonfiction
CON
BUCHANAN-BROWN, John ('John
Warland'), 1929- , British;
nonfiction CON
BUCHDAHL, Gerd, 1914- ,
German-English; nonfiction
CON
BUCHELE, William Martin,
1895- , American; nonfiction
CON
BUCHER, Glenn Richard, 1940- ,
American; nonfiction CON
BUCHER, Magnus, 1927- ,
German-American; nonfiction
CON
BUCHHEIM, Othar-Guenther,
1918- , German; nonfiction,
fiction CON
BUCHHEIT, Lee Charles, 1950- ,

American; nonfiction CON
BUCHHOLTZ, Andreas Heinrich,
1607-71, German; fiction,
poetry BU
BUCHHOLTZ, Johannes, 1882-1940,
Danish; fiction BU
BUCHINSKAYA, Nadezhda A. see
'TEFFY'
BUCHMAN, Dian Dincin, American;
nonfiction CON
BUCHMAN, Herman, 1920- ,
German-American; nonfiction
CON
BUCHMAN, Randall Loren, 1929- ,
American; nonfiction CON
BUCHMAN, Sidney, 1902-75, Amer-
ican; plays CON
BUCHNER, Augustus, 1591-1661,
German; poetry BU
BUCHWALD, Ann McGarry, Amer-
ican; juveniles WAR
BUCHWALD, Art, 1925- , Amer-
ican; journalism, juveniles
BR CO WA WAR
BUCHWALD, Emilie, 1935- ,
Austrian-American; nonfiction,
juveniles CO CON
BUCK, Ashley, -1980, American;
plays, nonfiction, fiction CON
BUCK, Doris Pitkin, 1898?-1980,
American; fiction, poetry CON
NI
BUCK, George Crawford, 1918- ,
American; translations CON
BUCK, John Lossing, 1890-1975,
American; nonfiction CON
BUCK, Lewis, 1925- , American;
juveniles, nonfiction CO CON
BUCK, Margaret Waring, 1910- ,
American; juveniles CO
BUCK, Paul Herman, 1899-1978,
American; nonfiction CON
BUCK, Pearl Sydenstricker, 1892-
1973, American; fiction, plays,
poetry, juveniles, nonfiction
BR BU CO CON MAG VN
BUCK, Peggy Sullivan, 1930- ,
American; poetry CON
BUCK, Philip Wallenstein, 1900- ,
American; nonfiction CON
BUCK, Robert N., 1914- , Amer-
ican; nonfiction CON
BUCKERRIDGE, Anthony Malcolm,
1912- , English; juveniles,
plays, fiction CO CON KI
BUCKEYE, Donald Andrew, 1930- ,
American; nonfiction CON
BUCKHOLDT, David R., 1942- ,

American; nonfiction CON
BUCKHOUT, Robert, 1935- ,
American; nonfiction CON
BUCKINGHAM, Burdette H.,
1907?-77, American; nonfic-
tion CON
BUCKINGHAM, Walter Samuel
Jr., 1924-67, American; non-
fiction CON
BUCKINGHAM, 2nd Duke of see
VILLIERS, George
BUCKINX, Pieter Geert, 1903- ,
Flemish; poetry BU
BUCKLAND, Michael Keeble,
1941- , Anglo-American;
nonfiction CON
BUCKLAND, Raymond ('Tony
Earll'; 'Jessica Wells'),
1934- , British; nonfiction
CON
BUCKLE, Henry Thomas, 1821-
62, English; nonfiction BU
DA
BUCKLE, Richard, 1916- , Brit-
ish; plays, nonfiction CON
BUCKLER, Ernest Redmond,
1908- , Canadian; fiction,
nonfiction BU VCN
'BUCKLEY, Doris H.' see BUCK-
LEY NEVILLE, Heather
'BUCKLEY, Fiona' see ANAND,
Valerie
BUCKLEY, James Lane, 1923- ,
American; nonfiction CON
BUCKLEY, Julian Gerard, 1905- ,
American; nonfiction CON
BUCKLEY, Mary Lorraine, Amer-
ican; nonfiction CON
BUCKLEY, Michael F., 1880?-
1977, American; journalism
CON
BUCKLEY, Michael Joseph,
1931- , American; nonfic-
tion CON
BUCKLEY, Priscilla, 1921- ,
American; fiction CON
BUCKLEY, Roger Norman,
1937- , American; nonfic-
tion CON
BUCKLEY, Shawn, 1943- ,
American; nonfiction CON
BUCKLEY, Vincent Thomas,
1925- , Australian; po-
etry, nonfiction CON DA
VCP
BUCKLEY, William F., Jr.,
1925- , American; fiction,
nonfiction MCC WA

BUCKLEY NEVILLE, Heather
('Doris Heather Buckley'),
1910- , American; nonfiction
CON
BUCKLIN, Louis Pierre, 1928- ,
American; nonfiction CON
BUCKMAN, Peter, 1941- , Eng-
lish; nonfiction CON
BUCKMASTER, Henrietta see
HENKLE, Henrietta
BUCKNER, Sally Beaver, 1931- ,
American; plays CON
BUCKSTEAD, Richard Chris,
1929- , American; nonfiction
CON
BUCKSTONE, John Baldwin, 1802-
79, English; plays VD
BUCZKOWSKI, Leopold, 1905- ,
Polish; fiction, nonfiction BU
CL CON
BUDAI-DELEANU, Ivan, 1760-
1820, Rumanian; nonfiction
BU
BUDANTSEV, Sergey Fëdorovich,
1896- , Russian; fiction BU
BUDBERG, Moura, 1892?-1974,
Russian-British; translations
CON
BUDBILL, David, 1940- , Amer-
ican; plays, juveniles, poetry,
fiction CON
BUDD, Elaine, 1925- , American;
journalism, nonfiction CON
BUDD, Lillian Peterson, 1897- ,
American; juveniles CO
BUDD, Mavis ('Sully Denham'),
British; nonfiction CON
BUDD, William Claude, 1923- ,
American; nonfiction CON
BUDDEE, Paul Edgar, 1913- ,
British; juveniles, poetry,
journalism CON
BUDDHAGHOSA, 5th century, In-
dian; nonfiction PRU
BUDE, Guillaume, 1468-1540,
French; nonfiction BU TH
'BUDE, John' (Ernest Carpenter
Elmore), 1901-57, British;
fiction, juveniles REI
BUDENZ, Louis Francis, 1891-
1972, American; nonfiction
CON
BUDGELL, Eustace, 1686-1737,
English; nonfiction BU DA
BUDICH, Carl, 1904- , German;
poetry, plays BU
BUDIMER, Simo Velimir, 1926- ,
Yugo-American; journalism CON

BUDRY, Paul, 1883-1949, Swiss;
nonfiction, fiction BU
'BUDRYS' (Algirda Jonas
Budrys, 'Alger Rome'),
1931- , American; fiction
AS COW NI
BUECHNER, Carl Frederick,
1926- , American; fiction,
nonfiction VCN WA
BÜCHNER, Karl George, 1813-
37, German; plays BU MAG
MCG TH
BUECHNER, Thomas Scharman,
1926- , American; nonfic-
tion CON
BUEHR, Walter Franklin, 1897-
1971, American; juveniles
CO DE
BUEHRIG, Gordon M., 1904- ,
American; nonfiction CON
BUEL, Richard Van Wyck, Jr.,
1933- , American; nonfiction
CON
BUELER, Lois Eaton, 1940- ,
American; nonfiction CON
BUELL, Harold G., American;
juveniles WAR
BUELL, John, 1927- , Canadian;
fiction CR
BUELL, Jon A., 1939- , Amer-
ican; nonfiction CON
BUELL, Lawrence, 1939- ,
American; nonfiction CON
BUENKER, John David, 1937- ,
American; nonfiction CON
BUENO, Jose de la Torre, 1905?-
80, American; nonfiction CON
BÜRGER, Gottfried August, 1747-
94, German; poetry BU TH
BUERKLE, Jack Vincent, 1923- ,
American; nonfiction CON
BUERO VALLEJO, Antonio,
1916- , Spanish; plays,
BU CL MCG TH
BUETOW, Harold Andrew,
1919- , American; nonfic-
tion CON
BUETTNER-JANUSCH, John,
1924- , American; nonfic-
tion CON
BUFERD, Norma Bradley,
1937- , American; nonfic-
tion CON
BUFF, Conrad, 1886-1975, Swiss-
American; juveniles CO
BUFF, Mary Marsh, 1890-1970,
American; juveniles CO KI
BUFFALOE, Neal Dollison,

1924- , American; nonfiction
CON
BUFFON, Georges-Louis Leclerc,
Comte de, 1707-88, French;
nonfiction BU TH
BUFKIN, Ernest Claude, Jr.,
1929- , American; nonfiction
CON
BUGAEV, Boris N. see 'BELY,
Andrey'
BUGAJ, Jan see BACZYNSKI,
Krzysztof K.
BUGG, Ralph, 1922- , American;
nonfiction CON
BUGGIE, Frederick Denman,
1929- , American; nonfic-
tion CON
BUGLIARELLO, George, 1927- ,
Italian-American; nonfiction
CON
BUGLIOSI, Vincent T., 1934- ,
American; nonfiction CON
BUHITE, Russell Devere, 1938- ,
American; nonfiction CON
BUHRY, Hemedi Bin Abdalla,
-1922, Swahili; poetry BU
BUHTURI, 821-97, Syrian; poetry
BU PRU
BUIES, Arthur, 1840-1901, Ca-
nadian; nonfiction BU
BUIRETTE, Pierre L., see 'BEL-
LOY, Dormont de'
BUIST, Vincent, 1919?-79, British;
journalism CON
BUKALSKI, Peter Julian, 1941- ,
American; nonfiction CON
BUKENYA, Austin S. (Agustine),
1944- , Ugandan; plays, fic-
tion HER JA
BUKER, George Edward, 1923- ,
American; nonfiction CON
BUKOWSKI, Charles, 1920- ,
German-American; poetry, fic-
tion BR SEY VCP WAK
BULATOVIC, Miodrag, 1930- ,
Yugoslav; fiction, plays BU
TH WAK
BULGAKOV, Mikhail Afanasyevich,
1891-1940, Russian; fiction,
plays BU CL MCG NI SEY
TH WA
BULGAKOV, Sergey Nikolayevich,
1789-1859, Russian; nonfiction
BU
BULGARIN, Faddey Venediktovich,
1789-1959, Russian; journalism,
fiction BU
BULGER, William Thomas, 1927- ,

American; nonfiction, fiction
CON
BULL, Angela Mary, 1936- ,
British; juveniles KI
BULL, John, 1914- , American;
nonfiction CON
BULL, Norman John, 1916- ,
American; juveniles, nonfic-
tion CON
BULL, Odd, 1907- , Norwegian;
nonfiction CON
BULL, Olaf Jacob Martin Luther,
1883-1933, Norwegian; poetry,
fiction, plays BU CL TH
BULL, Robert Jehu, 1920- ,
American; nonfiction CON
BULLA, Clyde Robert, 1914- ,
American; juveniles, fiction
KI
BULLARD, Oral, 1922- , Amer-
ican; fiction, nonfiction CON
BULLE, Florence Elizabeth,
1925- , American; nonfiction
CON
BULLEN, Dana Ripley, 1931- ,
American; journalism CON
BULLEN, Frank Thomas, 1857-
1915, English; nonfiction
MAG
'BULLEN, Leonard' see KEN-
NEDY, Leo
BULLEN, Robert, 1926?-76,
American; journalism, trans-
lations, nonfiction CON
BULLER, Herman, 1923- , Ca-
nadian; fiction CON
BULLHE, Shah (Sah), 1680-1758,
Punjabi; poetry BU PRU
BULLIET, Richard Williams ('Clar-
ence J.-L. Jackson'), 1940- ,
American; nonfiction CON
BULLINGER, Heinrich, 1504-75,
Swiss; plays BU
BULLINS, Ed, 1935- , American;
poetry, fiction, nonfiction, plays
CON MCN SH VCD VD WAK
BULLIS, Jerald, 1944- , Amer-
ican; poetry CON
BULLITT, Orville Horwitz, 1894-
1979, American; nonfiction
CON
BULLITT, William Christian,
1891-1967, American; nonfic-
tion CON
BULLIVANT, Cecil Henry, 1882- ,
English; fiction ST
BULLOCK, Alice, 1904- , Amer-
ican; nonfiction CON

BULLOCK, Clarence Hassell,
1930- , American; nonfiction
CON
BULLOCK, Henry Allen, 1907?-73,
American; nonfiction CON SH
BULLOCK, Michael Hale, 1918- ,
British; poetry, fiction, trans-
lations VCP
BULLOCK, Shan F., 1865-1935,
Irish; fiction HO
BULLOCK-WILSON, Barbara,
1945- , American; nonfiction
CON
BULLOUGH, Bonnie, 1927- ,
American; nonfiction CON
BULLOUGH, William Alfred, 1933- ,
American; nonfiction CON
BULMAN, Joan Carroll, 1904- ,
British; nonfiction, translations
CON
BULMAN, Oliver Meredith, 1902-
74, British; nonfiction CON
BULMER, Kenneth (H. K.; 'Alan
Burt Akers'; 'Frank Brandon';
'Rupert Clinton'; 'Ernest Cor-
ley'; 'Peter Green'; 'Philip
Kent'; 'Chesman Scot'; 'Nelson
Sherwood'; 'H. Philip Stratford';
'Tully Zetford'; 'Kenneth Johns';
'Karl Maras'), 1921- , Eng-
lish; fiction AS NI
BULOSAN, Carlos, 1914-56, Fil-
ipino; fiction, poetry PRU
BULTMANN, Rudolf Karl, 1884-
1976, German; nonfiction CON
WA
BULWER-LYTTON, Edward George,
1803-73, English; fiction, po-
etry, nonfiction, translations
MAG VN
BUMAGIN, Victoria E., 1923- ,
Polish-American; nonfiction
CON
BUMPPO, Nathaniel John ('Natty
Bumppo' 'John Dean'), 1940- ,
American; journalism, nonfic-
tion CON
BUMPUS, Jerry, 1937- , Amer-
ican; fiction CON
BUMSTED, John Michael, 1938- ,
American-Canadian; nonfiction
CON
BUNCE, Alan, 1939- , American;
journalism CON
BUNCH, Clarence, American; non-
fiction CON
BUNCH, David R., American; po-
etry, fiction AS NI

153   BUNDY

BUNDY, Clarence Everett,
1906- , American; nonfic-
tion CON
BUNIC-VICICEVIC, Ivan, 1597-
1658, Ragusan; poetry BU
BUNIM, Irving M., 1901?-80,
Russian-American; nonfiction
CON
BUNIN, Catherine, 1967- , Amer-
ican; juveniles CON
BUNIN, Ivan Alexeyevich, 1870-
1953, Russian; nonfiction, fic-
tion, poetry BU CL MAG
SEY TH
BUNIN, Sherry, 1925- , Amer-
ican; nonfiction, juveniles
CON
BUNING, Johan Willem Frederik,
1891-1958, Dutch; poetry BU
BUNKER, Edward, 1933- , Amer-
ican; nonfiction CON
BUNN, Thomas, 1944- , Amer-
ican; fiction CON
BUNSEKI, A. Fukiau, 1934- ,
Zairian; poetry, nonfiction
HER
BUNT, Lucas Nicolaas H., 1905- ,
Dutch-American; nonfiction
CON
BUNTING, Anne Evelyn ('Evelyn
Bolton'; 'A. E. Bunting'; 'Eve
Bunting'), 1928- , American;
fiction, juveniles CO CON
WAR
BUNTING, Bainbridge, 1913- ,
American; nonfiction CON
BUNTING, Basil, 1900- , Brit-
ish; poetry CON SEY VCP
VP WA
'BUNTING, Eve' see BUNTING,
Anne E.
BUNTING, Glenn Davison, 1957- ,
American; juveniles CO
BUNTING, Josiah, 1939- , Amer-
ican; fiction CON
BUNUEL, Luis, 1900- , Spanish;
film CON
BUNYAN, John, 1628-88, English;
nonfiction, fiction BRI BU
DA MAG PO RU VN
BUOL, Stanley Walter, 1934- ,
American; nonfiction CON
BUONAROTTI, Michelangelo,
1475-1564, Italian; poetry
BO BU MAG TH
BUONAROTTI, Michelangelo the
Younger, 1568-1642, Italian;
plays, poetry BO BU MCG

BUONCOMPAGNO da SEGNA,
-1240, Italian; nonfiction BU
BURACK, Abraham Saul, 1908-78,
American; plays, nonfiction
CON
BURANELLI, Marguerite, Amer-
ican; juveniles WAR
BURBANK, Garin, 1940- , Ameri-
can-Canadian; nonfiction CON
BURBRIDGE, Branse, 1921- ,
British; nonfiction CON
BURBY, Raymond Joseph II, 1942- ,
American; nonfiction CON
BURCH, Claire R., 1925- ,
American; poetry, nonfiction
CON
BURCH, Monte G. ('Mark Gregory'),
1943- , American; nonfiction
CON
BURCH, Pat, 1944- , American;
fiction CON
BURCH, Preston M., 1884-1978,
American; nonfiction CON
BURCH, Robert Joseph, 1925- ,
American; juveniles, transla-
tions DE KI
BURCHAM, Nancy Ann, 1942- ,
American; nonfiction CON
BURCHARD, John Ely, 1898-1975,
American; nonfiction CON
BURCHARD, Peter Duncan, 1921- ,
American; juveniles CO DE
BURCHARD, Marshall, American;
juveniles WAR
BURCHARD, Sue Huston, 1937- ,
American; juveniles CO CON
WAR
BURCHARDT, Nellie, 1921- ,
American; juveniles CO
BURCHARDT, William Robert,
1917- , American; fiction
CON
BURCHELL, S. C., American;
juveniles WAR
BURCHETT, Randall E., -1971,
American; nonfiction CON
BURCHETT, Wilfred, 1911- ,
Australian; nonfiction CON
BURCHFIELD, Joe Donald, 1937- ,
American; nonfiction CON
BURCHFIELD, Robert William,
1923- , English; nonfiction
CON
BURCHIELLO, Domenico da Gio-
vanni, 1404-49, Italian; poetry
BO BU
BURCHWOOD, Katharine Tyler,
American; nonfiction CON

BURCIAGA, Jose Antonio, 1940- ,
American; poetry MAR
BURCKEL, Nicholas Clare,
1943- , American; nonfic-
tion CON
BURCKHARDT, Carl Jakob, 1891-
1974, Swiss; nonfiction CON
BURCKHARDT, Jakob, 1818-97,
Swiss; nonfiction BU
BURD, Van Akin, 1914- , Amer-
ican; nonfiction CON
BURDA, Robert Warren, 1932- ,
American; fiction, plays
CON
BURDEN, William Douglas, 1898-
1978, American; nonfiction
CON
BURDETT, Charles, 1815-?,
American; journalism, fiction
ST
BURDETTE, Franklin L., 1911-
75, American; nonfiction CON
BURDGE, Rabel James, 1937- ,
American; nonfiction CON
BURDICK, Donald Walter, 1917- ,
American; nonfiction CON
BURDICK, Dorraine, 1929- ,
American; juveniles CON
BURDICK, Eugene Leonard, 1918-
65, American; fiction, juven-
iles AS CO NI WA
BUREAU, William Hobbs, 1913- ,
American; nonfiction CON
BURENIN, Viktor Petrovich,
1841-1926, Russian; nonfic-
tion BU
'BURFIELD, Eva' see EBBETT,
Eva
BURFORD, Eleanor, see HIB-
BERT, Eleanor
BURFORD, Lolah, American; non-
fiction, poetry CON
BURFORD, Roger Lewis, 1930- ,
American; nonfiction CON
BURFORD, William Skelly, 1927- ,
American; poetry, transla-
tions VCP
BURGE, Ethel, 1916- , Amer-
ican; nonfiction CON
BURGE, Milward R. K. see
'KENNEDY, Milward'
BURGER, Angela Sutherland
Brown, 1936- , American;
nonfiction CON
BURGER, Carl, 1888-1967, Amer-
ican; juveniles CO
BURGER, Dionys, Dutch; fiction
NI

BURGER, George Vanderkaar,
1927- , American; nonfiction
CON
BURGER, Henry G., 1923- ,
American; nonfiction CON
BURGER, John Robert, 1924- ,
American; nonfiction, fiction
CON
BURGER, Robert Eugene, 1931- ,
American; nonfiction CON
BURGER, Sarah Greene, 1935- ,
American; nonfiction CON
BURGERSDIJK, Leendert Alexander
Johannes, 1828-1900, Dutch;
translations BU
'BURGESS, Ann Marie' see GER-
SON, Noel B.
'BURGESS, Anthony' (John Anthony
Burgess Wilson; 'Joseph Kell'),
1917- , English; fiction, jour-
nalism, nonfiction, plays AS
BU DA NI PO SEY VCN WA
'BURGESS, Em' see BURGESS,
Mary W.
BURGESS, Eric Alexander, 1912- ,
British; fiction, nonfiction
CON
BURGESS, Frank Gelett, 1866-
1951, American; fiction, plays,
poetry, journalism, nonfiction
REI ST
BURGESS, Linda Cannon, 1911- ,
American; nonfiction CON
BURGESS, M. R. see 'REGINALD,
Robert'
BURGESS, Mary Wycke ('Em Bur-
gess'), 1916- , American;
juveniles, nonfiction CO CON
'BURGESS, Michael' see GERSON,
Noel B.
BURGESS, Robert Forrest, 1927- ,
American; juveniles CO WAR
BURGESS, Thornton Waldo ('W. B.
Thornton'), 1874-1965, Amer-
ican; juveniles, nonfiction CO
CON
'BURGESS, Trevor' see TREVOR,
Elleston
BURGESS, Warren Randolph, 1889-
1978, American; nonfiction
CON
BURGESS-KOHN, Jane, 1928- ,
American; nonfiction CON
BURGGRAF, Woldfried see 'FOR-
STER, Friedrich'
BURGH, Jacob van der, 1600-59,
Dutch; poetry BU
BURGIN, Charles David, 1939- ,

American; journalism CON
BURGOS, Francisco Javier de,
1842-1902, Spanish; plays
BU
BURGOS, Julia, 1914-53, Puerto
Rican; poetry, journalism
HIL
BURGOYNE, John, 1722-92, Eng-
lish; plays, nonfiction VD
BURGWYN, Mebane Holoman,
1914- , American; juveniles
CO CON
BURHANEDDIN, Kadi Ahmed,
1344-98, Turkish; poetry
PRU
BURICK, Simon, 1909- , Amer-
ican; journalism, nonfiction
CON
BURIDAN, Jean, 1300-68, French;
nonfiction BU
BURK, Bill Eugene, 1932- ,
American; nonfiction CON
BURK, Bruce, 1917- , American;
nonfiction CON
BURKE, Carol, 1950- , Amer-
ican; poetry, nonfiction CON
BURKE, Cletus Joseph, 1917-73,
American; nonfiction CON
BURKE, Edmund, 1729-97, Irish;
nonfiction BRI BU DA HO
MAG PO VN
BURKE, Gerald, 1914- , English;
nonfiction CON
BURKE, Jackson F., 1915- ,
American; fiction, poetry
CON
BURKE, James see DE BURCA,
Seamus
BURKE, James, 1936- , Irish;
tv, nonfiction CON
BURKE, James Wakefield, 1916- ,
American; nonfiction CON
'BURKE, John' see O'CONNOR,
Richard
BURKE, John Frederick ('Jonathan
Burke'; 'Owen Burke'; 'Har-
riet Esmond'; 'Jonathan
George'; 'Joanna Jones'; 'Sara
Morris'; 'Martin Sands'),
1922- , British; fiction,
plays, nonfiction AS NI REI
BURKE, John Garrett, 1917- ,
American; nonfiction CON
'BURKE, Jonathan' see BURKE,
John Frederick
BURKE, Joseph Terence, 1913- ,
British; nonfiction CON
BURKE, Kenneth Duva, 1897- ,

American; fiction, nonfiction,
poetry AM BOR BR BU PO
SEY VCN VCP
'BURKE, Leda' see GARNETT,
David
'BURKE, Noel' see 'OLSEN, D. B.'
BURKE, Omar Michael, 1927- ,
British; nonfiction CON
'BURKE, Owen' see BURKE, John F.
'BURKE, Ralph' see SILVERBERG,
Robert
BURKE, Richard Cullen, 1932- ,
American; nonfiction CON
BURKE, Samuel Martin, 1906- ,
American; nonfiction CON
'BURKE, Shifty' see BENTON,
Peggie
BURKE, Stanley, 1923- , Amer-
ican; fiction CON
BURKE, Ted, 1934?-78, American;
journalism CON
BURKE, Thomas, 1747?-83, Amer-
ican; poetry BA
BURKE, Thomas, 1886-1945, Brit-
ish; fiction, plays, juveniles,
nonfiction REI ST
BURKE, Tom, American; nonfic-
tion CON
BURKE, Velma Whitgrove (Vee),
1921- , American; nonfiction
CON
BURKE, Virginia M., 1916- ,
American; nonfiction CON
BURKERT, Nancy Ekholm, 1933- ,
juveniles CO DE
BURKERT, Walter, 1931- , Ger-
man; nonfiction CON
BURKETT, David Young, III,
1934- , American; nonfiction
CON
BURKETT, Jack, 1914- , British;
nonfiction CON
BURKETT, Molly, 1932- , English;
nonfiction CON
BURKETT, William R., Jr.,
1943- , American; fiction,
journalism NI
BURKEY, Richard Michael, 1930- ,
American; nonfiction CON
BURKHARD von HOHENFELS, fl.
1225, Swiss; poetry BU
BURKHART, Erika, 1922- , Swiss;
poetry, fiction CL
BURKHART, Kathryn Watterson
('Kitsi Burkhart'), 1942- ,
American; nonfiction CON
BURKS, Arthur J., 1898-1974,
American; fiction AS NI

BURKS, Arthur Walter, 1915- ,
American; nonfiction CON
BURL, Aubrey, 1926- , British;
nonfiction CON
BURLA, Yehuda, 1886-1969, Is-
raeli; fiction BU
BURLAND, Cottie Arthur, 1905- ,
English; juveniles CO
BURLEY, William John, 1914- ,
British; fiction, nonfiction
REI
BURLINGAME, Roger, 1889-1967,
American; juveniles WAR
BURLINGHAM, Dorothy Tiffany,
1891-1979, British; nonfiction
CON
BURLYUK, David Davidovich,
1882-1967, Russian; poetry
CL
BURMAN, Alice, (Caddy), 1896?-
1977, American; juveniles
CO
BURMAN, Ben Lucian, 1896- ,
American; juveniles CO
BURMAN, Petrus, Jr., 1713-78,
Dutch; poetry, nonfiction BU
BURMEISTER, Lou Ella, 1928- ,
American; nonfiction CON
BURMESTER, Heinrich, 1839-89,
German; fiction BU
BURN, Barbara, 1940- , Amer-
ican; nonfiction CON
BURNAM, Tom, 1913- , Amer-
ican; nonfiction, fiction CON
'BURNE, Glen' see GREEN, Alan
B.
BURNES, Chester Ray, 1937- ,
American; nonfiction CON
BURNES, Edward McNall, 1897-
1972, American; nonfiction
CON
BURNESS, Wallace Binny (Tad),
1933- , American; nonfic-
tion CON
BURNET, Frank Macfarlane,
1899- , Australian; nonfic-
tion CON
BURNET, Gilbert, 1643-1715,
Scots; nonfiction BU DA PO
BURNET, Mary Edith, 1911- ,
American; nonfiction CON
BURNET, Thomas, 1635-1715,
English; nonfiction, transla-
tions BU DA
BURNETT, Alfred David, 1937- ,
Scots; poetry, nonfiction
CON
BURNETT, Avis, 1937- ,

American; nonfiction CON
BURNETT, Frances Eliza Hodgson,
1849-1924, Anglo-American;
juveniles, fiction, plays BA
BR COM DA KI VN
BURNETT, James, 1714-99, Scots;
nonfiction DA
BURNETT, Janet, 1915- , Amer-
ican; nonfiction CON
BURNETT, John, 1925- , English;
nonfiction CON
BURNETT, Laurence, 1907- ,
American; nonfiction CON
BURNETT, Whit, 1899-1973, Amer-
ican; fiction, nonfiction CON
BURNETT, William Riley ('John
Monahan'; 'James Updyke'),
1899-1982, American; fiction,
plays, nonfiction BR REI ST
BURNEY, Charles, 1726-1814,
English; nonfiction BU
BURNEY, Fanny (Frances d'Arb-
lay), 1752-1840, English; fic-
tion, diary BU DA MAG PO
VN
BURNFORD, Sheila ('S. D. Burn-
ford'; 'Philip Cochrane Every'),
1918- , Scots; juveniles, fic-
tion, nonfiction CO DEM KI
BURNHAM, Dorothy Edith, 1921- ,
American; poetry CON
BURNHAM, James, 1905- , Amer-
ican; nonfiction BR
BURNHAM, Sophy, 1936- , Amer-
ican; nonfiction CON
BURNHAM, Walter Dean, 1930- ,
American; nonfiction CON
BURNIAUX, Constant, 1892-1975,
Belgian; fiction, poetry CL
BURNINGHAM, John Mackintosh,
1936- , British; juveniles
CO CON DE KI
BURNLEY, Judith, British; fiction
CON
BURNS, Alan, 1929- , British;
fiction, plays VCN
BURNS, Alan Cuthbert, 1887-1980,
British; nonfiction CON
BURNS, Alma ('Claire Dalton'),
American; fiction CON
'BURNS, Bobby' see BURNS, Vin-
cent G.
BURNS, James MacGregor, 1918- ,
American; nonfiction WA
BURNS, Jean Ellen, 1934- ,
American; nonfiction CON
BURNS, Jim, 1936- , British; po-
etry, nonfiction CON VCP

BURNS, Joan Simpson, 1927- ,
American; nonfiction CON
BURNS, John Horne, 1916-53,
American; fiction BR PO
BURNS, Norman Thomas, 1930- ,
American; nonfiction CON
BURNS, Paul C., American; ju-
veniles CO
BURNS, Raymond Howard, 1924- ,
American; juveniles CO
BURNS, Rex Raoul, 1935- ,
American; fiction, nonfiction
CON REI
BURNS, Richard Webster, 1920- ,
American; nonfiction CON
BURNS, Robert, 1759-96, Scots;
poetry BRI BU DA MAG PO
VP
BURNS, Robert Milton Clark, Jr.,
('Scott Burns'), 1940- ,
American; nonfiction CON
BURNS, Thomas, Jr., 1928- ,
American; nonfiction CON
BURNS, Thomas Stephen, 1927- ,
American; nonfiction CON
BURNS, Vincent Godfrey ('Bobby
Burns'), 1893-1979, Amer-
ican; nonfiction, plays, po-
etry CON
BURNS, William Aloysius, 1909- ,
American; juveniles CO WAR
BURNSHAW, Stanley, 1906- ,
American; poetry, plays, fic-
tion, nonfiction VCP WA
BURNSIDE, Wesley Mason, 1918- ,
American; nonfiction CON
BURNS-NCAMASHE, Sipo, 1920- ,
South African; poetry HER
BUROS, Oscar Krisen, 1905-78,
American; nonfiction CON
BURR, Charles, 1922?-76, Amer-
ican; journalism, nonfiction
CON
BURR, Gray, 1919- , American;
poetry CON
BURR, John Roy, 1933- , Amer-
ican; nonfiction CON
BURR, Lonnie, 1943- , Amer-
ican; plays CON
BURRELL, Berkeley Graham,
1919-79, American; nonfic-
tion CON
BURRELL, Evelyn Patterson,
American; poetry CON
BURRIDGE, Kenelm Oswald,
1922- , Canadian; nonfic-
tion CON
BURRINGTON, David E.,

1931- , American; journalism
CON
BURRIS-MEYER, Harold, 1902- ,
American; nonfiction CON
BURROS, Marian Fox, American;
nonfiction CON
BURROUGHS, Benjamin F., 1918- ,
American; nonfiction CON
BURROUGHS, Edgar Rice, 1875-
1950, American; fiction AS
BR COW NI VN
BURROUGHS, Jean Mitchel, 1908- ,
American; juveniles, nonfiction
CON
BURROUGHS, John, 1837-1921,
American; nonfiction BR
BURROUGHS, John Coleman,
1913- , American; fiction
NI
BURROUGHS, Margaret T. G.,
1917- , American; juveniles
SH
BURROUGHS, William, Jr.,
1947- , American; fiction,
nonfiction CON
BURROUGHS, William Seward
('William Lee'), 1914- ,
American; fiction, plays, po-
etry, nonfiction AS BR BU
COW HE NI PO SEY VCN VN
WA
BURROW, John Anthony, 1932- ,
British; nonfiction CON
BURROWAY, Janet Gay, 1936- ,
American; fiction, plays, po-
etry, juveniles CO KIB VCN
WAR
BURROWES, Michael Anthony,
1937- , British; fiction CON
BURROWS, Abe, 1910- , Amer-
ican; plays VCD
BURROWS, David James, 1936- ,
American; nonfiction CON
BURROWS, Edwin Gladding, 1917- ,
American; journalism, poetry
CON
BURROWS, Fredrika Alexander,
1908- , American; nonfiction
CON
BURROWS, John, 1945- , British;
plays CON VCD
BURROWS, Millar, 1889-1980,
American; nonfiction CON
BURROWS, William E., 1937- ,
American; nonfiction CON
BURSK, Christopher, 1943- ,
American; poetry CON
BURSSENS, Gaston, 1896-1965,

Flemish; poetry BU CL
BURSTEIN, Alvin George, 1931- ,
American; nonfiction CON
BURSTEIN, John, 1949- , American; juveniles CON
BURSTON, W. H., 1915-81, British; nonfiction CON
BURT, Frances Riemer, 1917- ,
American; nonfiction, plays
CON
BURT, Jesse Clefton, 1921-76,
American; juveniles CO
BURT, Olive Woolley, 1894- ,
American; juveniles CO
BURT, Robert Amsterdam,
1939- , American; nonfiction CON
BURTIS, Charles Edward, 1907- ,
American; nonfiction CON
BURTON, Alice Elizabeth ('Susan
Alice Kerby'), 1908- , English; fiction, nonfiction CON
BURTON, Anthony, 1933- , Anglo-
Canadian; nonfiction CON
BURTON, David Henry, 1925- ,
American; nonfiction CON
BURTON, Dwight Lowell, 1922- ,
American; nonfiction CON
BURTON, Gabrielle, 1939- ,
American; fiction CON
BURTON, Harold Bernard, 1908- ,
American; journalism, non-
fiction, juveniles CON
BURTON, Harry McGuire Philip,
1898?-1979, British; nonfiction CON
BURTON, Hester Wood-Hill,
1913- , British; juveniles
CO DE KI WAR
BURTON, John Andrew, 1944- ,
American; nonfiction CON
BURTON, John Hill, 1909-81,
Scots; nonfiction BU DA
BURTON, John Wear, 1915- ,
Australian; nonfiction CON
BURTON, Katherine Kurz, 1890-
1969, American; nonfiction
CON
BURTON, Lloyd E., 1922- ,
American; nonfiction CON
BURTON, Maurice, 1898- ,
English; nonfiction, juven-
iles CO CON
BURTON, Nelson, Jr., 1942- ,
American; nonfiction CON
BURTON, Richard, 1577-1640,
English; nonfiction MAG
BURTON, Sir Richard Francis,

1821-90, English; nonfiction,
translations BU DA PO
BURTON, Robert ('Democritus,
Jr.'), 1576/77-1639/40, Eng-
lish; nonfiction, plays, fiction
BU DA PO RU VN
BURTON, Robert Edward, 1927- ,
American; nonfiction CON
BURTON, Robert Wellesley, 1941- ,
English; juveniles, nonfiction
CO CON
BURTON, Roger Vernon, 1928- ,
American; nonfiction CON
BURTON, Samuel Holroyd, 1919- ,
British; nonfiction CON NI
BURTON, Virginia Lee, 1909-68,
American; juveniles KI
BURTON, William Henry, 1890-
1964, American; juveniles CO
BURTON-BRADLEY, Burton Gyrth,
1914- , Australian; nonfiction
CON
BURTT, George, 1914- , Canadian-
American; nonfiction CON
'BURY, Frank' see HARRIS, Her-
bert
BURY, John Bagnell, 1861-1927,
Irish; nonfiction DA
BURY, Richard Aungerville de,
1287?-1345, English; nonfiction
BU
BURYN, Edward Casimir, 1934- ,
American; nonfiction CON
BUS, Gervais du, -1339, French;
nonfiction BU
BUSBEE, Shirlee Elaine, 1941- ,
American; fiction CON
BUSBY, F. M., 1921- , Amer-
ican; fiction CON NI
BUSBY, Roger Charles, 1941- ,
British; fiction REI
BUSCH, Francis Xavier, 1879-
1975, American; nonfiction
CON
BUSCH, Frederick, 1941- , Amer-
ican; fiction, nonfiction KIB
VCN
BUSCH, Julia, 1940- , American;
nonfiction CON
BUSCH, Noel Fairchild, 1906- ,
American; nonfiction CON
BUSCH, Wilhelm, 1832-1908, Ger-
man; poetry BU TH
BUSCH(E), Hermann von dem,
1468-1534, German; nonfiction
BU
BUSE, Renee ('R. F. Buse'; 'Robert
Benton'; 'Michael King'), 1914?-

79, American; nonfiction
CON
BUSH, Barbara Holstein, 1935- ,
American; nonfiction CON
'BUSH, Christopher' (Charlie
Christmas Bush; 'Michael
Home'), 1888?-1973, Brit-
ish; fiction, nonfiction REI
ST
BUSH, Eric, 1899- , American;
nonfiction CON
BUSH, Jim, 1926- , American;
nonfiction CON
BUSH, Lewis William, 1907- ,
British; nonfiction CON
BUSH, Sargent, Jr., 1937- ,
American; nonfiction CON
BUSH, Vannevar, 1890-1974,
American; nonfiction CON
BUSH-BROWN, Louise, 1896?-
1973, American; nonfiction
CON
BUSHA, Charles Henry, 1931- ,
American; nonfiction CON
BUSHINSKY, Jay Joseph, 1932- ,
American; nonfiction, jour-
nalism CON
BUSHNELL, David Sherman,
1927- , American; nonfic-
tion CON
BUSHYAGER, Linda Eyster,
1947- , American; fiction
CON
BUSIA, Kofi Abrefa, 1913/14- ,
Ghanaian; nonfiction CON
HER
BUSIRI, 1213-96, Arab; poetry
BU
BUSKIN, Martin, 1930-76, Amer-
ican; journalism, nonfiction
CON
BUSLAYEV, Fëdor Ivanovich,
1818-97, Russian; nonfiction
BU
BUSON, see YOSA BUSON
BUSONI, Rafaello, 1900-62,
German-American; juveniles
CO
BUSSE, Thomas Valentine, 1941- ,
American; nonfiction CON
BUSSEY, Ellen Marion, 1926- ,
American; nonfiction CON
BUSSIERES, Simone, 1918- ,
Canadian; nonfiction, fiction
CON
'BUSTA, Christine' ('C. Dimt'),
1915- , Austrian; poetry
TH

BUSTAMANTE, Jorge A., 1938- ,
American; nonfiction MAR
BUSTANI, Butrus, 1819-83, Leban-
ese; journalism PRU
BUSTANOBY, Andre Steven, 1930- ,
American; nonfiction CON
BUSTARD, Robert, 1938- , Eng-
lish; nonfiction CON
BUSTEED, Marilyn, 1937- , Amer-
ican; nonfiction CON
BUTCHER, Anne Judith, 1927- ,
English; nonfiction CON
BUTCHER, Margaret Just, 1913- ,
American; nonfiction SH
BUTCHER, Phillip, 1918- , Amer-
ican; nonfiction SH
BUTCHER, Russell Devereux,
1938- , American; nonfiction
CON
'BUTCK, Zulie' see JONES, Thomas
W.
BUTH, Lenore, 1932- , American;
nonfiction CON
BUTHELEZI, Gatsha, 1928- ,
South African; nonfiction CON
BUTKOV, Yakov Petrovich, 1815-
56, Russian; fiction BU
BUTLER, Beverly Kathleen, 1932- ,
American; juveniles CO
BUTLER, Bill, 1934- , American;
poetry BR
BUTLER, David Francis, 1928- ,
American; nonfiction CON
BUTLER, David Jonathon, 1946- ,
American; juveniles, nonfiction
CON
BUTLER, Edgar Wilbur, 1929- ,
American; nonfiction CON
BUTLER, Ellis Parker, 1869-1937,
American; fiction PAL ST
BUTLER, Frederick Guy, 1918- ,
South African; poetry, plays,
fiction BU CON DA VCP VP
BUTLER, George Tyssen, 1943- ,
British; nonfiction CON
BUTLER, Gwendoline William
('Jennie Melville'), British;
fiction, plays REI
BUTLER, Hal, 1913- , American;
nonfiction CON
'BUTLER, Ivan' see BEUTTLER,
Edward I.
BUTLER, James Harmon, 1908- ,
American; nonfiction CON
BUTLER, Jean (Rouverol), 1916- ,
American; nonfiction, juveniles,
film CON
BUTLER, Jeffrey Ernest, 1922- ,

BUTLER 160

South African-American; non-
fiction CON
BUTLER, Jerry P., 1944- ,
American; nonfiction CON
'BUTLER, Joan' see ALEXANDER,
Robert W.
BUTLER, Joseph, 1692-1752, Eng-
lish; nonfiction BU DA PO
BUTLER, Joyce, 1933- , Amer-
ican; nonfiction CON
BUTLER, Lucius Albert, Jr.,
1928- , American; nonfiction
CON
BUTLER, Marilyn Speers, 1937- ,
British; nonfiction CON
BUTLER, Mildred Allen, 1897- ,
American; juveniles WAR
BUTLER, Natalie Sturges, 1908- ,
American; nonfiction CON
'BUTLER, Nathan' see SOHL,
Jerry
BUTLER, Octavia Estelle, 1947- ,
American; fiction CON
'BUTLER, Richard' see ALL-
BEURY, Ted
BUTLER, Richard, 1925- ,
English; fiction CON
BUTLER, Rick, 1946- , Canadian;
nonfiction CON
BUTLER, Robert Albert, 1934- ,
American; nonfiction CON
BUTLER, Robert Lee, 1918- ,
American; nonfiction CON
BUTLER, Robert Niel, 1927- ,
American; nonfiction CON
BUTLER, Ronald William, 1934- ,
American; nonfiction CON
BUTLER, Samuel, 1612/13-80,
English; poetry, nonfiction
BU DA MAG PO VP
BUTLER, Samuel, 1835-1902, Eng-
lish; fiction, nonfiction BU
DA MAG NI PO VN
BUTLER, Stanley, 1914- , Amer-
ican; nonfiction CON
BUTLER, Suzanne, Canadian; ju-
veniles WAR
'BUTLER, Walter C.' see
'BRAND, Max'
BUTLER, William, 1929- ,
American; juveniles, fiction
NI WAR
BUTLER, William Muxford
('Hassan i Sabbah'), 1934- ,
American; poetry CON
BUTON RINCHENDUP, 1290-1364,
Tibetan; nonfiction PRU
BUTOR, Michel, 1926- , French;

fiction, nonfiction, poetry BU
CL NI REI SEY TH WA
BUTRY, Zofia Teresa, 1927- ,
Polish-British; nonfiction CON
BUTSCHER, Edward, 1943- ,
American; nonfiction CON
BUTT, Howard Edward, Jr.,
1927- , American; nonfiction
CON
BUTT, Susan, 1938- , Canadian;
nonfiction CON
BUTTACI, Salvatore St. John,
1941- , American; plays, po-
etry CON
BUTTEL, Robert William, 1923- ,
American; nonfiction CON
BUTTERFIELD, Roger Place,
1907-81, American; journal-
ism, nonfiction CON
BUTTERFIELD, Stephen Thomas,
1942- , American; nonfiction
CON
'BUTTERFLY, Red' see 'LAURIT-
SEN, John P.'
BUTTERS, Dorothy (Gilman),
1923- , American; juveniles
CO REI
BUTTERWORTH, Michael, 1947- ,
English; fiction NI
BUTTERWORTH, Oliver, 1915- ,
American; juveniles DEM
WAR
BUTTERWORTH, William Edmund
III ('Webb Beach'; 'Walker E.
Blake'; 'James McM. Douglas';
'Edmund O. Scholefield'; 'Pat-
rick J. Williams'), 1929- ,
American; juveniles CO WAR
BUTTET, Marc Claude de, 1530-
86, French; poetry BU
BUTTI, Enrico Annibale, 1868-
1912, Italian; plays, fiction
BU MCG
BUTTITTA, Anthony, 1907- ,
American; plays, fiction CON
BUTTON, Daniel Evan, 1917- ,
American; nonfiction CON
BUTTON, Henry Warren, 1922- ,
American; nonfiction CON
BUTTON, James Wickham, 1942- ,
American; nonfiction CON
BUTTON, Kenneth John, 1948- ,
British; nonfiction CON
BUTTREY, Douglas Norton see
'BARR, Densil Neve'
BUTTRICK, George Arthur, 1892-
1980, Anglo-American; nonfic-
tion CON

161

BUTTERICK

BUTTERICK, George F., 1942- ,
American; poetry, nonfiction
CON
'BUTTS, Jane R.' see ROBERTS,
Jane
BUTTS, Porter Freeman, 1903- ,
American; nonfiction CON
BUTWELL, Richard, 1929- ,
American; nonfiction CON
BUTZ, Caspar, 1828-85, German-
American; poetry BU
BUULTJENS, Edward Ralph,
1936- , American; nonfic-
tion CON
BUXBAUM, Melvin H., 1934- ,
American; nonfiction CON
BUXBAUM, Robert Courtney,
1930- , American; nonfiction
CON
BUXTON, Bonnie, 1940- , Ca-
nadian; nonfiction CON
BUXTON, Charles Roberts,
1913- , American; nonfic-
tion CON
BUXTON, Edward Fulton, 1917- ,
American; nonfiction CON
BUXTON, Thomas Hamilton,
1940- , American; nonfiction
CON
BUYANNEMEKH, Sonombaljiryn,
1901/02-37, Mongolian; po-
etry, fiction, plays, nonfic-
tion PRU
BUYS, Donna, 1944- , American;
nonfiction CON
BUYSERO, Dirak, 1644-1707/08,
Dutch; poetry BU
BUYSSE, Cyriel, 1859-1932, Flem-
ish; fiction BU CL
BUZO, Alexander J., 1944- ,
Australian; plays CON VCD
BUZZATI-TRAVERSO, Dino, 1906-
72, Italian; fiction, plays,
journalism BO BU CL NI
SEY TH WA
'BUZZLE, Buck' see RUBIN,
Charles J.
BYARS, Betsy Cromer, 1928- ,
American; juveniles CO
DE KI
BYATT, Antonia Susan, 1936- ,
British; fiction VCN
BYE, Beryl Joyce, 1926- ,
English; nonfiction CON
BYE, Ranulph de Bayeux, 1916- ,
American; nonfiction CON
BYERLY, Henry Clement, 1935- ,
American; nonfiction CON

BYERS, David Milner, 1941- ,
American; nonfiction CON
BYERS, Richard McCulloch, 1913- ,
American; fiction CON
BYFIELD, Barbara Ninde, 1930- ,
American; juveniles CO
BYKAU, Vasil Uladzimiravic (By-
kov), 1924- , Byelorrussian;
fiction BU CL CON
BYLES, Mather, 1707-88, Amer-
ican; poetry BR
BYLINSKY, Gene Michael, 1930- ,
Yugoslav-American; journalism,
nonfiction CON
BYNNER, Witter, 1881-1968, Amer-
ican; poetry BR BU
BYNUM, Terrell Ward, 1941- ,
American; translations, nonfic-
tion CON
BYRD, Eldon Arthur, 1939- ,
American; nonfiction CON
BYRD, Richard Edward, 1931- ,
American; nonfiction CON
BYRD, Robert James ('Bobby
Byrd'), 1942- , American;
poetry CON
BYRD, William, 1543-1623, Eng-
lish; songs RU
BYRD, William II, 1674-1744,
American; nonfiction BA BR
BU PO
BYRNE, Donald Edward, Jr.,
1942- , American; nonfiction
CON
BYRNE, Donn (Brian Oswald Donn-
Byrne), 1889-1928, American;
fiction, nonfiction HO MAG
BYRNE, Frank Loyola, 1928- ,
American; nonfiction CON
BYRNE, Gary C., 1942- , Amer-
ican; nonfiction CON
BYRNE, James E., 1945- , Amer-
ican; nonfiction CON
BYRNE, John Keyess see 'LEO-
NARD, Hugh'
BYRNE, Peter, 1925- , American;
nonfiction CON
BYRNE, Robert 1930- , American;
nonfiction CON
BYRNE, Seamus, 1904-68, Irish;
plays HO
BYRNE, Stuart James ('Rothayne
Amare'; 'John Bloodstone'),
1913- , American; fiction
CON
BYRNES, Edward Thomas, 1929- ,
American; nonfiction CON
BYRNES, Eugene F., 1890?-1974,

American; nonfiction CON
BYROM, John, 1692-1763, English; poetry, nonfiction DA VP
BYRON, Carl Roscoe, 1948- , American; nonfiction CON
BYRON, Christopher M., 1944- , American; journalism CON
BYRON, George Gordon, 1788-1824, English; poetry, plays, BU DA MAG MCG PO VP
BYRON, Henry James, 1834-84, English; plays, fiction VD
'BYRON, John' see ARMSTRONG, John B.
BYRON, William James, 1927- , American; nonfiction CON
BYWATER, Hector Charles, 1884-1940, American; fiction NI
BYWATER, William Glen, Jr., 1940- , American; nonfiction CON

C

'CABALLERO, Fernán' (Cecilia Böhl de Faber), 1796-1877, Spanish; fiction BU TH
CABALLERO BONALD, José Manuel, 1926- , Spanish; poetry, fiction, nonfiction CL
CABALLERO CALDERON, Eduardo, 1910- , Colombian; fiction, journalism BR
CABANIS, José, 1922- , French; fiction, nonfiction CL
CABARGA, Leslie, 1954- , American; nonfiction CON
CABASSA, Victoria, 1912- , American; juveniles CON
CABBELL, Paul, 1942- , American; nonfiction CON
CABELL, James Branch, 1879-1958, American; poetry, fiction AS BA BR BU MAG NI PO VN
CABELLO-ARGADOÑA, Roberto, 1939- , American; nonfiction MAR
CABIBI, John Frank Joseph, 1912- , American; nonfiction MAR
CABLE, George Washington, 1844-1925, American; fiction BA BR BU MAG PO VN
CABLE, James Eric, 1920- ,

British; nonfiction CON
CABLE, John Laurence, 1934- , American; nonfiction CON
CABLE, Mary, 1920- , American; juveniles CO
CABOT, Blake, 1905?-74, American; nonfiction CON
CABOT, John Moors, 1901-81, American; nonfiction CON
CABOT, Thomas Dudley, 1897- , American; nonfiction CON
CABOT, Tracy, 1941- , American; nonfiction CON
'CABRAL, Alberto' see WHITE, Richard A.
CABRAL, Alexandre, 1917- , Portuguese; fiction, nonfiction CL
CABRAL de MELO NETO, João, 1920- , Brazilian; poetry BR BU
CABRERA, Fray Alonso de, 1546?-98, Spanish; nonfiction BU
CABRERA, Arturo Y., American; nonfiction MAR
CABRERA, Infante Guillermo ('G. Cain'), 1929- , Cuban; fiction, translations, film, nonfiction BR BU CON WAK
CABRERA de CORDOBA, Luis, 1559-1623, Spanish; nonfiction BU
CACOYANNIS, Michael, 1922- , Greek; film CON
CADALSO y VAZQUEZ, José de, 1741-82, Spanish; plays, poetry BU TH
CADARAINIS, Aleksandrs see 'CAKS, Aleksandrs'
'CADBURY, Mrs.' see JABAVU, Noni H. N.
CADBURY, Henry Joel, 1883-1974, American; nonfiction CON
CADDEN, Joseph E., 1911?-80, American; journalism CON
CADDY, Alice see BURMAN, Alice
'CADE, Robin' see NICOLE, Christopher R.
CADELL, Violet Elizabeth ('Harriet Ainsworth'), 1903- , British; fiction, juveniles CON
CADENHEAD, Ivie Edward, Jr., 1923- , American; nonfiction CON
CADERAS, Gian Fadri, 1830-91, Raeto-Romansch; poetry BU
CADET, John ('Charles Brown'; 'Fred Greene'), 1935- ,

British; nonfiction, fiction
CON
CADIEUX, Charles L., 1919- ,
American; nonfiction CON
CADIEUX, Lorenzo, 1903-76,
Canadian; nonfiction CON
CADILLA de MARTINEZ, Maria
('Triana'), 1886-1951, Puerto
Rican; poetry, nonfiction HIL
CADILLA de RUIBAL, Carmen
Alicia, 1908- , Puerto Rican;
poetry, journalism HIL
CADLUBONIS, Vincentius see KA-
DUBEK, Wincenty
CADOU, René Guy, 1920-51,
French; poetry BU CL WA
CADWALLADER, Sharon, 1936- ,
American; nonfiction, juven-
iles CO CON
CADY, Jack Andrew, 1932- ,
American; fiction CON
CADY, Steve Noel, 1927- ,
American; nonfiction CON
CADY, Walter Harrison, 1877/79-
1970, American; juveniles
CO
CAECILISU (Quintus C. Statius),
220-168 B.C., Latin; trans-
lations, plays BU GR LA
CAEDMON, -670/80, English;
poetry BU DA
CAELIUS, fl. 400, Latin; nonfic-
tion GR
CAELIUS RUFUS, Marcus, 83-48
B.C., Roman; nonfiction LA
CAEN, Herb, 1916- , American;
juveniles WAR
CAESAR, Gaius Julius, 102/100-
44 B.C., Roman; nonfiction
BU GR LA MAG
CAESARIUS of HEISTERBACH,
1180?-1240, German; nonfic-
tion BU TH
CAFFERTY, Bernard, 1934- ,
English; translations, nonfic-
tion CON
CAFFEY, David Luther, 1947- ,
American; nonfiction CON
CAFFREY, Kate (Toller), Eng-
lish; nonfiction CON
CAFLISCH, Artur, 1893-1971,
Raeto-Romansch; poetry,
plays, fiction BU
'CAGAT, Benat le' see 'TRE-
VANIAN'
CAGE, John, 1912- , American;
nonfiction BR WAK
CAGLE, William Rea, 1933- ,

American; nonfiction CON
CAHALAN, John Donald, 1912- ,
American; nonfiction CON
CAHAN, Abraham, 1860-1951,
American; fiction, journalism
BR BU VN
CAHAN, Yaakov, 1881-1960, Is-
raeli; poetry BU
CAHID SIDKI TARANCI, 1910-56,
Turkish; poetry BU
CAHILL, Daniel Joseph, 1929- ,
American; nonfiction CON
CAHILL, Kevin Michael, 1936- ,
American; nonfiction CON
CAHILL, Thomas Quinn, 1940- ,
American; fiction, nonfiction
CON
CAHN, Rhoda, 1922- , American;
nonfiction, juveniles CON
CAHN, Sammy, 1913- , Amer-
ican; nonfiction CON
CAHN, William, 1912-76, Amer-
ican; journalism, nonfiction
CON
CAHNMAN, Werner Jacob, 1902- ,
German-American; nonfiction
CON
CAIADO, Henrique (Henricus; Her-
micus Caiadus), -1508?, Por-
tuguese; poetry BU
CAIDIN, Martin, 1927- , Amer-
ican; fiction, juveniles AS NI
CAILLAVET, Gaston de, 1869/70-
1915, French; journalism,
plays CL MCG
CAILLIEU, Colijn, -1484?, Dutch;
poetry BU
CAILLOIS, Roger, 1913-78, French;
nonfiction CON
'CAILLOU, Alan' (Alan Lyle-
Smythe), 1914- , British;
fiction, nonfiction, film CON
REI
CAIN, Arthur Homer ('Arthur King'),
American; juveniles CO WAR
'CAIN, Christopher' see FLEMING,
Thomas J.
'CAIN, G.' see CABRERA, Infante
G.
CAIN, George, American; nonfic-
tion SH
CAIN, James Mallahan, 1892-1977,
American; fiction, journalism,
film BR CON MAG PO REI
ST VCN VN
CAIN, Julien, 1887-1974, French;
nonfiction ENG
CAIN, Maureen, 1938- , British;

nonfiction CON
CAIN, Michael Peter, 1941- ,
American; nonfiction CON
CAIN, Robert Owen, 1934- ,
American; nonfiction CON
CAIN, Thomas Henry, 1931- ,
Canadian; nonfiction CON
CAINE, Jeffrey Andrew, 1944- ,
British; fiction CON
'CAINE, Mitchell' see SPARKIA,
Roy B.
CAINE, Stanley Paul, 1940- ,
American; nonfiction CON
CAINE, Sir Thomas Henry Hall,
1853-1931, English; fiction
NI
CAIRD, Edward, 1835-1908, Scots;
nonfiction BU
CAIRD, George Bradford, 1917- ,
English; nonfiction CON
CAIRD, Janet, 1913- , English;
juveniles, fiction, poetry
CON
CAIRE, Janet Hinshaw, 1913- ,
British; fiction, poetry, ju-
veniles REI
CAIRNCROSS, Alexander Kirkland,
1911- , Scots; nonfiction
CON
CAIRNCROSS, Frances Anne,
1944- , English; nonfiction
CON
CAIRNS, David, 1904- , Scots;
nonfiction, translations CON
CAIRNS, Huntington ('Ralph Utley'),
1904- , American; nonfiction
CON
'CAIRNS, Kate' see BOSHER,
Kate L.
CAIRNS, Trevor, 1922- , Eng-
lish; juveniles CO
CAJAK, Ján, 1863-1944, Slovak;
fiction BU
'CAKE, Patrick' see WELCH,
Timothy L.
CAKRABARTI, Amiya (Chadravar-
ty), 1901- , Bengali; poetry
PRU
'CAKS, Aleksandrs' (Aleksandrs
Cadarainis), 1901-50, Lat-
vian; poetry CL
CALA A. M. de see NEBRIJA,
Elio A. de
CALABRESE, Alphonse F. X.,
1923- , American; nonfic-
tion CON
CALABRESE, Anthony, 1938- ,
American; nonfiction, tv CON

CALABRESI, Guido, 1932- ,
Italian-American; nonfiction
CON
CALAFERTE, Louis, 1928- ,
Italian; plays, fiction, nonfic-
tion CON
CALAMANDREI, Mauro, 1925- ,
Italian; nonfiction CON
CALAMNIUS, see KIANTO, Ilmari
CALASIBETTA, Charlotte Mankey,
1917- , American; nonfiction
CON
CALCAGNINI, Celio, 1479-1541,
Italian; nonfiction BU
CALCAR, Elisa Carolina Ferdinanda
van Schiötling, 1822-1904, Dutch;
fiction BU
CALDARELLI, Nazareno see 'CAR-
DARELLI, Vincenzo'
CALDE, Mark Augustine, 1945- ,
American; fiction, film CON
CALDECOTT, Moyra, 1927- ,
British; nonfiction, fiction,
plays CO CON
CALDECOTT, Randolph J., 1846-
86, English; juveniles CO
CALDER, Clarence Roy, Jr.,
1928- , American; nonfiction
CON
CALDER, Daniel Gillmore, 1939- ,
American; nonfiction CON
CALDER, Jenni, 1941- , Amer-
ican; nonfiction CON
CALDER, Robert Lorin, 1941- ,
Canadian; nonfiction CON
CALDER-MARSHALL, Arthur,
1908- , British; fiction,
plays, juveniles, nonfiction
CON VCN WA
CALDERON de la BARCA, Pedro,
1600-81, Spanish; plays, po-
etry BU MAG MCG TH
CALDERWOOD, David, 1575-1650,
Scots; nonfiction BU
CALDERWOOD, Ivan E., 1899- ,
American; fiction CON
CALDWELL, Edward Sabiston,
1928- , American; nonfiction,
fiction CON
CALDWELL, Erskine Preston,
1903- , American; fiction,
nonfiction AM BA BR BU
MAG PO SEY VCN VN
CALDWELL, Helen F., 1904- ,
American; nonfiction, transla-
tions CON
CALDWELL, Inga Gilson, 1897- ,
American; poetry CON

CALDWELL, Irene Catherine,
1908-79, American; nonfic-
tion CON
'CALDWELL, James' see LOW-
RY, Robert J.
CALDWELL, John, 1928- , Amer-
ican; nonfiction CON
CALDWELL, John Cope, 1913- ,
American; juveniles CO
CALDWELL, Kathryn Smoot
('Kathryn Alexander'), 1942- ,
American; nonfiction, film
CON
CALDWELL, Louis Oliver, 1935- ,
American; nonfiction CON
CALDWELL, Marge, 1914- ,
American; nonfiction CON
CALDWELL, Robert Granville,
1882-1976, American; nonfic-
tion CON
CALDWELL, Taylor, 1900- ,
American; fiction NI
CALEF, Robert, 1648-1719,
American; nonfiction BR
CALHOON, Richard Percival,
1909- , American; nonfiction
CON
CALHOON, Robert M., 1935- ,
American; nonfiction CON
CALHOUN, Daniel Fairchild,
1929- , American; nonfiction
CON
CALHOUN, Don Gilmore, 1914- ,
American; fiction, nonfiction
CON
'CALHOUN, Eric' see TURNER,
Robert H.
CALHOUN, Frances Boyd, 1867-
1909, American; fiction BA
CALHOUN, John Caldwell, 1782-
1850, American; nonfiction
MYE
CALHOUN, Mary, 1926- , Amer-
ican; juveniles DE
CALHOUN, Thomas, 1940- ,
American; nonfiction CON
CALIA, Vincent Frank, 1926- ,
American; nonfiction CON
'CALIBAN' see REID, John C.
CALIFANO, Joseph Anthony, Jr.,
1931- , American; nonfiction
CON
CALINESCU, George, 1899-1965,
Rumanian; nonfiction, fiction,
poetry BU CL
CALISHER, Hortense, 1911- ,
American; fiction, nonfiction
BR HE NI VCN VN WA

CALKIN, Homer Leonard, 1912- ,
American; nonfiction CON
CALKIN, Ruth Harms, 1918- ,
American; nonfiction CON
CALL, Frank Oliver, 1878-1956,
Canadian; poetry, nonfiction
CR
CALLADINE, Andrew Garfield,
1941- , Canadian-American;
nonfiction CON
CALLADINE, Carole Elizabeth,
1942- , American; nonfiction
CON
CALLAERT, Vrancke, 14th century,
Dutch; nonfiction BU
CALLAGHAN, Barry, 1937- ,
Canadian; nonfiction, poetry
CON
CALLAGHAN, Morley Edward,
1903- , Canadian; fiction,
plays, nonfiction BU DA SEY
VCN VN
'CALLAHAN, John' see GALLUN,
Raymond Z.
CALLAHAN, Philip Serna, 1923- ,
American; nonfiction, juven-
iles CO CON WAR
CALLAHAN, Raymond Aloysius,
1938- , American; nonfiction
CON
CALLAN, Richard Jerome, 1932- ,
American; nonfiction CON
CALLANAN, Jeremiah Joseph,
1795-1829, Irish; poetry,
translations BU HO
CALLAPADHYAY, Bankimchandra
see CHATTERJI, Bankimchand-
ra
'CALLAS, Theo' see 'CORY, Des-
mond'
CALLAWAY, Joseph Atlee, 1920- ,
American; nonfiction CON
CALLCOTT, Margaret Law, 1929- ,
American; nonfiction CON
CALLEN, Lawrence Willard, Jr.,
1927- , American; juveniles
CO CON
CALLENBACH, Ernest, 1929- ,
American; nonfiction CON
CALLENDER, Charles, 1928- ,
American; nonfiction CON
'CALLENDER, Julian' see 'AUST-
WICK, John'
CALLIMACHUS, 305-240 B.C.,
Greek; poetry, nonfiction BU
GR LA
CALLINUS, 7th century B.C.,
Greek; poetry, nonfiction

BU LA
CALLIS, Helmut Gunther, 1906- ,
American; nonfiction CON
CALLISTHENES, 370-28 B.C.,
Greek; nonfiction GR LA
CALLMANN, Rudolf, 1892-1976,
American; nonfiction CON
CALLOW, James Thomas, 1928- ,
American; nonfiction CON
CALLOW, Philip Kenneth, 1924- ,
British; fiction, plays VCN
CALLWOOD, June see FRAYNE,
June
CALMANN, John, 1935-80, Ger-
man; journalism, nonfiction
CON
CALMER, Edgar, 1907- , Amer-
ican; fiction RO
CALMER, Ned, 1907- , Amer-
ican; fiction CON
CALMO, Andrea, 1510-71, Italian;
plays BU
CALNE, Roy Yorke, 1930- , Eng-
lish; nonfiction CON
CALPURNIUS SICULUS, Titus,
fl. 54-68, Latin; poetry BU
GR LA
CALTER, Paul William, 1934- ,
American; nonfiction CON
CALUZA, Reuben Tolakele, 1900-
65, Zulu; songs HER
CALVERLEY, Charles Stuart,
1831-84, English; translations,
poetry, fiction DA PO VP
CALVERT, George Henry, 1803-89,
American; nonfiction, plays,
poetry MY
'CALVERT, John' see LEAF, Mun-
ro
CALVERT, Mary ('Mary Danby'),
1941- , British; juveniles
CON
'CALVERTON, Victor Francis'
(George Goetz), 1900-40,
American; nonfiction BR
CALVEZ, Jean-Yves, 1927- ,
French; nonfiction CON
'CALVIN, Henry' see HANLEY,
Clifford
CALVIN, Jean, 1509-64, French;
nonfiction BU
CALVINO, Italo, 1923- , Italian;
fiction, translations BO BU
CL CON NI SEY TH WA
CALVOCORESSI, Peter John,
1912- , English; nonfiction
CON
CALVO-SOTELO, Joaquín,

1905- , Spanish; journalism,
plays CL MCG
CALVUS, Gaius Licinius Macer,
82-47 B.C., Roman; poetry
LA
CALZABIGI, Ranieri de, 1714-95,
Italian; poetry BU
CAMARA, Juan de la see RODRI-
GUEZ del PADRON, Juan
CAMARA, Helder Pessoa ('Dom
Helder'), 1909- , Brazilian;
nonfiction CON
CAMARA LAYE, 1928- , African;
fiction BU
CAMARILLO, Alberto M., 1948- ,
nonfiction MAR
CAMARILLO, Mateo, 1941- ,
American; nonfiction MAR
CAMBA, Julio, 1884-1962, Spanish;
nonfiction BU CL
CAMBACERES, Eugenio, 1843-88,
Argentinian; fiction BR BU
CAMBLAK, Grigorije, 1364- ,
Serbian; nonfiction BU
CAMDEN, William, 1551-1623,
English; nonfiction BU DA
CAMENIATES, John, early 10th
century, Byzantine; nonfiction
LA
CAMERINI, Mario, 1895-1981,
Italian; film CON
CAMERON, Alan Douglas Edward,
1938- , English; nonfiction
CON
CAMERON, Allan Gillies, 1930- ,
British; nonfiction CON
CAMERON, Angus de Mille, 1913- ,
Canadian; nonfiction CON
CAMERON, Ann, 1943- , Amer-
ican; juveniles CON
CAMERON, Archibald James,
1920- , Scots; nonfiction CON
CAMERON, Betsy, 1949- , Amer-
ican; juveniles CON
CAMERON, Constance Carpenter,
1937- , American; fiction
CON
'CAMERON, D. Y.' see COOK,
Dorothy M.
CAMERON, David Robertson,
1941- , Canadian; nonfiction
CON
CAMERON, Edna M., 1905- ,
American; juveniles CO
CAMERON, Eleanor Butler, 1912- ,
American; juveniles CO DE KI
CAMERON, Eleanor Elford, 1910- ,
American; fiction CON

CAMERON, Elizabeth see NO-
WELL, Elizabeth
CAMERON, Elizabeth Jane ('Jane
Duncan'; 'Janet Sandison'),
1910-76, Scots; juveniles, non-
fiction CON WAR
CAMERON, George Glenn, 1905-
79, American; nonfiction CON
CAMERON, Harold W., 1905- ,
American; nonfiction CON'
'CAMERON, Ian' (Donald Gordon
Payne), 1924- , English;
fiction NI
CAMERON, John, American;
fiction NI
CAMERON, Kenneth, 1922- ,
British; nonfiction CON
CAMERON, Norman, 1905-53,
Scots; poetry, translations
SEY WA
CAMERON, Polly, 1928- , Amer-
ican; juveniles DEM
CAMINO, León Felipe, 1884- ,
Spanish; poetry BU
CAMMARATA, Jerry Frank,
1947- , American; nonfic-
tion CON
CAMMER, Leonard, 1913- ,
American; nonfiction CON
CAMOËNS, Luis de (Luis Vaz de
Camões), 1524-80?, Portu-
guese; poetry, plays BU
MAG TH
CAMOIN, Francois Andre, 1939- ,
Franco-American; fiction
CON
CAMP, Candace Pauline ('Lisa
Gregory'; 'Kristin James'),
1949- , American; fiction
CON
CAMP, Charles L., 1893-1975,
American; nonfiction, juven-
iles CON
CAMP, Dalton Kingsley, 1920- ,
Canadian; nonfiction CON
CAMP, Fred Valterma, 1911- ,
American; nonfiction, juven-
iles CON
CAMP, John Michael, 1915- ,
American; nonfiction CON
CAMP, Roderic Ai, 1945- ,
American; nonfiction CON
CAMP, Walter Chauncey, 1859-
1925, American; fiction, non-
fiction CON
CAMP, William Newton, 1926- ,
English; fiction, nonfiction
CON

CAMPA, Arthur Leon, 1905- ,
Mexican-American; nonfiction
CON
CAMPANA, Dino, 1885-1932,
Italian; poetry BO BU CL
SEY TH WA
CAMPANELLA, Francis B., 1936- ,
American; nonfiction CON
CAMPANELLA, Tommaso, 1568-
1639, Italian; nonfiction, po-
etry, fiction BO BU NI TH
CAMPANILE, Achille, 1899-1976,
Italian; fiction, plays, journal-
ism CL CON
CAMPANTAR, 7th century, Tamil;
poetry PRU
CAMPBELL, Alexander, 1912-77,
Scots; nonfiction, journalism
CON
CAMPBELL, Alistair, 1925- ,
New Zealander; poetry, plays,
juveniles VCP VP
'CAMPBELL, Angus' see CHET-
WYND-HAYES, Ronald H.
CAMPBELL, Ann R., 1925- ,
American; juveniles CO
CAMPBELL, Beatrice M. see
MURPHY, Beatrice M.
CAMPBELL, Carlos Cardozo,
1937- , American; nonfiction
CON
CAMPBELL, Charles Arthur,
1897-1974, Scots; nonfiction
CON
CAMPBELL, Charles Soutter,
1911- , American; nonfiction
CON
'CAMPBELL, Clyde Crane' see
GOLD, Horace
CAMPBELL, Cyril Calvin, 1925- ,
American; nonfiction CON
CAMPBELL, David Watt, 1915-79,
Australian; poetry, fiction BU
CON VCP WA
CAMPBELL, Dennis Marion, 1945- ,
American; nonfiction CON
CAMPBELL, Donald, 1940- ,
Scots; poetry, plays CON VCP
CAMPBELL, E. Simms, 1906-71,
American; cartoons, juveniles,
nonfiction CON
CAMPBELL, Ewing, 1940- ,
American; fiction CON
CAMPBELL, Fenton Gregory, Jr.,
1939- , American; nonfiction
CON
CAMPBELL, Gabrielle M. V. see
'SHEARING, Joseph'

CAMPBELL, George Frederick,
1915- , American; nonfiction
CON
CAMPBELL, Grace MacLennan
Grant, 1895-1963, Canadian;
fiction, nonfiction CR
CAMPBELL, Graeme, 1931- ,
Scots; plays CON
CAMPBELL, Herbert J., 1925- ,
American; fiction, nonfiction
AS CON NI
CAMPBELL, Hope ('Virginia
Hughes'; 'G. McDonald Wal-
lis'), American; fiction, ju-
veniles CO CON NI
CAMPBELL, Howard Ernest,
1925- , American; nonfiction
CON
CAMPBELL, Ian, 1899-1978,
American; nonfiction CON
CAMPBELL, Ian, 1942- , Eng-
lish; nonfiction CON
CAMPBELL, James, 1920- ,
Scots; nonfiction, fiction
CON
CAMPBELL, James Arthur,
1916- , American; nonfiction
CON
CAMPBELL, James Marshall,
1895-1977, American; nonfic-
tion CON
CAMPBELL, Jane see EDWARDS,
Jane
CAMPBELL, Jane, 1934- , Ca-
nadian; nonfiction CON
CAMPBELL, Jefferson Holland,
1931- , American; nonfiction
CON
'CAMPBELL, Jeffrey' see BLACK,
Campbell
CAMPBELL, John Campbell, 1779-
1861, Scots; nonfiction BU
CAMPBELL, John Ramsey ('Mont-
gomery Comfort'), 1946- ,
American; fiction CON
CAMPBELL, John Roy, 1933- ,
American; nonfiction CON
CAMPBELL, John Wood, Jr.
('Don A. Stuart'), 1910-71,
American; fiction, nonfiction
AS COW NI WA
CAMPBELL, Joseph ('Ultach'),
1879-1944, Irish; poetry,
plays BU HO
'CAMPBELL, Karen' see BEATY,
Betty
CAMPBELL, Karly Kohrs, 1937- ,
American; nonfiction CON

CAMPBELL, Ken ('Henry Pilk'),
1941- , British; plays CON
CAMPBELL, Kenneth, 1901?-79,
American; nonfiction CON
'CAMPBELL, Luke' see MADISON,
Thomas A.
CAMPBELL, M. Rudolph, Amer-
ican; juveniles WAR
CAMPBELL, Malcolm James,
1930- , American; nonfiction
CON
CAMPBELL, Margaret, British;
nonfiction CON
CAMPBELL, Maria, 1940- , Ca-
nadian; nonfiction, film CON
CAMPBELL, Marjorie Wilkins,
British; nonfiction CON
CAMPBELL, Michael Mussen,
1924- , Irish; fiction CON
HO
CAMPBELL, Patricia Jean, 1930- ,
American; nonfiction CON
CAMPBELL, Patrick Gordon, 1913-
80, American; nonfiction, tv
CON
CAMPBELL, Peter, New Zealander;
juveniles WAR
'CAMPBELL, R. T.' see TODD,
Ruthven
CAMPBELL, R. Wright, 1927- ,
American; fiction MCC
CAMPBELL, Randolph Bluford,
1940- , American; nonfiction
CON
CAMPBELL, Rex R., 1931- ,
American; nonfiction CON
CAMPBELL, Rita Ricardo, 1920- ,
American; nonfiction CON
CAMPBELL, Robert, 1922-77,
American; nonfiction CON
CAMPBELL, Robert Blair, 1923- ,
American; nonfiction CON
CAMPBELL, Robert Charles,
1924- , American; nonfiction
CON
CAMPBELL, Robert Wright, 1927- ,
American; film, fiction CON
CAMPBELL, Roy, 1901-57, South
African; poetry BU DA PO
SEY VP
CAMPBELL, Sheldon, 1919- ,
American; nonfiction CON
CAMPBELL, Stanley Wallace,
1926- , American; nonfiction
CON
CAMPBELL, Stephen Kent, 1935- ,
American; nonfiction CON
CAMPBELL, Thomas, 1777-1844,

169

CAMPBELL

Scots; poetry, journalism BU
DA PO VP
CAMPBELL, Thomas Moody,
1936- , American; nonfic-
tion CON
CAMPBELL-JOHNSON, Alan,
1913- , English; nonfiction
CON
CAMPEN, Richard Newman,
1912- , American; nonfic-
tion CON
CAMPERT, Remco Wouter, 1929- ,
Dutch; poetry BU
'UN CAMPESINO' see MORALES,
José P.
CAMPHUYSEN, Dirck Rafaelsz,
1586-1627, Dutch; poetry BU
TH
CAMPION, John Thomas, 1814-
9?; Irish; poetry, fiction HO
CAMPION, Nardi Reeder, 1917- ,
American; juveniles CO
CAMPION, Thomas, 1567-1619/20,
English; poetry, nonfiction,
songs BU DA MAG PO RU
VP
CAMPISTRON, Jean Galbert de,
1656?-1723, French; plays
BU
CAMPLIN, Jamie Robert, 1947- ,
American; nonfiction CON
CAMPO, Estanislao del, 1834-80,
Argentinian; poetry BR BU
CAMPOAMOR, Ramón de, 1817-
1901, Spanish; poetry BU TH
CAMPOLO, Anthony, Jr., 1935- ,
American; nonfiction CON
CAMPTON, David, 1924- , Brit-
ish; plays MCG VCD
CAMUS, Albert ('Bauchart'; 'Sae-
tone'; 'Albert Mothe'), 1913-
60, French; fiction, nonfic-
tion, plays, journalism BU
CL CON MAG MCG SEY TH
CAMUS, Jean Pierre, 1584-1652,
French; nonfiction, fiction
BU
CAMUS, Raoul Francois, 1930- ,
American; nonfiction CON
CAMUTI, Louis Joseph, 1893-
1981, Italian-American; non-
fiction CON
CANADA, Lena, 1920- , Swedish-
American; nonfiction CON
CANADAY, John Edwin see
'HEAD, Matthew'
CANALES, Nemesio R., 1878-
1923, Puerto Rican; poetry,

journalism, plays HIL
CANAN, James William, 1929- ,
American; nonfiction CON
CANAWAY, William Hamilton,
1925- , British; fiction, plays,
nonfiction CON VCN
CANBY, Henry Seidel, 1878-1961,
American; nonfiction CON
CANBY, Vincent, 1924- , Amer-
ican; journalism, fiction,
plays CON
CANCER y VELASCO, Jerónimo
de, 1600?-55, Spanish; poetry,
plays BU
CANCIAN, Francesca Micaela,
1937- , American; nonfiction
CON
CANCIAN, Francis Alexander
(Frank), 1934- , American;
nonfiction CON
CANDELARIA, Cordelia Chavez,
American; nonfiction MAR
CANDELARIA, Nash, 1928- ,
American; fiction, nonfiction
CON MAR
CANDELL, Victor, 1903-77,
Hungarian-American; juveniles
CON
CANDIDAS, Bengali; poetry PRU
CANDIDO, Antonio, 1918- , Bra-
zilian; nonfiction BR
CANDLER, Julie, 1919- , Amer-
ican; nonfiction CON
CANDLIN, Enid Saunders, 1909- ,
American; nonfiction CON
'CANDY, Edward' (Barbara Alison
Neville), 1925- , British;
fiction REI
CANE, Melville Henry, 1879-1980,
American; poetry, nonfiction
CON
CANE, Miguel, 1851-1905, Argen-
tinian; fiction BU
CAÑEDO, Oscar O., 1940- ,
American; nonfiction MAR
CANEMAKER, John, 1943- ,
American; nonfiction, film
CON
CANETTI, Elias, 1905- , Spanish-
English; fiction, plays BU
CL TH WA
CANFIELD, Cass, 1897- , Amer-
ican; nonfiction CON
CANFIELD, Dorothy see FISHER,
Dorothy
CANHAM, Kingsley, 1945- ,
South African; nonfiction CON
CANIFF, Milton Arthur, 1907- ,

American; cartoons CON
CANITZ, Friedrich Rudolf, Frei-
herr von, 1654-99, German;
poetry BU
CAÑIZARES, José de, 1676-1750,
Spanish; plays BU MCG
CANKAR, Ivan, 1876-1918, Slo-
vene; fiction, plays BU CL
CANKAR, Izidor, 1886-1958, Slo-
vene; nonfiction, fiction BU
CANN, Marjorie Mitchell, 1924- ,
Canadian-American; nonfiction
CON
CANNAN, Denis, 1919- , Brit-
ish; plays CON VCD
CANNAN, Joanna Maxwell, 1898-
1961, British; fiction, juven-
iles REI
CANNELL, Kathleen, 1891-1970,
American; journalism RO
CANNING, George, 1770-1827,
English; nonfiction BU
CANNING, Jeffrey Michael,
1947- , American; journal-
ism, nonfiction CON
CANNING, John, 1920- , British;
nonfiction CON
CANNING, Ray Russell, 1920- ,
American; nonfiction CON
CANNING, Victor ('Alan Gould'),
1911- , English; fiction
MCC REI ST WA
CANNON, Beth, 1951- , Amer-
ican; nonfiction CON
CANNON, C. E., American; non-
fiction SH
'CANNON, Curt' see 'HUNTER,
Evan'
CANNON, Harold Charles, 1930- ,
Anglo-American; translations
CON
CANNON, Helen ('Lincoln Pros-
per'), 1921- , American;
fiction CON
CANNON, James P., 1890-1974,
American; nonfiction CON
CANNON, John Ashton, 1918- ,
English; fiction, nonfiction
CON
CANNON, Le Grand, Jr., 1899-
1979, American; fiction CON
'CANNON, Ravenna' see MAY-
HAR, Ardath
CANNY, Nicholas Patrick, 1944- ,
Irish; nonfiction CON
CANO, Yvonne, American; non-
fiction MAR
CANO-BALLESTA, Juan, 1932- ,

Spanish-American; nonfiction
CON
CANON, Lance Kirkpatrick, 1939- ,
American; nonfiction CON
CANOVAN, Margaret, 1939- ,
British; nonfiction CON
CANOVAS del CASTILLO, Antonio,
1828-97, Spanish; nonfiction,
fiction BU
CANSEVER, Edip, 1928- , Turk-
ish; poetry PRU
CANSINOS-ASSENS, Rafael, 1883-
1964, Spanish; fiction, nonfic-
tion CL
CANTACUZENE, Julia, 1876-1975,
American; nonfiction CON
CANTACUZENUS, John VI, -1382,
Byzantine; nonfiction LA
CANTACUZINO, Constantin Stolnicul,
1650-1716, Rumanian; nonfic-
tion BU
CANTEMIR, Dimitrie, 1673-1723,
Russian; nonfiction BU
CANTERBERY, Estes Ray, 1935- ,
American; nonfiction CON
CANTH, Minna Ulrika Johansson,
1844-97, Finnish; fiction, plays
BU TH
CANTIN, Eileen, 1931- , Amer-
ican; nonfiction CON
CANTIN, Eugene Thorpe, 1944- ,
American; nonfiction CON
CANTONI, Alberto, 1841-1904,
Italian; fiction BU
CANTOR, Eli ('Agnes Wheatley'),
1913- , American; fiction,
plays CON
CANTOR, Leonard Martin, 1927- ,
British; nonfiction CON
CANTOR, Norman Frank, 1929- ,
Canadian-American; nonfiction
CON
CANTOR, Paul Arthur, 1945- ,
American; nonfiction CON
CANTOR, Paul David, 1916-79,
American; nonfiction CON
CANTU, Cesare, 1804-95, Italian;
nonfiction, fiction BU
CANTU, Roberto, 1943- , Amer-
ican; nonfiction MAR
CANTU MENON, Oyyarattu (Chandu
Menon), 1847-99, Malayalam;
fiction LA PRU
CANTWELL, Dennis Patrick,
1940- , American; nonfiction
CON
CANTWELL, Robert Emmett,
1908-78, American; fiction,

nonfiction, translations CON
VCN
CANTY, Mary, American; juveniles, poetry WAR
'CANUSI, José' see BARKER, S.
Omar
'CAPE, Judith' see PAGE, Patricia K.
CAPECI, Dominic Joseph, Jr.,
1940- , American; nonfiction CON
CAPEK, Josef, 1887-1945, Czech;
plays, fiction BU CL
CAPEK, Karel, 1890-1938, Czech;
plays, fiction, nonfiction AS
BU CL MAG MCG NI SEY TH
CAPEK-CHOD, Karel Matej, 1860-
1927, Czech; fiction BU CL
TH
CAPELLANUS, Johannes see WAL-
TON, John
CAPELLEN tot den POL, Joan
Derk van der, 1741-84,
Dutch; nonfiction BU
CAPETANAKIS, Demetrios, 1912-
44, Greek; poetry, nonfiction
TH WAK
CAPGRAVE, John, 1393-1464, Eng-
lish; nonfiction BU
CAPITEIN, Jacobus Eliza Joan-
nes, 1717-45, Ghanaian; non-
fiction HER JA
CAPIZZI, Michael, 1941- , Amer-
ican; nonfiction, fiction CON
CAPLAN, Edwin Harvey, Amer-
ican; nonfiction CON
CAPLIN, Alfred Gerald ('Al Capp'),
1909-79, American; fiction
CO CON
CAPLOVITZ, David, 1928- ,
American; nonfiction CON
CAPON, Harry Paul, 1912-69,
British; fiction AS CON NI
CAPORALI, Cesare, 1531-1601,
Italian; poetry BU
CAPOTE, Truman (Truman
Streckfus Persons), 1924- ,
American; fiction, plays,
nonfiction BA BR BU HE
PO SEY VCN VN
'CAPP, Al', see CAPLIN, Al-
fred G.
CAPP, Richard, 1935- , Amer-
ican; fiction CON
CAPPEL, Constance ('Constance
Montgomery'), 1936- ,
American; juveniles CO
CAPPER, Douglas Parode, 1898?-

1979, Australian; nonfiction
CON
CAPPO, Joseph, 1936- , Amer-
ican; nonfiction CON
CAPPONI, Gino, 1350?-1421, Ital-
ian; nonfiction BU
CAPPONI, Gino, 1792-1876, Italian;
nonfiction BU
CAPPS, Benjamin Franklin,
1922- , American; juveniles
CO
CAPPS, Carroll M., see MacAPP,
C. C.'
CAPRA, Frank, 1897- , Italian-
American; nonfiction CON
CAPRIO, Frank Samuel, 1906- ,
American; nonfiction CON
CAPRON, Walter Clark, 1904-79,
American; nonfiction CON
CAPSTICK, Peter Hathaway,
1940- , American; nonfic-
tion CON
CAPUANA, Luigi, 1839-1915,
Italian; fiction, nonfiction,
journalism BO BU MCG TH
CAPUS, Alfred, 1858-1922, French;
journalism, fiction, plays
MCG
CAPUTO, David Armand, 1943- ,
American; nonfiction CON
CAPUTO, Philip, 1941- , Amer-
ican; fiction CON
CAPUTO, Robert, 1949- , Amer-
ican; juveniles CON
'CARAFOLI, Marci' see RIDLON,
Marci
CARAGIALE, Ion Luca, 1852-1912,
Rumanian; plays, fiction, jour-
nalism BU CL MCG TH
CARAGIALE, Mateiu, 1885-1936,
Rumanian; fiction BU
CARALEY, Demetrios, 1932- ,
American; nonfiction CON
CARAS, Roger Andrew, ('Roger
Sarac'), 1928- , American;
juvenile, fiction CO NI
CARBAUGH, Robert John, 1946- ,
American; nonfiction CON
'CARBERY, Ethna' (Anna Isabel
Johnston), 1866-1902, Irish;
poetry HO
CARBONNIER, Jeanne, Franco-
American; juveniles CO
'CARBURY, A. B.' see CARR,
Albert Z.
CARCANO, Giulio, 1812-82, Italian;
fiction, poetry BU
CARCINUS, 4th century B.C.,

Greek; poetry BU
'CARCO, Francis' (Francois Car-
copino-Tusoli), 1886-1958,
French; poetry, fiction BU
CL TH
CARD, Orson Scott, 1951- ,
American; fiction, nonfiction,
plays CON
CARDARELLI, Joseph, 1944- ,
American; nonfiction CON
'CARDARELLI, Vincenzo' (Naza-
reno Caldarelli), 1887-1959,
Italian; poetry, nonfiction BO
BU CL TH
CARDEN, Karen Wilson, 1946- ,
American; nonfiction CON
CARDEN, Maren Lockwood, Anglo-
American; nonfiction CON
CARDEN, Patricia, 1935- ,
American; nonfiction CON
CARDENAL, Ernesto, 1925- ,
Nicaraguan; poetry BR BU
CON SEY WAK
CARDENAS, Daniel Negrete,
1917- , American; nonfic-
tion CON MAR
CARDENAS, Gilbert, 1947- ,
American; nonfiction CON
MAR
CARDENAS, Isaac, 1943- , Amer-
ican; nonfiction MAR
CARDENAS, Reyes, 1948- ,
American; poetry, fiction
MAR
CARDEW, Michael Ambrose,
1901- , English; nonfiction
CON
CARDIFF, Gray Emerson, 1949- ,
American; nonfiction CON
CARDINAL, Roger Thomas ('Peter
Bridgecross'), 1940- , Eng-
lish; nonfiction CON
CARDOSO, Antonio, 1933- , Ango-
lan; poetry, journalism, fiction
HER JA
CARDOSO, Lawrence A., 1940- ,
American; nonfiction MAR
CARDOSO, Pedro Monteiro, 1890?-
1942, Cape Verde Islander;
poetry, fiction HER
CARDOZA y ARAGON, Luis,
1904- , Guatemalan; poetry,
nonfiction BR
CARDOZO, Arlene Rossen, 1938- ,
American; nonfiction CON
CARDOZO, Nancy, American; po-
etry CON
CARDOZO, Peter, 1916- ,

American; juveniles, fiction
CON
CARDOZO-FREEMAN, Inez, 1928- ,
American; nonfiction MAR
CARDUCCI, Giosuè, 1835-1907,
Italian; poetry, nonfiction BO
BU MAG SEY TH
CARDUS, Neville, 1889-1975, Brit-
ish; journalism, nonfiction
CON
CARDWELL, Donald Stephen Lowell,
1919- , British; nonfiction
CON
CARDWELL, Paul, American; ju-
veniles WAR
CARELESS, James Maurice Stock-
ford, 1919- , Canadian; non-
fiction CON
CARÊME, Maurice, 1899-1977,
Belgian; poetry, fiction BU
CL
CARENS, James Francis, 1927- ,
American; nonfiction CON
CARETTE, Louise see MARCEAU,
Felicien'
CAREW, Dorothy, 1910?-73, Amer-
ican; journalism, nonfiction
CON
CAREW, Dudley Charles, 1903-81,
British; journalism, nonfiction
CON
CAREW, Jan Rynveld, 1925- ,
Guyanan; fiction, plays, juven-
iles BU CON VCN
CAREW, Richard, 1555-1620, Eng-
lish; translations, nonfiction
BU
CAREW, Thomas, 1594/95-1639/40,
English; poetry, plays BRI
BU DA MAG PO RU VP
CAREY, Bonnie, 1941- , Amer-
ican; juveniles CO
CAREY, Gary, 1938- , American;
nonfiction CON
CAREY, Henry, 1687?-1743, Eng-
lish; plays, poetry, nonfiction
BU DA VD
CAREY, Jane Perry Clark, 1898-
1981, American; nonfiction CON
CAREY, John, 1934- , English;
nonfiction CON
CAREY, Mary Virginia, 1925- ,
Anglo-American; juveniles
CON
CAREY, Michael Lawrence, 1948- ,
American; nonfiction CON
CAREY, Miriam E., 1858- ,
American; nonfiction ENG

CAREY, Richard John, 1925- ,
American; nonfiction CON
CARFAGNO, Vincent R. , 1935- ,
American; translations, non-
fiction CON
'CARFAX, Catherine' see FAIR-
BURN, Eleanor
CARGO, David Niels, 1932- ,
American; nonfiction CON
CARGON, Robert T. , 1933- ,
American; nonfiction CON
CARHART, Arthur H. ('Hart
Thorne'), 1892- , Amer-
ican; fiction, nonfiction PAL
'EL CARIBE' see PADILLA, José
G.
CARIGIET, Alois, 1902- , Swiss;
juveniles CO CON DE
CARINI, Edward, 1923- , Amer-
ican; juveniles, nonfiction
CO CON
CARITEO, Gareth Benedetto,
1450?-1514, Italian; poetry
BO BU
CARKEET, David, 1946- , Amer-
ican; fiction, nonfiction CON
CARL, Beverly May, 1932- ,
American; nonfiction CON
CARLE, Eric, 1929- , Amer-
ican; juveniles CO DEM
CARLEN, Emilie Flygare Smith,
1807-92, Swedish; fiction BU
'CARLETON, Captain L. C.' see
ELLIS, Edward S.
CARLETON, Reginal Milton,
1899- , American; nonfic-
tion, juveniles CON WAR
CARLETON, William, 1794-1869,
Irish; fiction BU HO MAG
VN
CARLETTI, Ercole, 1877-1946,
Friulian; poetry, plays BU
CARLEY, Van Ness Royal, 1906-
76, American; juveniles CO
CARLI, Angelo, 1937- , Amer-
ican; nonfiction CON
CARLILE, Clark Stites, 1912- ,
American; nonfiction CON
CARLING, Finn, 1925- , Nor-
wegian; plays, fiction CL
CARLINO, Lewis John, 1932- ,
American; plays, fiction CON
VCD
'CARLISLE, Clark' see HOLD-
ING, James
'CARLISLE, D. M.' see COOK,
Dorothy M.
CARLISLE, Douglas Hilton,

1921- , American; nonfiction
CON
CARLISLE, Ervin Fred, 1935- ,
American; nonfiction CON
CARLISLE, Fred ('K. F. Murray'),
1915- , British; fiction, non-
fiction CON
CARLISLE, Howard Myron, 1928- ,
American; nonfiction CON
CARLISLE, Lilian Baker, 1912- ,
American; nonfiction CON
CARLISLE, Olga Andreyev, 1930- ,
French; juveniles WAR
CARLISLE, Regis, 1955- , Amer-
ican; fiction, nonfiction CON
CARLISLE, Rodney P. , 1936- ,
American; nonfiction CON
CARLISLE, Thomas Fiske ('Bal-
thazar Kahn'), 1944- ., Amer-
ican; fiction CON
CARLISLE, Thomas John, 1913- ,
American; poetry CON
CARLOS, Manuel L. , 1937- ,
American; nonfiction MAR
CARLOVA, Vasile, 1809-31, Ru-
manian; poetry BU
CARLSEN, Ruth Christoffer, 1918- ,
American; juveniles WAR
CARLSON, Avis Dungan, 1896- ,
American; nonfiction CON
CARLSON, Bernice Wells, 1910- ,
American; juveniles CO
CARLSON, Carl Walter, 1907- ,
American; nonfiction CON
CARLSON, Dale Bick, 1935- ,
American; juveniles WAR
CARLSON, Elof Azel, 1931- ,
American; nonfiction CON
CARLSON, Lewis Herbert, 1934- ,
American; nonfiction CON
CARLSON, Nathalie Savage, 1906- ,
American; juveniles KI
CARLSON, Paul Robins, 1928- ,
American; nonfiction CON
CARLSON, Richard, 1912?-77,
American; fiction CON
CARLSON, Richard Stocks, 1942- ,
American; poetry CON
CARLSON, Rick J. , 1940- , Amer-
ican; nonfiction CON
CARLSON, Robert Eugene, 1922- ,
American; nonfiction CON
CARLSON, Roy Lincoln, 1930- ,
American; nonfiction CON
CARLSON, Theodore Leonard,
1905- , American; nonfiction
CON
CARLSON, Vada F. ('Florella

Rose'), 1897- , American;
journalism, juveniles CO
WAR
'CARLTON, Alva' see DELK,
Robert C.
CARLTON, Charles, 1941- ,
Anglo-American; nonfiction
CON
CARLTON, Charles Merritt,
1928- , American; nonfic-
tion CON
CARLTON, David, 1938- , Brit-
ish; nonfiction CON
CARLTON, Henry Fisk, 1893?-
1973, American; plays, radio
CON
CARLTON, Lessie, 1903- ,
American; nonfiction CON
CARLTON, Roger, English; fic-
tion NI
CARLTON, Wendy, 1949- ,
American; nonfiction CON
CARLYLE, Alexander, 1722-1805,
Scots; nonfiction DA
CARLYLE, Thomas, 1795-1881,
Scots; nonfiction, translations
BU DA MAG PO VN
CARMACK, Robert M., 1934- ,
American; nonfiction CON
CARMAN, Robert Archibald,
1931- , American; nonfic-
tion CON
CARMAN, William Bliss ('Louis
Norman'), 1861-1929, Ca-
nadian; poetry, nonfiction
BR BU CR VP
CARMEL, Catherine, 1939- ,
American; nonfiction CON
CARMEL, Hesi, 1937- , Aus-
trian; nonfiction CON
CARMEN, Arlene, 1936- , Amer-
ican; nonfiction CON
CARMER, Carl Lamson, 1893-
1976, American; journalism,
nonfiction, fiction CON
CARMER, Elizabeth Black, 1904- ,
American; juveniles CO
'CARMI, T.' (Carmi Charny),
1925- , Hebrew; poetry,
translations WAK
CARMICHAEL, Calum M., 1938- ,
Scots; nonfiction CON
'CARMICHAEL, Harry' (Leopold
Horace Ognall; 'Hartley
Howard'), 1908-79, British;
fiction REI
CARMICHAEL, Joel, 1915- ,
American; juveniles WAR

CARMICHAEL, Leonard, 1898-
1973, American; nonfiction
CON
CARMICHAEL, Stokely, 1941- ,
American; nonfiction CON
CARMIGGELT, Simon Johannes
('Kronkel'; 'Karel Bralleput'),
1913- , Dutch; journalism
BU
CARMILLY, Moshe, 1908- ,
Hungarian-American; nonfic-
tion CON
CARMINES, Alvin Allison, 1936- ,
American; plays CON
CARMODY, Denise Lardner,
1935- , American; nonfiction
CON
CARMODY, Jay, 1900?-73, Amer-
ican; nonfiction CON
CARMONA, Roel Guerra, 1935- ,
American; nonfiction MAR
CARMOY, Guy de, 1907- , French;
nonfiction CON
'CARNAC, Carol' (Edith Caroline
Rivett; 'E. C. R. Lorac'),
1894-1958, British; fiction
REI ST
CARNAP, Rudolf, 1891-1970, Amer-
ican; nonfiction WA
CARNEGIE, Andrew, 1835-1919,
American; nonfiction BR ENG
CARNEGIE, Dale, 1888-1955, Amer-
ican; nonfiction BR
CARNEGY, Patrick, 1940- , Brit-
ish; nonfiction CON
CARNELL, Corbin Scott, 1929- ,
American; nonfiction CON
CARNELL, Edward John, 1912-72,
British; fiction AS NI
CARNER, Josep, 1884-1970/71,
Catalan; poetry BU CL
CARNES, Conrad Dew, 1936- ,
American; nonfiction CON
CARNES, Paul Nathaniel, 1921-79,
American; nonfiction CON
CARNEVALI, Doris Lorrain, Amer-
ican; nonfiction CON
CARNEY, John Joseph, Jr.,
1932- , American; nonfic-
tion CON
CARNEY, Thomas Francis, 1931- ,
American; nonfiction CON
CARNICELLI, Domenick D., 1931- ,
American; nonfiction, transla-
tions CON
CARNOT, Joseph Barry, 1941- ,
American; nonfiction CON
CARNOY, Martin, 1938- , Polish-

American; nonfiction CON
CARO, Annibal, 1507-66, Italian;
poetry, translations BO BU
TH
CARO, Francis George, 1936- ,
American; nonfiction CON
CARO, José Eusebio, 1817-53,
Colombian; poetry BR BU
CARO, Joseph see KARO, Joseph
CARO, Robert A., American;
journalism, nonfiction CON
CARO, Rodrigo, 1573-1647, Span-
ish; poetry BU TH
CARO BAROJA, Julio, 1914- ,
Spanish; nonfiction CL
'CAROL, Bill J.' see KNOTT,
William C., Jr.
CAROLAN, T. see O CEAR-
BHALLAIN, Toirdhealbach
CAROLL, Nonie (Murphy), 1926- ,
American; fiction CON
CARON, Roger, 1938- , Cana-
dian; nonfiction CON
CARONIA, Giuseppe, 1884?-1977,
Italian; nonfiction CON
CAROSELLI, Remus Francis,
1916- , American; nonfic-
tion, juveniles CON
CAROSSA, Hans, 1878-1956, Ger-
man; poetry, fiction BU CL
TH
CAROTHERS, J. Edward, 1907- ,
American; nonfiction CON
CAROTHERS, Robert Lee, 1942- ,
American; poetry CON
CAROUSSO, Georges, 1909- ,
American; nonfiction, fiction
CON
CAROZZI, Albert Victor, 1925- ,
Swiss-American; nonfiction,
translations CON
CARPELAN, Bo Gustaf, 1926- ,
Finnish; poetry, juveniles
CO CON TH
CARPENTER, Alexander (Alex-
ander Anglus), fl. 1429, Eng-
lish; nonfiction BU
CARPENTER, Allan, 1917- ,
American; juveniles CO
CARPENTER, Andrew, 1943- ,
British; nonfiction CON
CARPENTER, Clarence Ray,
1905-75, American; nonfic-
tion CON
CARPENTER, Donald Richard,
1931- , American; fiction
CON
'CARPENTER, Duffy ' see 'RAF-

FERTY, S. S.'
CARPENTER, Edmund Snow,
1922- , American; poetry,
juveniles WAR
CARPENTER, Edward, 1844-1929,
English; nonfiction DA SEY
CARPENTER, Elizabeth Suther-
land, 1920- , American; non-
fiction CON
CARPENTER, Elmer J., American;
fiction NI
CARPENTER, Frances, 1890- ,
American; juveniles CO
CARPENTER, Francis Ross,
1925- , American; nonfiction
CON
'CARPENTER, Fred' see HAND,
Andrus J.
CARPENTER, Humphrey, 1946- ,
British; nonfiction CON
CARPENTER, John, 1936- , Amer-
ican; poetry, translations CON
CARPENTER, John Alcott, 1921-78,
American; nonfiction CON
'CARPENTER, John J.' see REESE,
John H.
CARPENTER, Marjorie, 1896- ,
American; nonfiction CON
CARPENTER, Patricia Healy
(Evans), 1920- , American;
juveniles CO
CARPENTER, Rhys, 1889-1980,
American; nonfiction, poetry
CON
CARPENTIER y VALMONT, Alejo,
1904-80, Cuban; fiction, jour-
nalism, poetry BR BU CON
WA
CARPER, L. Dean, 1931- , Amer-
ican; fiction CON
CARR, A. H. Z., 1902-71, Amer-
ican; fiction ST
CARR, Albert Zotalkoff ('A. B.
Carbury'), 1902-71, American;
fiction, nonfiction REI
CARR, Arthur Japheth, 1914- ,
American; nonfiction CON
CARR, Charles, English; fiction
NI
CARR, Charles Telford, 1905-76,
British; nonfiction CON
CARR, Edward Hallet, 1892- ,
English; nonfiction CON
CARR, Edwin George, 1937- ,
Australian; nonfiction CON
'CARR, Glyn' see STYLES, Frank
S.
CARR, Gwen R., 1924- , Amer-

ican; nonfiction CON
CARR, Harriett Helen, 1899- ,
American; juveniles CO
CARR, James Lloyd, 1912- ,
British; fiction, nonfiction,
juveniles CON
CARR, Jay Phillip, 1936- ,
American; journalism CON
CARR, John Charles, 1929- ,
American; nonfiction CON
CARR, John Dickson ('Carter
Dickson'; 'John Rhode'),
1905/06-77, American; fic-
tion CON DA NI REI ST
CARR, John Laurence, 1916- ,
English; nonfiction CON
CARR, Lois Green, 1922- ,
American; nonfiction CON
CARR, Margaret ('Martin Car-
roll'; 'Carole Kerr'), 1935- ,
British; fiction REI
CARR, Pat Moore (Pat M. Es-
slinger), 1932- , American;
fiction, nonfiction CON
CARR, Rachel, American; juven-
iles WAR
CARR, Robert Kenneth, 1908-79,
American; nonfiction CON
CARR, Robert Spencer, 1909- ,
American; fiction NI
CARR, Stephen Lamoni, American;
nonfiction CON
CARR, Terry ('Norman Edwards'),
1937- , American; fiction,
nonfiction AS CON NI
CARR, Virginia Spencer, 1929- ,
American; nonfiction CON
CARR, William, 1921- , British;
nonfiction CON
CARR, William George, 1901- ,
Anglo-American; nonfiction
CON
CARRANCO, Lynwood, 1922- ,
American; nonfiction CON
CARRAS, Mary Calliope, Amer-
ican; nonfiction CON
CARRASCO, Pedro, 1921- ,
American; nonfiction MAR
CARRASQUILLA, Tomás, 1858-
1940, Colombian; fiction
BR BU
'CARREL, Mark' see PAINE,
Lauran B.
CARRER, Luigi, 1801-50, Italian;
poetry, translations BO
CARRERA ANDRADE, Jorge,
1902/03-78, Ecuadorian; non-
fiction, poetry BR BU CON

CARRERAS, Carlos N., 1895-1959,
Puerto Rican; poetry, journal-
ism, fiction HIL
CARRERE, Emilio, 1880-1947,
Spanish; poetry BU
CARRICK, Carol, 1935- , Amer-
ican; juveniles CO CON DEM
CARRICK, Donald, 1929- , Amer-
ican; juveniles CO CON DEM
CARRICK, Malcolm, 1945- ,
Welsh; juveniles, tv CON
CARRIER, Jean-Guy, 1945- ,
Canadian; fiction, nonfiction
CON
CARRIGAN, Andrew Gardner,
1935- , American; nonfiction,
poetry CON
CARRIGAN, Nancy, American; fic-
tion NI
CARRIGAN, Richard, American;
fiction NI
CARRIGHAR, Sally, American;
fiction, plays, nonfiction,
film CO CON
CARRIKEER, Robert Charles,
1940- , American; nonfiction
CON
CARRILLO, Bert B., 1935- ,
American; nonfiction MAR
CARRILLO de y SOTOMAYOR,
Luis, 1583?-1610, Spanish;
poetry BU TH
CARRINGER, Robert L., 1941- ,
American; nonfiction CON
CARRINGTON, Frank Gamble, Jr.,
1936- , American; nonfiction
CON
CARRINGTON, Harold, American;
fiction SH
CARRIO de la VANDERA ('Conco-
lorcorvo'), 1715?-78?, Span-
ish; nonfiction BR BU
CARRION MADURO, Tomas ('Cum-
ba'), 1870-1920, Puerto Rican;
poetry, journalism HIL
CARRITHERS, Gale Hemphill, Jr.,
1932- , American; nonfiction
CON
'CARROL, Shana' see NEWCOMB,
Kerry; SCHAEFER, Frank
'CARROLL, Ann Kristin' see
DENIS, Barbara J.
CARROLL, Archer Latrobe, 1894- ,
American; juveniles CO
CARROLL, Berenice Anita, 1932- ,
American; nonfiction CON
CARROLL, Billy Dan, 1940- ,
American; nonfiction CON

CARROLL, Carroll, 1902- ,
American; nonfiction CON
CARROLL, Charles Francis,
1936- , American; nonfic-
tion CON
'CARROLL, Curt' see BISHOP,
Curtis K.
CARROLL, Daniel Bernard, 1928- ,
American; nonfiction CON
CARROLL, Jackson Walker, 1932- ,
American; nonfiction CON
CARROLL, James P., 1943?- ,
American; plays, poetry, fic-
tion, nonfiction CON
CARROLL, Jeffrey, 1950- ,
American; fiction CON
CARROLL, Jim, 1951- , Amer-
ican; nonfiction, poetry CON
CARROLL, John, 1944- , Eng-
lish; nonfiction CON
CARROLL, Joseph Thomas, 1935- ,
Irish; nonfiction CON
CARROLL, Joy, 1924- , Cana-
dian; nonfiction CON
'CARROLL, Laura' see PARR,
Lucy
'CARROLL, Lewis' (Charles Lut-
widge Dodgson), 1832-98, Eng-
lish; juveniles, poetry BU
DA KI MAG NI PO VN
CARROLL, Loren, 1904-78, Amer-
ican; nonfiction CON
'CARROLL, Martin' see CARR,
Margaret
CARROLL, Paul, 1927- , Amer-
ican; poetry MAL
CARROLL, Paul Vincent, 1900-68,
Irish; plays, poetry BU HO
MCG VCP
CARROLL, Peter Neil, 1943- ,
American; nonfiction CON
CARROLL, Stephen John, Jr.,
1930- , American; nonfiction
CON
CARROLL, Theodus, 1928- ,
American; fiction CON
CARROLL, Thomas J., 1909-71,
American; nonfiction CON
CARROLL, Tom M., 1950- ,
American; fiction CON
CARROLL, Vern, 1933- ,
American; nonfiction CON
CARROTT, Richard G., 1924- ,
American; nonfiction CON
'CARROUGES, Michel' see
COUTURIER, Louis J.
CARR-SAUNDERS, Alexander,
1886-1966, British; nonfic-

tion CON
CARRUTH, Ella Kaiser, American;
juveniles WAR
CARRUTH, Gorton Veeder, 1925- ,
American; nonfiction CON
CARRUTH, Hayden, 1921- , Amer-
ican; poetry, nonfiction, fiction
VCP WA
CARRUTHERS, Malcolm Euan,
1938- , British; nonfiction
CON
'CARRYAWAY, Nick' see MURRAY,
John F.
'CARSAC, Francis' see BORDES,
Francois
CARSE, Robert, 1902-71, Amer-
ican; juveniles CO
CARSON, Ciaron, 1948- , Irish;
poetry HO
'CARSON, Kit' see CARSON, Xan-
thus
CARSON, Lular, 1921- , Amer-
ican; fiction, plays SH
CARSON, Mary, 1934- , Amer-
ican; nonfiction CON
CARSON, Rachel Louise, 1907-64,
American; nonfiction CO CON
CARSON, Ray Fritziof, 1939- ,
American; nonfiction CON
CARSON, Robert B., 1934- ,
American; nonfiction CON
'CARSON, Sylvia' see DRESSER,
Davis
CARSON, Xanthus ('Kit Carson';
'Kit Wade'), 1910- , Amer-
ican; nonfiction CON
CARSTAIRS, George Morrison,
1916- , British; nonfiction
CON
'CARSTAIRS, Kathleen' see PEN-
DOWER, Jacques
CARSWELL, Catherine Roxburgh,
1870-1946, Scots; fiction, non-
fiction DA
CARSWELL, Evelyn Medicus,
1919- , American; nonfiction
CON
'CARSWELL, Leslie' see STEPH-
ENS, Rosemary
CARTAGENA, Alfonso de, 1385/86-
1456, Spanish; nonfiction, trans-
lations BU
CARTE, Gene Edward, 1938- ,
American; nonfiction CON
CARTE, Thomas, 1686-1754, Eng-
lish; nonfiction BU
CARTER, Angela, 1940- , Eng-
lish; fiction, juveniles, non-

fiction CON NI
'CARTER, Ashley' see WHITTING-
TON, Harry
CARTER, Barbara Ellen, 1925- ,
American; nonfiction CON
'CARTER, Bruce' see HOUGH,
Richard A.
CARTER, Burnham, 1901?-79,
American; fiction CON
CARTER, Carolle Jeane, 1934- ,
American; nonfiction CON
CARTER, Dan T., 1948- , Amer-
ican; nonfiction CON
CARTER, David Charles ('Charles
Bertrand'; 'David Doyle';
'Lang Reade'), 1946- , Amer-
ican; nonfiction CON
CARTER, Don Carl, 1917- ,
American; journalism CON
CARTER, Dorothy Sharp, 1921- ,
American; juveniles CO CON
CARTER, Elizabeth, 1717-1806,
English; poetry BU
CARTER, Elliott Cook, 1908- ,
American; nonfiction CON
CARTER, Felicity W., see 'BON-
ETT, John and Emery'
CARTER, Helene, 1887-1960,
Canadian-American; juveniles
CO
CARTER, Henry Hare, 1905- ,
American; nonfiction CON
CARTER, Hodding, 1907-72, Amer-
ican; nonfiction, journalism,
fiction, poetry BA
CARTER, James Earl, Jr., 1924- ,
American; nonfiction CON
CARTER, James Edward, 1935- ,
American; nonfiction CON
CARTER, John Anthony, 1943- ,
English; nonfiction CON
CARTER, John Mack, 1928- ,
American; journalism CON
CARTER, John Waynflete, 1905-
75, British; journalism, non-
fiction CON
CARTER, Joseph, 1912- , Amer-
ican; fiction, nonfiction CON
CARTER, Lief Hastings, 1940- ,
American; nonfiction CON
CARTER, Linwood Vrooman,
1930- , American; fiction,
nonfiction AS CON NI
CARTER, Lonnie, 1942- , Amer-
ican; plays CON VCD
CARTER, Luther Jordan, 1927- ,
American; nonfiction CON
'CARTER, Mark' see BANNER-

MAN, James
CARTER, Martin Wylde, 1927- ,
Guyanan; poetry CON VCP
CARTER, Mary Kennedy, 1934- ,
American; juveniles, nonfiction
CON SH
'CARTER, Nevada' see PAINE,
Lauran B.
'CARTER, Nick' see AVALLONE,
Michael A., Jr.; BALLARD,
Willis T.; 'COLLINS, Michael';
DEY, Frederic V. R.; GRAN-
BECK, Marilyn; WALLMANN,
Jeffrey M.
CARTER, Page, American; juven-
iles WAR
CARTER, Peter, 1929- , British;
juveniles, fiction CON KI
'CARTER, Phyllis Ann' see EBERLE,
Irmengarde
CARTER, Randolph, 1914- , Amer-
ican; plays CON
CARTER, Richard ('Tom Ainslie'),
1918- , American; nonfiction,
fiction CON
CARTER, Samuel III, 1904- ,
American; nonfiction CON
CARTER, Thomas Pelham, 1927- ,
American; nonfiction MAR
CARTER, Wilmoth A., American;
nonfiction SH
CARTER, Worrall Reed, 1885?-
1975, American; nonfiction
CON
CARTERETTE, Edward Calvin,
1921- , American; nonfiction
CON
CARTER-RUCK, Peter Frederick,
1914- , British; nonfiction
CON
CARTEY, Wilfred, 1931- , British;
nonfiction CON
CARTIER, Edd, American; illustra-
tions AS
CARTLIDGE, Michelle, 1950- ,
British; juveniles CON
CARTMILL, Cleve, 1908-64, Amer-
ican; fiction, journalism AS
NI
CARTNER, William Carruthers,
1910- , English; juveniles
CO CON
'EL CARTUJANO' see PADILLA,
Juan de
CARTWRIGHT, Desmond Spencer,
1924- , Anglo-American; non-
fiction CON
CARTWRIGHT, Gary, 1934- ,

American; fiction, film CON
CARTWRIGHT, Joseph H., 1939- ,
American; nonfiction CON
'CARTWRIGHT, N.' see SCO-
FIELD, Norma M. C.
CARTWRIGHT, Peter, 1785-1872,
American; nonfiction BR
CARTWRIGHT, Rosaline (Dymond),
1922- , American; nonfiction
CON
CARTWRIGHT, Sally, 1923- ,
American; juveniles CO CON
WAR
CARTWRIGHT, Thomas, 1535-
1603, English; nonfiction BU
CARTWRIGHT, William, 1611-43,
English; poetry, plays BU
DA RU VD
CARTY, James William, Jr.,
1925- , American; nonfiction
CON
CARUBA, Alan ('Monica Jordan'),
1937- , American; fiction
CON
CARUS, Paul, 1852-1919, German-
American; nonfiction, poetry
BU
CARUTHERS, William Alexander,
1800-46, American; fiction
BA BR MYE
CARVAJAL (Carvajales), mid
15th century, Spanish; poetry
BU
CARVAJAL, Micael de, -1575,
Spanish; plays BU
CARVAJAL y MENDOZA, Luisa
de, 1566-1614, Spanish; po-
etry BU
CARVALHO, Maria Judite de,
1921- , Portuguese; fiction
CL
CARVALHO, Rómulo de see
'GEDEÃO, Antonio'
CARVALHO, Ronald de, 1893-
1935, Brazilian; poetry BR
CARVALHO, Vicente, 1866-1924,
Brazilian; poetry BR
CARVALHO-NETO, Paulo de,
1923- , Brazilian-American;
nonfiction, fiction CON
'CARVER, Dave' see BENGLEY,
David E.
CARVER, Frank Gould, 1928- ,
American; nonfiction CON
CARVER, Jeffrey Allan, 1949- ,
American; fiction CON
'CARVER, John' see GARDNER,
Richard

CARVER, Jonathan, 1710-80, Amer-
ican; nonfiction BR
CARVER, Michael, 1915- , Brit-
ish; nonfiction CON
CARVER, Norman F., Jr., 1928- ,
American; nonfiction CON
CARVIC, Heron, -1980, English;
fiction, plays CON REI
CARY, Barbara Knapp, 1912?-75,
American; juveniles CON
CARY, Diana see CARY, Peggy-
Jean M.
CARY, Elizabeth Tanfield, Vis-
countess Falkland, 1585?-1639,
English; poetry, translations,
plays BU
CARY, Henry Francis, 1772-1844,
English; translations BU
CARY, Joyce ('Arthur Cary'),
1885-1957, Irish; fiction, po-
etry BU DA HO MAG PO
SEY VCN VN
'CARY, Jud' see TUBB, Edwin C.
CARY, Louis Favreau, 1915- ,
American; juveniles CO
CARY, Lucius, 1609/10-43, Eng-
lish; poetry, nonfiction BU
CARY, Otis, 1921- , American;
nonfiction, translations CON
CARY, Patrick, 1624-56, English;
poetry BU
CARY, Peggy-Jean Montgomery
('Diana Serra Cary'; 'Diana
Cary'), 1918- , American;
nonfiction CON
CARY, Phoebe, 1824-71, Amer-
ican; poetry BR
'CARYL, Jean' see KAPLOY, Jean
C. K.
CASA, Giovanni della, 1503-56,
Italian; nonfiction, translations,
poetry BU
CASADO, Pablo Gil, 1931- ,
Spanish-American; nonfiction
CON
CASAL, Julián del, 1863-93, Cuban;
poetry BR BU
CASALE, John Therese ('John C.
Watkins'), 1935- , American;
nonfiction CON
CASALS, Pablo, 1876-1973, Span-
ish; poetry, nonfiction CON
CASANOVA de SEINGALT, Giacomo
Girolamo, 1725-98, Italian;
fiction, nonfiction BO BU
MAG NI TH
CASAS, Jesus Manuel, 1941- ,
American; nonfiction MAR

CASAVANTES, Edward Joseph,
1929- , American; nonfiction
MAR
CASCALES, Francisco, 1567-1642,
Spanish; nonfiction BU
CASCIO, Chuck, 1946- , Amer-
ican; nonfiction, journalism
CON
CASDORPH, Herman Richard,
1928- , American; nonfic-
tion CON
CASE, Geoffrey, British; plays,
tv CON
'CASE, Justin' see GLEADOW,
Rupert S.
CASE, Marshall Taylor, 1941- ,
American; juveniles, nonfic-
tion CO CON
'CASE, Michael' see HOWARD,
Robert W.
CASEBIER, Allan Frank, 1934- ,
American; nonfiction CON
CASEBIER, Virginia Eleanor,
1918- , American; nonfic-
tion CON
CASELEYR, Camille A. M. see
'DANVERS, Jack'
CASELLA, Alberto, 1891- ,
Italian; plays MCG
CASELY-HAYFORD, Adelaide
Smith, 1868-1959, Ghanaian;
fiction, nonfiction HER
CASELY-HAYFORD, Gladys May
('Aquah Laluah'), 1904-50,
Sierra Leonese; poetry, fic-
tion HER JA LA
CASELY-HAYFORD, Joseph
Ephraim, 1866-1930, Ghan-
aian; journalism, fiction
HER JA
CASEMORE, Robert, 1915- ,
American; nonfiction, plays
CON
CASEWIT, Curtis ('D. Green';
'D. Vernor'; 'K. Werner'),
1922- , German-American;
juveniles CO NI
CASEY, Brigid, 1950- , Amer-
ican; juveniles, nonfiction
CO CON
CASEY, Daniel Joseph ('Donal
O'Cathasaigh'), 1937- ,
American; nonfiction CON
CASEY, Edward Scott, 1939- ,
American; translations, non-
fiction CON
CASEY, John, 1939- , Amer-
ican; fiction CON

CASEY, John Keegan, 1846-70,
Irish; poetry HO
CASEY, Juanita, 1925- , Irish;
fiction, poetry CON HO
CASEY, Kevin, 1940- , Irish;
fiction, plays HO
CASEY, Lawrence B., 1905-77,
American; journalism, nonfic-
tion CON
CASEY, Michael, 1947- , Amer-
ican; poetry CON VCP
'CASEY, Richard' Ziff-Davis house
name NI
CASEY, Richard Gardiner, 1890-
1976, Australian; nonfiction
CON
CASEY, Robert Joseph, 1890-1962,
American; nonfiction CON
CASEY, Rosemary, 1904-76, Amer-
ican; plays CON
CASEY, Warren, 1935- , Amer-
ican; plays CON
CASEY, William Francis, 1884-
1957, Irish; journalism, fic-
tion, plays HO
CASEY, William Van Etten, 1914- ,
American; nonfiction CON
CASGRAIN, Henri Raymond, 1831-
1904, Canadian; nonfiction BU
CASH, Anthony, 1933- , British;
translations, nonfiction CON
CASH, Joseph Harper, 1927- ,
American; nonfiction CON
CASH, Kevin, 1926- , American;
nonfiction CON
CASH, Wilbur Joseph, 1900-41,
American; nonfiction, journal-
ism BA WA
'CASHMAN, John' see DAVIS, Tim-
othy F. T.
CASIA, (Ikasia), early 9th century,
Byzantine; poetry LA
CASLER, Lawrence Ray, 1932- ,
American; nonfiction CON
CASO, Adolph, 1934- , American;
fiction, nonfiction CON
CASON, Mabel Earp ('Emily Mary
Bell'), 1892-1965, American;
juveniles CO
'CASONA, Alejandro' (Alejandro
Rodriguez Alvarez), 1903-65,
Spanish; plays, poetry BU CL
CON MCG TH
CASOTTI, Fred, 1923- , Amer-
ican; nonfiction CON
CASPARI, Ernest Wolfgang, 1909- ,
German-American; nonfiction
CON

CASPARY, Vera, 1899/1904- ,
American; fiction, film, non-
fiction REI ST
CASPER, Barry Michael, 1939- ,
American; nonfiction CON
CASPER, Jonathan David, 1942- ,
American; nonfiction CON
CASPER, Joseph Andrew, 1941- ,
American; nonfiction CON
CASS, James Michael, 1915- ,
American; nonfiction CON
CASSADY, Ralph, Jr., 1900-78,
American; nonfiction CON
CASSARA, Ernest, 1925- , Amer-
ican; nonfiction CON
CASSAVETES, John, 1929- ,
American; film CON
CASSEDY, Sylvia, American;
poetry, juveniles WAR
CASSEL, Lili see WRONKER, Lili
CASSEL, Mana-Zucca ('Mana-Zuc-
ca'), 1891-1981, American;
composer CON
'CASSELLS, John' see DUNCAN,
William M.
CASSELS, Louis, 1922-74, Amer-
ican; journalism, nonfiction
CON
CASSERLEY, Henry Cyril, 1903- ,
American; nonfiction CON
'CASSIDY, Claude' see PAINE,
Lauran B.
CASSIDY, John Rufus, 1922- ,
American; nonfiction CON
CASSIDY, Michael, 1936- , South
African; nonfiction CON
CASSIDY, William Lawrence ('Wil-
liam Schwabe'), American;
nonfiction CON
CASSILL, Kay, American; nonfic-
tion CON
CASSILL, Ronald Verlin, 1919- ,
American; fiction, nonfiction
KIB PAL VCN WA
CASSIN, Rene Samuel, 1887-1966,
French; nonfiction CON
CASSIODORUS (Flavius Magnus
Aurelius), 480-580, Roman;
nonfiction, letters BU GR
LA TH
CASSIRER, Ernst, 1874-1945,
German; nonfiction TH
CASSIUS DIO COCCEIANUS, 155-
235, Greek; nonfiction BU
CASSIUS HEMINA, Lucius, fl.
146 B.C., Roman; nonfic-
tion LA
CASSO, Evans Joseph, 1914- ,

American; nonfiction CON
CASSO, Henry J., 1931- , Amer-
ican; nonfiction MAR
CASSOLA, Carlo, 1917- , Italian;
fiction, journalism BO CL
CON TH WA
CASSON, Hugh Maxwell, 1910- ,
British; nonfiction CON
CASSOU, Jean, 1897- , French;
fiction, nonfiction, poetry BU
CL
CASSYERE, Jacob Jacobsoon, 16th
century, Dutch; poetry BU
CASTAÑEDA, Alfredo, 1923- ,
American; nonfiction MAR
CASTANEDA, Carlos, 1925- ,
Peruvian; nonfiction WAK
CASTANEDA, James Agustin,
1933- , American; nonfiction
CON
CASTANHEDA, Fernão Lopes de,
1500?-59, Portuguese; nonfic-
tion BU TH
CASTELAR, Emilio, 1832-99,
Spanish; nonfiction BU
CASTELEIN, Matthijs de, 1485-
1550, Dutch; poetry BU
'CASTELHUN, Friedl von' see
MARION, Frieda
CASTELLANO, Giuseppe, 1893-
1977, Italian; nonfiction CON
CASTELLANOS, Jane Mollie Robin-
son, 1913- , American; juven-
iles CO WAR
CASTELLANOS, Juan de, 1522-
1605/07, Spanish; poetry BR
BU
CASTELLANOS, Rosario, 1915/25-
74, Mexican; poetry, fiction
BR BU CON
CASTELLET i DIEZ de COSSIO,
Josep Maria, 1926- , Catalan;
nonfiction CL
CASTELLS, Matilde Olivella,
1929- , Cuban-American;
nonfiction CON
CASTELO BRANCO, Camilo, 1825-
90, Portuguese; fiction BU TH
CASTELVETRO, Lodovico, 1505?-
71, Italian; nonfiction BO BU
TH
CASTERET, Norbert, 1897- ,
French; fiction NI
CASTI, Giambattista, 1724-1803,
Italian; poetry BU
CASTIGLIONE, Baldassare, 1478-
1529, Italian; nonfiction, poetry
BO BU MAG RU TH

CASTILHO, Antonio Feliciano de, 1800-75, Portuguese; poetry BU TH

CASTILLA del PINO, Carlos, 1922- , Spanish; nonfiction CL

CASTILLEJO, Cristóbal de, 1492-1550, Spanish; poetry BU TH

CASTILLO, Ana, 1953- , American; nonfiction, poetry MAR

CASTILLO, Pedro, 1942- , American; nonfiction MAR

CASTILLO ANDRACA y TAMAYO, Francisco del, 1716-70, Peruvian; poetry BR

CASTILLO PUCHE, José Luis, 1919- , Spanish; fiction CL

CASTILLO SOLORZANO, Alonso de, 1584-1648?, Spanish; fiction, plays BU TH

CASTLE, Coralie, 1924- , American; nonfiction CON

'CASTLE, Damon' see SMITH, Richard R.

'CASTLE, Frances' see LEADER, Evelyn B.

CASTLE, Jeffery Lloyd, 1898- , English; fiction NI

'CASTLE, Lee' see OGAN, George F.; OGAN, Margaret E. N.

CASTLE, Mort, 1946- , American; fiction, poetry, nonfiction CON

CASTLE, William, 1914-77, American; nonfiction, plays CON

CASTLETON, Virginia (Thomas), 1925- , American; nonfiction CON

CASTRO, Antonio (Tony), 1946- , American; nonfiction CON

CASTRO, Eugénio de, 1869-1944, Portuguese; poetry BU TH

CASTRO, Francisco de, late 17th century, Mexican; poetry BR

CASTRO, Jose Maria Ferreira de, 1898-1974, Portuguese; journalism, fiction BU CL CON

CASTRO, Raymond E., 1948- , American; nonfiction MAR

CASTRO, Rosalia de, 1837-85, Spanish; poetry BU TH

CASTRO, Tomas de Jesus, 1902- , Puerto Rican; journalism, nonfiction HIL

CASTRO ALVES, Antonio de, 1847-71, Brazilian; poetry BR BU

CASTRO-KLAREN, Sara, 1942- , American; nonfiction CON

CASTRO QUESADA, Américo, 1885-1972, Spanish; nonfiction BU CL

CASTRO y BELLVIS, Guillén de, 1569-1631, Spanish; plays, poetry BU MCG TH

CASWELL, Helen Rayburn, 1923- , American; juveniles CO WAR

CATALA, Rafael, 1942- , Cuban-American; nonfiction, poetry CON

'CATALA, Victor' see ALBERT i PARADIS, Catarina

CATALANO, Donald Bernard, 1920- , American; song, fiction, journalism CON

CATALANO, Joseph Stellario, 1928- , American; nonfiction CON

CATARINA da SIENA, see CATHERINE of Siena

CATE, Benjamin Wilson, 1931- , Franco-American; journalism CON

CATE, Curtis Wolsey, 1884-1976, American; nonfiction, journalism CON

CATE, Richard Edward Nelson, 1932- , British; juveniles CON

CATHCART, Robert Stephen, 1923- , American; nonfiction CON

CATHER, Willa Sibert, 1876-1947, American; fiction, journalism, poetry AM BR BU MAG PO SEY VN

CATHERALL, Arthur ('A. R. Channel'; 'Dan Corby'; 'Peter Hallard'), 1906- , English; juveniles, fiction, plays CO KI

CATHERINE II (the Great), 1729-96, Russian; nonfiction BU

CATHERINE of SIENA (Catarina), 1347-80, Italian; nonfiction BO BU

CATLEDGE, Turner, 1901- , American; nonfiction CON

CATLIN, George, 1796-1872, American; nonfiction BU

CATLIN, George Edward Gordon, 1896-1979, British; nonfiction CON

CATLIN, Warren Benjamin, 1881-1968, American; nonfiction CON

CATLIN, Wynelle, 1930- , American; juveniles CO CON
CATO the ELDER, Marcus Porcius, 234-149 B.C., Roman; nonfiction BU GR LA
CATO the YOUNGER, Marcus Portius, 95-46 B.C., Roman; nonfiction BU
CATON, Hiram, 1936- , American; nonfiction CON
CATRON, Louis E., 1932- , American; plays, poetry CON
CATS, Jacob, 1577-1660, Dutch; poetry BU TH
CATTANAR, 6-8th century?, Tamil; poetry LA PRU
CATTAPADHYAY see CHATTERJI, Bankimcandar
CATTAPADHYAY, Saratcandra (Chatterji), 1876-1937, Bengali; fiction PRU
CATTELL, Psyche, 1893- , American; nonfiction CON
CATTON, Bruce, 1899-1978, American; journalism, nonfiction BR CO CON
CATUDAL, Honore Marc, Jr., 1944- , American; nonfiction CON
CATULLUS, Gaius Valerius, 84-54 B.C., Latin; poetry BU GR LA MAG
CATULUS, Quintus Lutatius, -87 B.C., Roman; nonfiction LA
'CATZ, Max' see GLASER, Milton
CAU, Jean, 1925- , French; fiction, journalism WA
CAUDILL, Rebecca, 1899- , American; juveniles KI
'CAUDWELL, Christopher' (Christopher St. John Sprigg), 1907-37, English; fiction, poetry, nonfiction BOR DA PO REI ST
CAULEY, John Rowan, 1908-76, American; journalism, nonfiction CON
CAULEY, Lorinda Bryan, 1951- , American; juveniles CON
CAULFIELD, Malachy Francis ('Max Caulfield'; 'Malachy McCoy'), 1915- , Irish; journalism, fiction, nonfiction CON
CAUSLEY, Charles Stanley, 1917- , British; juveniles, plays, poetry, fiction CO KI PO VCP WA
CAUTE, John David, 1936- ,

English; nonfiction, fiction, plays VCD VCN WAK
CAVACCHIOLI, Enrico, 1885-1954, Italian; plays, journalism MCG
CAVAFY, Constantine P. (Kavafis), 1863-1933, Greek; poetry BU CL MAG SEY TH
CAVAIANI, Mabel, 1919- , American; nonfiction CON
CAVALCA, Domenico, 1270-1342, Italian; translations, poetry BU
CAVALCANTI, Bartolomeo, 1503-62, Italian; nonfiction BU
CAVALCANTI, Guido, 1260-1300, Italian; poetry BO BU TH
CAVALIER, Julian, 1931- , Canadian; nonfiction CON
CAVALIERO, Glen, 1927- , British; nonfiction, poetry CON
CAVALLO, Diana, 1931- , American; juveniles CO
CAVALLO, Robert M., 1932- , American; nonfiction CON
CAVAN, Romilly, 1914?-75, British; plays, fiction, film CON
CAVANAGH, Gerald Francis, 1931- , American; nonfiction CON
CAVANNA, Betty ('Elizabeth Headley'; 'Betsy Allen'), 1909- , American; juveniles KI
CAVELL, Stanley Louis, 1926- , American; nonfiction CON
CAVENDISH, George, 1500?-61?, English; poetry, nonfiction BU MAG RU
CAVENDISH, Margaret Lucas, Duchess of Newcastle, 1623/24-73/74, English; poetry, plays BU RU
CAVENDISH, William, Duke of Newcastle, 1593-1676, English; poetry, plays BU RU
CAVENEY, Philip Richard, 1951- , Welsh; fiction CON
'CAVERHILL, Nicholas' see KIRKGREENE, Anthony
CAVIN, Ruth Brodie, 1918- , American; nonfiction CON
CAWEIN, Madison Julius, 1865-1914, American; poetry BA
CAWLEY, Robert Ralston, 1893-1973, American; nonfiction CON
CAWLEY, Winifred, 1915- , English; juveniles, fiction CO CON KI

CAWTHORN, James ('Philip James'), 1929- , English; fiction NI
CAWTHORNE, Graham, 1906?-80, British; journalism, nonfiction CON
'CAXTON, Pisistratus' see LYTTON, Edward B.
CAXTON, William, 1422-91, English; printer, translations BU DA PO
CAYANKONTAR, 11-12th centuries, Tamil; poetry PRU
CAYLEY, Michael Forde, 1950- , English; poetry, nonfiction CON
CAYROL, Antoni see 'CERDA, Jordi-Pere'
CAYROL, Jean, 1911- , French; poetry, fiction, nonfiction, film BU CL CON TH WA
CAZAMIAN, Louis Francois, 1877-1960, French; nonfiction CON
CAZDEN, Elizabeth, 1950- , American; nonfiction CON
CAZEAU, Isabelle, 1926- , American; nonfiction CON
CAZELLES, Brigitte Jacqueline, 1944- , American; fiction, nonfiction CON
CAZEMAJOU, Jean, 1924- , French; nonfiction CON
CA'ZORZI, Giacomo see 'NOVENTA, Giacomo'
CEARD, Henri, 1851-1924, French; fiction BU
CEBOLLERO, Pedro, 1896- , Puerto Rican; poetry, nonfiction HIL
CEBULASH, Mel ('Ben Farrell'; 'Glenn Harlan'; 'Jared Jansen'; 'Jeanette Mara'), 1937- , American; juveniles CO
CECAUMENUS, mid 11th century, Byzantine; nonfiction BU LA
CECCHI, Emilio, 1884-1966, Italian; nonfiction BO BU CL TH
CECCHI, Giamaria, 1518-87, Italian; nonfiction, plays BU MCG
CECH, Svatopluk, 1846-1908, Czech; poetry, fiction, plays BU TH
CECIL, Lord David, 1902- , English; nonfiction BOR CON DA
'CECIL, Henry' (Henry Cecil

Leon), 1902-76, English; fiction, plays, nonfiction REI ST WA
'CECIL, R. H.' see HEWITT, Cecil R.
CECIL, Robert, 1913- , English; poetry, nonfiction CON
CEDER, Georgiana Dorcas ('Ana Dor'), American; juveniles CO
CEDERBORGH, Fredrik, 1784-1835, Swedish; fiction, plays BU
CEDRENUS, George, 11th century, Byzantine; nonfiction LA
CEIDE, Amelia, 1908- , Puerto Rican; poetry, journalism HIL
'CEIRIOG' see HUGHES, John C.
CEITINN, Séathrún (Geoffrey Keating), 1570-1650, Irish; poetry, nonfiction DA
CEKKILAR, 11th century, Tamil; poetry PRU
CELA, Camilo José, 1916- , Spanish; fiction, nonfiction, poetry BU CL MAG SEY WA
CELAKOVSKY, Frantisek Ladislav, 1799-1852, Czech; poetry BU
'CELAN, Paul' (Paul Antschel), 1920-70, German-French; poetry, translations, nonfiction BU CL CON SEY TH WA
'CELAYA, Gabriel' (Rafael Múgica), 1911- , Spanish; poetry BU CL TH
CELEBI DEDE, Suleyman, -1421/22, Turkish; poetry PRU
CELESTE, Sr. Marie, American; nonfiction CON
CELINE, Louis Ferdinand (Henri Louis Destouches), 1894-1961, French; fiction BU CL CON MAG SEY TH
CELL, John Whitson, 1935- , American; nonfiction CON
CELLAPPA, Ci Cu, 1912- , Tamil; poetry, nonfiction PRU
CELLE, Giovanni dalle, 1310?-94, Italian; nonfiction BU
'CELLIERS, Jan' (Johannes Francois Elias), 1865-1940, Afrikaans; poetry BU
CELLINI, Benvenuto, 1500-71, Italian; nonfiction BO BU MAG TH
CELORIA, Francis S. C., 1926- , British; nonfiction CON
CELOSSE, Jacobus, 1560-1631,

Dutch; poetry, plays BU
CELSUS, Aulus Cornelius, fl. 14-
37 A.D., Latin; nonfiction
BU GR LA
CELTIS, Conrad, 1459-1508, Ger-
man; nonfiction BU TH
CEM SULTAN, 1459-92, Turkish;
poetry PRU
CEMACH, Harry Paul, 1917- ,
Austrian-English; nonfiction
CON
CEMAL SÜREYA, 1931- , Turk-
ish; poetry PRU
'CENDRARS, Blaise' (Frédéric
Sauser Hall), 1887-1961, Swiss;
fiction, poetry BU CL CON
SEY TH
CENICEROZ, Raymond G., 1934- ,
American; nonfiction MAR
'CENTE, H. F.' see ROCKLIN,
Ross L.
CENTLIVRE, Susanna Freeman,
1667-1723, English; plays
BU MCG PO VD
'CENTO' see COBBING, Bob
CEP, Jan, 1902-74, Czech; fic-
tion BU CL
CEPHALAS, Constantius, 9-10th
centuries, Greek; anthologist;
GR
CEPOLLA, Joan see BAGNEL,
Joan
'CERAM, C. W.' see MAREK,
Kurt W.
CERAVOLO, Joseph, 1934- ,
American; poetry CON VCP
CERCIDAS of MEGALOPOLIS, 290-
20 B.C., Greek; poetry, non-
fiction BU GR LA
'CERDA, Jordi-Pere' (Antoni Cay-
rol), 1920- , French-
Catalan; fiction CL
CERF, Bennett Alfred, 1898-1971,
American; juveniles, nonfic-
tion CO
CERF, Jay Henry, 1923-74, Amer-
ican; nonfiction CON
CERMAK, Laird Scott, 1942- ,
American; nonfiction CON
'CERNA, Panait' (Panait Stan-
ciof), 1881-1913, Rumanian;
poetry BU
CERNUDA y BIDON, Luis, 1902/04-
63, Spanish; poetry, nonfiction,
translations, fiction BU CL
CON SEY TH WA
CERRA, Frances, 1946- , Amer-
ican; nonfiction CON

CERRI, Lawrence J. ('Lawrence
Cortesi'), 1923- , American;
fiction, juveniles, nonfiction
CON
CERRUTI, James Smith, 1918- ,
American; nonfiction CON
CERTNER, Simon, 1909?-79, Amer-
ican; fiction CON
CERUTTY, Percy Wells, 1895-
1975, Australian; nonfiction
CON
CERVANTES, Lorna Dee, 1954- ,
American; poetry MAR
CERVANTES, Robert A., 1941- ,
American; nonfiction MAR
CERVANTES SAAVEDRA, Miguel
de, 1547-1616, Spanish; fiction,
plays, poetry BU MAG MCG
TH
CERVANTES y SALAZAR, Fran-
cisco, 1514?-75, Spanish; non-
fiction BU
CERVERI, Doris, 1914- , Amer-
ican; nonfiction CON
CERVERI de GIRONA (Guillem de
Cervera), -1285?, Catalan;
poetry BU
'CERVON, Jacqueline' see MOS-
SARD, Jacqueline
CESAIRE, Aimé Fernand, 1913- ,
French; poetry, plays, nonfic-
tion BU CL CON HER SEY
TH WA
CESAREC, August, 1893-1941,
Croatian; fiction, plays, trans-
lations BU TH
CESARI, Antonio, 1760-1828, Italian;
nonfiction BU
CESARIC, Dobrisa, 1902- , Croa-
tion; poetry BU CL TH
CESAROTTI, Melchiorre, 1730-
1808, Italian; poetry, nonfiction,
translations BO BU TH
'CESBRON, Gilbert' (Jean Guyon),
1913- , French; fiction BU
CESPEDES, Alba de, 1911- ,
Italian; fiction, journalism
CL WA
CESPEDES, Augusto, 1904- ,
Bolivian; journalism, fiction
BR
CESPEDES y MENESES, Gonzalo
de, 1585?-1638, Spanish; fic-
tion, nonfiction BU
CESTERO, Ferdinand R. ('Benja-
min Duval'; 'Ferdinand'), 1864-
1945, Puerto Rican; poetry
HIL

CETINA, Gutierre de, 1514/7-
54/57, Spanish; poetry BU
TH
CETTA, Lewis Thomas, 1933- ,
American; nonfiction CON
CEUPPENS, Rik see 'MICHIELS,
Ivo'
CHAADAYEV, Peter Yakovlevich
(Chaadaev), 1793-1856, Rus-
sian; nonfiction BU
CHABE, Alexander Michael, 1923- ,
American; nonfiction CON
'CHABER, M. E.' see CROSSEN,
Kendell F.
CHABOT, Cécile, 1907- , Ca-
nadian; poetry, fiction, trans-
lations CR
CHACE, William Murdough, 1938- ,
American; nonfiction CON
CHACEL, Rosa, 1898- , Spanish;
fiction, poetry CL
CHACHA, Tom, 1940?- , Tan-
zanian; fiction HER
CHACHOLIADES, Miltiades, 1937- ,
American; nonfiction CON
CHACKO, David, 1942- , Amer-
ican; fiction, nonfiction CON
CHACKO, George Kuttickal, 1930- ,
Indian; nonfiction CON
CHACONAS, Doris J. Kozak,
1938- , American; juven-
iles WAR
CHADEAYNE, Lee, 1933- ,
American; translations, non-
fiction CON
CHADOURNE, Marc, 1896?-1975,
French; nonfiction CL CON
CHADWICK, Bruce Albert, 1940- ,
American; nonfiction CON
CHADWICK, Janet Bachand, 1933- ,
American; nonfiction CON
CHADWICK, Lee, 1909- , Brit-
ish; nonfiction CON
CHADWICK, Philip George, Brit-
ish; fiction NI
CHAET, Bernard, 1924- ,
American; nonfiction CON
CHAFE, William Henry, 1942- ,
American; nonfiction CON
CHAFETZ, Henry, 1916-78, Amer-
ican; nonfiction, juveniles
CON
CHAFETZ, Janet Saltzman,
1942- , American; nonfic-
tion CON
CHAFFEE, Allen, American;
juveniles CO
CHAFFEE, John, 1946- , Amer-

ican; nonfiction CON
CHAFFIN, Lillie Dorton, 1925- ,
American; juveniles, poetry
WAR
CHAFIN, Andrew, 1937- , Amer-
ican; nonfiction CON
CHAFULUMIRA, English William,
1908/30- , Malawian; nonfic-
tion HER JA
'CHAGAS, Antonio das' (Antonio
da Fonseca Soares), 1631-82,
Portuguese; nonfiction, poetry
BU TH
CHAIKIN, Miriam, 1928- , Amer-
ican; juveniles CO CON
CHAIRIL ANWAR, 1922-49, Indo-
nesian; poetry LA
CHAIS, Pamela Herbert, 1930- ,
American; tv, fiction CON
CHAKAIPA, Patrick, 1932- ,
Rhodesian; fiction JA
CHAKERIAN, Charles Garabed,
1904- , Turkish-American;
nonfiction CON
CHAKHRUKHADZE, 12-13th cen-
turies, Georgian; poetry PRU
CHAKRAVARTY, Amiya see CAK-
RABARTI, Amiya
CHAKRAVARTY, Birendra Narayan,
1904-80?, Indian; nonfiction
CON
CHALCOCONDYLES, Laonicus,
1423?-90?, Byzantine; nonfic-
tion LA
CHALHOUB, Michael ('Omar Shar-
if'), 1932- , Egyptian; nonfic-
tion CON
CHALIDZE, Valery Nikolaevich,
1938- , Russian-American;
nonfiction CON
CHALK, John Allen, 1937- ,
American; nonfiction CON
CHALK, Ocania, 1927- , Amer-
ican; nonfiction CON SH
CHALKER, Jack Laurence, 1944- ,
American; fiction, nonfiction
CON NI
CHALKHILL, John, fl. 1600, Eng-
lish; poetry BU
CHALLANS, Mary see 'RENAULT,
Mary'
CHALLINOR, John, 1894- , Brit-
ish; nonfiction CON
'CHALLES, George' see 'BRAND,
Max'
'CHALLONE, H. K.' see MILLS,
Janet M. A.
CHALMERS, Eric Brownlie, 1929- ,

187

CHALMERS

Scots; nonfiction CON
CHALMERS, George, 1742-1825,
Scots; nonfiction BU
CHALMERS, John W., 1910- ,
Canadian; nonfiction CON
CHALMERS, Mary Eileen, 1927- ,
American; juveniles CO DE
CHALON, Jean, 1935- , French;
journalism, nonfiction CON
CHALONER, John Seymour (Jon),
1924- , British; fiction, ju-
veniles CON
CHALUPKA, Ján, 1791-1871, Slo-
vak; plays BU
CHALUPKA, Samo, 1812-83, Slo-
vak; poetry BU
CHAMBERLAIN, Anne, 1917- ,
American; fiction CON
CHAMBERLAIN, John, 1553-1627,
English; letters RU
CHAMBERLAIN, John Rensselaer,
1903- , American; nonfiction
CON
CHAMBERLAIN, Jonathan Mack,
1928- , American; nonfic-
tion CON
CHAMBERLAIN, Muriel Evelyn,
1932- , British; nonfiction
CON
CHAMBERLAIN, Samuel ('Phineas
Beck'), 1895-1975, American;
nonfiction CON
CHAMBERLAIN, William, 1903- ,
American; fiction NI
'CHAMBERLAIN, Wilson' see
CRANDALL, Norma
CHAMBERLAIN, Wilton Norman,
1936- , American; nonfiction
CON
CHAMBERLAND, Paul, 1939- ,
Canadian; poetry, nonfiction
BU
CHAMBERLAYNE, William, 1619-
89, English; poetry BU
CHAMBERLIN, Eric Russell,
1926- , British; nonfiction
CON
CHAMBERLIN, J. Edward, 1943- ,
American; nonfiction CON
CHAMBERLIN, Judi, 1944- ,
American; nonfiction CON
CHAMBERLIN, Leslie Joseph,
1926- , American; nonfic-
tion CON
CHAMBERLIN, M. Hope, 1920-
74, American; nonfiction
CON
CHAMBERLIN, Mary, 1914- ,

American; nonfiction CON
CHAMBERLIN, Waldo, 1905- ,
American; nonfiction CON
CHAMBERS, Bradford, American;
juveniles WAR
CHAMBERS, Clarke Alexander,
1921- , American; nonfiction
CON
CHAMBERS, Sir Edmund Kerchever,
1866-1954, English; nonfiction
BU DA
'CHAMBERS, Howard V.' see LOW-
ENKOPF, Shelley A.
CHAMBERS, Jane, 1937- , Amer-
ican; fiction, plays, film CON
CHAMBERS, Robert, 1802-71,
Scots; nonfiction BU DA
CHAMBERS, Robert William, 1865-
1933, American; fiction NI
CHAMBERS, Robin Bernard, 1942- ,
British; nonfiction CON
CHAMBERS, Whittaker, 1901-61,
American; journalism, trans-
lations, nonfiction CON WA
CHAMBERS, William, 1800-83,
Scots; nonfiction BU
CHAMBERS, William E., 1943- ,
American; fiction CON
'CHAMBERTIN, Ilya' see von
BLOCK, Sylvia
CHAMBLISS, William C. 1908?-75,
American; nonfiction CON
CHAMELIN, Neil Charles, 1942- ,
American; nonfiction CON
CHAMFORT, Sébastien Roch Nico-
las, 1741-94, French; nonfic-
tion, plays BU TH
CHAMIER, George, 1842-1915?,
English; fiction BU
'CHAMISSO, Adalbert von' (Louis
Charles Chamisso de Bon-
court), 1781-1838, French-
German; poetry BU TH
'CHAMPFLEURY' (Jules Husson;
Fleury), 1821-89, French;
fiction BU TH
CHAMPIER, Symphorien, 1472-
1539, French; nonfiction BU
CHAMPION, Richard Gordon,
1931- , American; nonfiction
CON
CHAMPLIN, Charles Davenport,
1926- , American; nonfiction
CON
CHAMPLIN, Joseph Masson, 1930- ,
American; nonfiction CON
CHAMSON, André, 1900- ,
French; fiction BU CL TH

'CHAMUDOT, Daniel Y.' see LIE-
BERMANN, Aharon S.
CHAN, Loren Briggs, 1943- ,
American; nonfiction CON
'CHANAN, Ben' see YAFFE,
Richard
CHANAN, Gabriel, 1942- , Eng-
lish; fiction CON
CHANCE, John Newton ('J. Drum-
mond'; 'John Lymington'; 'Da-
vid C. Newton'; 'Jonathan
Chance'), 1911- , British;
fiction, nonfiction, juveniles
AS CON NI REI
CHANCE, Michael Robin Alexan-
der, 1915- , British; non-
fiction CON
'CHANCE, Stephen' see TURNER,
Philip W.
CHANCELLOR, Paul, 1900-75,
American; nonfiction CON
CHAND BARDAI, Hindi; poetry
BU
CHANDAR, Krishan, 1914- ,
Urdu; fiction PRU
CHANDIDAS, 1417-77, Vaishna-
van; poetry BU
CHANDLER, Alice, 1931- ,
American; nonfiction CON
CHANDLER, Arthur Bertram,
1912- , English; fiction
AS NI
CHANDLER, Caroline Augusta,
1906-79, American; juveniles,
ficiton CO CON
CHANDLER, David Leon, Amer-
ican; nonfiction CON
CHANDLER, David Porter, 1933- ,
American; nonfiction CON
CHANDLER, Edna Walker, 1908- ,
American; juveniles CO
CHANDLER, Edwin Russell, Jr.,
1932- , American; nonfic-
tion CON
'CHANDLER, Frank' see HARK-
NETT, Terry
CHANDLER, Norman, 1899-1973,
American; journalism CON
CHANDLER, Raymond Thornton,
1888-1959, American; fic-
tion BR BU PO REI SEY
ST VN
CHANDLER, Robert Wilbur,
1921- , American; jour-
nalism CON
CHANDLER, Ruth Forbes, 1894-
1978, American; juveniles
CON

CHANDLER, Sue Pinkston, Amer-
ican; nonfiction SH
CHANDLER, Tertius, 1915- ,
American; nonfiction CON
CHANDONNET, Ann, 1943- ,
American; poetry, nonfiction
CON
'CHANDOS, John' see McCONNELL,
John L. C.
CHANDRA, Pramod, 1930- , In-
dian; nonfiction CON
CHANDRASEKHAR, Sripati, 1918- ,
Indian; nonfiction CON
CHANELES, Sol, 1926- , Amer-
ican; juveniles, nonfiction
CON WAR
CHANG, Constance Dan, 1917- ,
Chinese; nonfiction CON
CHANG, Dae Hong, 1928- , Amer-
ican; nonfiction CON
CHANG, Eileen see CHANG AI-
LING
CHANG, Kwang-chih, 1931- ,
Chinese-American; nonfiction
CON
'CHANG, Lee' see 'JORDAN, Leon-
ard'
CHANG, Parris Hsu-cheng, 1936- ,
Chinese-American; nonfiction
CON
CHANG, Richard Taiwon, 1933- ,
Korean-American; nonfiction
CON
CHANG AI-LING (Eileen Chang),
1920- , Chinese; fiction PRU
WA
CHANG CHI, 768-830, Chinese;
poetry BU
CHANG HÊNG, 78-139, Chinese;
nonfiction, poetry BU PRU
CHANG HSIEN, 990-1078, Chinese;
poetry, nonfiction PRU
CHANG HSÜEH-CH'ÊNG, 1738-
1801, Chinese; nonfiction BU
CHANG K'O-CHIU, 1270-1350,
Chinese; poetry BU
CHANG PING'LIN, 1868-1936,
Chinese; nonfiction BU
CHANG T'IEN-I, 1907- , Chinese;
fiction BU PRU
CHANG TSAI, 1020-77, Chinese;
nonfiction BU
CHANG TSU, 658-730, Chinese;
nonfiction BU PRU
'CHANGAMJNIZHA' see KRSNA
PILLA, Cannampuza
CHANIN, Abraham Solomon, 1921- ,
American; nonfiction CON

CHANKIN, Donald Oliver, 1934- ,
American; nonfiction CON
'CHANNEL, A. R. ' see CATH-
ERALL, Arthur
CHANNELS, Vera Grace, 1915- ,
American; nonfiction CON
CHANNING, Edward Tyrell, 1790-
1856, American; nonfiction
BR MY
CHANNING, William Ellery, 1780-
1842, American; nonfiction
BR BU MY
CHANNING, William Ellery II,
1817-1901, American; poetry,
nonfiction BR MY VP
CHANNING, William Henry, 1810-
84, American; juveniles MY
CHANOVER, Hyman, 1920- ,
Polish-American; nonfiction
CON
CHANT, Barry Mostyn, 1938- ,
Australian; nonfiction CON
CHANT, Donald Alfred, 1928- ,
Canadian; nonfiction CON
CHANT, Eileen Joyce (Joy),
1945- , English; fiction,
nonfiction CON
CHANT, Kenneth David, 1933- ,
Australian; nonfiction CON
CHANTILES, Velma Liacouras,
1925- , American; nonfiction
CON
CHANTLER, David Thomas, 1925- ,
American; fiction, film CON
CHAO, Buwei Yang, 1889- ,
Chinese-American; transla-
tions, nonfiction CON
CHAO CHIH-HSIN, 1662-1744,
Chinese; poetry BU
CHAO CHING-SHEN, late 19th
century, Chinese; translations,
nonfiction, poetry PRU
CHAO I, 1727-1814, Chinese; non-
fiction, poetry BU
CHAO MÊNG-FU, 1254-1322,
Chinese; poetry BU
CHAO SHU-LI, 1906- , Chinese;
fiction BU PRU
CHAPARADZA, L. Washington,
1926-64, Rhodesian; journal-
ism JA
CHAPDELAINE, Perry A., 1925- ,
American; fiction NI
CHAPELAIN, Jean, 1595-1674,
French; poetry, nonfiction
BU TH
CHAPELLE, Howard Irving, 1901-
75, American; nonfiction CON

CHAPIN, Dwight Allan, 1938- ,
American; nonfiction CON
CHAPIN, Henry, 1893- , Amer-
ican; poetry, juveniles CON
CHAPIN, Katherine Garrison see
BIDDLE, Katherine G.
CHAPIN, Kim, 1942- , American;
nonfiction CON
CHAPIN, Louis Le Bourgeois, Jr.,
1918-81, American; nonfiction
CON
CHAPIN, Schuyler Garrison,
1923- , American; nonfiction
CON
CHAPLIN, Charlie, 1889-1977,
British; nonfiction CON
CHAPLIN, George, 1914- , Amer-
ican; nonfiction CON
CHAPLIN, Sidney, 1916- , British;
fiction, plays VCN
CHAPLIN, W. W. (Bill), 1895?-
1978, American; journalism
CON
CHAPMAN, Abraham, 1915- ,
American; nonfiction CON
CHAPMAN, Carleton Burke, 1915- ,
American; nonfiction CON
CHAPMAN, Charles Frederic,
1881-1976, American; nonfic-
tion CON
CHAPMAN, Christine, 1933- ,
American; nonfiction CON
CHAPMAN, Constance Elizabeth
Mann, 1919- , English; ju-
veniles CO
CHAPMAN, Dorothy Hilton, 1934- ,
American; nonfiction CON
CHAPMAN, George, 1559?-1634,
English; poetry, plays, trans-
lations BRI BU DA MAG MCG
PO RU VD VP
CHAPMAN, Guy Patterson, 1889-
1972, English; nonfiction, fic-
tion CON WA
CHAPMAN, Hester Wolferstan,
1899-1976, British; fiction,
nonfiction CON
CHAPMAN, James Keith, 1919- ,
Canadian; nonfiction CON
CHAPMAN, Jean, Australian; ju-
veniles CON
CHAPMAN, John Jay, 1862-1933,
American; poetry, plays BR
CHAPMAN, John Roy, 1927- ,
British; plays, film CON
CHAPMAN, Joseph Irvine, 1912- ,
American; nonfiction CON
CHAPMAN, Karen C., 1942- ,

CHAPMAN   190

American; translations,
plays CON
CHAPMAN, Loren James, 1927- ,
American; nonfiction CON
CHAPMAN, Marie Manire, 1917- ,
American; nonfiction CON
CHAPMAN, Mary Winslow, 1903- ,
American; poetry CON
CHAPMAN, Rick M., 1943- ,
American; nonfiction CON
CHAPMAN, Samuel, American;
fiction NI
CHAPMAN, Steven, American;
nonfiction CON
CHAPMAN, Vera ('Belladonna
Took'), 1898- , British; fic-
tion CON
CHAPMAN, Victoria Lynn, 1944- ,
American; juveniles CON
'CHAPMAN, Walker' see SILVER-
BERG, Robert
CHAPNICK, Howard, 1922- ,
American; nonfiction CON
CHAPONE, Hester Mulso, 1727-
1801, English; poetry, non-
fiction BU
CHAPPEL, Bernice Marie, 1910- ,
American; juveniles, nonfic-
tion CON
CHAPPELL, Clovis Gillham, 1882-
1972, American; nonfiction
CON
CHAPPELL, Fred, 1936- , Amer-
ican; poetry, fiction BA KIB
CHAPPELL, Gordon Stelling,
1939- , American; nonfiction
CON
CHAPPELL, Jeannette see KALT,
Jeannette
CHAPPELL, Mollie, ?; fiction
CON
CHAPPELL, Warren, 1904- ,
American; juveniles CO DE
CHAPPELOW, Allan Gordon, Dan-
ish; nonfiction CON
CHAPPLE, Eliot Dismore, 1909- ,
American; nonfiction CON
CHAPPLE, Steve, 1949- , Amer-
ican; nonfiction CON
CHAPYGIN, Alexey Pavlovich,
1870-1937, Russian; fiction
BU CL
CHAR, René, 1907- , French;
poetry BU CL SEY TH WA
CHAR, Tin-Yuke, 1905- , Amer-
ican; nonfiction CON
'CHAR, Yum' see BARRETT,
Dean

CHARASHA, Tembot, 1902- ,
Circassian; fiction PRU
CHARBONNEAU, Jean, 1875-1960,
Canadian; poetry CR
CHARBONNEAU, Louis Henry
('Carter Travis Young'), 1924- ,
American; fiction, journalism
AS CON NI
CHARBONNEAU, Robert, 1911-67,
Canadian; fiction, poetry, non-
fiction BU
CHARD, Judy ('Doreen Gordon'),
1916- , British; nonfiction
CON
CHARDIET, Bernice Kroll, 1927?- ,
American; juveniles CON
CHARDON de CROISILLES (de
Reims), fl. 1235, French; po-
etry BU
'CHARDONNE, Jacques' (Jacques
Boutelleau), 1884-1968, French;
fiction, nonfiction BU CL TH
CHARDRY, 13th century, Anglo-
Norman; poetry BU
CHARGAFF, Erwin, 1905- ,
Austrian-American; nonfiction
CON
CHARIK, Izy, 1898-1937, Yiddish;
poetry BU
CHARINHO, Payo Gomes, 13th
century, Galician; poetry BU
CHARITON, 2nd century, Greek;
fiction GR
CHARKIN, Paul, 1907- , English;
fiction NI VCN
CHARLAND, William Alfred, Jr.,
1937- , American; nonfiction
CON
CHARLES IV, Holy Roman Em-
peror, 1316-78, Bohemian;
nonfiction BU
CHARLES, Carol Morgan, 1931- ,
American; nonfiction CON
'CHARLES, David' see MONDEY,
David C.
'CHARLES, Franklin' see ADAMS,
Cleve F.; BELLEM, Robert L.
CHARLES, Gerda, English; fiction
WA
'CHARLES, Mark' see BICKERS,
Richard L. T.
'CHARLES, Nicholas' see KUSKIN,
Karla
'CHARLES, Robert' see SMITH,
Robert C.
CHARLES d'ORLEANS, 1394-1465,
French; poetry TH
CHARLES-ROUX, Edmonde, 1920- ,

French; fiction CON
CHARLESTON, Robert Jesse,
1916- , British; translations,
nonfiction CON
CHARLESWORTH, Arthur Riggs,
1911- , American; nonfiction
CON
CHARLESWORTH, James Clyde,
1900-74, American; nonfic-
tion CON
CHARLIP, Remy, 1929- , Amer-
ican; juveniles CO DE
CHARLOT, Jean, 1898- , French;
juveniles CO
CHARLTON, James Mervyn, 1939- ,
American; fiction CON
CHARMATZ, Bill, 1925- , Amer-
ican; juveniles CO
'CHARNANCE, L. P.' see HAN-
NAWAY, Patricia H.
CHARNAS, Suzy McKee, 1939- ,
American; fiction, nonfiction
CON NI
CHARNEY, Ann, Polish-Canadian;
fiction, film CON
CHARNEY, David H., 1923- ,
American; nonfiction CON
CHARNEY, George, 1905?-75,
Russian-American; nonfiction
CON
CHARNEY, Hanna Kurz, 1931- ,
American; nonfiction CON
CHARNI, Shmuel see 'NIGER,
Shmuel'
CHARNIN, Martin Jay, 1934- ,
American; lyrics, juveniles,
plays CON
CHARNLEY, Mitchell Vaughn,
1898- , American; nonfic-
tion CON
CHARNY, Carmi see CARMI, T.
CHARNY, Israel Wolf, 1931- ,
American; nonfiction CON
CHAROSH, Mannis, 1906- ,
American; juveniles CO
CHARQUES, Dorothy Taylor
('R. D. Dorothy'), 1899-1976,
British; nonfiction, fiction
CON
CHARRIERE, Henri, 1907?-73,
French; nonfiction CON
CHARRIERE, Isabelle de van
Tuyll van Zuylen, 1740-1805,
Franco-Swiss; nonfiction, fic-
tion BU
CHARRON, Pierre, 1541-1603,
French; nonfiction BU TH
CHARRON, Shirley, 1935- ,

American; nonfiction CON
CHARRY, Elias, 1906- , Amer-
ican; nonfiction CON
CHARTERIS, Hugo, 1922-70, Eng-
lish; fiction, journalism, tv
CON WA
'CHARTERIS, Leslie' (Leslie
Charles Bowyer Yin), 1907- ,
Anglo-American; fiction MCC
REI ST
CHARTIER, Alain, 1390?-1440?,
French; poetry BU TH
CHARTIER, Emile Auguste see
'ALAIN'
'CHARTIER, Emilio' see ESTENS-
SORO, Hugo
CHARTIER, Jean, -1464, French;
nonfiction BU
CHARVET, John, 1938- , British;
nonfiction CON
CHARY, Frederick Barry, 1939- ,
American; nonfiction CON
CHARYN, Jerome, 1937- , Amer-
ican; fiction, plays VCN
'CHASE, Adam' see THOMSON,
James C.
'CHASE, Alice' see McHARGUE,
Georgess
CHASE, Cleveland Bruce, 1904?-
75, American; nonfiction CON
CHASE, Cora Gingrich, 1898- ,
American; nonfiction CON
CHASE, Donald, 1943- , Amer-
ican; nonfiction CON
'CHASE, Glen' see 'JORDAN,
Leonard'
CHASE, Ilka, 1905?-78, American;
nonfiction, fiction CON
'CHASE, James Hadley' (Rene Bra-
bazon Raymond; 'James L.
Docherty'; 'Ambrose Grant';
'Raymond Marshall'), 1906- ,
British; fiction, plays REI
ST
CHASE, James Staton, 1932- ,
American; nonfiction CON
CHASE, Judith Wragg, 1907- ,
American; nonfiction CON
CHASE, Lawrence, 1943- , Amer-
ican; nonfiction CON
CHASE, Loriene Eck, American;
nonfiction CON
CHASE, Mary Coyle, 1907-81,
American; plays, juveniles
CO CON MCG VCD
CHASE, Mary Ellen, 1887-1973,
American; juveniles, fiction,
nonfiction BR CO CON DEM

CHASE, Otta Louise, 1909- ,
American; poetry CON
CHASE, Richard, 1904- , Amer-
ican; juveniles, nonfiction
CON WAR
CHASE, Richard Volney, 1914-
63/66, American; nonfiction
BOR BR
CHASE, Stuart, 1888- , Amer-
ican; nonfiction CON
CHASEK, Judith, American; juven-
iles WAR
CHASIN, Barbara, 1940- , Amer-
ican; nonfiction CON
CHASINS, Abram, 1903- , Amer-
ican; juveniles WAR
CHASSIGNET, Jean Baptiste,
1571/78-1635?, French; po-
etry BU TH
CHASTAIN, Madye Lee, 1908- ,
American; juveniles CO
CHATELAIN, Nicolas, 1913-76,
French; journalism, nonfic-
tion CON
CHASTELAIN de COUCI, Le,
-1203, French; poetry BU
CHASTELLAIN, Georges, 1415-
75, French; nonfiction, po-
etry BU
CHASTELLAIN, Pierre ('Vaillant'),
-1408?, French; poetry BU
CHASTENET de CASTAING,
Jacques, 1893-1978, French;
journalism, nonfiction CON
CHASTON, Gloria Duncan, 1929- ,
American; nonfiction CON
CHATEAUBRIAND, Francois René,
1768-1848, French; nonfiction,
fiction BU MAG TH
CHÂTEAUBRIANT, Alphonse de,
1882-1951, French; fiction
CL TH
CHATHAM, Douglas M., 1938- ,
American; nonfiction CON
CHATHAM, Josiah George, 1914- ,
American; nonfiction CON
CHATHAM, Russell, 1939- ,
American; nonfiction CON
CHÂTILLON, Walter of, 1135-84,
French; nonfiction, poetry
BU
CHATRAIN, Alexandre see
'ERCKMANN-CHATRAIN'
CHATT, Orville Keith, 1924- ,
American; nonfiction CON
CHATTERJE, Sarat Chandra,
1876-1936, Bengali; fiction
BU

CHATTERJI, Bankimchandra (Calla-
padhyay), 1838-94, Bengali;
fiction BU LA PRU
CHATTERJI, Suniti Kumar, 1890- ,
Indian; nonfiction CON
CHATTERTON, Thomas, 1752-70,
English; poetry BU DA MAG
PO VP
CHATTOPADHYAY, Harindranath,
1898- , Indian; plays PRU
CHATWIN, Charles Bruce, 1940- ,
British; nonfiction CON
CHAUCER, Geoffrey, 1340-1400,
English; poetry, fiction BRI
BU DA MAG PO VP
CHAUDHURI, Nirad Chandra,
1897- , Indian; nonfiction,
journalism BU DA PRU WAK
CHAUDHURI, Sukanta, 1950- ,
Indian; poetry CON
CHAUNCY, Nancen Beryl Master-
man, 1900-70, British; juven-
iles CO DE KI
CHAUNDLER, Christine ('Peter
Martin'), 1887-1972, British;
juveniles CO
CHAVARRIA, Jesus, 1935- ,
American; nonfiction MAR
CHAVCHAVADZE, Aleksander,
1786-1846, Georgian; poetry
PRU
CHAVCHAVADZE, Ilia, 1837-1907,
Georgian; fiction, poetry, non-
fiction LA PRU
CHAVEE, Achille, 1906-70, Bel-
gian; poetry CL
CHAVEL, Charles Ber, 1906- ,
Polish-American; nonfiction
CON
CHAVES, Jonathan, 1943- , Amer-
ican; nonfiction CON
CHAVEZ, Fray Angelico, 1910- ,
American; poetry, fiction
CON MAR
CHAVEZ, Arnold, 1945- , Amer-
ican; nonfiction MAR
CHAVEZ, Cesar, 1927- , Amer-
ican; nonfiction MAR
CHAVEZ, Nelba R., American;
nonfiction MAR
CHAVEZ, Patricia, 1934- , Amer-
ican; nonfiction CON
CHAYEFSKY, Paddy, 1923-81,
American; tv, film, plays,
BR MCG MCN SEY VCD VD
WA
CHAYES, Abram, 1922- , Amer-
ican; nonfiction CON

CHAZAL, Malcolm de, 1902- ,
French; nonfiction TH
CHEATHA, Karyn Follis ('Long-
neck Woman'), 1943- , Amer-
ican; poetry, fiction CON
CHEAVENS, Martha Louis, 1898-
1975, American; fiction, po-
etry CON
CHEDID, Andrée, 1921- , French;
fiction, poetry, plays BU
CHEEK, Frances Edith, 1923- ,
Canadian-American; nonfiction
CON
'CHËRNY, Sasha' see CHORNY,
Sasha
CHEESMAN, Paul R., 1921- ,
American; nonfiction CON
CHEETHAM, Nicholas John,
1910- , British; nonfiction
CON
CHEEVER, John, 1912-82, Amer-
ican; fiction AM BR BU HE
MAG PO SEY VCN VN WA
CHEEVER, Susan, 1943- , Amer-
ican; journalism, fiction CON
CHEFFINS, Ronald I., 1930- ,
Canadian; nonfiction CON
CHEIFETZ, Dan, 1926- , Amer-
ican; fiction, nonfiction CON
CHEIFETZ, Philip Morris, 1944- ,
American; nonfiction CON
CHEKE, Sir John, 1514-57, Eng-
lish; nonfiction BU DA
CHEKHOV, Anton Pavlovich, 1860-
1904, Russian; fiction, poetry,
plays BU CL MAG MCG TH
CHEKHOVA, Olga, 1897-1980,
Russian; nonfiction CON
CHEKKI, Danesh Ayyappa, 1935- ,
Indian-Canadian; nonfiction
CON
CHELCECKY, Petr, 1390?-1460,
Czech; nonfiction BU TH
CHELMINSKI, Rudolph, 1934- ,
American; journalism CON
CHELWOOD, Tufton Victor ('Tuf-
ton Victor Beamish'), 1917- ,
American; nonfiction CON
CHEMNITZER, Ivan I., see
KHEMNITSER, Ivan I.
CHEN, Anthony, 1929- , Amer-
ican; juveniles, journalism
CON
CHEN, Chung-Hwan, 1906- ,
Chinese-American; nonfiction
CON
CHEN, Jack, 1908- , English;
nonfiction CON

CHEN, Janey, 1922- , Chinese-
American; nonfiction CON
CHEN, Kan, 1928- , American;
nonfiction CON
CHEN, King Ching, 1926- ,
Chinese-American; nonfiction
CON
CHEN, Kuan I., 1926- , Chinese-
American; nonfiction CON
CHEN, Lincoln Chih-ho, 1942- ,
Chinese; nonfiction CON
CHEN, Samuel Shih-Tsai, 1915- ,
Chinese-American; nonfiction
CON
CH'ÊN, Shih-Tao, 1053-1102, Chi-
nese; poetry BU
CHEN, Tony, 1929- , American;
juveniles CO
CH'ÊN, Tu-hsiu, 1879-1942, Chi-
nese; nonfiction BU
CH'ÊN, Tzu-ang, 661-702, Chi-
nese; poetry, nonfiction BU
PRU
CHÊNEDOLLE, Charles Julien
Lioult de, 1769-1833, French;
poetry BU TH
CHENERY, Janet Dai, 1923- ,
American; juveniles CO CON
CHENERY, William Ludlow, 1884-
1974, American; journalism
CON
CHENEVIERE, Jacques, 1886- ,
Swiss; fiction BU
CHENEY, Anne, 1944- , Amer-
ican; nonfiction CON
CHENEY, Brainard Bartwell,
1900- , American; fiction
BA
CHENEY, Cora, 1916- , Amer-
ican; juveniles CO
CHENEY, Ednah Dow Littlehale,
1824-1904, American; nonfic-
tion MY
CHENEY, Lynne, 1941- , Amer-
ican; fiction CON
CHENEY, Margaret, 1921- ,
American; nonfiction CON
CHENEY, Roberta Carkeek, 1912- ,
American; nonfiction CON
CHENEY, Sheldon Warren, 1886-
1980, American; nonfiction
CON
CHENEY, Theodore Albert, (Ted),
1928- , American; juveniles
CO CON
CHENEY, Thomas E., 1901- ,
American; nonfiction CON
CHENEY-COKER, Syl, 1945- ,

?; journalism, poetry CON
CHENG, Hang-sheng, 1927- ,
Chinese-American; nonfiction
CON
CHENG, Hou-tien, 1944- , Chinese-
American; nonfiction CON
CHENG, Ronald Ye-lin, 1933- ,
Chinese-American; nonfiction
CON
CHENG, Ying-wan, American;
nonfiction CON
CHENG CHEN-TO, 1898-1958,
Chinese; nonfiction, fiction
PRU
CH'ÊNG HAO, 1032-85, Chinese;
nonfiction BU
CH'ÊNG I, 1033-1107, Chinese;
nonfiction BU
CHENG PAN-CH'IAO, 1693-1766,
Chinese; poetry BU
CHENIER, Andre Marie, 1762-94,
French; poetry BU TH
CHENIER, Marie Joseph, 1764-
1811, French; plays, poetry
BU TH
CHENNAULT, Anna Chan, 1925- ,
Chinese-American; nonfiction
CON
CHERASKIN, Emanuel, 1916- ,
American; nonfiction CON
CHERIM, Stanley Marshall, 1929- ,
American; nonfiction CON
CHERINGTON, Paul Whiton, 1818-
74, American; nonfiction CON
CHERITON, Odo of, -1247, Eng-
lish; fiction BU
CHERMAYEFF, Ivan, 1932- ,
Anglo-American; nonfiction,
juveniles CON
CHERNAIK, Judith, 1934- , Amer-
ican; fiction, nonfiction CON
CHERNIAVSKY, Michael, 1923?-
73, American; nonfiction CON
CHERNISS, Harold, 1904- , Amer-
ican; nonfiction CON
'CHERNOFF, Dorothy A.' see
ERNST, Lyman J.
CHERNOFF, Goldie Taub, 1909- ,
Austrian-American; juven-
iles CO
CHERNOFSKY, Jacob L., 1928- ,
American; journalism CON
CHERNOW, Carol, 1934- , Amer-
ican; nonfiction CON
CHERNOW, Fred B., 1932- ,
American; nonfiction CON
CHERNOWITZ, Maurice E., 1909-
77, American; nonfiction CON

CHERNYSHEVSKY, Nikolay Gavrilo-
vich, 1828-89, Russian; non-
fiction, fiction BU TH
CHERRY, Andrew, 1762-1812,
Irish; plays, songs HO
CHERRY, Caroline Lockett, 1942- ,
American; nonfiction CON
CHERRY, Carolyn J. see 'CHER-
RYH, C. J.'
CHERRY, Charles Lester, 1942- ,
American; nonfiction CON
CHERRY, Colin, 1914-79, British;
nonfiction CON
CHERRY, Gwendolyn, American;
nonfiction SH
CHERRY, Kelly, American; non-
fiction, fiction, poetry CON
CHERRY, Sheldon Harold, 1934- ,
American; nonfiction CON
'CHERRYH, C. J.' (Carolyn Janice
Cherry), 1942- , American;
fiction CON NI
'CHERRYHOLMES, Anne' see
PRICE, Olive
CHERVIN, Ronda, 1937- , Amer-
ican; nonfiction CON
CHERVINSKAYA, Lidiya Davydovna,
1907- , Russian; poetry CL
CHESBRO, George Clark, 1940- ,
American; fiction CON
'CHESHAM, Henry' see BINGLEY,
David E.
CHESHER, Kim, 1955- , British;
juveniles CON
CHESHIRE, David, 1944- , Brit-
ish; nonfiction CON
CHESLER, Phyllis, 1940- , Amer-
ican; nonfiction CON
CHESNEY, Sir George Tomkyns,
1830-95, English; fiction NI
CHESNEY, Inga L., 1928- ,
German-American; nonfiction
CON
CHESNUT, Mary Boykin Miller,
1823-86, American; nonfiction
BA
CHESNUTT, Charles Waddell, 1858-
1932, American; fiction, non-
fiction BA BU MAG VN
CHESS, Stella, 1914- , American;
nonfiction CON
CHESSER, Eustace, 1902-73, Brit-
ish; nonfiction CON
CHESSEX, Jacques, 1934- , Swiss;
nonfiction, poetry CL CON
CHESSMAN, Caryl Whittier, 1921-
60, American; nonfiction CON
CHESSON, Nora Hopper, 1871-1906,

Irish; poetry, fiction HO
CHESTER, Deborah, 1957- ,
American; fiction, juveniles
CON
CHESTER, George Randolph, 1869-
1924, American; fiction, film
NI ST
CHESTER, Laura, 1949- , Amer-
ican; poetry, fiction CON
CHESTER, Sir Robert, 1566-1640,
English; poetry BU
CHESTER, William L., 1907- ,
American; fiction NI
CHESTERFIELD, Philip Dormer
Stanhope, 1694-1733, English;
nonfiction, letters BU DA
MAG PO
CHESTERTON, Gilbert Keith,
1874-1936, English; fiction,
poetry, nonfiction BU DA
MAG MCC NI PO REI SEY
ST VN
CHETIN, Helen, 1922- , Amer-
ican; juveniles CO
CHETTLE, Henry, 1560-1607, Eng-
lish; plays BU DA RU VD
CHETWODE, Penelope, 1910- ,
British; nonfiction CON
CHETWYND, Bridget, British;
fiction NI
CHETWYND, Tom, 1938- , Eng-
lish; fiction, nonfiction CON
CHETWYND-HAYES, Ronald Henry
('Angus Campbell'), 1919- ,
English; fiction CON
CHEUSE, Alan, 1940- , Amer-
ican; nonfiction CON
CHEVALIER, Haakon Maurice,
1902- , American; fiction,
translations CON NI
CHEVALIER, Louis, 1911- ,
French; nonfiction CON
CHEVALLIER, Gabriel, 1895-1969,
French; fiction BU
CHEVALLIER, Raymond, 1929- ,
French; nonfiction CON
CHEVIGNY, Bell Gale, 1936- ,
American; nonfiction CON
CHEVIGNY, Paul G., 1935- ,
American; nonfiction CON
CHEVILLE, Roy Arthur, 1897- ,
American; nonfiction CON
CHEW, Peter, 1924- , American;
nonfiction CON
CHEW, Ruth ('Ruth Silver'),
1920- , American; juven-
iles CO CON
CHEYETTE, Irving, 1904- ,

American; nonfiction CON
CHEYNEY, Peter, 1896-1951, Eng-
lish; fiction, journalism, plays
MCC REI
CHEYNEY, Reginald Evelyn Peter
S., 1896-1951, English; fiction,
journalism ST
CHEYNEY-COKER, Syl, 1945- ,
Sierra Leonese; poetry VCP
CHI, Madeleine, 1930- , Chinese-
American; nonfiction CON
CHI K'ANG, 223-62, Chinese; non-
fiction, poetry PRU
CHI YÜN, 1724-1805, Chinese; non-
fiction BU
CHIA I, 201-169, B.C., Chinese;
poetry, nonfiction BU PRU
CHIABRERA, Gabriello, 1552-1638,
Italian; poetry BO BU TH
CHIADO, Antonio Ribeiro, -1591,
Portuguese; plays BU
CHIAMPEL, Durich, 1510-82,
Raeto-Romansch, poetry,
translations BU
CHIANG, Yee, 1903-77, Chinese-
American; nonfiction, poetry
CON
CHIANG HAI-CH'ÊNG, see 'AI
CH'ING'
CHIANG KUANG-TZ'U, 1901-31,
Chinese; fiction, poetry, non-
fiction, translations PRU
CHIANG K'UEI, 1155-1221, Chinese;
poetry BU
CHIANG PAI-SHIH, 1155-1230, Chi-
nese; poetry, nonfiction PRU
CHIANG SHIH-CH'ÜAN, 1725-85,
Chinese; poetry, plays BU
CH'IAO CHI, 1280-1345, Chinese;
poetry, plays BU
CHIARA, Piero, 1913- , Italian;
fiction, poetry, nonfiction
CON
CHIARELLI, Luigi, 1880-1947,
Italian; journalism, fiction,
plays BO CL MCG
CHIARI, Pietro, 1711-85, Italian;
fiction, plays BU
CHIARINI, Giuseppe, 1833-1908,
Italian; poetry, nonfiction BU
CHIAROMONTE, Nicola, 1905-72,
Italian; nonfiction CL
CHICAGO, Judy (Cohen), 1939- ,
American; nonfiction CON
CHICKERING, Marjorie, American;
juveniles WAR
CHICKERING, Roger Philip, 1942- ,
American; nonfiction CON

CHICKOS, James Speros, 1941- ,
American; nonfiction CON
CHICOREL, Marietta, Austrian-
American; nonfiction CON
CHIDSEY, Donald Barr, 1920-81,
American; journalism, fiction,
nonfiction CO CON
CHIDYAUSIKU, Paul, 1927/35- ,
Rhodesian; fiction, plays,
journalism HER JA
CHIELENS, Edward Ernest,
1943- , American; nonfiction
CON
CH'IEN CH'IEN-I, 1582-1664,
Chinese; poetry BU
CH'IEN CHUNG-SHU, 20th cen-
tury, Chinese; nonfiction, fic-
tion PRU
CH'IEN HSING-TSUN see A YING
CHIESA, Francesco, 1871-1973,
Swiss; poetry, fiction BU CL
CHIGOUNIS, Evans, 1931- ,
American; poetry CON
CHIKAKO, (Shinshi), 13th century,
Japanese; poetry HI
CHIKAMATSU HANJI, 1725-83,
Japanese; plays HI
'CHIKAMATSU MONZAEMON' (Sugi-
mori Nobumori), 1653-1725,
Japanese; plays BU HI LA
MAG MCG PRU
CHIKOVANI, Svimon, 1902- ,
Georgian; poetry PRU
CHILADZE, Tamaz, 1931- ,
Georgian; nonfiction PRU
CHILCOTT, John Henry, 1924- ,
American; nonfiction CON
'CHILD, Charles B.' (C. Vernon
Frost), 1903- , English; fic-
tion ST
CHILD, Francis James, 1825-96,
American; nonfiction MY
CHILD, Irvin Long, 1915- ,
American; nonfiction CON
CHILD, John, 1922- , New Zeal-
ander; nonfiction CON
CHILD, Julia, 1912- , Amer-
ican; nonfiction CON
CHILD, Lydia Maria Francis,
1802-80, American; fiction,
juveniles, nonfiction BU
CHILD, Philip Albert, 1898- ,
Canadian; fiction, poetry
BU
CHILD, Richard Washburn, 1881-
1935, American; fiction ST
CHILDERS, Robert Erskine,
1870-1922, Anglo-Irish; fic-

tion HO MCC NI REI ST
CHILDRESS, Alice, 1920- , Amer-
ican; plays, juveniles, nonfic-
tion CO CON MCN SH VCD
WAR
CHILDRESS, James Franklin,
1940- , American; nonfiction
CON
CHILDRESS, William, 1933- ,
American; nonfiction, fiction,
poetry CON
CHILDS, Fay, 1890-1971, Amer-
ican; juveniles CO
CHILDS, James Bennett, 1896-
1977, American; nonfiction
CON
CHILDS, Marquis, 1903- , Amer-
ican; journalism, nonfiction
CON PAL
CHILDS, Timothy, 1941- , Amer-
ican; fiction CON
CHILINGIROV, Stiliyan, 1881-1962,
Bulgarian; fiction BU
CHILL, Dan Samuel, 1945- ,
American; nonfiction CON
CHILSON, Richard William, 1943- ,
American; nonfiction CON
CHILSON, Robert, 1945- , Amer-
ican; fiction CON NI
CHILTON, Charles Frederick Wil-
liams, 1927- , English; fic-
tion AS NI
CHILTON, Irma, 1930- , Welsh;
juveniles CON
CHILTON, John James, 1932- ,
English; nonfiction CON
CHILTON, Shirley Ray, 1923- ,
American; nonfiction, juveniles
CON
'CHIMMOY' see GHOSE, Sri C. K.
CHIN, Robert, 1918- , American;
nonfiction CON
CHINAKA, B. A. see STEPHEN,
Félix N.
CHINAS, Beverly Newbold, 1924- ,
American; nonfiction CON
CHINERY, Michael, 1938- , Brit-
ish; nonfiction, juveniles CON
CHING, Julia Chia-yi, 1934- ,
Chinese-American; nonfiction
CON
CHINN, Laurene Chambers, 1902-
78, American; nonfiction CON
CHINN, Robert Edward, 1928- ,
American; nonfiction CON
CHINNOV, Igor Vladimirovich,
1909- , Russian; poetry CL
CHINOY, Ely, 1921-75, American;

nonfiction CON
CHINWEIZU, 1943- , Nigerian;
nonfiction CON
CHIPPERFIELD, Joseph Eugene,
1912- , British; juveniles
KI
CHIRENJE, J. Mutero, 1935- ,
Rhodesian; nonfiction CON
CHIRICO, Andrea De see 'SA-
VINIO, Alberto'
CHIRIKOV, Evgeny Nikolayevich,
1864-1932, Russian; fiction
BU
CHIROVSKY, Nicholas L., 1919- ,
American; nonfiction CON
CHISHOLM, K. Lomneth, 1919- ,
American; nonfiction CON
'CHISHOLM, Matt' see WATTS,
Peter C.
CHISHOLM, Roderick Milton,
1916- , American; nonfic-
tion CON
CHISHOLM, Shirley Anita, 1924- ,
American; nonfiction SH
CHISHOLM, William Sherman,
Jr., 1931- , American; non-
fiction CON
CHISSELL, Joan Olive, English;
nonfiction CON
CHITEPO, Herbert Wiltshire,
1923- , Rhodesian; poetry
HER
CHITHAM, Edward Harry, 1932- ,
British; nonfiction, juveniles
CON
CHITRABHANU, Gurudev Shree,
1922- , Indian-American;
nonfiction CON
CHITTENDEN, Elizabeth F.,
1903- , American; juveniles,
nonfiction CO CON
CHITTENDEN, Margaret, 1935- ,
American; juveniles, fiction
CON
CHITTICK, William Oliver, 1937- ,
American; nonfiction CON
CHITTUM, Ida Hoover, 1918- ,
American; juveniles CO
WAR
CHITTY, Arthur Benjamin,
1914- , American; nonfic-
tion CON
CHITTY, Sir Thomas W., see
'HINDE, Thomas'
CHITWOOD, Billy James, 1931- ,
American; nonfiction CON
CHIU, Hong-Yee, 1932- , Amer-
ican; nonfiction CON

CHIVERS, Thomas Holley, 1809-58,
American; poetry, plays, non-
fiction BA BR BU MYE VP
CHLUMBERG, Hans, 1897-1930,
Austrian; plays MCG
CHMAJ, Betty E., 1930- , Amer-
ican; nonfiction CON
CHO KI-CH'ON, 1913-51, Korean;
poetry PRU
CHOATE, Ernest Alfred, 1900- ,
American; nonfiction CON
CHOCANO, José Santos, 1875-1934,
Peruvian; poetry BR BU
CHODASIEWICZ, Vladislav F., see
KHODASEVICH, Vladislav F.
CHODERLOS de LACLOS, Pierre
Ambroise Francois, 1741-1803,
French; fiction BU
CHODES, John, 1939- , American;
nonfiction CON
CHODOROV, Edward, 1904- ,
American; plays, film CON
CHODOROV, Jerome, 1911- ,
American; plays, film CON
MCG
CHODZIESNER, G. see 'KOLMAR,
Gertrud'
CH'OE CH'I-UON ('Koun'), 857- ,
Korean; poetry PRU
CH'OE NAM-SON ('Yuktang'), 1890-
1957, Korean; nonfiction PRU
CHÖNZ, Selina, Swiss; juveniles
DEM
CHOMETTE, Rene Lucien ('Rene
Clair'), 1898-1981, French;
journalism, fiction CON
CHOMSKY, Noam, 1928- , Amer-
ican; nonfiction BR WAK
CHOMSKY, William, 1896-1977,
Russian-American; nonfiction,
translations CON
CHONA, Mainza Mathias, 1930- ,
Zambian; fiction JA
CHONG CHI-YONG, 1903- , Ko-
rean; poetry PRU
CHONG CH'OL, 1536-93/94, Ko-
rean; poetry BU PRU
CHONG YAG-YONG, 1762-1836,
Korean; nonfiction PRU
CHONIATES, Michael (Michael
Acominatus), 1138?-1222?,
Byzantine; nonfiction LA
CHONIATES, Nicetas (Nicetas
Acominatus), 1150?-1213,
Byzantine; nonfiction LA
CHOPIN, Kate O'Flaherty, 1851-
1904, American; fiction AM
BA BR BU VN

CHOQUETTE, Adrienne, 1915- ,
Canadian; nonfiction, fiction
CR
CHOQUETTE, Robert ('Guy de
Vaudreuil'), 1905- , Cana-
dian; poetry, plays, fiction
BU CR
CHORAO, Ann McKay Sproat,
1936- , American; juveniles
CO CON
CHORAO, Kay, 1937- , Amer-
ican; juveniles DEM
CHORBAJIYSKI, Dimitur H. see
'CHUDOMIR'
CHORELL, Walentin, 1912- ,
Swedish-Finnish; plays, fic-
tion TH
CHORNY, Merron, 1922- , Ca-
nadian; nonfiction CON
'CHORNY, Sasha' (Aleksandr Mik-
haylovich Glikberg; Chěrny),
1880-1932, Russian; poetry,
fiction BU CL
CHOROMANSKI, Michal, 1904- ,
Polish; fiction, plays BU TH
CHORPENNING, Charlotte Lee
Barrows, 1872-1955, Amer-
ican; plays KI
CHOTZINOFF, Samuel, 1889-1964,
Russian-American; journalism
CON
CHOU, Ya-luu, 1923- , Chinese-
American; nonfiction CON
CHOU LI-PO, 1908- , Chinese;
fiction BU PRU
CHOU PANG-YEN, 1056-1121,
Chinese; poetry BU PRU
CHOU SHU-JÊN, see 'Lu Hsün'
CHOU, TSO-JÊN, 1885-1966,
Chinese; nonfiction, transla-
tions BU PRU
CHOU TUN-I, 1017-73, Chinese;
nonfiction BU
CHOU YANG, 1908- , Chinese;
nonfiction PRU
CHOUCRI, Nazli, 1943- ,
Egyptian-American; nonfic-
tion CON
CHOUROQUI, Andre Nathanael,
1917- , Algerian-Israeli;
nonfiction, poetry, transla-
tions CON
CHOWDER, Ken, 1950- , Amer-
ican; fiction CON
CHOY, Bong-youn, 1914- ,
Korean-American; nonfiction
CON
CHOYNOWSKI, Piotr, 1885-1935,

Polish; fiction TH
CHRAÏBI, Driss, 1926- , Moroc-
can; journalism, fiction PRU
CHRETIEN de TROYES, fl. 1160-
80, French; poetry BU MAG
TH
CHRETIEN li GOIS, French; po-
etry BU
CHRISLOCK, Carl Hendrick, 1917- ,
American; nonfiction CON
CHRISMAN, Arthur Bowie, 1889-
1953, American; juveniles
COM
CHRIST, Carol Tecla, 1944- ,
American; nonfiction CON
'CHRISTEN, Ada' (Christiane von
Breden Frideriks), 1844-1901,
Austrian; poetry, fiction BU
CHRISTENSEN, Clyde M., 1905- ,
American; nonfiction CON
CHRISTENSEN, Eleanor Ingalls,
1913- , American; nonfiction
CON
CHRISTENSEN, Harold Taylor,
1909- , American; nonfiction
CON
CHRISTENSEN, Inger, 1935- ,
Danish; fiction, poetry CL
CHRISTENSEN, Jack Arden, 1927- ,
American; nonfiction, poetry
CON
CHRISTENSEN, James Lee, 1922- ,
American; nonfiction CON
CHRISTENSEN, Paul, 1943- ,
American; poetry CON
CHRISTENSEN, Yolanda Maria
(Jo), 1943- , American; non-
fiction CON
CHRISTENSON, Larry, 1928- ,
American; nonfiction CON
CHRISTESEN, Clement Byrne,
1911- , Australian; journal-
ism, nonfiction, translations,
poetry CON
CHRISTGAU, Alice Erickson,
1902- , American; juveniles
CO
CHRISTGAU, John Frederick,
1934- , American; nonfiction
CON
CHRISTGAU, Robert Thomas,
1942- , American; nonfiction
CON
CHRISTIAN, 10th century, Czech;
nonfiction BU
'CHRISTIAN, A. B.' see YABES,
Leopoldo
CHRISTIAN, Carol Cathay, 1923- ,

English; nonfiction, fiction
CON
CHRISTIAN, George Eastland,
1927- , American; nonfic-
tion CON
CHRISTIAN, James Lee, 1927- ,
American; nonfiction CON
'CHRISTIAN, Jill' see DILCOCK,
Noreen
'CHRISTIAN, John' see DIXON,
Roger
'CHRISTIAN, Louise' see GRILL,
Nannette L.
CHRISTIAN, Marcus Bruce,
1900- , American; poetry,
nonfiction CON SH
CHRISTIAN, Mary Blount, 1933- ,
American; juveniles CO CON
CHRISTIAN, Portia, 1908- ,
American; nonfiction CON
CHRISTIAN, Roy Cloberry, 1914- ,
British; nonfiction CON
CHRISTIAN, Samuel T., Amer-
ican; juveniles WAR
CHRISTIANSEN, Arne Einar, 1861-
1939, Danish; plays, poetry,
fiction BU
CHRISTIANSEN, Harley Duane,
1930- , American; nonfiction
CON
CHRISTIANSEN, Sigurd Wesley,
1891-1947, Norwegian; fic-
tion, plays BU CL TH
CHRISTIANSON, Gale E., 1942- ,
American; nonfiction CON
CHRISTIE, Agatha Mary Miller
('Mary Westmacott'), 1890-
1976, English; fiction, plays
BU CON DA REI ST VCD
VCN VN
'CHRISTIE, Hugh' see CHRISTIE-
MURRAY, David H. A.
CHRISTIE, Jean, 1912- , Amer-
ican; nonfiction CON
CHRISTIE, John Aldrich, 1920- ,
American; nonfiction CON
CHRISTIE, Lindsay H., 1906?-
76, American; nonfiction
CON
CHRISTIE-MURRAY, David Hugh
Arthur ('Hugh Arthur'; 'Hugh
Christie'), 1913- , English;
nonfiction CON
CHRISTIN, Pierre, 1938- ,
French; fiction NI
CHRISTINE de PISAN, 1365-
1430?, French; poetry BU
TH

CHRIST-JANER, Albert W., 1910-
73, American; nonfiction CON
CHRISTMAN, Elizabeth, 1914- ,
American; fiction CON
CHRISTMAN, Henry Max, 1932-80,
American; nonfiction CON
CHRISTMAN, Raymond John, 1919- ,
American; nonfiction CON
CHRISTOFOROV, Assen, 1910-70,
Bulgarian; nonfiction BU
CHRISTOPHER, Joe Randell, 1935- ,
American; nonfiction, poetry
CON
'CHRISTOPHER, John' (Christopher
Samuel Youd; 'Hilary Ford';
'Peter Graaf'; 'Peter Nichols;
'Anthony Rye'), 1922- , Eng-
lish; fiction, juveniles AS
CON DEM KI NI WA
CHRISTOPHER, Maurine Brooks,
American; nonfiction CON
CHRISTOPHER, Robert Collins,
1924- , American; journal-
ism CON
CHRISTOPHER of MYTILENE,
1000-50, Byzantine; poetry
BU LA
CHRISTOPHERSEN, Paul Hans,
1911- , Danish; nonfiction
CON
CHRISTOWE, Stoyan, 1898- ,
American; nonfiction, fiction
CON
CHRISTY, Betty, 1924- , Amer-
ican; nonfiction CON
CHRISTY, Howard Chandler, 1873-
1952, American; juveniles CO
CHRISTY, Marian, 1932- , Amer-
ican; nonfiction CON
CHRISTY, Teresa Elizabeth,
1927- , American; nonfic-
tion CON
CHROBAK, Dobroslav, 1907-51,
Slovak; fiction BU
CHROMAN, Eleanor, 1937- ,
Austrian-American; juveniles
CON
CHROMAN, Nathan, 1929- ,
American; nonfiction CON
CHRYSIPPUS, 280-207/06 B.C.,
Greek; nonfiction BU GR LA
CHRYSOSTOM, John, 350-407,
Greek; nonfiction LA
CHU, Arthur T. S. ('W. R. Chu'),
1916- , American; nonfiction
CON
CHU, Daniel, 1933- , American;
juveniles CO

CHU

CHU, Grace Goodyear, 1916- ,
American; nonfiction CON
CHU, Kong, 1926- , Chinese-
American; nonfiction CON
CHU, Samuel C., 1929- ,
Chinese-American; nonfiction
CON
'CHU, W. R.' see CHU, Arthur
T. S.
'CHU CH'AN' see BLOFELD,
John E.
'CHU CHUNG-YU' see HSU, Bene-
dict
CHU HSI, 1130-1200, Chinese;
nonfiction BU PRU
CHU HSIANG, 1904-33, Chinese;
poetry, nonfiction BU PRU
CHU I-TSUN, 1629-1709, Chinese;
nonfiction, poetry BU
CHU TZU-CH'ING, 1898-1948,
Chinese; nonfiction, poetry
BU PRU
CHUANG-TZU, 369?-286? B.C.,
Chinese; poetry, nonfiction
BU LA PRU
CHUBAK, Sadeq, 1916- , Iranian;
fiction BU PRU
CHUDACOFF, Howard Peter,
1943- , American; nonfic-
tion CON
'CHUDOMIR' (Dimitur Hajihristov
Chorbajiyski), 1890-1967, Bul-
garian; fiction BU
CH'Ü CH'IU-PAI, 1899-1935, Chi-
nese; nonfiction, translations
PRU
CH'Ü YU, 1341-1427, Chinese;
poetry, fiction BU
CH'Ü YÜAN, 343-277 B.C., Chi-
nese; poetry BU
CHUGHTAI, Ismat, 1915- , Urdu;
fiction, plays, nonfiction PRU
CHUKOVSKAYA, Lidiya, 1907- ,
Russian; fiction, nonfiction
CL WA
'CHUKOVSKY, Kornei' (Nikolai
Iwanovich Korneichuk), 1882-
1969, Russian; juveniles, non-
fiction BU CL CO TH WA
CHULKOV, Georgy Ivanovich,
1879- , Russian; poetry BU
CHULKOV, Mikhail Dmitrievich,
1743-93, Russian; fiction BU
CHUM, Haji, 1920?- , Kenyan;
fiction HER
CHUMACERO, Alí, 1918- , Mex-
ican; poetry BR
CHUMAN, Frank Fujio, 1917- ,

American; nonfiction CON
CHUN, Jinsie Kyung ('P. M. Sung'),
1902- , Chinese-American;
fiction, nonfiction CON
CHUN, Richard, 1935- , Korean-
American; nonfiction CON
CHUNG, Hyung Chan, 1931- ,
Korean-American; nonfiction
CON
CHUNG, Joseph Sang-hoon, 1929- ,
Korean-American; nonfiction
CON
CHUNG HUNG, 468-518, Chinese;
nonfiction PRU
CHUPACK, Henry, 1915- , Amer-
ican; nonfiction CON
CHURCH, Carol Bauer, American;
juveniles WAR
CHURCH, Richard Thomas, 1893-
1972, English; juveniles, po-
etry, nonfiction, fiction CO
DA KI
CHURCH, Richard William, 1815-
90, English; nonfiction BU
CHURCH, Robert Le Valley, 1938- ,
American; nonfiction CON
CHURCHILL, Allen, 1911- , Amer-
ican; nonfiction CON
CHURCHILL, Caryl, 1938- , Brit-
ish; plays CON VCD
CHURCHILL, Charles, 1731/32-
64, English; poetry, nonfiction
BU DA PO VP
CHURCHILL, Creighton, 1912- ,
American; nonfiction CON
CHURCHILL, E. Richard, 1937- ,
American; juveniles CO
'CHURCHILL, Joyce' see HARRI-
SON, Michael J.
CHURCHILL, Randolph, 1911-68,
British; journalism CON
CHURCHILL, Reginald Charles,
1916- , English; fiction NI
CHURCHILL, Winston, 1871-1947,
American; fiction, plays BR
BU CON MAG PO VN
CHURCHILL, Sir Winston, 1874-
1965, English; journalism,
fiction, nonfiction BU DA
MAG PO
CHURCHYARD, Thomas, 1520-1604,
English; poetry BU DA RU VP
CHUTE, Marchette Gaylord, 1909- ,
juveniles, plays, nonfiction KI
CHWAST, Jacqueline, 1932- ,
American; juveniles CO CON
DEM
CHWAST, Seymour, 1931- ,

American; juveniles CO DEM
CHWAT, Aleksander see 'WAT,
Aleksander'
CIARDI, John, 1916- , Amer-
ican; nonfiction, poetry,
translations, juveniles BR
BU DE KI PO VCP
CIBBER, Colley, 1671-1757,
English; poetry, plays BU
DA MAG MCG PO VD
CICCORELLA, Aubra Dair, Amer-
ican; nonfiction CON
CICELLIS, Kay, 1926- , French;
fiction, translations NI VCN
CICERO, Marcus Tullius, 106-
43 B.C., Roman; nonfiction
BU GR LA MAG
CICERO, Quintus Tullius, 102-
43 B.C., Roman; nonfiction
LA
CICOGNANI, Amleto Giovanni,
1883-1973, Italian; nonfiction
CON
CICOGNANI, Bruno, 1879-1972,
Italian; fiction, plays BU
CL TH
CICOUREL, Aaron V., 1928- ,
American; nonfiction CON
CID PEREZ, Jose Diego, 1906- ,
Cuban-American; nonfiction,
fiction, plays CON
CIECHANOWSKI, Jan, 1888-1973,
Polish; nonfiction CON
CIELO d'ALCAMO, 13th century,
Italian; poetry BO
CIENCIALA, Anna Maria, 1929- ,
Polish-American; nonfiction
CON
CIENFUEGOS, Nicasio Alvarez de,
1764-1809, Spanish; poetry
TH
CIEPLAK, Tadeusz Nowak, 1918- ,
Polish-American; nonfiction
CON
CIETAK, Ján see 'SMREK, Ján'
CIEZA de LEON, Pedro, 1518?-60,
Spanish; nonfiction BU
CIFRE de LOUBRIEL, Estella,
Puerto Rican; nonfiction HIL
'CILFFRIW, Gwynfor' see GRIFF-
ITH, Thomas G.
CIMBOLLEK, Robert Carl, 1937- ,
American; nonfiction CON
CIMENT, Michel, 1938- ,
French; nonfiction CON
'CIMINELLI, Serafino de' (Sera-
fino Aquilano), 1466-1500,
Italian; poetry BU TH

CIMINO, Maria, American; juven-
iles WAR
CINBERG, Bernard L., 1905-79,
American; nonfiction CON
CINGRIA, Charles Albert, 1883-
1954, Swiss; nonfiction BU
CINNA, Gaius Helvius, 70-44 A.D.,
Latin; poetry BU GR LA
CINNAMUS, John, 1144?-1203?,
Byzantine; nonfiction LA
CINO da PISTOIA, 1270-1336/37,
Italian; poetry BO BU
'IL CINZIO' see GIRALDI, Giam-
battista
CIORAN, Emile M., 1911- , Ru-
manian; nonfiction CL WA
CIPALUNKAR, Visnusastri, 1850-
82, Marathi; nonfiction, juven-
iles BU PRU
CIPRIANO, Anthony John, 1941- ,
American; juveniles CON
CIRIA, Alberto, 1934- , Argentian-
Canadian; nonfiction, transla-
tions, journalism CON
CIRIACO d'ANCONA, 1391-1452,
Italian; fiction BU
CIRINO, Linda Davis, 1941- ,
American; nonfiction CON
CIRINO, Robert, 1937- , Amer-
ican; nonfiction CON
CISMARU, Alfred, 1933- , Amer-
ican; nonfiction CON
CISSE, Emile, 1930?- , Guinean;
fiction HER
'CISSMANN, Anne' see CLUNE,
Anne
CISSOKO, Siriman, 1934/40- ,
Malian; poetry HER JA
CITASHE, I. W. W., 1845?-1930?,
Xhosan; poetry HER
CITATI, Pietro, 1930- , Italian;
nonfiction CON
'CITTAFINO, Ricardo' see BICK-
ERS, Richard L. T.
CIUBA, Edward Joseph, 1935- ,
American; nonfiction CON
CIVILLE, John Raphael, 1940- ,
American; nonfiction CON
CIXOUS, Hélène, 1937- , French;
fiction, nonfiction CL
CLABAUGH, Gary Kenneth, 1940- ,
American; nonfiction CON
CLAERBAUT, David, 1946- ,
American; nonfiction CON
CLAES, Ernest, 1885-1968, Flem-
ish; fiction BU
CLAFLIN, Edward, 1949- , Amer-
ican; nonfiction CON WAR

CLAGHORN, Charles Eugene,
1911- , American; nonfic-
tion CON
CLAGUE, Maryhelen, 1930- ,
American; fiction CON
CLAIN, Samuil (Micu), 1745-1806,
Russian; nonfiction BU
CLAIR, Andrée, French; juven-
iles CO
CLAIR, Bernard Eddy, 1951- ,
American; nonfiction CON
'CLAIR, Rene' see CHOMETTE,
Rene L.
CLAIRE, William Francis, 1935- ,
American; poetry CON
CLAMMER, David, 1943- , Brit-
ish; nonfiction CON
CLANCY, Joseph P., American;
juveniles, translations CON
WAR
CLANTON, Gordon, 1942- , Amer-
ican; nonfiction CON
CLANTON, Orval Gene, 1934- ,
American; nonfiction CON
CLANVOWE, Sir John, 1341-91,
English; poetry BU
CLAPP, Henry, 1814-75, Amer-
ican; journalism BR
CLAPP, Margaret, 1910-74, Amer-
ican; nonfiction CON
CLAPP, Patricia, 1912- , Amer-
ican; juveniles, plays CO KI
CLARDY, Andrea Fleck, 1943- ,
American; nonfiction CON
'CLARE, Adap (Jane McElheney),
1836-74, American; fiction,
poetry BR
'CLARE, Elizabeth' see COOK,
Dorothy M.
'CLARE, Helen' see HUNTER
BLAIR, Pauline C.
CLARE, John, 1793-1864, English;
poetry BU DA MAG PO VP
CLARE, Josephine, 1933- ,
German-American; nonfiction,
translations CON
CLARENDON, Edward see HYDE,
Edward
CLARESON, Thomas D., 1926- ,
American; nonfiction NI
CLARFIELD, Gerard Howard,
1936- , American; nonfic-
tion CON
CLARI, Robert de, -1217?,
French; nonfiction BU
CLARIE, Thomas Cashin, 1943- ,
American; nonfiction CON
'CLARIN' see ALAS y UREÑA,

Leopoldo
CLARK, Admont Gulick, 1919- ,
American; nonfiction CON
CLARK, Alfred A. G. see
'HARE, Cyril'
CLARK, Alice Sandell, 1922- ,
American; nonfiction CON
CLARK, Ann Nolan, 1896/98- ,
American; juveniles, poetry
CO KI
CLARK, Anna, 1919- , British;
fiction REI
CLARK, Austin, 1896-1974, Irish;
poetry, plays, fiction, nonfic-
tion VP
CLARK, Ben T., 1928- , Amer-
ican; nonfiction CON
CLARK, Brian, 1932- , English;
plays CON
CLARK, Bruce Budge, 1918- ,
American; nonfiction CON
CLARK, Carol Lois, 1948- ,
American; nonfiction CON
CLARK, Catherine Anthony Smith,
1892-1977, Canadian; juveniles,
poetry, fiction CR KI
CLARK, Charles Manning Hope,
1915- , Australian; nonfiction
CON
CLARK, China Debra, 1950- ,
American; nonfiction, plays
CON
CLARK, Clifford Edward, Jr.,
1941- , American; nonfiction
CON
CLARK, Colin Grant, 1905- ,
English; nonfiction CON
'CLARK, Curt' see WESTLAKE,
Donald E.
'CLARK, David Allen' see ERNST,
Lyman J.
CLARK, David Gillis, 1933- ,
American; nonfiction CON
CLARK, Donald Rowlee, 1925- ,
American; nonfiction CON
CLARK, Dora Mae, 1893- , Amer-
ican; nonfiction CON
CLARK, Eleanor, 1913- , Amer-
ican; nonfiction, fiction, juven-
iles, translations KIB VCN
CLARK, Electa, 1910- , American;
juveniles CON WAR
CLARK, Eliot Candee, 1883-1980,
American; nonfiction CON
CLARK, Ellery Harding, Jr.,
1909- , American; nonfiction
CON
CLARK, Emily Tapscott, 1892-1953,

American; journalism BA
CLARK, Eri, 1937- , British;
journalism, nonfiction, fiction CON
CLARK, Eugenie, 1922- , American; nonfiction CON
CLARK, Frank James, 1922- , American; juveniles CO
CLARK, Gail (Maggie MacKeever';
'Grace South'), 1944- , American; fiction CON
'CLARK, Garel' see GARELICK, May
CLARK, George Norman, 1890-1979, British; nonfiction CON
CLARK, Gregory, 1892-1977, Canadian; nonfiction, fiction CON CR
CLARK, Harry, 1917- , American; nonfiction CON
CLARK, James Anthony, 1907- , American; nonfiction CON
CLARK, Jean Cashman, 1920- , American; fiction CON
CLARK, Jerry Eugene, 1942- , American; nonfiction CON
CLARK, Joan, 1934- , Canadian; juveniles CON
CLARK, John Desmond, 1916- , American; nonfiction CON
CLARK, John Grahame Douglas, 1907- , English; nonfiction CON
CLARK, John Pepper, 1935- , Nigerian; poetry, plays, nonfiction BU CON HER JA LA VCD VCP VP WAK
CLARK, John Ralph Kukeakalani, 1946- , American; nonfiction CON
CLARK, Sir Kenneth, 1903- , English; nonfiction BU CON
CLARK, Kenneth B., 1914- , American; nonfiction SH
CLARK, Leonard, 1905-81, British; poetry, nonfiction, juveniles KI VCP
CLARK, Leonard Hill, 1915- , American; nonfiction CON
CLARK, Leroy D., American; nonfiction CON
CLARK, Lewis Gaylord, 1808-73, American; nonfiction MYE
CLARK, Lindley Hoag, Jr., 1920- , American; nonfiction CON
CLARK, Mabel Margaret (Cowie;

'Lesley Storm'), 1903-75, British; fiction, plays, films CON
CLARK, Marden J., 1916- , American; nonfiction CON
CLARK, Margaret Goff, 1913- , American; juveniles CO
CLARK, Marion L., 1943-77, American; nonfiction CON
CLARK, Mary Higgins, 1931- , American; nonfiction, fiction CON
CLARK, Mary Jane, 1915- , American; nonfiction CON
CLARK, Mary Twibill, American; nonfiction CON
CLARK, Mavis Thorpe ('Mavis Latham'), Australian; juveniles, fiction, nonfiction CO CON KI
'CLARK, Merle' see GESSNER, Lynne
CLARK, Naomi, 1932- , American; nonfiction CON
CLARK, Norman Harold, 1925- , American; nonfiction CON
'CLARK, Parlin' see TRIGG, Harry D.
CLARK, Patricia Finrow, 1929- , American; juveniles CO
CLARK, Robert Alfred, 1908- , American; nonfiction CON
CLARK, Robert Eugene, 1912- , American; nonfiction CON
CLARK, Robert Lloyd, Jr., 1945- , American; nonfiction CON
CLARK, Ronald William, 1916- , English; fiction, journalism NI
CLARK, Ruth Campbell ('Alan Porter'), 1920- , American; nonfiction CON
CLARK, Samuel, 1945- , American; nonfiction CON
CLARK, Stephen Richard Lyster, 1945- , British; nonfiction CON
CLARK, Sue Cassidy, 1935- , American; nonfiction CON
CLARK, Sydney Alylmer, 1890-1975, American; nonfiction CON
CLARK, Thomas Willard, 1941- , American; poetry, plays, fiction CON
CLARK, Tom, 1941- , American; poetry, plays VCP
CLARK, Truman Ross, 1935- , American; nonfiction CON
'CLARK, Virginia' see GRAY,

Patricia C.
CLARK, Walter Van Tilburg,
1909-71, American; fiction
BR CO MAG VCN VN
CLARK, William, 1770-1838,
American; nonfiction MAG
CLARKE, Anna, 1919- , South
African; translations, nonfic-
tion CON
CLARKE, Arthur Charles, 1917- ,
British; fiction, plays, non-
fiction AS CO DEM NI VCN
CLARKE, Austin, 1896-1974,
Irish; poetry, plays, fiction
BU CON HO VCN VCP
CLARKE, Basil Fulford, 1908-78,
British; nonfiction CON
CLARKE, Brenda Margaret Lilian
('Brenda Honeyman'), 1926- ,
British; fiction CON
CLARKE, Charles Cowden, 1787-
1877, English; nonfiction BU
CLARKE, Clorinda, 1917- ,
American; juveniles CO
CLARKE, Derrick Harry, 1919- ,
British; nonfiction CON
CLARKE, Duncan Lynn, 1941- ,
American; nonfiction CON
CLARKE, Dwight Lancelot, 1885-
1961, American; nonfiction
CON
CLARKE, Ernest George, 1927- ,
Canadian; nonfiction CON
CLARKE, Fred G., -1964,
American; juveniles WAR
CLARKE, Garry Evans, 1943- ,
American; nonfiction CON
CLARKE, Henry Charles ('Hock-
ley Clarke'), 1899- , Brit-
ish; nonfiction CON
CLARKE, Hugh Vincent, 1919- ,
American; nonfiction, fiction
CON
CLARKE, Ignatius Frederic,
1918- , Scots; nonfiction
AS NI
'CLARKE, Captain Jafar' see
NEWSMITH, Robert I.
CLARKE, James Franklin,
1906- , American; nonfic-
tion CON
CLARKE, James Freeman,
1810-88, American; trans-
lations, nonfiction MY
CLARKE, Joan, British; ju-
veniles KI
'CLARKE, John' see LAKLAN,
Carli

CLARKE, John Henrik, 1915- ,
American; nonfiction, journal-
ism, poetry BA CON SH
CLARKE, Lige, 1942- , Amer-
ican; nonfiction CON
CLARKE, Marcus Hislop, 1846-81,
Australian; fiction, journalism,
plays BU DA VN
CLARKE, Mary Stetson, 1911- ,
American; juveniles CO
CLARKE, Mavis Thorpe, Austral-
ian; juveniles DEM
'CLARKE, Michael' see NEWTON,
Clarke
CLARKE, Pauline see HUNTER
BLAIR, Pauline C.
CLARKE, Peter E., see KUMALO,
Peter E.
CLARKE, Peter Frederick, 1942- ,
British; nonfiction CON
'CLARKE, Richard' see PAINE,
Lauran B.
CLARKE, Samuel, 1675-1729, Eng-
lish; nonfiction BU
CLARKE, Stephan Paul, 1945- ,
American; nonfiction CON
CLARKE, Thomas Emmet, 1918- ,
American; nonfiction CON
CLARKE, Thomas Ernest Bennett,
1907- , British; nonfiction,
plays, film CON
CLARKE, Thurston, 1946- ,
American; nonfiction CON
CLARKE, William Malpas, 1922- ,
English; nonfiction CON
CLARKE, William Thomas, 1932- ,
Canadian; nonfiction CON
CLARKIN, Sean, 1941- , Irish;
poetry HO
CLARKSON, Adrienne, 1939- ,
American; fiction CON
CLARKSON, Ewan, 1929- , Brit-
ish; juveniles, plays CO KI
CLARKSON, Helen see 'McCloy,
Helen W.
'CLARKSON, J. F.' see TUBB,
Edwin C.
CLARKSON, Jan Nagel, 1943- ,
American; juveniles, journal-
ism CON
CLARKSON, Jesse Dunsmore,
1897-1973, American; nonfic-
tion CON
CLARKSON, Leslie Albert, 1933- ,
British; nonfiction CON
CLARKSON, Stephen, 1937- ,
English; nonfiction CON
CLARKSON, Tom, 1913- , Brit-

ish; nonfiction, poetry CON
'CLARO OSCURO' see ASENJO,
Federico
CLARY, Jack, 1932- , American;
nonfiction CON
CLASEN, Claus Peter, 1931- ,
German-American; nonfiction
CON
CLASPY, Everett M., 1907?-73,
American; nonfiction CON
CLAUDEL, Alice Moser, 1918- ,
American; nonfiction, poetry
CON
CLAUDEL, Paul, 1868-1955,
French; poetry, plays, non-
fiction BU CL MAG MCG
SEY TH
'CLAUDIA, Susan' see JOHNSTON,
William
CLAUDIAN (Claudius Claudianus),
370-404/08, Latin; poetry
BU GR LA
CLAUDIUS (Tiberius Claudius Nero
Germanicus), 10 B.C.-54 A.D.,
Roman; nonfiction GR LA
CLAUDIUS, Hermann, 1878- ,
German; poetry, fiction BU
CLAUDIUS, Matthias, 1740-1815,
German; poetry BU TH
CLAUDIUS QUADRIGARIUS, Quin-
tus, fl. 80 B.C., Roman;
nonfiction BU LA
CLAUDY, Carl H., 1879-1957,
American; fiction NI
CLAUS, Hugo Maurice, 1929- ,
Belgian; poetry, fiction,
plays, film BU CL WAK
CLAUSEN, Aage R., 1932- ,
American; nonfiction CON
CLAUSEN, Sven, 1893-1961, Dan-
ish; plays, poetry, nonfiction
BU
CLAUSSEN, Sophus Niels Christen,
1865-1931/32, Danish; poetry
BU CL TH
CLAVEL, Bernard Charles, 1923- ,
French; fiction, nonfiction
CON
CLAVEL, Maurice, 1920-79,
French; nonfiction, plays,
fiction CL CON
'CLAVERS, Mrs. Mary' see
KIRKLAND, Caroline
CLAVIJO y FAJARDO, José de,
1730-1806, Spanish; nonfiction
BU
CLAWSON, Marion, 1905- ,
American; nonfiction CON

CLAY, Charles, 1906- , Canadian;
juveniles, fiction CR
CLAY, Charles Travis, 1885-1978,
British; nonfiction CON
CLAY, Comer, 1910- , American;
nonfiction CON
CLAY, Floyd Martin, 1927- ,
American; nonfiction CON
CLAY, Grady E., 1916- , Amer-
ican; nonfiction CON
CLAY, Lucius DuBignon, 1897-
1978, American; nonfiction
CON
CLAY, Marie Mildred, 1926- ,
New Zealander; nonfiction
CON
CLAYBAUGH, Amos Lincoln,
1917- , American; nonfiction
CON
CLAYDON, Leslie Francis, 1923- ,
English; nonfiction CON
CLAYRE, Alasdair, 1935- , Brit-
ish; fiction, poetry, nonfiction
CON
'CLAYTON, Barbara' see PLUFF,
Barbara L.
CLAYTON, Bruce, 1939- , Amer-
ican; nonfiction CON
CLAYTON, Charles Curtis, 1902- ,
American; nonfiction CON
CLAYTON, Donald Delbert, 1935- ,
American; nonfiction CON
CLAYTON, Howard, 1929- ,
American; nonfiction CON
CLAYTON, Jo, 1939- , American;
fiction CON NI
'CLAYTON, John' see BEEVERS,
John L.
CLAYTON, John, 1892-1979, Amer-
ican; journalism CON
CLAYTON, John Bell, 1906-55,
American; fiction BA
CLAYTON, Paul Clark, 1932- ,
American; nonfiction CON
CLAYTON, Richard see 'HAGGARD,
William'
CLAYTON, Sylvia, British; fiction
CON
CLAYTON, Thomas Swoverland,
1932- , American; nonfiction
CON
CLAYTON, Thompson Bowker,
1904- , American; nonfiction
CON
CLAYTOR, Gertrude Boatwright,
1890?-1973, American; poetry
CON
CLEAGE, Albert B., Jr., 1911- ,

American; nonfiction CON
SH
CLEANTHES of ASSOS, 331-232
B.C. , Greek; nonfiction BU
GR LA
CLEARE, John, 1936- , English;
nonfiction CON
CLEARY, Beverly Bunn, 1916- ,
American; juveniles, poetry,
plays KI
CLEARY, Florence Damon, 1896- ,
American; nonfiction CON
CLEARY, Jon, 1917- , Austral-
ian; fiction, plays, film REI
VCN WA
CLEARY, Robert Edward, 1932- ,
American; nonfiction CON
CLEATOR, Philip Ellaby, 1908- ,
British; nonfiction CON
CLEAVER, Bill, 1920- , Amer-
ican; juveniles CO CON DEM
KI
CLEAVER, Carole, 1934- ,
American; juveniles CO
CON
CLEAVER, Eldridge, 1935- ,
American; nonfiction PO SH
CLEAVER, Elizabeth M. , 1939- ,
Canadian; juveniles CO CON
DEM
CLEAVER, Hylton Reginald ('Reg-
inald Crunden'), 1891-1961,
British; juveniles, fiction
CON
CLEAVER, Vera, 1919- , Amer-
ican; juveniles, fiction CO
CON DEM KI
CLEAVES, Peter Shurtleff, 1943- ,
American; nonfiction CON
CLECAK, Peter E. , 1938- ,
American; nonfiction CON
CLEEVE, Brian Talbot, 1921- ,
English; nonfiction, fiction,
journalism CON HO REI
CLEGG, Alexander Bradshaw,
1909- , British; nonfiction
CON
CLEGG, Jerry Stephen, 1933- ,
American; nonfiction CON
CLEGG, Stewart Roger, 1947- ,
American; nonfiction CON
CLEIDEMUS, fl. 350 B.C. ,
Greek; nonfiction LA
'CLEISHBOTHAM, Jebediah' see
SCOTT, Sir Walter
CLEITARCHUS, 4-3rd centuries
B.C. , Greek; nonfiction GR
LA

CLELAND, Charles Carr, 1924- ,
American; nonfiction CON
CLELAND, John, 1709/10-89, Eng-
lish; fiction, plays BU VN
CLELAND, Mabel see WIDDENER,
Mabel C.
'CLELLAND, Catherine' see TOWN-
SEND, Doris McF.
CLEMENS, Alphonse H. , 1905-77,
American; nonfiction CON
CLEMENS, Bryan T. , 1934- ,
American; nonfiction CON
CLEMENS, Samuel Langhorne see
'TWAIN, Mark'
CLEMENS, Virginia Phelps 1941- ,
American; juveniles CON
CLEMENT, Evelyn Geer, 1926- ,
American; nonfiction CON
'CLEMENT, Hal' (Harry Clement
Stubbs), 1922- , American;
fiction, nonfiction AS COW NI
CLEMENT, Herbert Flint, 1927- ,
American; nonfiction CON
CLEMENT, Roland Charles, 1912- ,
American; nonfiction CON
CLEMENT of ALEXANDRIA (Titus
Flavius Clemens), 150-212/14,
Greek; nonfiction BU GR LA
CLEMENT of ROME (Pope Clement
I), Greek; nonfiction GR
CLEMENTIS, Vladimir, 1902-52,
Slovak; journalism BU
CLEMENTS, Barbara Evans,
1945- , American; nonfic-
tion CON
CLEMENTS, Bruce, 1931- , Amer-
ican; juveniles, fiction CON
WAR
CLEMENTS, Frank A. , 1942- ,
Scots; nonfiction CON
CLEMENTS, Harold M. , Sr. ,
1907- , American; nonfiction
CON
CLEMENTS, John, 1916- , Amer-
ican; nonfiction CON
CLEMENTS, Traverse, 1900?-77,
American; nonfiction CON
CLEMHOUT, Simone, 1934- ,
Belgian-American; nonfiction
CON
CLEMMONS, Francois, 1945- ,
American; nonfiction CON
CLEMMONS, William Preston,
1932- , American; nonfiction
CON
CLEMO, Jack, 1916- , British;
poetry, fiction, nonfiction
VCP

CLEMO, Richard Frederick, 1920-76, American; nonfiction CON

CLEMOES, Peter Alan Martin, 1920- , British; nonfiction CON

'CLEMONS, Elizabeth' see NOWELL, Elizabeth

CLEMONS, Lulamae, 1917- , American; nonfiction CON SH

CLEPPER, Henry Edward, 1901- , American; nonfiction CON

CLEPPER, Irene Elizabeth, American; nonfiction, juveniles CON

CLERICI, Gianni, 1930- , Italian; nonfiction, fiction CON

CLERQ, Willem de, 1795-1844, Dutch; nonfiction BU

CLERY, Reginald Valentine ('Janus'), 1924- , Canadian; nonfiction CON

'CLEVE, John' see OFFUTT, Andrew J.

CLEVELAND, Carles, 1952- , American; plays, fiction CON

CLEVELAND, E. E., American; nonfiction SH

CLEVELAND, John (Cleiveland), 1613-58, English; poetry, nonfiction BU DA PO RU VP

CLEVELAND, Leslie, 1921- , Australian; poetry, nonfiction CON

CLEVENGER, Ernest Allen, Jr. ('Ben Rovin'), 1929- , American; nonfiction CON

CLEVENGER, Theodore, Jr., 1929- , American; nonfiction CON

CLEVER, Warren Glenn, 1918- , Canadian; poetry CON

CLEVIN, Joergen, 1920- , Danish; juveniles CO

CLEW, Jeffrey Robert, 1928- , English; nonfiction CON

CLEW, William Joseph, 1904- , American; journalism CON

CLEWES, Dorothy Mary, 1907- , British; juveniles, fiction KI

CLEWS, Roy, 1937- , English; fiction CON

CLICK, John William, 1936- , American; nonfiction CON

CLIFFORD, Eth see ROSENBERG, Ethel C.

'CLIFFORD, Francis' (Arthur Bell Thompson), 1917-75, British; fiction CON MCC REI VCN WAK

CLIFFORD, Harold B. ('Burt Farnham'), 1893- , American; juveniles CO

CLIFFORD, James Lowry, 1901-78, American; nonfiction CON

CLIFFORD, John Garry, 1942- , American; nonfiction CON

CLIFFORD, John McLean, 1904-79, American; journalism CON

'CLIFFORD, Martin' see HAMILTON, Charles H. S.

CLIFFORD, Mary Louise Beneway, 1926- , American; juveniles WAR

'CLIFFORD, Theodore' see von BLOCK, Sylvia

CLIFT, Virgil A., 1912- , American; nonfiction SH

'CLIFTON, Harry' see HAMILTON, Charles H. S.

'CLIFTON, Lewis' see LINEDECKER, Clifford L.

CLIFTON, Lucille, 1936- , American; poetry, juveniles CO CON KI VCP

CLIFTON, Mark, 1906-63, American; fiction AS NI

CLINE, C. Terry, Jr., 1935- , American; nonfiction CON

CLINE, Charles William, 1937- , American; nonfiction, poetry CON

CLINE, Edward, 1946- , American; nonfiction CON

'CLINE, Joan' see HAMILTON, Joan L.

CLINE, Linda, 1941- , American; juveniles CON

CLINE, Rodney, 1903- , American; nonfiction CON

CLINE, Victor Bailey, 1925- , American; nonfiction CON

CLINGERMAN, Mildred McElroy, 1918- , American; fiction AS NI

'CLINTON, Jon' see PRINCE, Jack H.

CLINTON, Richard Lee, 1938- , American; nonfiction CON

'CLINTON, Rupert' see BULMER, Kenneth

CLINTON-BADDELEY, Victor Clinton, 1900-70, British; fiction, plays, poetry REI

CLIPPER, Lawrench John, 1930- ,

American; nonfiction CON
'CLISTIER, Adeline' see DENNY,
Alma
'CLIVE, Clifford' see HAMILTON,
Charles H. S.
CLIVE, John, 1933- , British;
fiction CON
CLIVE, John Leonard, 1924- ,
German-American; nonfiction
CON
'CLIVE, William' see BASSETT,
Ronald
CLODFELTER, Michael, 1946- ,
American; nonfiction CON
CLODFELTER, William Franklin,
1911- , American; nonfic-
tion CON
CLODIUS LICINUS, Gaius, fl. 4
A.D., Roman; nonfiction LA
CLOEREN, Hermann Josef,
1934- , German-American;
nonfiction CON
CLOETE, Stuart Graham, 1897-
1976, South African; fiction,
poetry, nonfiction BU CON
VCN
CLOETTA, Gian Gianet, 1874-
1965, Raeto-Romansch; po-
etry, fiction BU
CLOFFORD, Mary Louise, 1926- ,
American; juveniles CO
CLOKE, Richard, 1916- , Amer-
ican; fiction, poetry CON
CLONES, Nicholas J. ('N. I.
Klonis'), American; nonfic-
tion CON
CLOR, Harry Mortimer, 1929- ,
American; nonfiction CON
CLOSE, A. Kathryn, 1908?-73,
American; nonfiction CON
'CLOSE, Upton' see HALL, Jo-
sef W.
CLOSS, Elizabeth, see TRAU-
GOTT, Elizabeth
CLOSSON, Herman, 1901- ,
Belgian; plays CL
CLOTFELTER, Beryl Edward,
1926- , American; nonfic-
tion CON
CLOTFELTER, Cecil F., 1929- ,
American; nonfiction CON
CLOTFELTER, Mary Eunice
Long, American; nonfiction
CON
CLOTHIER, Peter Dean, 1936- ,
American; poetry, fiction,
nonfiction CON
CLOUD, Preston Ercelle, 1912- ,

American; nonfiction CON
'CLOUD, Yvonne' see KAPP,
Yvonne M.
CLOUDSLEY-THOMPSON, John
Leonard, 1921- , English;
juveniles CO
CLOUGH, Arthur Hugh, 1819-61,
English; poetry BU DA PO
VP
CLOUGH, William, 1911?-76,
American; nonfiction CON
CLOUSER, John William, 1932- ,
American; nonfiction CON
CLOUSTON, Joseph Storer, 1870-
1944, Scots; fiction, nonfiction
DA NI
CLOUT, Hugh Donald, 1944- ,
English; nonfiction CON
CLOUTIER, Cecile ('Cecile de
Lantagne'), 1930- , Canadian;
poetry CON CR
CLOUTIER, David, 1951- , Amer-
ican; nonfiction CON
CLOUTIER, Eugène, 1921- , Ca-
nadian; fiction, nonfiction CR
CLOUTS, Sydney David, 1926- ,
South African; poetry VCP
CLOVER, Frank Metlar III, 1940- ,
American; nonfiction CON
CLOWARD, Richard Andrew,
1926- , American; nonfic-
tion CON
CLOWER, Robert Wayne, 1926- ,
American; nonfiction CON
CLUBB, Louise George, 1930- ,
American; nonfiction CON
CLUCHEY, Douglas Rickland,
1933- , American; plays
VCD
CLUFF, Charles E., 1937- ,
American; nonfiction CON
CLUGSTON, Richard, 1938- ,
Irish; nonfiction CON
CLUM, John MacKenzie, 1941- ,
American; plays, nonfiction
CON
'CLUN, Arthur' see POLSBY, Nel-
son W.
CLUNE, Anne ('Anne Cissmann'),
1945- , Irish; nonfiction CON
CLUNIES ROSS, Anthony Ian,
1932- , Australian; nonfic-
tion CON
CLURMAN, Harold, 1901-80, Amer-
ican; nonfiction BR CON
CLUSTER, Dick, 1947- , Amer-
ican; nonfiction CON
CLUTE, John, 1940- , Canadian;

fiction NI
CLUTE, Robert Eugene, 1924- ,
American; nonfiction CON
CLUVIUS RUFUS, 1st century,
Roman; nonfiction GR
CLUYSENAAR, Anne A. , 1936- ,
Irish; poetry, nonfiction CON
VCP
CLYDE, Norman Asa, 1885- ,
American; nonfiction CON
CLYMER, Eleanor ('Janet Bell';
'Elizabeth Kinsey'), 1906- ,
American; juveniles CO CON
DEM KI
CLYNE, James F. , 1898?-1977,
American; nonfiction CON
CLYNE, Patricia Edwards, Amer-
ican; journalism, juveniles
CON WAR
COAD, Frederick Roy, 1925- ,
British; nonfiction CON
COAD, Oral Sumner, 1887- ,
American; nonfiction CON
COAKLEY, Lakme, 1912- ,
American; nonfiction CON
COALE, Samuel Chase, 1943- ,
American; fiction CON
COALSON, Glo, 1946- , Amer-
ican; juveniles CON
COAN, Richard Welton, 1928- ,
American; nonfiction CON
COATES, Austin, 1922- , Brit-
ish; nonfiction, translations
CON
COATES, Donald Robert, 1922- ,
American; nonfiction CON
COATES, Robert Myron, 1897-
1973, American; fiction, BR
CON NI RO
COATES, Ruth Allison, 1915- ,
American; juveniles, fiction
CO CON
COATES, Willson Havelock, 1899-
1976, Canadian; nonfiction
CON
COATS, Alice Margaret, 1905- ,
English; juveniles, nonfiction
CO CON
COATS, Peter, 1910- , Scots;
nonfiction CON
COATSWORTH, Elizabeth Jane,
American; juveniles, poetry,
fiction KI
COBB, Charlie, American; non-
fiction SH
COBB, Geoffrey Belton, 1892-
1971, British; fiction, juven-
iles, nonfiction REI

COBB, Irvin Shrewsbury, 1876-
1944, American; fiction, jour-
nalism BA ST
COBB, Jane see BERRY, Jane
COBB, Jonathan, 1946- , Amer-
ican; nonfiction CON
COBB, Robert A. , 1941- , Amer-
ican; nonfiction CON
COBB, Sylvanus, Jr. , 1823-87,
American; fiction ST
COBB, Vicki Wolf, 1938- , Amer-
ican; juveniles CO WAR
'COBBETT, Richard' see PLUCK-
ROSE, Henry A.
COBBETT, William ('Peter Porcu-
pine'), 1762/63-1835, English;
journalism, nonfiction BU DA
PO
COBBING, Bob ('Cento'), 1920- ,
British; poetry CON VCP
COBBLEDICK, James R. , 1935- ,
American; nonfiction CON
COBBS, Price M. , American; non-
fiction SH
COBER, Alan Edwin, 1935- ,
American; juveniles CO DEM
'COBHAM, Sir Alan' see HAMIL-
TON, Charles H. S.
COBLEIGH, Ira Underwood, 1903- ,
American; nonfiction CON
COBLENTZ, Stanton Arthur, 1896- ,
American; fiction, poetry AS
NI
COBURN, Andrew, 1932- , Amer-
ican; nonfiction CON
COBURN, Donald Lee, 1938- ,
American; plays CON
COBURN, John Bowen, 1914- ,
American; juveniles WAR
COBURN, Karen Levin, 1941- ,
American; nonfiction CON
COBURN, Kathleen, 1905- , Ca-
nadian; nonfiction CON
COCAGNAC, Augustin Maurice
Jean ('J. M. Warbler'), 1924- ,
French; juveniles CO
COCCIO, Marcantonio see 'SABEL-
LICO, Marcantonio
COCCIOLI, Carlo, 1920- , Italian;
fiction CL
COCHARD, Thomas Sylvester,
1893- , American; nonfiction
CON
COCHET, Gabriel, 1888-1973,
French; nonfiction CON
COCHRAN, Bert, 1917- , Amer-
ican; nonfiction CON
COCHRAN, Bobbye A. , 1949- ,

American; juveniles CO
COCHRAN, Charles Leo, 1940- ,
American; nonfiction CON
COCHRAN, Hamilton, 1898-1977,
American; nonfiction CON
COCHRAN, Jacqueline, 1910?-80,
American; journalism CON
COCHRAN, John Robert, 1937- ,
American; nonfiction CON
COCHRAN, Leslie Hershel, 1939- ,
American; nonfiction CON
COCHRAN, Thomas Childs, 1902- ,
American; nonfiction CON
COCHRANE, Eric, 1928- , Amer-
ican; nonfiction CON
COCHRANE, Glynn, 1940- ,
American; nonfiction CON
COCHRANE, Hugh Ferrier, 1923- ,
Canadian; nonfiction CON
COCHRANE, Ian, 1942- , Irish;
fiction HO
COCHRANE, Jennifer Ann, 1936- ,
British; juveniles CON
COCHRANE, William E. ('S. Kye
Boult'; 'Leo Paige'), 1926- ,
American; fiction CON
COCKBURN, Alison (Alicia), 1713-
94, Scots; poetry DA
COCKBURN, Claud ('James Hel-
vick'; 'Frank Pitcairn'),
1904-81, British; nonfiction,
fiction, journalism CON WA
COCKETT, Mary, 1915- , Brit-
ish; juveniles CO KI
COCKING, John Martin, 1914- ,
English; nonfiction CON
COCKRELL, Amanda, see CROWE,
Amanda
COCTEAU, Jean, 1889-1963,
French; poetry, fiction,
plays BU CL MAG MCG
SEY TH
CODE, Grant Hyde, 1896-1974,
American; poetry, plays, fic-
tion, nonfiction CON
CODEL, Martin, 1903?-73, Amer-
ican; nonfiction CON
CODEL, Michael Richard, 1939- ,
American; nonfiction CON
CODERE, Helen Frances, 1917- ,
Canadian-American; nonfiction
CON
CODEVILLA, Maria Angelo,
1943- , Italian-American;
nonfiction CON
CODJOE, Thomas A., 1925?- ,
Ghanaian; poetry, journalism
HER

CODY, Charles S., 1923- , Amer-
ican; fiction CON
CODY, Douglas Thane Romney,
1932- , Canadian-American;
nonfiction CON
CODY, John, 1925- , American;
nonfiction CON
CODY, Martin Leonard, 1941- ,
English; nonfiction CON
CODY, William F., 1846-1917,
American; fiction, nonfiction
PAL
COE, Charles Francis, 1890-1956,
American; fiction ST
COE, Frederick, 1914-79, Amer-
ican; tv CON
COE, Lloyd, 1899?-1976, Amer-
ican; cartoons CON
COE, Richard Livingston, 1916- ,
American; nonfiction CON
COE, Rodney Michael, 1933- ,
American; nonfiction CON
'COE, Tucker' see WESTLAKE,
Donald E.
COELHO, George Victor, 1918- ,
American; nonfiction CON
COELHO, Joaquim G. G. see
'DINIS, Júlio'
COELHO, José Francisco Trindade,
1861-1908, Portuguese; fiction
BU
COELHO NETO, Henrique Max-
imiano, 1864-1934, Brazilian;
fiction BR
COELIUS ANTIPATER, Lucius,
fl. 120 B. C., Roman; non-
fiction BU LA
COELLO y OCHOA, Antonio,
1600/11-52/53, Spanish; plays
BU MCG
COEN, Rena Neumann, 1925- ,
American; juveniles CO
COENEN, Frans, 1886-1936, Dutch;
nonfiction BU
COERR, Eleanor (Page; 'Eleanor
B. Hicks'), 1922- , Canadian;
juveniles WAR
COETZEE, John M., 1940- ,
American; fiction, translations
CON
'COFFEY, Brian' see KOONTZ,
Dean R.
COFFEY, Brian, 1905- , Irish;
poetry HO
COFFEY, Dairine, 1933- , Irish;
juveniles WAR
COFFEY, John Will, Jr., 1925- ,
American; nonfiction CON

COFFEY, Joseph Irving, 1916- ,
American; nonfiction CON
COFFEY, Marilyn, American;
poetry, fiction CON
COFFEY, Robert Edward, 1931- ,
American; nonfiction CON
COFFEY, Thomas, 1925- ,
Irish; plays HO
COFFIN, Charles, 1676-1749,
French; hymns, poetry BU
TH
'COFFIN, Geoffrey' see MASON,
Francis V. W.
COFFIN, Joseph John, 1899- ,
American; juveniles, nonfic-
tion CON WAR
COFFIN, Lewis Augustus III,
1932- , American; nonfic-
tion CON
COFFIN, Patricia, 1912-74,
American; nonfiction CON
'COFFIN, Peter' see LATIMER,
Jonathan W.
COFFIN, Robert Peter Tristram,
1892-1955, American; poetry,
fiction BR
COFFIN, William Sloane, Jr.,
1924- , American; nonfic-
tion CON
COFFINET, Julien, 1907- ,
French; nonfiction CON
COFFMAN, Charles DeWitt,
1909- , American; nonfic-
tion CON
COFFMAN, Ramon Peyton ('Uncle
Ray'), 1896- , American;
juveniles CO
COFFMAN, Virginia Edith ('Victor
Cross'; 'Virginia C. DuVaul'),
1914- , American; fiction
CON
COGHILL, Neville Henry, 1899-
1980?, British; nonfiction
CON
COGLEY, John, 1916-76, Amer-
ican; journalism CON
COGSWELL, Frederick William,
1917- , Canadian; poetry,
translations BU VCP
COGSWELL, Theodore Rose,
1918- , American; fiction
AS NI
COHAN, Avery Berlow, 1914-
77, American; nonfiction
CON
COHAN, George Michael, 1878-
1942, American; plays, po-
etry MCG VD

COHANE, John Philip, 1911- ,
American; nonfiction CON
COHART, Mary, 1911- , Amer-
ican; nonfiction CON
COHEN, Aharon, 1910- , Russian-
American; nonfiction CON
COHEN, Amnon, 1936- , Israeli;
nonfiction CON
COHEN, Anne Billings, 1937- ,
American; nonfiction CON
COHEN, Anthea, 1913- , British;
nonfiction CON
COHEN, Barbara Nash, 1932- ,
American; juveniles CO CON
WAR
COHEN, Benjamin Jerry, 1937- ,
American; nonfiction CON
COHEN, Bernard, 1937- , Amer-
ican; nonfiction CON
COHEN, Bernard P., 1930- ,
American; nonfiction CON
COHEN, Bruce J., 1938- , Amer-
ican; nonfiction CON
COHEN, Daniel, 1936- , American;
journalism, juveniles CO CON
WAR
COHEN, David Steven, 1943- ,
American; nonfiction CON
COHEN, Edmund David, 1943- ,
American; nonfiction CON
COHEN, Elie Aron, 1909- , Dutch-
American; nonfiction CON
COHEN, Gary C., 1934- , Amer-
ican; nonfiction, fiction CON
COHEN, George Michael, 1931- ,
American; nonfiction CON
COHEN, I. Bernard, 1914- ,
American; nonfiction CON
COHEN, Jerome Alan, 1930- ,
American; nonfiction CON
COHEN, Joan Lebold, 1932- ,
American; juveniles CO
COHEN, Joel H., American; ju-
veniles WAR
COHEN, Joseph, 1926- , Amer-
ican; nonfiction CON
COHEN, Judy, see CHICAGO, Judy
COHEN, Kathleen Rogers, 1933- ,
American; nonfiction CON
COHEN, Keith, 1945- , American;
nonfiction CON
COHEN, Lawrence Jonathan, 1923- ,
English; nonfiction CON
COHEN, Leonard Norman, 1934- ,
Canadian; poetry, fiction,
plays BU CR VCN VCP WAK
COHEN, Matthew, 1942- , Cana-
dian; fiction, poetry CON VCN

COHEN, Morris Leo, 1927- , American; nonfiction CON
COHEN, Morton, N. ('John Moreton'), 1921- , American; juveniles WA
COHEN, Nathan, 1923-71, Canadian; nonfiction, translations CR
COHEN, Octavus Roy, 1891-1959, American; fiction, plays REI ST
COHEN, Peter Zachary, 1931- , American; juveniles CO
COHEN, Richard Murry, 1938- , American; nonfiction CON
COHEN, Robert Carl, 1930/38- , American; juveniles, nonfiction CO CON WAR
COHEN, Roberta G., 1937- , American; nonfiction CON
COHEN, Ronald Jay, 1949- , American; nonfiction CON
COHEN, Sara Kay Sherman, 1943- , American; nonfiction CON
COHEN, Sarah Blacher, 1936- , American; nonfiction CON
COHEN, Sharleen Cooper, American; fiction CON
COHEN, Sherry Suib, 1934- , American; poetry, nonfiction CON
COHEN, Stephen Frand, 1938- , American; nonfiction CON
COHEN, Stephen Marshall, 1929- , American; nonfiction CON
COHEN, Stewart, 1940- , American; nonfiction CON
COHEN, Susan ('Elizabeth St. Clair'), 1938- , American; nonfiction, fiction CON
COHEN, William Alan, 1937- , American; nonfiction CON
COHN, Angelo, 1914- , Rumanian-American; juveniles CO
COHN, Clara see VIEBIG, Clara
COHN, Dorrit, 1924- , Austrian-American; nonfiction CON
COHN, Elchanan, 1941- , Israeli-American; nonfiction CON
COHN, Haim Herman, 1911- , German-Israeli; nonfiction CON
COHN, Helen Desfosses, 1945- , American; nonfiction CON
COHN, Jan Kadetsky, 1933- , American; nonfiction CON
COHN, Nik, 1946- , British; fiction, nonfiction CON WAR
COHN, Norman, 1915- , English; nonfiction CON
COHN, Rubin Goodman, 1911- , American; nonfiction CON
COHN, Ruby, 1922- , American; nonfiction CON
COHN, Theodore, 1923- , American; nonfiction CON
COHN, Vera ('Vera Broido'), 1907- , Russian-British; nonfiction CON
COHN, Victor Edward, 1919- , American; nonfiction CON
COIGNEY, Virginia (Travers), 1917- , American; nonfiction CON
COIMIN, Mícheál (Michael Comyn), 1688-1760, Irish; poetry, fiction DA
COKAYNE, Sir Aston, 1608-83/84, English; poetry, plays, translations BU VD
COKER, Elizabeth Boatwright, 1909- , American; fiction, poetry CON
COKER, Gylbert, 1944- , American; juveniles CON
COL, Gontier, 1354?-1418, French; nonfiction BU
'EL COLABORODOR' see MORALES, José P.
COLANERI, John Nunzio, 1930- , American; nonfiction CON
COLBACH, Edward Michael, 1939- , American; nonfiction CON
COLBERG, Juan Enrique, 1917-64, Puerto Rican; nonfiction, journalism, poetry, fiction HIL
COLBERT, Anthony, 1934- , English; juveniles CO CON
COLBERT, Douglas Albert, 1933- , American; nonfiction CON
COLBERT, Edwin Harris, 1905- , American; nonfiction CON
COLBERT, Evelyn Speyer, 1918- , American; nonfiction CON
COLBERT, Roman, 1921- , Belgian-American; nonfiction CON
COLBURN, George Abbott, 1938- , American; nonfiction CON
COLBY, Benjamin Nick, 1931- , American; nonfiction CON
COLBY, Carroll Burleigh, 1904- , American; juveniles CO
COLBY, Jean Poindexter, 1909- , American; juveniles CO WAR

COLBY, Joan, 1939- , American; journalism, poetry CON
COLBY, Robert Alan, 1920- , American; nonfiction CON
COLBY, William Egan, 1920- , American; nonfiction CON
COLCHIE, Elizabeth Schneider, 1943- , American; nonfiction CON
COLDWELL, Michael J., 1888-1974, Canadian; nonfiction CON
COLE, Andrew Thomas, Jr., 1933- , American; nonfiction CON
COLE, Ann, 1937- , American; juveniles CON
'COLE, Annette' see STEINER, Barbara A.
COLE, Arthur Charles, 1886-1976, American; nonfiction CON
COLE, Barry, 1936- , British; fiction, poetry VCN VCP
COLE, Bruce, 1938- , American; nonfiction CON
'COLE, Burt' (Thomas Dixon), 1930- , American; fiction, nonfiction, journalism CON NI
'COLE, Cannon' see COOK, Arlene E.
COLE, Charles Leland, 1927- , American; nonfiction CON
COLE, Charles Robert, 1939- , American; nonfiction CON
COLE, Charles Woolsey, 1906-78, American; nonfiction CON
COLE, Cyrus, American; fiction NI
COLE, Doris, 1938- , American; nonfiction CON
COLE, Eddie-Lou, 1909- , American; poetry CON
COLE, Edmund Keith, 1919- , Australian; nonfiction CON
COLE, Eugene Roger, 1930- , American; nonfiction, poetry, fiction, plays CON
COLE, Everett B., 1910- , American; fiction AS NI
COLE, Frank Raymond, 1892- , American; nonfiction CON
COLE, George Douglas Howard, 1889-1959, English; fiction, poetry, nonfiction REI ST
COLE, George Fraser, 1935- ,

American; nonfiction CON
COLE, Howard Chandler, 1934- , American; nonfiction CON
'COLE, Jack' see STEWART, John W.
'COLE, Jackson' see SCHISGAL, Oscar
'COLE, Janet' see HUNTER, Kim
COLE, John Nelson, 1923- , American; nonfiction CON
COLE, John Young, Jr., 1940- , American; nonfiction CON
COLE, Jonathan Richard, 1942- , American; nonfiction CON
COLE, Larry, 1936- , American; nonfiction CON
COLE, Leonard Aaron, 1933- , American; nonfiction CON
COLE, Leonard Leslie ('Cole Lesley'), 1909-80, British; nonfiction CON
COLE, Lois Dwight ('Caroline Arnett'; 'Lynn Avery'; 'Nancy Dudley'; 'Allan Dwight'; 'Anne Eliot'), 1903-79, American; juveniles CO
COLE, Margaret Isabel Postgate, 1893-1980, English; fiction, poetry, nonfiction CON REI ST
'COLE, Mary' see HANNA, Mary T.
COLE, Michael, 1938- , American; nonfiction CON
COLE, Robert Evan, 1937- , American; nonfiction CON
COLE, Robert Wellesley, 1907- , Sierra Leonese; nonfiction, fiction HER JA
COLE, Robert William, British; fiction NI
COLE, Sheila Rotenberg, 1939- , Canadian-American; fiction, juveniles, nonfiction CO CON
COLE, Sonia Mary, 1918- , British; nonfiction CON
COLE, Sylvan, Jr., 1918- , American; nonfiction CON
COLE, Walter Randall, 1933- , American; nonfiction NI
COLE, William Rossa, 1919- , American; juveniles, poetry CO DEM
COLE, William Shadrack, 1937- , American; nonfiction CON
COLECCHIA, Francesca Maria, American; nonfiction CON
COLEGROVE, Kenneth, 1886-1975, American; nonfiction CON

COLEMAN, Allan Douglass,
1943- , American; nonfic-
tion, journalism CON
COLEMAN, Arthur, 1924- ,
American; nonfiction, fiction
CON
COLEMAN, Dorothy Gabe, 1935- ,
Welsh; nonfiction CON
COLEMAN, Elliott, 1906-80,
American; poetry, transla-
tions CON VCP
COLEMAN, Emily Holmes, 1899-
1974, American; fiction RO
COLEMAN, Felicia Slatkin, 1916?-
81, American; nonfiction CON
COLEMAN, James Nelson, Amer-
ican; fiction NI
COLEMAN, John Winton, Jr.,
1898- , American; nonfiction
CON
COLEMAN, Lonnie, 1920-82, Amer-
ican; fiction, plays CON
COLEMAN, Lucile, American; po-
etry, juveniles, plays CON
COLEMAN, Merton H., 1889- ,
American; nonfiction SH
COLEMAN, Raymond James,
1923- , American; nonfic-
tion CON
COLEMAN, Richard James, 1941- ,
American; nonfiction CON
COLEMAN, Thomas R., 1942- ,
American; fiction CON
COLEMAN, Vernon ('Edward Ver-
non'), 1946- , British; non-
fiction CON
COLEMAN, William LeRoy,
1938- , American; nonfic-
tion CON
COLEMAN, William Vincent,
1932- , American; nonfic-
tion CON
COLEN, B. D., 1946- , Amer-
ican; nonfiction CON
COLENSO, John William, 1814-
83, English; nonfiction DA
COLERIDGE, Hartley, 1796-1849,
English; poetry, journalism
BU
COLERIDGE, Mary Elizabeth,
1861-1907, English; poetry,
fiction BU
COLERIDGE, Samuel Taylor, 1772-
1834, English; poetry, nonfiction BU DA MAG PO VP
COLERIDGE, Sara, 1802-52, English; nonfiction, translations
BU

COLES, Flournoy Arthur, Jr.,
1915- , American; nonfiction
CON
'COLES, Manning' (Cyril Henry
COLES, 1889-1965; Adelaide
Frances Oke Mann MANNING,
1891-1959), English; fiction
REI ST
COLES, Robert Martin, 1929- ,
American; nonfiction, fiction,
juveniles CO CON WAK WAR
COLES, William E. Jr., 1932- ,
American; nonfiction CON
COLET, John, 1467-1519, English;
nonfiction BU
COLETTA, Paolo Enrico, 1916- ,
American; nonfiction CON
COLETTE, Jacques, 1929- , Bel-
gian; nonfiction CON
COLETTE, Sidonie Gabrielle ('Wil-
ly'), 1873-1954, French; fic-
tion, nonfiction BU CL MAG
SEY TH
'COLIN, Jean' see BELL, Joyce
'COLIN MUSET' fl. 1230-50,
French; poetry BU TH
COLINAS, Antonio, 1946- , Span-
ish; poetry, nonfiction CL
COLINVAUX, Paul Alfred, 1930- ,
American; nonfiction CON
COLL y TOSTE, Cayetano, 1850-
1930, Puerto Rican; nonfiction,
journalism, poetry HIL
COLL VIDAL, Antonio, 1898- ,
Puerto Rican; poetry, plays,
journalism HIL
COLLADO MARTELL, Alfredo,
1900-30, Puerto Rican; jour-
nalism, poetry, fiction HIL
COLLARD, Edgar Andrew, 1911- ,
Canadian; journalism, nonfic-
tion CON
COLLENUCCIO, Pandolfo, 1444-
1504, Italian; nonfiction BU
COLLETT, Camilla Wergeland,
1813-95, Norwegian; fiction
BU
COLLETT, Rosemary King, 1931- ,
American; nonfiction CON
COLLEY, Iain ('Basil Ransome-
Davies'), 1940- , British;
nonfiction CON
COLLIANDER, Tito, 1904- ,
Swedish-Finnish; fiction TH
COLLIAS, Joe G., 1928- , Amer-
ican; nonfiction CON
COLLIE, Michael John, 1929- ,
Anglo-Canadian; poetry, non-

fiction CON
COLLIER, Boyd Dean, 1938- ,
American; nonfiction CON
COLLIER, Christopher, 1930- ,
American; juveniles CO WAR
COLLIER, David, 1942- , Amer-
ican; nonfiction CON
COLLIER, Ethel, 1903- , Amer-
ican; juveniles CO CON
COLLIER, Eugenia, 1928- ,
American; nonfiction CON
SH
COLLIER, Gaydell Maier, 1935- ,
American; nonfiction CON
COLLIER, Herbert Leon, 1933- ,
American; nonfiction CON
COLLIER, James Lincoln ('Charles
Williams'), 1928- , Amer-
ican; juveniles CO WAR
'COLLIER, Jane' see COLLIER,
Zena
COLLIER, Jeremy, 1650-1726,
English; nonfiction BU DA
PO
COLLIER, John, 1901-80, Eng-
lish; fiction, poetry, nonfic-
tion, plays BR CON NI REI
ST VCN
'COLLIER, Joy' see MILLAR, Joy
COLLIER, Kenneth Gerald, 1910- ,
British; nonfiction CON
'COLLIER, Margaret' see TAY-
LOR, Margaret S.
COLLIER, Peter, 1939- , Amer-
ican; nonfiction CON
COLLIER, Zena ('Jane Collier';
'Zena Shumsky'), 1926- ,
British; juveniles CO
COLLIGNON, Joseph, 1930- ,
American; nonfiction CON
COLLIN, Heinrich Joseph von,
1772-1811, Austrian; plays
BU
COLLINGS, Ellsworth, 1887- ,
American; nonfiction CON
COLLINGWOOD, Robin George,
1889-1943, English; nonfic-
tion BU DA
COLLINS, Alice Hesslein,
1907- , American; nonfic-
tion CON
COLLINS, Arnold Quint, 1935- ,
American; journalism CON
COLLINS, Barbara J., 1929- ,
American; nonfiction CON
COLLINS, Barry, 1941- , Brit-
ish; plays CON VCD
COLLINS, Charles William,

1880-1964, American; journal-
ism CON
COLLINS, Christopher, 1936- ,
American; nonfiction CON
'COLLINS, Cindy' see SMITH,
Richard R.
COLLINS, David Raymond, 1940- ,
American; juveniles CO WAR
COLLINS, Desmond, 1940- , Brit-
ish; nonfiction CON
COLLINS, Fletcher, Jr., 1906- ,
American; nonfiction CON
COLLINS, Gary Ross, 1934- ,
Canadian-American; nonfiction
CON
'COLLINS, Harry C.' see ALTH,
Max O.
'COLLINS, Hunt' see 'HUNTER
Evan'
COLLINS, Jackie, British; fiction
CON
COLLINS, John Churton, 1848-1908,
English; nonfiction BU
COLLINS, John Martin, 1921- ,
American; nonfiction CON
COLLINS, Joseph B., 1898?-1975,
American; nonfiction CON
COLLINS, Judy Marjorie, 1939- ,
American; nonfiction CON
COLLINS, Larry, 1929- , Amer-
ican; nonfiction CON
COLLINS, Lorraine Hill, 1931- ,
American; nonfiction CON
COLLINS, Margaret ('Susan Welsh'),
1909- , American; nonfiction,
plays CON
COLLINS, Marie Margaret, 1935- ,
American; translations, non-
fiction CON
COLLINS, Marjorie Ann, 1930- ,
American; nonfiction CON
COLLINS, Max Allan, Jr., 1948- ,
American; fiction CON
COLLINS, Meghan, 1926- , Amer-
ican; fiction CON
COLLINS, Michael ('Dennis Lynds';
'William Arden'; 'Nick Carter';
'John Crowe'; 'Maxwell Grant';
'Mark Sadler'), 1924/30- ,
American; fiction, journalism,
juveniles CON NI REI ST
COLLINS, Myrtle Telleen, 1915- ,
American; nonfiction CON
COLLINS, Orvis Floyd, 1918- ,
American; nonfiction CON
COLLINS, Peter Sheridan, 1942- ,
?; nonfiction CON
COLLINS, Robert, 1924- , Ca-

nadian; journalism, nonfiction,
juveniles CON
COLLINS, Robert Emmet, 1927- ,
American; nonfiction CON
COLLINS, Ruth Philpott, 1890-
1975, American; juveniles,
nonfiction CON
COLLINS, Thomas Hightower
('Paul Hightower'), 1910- ,
American; journalism, non-
fiction CON
'COLLINS, Tom' see FURPHY,
Joseph
COLLINS, Wilkie, 1824-89, Eng-
lish; fiction, plays, nonfiction
BU DA MAG PO REI ST VN
COLLINS, William, 1721-59, Eng-
lish; poetry BRI BU DA MAG
PO VP
COLLINS, William Alexander
Roy, 1900-76, British; pub-
lisher CON
COLLINSON, Laurence Henry,
1925- , British; poetry,
juveniles, plays, tv CON
VCD VCP
'COLLINSON, Peter' see HAM-
METT, Dashiell
COLLIS, John Stewart, 1900- ,
Irish; fiction, nonfiction CON
COLLIS, Maurice, 1889-1973,
Irish; nonfiction CON
COLLISON, Koder Macklin,
1910- , American; nonfic-
tion CON
'COLLODI, Carlo' (Carlo Loren-
zini), 1826-90, Italian; juven-
iles BO BU
COLLOM, Jack, 1931- , Amer-
ican; poetry CON
COLLOMS, Brenda, 1919- , Eng-
lish; nonfiction CON
COLLOREDO, Hermes, Count of
Waldsee, 1622-92, Raeto-
Romansch; poetry BU
COLLYMORE, Frank Appleton,
1893- , British; poetry VCP
COLLYNS, Robin, 1940- , New
Zealander; nonfiction CON
COLM, Gerhard, 1897-1968,
German-American; nonfiction
CON
COLM, Jan S., 1575-1637, Dutch;
plays BU
COLMAN, Benjamin, 1673-1747,
English; poetry BR
COLMAN, Ernest Adrian Mac-
kenzie, 1930- , Scots;

nonfiction CON
COLMAN, George, the Elder,
1732-94, English; plays, po-
etry, translations BU DA
MCG PO VD
COLMAN, George, the Younger,
1762-1836, English; plays
BU DA PO VD
COLMAN, Hila Crayder, Amer-
ican; juveniles DE
COLMAN, Juliet Benita, 1944- ,
American; nonfiction CON
COLMAN, Morris, 1899?-1981,
American; juveniles CO
COLMER, John Anthony, 1921- ,
British; nonfiction CON
COLMER, Michael J., 1942- ,
British; journalism, nonfiction
CON
COLOMA, Carlos, 1566-1637,
Spanish; nonfiction BU
COLOMA y ROLDAN, Luis, 1851-
1915, Spanish; fiction, journal-
ism BU
COLOMB, Catherine, 1899-1965,
Swiss; fiction BU
COLOMBINI, Giovanni, 1304?-67,
Italian; nonfiction BU
COLOMBO, John Robert, 1936- ,
Canadian; poetry, translations
VCP
COLON, Cristobal see COLUMBUS,
Christopher
COLONIUS, Lillian, 1911- , Amer-
ican; juveniles CO
COLONNA, Francesco, 1432?-
1527?, Italian; nonfiction, po-
etry BO BU TH
COLONNA, Vittoria, 1492-1547,
Italian; poetry BO BU TH
COLONNE, Guido delle, 1215-85,
Italian; poetry BU
COLORADO, Antonio J., 1903- ,
Puerto Rican; translations,
nonfiction, juveniles CO HIL
COLQUHOUN, Archibald, 1912-64,
British; translations, nonfiction
CON WA
COLQUHOUN, Keith, 1927- ,
British; journalism, fiction
CON
COLQUITT, Betsy Feagan, 1926- ,
American; nonfiction CON
COLSON, Charles Wendell, 1931- ,
American; nonfiction CON
COLSON, Elizabeth, 1917- ,
American; nonfiction CON
'COLSON, Frederick' see GEIS,

Richard E.
COLSTON, Lowell Gwen, 1919- ,
American; nonfiction CON
COLTER, Cyrus, 1910- , Amer-
ican; fiction CON SH VCN
'COLTMAN, Will' see BINGLEY,
David E.
COLTON, Helen, 1918- , Amer-
ican; nonfiction CON
'COLTON, James' see HANSEN,
Joseph
COLTON, John, 1889-1946, Anglo-
American; plays MCG
'COLTRANE, James' see WOHL,
James P.
COLUM, Mary, 1887-1957, Irish;
nonfiction HO
COLUM, Padraic, 1881-1972,
Irish; poetry, plays, nonfic-
tion, fiction, juveniles BU CO
CON DA HO KI MCG PO VP
COLUMBA, St., 521-97, Irish;
nonfiction, poetry BU DA
COLUMBANUS, Abbot of Bobbio,
543-615, Latin; nonfiction,
poetry BU DA TH
COLUMBUS, Christopher (Cris-
tobal Colón), 1451?-1506,
Italian; nonfiction BR BU
COLUMBUS, Samuel Jonae, 1642-
79, Swedish; poetry BU
'COLUMELLA' see MOORE,
Clement C.
COLUMELLA, Lucius Junius Mo-
deratus, 1st century, Latin;
nonfiction BU GR LA
COLVER, Alice Mary Ross
('Mary Randall'), 1892- ,
American; juveniles, nonfic-
tion, fiction CON
COLVER, Anne ('Polly Anne
Graff'; 'Colver Harris'),
1908- , American; juven-
iles, fiction CO CON
COLVER, Anthony Wayne, 1923- ,
American; nonfiction CON
COLVETT, Latayne see SCOTT,
Latayne
COLVILLE, John Rupert, 1915- ,
English; nonfiction CON
COLVIN, Howard Montagu, 1919- ,
English; nonfiction CON
COLVIN, Ian, 1912-75, British;
fiction, journalism, nonfic-
tion CON NI
'COLVIN, James' house name
NI
'COLVIN, James' see MOOR-

COCK, Michael
COLWELL, Charles Carter, 1932- ,
American; nonfiction CON
COLWELL, Ernest Cadman, 1901-
74, American; nonfiction CON
COLWELL, Richard James, 1930- ,
American; nonfiction CON
COLWIN, Laurie, 1945- , Amer-
ican; fiction, nonfiction CON
COLYER, Penrose, 1940- , Eng-
lish; nonfiction CON
COMAN, Dale Rex, 1906- , Amer-
ican; nonfiction CON
COMAY, Joan, South African; non-
fiction CON
COMBE, William, 1742-1823, Eng-
lish; nonfiction, poetry BU
PO VP
COMBER, Elizabeth see 'HAN SU-
YIN'
COMBS, Elisha Trammell, Jr.,
1924- , American; poetry
BR
COMBS, James Everett, 1941- ,
American; nonfiction CON
COMDEN, Betty, 1919- , Amer-
ican; plays CON
COMEAU, Arthur M., 1938- ,
American; nonfiction, poetry
CON
COMELLA y VILLAMITJANA,
Luciano Francisco, 1751-1812,
Spanish; plays BU
'EL COMENDADOR GRIEGO' see
NUÑEZ de GUZAMAN, Hernán
COMENIUS, Johannes A., see KO-
MENSKY, Jan A.
COMER, James Pierpont, 1934- ,
American; nonfiction CON
COMEY, James Hugh, 1947- ,
American; nonfiction CON
COMFORT, Alexander, 1920- ,
British; fiction, poetry, non-
fiction, translations DA VCN
VCP
COMFORT, Mildred Houghton,
1886- , American; juveniles
CO
'COMFORT, Montgomery' see
CAMPBELL, John R.
'COMIDAS, Chinas' see GENSER,
Cynthia
COMINI, Alessandra, 1934- ,
American; nonfiction CON
COMINS, Ethel Mae, 1901- ,
American; fiction, plays, ju-
veniles CO CON
COMINS, Jeremy, 1933- , Amer-

ican; nonfiction CON
COMISSO, Giovanni, 1895-1969,
Italian; fiction, journalism
BU
COMMAGER, Henry Steele, 1902- ,
American; nonfiction BR CO
COMMINES, Philippe de (Com-
mynes), 1445?-1511, French;
nonfiction BU TH
COMMIRE, Anne, American;
plays CON
COMMIRE, Jean, 1626-1702,
French; poetry BU
COMMITTEE, Thomas C. , 1922- ,
American; nonfiction CON
COMMODIANUS, 3-5th century,
Latin; nonfiction BU
COMMONER, Barry, 1917- ,
American; nonfiction CON
COMMYNES, Philippe de see
COMMINES, Philippe de
COMO, Michael William, 1925- ,
American; nonfiction, jour-
nalism CON
COMPAGNI, Dino, 1255?-1324,
Italian; nonfiction, poetry
BO BU TH
COMPARETTI, Domenico, 1835-
1927, Italian; nonfiction BU
COMPIUTA DONZELLA, mid 13th
century, Florentine; poetry
BO BU
COMPLO, Sr. Jannita Marie,
1935- , American; nonfic-
tion CON
COMPRONE, Joseph John, 1943- ,
American; nonfiction CON
COMPTON, David Guy, 1930- ,
English; fiction AS NI
COMPTON-BURNETT, Ivy 1892-
1969/70, English; fiction BU
DA MAG PO SEY VN
'COMRADE, Robert W.' see
'GRAY, Berkeley'
COMSTOCK, Helen, 1893-1970,
American; nonfiction CON
COMSTOCK, William Richard,
1928- , American; nonfic-
tion CON
COMTE, Auguste, 1798-1857,
French; nonfiction BU
COMYN, Michael see COIMIN,
Míchéal
CONAN, Laure, 1845-1924, Ca-
nadian; fiction, nonfiction
CR
CONAN DOYLE, Arthur see
DOYLE, Sir Arthur C.

CONANT, Eaton H. , 1930- ,
American; nonfiction CON
CONANT, James Bryant, 1893-
1978, American; nonfiction
CON
CONARROE, Richard Riley, 1928- ,
American; nonfiction CON
'CONCOLORCORVO' see CARRIO
de la VANDERA
CONCONI, Charles N. , 1938- ,
American; nonfiction CON
CONDE, Carmen, 1907- , Span-
ish; poetry, fiction, nonfiction
CL
CONDE, Jesse Clay, 1912- ,
American; nonfiction CON
CONDILLAC, Etienne Bonnot,
1714-80, French; nonfiction
BU TH
CONDIT, Martha Olson, 1913- ,
American; juveniles CON
CONDON, Eddie, 1905-73, Amer-
ican; nonfiction CON
CONDON, George Edward, 1916- ,
American; journalism, nonfic-
tion CON
CONDON, Richard Thomas, 1915- ,
American; fiction, plays, non-
fiction BR MCC NI REI VCN
WA
CONDORCET, Marie Jean Antoine,
1743-94, French; nonfiction
BU
CONDRY, William Moreton, 1918- ,
British; nonfiction CON
CONE, Fairfax Mastick, 1903-77,
American; nonfiction CON
CONE, James H. , 1938- , Amer-
ican; nonfiction SH
CONE, Molly, 1918- , American;
juveniles DE
CONE, William F. , 1919- , Amer-
ican; nonfiction CON
CONEGLIANO, Emanuele see 'DA
PONTE, Lorenzo'
CONEY, Michael G. , 1932- ,
British; fiction CON NI
CONFORD, Ellen Schaffer, 1942- ,
American; juveniles CO WAR
'CONFUCIUS' see LUND, Philip R.
CONFUCIUS (K'ung Fu-Tzu),
551-479 B.C. , Chinese; non-
fiction BU LA PRU
CONGDON, Kirby, 1924- , Amer-
ican; poetry BR
'CONGER, Lesley' see SUTTLES,
Shirley S.
CONGRAINS MARTIN, Enrique,

1932- , Peruvian; fiction
BR
CONGRAT-BUTLER, Stefan, 1914?-
79, American; nonfiction,
journalism CON
CONGREVE, Willard John, 1921- ,
American; nonfiction CON
CONGREVE, William, 1669/70-
1729, Irish; nonfiction, plays
BRI BU DA HO MAG MCG
PO VD
CONINE, Odie Ernest, 1925- ,
American; journalism CON
CONKLE, Ellsworth Prouty,
1899- , American; plays
CON
CONKLIN, Gladys, 1903- , Amer-
ican; juveniles DEM
CONKLIN, Groff, 1904-68, Amer-
ican; anthologist AS
CONKLIN, Paul, American; ju-
veniles WAR
CONKLING, Hilda, 1910- , Amer-
ican; juveniles CO
CONLEY, Enid Mary, 1917- ,
Australian; nonfiction CON
CONLEY, Ellen Alexander, 1938- ,
American; fiction CON
CONLEY, Everett Nathaniel,
1949- , American; nonfic-
tion SH
CONLEY, John Allan, 1912- ,
American; nonfiction, fiction
CON
CONLEY, Phillip Mallory, 1887- ,
American; nonfiction CON
CONLEY, Robert Jackson, 1940- ,
American; nonfiction CON
CONLIN, Joseph R., 1940- ,
American; nonfiction CON
CONLY, Robert L. see 'O'BRIEN,
Robert C.'
CONN, Canary Denise, 1949- ,
American; nonfiction CON
CONN, Charles Paul, 1945- ,
American; nonfiction CON
CONN, Frances Goldberg, 1925- ,
American; juveniles WAR
CONN, Martha Orr, 1935- ,
American; journalism, juven-
iles CON
CONN, Stewart, 1936- , Brit-
ish; plays, poetry VCD VCP
CONNABLE, Alfred, 1931- ,
American; fiction, nonfiction
CON
CONNALLY, Eugenia Horstman,
1931- , American; nonfic-

tion CON
CONNELL, Evan Shelby, Jr.,
1924- , American; fiction,
poetry, nonfiction BR HE
MAG SEY VCN WA
CONNELL, Jon, 1952- , Scots;
journalism, nonfiction CON
CONNELL, Richard Edward, 1893-
1949, American; fiction ST
CONNELL, Vivian, 1905- , Irish;
fiction, plays HO
CONNELLAN, Leo, 1928- , Amer-
ican; poetry, film CON
CONNELLY, Marc, 1890-1980,
American; plays, journalism
BR CO CON MCG MCN VCD
VD
CONNER, Berenice Gillete, 1908- ,
American; nonfiction CON
CONNER, Reardon, 1907- , Irish;
fiction HO
CONNERS, Bernard F., 1926- ,
American; fiction CON
CONNERY, Robert Howe, 1907- ,
American; nonfiction CON
CONNIFF, Frank, 1914-71, Amer-
ican; journalism CON
'CONNINGTON, J. J.' (Alfred Wal-
ter Stewart), 1880-1947, Eng-
lish; fiction NI REI ST
CONNOLLY, Cyril Vernon, 1903-
74, British; nonfiction, fiction,
translations BOR BU CON DA
MCC PO
CONNOLLY, James, 1868-1916,
Irish; nonfiction HO
CONNOLLY, Jerome Patrick,
1931- , American; juveniles
CO
'CONNOLLY, Paul' see WICKER,
Thomas G.
CONNOLLY, Peter, 1935- , Brit-
ish; juveniles, nonfiction CON
CONNOLLY, Ray, 1940- , Brit-
ish; journalism, fiction, film
CON
CONNOLLY, Robert Duggan, Jr.,
('Pat Duggans'), 1917- ,
American; nonfiction, journal-
ism CON
CONNOLLY, Vivian, 1925- ,
American; fiction CON
CONNOR, James, American; ju-
veniles WAR
CONNOR, Joyce Mary see MAR-
LOW, Joyce
CONNOR, Lawrence Stanton, 1925- ,
American; journalism CON

'CONNOR, Ralph' (Charles William Gordon), 1860-1937, Canadian; fiction, juveniles BU CR KI
CONNOR, Seymour Vaughan, 1923- , American; nonfiction CON
CONNOR, Tony, 1930- , British; poetry, plays, translations VCP
CONNOR, Walter Robert, 1934- , American; nonfiction CON
'CONNORS, Bruton' see ROHEN, Edward
CONNORS, Dorsey, American; nonfiction CON
CONON de BETHUNE, 1150-1219/20, French; poetry BU TH
CONOT, Robert E., 1929- , American; nonfiction CON
CONOVER, Carole, 1941- , American; nonfiction CON
CONOVER, Chris, American; juveniles WAR
CONQUEST, George Robert Ackworth, 1917- , English; fiction, poetry, nonfiction AS NI VCP WA
CONQUEST, Owen' see HAMILTON, Charles H. S.
CONRAD, Barnaby, Jr., 1922- , American; fiction, nonfiction WA
'CONRAD, Brenda' see 'FORD, Leslie'
'CONRAD, C.' see BENJAMIN, Walter
CONRAD, Earl, 1912- , American; fiction NI
CONRAD, John Wilfred, 1935- , American; nonfiction CON
CONRAD, Joseph (Teodor Jozef Konrad Korzieniowski), 1857-1924, Polish; fiction BU DA MAG MCC NI PO SEY ST VN
'CONRAD, Paul' (Albert King), 1924- , British; fiction, journalism NI
CONRAD, Robert, 1928- , American; nonfiction CON
CONRAD, Robert Taylor, 1810-58, American; poetry, journalism, plays MCG
'CONRADI, Hermann' (Hermann Costa), 1862-90, German; poetry, fiction BU
CONRAN, Anthony, 1931- , Welsh; poetry, translations

CON VCP
CONRAN, Shirley Ida, 1932- , British; nonfiction CON
CONRAN, Terence Orby, 1931- , American; nonfiction CON
CONRART, Valentin, 1603-75, French; nonfiction BU
CONROW, Robert, 1942- , American; nonfiction CON
CONROY, Frank, 1936- , American; nonfiction CON
CONROY, Jack Wesley ('John Conroy; 'Tim Brennan'; 'John Norcross'), 1899- , American; juveniles, fiction CO VCN
CONROY, Michael Ralph, 1945- , American; nonfiction CON
CONROY, Patricia, 1941/45- , American; nonfiction CON KIB
CONROY, Peter Vincent, Jr., 1944- , American; nonfiction CON
CONRY, F. see O MAOIL CHONAIRE, Flaithrí
CONSCIENCE, Hendrik, 1812-83, Flemish; fiction BU CL MAG
CONSIDINE, Douglas Maxwell, 1915- , American; nonfiction CON
CONSIDINE, Robert Bernard, 1906-75, American; journalism, nonfiction, film CON
CONSILVIO, Thomas, 1947- , American; nonfiction CON
CONSTABLE, Henry, 1562-1613, English; poetry BU DA RU VP
CONSTABLE, John W., 1922- , American; nonfiction CON
CONSTABLE, Trevor James ('Trevor James'), 1925- , New Zealander-American; nonfiction CON
CONSTABLE, William George, 1887-1976, British; nonfiction CON
CONSTANT, Alberta Wilson, 1908- , American; juveniles, poetry CO WAR
CONSTANT de REBECQUE, Benjamin, 1767-1830, French; fiction, nonfiction BU MAG TH
CONSTANTIN, Mary McCaffrey, 1935- , American; fiction CON
CONSTANTINE VII, Porphyrogenitus, 905-59, Byzantine; nonfiction BU GR LA

CONSTANTINE, Larry LeRoy,
1943- , American; nonfic-
tion CON
CONSTANTINE, Murray, English;
fiction NI
CONSTANTINE MANASSES, -1187?,
Byzantine; nonfiction, poetry
BU LA
CONSTANTINE of RHODES, early
10th century, Byzantine; po-
etry LA
CONTI, Antonio, 1677-1749, Ital-
ian; poetry, plays BU
CONTI, Guisto de, 1389?-1449,
Italian; poetry BU
CONTON, William, 1925- , Gam-
bian; fiction HER JA LA
'CONTRADUC, A.' see HOEN,
Pieter 'T
CONTRERAS, Alonso de, 1582-
1640?, Spanish; nonfiction
BU
CONTRERAS, Francisco, 1877-
1933, Chilean; nonfiction BR
CONTRERAS, Jerónimo de, late
16th century, Spanish; fiction
BU
CONVERSE, John Marquis, 1909-
80, American; nonfiction CON
'The CONVICT WRITER' see TOR-
OK, Lou
CONWAY, Gerard F., American;
fiction NI
'CONWAY, Gordon' see HAMIL-
TON, Charles H. S.
CONWAY, Joan Ditzel, 1933- ,
American; fiction CON
CONWAY, Moncure Daniel, 1832-
1907, American; nonfiction,
fiction BA BR MY
'CONWAY, Olive' see BRIGHOUSE,
Harold
CONWAY, Theresa Ann, 1951- ,
American; fiction CON
'CONWAY, Troy' see AVALLONE,
Michael A., Jr.
CONYERS, James E., 1932- ,
American; nonfiction CON
CONYNGHAM, William Joseph,
1924- , American; nonfic-
tion CON
COOGLER, James Gordon, 1865-
1901, American; journalism,
poetry BA
COOK, Adrian, 1940- , English;
nonfiction CON
COOK, Albert Spaulding, 1925- ,
American; nonfiction, poetry,

plays, translations WA
COOK, Alice Rice, 1899-1973,
American; nonfiction CON
COOK, Arlene Ethel ('Cannon
Cole'), 1936- , American;
nonfiction CON
COOK, Bernadine, 1924- , Amer-
ican; juveniles CO
COOK, Blanche Wiesen, 1941- ,
American; nonfiction CON
COOK, Christopher, 1945- , Eng-
lish; nonfiction CON
COOK, Daniel Joseph, 1938- ,
American; nonfiction CON
COOK, David, 1940- , British;
tv, fiction CON
COOK, David Charles III, 1912- ,
American; nonfiction CON
COOK, David T., 1946- , Amer-
ican; nonfiction CON
COOK, Don Lewis, 1928- , Amer-
ican; nonfiction CON
COOK, Dorothy Mary ('D. Y.
Cameron'; 'D. M. Carlisle';
'Elizabeth Clare'), 1907- ,
British; fiction CON
COOK, Ebenezer, 1672?-1732,
American; poetry BR
COOK, Frederick P., 1937- ,
American; nonfiction CON
COOK, Geoffrey, 1946- , Amer-
ican; poetry, nonfiction CON
COOK, George S., 1920- , Amer-
ican; nonfiction CON
COOK, Harold James, 1926- ,
American; journalism CON
COOK, Hugh Christopher Bult,
1910- , English; nonfiction
CON
COOK, James Graham, 1925-66,
American; journalism, nonfic-
tion CON
COOK, James Wyatt, 1932- ,
American; nonfiction, poetry
CON
COOK, Jeffrey, 1934- , Canadian;
nonfiction CON
COOK, Joan Marble, 1920- ,
American; nonfiction CON
COOK, John Augustine (Jack),
1940- , American; nonfiction
CON
'COOK, John Estes' see BAUM,
Lyman F.
COOK, Joseph Jay, 1924- ,
American; juveniles CO
COOK, Luther Townsend, 1901- ,
American; nonfiction CON

COOK   222

'COOK, Lyn see WADDELL,
Evelyn M.
COOK, Marjorie, 1920- , Amer-
ican; juveniles, nonfiction,
fiction CON
COOK, Mary Jane, 1929- , Amer-
ican; poetry CON
COOK, Melvin Alonzo, 1911- ,
American; nonfiction CON
COOK, Mercer, 1903- , Amer-
ican; nonfiction CON SH
COOK, Michael, 1933- , Cana-
dian; plays, fiction CON VCD
COOK, Petronelle Marguerite Mary
('Margot Arnold'), 1925- ,
Anglo-American; fiction CON
COOK, Ramsay, 1931- , Cana-
dian; nonfiction CON
COOK, Raymond Allen, 1919- ,
American; nonfiction, poetry
CON
COOK, Reginald L., 1903- ,
American; nonfiction CON
COOK, Stanley, 1922- , British;
poetry CON VCP
COOK, Sylvia Carol, 1938- , Eng-
lish; nonfiction CON
COOK, Terry, 1942- , American;
nonfiction CON
COOK, William Wallace, 1867-
1933, American; fiction NI
COOKE, Alistair, 1908- , Anglo-
American; nonfiction CON
'COOKE, Barbara' see ALEXAN-
DER, Anna B.
COOKE, Barclay, 1912-81, Amer-
ican; nonfiction CON
COOKE, Charles, American; ju-
veniles WAR
COOKE, Charles Harris, 1904?-
77, American; nonfiction CON
COOKE, Ebenezer, 1671?-1732,
English; poetry BA VP
COOKE, Edward Francis, 1923- ,
American; nonfiction CON
COOKE, Hereward Lester, 1916-
73, American; nonfiction CON
COOKE, John, 17th century, Eng-
lish; plays BU
COOKE, John Esten, 1830-86,
American; fiction, nonfiction
BA BR BU MAG MYE VN
COOKE, Joseph Robinson, 1926- ,
American; nonfiction CON
COOKE, Philip Pendleton, 1816-
50, American; poetry, fic-
tion BA MYE
COOKE, Robert Gordon, 1930- ,

Welsh; journalism, nonfiction
CON
COOKSON, Catherine (McMullen;
'Catherine Marchant'), 1906- ,
English; juveniles CO
COOKSON, Frank Barton, 1912-77,
American; nonfiction CON
COOKSON, Peter W., 1913- ,
American; fiction, plays CON
COOKSON, William, 1939- , Amer-
ican; nonfiction CON
'COOL, Clyde' see FRAZIER, Wal-
ter
COOL, Ola C., 1890?-1977, Amer-
ican; nonfiction CON
COOLEY, Peter, 1940- , Amer-
ican; poetry CON
COOLIDGE, Clark, 1939- , Amer-
ican; poetry, plays VCP
COOLIDGE, Olivia, 1908- , Amer-
ican; juveniles KI
'COOLIDGE, Susan' (Sarah Chauncy
Woolsey), 1835-1905, Amer-
ican; juveniles, poetry KI
COOLING, Benjamin Franklin,
1938- , American; nonfiction
CON
'COOLUS, Romain' (Max René
Weil), 1868-1952, French;
plays MCG
COOMBES, B. L., 1894?-1974,
British; nonfiction CON
COOMBS, Charles Ira, 1914- ,
American; juveniles CO
COOMBS, H. Samm, 1928- ,
American; nonfiction CON
COOMBS, Herbert Cole, 1906- ,
Australian; nonfiction CON
'COOMBS, Murdo' see DAVIS,
Frederick C.
COOMBS, Orde, American; nonfic-
tion CON SH
COOMBS, Patricia, 1926- , Amer-
ican; juveniles CO
COOMBS, Robert Holman, 1934- ,
American; nonfiction CON
COOMER, Anne, American; juven-
iles WAR
COON, Carleton Stevens, 1904-81,
American; nonfiction WA
COON, Gene Lee, 1924-73, Amer-
ican; journalism, film CON
COON, Horace, 1897-1961, Amer-
ican; fiction NI
COON, Nelson, 1895- , American;
nonfiction CON
COON, Stephen, 1948- , Amer-
ican; nonfiction CON

COONEY, Barbara, 1917- ,
American; juveniles CO
COONEY, Caroline B. , 1947- ,
American; fiction, juveniles
CON
COONEY, Eugene Jerome, 1931- ,
Canadian; nonfiction CON
COONEY, Seamus Anthony, 1933- ,
American; nonfiction CON
COONS, William Richard, 1934- ,
American; fiction, nonfiction
CON
COOPE, Rosalys, 1921- , Eng-
lish; nonfiction CON
COOPER, Anthony Ashley, 1670/71-
1712/13, English; nonfiction
BU
COOPER, Bernarr, 1912- , Amer-
ican; nonfiction CON
COOPER, Brian Newman, 1919- ,
British; fiction REI
'COOPER, Charles E.' see KAR-
LEE, Varfelli
COOPER, Charles Muhlenberg,
1909- , American; nonfiction
CON
COOPER, Clarence, American;
fiction SH
COOPER, Colin Symons ('Daniel
Benson'), 1926- , British;
fiction, plays, radio CON
NI
COOPER, Darien Birla, 1937- ,
American; nonfiction CON
COOPER, David E. , 1942- ,
English; nonfiction CON
COOPER, David Graham, 1931- ,
South African; nonfiction
CON
COOPER, Derek Macdonald,
1925- , British; nonfiction
CON
COOPER, Dominic Xavier, 1944- ,
American; fiction CON
COOPER, Duff, 1890-1954, Eng-
lish; fiction MCC
COOPER, Edith E. see 'FIELD,
Michael'
COOPER, Edmund, 1926- ,
British; fiction AS MCC NI
COOPER, Elizabeth K. , 1916- ,
American; juveniles DEM
COOPER, Emmanuel ('Jonathan
Sidney'), 1940- , English;
nonfiction CON
COOPER, Gordon John, 1932- ,
British; juveniles CO CON
KI WAR

COOPER, Grace Rogers, 1924- ,
American; nonfiction CON
COOPER, Harold Eugene, 1928- ,
American; nonfiction CON
COOPER, Harold H. , 1911?-76,
American; nonfiction, fiction
CON
COOPER, Harold R. , 1911?-78,
American; journalism CON
COOPER, Henry Spotswood Feni-
more, Jr. , 1933- , Amer-
ican; nonfiction CON
COOPER, Irving Spencer, 1922- ,
American; nonfiction CON
COOPER, James Fenimore ('Jane
Morgan'), 1789-1851, Amer-
ican; nonfiction, fiction AM
BR BU CO MAG MCC MYE
PO VN
COOPER, James Louis, 1934- ,
American; nonfiction CON
COOPER, James M. , 1939- ,
American; nonfiction CON
COOPER, Jane Marvel, 1924- ,
American; poetry VCP
COOPER, Jeff ('John Dean Cooper'),
1920- , American; nonfiction
CON
COOPER, Jeremy Francis, 1946- ,
British; nonfiction CON
COOPER, John Irwin, 1905- ,
Canadian; nonfiction CON
COOPER, John Owen, 1938- ,
American; nonfiction CON
COOPER, Joseph David, 1917-75,
American; nonfiction CON
COOPER, Kay, 1941- , American;
juveniles, nonfiction CO CON
COOPER, Kent, 1880-1965, Amer-
ican; journalism CON
COOPER, Lee Pelham, American;
juveniles CO
COOPER, Leslie Muir, 1930- ,
American; nonfiction CON
COOPER, Lettice Ulpha, 1894- ,
British; fiction, juveniles KI
VCN
COOPER, Martin Du Pre, 1910- ,
British; nonfiction CON
COOPER, Matthew Heald, 1952- ,
British; nonfiction CON
COOPER, Michele Freda, 1941- ,
American; nonfiction CON
COOPER, Parley Joseph, 1937- ,
American; fiction CON
COOPER, Patricia Jean, 1936- ,
American; nonfiction CON
COOPER, Paul, 1926- , Amer-

ican; nonfiction CON
COOPER, Phyllis, 1939- ,
American; nonfiction CON
COOPER, Sandi E., 1936- ,
American; translations, non-
fiction CON
COOPER, Signe Skott, 1921- ,
American; nonfiction CON
COOPER, Susan Mary, 1935- ,
English; journalism, fiction,
juveniles CO DEM KI NI
WAR
COOPER, Thomas, 1805-92, Eng-
lish; poetry BU
COOPER, Wayne, 1938- , Amer-
ican; nonfiction CON
COOPER, Wilhelmina Behmenburg
('Wilhelmina'), 1939?-80,
Dutch; nonfiction CON
COOPER, Will, 1929- , Amer-
ican; fiction, nonfiction CON
'COOPER, William' (Harry Sum-
merfield Hoff), 1910- , Brit-
ish; fiction, plays, nonfiction
DA VCN WA
COOPER, William Frazier, 1932- ,
American; translations, fiction
CON
COOPER, William Hurlbert,
1924- , American; nonfic-
tion CON
COOPER, William James, Jr.,
1940- , American; nonfiction
CON
COOPER, Wyatt Emory, 1927-78,
American; nonfiction CON
COOPERMAN, Stanley, 1929- ,
Canadian; poetry, nonfiction
VCP
COOPERSMITH, Jerome, 1925- ,
American; tv, juveniles CON
WAR
COORNHERT, Dirck Volckerts-
zoon, 1522-90, Dutch; poetry,
nonfiction BU TH
COOVER, James Burrell ('C. B.
James'), 1925- , American;
nonfiction CON
COOVER, Robert Lowell, 1932- ,
American; fiction, plays BR
CON HE NI VCN WAK
COPANI, Peter, 1942- , Amer-
ican; plays CON
'COPE, Abiezer' see TAYLOR,
John A.
COPE, Jack, 1913- , South
African; fiction, poetry, non-
fiction, translations BU VCN

COPE, Jackson Irving, 1925- ,
American; nonfiction CON
COPE, Myron, 1929- , American;
nonfiction CON
COPEAU, Jacques, 1879-1949,
French; plays CL MCG
COPELAND, Bonnie Chapman,
1919- , American; fiction
CON
COPELAND, Carolyn Faunce,
1930- , American; nonfiction
CON
COPELAND, Helen, 1920- , Amer-
ican; juveniles CO
COPELAND, Melvin T., 1884-1975,
American; nonfiction CON
COPELAND, Paul W., American;
juveniles CO
COPELAND, Thomas Wellsted,
1907-79, American; nonfiction
CON
COPERNICUS, Nicolaus, 1473-1543,
Polish; nonfiction BU
'COPIA, Isis' see 'MAYY'
COPIC, Branko, 1915- , Serbian;
fiction BU TH
COPLAND, Robert, 1508?-47?,
English; printer BU
COPLEY, Frank Barkley, Amer-
ican; fiction NI
COPMAN, Louis, 1934- , Amer-
ican; nonfiction, fiction CON
COPP, E. Anthony, 1945- , Amer-
ican; nonfiction CON
COPPARD, Alfred Edgar, 1878-
1957, English; fiction, poetry,
nonfiction, juveniles COM DA
MAG REI SEY VN
COPPEE, Francis Joachim Edouard,
1842-1907/08, French; poetry,
plays, fiction BU MCG TH
COPPEL, Alec, 1909?-72, Aus-
tralian; fiction, plays, film
REI
'COPPEL, Alfred' (Alfred José de
Marini y Coppel; 'Robert Cham
Gilman'; 'Sol Galaxan'), 1921- ,
American; fiction AS NI
COPPER, Arnold, 1934- , Amer-
ican; nonfiction CON
COPPER, Basil ('Lee Falk'),
1924- , British; fiction, non-
fiction REI
COPPER, John Franklin, 1940- ,
American; translations, nonfic-
tion CON
COPPER, Marcia Snyder, 1934- ,
American; nonfiction, fiction CON

COPPERMAN, Paul, 1947- ,
American; nonfiction CON
COPPOCK, John Terence, 1921- ,
Welsh; nonfiction CON
COPPOCK, Joseph David, 1909- ,
American; nonfiction CON
COPPOLA, Francis Ford, 1939- ,
American; film CON
COPPOLA, Raymond Thomas,
1947- , American; nonfic-
tion CON
COQUILLART, Guillaume, 1450?-
1510, French; poetry, plays
BU
'CORAM, Christopher' see WALK-
ER, Peter N.
CORAX, fl. 465 B.C., Greek;
nonfiction BU
CORAZZINI, Sergio, 1886-1907,
Italian; poetry BO BU TH
CORBET(T), Richard, 1582-1635,
English; poetry BU DA PO
RU
CORBETT, Elizabeth Frances,
1887-1981, American; fiction,
poetry, nonfiction CON
CORBETT, James, British; fic-
tion NI
CORBETT, James Arthur, 1908- ,
American; nonfiction CON
CORBETT, Richard, 1582-1635,
English; poetry VP
CORBETT, Scott, 1913- , Amer-
ican; juveniles, nonfiction
DEM KI
CORBETT, Thomas Henry, 1938- ,
American; nonfiction CON
CORBETT, William, 1763-1835,
English; nonfiction, poetry,
plays VN
CORBIERE, Edouard Joachim
('Tristan'), 1845-75, French;
poetry BU MAG TH
CORBIN, Claire, 1913- , Amer-
ican; nonfiction CON
CORBIN, Hayman Dan, 1912- ,
American; nonfiction CON
'CORBIN, Sabra L.' see MAL-
VERN, Gladys
'CORBIN, William' see Mc-
GRAW, William C.
CORBISHLEY, Thomas, 1903-
76, British; nonfiction CON
CORBITT, Helen Lucy, 1906-78,
American; nonfiction CON
'CORBY, Dan' see CATHERALL,
Arthur
CORCHADO, Manuel, 1840-84,

Puerto Rican; journalism, plays,
poetry HIL
CORCORAN, Barbara ('Paige Dixon';
'Gail Hamilton'), 1911- , Amer-
ican; juveniles CO WAR
CORCOS, Lucille, 1908-73, Amer-
ican; juveniles CO
'CORDELL, Alex' (Alex Graber),
1914- , British; juveniles,
fiction CO KI
CORDER, Brice Wood, 1936- ,
American; nonfiction CON
CORDIER, Mathurin, 1479-1564,
French; nonfiction BU
CORDINGLY, David, 1938- , Brit-
ish; nonfiction CON
CORDOBA, Martín Alfonso de,
-1476?, Spanish; nonfiction
BU
CORDOVA, Ignacio R., 1940- ,
American; nonfiction MAR
CORDTZ, Dan, 1927- , Amer-
ican; journalism CON
CORDUS, Euricus, 1486-1535,
German; poetry BU
CORDWELL, Miriam, 1908- ,
American; nonfiction CON
COREA, Genoveffa (Gena), 1946- ,
American; nonfiction CON
'CORELLI, Marie' (Mary Mackay),
1855?-1924, British; fiction
DA NI VN
COREN, Alan, 1938- , British;
fiction, juveniles, tv, radio
CON
CORESI, -1583, Rumanian; printer
BU
COREY, Dorothy, Canadian; juven-
iles CO CON
COREY, Paul Frederick, 1903- ,
American; fiction, nonfiction
NI PAL
CORFE, Thomas Howell, 1928- ,
British; nonfiction CON
CORFMAN, Eunice Luccock, 1928-
80, American; fiction, nonfic-
tion CON
CORINA, Maurice, 1936- , Eng-
lish; nonfiction CON
CORINNA, 5th century B.C., Greek;
poetry BU GR LA
CORIPPUS, Flavius Cresconius,
6th century, African-Latin;
nonfiction BU TH
CORKE, Hilary, 1921- , British;
poetry, translations CON VCP
CORKERY, Daniel, 1878-1964,
Irish; poetry, fiction, nonfiction

CORLETT

226

BU HO
CORLETT, William, 1938- ,
British; juveniles, plays
CON KI
CORLEY, Edwin, 1931-81, Amer-
ican; fiction NI
'CORLEY, Ernest' see BULMER,
Kenneth
CORLEY, James, 1947- , Eng-
lish; fiction NI
CORLISS, Charlotte Nuzum, 1932- ,
American; nonfiction CON
CORLISS, William Roger, 1926- ,
American; nonfiction CON
CORMACK, Alexander James Ross
(Sandy), 1942- , American;
nonfiction CON
CORMACK, Margaret Grant,
1913- , American; juveniles
CO
CORMAN, Avery, 1935- , Amer-
ican; nonfiction, fiction CON
CORMAN, Cid (Sidney), 1924- ,
American; poetry, transla-
tions CON VCP
CORMAN, Roger, 1926- , Amer-
ican; film NI
CORMIER, Ramona, 1923- ,
American; nonfiction CON
CORMIER, Raymond Joseph,
1938- , American; nonfiction
CON
CORMIER, Robert Edmond ('John
Fitch IV'), 1925- , American;
juveniles CO
CORMILLOT, Albert E. J.,
1938- , Argentinian; nonfic-
tion CON
CORN, Ira George, Jr., 1921- ,
American; nonfiction CON
CORNAZZANO, Antonio, 1429-84,
Italian; poetry BU
CORNEHLS, James Vernon, 1936- ,
American; nonfiction CON
CORNEILLE, Pierre, 1606-84,
French; plays BU MAG MCG
TH
CORNEILLE, Thomas, 1625-1709,
French; plays BU MCG TH
CORNEJO, Ricardo J., American;
nonfiction MAR
CORNELIUS NEPOS, 100-25 B.C.,
Roman; nonfiction BU LA
CORNELL, Francis Griffith, 1906-
79, American; nonfiction CON
CORNELL, Frederick Carruthers,
1867-1921, South African; non-
fiction, poetry, fiction BU

CORNELL, James Clayton, Jr.,
1938- , American; nonfiction
CON
CORNELL, Jean Gay, 1920- ,
American; nonfiction CO CON
CORNELL, Jeffrey (J. Cornell),
1945- , American; juveniles
CO
CORNER, George Washington,
1889-1981, American; nonfic-
tion CON
CORNETT, Joe Delayne, 1935- ,
American; nonfiction CON
CORNFELD, Gaalyahu, 1902- ,
Israeli; nonfiction CON
CORNFORD, Frances Crofts Dar-
win, 1886-1960, English; po-
etry DA
CORNFORD, Rupert John, 1915-
36, English; poetry, nonfiction
DA
CORNFORTH, Maurice, 1909-80,
British; nonfiction CON
CORNIER, Vincent, 1898- , Eng-
lish; fiction ST
CORNIFICIUS QUINTUS, 1st cen-
tury B.C., Latin; poetry LA
CORNISH, John Buckley, 1914- ,
Canadian; fiction CR
CORNISH, Samuel James, 1935- ,
American; poetry, juveniles
CO CON SH VCP
CORNMAN, James Welton, 1929- ,
American; nonfiction CON
'CORNWALL, Barry' see PROCTER,
Bryan W.
CORNWALL, Espie Judson, 1924- ,
American; nonfiction CON
CORNWELL, David J. M. see 'LE
CARRE, John'
'CORNWELL, Smith' see SMITH,
David J.
COROMINES, Pere, 1870-1939,
Catalan; nonfiction CL
CORONA, Bert N., 1918- , Amer-
ican; nonfiction MAR
CORONADO, Carolina, 1823-1911,
Spanish; poetry, fiction, plays
BU TH
CORONEL, Soledad Santa Cruz,
1933- , American; nonfiction
MAR
CORPI, Lucha, 1945- , American;
fiction, poetry MAR
CORRAL, Pedro del, 15th century,
Spanish; nonfiction BU
CORREA, Gustavo, 1914- , Co-
lombian; nonfiction CON

CORREGGIO, Niccolò de, 1450-
1508, Italian; poetry BU
CORREIA, Gaspar, 1495?-1565?,
Portuguese; nonfiction BU
TH
CORREIA, Raimundo, 1860-1911,
Brazilian; poetry BR
'EL CORRESPONSAL' see MOR-
ALES, José P.
CORRETJER, Juan Antonio, 1908- ,
Puerto Rican; poetry, journal-
ism, nonfiction HIL
'CORREY, Lee' see STINE, George
H.
CORRIGAN, Adeline, 1909- ,
American; juveniles, nonfic-
tion CO CON
CORRIGAN, Barbara, 1922- ,
American; juveniles, nonfic-
tion CO CON
CORRIGAN, John Davitt, Amer-
ican; nonfiction CON
CORRIGAN, John Thomas, 1936- ,
American; nonfiction CON
'CORRIGAN, Mark' (Norman Lee;
'Raymond Armstrong'; 'Rob-
ertson Hobart'), 1905-62,
British; fiction, plays, non-
fiction REI
CORRINGTON, John William,
1932- , American; poetry,
fiction, film, nonfiction BA
KIB VCP
CORRIVEAU, Monique, 1927- ,
Canadian; juveniles CON
CORSARO, Francesco Andrea
(Frank), 1924- , American;
plays CON
CORSI, Jerome Robert, 1946- ,
American; nonfiction, juven-
iles, plays CON
CORSO, Gregory Nunzio, 1930- ,
American; poetry, plays, fic-
tion BR BU MAL PO VCP
WAK
CORSON, Richard, American; non-
fiction CON
CORSTON, Michael George,
1932- , British; fiction NI
'CORTADILLO' see RODRIQUEZ
CABRERO, Luis
CORTAZAR, Julio ('Julio Denis'),
1914- , Argentinian; fiction
BR BU SEY WA
CORTE REAL, Jerónimo, 1533?-
88?, Portuguese; poetry BU
CORTES, Carlos, 1934- , Amer-
ican; nonfiction CON MAR

CORTES, Hernán, 1485-1547, Span-
ish; nonfiction BR BU
CORTESÃO, Jaime, 1884-1960,
Portuguese; poetry, plays, non-
fiction CL
CORTESE, Anthony James, 1917- ,
Canadian-American; nonfiction
CON
'CORTESI, Lawrence' see CERRI,
Lawrence J.
CORTEZ, Alfredo, 1880-1946,
Portuguese; plays CL
CORTEZ, Jayne, 1937- , Amer-
ican; fiction, poetry CON SH
CORTON, Antonio ('Lord Harrison';
'Quijotin'), 1854-1913, Puerto
Rican; journalism, nonfiction
HIL
CORTRIGHT, David, 1946- , Amer-
ican; nonfiction CON
CORVER, Marten, 1727-94, Dutch;
nonfiction BU
CORVO, Baron, see ROLFE, Fred-
erick W.
CORWEN, Leonard, 1921- , Amer-
ican; nonfiction CON
CORWIN, Judith Hoffman, 1946- ,
American; juveniles CO
'CORY, Desmond' (Shaun Lloyd
McCarthy; 'Theo Callas'),
1928- , British; fiction, plays,
juveniles REI
'CORY, Howard L.', (Jack Owen
JARDINE, 1931- ; Julie Ann
JARDINE, 1926- ,), American;
fiction NI
CORY, Irene E. ('Corrine Cory';
'I. E. Corya'), 1910- , Amer-
ican; nonfiction CON
CORY, Jean-Jacques, 1947- ,
American; nonfiction CON
'CORY, William' (William Johnson),
1823-92, English; poetry BU
CORYATE, Thomas (Coryatt),
1577?-1617, English; nonfiction
BU DA
COSBUC, Gheorghe, 1866-1918,
Rumanian; poetry BU CL TH
COSBY, Bill, 1937- , American;
nonfiction CON
COSBY, Yvonne Shepard ('Everett
Young'), 1886?-1980, Franco-
American; fiction CON
COSGRAVE, John O'Hara II, 1908-
68, American; juveniles CO
COSGROVE, Margaret, 1926- ,
American; juveniles DEM
COSGROVE, Mark P., 1947- ,

American; nonfiction CON
COSGROVE, Maynard Giles,
1895- , American; nonfic-
tion CON
COSGROVE, Rachel, see PAYES,
Rachel C.
COSGROVE, Stephen Edward ('Ed-
ward Stevens'), 1945- ,
American; juveniles CON
COSIC, Bora, 1932- , Serbian;
fiction, nonfiction, film,
translations BU
COSIC, Branimir, 1901-34, Ser-
bian; fiction BU
COSIC, Dobrica, 1921- , Ser-
bian; fiction BU CL TH
COSKEY, Evelyn, 1932- , Amer-
ican; juveniles CO CON WAR
COSLOW, Sam, 1905- , Amer-
ican; nonfiction, film, song
CON
COSMAS INDICOPLEUSTES, early
6th century, Greek; nonfiction
BU GR LA
COSMAS of JERUSALEM, 8th cen-
tury, Byzantine; poetry BU
COSMAS of PRAGUE, 1045?-1125,
Czech; nonfiction BU TH
COSNECK, Bernard Joseph,
1912- , American; nonfic-
tion CON
COSSA, Pietro, 1830-81, Italian;
poetry, plays BO BU MCG
COSSEBOOM, Kathy G. see EL-
MESSIDI, Kathyanne G.
COSSI, Olga, 1921- , Amer-
ican; journalism, juveniles
CON
COSSIO, Josep M. see CASTE-
LLET i DIEZ de COSSIO,
Josep M.
COSSIO, Manuel Bartolomé, 1858-
1935, Spanish; nonfiction BU
'COST, March' see MORRISON,
Margaret M.
COSTA, Cláudio Manuel da, 1729-
89, Brazilian; poetry BR
COSTA, Hermann see 'CONRADI,
Herman'
COSTA, Paolo, 1771-1836, Italian;
plays BU
COSTA ALEGRE, Caetano da, see
ALEGRE, Caetano da C.
'COSTA ANDRADE, Fernando' see
ANDRADE, Costa
COSTA i LLOBERA, Miguel, 1854-
1922, Catalan; poetry BU CL
COSTA y MARTINEZ, Joaquin,

1846-1911, Spanish; nonfiction
BU CL TH
COSTANZO, Angelo di, 1507-91?,
Italian; nonfiction, poetry BU
COSTAS, Orlando Enrique, 1942- ,
Puerto Rican; nonfiction CON
COSTAS, Procope, 1900?-74, Amer-
ican; nonfiction CON
COSTELLO, Anne, 1937- , Amer-
ican; fiction CON
COSTELLO, David Francis, 1904- ,
American; juveniles CO
COSTELLO, John Edward, 1943- ,
Scots; nonfiction CON
'COSTELLO, P. F.' Ziff-Davis
house name NI
COSTELLO, Peter, 1946- , Irish;
nonfiction CON
COSTELLO, William Aloysious,
1904-69, American; journalism,
nonfiction CON
COSTELLOE, Martin Joseph,
1914- , American; transla-
tions, nonfiction CON
COSTER, Charles de, 1827-79,
Belgian; fiction MAG
COSTER, Dirk, 1887-1956, Dutch;
nonfiction BU
'COSTER, Robert' see BARLTROP,
Robert
COSTER, Samuel, 1579-1665,
Dutch; plays BU
COSTIGAN, James, 1928- , Amer-
ican; poetry CON
COSTIN, Miron, 1633-91, Mol-
davian; nonfiction BU
COSTIN, Nicolae, 1660-1712, Mol-
davian; nonfiction BU
'COSTINESU, Tristan' see GROSS,
Terence
COSTIS, Harry George, 1928- ,
Greek-American; nonfiction
CON
COSTLEY, William Kirkwood,
Jr., 1942- , American; po-
etry CON
COSTONIS, John Joseph, 1937- ,
American; nonfiction CON
COTA, Rodrigo, -1504?, Spanish;
poetry BU
COTA CARDENAS, Margarita,
1941- , American; poetry,
fiction MAR
COTE, Richard George, 1934- ,
American; nonfiction CON
COTERA, Martha P., 1938- ,
American; nonfiction MAR
COTES, Sara Jeannette Duncan

('Garth Grafton'), 1861-1922,
Canadian; nonfiction, juven-
iles CR
COTHRAN, Jean, 1910- , Amer-
ican; juveniles CON
COTIN, Charles, 1604-82, French;
poetry TH
COTLER, Sherwin Barry, 1941- ,
American; nonfiction CON
COTLOW, Lewis Nathaniel, 1898- ,
American; nonfiction CON
COTRUS, Aron, 1891-1961, Ru-
manian; poetry BU
COTT, Jonathan, 1942- , Amer-
ican; juveniles, poetry, non-
fiction CO CON WAR
COTT, Nancy F., 1945- , Amer-
ican; nonfiction CON
COTTAM, Clarence, 1899-1974,
American; nonfiction CO CON
COTTAM, Keith M., 1941- ,
American; nonfiction CON
COTTER, Janet Merrill, 1914- ,
American; nonfiction CON
COTTER, Richard Vern, 1930- ,
American; nonfiction CON
COTTERELL, Alan Geoffrey,
1919- , English; fiction WA
COTTERELL, Francis Peter,
1930- , American; nonfic-
tion CON
'COTTLE, Charles' see ANDER-
SON, Robert C.
COTTLE, William Cullen, 1913- ,
American; nonfiction CON
COTTLER, Joseph, 1899- ,
American; juveniles CO
COTTO THORNER, Giullermo,
1916- , Puerto Rican; fic-
tion HIL
COTTON, Charles, 1630-86/87,
English; poetry, translations,
nonfiction BU DA PO VP
COTTON, John, 1584-1652, Amer-
ican; nonfiction BR
COTTON, John, of Queen's Creek,
Va., 1643?-80?, American;
nonfiction BA
COTTON, John, 1925- , British;
poetry CON VCP
COTTON, Norris, 1900- , Amer-
ican; nonfiction CON
COTTON, Sir Robert Bruce,
1570/71-1631, English; non-
fiction BU
COTTRELL, Alan Howard,
1919- , English; nonfiction
CON

COTTRELL, Leonard, 1913-74,
English; juveniles, nonfiction,
journalism CO DEM WA
COTTRELL, Robert Duane, 1930- ,
American; nonfiction CON
COUCH, William, Jr., American;
nonfiction SH
COUCHORO, Félix, 1900/05-68,
Dahoman; fiction, journalism,
HER JA
COUGER, J. Daniel, 1929- ,
American; nonfiction CON
COUGHLAN, John Robert, 1914- ,
American; nonfiction CON
COUGHLAN, Margaret N., Amer-
ican; juveniles WAR
COUGHLIN, Charles Edward, 1891-
1979, American; nonfiction CON
COUGHLIN, Violet Louise, Cana-
dian; nonfiction CON
COULET du GARD, Rene ('Andre
Algery'; 'Raphael Anduze-
Dufy'), 1919- , American;
nonfiction, fiction CON
COULETTE, Henri Anthony, 1927- ,
American; nonfiction, poetry
CON VCP
COULIBALY, Augustin Sondé,
1933- , Upper Voltan; poetry,
nonfiction, journalism HER
JA
COULLING, Sidney Baxter, 1924- ,
American; nonfiction CON
COULSON, John H. A. see 'BON-
ETT, John and Emery'
COULSON, Juanita ('John Jay
Wells'), 1933- , American;
fiction AS NI
COULSON, Robert, 1924- , Amer-
ican; nonfiction, fiction CON
NI
COULSON, William Donald, 1942- ,
Anglo-American; nonfiction
CON
COULTER, John William, 1888- ,
Canadian; poetry, fiction, non-
fiction, plays CR HO
COULTER, Norman Arthur, Jr.,
1920- , American; nonfiction
CON
COULTER, Stephen ('James Mayo'),
1914- , English; fiction MCC
REI
COUNCIL, Norman Briggs, 1936- ,
American; nonfiction CON
COUNSELL, John William, 1905- ,
English; nonfiction CON
'THE COUNTRYMAN' see WHIT-

LOCK, Ralph
COUNTS, Charles Richard, 1934- ,
American; nonfiction CON
COUNTS, George Sylvester, 1889-
1974, American; nonfiction
CON
COUPER, John Mill, 1914- ,
American; nonfiction, poetry
CON
COUPERUS, Louis Marie Anne,
1863-1923, Dutch; nonfiction,
fiction BU CL MAG SEY TH
COUR, Paul Arvid, 1902-56, Dan-
ish; poetry, nonfiction BU
COURAGE, James Francis, 1903-
63, New Zealander; fiction,
plays BU CON VCN VN
COURCY, Jean de, 1360-1431,
French; nonfiction BU
COURIER, Paul Louis, 1772-1825,
French; nonfiction TH
COURLANDER, Harold, 1908- ,
American; juveniles CO
COUROUBLE, Leópold, 1861-1937,
Belgian; fiction, poetry BU
COURSE, Edwin, 1922- , British;
nonfiction CON
COURSEN, Herbert Randolph, Jr.,
1932- , American; nonfiction
CON
COURT, Wesli, 1940- , Amer-
ican; poetry, juveniles CON
COURTADE, Pierre, 1915-63,
French; fiction BU
'COURTELINE, Georges' (G. Moi-
neaux), 1858-1929, French;
fiction, plays BU CL MCG
TH
COURTER, Gay, 1944- , Amer-
ican; nonfiction CON
COURTHION, Pierre Barthelemy,
1902- , Swiss; nonfiction
CON
COURTIER, Sidney Hobson, 1904-
74, Australian; fiction REI
ST
COURTINE, Robert ('La Reyniere';
'Savarin'), 1910- , French;
nonfiction CON
COURTNEY, Ragan, 1941- , Amer-
ican; nonfiction CON
'COURTNEY, Robert' see ROBIN-
SON, Frank M.
COURTNEY, William John, 1921- ,
American; nonfiction CON
COURVILLE, Donovan Amos,
1901- , American; nonfiction
CON

COURY, Phil, American; fiction
NI
COUSER, Giffith Thomas, 1946- ,
American; nonfiction CON
COUSIN, Victor, 1792-1867, French;
nonfiction BU
COUSINS, Albert Newton, 1919- ,
American; nonfiction CON
COUSINS, James Henry, 1873-1956,
Irish; poetry, plays HO
COUSSE, Raymond, 1942- , French;
fiction CON
COUSTEAU, Jacques-Yves, 1910- ,
French; nonfiction CON
COUSTEAU, Philippe Pierre, 1940-
79, French; nonfiction CON
COUSTILLAS, Pierre, 1930- ,
French; nonfiction CON
COUTINHO, Joaquim, 1886?-1978,
Portuguese; nonfiction CON
COUTO, Diogo do, 1542/43-1616,
Portuguese; nonfiction BU TH
COUTO, Richard A., 1941- ,
American; nonfiction CON
COUTO, Rui Ribeiro, 1898-1963,
Brazilian; fiction, poetry BR
COUTURE, Andrea, 1943- , Amer-
ican; journalism, nonfiction
CON
'COUTURE, Sévére' see DESMAR-
CHAIS, Rex
COUTURIER, Louis Joseph ('Michel
Carrouges'), 1910- , French;
nonfiction, fiction CON
COUZYN, Jeni, 1942- , South
African; poetry CON VCP
COVARRUBIAS y OROZCO, Se-
bastián de, 1539?-1613?, Span-
ish; nonfiction BU
COVATTA, Anthony Gallo, 1944- ,
American; nonfiction CON
COVE, Joseph Walter see 'GIBBS,
Lewis'
COVELL, Jon Carter, 1910- ,
American; nonfiction CON
COVENY, James, 1920- , English;
nonfiction CON
COVENTRY, John, 1915- , Brit-
ish; nonfiction CON
COVER, Arthur Byron, 1950- ,
American; fiction NI
COVER, Robert M., 1943- ,
American; nonfiction CON
COVERDALE, John Foy, 1940- ,
American; nonfiction CON
COVERDALE, Miles, 1488-1568,
English; translations, nonfiction
BU DA PO

COVERT, Paul, 1941- , American; fiction, film CON
COVILLE, Bruce, 1950- , American; juveniles CON
COVIN, Theron Michael, 1947- , American; nonfiction CON
COVINA, Gina, 1952- , American; nonfiction CON
COVINGTON, John, American; juveniles WAR
COVINO, Frank, 1931- , American; nonfiction CON
COWAN, Charles Donald, 1923- , British; nonfiction CON
COWAN, Edward James, 1944- , Scots; nonfiction CON
COWAN, Frank, 1844-1905, American; poetry, fiction NI
COWAN, Geoffrey, 1942- , American; nonfiction CON
COWAN, George McKillop, 1916- , American; nonfiction CON
COWAN, Gregory Mac, 1935- , American; nonfiction CON
COWAN, Henry Jacob, 1919- , Polish-Australian; nonfiction CON
COWAN, Ian Borthwick, 1932- , Scots; nonfiction CON
COWAN, James, 1870-1943, American; fiction NI
COWAN, Janice, 1941- , British; juveniles CON
COWAN, Peter, 1914- , Australian; fiction VCN
COWAN, Richard Olsen, 1934- , American; nonfiction CON
COWAN, Wood Messick, 1896-1977, American; nonfiction, journalism CON
COWARD, Sir Noel, 1899-1973, English; plays, fiction, nonfiction, poetry BU CON DA MAG MCG PO VD
COWDEN, Dudley Johnstone, 1899- , American; nonfiction CON
COWDEN, Jeanne, 1918- , South African; film, nonfiction CON
COWDEN, Joanna Dunlap, 1933- , American; nonfiction CON
COWELL, Frank Richard, 1897- , American; nonfiction CON
COWELL, John Adrian, 1934- , British; nonfiction CON
COWEN, Emory Leland, 1926- , American; nonfiction CON
'COWEN, Eve' see WERNER, Herma

COWEN, Frances ('Eleanor Hyde'), 1915- , British; fiction, juveniles REI
COWEN, Ida, 1898- , Polish-American; nonfiction CON
COWEN, Ronald, 1944- , American; plays CON VCD
COWIE, Hamilton Russell, 1931- , New Zealander; nonfiction CON
COWIE, Leonard Wallace, 1919- , English; juveniles CO
COWIE, Margaret see CLARK, Mabel M.
COWIE, Peter, 1939- , English; nonfiction CON
COWLE, Jerome Milton, 1917- , American; nonfiction CON
COWLES, Frank, Jr., 1918- , American; nonfiction CON
COWLES, Ginny, 1924- , American; juveniles CON
COWLES, Lois Thornburg, 1909-80, American; journalism CON
COWLES, Raymond Bridgeman, 1896-1975, South African-American; nonfiction CON
COWLES, Virginia Spencer, 1912- , American; nonfiction CON
COWLEY, Abraham, 1618?-67, English; poetry, nonfiction, plays BRI BU DA MCG PO RU VP
COWLEY, Cassia Joy, 1936- , New Zealander; fiction, juveniles CO WAR
COWLEY, Hannah Parkhurst (Parkhouse), 1743-1809, English; poetry, plays DA VD
COWLEY, Malcolm, 1898- , American; nonfiction, poetry, translations BOR BR RO VCP
'COWPER, Richard' (John Middleton Murry, Jr.), 1926- , British; fiction AS NI
COWPER, William, 1731-1800, English; poetry, translations, letters BRI BU DA MAG PO VP
COX, Albert Wesley, 1921- , American; nonfiction CON
COX, Allan, 1937- , American; nonfiction CON
COX, Anthony Berkeley see 'BERKELEY, Anthony'
COX, Archibald, 1912- , American; nonfiction CON
COX, Barry, 1931- , British; nonfiction CON

COX, C. Benjamin, 1925- ,
American; nonfiction CON
COX, Donald William, 1921- ,
American; juveniles CO
COX, Edith Muriel ('Muriel Goa-
man'), British; nonfiction, ju-
veniles CON
COX, Erle, 1873-1950, Australian;
fiction, journalism NI
COX, Frederick Moreland, 1928- ,
American; nonfiction CON
COX, Geoffrey Sandford, 1910- ,
New Zealander; nonfiction
CON
COX, Harvey Gallagher, Jr. ,
1929- , American; nonfic-
tion CON
COX, James Middleton, Jr. ,
1903-74, American; journal-
ism CON
COX, Joan Irene, 1942- , Amer-
ican; fiction CON
COX, John Roberts ('Jack Cox';
'David Roberts'; 'John Haven-
hand'), 1915- , English; ju-
veniles CO
COX, Joseph A. , 1896?-1980,
American; nonfiction CON
COX, Joseph Mason Andrew,
1923- , American; fiction,
nonfiction, poetry CON
COX, Joseph William, 1937- ,
American; nonfiction CON
COX, Keith John, 1931- , Amer-
ican; nonfiction CON
COX, Luther, American; fiction
NI
COX, Oliver Cromwell, 1901-74,
British; nonfiction CON
COX, Palmer, 1840-1924, Cana-
dian; juveniles CO WAR
COX, Patrick Brian ('Kenneth
Stuart'; 'Tantrist'; 'Bjoern
Kenneth Wesander'), 1914- ,
Australian; nonfiction, poetry
CON
COX, Thomas Richard, 1933- ,
American; nonfiction CON
COX, Wally, 1924-73, American;
plays, fiction, juveniles CO
CON
COX, Warren Earle, 1895-1977,
American; nonfiction CON
COX, William Harvey, 1939- ,
English; nonfiction CON
COX, William T. see 'TREVOR,
William'
COXE, George Harmon, 1901- ,
American; film, fiction, non-

fiction CON REI ST WA
COXE, Louis Osborne, 1918- ,
American; poetry, plays MCG
VCP WA
COXHEAD, Elizabeth, 1909?-79,
American; fiction, nonfiction
CON
'COX-JOHNSON, Ann' see SAUN-
DERS, Ann L.
COY, Harold, 1902- , American;
juveniles CO
COYLE, David Cushman, 1887-
1969, American; nonfiction
CON
COYLE, Lee Perry, 1925- ,
American; nonfiction CON
COYNE, John, American; fiction,
nonfiction CON
COYSH, Arthur Wilfred, 1905- ,
British; nonfiction CON
COYSH, Victor, 1906- , English;
nonfiction CON
COZE, Paul, 1903?-74, Franco-
American; nonfiction CON
COZZANI, Ettore, 1884- , Italian;
poetry, fiction BU
COZZENS, James Gould, 1903-78,
American; fiction AM BR BU
CON MAG PO VCN VN
CRABB, Alfred Leland, 1884- ,
American; fiction, nonfiction
BA
CRABB, Lawrence James, Jr. ,
1944- , American; nonfiction
CON
CRABBE, Buster, 1908- , Amer-
ican; nonfiction CON
CRABEE, George, 1754-1832,
English; poetry BRI BU DA
MAG PO VP
CRACKNELL, Basil Edward,
1925- , British; nonfiction
CON
CRACRAFT, James Edward,
1939- , American; nonfiction
CON
CRACROFT, Richard Holton,
1936- , American; nonfic-
tion CON
'CRADDOCK, Charles E.' see
MURFREE, Mary N.
CRADDOCK, Patricia Bland,
1938- , American; nonfic-
tion CON
CRADDOCK, Thomas, 1718-70,
American; poetry, nonfiction
BA
CRADDOCK, William James ('Wil-
liam James'), 1946- , Amer-

ican; fiction, nonfiction CON
CRAFT, Maurice, 1932- , Eng-
lish; nonfiction CON
CRAFT, Robert Lawson, 1923- ,
American; nonfiction WAK
CRAFT, Ruth, New Zealander;
tv, juveniles WAR
CRAFTS, William, 1787-1826,
American; poetry, nonfiction
BA
CRAGG, Gerald Robertson, 1906- ,
Canadian; nonfiction CON
CRAGHAN, John Francis, 1936- ,
American; nonfiction CON
CRAIB, Ian, 1945- , British; non-
fiction CON
CRAIG, Alex, American; fiction
NI
CRAIG, Charlotte Marie, 1929- ,
Czech-American; nonfiction
CON
CRAIG, David, 1932- , Scots;
nonfiction CON
CRAIG, Donald Laurence, 1946- ,
American; journalism CON
CRAIG, Edward Gordon, 1872-
1966, English; plays DA
CRAIG, Eleanor, 1929- , Amer-
ican; juveniles CON
CRAIG, Elizabeth Josephine, 1883?-
1980, British; journalism, non-
fiction CON
CRAIG, Elizabeth May, 1889?-
1975, American; journalism
CON
CRAIG, Evelyn Quita ('Eve Lang-
dale'), 1917- , American;
nonfiction CON
CRAIG, Henry Armitage Llewelyn,
1921-78, Irish; fiction, film
CON
CRAIG, James, 1930- , Canadian-
American; nonfiction CON
CRAIG, John Ernest, 1921- ,
Canadian; juveniles, fiction,
tv CO CON KI
CRAIG, M. Jean, 1915- , Amer-
ican; juveniles CO CON DEM
CRAIG, Margaret Maze, 1911-64,
American; juveniles CO
CRAIG, Mary Francis (SHURA),
1923- , American; juveniles
CO DE
CRAIG, Maurice James, 1919- ,
Irish; poetry, nonfiction HO
CRAIG, Richard Blythe, 1935- ,
American; nonfiction CON
CRAIG, Robert Bruce, 1944- ,

American; nonfiction CON
CRAIG, Robert Dean, 1934- ,
American; nonfiction CON
'CRAIG, Webster' see RUSSELL,
Eric F.
CRAIGHEAD, Frank Cooper, Jr.,
1916- , American; nonfiction
CON
CRAIK, Dinah M. M. see MULOCK,
Dinah M.
CRAIK, Kenneth Henry, 1936- ,
American; nonfiction CON
CRAIN, John, 1926?-79, American;
editor CON
CRAIN, Sharie, 1942- , Amer-
ican; nonfiction CON
'CRAINIC, Nichifor' (Ion Dobre),
1889- , Rumanian; poetry
BU
CRAM, Mildred, 1889- , Amer-
ican; fiction CON
CRAMER, Richard Louis, 1947- ,
American; nonfiction CON
CRAMPTON, Georgia (Ronan),
1925- , American; nonfiction
CON
CRANCH, Christopher Pearse,
1813-92, American; poetry,
juveniles, translations BU MY
CRANDALL, James Edward, 1930- ,
American; nonfiction CON
'CRANDALL, Joy' see MARTIN,
Joy
CRANDALL, Norma ('Norma Mc-
Carty'; 'Wilson Chamberlain'),
1907- , American; nonfiction,
poetry, translations CON
CRANDELL, Richard F., 1901-74,
American; journalism, non-
fiction CON
CRANE, Caroline, 1930- , Amer-
ican; plays, juveniles CO
WAR
CRANE, Catherine Cowle, 1940- ,
American; nonfiction CON
CRANE, Diana, 1933- , Canadian-
American; nonfiction CON
CRANE, Donald Paul, 1933- ,
American; nonfiction CON
CRANE, Frances Kirkwood, 1896- ,
American; fiction REI ST
CRANE, Frank H., 1912- , Amer-
ican; nonfiction CON
CRANE, Hart, 1899-1932, Amer-
ican; poetry AM BR BU MAG
PO RO SEY VP
CRANE, Joan St. Clair, 1927- ,
American; nonfiction CON

CRANE, Julia Gorham, 1925- ,
American; nonfiction CON
CRANE, Maureen, see WARTSKI,
Maureen A.
CRANE, Richard Arthur, 1944- ,
British; plays, tv CON
'CRANE, Robert' see SELLERS,
Connie L. , Jr.
CRANE, Robert' (Bernard Glem-
ser), 1908- , English; fiction
NI
CRANE, Robert Dickson, 1929- ,
American; nonfiction CON
CRANE, Ronald Salmon, 1886-
1967, English; nonfiction BOR
BR BU CON
CRANE, Royston Campbell (Roy),
1901-77, American; juveniles
CO CON
CRANE, Stephen Townley ('Johns-
ton Smith'), 1871-1900, Amer-
ican; fiction, journalism, ju-
veniles, poetry AM BR BU
COM MAG PO VN
CRANE, Theodore Rawson, 1929- ,
American; nonfiction CON
CRANE, Walter, 1845-1915, Eng-
lish; juveniles CO
CRANE, Wilder Willard, 1928- ,
American; nonfiction CON
CRANE, William Earl, 1899- ,
American; nonfiction CON
CRANIN, Abraham Norman, 1927- ,
American; nonfiction CON
CRANMER, Thomas, 1489-1556,
English; nonfiction BU DA
PO
'CRANSTON, Edward' see FAIR-
CHILD, William
CRANSTON, Mechthild ('Michele
Delorme'), German-American;
nonfiction CON
CRANWELL, John Philips, 1904- ,
American; nonfiction CON
CRAON, Amauri, fl. 1180-1220,
French; poetry BU
CRAON, Maurice, fl. 1180-1220,
French; poetry BU
CRAON, Pierre, fl. 1180-1220,
French; poetry BU
CRAPANZANO, Vincent Bernard,
1939- , American; nonfic-
tion CON
CRAPOL, Edward Paul, 1936- ,
American; nonfiction CON
CRAPPS, Robert W. , 1925- ,
American; nonfiction CON
CRARY, Margaret Coleman,

1906- , American; juveniles
CO
CRASHAW, Richard, 1612/13-49,
English; poetry, translations
BRI BU DA MAG PO RU VP
CRASSUS, Lucius Licinius, 140-
91 B.C. , Roman; nonfiction
LA
CRATES, fl. 450-25 B.C. , Greek;
plays BU
CRATES of MALLUS, 2nd century
B.C. , Greek; nonfiction GR
CRATES of THEBES, 365-285 B.C. ,
Greeks; nonfiction BU
CRATINUS, 510/490-23?, B.C. ,
Greek; plays, poetry BU
CRATON, Michael John, 1931- ,
American; nonfiction CON
CRAVEIRINHA, José ('José Gr.
Vetrinha'), 1922- , Mozam-
bican; fiction, poetry, journal-
ism CL HER JA
CRAVEN, George Milton, 1929- ,
American; nonfiction CON
CRAVEN, Margaret, 1901-80,
American; fiction, nonfiction
CON
CRAVEN, Roy C. , Jr. , 1924- ,
American; nonfiction CON
CRAVEN, Thomas, 1889-1969,
American; juveniles, fiction,
nonfiction CO CON
CRAVEN, Wesley Frank, Jr. ,
1905-81, American; nonfiction
CON
CRAVENS, Gwyneth, American;
nonfiction CON
CRAVENS, Hamilton, 1938- ,
American; nonfiction CON
CRAWFORD, Alan, 1953- , Amer-
ican; nonfiction CON
CRAWFORD, Char ('Charlene John-
son'), 1935- , American; fic-
tion, nonfiction CON
CRAWFORD, Charles Merle, 1924- ,
American; nonfiction CON
CRAWFORD, Charles P. , 1945- ,
American; nonfiction CON
CRAWFORD, Charles Wann, 1931- ,
American; nonfiction CON
CRAWFORD, Christian, 1939- ,
American; nonfiction CON
CRAWFORD, Clan, Jr. , 1927- ,
American; nonfiction CON
CRAWFORD, David L. , 1890-1974,
American; nonfiction CON
CRAWFORD, Deborah, 1922- ,
American; juveniles, nonfiction

CO CON
CRAWFORD, Donald Wesley,
1938- , American; nonfiction
CON
CRAWFORD, Francis Marion,
1854-1909, American; fiction
BR VN
CRAWFORD, Fred Roberts, 1924- ,
American; nonfiction CON
CRAWFORD, Isabella Valancy,
1850-87, Canadian; poetry,
fiction BU VP
CRAWFORD, James M., 1925- ,
American; nonfiction CON
CRAWFORD, John Edmund, 1904-
71, American; juveniles CO
CRAWFORD, John R., 1915?-76,
American; nonfiction CON
CRAWFORD, John William, 1936- ,
American; nonfiction, poetry
CON
CRAWFORD, Kenneth Gale, 1902- ,
American; nonfiction CON
CRAWFORD, Linda, 1938- ,
American; fiction CON
CRAWFORD, Max, 1938- , Amer-
ican; fiction CON
CRAWFORD, Oliver, 1917- ,
American; film, fiction CON
CRAWFORD, Patricia, American;
nonfiction CON
CRAWFORD, Phyllis ('Josie Tur-
ner'), 1899- , American; ju-
veniles CO
CRAWFORD, Richard Arthur,
1935- , American; nonfiction
CON
'CRAWFORD, Robert' see RAE,
Hugh C.
CRAWFORD, Stanley Gottlieb,
1937- , American; fiction
CON
CRAWFORD, William L., 1911- ,
American; nonfiction NI
CRAWLEY, Aidan Merivale,
1908- , English; journalism,
nonfiction CON
CRAY, Edward, 1933- , Amer-
ican; nonfiction CON
CRAYDER, Dorothy, 1906- ,
American; juveniles, radio,
tv, fiction CO WAR
CRAYENCOUR, Marguerite de
see 'YOURCENAR, Mar-
guerite'
'CRAYON, Geoffrey' see IRVING,
Washington
'CRAYON, Porte' see STROTHER,

David H.
CRAZ, Albert G., 1926- , Amer-
ican; juveniles CO
CREAN, John Edward, Jr., 1939- ,
American; nonfiction CON
CREANGA, Ion, 1837-89, Ruman-
ian; nonfiction BU TH
CREASEY, John ('J. J. Marric';
'Anthony Morton'; 'Gordon
Ashe'; 'Norman Deane'; 'Mich-
ael Halliday'; 'Kyle Hunt'; 'Pe-
ter Manton'; 'Richard Martin';
'Jeremy York'; 'Ken Ranger';
'William K. Reilly'; 'Tex Reil-
ly'), 1908-73, English; fiction
CON MCC NI REI ST WA
CREASY, Sir Edward Shepherd,
1812-78, English; nonfiction
BU
CREBILLON, Fils, Claude Prosper
Jolyot de, 1707-77, French;
fiction BU TH
CREBILLON, Père, Prosper Jolyot
de, 1674-1762, French; plays
BU MAG MCG TH
CRECINE, John Patrick, 1939- ,
American; nonfiction CON
'CRECY, Jeanne' see WILLIAMS,
Jeanne
CREDLAND, Peter Francis, 1946- ,
British; nonfiction CON
CREEKMORE, Betsey Beeler,
1915- , American; nonfiction
CON
CREEKMORE, Hubert, 1907-66,
American; poetry, fiction BA
CREEL, Herrlee Glessner, 1905- ,
American; journalism, nonfic-
tion CON
CREEL, Stephen Melville ('E. B.
Sachem'), 1938- , American;
fiction CON
CREELEY, Robert White, 1926- ,
American; poetry, fiction, non-
fiction BR BU MAL PO SEY
VCP VP WA
CREER, Thomas Laselle, 1934- ,
American; nonfiction, juveniles
CON
CREETH, Edmund Homer, 1928- ,
American; nonfiction CON
CREGAN, David Appleton, 1931- ,
British; plays, fiction CON
VCD
CREGIER, Don Mesick, 1930- ,
American; nonfiction CON
CREIGHTON, Donald Grant, 1902-
79, Canadian; nonfiction CON

CREIGHTON
CREIGHTON, Joanne Vanish, 1942- , American; nonfiction CON
CREIGHTON, Mary Helen, 1899- , Canadian; nonfiction CON
CRELLIN, John, 1916- , American; nonfiction CON
CREMAZIE, Joseph Octave, 1827-79, Canadian; poetry BU
CREMER, Jacobus Jan, 1827-80, Dutch; nonfiction BU
CREMER, Jan, 1940- , Dutch; fiction, plays BU
CREMER, Robert Roger, 1947- , American; nonfiction CON
CREMIEUX, Benjamin, 1888-1944, French; nonfiction CL
CREMUTIUS, Cordus Aulus, -25 A.D., Roman; nonfiction GR LA
CRENNE, Hélisenne de, fl. 1540, French; fiction BU
CRENSHAW, Mary Ann, American; nonfiction CON
CRESCAS, Hasdai, 1340-1410, Hebrew; nonfiction BU TH
CRESSON, Bruce Collins, 1930- , American; nonfiction CON
CRESSWELL, Helen, 1934/36- , English; juveniles, tv, plays DEM KI
CRETAN, Gladys Yessayan, 1921- , American; juveniles WAR
CRETIN, Guillaume, 1460?-1525, French; poetry BU TH
CREUTZ, Count Gustaf Philip, 1731-85, Swedish; poetry BU TH
CREVECOEUR, Michel Guillaume Jean de, 1735-1813, American; nonfiction AM BR BU MAG PO
CREVEL, René, 1900-35, French; nonfiction, fiction CL
CREW, Helen Cecilia Coale, 1866-1941, American; juveniles, poetry, fiction COM
CREW, Louie, 1936- , American; nonfiction CON
CREWS, Frederick Campbell, 1933- , American; nonfiction BOR
CREWS, Harry Eugene, 1935- , American; fiction KIB WAK
CREWS, Judson, 1917- , American; poetry VCP

CRICHLOW, Ernest, 1914- , American; juveniles DEM
CRICHTON, Kyle Samuel ('Robert Forsythe'), 1896-1960, American; nonfiction, fiction CON
CRICHTON, Michael ('John Lange'; 'Jeffery Hudson'; 'Michael Douglas'), 1942- , American; fiction AS CO NI REI VCN WAK
CRICK, Donald Herbert, 1916- , Australian; fiction CON
CRIDEN, Joseph, 1916- , American; nonfiction CON
CRILE, George, Jr. (Barney), 1907- , American; nonfiction CON
CRIM, Mort, 1935- , American; nonfiction CON
CRINER, Beatrice, American; juveniles WAR
CRINER, Calvin, American; juveniles WAR
CRIPE, Helen, 1932- , American; nonfiction CON
CRIPPS, Louise Lilian (Louise Cripps Samoiloff), 1914- , British; nonfiction CON
CRIPPS, Thomas Robert, 1932- , American; nonfiction CON
CRISINEL, Edmond Henri, 1897-1948, Swiss; poetry BU
CRISOLORA, Maneule, 1350?-1415, Byzantine; nonfiction, translations BU
CRISP, Anthony Thomas ('Mark Western'), 1937- , British; nonfiction CON
CRISP, Frank Robson, 1915- , British; fiction NI
CRISP, Norman James, 1923- , American; fiction, plays, tv CON
'CRISPIN, Edmund' (Robert Bruce Montgomery), 1921-78, British; fiction AS NI REI ST WA
CRISPIN, John, 1936- , Belgian-American; nonfiction, translations CON
CRISPIN, Ruth Helen Katz, 1940- , American; nonfiction CON
CRIST, Judith, 1922- , American; nonfiction CON
CRIST, Lyle Martin, 1924- , American; nonfiction CON
CRIST, Raymond E., 1904- , American; nonfiction CON
CRIST, Steven Gordon, 1956- ,

American; nonfiction CON
'CRISTABEL' see ABRAHAMSEN,
Christine E.
CRISTOFER, Michael, 1946- ,
American; plays MCN
'CRISTOFILO Sardanapalo' see
TAPIA y RIVERA, Alejandro
CRITCHFIELD, Howard John,
1920- , American; nonfiction
CON
CRITCHFIELD, Richard, 1931- ,
American; nonfiction CON
CRITCHLEY, Julian Michael ('Wil-
liam Beaufitz'), 1930- , Brit-
ish; nonfiction CON
CRITES, Ronald Wayne, 1945- ,
American; nonfiction CON
CRITES, Stephen Decatur, 1931- ,
American; nonfiction, trans-
lations CON
CRITIAS of ATHENS, -403 B.C.,
Greek; nonfiction BU
CRITOBULUS, Michael, 1400?-67,
Byzantine; nonfiction LA
CRITTENDEN, Mabel Buss,
1917- , American; nonfic-
tion CON
CRNJANSKI, Miloš, 1893- , Ser-
bian; poetry, plays, fiction,
journalism BU CL TH WAK
CROCE, Benedetto, 1866-1952,
Italian; nonfiction BO BU CL
MAG TH
CROCE, Giulio Cesare, 1550-1609,
Italian; fiction, poetry BO
CROCETTI, Guido M., 1920-79,
American; nonfiction CON
CROCKER, Helen Bartter, 1929- ,
American; nonfiction CON
CROCKER, Mary Wallace, 1941- ,
American; nonfiction CON
CROCKETT, Albert Stevens, 1873-
1969, American; journalism,
nonfiction CON
CROCKETT, David, 1786-1836,
American; nonfiction BA BR
MAG MYE
CROCKETT, James Underwood,
1915-79, American; nonfiction
CON
CROCKETT, Samuel Rutherford,
1860-1914, British; juveniles,
fiction, poetry BU DA KI
CROCUS, Cornelius, 1500-50,
Dutch; plays BU
'CROFT, Sutton' see LUNN,
Arnold
CROFT-COOKE, Rupert ('Leo

Bruce'), 1903-79, British;
nonfiction, fiction CON REI
CROFT-MURRAY, Edward, 1907-
80, British; nonfiction CON
CROFTS, Freeman Wills, 1879-
1957, Irish; fiction DA REI
ST
CROFUT, William E., III, 1934- ,
American; juveniles CO
'CROISSET, Francis de' (Frantz
Wiener), 1877-1937, French;
plays MCG
CROIZIER, Ralph, 1935- , Ca-
nadian; nonfiction CON
CROKER, John Wilson, 1780-1857,
Irish; nonfiction, journalism
BU DA HO PO
CROKER, Thomas Crofton, 1798-
1854, Irish; nonfiction BU HO
CROLY, Rev. George, 1780-1860,
English; fiction NI
CROMAN, Dorothy Y. see PICARD,
Dorothy Y.
CROMIE, Alice Hamilton ('Vivian
Mort'), 1914- , American;
juveniles CO WAR
CROMIE, Robert, 1856-1907, Eng-
lish; fiction NI
CROMIE, William Joseph, 1930- ,
American; juveniles CO WAR
CROMMELYNCK, Fernand, 1885/88-
1969/70, Belgian; plays BU
CL CON MCG TH WA
CROMPTON, Anne Eliot, 1930- ,
American; juveniles CO WAR
'CROMPTON, Richmal' see LAM-
BURN, Richmal C.
CROMWELL, Chester R., 1925- ,
American; nonfiction CON
'CROMWELL, Elsie' see LEE,
Elsie
CROMWELL, John, 1887-1979,
American; director, producer
CON
CROMWELL, John, 1914?-79,
British; fiction, plays CON
CROMWELL, Otelia, American;
nonfiction SH
CROMWELL, Richard Sidney,
1925- , American; nonfiction
CON
CRONBACH, Abraham, 1882-1965,
American; juveniles CO
CRONE, Anne, 1915- , Irish;
fiction HO
CRONE, Ruth, 1919- , American;
juveniles CO
CRONEGK, Johann Friedrich von,

1731-58, German; plays BU
TH
CRONIN, Anthony, 1926- , Irish;
poetry, nonfiction, fiction HO
CRONIN, Archibald Joseph, 1896-
1981, British; fiction, plays,
nonfiction BU CO CON DA
VCN
CRONIN, Charles B. <u>see</u> 'NORTH,
Eric'
CRONIN, George, 1933- , Amer-
ican; fiction CON
CRONIN, James Emmett, 1908- ,
American; nonfiction CON
CRONIN, Joseph Marr, 1935- ,
American; nonfiction CON
CRONIN, Sylvia, 1929- , Amer-
ican; journalism CON
CRONIN, Thomas Edward, 1940- ,
American; nonfiction CON
CRONKITE, Walter Leland, Jr.,
1916- , American; nonfiction
CON
CRONLEY, Jay, 1943- , Amer-
ican; fiction, nonfiction CON
CRONNE, Henry Alfred, 1904- ,
British; nonfiction CON
CROOK, Bette Jean ('San Leslie'),
1921- , American; poetry,
journalism CON
CROOK, Compton N. <u>see</u> 'TALL,
Stephen'
CROOK, David, 1910- , British;
nonfiction CON
CROOK, Isabel, 1915- , British;
nonfiction CON
CROOK, Joseph Mordaunt, 1937- ,
English; nonfiction CON
CROOK, William, 1933- , Brit-
ish; nonfiction CON
CROOKENDEN, Napier, 1915- ,
British; nonfiction CON
CROPPER, Margaret, 1886-1980,
British; poetry CON
CROS, Charles, 1842-88, French;
poetry BU TH
CROSBIE, John Shaver, 1920- ,
Canadian; nonfiction CON
CROSBIE, Sylvia (Kowitt), 1938- ,
American; fiction, nonfiction
CON
CROSBY, Alexander L., 1906-80,
American; journalism, nonfic-
tion CO CON
CROSBY, Caresse, 1892-1970,
American; poetry RO
CROSBY, Donald Allen, 1932- ,
American; nonfiction CON

CROSBY, Donald Francis, 1933- ,
American; nonfiction CON
CROSBY, Harry, 1898-1929, Amer-
ican; poetry, diary RO
CROSBY, Harry C., Jr. <u>see</u> 'AN-
VIL, Christopher'
CROSBY, James O'Hea, 1942- ,
American; nonfiction CON
CROSBY, Philip Bayard, 1926- ,
American; nonfiction CON
CROSBY, Ruth, 1897- , American;
nonfiction CON
CROSHER, Geoffrey Robins ('G. R.
Kestevan'), 1911- , English;
juveniles CO CON
CROSLAND, Andrew Tate, 1944- ,
American; nonfiction CON
CROSLAND, Anthony, 1918-77,
British; nonfiction CON
CROSLAND, Margaret, 1920- ,
English; nonfiction, transla-
tions, poetry CON
CROSS, Alan Beverley, 1931- ,
British; plays, fiction CON
VCD
'CROSS, Amanda' <u>see</u> HEILBRUN,
Carolyn G.
CROSS, Donna Woolfolk, 1947- ,
American; nonfiction CON
CROSS, Eric, 1903- , Irish; fic-
tion HO
CROSS, Frank Moore, Jr., 1921- ,
American; nonfiction CON
CROSS, Helen <u>see</u> BROADHEAD,
Helen
CROSS, Herbert James, 1934- ,
American; nonfiction CON
CROSS, Ian, 1925- , New Zeal-
ander; fiction, plays DA VCN
CROSS, John Keir ('Stephen Mac-
Farlane'; 'Susan Morley'),
1914-67, Scots; juveniles, fic-
tion CON NI
CROSS, Leslie Frank, 1909-77,
American; nonfiction CON
CROSS, Milton John, 1897-1975,
American; nonfiction CON
CROSS, Ralph Donald, 1931- ,
American; nonfiction CON
CROSS, Robert, 1912-80, British;
nonfiction CON
CROSS, Samuel Stephen, 1919- ,
American; nonfiction CON
CROSS, Theodore Lamont, 1924- ,
American; nonfiction CON
'CROSS, Victor' <u>see</u> COFFMAN,
Virginia E.
CROSSAN, Darryl' <u>see</u> SMITH,

Richard R.
CROSSCUP, Richard, 1905- ,
American; juveniles WAR
CROSSEN, Kendell Foster
('Bennet Barlay'; 'M. E.
Chaber'; 'Richard Foster';
'Christopher Monig'; 'Clay
Richards'), 1910- , Amer-
ican; fiction AS NI REI
CROSSLEY-HOLLAND, Kevin
John, 1941- , British; poetry,
juveniles, translations CO
CON DEM KI VCP WAR
CROSSMAN, Richard Howard Staf-
ford, 1907-74, British; non-
fiction CON WA
CROTHERS, Rachel, 1878-1958,
American; plays MCG MCN
VD
'CROTUS RUBEANUS' (Johann
Jäger), 1480-1539?, German;
nonfiction BU
CROUCH, Harold Arthur, 1940- ,
Australian; nonfiction CON
CROUCH, Marcus, 1913- , Eng-
lish; juveniles CO
CROUCH, Stanley, American;
fiction SH
CROUCH, Steve, 1915- , Amer-
ican; nonfiction CON
CROUCH, Thomas William,
1932- , American; nonfiction
CON
CROUCH, William George Alfred,
1903-70, British; nonfiction
CON
CROUSE, Russel, 1893-1966,
American; journalism, plays
CON MCG
CROUSE, Timothy, 1947- ,
American; journalism CON
CROUT, George Clement, 1917- ,
American; juveniles CO
CROW, Charles Patrick, 1938- ,
American; journalism, fiction
CON
CROW, Duncan, 1920- , Scots;
nonfiction CON
CROW, Elizabeth Smith, 1946- ,
American; journalism CON
CROW, Jeffrey Jay, 1947- ,
American; nonfiction CON
CROW, Mark Alan, 1948- ,
American; poetry CON
CROW, William Bernard, 1895-
1976, British; nonfiction
CON
'CROWBATE, Ophelia Mae' see

SMITH, C. U.
CROWCROFT, Peter ('Jane Crow-
croft'; 'James Muntz'; 'Max
Orloff'), 1923- , Anglo-
American; fiction CON NI
CROWDER, Christopher, M. D.,
1922- , British; nonfiction CON
CROWE, Amanda (Cockrell),
1948- , American; journalism,
fiction CON
CROWE, Bettina Lum ('Peter
Lum'), 1911- , American;
juveniles CO
CROWE, Catherine Stevens, 1800-
76, English; fiction BU
CROWE, Charles Monroe, 1902-78,
American; nonfiction CON
'CROWE, F. J.' see JOHNSTON,
Jill
'CROWE, John' see 'COLLINS,
Michael'
CROWE, Kenneth Charles, 1934- ,
American; nonfiction CON
CROWE, Philip Kingsland, 1908-
76, American; nonfiction CON
CROWE, Robert Lee, 1937- ,
American; nonfiction CON
CROWE-CARRACO, Carol, 1943- ,
American; nonfiction CON
CROWELL, Ann, American; juve-
niles WAR
CROWELL, Joan, 1921- , Amer-
ican; fiction, nonfiction CON
CROWELL, Muriel Beyea, 1916- ,
American; nonfiction CON
'CROWFIELD, Christopher' see
STOWE, Harriet B.
CROWLEY, Ellen Teresa, 1943- ,
American; nonfiction CON
CROWLEY, John, 1942- , Amer-
ican; fiction CON NI
CROWLEY, John Edward, 1943- ,
American; nonfiction CON
CROWLEY, John William, 1945- ,
American; nonfiction CON
CROWLEY, Mart, 1935- , American;
plays CON MCG MCN VCD
CROWLEY, Mary C., 1915- ,
American; nonfiction CON
CROWLEY, Robert, 1518?-88,
English; printer BU
CROWNE, John, 1640?-1703/12,
English; plays BU DA MCG
PO VD
CROWNFIELD, Gertrude, 1867-
1945, American; fiction, poetry,
juveniles COM
CROWSON, Paul Spiller, 1913- ,

CROWTHER 240

English; nonfiction CON
CROWTHER, Betty, 1939- ,
American; nonfiction CON
CROWTHER, Bosley, 1905-81,
American; journalism, plays,
nonfiction CON
'CROWTHER, Brian' see GRIER-
SON, Edward D.
CROWTHER, James Gerald,
1899- , English; juveniles
CO CON
CROWTHER, Samuel Adjai, 1807-
91, Nigerian; nonfiction JA
CROXFORD, Leslie, 1944- ,
American; fiction CON
CROXTON, Anthony Hugh, 1902- ,
English; nonfiction CON
CROY, Homer, 1883-1965, Amer-
ican; journalism, fiction,
nonfiction CON RO
CRUICKSHANK, Allan Dudley,
1907-74, American; nonfiction
CON
CRUICKSHANK, Helen Burness,
1886/96- , Scots; poetry
DA VCP
CRUICKSHANK, William Mellon,
1915- , American; nonfiction
CON
CRUIKSHANK, George, 1792-1878,
English; juveniles CO
CRUL, Cornelis, 1500-50, Dutch;
poetry BU
CRUMBAKER, Alice ('Allison
Baker'), 1911- , American;
fiction CON
CRUMLEY, James, 1939- ,
American; fiction CON
CRUMM, Lloyd Carlton, Jr.,
1927- , American; nonfiction
CON
CRUMP, Fred H., Jr., 1931- ,
American; juveniles CO
CRUMP, Galbraith Miller, 1929- ,
American; nonfiction CON
CRUMP, James Irving, 1887-
1979, American; juveniles,
journalism CO CON
CRUMP, Stephen Thomas, 1929- ,
English; nonfiction CON
CRUMPLER, Frank Hunter,
1935- , American; nonfiction
CON
CRUMPLER, Gus Hunt, 1911- ,
American; nonfiction CON
CRUNDEN, Frederick Morgan,
1847-1911, American; nonfic-
tion ENG

'CRUNDEN, Reginald' see CLEAV-
ER, Hylton
CRUSE, Harold W., American;
nonfiction CON SH
CRUSENSTOLPE, Magnus Jacob,
1795-1865, Swedish; journalism,
nonfiction, fiction BU
CRUSO, Thalassa, 1909- , Anglo-
American; nonfiction CON
CRUZ, Agostinho da, 1540-1619,
Portuguese; poetry BU
CRUZ, Bernardo Roberto, 1941- ,
American; nonfiction MAR
CRUZ, Gilbert R., 1929- , Amer-
ican; nonfiction, plays MAR
CRUZ, Joan Carroll, 1931- ,
American; fiction, nonfiction
CON
CRUZ, Sor Juana Inés de la (Juana
d. de Asbaje y Ramírez de
Santillana), 1648/51-95, Span-
ish; poetry, plays, nonfiction
BR BU MAG
CRUZ, Martha O., 1943- , Amer-
ican; nonfiction MAR
CRUZ, Raymond, 1933- , Amer-
ican; juveniles CO
CRUZ, Tomaz Vieira da, 1900- ,
Angolan; poetry JA
CRUZ, Victor Hernandez, 1949- ,
Puerto Rican; poetry CON
MAL VCP
CRUZ, Viriato da, 1928- , Ango-
lan; poetry JA
CRUZ CANO y OLMEDILLA, Ramón
de la, 1731-94, Spanish; plays,
translations, poetry BU MCG
TH
CRUZ e SILVA, Antonio Dinis da,
1731-99, Portuguese; poetry
BU
CRUZ e SOUSA, João de, 1861-98,
Brazilian; poetry BR BU
CRUZ MONCLOVA, Lidio, 1899- ,
Puerto Rican; nonfiction HIL
CRUZ y NIEVES, Antonio, 1907- ,
Puerto Rican; poetry, journal-
ism HIL
CRYSTAL, John Curry, 1920- ,
American; nonfiction CON
CSEZMICZEY, János, 1434-72,
Hungarian; poetry BU
CSIKOS-NAGY, Bela, 1915- ,
Hungarian; nonfiction CON
CSIKY, Gergely, 1842-91, Hungar-
ian; plays MCG
CSOKONAI VITEZ, Mihály, 1773-
1805, Hungarian; poetry, plays

BU TH
CSOKOR, Franz Theodor, 1885-
1969, Austrian; fiction, po-
etry, plays MCG
CTESIAS, fl. 400 B.C. , Greek;
nonfiction BU GR LA
CTVRTEK, Václav, 1911-76,
Czech; juveniles DEM
CUADRA, José de la, 1903-41,
Ecuadorian; fiction BR
CUADRA, Pablo Antonio, 1912- ,
Nicaraguan; poetry, plays
BR
CUBILLO de ARAGON, Alvaro,
1596?-1661, Spanish; plays,
poetry BU MCG
CUBRANOVIC, Andrija, 1480-
1520, Ragusan; poetry BU
CUCHI COLL, Isabel, 1904- ,
Puerto Rican; journalism,
poetry, plays HIL
CUDAHY, Brian James, 1936- ,
American; nonfiction CON
CUDDIHY, John Murray,
1922- , American; nonfiction
CON
CUDDY, Don, 1925- , American;
nonfiction CON
CUDWORTH, Ralph, 1617-88,
English; nonfiction BU
CUELHO, Art, 1943- , Ameri-
can; poetry CON
CUELLAR, Alfredo, American;
nonfiction MAR
CUELLAR, Jose B. , American;
nonfiction MAR
CUEVA, Juan de la, 1550?-
1610, Spanish; poetry, plays
BU MCG TH
CUEVAS, Clara ('Isa de Rival'),
1933- , Puerto Rican; poetry,
fiction CON
'CUFF, Barry' see KOSTE, Robert
F.
CUFFARI, Richard, 1925-78,
American; juveniles CO
CUGOANA, Ottabah, 1745/48-90?,
Ghanaian; nonfiction HER
JA
CUISENAIRE, Emile Georges,
1891?-1976, Belgian; nonfic-
tion CON
CUISENIER, Jean, 1927- ,
French; nonfiction CON
CULBERT, Samuel Alan, 1938- ,
American; nonfiction CON
CULBERTSON, Hugh M. , Amer-
ican; nonfiction CON

CULBERTSON, Judi, 1941- ,
American; journalism, nonfic-
tion CON
CULBERTSON, Manie, 1927- ,
American; nonfiction CON
CULL, John Guinn, Jr. , 1934- ,
American; nonfiction CON
CULLEN, Charles Thomas,
1940- , American; nonfiction
CON
CULLEN, Countee, 1903-46, Amer-
ican; poetry BR BU CO DEM
PO RO VP
CULLEN, George Francis, 1901-
80, American; journalism
CON
CULLEN, Joseph Patrick, 1920- ,
American; nonfiction CON
CULLEN, Lee Stowell, 1922- ,
American; journalism CON
CULLEN, Maurice Raymond, Jr. ,
1927- , American; journalism
CON
'CULLEN, Peta' see PYLE, Hilary
CULLER, Annette see PENNEY,
Annette
CULLIFORD, Stanley George,
1920- , New Zealander; non-
fiction CON
CULLIGAN, Matthew Joseph,
1918- , American; nonfiction
CON
CULLINANE, Leo Patrick, 1907?-
78, American; journalism, non-
fiction CON
CULLINEY, John L. , 1942- ,
American; nonfiction CON
'CULLINGFORD, Guy' (Constance
Lindsay Taylor), 1907- ,
British; fiction, tv REI
CULLUM, Albert, American; juve-
niles WAR
CULP, Paula, 1941- , American;
poetry CON
CULPEPPER, Robert Harrell,
1924- , America; nonfiction
CON
CULSHAW, John Royds, 1924-80,
British; nonfiction CON
'CULVER, Kathryn' see DRESSER,
Davis
CULVER, Kenneth Leon, 1903- ,
American; nonfiction CON
'CULVER, Timothy J. ' see
WESTLAKE, Donald E.
CUMALI, Necati, 1921- , Turk-
ish; poetry, fiction, plays
BU

'CUMBA' see CARRION MADURO, Tomas
CUMBERLAND, Kenneth Brailey, 1913- , English; nonfiction CON
CUMBERLAND, Marten ('Kevin O'Hara'), 1892-1972, British; fiction, plays REI
CUMBERLAND, Richard, 1732-1811, English; plays BU DA MCG PO VD
CUMBERLEGE, Marcus Crossley, 1938- , British; poetry, nonfiction CON VCP
CUMBERLEGE, Vera, 1908- , British; juveniles, plays CON
CUMBLER, John Taylor, 1946- , American; nonfiction CON
CUMBO, Kattie, 1938- , American; poetry SH
CUMES, James William Crawford ('C. W. James'), 1922- , Australian; nonfiction CON
CUMMING, Patricia Arens, 1932- , American; poetry, nonfiction, plays CON
CUMMING, Primrose Amy, 1915- , British; juveniles CO
CUMMINGS, Arthur J., 1920?-79, American; fiction, nonfiction CON
CUMMINGS, Betty Sue, 1918- , American; juveniles, fiction CO CON
CUMMINGS, Donald Wayne, 1935- , American; nonfiction CON
CUMMINGS, Edward Estlin, 1894-1962, American; poetry, fiction, plays AM BR BU CON MAG MCG PO RO SEY VP
'CUMMINGS, Florence' see BONIME, Florence
CUMMINGS, Larry Lee, 1937- , American; nonfiction CON
CUMMINGS, Monette A., American; fiction NI
CUMMINGS, Raymond King, 1887-1957, American; fiction AS COW NI
'CUMMINGS, Richard' see GARDNER, Richard
CUMMINGS, Richard Le Roy, 1933- , American; nonfiction CON
CUMMINGS, Thomas Gerald, 1944- , American; nonfiction CON

CUMMINGS, Violet May, 1905- , American; nonfiction CON
CUMMINS, Geraldine Dorothy, 1890- , Irish; plays, fiction HO
CUMMINS, Harle Owen, American; fiction NI
CUMMINS, Maria Susanna, 1827-66, American; juveniles COM
CUMMINS, Walter Merrill, 1936- , American; fiction, nonfiction CON
CUNEO, Gilbert Anthony, 1913-78, American; nonfiction CON
CUNEO, John Robert, 1911- , American; nonfiction CON
CUNHA, Euclides Rodrigues Pimenta da, 1866-1909, Brazilian; nonfiction BR BU
CUNHA, José Anastácio da, 1744-87, Portuguese; poetry BU
CUNIGGIM, Merrimon, 1911- , American; nonfiction CON
CUNLIFFE, Barrington Windsor (Barry), 1939- , English; nonfiction CON
CUNLIFFE, John Arthur, 1933- , English; juveniles CO CON
CUNNINGHAM, Aline, American; juveniles CON
CUNNINGHAM, Allan, 1784-1842, Scots; nonfiction, poetry BU DA
CUNNINGHAM, Barry, 1940- , American; nonfiction CON
CUNNINGHAM, Chet ('Cathy Cunningham'), 1928- , American; fiction, juveniles CO CON
CUNNINGHAM, Dale Speers, 1932- , American; juveniles CO
CUNNINGHAM, Donald Hayward, 1935- , American; nonfiction CON
'CUNNINGHAM, E. V.' see FAST, Howard
'CUNNINGHAM, Captain Frank' see GLICK, Carl C.
CUNNINGHAM, Imogen, 1883-1976, American; nonfiction CON
CUNNINGHAM, James Vincent, 1911- , American; poetry, nonfiction BOR VCP WA
CUNNINGHAM, John, 1727-73, Scots; poetry, plays VP
CUNNINGHAM, Joseph F. X., 1925- , American; nonfiction

CON
CUNNINGHAM, Joseph Sandy,
1928- , English; nonfiction
CON
CUNNINGHAM, Julia Woolfolk,
1916- , American; juveniles
DE KI
CUNNINGHAM, Laura, 1947- ,
American; nonfiction, fiction
CON
CUNNINGHAM, Lawrence, 1935- ,
American; nonfiction CON
CUNNINGHAM, Michael Alan,
1945- , American; nonfiction
CON
CUNNINGHAM, Noble E. , Jr. ,
1926- , American; nonfiction
CON
CUNNINGHAM, Paul James, Jr. ,
1917- , American; journalism
CON
CUNNINGHAM, Richard, 1939- ,
American; fiction CON
CUNNINGHAM, Robert Louis,
1926- , American; nonfiction
CON
CUNNINGHAM, Robert Maris,
Jr. , 1909- , American; non-
fiction CON
CUNNINGHAM, Robert Stanley,
1907- , American; nonfiction
CON
CUNNINGHAM, Ronnie Walter,
1932- , American; nonfiction
CON
CUNNINGHAM, Veronica, 1952- ,
American; poetry MAR
CUNNINGHAME GRAHAM, Robert
Bontine, 1852-1936, Scots;
nonfiction BU
CUNNINGTON, Phillis, 1887-
1974, British; nonfiction
CON
CUNQUIERO, Alvaro, 1911- ,
Spanish; fiction, nonfiction
CL
CUNTARAM PILLAI, Alappurai
Perumal, 1853-97, Tamil; non-
fiction, poetry PRU
CUNTARAR, 9th century, Tamil;
poetry PRU
CUOCO, Vincenzo, 1770-1823,
Italian; nonfiction BU
CUOMO, Mario Matthew, 1932- ,
American; nonfiction CON
CUPITT, Don, 1914- , English;
nonfiction CON
CUPPIRAMANIYA AIYAR, Vara-

kaneri V. , 1881-1925, Tamil;
nonfiction, fiction PRU
CUPPURATTINAM, Kanaka
('Bharathithasan'), 1891-1964,
Tamil; poetry PRU
CURE, Karen, 1940- , American;
nonfiction CON
CUREL, Francois de, 1854-1928,
French; plays, fiction BU CL
MCG TH
CURIATUS MATERNUS, 1st cen-
tury, Roman; poetry LA
'EL CURIOSO PARLANTE' see
MESONERO ROMANOS, Ramon
de
CURL, David H. , 1932- , Amer-
ican; nonfiction CON
CURLER, Mary Bernice (Davis),
1915- , American; nonfiction,
plays, fiction CON
CURLEY, Charles, 1949- , Amer-
ican; nonfiction CON
CURLEY, Daniel, 1918- , Amer-
ican; juveniles CO
CURLEY, Walter Joseph Patrick,
1922- , American; nonfiction
CURLING, Audrey, English; fiction,
nonfiction CON
CURLING, Bryan William Richard
('Bill Curling'; 'Hotspur';
'Julius'), 1911- , British; non-
fiction, journalism CON
CURNOW, Allen, 1911- , New
Zealander; poetry, nonfiction,
plays, poetry BU CON DA
VCD VCP VP WA
CURRAN, Dolores, 1932- , Amer-
ican; nonfiction CON
CURRAN, Donald J. , 1926- ,
American; nonfiction CON
CURRAN, Jan (Goldberg), 1937- ,
American; journalism, nonfic-
tion CON
CURRAN, Joseph Maroney, 1932- ,
American; nonfiction CON
CURRAN, Peter Malcolm, 1922- ,
American; nonfiction CON
CURRAN, Philip Read, 1911- ,
American; journalism CON
CURRAN, Robert, 1923- , Amer-
ican; journalism, nonfiction
CON
CURRAN, Thomas Joseph, 1929- ,
American; nonfiction CON
CURRAN, Ward Schenk, 1935- ,
American; nonfiction CON
CURRER-BRIGGS, Noel, 1919- ,

British; nonfiction CON
CURREY, Ralph Nixon, 1907- ,
British; poetry CON VCP
CURRIE, Anne, 1922?-80, Amer-
ican; fiction CON
CURRIE, Lauchlin, 1902- ,
Canadian-American; nonfiction
CON
CURRIER, Frederick Plumer,
1923- , American; nonfiction
CON
CURRIER, Richard Leon, 1940- ,
American; nonfiction CON
CURRIMBHOY, Asif, 1928- ,
Indian; plays PRU
CURROS ENRIQUEZ, Manuel,
1851-1908, Spanish; poetry,
journalism CL
CURRY, Andrew, 1931- ,
American; nonfiction CON
'CURRY, Avon' see BOWDEN, Jean
CURRY, David, 1942- , Amer-
ican; poetry CON
CURRY, George Edward, 1947- ,
American; nonfiction CON
CURRY, Jane Louise, 1932- ,
American; juveniles DEM
KI
CURRY, Jennifer, 1934- , Brit-
ish; juveniles, plays CON
CURRY, Martha Mulroy, 1926- ,
American; nonfiction CON
CURRY, Paul, 1917- , American;
nonfiction CON
CURRY, Peggy Simson, 1911- ,
Scots-American; juveniles
CO
CURRY, Thomas A., 1901?-76,
American; fiction, nonfiction
CON
CURRY-LINDAHL, Kai, 1917- ,
Swedish; nonfiction CON
CURTAYNE, Alice, 1898- ,
Irish; fiction, nonfiction,
translations CON
CURTEIS, Ian Bayley, 1935- ,
British; plays, tv CON
CURTIN, Mary Ellen, 1922- ,
American; nonfiction CON
'CURTIN, Philip' see LOWNDES,
Marie A. B.
CURTIN, William Martin,
1927- , American; nonfiction
CON
CURTIS, Anthony, 1926- ,
British; nonfiction CON
CURTIS, Carol Edwards, 1943- ,
American; journalism CON

CURTIS, Donald, 1915- , Amer-
ican; nonfiction CON
CURTIS, Edith Roelker, 1893-1977,
American; nonfiction CON
CURTIS, Edmund, 1881-1943, Irish;
nonfiction HO
CURTIS, George William, 1824-
92, American; nonfiction BU
MY
CURTIS, Jack, 1922- , American;
fiction, poetry CON
CURTIS, Jackie, 1947- , Ameri-
can; plays CON VCD
CURTIS, Jared Ralph, 1936- ,
American; nonfiction CON
'CURTIS, Jean Louis' (Louis La-
fitte), 1917- , French; fiction
BU NI TH
CURTIS, Lewis Perry, 1900-76,
American; nonfiction CON
CURTIS, Lindsay Raine, 1916- ,
American; nonfiction CON
CURTIS, Lynn Alan, 1943- ,
American; nonfiction CON
CURTIS, Michael Raymond,
1923- , British; nonfiction
CON
CURTIS, Norman, 1917- , Amer-
ican; nonfiction CON
CURTIS, Patricia, 1921- , Amer-
ican; juveniles CO
CURTIS, Patricia, 1924- , Amer-
ican; nonfiction CON
'CURTIS, Paul' see CZURA, Roman
P.
'CURTIS, Peter' see LOFTS, Norah
R.
CURTIS, Richard Alan, 1937- ,
American; fiction NI WAR
CURTIS, Robert H., American;
juveniles WAR
CURTIS, Rosemary Ann Stevens,
1935- , Anglo-American;
juveniles WAR
CURTIS, Thomas Bradford, 1911- ,
American; nonfiction CON
'CURTIS, Tom' see PENDOWER,
Jacques
CURTIS, Tony, 1925- , American;
nonfiction CON
'CURTIS, Wade' see POURNELLE,
Jerry E.
CURTIS, Wardon Allan, 1867- ,
American; fiction NI
CURTISS, Ursula Reilly, 1923- ,
American; fiction REI ST
CURTIUS, Ernst Robert, 1886-1956,
German; nonfiction WA

CURTIUS RUFUS, Quintus, 1st
century, Roman; nonfiction
BU GR LA
CURTLER, Hugh Mercer, 1937- ,
American; nonfiction CON
'CURVAL, Philippe' (Philippe
Tronche), 1929- , French;
fiction NI
CURVERS, Alexis, 1906- ,
Belgian; fiction CL
CURWIN, Richard Leonard,
1944- , American; nonfiction
CON
CURWOOD, James Oliver, 1878-
1927, Canadian; fiction, non-
fiction CR
CURZON, Daniel ('Daniel Rus-
sell Brown'), American; fic-
tion, plays, poetry CON
'CURZON, Lucia' see STEVEN-
SON, Florence
CUSACK, Michael Joseph ('Samuel
F. O'Gorman'), 1928- ,
Irish-American; nonfiction
CON
CUSHING, Barry Edwin, 1945- ,
American; nonfiction CON
CUSHING, Mary Watkins, 189?-
1974, American; journalism,
nonfiction CON
CUSHION, John Patrick, 1915- ,
British; nonfiction CON
CUSHMAN, Clarissa Fairchild,
1889-1980, American; fiction
CON
CUSHMAN, Jerome, American;
juveniles WAR
CUSHMAN, Robert Fairchild,
1918- , American; nonfiction
CON
CUSICK, Philip A., 1937- ,
American; nonfiction CON
CUSKEY, Walter, 1934- ,
American; nonfiction CON
CUSSLER, Clive Eric, 1931- ,
American; fiction CON
CUSTER, Chester Eugene, 1920- ,
American; nonfiction CON
'CUSTER, Clint' see PAINE,
Lauran B.
CUSTIS, George Washington
Parke, 1781-1857, American;
plays BA
CUTCHEN, Billye Walker ('Billye
Walker Brown'), 1930- ,
American; juveniles CO CON
CUTHBERTSON, Gilbert Morris,
1937- , American; nonfiction

CON
CUTHBERTSON, Tom, 1945- ,
American; nonfiction CON
CUTLER, Carl Custer, 1878-1966,
American; nonfiction CON
CUTLER, Carol, 1926- , Ameri-
can; nonfiction CON
CUTLER, Charles Locke, Jr.,
1930- , American; nonfiction
CON
CUTLER, Ivor ('Knifesmith'),
1923- , British; juveniles CO
CUTLER, May Ebbitt, 1923- ,
Canadian; juveniles, nonfiction
CO CON WAR
CUTLER, Roland, 1938- , Amer-
ican; fiction, film CON
'CUTLER, Samuel' see FOLSOM,
Franklin B.
CUTLER, William Worcester III,
1941- , American; nonfiction
CON
CUTLIFFE, Stephen Hosmer,
1947- , American; nonfiction
CON
CUTRIGHT, Paul Russell, 1897- ,
American; nonfiction CON
CUTSUMBIS, Michael Nicholas,
1935- , American; nonfiction
CON
CUTT, William Towrie, 1898- ,
Canadian; juveniles, nonfiction
CO CON KI
CUTTER, Charles Ammi, 1837-
1907, American; nonfiction
ENG
CUTTER, Fred, 1924- , American;
nonfiction CON
CUTTER, Robert Arthur, 1930- ,
American; nonfiction CON
CUTTLE, Evelyn Roeding, Ameri-
can; nonfiction CON
CUTTS, John P., 1927- , Amer-
ican; nonfiction CON
CUTUL, Ann-marie, 1945- ,
Swedish-American; nonfiction
CON
CUVAMINATA AIYAR, U. V., 1855-
1942, Tamil; nonfiction PRU
'CUYLER, Stephen' see BATES,
Barbara S.
CUYLER, Susanna Stevens, 1946- ,
American; nonfiction CON
CVIRKA, Petras, 1909-47, Lithu-
anian; poetry, fiction BU
CYDONES, Demetrius, 1324?-97/
98, Byzantine; nonfiction LA
CYNDDELW BRYDYDD MAWR, fl.

1155-1200, Welsh; poetry BU
CYNEWULF, 9th century, Anglo-
Saxon; poetry BU DA VP
CYPRIAN, St. (Thascius Calcilius
Cyprianus), 1200-58, Latin;
nonfiction BU GR LA
CYR, Donald Joseph, 1935- ,
American; nonfiction CO
CYR, John Edwin, 1915- ,
American; nonfiction CON
CYRANO de BERGERAC, Savinien,
1619-55, French; nonfiction,
plays, fiction BU NI TH
CYRIL, St. , 826/27-69, Roman;
nonfiction BU
CYRIL, Bishop of Turov, fl.
1150, Russian; nonfiction
BU
CYRIL of ALEXANDRIA, -444,
Greek; nonfiction BU
CYRIL of JERUSALEM, 313-86,
Greek; nonfiction BU
CYRIL of SCYTHOPOLIS, 524?-
60?, Byzantine; nonfiction
BU LA
CZAJA, Michael, 1911- , Amer-
ican; nonfiction CON
CZAJKOWSKI, Michael, 1804-86,
Polish; fiction BU
CZAPLINSKI, Suzanne, 1943- ,
American; nonfiction CON
CZARTORYSKI, Adam Jerzy,
1770-1861, Polish; poetry BU
'CZASZKA, Tomasz' see RITT-
NER, Tadeusz
CZAYKOWSKI, Bogdan, 1932- ,
Polish; poetry, nonfiction,
translations CL
CZECHOWICZ, Józef, 1903-39,
Polish; poetry BU CL TH
'CZEPIEL, Adam' see BRZOZOW-
SKI, Leopold S. L.
CZEPKO von REIGERSFELD,
Daniel, 1605-60, German;
poetry BU
CZERNIAWSKI, Adam, 1934- ,
Polish; poetry, nonfiction,
translations CL
CZERNY, Peter Gerd, 1941- ,
German-American; nonfiction
CON
CZUCHNOWSKI, Marian, 1909- ,
Polish; poetry, fiction CL
CZURA, Roman Peter ('Paul Cur-
tis'; 'Roman Dale'), 1913- ,
American; nonfiction CON

D

'DAALBERG, Bruno' (Petrus de
Wakker van Zon), 1758-1818,
Dutch; fiction, nonfiction BU
DAANE, Calvin John, 1925- ,
American; nonfiction CON
DABBS, James McBride, 1896-1970,
American; nonfiction BA
DABIT, Eugène, 1908-36, French;
fiction BU CL
DABKIN, Edwin Franden, 1898?-
1976, American; nonfiction
CON
DABNEY, Dick, 1933-81, American;
fiction, nonfiction CON
DABNEY, Joseph Earl, 1929- ,
American; nonfiction CON
DABNEY, Richard, 1787-1825,
American; poetry, translations
BA
DABNEY, Virginius, 1901- ,
American; nonfiction CON
DABROWSKA, Maria Szumska, 1889-
1965, Polish; fiction, plays
BU CL TH
DACE, Edwin Wallace, 1920- ,
American; nonfiction, plays
CON
DACH, Simon, 1605-59, German;
poetry BU TH
DACHS, David ('Dave Stanley'),
1922- , American; nonfiction
CON
DA COSTA, Isaac, 1798-1860,
Dutch; poetry BU
DA CRUZ, Viriato, 1928- , Ango-
lan; poetry, journalism HER
DADIE, Bernard Binlin, 1916- ,
Ivory Coaster; plays, poetry,
fiction BU HER JA LA
DADU, 1544-1603, Indian; poetry
BU
DAEMMRICH, Horst S. , 1930- ,
German-American; nonfiction
CON
DAENZER, Bernard John, 1916- ,
American; nonfiction CON
DÄUBLER, Theodor, 1876-1934,
German; poetry CL TH
DAFYDD ab EDMWND, fl. 1450-80,
Welsh; poetry BU
DAFYDD ap GWILYM, fl. 1340-70,
Welsh; poetry BU DA
DAFYDD NANMOR, fl. 1450-80,
Welsh; poetry BU DA
DAGENAIS, James Joseph, 1928- ,
American; nonfiction CON

DAGENAIS, Pierre, Canadian;
plays CR
DAGER, Edward Zicca, 1921- ,
American; nonfiction CON
DAGERMAN, Stig Halvard,
1923-54, Swedish; fiction,
plays, poetry BU CL MCG
SEY TH WAK
DAGG, Anne Innis, 1933- ,
Canadian; nonfiction CON
DAGH DIHLAVI, Navab Khan,
1831-1905, Urdu; poetry PRU
DAGLARCA, Tazil Hüsnü, 1914- ,
Turkish; poetry CL PRU
DAGLISH, Eric Fitch, 1892-1966,
British; nonfiction CON
DAGMAR, Peter, English; fiction
NI
D'AGOSTINO, Giovanna P.,
1914- , American; nonfiction
CON
D'AGOSTINO, Joseph David,
1929- , American; nonfiction
CON
DAHINDEN, Justus, 1925- ,
Swiss-American; nonfiction
CON
DAHL, Borghild, 1890- , Amer-
ican; juveniles CO DE
DAHL, Charles Curtis, 1851-1902,
American; fiction NI
DAHL, Georg, 1905- , Swedish;
nonfiction CON
DAHL, Gordon J., 1932- ,
American; nonfiction CON
DAHL, Mary B., American; juve-
niles WAR
DAHL, Nils Alstrup, 1911- ,
Norwegian; nonfiction CON
DAHL, Roald, 1916- , British;
fiction, film, juveniles AS
DE KI NI REI VCN WA
DAHL, Robert Alan, 1915- ,
American; nonfiction CON
'DAHL, Vladimir Ivanovich' (Kazak
Lugansky), 1801-72, Russian;
fiction BU
DAHLBERG, Edward, 1900-77,
American; fiction, nonfiction
BR CON VCN VN
DAHLGREN, Fredrik August,
1816-95, Swedish; nonfiction
BU
DAHLSTEDT, Marden Armstrong,
1921- , American; juveniles
CO CON WAR
DAHLSTIERNA, Gunno, 1661-1709,
Swedish; poetry BU TH

DAHMS, Alan Martin, 1937- ,
American; nonfiction CON
DAHN, Felix, 1834-1912, German;
fiction BU
DAICHES, David, 1912- , British;
nonfiction BOR
DAILEY, Charles Alvin, 1923- ,
American; nonfiction CON
DAILEY, Janet, 1944- , American;
fiction CON
DAIN, Alex, American; fiction NI
DAIN, Phyllis, 1929- , American;
nonfiction CON
'DAISNE, Johan' (Herman Thiery),
1912- , Flemish; poetry, fic-
tion, plays BU CL
DAKE, Charles Romyn, American;
fiction NI
DAKERS, Elaine Kidner ('Jane
Lane'), 1905-78, British; fic-
tion, juveniles, nonfiction
CON NI
DAKIN, David Martin, 1908- ,
British; nonfiction CON
D'ALCAMO, Cielo, early 13th cen-
tury, Italian; poetry BU
DALE, Edwin L., Jr., 1923- ,
American; nonfiction CON
'DALE, Jack' see HOLLIDAY,
Joseph
DALE, Jan van den, 1460-1522,
Dutch; poetry BU
'DALE, Norman' see DENNY,
Norman G.
DALE, Peter John, 1938- , Brit-
ish; poetry, nonfiction, transla-
tions CON VCP
'DALE, Roman' see CZURA, Roman
P.
DALE, Thomas, 1700-50, American;
nonfiction BA
DA LENTINO, Giacomo, 13th cen-
tury, Italian; poetry BO
DALES, Richard Clark, 1926- ,
American; nonfiction CON
D'ALESSANDRO, Robert Philip,
1942- , American; nonfiction
CON
DALEY, Arthur John, 1904-74,
American; journalism CON
DALEY, Joseph Andrew, 1927- ,
American; fiction CON
DALFIN d'ALVERNHA (Dauphin
d'Auvernge), 1167-1235, Pro-
vencal; poetry BU
DALGLIESH, Alice, 1893-1979,
American; juveniles CO CON
KI

DALIN, Olof von, 1708-63, Swedish; nonfiction BU
DALL, Caroline Wells Healey, 1822-1912, American; nonfiction MY
DALLAS, Eneas Sweetland, 1828-79, English; journalism, nonfiction PO
'DALLAS, John' see DUNCAN, William M.
DALLAS, Philip, 1921- , Anglo-Italian; nonfiction, translations CON
DALLAS, Ruth, 1919- , New Zealander; poetry, juveniles CON KI VCP
DALLAS-DAMIS, Athena Gianakas, 1925- , American; journalism, translations, film CON
'D'ALLENGER, Hugh' see KERSHAW, John H.
DALLING and BULWER, William Henry Lytton, 1801-72, English; nonfiction DA
DALLMAYR, Fred Reinhard, 1928- , German-American; nonfiction CON
DALL' ONGARO, Francesco, 1808-73, Italian; plays, poetry BU
'DALMAS, John' see MANDEL, Leon
DALMAU CANET, Sebastian, 1884-1937, Puerto Rican; journalism HIL
DAL POGGETTO, Newton Francis, 1922- , American; fiction CON
DALRYMPLE, Byron William, 1910- , American; nonfiction CON
DALRYMPLE, Douglas Jesse, 1934- , American; nonfiction CON
'DALTON, Claire' see BURNS, Alma
DALTON, Elizabeth, 1936- , American; nonfiction CON
D'ALTON, John, 1792-1867, Irish; poetry, nonfiction HO
DALTON, John David, 1944- , British; nonfiction CON
D'ALTON, Louis Lynch, 1900-51, Irish; plays, fiction HO
'DALTON, Priscilla' see AVALLONE, Michael A., Jr.
DALTON, Richard, 1930- , American; juveniles CON

DALTON, Stephen, 1937- , British; nonfiction CON
DALY, Augustin, 1838-99, American; plays MCG VD
DALY, Carroll John, 1889-1958, American; fiction REI ST
DALY, Donald Fremont, American; nonfiction CON
DALY, Elizabeth, 1879-1967, American; fiction REI ST
DALY, Faye Kennedy, 1936- , American; fiction CON
DALY, Herman E., 1938- , American; nonfiction CON
DALY, John Jay, 1888?-1976, American; journalism, poetry, nonfiction CON
DALY, Kathleen N., Anglo-American; juveniles WAR
DALY, Mary Tinley, 1904?-79, American; journalism CON
DALY, Maureen, American; juveniles, nonfiction KI
DALY, Padraig J., 1943- , Irish; poetry HO
DALY, Robert Welter, 1916-75, American; nonfiction CON
DALY, Saralyn Ruth, 1924- , American; nonfiction CON
DALZELL, Robert Fenton, Jr., 1937- , American; nonfiction CON
DAM, Hari Narayan, 1921- , Indian-American; nonfiction CON
DAM, Kenneth W., 1932- , American; nonfiction CON
DAM, Niels Albert, 1880-1972, Danish; fiction BU CL TH
DAMACHI, Godwin Ukandi, 1942- , Nigerian; nonfiction CON
DAMAS, León Gontran, 1912-78, French Guianan; poetry, fiction, anthology BU CON HER
DAMASUS I, Pope, fl. 366-81, Latin; nonfiction LA
d'AMATO, Alexander, 1919- , American; juveniles, nonfiction CO CON WAR
D'AMATO, Barbara, 1938- , American; plays, nonfiction CON
D'AMATO, Janet Potter, 1925- , American; juveniles, nonfiction CO CON WAR
da MATTA, Joaquim Dias Cordeiro, 1857-94, Angolan; poetry, fiction HER JA

D'AMBRA, Francesco, 1499-
1558, Italian; plays BU
'D'AMBRA, Lucio' (Renato Edu-
ardo Manganella), 1880-1939,
Italian; fiction, plays BU
D'AMBROSIO, Richard Anthony,
1927- , American; nonfiction
CON
D'AMBROSIO, Vinnie-Marie,
1928- , American; nonfiction
CON
DAMDINSÜREN, Tsendün, 1908- ,
Mongolian; nonfiction, poetry,
fiction PRU
DAMERON, John Lasley, 1925- ,
American; nonfiction CON
DAMIANI, Bruno Mario, 1942- ,
Italian-American; nonfiction
CON
DAMIÃO de GOIS, 1501-74, Portu-
guese; nonfiction TH
DAMJAN, Mischa, 1914- ,
American; juveniles WAR
DAMLE, Krsnaji K. see
'KESAVSUT'
DAMODARAGUPTA, 8-9th cen-
turies, Indian; poetry PRU
DAMON, Samuel Foster,   -1971,
American; nonfiction CON
'DAMOR, Hakji' see LESSER,
Roger H.
DAMORE, Leo, 1929- , Canadian-
American; nonfiction CON
DAMPIER, William, 1652-1715,
English; nonfiction DA
DAMROSCH, Helen see TEE-VAN,
Helen
DAMROSCH, Leopold, Jr.,
1941- , American; nonfiction
CON
DAMTOFT, Walter Atkinson,
1922- , American; nonfiction
CON
'DANA, Amber' see PAINE, Lauran
B.
DANA, Barbara, 1940- , Amer-
ican; juveniles CO
DANA, Charles Anderson, 1819-
97, American; journalism,
nonfiction MYE
DANA, John Cotton, 1856-1929,
American; nonfiction ENG
'DANA, Richard' see PAINE,
Lauran B.
DANA, Richard Henry, Sr., 1787-
1879, American; poetry, jour-
nalism BR
DANA, Richard Henry, 1815-82,

American; nonfiction BR BU
MAG MY PO VN
DANA, Richard Henry, 1927- ,
American; nonfiction CON
DANA, Robert Patrick, 1929- ,
American; poetry VCP
'DANA, Rose' see ROSS, William
E. D.
DANAHER, Kevin ('Caoimhin O.
Danachair'), 1913- , Irish;
juveniles CO
DANAN, Alexis, 1889?-1979,
French; journalism CON
'DANBY, Mary' see CALVERT,
Mary
DANCE, Stanley Peter, 1932- ,
British; nonfiction CON
D'ANCONA, Alessandro, 1835-1914,
Italian; nonfiction BU
D'ANCONA, Mirella Levi, 1919- ,
Italian-American; nonfiction
CON
DANCOURT, Florent Carton, 1661-
1725, French; plays BU MCG
DANDIN, 7th century, Sanskrit;
fiction, poetry BU LA PRU
'D'ANDREA, Kate' see STEINER,
Barbara A.
DANDRIDGE, Danske, 1854-1913,
American; poetry, nonfiction
BA
'DANE, Clemence' (Winifred Ash-
ton), 1888-1965, English; fic-
tion, plays CON MCG REI
VD
DANE, Leslie A., 1925- , Amer-
ican; journalism, nonfiction
CON
'DANE, Mark' see AVALLONE,
Michael A., Jr.
'DANE, Mary' see MORLAND,
Nigel
DANE, Nathan, 1916-80, American;
nonfiction CON
DANENBERG, Leigh, 1893-1976,
American; publisher CON
DANESH, Ahmad see DONISH, Ah-
mad
DANFORTH, Mildred E., English;
fiction NI
DANGAARD, Colin Edward, 1942- ,
Australian-American; fiction,
nonfiction CO
DANGERFIELD, George, 1904- ,
American; nonfiction WA
DANGERFIELD, Rodney ('Jack
Roy'), 1922?- , American;
nonfiction CON

DANIEL, Anita ('Anita'), 1893?-
1978, Rumanian-American;
journalism, juveniles, nonfic-
tion CO CON
'DANIEL, Anne' see STEINER,
Barbara A.
DANIEL, Emmett Randolph,
1935- , American; nonfiction
CON
DANIEL, George, 1616-57, Eng-
lish; poetry BU
DANIEL, Glyn Edmund ('Dilwyn
Rees'), 1914- , English;
nonfiction, translations CON
REI ST
DANIEL, Hawthorne, 1890- ,
American; juveniles CO
DANIEL, James, 1916- , Amer-
ican; nonfiction CON
DANIEL, Milly Hawk, American;
juveniles WAR
DANIEL, Norman Alexander,
1919- , English; nonfiction
CON
'DANIEL, Pierre' see ELIE,
Robert
DANIEL, Price, Jr., 1941-81,
American; nonfiction CON
DANIEL, Ralph Thomas, 1921- ,
American; nonfiction CON
DANIEL, Samuel, 1562/63-1619,
English; poetry, plays, non-
fiction BU DA MAG PO RU
VP
DANIEL, William Roland ('Sonia
Anderson'), 1880-1969, Brit-
ish; fiction, plays REI
DANIEL, Yuli, 1925- , Russian;
fiction CL NI
'DANIEL von SOEST', fl. 1534-
39, German; fiction BU
DANIELE, Joseph William, 1927- ,
American; nonfiction CON
'DANIELL, David Scott' (Albert
Scott Daniell), 1906-65, Brit-
ish; juveniles, plays, fiction
KI
DANIELLO, Bernardino, 1500?-
65, Italian; translations, po-
etry, nonfiction BO
DANIELLS, Lorna McLean,
1918- , American; nonfiction
CON
DANIELLS, Roy, 1902- , Cana-
dian; poetry, nonfiction CON
CR VCP
DANIELOU, Alain, 1907- ,
French; nonfiction CON

DANIELOU, Jean, 1905-74, French;
nonfiction CON
'DANIEL-ROPS' (Henry Jules
Charles Petiot), 1901-65,
French; fiction, nonfiction,
poetry CL
DANIELS, David, 1933- , Amer-
ican; nonfiction CON
DANIELS, Dorothy ('Danielle Dor-
sett'; 'Angela Gray'; 'Cynthia
Kavanaugh'; 'Helaine Ross';
'Suzanne Somers'; 'Geraldine
Thayer'; 'Helen Gray Weston'),
1915- , American; fiction
CON
DANIELS, Draper, 1913- , Amer-
ican; nonfiction CON
DANIELS, Guy, 1919- , American;
juveniles, poetry CO WAR
DANIELS, Jonathan, 1902-81,
American; fiction, nonfiction
CON
DANIELS, Leslie Noel III, 1943- ,
American; nonfiction CON
DANIELS, Mary, 1937- , Ameri-
can; journalism, nonfiction
CON
DANIELS, Norman ('Peter Brady';
'Harrison Judd'), American;
fiction CON
DANIELS, Pamela, 1937- , Amer-
ican; nonfiction CON
DANIELS, Randy Allan, 1949- ,
American; nonfiction CON
DANIELS, Robertson Balfour,
1900- , American; nonfiction
CON
'DANIELSON, J. D.' see
'JAMES, M. R.'
DANIELSON, Wayne Allen, 1929- ,
American; nonfiction CON
DANIIL, 12th century, Russian;
nonfiction BU
DANIIL the EXILE, 13th? century,
Russian; nonfiction BU
DANIIL the PRISONER, 12-13th
centuries, Russian; nonfiction
TH
DANILEVSKY, Grigory Petrovich,
1829-90, Russian; fiction BU
DANILEVSKY, Nikolay Yakolevich,
1822-85, Russian; nonfiction
BU
DANILOFF, Nicholas, 1934- ,
French; nonfiction CON
DANINOS, Pierre Charles, 1913- ,
French; fiction, journalais
BU CON WA

251

DANISH

DANISH, Barbara, 1948- , American; poetry CON
DANK, Milton, 1920- , American; nonfiction CON
DANKEY, James Philip, 1947- , American; nonfiction CON
DANN, Jack, 1945- , American; fiction, nonfiction CON NI
DANNAY, Frederic see 'QUEEN, Ellery'
DANNER, Margaret, 1915- , American; poetry SH
D'ANNUNZIO, Gabriele, 1863-1938, Italian; poetry, plays, fiction BO BU CL MAG MCG SEY TH
DANOFF, I. Michael, 1940- , American; nonfiction CON
DANQUAH, Joseph Kwame Kyeretwie Boakye, 1895-1965, Ghanaian; nonfiction, plays HER JA
DANQUAH, Mabel Dove, 1910?- , Ghanaian; fiction, journalism HER
DANSON, Lawrence Neil, 1942- , American; nonfiction CON
DANTE ALIGHIERI, 1265-1321, Italian; poetry, fiction BO BU MAG NI TH
DANTE de MAIANO, late 13th century, Italian; poetry BU
'd'ANTIBES, Germain' see SIMENON, Georges
DANTO, Bruce L., 1927- , American; nonfiction CON
'DANTON, Rebecca' see ROBERTS, Janet L.
DANTZIC, Cynthia Maris, American; juveniles CON
'DANVERS, Jack' (Camille Auguste Marie Caseleyr), 1909- , Belgian; fiction NI
DANZIG, Allan Peter, 1931- , American; nonfiction CON
DANZIG, Fred Paul, 1925- , American; nonfiction CON
DANZIGER, Edmund Jefferson, Jr., 1938- , American; nonfiction CON
DANZIGER, Kurt, 1926- , German-Canadian; nonfiction CON
'DA PONTE, Lorenzo' (Emanuele Conegliano), 1749-1838, Italian; poetry, nonfiction BO BU
DA PORTO, Luigi (Porta), 1485-

1529, Italian; poetry, nonfiction, fiction BO BU TH
DAQIQI of TUS, Abu Mansur, -952/77, Persian; poetry BU PRU
DARA SHIKOH, Muhammad, 1615-58, Indo-Persian; poetry PRU
DARBEN, Althea Gibson, 1927- , American; nonfiction SH
'DARBY, J. N.' see GOVAN, Christine N.
DARBY, Patricia Paulsen, American; juveniles, nonfiction CO CON
DARBY, Raymond K., 1912- , Canadian; juveniles CO
DARCY, Clare, American?; fiction CON
'DARCY, Jean' see LEPLEY, Jean E.
D'ARCY, Martin Cyril, 1888-1976, British; nonfiction CON
DARD, Khvaja Mir, 1721-85, Urdu; poetry PRU
DARDEN, William Raymond, 1936- , American; nonfiction CON
DARDESS, John Wolfe, 1937- , American; nonfiction CON
DARDIG, Jill Carolyn, 1948- , American; nonfiction CON
DARDIS, Tom, 1926- , American; nonfiction CON
DAREFF, Hal ('Scott Foley'), 1920- , American; nonfiction, juveniles CON
DARES PHRYGIUS, 5th century, Greek; nonfiction BU
DARGAN, Olive Tilford, 1869-1968, American; poetry, plays, fiction BA
'DARIO, Rubén' (Félix Rubén García Sarmiento), 1867-1916, Nicaraguan; fiction BR BU MAG SEY
DARITY, William A., Jr., 1953- , American; nonfiction SH
DARK, Eleanor, 1901- , Australian; fiction BU
DARK, Harris Edward, 1922- , American; nonfiction CON
DARK, Philip John Crosskey, 1918- , Anglo-American; nonfiction CON
DARKE, Marjorie, 1929- , British; juveniles, nonfiction CO CON KI
DARLEY, George, 1795-1846, Irish; poetry, nonfiction BU DA HO

DARLEY 252

PO VP
DARLEY, John McConnon, 1938- ,
American; nonfiction CON
DARLING, Edward, 1907-74,
American; nonfiction CON
DARLING, Jay Norwood ('J. N.
Ding'), 1876-1962, American;
cartoons CON
DARLING, John Rothburn, 1937- ,
American; nonfiction CON
DARLING, Lois MacIntyre,
1917- , American; juveniles
CO
DARLING, Louis, Jr., 1916-70,
American; juveniles CO CON
DARLING, Mary Kathleen, 1943- ,
American; juveniles CO CON
DARLING, Richard Lewis, 1925- ,
American; nonfiction WAR
DARLINGTON, Alice Benning,
1906-73, American; nonfiction
CON
DARLINGTON, Joy, 1947- ,
American; fiction CON
'DARLTON, Clark' (Walter Ern-
sting; 'F. MacPatterson'),
1920- , German; fiction,
translations AS NI
DARNAY, Arsen, American;
fiction NI
DARR, Ann, 1920- , American;
poetry, nonfiction CON
DARRAH, William Culp, 1909- ,
American; nonfiction CON
DARRINGTON, Hugh, English;
fiction NI
DARROCH, Sandra (Jobson),
1942- , Australian; jour-
nalism, juveniles, nonfiction
CON
DARROW, Ralph Carroll, 1918- ,
American; nonfiction CON
DARROW, Whitney, 1909- ,
American; juveniles, car-
toons, nonfiction CO CON
WAR
DART, John, 1936- , American;
nonfiction CON
DARVAS, Nicholas, 1920- ,
Hungarian; nonfiction CON
DARVEAUX, Terry Alan, 1943- ,
American; nonfiction CON
DARVILL, Fred Thomas, Jr.,
1927- , American; nonfiction
CON
DARWIN, Charles Robert, 1809-
82, English; nonfiction BU
DA MAG PO

DARWIN, Erasmus, 1731-1802,
English; nonfiction, poetry BU
DA NI PO VP
DARWIN, Leonard, 1916- , Amer-
ican; juveniles CO
'DARWIN, M. B.' see McDAVID,
Raven I., Jr.
DARYUSH, Elizabeth, 1887- ,
English; poetry CON
DAS, Deb Kumar, 1935- , Indian;
poetry, nonfiction, translations
CON VCP
DAS, Durga, 1900-74, Indian; jour-
nalism CON
DAS, Jagannath Prasad, 1931- ,
Indian-Canadian; nonfiction
CON
DAS, Jihanananda, 1899-1954,
Bengali; poetry PRU
DAS, Kamala ('Madhavikutty'),
1934- , Indian; poetry, fiction,
juveniles BU CON VCP
DAS, Sarala, 14th century, Oriyan;
poetry PRU
DAS GUPTA, Jyotirinda, 1933- ,
Indian-American; nonfiction
CON
DASH, Joan, 1925- , American;
nonfiction CON
DASHIELL, Alfred Sheppard, 1901-
70, American; journalism, non-
fiction CON
DASHKOVA, Ekaterina Romanovna,
1743-1810, Russian; plays, non-
fiction BU
DASHTI, Ali, 1894- , Persian;
fiction, nonfiction, translations
BU CON PRU
'DA SILVA, Leon' see WALLMANN,
Jeffrey M.
da SILVEIRA, Onésimo, 1935- ,
Cape Verde Islander; poetry,
nonfiction HER
DASKALOS, Alexandre, 1924-61,
Angolan; poetry HER JA
DASKAM, Josephine see BACON,
Josephine D.
DASS, Petter, 1647-1707, Nor-
wegian; poetry, hymns BU
TH
'DASS, Ram' see ALPERT, Richard
DASSONVILLE, Michel Auguste,
1927- , Franco-American;
nonfiction CON
DATER, Henry M., 1909?-74,
American; nonfiction CON
DATESH, John Nicholas, 1950- ,
American; fiction CON

DATHENUS, Petrus (Pieter Dae-
ten; Daets), 1531/32-88,
Dutch; poetry BU
DATHORNE, Oscar Ronald,
1934- , British; fiction, non-
fiction CON VCN
DATI, Giuliano,   -1524, Italian;
poetry BU
DATI, Gregorio, 1362-1435,
Italian; nonfiction BU
DATI, Leonardo di Piero, 1408-
72, Italian; poetry BU
DA TODI, Jacopone, 1236-1306,
Italian; poetry BO
DATSKI, Hamlet P. see POD-
VURZACHOV, Dimitur
DATTA, Michael Madhusudan
see DUTT, Michael M.
DATTA, Sudhindranath (Dutt),
1901-60, Bengali; poetry,
nonfiction PRU
DAUBENY, Peter Lauderdale,
1921-75, German-English;
nonfiction CON
D'AUBIGNE, Théodore Agrippa,
1552-1630, French; poetry,
nonfiction TH
DAUBON, José Antonio, 1840-
1922, Puerto Rican; poetry,
journalism HIL
DAUDET, Alphonse, 1840-97,
French; fiction, juveniles,
plays MAG MCG TH WAR
DAUDET, Léon, 1867-1942,
French; fiction BU CL
DAUDET, Louis Marie Alphonse,
1840-97, French; fiction
BU
DAUER, Manning Julian, 1909- ,
American; nonfiction CON
DAUER, Rosamond, 1934- ,
American; juveniles CO CON
DAUGHDRILL, James Harold,
Jr., 1934- , American; non-
fiction CON
DAUGHERTY, Charles Michael,
1914- , American; juveniles,
nonfiction CON CO
DAUGHERTY, James Henry, 1889-
1974, American; juveniles,
nonfiction CO CON KI
d'AULAIRE, Edgar Parin, 1898- ,
American; juveniles CO CON
KI
d'AULAIRE, Ingri Mortenson
Paris, 1904-80, American;
juveniles CO CON KI
D'AULNOY, Marie,   -1705,

French; juveniles WAR
DAUMAL, René, 1908-44, French;
poetry, fiction, nonfiction
CL TH
DAUENHAUER, Richard Leonard,
1942- , American; transla-
tions, poetry CON
DAUSTER, Frank Nicholas, 1925- ,
American; nonfiction CON
DAUTHENDEY, Max, 1867-1918,
German; poetry, fiction TH
DAUTZENBERG, Johan Michel,
1808-69, Flemish; poetry BU
DAUW, Dean Charles, 1933- ,
American; nonfiction CON
DAVANZATI, Bernardo, 1529-1606,
Italian; nonfiction, translations
BU
DAVANZATI, Chiaro, 1230/40-
1303/04, Florentine; poetry
BO BU
D'AVANZO, Mario Louis, 1931- ,
American; nonfiction CON
DAVAR, Ashok, Indian-American;
juveniles, nonfiction CON
'DAVE, Shyam' see GANTZER,
Hugh
DAVELUY, Marie Claire, 1880-
1968, Canadian; nonfiction,
juveniles CR
DAVELUY, Paule Cloutier, 1919- ,
Canadian; juveniles CO
DAVENANT, Sir William (D'Ave-
nant), 1605/06-68, English;
poetry, plays BU DA MAG
MCG PO RU VD
DAVENPORT, Basil, 1905-66,
American; anthology, nonfiction
AS NI
DAVENPORT, Benjamin Rush,
American; fiction NI
DAVENPORT, Elaine, 1946- ,
American; journalism, nonfic-
tion CON
DAVENPORT, Robert, fl. 1624-40,
English; plays DA
DAVENPORT, Thomas Rodney Hope,
1926- , British; nonfiction
CON
DAVENTRY, Leonard John, 1915- ,
British; fiction AS NI
DAVES, Delmer Lawrence,
1904/07- , American; film
CON
DAVES, Francis Marion, 1903- ,
American; fiction, poetry
CON
DAVES, Jessica, 1898?-1974,

American; nonfiction CON
DAVES, Michael, 1938- , American; juveniles WAR
DAVEY, Frankland Wilmot, 1940- , American; poetry CON
'DAVEY, Jocelyn' see RAPHAEL, Chaim
'DAVEY, John' see RICHEY, David
DAVIAU, Donald George, 1927- , American; nonfiction CON
DAVICO, Oskar, 1909- , Serbian; poetry, fiction BU CL TH
DAVID, fl. 1000-961 B. C. , Israeli; nonfiction PRU
DAVID, Alfred, 1929- , German-American; nonfiction, juveniles CON
'DAVID, Jonathan' see AMES, Lee J.
DAVID, Michael Robert, 1932- , American; plays CON
DAVID, Paul Allan, 1935- , American; nonfiction CON
DAVIDESCU, Nicolae, 1888-1954, Rumanian; poetry BU
DAVIDOW, Mike, 1913- , Russian-American; nonfiction CON
DAVIDS, Anthony, 1923- , American; nonfiction CON
DAVIDS, Richard Carlyle, 1913- , American; nonfiction CON
DAVIDSOHN, Hans see 'HODDIS, Jakob van'
DAVIDSON, Abraham A. , 1935- , American; nonfiction CON
DAVIDSON, Alan Eaton, 1924- , Irish; nonfiction CON
DAVIDSON, Angus Henry, 1898-1980, British; nonfiction, translations CON
DAVIDSON, Avram, 1923- , American; fiction, nonfiction AS CON COW NI
DAVIDSON, Basil, 1914- , English; fiction, nonfiction, journalism WA
DAVIDSON, Bill, 1914- , English; juveniles CO
DAVIDSON, Chandler, 1936- , American; nonfiction CON
'DAVIDSON, Clarissa S. ' see LIPPERT, Clarissa S.
DAVIDSON, Clifford, 1932- , American; poetry, nonfiction

CON
DAVIDSON, David, 1908- , American; fiction CON
DAVIDSON, Donald Grady, 1893-1968, American; poetry, nonfiction BA BR VP
DAVIDSON, Donald Herbert, 1917- , American; nonfiction CON
DAVIDSON, Ellen Prescott, American; fiction CON
DAVIDSON, Eva Rucker, 1894?-1974, American; nonfiction CON
DAVIDSON, Glen William, 1936- , American; nonfiction CON
DAVIDSON, Harold Gordon, 1912- , Canadian; nonfiction CON
DAVIDSON, Henry Alexander, 1905-73, American; nonfiction CON
DAVIDSON, Hugh MacCullough, 1918- , American; nonfiction CON
DAVIDSON, James West, 1946- , American; nonfiction CON
DAVIDSON, Jessica, 1915- , American; juveniles, nonfiction CO CON
'DAVIDSON, John' see REID, Charles S.
DAVIDSON, John, 1857-1909, Scots; poetry, plays, fiction BU DA PO VP
DAVIDSON, Julian M. , 1931- , Irish-American; nonfiction CON
DAVIDSON, Lionel, 1922- , British; fiction NI REI
DAVIDSON, Margaret Compere, 1936- , American; juveniles CO WAR
'DAVIDSON, Marion' see GARIS, Howard R.
DAVIDSON, Mary R. , 1885-1973, American; juveniles CO
DAVIDSON, Max D. , 1899?-1977, American; nonfiction CON
'DAVIDSON, Michael' see RORVIK, David M.
DAVIDSON, Mildred, 1935- , British; nonfiction, juveniles CON
DAVIDSON, Morris, 1898-1979, American; nonfiction CON
'DAVIDSON, Peter' see BANNERMAN, James
DAVIDSON, Philip Grant, 1902- , American; nonfiction CON

DAVIDSON, Robert Franklin,
1902-   , American; nonfiction
CON
DAVIDSON, Rosalie, 1921- ,
American; juveniles CO CON
DAVIDSON, Sandra Calder,
1935- , American; nonfic-
tion, translations, juveniles
CON WAR
DAVIDSON, Sara, 1943- , Amer-
ican; fiction CON
DAVIDSON, William, 1918- ,
American; journalism, non-
fiction CON
DAVIE, Donald Alfred, 1922- ,
British; nonfiction, transla-
tions, poetry BOR BU SEY
VCP VP WA
DAVIE, Ian, 1924- , Scots;
poetry CON
DAVIE, Michael, 1924- , Eng-
lish; nonfiction CON
DAVIES, Alfred Mervyn, 1899-
1976, British; nonfiction
CON
DAVIES, Bettilu Donna, 1942- ,
American; juveniles CON
'DAVIES, Colin' see ELLIOT, Ian
DAVIES, David I. see 'NOVELLO,
Ivor'
DAVIES, David Jacob, 1916-74,
Welsh; poetry, journalism,
translations CON
DAVIES, Edward Tegla, 1880-
1967, Welsh; fiction BU
DAVIES, Evelyn, 1924- , Eng-
lish; juveniles CON
DAVIES, Evelyn Adele, 1915- ,
American; nonfiction CON
'DAVIES, Fredric' see ELLIK,
Ronald C.
DAVIES, Harriet Vaughn, 1879?-
1978, American; nonfiction
CON
DAVIES, Howell see 'MARVELL,
Andrew'
DAVIES, Hugh Sykes, 1909- ,
English; fiction, poetry, non-
fiction NI WA
DAVIES, Hunter, 1936- , Scots;
fiction, nonfiction CON
DAVIES, Ivor Kevin, 1930- ,
English; nonfiction CON
DAVIES, J. Kenneth, 1925- ,
American; nonfiction CON
DAVIES, James Chowning, 1918- ,
American; nonfiction CON
DAVIES, John, 1565/69-1618/26,

English; poetry BU DA PO
RU VP
DAVIES, John, of Hereford, 1565?-
1618?, English; poetry BU DA
DAVIES, John Christopher, 1941- ,
British; nonfiction CON
DAVIES, John E. W. see
'MATHER, Berkly'
DAVIES, John Gordon, 1919- ,
British; nonfiction, translations
CON
DAVIES, Laurence, 1926- ,
Welsh; nonfiction CON
DAVIES, Leslie Purnell ('Leslie
Vardre'), 1914- , British;
fiction NI REI
DAVIES, Martin Brett, 1936- ,
British; nonfiction CON
DAVIES, Merton Edward, 1917- ,
American; nonfiction CON
DAVIES, Nigel, 1920- , British;
nonfiction CON
DAVIES, Norman, 1939- , Eng-
lish; nonfiction CON
DAVIES, Peter, 1937- , Anglo-
Canadian; fiction CON
DAVIES, Piers, 1941- , Australian;
poetry, film CON
DAVIES, Rhys, 1903-78, Anglo-
Welsh; poetry, fiction BU
CON DA VCN
DAVIES, Robertson, 1913- ,
Canadian; nonfiction, plays,
fiction BU CR DA MCG VCD
VCN VN WA
DAVIES, Rod, 1941- , Anglo-
Canadian; nonfiction CON
DAVIES, Rosemary Reeves,
1925- , American; nonfiction
CON
DAVIES, Samuel, 1723-61, Amer-
ican; poetry, nonfiction BA
DAVIES, Stan Gebler, 1943- ,
Irish-American; nonfiction
CON
DAVIES, Thomas Mockett, Jr.,
1940- , American; nonfiction
CON
DAVIES, William Henry, 1871-1940,
Anglo-Welsh; poetry, fiction,
nonfiction, plays BU DA PO
SEY VP
DAVILA, Alexandru, 1862-1929,
Rumanian; plays BU
DAVILA, Arturo, Puerto Rican;
nonfiction HIL
DAVILA, Enrico Caterino, 1576-
1631, Italian; nonfiction BU

DAVILA, José Antonio, 1898-
1941, Puerto Rican; poetry
HIL
DAVILA, Luis, American; non-
fiction MAR
DAVILA, Virgilio, 1869-1943,
Puerto Rican; poetry HIL
DAVIN, Daniel Marcus, 1913- ,
British; fiction, nonfiction
DA VCN VN WA
DA VINCI, Leonardo, 1452-1519,
Italian; nonfiction BO BU
MAG TH
'DAVIOT, Gordon' see 'TEY,
Josephine'
DAVIS, Adelle ('Jane Dunlap'),
1904-74, American; nonfic-
tion CON
DAVIS, Allison, 1902- , Amer-
ican; nonfiction SH
DAVIS, Angelo Yvonne, 1944- ,
American; nonfiction CON
DAVIS, Ann Elizabeth, 1932- ,
American; nonfiction CON
DAVIS, Arthur H. see 'RUDD,
Steele'
DAVIS, Arthur Paul, 1904- ,
American; nonfiction, fiction
CON SH
'DAVIS, Audrey' see PAINE,
Lauran B.
DAVIS, Ben Reeves, 1927- ,
American; journalism CON
DAVIS, Berrie, 1922- , Anglo-
American; fiction, plays
CON
DAVIS, Bette, 1908- , Amer-
ican; nonfiction CON
DAVIS, Bette J., 1923- , Amer-
ican; juveniles CO CON
DAVIS, Burke, 1913- , Amer-
ican; juveniles CO
DAVIS, Christopher, 1928- ,
American; poetry, juveniles
CO WAR
'DAVIS, Cliff' see SMITH, Richard
R.
DAVIS, Creath, 1939- , Amer-
ican; nonfiction CON
DAVIS, Daniel Sheldon, 1936- ,
American; nonfiction CO
CON
DAVIS, Daphne, American; tv
CON
DAVIS, David Howard, 1941- ,
American; nonfiction CON
'DAVIS, Don' see DRESSER, Davis
DAVIS, Donald Gordon, Jr.,

1939- , American; nonfiction
CON
DAVIS, Dorothy Salisbury, 1916- ,
American; fiction REI ST WA
DAVIS, Earle Rosco, 1905- ,
American; poetry, nonfiction
CON
DAVIS, Elise Miller, 1915- ,
American; nonfiction CON
'DAVIS, Elizabeth' see DAVIS,
Lou E.
DAVIS, Elizabeth G., 1910?-74,
American; nonfiction CON
DAVIS, Fitzroy, 1912-80, Amer-
ican; fiction, plays CON
DAVIS, Flora, 1934- , American;
nonfiction CON
DAVIS, Forest Kendall, 1918- ,
American; nonfiction CON
DAVIS, Frank Greene, 1915- ,
American; nonfiction CON
DAVIS, Frederick Clyde ('Murdo
Coombs'; 'Stephen Ransome';
'Curtis Steele'), 1902-77,
American; fiction, nonfiction
REI
DAVIS, Garold Neil, 1932- ,
American; nonfiction CON
DAVIS, Genevieve, 1928- , Amer-
ican; fiction CON
DAVIS, George, 1939- , American;
fiction, nonfiction, journalism
CON SH
DAVIS, George Littleton, Sr.,
1921- , American; nonfiction
CON
DAVIS, Gerry, British; tv, fiction
NI
'DAVIS, Gordon' see HUNT, Ever-
ette H.
DAVIS, Gordon Bitter, 1930- ,
American; nonfiction CON
DAVIS, Grania ('Mama G.'),
1943- , American; juveniles,
fiction CON
DAVIS, Harold Lenoir, 1896-1960,
American; fiction, poetry, non-
fiction CON MAG
DAVIS, Harold Seaton, 1919- ,
American; nonfiction CON
DAVIS, Harriet Eager, 1892?-1974,
American; nonfiction CON
DAVIS, Hope Harding, 1915?-76,
American; nonfiction, film
CON
DAVIS, Horance Gibbs, Jr.,
1924- , American; nonfiction
CON

DAVIS, Hubert, American; juveniles WAR
DAVIS, Irene Mary, 1926- , English; nonfiction CON
DAVIS, James H., 1932- , American; nonfiction CON
DAVIS, James Richard, 1936- , American; nonfiction CON
DAVIS, James Robert, 1945- , American; journalism CON
DAVIS, James William, 1908- , American; nonfiction CON
DAVIS, Jan Haddle, 1950- , American; nonfiction CON
DAVIS, Jean Reynolds, 1927- , American; juveniles, nonfiction CON
DAVIS, Jerome, 1891-1979, American; nonfiction CON
'DAVIS, Jim' see SMITH, Richard R.
DAVIS, Joe Lee, 1906-74, American; poetry, nonfiction CON
DAVIS, Johanna, 1937-74, American; journalism, nonfiction CON
DAVIS, John Cary, 1905- , American; nonfiction CON
DAVIS, Joseph Cole, 1908- , American; nonfiction CON
DAVIS, Joseph Stancliffe, 1885-1975, American; nonfiction CON
DAVIS, Julia ('F. Draco'), 1904- , American; juveniles CO
DAVIS, Julian, 1902?-74, American; poetry CON
DAVIS, Julie, English; editor AS
DAVIS, Kenneth Pickett, 1906- , American; nonfiction CON
DAVIS, Lance Edwin, 1928- , American; nonfiction CON
DAVIS, Lanny Jesse, 1945- , American; nonfiction CON
DAVIS, Lawrence Bennion, 1939- , American; nonfiction CON
DAVIS, Lenwood, 1939- , American; nonfiction SH
DAVIS, Lloyd Moore, 1931- , American; poetry, nonfiction CON
DAVIS, Lou Ellen ('Pat Bannister'; 'Elizabeth Davis'), 1936- , American; nonfiction,

fiction CON WAR
DAVIS, Louis Elkin, 1918- , American; nonfiction CON
DAVIS, Louise Littleton, American; nonfiction CO CON
DAVIS, Margaret Thomson, 1926- , Scots; nonfiction, fiction CON
DAVIS, Martha, 1942- , American; nonfiction CON
DAVIS, Mary B. see CURLER, Mary B.
DAVIS, Mary Lee, 1935- , American; juveniles CO CON WAR
DAVIS, Mary Octavia ('Dutz'), 1901- , American; juveniles CO
DAVIS, Melton Samillow, 1910- , American; nonfiction, translations CON
DAVIS, Michael Justin, 1925- , British; nonfiction CON
DAVIS, Mildred, American; nonfiction, fiction CON
DAVIS, Millard C., 1930- , American; nonfiction CON
DAVIS, Monte, 1949- , American; nonfiction CON
DAVIS, Morris, 1933- , American; nonfiction CON
DAVIS, Morton David, 1930- , American; nonfiction CON
DAVIS, Murray Stuart, 1940- , American; nonfiction CON
DAVIS, Myrna Mushkin, 1936- , American; nonfiction CON
DAVIS, Natalie Zemon, 1928- , American; nonfiction CON
DAVIS, Nolan, 1942- , American; fiction CON
DAVIS, Norman Maurice, 1936- , American; nonfiction CON
DAVIS, Olivia, 1922- , Anglo-American; fiction CON
DAVIS, Ossie, 1917- , American; plays, film BA MCN SH VCD WAK
DAVIS, Owen, 1874-1956, American; plays MCG
DAVIS, Patrick David, 1925- , British; nonfiction CON
DAVIS, Paxton, 1925- , American; juveniles CO
DAVIS, Philip Edward, 1927- , American; nonfiction CON
DAVIS, Polly Ann, 1931- , American; nonfiction CON
DAVIS, R. G., 1933- , American; nonfiction CON

DAVIS, Rebecca Harding, 1831-
1910, American; fiction,
journalism BA VN
DAVIS, Richard, English; fiction
CON
DAVIS, Richard Harding, 1864-
1916, American; journalism,
nonfiction, fiction, plays
BR BU PO ST VN
DAVIS, Robert, 1881-1949, Amer-
ican; juveniles COM
'DAVIS, Robert H.' see WHIT-
TINGTON, Harry
DAVIS, Rocky, 1927- , Amer-
ican; nonfiction CON
DAVIS, Russell Gerard, 1922- ,
American; juveniles CO
'DAVIS, Suzanne' see SUGAR,
Bert R.
DAVIS, Thomas Joseph, 1946- ,
American; nonfiction CON
DAVIS, Thomas Osborne, 1814-
45, Irish; poetry, nonfiction
BU DA HO
DAVIS, Timothy Francis Tot-
hill ('John Cashman'), 1941- ,
British; fiction CON
DAVIS, Tom Edward, 1929- ,
American; nonfiction CON
DAVIS, Verne Theodore, 1889-
1973, American; juveniles
CO
DAVIS, Walter Richardson, 1928- ,
American; nonfiction CON
DAVIS, William, 1933- , Eng-
lish; nonfiction CON
DAVIS, William Charles, 1946- ,
American; nonfiction CON
DAVIS, William Newell, Jr.,
1915- , American; nonfic-
tion CON
DAVIS-GOFF, Annabel, 1942- ,
Irish-American; nonfiction
CON
DAVISON, Frank Dalby, 1893-
1970, Australian; fiction BU
DAVISON, Jean, 1937- , Amer-
ican; fiction, nonfiction CON
DAVISON, Ned J., 1926- ,
American; nonfiction, poetry,
translations CON
DAVISON, Peter Hubert, 1928- ,
American; poetry VCP
WAK
DAVISON, Verne Elbert, 1904- ,
American; nonfiction CON
DAVIS-WEYER, Caecilia, 1929- ,
German-American; nonfiction

CON
DAVOYAN, Razmik, 1940- ,
Armenian; poetry PRU
DAVYDOV, Denis Vasilyevich,
1784-1839, Russian; poetry
BU
DAWDY, Doris Ostrander, Amer-
ican; nonfiction CON
DAWE, Donald Bruce, 1930- ,
Australian; poetry CON VCP
DAWE, Gerald, 1952- , Irish;
poetry HO
DAWES, Frank, 1933- , British;
nonfiction CON
DAWES, Nathaniel Thomas, Jr.,
1937- , American; nonfiction
CON
DAWIS, René Villaneuva, 1928- ,
Filipino; nonfiction CON
DAWISHA, Adeed Isam, 1944- ,
Iraqi; nonfiction CON
DAWKINS, Richard, 1941- , Brit-
ish; nonfiction CON
DAWLEY, David, 1941- , Amer-
ican; nonfiction CON
DAWLEY, Powel Mills, 1907- ,
American; nonfiction CON
'DAWLISH, Peter' see KERR,
James L.
DAWN, Clarence Ernest, 1918- ,
American; nonfiction CON
DAWOOD, Nessim Joseph, 1927- ,
English; translations, nonfiction
CON
DAWSON, Alan David, 1942- ,
Canadian; nonfiction CON
DAWSON, Carl, 1938- , English;
nonfiction CON
DAWSON, Fielding, 1930- ,
American; nonfiction, fiction
CON
DAWSON, Frank Gates, Jr.,
1925- , American; nonfiction
CON
DAWSON, Howard A., 1895?-1979,
American; nonfiction CON
DAWSON, Jan, 1939?-80, British;
nonfiction CON
DAWSON, Jennifer, 1952- , Brit-
ish; fiction CON VCN
DAWSON, Mary, 1919- , English;
juveniles CO
DAWSON, Minnie E., 1906-78,
American; nonfiction CON
DAWSON, Richard Evans, 1939- ,
American; nonfiction CON
DAWSON, William, 1704-52,
American; poetry BA

DAY, Albert Edward, 1884-1973, American; nonfiction CON
DAY, Albert M., 1897-1979, American; nonfiction CON
DAY, Beth Feagles, 1924- , American; juveniles, nonfiction WAR
DAY, Bradford Marshall, 1916- , American; nonfiction, fiction AS NI
DAY, Clarence, 1874-1935, American; nonfiction BR MAG
DAY, David, 1944- , British; nonfiction CON
'DAY, Donald' see HARDING, Donald E.
DAY, Donald Byrne, 1909-78, American; nonfiction AS NI
DAY, Dorothy, 1897-1980, American; nonfiction CON
DAY, John (Daye; Daie), 1522-84, English; printer RU
DAY, John, 1574-1640, English; plays BU DA PO RU VD
DAY, John Laurence, 1934- , American; nonfiction CON
DAY, Michael Herbert, 1927- , American; nonfiction CON
DAY, Price, 1907-78, American; journalism CON
DAY, Richard Bruce, 1942- , Canadian; nonfiction CON
DAY, Robert Adams, 1924- , American; nonfiction CON
DAY, Thomas, 1748-89, English; fiction, nonfiction, juveniles, poetry BU COM DA MAG
DAY, Truman Owen, 1890- , American; nonfiction CON
DAY LEWIS, Cecil see LEWIS, Cecil D.
DAYAN, Yaël, 1939- , Israeli; journalism, fiction, diary CON WA
DAYANANDA, James Yesupriya, 1934- , Indian; nonfiction CON
DAYARAMA, 1767-1852, Gujarati; poetry BU
DAYTON, Donald Wilber, 1942- , American; nonfiction CON
DAYTON, Edward Risedorph, 1924- , American; nonfiction CON
DAYTON, Irene, 1922- , American; poetry CON
'DAZAI OSAMU' (Tsushima Shuji),

1909-48, Japanese; fiction BU LA PRU SEY WA
DAZANA, S., 1905- , South African; fiction HER
D'AZEGLIO, Massimo Tapparelli, 1798-1866, Italian; fiction BO
D'AZEVEDO, Warren L., 1920- , American; nonfiction CON
DAZEY, Agnes Johnston, American; film, juveniles WAR
DAZEY, Frank M., American; film juveniles WAR
DE, Bisnu, 1909- , Bengali; poetry PRU
DEACON, Joseph John, 1920- , American; nonfiction CON
'DEACON, Richard' see McCORMICK, George D. K.
DEACON, Ruth E., 1923- , American; nonfiction CON
DEACON, William Arthur, 1890-1964, Canadian; journalism, nonfiction CON
DEAGON, Ann Fleming, 1930- , American; poetry CON
DEAK, Edward Joseph, Jr., 1943- , American; nonfiction CON
DEAKINS, Roger Lee, 1933- , American; nonfiction, translations CON
DEAL, Borden, 1922- , American; fiction KIB
de ALMEIDA, José Maria (Francisco Viana; Viana de Almeida), 1903- , Angolan; fiction, journalism HER
DE AMICIS, Edmondo, 1846-1908, Italian; fiction BO BU TH
DEAN, Alfreda Joan, 1925- , British; nonfiction CON
DEAN, Amber, 1902- , American; fiction REI
DEAN, Anabel, 1915- , American; juveniles CO
DEAN, Basil, 1888- , British; nonfiction, plays CON
DEAN, Burton Victor, 1924- , American; nonfiction CON
DEAN, E. Douglas, 1916- , British; nonfiction CON
DEAN, Howard Edward, 1916- , American; nonfiction CON
'DEAN, Ida' see GRAE, Ida
'DEAN, John' see BUMPPO, Nathaniel J.
DEAN, John Aurie, 1921- , American; nonfiction CON

DEAN, Leigh, American; juveniles WAR
DEAN, Luella Jo, 1908?-77, American; nonfiction CON
DEAN, Morton, 1935- , American; journalism CON
DEAN, Nancy, 1930- , American; nonfiction CON
DEAN, Roy, 1925- , English; nonfiction CON
DEAN, Stanley Rochelle, 1908- , American; nonfiction CON
DEAN, Winton Basil, 1916- , English; nonfiction CON
DEANDA, Joseph, American; nonfiction MAR
DE ANDRADE, Mário Coelho Pinto, 1928- , Angolan; poetry, nonfiction HER
De ANDREA, William Louis, 1952- , American; fiction CON
DEANE, Dee Shirley, 1928- , American; nonfiction CON
'DEANE, Elisabeth' see BEILENSON, Edna
DEANE, James Garner, 1923- , American; journalism CON
DEANE, John F., 1943- , Irish; poetry HO
'DEANE, Norman' see CREASEY, John
DEANE, Seamus Francis, 1940- , Irish; poetry HO
DE ANGELI, Marguerite Lofft, 1889- , American; juveniles KI
DEARDORFF, Robert, 1912- , American; nonfiction CON
DEARDORFF, Tom, 1940- , American; nonfiction CON
DEARLOVE, John, 1944- , British; nonfiction CON
DE ARMAND, Frances Ullman, American; juveniles CO
DEARMENT, Robert Kendall, 1925- , American; nonfiction CON
DEARSTYNE, Howard Best, 1903-79, American; nonfiction CON
DEASON, Hilary John, 1903- , American; nonfiction CON
d'EASUM, Cedric Godfrey (Dick), 1907- , Canadian-American; journalism CON
DEASY, Cornelius Michael, 1918- , American; nonfiction CON

DEATON, Charles W., 1942- , American; nonfiction CON
DEATON, John Graydon, 1939- , American; nonfiction CON
DEATS, Randy, 1954- , American; nonfiction CON
DE AVILA, Edward A., 1937- , American; nonfiction MAR
DeBAKEY, Michael Ellis, 1908- , American; nonfiction CON
DE BANKE, Cecile, 1889-1965, English; juveniles CO
deBARY, William Theodore, 1919- , American; nonfiction CON
DeBEAUBIEN, Philip Francis ('Homer Holiday'), 1913-79, American; journalism CON
DEBELYANOV, Dimcho, 1887-1916, Bulgarian; poetry BU TH
DeBENEDETTI, Charles Louis, 1943- , American; nonfiction CON
DeBERARD, Ella, 1900- , American; plays, fiction, nonfiction CON
DEBERDT-MALAQUAIS, Elisabeth, 1937- , French; translations, nonfiction CON
de BEUS, Jacobus Gysbertus, 1909- , Swiss; nonfiction CON
DE BLASIS, Celeste, 1946- , American; fiction, poetry CON
DEBLASSIE, Richard Roland, 1932- , American; nonfiction MAR
DEBO, Angie, 1890- , American; nonfiction CON
DE BONA, Maurice, Jr., 1926- , American; nonfiction CON
DeBONVILLE, Bob, 1926- , American; nonfiction CON
DE BORCHGRAVE, Arnaud, 1926- , Belgian-American; journalism, nonfiction CON
De BOSIS, Adolfo, 1863-1924, Italian; poetry BU
De BOW, James Dunwoody Brownson, 1820-67, American; nonfiction, journalism BA MYE
DE BREFFNY, Brian, 1931- , Irish; nonfiction CON
'De BRETT, Hal' see DRESSER, Davis
DEBROT, Cola, 1902- , Dutch; poetry, nonfiction BU
De BRUYN, Monica Jean, 1952- ,

American; juveniles CO CON
De BURCA, Seamus (James
Burke), 1912- , Irish; plays
HO
De CAMP, Catherine Crook,
1907- , American; juveniles
CO
DeCAMP, Graydon, 1934- ,
American; journalism CON
De CAMP, Lyon Sprague ('Lyman
R. Lyon'; 'J. Wellington
Wells'), 1907- , American;
fiction, nonfiction AS CO
COW NI WA
de CAMPI, John Webb, 1939- ,
American; nonfiction CON
De CANIO, Stephen John, 1942- ,
American; nonfiction CON
De CAPOULET-JUNAC, Edward
Georges, 1930- , French;
fiction NI
DECARIE, Therese Gouin, 1923- ,
Canadian; nonfiction CON
DeCARL, Lennard, 1940- ,
American; nonfiction CON
de CASTRO, Fernando Jose,
1937- , Cuban-American;
nonfiction CON
'DECAUX, Lucile' see BIBESCO,
Marthe L.
DECEMBRIO, Pier Candido, 1392-
1477, Italian; nonfiction,
translations BU
De CESPEDES, Alba, 1911- ,
Cuban; fiction, journalism,
plays, poetry BO
de CHAIR, Somerset Struben
('Hon. Member for X'),
1911- , English; fiction,
translations, nonfiction CON
De CHANT, John Aloysius, 1917-
74, American; nonfiction
CON
de CHARMS, Richard IV, 1927- ,
American; nonfiction CON
de CHIRICO, Giorgio, 1888-1978,
Italian; fiction, nonfiction
CON
DE CHRISTOFORO, Ronald,
1951- , American; fiction
CON
DECI, Edward Lewis, 1942- ,
American; nonfiction CON
DECK, Allan Figueroa, 1945- ,
American; nonfiction MAR
DECKER, Beatrice, 1919- ,
American; nonfiction CON
DECKER, Duane ('Richard Wayne'),

1910-64, American; juveniles
CO
DECKER, Hannah Shulman, 1937- ,
American; nonfiction CON
DECKER, Jeremias de, 1609-66,
Dutch; poetry BU
DECKER, Robert Owen, 1927- ,
American; nonfiction CON
De COCK, Liliane, 1939- ,
Belgian-American; nonfiction
CON
'DECOLTA, Ramon' see WHIT-
FIELD, Raoul
de COSTA, George Rene, 1939- ,
American; nonfiction CON
De COSTER, Charles Theodore
Henri, 1827-79, Belgian; fic-
tion BU
De COSTER, Cyrus Cole, 1914- ,
American; nonfiction CON
de COY, Robert H., American;
nonfiction SH
de CRESPIGNY, Richard Rafe,
1936- , Australian; nonfiction
CON
DECTER, Midge Rosenthal,
1927- , American; nonfiction
CON
DEDEKIND, Friedrich, 1525-98,
German; fiction, plays BU
DEDINI, Eldon, 1921- , American;
nonfiction CON
de DIENES, Andre, 1913- , Hun-
garian-American; nonfiction
CON
DEE, John, 1527-1608, English;
nonfiction RU
'DEE, Roger' (Roger Dee Aycock),
1914- , American; fiction
NI
DEEDY, John, 1923- , American;
juveniles CO
'DEEGAN, Jon J.' Hamilton house
name NI
DEEGAN, Paul Joseph, 1937- ,
American; juveniles CON
DEEKEN, Alfons, 1932- , Ger-
man; nonfiction CON
DEELEY, Roger, 1944- , Amer-
ican; fiction CON
DEEMER, Charles Robert, Jr.,
1939- , American; plays, fic-
tion CON
DEEPING, George Warwick, 1877-
1950, English; fiction DA
DEETER, Allen C., 1931- ,
American; nonfiction CON
DEEVY, Teresa, -1963, Irish;

plays HO
DeFANTI, Charles, 1942- , Amer-
ican; nonfiction CON
DE FELICE, Louise Paula, 1945- ,
American; nonfiction CON
DE FELITTA, Frank Paul, 1921- ,
American; fiction, film, tv
CON
DE FERRARIIS, Antonio ('Il Gala-
teo'), 1444-1517, Italian;
nonfiction BU
De FILIPPO, Eduardo, 1900- ,
Italian; plays, poetry BO
CL MCG
DEFOE, Daniel, 1660-1731, Eng-
lish; fiction, journalism
BRI BU CO DA MAG NI PO
VN
deFONTAINE, Wade Hampton,
1893-1969, American; jour-
nalism, nonfiction CON
DEFONTENAY, Charlemagne
Ischir, French; fiction NI
de FORD, Miriam Allen, 1888-
1975, American; fiction, jour-
nalism, poetry AS NI REI
ST
De FOREST, Charlotte B.,
1879- , American; juveniles,
poetry WAR
De FOREST, John William, 1826-
1906, American; fiction, non-
fiction BR BU MAG PO ST
VN
de FOSSARD, Ronald Alfred,
1929- , English; nonfiction
CON
DEGANI, Meir Hershtenkorn,
1909- , Polish-American;
nonfiction CON
DeGARMO, Kenneth Scott, 1943- ,
American; journalism CON
De GARZA, Patricia, ?; film,
juveniles WAR
DEGENSHEIN, George A., 1918?-
79, American; nonfiction
CON
De GERING, Etta Fowler, 1898- ,
American; juveniles CO
DEGETAU, Federico, 1862-1914,
Puerto Rican; poetry, jour-
nalism, fiction HIL
DEGH, Linda, 1920- , Hungarian-
American; nonfiction CON
DEGNAN, James Philip, 1933- ,
American; nonfiction CON
'De GRAEF, Allen' (Albert Paul
Blaustein), 1921- , American;

nonfiction NI
DeGRAFT, Joseph Coleman,
1932?- , Ghanaian; plays,
poetry, fiction CON HER VCD
de GRAMONT, Sanche ('Ted Mor-
gan'), 1932- , Swiss-American;
nonfiction, fiction CON MCC
De GRAZIA, Ettore (Ted), 1909-82,
American; nonfiction CON
De GRAZIA, Sebastian, 1917- ,
American; nonfiction CON
de GRUMMOND, Lena Young,
American; juveniles CO
DEGUINE, Jean Claude, 1943- ,
French; juveniles CON
de GUINGAND, Francis Wilfred,
1900-79, British; nonfiction
CON
DEGUY, Michel, 1930- , French;
poetry WAK
deGUZMAN, Daniel, 1910- ,
American; journalism, nonfic-
tion CON
De HAAN, Margaret see FREED,
Margaret
De HAAS, Elsa, 1901- , American;
nonfiction CON
de HAMEL, Joan Littledale,
1924- , British; juveniles, tv
CON
de HARTMANN, Olga, 1883?-1979,
Russian-American; nonfiction
CON
De hdde, Dubhghlas see HYDE,
Douglas
DEHKHODA, Ali Akbar (Dihkuda),
1879-1956, Iranian; poetry
BU PRU
DEHMEL, Richard, 1863-1920,
German; poetry, plays, nonfic-
tion BU CL TH
DEHN, Paul Edward, 1912-76,
British; poetry, plays CON
VCP
De HOYOS, Arturo, 1925- ,
American; nonfiction MAR
DEI, Benedetto, 1418-92, Italian;
nonfiction BU
DEI-ANANG, Michael Francis,
1909- , Ghanaian; poetry,
plays, fiction CON HER JA
LA
DEIBLER, William E., 1932- ,
American; journalism CON
DEIGHTON, Len, 1929- , English;
fiction, nonfiction MCC NI
REI ST VCN WA
DEINDORFER, Scott, 1967- ,

263DEISS

American; nonfiction CON
DEISS, Joseph Jay, 1915- ,
American; juveniles CO
De JAEGHER, Raymond Joseph
('Lei Chen Yuan'), 1905-80,
Belgian; journalism, nonfiction
CON
DE JONG, Arthur Jay, 1934- ,
American; nonfiction CON
De JONG, David Cornel ('Tjal-
mar Breda'), 1905-67, Dutch-
American; juveniles CO
de JONG, Dola, Dutch-American;
juveniles CO
De JONG, Gerald Francis, 1921- ,
American; nonfiction CON
DeJONG, Meindert, 1906- ,
Dutch-American; juveniles
BU KI
DE JONG, Peter, 1945- , Amer-
ican; nonfiction CON
de JONGE, Alex, 1938- , Eng-
lish; nonfiction CON
de JONGH, James, 1942- ,
American; plays CON
DEJU, Raul Antonio, 1946- ,
American; nonfiction CON
'DEKALB, Lorimer' see KNORR,
Marian L.
de KAY, Ormonde, Jr., 1923- ,
American; nonfiction CO
DEKEN, Agatha, 1741-1804, Dutch;
fiction BU
'DEKKER, Carl' see LAFFIN,
John A.
DEKKER, Eduard D. see
'Multali'
DEKKER, Maurits Rudolph Joëll,
1896-1962, Dutch; plays, fic-
tion BU
DEKKER, Thomas, 1572-1632,
English; plays, nonfiction
BU DA MAG MCG PO RU VD
DEKNATEL, Frederick Brockway,
1905-73, American; nonfiction
CON
DEKOBRA, Maurice, 1885-1973,
French; fiction, journalism
CON
De KOENIGSWERTHER, Edwin
Raymond, 1930- , American;
nonfiction CON
DeKOSKY, Robert K., 1945- ,
American; nonfiction CON
DE KOVEN, Bernard, 1941- ,
American; plays CON
de KRUIF, Paul Henry, 1890-1971,

American; juveniles, nonfiction
CO
DELACATO, Carl Henry, 1923- ,
American; nonfiction CON
De La Cruz, Jesse Elias, 1945- ,
American; nonfiction MAR
de la GARZA, Rodolfo Oropea,
1942- , American; nonfiction
CON
De LAGE, Ida, 1918- , American;
juveniles CO CON
DE LA GRANGE, Henry Louis,
1924- , French; nonfiction
CON
de LAGUNA, Grace Mead Andrus,
1878-1978, American; nonfiction
CON
de la MARE, Walter, 1873-1956,
British; juveniles, plays, po-
etry, fiction, nonfiction BU
CO DA KI MAG PO SEY VP
'DE LAMARTER, Jeanne' see
BONNETTE, Jeanne
De LAMOTTE, Roy Carroll ('Greg-
ory Wilson'), 1917- , Ameri-
can; fiction CON
DeLANCEY, Mark Wakeman,
1939- , American; nonfiction
CON
DELAND, Margaretta Wade Camp-
bell, 1857-1945, American;
fiction, plays, poetry, nonfiction
VN
DELANEY, Daniel Joseph, 1938- ,
American; nonfiction CON
DELANEY, Francis, Jr. (Bud),
1931- , American; nonfiction
CON
DELANEY, Harry, 1932- , Eng-
lish; juveniles CO
DeLANEY, Joseph Lawrence,
1917- , American; nonfiction,
fiction CON
DELANEY, Lolo Mae, 1937- ,
American; nonfiction CON
'DELANEY, Marshall' see FUL-
FORD, Robert
DELANEY, Mary Murray ('Mary D.
Lane'), 1913- , American;
fiction, nonfiction CON
DELANEY, Ned, 1951- , American;
juveniles CON
DELANEY, Shelagh, 1939- , Eng-
lish; plays DA MCG VCD WA
de LANGE, Nicholas Robert,
1944- , British; translations,
nonfiction CON
DELANO, Anthony, 1930- , Amer-

ican; journalism, fiction, non-
fiction CON
DELANO, Hugh, 1933- , Amer-
ican; juveniles, nonfiction
CO CON
DELANO, Kenneth Joseph, 1934- ,
American; nonfiction CON
DELANO, Oloye I. O., 1904- ,
Nigerian; nonfiction JA
DELANY, Kevin Francis, 1927- ,
American; journalism CON
DELANY, Samuel Ray, 1942- ,
American; fiction AS CON
COW NI SH VCN WAK
DELAPORTE, Ernest Pierre,
1924- , French; nonfiction
CON
de la PORTILLA, Marta Rosa,
1927- , Cuban-American;
nonfiction CON
De LAPP, Ardyce Lucile, 1903- ,
American; fiction CON
DeLAPP, George Leslie, 1895- ,
American; nonfiction CON
De La RAMEE, Marie Louise
see 'OUIDA'
De la ROCHE, Mazo, 1879-1961,
Canadian; fiction, juvenile,
plays, nonfiction BU CON
DA MAG VN
'de la TORRE, Lilian' (Lillian
McCue), 1902- , American;
fiction, plays, nonfiction,
juveniles REI ST
de LAUBENFELS, David John,
1925- , American; nonfiction
CON
DELAUNE, Jewel Lynn de Grum-
mond, American; juveniles
CO
De LAURENTIS, Louise Budde,
1920- , American; juveniles
CO
DELAVIGNE, Casimir Jean Fran-
cois, 1793-1843, French;
poetry, plays BU MCG
'DELAVRANCEA, Barbu' (Barbu
Stefanescu), 1858-1918,
Rumanian; nonfiction, plays
BU MCG
DELAY-BAILLEN, Claude ('Claude
Baillen'), 1934- , American;
nonfiction CON
Del BAGNO, Panuccio, 1215/34-
76?, Italian; poetry BO
DELBANCO, Nicholas, 1942- ,
American; fiction KIB
Del BENE, Bartolomeo, 1514-87?,

Italian; poetry BU
DELBLANC, Sven, 1931- , Swed-
ish; fiction, plays CL
DEL CASTILLO, Michel, 1933- ,
Spanish; fiction WA
DELCROIX, Carlo, 1896-1977,
Italian; nonfiction CON
DELDERFIELD, Eric Raymond,
1909- , American; nonfiction,
fiction CO CON
DELDERFIELD, Ronald Frederick,
1912-72, English; juveniles,
plays CO CON
DELEAR, Frank J., 1914- ,
American; journalism, juveniles
WAR
DELEDDA, Grazia, 1875-1936,
Italian; fiction BO BU CL
MAG SEY TH
de LEEUW, Hendrik, 1891-1977,
Dutch-American; nonfiction
CON
de LEIRIS, Alain, 1922- , Franco-
American; nonfiction CON
de LEON, Arnoldo, 1945- ,
American; nonfiction MAR
De LEON, Edwin, 1818-91, Amer-
ican; nonfiction BA
De LEON, Nephtali, 1945- ,
American; poetry MAR
De LEON, Thomas Cooper, 1839-
1914, American; poetry, fiction
BA
de LERMA, Dominique Rene,
1928- , American; nonfiction
CON
DELF, Dirc van, 1365- , Dutch;
nonfiction BU
DELGADO, Abelardo ('Lalo'),
1931- , American; poetry,
plays MAR
DELGADO, Emilio, 1904-67, Puerto
Rican; poetry, journalism
HIL
DELGADO, Ramon Louis, 1937- ,
American; plays, nonfiction,
poetry CON
D'ELIA, Donald John, 1933- ,
American; nonfiction CON
DELIBES SETIEN, Miguel, 1920- ,
Spanish; fiction, nonfiction
BU CL CON WAK
DELICADO, Francesco (Delgado),
early 16th century, Spanish;
fiction BU TH
DELIGIORGIS, Stavros George,
1933- , Rumanian-American;
translations, nonfiction CON

DELILLE, Jacques, 1738-1813,
French; poetry, translations
BU TH
DELILLO, Don, 1936- , Amer-
ican; fiction CON KIB NI
de LIMA, Agnes, 1887?-1947,
American; nonfiction CON
De LIMA, Clara Rosa ('Penelope
Driftwood'), 1922- , American;
poetry, fiction CON
De LIMA, Sigrid, 1921- , Amer-
ican; fiction WA
DELISLE, Francoise, 1886?-
1974, American; nonfiction
CON
DELISLE, Leopold Victor, 1824-
1910, Italian; nonfiction
ENG
De LISSER, Herbert George,
1878-1944, West Indian; jour-
nalism, fiction BU
DELIUS, Anthony, 1916- ,
South African; poetry, plays,
nonfiction BU DA NI VCP
DELK, Robert Carlton ('Alva
Carlton'; 'George Tenness'),
1920- , Canadian-American;
nonfiction CON
'DELL, Belinda' see BOWDEN,
Jean
DELL, Christopher, 1927- ,
American; nonfiction CON
DELL, Edmund, 1921- , British;
nonfiction CON
DELL, Floyd, 1887-1969, Amer-
ican; fiction, plays BR CON
VN
DELL, Roberta Elizabeth,
1946- , American; nonfiction
DELLA CASA, Giovanni, 1503-56,
Italian; poetry BO TH
DELLA MIRANDOLA, Giovanni
Pico, 1463-94, Italian; non-
fiction BO
DELLA-PIANA, Gabriel M.,
1926- , American; nonfiction
CON
DELLA PORTA, Giambattista,
1535-1615, Italian; plays
BO BU MCG
DELLA VALLE, Federico, 1560-
1628, Italian; plays, poetry
BO BU MCG TH
DELLIN, Lubomir A. D.,
1920- , Bulgarian-American;
nonfiction CON
DELLINGER, David T., 1915- ,

American; nonfiction CON
'DELMAR, Roy' see WEXLER,
Jerome L.
DELMAR, Vina Croter, 1905- ,
American; fiction, plays CON
'DEL MARIA, Astron' Gaywood
Press house name NI
De LOACH, Allen Wayne, 1939- ,
American; poetry, nonfiction
CON
De LOACH, Clarence, Jr., 1936- ,
American; nonfiction CON
De LOLME, John Louis, 1740-
1807, Swiss; nonfiction BU
Del OLMO, Frank P., 1948- ,
American; nonfiction MAR
DELON, Floyd Gurney, 1929- ,
American; nonfiction CON
DE LONE, Richard H., 1940- ,
American; nonfiction CON
De LONE, Ruth see RANKIN, Ruth
DELONEY, Thomas, 1543?-1600,
English; fiction, nonfiction,
poetry BU DA MAG PO RU
VN
De LORA, Joann Schepers, 1935- ,
American; nonfiction CON
DELORIA, Vine Victor, Jr.,
1933- , American; nonfiction
CO CON
'DELORME, Andre' see JULIEN,
Charles A.
'DELORME, Michele' see CRAN-
STON, Mechthild
DELORT, Robert, 1932- , French;
nonfiction CON
de los REYES, Gabriel, Cuban-
American; nonfiction CON
De Los SANTOS, Alfredo Guada-
lupe, Jr., American; nonfiction
MAR
DELP, Michael William, 1948- ,
American; poetry, nonfiction
CON
DELPAR, Helen, 1936- , Amer-
ican; nonfiction CON
del RAY, Lester ('John Alvarez';
'Marion Henry'; 'Philip James';
'Wade Kaempfert'; 'Henry
Marion'; 'Edson McCann';
'Philip St. John'; 'Erik Van
Lhin'; 'Kenneth Wright'),
1915- , American; fiction,
juveniles AS CO CON COW
DE NI
'DELTA' see MOIR, David M.
DELTON, Judy, 1931- , American;
nonfiction, juveniles CO CON

WAR
De LUCA, Charles J., 1927- ,
American; nonfiction CON
De LUCCA, John, 1920- ,
American; nonfiction, trans-
lations CON
DELULIO, John, 1938- , Amer-
ican; juveniles CO
DELUMEAU, Jean, 1923- ,
French; nonfiction CON
De LUNA, Frederick Adolph,
1928- , American; nonfiction
CON
DELUPIS, Ingrid ('Ingrid Detter';
'Ingrid Doimi di Delupis'),
1939- , Swedish; nonfiction
CON
DEL'VIG, Anton Antonovich, 1798-
1831, Russian; poetry BU
'DELVING, Michael' see WIL-
LIAMS, Jay
DeLYNN, Jane, 1946- , Amer-
ican; fiction CON
DEMADES, fl. 350-19 B. C.,
Greek; nonfiction BU
DEMAND GOH, Gaston, 1940- ,
Ivory Coaster; plays JA
De MANIO, Jack, 1914- , Eng-
lish; nonfiction CON
De MARCHI, Emilio, 1851-1901,
Italian; fiction BO BU TH
De MARCO, Donald, 1937- ,
American; nonfiction CON
'DEMAREST, Doug' see BARKER,
Will
DEMARET, Pierre, 1943- ,
French; nonfiction CON
De MARINIS, Rick, 1934- ,
American; fiction CON
DEMARIS, Ovid, 1919- , Amer-
ican; fiction, nonfiction REI
DEMAS, Vida, 1927- , Ameri-
can; fiction, juveniles CO
CON
de MAUSE, Lloyd, 1931- , Amer-
ican; nonfiction CON
DEMBELE, Sidiki, 1930?- ,
Malian; fiction, plays HER
JA
DEMBER, Jean Wilkins, Amer-
ican; poetry SH
DEMBY, William, 1922- ,
American; fiction, nonfiction
BR CON SH
DEMEDTS, André, 1906- ,
Flemish; fiction, poetry, plays
BU
DEMEERS, James, 1942- ,

Canadian; fiction, film CON
de MESNE, Eugene Frederick
('Julian Ocean'), English; fic-
tion CON
DEMETER, Dimitrija, 1811-72,
Croatian; plays BU
DEMETILLO, Ricaredo, 1920- ,
Filipino; poetry, plays CON
VCP
DEMETRIUS, Lucia, 1910- ,
Rumanian; plays, fiction BU
DEMETRIUS CYDONES, -1400,
Byzantine; nonfiction BU
DEMETRIUS of PHALERUM, 350-
283 B. C., Greek; nonfiction
BU GR LA
DEMETRIUS TRICLINIUS, 1280?-
1340?, Byzantine; nonfiction
LA
DEMETZ, Peter, 1922- , Czech-
American; nonfiction CON
'DEMIJOHN, Thom' see DISCH,
Thomas M.; SLÁDEK, John T.
de MILLE, Agnes see PRUDE,
Agnes G.
DEMILLE, Darcy, 1929- , Amer-
ican; nonfiction SH
De MILLE, James, 1837-80, Cana-
dian; fiction NI
'DE MILLE, Nelson' see 'JORDAN,
Leonard'
De MILLE, Nelson, 1943- ,
American; fiction CON
DEMING, Barbara, 1917- , Amer-
ican; nonfiction, poetry, fiction
CON
DEMING, Louise Macpherson, 1916-
76, American; nonfiction CON
DEMING, Richard ('Max Franklin';
'Emily Moor'; 'Nick Morino'),
1915- , American; fiction,
nonfiction CO REI WAR
DeMIRJIAN, Arto, Jr., 1931- ,
American; fiction CON
DEMIRTSHIAN, Derenik, 1877-1956,
Armenian; poetry, plays PRU
DEML, Jakob, 1878-1961, Czech;
poetry BU
'DEMOCRITO' see MUÑOZ RIVERA,
Luis
DEMOCRITUS, 460-370 B. C.,
Greek; nonfiction BU GR
'DEMOCRITUS, Jr.' see BURTON,
Robert
DEMOLDER, Eugène, 1862-1919,
Belgian; fiction BU
De MOLEN, Richard Lee, 1938- ,
American; nonfiction CON

De MONFRIED, Henri, 1879?-
1974, French; nonfiction
CON
de MONTEBELLO, Guy-Philippe
Lannes, 1936- , Franco-
American; nonfiction CON
DEMOREST, Stephen, 1949- ,
American; nonfiction CON
De MORGAN, William, 1839-
1917, English; fiction BU DA
MAG VN
DEMOTHENES, 384-22 B. C.,
Greek; nonfiction BU GR
LA MAG
De MOTT, Benjamin, 1924- ,
American; fiction, nonfiction
WA
De MOTT, Donald Warren, 1928- ,
American; nonfiction CON
DEMPSEY, Hugh Aylmer, 1929- ,
Canadian; nonfiction CON
DEMPSEY, Jack, 1895- , Amer-
ican; nonfiction CON
DEMPSEY, Lotta, Canadian;
journalism CON
DEMPSEY, Richard Allen, 1932- ,
American; nonfiction CON
DEMPSTER, Roland Tombekai,
1910-65, Liberian; poetry
HER JA LA
DEMURA, Fumio, 1940- ,
Japanese-American; nonfiction
CON
DEMUTH, Michel, 1939- ,
French; fiction NI
'DENBIE, Roger' see GREEN,
Alan B.
DEN BOER, James, 1937- ,
American; poetry VCP
DENDEL, Esther see WARNER,
Esther
DENE, Edewaerd de, 1505-78,
Dutch; poetry BU
DeNEEF, Arthur Leigh, 1942- ,
American; nonfiction CON
DENEEN, James R., 1928- ,
American; nonfiction CON
de NEUFVILLE, Richard, 1939- ,
American; nonfiction CON
DENEVEN, William Maxfield,
1931- , American; nonfiction
CON
DENEVI, Marco, 1922- , Ar-
gentinian; fiction BR
DENFELD, Duane, 1939- ,
American; nonfiction CON
DENGLER, Dieter, 1938- ,
German-American; nonfiction

CON
DENGLER, Marianna Herron,
1935- , American; fiction
CON
DENHAM, Bertie, 1927- , British;
fiction CON
DENHAM, Henry Magles, 1897- ,
American; nonfiction CON
DENHAM, Sir John, 1615-69, Eng-
lish; poetry, plays BU DA PO
VP
DENHAM, Robert Dayton, 1938- ,
American; nonfiction CON
'DENHAM, Sully' see BUDD, Mavis
DENHARDT, Robert Moorman,
1912- , American; nonfiction
CON
DENHOLTZ, Elaine, 1932- ,
American; plays, film CON
DENIS, King of Portugal, 1261-
1325, Portuguese; poetry BU
DENIS, Barbara J. ('Anne Kristin
Carroll'), 1940- , American;
nonfiction CON
DENIS, Johan Nepomuk Cosmas
('Sined der Barde'), 1729-1800,
Austrian; poetry BU
'DENIS, Julio' see CORTAZAR,
Julio
DENISON, Dulcie W. C. see
'GRAY, Dulcie'
DENISON, Merrill, 1893- , Cana-
dian; fiction, nonfiction, plays
CR MCG
DENISON, Muriel Goggin ('Frances
Newton'), 1885-1954, Canadian;
fiction, juvenile, nonfiction
CR
DENISON, Norman, 1925- , Eng-
lish; nonfiction, fiction CON
DENKLER, Horst, 1935- , Ger-
man; nonfiction CON
DENKSTEIN, Vladimir, 1906- ,
Czech; nonfiction CON
DENMAN, Donald Robert, 1911- ,
English; nonfiction CON
DENMARK, Florence L., 1932- ,
American; nonfiction CON
DENNES, William Ray, 1898- ,
American; nonfiction CON
DENNETT, Daniel C., 1942- ,
American; nonfiction CON
DENNEY, Diana ('Gri'; 'Diana
Ross'), 1910- , British;
juveniles CO KI
DENNEY, Myron Keith, 1930- ,
American; nonfiction CON
DENNIE, Joseph, 1768-1812,

American; nonfiction BR BU
'DENNING, Melita' see GODFREY,
Vivian
DENNIS, Benjamin G., 1929- ,
Liberian-American; nonfiction
CON
DENNIS, Carl, 1939- , American;
poetry CON
DENNIS, Clarence James, 1876-
1938, Australian; poetry BU
DENNIS, Everette E., 1942- ,
American; nonfiction CON
DENNIS, Henry Charles, 1918- ,
American; nonfiction CON
DENNIS, James Munn, 1932- ,
American; nonfiction CON
DENNIS, John, 1657-1734, Eng-
lish; nonfiction, poetry, plays
BU DA PO VD
DENNIS, Landt, 1937- , Amer-
ican; nonfiction CON
DENNIS, Lane Timothy, 1943- ,
American; nonfiction CON
DENNIS, Lawrence, 1893-1977,
American; nonfiction CON
DENNIS, Morgan, 1891?-1960,
American; juveniles CO
DENNIS, Nigel Forbes, 1912- ,
English; fiction, plays, jour-
nalism DA PO VCD VCN
WA
'DENNIS, Patrick' see TANNER,
Edward E. III
DENNIS, Peggy, 1909- , Amer-
ican; nonfiction CON
DENNIS, Peter John, 1945- ,
Australian; nonfiction CON
DENNIS, Robert C., 1920- ,
American; fiction, film, plays
CON
DENNIS, Wayne, 1905-76, Amer-
ican; nonfiction CON
DENNIS, Wesley, 1903-66, Amer-
ican; juveniles CO
DENNIS-JONES, Harold ('Paul
Hamilton'; 'Dennis Hessing'),
1915- , English; translations,
nonfiction CON
DENNISON, Alfred Dudley, Jr.,
1914- , American; nonfiction
CON
DENNISON, George Harris, 1925- ,
American; nonfiction CON
DENNISON, George Marshel,
1935- , American; nonfiction
CON
DENNISON, Shane, 1933- ,
Canadian; nonfiction CON

DENNISTON, Denise, 1946- ,
American; nonfiction CON
DENNISTON, Elinore ('Rae Foley';
'Dennis Allan'), 1900-78,
American; fiction, juveniles
CO CON REI
DENNISTON, Lyle William, 1931- ,
American; nonfiction CON
DENNY, Alma ('Adeline Clistier'),
1912- , American; nonfiction
CON
'DENNY, Brian' see DOUGHTY,
Bradford
DENNY, Maurice Ray, 1918- ,
American; nonfiction CON
DENNY, Norman George ('Norman
Dale'), 1901- , American;
juveniles, translations WAR
DENNY-BROWN, Derek Ernest,
1901-81, New Zealander; non-
fiction CON
DENNYS, Rodney Onslow, 1911- ,
British; nonfiction CON
DENOEU, Francois, 1898-1975,
French; fiction, nonfiction
CON
DENOON, Donald John, 1940- ,
Scots; nonfiction CON
de NORONHA, Rui, 1909-43,
Mozambican; poetry HER
DENSEN-GERBER, Judianne,
1934- , American; juveniles
WAR
DENSLOW, William Wallace, 1856-
1915, American; juveniles CO
DEM
DENT, Guy, British; fiction NI
DENT, Harry Shuler, 1930- ,
American; nonfiction CON
DENT, Lester ('Kenneth Robeson';
'Tim Ryan'), 1904-59, Ameri-
can; fiction, film NI REI
DENT, Tom, American; nonfiction
SH
'DENTINGER, Stephen' see HOCH,
Edward D.
DENTON, Jeffery Howard, 1939- ,
English; nonfiction CON
DENTON, Jeremiah Andrew, Jr.,
1924- , American; nonfiction
CON
DENUES, Celia, 1915- , Ameri-
can; nonfiction CON
DENZEL, Justin Francis, 1917- ,
American; nonfiction CON
DENZER, Ann W. see WISEMAN,
Ann S.
de PAOLA, Thomas Anthony,

1934- , American; juveniles
CO CON
DEPAS, Spencer, 1925- ,
Haitian-American; nonfiction
CON
DE PAUW, Linda Grant, 1940- ,
American; juveniles CO
WAR
DEPEL, Jim, 1936- , American;
nonfiction CON
DEPEW, Arthur McKinley, Amer-
ican; nonfiction CON
De PIETRO, Albert, 1913- ,
American; poetry CON
DE POLNAY, Peter, 1906- ,
British; nonfiction, juveniles
CON
DePORTE, Michael Vital, 1939- ,
American; nonfiction CON
DEPP, Robert J., 1947- ,
American; nonfiction CON
'de PRE, Jean-Anne' see AVAL-
LONE, Michael A., Jr.
DePREE, Gladis Lenore, 1933- ,
American; fiction, nonfiction,
poetry CON
DePREE, Gordon, 1930- , Amer-
ican; nonfiction CON
DEPTA, Victor Marshall, 1939- ,
American; poetry CON
De PUY, Norman Robert,
1929- , American; nonfiction
CON
De QUINCEY, Thomas, 1785-
1859, English; nonfiction,
journalism BU DA MAG PO
VN
D'ERASMO, Martha, 1939- ,
American; nonfiction CON
DERBY, Pat, 1942- , British;
nonfiction CON
de REGNIERS, Beatrice Schenck,
1914- , American; juveniles,
poetry KI
'DEREME, Tristan' (Philippe
Huc), 1889-1941, French;
poetry CL
DERENBERG, Walter Julius,
1903-75, German-American;
nonfiction CON
de REYNA, Rudy, 1914- ,
Spanish-American; nonfiction
CON
'DERIN, P. I.' see LANSEL,
Peider
De RISI, William Joseph, 1938- ,
American; nonfiction CON
de RIVERA, Joseph Hosmer,

1932- , American; nonfiction
CON
DERLETH, August ('Stephen Gren-
don'; 'Tally Mason'), 1909-71,
American; fiction, poetry AS
CO REI ST NI
DERMAN, Lou, 1914?-76, Ameri-
can; tv CON
DERMAN, Sarah Audrey, 1915- ,
American; juveniles CO
DERMID, Jack, 1923- , American;
nonfiction CON
DERMODY, Thomas, 1775-1802,
Irish; poetry BU HO
DERN, Karl Ludwig, 1894- ,
American; nonfiction CON
DER NERSESSIAN, Sirarpie,
1896- , Turkish-American;
nonfiction CON
De ROUEN, Reed Randolph, 1917- ,
American; fiction NI
DERMOUT, Maria Ingerman, 1888-
1962, Dutch; fiction, nonfiction
BU WA
De ROBERTIS, Giuseppe, 1888-1963,
Italian; nonfiction BU
De ROBERTO, Federico, 1866-1927,
Italian; journalism, fiction
BO BU CL TH
De ROIN, Nancy ('Nancy Ross'),
1934- , American; nonfiction
CON
de ROO, Anne Louise, 1931- ,
New Zealander; juveniles, plays
CO CON KI
De' ROSSI, Azariah, 1513-78,
Italian; poetry, nonfiction BU
DE ROSSI, Claude Joseph, 1942- ,
American; nonfiction CON
de ROTHSCHILD, Pauline, 1908?-
76, American; nonfiction CON
DEROULEDE, Paul, 1846-1914,
French; poetry, plays BU TH
DERR, Richard Luther, 1930- ,
American; nonfiction CON
DERR, Thomas Sieger, 1931- ,
American; nonfiction CON
'DERRICK, Graham' see RABY,
Derek G.
DERRIDA, Jacques, 1930- ,
French; nonfiction CL
'DERRY, Derry Down' see LEAR,
Edward
'DERSONNES, Jacques' see SIM-
ENON, Georges
DERVIN, Daniel Arthur, 1935- ,
American; nonfiction CON
DERWENT, Lavinia, Scots; juveniles,

nonfiction CO CON
DERY, Tibor, 1884/94-1977, Hungarian; fiction, plays, nonfiction BU CL CON TH WA
DERZHAVIN, Gavril Romanovich, 1743-1816, Russian; poetry BU TH
DESOI, Anita, 1937- , Indian; fiction, juveniles BU CON VCN
DESAI, Rupin Walter, 1934- , Burmese; nonfiction CON
de ST. JORRE, John, 1936- , American; nonfiction CON
de STE. Croix, Geoffrey Ernest Maurice, 1910- , British; nonfiction CON
deSALVO, Joseph Salvatore, 1938- , American; nonfiction CON
DeSALVO, Louise Anita, 1942- , American; nonfiction CON
DESAN, Wilfrid, 1908- , Belgian-American; nonfiction CON
De SANCTIS, Francesco, 1817-83, Italian; nonfiction BO BU TH
DESANI, Govindas Vishnoodas, 1909- , British; fiction, plays BU CON VCN
DESATNICK, Robert Lawrence, 1931- , American; nonfiction CON
DES AUTELS, Guillaume, 1529-81?, French; poetry BU
DESBORDES-VALMORE, Marceline, 1786-1859, French; poetry BU TH
DESCARTES, René, 1596-1650, French; nonfiction BU MAG TH
DESCAVES, Lucien, 1861-1949, French; fiction, plays CL MCG
DESCHAMPS, Antony, 1800-69, French; poetry TH
DESCHAMPS, Emile, 1791-1871, French; nonfiction, poetry BU TH
DESCHAMPS, Eustache ('Morel'), 1346-1406?, French; poetry BU TH
DESCHARNES, Robert Pierre, 1926- , French; nonfiction CON
DESCHENAUX, Jacques, 1945- , Swiss; nonfiction CON

DESCHLER, Lewis, 1905-76, American; nonfiction CON
DESCHNER, Hans Guenther, 1941- , German; nonfiction CON
DESCHNER, John, 1923- , American; nonfiction CON
De SCHWEINITZ, Karl, 1887-1975, American; juveniles, nonfiction CON WAR
DESCLOT, Bernat, 13th century, Catalan; nonfiction BU
De SELINCOURT, Aubrey, 1894-1962, English; juveniles, translations, nonfiction CO CON
de SENA, Jorge, 1919-78, Portuguese; nonfiction, poetry, plays CON
DESEWO, P. M., 1925?- , Ghanaian; fiction HER
DESFONTAINES, Pierre Francois Guyot, 1685-1745, French; journalism TH
DES GAGNIERS, Jean, 1929- , Canadian; nonfiction CON
DeSHAZO, Edith Kind, 1920- , American; nonfiction CON
DESHEN, Shlomo, 1935- , Israeli; nonfiction CON
DESHLER, George Byron, 1903- , American; nonfiction CON
DESHOUHIERES, Antoinette Du Ligier de la Garde, 1638-94, French; poetry BU
DESILETS, Guy, 1928- , Canadian; poetry CR
DESJARDINS, Paul, 1859-1940, French; nonfiction CL
DESMARCHAIS, Rex ('A. Sainte-Croix'; 'Hugues Bergeret'; 'Sévère Couture'; 'Alain Després'; 'Xavier Durand'; 'Charles Lancret'; 'Jacques Meilleur'), 1908- , Canadian; fiction, nonfiction CR
Des MARESTS de SAINT-SORLIN, Jean, 1595-1676, French; fiction, poetry, plays, nonfiction BU MCG TH
Des MASURES, Louis, 1515-74, French; poetry, plays BU TH
DESMOND, Adrian John, 1947- , English; nonfiction CON
DESMOND, Alice Curtis, 1897- , American; juveniles CO
DESMOND, Hugh, British; fiction REI
DESMOND, John, 1909?-77, Amer-

ican; journalism CON
DESMOND, Robert William,
1900- , American; nonfiction
CON
DESMOND, Shaw, 1877-1960,
Irish; fiction, poetry CON NI
DESNICA, Vladan, 1905-67, Croat-
ian; fiction BU TH
DESNOES, Edmundo, 1930- ,
Cuban; fiction BR
DESNOS, Robert, 1900-45, French;
poetry, fiction BU CL SEY
TH WA
DESNOUES, Lucienne, 1921- ,
Belgian; poetry CL
DE SOLA, Ralph, 1908- , Amer-
ican; juveniles, nonfiction
CON
De SOUSA, Noêmia Carolina
('Vera Micaia'), 1927- ,
Mozambican; poetry HER JA
DES PERIERS, Bonaventure,
1510-44, French; fiction, non-
fiction BU TH
DESPERT, Juliette Louise,
1892- , French; nonfiction
CON
DESPLAND, Michel, 1936- ,
Swiss-Canadian; nonfiction
CON
DESPORTES, Philippe, 1547-
1606, French; poetry BU TH
DESPREAUX see BOILEAU, Nico-
las
'DESPRES, Alain' see DE-
MARCHAIS, Rex
DES PRES, Terrence, 1939- ,
American; nonfiction CON
DESROCHERS, Alfred, 1901- ,
Canadian; poetry CR
DESSAUER, John Paul, 1924- ,
American; nonfiction CON
DESSEL, Norman Frank, 1932- ,
American; nonfiction CON
DESSEN, Alan Charles, 1935- ,
American; nonfiction CON
DESSI, Giuseppe, 1901/09-77,
Italian; fiction, plays BO
CON
De STEUCH, Harriet (Henry),
1897?-1974, American; fic-
tion CON
DESTLER, Irving McArthur,
1939- , American; nonfiction
CON
DESTOUCHES, Henri Louis see
'CELINE'
DESTOUCHES, Philippe Néricault,

1680-1754, French; plays BU
MCG TH
DESTREE, Jules, 1863-1936, Bel-
gian; fiction, nonfiction BU
CL
DE SWAAN, Abram, 1942- ,
Dutch; nonfiction CON
de SYLVA, Donald Perrin, 1928- ,
American; nonfiction CON
de TABLEY, Lord (John Byrne
Leiscester Warren), 1835-95,
English; poetry VP
De TARDE, Gabriel, 1843-1904,
French; fiction NI
DETER, Dean Allen, 1945- ,
American; poetry, fiction CON
DETHIER, Vincent Gaston, 1915- ,
American; nonfiction, fiction
CON
De TIMMS, Graeme, American;
fiction NI
'DETINE, Padre' see OLSEN, Ib S.
de TIRTOFF, Romain ('Erte'),
1892- , Russian-British; non-
fiction CON
DE TOLNAY, Charles Erich ('Karoly
Tolnai'; 'Vagujhelyi Karoly Tol-
nai'), 1899- , Hungarian-
American; nonfiction CON
DETRO, Gene, 1935- , American;
poetry, fiction CON
'DETTER, Ingrid' see DELUPIS,
Ingrid
DETZER, David William, 1937- ,
American; nonfiction CON
'DETZER, Diane' (Diane Detzer de
Reyna; 'Adam Lukens'; 'Jorge
de Reyna'), 1930- , American;
fiction NI
DEUS, João de, 1830-96, Portu-
guese; poetry TH
'DEUTSCH' see MANUEL, Niklaus
DEUTSCH, Arnold R., 1919- ,
Hungarian-American; nonfiction
CON
DEUTSCH, Babette, 1895- ,
American; poetry, nonfiction,
fiction, juveniles, translations
BR VCP
DEUTSCH, Eberhard Paul, 1897-
1980, American; nonfiction
CON
DEUTSCH, Eliot Sandler, 1931- ,
American; translations, nonfic-
tion CON
DEUTSCH, Herbert Arnold, 1932- ,
American; nonfiction CON
DEUTSCH, Hermann Bacher, 1889-

1970, Austrian-American;
journalism, fiction CON
DEUTSCH, Karl Wolfgang, 1912- ,
Czech-American; nonfiction
CON
DEUTSCH, Marilyn Weisberg,
1950- , American; nonfiction
CON
DEUTSCHER, Isaac, 1907-67,
Anglo-Polish; journalism,
nonfiction WA
DEUTSCHER, Max, 1916?-79,
American; nonfiction CON
DEVAHUTI, D., 1929- , Indian;
nonfiction CON
'DEVAJEE, Ved' see GOOL,
Reshard
DEVAL, Govind Ballal, 1855-
1916, Marathi; plays PRU
'DEVAL, Jacques' (Jacques Bou-
laran), 1894- , French;
film, plays MCG TH
DE VALERA, Eamon, 1882-1975,
Irish; nonfiction CON
DE VALERA, Sinead, 1879?-
1975, Irish; juveniles CON
DEVANEY, John, 1926- ,
American; juveniles CO
WAR
DEVARAKSITA JAYABAHU
DHARMAKIRTI, 14-15th cen-
turies, Sinhalese; nonfiction
PRU
DE VEAUX, Alexis, 1948- ,
American; juveniles, fiction,
plays CON
DEVENTER, Emma M. Van see
'LYNCH, Lawrence L.'
DE VERE, Sir Aubrey, 1788-
1846, Irish; poetry, plays
HO
DE VERE, Aubrey Thomas, 1814-
1902, Irish; poetry BU DA
HO PO VP
DEVEREUX, Frederick Leonard,
Jr., 1914- , American;
nonfiction, juveniles CO CON
DEVEREUX, George, 1908- ,
Hungarian-American; nonfic-
tion CON
DEVEREUX, Robert, 1567-1600/
01, English; poetry BU
DEVEREUX, Walter, 1541-76,
English; poetry BU
DE VET, Charles V., 1911- ,
American; fiction, nonfiction
CON NI
DEVIEW, Lucille, 1920- ,

American; nonfiction, poetry
CON
de VILLIERS, Gerard, 1929- ,
French; nonfiction, fiction
CON
de VINCK, Antoine, 1924- , Bel-
gian; juveniles CON
de VINCK, Catherine, 1922- ,
Belgian-American; poetry CON
DEVINE, David McDonald ('Dominic
Devine'), 1920- , British;
fiction, radio REI ST
DEVINE, Donald J., 1937- ,
American; nonfiction CON
DEVINE, George, 1941- , Amer-
ican; nonfiction CON
DEVINE, Janice, 1909?-73, Amer-
ican; nonfiction CON
DEVINE, Joseph Lawrence, 1935- ,
American; journalism CON
DE VINNEY, Richard, 1936- ,
American; nonfiction CON
DeVITO, Joseph Anthony, 1938- ,
American; nonfiction CON
DEVKOTA, Laksmi Prasad, 1909-
59, Nepalese; poetry, nonfiction
PRU
DEVLETOGLOU, Nicos E., 1936- ,
Greek; nonfiction CON
DEVLIN, Denis, 1908-59, Irish;
poetry, translations BU HO
WA
DEVLIN, Dorothy Wende, 1918- ,
American; juveniles CO CON
DEVLIN, Harry, 1918- , Ameri-
can; juveniles CO CON
DEVLIN, L. Patrick, 1939- ,
American; nonfiction CON
DEVLIN, Patrick Arthur, 1905- ,
British; nonfiction CON
DEVLIN, Thomas, American; juven-
iles WAR
DE VOE, Shirley Spaulding, 1899- ,
American; nonfiction CON
DEVOL, Kenneth Stowe, 1929- ,
American; nonfiction CON
De VOS, Karen Helder, 1939- ,
American; nonfiction CON
De VOS, Luk, Belgian; nonfiction
NI
De VOTO, Bernard, 1897-1955,
American; nonfiction BR
De VRIES, Carrow, 1906- ,
American; nonfiction, poetry
CON
de VRIES, Egbert, 1901- , Dutch;
nonfiction CON
de VRIES, Jan, 1943- , Dutch-

American; nonfiction CON
De VRIES, Peter, 1910- , American; fiction, plays BR KIB
SEY VCN WA
De VRIES, Simon John, 1921- ,
American; nonfiction CON
DE VRIES, Walter Dale, 1929- ,
American; nonfiction CON
DEW, Edward MacMillan, 1935- ,
American; nonfiction CON
de WAAL MALEFIJT, Annemarie,
1914- , Dutch-American;
nonfiction CON
De WAARD, Elliott John, 1935- ,
American; nonfiction, juveniles
CO CON
DEWDNEY, John Christopher,
1928- , British; nonfiction
CON
DEWDNEY, Selwyn Hanington,
1909- , Canadian; fiction,
nonfiction, juveniles CON
DeWEERD, Harvey A., 1902- ,
American; nonfiction CON
DeWEESE, Gene, American; non-
fiction NI
DeWEESE, Thomas Eugen ('Jean
DeWeese'; 'Thomas Stratton'),
1934- , American; nonfic-
tion, fiction CON
DEWEY, Ariane (Aruego), 1937- ,
American; juveniles CO CON
DEM
DEWEY, Edward Russell, 1895- ,
American; nonfiction CON
DEWEY, Godfrey, 1887-1977,
American; nonfiction CON
DEWEY, John, 1859-1952, Amer-
ican; nonfiction BR BU PO
SEY
DEWEY, Melvil, 1851-1931,
American; nonfiction ENG
DEWEY, Thomas Blanchard ('Tom
Brandt'; 'Cord Wainer'),
1915- , American; fiction,
nonfiction REI ST
DEWHIRST, Ian, 1936- , British;
nonfiction CON
DEWHURST, Keith, 1931- ,
British; plays CON VCD
DEWSBURY, Donald Allen, 1939- ,
American; nonfiction CON
DEXIPPUS, Publius Herennius,
200/10- , Greek; nonfiction
GR
DEXTER, Ellen Patricia Egan,
American; fiction, juveniles
CON

'DEXTER, John' see PLOTNICK,
Arthur
DEXTER, Norman Colin, 1930- ,
English; nonfiction, fiction
CON
'DEXTER, William' (William Thomas
Pritchard), 1909- , English;
fiction NI
DEY, Frederic Van Rensselaer
('Nicholas and Nick Carter';
'Marmaduke Dey'; 'Frederic
Ormond'; 'Varick Vanardy'),
1865-1922, American; fiction,
plays REI
DEYENKA, Anita, 1943- , Amer-
ican; juveniles, nonfiction CO
CON
DEYRUP, Astrith Johnson, 1923- ,
American; nonfiction, juveniles
CO CON WAR
'DEYSSEL, Lodewijk van' (Karel
Joan L. A. Thijm), 1864-1952,
Dutch; nonfiction BU CL TH
DEZA, Ernest C., 1923- , Amer-
ican; poetry CON
D'HAEN, Christine, 1923- ,
Belgian; poetry CL
D'HALMAR, Augusto, 1880-1950,
Chilean; journalism, fiction
BR
DHAMMARAJA, Sri, early 18th
century, Cambodian; poetry
PRU
DHARMASENA, 13th century, Sin-
halese; translations PRU
DHARTA, A. S., 1924- , Indo-
nesian; poetry PRU
DHIEGH, Khigh Alexander, Amer-
ican; nonfiction CON
DHLOMO, Herbert Isaac Ernest,
1903/05-56, Zulu; fiction, po-
etry, plays HER JA LA
DHLOMO, Rolfus Reginald Ray-
mond, 1901-71, Zulu; fiction,
journalism HER JA LA
DHOKALIA, Ramaa Prasad, 1925- ,
Indian; nonfiction CON
DHÔTEL, André, 1900- , French;
fiction BU CL WA
DIA, Amadou Cissé, 1915- ,
Senegalese; plays JA
DIABATE, Massa Makan, 1938- ,
Malian; fiction JA
'DIABOLIN' see RODRIQUEZ
CABRERO, Luis
DIAGNE, Ahmadou Mapaté, 1894/
99- , Senegalese; fiction
HER JA

DIAKHATE, Lamine, 1928- ,
Senegalese; poetry, plays
HER JA
DIAL, Joan ('Katherine Kent';
'Amanda York'), 1937- ,
British; fiction CON
DIALLO, Assane Y., 1940?- ,
Senegalese; poetry HER
DIALLO, Bakary, 1892- , Sene-
galese; fiction, poetry, non-
fiction HER JA
'DIALLO, Georges' (Rev. Georges
Janssens), French?; fiction
JA
DIALLO, Mamadou, 1920- ,
Ivory Coaster; poetry JA
DIAMANTE, Juan Bautista, 1625?-
87?, Spanish; plays BU
MCG
DIAMOND, Betty, 1947- , Amer-
ican; nonfiction MAR
DIAMOND, Graham ('Rochelle
Leslie'), 1945- , Anglo-
American; fiction CON
DIAMOND, Isidore A. L., 1920- ,
Rumanian-American; film CON
DIAMOND, Jay, 1934- , Amer-
ican; nonfiction CON
DIAMOND, John, 1934- , Aus-
tralian; nonfiction CON
DIAMOND, Martin, 1919-77, Amer-
ican; nonfiction CON
DIAMOND, Milton, 1934- , Amer-
ican; nonfiction CON
DIAMOND, Sander A., 1942- ,
American; nonfiction CON
DIAMOND, Solomon, 1906- ,
American; nonfiction CON
DIAMOND, Stanley, 1922- ,
American; nonfiction CON
DIAMOND, Stephen Arthur,
1946- , American; nonfiction
CON
DIAMOND, William, 1917- ,
American; nonfiction CON
DIAMONSTEIN, Barbaralee D.,
American; nonfiction, film
CON
DIAPER, William, 1685-1717,
English; poetry, translation
VP
DIARA, Agadem Lumumba,
1947- , American; nonfiction
CON
DIARA, Schavi Mali, 1948- ,
American; fiction, poetry
CON
DIAS, João, 1926-49, Angolan;

fiction HER
DIAS, Joao Pedro Grabata', (An-
tonio Quadros), 1933- , Por-
tuguese; poetry CL
DIAZ, Eugenio Muñoz see 'NOEL,
Eugenio'
DIAZ, Janet Winecoff, 1935- ,
American; nonfiction CON
DIAZ ALFARO, Abelardo M.,
1920- , Puerto Rican; fiction
HIL
DIAZ ARRIETA, Hernán ('Alone'),
1891- , Chilean; nonfiction
BR
DIAZ de TOLEDO, Pero, 1418-66,
Spanish; translations, nonfiction
BU
DIAZ del CASTILLO, Bernal,
1498?-1568/84, Spanish; non-
fiction BR BU TH
DIAZ-GUERRERO, Rogelio, 1918- ,
American; nonfiction CON
MAR
DIAZ MIRON, Salvador, 1853-1928,
Mexican; poetry BR BU
DIAZ MONTERO, Anibal, 1911- ,
Puerto Rican; journalism, fic-
tion HIL
DIAZ RODRIGUEZ, Manuel, 1868-
1927, Venezuelan; fiction, non-
fiction BR BU
DIAZ SOLER, Luis M., 1916- ,
Puerto Rican; nonfiction HIL
DIAZ VALCARCEL, Emilio,
1929- , Puerto Rican; fiction
HIL
DIB, Mohammed, 1920- , Alger-
ian; fiction, poetry BU PRU
DIBB, Paul, 1939- , English;
nonfiction CON
DIBBLE, Nancy Ann ('Ansen
Dibell'), 1942- , American;
fiction CON
DIBDIN, Charles, 1745-1814, Eng-
lish; plays, fiction, poetry
BU VD
DIBDIN, Michael, 1947- , British;
fiction, plays CON
DI BREME, Ludovico, 1781-1820,
Italian; nonfiction BO
DICAERCHUS, late 4th century
B.C., Greek; nonfiction GR
LA
DI CAVALCANTI, Emiliano, 1898?-
1976, Brazilian; nonfiction
CON
DICE, Lee R., 1889?-1976, Amer-
ican; nonfiction CON

DICENTA y BENEDICTO, Joaquin, 1863-1917, Spanish; fiction, plays BU CL MCG

DI CICCO, Pier Giorgio, 1949- , American; poetry CON

DICK, Daniel T., 1946- , American; nonfiction CON

DICK, Kay, 1915- , English; fiction NI

DICK, Philip Kindred ('Richard Phillips'), 1928-82, American; fiction AS CON COW NI VCN

'DICK, R. A.' see LESLIE, Josephine A. C.

DICK, Trella Lamson, 1889-1974, American; juveniles CO

DICK, William Milner, 1933- , Scots-Canadian; nonfiction CON

DICKE, Robert Henry, 1916- , American; nonfiction CON

DICKENS, Arthur Geoffrey, 1910- , English; nonfiction CON

DICKENS, Charles, 1812-70, English; fiction BR BU CO DA MAG MCC PO REI ST VN

DICKENS, Monica Enid, 1915- , English; fiction, juveniles, nonfiction, journalism CO DA VCN WA WAR

'DICKENS, Norman' see EISENBERG, Lawrence B.

DICKENS, Roy Selman, Jr., 1938- , American; nonfiction CON

DICKENSON, James R., 1931- , American; journalism CON

DICKENSON, John, fl. 1594, English; poetry, fiction BU

DICKER, Ralph Leslie, 1914- , American; nonfiction CON

DICKERSON, John, 1939- , English; nonfiction CON

DICKERSON, Martha Ufford, 1922- , American; nonfiction CON

DICKERSON, Nancy Hanschman, 1930- , American; nonfiction CON

DICKERSON, Roy Ernest, 1886-1965, American; journalism CON

DICKEY, Charley, 1920- , American; nonfiction CON

DICKEY, Glenn, 1936- , American; nonfiction CON

DICKEY, James, 1923- , American; poetry, fiction BA BR MAG MAL PO SEY VCP VP WA

'DICKEY, Lee' see BREMYER, Jayne D.

DICKEY, Robert Preston, 1936- , American; poetry, plays VCP

DICKEY, William, 1928- , American; poetry VCP WA

DICKIE, James, 1934- , Scots; nonfiction CON

DICKINSON, Alan Edgar Frederic, 1899- , British; nonfiction CON

DICKINSON, Edward Clive, 1938- , English; nonfiction CON

DICKINSON, Eleanor, 1931- , American; nonfiction CON

DICKINSON, Emily Elizabeth, 1830-86, American; poetry AM BR BU MAG MY PO VP

DICKINSON, John, 1732-1808, American; nonfiction BR

'DICKINSON, Margaret' see MUGGESON, Margaret E.

DICKINSON, Patric Thomas, 1914- , British; poetry, plays, nonfiction, translations VCP

DICKINSON, Peter Allen, 1926- , American; nonfiction CON

DICKINSON, Peter ('Malcolm de Brissac'), 1927- , British; juveniles, plays, fiction CO CON DEM KI NI REI ST WAK WAR

DICKINSON, Susan, 1931- , English; juveniles, nonfiction CO CON

DICKINSON, Thorold Barron, 1903- , English; nonfiction CON

DICKINSON, William Boyd, 1908-78, American; journalism CON

DICKINSON, William Croft, 1897-1963, English; juveniles CO

DICK-LAUDER, George ('George Lauder'), 1917- , British; fiction CON

DICKMANN, Max, 1902- , Argentinian; journalism, fiction BR

DICKS, Henry Victor, 1900- , British; nonfiction CON

'DICKSON, Carter' see CARR, John D.

DICKSON, Franklyn, 1941- , American; nonfiction CON

DICKSON, George Edmond, 1918- ,
American; nonfiction CON
DICKSON, Gordon Rupert, 1923- ,
Canadian-American; fiction
AS COW NI
'DICKSON, Helen' see REYNOLDS,
Helen M. G.
DICKSON, Naida ('Grace Lee
Richardson'), 1916- , Amer-
ican; juveniles CO
DICKSON, Samuel Henry, 1798-
1872, American; poetry BA
DICKSON, Stanley, 1927- ,
American; nonfiction CON
DICKSTEIN, Morris, 1940- ,
American; nonfiction CON
DICTYS CRETENSIS, Greek; non-
fiction BU
DICUIL, -825, Irish; poetry
BU
DIDEROT, Denis, 1713-84, French;
nonfiction, fiction BU MAG
MCG NI TH
DIDINGER, Ray, 1946- , Amer-
ican; nonfiction CON
DIDION, Joan, 1934- , Amer-
ican; fiction, journalism, film
HE VCN WAK
di DONATO, Georgia, 1932- ,
American; fiction CON
di DONATO, Pietro, 1911- ,
American; fiction, plays,
nonfiction CON
DIDYMUS, 80-10 B.C., Greek;
nonfiction BU GR LA
DIEBOLD, John Theurer, 1926- ,
American; nonfiction CON
DIECKELMANN, Heinrich, 1898- ,
German; poetry, plays BU
DIECKMANN, Liselotte, 1902- ,
German-American; nonfiction
CON
DIEDERICH, Bernard, 1926- ,
New Zealander; nonfiction
CON
DIEGO, Gerardo, 1896- ,
Spanish; poetry BU CL TH
DIEGO, Jose de ('Leon Americano'),
1866-1918, Puerto Rican; po-
etry, journalism HIL
DIEGO PADRO, José I. de ('Raul
de la Vega'), 1896- , Puerto
Rican; poetry, fiction, jour-
nalism HIL
DIEHL, James Michael, 1938- ,
American; nonfiction CON
DIEHL, Robert Digby, 1940- ,
American; nonfiction CON

DIEHL, William Francis, Jr.,
1924- , American; journal-
ism, nonfiction, fiction CON
DIEKHOFF, John Siemon, 1905-76,
American; nonfiction CON
DIEL, Paul, 1893- , Austrian;
nonfiction CON
DIENES, Charles Thomas, 1940- ,
American; nonfiction CON
DIENSTAG, Eleanor, 1938- ,
American; nonfiction CON
DIERICKX, Charles Wallace,
1921- , American; nonfiction
CON
DIERX, Marais Victor Léon, 1838-
1912, French; poetry BU
DIETMAR von ELST (Aist), fl.
1160-70, Austrian; poetry BU
TH
DIETRICH, Noah, 1889- , Amer-
ican; nonfiction CON
DIETRICH, Richard Vincent ('R.
Dirk'), 1924- , American;
nonfiction CON
'DIETRICH, Robert' see HUNT,
Everette H.
DIETZ, David Henry, 1897- ,
American; juveniles CO
DIETZ, Elisabeth H., 1908- ,
American; juveniles WAR
DIETZ, Howard, 1896- , Amer-
ican; journalism, nonfiction
CON
DIETZ, Lew, 1907- , American;
juveniles CO
DIETZ, Marjorie Johnson, 1918- ,
American; nonfiction CON
DIETZE, Charles Edgar, 1919- ,
American; nonfiction CON
DIEZ CANEDO, Enrique, 1879-
1944, Spanish; poetry, nonfic-
tion BU CL
DIEZ de GAMES, Gutierre, 1378?-
1448?, Spanish; nonfiction BU
DIFFIN, Charles Willard, Ameri-
can; fiction NI
Di FRANCO, Fiorenza, 1932- ,
Hungarian-American; nonfiction
CON
DIGBY, Sir Kenelm, 1603-65,
English; nonfiction DA RU
DIGENNARO, Joseph, 1939- ,
American; nonfiction CON
DIGGES, Leonard, 1588-1635, Eng-
lish; poetry, translations BU
DIGGLE, James, 1944- , English;
nonfiction CON
Di GIACOMO, Salvatore, 1860-1934,

Italian; poetry, fiction BO
BU CL MCG
Di GIROLAMO, Vittorio, 1928- ,
American; nonfiction CON
DIHKHUDA, Ali Akbar see
DEHKHODA, Ali A.
DIHOFF, Gretchen, 1942- ,
American; nonfiction CON
DIKSHIT, Ramesh Dutta; 1939- ,
Indian; nonfiction CON
DIKTONIUS, Elmer, 1896-1961,
Finnish-Swedish; poetry, non-
fiction BU CL TH
DIKTY, Thaddeus Eugene, 1920- ,
American; nonfiction AS NI
DILCOCK, Noreen ('Norrey Ford';
'Jill Christian'; 'Christian
Walford'), 1907- , British;
fiction CON
Di LELLO, Richard, 1945- ,
American; nonfiction CON
DILES, Dave, 1931- , Amer-
ican; nonfiction CON
DILKE, Charles Wentworth, 1789-
1964, English; nonfiction BU
DILKE, Oswald Ashton Wentworth,
1915- , British; nonfiction
CON
DILKS, David Neville, 1938- ,
English; nonfiction CON
DILLARD, Annie, 1945- ,
American; poetry, nonfiction,
juveniles CO CON
DILLARD, Emil Lee, 1921- ,
American; poetry CON
DILLARD, Joey Lee, 1924- ,
American; nonfiction CON
DILLARD, Polly Hargis, 1916- ,
American; juveniles CO
DILLARD, Richard Henry Wilde,
1937- , American; poetry,
plays, fiction VCP
DILLER, Edward, 1925- ,
American; nonfiction CON
DILLER, Phyllis Ada, 1917- ,
American; journalism, non-
fiction CON
DILLING, Judith see RHOADES,
Judith
DILLINGHAM, Beth, 1927- ,
American; nonfiction CON
DILLON, Bert, 1937- , Amer-
ican; nonfiction CON
DILLON, David, 1941- , Amer-
ican; nonfiction CON
DILLON, Diane, 1933- , Amer-
ican; juveniles CO WAR
DILLON, Eilis, 1920- , Irish;

fiction, juveniles DE HO KI
DILLON, George, 1906-68, Amer-
ican; poetry, translations
CON
DILLON, John Myles ('The Western
Spy'), 1939- , American; non-
fiction CON
DILLON, Lawrence Samuel,
1910- , American; nonfiction
CON
DILLON, Leo, 1933- , American;
juveniles CO WAR
DILLON, Martin, 1949- , Irish;
nonfiction, plays CON
DILLON, Millicent, 1925- , Amer-
ican; fiction CON
DILMEN, Güngör, 1930- , Turk-
ish; plays CL
DILTHEY, Wilhelm, 1833-1911,
German; nonfiction BU TH
DILTZ, Bert Case, 1894- , Cana-
dian; poetry, fiction, nonfiction
CON
Di MARCO, Luis Eugenio, 1937- ,
Argentinian; nonfiction CON
DIMBERG, Ronald Gilbert, 1938- ,
American; nonfiction CON
Di MEGLIO, Clara, 1933- , Ital-
ian; journalism, nonfiction
CON
DiMEGLIO, John Edward, 1934- ,
American; nonfiction CON
DIMENT, Adam, ?; fiction REI
DiMENTO, Joseph Frank, 1947- ,
American; nonfiction CON
di MICHELE, Mary, 1949- ,
Canadian; poetry CON
DIMITROVA, Blaga, 1922- ,
Bulgarian; poetry BU
DIMOND, Edmunds Grey, 1918- ,
American; nonfiction CON
DIMOND, Mary Clark, American;
nonfiction CON
DIMONT, Madelon, 1938- , Aus-
trian; nonfiction CON
'DIMONT, Penelope' see MORTI-
MER, Penelope R.
DIMOV, Dimitur, 1909-66, Bul-
garian; fiction BU
'DIMSON, Wendy' see BARON,
Ora W.
DIMT, C. see 'BUSTA, Christine'
DINARCHUS, 360-292? B.C.,
Greek; nonfiction BU
DINEKOV, Petur, 1910- , Bul-
garian; nonfiction BU
DINELEY, David Lawrence,
1927- , American; nonfiction

CON
DINER, Hasia Rena, 1946- ,
American; nonfiction CON
DINERMAN, Helen Schneider,
1921-74, American; nonfiction
CON
DINES, Harry Glen, 1925- ,
American; juveniles CO
DINES, Michael, 1916- , British;
nonfiction, plays, fiction
CON
DINESEN, Isak see BLIXEN,
Karen
'DING, J. N.' see DARLING,
Jay N.
DINGES, John Charles ('Ramon
Marsano'), 1941- , American;
nonfiction, translations CON
DINGMAN, Roger, 1938- ,
American; nonfiction CON
DINGS, John Garetson, 1939- ,
American; nonfiction CON
DINGWALL, Eric John, British;
nonfiction CON
'DINIS, Júlio' (Joaquim Guilherme
Gomes Coelho), 1839-71,
Portuguese; fiction BU TH
DINKAR, 1908- , Hindi; poetry,
nonfiction PRU
DINKMEYER, Don C. , 1924- ,
American; nonfiction CON
DINNAN, James A. , 1929- ,
American; nonfiction CON
DINNEEN, Betty, 1929- ,
Anglo-American; juveniles
CON
DINSDALE, Tim, 1924- , Welsh;
juveniles CO
DINSKY, Lazar, 1891?-1976,
American; poetry, nonfiction
CON
DINSMORE, Herman H. , 1900?-
80, American; journalism,
nonfiction CON
DIO CASSIUS (Cassius Dio Coc-
ceianus), 163/64-229, Greek;
nonfiction GR LA
DIO CHRYSOSTOM (Dio Coccei-
anus), 40/50-112/15, Roman?;
nonfiction BU GR LA
DIODORUS, Siculus, -21 B. C. ,
Greek; nonfiction BU GR
LA
'DIOGENES' see MUÑOZ RIVERA,
Luis
DIOGENES LAERTIUS, 3rd cen-
tury, Greek; nonfiction BU
GR LA

DIOGENES of APOLLONIA, fl.
440-30 B. C. , Greek; nonfiction
LA
DIOLE, Philippe V. , 1908- ,
French; nonfiction, journalism
CON
DION, Gerard, 1912- , Canadian;
nonfiction CON
DIONE, Robert Lester, 1922- ,
American; nonfiction CON
DIONYSIUS of HALICARNASSUS,
1st century B. C. , Greek; non-
fiction BU GR LA
DIONYSIUS the AREOPAGITE, late
5th century, Byzantine; non-
fiction BU
DIONYSIUS the CARTHUSIAN, 1402-
71, Latin; nonfiction BU
DIONYSIUS THRAX, 150/70-90
B. C. , Greek; nonfiction BU
GR LA
DIOP, Alioune, 1910- , Senegal-
ese; nonfiction JA
DIOP, Birago Ismaïl, 1906- ,
Senegalese; fiction, poetry BU
CL HER JA LA
DIOP, Cheikh Anta (Sheikh),
1923- , Senegalese; nonfic-
tion JA LA
DIOP, David Mandessi, 1927-60,
Senegalese; poetry HER JA
LA
DIOP, Massyla, 1886?-1932,
Senegalese; fiction, journalism
HER JA
DIOP, Ousmane S. see SOCE,
Ousmane D.
DIOP, Sheikh Anta see DIOP,
Cheikh A.
Di ORIO, Al, 1950- , American;
nonfiction CON
DIOSCORIDES, late 3rd century,
Greek; poetry BU
DIOSCORIDES, Pedanius, 1st cen-
tury, Greek; nonfiction GR
DIOSCORIDES of ANABARZUS, fl.
50, Greek; nonfiction LA
Di PASQUALE, Dominic, 1932- ,
American; nonfiction CON
DiPEGO, Gerald Francis, 1941- ,
American; journalism, film
fiction CON
Di PESO, Charles Corradino,
1920- , American; nonfiction
CON
DIPHILUS, 355?-288 B. C. , Greek;
poetry, plays BU GR LA
DIPOKO, Mbella Sonne, 1936- ,

Cameroonian; fiction, poetry
HER JA
DIPPER, Alan, 1922- , English;
fiction CON
di PRIMA, Diane, 1934- , Amer-
ican; poetry, plays, fiction,
translations VCP
Di RENZO, Gordon James, 1934- ,
American; nonfiction CON
DIRANAS, Ahmet Muhip (Dranas),
1909- , Turkish; poetry
CL
DIRINGER, David, 1900-75, Uk-
rainian; nonfiction CON
'DIRK, R.' see DIETRICH, Rich-
ard V.
DIRKSEN, Everett McKinley,
1896-1969, American; juven-
iles WAR
DIRKSEN, Louella Carver, 1899-
1979, American; nonfiction
CON
DIRLIK, Arif, 1940- , Turkish-
American; nonfiction CON
DISALVO, Cristina Chiriboga,
1948- , American; nonfiction
MAR
DISCH, Thomas Michael ('Thom
Demijohn'), 1940- , Amer-
ican; fiction AS COW NI
DISENGOMOKO, A. Emile, 1915-
65, Kikongo; fiction, poetry,
nonfiction HER
DISKA, Pat, American; juveniles
WAR
DISLON, Jesse, 1914- , Amer-
ican; juveniles CO
'd'ISLY, Georges' see SIMENON,
Georges
DISNEY, Doris Miles, 1907-76,
American; fiction CON REI
ST
DISNEY, Dorothy Cameron,
1903- , American; fiction,
nonfiction REI
DISON, Norma, 1928- , Amer-
ican; nonfiction CON
DISPENZA, Joseph Ernest,
1942- , American; nonfic-
tion, plays CON
DISRAELI, Benjamin, 1804-81,
British; fiction BU DA
MAG PO VN
D'ISRAELI, Isaac, 1766-1848,
English; nonfiction BU DA
DISSTON, Harry ('H. D. N. Hill'),
1899- , American; nonfiction,
juveniles CON

DITCHBURN, Robert William,
1903- , British; nonfiction
CON
DITLEVSEN, Tove, 1918-76, Dan-
ish; poetry, fiction BU CL TH
DITSKY, John Michael, 1938- ,
American; nonfiction CON
DITTES, James Edward, 1926- ,
American; nonfiction CON
DITTMER, Lowell, 1941- , Amer-
ican; nonfiction CON
DITZEL, Paul Calvin, 1926- ,
American; juveniles, nonfiction
CON WAR
DITZEN, Rudolf see 'FALLADA,
Hans'
DITZION, Sidney, 1908-75, Amer-
ican; nonfiction CON
Di VALENTIN, Maria Messuri,
1911- , American; juveniles
CO
DIVINE, Arthur Durham ('David
Divine'; 'David Rame'),
1904- , South African; fiction
CON
DIX, Dorothea Lynde, 1802-87,
American; nonfiction MY
DIX, William Shepherd, 1910-78,
American; nonfiction CON
DIXON, Bernard, 1938- , English;
nonfiction CON
DIXON, Jeane, 1918- , American;
nonfiction CON
DIXON, Joseph Lawrence, 1896- ,
American; nonfiction, poetry
CON
'DIXON, Paige' see CORCORAN,
Barbara
DIXON, Peter Lee, 1931- ,
American; juveniles, nonfiction,
fiction CO CON
DIXON, Richard Watson, 1833-1900,
English; poetry, nonfiction
BU PO VP
DIXON, Robert Galloway, 1920-80,
American; nonfiction CON
DIXON, Roger ('John Christian';
'Charles Lewis'), 1930- ,
English; nonfiction, fiction
CON NI
DIXON, Stephen, 1936- , Amer-
ican; fiction CON
DIXON, Sydney Lawrence, 1930- ,
British; nonfiction CON
DIXON, Thomas see 'COLE, Burt'
DIXON, Thomas, 1864-1946, Amer-
ican; fiction, plays, nonfiction
BA BU NI PO

DIXON, William Hepworth, 1821-79, English; nonfiction BU
DIZDAR, Mak, 1917- , Croatian; poetry BU
DIZINZO, Charles John, 1938- , American; plays, juveniles VCD
DJALSKI, Ksaver Sandor, 1854-1935, Croatian; fiction BU
DJILAS, Milovan, 1911- , Yugoslav; nonfiction WA
DJOLETO, Amu, 1929- , Ghanaian; fiction, poetry HER JA
DJONOVICH, Dusan J., 1920- , Yugoslav-American; nonfiction CON
DJURDJEVIC, Ignjat (Djardjič), 1675-1737, Ragusan; poetry BU
DJURDJEVIC, Stijepo, 1579-1632, Ragusan; poetry BU
DLUGOSZ, Jan, 1415-80, Polish; nonfiction BU
DLUZNOWSKY, Moshe, 1906-77, Polish; fiction, plays, nonfiction CON
DMITRIEV, Ivan Ivanovich, 1760-1837, Russian; poetry BU
DMITRY, Rostovsky (Demetrius of Rostov), 1561-1709, Russian; nonfiction, plays BU
DMOCHOWSKI, Franciszek Ksawery, 1762-1808, Polish; poetry BU
DOAK, Dearle Donnell, 1930- , American; journalism CON
DOAK, Wade Thomas, 1940- , New Zealander; nonfiction CON
DOAN, Daniel, 1914- , American; fiction, nonfiction CON
DOANE, Donald Paul, 1910- , American; journalism CON
DOANE, Pelagie, 1906-66, American; juveniles CO
DOAN-thi-DIEM, 1705-48, Vietnamese; poetry LA PRU
DOBB, Maurice Herbert, 1900-76, British; nonfiction CON
DOBBIN, John E., 1914-79, American; nonfiction, journalism CON
DOBBINS, Austin Charles, 1919- , American; nonfiction CON
DOBBINS, Dorothy Wyeth, 1929- , American; juveniles CON
DOBBINS, Marybelle King, 1900- ,

American; nonfiction, juveniles CON
DOBBS, Betty Jo Teeter, 1930- , American; nonfiction CON
DOBBS, Farrell, 1907- , American; nonfiction CON
DOBBS, Greg, 1946- , American; journalism CON
DOBBS, Kildare Robert Eric, 1923- , Canadian; nonfiction, poetry, fiction CR
DOBBYN, John Francis, 1937- , American; nonfiction CON
DOBELL, Isabel Marian (Barclay), 1909- , Canadian-American; juveniles CO
DOBELL, Sydney Thompson, 1824-74, English; poetry BU DA VP
DOBIE, Bertha McKee, 1890?-1974, American; nonfiction CON
DOBIE, Edith, 1894-1975, American; nonfiction CON
DOBIE, James Frank, 1888-1964, American; nonfiction BA
DOBIN, Abraham, 1907- , American; nonfiction CON
DOBKIN, Alexander, 1908-75, American; nonfiction CON
DOBKIN de RIOS, Marlene, 1939- , American; nonfiction CON
DOBKINS, James Dwight, 1943- , American; nonfiction CON
DOBLER, Bruce, 1939- , American; fiction CON
DOBLER, Lavinia G., 1910- , American; juveniles CO
DOBNEY, Frederick John, 1943- , American; nonfiction CON
DOBRACZYNSKI, Jan, 1910- , Polish; fiction CL TH
DOBRE, Ion see 'CRAINIC, Nichifor'
DOBREE, Bonamy, 1891-1974, English; nonfiction CON
DOBRIN, Arnold, 1928- , American; juveniles CO WAR
DOBRIN, Arthur, 1943- , American; nonfiction CON
DOBRINER, William Mann, 1922- , American; nonfiction CON
DOBROGEANU-GHEREA, Constantin, 1855-1920, Rumanian; nonfiction BU
DOBROLYUBOV, Aleksandr Mikhaylovich, 1876- , Russian; poetry TH
DOBROLYUBOV, Nikolay Alek-

sandrovich, 1836-61, Russian;
nonfiction BU TH
DOBROVSKY, Josef, 1753-1829,
Czech; nonfiction BU TH
DOBROWOLSKI, Tomasz B.,
1914?-76, Polish-American;
nonfiction, journalism CON
DOBSCHINER, Johanna-Ruth,
1925- , German-British;
nonfiction CON
DOBSON, Christopher Joseph,
1927- , British; journalism,
nonfiction CON
DOBSON, Henry Austin, 1840-
1921, English; poetry, non-
fiction BU DA PO VP
DOBSON, Julia Margaret, 1937- ,
American; nonfiction CON
DOBSON, Margaret June, 1931- ,
American; nonfiction CON
DOBSON, Rosemary de Brissac,
1920- , Australian; poetry
CON SEY VCP VP
DOBSON, Terry, 1937- , Amer-
ican; nonfiction CON
DOBYNS, Stephen, 1941- ,
American; poetry, fiction
CON
DOBZHANSKY, Theodosius, 1900-
75, Russian-American; non-
fiction CON
'DOCHERTY, James L.' see
'CHASE, James H.'
DOCKERAY, James Carlton,
1907- , American; nonfiction
CON
DOCTOROW, Edgar Laurence,
1931- , American; fiction,
nonfiction CON HE NI WAK
DOCTORS, Samuel Isaac, 1936- ,
American; nonfiction CON
DODD, Anne Westcott, 1940- ,
American; nonfiction, poetry
CON
DODD, Arthur Herbert, 1893?-
1975, American; nonfiction
CON
DODD, Charles Harold, 1884-
1973, British; nonfiction CON
DODD, Donald Bradford, 1940- ,
American; nonfiction CON
DODD, Edward Benton, 1902- ,
American; juveniles, nonfiction
CO CON
DODD, Edward Howard, Jr.
('W. M. Hill'), 1905- ,
American; nonfiction CON
DODD, James Harvey, 1892-1969,

American; nonfiction CON
DODD, Stuart Carter, 1900- ,
American; nonfiction CON
DODD, William, 1729-77, English;
nonfiction BU
DODDERIDGE, Esme, 1916- ,
Welsh; nonfiction CON
DODDRIDGE, Philip, 1702-51, Eng-
lish; nonfiction DA
DODDS, Eric Robertson, 1893-1979,
Irish; translations, nonfiction
CON
DODDS, John Wendell, 1902- ,
American; juveniles WAR
DODDS, Tracy, 1952- , American;
journalism, nonfiction CON
DODERER, Heimito von, 1896-1966,
Austrian; fiction, poetry, non-
fiction BU CL SEY TH WA
DODGE, Bertha Sanford, 1902- ,
American; juveniles CO
DODGE, Calvert Renaul, 1931- ,
American; nonfiction CON
DODGE, David Francis, 1910- ,
American; fiction, nonfiction
CON REI WA
DODGE, Dick, 1918?-74, Ameri-
can; juveniles CON
DODGE, Dorothy Rae, 1927- ,
American; nonfiction CON
DODGE, Ernest Stanley, 1913-80,
American; nonfiction CON
'DODGE, Fremont' see GRIMES,
Lee
DODGE, Marshall, 1935- , Amer-
ican; nonfiction CON
DODGE, Mary Mapes, 1831-1905,
American; juveniles, poetry
CO KI
DODGE, Nicholas A., 1933- ,
American; nonfiction CON
DODGE, Wendell Phillips, 1883-
1976, American; nonfiction
CON
DODGSON, Charles L. see 'CAR-
ROLL, Lewis'
DODSLEY, Robert, 1703?-64, Eng-
lish; plays, poetry BU VD
DODSON, James L., 1910- ,
American; nonfiction CON
DODSON, Kenneth MacKenzie,
1907- , American; juveniles
CO
DODSON, Owen Vincent, 1914- ,
American; poetry, plays, fic-
tion BR CON SH
DODSON, Susan, 1941- , Ameri-
can; juveniles CON

DOEBLER, John Willard, 1932- ,
American; nonfiction CON
DÖBLIN, Alfred ('Linke Poot'),
1878-1957, German; fiction,
plays, nonfiction BU CL
SEY TH
DOENITZ, Karl, 1891-1980, Ger-
man; nonfiction CON
DOERINGER, Peter Brantley,
1941- , American; nonfiction
CON
DOERNENBURG, Emil, 1880-
1935, German-American;
poetry BU
DOERR, Arthur Harry, 1924- ,
American; nonfiction CON
DOERSCHUK, Anna Beatrice,
1880?-1974, American; non-
fiction CON
DOESBORCH, Jan van, 16th cen-
tury, Dutch; fiction BU
DOESER, Linda Ann, 1950- ,
British; nonfiction CON
DOGEN, 1200-53, Japanese; non-
fiction HI
DOGHEH-DAVID, Richard G.,
1935?- , Dahoman; poetry
HER JA
DOHAN, Mary Helen, 1914- ,
American; nonfiction, fiction
CON
DOHERTY, Catherine de Hueck,
1900- , Russian-Canadian;
nonfiction CON
DOHERTY, Charles Hugh, 1913- ,
English; juveniles CO
DOHERTY, Edward Joseph, 1890-
1975, American; journalism,
nonfiction CON
DOHERTY, Geoffrey Donald,
1927- , British; anthology,
fiction AS NI
DOHERTY, William Thomas, Jr.,
1923- , American; nonfiction
CON
DOI (Tsuchii) BANSUI, 1871-1952,
Japanese; nonfiction, poetry
HI
DOIG, Desmond, 1921- , British;
nonfiction CON
DOIG, Ivan, 1939- , American;
nonfiction CON
'DOKMAI SOT' (Mom Luong Bub-
pha Nimmanhemint), 1906-
62/63, Thai; fiction LA PRU
DOLAMO, Elon Ramarisane,
1927- , South African; poetry
JA

DOLAN, Anthony Rossi, 1948- ,
American; nonfiction CON
DOLAN, Edward Francis, 1924- ,
American; juveniles WAR
DOLAN, Jay Patrick, 1936- ,
American; nonfiction CON
DOLAN, Josephine Aloyse,
1913- , American; nonfiction
CON
DOLAN, Winthrop Wiggin, 1909- ,
American; nonfiction CON
DOLBIER, Maurice Wyman,
1912- , American; juveniles,
fiction CON
DOLBY, James Louis, 1926- ,
American; nonfiction CON
DOLCE, Ludovico, 1508-68, Ital-
ian; translations, plays, non-
fiction BU MCG
DOLCE, Philip Charles, 1941- ,
American; nonfiction CON
DOLCI, Danilo, 1924- , Italian;
nonfiction WA
DOLE, Gertrude Evelyn, American;
nonfiction CON
DOLEZEL, Lubomir, 1922- ,
Czech-Canadian; nonfiction
CON
DOLGIN, Yoseph see ARICHA,
Yoseph
DOLGORUKOVA, Natalie Borisovna,
1714-71, Russian; nonfiction
BU
DOLIBER, Earl Lawrence, 1947- ,
American; nonfiction CON
DOLIN, Edwin, 1928- , American;
nonfiction, translations CON
'DOLININ, A.' (Arkadiy Semëno-
vich), 1883- , Russian; non-
fiction BU
DOLINSKY, Mike (Meyer), 1923- ,
American; fiction CON NI
DOLIT, Alan, 1934- , American;
nonfiction CON
DOLITZKI, Menachem Mendel,
1856-1931, Hebrew; poetry,
fiction TH
DOLLAR, Truman E., 1937- ,
American; nonfiction CON
DOLLOFF, Eugene Dinsmore,
1890-1972, American; nonfic-
tion CON
DOLMATCH, Theodore Bieley
('Stephen Josephs'), 1924- ,
American; nonfiction CON
DOLMATOVSKY, Evgeny Aronovich,
1915- , Russian; poetry BU
DOLS, Michael Walters, 1942- ,

American; nonfiction CON
DOLSON, Hildegarde (Lockridge),
1908-81, American; juveniles,
fiction, nonfiction CO CON
REI
DOMACHEVITSKY, Isaiah see
'BERSHADSKY, Isaiah'
DOMAN, Glenn Joseph, 1919- ,
American; nonfiction CON
'DOMAN, June' see BEVERIDGE,
Meryle
DOMANOVIC, Radoje, 1873-1908,
Serbian; fiction TH
DOMANSKA, Janina, Polish-
American; juveniles CO DE
DOMARADZKI, Theodore Felix,
1910- , Polish-Canadian;
nonfiction CON
DOMBROVSKY, Yury Osipovich,
1909-78, Russian; fiction CL
DOMENICHI, Ludovico, 1515-64,
Italian; poetry, plays, trans-
lations, nonfiction BU
DOMENICHINA, Juan José, 1898-
1959, Spanish; poetry CL
DOMETT, Alfred, 1811-87, New
Zealander; poetry, nonfiction
BU VP
DOMHOFF, George William,
1936- , American; nonfiction
CON
DOMIN, Hilde, 1912- , German;
poetry, nonfiction CL
DOMINGUES, Mário, 1899- ,
Portuguese; fiction HER
DOMINGUEZ, José de Jesus
('Gerardo Alcides'), 1843-98,
Puerto Rican; journalism,
plays, poetry HIL
DOMINGUEZ de CAMARGO, Her-
nando, -1657, Colombian;
poetry BR
'DOMINIC, R. B.' see HENNISART,
Martha; LATSIS, Mary Jane
DOMINICI, Giovanni, 1356-1419,
Italian; nonfiction BU
DOMINOWSKI, Roger L., 1939- ,
American; nonfiction CON
DOMITIUS, Marsus, 54-4 B. C.,
Latin; nonfiction LA
DOMJAN, Joseph, 1907- ,
Hungarian-American; juveniles
CO
DOMVILLE, Eric, 1929- , Eng-
lish; nonfiction CON
DONABEDIAN, Avedis, 1919- ,
American; nonfiction CON
DONAGHY, Henry James, 1930- ,

American; nonfiction CON
DONAGHY, John Lyle, 1902-47,
Irish; poetry HO
DONAGHY, William A., 1910?-75,
American; nonfiction CON
DONAHUE, Don, 1942- , Amer-
ican; nonfiction CON
DONAHUE, Jack, 1917- , Amer-
ican; fiction CON
DONAHUE, Roy Luther, 1908- ,
American; nonfiction CON
DONALD, David Herbert, 1920- ,
American; nonfiction WA
DONALD, Larry Watson, 1945- ,
American; journalism CON
DONALD, Maxwell, 1897-1978,
British; nonfiction CON
'DONALDS, Gordon' see SHIR-
REFFS, Gordon D.
DONALDSON, Betty, 1923- ,
Anglo-American; nonfiction
CON
DONALDSON, Charles Ian Edward,
1935- , Australian; nonfiction
CON
DONALDSON, Charles William,
1935- , British; nonfiction
CON
DONALDSON, Elvin F., 1903-72,
American; nonfiction CON
DONALDSON, Ethelbert Talbot,
1910- , American; nonfiction
CON
DONALDSON, Frances Annesley,
1907- , English; nonfiction
CON
DONALDSON, John W., 1893?-
1979, American; nonfiction
CON
DONALDSON, Kenneth, 1908- ,
American; nonfiction CON
DONALDSON, Margaret (Margaret
Lennox Salter), 1926- , Scots;
nonfiction, juveniles CON
DONALDSON, Robert Herschel,
1943- , American; nonfiction
CON
DONALDSON, Stephen R. ('Reed
Stephens'), 1947- , American;
fiction CON
DONATUS, Aelius, 4th century,
Latin; nonfiction BU GR LA
'DONOVAN, John' see MORLAND,
Nigel
DONCEVIC, Ivan, 1909- , Croat-
ian; fiction BU
DONCHESS, Barbara Briggs,
1922- , American; nonfiction

CON
DONDEY, Theophile see 'O'NEDDY,
Philothée'
DONDIS, Donis Asnin, 1924- ,
American; nonfiction CON
DONELAITIS, Krustijonas (Dona-
litius), 1714-80, Lithuanian;
poetry BU
DONELSON, Kenneth Lavern,
1927- , American; nonfiction
CON
DONGMO, Jean Louis, 1945?- ,
Cameroonian; poetry HER
DONI, Anton Francesco, 1513-74,
Italian; nonfiction, journalism
BO BU TH
DONICHT, Mark Allen ('Marcus
Allen'; 'Mark Allen'), 1946- ,
American; nonfiction, poetry,
fiction CON
DONIN, Hayim Halevy, 1928- ,
American; nonfiction CON
DONIS, Miles, 1937-79, American;
fiction, film CON
DONISH, Ahmad (Danesh; Makh-
dum Kalla), 1827-97, Tajik;
nonfiction PRU
'DONKER, Anthonie' (Nicolaas
Anthonie Donkersloot), 1902-
65, Dutch; poetry, nonfiction
BU
DONKIN, Nance Clare, 1915- ,
Australian; journalism, juven-
iles CON KI
DONLEAVY, James Patrick,
1926- , American; fiction,
plays BR HO KIB PO SEY
VCD VCN WA
DONLEY, Marshall Owen, Jr.,
1932- , American; nonfiction
CON
'DONN, Rob' (Robert Mackay),
1714-78, Scots; poetry DA
DONNA, Natalie, 1934- , Amer-
ican; juveniles CO
DONNADIEU, Marguerite see
'DURAS, Marguerite'
DONNAY, Maurice, 1859-1945,
French; plays CL MCG TH
DONNE, John, 1572-1631, Eng-
lish; poetry BRI BU DA
MAG PO RU VP
'DONNE, Maxim' see DUKE,
Madelaine
DONNEAU de VISE, Jean, 1638-
1710, French; nonfiction BU
DONNELL, John Corwin, 1919- ,
American; nonfiction CON

DONNELL, John Douglas, 1920- ,
American; nonfiction CON
DONNELLY, Ignatius, 1831-1901,
American; fiction BR BU NI
PO VN
DONNELLY, James Stephen, Jr.,
1943- , American; nonfiction
CON
DONNELLY, John, 1941- , Amer-
ican; nonfiction CON
DONNELLY, John Patrick, 1934- ,
American; nonfiction CON
DONNELY, Joseph Peter, 1905- ,
American; nonfiction CON
DONNER, Stanley Temple, 1910- ,
American; nonfiction CON
DONNISON, Jean, 1925- , British;
nonfiction CON
DONOGHUE, Denis, 1928- , Irish;
nonfiction BOR HO WAK
DONOHOE, Thomas, 1917- ,
American; nonfiction CON
DONOHUE, James Fitzgerald,
1934- , American; journalism,
fiction CON
DONOHUE, Joseph Walter, Jr.,
1935- , American; nonfiction
CON
DONOHUE, Mark, 1937-75, Amer-
ican; nonfiction CON
DONOSO, José, 1924- , Chilean;
fiction BR CON WAK
DONOSO CORTES, Juan, 1809-53,
Spanish; nonfiction BU
DONOVAN, Bonita R., 1947- ,
American; nonfiction CON
'DONOVAN, Dick' (Joyce Emmerson
Preston Muddock), 1843-1934,
English; fiction, journalism
REI ST
DONOVAN, Frank Robert, 1919-75,
American; nonfiction, juveniles
CON
DONOVAN, James Britt, 1916-70,
American; nonfiction CON
DONOVAN, John, 1928- , Amer-
ican; juveniles, plays CON KI
DONOVAN, Timothy Paul, 1927- ,
American; nonfiction CON
'DONOVAN, William' see BERKE-
BILE, Fred D.
DONS, Aage, 1903- , Danish;
fiction BU TH
DONSKOI, Mark Semyonovich, 1901-
81, Russian; film, nonfiction
CON
DONSON, Dyril, 1919- , British;
fiction NI

DONZE, Sara Lee, American;
juveniles WAR
DOOB, Leonard William, 1909- ,
American; juveniles CO
WAR
DOOB, Penelope Billings Reed,
1943- , American; nonfiction
CON
DOODY, Margaret Anne, 1939- ,
Canadian; nonfiction CON
DOOLEY, Howard John, 1944- ,
American; nonfiction CON
DOOLEY, Patrick Kiaran, 1942- ,
American; nonfiction CON
DOOLEY, Peter Chamberlain,
1937- , American; nonfiction
CON
DOOLEY, Thomas Anthony, 1927-
61, American; journalism,
nonfiction CON
DOOLEY, William Germain,
1905?-75, American; nonfic-
tion CON
DOOLITTLE, Hilda ('H. D. ';
'John Helforth'), 1886-1966,
American; poetry AM BR
BU CON MAG PO RO SEY
VP
DOOLITTLE, Jerome Hill, 1933- ,
American; nonfiction CON
DOORNKAMP, John Charles,
1938- , English; nonfiction
CON
DOPUCH, Nicholas, 1929- ,
American; nonfiction CON
'DOR, Ana' see CEDER, Geor-
giana D.
DORAN, Charles Francis,
1943- , American; nonfiction
CON
DORAY, Maya, 1922- , Austrian-
American; nonfiction CON
DORE, Gustave, 1832-83, French;
juveniles CO
DORE, Ronald Philip, 1925- ,
British; nonfiction CON
DOREIAN, Patrick, 1942- ,
Anglo-American; nonfiction
CON
DORESKI, William, 1946- ,
American; poetry, plays CON
DORFMAN, John, 1947- ,
American; nonfiction CON
DORFMAN, Joseph, 1904- ,
Russian-American; nonfiction
CON
DORFMAN, Nancy Schelling,
1922- , American; nonfiction

CON
DORFMAN, Nat N. , 1895-1977,
American; journalism, plays
CON
'DORGELES, Roland' (Roland Lé-
cavelé), 1886-1973, French;
fiction BU CL LA
DORIA, Charles, 1938- , Amer-
ican; nonfiction CON
DORIAN, Edith McEwen, 1900- ,
American; juveniles CO
'DORIAN, Harry' see HAMILTON,
Charles H. S.
DORIAN, Marguerite, Rumanian-
American; juveniles, poetry
CO
'DORIDA MESENIA' see EULATE
SANJURJO, Carmen
DORIN, Patrick Carberry, 1939- ,
American; nonfiction CON
DORIS, John Lawrence, 1923- ,
American; nonfiction CON
DORLAND, Michael, 1948- ,
Canadian; fiction CON
DORLANT, Pieter (Petrus Dor-
landus), 1454-1507, Dutch;
nonfiction BU
DORLING, Henry T. see 'TAF-
FRAIL'
DORMAN, Michael ('Jack Bishop'),
1932- , American; juveniles
CO WAR
DORMAN, Sonya, 1924- , Amer-
ican; fiction, juveniles, poetry
AS CON NI
DORN, Edward Merton, 1929- ,
American; poetry, fiction, non-
fiction BR CON MAL PO
VCP WAK
DORN, Phyllis Moore, 1910?-78,
American; nonfiction, fiction
CON
DORN, Sylvia O'Neill, 1918- ,
American; nonfiction CON
DORN, William S. ('Ian Malcolm
Earlson'), 1928- , American;
nonfiction CON
DORNAN, James E. , Jr. , 1938?-
79, American; nonfiction CON
DORNBERG, John Robert, 1931- ,
German; juveniles WAR
DORO, Marion Elizabeth, 1928- ,
American; nonfiction CON
DOROSH, Yefim Yakovlevich, 1908-
72, Russian; nonfiction CL
DOROSHEVICH, Vlas Mikhaylovich,
1864-1922, Russian; journalism
BU

'DOROTHY, R. D.' see
  CHARQUES, Dorothy T.
DORRIS, Michael Anthony, 1945- ,
  American; nonfiction CON
D'ORS y ROVIRA, Eugenio, 1882-
  1954, Spanish; nonfiction CL
'DORSAN, Luc' see SIMENON,
  Georges
'DORSANGE, Jeane' see SIMENON,
  Georges
DORSCH, Eduard, 1822-87,
  German-American; poetry
  BU
DORSET, Charles Sackville,
  1638-1705/06, English; poetry
  BRI BU DA VP
'DORSET, Ruth' see ROSS, Wil-
  liam E. D.
DORSET, Thomas Sackville, 1536-
  1608, English; poetry, plays
  BU
'DORSETT, Danielle' see DANIELS,
  Dorothy
DORSONVILLE, Max, 1943- ,
  Canadian; nonfiction CON
DORST, Tankred, 1925- , Ger-
  man; plays, translations
  CON MCG
DORWART, Jeffrey Michael,
  1944- , American; nonfiction
  CON
DORWART, Reinhold August,
  1911- , American; nonfiction
  CON
DOSA, Marta (Leszlei), Hun-
  garian-American; translations,
  fiction, nonfiction CON
DOSKOCILOVA, Hana, 1936- ,
  Czech; juveniles CON
DOSOFTEI, 1624-93, Moldavian;
  translations BU
DOS PASSOS, John Roderigo,
  1896-1970, American; fiction,
  plays, nonfiction AM BR
  BU MAG PO RO SEY VN
DOSS, Helen Grigsby, 1918- ,
  English; juveniles CO
DOSS, Margot Patterson, Amer-
  ican; juveniles CO WAR
'DOSSAGE, Jean' see SIMENON,
  Georges
DOS SANTOS, Marcelino ('Kalung-
  ano'; 'Lilinho Micaia'),
  1929- , Mozambican; poetry
  HER
'DOSSI, Carlo' (Alberto Pisani
  Dossi), 1849-1910, Italian;
  journalism, nonfiction CL

DOSSICK, Philip, 1941- , Amer-
  ican; film, nonfiction CON
DOSTOYEVSKY, Fëdor Mikhailo-
  vich, 1821-81, Russian; fiction,
  juveniles BU CL MAG NI ST
  TH WAR
DOTHARD, Robert Loos, 1909?-
  79, American; nonfiction CON
DOTT, Robert Henry, Jr., 1929- ,
  American; nonfiction CON
DOTTS, M. Franklin, 1929- ,
  American; nonfiction CON
DOTY, Charles Stewart, 1928- ,
  American; nonfiction CON
DOTY, Gladys ('Marcia Kent Doug-
  lass'), 1908- , American;
  nonfiction CON
DOTY, Gresdna Ann, 1931- ,
  American; nonfiction CON
DOTY, Jean Slaughter, 1929- ,
  Anglo-American; juveniles
  CON WAR
DOTY, Robert McIntyre, 1933- ,
  American; nonfiction CON
DOTY, Roy, 1922- , American;
  nonfiction CON
DOTY, William Guy, 1939- ,
  American; nonfiction CON
DOUAY, Dominique, 1944- ,
  French; fiction NI
DOUBLEDAY, Neal Frank, 1905- ,
  American; nonfiction CON
DOUCET, Louis Joseph, 1874-
  1959, Canadian; poetry CR
DOUGAN, Michael Bruce, 1944- ,
  American; nonfiction CON
DOUGHERTY, Betty ('Elisabeth
  Mount'), 1922- , English;
  nonfiction CON
DOUGHERTY, Charles, 1922- ,
  American; juveniles CO
DOUGHTERTY, Jude Patrick,
  1930- , American; nonfiction
  CON
DOUGHTIE, Edward Orth, 1935- ,
  American; nonfiction CON
DOUGHTY, Bradford ('Brian Den-
  ny'), 1921- , American; fic-
  tion CON
DOUGHTY, Charles Montagu, 1843-
  1926, English; poetry, nonfic-
  tion, fiction BU DA MAG NI
DOUGHTY, Nina Beckett, 1911- ,
  American; poetry CON
DOUGHTY, Paul Larrabee, 1930- ,
  American; nonfiction CON
DOUGLAS, Lord Alfred Bruce,
  1870-1945, English; poetry DA

DOUGLAS, David Charles,
1898- , British; nonfiction
CON
'DOUGLAS, Ellen' (Josephine
Ayres Haxton), 1921- ,
American; fiction BA
DOUGLAS, Gavin, 1474/74-1522,
Scots; poetry BU DA PO
VP
'DOUGLAS, George' (George Doug-
las Brown), 1869-1902, Scots;
fiction BU DA MAG
DOUGLAS, George Halsey,
1934- , American; nonfiction
CON
'DOUGLAS, Glenn' see DUCKETT,
Alfred
DOUGLAS, Helen (Gahagan), 1900-
80, American; nonfiction
CON
DOUGLAS, Helen L. see BEE,
Helen L.
DOUGLAS, James, 1929- ,
Irish; plays, fiction HO
'DOUGLAS, James McM.' see
BUTTERWORTH, William E.
'DOUGLAS, Kathryn' see
EWING, Kathryn
DOUGLAS, Keith Castellain,
1920-44, English; poetry
DA PO SEY VP WA
DOUGLAS, Lloyd C., 1877-1951,
American; fiction BR MAG
DOUGLAS, Marjory Stoneman,
1890- , American; juveniles
CO
DOUGLAS, Mary Tew, 1921- ,
American; nonfiction CON
'DOUGLAS, Michael' see
BRIGHT, Robert; CRICHTON,
Michael
DOUGLAS, Mike, 1925- ,
American; nonfiction CON
DOUGLAS, Norman, 1868-1952,
Scots; nonfiction, fiction
BU DA MAG NI PO SEY VN
DOUGLAS, Paul Howard, 1892-
1976, American; nonfiction
CON
DOUGLAS, Roy Ian, 1924- ,
British; nonfiction CON
'DOUGLAS, Thorne' see HAAS,
Benjamin L.
DOUGLAS, William Allison,
1934- , American; nonfic-
tion CON
DOUGLAS, William Orville, 1898-
1980, American; nonfiction

CON
'DOUGLAS-HOME, Alec' see
HOME, Alexander F.
DOUGLAS-HOME, Henry, 1907-80,
British; nonfiction CON
'DOUGLASS, Amanda Hart' see
WALLMANN, Jeffrey M.
DOUGLASS, Donald McNutt, 1890-
1975, American; nonfiction
CON
DOUGLASS, Elisha Peairs,
1915- , American; nonfiction
CON
DOUGLASS, Ellsworth, English?;
fiction NI
DOUGLASS, Frederick, 1817?-95,
American; journalism, nonfic-
tion MY PO
DOUGLASS, Herbert Edgar,
1927- , American; fiction,
nonfiction CON
DOUGLASS, Malcolm Paul, 1923- ,
American; nonfiction CON
'DOUGLASS, Marcia Kent' see
DOTY, Gladys
DOUGLASS, Robert W., 1934- ,
American; nonfiction CON
DOUGLASS, William Anthony,
1939- , American; nonfiction
CON
DOULATSHAH, -1494/95, Per-
sian; nonfiction PRU
DOUMATO, Lamia, 1947- ,
Syrian-American; nonfiction
CON
DOUSA, Janus, 1545-1609, Dutch;
poetry BU
DOUTEO, Bertin B., 1927- ,
Ivory Coaster; poetry JA
DOUTY, Esther Morris, 1911-78,
American; juveniles CO CON
WAR
DOUTY, Norman Franklin, 1899- ,
American; nonfiction CON
D'OVIDIO, Francesco, 1849-1925,
Italian; nonfiction BU
DOVIZI, Bernardo (Il Bibiena),
1470-1520, Italian; plays BO
BU MCG
'DOVLOS, Jay' see JOYCE, Jon L.
DOW, Blanche Hinnan, 1893-1973,
American; nonfiction CON
DOW, Emily R., 1904- , Amer-
ican; juveniles CO
DOWD, Herle Edward, 1918- ,
American; nonfiction CON
DOWDELL, Dorothy Florence
Karns, 1910- , American;

juveniles CO
DOWDEN, Anne Ophelia (Todd),
1907- , American; juveniles
CO
DOWDEN, Edward, 1843-1913,
Irish; nonfiction DA
DOWDEN, George, 1932- , Amer-
ican; poetry CON
DOWDEY, Clifford, 1904- ,
American; fiction, nonfiction
BA
DOWDEY, Landon Gerald, 1923- ,
American; juveniles, nonfiction
CO CON
DOWDY, Andrew, 1936- , Amer-
ican; fiction CON
DOWELL, Jack Larder, 1908- ,
Canadian; nonfiction CON
'DOWER, Penn' see PENDOWER,
Jacques
DOWIE, James Iverne, 1911- ,
American; nonfiction CON
DOWIE, Mark, 1939- , Canadian-
American; nonfiction CON
DOWLEY, Timothy Edward,
1946- , British; nonfiction
CON
DOWLING, Basil Cairns, 1910- ,
British; poetry CON VCP
DOWLING, Eddie, 1894-1976,
American; plays CON
DOWLING, Harry Filmore, 1904- ,
American; nonfiction CON
DOWLING, Richard, 1846-98,
Irish; journalism, fiction
HO
DOWLING, Thomas, Jr., 1921- ,
American; nonfiction CON
DOWNARD, William L., 1940- ,
American; nonfiction CON
DOWNER, Marion, 1892?-1971,
American; juveniles CO
'DOWNES, Quentin' see HARRISON,
Michael
DOWNES, Randolph Chandler,
1901-75, American; nonfiction
CON
DOWNEY, Fairfax Davis, 1893- ,
American; juveniles, nonfic-
tion CO
DOWNEY, Harris, 1907- ,
American; fiction BA
DOWNEY, James, 1939- , Cana-
dian; nonfiction CON
DOWNIE, Leonard, Jr., 1942- ,
American; nonfiction CON
DOWNIE, Mary Alice ('Dawe
Hunter'), 1934- , American;

juveniles CO KI
DOWNING, Christine, 1931- ,
German-American; nonfiction
CON
DOWNING, J. Hyatt, 1887- ,
American; fiction PAL
'DOWNING, Major Jack' see
SMITH, Seba
DOWNING, John Allen, 1922- ,
Anglo-Canadian; nonfiction
CON
DOWNING, Warwick, 1931- ,
American; fiction CON
DOWNS, Anthony, 1930- , Amer-
ican; nonfiction CON
DOWNS, Cal W., 1936- , Amer-
ican; nonfiction CON
DOWNS, Hugh Malcolm, 1921- ,
American; nonfiction CON
DOWNS, James Francis, 1926- ,
American; journalism, nonfic-
tion CON
DOWNS, Robert Bingham, 1903- ,
American; nonfiction ENG
DOWNS, Robert C. S., 1937- ,
American; fiction CON
DOWNS, William Randall, Jr.,
1914-78, American; journalism
CON
DOWSON, Ernest Christopher,
1867-1900, English; poetry,
fiction BU DA MAG PO VP
'DOX' (Jean Verdi Salomon Razu-
kandrainy), 1913- , Madagas-
can; poetry, plays JA
DOXEY, Roy Watkins, 1908- ,
American; nonfiction CON
DOXEY, William Sanford, Jr.,
1935- , American; poetry,
fiction CON
DOXIADIS, Constantinos Apostolos,
1913-75, Greek; nonfiction
CON
DOYLE, Sir Arthur Conan, 1859-
1930, English; fiction AS BU
CO DA MAG MCC NI PO REI
SEY ST VN
DOYLE, Brian, 1930- , English;
nonfiction CON
DOYLE, Charles Desmond ('Mike
Doyle'), 1928- , British;
poetry VCP
DOYLE, Charlotte Lackner,
1937- , Austrian-American;
nonfiction CON
'DOYLE, David' see CARTER,
David C.
DOYLE, Don Harrison, 1946- ,

American; nonfiction CON
'DOYLE, Donovan' see BOEGE-
HOLD, Betty D.
DOYLE, Esther M. , 1910- ,
American; nonfiction CON
DOYLE, James Stephen, 1935- ,
American; nonfiction CON
'DOYLE, Lynn' (Leslie Alexander
Montgomery), 1873-1961,
Irish; fiction, plays BU HO
'DOYLE, Mike' see DOYLE,
Charles D.
DOYLE, Richard, 1824-83, Eng-
lish; juveniles CO
DOYLE, Richard, 1948- ,
British; fiction CON
DOYLE, Richard James, 1923- ,
Canadian; nonfiction CON
DOYLE, Robert Vaughn, 1916- ,
American; nonfiction CON
DOZIER, Craig Lanier, 1920- ,
American; nonfiction CON
DOZOIS, Gardner R. , 1947- ,
American; fiction, anthology
AS NI
DRABBLE, Margaret, 1939- ,
British; fiction, plays, non-
fiction SEY VCN WAK
DRABBLE, Phil, 1914- , Brit-
ish; nonfiction CON
DRABEK, Jan, 1935- ,
Czech-Canadian; journalism,
nonfiction CON
DRABEK, Thomas Edward,
1940- , American; nonfic-
tion CON
DRACH, Ivan, 1936- , Ukrain-
ian; poetry CL
DRACHLER, Jacob, 1909- ,
American; nonfiction CON
DRACHLER, Rose, 1911- ,
American; poetry CON
DRACHMAN, Julian Moses ('Ben
Adam'; 'Melanie Goodall';
'Octopus'), 1894- , Amer-
ican; nonfiction CON
DRACHMAN, Theodore Solomon,
1904- , American; fiction
CON
DRACHMANN, Holger Henrik
Herholdt, 1846-1908, Danish;
poetry, fiction BU CL TH
'DRACO, F. ' see DAVIS, Julia
DRACONTIUS, Blossius Aemilius,
late 5th century, Latin; poetry
BU LA TH
DRAGER, Marvin, 1920- ,
American; nonfiction CON

DRAGNICH, Alexander N. , 1912- ,
American; nonfiction CON
DRAGO, Harry Sinclair ('Will Er-
mine'; 'Bliss Lomax'), 1888-
1979, American; journalism,
nonfiction, film CON
DRAGOJEVIC, Danijel, 1934- ,
Croatian; poetry BU
DRAGONETTE, Jessice,   -1980,
American; nonfiction CON
DRAGONWAGON, Crescent, 1952- ,
American;.juveniles CO CON
DRAGOUMIS, Ion, 1878-1920,
Greek; nonfiction BU
DRAITSER, Emil ('Emil Abramov'),
1937- , Russian-American;
nonfiction CON
DRAKE, Alice Hutchins, 1889?-
1975, American; nonfiction
CON
DRAKE, David Allen, 1945- ,
American; fiction CON
DRAKE, Donald Charles, 1935- ,
American; journalism, plays,
nonfiction CON
'DRAKE, Frank' see HAMILTON,
Charles H. S.
DRAKE, George Randolph, 1938- ,
American; nonfiction CON
DRAKE, Harold Allen, 1942- ,
American; nonfiction CON
DRAKE, John Gibbs St. Clair,
1911- , American; nonfiction
CON SH
DRAKE, Joseph Rodman, 1795-
1820, American; poetry BR
VP
'DRAKE, Kimbal' see GALLAGHER,
Rachel
DRAKE, St. Clair see DRAKE,
John St. C.
DRAKE, Stillman, 1910- , Amer-
ican; translations, nonfiction
CON
DRAKE, Walter Raymond, 1913- ,
English; fiction CON
DRAKE, William Daniel, 1941- ,
American; nonfiction CON
DRAKE, Winbourne Magruder,
1914- , American; nonfiction
CON
DRAMANI, Bazini Zakari, 1940- ,
Dahoman; poetry JA
DRANAS, Ahmet M. see DIRANAS,
Ahmet M.
DRANE, John William, 1946- ,
British; nonfiction CON
'DRAPER, Canyon' see HARRISON,

Hank
'DRAPER, Hastings' see JEFF-
RIES, Roderic
DRAPER, James Thomas, Jr.,
1935- , American; nonfic-
tion CON
DRAPER, John William, 1893-
1976, American; nonfiction,
poetry CON
DRAPER, Norman Richard,
1931- , American; nonfiction
CON
DRAPER, Ronald Philip, 1928- ,
British; plays, nonfiction
CON
'DRAPIER, M. B.' see SWIFT,
Jonathan
DRAPKIN, Israel, 1906- ,
Argentinian-Israeli; nonfiction
CON
DRASKOVICH, Slobodan M.,
1910- , Serbian-American;
nonfiction CON
DRATH, Viola Herms, 1926- ,
German-American; plays,
nonfiction CON
DRAWBELL, James Wedgwood,
1899- , American; nonfiction
CON
DRAWSON, Blair, 1943- ,
Canadian-American; juveniles
CO CON
DRAYTON, Henry Sinclair, 1839- ,
American; fiction NI
DRAYTON, Michael, 1563-1631?,
English; poetry, plays BU
DA MAG MCG PO RU VP
DRDA, Jan, 1915- , Czech;
fiction, plays BU TH
DREBINGER, John, 1891?-1979,
American; journalism CON
DREGER, Ralph Mason, 1913- ,
American; nonfiction CON
DREHER, Carl, 1896-1976,
Austrian-American; nonfiction
CON
DREIER, Frederik Henrik Hen-
nings, 1827-53, Danish; non-
fiction BU
DREIFORT, John E., 1943- ,
American; nonfiction CON
DREIFUS, Claudia, 1944- ,
American; nonfiction CON
DREISER, Theodore, 1871-1945,
American; fiction, nonfiction,
plays, poetry AM BR BU
MAG PO SEY ST VN
DREISER, Vera, American; non-

fiction, journalism CON
DREISS-TARASOVIC, Marcia Mar-
garet, 1943- , American;
poetry CON
DREITZEL, Hans Peter, 1935- ,
German; nonfiction CON
DRENNAN, William, 1754-1820,
Irish; poetry HO
DRESANG, Eliza Carolyn, 1941- ,
American; juveniles CO CON
DRESCHER, John Mummau,
1928- , American; nonfiction
CON
DRESCHER, Martin, 1863-1920,
German-American; poetry BU
DRESCHER, Sandra, 1957- ,
American; nonfiction CON
DRESSER, Davis ('Asa Baker';
'Matthew Blood'; 'Sylvia Car-
son'; 'Kathryn Culver'; 'Don
Davis'; 'Hal DeBrett'; 'Brett
Halliday'; 'Anthony Scott';
'Peter Shelley'; 'Anderson
Wayne'), 1904-77, American;
fiction CON REI ST WA
DREUX, William Behan, 1911- ,
Franco-American; nonfiction
CON
DREW, Donald J., 1920- , Eng-
lish; nonfiction CON
DREW, Patricia Mary, 1938- ,
English; juveniles CO CON
DREWERY, Mary, 1918- , Eng-
lish; juveniles CO
DREWRY, Henry N., 1924- ,
American; nonfiction CON
'DREXEL, Jay B.' see BIXBY,
Jerome L.
DREXLER, Arthur, 1925- ,
American; nonfiction CON
'DREXLER, J. F.' see PAINE,
Lauren B.
DREXLER, Rosalyn ('Julia Sorel'),
1926- , American; plays, fic-
tion CON VCD WAK
DREYER, Peter Richard, 1939- ,
American; fiction, nonfiction,
translations, poetry CON
DREYFACK, Raymond, 1919- ,
American; nonfiction CON
'DREYFUS, Fred' see ROSEN-
BLATT, Fred
DREYFUSS, Henry, 1904-72,
American; nonfiction CON
DREYFUSS, Joel, 1945- , Amer-
ican; nonfiction CON
DREYFUSS, Larry, 1928- , Amer-
ican; nonfiction CON

DREYFUSS, Randolph Lowell,
1956- , American; nonfiction
CON
DRIBERG, Thomas Edward Neil,
1905- , American; nonfiction
CON
DRIEU LA ROCHELLE, Pierre
Eugene, 1893-1945, French;
fiction, poetry BU CL TH
WAK
'DRIFTWOOD, Penelope' see DE
LIMA, Clara R.
DRIMMER, Frederick, 1916- ,
American; nonfiction CON
'DRINAN, Adam' see MACLEOD,
Joseph T.
DRINKLE, Ruth Wolfley, 1903- ,
American; nonfiction CON
'DRINKROW, John' see HARD-
WICK, Michael
DRINKWATER, John, 1882-1937,
English; poetry, plays BU
DA MCG PO VD
DRINKWATER, Terry, 1936- ,
American; journalism CON
DRISCOLL, Gertrude, 1898?-
1975, American; nonfiction
CON
DRISCOLL, Peter John, 1942- ,
English; fiction CON REI
DRISCOLL, Robert Eugene,
1949- , American; nonfiction
CON
DRISKELL, David Clyde, 1931- ,
American; nonfiction CON
DRIVER, Charles Jonathan,
1939- , British; fiction VCN
DRIVER, Christopher Prout,
1932- , English; nonfiction
CON
DRIVER, Godfred Rolles, 1892-
1975, British; nonfiction
CON
DRODE, Daniel, 1932- , French;
fiction NI
'DRORA, Bar' see LIEBERMANN,
Aharon S.
DROST, Aarnout, 1810-34, Dutch;
nonfiction, fiction BU TH
DROSTE, Coenraat, 1642-1734,
Dutch; nonfiction BU
DROSTE, Georg, 1866-1935,
German; fiction BU
DROSTE-HÜLSHOFF, Annette,
1797-1848, German; poetry,
fiction BU TH
DROUART la VACHE, late 13th
century, French; translations

BU
DROWATZKY, John Nelson, 1936- ,
American; nonfiction CON
DROWN, Harold James, 1904- ,
American; nonfiction CON
DROZHZHIN, Spiridon Dmitrievich,
1848-1930, Russian; poetry
BU
DRUBERT, John II., 1925- ,
American; nonfiction CON
DRUCKER, Malka, 1945- , Amer-
ican; nonfiction, juveniles
CON
DRUCKER, Peter Ferdinand,
1909- , American; nonfiction
CON WAK
DRUMEV, Vassil (Kliment, Metro-
politan of Turnovo), 1840-1901,
Bulgarian; nonfiction, plays
BU
DRUMHELLER, Sidney John,
1923- , American; nonfiction
CON
DRUMMOND, A. H., American;
juveniles WAR
'DRUMMOND, Charles' see 'Mc-
GIRR, Edmund'
DRUMMOND, Dorothy Weitz,
1928- , American; nonfiction
CON
'DRUMMOND, Ivor' (Roger Erskine
Longrigg; 'Rosaline Erskine'),
1929- , British; fiction, radio,
tv, nonfiction REI
'DRUMMOND, J.' see CHANCE,
John Newton
DRUMMOND, Jack ('George Red-
der'), 1923?-78, American;
fiction CON
DRUMMOND, John Dodds, 1944- ,
British; nonfiction CON
DRUMMOND, June, 1923- , Eng-
lish; fiction NI REI
DRUMMOND, Richard Henry,
1916- , American; nonfiction
CON
DRUMMOND, Violet Hilda, 1911- ,
British; juveniles, tv CO DE
KI
'DRUMMOND, Walter' see SILVER-
BERG, Robert
DRUMMOND, William, 1585-1649,
Scots; poetry, nonfiction, plays
BU DA PO RU VP
DRUMMOND, William Hamilton,
1778-1865, Irish; poetry HO
DRUMMOND, William Henry, 1854-
1907, Canadian; poetry CR

DRUMMOND, William Joe, 1944- ,
American; journalism, nonfic-
tion CON
DRUMMOND de ANDRADE, Car-
los, 1920- , Brazilian;
poetry, journalism, fiction
BR BU SEY WAK
'DRUMMONT,_ Judith' see MELEN-
DEZ MUÑOZ, Miguel
DRUMOND, Maldwin Andrew
Cyril, 1932- , British; non-
fiction CON
'DRUON, Maurice' (Maurice Kes-
sel), 1918- , French; fiction
BU TH WA
DRURY, Allen Stuart, 1918- ,
American; fiction, journalism,
nonfiction CON NI VCN WA
DRURY, Margaret Josephine,
1937- , American; nonfiction
CON
DRURY, Michael, American; non-
fiction CON
DRURY, Roger Wolcott, 1914- ,
American; juveniles CO
CON WAR
DRURY, Tresa Way, 1937- ,
American; nonfiction CON
DRUTMAN, Irving, 1910-78,
American; nonfiction CON
DRUXMAN, Michael Barnett,
1941- , American; nonfiction
CON
DRUYANOV, Alter ('Abgad Haed-
reyi'), 1870-1938, Israeli;
nonfiction BU TH
DRUZBACKA, Elzbieta Kowalska,
1695-1765, Polish; poetry
BU
DRUZHININ, Alexander Vasilye-
vich, 1824-64, Russian; non-
fiction BU
DRVOTA, Mojmir, 1923- ,
American; fiction, plays
CON
DRYANSKY, G. Y., American;
fiction CON
DRYDEN, Edgar A., 1937- ,
American; nonfiction CON
DRYDEN, John, 1631-1700,
English; plays, poetry, trans-
lations, nonfiction BRI BU
DA MAG MCG PO VD VP
'DRYDEN, Lennox' see STEEN,
Marguerite
DRYSDALE, Frank Reiff, 1943- ,
American; nonfiction CON
DRZIC, Dzôre, 1461-1501,

Ragusan; poetry BU
DRZIC, Marin, 1508-67, Ragusan;
plays BU
DU'AJI, Ali, 1909-49, Tunisian;
poetry, plays PRU
'DUANE, Jimm' see HURLEY, Vic
DUARTE, King of Portugal, 1391-
1438, Portuguese; nonfiction
BU TH
DUARTE, Fausto Castilho, 1903-
53, Cape Verde Islander; fic-
tion HER
DUARTE, Joseph Simon, 1913- ,
American; nonfiction CON
DU BARTAS, Guillaume de Sal-
luste, 1544-90, French; poetry
BU TH
DUBAY, Robert W., 1943- ,
American; nonfiction CON
DUBE, John Langalibalele, 1871-
1946, Zulu; fiction HER JA
LA
DUBE, Marcel, 1930- , Canadian;
plays, tv, translations, fiction
BU CR MCG
DUBE, Pierre Herbert, 1943- ,
Canadian; nonfiction CON
DUBE, Rodolphe see HERTEL,
Francois
DU BELLAY, Guillaume, 1491-1543,
French; poetry BU
DU BELLAY, Joachim, 1522-60,
French; poetry BU TH
DUBERMAN, Lucile, 1926- ,
American; nonfiction CON
DUBERMAN, Martin, 1930- ,
American; plays, nonfiction
VCD
DUBERSTEIN, Helen, 1926- ,
American; plays, poetry, fic-
tion CON
DUBIE, Norman Evans, 1945- ,
American; poetry CON
DUBILLARD, Roland, 1923- ,
French; plays CL TH
DUBIN, Robert, 1916- , Ameri-
can; nonfiction CON
DUBKIN, Lois Knudson, 1911- ,
American; juveniles WAR
DUBLIN, Thomas Louis, 1946- ,
American; nonfiction CON
DUBOFSKY, Melvyn, 1934- ,
American; nonfiction CON
DU BOIS, David Graham, 1925- ,
American; nonfiction CON
'DUBOIS, M.' see KENT, Arthur
W. C.
DUBOIS, Paul Martin, 1945- ,

American; nonfiction CON
DU BOIS, Shirley Graham, 1907-
77, American-Ghanaian;
nonfiction, plays, juveniles
CO CON SH
Du BOIS, Theodora McCormick,
1890- , American; fiction
NI
Du BOIS, William Edward Burg-
hart, 1868-1963, American;
poetry, fiction, nonfiction
BR BU CON PO VN
du BOIS, William Pène, 1916- ,
American; juveniles, fiction
CO KI NI
Du BOISGOBEY, Fortuné, 1821-
91, French; fiction ST
Du BOS, Charles, 1882-1939,
French; nonfiction CL
DUBOUT, Charles Albert, 1905-
76, French; nonfiction CON
DUBOV, Gwen (Bagni; Gwen
Bagni Gielgud), American;
fiction, film, tv CON
DUBOV, Paul, -1979, American;
film, fiction, tv CON
Du BRIN, Andrew John, 1935- ,
American; nonfiction CON
DUBROVIN, Vivian, 1931- ,
American; juveniles CON
Du CANGE, Charles du Fresne,
1610-88, French; nonfiction
BU
DUCAS, 1400?-70?, Byzantine;
nonfiction BU LA
'DUCASSE, Isidore L.' see
'LAURTEAMONT, Le Comte
de'
DUCHARME, Réjean, 1941- ,
Canadian; fiction, plays BU
DUCHER, Bruce, 1938- , Amer-
ican; fiction, nonfiction CON
'DUCHESNE, Antoinette' see
PAINE, Lauran B.
DUCIC, Jovan, 1871-1943, Ser-
bian; poetry BU CL TH
DUCIS, Jean Francois, 1733-
1816, French; translations,
plays BU
DUCK, Stephen, 1705-56, English;
poetry VP
DUCKERT, Mary ('Ann Hall'),
1929- , American; nonfiction
CON
DUCKETT, Alfred ('Glenn Doug-
las'), 1917- , American;
juveniles CON
DUCKETT, Eleanor Shipley,

1880?-1976, Anglo-American;
nonfiction CON
DUCKHAM, Alec Narraway,
1903- , British; nonfiction
CON
DUCKHAM, Baron Frederick,
1933- , British; nonfiction
CON
DUCKWORTH, Alistair McKay,
1936- , Scots; nonfiction
CON
DUCLOS, Charles Pinot, 1704-72,
French; fiction, nonfiction BU
TH
DUCORNET, Erica ('Rikki'),
1943- , American; juveniles
CO CON WAR
DUCORNET, Guy, 1943- , Amer-
ican; juveniles WAR
DUDA, Margaret Barbalich,
1941- , American; nonfiction,
plays CON
DUDEK, Louis, 1918- , Canadian;
poetry, nonfiction BU CON
VCP
DUDINTSEV, Vladimir, 1918- ,
Russian; fiction CL NI TH
WA
DUDLEY, Barbara Hudson (Bar-
bara Hudson Powers), 1921- ,
American; juveniles, plays
CON
DUDLEY, Edward, 1926- ,
American; nonfiction CON
DUDLEY, Guilford Allerton, 1921-
72, American; nonfiction CON
DUDLEY, Louise, 1884- , Amer-
ican; nonfiction CON
'DUDLEY, Nancy' see COLE, Lois
D.
'DUDLEY, Robert' see BALDWIN,
James
DUDLEY, Ruth Hubbell, 1905- ,
American; juveniles, nonfiction
CO CON
'DUDLEY-SMITH, T.' see TREVOR,
Elleston
DUDLEY-SMITH, Timothy, 1926- ,
British; nonfiction CON
DUDMAN, Richard Beebe, 1918- ,
American; nonfiction CON
DUEKER, Christopher Wayne,
1939- , American; nonfiction
CON
DUEKER, Joyce Sutherlin, 1942- ,
American; nonfiction CON
DUEÑAS, Juan de, -1460, Span-
ish; poetry BU

DUEÑAS GONZALEZ, Roseann,
1948- , American; nonfiction
MAR
DUERR, Edwin, 1904- , Amer-
ican; nonfiction CON
DÜRRENMATT, Friedrich,
1921- , Swiss-German;
plays, fiction BU CL MCG
REI SEY TH WA
Du FAIL, Noël, 1520-91, French;
fiction BU
DUFAULT, Joseph E. N. see
'JAMES, Will'
DUFF, Gerald, 1938- , Amer-
ican; nonfiction, poetry, fic-
tion CON
DUFF, John B., 1931- , Amer-
ican; nonfiction CON
DUFFERIN, Lady Helen Selina
Sheridan, 1807-67, Irish;
poetry, fiction HO
DUFFET, Thomas, fl. 1675,
English; plays BU
DUFFEY, Margery, 1926- ,
American; nonfiction CON
DUFFUS, Robert Luther, 1888-
1972, American; fiction,
nonfiction CON
DUFFY, Bernard, -1952,
Irish; plays, fiction HO
DUFFY, Sir Charles Gavan,
1816-1903, Irish; journalism,
poetry DA HO
DUFFY, Edmund, 1899-1962,
American; journalism CON
DUFFY, Francis Ramon, 1915- ,
American; nonfiction CON
DUFFY, James, 1809?-71,
Irish; printer HO
DUFFY, John Joseph, 1934- ,
American; nonfiction CON
DUFFY, Maureen, 1933- ,
British; fiction, plays, poetry,
translations SEY VCD VCN
DUFRESNY, Charles Rivière,
1654-1724, French; plays
BU MCG
DUFTY, William, 1916- ,
American; nonfiction, film
translations CON
DUGAN, Alan, 1923- , Amer-
ican; poetry BR CON MAL
VCP WA
DUGAN, Michael Gray, 1947- ,
Australian; juveniles, poetry
CO CON
DUGARD, C. John R., 1936- ,
South African; nonfiction

CON
DUGAS, Marcel, 1883-1947, Cana-
dian; nonfiction CR
DUGDALE, Sir William, 1605-
85/86, English; nonfiction BU
DUGGAN, Alfred, 1903-64, English;
juveniles, fiction, nonfiction
CO CON DEM MAG
DUGGAN, Eileen May, 1894-1972,
New Zealander; poetry VP
DUGGAN, Maurice Noel, 1922-75,
New Zealander; juveniles, fic-
tion BU CON KI VCN VN
DUGGAN, William Redman,
1915- , American; nonfiction
CON
'DUGGANS, Pat' see CONNOLLY,
Robert D., Jr.
DUGONICS, András, 1740-1818,
Hungarian; fiction, plays BU
DUGUID, John Bright, 1895-1980,
Scots; nonfiction CON
Du GUILLET, Pernette, 1520-45,
French; poetry BU TH
'DUHAMEL, Georges' (Denis Thé-
venin), 1884-1966, French;
nonfiction, poetry, fiction BU
CL CON SEY TH
DUHAMEL, Roger, 1916- , Cana-
dian; nonfiction, journalism,
translations BU CR
DUIKER, William J., 1932- ,
American; nonfiction CON
DUIM, Frederik, 1674-1750?,
Dutch; plays BU
'DUINKERKEN, Anton van' (Willem
Johannes Asssebergs), 1903-68,
Dutch; poetry, nonfiction BU
DUJARDIN, Edouard, 1861-1949,
French; fiction, poetry, plays,
nonfiction CL
Du JARDIN, Rosamond Neal, 1902-
63, American; juveniles, fiction
CON WAR
DUKE, Alvah Carter, 1908- ,
American; nonfiction CON
DUKE, Benjamin, 1931- , Amer-
ican; nonfiction CON
DUKE, Charles Richard, 1940- ,
American; nonfiction CON
DUKE, Forrest Reagan, 1918- ,
American; journalism CON
DUKE, James Taylor, 1933- ,
American; nonfiction CON
DUKE, Madelaine ('Maxim Donne';
'Alex Duncan'), 1925- ,
Swiss-English; fiction, juveniles
CON NI

DUKE, Richard De La Barre,
1930- , American; nonfic-
tion CON
'DUKE, Will' see GAULT, William
C.
DUKE, Winifred, -1962, Eng-
lish; fiction, nonfiction ST
DUKE-ELDER, Stewart, 1896-
1978, British; nonfiction CON
DUKER, Abraham Gordon, 1907- ,
Polish-American; nonfiction
CON
DUKER, Sam, 1905-78, American;
nonfiction CON
'DUKES, Philip' see BICKERS,
Richard L. T.
DULAC, Edmund, 1882-1953,
French; juveniles CO
DULANEY, Daniel the Elder,
1685-1753, American; non-
fiction BA
DULANEY, Daniel the Younger,
1722-97, American; nonfiction
BA
DULANY, Don E., Jr., 1928- ,
American; nonfiction CON
DULK, Albert Friedrich Benno,
1819-84, German; plays BU
DULL, Jonathan Romer, 1942- ,
American; nonfiction CON
DULLAERT, Heiman, 1636-84,
Dutch; poetry BU
DULLIN, Charles, 1865-1949,
French; plays CL
'DULOUP, Victor' see VOLKOFF,
Vladimir
DUMARCHEY, Pierre see 'Mac-
ORLAN, Pierre'
DUMAS, Alexandre Père, 1802-70,
French; fiction, plays BU
CO MAG MCG TH
DUMAS, Alexandre fils, 1824-95,
French; plays, fiction BU
MAG MCG TH
DUMAS, Andre, 1918- , French;
nonfiction CON
'DUMAS, Claire' see VAN WED-
DINGEN, Marthe
DUMAS, Frederic, 1913- ,
French; nonfiction CON
DUMAS, Henry L., 1934-68,
American; poetry, nonfiction,
fiction CON
Du MAURIER, Daphne, 1907- ,
English; fiction, plays, non-
fiction DA MAG NI REI ST
VCN VN
Du MAURIER, George Louis,

1834-96, English; fiction BU
DA MAG NI VN
DUMBLETON, Joseph, fl. 1740,
American; poetry BA
DUMERY, Henry, 1920- , French;
nonfiction CON
DUMITRIU, Petru, 1924- , Ru-
manian; fiction, plays BU
MAG WA
DUMMETT, Michael Anthony Eard-
ley, 1925- , British; nonfic-
tion CON
DUMOND, Dwight Lowell, 1895-
1976, American; nonfiction
CON
DUMONT, Jean-Paul, 1940- ,
French; nonfiction CON
DUNAN, Dougal, 1921- , British;
nonfiction CON
DUNASH ben LABRAT (Adonis Ha-
Levi), 920-80?, Hebrew; po-
etry, nonfiction BU
DUNATHAN, Arni Thomas, 1936- ,
American; nonfiction CON
DUNAWAY, John Marson, 1945- ,
American; nonfiction CON
DUNBABIN, John Paul Delacour,
1938- , British; nonfiction
CON
DUNBAR, Maxwell John, 1914- ,
Scots; nonfiction CON
DUNBAR, Paul Laurence, 1872-
1906, American; fiction, po-
etry BR BU PO VP
DUNBAR, Robert Everett, 1926- ,
American; nonfiction CON
DUNBAR, William, 1460-1513/20,
Scots; poetry BU DA PO VP
DUNBAUGH, Frank Montgomery,
1895- , American; nonfiction
CON
'DUNCAN, Alex' see DUKE, Made-
laine
DUNCAN, Alistair Charteris,
1927- , English; juveniles
CON
DUNCAN, Archibald Alexander,
1926- , Scots; nonfiction
CON
DUNCAN, Bruce, American; fiction
NI
DUNCAN, Chester, 1913- , Cana-
dian; nonfiction CON
DUNCAN, David, 1913- , Amer-
ican; fiction AS NI
DUNCAN, Delbert James, 1895- ,
American; nonfiction CON
DUNCAN, Elmer Hubert, 1933- ,

American; nonfiction CON
DUNCAN, Florence Belle, 1917?-
80, American; nonfiction
CON
DUNCAN, Frances Mary, 1942- ,
Canadian; juveniles CON
'DUNCAN, Gregory' see Mc-
CLINTOCK, Marshall
DUNCAN, Irma, 1897- , Amer-
ican; nonfiction CON
'DUNCAN, Jane' see CAMERON,
Elizabeth J.
DUNCAN, Julia C. see SATHER,
Julia C.
DUNCAN, Marion Moncure, 1913-
78, American; nonfiction
CON
DUNCAN, Norman, 1871-1916,
Canadian; juveniles, fiction
COM KI
DUNCAN, Reid Bingham, 1911- ,
American; nonfiction CON
DUNCAN, Robert Edward,
1919- , American; poetry,
plays, nonfiction BR BU
MAL PO VCP VP WA
DUNCAN, Robert L. see
'ROBERTS, James H.'
DUNCAN, Ronald Frederick
Henry, 1914- , British;
plays, fiction, poetry, non-
fiction, translation NI VCD
VCP VD
DUNCAN, T. Bentley, 1929- ,
American; nonfiction CON
DUNCAN, Thomas W., 1905- ,
American; nonfiction, fiction
PAL
DUNCAN, W. Raymond, 1936- ,
American; nonfiction CON
DUNCAN, William Murdoch
('John Cassells'; 'John Dallas';
'Neill Graham'; 'Martin
Locke'; 'Peter Malloch';
'Lovat Marshall'), 1909-76,
British; fiction REI
DUNCANSON, Michael Edwards,
1948- , American; nonfic-
tion CON
DUNCOMBE, Frances Riker,
1900- , American; juveniles
CO
'DUNDEE, Robert' see KIRSCH,
Robert R.
DUNDY, Elaine, 1937- , Amer-
ican; fiction, plays CON
VCN
DUNHAM, Bertha Mabel, 1881-

1957, Canadian; juveniles, fic-
tion KI
DUNHAM, Katherine ('Kay Dunn'),
1910- , American; nonfiction
CON SH
DUNHAM, Robert ('Bob Dunham';
'Dan Yuma'), 1931- , Amer-
ican; fiction, plays CON
DUNHAM, William Huse, Jr.,
1901- , American; nonfiction
CON
DUNKEL, Richard Hadley, 1933- ,
American; journalism CON
DUNKERLEY, Elsie J. see
'OXENHAM, Elsie'
DUNKLE, William Frederick, Jr.,
1911- , American; nonfiction
CON
DUNKLING, Leslie Alan, 1935- ,
British; nonfiction, radio, tv
CON
DUNLAP, George Dale, 1923- ,
American; nonfiction CON
DUNLAP, Jan, American; nonfic-
tion CON
'DUNLAP, Jane' see DAVIS, Adelle
DUNLAP, Joseph Riggs, 1913- ,
American; nonfiction CON
DUNLAP, William, 1766-1839,
American; plays, nonfiction
BR BU MCG PO VD
DUNLEAVY, Janet (Egleson; 'Janet
Frank'), 1928- , American;
fiction, translations, juveniles
CON
DUNLOP, Agnes M. R. ('Elisabeth
Kyle'; 'Jan Ralston'), Scots;
fiction, juveniles CO KI
DUNLOP, Derrick Melville, 1902-
80, American; nonfiction CON
DUNLOP, Eileen Rhona, 1938- ,
Scots; juveniles CO CON
DUNLOP, John Barrett, 1942- ,
American; nonfiction CON
DUNN, Alan Cantwell, 1900-74,
American; nonfiction CON
DUNN, Charles William, 1915- ,
Scots-American; nonfiction
CON
DUNN, Douglas Eaglesham, 1942- ,
Scots; poetry CON VCP WAK
DUNN, Edward D., 1883?-1978,
American; plays CON
DUNN, Esther Cloudman, 1891-
1977, American; nonfiction
CON
DUNN, Halbert Louis, 1896-1975,
American; nonfiction CON

DUNN, Henry Hampton, 1916- ,
American; nonfiction CON
DUNN, James Douglas Grant,
1939- , British; nonfiction
CON
DUNN, John Montfort, 1940- ,
British; nonfiction CON
DUNN, Judith see SPANGENBERG,
Judith
'DUNN, Judith F.' see BERNAL,
Judith F.
'DUNN, Kay' see DUNHAM, Kath-
erine
DUNN, Lloyd W., 1906- ,
American; nonfiction CON
DUNN, Mary Lois, 1930- ,
American; juveniles CO
CON WAR
DUNN, Nell see 'SANDFORD,
Nell M.'
'DUNN, Saul' (Philip M. Dunn),
1946- , English; fiction NI
DUNN, Si, 1944- , American;
journalism, poetry, nonfiction
CON
DUNN, Stuart, 1900- , American;
nonfiction CON
DUNN, Walter Scott, Jr., 1928- ,
American; nonfiction CON
DUNNAHOO, Terry, 1927- ,
American; juveniles CO
CON
DUNNAM, Maxie Denton, 1934- ,
American; nonfiction CON
DUNNE, Christopher Lee,
1934- , Irish; fiction HO
DUNNE, Finley Peter, 1867-1936,
American; journalism BR
VN
DUNNE, Gerald T., 1919- ,
American; nonfiction CON
DUNNE, John Gregory, 1932- ,
American; fiction, film, non-
fiction REI
DUNNE, Mary Collins ('Regina
Moore'), 1914- , Irish-
American; juveniles, nonfic-
tion CO CON WAR
DUNNE, Robert William, 1895-
1977, American; nonfiction
CON
DUNNELL, Robert Chester,
1942- , American; nonfiction
CON
DUNNETT, Alastair MacTavish,
1908- , Scots; nonfiction,
plays CON
DUNNETT, Dorothy Halliday,

1923- , British; fiction REI
DUNNIG, Ralph Cheever, 1878-
1930, American; poetry RO
DUNNING, Arthur Stephen,
1924- , American; juveniles
WAR
DUNNING, Brad, 1957- , Amer-
ican; nonfiction CON
DUNNING, Bruce, 1940- , Amer-
ican; journalism CON
DUNNING, John, 1942- , Amer-
ican; fiction, nonfiction CON
DUNNING, Lawrence, 1931- ,
American; fiction CON
DUNNING, Philip, 1891-1957,
American; plays MCG
DUNNING, Robert William, 1938- ,
English; nonfiction CON
DUNS SCOTUS, Johannes, 1265-
1308, Scots; nonfiction BU
DUNSANY, Edward John Moreton
(Plunkett), 1878-1957, Irish;
plays, fiction, poetry BU DA
HO MCG NI ST VD
DUNSTER, Mark, 1927- , Amer-
ican; plays CON
DUNTON, Samuel Cady, 1910?-75,
American; nonfiction CON
DUODU, Cameron, 1937- ,
Ghanaian; fiction, journalism,
poetry HER JA
DUPEE, Frederick Wilcox, 1904-
79, American; nonfiction CON
Du PERRIER, Charles (Dupérier),
1622-92, French; poetry BU
Du PERRON, Jacques Davy, 1556-
1618, French; poetry BU
'du PERRY, Jean' see SIMENON,
Georges
'DUPIN, August D.' see TAYLOR,
John A.
DUPIN, Jacques, 1927- , French;
poetry, nonfiction WA
Du PLESSIS, Izak Dawid, 1900- ,
Afrikaans; poetry, fiction BU
DUPRE, Josef Stefan, 1936- ,
Canadian; nonfiction CON
DUPREE, Louis, 1925- , Amer-
ican; nonfiction CON
'DUPRES, Henri' see FAWCETT,
Frank D.
DUPUY, Richard Ernest, 1887-
1975, American; nonfiction
CON
DUPUY, Trevor Nevitt, 1916- ,
American; juveniles CO
'DURAC, Jack' see RACHMAN,
Stanley J.

DURACK, Mary, 1913- , Australian; juveniles, plays, poetry, fiction CON KI
DURAM, James Carl, 1939- , American; nonfiction CON
DURAN, Daniel Flores, 1946- , American; nonfiction MAR
DURAN, Simeon ben Zemah (Rashbaz), 1361-1444, Spanish; poetry, nonfiction BU
DURAND, John Dana, 1913- , American; nonfiction CON
DURAND, Robert, 1944- , American; poetry CON
'DURAND, Xavier' see DESMARCH-AIS, Rex
DURANT, David Norton, 1952- , British; nonfiction CON
DURANTE, Jimmy, 1893-1980, American; nonfiction CON
DURÃO, Frei José de Santa Rita, 1702?-84, Brazilian; poetry BU
'DURAS, Marguerite' (Marguerite Donnadieu), 1914- , French; fiction, plays, journalism BU CL MCG SEY TH WA
DURAYD b. As-SIMMA, 530-630, Arab; poetry PRU
DURBAHN, Walter E., 1895?-1981, American; nonfiction CON
DURBIN, Richard Louis, 1928- , American; nonfiction CON
DURBRIDGE, Francis Henry ('Paul Temple'), 1912- , English; fiction, plays CON REI ST
D'URFE, Honoré, 1567-1625, French; nonfiction TH
DURCAN, Paul, 1944- , Irish; poetry HO
D'URFEY, Thomas, 1653-1723, English; poetry, plays, songs BU DA VD
'DURHAM, David' see VICKERS, Roy C.
'DURHAM, John' see PAINE, Lauran B.
DURHAM, Mae see ROGER, Mae
DURHAM, Marilyn, 1930- , American; fiction CON
DURIAN, Petros, 1852-72, Armenian; poetry, plays PRU
DURIS, 340-260 B.C., Greek; nonfiction BU GR LA
DURKA, Gloria, 1939- , American; nonfiction CON

DURKHEIM, Emile, 1858-1917, French; nonfiction CL
DURKIN, Henry Paul, 1940- , Czech-American; nonfiction CON
DURLAND, William Reginald, 1931- , American; nonfiction CON
DURRAK, Jam, -1706, Baluchi; poetry PRU
'DURRANT, Theo' see OFFORD, Lenore G.
DURRELL, Gerald, 1925- , English; nonfiction CO WA
DURRELL, Lawrence, 1912- , English; poetry, fiction, nonfiction, translations, plays BU DA MAG NI PO SEY VCD VCN VCP VN
DURRELL, Zoe Compton, 1910- , American; nonfiction CON
DURRENMATT, Friedrich see DÜRRENMATT, Friedrich
DURSLAG, Melvin, 1921- , American; journalism CON
'DURTAIN, Luc' (André Nepveu), 1881-1959, French; fiction, poetry, plays, nonfiction CL
DURYCH, Jaroslav, 1886-1962, Czech; nonfiction BU CL TH
Du RYER, Pierre, 1600-58, French; plays, translations BU MCG
DURZAK, Manfred, 1938- , German-American; nonfiction CON
DUSCHA, Julius Carl, 1924- , American; nonfiction CON
DUSHKIN, Alexander Mordecai, 1890-1976, Polish-Israeli; nonfiction CON
DUSKA, Ronald, 1937- , American; nonfiction CON
DUSKY, Lorraine, 1942- , American; journalism, nonfiction CON
Du SOE, Robert C., 1892-1958, American; juveniles COM
DUSSEL, Enrique D., 1934- , Argentinian; nonfiction CON
DUSSERE, Carolyn Thomas, 1942- , American; nonfiction con
DUSTER, Alfreda M. Barnett, 1904- , American; nonfiction SH
DUSTER, Troy, 1936- , American; nonfiction SH

DUTOURD, Jean Hubert, 1920- , French; nonfiction, fiction, plays BU CON MCG
DUTT, Michael Madhusudan, 1824-73, Bengali; poetry, plays BU PRU
DUTT, Rajani Palme, 1896-1974, British; nonfiction CON
DUTT, Sudhindranath see DATTA, Sudhindranath
DUTT, Toru, 1856-77, Indian; poetry BU DA
DUTTA, Reginald (Rex), 1914- , English; nonfiction CON
DUTT(A), Romesh Chandra, 1848-1909, Bengali; nonfiction, fiction BU
DUTT(A), Satyen, fl. 1882-1922, Bengali; poetry BU
DUTTON, Geoffrey Piers, 1922- , Australian; poetry, nonfiction, fiction, juveniles, translations BU CON VCN VCP VP
DUTTON, John Mason, 1926- , American; nonfiction CON
'DUTZ' see DAVIS, Mary O.
DUUH, Ali, -1910?, Somali; poetry HER
DUUN, Ole Julius (Olav), 1876-1939, Norwegian; fiction BU CL MAG TH
DUUS, Masayo, 1938- , Japanese-American; nonfiction CON
Du VAIR, Guillaume, 1556-1621, French; nonfiction BU TH
'DUVAL, Armando' see MONTEAGUDO, Joaquin
'DUVAL, Benjamin' see CESTERO, Ferdinand R.
DUVAL, Colette see 'VIVIER, Colette'
DUVAL, Jean-Jacques, 1930- , Franco-American; nonfiction CON
'DUVAL, Margaret' see ROBINSON, Patricia C.
DUVALL, Evelyn Millis, 1906- , American; juveniles CO
DUVALL, Richard M., 1934- , American; nonfiction CON
'Du VAUL, Virginia C.' see COFFMAN, Virginia E.
DUVEEN, Geoffrey, 1883-1975, British; nonfiction CON
DUVERGER, Maurice, 1917- , French; nonfiction CON
'DUVERNOIS, Henri' (H. Simon Schwabacher), 1875-1937, French; fiction, plays MCG
DUVOISIN, Roger Antoine, 1904-80, American; juveniles CO CON KI
Du WORS, Richard Edward, 1914- , American; nonfiction CON
DUY, Pham, 1927- , Vietnamese-American; nonfiction CON
DUYCKINCK, Evert Augustus, 1816-78, American; nonfiction BR MYE
DUYCKINCK, Evert A., 1823-63, American; nonfiction BR
DUYCKINCK, George Long, 1823-63, American; nonfiction MYE
DUYM, Jonkheer Jacob, 1547-1624, Dutch; poetry BU
DUYSE, Prudens van, 1804-59, Flemish; poetry BU
DVIVEDI, Mahavvirprasad, 1864-1938, Hindi; nonfiction PRU
DVORNIK, Francis, 1893-1975, Czech-American; nonfiction CON
DWIGGINS, Don, 1913- , American; juveniles CO WAR
'DWIGHT, Allan' see COLE, Lois D.
DWIGHT, John Sullivan, 1813-93, American; nonfiction MY
DWIGHT, Timothy, 1752-1817, American; nonfiction, poetry BR BU PO VP
DWORKIN, Andrea, 1946- , American; nonfiction CON
DWORKIN, Gerald, 1937- , American; nonfiction CON
DWOSKIN, Charles, 1922?-80, American; fiction CON
DWOSKIN, Stephen, 1939- , British; nonfiction CON
DWYER, Carlota Cardenas de, 1940- , American; nonfiction MAR
'DWYER, K. M.' see KOONTZ, Dean R.
DWYER-JOYCE, Alice, 1913- , Irish; fiction CON
DYBEK, Stuart, 1942- , American; fiction, poetry CON
DYCE, Alexander, 1798-1869, Scots; nonfiction BU
DYCK, Cornelius John, 1921- , Russian-American; nonfiction CON
DYCK, Harvey Leonard, 1934- ,

Canadian; nonfiction CON
DYCK, J. William, 1918- ,
Canadian; nonfiction CON
DYCK, Martin, 1927- , Canadian; nonfiction CON
'DYE, Anne G.' see PHILLIPS, Anne G.
DYE, Charles, 1926-60?, American; fiction NI
DYE, Frank Charles, 1930- , British; nonfiction CON
DYE, Hershel Allan, 1931- , American; nonfiction CON
DYE, Margaret, 1932- , British; nonfiction CON
DYEN, Isidore, 1913- , American; nonfiction CON
DYER, Beverly, 1921- , American; nonfiction CON
DYER, Charles Raymond, 1928- , British; plays, fiction VCD
DYER, Sir Edward, 1543-1607, English; poetry BU RU
DYER, Esther Ruth, 1950- , American; nonfiction CON
DYER, George Bell, 1903-78, American; nonfiction CON
DYER, James Frederik, 1934- , British; nonfiction CON
DYER, John, 1700-58, English; poetry BU DA PO VP
DYER, John Percy, 1902-75, American; nonfiction CON
DYER, Thomas Allan, 1947- , American; juveniles CON
DYER, Wayne Walter, 1940- , American; nonfiction CON
DYER, William Gibb, 1925- , American; nonfiction CON
DYGARD, Thomas J., 1931- , American; fiction CO CON
DYGASINSKI, Tomasz Adolf ('Dygas'), 1839-1902, Polish; fiction BU CL
DYGAT, Stanislaw, 1914-78, Polish; fiction BU CL
DYGERT, James Herbert, 1934- , American; nonfiction CON
DYK, Viktor, 1877-1931, Czech; nonfiction, poetry, fiction, plays BU CL
DYKEMAN, Richard Mills, 1943- , American; nonfiction CON
DYKHUIZEN, George, 1899- , American; nonfiction CON
DYKSTRA, Gerald, 1922- , American; nonfiction CON

DYKSTRA, Waling, 1821-1914, Frisian; nonfiction BU
'DYLAN, Bob' (Robert Zimmerman), 1941- , American; poetry, nonfiction CON VCP
DYMALLY, Mervyn Malcolm, 1926- , West Indian; nonfiction CON
DYMOND, Rosaline see CARTWRIGHT, Rosaline
DYMSZA, William Alexander, 1922- , American; nonfiction CON
DYROFF, Jan Michael, 1942- , American; poetry, plays, nonfiction CON
DYSON, Anthony Edward, 1928- , English; nonfiction CON
DYSON, Freeman John, 1923- , English; nonfiction CON NI
DYWASUK, Colette Taube, 1941- , American; nonfiction CON
DZANAYTY, Ivan see 'NIGER'
DZIATZKO, Karl, 1842-1903, German; nonfiction ENG
DZOVO, Emmanuel Victor K., 1915?- , Ghanaian; fiction HER
DZYUBA, Ivan, 1931- , Ukrainian; nonfiction BU CL
DZYUBIN, E. see 'BAGRITSKY, Eduard G.'

E

EADMER, -1124, English; nonfiction BU
EAGAN, Andrea Boroff, 1943- , American; plays, nonfiction CON
EAGAR, Frances, 1940- , English; juveniles CO CON
EAGER, Edward McMaken, 1911-64, American; juveniles, plays CO CON KI
EAGLE, Chester Arthur, 1933- , Australian; fiction, nonfiction CON
EAGLE, Mike, 1942- , American; juveniles CO
'EAGLESFIELD, Francis' see GUIRDHAM, Arthur
EAGLESON, John, 1941- , American; translations, nonfiction CON
EAGLETON, Terence Francis (Terry), 1943- , English;

nonfiction CON
EAGLY, Robert Victor, 1933- ,
American; nonfiction CON
EAKIN, Frank Edwin, Jr.,
1936- , American; nonfiction
CON
EAKIN, Richard Marshall, 1910- ,
American; nonfiction CON
EAKIN, Sue, 1918- , American;
nonfiction CON
EAKINS, David Walter, 1923- ,
American; nonfiction CON
EALHWINE see ALCUIN
EAMES, David, 1934- , Amer-
ican; fiction CON
EAMES, Edwin, 1930- , Amer-
ican; nonfiction CON
EAMES, Hugh, 1917- , American;
nonfiction CON
EAMES, John Douglas, 1915- ,
British; nonfiction CON
EAMES, Samuel Morris, 1916- ,
American; nonfiction CON
EAMES, Wilberforce, 1855-1937,
American; nonfiction ENG
EARDLEY, George Charles,
1926- , American; nonfiction
CON
EARL, Donald Charles, 1931- ,
English; nonfiction CON
EARL, Johnrae, 1919?-78, Amer-
ican; journalism CON
EARL, Paul Hunter, 1945- ,
American; nonfiction CON
EARLE, Alice Morse, 1853-1911,
American; juveniles WAR
EARLE, John, 1601?-65, Eng-
lish; poetry, nonfiction BU
DA PO
'EARLE, Marilee' see ZDENEK,
Marilee
EARLE, Olive Lydia, English;
juveniles CO
'EARLE, William' see JOHNS,
William E.
EARLE, William Alexander,
1919- , American; nonfiction
CON
EARLEY, George Whiteford,
1927- , American; anthology
NI
'EARLL, Tony' see BUCKLAND,
Raymond
'EARLSON, Ian M.' see DORN,
William S.
EARLY, James, 1923- , Amer-
ican; nonfiction CON
EARLY, Richard Elliott, 1908- ,

British; nonfiction CON
EARLY, Robert, 1940- , Ameri-
can; fiction CON
EARNEY, Fillmore Christy Fidelia,
1931- , American; nonfiction
CON
EARNSHAW, Anthony, 1924- ,
English; fiction CON NI
EARNSHAW, Brian, 1929- , Eng-
lish; juveniles CO NI
EASMON, Raymond Sarif, 1930?- ,
Sierra Leonese; fiction, plays
HER JA VCD
EASON, Ruth P., 1898?-1978,
American; nonfiction CON
EASSON, James, 1895-1979, Scots;
nonfiction CON
EASSON, William McAlpine,
1931- , American; nonfiction
CON
'EAST, Michael' see WEST, Mor-
ris L.
EAST, P. D., 1921-71, American;
journalism CON
EAST, William Gordon, 1902- ,
British; nonfiction CON
EASTHAM, Thomas ('Thomas Har-
ling'), 1923- , American;
nonfiction CON
EASTHOPE, Gary, 1945- , Brit-
ish; nonfiction CON
EASTIN, Roy Brandon, 1917- ,
American; nonfiction CON
EASTLAKE, William Derry,
1917- , American; fiction
BR KIB VCN WA
EASTLAND, Terry, 1950- ,
American; journalism, nonfic-
tion CON
EASTMAN, Addison J., 1918- ,
American; nonfiction CON
EASTMAN, Charles Alexander,
1858-1939, American; juveniles
COM
'EASTMAN, G. Don' see OOSTER-
MAN, Gordon
EASTMAN, Max Forrester, 1883-
1969, American; nonfiction,
poetry, translations BR BU
EASTMAN, Robert E., 1913- ,
American; fiction CON
EASTMAN, Roger Herbert, 1931- ,
American; nonfiction CON
EASTON, Allan, 1916- , Amer-
ican; nonfiction CON
EASTON, Carol, 1933- , Amer-
ican; nonfiction CON
EASTWICK, Ivy Ethel, American;

juveniles CO
EATOCK, Marjorie, 1927- ,
American; fiction CON
EATON, Charles Edward, 1916- ,
American; poetry, plays,
fiction, nonfiction VCP
EATON, Evelyn Sybil, 1902- ,
Swiss-American; fiction
CON
EATON, Faith Sybil, 1927- ,
British; nonfiction CON
'EATON, George L.' see VER-
RAL, Charles S.
EATON, Jeanette, 1886-1968,
American; juveniles CO CON
WAR
EATON, Theodore Hildreth, Jr.,
1907- , American; nonfic-
tion CON
EATON, Tom, 1940- , Amer-
ican; nonfiction, juveniles
CO CON
EATON, William Edward, 1943- ,
American; nonfiction CON
EAVES, Thomas Cary Duncan,
1918- , American; nonfiction
CON
EBAN, Abba Solomon ('Aubrey
Eban'), 1915- , Israeli;
nonfiction, translations CON
EBB, Fred, 1935- , American;
film, plays, tv CON
EBBESEN, Ebbe Bruce, 1944- ,
American; nonfiction CON
EBBETT, Eva ('Eva Burfield'),
1925- , British; nonfiction,
fiction CON
EBEL, Alex, 1927- , American;
juveniles CO
EBEL, Henry, 1938- , American;
nonfiction CON
EBEL, Robert Louis, 1910- ,
American; nonfiction CON
'EBEL, Suzanne' see GOODWIN,
Suzanne
EBENSTEIN, Ronnie Sue, 1946- ,
American; nonfiction CON
EBENSTEIN, William, 1910-76,
Austrian; nonfiction CON
EBER, Dorothy Margaret Harley,
1930- , English; nonfiction
CON
EBER, Irene, 1929- , German-
American; nonfiction CON
EBERHARD, Wolfram, 1909- ,
German-American; nonfiction
CON
EBERHARD of BETHUNE

(Bourges), fl. 1210, French;
nonfiction TH
EBERHARD von CERSNE, fl. 1400,
German; fiction BU
EBERHARD von GANDERSHEIM,
early 13th century, German;
poetry BU
'EBERHARDT, Peter' see ADAMS,
Robert F.
EBERHART, Dikkon, 1946- ,
American; fiction CON
EBERHART, Mignon Good, 1899- ,
American; fiction, plays CON
REI ST
EBERHART, Richard, 1904- ,
American; poetry, plays AM
BR BU MAG PO SEY VCP VP
EBERLE, Irmengarde ('Allyn Al-
len'; 'Phyllis Ann Carter'),
1898-1979, American; juveniles
CO CON
EBERLE, Paul, 1928- , American;
juveniles, nonfiction CON
EBERLIN von GÜNTZBERG, Johann,
1465-1530, German; fiction BU
EBERS, Georg Moritz, 1837-98,
German; nonfiction, fiction
BU
EBERSHOFF-COLES, Susan Vaughan,
1941- , American; nonfiction
CON
EBERSOHN, Wessel Schalk, 1940- ,
American; fiction CON
EBERSTADT, Charles F., 1914?-
74, American; nonfiction CON
EBERT, Alan, 1935- , American;
nonfiction CON
EBERT, Arthur F. see 'ARTHUR,
Frank'
EBERT, Friedrich Adolf, 1791-
1834, German; nonfiction
ENG
EBERT, Johann Arnold, 1723-95,
German; translations BU
EBERT, Roger Joseph, 1942- ,
American; journalism, film
CON
EBLE II de VENTADORN, 1100-40,
Provencal; poetry BU
EBLE GUI, fl. 1190-1240, Proven-
cal; poetry BU
'EBNE YAMIN' (Amir Mahmud),
1286-1368, Persian; poetry
PRU
EBNER, Margarethe, 1291-1351,
German; nonfiction BU
EBNER-ESCHENBACH, Marie von,
1830-1916, Austrian; fiction,

poetry BU TH
EBREO, Leone see ABARBANEL,
Judah
EBSEN, Buddy, 1908- , American; plays, nonfiction, tv
CON
EÇA de QUEIROS, José Maria de, 1845-1900, Portuguese; fiction, nonfiction TH
'ECCLES' see WILLIAM, Ferelith E.‾‾
ECCLES, David McAdam, 1904- , English; nonfiction CON
ECCLES, Frank, 1923- , British; juveniles CON
ECCLES, John Carew, 1903- , Australian; nonfiction CON
ECCLI, Sandra Fulton, 1936- , American; nonfiction CON
ECHEGARAY y ELIZAGUIRRE, José, 1832-1916, Spanish; plays BU CL MAG MCG TH
ECHERUO, Kevin, 1946-69, Nigerian; poetry HER
ECHERUO, Michael Joseph, 1937- , Nigerian; poetry, nonfiction CON HER JA VCP
ECHEVERRIA, Esteban, 1805-51, Argentinian; poetry BR BU
ECHEWA, Thomas Obinkaram, 1940- , Nigerian-American; fiction, plays CON
ECHOLS, Margit, 1944- , American; nonfiction CON
ECKAUS, Richard Samuel, 1926- , American; nonfiction CON
ECKBLAD, Edith Berven, 1923- , American; juveniles CO
ECKE, Wolfgang, German; radio, juveniles WAR
ECKEL, Malcolm William, 1912- , American; nonfiction CON
ECKELS, Jon (Askia Akhnaton), American; nonfiction, poetry CON SH
ECKERMANN, Johann Peter, 1792-1854, German; nonfiction BU MAG
ECKER-RACZ, L. Laszlo, 1906- , Czech-American; nonfiction CON
ECKERT, Allan W., 1931- , American; juveniles DEM WAR
ECKERT, Edward Kyle, 1943- , American; nonfiction CON

ECKERT, Horst ('Janosch'), 1931- , Polish; juveniles CO DEM
ECKES, Alfred Edward, Jr., 1942- , American; nonfiction CON
ECKHARDT, Robert Christian, 1913- , American; nonfiction CON
ECKHART, Johannes (Meister), 1260?-1327, German; nonfiction BU TH
ECKHOLM, Erik Peter, 1949- , American; nonfiction CON
ECKLEY, Grace, 1932- , American; nonfiction CON
ECKLEY, Mary M., American; journalism, juveniles CON
ECKLEY, Wilton Earl, Jr., 1929- , American; nonfiction CON
ECKMAN, Lester Samuel, 1937- , Polish-American; nonfiction CON
ECKSTEIN, Alexander, 1915-76, Yugoslav-American; nonfiction CON
ECKSTEIN, Gustav, 1890-1981, American; nonfiction, fiction CON
ECKSTROM, Jack Dennis, American; fiction NI
ECO, Umberto, 1932- , Italian; nonfiction BO CON
ECONOMOU, George, 1934- , American; poetry, nonfiction VCP
EDARI, Ronald Samuel, 1943- , Kenyan-American; nonfiction
EDBERG, Rolf, 1912- , Swedish; nonfiction CON
EDDINGS, Claire Neff, American; juveniles WAR
EDDIS, William, 1738-1825, English; nonfiction BA
EDDISON, Eric Rucker, 1882-1945, English; fiction NI WA
EDDISON, John, 1916- , English; nonfiction CON
EDDY, Edward Danforth, 1921- , American; nonfiction CON
EDDY, John, 1932- , American; nonfiction CON
EDDY, John Jude, 1933- , Australian; nonfiction CON
EDDY, John Percy, 1881-1975, British; nonfiction CON

EDDY, Paul, 1944- , British;
nonfiction CON
EDEL, Leon, 1907- , American;
nonfiction BOR WA
EDELBERG, Cynthia Dubin,
1940- , American; nonfiction
CON
EDELEN, Georges, 1924- ,
American; nonfiction CON
EDELL, Celeste, American;
juveniles CO
EDELMAN, Lily Judith, 1915-81,
American; juveniles, nonfic-
tion CO CON
EDELMAN, Maurice, 1911-75,
English; fiction, nonfiction,
journalism CON MCC VCN
WA
EDELSON, Edward, 1932- ,
American; juveniles WAR
EDELSTEIN, Arthur, 1923- ,
American; nonfiction CON
EDELSTEIN, David Simeon,
1913- , American; nonfiction
CON
EDELSTEIN, J. M., 1924- ,
American; nonfiction CON
EDELSTEIN, Morton A., 1925- ,
American; journalism CON
EDEN, Alvin Noam, 1926- ,
American; nonfiction CON
EDEN, Anthony, 1897-1977,
British; nonfiction CON
EDEN, Dorothy ('Mary Paradise'),
1912-82, British; fiction
CON REI
EDEN, Robert Anthony, 1897-
1977, British; nonfiction
CON
EDER, George Jackson, 1900- ,
American; nonfiction CON
EDEY, Maitland Armstrong,
1910- , American; nonfiction
CO CON
EDFELT, Johannes, 1904- ,
Swedish; poetry, nonfiction,
translations BU CL
EDGAR, David, 1948- , British;
plays CON VCD
EDGAR, David, 1948- , British;
plays CON VCD
EDGAR, Frank Terrell R. ('Bill
Ritchie'), 1932- , American;
nonfiction CON
'EDGAR, Josephine' see MUSSI,
Mary
EDGAR, Ken, 1925- , American;
fiction, juveniles CON

EDGAR, Neal Lowndes, 1927- ,
American; nonfiction CON
EDGAR, Oscar Pelham, 1871-1948,
Canadian; nonfiction BU
'EDGAR, Peter' (Peter King-Scott),
English; fiction NI
EDGE, David Owen, 1932- , Brit-
ish; nonfiction, tv CON
EDGERTON, Harold Eugene,
1903- , American; nonfiction
CON
EDGERTON, Robert Breckenridge,
1931- , American; nonfiction
CON
EDGEWORTH, Maria, 1767-1849,
Irish; fiction BU CO DA HO
MAG PO VN
EDGLEY, Charles Kenneth,
1943- , American; nonfiction
CON
EDINBOROUGH, Arnold, 1922- ,
British; nonfiction CON
EDINGER, Edward Ferdinand,
1922- , American; nonfiction
CON
EDINGTON, Andrew, 1914- ,
American; nonfiction CON
EDKINS, Anthony, 1927- , British;
nonfiction, translations CON
EDKINS, Diana Maria, 1947- ,
American; nonfiction CON
EDLIN, Herbert Leeson, 1913-76,
English; nonfiction CON
EDMISTON, Susan, 1940- ,
American; journalism, nonfic-
tion CON
'EDMOND, Jay' see JONES, Jack
EDMONDS, Arthur Denis ('Alan
Arthur'; 'Elizabeth Graham'),
1932- , British; nonfiction,
journalism CON
EDMONDS, Harry, English; fiction
NI
EDMONDS, Helen Grey, 1911- ,
American; nonfiction CON SH
EDMONDS, Helen W. see
'KAVAN, Anna'
EDMONDS, Ivy Gordon ('Gary Gor-
don'), 1917- , American;
juveniles CO WAR
EDMONDS, Margaret Hammett
('Margot Edmonds'), American;
nonfiction CON
EDMONDS, Randolph, 1900- ,
American; plays BA
EDMONDS, Robert H. G. ('Robin
Edmonds'), 1920- , British;
nonfiction CON

EDMONDS, Walter Dumaux,
1903- , American; juveniles,
fiction, nonfiction BR KI
MAG
EDMONDSON, Clifton Earl,
1937- , American; nonfiction
CON
EDMONDSON, G. C., 1922- ,
Mexican-American; fiction,
translations AS CON NI
EDMONDSON, Madeleine, Amer-
ican; juveniles WAR
EDMONSON, Harold Arthur,
1937- , American; nonfiction
CON
'EDMUND, Sean' see PRINGLE,
Laurence
EDMUNDS, Malcolm, 1938- ,
British; nonfiction CON
EDMUNDS, Stahrl William,
1917- , American; nonfiction
CON
EDMUNDS, Thomas Murrell,
1898- , American; fiction,
plays, poetry BA
EDOGAWA RAMPO, 1894- ,
Japanese; fiction LA
EDQVIST, Dagmar Jansson,
1903- , Swedish; fiction BU
EDSALL, Marian Stickney, 1920- ,
American; juveniles, nonfic-
tion CO CON WAR
'EDSCHMID, Kasimir' (Eduard
Schmid), 1890-1966, German;
fiction, nonfiction BU CL
TH
EDSON, Peter, 1896-1977, Amer-
ican; journalism CON
EDSON, Russell, 1935- , Amer-
ican; poetry, plays VCP
'EDWARDES, Allen' see KINS-
LEY, Daniel A.
EDWARDES, Michael F. H.,
1923- , English; nonfiction
CON
EDWARDS, A. W. F., 1935- ,
British; nonfiction CON
EDWARDS, Anne, 1927- , Amer-
ican; nonfiction, juveniles
CON
EDWARDS, Anne-Marie, 1932- ,
British; nonfiction CON
EDWARDS, Audrey, 1947- ,
American; juveniles CON
'EDWARDS, Bertram' see ED-
WARDS, Herbert G.
EDWARDS, Blake, 1922- , Amer-
ican; film CON

'EDWARDS, Bronwen E.' see
ROSE, Wendy
EDWARDS, Carl Normand, 1943- ,
American; nonfiction CON
EDWARDS, Cecile Pepin, 1916- ,
American; juveniles CO
EDWARDS, Charles, 1628-91,
Welsh; nonfiction BU
EDWARDS, Charles Mundy, Jr.,
1903- , American; nonfiction
CON
EDWARDS, Charleszime Spears,
1907- , American; nonfiction
SH
EDWARDS, Clifford Duane, 1934- ,
American; nonfiction CON
EDWARDS, Corwin D., 1901-79,
American; nonfiction CON
EDWARDS, David, American; fic-
tion NI
EDWARDS, David Charles, 1937- ,
American; nonfiction CON
'EDWARDS, Donald Earl' see
HARDING, Donald E.
EDWARDS, Donald Isaac, 1904- ,
English; nonfiction CON
EDWARDS, Dorothy, British;
juveniles, plays, poetry CO
KI
EDWARDS, Edward, 1812-86,
American; nonfiction ENG
'EDWARDS, Elizabeth' see
INDERLIED, Mary E.
EDWARDS, Elwyn Hartley ('Edward
Leyhart'), 1927- , English;
nonfiction CON
EDWARDS, George, 1914- , Amer-
ican; nonfiction CON
EDWARDS, Harry, American; non-
fiction SH
EDWARDS, Harry Stillwell, 1855-
1938, American; fiction, jour-
nalism BA
EDWARDS, Harvey, 1929- ,
American; juveniles CO WAR
EDWARDS, Herbert Charles ('Bert-
ram Edwards'), 1912- , Eng-
lish; juveniles CO
EDWARDS, Hilton, 1903- , Eng-
lish; nonfiction CON
EDWARDS, Hugh, 1878-1952, Eng-
lish; fiction SEY
EDWARDS, Jane (Campbell),
1932- , American; juveniles
CO
EDWARDS, Jaroldeen, 1932- ,
Canadian; fiction CON
EDWARDS, Jonathan, 1703-58,

American; nonfiction AM BR
BU MAG PO
'EDWARDS, Julie' see ANDREWS,
Julie
'EDWARDS, June' see BHATIA,
Jamunadevi
EDWARDS, Lynne, 1943- , Brit-
ish; fiction CON
EDWARDS, Malcolm John, 1949- ,
British; fiction NI
EDWARDS, Marie Babare, Amer-
ican; nonfiction CON
EDWARDS, Mark Ulin, Jr.,
1946- , American; nonfiction,
translations CON
EDWARDS, Michael, 1932- ,
British; nonfiction CON
EDWARDS, Monica le Doux,
1912- , British; juveniles,
plays, fiction CO KI
'EDWARDS, Norman' see CARR,
Terry
EDWARDS, Otis Carl, Jr.,
1928- , American; nonfiction
CON
EDWARDS, Owen Dudley, 1938- ,
Irish; nonfiction CON
EDWARDS, Sir Owen Morgan,
1858-1920, Welsh; nonfiction
BU
EDWARDS, Page L., Jr., 1941- ,
American; nonfiction, fiction
CON
EDWARDS, Paul, 1923- , Aus-
trian-American; nonfiction
CON
EDWARDS, Paul Geoffrey,
1926- , English; nonfiction,
translations CON
EDWARDS, Paul Madison, 1933- ,
American; nonfiction CON
EDWARDS, Peter, 1946- , Eng-
lish; fiction NI
EDWARDS, Richard, 1523?-66,
English; poetry, plays BU
EDWARDS, Richard Alan, 1934- ,
American; nonfiction CON
EDWARDS, Richard C., 1944- ,
American; nonfiction CON
EDWARDS, Sally Cary, 1929- ,
American; juveniles CO
'EDWARDS, Samuel' see GERSON,
Noel B.
EDWARDS, Thomas (Twm O'r
Nant), 1738/39-1810, Welsh;
poetry BU
EDWARDS, Tilden Hampton,
Jr., 1935- , American;

nonfiction CON
EDWARDS BELLO, Joaquín, 1887-
1968, Chilean; fiction BR BU
EDYANG, Ernest, 1935?- , Ni-
gerian; plays HER
EEDEN, Frederik Willem van,
1860-1932, Dutch; poetry, non-
fiction, fiction, plays BU CL
TH
EEKHOUD, Georges, 1854-1927,
Belgian; fiction, nonfiction BU
EEKMAN, Thomas, 1923- , Dutch-
American; nonfiction CON
EELLS, Robert James, 1944- ,
American; nonfiction CON
EFFEN, Justus van, 1684-1735,
Dutch; nonfiction, fiction BU
TH
EFFINGER, George Alec, 1947- ,
American; fiction AS COW
'EFRAT, Israel' see EFROS, Israel
EFREMOV, Ivan S. see YEFREMOV,
Ivan A.
EFRON, Arthur, 1931- , Ameri-
can; nonfiction CON
EFRON, Edith Carol, 1922- ,
American; journalism, nonfic-
tion CON
EFROS, Israel Isaac ('Efrat'), 1891-
1981, Polish-Israeli; transla-
tion, poetry, nonfiction BU
EFTIMIU, Victor, 1889- , Ruman-
ian; poetry, plays BU
EGAMI, Tomi, 1899- , Japanese;
nonfiction CON
EGAN, David Ronald, 1943- ,
American; nonfiction CON
EGAN, Desmond, 1940?- , Irish;
poetry HO
'EGAN, Lesley' see LININGTON,
Elizabeth
EGAN, Melinda Anne, 1950- ,
American; nonfiction CON
EGAN, Michael, 1941- , South
African-American; nonfiction
CON
EGAN, Pierce the Elder, 1772-
1849, English; journalism, po-
etry, nonfiction BU MAG VN
EGAN, Robert, 1945- , American;
nonfiction CON
'EGBERT, H. M.' see 'ROUSSEAU,
Victor'
EGBUNA, Obi Benu, 1942?- ,
Nigerian; plays, fiction CON
HER JA VCD
EGELHOF, Joseph Baird, 1919?-

80, American; journalism CON

EGEN von BAMBERG, fl. 1320-40, German; poetry BU

EGER, Ernestina N., 1942- , American; nonfiction MAR

EGERIA, (Aetheria), fl. 414-16, Gaulish; nonfiction TH

EGERTON, George William, 1942- , Canadian; nonfiction CON

EGERTON, John Walden, 1935- , American; nonfiction CON

'EGERTON, Lucy' see MALLESON, Lucy B.

EGGE, Peter, 1869-1959, Norwegian; fiction, plays BU CL TH

EGGELING, Hans Friedrich, 1878-1977, Scots; nonfiction CON

EGGENBERGER, David, 1918- , American; juveniles CO

EGGER, Maurice David, 1936- , American; nonfiction CON

EGGLESTON, Edward, 1837-1902, American; fiction, nonfiction BR BU MAG PO VN

EGGLESTON, George Cary, 1839-1911, American; fiction, nonfiction, juveniles, journalism BA

EGHAREVBA, Jacob Uwadiae, 1920?- , Nigerian; poetry, nonfiction HER JA

EGIELSKI, Richard, 1952- , American; juveniles CO

EGLESON, Janet see DUNLEAVY, Janet

EGLETON, Clive Frederick ('Patrick Blake'; 'John Tarrant'), 1927- , British; fiction CON MCC REI

'EGLINTON, John' (William Kirkpatrick Magee), 1868-1961, Irish; nonfiction HO

EGREMONT, Max, 1948- , British; nonfiction CON

EGUCHI, Shinichi, 1914-79, Japanese; poetry CON

EGUDU, Romanus, 1930?- , Nigerian; poetry, nonfiction HER

EGUREN, José María, 1882-1942, Peruvian; poetry BR BU

EGYPT, Ophelia Settle, 1903- , American; nonfiction, juveniles CO CON SH

EHRE, Milton, 1933- , American;

nonfiction CON

EHRENBERG, Victor Leopold, 1891-1976, German-British; nonfiction CON

EHRENBURG, Ilya see ERENBURG, Ilya G.

EHRENCRON-KIDDE, Astrid Margarethe, 1874-1960, Danish; fiction BU

EHRENFELD, David William, 1938- , American; nonfiction CON

EHRENPREIS, Anne Henry, 1927- , American; nonfiction CON

EHRENREICH, Barbara, 1941- , American; nonfiction CON

EHRENSTEIN, Albert, 1886-1950, Austrian; poetry TH

EHRENSVÄRD, Carl August, 1745-1800, Swedish; nonfiction BU

EHRENVAERD, Goesta Carl, 1910- , Swedish-American; nonfiction CON

EHRENWALD, Jan, 1900- , Czech-American; nonfiction CON

EHRESMANN, Donald Louis, 1937- , American; nonfiction CON

EHRHART, William Daniel, 1948- , American; poetry CON

EHRKE, Hans, 1898- , German; poetry, fiction BU

EHRLE, Francesco (Franz), 1845-1934, German; nonfiction ENG

EHRLICH, Amy, 1942- , American; juveniles CO

EHRLICH, Anne Howland, 1933- , American; nonfiction CON

EHRLICH, Cyril, 1925- , British; nonfiction CON

EHRLICH, Leonard Harry, 1924- , Austrian-American; nonfiction CON

EHRLICH, Max Simon, 1909- , American; fiction NI

EHRLICH, Nathaniel Joseph, 1940- , American; nonfiction CON

EHRLICH, Otto Hild, 1892-1979, American; nonfiction CON

EHRLICH, Paul Ralph, 1932- , American; nonfiction CON

EHRLICH, Walter, 1921- , American; nonfiction CON

EHRLICHMAN, John Daniel,

1923- , American; fiction CON

EHRMAN, Lee, 1935- , American; nonfiction CON

EHRSAM, Theodore George, 1909- , American; nonfiction CON

EIBY, George, 1918- , New Zealander; nonfiction, plays CON

EICH, Günter ('Erich Guenter'), 1907-72, German; poetry, fiction, radio BU CL CON SEY TH WA

EICHELBAUM, Stanley, 1926- , American; journalism CON

EICHELBERGER, Clarkmell, 1896-1980, American; nonfiction CON

EICHELBERGER, Clayton L., 1925- , American; nonfiction CON

EICHELBERGER, Rosa Kohler, 1896- , American; juveniles CON

EICHENBAUM, Boris Mikhaylovich, 1886- , Russian; nonfiction BU

EICHENBERG, Fritz, 1901- , German-American; juveniles CO CON

EICHENDORFF, Joseph, 1788-1857, German; poetry, translations, nonfiction, fiction BU MAG MCG TH

EICHER, Joanne Bubolz, 1930- , American; nonfiction CON

EICHNER, James A., 1927- , American; juveniles CO

EICHORN, Dorothy Hansen, 1924- , American; nonfiction CON

EICK, Draynder D. van see ENZINAS, Francisco de

EID, Leif, 1908?-76, American; journalism CON

EIDENBERG, Eugene, 1939- , American; nonfiction CON

EIDSVIK, Charles Vernon, 1943- , American; nonfiction CON

'EIFION WYN' (Eliseus Williams), 1867-1926, Welsh; poetry BU

EIFUKU MON-IN (Yofuku Monin), 1271-1342, Japanese; poetry HI

EIGNER, Lawrence Joel, 1927- , American; poetry, plays VCP

EIKE von REPGOWE, 1180-1235, German; nonfiction BU

EILAND, Murray Lee, 1936- , American; nonfiction CON

EILERS, Angelika see 'MECHTEL, Angelika'

EILHART von OBERG, fl. 1180, German; poetry BU TH

'EIN Geabonneerde op Het Bijblad' see HUET, Conrad B.

EINARSSON, Indridi, 1851-1939, Icelander; plays BU

EINHARD, 770-840, German; nonfiction BU GR TH

EINSEL, Naiad, American; juveniles CO

EINSEL, Walter, 1926- , American; juveniles CO

EINSTEIN, Albert, 1849-1955, German-American; nonfiction BU

EINSTEIN, Charles, 1926- , American; fiction, nonfiction, plays CON NI

EINSTEIN, Stanley, 1934- , American; nonfiction CON

EINSTOSS, Ron, 1930?-77, American; journalism CON

EINZIG, Paul, 1897-1973, Hungarian-British; journalism, nonfiction CON

'EIRELIN, Glenn' see EVANS, Glen

EISDORFER, Carl, 1930- , American; nonfiction CON

EISELE, Albert Alois, 1936- , American; nonfiction CON

EISELEY, Loren Corey, 1907-77, American; nonfiction, poetry CON WA

EISEMAN, Alberta, 1925- , American; juveniles CO CON WAR

EISEN, Carol see RINZLER, Carol

EISEN, Jack, 1925- , American; journalism CON

EISENBERG, Azriel Louis, 1903- , American; nonfiction CO CON

EISENBERG, Daniel Bruce, 1946- , American; nonfiction CON

EISENBERG, Gerson G., 1909- , American; nonfiction CON

EISENBERG, Howard, 1946- , Canadian; nonfiction CON

EISENBERG, Lawrence Benjamin ('Norma Dickens'), American; fiction AS CON

EISENBERG, Lee, 1946- , American; nonfiction CON

EISENBERG, Ralph, 1930-73, American; nonfiction CON
EISENBERG, Ronald Lee, 1945- , American; nonfiction CON
EISENBERGER, Kenneth, 1948- , American; nonfiction CON
EISENBUD, Jule, 1908- , American; nonfiction CON
EISENHOWER, Dwight David, 1890-1969, American; nonfiction CON
EISENHOWER, Milton Stover, 1899- , American; nonfiction CON
EISENSTEIN, Elizabeth Lewisohn, 1923- , American; nonfiction CON
EISENSTEIN, Phyllis, 1946- , American; fiction CON
EISENSTEIN, Samuel Abraham, 1932- , American; nonfiction, plays, fiction CON
EISERER, Leonard Arnold, 1948- , American; nonfiction CON
EISINDRATH, Craig R., 1936- , American; nonfiction CON
EISINGER, Peter Kendall, 1942- , American; nonfiction CON
EISLER, Colin Tobias, 1931- , German-American; nonfiction CON
EISLER, Paul Erich, 1922- , American; nonfiction CON
EISLER, Riane Tennenhaus, 1931- , Austrian-American; nonfiction, plays CON
EISMAN, Hy, 1927- , American; fiction CON
EISNER, Lotte Henriette, German; nonfiction CON
EISNER, Victor, 1921- , American; nonfiction CON
EISSENSTAT, Bernard W., 1927- , American; nonfiction CON
EISTER, Allan Wardwell, 1915- , American; nonfiction CON
EITEMAN, David Kurt, 1930- , American; nonfiction CON
EITINGER, Leo, 1912- , Norwegian; nonfiction CON
EITZEN, Allan, 1928- , American; juveniles CO
EITZEN, David Stanley, 1934- , American; nonfiction CON
EITZEN, Ruth Carper, 1924- , American; nonfiction, poetry,

juveniles CO CON
EIXIMENIS, Francesc, 1340-1409, Catalan; nonfiction BU
EIZYKMAN, Boris, 1949- , French; nonfiction NI
'EJIMA KISEKI' (Ejima Shigetomo), 1667-1736, Japanese; fiction BU HI
EKEH, Peter Palmer, 1937- , Nigerian; nonfiction CON
EKELÖF, Gunnar, 1907-68, Swedish; poetry, nonfiction, translations BU CL SEY TH WA
EKELUND, Vilhelm, 1880-1949, Swedish; poetry, nonfiction BU CL TH
EKKEHART I, 900?-73, Swiss; poetry, nonfiction BU TH
EKKEHART IV, 980-1060, Swiss; poetry, nonfiction BU TH
EKLUND, Gordon, 1945- , American; fiction AS NI
EKNATH, 1548-1608, Indian; hymns BU
EKREM RECAIZADE, 1847-1914, Turkish; nonfiction PRU
EKSTEINS, Modris, 1943- , Latvian-Canadian; nonfiction CON
EKWENSI, Cyprian, 1921- , Nigerian; juveniles, fiction BU HER JA KI LA SEY VCN VN WA
EKWERE, John, 1930?- , Nigerian; poetry, plays, fiction HER
ELA, Jean Marc, 1936- , Cameroonian; nonfiction JA
ELA, Jonathan Pell, 1945- , American; nonfiction CON
ELAM, Dorothy Allen Conley, 1904- , American; nonfiction SH
ELAM, Richard Mace, Jr., 1920- , American; juveniles, fiction CO CON
EL-AREF, Aref, -1973, Arab; nonfiction CON
ELASHOFF, Janet Dixon, 1942- , American; nonfiction CON
ELBERT, George A., 1911- , American; nonfiction CON
ELBERT, Virginie Fowler, 1912- , American; juveniles, nonfiction CON WAR
ELBIN, Paul Nowell, 1905- , American; nonfiction CON
ELBOW, Peter Henry, 1935- ,

American; nonfiction CON
'ELDER, Evelyn' see 'KENNEDY,
    Milward'
ELDER, Gary, 1939- , American;
    poetry CON
ELDER, Glennard Holl, Jr.,
    1934- , American; nonfiction
    CON
ELDER, Joseph, American; anthol-
    ogy NI
ELDER, Karl, 1948- , American;
    poetry, nonfiction CON
'ELDER, Leon' see YOUNG, Noel
ELDER, Lonne III, 1931- ,
    American; plays, film CON
    MCN SH VCD
ELDER, Mark, 1935- , Amer-
    ican; fiction CON
ELDER, Michael, 1931- , Eng-
    lish; fiction NI
ELDRED, Vince, 1924- ,
    American; nonfiction CON
ELDREDGE, Hanford Wentworth,
    1909- , American; nonfiction
    CON
ELDRIDG, Frank R., 1889?-
    1976, American; nonfiction
    CON
ELDRIDGE, Paul, 1888- ,
    American; fiction NI
ELEBE, Philippe ('Philippos'),
    1937- , Zairian; poetry,
    nonfiction JA
ELEK, Paul, 1906?-76, Hungarian-
    British; nonfiction CON
'ELEUTER' see IWASZKIEWICZ,
    Jaraslav
ELEVITCH, Morton D., 1925- ,
    American; nonfiction, fiction
    CON
'ELFED' (Howel Elvet Lewis),
    1860-1953, Welsh; poetry BU
ELFMAN, Blossom, 1925- ,
    American; juveniles, fiction
    CO CON
ELGAR, Frank, 1899- , French;
    nonfiction CON
ELGIN, Patricia Ann Suzette,
    1936- , American; fiction,
    nonfiction, poetry CON
ELGIN, Suzette Haden, 1936- ,
    American; poetry, fiction
    NI
ELGSTRÖM, Per, 1781-1810,
    Swedish; poetry BU
'ELIA' see LAMB, Charles
ELIADE, Mircea, 1907- , Ruman-
    ian; nonfiction BU CON WA

ELIAS, Albert J., 1920- , Amer-
    ican; fiction CON
ELIAS, Horace Jay, 1910- ,
    American; juveniles, nonfiction
    CON
ELIAS, Johannes F. see 'CELLI-
    ERS, Jan'
ELIAS, John Lawrence, 1933- ,
    American; nonfiction CON
ELIAS, Robert Henry, 1914- ,
    American; nonfiction CON
ELIASON, Joyce, 1934- , Amer-
    ican; nonfiction CON
ELIAV, Arie Lova ('Ben Ami'),
    1921- , Israeli; nonfiction
    CON
ELIAZ, Raphael, 1905- , Israeli;
    poetry BU
ELIE, Robert ('Pierre Daniel'),
    1915- , Canadian; plays, fic-
    tion, poetry BU CR
'ELIN PELIN' (Dimitar Ivanov),
    1878-1949, Bulgarian; fiction
    BU TH
ELINSON, Jack, 1917- , American;
    nonfiction CON
ELIOT, Alexander, 1919- , Amer-
    ican; nonfiction CON
'ELIOT, Anne' see COLE, Lois D.
'ELIOT, George' (Mary Ann Evans),
    1819-80, English; fiction BU
    DA MAG PO VN
ELIOT, John, 1604-90, American;
    nonfiction BR
'ELIOT, Mary Ann' see EVANS,
    Nancy
ELIOT, Sonny, 1926- , American;
    journalism CON
ELIOT, Thomas Hopkinson, 1907- ,
    American; nonfiction CON
ELIOT, Thomas Stearns, 1888-1965,
    American; poetry, plays, non-
    fiction AM BR BU DA MAG
    MCG MCN PO SEY VD VP
ELIOT HURST, Michael Eliot,
    1938- , Canadian; nonfiction
    CON
ELIS, Islwyn ffowe, 1924- ,
    Welsh; nonfiction, fiction
    CON
ELISABETH, Countess of Nassau
    and Saarbrucken, 1397-1456,
    German; fiction BU
ELISCU, Frank, 1912- , Amer-
    ican; nonfiction CON
'ELISIO, Filinto' see NASCIMENTO,
    Francesco M. do
ELISOFON, Eliot, 1911-73, Amer-

ican; juveniles, nonfiction CO
CON
ELISON, George, 1937- , Lithu-
anian-American; nonfiction
CON
ELIZABETH I, 1533-1603, English;
translations BU
ELIZONDO, Sergio D., 1930- ,
American; nonfiction MAR
ELIZONDO, Virgil P., American;
nonfiction MAR
ELKIN, Benjamin, 1911- , Amer-
ican; juveniles CO DEM
ELKIN, Frederick, 1918- ,
American; nonfiction CON
ELKIN, Judith Laikan, 1928- ,
American; nonfiction CON
ELKIN, Stanley Lawrence, 1930- ,
American; fiction, plays BR
HE VCN WAK
ELKIND, David, 1931- , Amer-
ican; nonfiction CON
ELKINS, Dov Peretz, 1937- ,
American; juveniles CO
ELKINS, Stanley Maurice, 1925- ,
American; nonfiction CON
ELKINS, Stephen Lloyd, 1941- ,
American; nonfiction CON
ELKON-HAMELCOURT, Juliette,
1912- , Belgian-American;
nonfiction CON
ELKOURI, Frank, 1921- , Amer-
ican; nonfiction CON
ELLACOTT, Samuel Ernest,
1911- , English; juveniles
CO
ELLEDGE, Jim, 1950- , Amer-
ican; nonfiction CON
ELLENS, Jay Harold, 1932- ,
American; nonfiction CON
ELLENSON, Gene, 1921- ,
American; nonfiction CON
ELLENTUCK, Shan, American;
juveniles WAR
ELLER, William, 1921- , Amer-
ican; nonfiction CON
ELLERMAN, Annie W. see
'BRYHER'
'ELLEY' (Seraphim Romanovich
Kulachikov), 1904- , Yakut;
poetry PRU
ELLIK, Ronald C. ('Fredric
Davies'), 1938-68, American;
fiction NI
ELLIN, Elizabeth Muriel, 1905- ,
New Zealander; juveniles KI
ELLIN, Stanley Bernard, 1916- ,
American; fiction, film

REI ST WA
ELLINGTON, Edward Kennedy
(Duke), 1899-1974, American;
nonfiction CON
ELLINGTON, Richard, 1915?-80,
American; fiction, radio CON
'ELLIOT, Daniel' see FELDMAN,
Leonard
'ELLIOT, Geraldine' see BING-
HAM, Evangeline M.
ELLIOT, Ian ('Colin Davies'),
1925- , American; journalism,
nonfiction, plays CON
ELLIOT, Jean (Jane), 1727-1805,
Scots; poetry DA
ELLIOT, John, 1918- , British;
fiction, tv NI
ELLIOTT, Alan Curtis, 1952- ,
American; nonfiction CON
ELLIOTT, Andrew Jackson, 1899-
1965, Canadian; fiction, nonfic-
tion CR
ELLIOTT, Aubrey George, 1917- ,
South African; nonfiction CON
ELLIOTT, Bruce ('Walter Levely';
'Bruce Stacy'; 'Walter Stacy'),
1915?-73, American; fiction,
nonfiction CON NI
ELLIOTT, David W., 1939- ,
American; fiction CON
ELLIOTT, Donald, 1928- , Amer-
ican; nonfiction CON
ELLIOTT, Ebenezer, 1781-1849,
English; poetry BU DA PO
VP
ELLIOTT, Emory, 1942- , Amer-
ican; nonfiction CON
ELLIOTT, Errol Thomas, 1894- ,
American; nonfiction CON
ELLIOTT, George Paul, 1918-80,
American; fiction, poetry, non-
fiction CON VCN VCP WA
ELLIOTT, Harley, 1940- , Amer-
ican; poetry CON
ELLIOTT, Harry Chandler, 1909- ,
Canadian-American; fiction NI
ELLIOTT, Lesley ('Lesley Gor-
don'), 1905- , British; fiction,
juveniles, nonfiction CON
ELLIOTT, Malissa Childs (Malissa
Redfield), 1929?-79, American;
fiction CON
ELLIOTT, Osborn, 1924- , Amer-
ican; journalism, nonfiction
CON
'ELLIOTT, Robert' see BANNER-
MAN, James
ELLIOTT, Roberta, New Zealander;

juveniles, plays CON KI
ELLIOTT, Russell Richard,
1912- , American; nonfiction
CON
ELLIOTT, Sarah Barnwell, 1848-
1928, American; fiction BA
ELLIOTT, Sarah McCarn, 1930- ,
American; juveniles, nonfic-
tion CO CON WAR
ELLIOTT, Thomas Joseph, 1941- ,
American; nonfiction, trans-
lations CON
ELLIOTT, Ward Edward Yandell,
1937- , American; nonfiction
CON
ELLIOTT, William III, 1788-
1863, American; nonfiction
BA MYE
ELLIOTT, William Douglas,
1938- , American; nonfiction
CON
ELLIOTT, William Yandell, 1896-
1979, American; nonfiction
CON
ELLIS, Alec Charles, 1932- ,
English; nonfiction CON
ELLIS, Audrey, English; non-
fiction CON
ELLIS, Brooks Fleming, 1897-
1976, American; nonfiction
CON
ELLIS, Byron Robert, 1940- ,
American; nonfiction CON
'ELLIS, Craig' house name NI
ELLIS, D. E., English; fiction
NI
ELLIS, Edward Sylvester ('B. H.
Belknap'; 'J. G. Bethune';
'Captain L. C. Carleton';
'Col. H. R. Gordon'; 'Captain
R. M. Hawthorne'; 'Lt. R.
H. Jayne'; 'C. E. Lassalle';
'Seward D. Lisle'; 'Billex
Muller'; 'Lt. J. H. Randolph';
'Seelin Robins'; 'Emerson
Rodman'; 'Captain Wheeler'),
1840-1916, American; juven-
iles, fiction COM NI
ELLIS, Ella Thorp, 1928- ,
American; juveniles CO CON
WAR
ELLIS, Florence Hawley (Flor-
ence M. Hawley; 'Florence
H. Senter'), 1906- , Amer-
ican; nonfiction CON
ELLIS, Frank Hale, 1916- ,
American; nonfiction CON
ELLIS, George, 1753-1815, Eng-

lish; nonfiction, fiction BU
DA
ELLIS, Harry Bearse, 1921- ,
American; juveniles CO
ELLIS, Henry Carlton, 1927- ,
American; nonfiction CON
ELLIS, Henry Havelock, 1859-
1939, English; nonfiction BU
ELLIS, Howard Sylvester, 1898- ,
American; nonfiction CON
ELLIS, J. Franklyn, 1904?-76,
American; nonfiction CON
ELLIS, Jack Clare, 1922- ,
American; nonfiction CON
ELLIS, Jody, 1925- , American;
nonfiction CON
ELLIS, John Marion, 1917- ,
American; nonfiction CON
ELLIS, John Martin, 1936- ,
Anglo-American; nonfiction
CON
ELLIS, John Oliver, 1917- ,
American; nonfiction CON
ELLIS, John Richard, 1938- ,
Australian; nonfiction CON
ELLIS, Joseph John, 1943- ,
American; nonfiction CON
ELLIS, Keith Stanley, 1927- ,
British; nonfiction CON
ELLIS, Madeleine Blanche, 1915- ,
Canadian; nonfiction CON
ELLIS, Mark Karl, 1945- , Brit-
ish; fiction CON
ELLIS, Melvin Richard, 1912- ,
American; juveniles CO
ELLIS, Peter Berresford ('Peter
Tremayne'), 1943- , British;
journalism, nonfiction, fiction
CON
ELLIS, Richard Emanuel, 1937- ,
American; nonfiction CON
ELLIS, Ronald Walter, 1941- ,
British; poetry CON
ELLIS, William, 1918- , Ameri-
can; fiction CON
ELLIS, William Donohue, 1918- ,
American; fiction, nonfiction
CON
ELLISON, Craig William, 1944- ,
American; nonfiction CON
ELLISON, Glenn, 1911- , Ameri-
can; nonfiction CON
ELLISON, Harlan Jay, 1934- ,
American; fiction AS COW NI
WAK
ELLISON, Katherine White,
1941- , American; nonfiction
CON

ELLISON, Lucile Watkins, 1907?-
79, American; juveniles CO
CON
ELLISON, Max, 1914- , Amer-
ican; poetry CON
ELLISON, Ralph Waldo, 1914- ,
American; fiction BA BR BU
HE MAG PO SEY SH VCN
VN WA
ELLISON, Virginia Howell ('Vir-
ginia Tier Howell'; 'Mary A.
Mapes'; 'Virginia T. H.
Mussey'; 'V. H. Soskin';
'Leong Gor Yung'), 1910- ,
American; juveniles CO WAR
ELLISON, William McLaren,
1919?-78, American; jour-
nalism CON
ELLISTON, Thomas Ralph, 1919-
77, American; journalism
CON
ELLITHORPE, Harold Earle,
1925- , American; nonfiction
CON
ELLMAN, Michael, 1942- ,
English; nonfiction CON
ELLMANN, Richard, 1918- ,
American; nonfiction BOR
HO WA
ELLSBERG, Daniel, 1931- ,
American; nonfiction CON
ELLSBERG, Edward, 1891- ,
American; juveniles CO
ELLSWORTH, Samuel George,
1916- , American; nonfiction
CON
ELLUL, Jacques, 1912- ,
French; nonfiction CON
ELLWOOD, Robert Scott, Jr.,
1933- , American; nonfiction
CON
ELMAN, Robert, 1930- , Amer-
ican; nonfiction, juveniles
CON
ELMANDJRA, Mahdi, 1933- ,
Morroccan; nonfiction CON
ELMEN, Paul H., 1931- ,
American; nonfiction CON
ELMENDORF, Mary Lindsay,
1917- , American; nonfiction
CON
ELMENDORF, Theresa West,
1855-1932, American; non-
fiction ENG
ELMER, Carlos Hall, 1920- ,
American; nonfiction CON
EL-MESSIDI, Kathyanne Groehn
(Kathy Groehn Cosseboom),

1946- , American; nonfiction
CON
ELMI, Bownderi see ILMI, Bown-
deri
ELMORE, Ernest C. see 'BUDE,
John'
ELMS, Alan Clinton, 1938- ,
American; nonfiction CON
ELMSLIE, Kenward, 1929- ,
American; plays, fiction, po-
etry VCP
ELOVITZ, Mark Harvey, 1938- ,
American; nonfiction CON
'ELPHINSTONE, Murgatroyd' see
KAHLER, Hugh M.
'ELPIDON' see BALUCKI, Michal
EL SAFFAR, Ruth Ann, 1941- ,
American; nonfiction CON
ELSASSER, Albert Bertrand,
1918- , American; nonfiction
CON
ELSASSER, Glen Robert, 1935- ,
American; journalism CON
ELSBERRY, Terence, 1943- ,
American; nonfiction CON
ELSE, Gerald Frank, 1908- ,
American; nonfiction CON
ELSKAMP, Max, 1862-1931, Bel-
gian; poetry BU CL
ELSNER, Gisela, 1937- , Ger-
man; fiction CL
ELSOM, John Edward, 1934- ,
English; nonfiction CON
ELSON, Lawrence McClellan,
1935- , American; nonfiction
CON
ELSON, Robert Truscott, 1906- ,
American; journalism, nonfic-
tion CON
'ELSPETH' see BRAGDON, Elspeth
M.
'ELSSCHOT, Willem' (Alfons de
Ridder), 1882-1960, Flemish;
fiction, poetry BU SEY TH
'ELSTAR, Dow' see GALLUN, Ray-
mond Z.
ELSTER, Kristian Mandrup, 1841-
81, Norwegian; fiction BU
ELSTOB, Elizabeth, 1663-1756,
English; translations, nonfiction
BU
ELSY, Winifred Mary, British;
nonfiction CON
ELTON, Edwin Joel, 1939- ,
American; nonfiction CON
'ELUARD, Paul' (Eugene Grindel),
1895-1952, French; poetry
BU CL SEY TH

ELVIN, Mark, 1938- , British; translation, nonfiction CON
ELWELL, Jerry MacElroy, 1922- , American; nonfiction, juveniles CON
ELWIN, Malcolm, 1903-73, British; journalism, nonfiction CON
ELWOOD, Catharyn, 1903?-75, American; nonfiction CON
ELWOOD, Roger, 1943- , American; juveniles, fiction AS CON NI WAR
ELY, David, 1927- , American; fiction, journalism CON NI VCN
ELY, James Wallace, Jr. , 1938- , American; nonfiction CON
ELY, John Hart, 1938- , American; nonfiction CON
ELY, Paul Henri, 1897-1975, American; nonfiction CON
ELYOT, Sir Thomas, 1490?-1546, English; nonfiction, translations BU DA PO RU
'ELYTIS, Odysseus' (Odysseus Alepoudelis), 1911/12- , Greek; poetry CL CON TH WA
ELZABURU, Manuel ('Américo Amador'; 'Fabian Montes'), 1851-92, Puerto Rican; journalism, poetry, translations HIL
ELZINGA, Kenneth Gerald, 1941- , American; nonfiction CON
EMANS, Robert, 1934- , American; nonfiction CON
EMANTS, Marcellus, 1848-1923, Dutch; poetry, plays, fiction BU CL
EMANUEL, James Andrew, Sr. , 1921/23- , American; poetry, nonfiction MAL SH VCP
EMANUEL, Victor R. see 'ROUSSEAU, Victor'
EMBER, Carol Ruchlis, 1943- , American; nonfiction CON
EMBERLEY, Barbara Anne, 1932- , American; juveniles CO DE
EMBERLEY, Edward Randolph, 1931- , American; juveniles CO DE
EMBIRIKOS, Andreas, 1901- , Greek; poetry TH
EMBODEN, William A. , Jr. ,

1935- , American; nonfiction CON
EMBRY, Margaret Jacob, 1919- , American; juveniles CO WAR
EMECHETA, Buchi, 1944- , Nigerian; fiction CON
EMENEGGER, Robert, 1933- , American; fiction CON
EMERICH, Kenneth Fred, 1925- , American; nonfiction CON
EMERSON, Caroline D. , 1891-1973, American; juveniles CON
EMERSON, Frank Creighton, 1936- , American; nonfiction CON
'EMERSON, Mary Lee' see KENNEDY, Mary
EMERSON, Ralph Waldo, 1803-82, American; poetry, nonfiction AM BR BU MAG MY PO VN VP
EMERSON, Rupert, 1899-1979, American; nonfiction CON
EMERSON, William Keith, 1925- , American; nonfiction, juveniles CO CON
EMERSON, Willis George, 1856-1918, American; fiction NI
EMERY, Alan Eglin H. , 1928- , British; nonfiction CON
EMERY, Edwin, 1914- , American; nonfiction CON
EMERY, Fred, 1933- , English; journalism CON
EMERY, Michael, 1940- , American; nonfiction CON
EMERY, Pierre-Yves, 1929- , Dutch; nonfiction CON
EMETT, Rowland, 1906- , British; juveniles CON
EMIG, Janet Ann, American; nonfiction, poetry CON
EMIN, Fëdor Alexandrovich, 1735?-70, Russian; fiction BU
EMIN, Gevorg, 1919- , Armenian; poetry PRU
EMINESCU, Mihai (Eminovici), 1850-89, Rumanian; poetry BU TH
'EMMANUEL, Pierre' (Jean Noël Mathieu), 1916- , French; poetry BU CL WA
EMMERSON, Donald Kenneth, 1940- , American; nonfiction CON
EMMERSON, John Kenneth, 1908- , American; nonfiction CON
EMMET, Robert, 1778-1803, Irish;

315 EMMETT

speeches HO
EMMETT, Bruce, 1949- , American; juveniles CON
EMMRICH, Kurt see 'BAMM, Peter'
EMORY, Alan Steuer, 1922- , American; journalism CON
EMPEDOCLES, 493-33 B.C., Greek; poetry, nonfiction BU GR LA
'EMPLOYEE X' see FAUTSKO, Timothy F.
EMPSON, William, 1906- , English; poetry, nonfiction BOR BU DA PO SEY VCP VP
EMRICH, Duncan (Blackie Macdonald), 1908- , American; juveniles, nonfiction CO CON WAR
'EMRYS ap IWAN' (Robert Ambrose Jones), 1851-1906, Welsh; nonfiction BU
'EMSH, Ed' (Edmund Alexander Emshwiller), 1925- , American; illustrator AS NI
EMSHWILLER, Carol, American; fiction AS CON NI
EMSLEY, Michael Gordon, 1930- , Anglo-American; nonfiction CON
'EMSLIE, M. L.' see SIMPSON, Myrtle L.
EMY, Hugh Vincent, 1944- , British; nonfiction CON
ENAHORO, Anthony, 1923- , Nigerian; nonfiction JA
ENAHORO, Peter ('Peter Pan'), 1935- , Nigerian; journalism, nonfiction JA
ENAMORADO CUESTA, José, 1892- , Puerto Rican; journalism, poetry HIL
ENCHI FUMIKO, 1905- , Japanese; fiction HI
ENCINA, Juan del, 1468-1529?, Spanish; poetry, plays BU MCG TH
ENCKELL, Rabbi Arnfinn, 1903-74, Finnish-Swedish; poetry, plays, nonfiction BU CL TH
ENDE, Jean, 1947- , American; nonfiction CON
ENDO, Mitsuko, 1942- , Japanese-American; nonfiction CON
ENDORE, Guy S., 1900-70, American; fiction, translations NI
ENDY, Melvin Becker, Jr., 1938- , American; nonfiction

CON
ENEA SILVIO Piccolomini, 1405-64, Italian; nonfiction BO
ENGDAHL, Sylvia Louise, 1933- , American; fiction, juveniles CO DEM KI NI WAR
ENGEBRECHT, Patricia Ann, 1935- , American; fiction, poetry, nonfiction CON
ENGEL, Aaron Lehman, 1910- , American; nonfiction CON
ENGEL, Leonard, 1916- , American; fiction NI
ENGEL, Lyle Kenyon ('Jeffrey Lord'), 1915- , American; fiction, nonfiction CON NI
ENGEL, Madeline Helena, 1941- , American; nonfiction CON
ENGEL, Marian, 1933- , Canadian; fiction, juveniles VCN
ENGEL, Peter H., 1935- , German-American; nonfiction, fiction CON
ENGEL, Srul Morris, 1931- , Polish-American; translations, nonfiction CON
ENGELBRETSDATTER, Dorothe, 1634-1716, Norwegian; poetry BU
ENGELKING, L. L., 1903-80, American; journalism CON
'ENGELMAN, Jan' (Johann Aloysius Antonius), 1900- , Dutch; poetry, nonfiction BU
ENGELMAN, Rose C., 1919-79, American; nonfiction CON
ENGELMANN, Hugo Otto, 1917- , Austrian-American; nonfiction CON
ENGELMANN, Larry, 1941- , American; nonfiction CON
ENGELS, Donald W., 1946- , American; nonfiction CON
ENGEN, Rodney Kent, 1948- , American; nonfiction CON
ENGERMAN, Stanley Lewis, 1936- , American; nonfiction CON
ENGH, John ('H. T. White'), 1938- , American; nonfiction con
ENGH, Mary Jane, 1933- , American; fiction, poetry CON NI
ENGHOLM, Eva, 1909- , British; nonfiction CON
ENGL, Lieselotte, 1918- , German; nonfiction CON
ENGL, Theodor, 1925- , German;

nonfiction CON
ENGLAND, Anthony Bertram, 1939- , British; nonfiction CON
ENGLAND, Barry, 1934- , British; plays, fiction VCD
'ENGLAND, E. Squires' see BALL, Sylvia P.
ENGLAND, George Allan, 1877-1936, American; fiction AS NI
ENGLE, Eloise Katherine, 1923- , American; juveniles CO
ENGLE, Jeffrey, 1947- , American; nonfiction CON
ENGLE, John David, Jr. ('David Johnn'), 1922- , American; poetry, plays CON
ENGLE, Paul Hamilton, 1908- , American; poetry, fiction, nonfiction, translations, plays PAL VCP WA
ENGLEBERT, Victor, 1933- , Belgian; juveniles CO CON
ENGLER, Larry, 1949- , American; nonfiction CON
'ENGLISH, Arnold' see HERSHMAN, Morris
'ENGLISH, Charles' see NUETZEL, Charles A.
ENGLISH, David, 1931- , British; journalism, nonfiction CON
ENGLISH, Deirdre Elena, 1948- , American; nonfiction CON
ENGLISH, E. Schuyller, 1899-1981, American; nonfiction CON
ENGLISH, Edward H., 19?- 73, American; poetry CON
ENGLISH, Fenwick Walter, 1939- , American; nonfiction CON
ENGLISH, Isobel, 1923- , British; fiction CON VCN
ENGLISH, John Wesley, 1940- , American; nonfiction CON
ENGLISH, Maurice, 1909- , American; poetry, nonfiction, translations VCP
ENGS, Robert Francis, 1943- , American; nonfiction CON
ENGSTRÖM, Albert, 1869-1940, Swedish; nonfiction BU
ENGSTROM, Ted Wilhelm, 1916- , American; nonfiction CON
ENGSTROM, Winfred Andrew, 1925- , American; nonfiction CON
ENIS, Ben Melvin, 1942- ,

American; nonfiction CON
ENKE, Stephen, 1916-74, Canadian-American; nonfiction CON
ENKING, Ottomar, 1867-1945, German; fiction BU
ENNES, James Marquis, Jr., 1933- , American; nonfiction CON
ENNIS, John, 1944- , Irish; poetry HO
ENNIUS, Quintus, 239-169 B. C., Roman; poetry BU GR LA
ENNODIUS, Magnus Felix, 473-521, Latin; nonfiction, poetry BU TH
ENO, Susan, American; nonfiction CON
ENO-BELINGA, Samuel Martin, 1935- , Cameroonian; poetry, nonfiction JA
ENOMOTO, Kikahu, 1661-1707, Japanese; poetry HI
ENQUIST, Per Olov, 1934- , Swedish; fiction CL
ENRIGHT, Dennis Joseph, 1920- , British; poetry, nonfiction, fiction BOR CO DA SEY VCN VCP WA
ENRIGHT, Elizabeth, 1909-68, American; juveniles, nonfiction, fiction CO CON KI
'ENRIQUE' see MORALES, José P.
ENRIQUEZ GOMEZ, Antonio, 1600-63, Spanish; poetry, plays, fiction BU TH
ENSIGN, Thomas (Tod), 1940- , American; nonfiction CON
ENSLIN, Theodore Vernon, 1925- , American; poetry BR CON VCP
ENSMINGER, Marion Eugene, 1908- , American; nonfiction CON
ENTERLINE, James Robert, 1932- , American; nonfiction CON
ENTHOVEN, Alain Charles, 1930- , American; nonfiction CON
ENTWISTLE, Noel James, 1936- , British; nonfiction CON
ENVALLSON, Carl Magnus, 1756-1806, Swedish; nonfiction, translations, plays BU
ENZ, Jacob John, 1919- , American; nonfiction CON
ENZENSBERGER, Hans Magnus, 1929- , German; poetry, nonfiction, translations BU CL

TH WA
ENZINAS, Francisco de (Drander
Du Chesne Van Eick), 1520?-
52, Spanish; nonfiction BU
ENZLER, Clarence J., 1910?-76,
American; nonfiction CON
ENZO, 1220-72, Italian; poetry
BU
EÖTVÖS, Baron József, 1813-
71/74, Hungarian; nonfiction,
poetry, fiction BU TH
EPAND, Len, 1950- , American;
journalism, nonfiction CON
EPANYA YONDO, Elolongué,
1930- , Cameroonian; poetry
HER JA
EPEE, Valère, 1938- , Camer-
oonian; poetry JA
EPHORUS, 405-330 B. C., Greek;
nonfiction BU GR LA
EPHRAEM, 13th century, By-
zantine; nonfiction BU
EPHREM the SYRIAN, St., 306-
73, Syriac; poetry, nonfiction
BU
EPHRON, Delia, 1944- , Amer-
ican; nonfiction CON
EPHRON, Henry, 1911- , Amer-
ican; nonfiction, plays, film
CON
EPHRON, Nora, 1941- , Amer-
ican; journalism, nonfiction
CON
EPICHARMUS, 530-440 B. C.,
Greek; plays, poetry BU
GR LA
EPICETETUS, 55-135, Greek;
nonfiction BU LA
EPICURUS, 341-270 B. C., Greek;
nonfiction BU GR LA
EPLER, Percy H., 1872-1975,
American; nonfiction CON
EPP, Margaret Agnes ('Agnes
Goossen'), Canadian; juveniles
CO
'EPPIE' see NAISMITH, Helen
EPPINGER, Josh, 1940- , Amer-
ican; journalism CON
EPPINK, Norman Roland, 1906- ,
American; nonfiction CON
EPPLE, Anne Orth, 1927- ,
American; juveniles CO
EPPS, Edgar Gustavas, 1929- ,
American; nonfiction CON
EPPS, Garrett, 1950- , Amer-
ican; fiction, nonfiction CON
EPSTEIN, Anne Merrick, 1931- ,
American; juveniles, fiction

CO CON
EPSTEIN, Benjamin Robert, 1912-
American; translations, nonfic-
tion CON
EPSTEIN, Charlotte, 1921- ,
American; nonfiction, fiction
CON
EPSTEIN, Daniel Mark, 1948- ,
American; poetry CON
EPSTEIN, David George, 1943- ,
American; nonfiction CON
EPSTEIN, Dena J., 1916- ,
American; nonfiction CON
EPSTEIN, Eugene, 1944- , Amer-
ican; nonfiction CON
EPSTEIN, Fritz Theodor, 1898- ,
German; nonfiction CON
EPSTEIN, Helen, 1947- , Czech-
American; nonfiction CON
EPSTEIN, Jason, 1928- , Amer-
ican; nonfiction CON
EPSTEIN, Judith Sue ('Judy Sue'),
1947- , American; poetry
CON
EPSTEIN, Julius, 1901-75, Amer-
ican; journalism, nonfiction
CON
EPSTEIN, June, Australian; nonfic-
tion, plays CON
EPSTEIN, Leslie, 1938- , Amer-
ican; fiction, nonfiction CON
EPSTEIN, Melech Michael, 1889?-
1979, American; journalism,
nonfiction CON
EPSTEIN, Morris, 1921-73, Amer-
ican; nonfiction CON
EPSTEIN, Perle Sherry, 1938- ,
American; nonfiction, juveniles
CON WAR
EPSTEIN, William, 1912- , Cana-
dian; nonfiction CON
EPSTEIN, William Henry, 1944- ,
American; nonfiction CON
EQUIANO, Olaudah, 1745/54-97/
1801, Ibo; nonfiction BU JA
EQUICOLA, Mario, 1470-1525,
Italian; nonfiction BU
ERAQI, Fakhroddin Ebrahim,
-1289, Persian; poetry PRU
ERASISTRATUS, early 3rd century
B. C., Greek; nonfiction GR
ERASMUS, Desiderius, 1467-1536,
Dutch; nonfiction BU MAG TH
ERATOSTHENES, 275-195 B. C.,
Greek; nonfiction, poetry BU
GR LA
ERAUSO, Catalina de ('La Monja
Alférez'), 1592-1650?, Spanish;

nonfiction BU
ERBEN, Karel Jaromír, 1811-70,
Czech; poetry BU TH
ERBSEN, Claude E., 1938- ,
Italian-American; nonfiction
CON
ERCELDOUNE, Thomas de (Thomas the Rhymer), 1220-97,
Scots; poetry BU DA
ERCILLA y ZUÑIGA, Alonso de,
1533-94, Spanish; poetry BU
TH
'ERCKMANN-CHATRIAN' (Emile
Erckman, 1822-99; Alexandre
Chatrian, 1826-90), French;
fiction, plays BU
ERDENE, Sengün, 1929- , Mongolian; fiction PRU
ERDMAN, Nikolay Robertovich,
1902/04-70, Russian; plays
CL TH
ERDMAN, Paul Emil, 1932- ,
Canadian-American; fiction
CON REI
ERDOES, Richard, 1912- ,
Austrian-American; nonfiction,
juveniles CON
ERENBURG, Ilya Grigryevich
(Ehrenburg), 1891-1967, Russian; fiction, poetry, journalism BU CL CON TH
ERENS, Patricia, 1938- , American; nonfiction CON
ERICKSON, Arthur Charles,
1924- , Canadian; nonfiction
CON
ERICKSON, Carolly, 1943- ,
American; nonfiction CON
ERICKSON, Edsel Lee, 1928- ,
American; nonfiction CON
ERICKSON, John, 1929- , American; nonfiction CON
ERICKSON, Marilyn T., 1936- ,
American; nonfiction CON
ERICKSON, Millard J., 1932- ,
American; nonfiction CON
ERICKSON, Milton Hyland, 1901-
80, American; nonfiction CON
ERICKSON, Russell Everett,
1932- , American; juveniles
CON WAR
ERICKSON, Stephen Anthony,
1940- , American; nonfiction
CON
ERICKSON, Walter Bruce, 1938- ,
American; nonfiction CON
ERICSON, Edward Einar, 1939- ,
American; nonfiction CON

ERICSON, Joe Ellis, 1925- ,
American; nonfiction CON
'ERICSON, Walter' see FAST,
Howard
ERICSSON, Emily Alice, 1904-76,
American; nonfiction CON
ERIGINA, John Scotus (Eriugena),
810-77, Latin; nonfiction GR
ERIKSON, Erik Homburger,
1902- , American; nonfiction
WAK
'ERIKSSON, Buntel' see BERGMAN, Ernst I.
ERIKSSON, Edward, 1941- ,
American; plays, tv CON
ERINNA, 4-3rd centuries B. C.,
Greek; poetry BU GR LA
ERLANGER, Ellen Louise, 1950- ,
American; nonfiction, juveniles
CON
ERLICH, Lillian Feldman, 1910- ,
American; juveniles CO
ERLINGSSON, Thorsteinn, 1858-
1914, Icelander; poetry BU
CL
'ERMAN, Jacques De Forest' see
ACKERMAN, Forrest J.
ERMENGEN, Franz van see
'HELLENS, Franz'
'ERMINE, Will' see DRAGO,
Harry S.
ERMOLD the BLACK, fl. 825-50,
Latin; poetry TH
'ERNEST, William' see BERKEBILE, Fred D.
ERNHARTH, Ronald Louis, 1936- ,
American; nonfiction CON
ERNST, Barbara, 1945- , American; nonfiction CON
ERNST, Carl Henry, 1938- ,
American; nonfiction CON
ERNST, Eldon Gilbert, 1939- ,
American; nonfiction CON
ERNST, Kathryn Fitzgerald,
1942- , American; nonfiction,
juveniles CO CON
ERNST, Lyman John ('Dorothy A.
Chernoff'; 'David Allen Clark'),
1940- , American; juveniles,
fiction CON
ERNST, Morris Leopold, 1888-
1976, American; nonfiction
CON
'ERNST, Otto' (O. E. Schmidt),
1862-1926, German; plays,
fiction BU
ERNST, Paul, 1866-1933, German;
plays, nonfiction, fiction BU

CL MCG TH
ERNST, Paul ('Paul Frederick
Stern'), 1902- , American;
fiction AS NI
ERNSTING, Walter see 'DARLTON,
Clark'
ERNY, Pierre Jean Paul, 1933- ,
French; nonfiction CON
ERSHOV, Peter Pavlovich, 1815-
69, Russian; poetry BU
ERSKINE, Laurie York, 1894?-
1976, Anglo-American; fiction
CON
'ERSKINE, Margaret' see WIL-
LIAMS, Margaret W.
'ERSKINE, Rosaline' see 'DRUM-
MOND, Ivor'
ERSKINE, Thomas, 1788-1870,
English; fiction NI
ERSKINE, Thomas Leonard,
1939- , American; nonfiction
CON
ERSKINE-LINDOP, Audrey Beatrice
N. , 1921- , British; fiction,
plays CON
ERSOY, Mehmet Akif (Mehmet
Akif), 1873-1936, Turkish;
poetry BU CL
'ERTE' see de TIRTOFF, Romain
ERTEL, Aleksandr Ivanovich,
1855-1908/09, Russian; fiction
BU CL TH
ERTER, Isaac, 1791-1851, Hebrew;
nonfiction BU
ERVIN, Janet Halliday, 1923- ,
American; juveniles CO
ERVINE, St. John Greer, 1883-
1971, Irish; plays, fiction,
nonfiction BU DA HO MCG
PO VD
ERVIN-TRIPP, Susan Moore,
1927- , American; nonfiction
CON
'ERWIN, Annabel' see BARRON,
Ann F.
ERWIN, Betty K. , American;
juveniles WAR
ESAD, Mehmed see 'GÂLIB DEDE,
Seyh'
ESAU, Helmut, 1941- , German-
American; nonfiction CON
ESCALERA, Faustino, Jr. ,
1942- , American; nonfiction
MAR
ESCOBEDO, Arturo Ernesto,
American; nonfiction MAR
ESCOSURA, Patricio de la, 1807-
78, Spanish; poetry, fiction

BU
ESCOTT, Jonathan ('Jack S. Scott'),
1922- , English; fiction CON
ESCOTT, Paul David, 1947- ,
American; nonfiction CON
ESCOUCHY, Mathieu d', 1420?-
82?, French; nonfiction BU
ESCRIVA, Juan, late 15th century,
Spanish; poetry BU
ESCRIVA de BALAGUER, Jose-
maria, 1902-75, Spanish; non-
fiction CON
ESDAILE, Arundell James Kennedy,
1880-1956, British; nonfiction
ENG
'ESEKI, Bruno' see MPHAHLELE,
Ezekiel
ESENIN, Sergey see YESENIN,
Sergei
ESHBACH, Lloyd Arthur, 1910- ,
American; fiction AS NI
ESHERICK, Joseph Wharton,
1942- , American; nonfiction,
juveniles CON WAR
ESHLEMAN, Clayton, 1935- ,
American; poetry BR VCP
ESHLEMAN, J. Ross, 1936- ,
American; nonfiction CON
ESHQI, Mohammad Reza, 1893/94-
1924, Iranian; poetry PRU
ESHUGBAYI, Ezekiel Aderogba,
Nigerian; juveniles WAR
ESKENAZI, Gerald, 1936- ,
American; nonfiction CON
ESKEY, Kenneth, 1930- , Amer-
ican; journalism CON
ESLER, William K. , 1930- ,
American; nonfiction CON
ESMAN, Aaron Hirsh, 1924- ,
American; nonfiction CON
ESMAN, Milton J. , 1918- , Amer-
ican; nonfiction CON
ESMEIN, Jean, 1923- , French;
nonfiction CON
'ESMOND, Harriet' see BURKE,
John F.
ESPANCA, Florbela, 1894-1930,
Portuguese; poetry, fiction
CL
ESPARZA, Moctesuma, American;
film MAR
ESPARZA, Ricardo, American; non-
fiction MAR
ESPENSHADE, Edward Bowman,
1910- , American; juveniles
WAR
ESPEY, John Jenkins, 1913- ,
American; fiction VCN

ESPINA, Antonio, 1894- , Spanish; nonfiction, fiction, poetry BU CL

ESPINA de SERNA, Concha, 1877-1955, Spanish; fiction, poetry BU CL

ESPINEL MARTINEZ, Vicente, 1550-1624, Spanish; fiction, poetry BU TH

ESPINO, Federico Licsi, Jr. ('Quixote de Extramuros'), 1939- , Filipino; poetry, fiction CON VCP

ESPINO CALDERON, Margarita, 1944- , American; nonfiction MAR

ESPINOSA, Pedro, 1578-1650, Spanish; poetry, nonfiction BU TH

ESPINOSA, Ruben William, 1948- , American; nonfiction MAR

ESPINOZA, Rudolph L., 1933- , American; fiction CON MAR

ESPIRITO SANTO, Alda do, 1926- , Portuguese; poetry, journalism HER JA

ESPRIU, Salvador, 1913- , Catalan; nonfiction, poetry, fiction, plays BU CL

ESPRONCEDA, José, 1808-42, Spanish; poetry BU TH

ESPY, Willard Richardson, 1910- , American; nonfiction CON

ESQUEDA, Carlos Garcia, 1929- , American; nonfiction MAR

ESQUENAZI-MAYO, Robert, 1920- , Cuban-American; nonfiction CON

ESQUIBEL, George Arthur, 1939- , American; nonfiction MAR

ESQUILACHE, Francisco de Borja y Acevedo, -1658, Spanish; poetry BU

ESSAME, Hubert, 1896-1976, British; nonfiction CON

ESSICK, Robert Newman, 1942- , American; nonfiction CON

ESSLIN, Martin Julius, 1918- , Austrian-British; nonfiction, translations BOR CON WAK

ESSLINGER, Dean Robert, 1942- , American; nonfiction CON

ESSLINGER, Pat M. see CARR, Pat Moore

ESTABROOK, Robert Harley, 1918- , American; nonfiction CON

ESTABROOKS, George H., 1896-1973, American; nonfiction CON

'ESTANG, Luc' (Lucien Bastard), 1911- , French; poetry, fiction, nonfiction CON TH WA

ESTARELLAS, Juan, 1918- , Spanish-American; nonfiction CON

ESTAUNIE, Edouard, 1862-1942, French; fiction CL

ESTAVER, Marguerite M., 1893- , Canadian; poetry CON

ESTEBANEZ CALDERON, Serafín, 1799-1867, Spanish; nonfiction, poetry, fiction BU TH

ESTELLA, Fr. Diego de (Diego de San Cristobal), 1524-78, Spanish; nonfiction BU

ESTENSSORO, Hugo ('Emilio Chartier'), 1946- , Bolivian; nonfiction CON

ESTEP, Irene Compton, American; juveniles CO

ESTES, Eleanor Ruth, 1906- , American; juveniles, plays, fiction CO KI

ESTES, John Edward, 1939- , American; nonfiction CON

ESTES, Steven Douglas, 1952- , American; nonfiction CON

ESTEVES, José de Jesus, 1882-1918, Puerto Rican; journalism HIL

ESTIENNE, Henri II, 1531?-98, French; nonfiction, printer BU TH

ESTLANDER, Carl Gustaf, 1834-1910, Finnish-Swedish; nonfiction BU

ESTLEMAN, Loren D., 1952- , American; journalism, fiction CON

'ESTORIL, Jean' see ALLAN, Mabel E.

ESTRADA, Diego, 1589-1647?, Spanish; nonfiction BU

ESTRIDGE, Robin see 'LORAINE, Philip'

ESTUÑIGA, Lope Ortiz de, 1407-77, Spanish; poetry BU

ESTUPINIAN, Rafael Herman, 1929- , American; nonfiction, poetry MAR

ESWARCHANDRA VIDYASAGAR, 1820-91, Sanskrit; nonfiction, plays BU

ETCHEBASTER, Pierre, 1894-
1980, French; nonfiction CON
ETCHESON, Warren Wade, 1920- ,
American; nonfiction CON
ETEROVICH, Adam Slav, 1930- ,
American; nonfiction CON
ETHELL, Jeffrey Lance, 1947- ,
American; nonfiction CON
ETHEREGE, Sir George, 1634/
35-91, English; poetry, plays
BRI BU DA MAG MCG PO
VD
ETHRIDGE, Mark Foster, 1896-
1981, American; journalism
CON
ETIEMBLE, René Joseph Ernest,
1909- , French; nonfiction,
fiction BU CL
ETIENNE de BOURBON, fl. 1190-
1261, French; nonfiction TH
ETIENNE de FOUGERES,
-1178, French; poetry BU
ETKIN, Anne Dunwody, 1923- ,
American; nonfiction CON
'ETLAR, Carit' see BROSBOEL,
Johan C. C.
'ETON, Robert' see MEYNELL,
Laurence W.
ETRA, Jonathan, 1952- , Amer-
ican; nonfiction CON
ETS, Marie Hall, 1893- ,
American; juveniles, poetry
KI
ETS-HOKIN, Judith Diane,
1938- , American; nonfiction
CON
ETTINGER, Solomon, 1799/1803-
55/56, Polish; plays MCG
TH
ETTINGHAUSEN, Richard, 1906-
79, German-American; non-
fiction CON
ETTLINGER, Gerard Herman,
1935- , American; nonfiction
CON
ETULAIN, Richard Wayne,
1938- , American; nonfiction
CON
ETZKORN, Klaus Peter, 1932- ,
German-American; nonfiction
CON
ETZOLD, Thomas Herman,
1945- , American; nonfiction
CON
EUBA, Femi, 1935?- , Nigerian;
plays HER
EUBANK, Nancy, 1934- , Amer-
ican; nonfiction CON

EUBULUS, fl. 375-30 B. C. , Greek;
plays, poetry BU
EUCLID, fl. 306-283 B. C. , Greek;
nonfiction BU GR LA
EUCLIDES of MEGARA, 450-380
B. C. , Greek; nonfiction BU
EUDOXUS, 390-40 B. C. , Greek;
nonfiction GR LA
EUGENIUS of PALERMO, 1130?-
1203, Greek; poetry LA
EUGENIUS of TOLEDO, 600?-58,
Visigoth; poetry TH
EUHEMERUS, fl. 301-297 B. C. ,
Greek; fiction GR
EULATE SANJURJO, Carmen
('Dórida Mesenia'), 1871-1961,
Puerto Rican; translations,
journalism, nonfiction, fiction
HIL
'EULENSPIEGEL, Alexander' see
SHEA, Robert J.
EULERT, Don, 1935- , American;
nonfiction, poetry, fiction CON
EUNAPIUS, 345-420, Greek; nonfic-
tion BU
EUNSON, Dale, 1904- , American;
juveniles, tv, fiction, plays
CO CON
EUNSON, Robert Charles, 1912-75,
American; nonfiction CON
EUNSON, Roby, American; juveniles
WAR
'EUPHEMIDES, Aristos' see von
KOERBER, Hans N.
EUPHROION, 276/75 B. C. - ,
Greek; poetry BU GR LA
EUPOLIS, 446?-12 B. C. , Greek;
plays, poetry BU GR LA
EURICH, Nell, 1919- , American;
nonfiction CON
EURIPEDES, 485-06 B. C. , Greek;
poetry, plays BU GR LA MAG
MCG
EUSDEN, John Dykstra, 1922- ,
American; nonfiction, transla-
tions CON
EUSDEN, Laurence, 1688-1730,
English; poetry DA
EUSEBIUS, 260/64-340, Greek;
nonfiction BU GR LA
EUSTACE, Cecil John, 1903- ,
Anglo-Canadian; nonfiction,
fiction CON
'EUSTACE, Robert' (Eustace Robert
Barton), 1854-1943, British;
fiction, plays REI
EUSTACHE, fl. 1170, French; po-
etry BU

EUSTACHE d'AMIENS, 12th cen-
tury, French; poetry BU
EUSTATHIUS of THESSALONICA,
-1195?, Byzantine; nonfiction
BU LA
EUSTIS, Alvin Allen, Jr.,
1917- , American; nonfiction
CON
EUSTIS, Helen White, 1916- ,
American; fiction, transla-
tions REI ST
'EUSTIS, Laurette' see MUR-
DOCK, Laurette P.
EUTROPIUS, 4th century, Roman;
nonfiction BU GR LA
EVAGRIUS of PONTUS, 345-99,
Latin; nonfiction BU
EVAGRIUS SCHOLASTICUS, 536-?,
Byzantine; nonfiction BU
EVAIN, Elaine, 1931- , Amer-
ican; fiction CON
EVANG, Karl, 1902- , Norwegian;
nonfiction CON
EVANS, Abbie Huston, 1881- ,
American; poetry CON VCP
WA
EVANS, Albert, 1917- , Amer-
ican; plays CON
EVANS, Anne A. see 'RAINE,
Allen'
EVANS, Arthur Bruce, 1948- ,
American; nonfiction CON
'EVANS, Bennett' see BERGER,
Ivan B.
EVANS, Bergen Baldwin, 1904-
78, American; nonfiction CON
EVANS, Bill, 1921- , American;
fiction NI
'EVANS, Caradoc' (David Evans),
1878-1945, Anglo-Welsh; fic-
tion BU PO SEY
EVANS, Charles, 1850-1935,
American; nonfiction ENG
EVANS, Christopher Riche,
1931-79, Welsh; nonfiction
CON
EVANS, Cyril Kenneth, 1917- ,
Welsh; fiction CON
EVANS, Dale see ROGERS, Dale
EVANS, David see 'EVANS,
Caradoc'
EVANS, David Allan, 1940- ,
American; nonfiction, poetry
CON
EVANS, David Stanley, 1916- ,
American; nonfiction CON
EVANS, Donald Dwight, 1927- ,
Canadian; nonfiction CON

EVANS, Donald Paul, 1930- ,
American; nonfiction CON
EVANS, Edward Everett, 1893-
1958, American; fiction AS
NI
EVANS, Edward Gordon, Jr.,
1916- , American; nonfiction
CON
EVANS, Eli N., 1936- , Amer-
ican; nonfiction CON
EVANS, Elizabeth, 1932- , Amer-
ican; nonfiction CON
EVANS, Eva Knox, 1905- , Amer-
ican; juveniles CON
'EVANS, Evan' see 'BRAND, Max';
'IEUAN GLAN GEIRIONYDD'
'EVANS, F. M. G.' see HIGHAM,
Florence M. G.
EVANS, George Ewart, 1909- ,
Welsh; fiction, plays, nonfic-
tion CON
EVANS, Glen ('Glenn Eirelin'),
1921- , American; nonfiction
CON
EVANS, Gwynfor, 1912- , Welsh;
nonfiction CON
EVANS, Harold Matthew, 1928- ,
English; nonfiction CON
EVANS, Herndon J., 1895-1976,
American; nonfiction CON
EVANS, Hubert Reginald, 1892- ,
Canadian; juveniles, poetry,
fiction CON KI
EVANS, Idrisyn Oliver, 1894-1977,
British; fiction, translations,
nonfiction AS NI
EVANS, Ilona, 1918?-80, American;
nonfiction CON
EVANS, J. Martin, 1935- , Welsh;
nonfiction CON
EVANS, Jay, 1925- , American;
nonfiction CON
EVANS, Jean ('Ruth Graham'),
1939- , British; fiction CON
EVANS, Joan, 1893-1977, British;
nonfiction CON
'EVANS, John' see BROWNE,
Howard
EVANS, John Lewis, 1930- ,
American; nonfiction CON
EVANS, John Robert, 1942- ,
American; nonfiction CON
EVANS, Joseph S., Jr., 1909?-78,
American; journalism CON
EVANS, Katherine Floyd, 1901-64,
American; juveniles CO
EVANS, Lawrence Watt (Lawrence
Watt-Evans), 1954- , Amer-

ican; fiction CON
EVANS, Lloyd ('Lloyd Thomas'),
1927- , New Zealander; non-
fiction CON
EVANS, Luther Harris, 1902- ,
American; nonfiction ENG
EVANS, Margiad, 1909- ,
Welsh; poetry BU
EVANS, Mari, 1923- , American;
poetry, juveniles CO CON
MAL SH VCP WAR
EVANS, Mark, American; nonfic-
tion, juveniles CO CON
EVANS, Marvin Russell, 1915- ,
American; poetry CON
EVANS, Mary Ann see 'ELIOT,
George'
EVANS, Medford Stanton, 1934- ,
American; nonfiction CON
EVANS, Nancy ('Mary Ann Eliot'),
1950- , American; nonfiction
CON
EVANS, Pamela see 'WYKHAM,
Helen'
EVANS, Patricia see CARPENTER,
Patricia H.
EVANS, Pauline Rush, American;
juveniles WAR
EVANS, Richard Louis, 1906-71,
American; nonfiction CON
EVANS, Robert Leonard, 1917- ,
American; nonfiction CON
EVANS, Rodney Earl, 1939- ,
American; nonfiction CON
EVANS, Sara, 1943- , American;
nonfiction CON
EVANS, Shirlee, 1931- , Amer-
ican; fiction CON
EVANS, Theophilus, 1693-1767,
Welsh; nonfiction BU DA
EVANS, Thomas William, 1930- ,
American; nonfiction CON
EVANS, Travers Moncure,
1938- , American; nonfiction
CON
EVANS, Wilbur, 1913- , Amer-
ican; journalism, nonfiction
CON
EVANS, William, 1895- , Welsh;
nonfiction CON
EVANS, William E. Webster,
1908- , English; nonfiction
CON
EVANS, William Glyn, 1918- ,
Welsh-American; nonfiction
CON
EVANS, Walker, 1903-75, Amer-
ican; nonfiction CON

EVANS DAVIES, Gloria, 1932- ,
British; poetry VCP
EVANS-PRITCHARD, Edward Evan,
1902-73, English; nonfiction
CON WA
EVARTS, Hal G., Jr., 1915- ,
American; juveniles, fiction
CO CON WAR
EVE, Barbara see REISS, Barbara
EVELAND, Wilbur Crane, 1918- ,
American; nonfiction CON
EVELING, Harry Stanley, 1925- ,
English; plays, poetry CON
VCD
EVELY, Louis, 1910- , Belgian;
nonfiction CON
EVELYN, John, 1620-1706, English;
nonfiction, diary, translations
BRI BU DA MAG PO
EVELYN, John M. see 'UNDER-
WOOD, Michael'
EVENSMO, Sigurd, 1912- , Nor-
wegian; fiction BU
EVERAERT, Cornelis, 1480-1556,
Dutch; poetry BU
EVERETT, Alexander Hill, 1790-
1847, American; poetry, non-
fiction BR
EVERETT, Arthur W., Jr.,
1914- , American; journalism
CON
EVERETT, Edward, 1794-1865,
American; nonfiction BR MY
EVERETT, Glenn D., 1921- ,
American; nonfiction CON
EVERETT, Peter, 1931- , Brit-
ish; fiction, plays, film CON
VCN
EVERETT, Walter, 1936- , Amer-
ican; nonfiction CON
EVERETT-GREEN, Evelyn, 1856-
1932, British; juveniles, fiction
KI
EVERHART, James William, Jr.,
1924- , American; nonfiction
CON
EVERITT, Bridget Mary, 1924- ,
English; fiction CON
EVERITT, Charles William F.,
1934- , Anglo-American;
nonfiction CON
EVERMAN, Welch Duane, 1946- ,
American; fiction CON
EVERNDEN, Margery, 1916- ,
American; juveniles CO
EVERSON, Ronald Gilmour, 1903- ,
Canadian; poetry CR VCP
EVERSON, William O. see

'ANTONINUS, Brother'
EVERWINE, Peter Paul, 1930- ,
American; poetry CON
'EVERY, Philip C.' see BURN-
FORD, Sheila
EVETTS, Julia, 1944- , British;
nonfiction CON
EVINS, Joseph Landon, 1910- ,
American; nonfiction CON
EVLIYA CELEBI, 1611/14-84,
Turkish; nonfiction BU LA
PRU
EVREINOV, Nikolay Nikolayevich,
1879- , Russian; plays BU
EVSLIN, Bernard, 1922- ,
American; fiction, juveniles
WAR
EVSLIN, Dorothy, 1923- ,
American; fiction, nonfiction
CON
EVTIMY of TURNOVO (Turovski),
1330-95, Bulgarian; nonfiction
BU
EVTUSHENKO, Yevgeny see
YEVTUSHENKO, Yevgeny
EWALD, Carl, 1856-1908, Danish;
fiction, nonfiction BU NI
EWALD, Herman Frederik, 1821-
1908, Danish; fiction BU
EWALD, Johannes, 1743-81,
Danish; poetry, plays BU TH
EWART, Gavin Buchanan,
1916- , British; poetry,
nonfiction CON VCP WA
EWBANK, Henry Lee, Jr.,
1924- , American; nonfiction
CON
EWEN, David, 1907- , Austrian-
American; juveniles CO
EWEN, Frederic, 1899- ,
Austrian-American; nonfiction
CON
EWEN, Stuart, 1945- , American;
nonfiction CON
EWERS, Hans Heinz, 1871-1943,
German; fiction NI
EWING, Donald M., 1895?-1978,
American; journalism CON
EWING, Elizabeth, 1904- ,
Scots; nonfiction CON
'EWING, Frederick R.' see
'STURGEON, Theodore'
EWING, George Wilmeth, 1923- ,
American; nonfiction CON
EWING, John Melvin, 1925- ,
American; nonfiction CON
EWING, Juliana Horatia (Gatty),
1841-85, English; juveniles,

poetry BU CO KI
EWING, Kathryn ('Kathryn Doug-
las'), 1921- , American;
plays, juveniles, fiction CO
CON WAR
EWING, Sherman, 1901-75, Amer-
ican; plays CON
EWTON, Ralph Waldo, Jr.,
1938- , American; nonfiction
CON
'EXCELLENT, Matilda' see FAR-
SON, Daniel N.
EXLEY, Frederick Earl, 1929- ,
American; fiction CON
EXMAN, Eugene, 1900-75, Ameri-
can; nonfiction CON
EXTON, Clive Jack, 1930- , Eng-
lish; plays, tv, film CON
EXTON, William, Jr., 1907- ,
American; nonfiction CON
'EXTRAMUROS, Quixote de' see
ESPINO, Federico L., Jr.
EYBERS, Elisabeth, 1915- ,
Afrikaans; poetry BU LA
EYCK, Pieter Nicolaas van (van
Eijk), 1887-1954, Dutch; poetry,
nonfiction BU CL
EYE, Glen Gordon, 1904- , Amer-
ican; nonfiction CON
EYEN, Tom, 1941- , American;
plays VCD
EYERLEY, Jeanette Hyde ('Jean-
nette Griffith'), 1908- ,
American; juveniles CO WAR
EYESTONE, Robert, 1942- ,
American; nonfiction CON
EYKMAN, Christoph, 1937- ,
German-American; nonfiction
CON
'EYRE, Annette' see WORBOYS,
Annette I.
EYRE, Richard Melvin, 1944- ,
American; nonfiction CON
EYTH, Max von, 1836-1906, Ger-
man; nonfiction BU
EYÜBOGLU, Bedri Rahmi,
1913- , Turkish; poetry BU
EZEKIEL, 6th century B.C., Is-
raeli; nonfiction PRU
EZEKIEL, Mordecai J. B., 1899?-
1974, American; nonfiction
CON
EZEKIEL, Nissim (Nizzim),
1924- , Indian; poetry, plays,
nonfiction BU CON PRU VCP
EZEKIEL, Raphael S., 1931- ,
American; nonfiction CON
EZELL, Harry Eugene, 1918-74,

American; nonfiction CON
EZELL, Macel D., 1934- ,
American; nonfiction CON
EZERGAILIS, Andrew, 1930- ,
Latvian-American; juveniles,
nonfiction CON
EZNIK of KOLB, 5th century, Armenian; nonfiction BU
EZORSKY, Gertrude, American;
nonfiction CON
EZRA, fl. 458-398 B. C., Israeli;
nonfiction PRU
EZUMA, Benjamin James, 1937?- ,
Nigerian; plays JA
EZZO, fl. 1065, German; poetry
BU

F

FAARAH, Nuur, 1850?-1930?,
Somali; poetry HER LA
FABBRI, Diego, 1911-80, Italian;
plays, journalism BO BU CL
MCG
FABBRI, Nancy Rash ('Mary Harrison'), 1940- , American;
nonfiction CON
FABE, Maxene, 1943- , American; juveniles, fiction, nonfiction CO CON
FABER, Adele, 1928- , American; nonfiction, tv CON
FABER, Cecilia B. de see
'CABALLERO, Fernán'
FABER, Doris Greenberg, 1924- ,
American; juveniles CO
FABER, Harold, 1919- , American; juveniles CO
FABER, Nancy Weingarten, 1909-
76, American; fiction, nonfiction CON
FABER, Peter Christian Frederik, 1810-77, Danish; poetry
BU
FABER, Richard Stanley, 1924- ,
English; nonfiction CON
FABER-KAISER, Andreas, 1944- ,
Spanish; nonfiction CON
FABIAN, Robert Honey, 1901-78,
British; nonfiction, fiction
CON
FABIO, Sarah Webster, 1928- ,
American; nonfiction, poetry
CON SH
FABISCH, Judith Patricia, 1938- ,
American; nonfiction CON
FABIUS PICTOR, Quintus, 3rd

century, Roman; nonfiction
BU GR LA
FABIUS RUSTICUS, 1st century,
Latin; nonfiction GR LA
FABO, Paul, Dahoman; plays JA
FABOS, Julius Gyula, 1920- ,
Hungarian-American; nonfiction
CON
FABRA i POC, Pompeu, 1868/69-
1948/51, Catalan; nonfiction
BU CL
FABRE, Emile, 1869-1955, French;
plays MCG TH
FABRE, Jean Henri Casimir, 1823-
1915, French; juveniles CO
FABRE, Michael Jacques, 1933- ,
American; nonfiction CON
'FABRE d'EGLANTINE' (Philippe
Fabre), 1755-94, French; nonfiction, plays BU
FABREGA, Horatio, 1934- , American; nonfiction CON MAR
FABRI, Pierre (Lefevre), 1460-
1520?, French; nonfiction BU
FABRI, Ralph, 1894-1975, Hungarian-American; nonfiction
CON
FABRICAND, Burton Paul, 1923- ,
American; nonfiction CON
FABRICIUS, Johan Johannes,
1899- , Dutch; nonfiction,
plays, fiction BU CON
FABRICIUS, Sara see 'SANDEL,
Cora'
FABRIZI, Cinzio Aloise, early
16th century, Italian; poetry
BU
'FABRIZIUS, Peter' see KNIGHT,
Max
FABRY, Rudolf, 1915- , Slovak;
poetry BU
FABUN, Don, 1920- , American;
nonfiction CON
FACCIO, Rina see 'ALERAMO,
Sibilla'
FACKLAM, Margery Metz, 1927- ,
American; juveniles CO WAR
FACOS, James Francis, 1924- ,
American; plays, poetry CON
FADAYEV, Alexander Alexandrovich, 1901-56, Russian; fiction
BU CL TH
FADER, Shirley Sloan, 1931- ,
American; journalism, juveniles,
nonfiction CON
FADIMAN, Clifton Paul, 1904- ,
American; nonfiction, juveniles,
translations CO CON

FAEGRE, Torvald, 1941- , American; nonfiction CON
FAFUNWA, A. Babs, 1923- , Nigerian; journalism HER
FAGAN, Brian Murray, 1936- , Anglo-American; nonfiction CON
FAGAN, Henry Allan, 1889- , South African; fiction NI
FAGEN, Stanley Alan, 1936- , American; nonfiction CON
FAGERBERG, Sven Gustaf, 1918- , Swedish; fiction BU
FAGERSTROM, Stan ('Stanley Scott'), 1923- , American; nonfiction CON
FAGG, John Edwin, 1916- , American; nonfiction CON
FAGG, William Buller, 1914- , British; nonfiction CON
FAGHANI, Baba, -1519, Persian; poetry BU
FAGUNDES VARELA, Luis Nicolau, 1841-75, Brazilian; poetry BR
FAGUNWA, Daniel Olorunfemi, 1910?-63, Nigerian; fiction BU HER JA LA SEY
'FAGUS' (Georges Eugène Faillet), 1872-1933, French; poetry CL
FAHEY, Frank Michael, 1917- , American; nonfiction CON
FAHEY, James Charles, 1903-74, American; nonfiction CON
FAHLSTROM, Oyvind Axel, 1928-76, Swedish; journalism, plays CON
FAHNESTOCK, Beatrice Beck, 1899?-1980, American; journalism, nonfiction CON
FAHS, Ivan J., 1932- , American; nonfiction CON
FAHS, Sophia Blanche Lyon, 1876-1978, American; juveniles, nonfiction CON
FA-HSIEN (Kung), -420, Chinese; nonfiction, translations BU PRU
FAHY, Christopher, 1937- , American; fiction, nonfiction, poetry CON
FAIKO, Alexey Mikhailovich, 1893- , Russian; plays BU
FAILLET, Georges E. see 'FAGUS'
FAINLIGHT, Ruth, American; poetry, plays, fiction VCP

FAINSTEIN, Norman Ira, 1944- , American; nonfiction CON
FAINSTEIN, Susan S., 1938- , American; nonfiction CON
FAINZELBERG, I. A. see 'IL'F'
'FAIR, A. A.' see GARDNER, Erle S.
FAIR, Harold Lloyd, 1924- , American; nonfiction CON
FAIR, Ronald, 1932- , American; nonfiction, fiction CON SH
FAIR, Sylvia, 1933- , Welsh; juveniles CO CON
'FAIR FAX' see MUÑOZ RIVERA, Luis
FAIRBAIRN, Garry L., 1947- , Canadian; journalism CON
FAIRBAIRN, Ian John, 1933- , Australian; nonfiction CON
FAIRBAIRNS, Zoe Ann, 1948- , British; nonfiction CON
FAIRBANKS, Carol ('C. F. Myers'; 'Carol Fairbanks Myers'), 1935- , American; nonfiction CON
FAIRBRIDGE, Kingsley Ogilvie, 1885-1924, South African; poetry BU
FAIRBURN, Arthur Rex Dugard, 1904-57, New Zealander; poetry BU DA VP WA
FAIRBURN, Eleanor ('Catherine Carfax'), 1928- , British; fiction CON
FAIRCHILD, Hoxie Neale, 1894-1973, American; nonfiction CON
FAIRCHILD, Mary Salome Cutler, 1855-1921, American; nonfiction ENG
FAIRCHILD, William ('Edward Cranston'), British; plays, fiction, film CON
'FAIRE, Zabrina' see STEVENSON, Florence
'FAIRFAX, Beatrice' see McCARROLL, Marion C.
FAIRFAX, Edward, 1635- , English; translations BU
FAIRFAX, John, 1930- , British; poetry, nonfiction CON VCP
FAIRFAX, John, 1937- , English; nonfiction CON
FAIRFAX, Thomas, 1612-71, English; poetry DA
FAIRFAX-BLAKEBOROUGH, John Freeman ('Hambletonian'), 1883-1978?, British; nonfiction

CON
FAIRFAX-LUCY, Brian Fulke,
1898- , Scots; juveniles CO
WAR
FAIRFIELD, Cicily I. see 'WEST,
Rebecca'
FAIRFIELD, Richard, 1937- ,
American; nonfiction CON
FAIRHALL, David Keir, 1934- ,
British; nonfiction CON
FAIRHOLME, Elizabeth, 1910- ,
British; juveniles CON
FAIRLEY, Irene R. , 1940- ,
American; nonfiction CON
FAIRLEY, James Stewart, 1940- ,
Irish; nonfiction CON
FAIRLIE, Gerard, 1899- , Eng-
lish; fiction, plays, nonfiction
MCC REI
FAIRMAN, Charles, 1897- ,
American; nonfiction CON
FAIRMAN, Honora C. , 1927?-
78, American; journalism
CON
FAIRMAN, Joan Alexandra,
1935- , American; juveniles
CO
FAIRMAN, Paul W. , 1916-77,
American; fiction AS NI
FAISON, Samson Lane, Jr. ,
1907- , American; nonfiction
CON
FAITHFULL, Gail (Gail Faithfull
Keller), 1936- , American;
juveniles CO CON
FAITINELLI, Pietro de' (Mug-
none), 1280/90-1349, Italian;
poetry BU
FAIZ, Ahmad Faiz, 1912- ,
Urdu; poetry PRU
FAIZI, Abu'l-Faiz, 1547-95, Per-
sian; poetry BR BU
FAKHR-al-DIN, Jurjani, As'ad,
11th century, Persian; poetry
BU
FAKHURI, Umar, 1895-1946,
Lebanese; nonfiction, journal-
ism PRU
FAKINOS, Aris, 1935- , Greek;
fiction CON
'FAKIR, Falstaff' see WALLIN-
GREN, Axel
FALAGUERA, Shemtob, 1225-95,
Spanish; poetry, nonfiction
BU
FALB, Lewis William, 1935- ,
American; nonfiction CON
FALCÃO, Cristóvão, 1515-53,

Portuguese; poetry BU TH
FALCK, Adrian Colin, 1934- ,
English; poetry CON VCP
'FALCO, João' see LISBOA, Irene
FALCO, Maria Josephine, 1932- ,
American; nonfiction CON
FALCOFF, Mark, 1941- , Amer-
ican; nonfiction CON
'FALCON' see NESTLE, John F.
'FALCONER, James' see KIRKUP,
James
FALCONER, William, 1732-69,
Scots; poetry, nonfiction BU
DA PO VP
FALES, Edward Daniel, Jr. ,
1906- , American; nonfiction
CON
FALETI, Adebayo, 1937- , Niger-
ian; plays, tv JA
FALIH RIF ki ATAY, 1894- ,
Turkish; journalism, nonfiction
BU
FALK, Kathryn, 1940- , Ameri-
can; nonfiction CON
'FALK, Lee' see COPPER, Basil
FALK, Lee Harrison, 1915- ,
American; nonfiction CON
FALK, Louis A. , 1896?-1979,
American; nonfiction CON
FALK, Robert, 1914- , American;
nonfiction CON
FALK, Roger Salis, 1910- , Eng-
lish; nonfiction CON
FALKBERGET, Johan Petter, 1879-
1967, Norwegian; fiction BU
CL TH
'FALKLAND, Samuel' see HEIJER-
MANS, Herman
FALKNER, John Meade, 1858-1932,
English; fiction, nonfiction NI
WA
FALKNER, Leonard, 1900- ,
American; juveniles CO
FALKNER, William Clark, 1825-
79/89, American; plays, fiction,
nonfiction BA BR
FALL, Bernard B. , 1926-67,
French; nonfiction, journalism
WA
FALL, Frieda Kay, 1913- ,
American; nonfiction CON
'FALL, Thomas' see SNOW, Donald
C.
FALLACI, Oriana, 1930- , Italian;
nonfiction CON
'FALLADA, Hans' (Rudolf Ditzen),
1893-1947, German; fiction,
nonfiction BU CL SEY TH

FALLER, Kevin, 1920- , Irish;
poetry, fiction CON
'FALLERE, Felicia' see KNIST,
Francis E.
FALLERS, Lloyd Ashton, Jr.,
1925-74, American; nonfiction
CON
FALLIS, Guadalupe Valdes, 1941- ,
American; nonfiction MAR
FALLON, Carlos, 1909- , Amer-
ican; nonfiction CON
FALLON, Frederic Michael, 1944-
70, American; fiction CON
'FALLON, George' see BINGLEY,
David E.
FALLON, John William, 1924- ,
American; nonfiction CON
'FALLON, Martin' see 'MARLOWE,
Hugh'
FALLON, Padraic, 1905-74, Irish;
poetry, plays, fiction CON
HO VCP
FALLON, Peter, 1951- , Irish;
poetry HO
FALLOWS, James Mackenzie,
1949- , American; nonfiction
CON
FALLS, Joe, 1928- , American;
journalism, nonfiction CON
FALLWELL, Marshall Leigh,
Jr. , 1943- , American;
nonfiction CON
'FALORP, Nelson O. ' see JONES,
Stephen P.
FALSTEIN, Louis, 1909- , Rus-
sian-American; fiction, juven-
iles CON
FALSTER, Christian, 1690-1752,
Danish; nonfiction BU
FALUDY, György, 1913- , Hun-
garian; poetry TH
FALWELL, Jerry, 1933- ,
American; nonfiction CON
FAMIGLIETTI, Eugene Paul,
1931?-80, American; journal-
ism, nonfiction CON
FAN CH'ÊNG-TA, 1126-93,
Chinese; poetry, nonfiction
BU
FAN CHUNG-YEN, 989-1052,
Chinese; nonfiction, poetry
BU
FANCHER, Ewilda, 1928- ,
American; nonfiction CON
FANCHER, Raymond Elwood, Jr. ,
1940- , American; nonfiction
CON
FANDEL, John, 1925- , Amer-

ican; nonfiction CON
FANDLEF, Juraj, 1750-1811,
Slovak; nonfiction BU
'FANE, Bron' see FANTHORPE,
Robert L.
FANE, Mildmay, 1602-64/65, Eng-
lish; poetry, plays BU
FANG, Irving E. , 1929- , Amer-
ican; nonfiction CON
FANG, Josephine Maria Riss,
1922- , Austrian-American;
nonfiction CON
FANG HSIAO-JU, 1357-1402,
Chinese; nonfiction BU
FANGEN, Ronald August, 1895-
1946, Norwegian; fiction, plays
BU TH
FANN, Kuang Tih, 1937- ,
Chinese-Canadian; nonfiction
CON
FANN, William Edwin, 1930- ,
American; nonfiction CON
FANNIN, Allen, 1939- , Ameri-
can; nonfiction CON
FANNING, Buckner, 1926- ,
American; nonfiction CON
FANNING, Charles Frederick, Jr. ,
1942- , American; nonfiction
CON
FANNING, Leonard Mulliken, 1888-
1967, American; juveniles CO
FANNING, Louis Albert, 1927- ,
American; nonfiction CON
FANNING, Michael, 1942- ,
American; nonfiction, poetry,
fiction CON
FANNING, Odom, 1920- , Amer-
ican; nonfiction CON
FANNING, Robbie, 1947- , Amer-
ican; nonfiction CON
FANNIUS, Gaius, fl. 122 B. C. ,
Roman; nonfiction LA
FANON, Frantz, 1925-61, French;
nonfiction CON WA
FANSHAWE, David, 1942- , Brit-
ish; nonfiction CON
FANSHAWE, Sir Richard, 1608-66,
English; translation, poetry
BU DA PO
'FANTASIS' see HUET, Conrad B.
FANTE, John Thomas, 1911- ,
American; fiction, juveniles
CON
FANTEL, Hans, 1922- , Austrian-
American; nonfiction CON
FANTHORPE, Patricia Alice,
1938- , British; nonfiction
CON

FANTHORPE, Robert Lionel ('Neil Balfort'; 'Othello Baron'; 'Erie Barton'; 'Lee Barton'; 'Thornton Bell'; 'Noel Bertram'; 'Leo Brett'; 'Bron Fane'; 'Phil Hobel'; 'Mel Jay'; 'Marston Johns'; 'Victor La Salle'; 'Oban Lerteth'; 'Robert Lionel'; 'John E. Muller'; 'Elton T. Neef'; 'Peter O' Flinn'; 'Peter O'Flynn'; 'Lionel Roberts'; 'Rene Rolant'; 'Deutero Spartacus'; 'Robin Tate'; 'Neil Thanet'; 'Trebor Thorpe'; 'Trevor Thorpe'; 'Pel Torro'; 'Olaf Trent'; 'Karl Zeigfreid'), 1935- , British; fiction AS CON NI

FANTINI, Mario D., American; nonfiction CON

FANTONI, Giovanni, 1755-1807, Italian; poetry BO BU

FARABEE, Barbara, 1944- , American; nonfiction, poetry CON

FARABI, Abu Nasr Muhammad, 870?-950, Islamic; nonfiction BU PRU

FARADAY, Ann, 1935- , Anglo-American; nonfiction CON

FARAGO, Ladislas, 1906-80, Hungarian-American; nonfiction CON

FARAH, Caesar Elie, 1929- , American; translations, nonfiction CON

FARAH, Madelain, 1934- , American; nonfiction CON

FARAH, Nuruddin, 1945- , Somalian; fiction, plays HER

FARALLA, Dana ('Dorothy W. Faralla'; 'Dana Wilma'), 1909- , American; juveniles, fiction CO CON

FARAZDAQ, 7-8th centuries, Arab; poetry BU

FARB, Peter, 1929-80, American; juveniles CO CON WAR

FARB, Stan Peters, 1929- , American; fiction, journalism, nonfiction WAK

FARBER, Leslie Hilel, 1912-81, American; nonfiction CON

FARBER, Marvin, 1901- , American; nonfiction CON

FARBER, Norma, 1909- , American; poetry, juveniles CO

CON WAR

FARBER, Seymour Morgan, 1912- , American; nonfiction CON

FARBER, Stephen E., 1943- , American; nonfiction CON

FARBER, Thomas David, 1944- , American; nonfiction CON

FARBERMAN, Harvey Alan, 1939- , American; nonfiction CON

FARCA, Marie C., 1935- , American; fiction NI

'FARELY, Alison' see POLAND, Dorothy

FARGUE, León Paul, 1876-1947, French; poetry, nonfiction BU CL SEY TH WA

FARHI, Moris, 1935- , Turkish-British; plays, film CON

FARIA, Anthony John, 1944- , American; nonfiction CON

FARIA, Otavio de, 1908- , Brazilian; fiction BR

FARIA e SOUSA, Manuel, 1590-1649, Portuguese; poetry BU

FARID, -1552, Panjabi; poetry PRU

FARIGOULE, Louis see 'ROMAINS, Jules'

FARINA, Richard, 1936?-66, American; plays, fiction CON

FARJEON, Benjamin Leopold, 1838-1903, English; fiction ST

FARJEON, Eleanor, 1881-1965, British; juveniles, plays, poetry, fiction BU KI

FARJEON, Eve Annabel ('Sarah Jefferson'), 1919- , English; juveniles CO CON

FARJEON, Herbert, 1887-1945, English; nonfiction DA

FARJEON, Joseph Jefferson, 1883-1955, English; fiction, plays NI

FARKAS, Emil, 1946- , Hungarian-American; nonfiction, film CON

FARKAS, Philip, 1914- , American; nonfiction CON

FARLEY, Carol ('Carol McDole'), 1936- , American; juveniles CO WAR

FARLEY, James Aloysius, 1888-1976, American; nonfiction CON

FARLEY, Miriam Southwell, 1907?-75, American; nonfiction CON

'Farley, Ralph Milne' (Roger Sherman Hoar), 1887-1963, American; fiction AS NI
FARLEY, Rawle, 1922- , American; nonfiction CON
FARLEY, Walter Lorimer, 1920- , American; juveniles KI
FARLEY, William Edward, 1929- , American; nonfiction CON
FARLEY-HILLS, David, 1931- , British; nonfiction CON
FARLIE, Barbara Leitzaw, 1936- , American; nonfiction CON
FARLIE, Robert (Farley), fl. 1638, Scots; poetry BU
FARMER, Charles Joseph, 1943- , American; nonfiction CON
FARMER, Don, 1938- , American; nonfiction CON
FARMER, Gary Ray, 1923- , American; nonfiction CON
FARMER, Herbert Henry, 1892-1981?, British; nonfiction CON
FARMER, Kathleen, 1946- , American; nonfiction CON
FARMER, Laurence, 1895?-1976, American; nonfiction CON
FARMER, Penelope, 1939- , British; juveniles, tv DEM KI
FARMER, Philip José ('Kilgore Trout'), 1918- , American; fiction, nonfiction AS COW NI WAK
FARMER, Richard, 1735-97, English; nonfiction DA
FARMILOE, Dorothy Alicia, 1920- , Canadian; poetry CON
FARNER, Donald Sankey, 1915- , American; nonfiction CON
'FARNHAM, Burt' see CLIFFORD, Harold B.
FARNHAM, Emily, 1912- , American; nonfiction CON
FARNHAM, Marynia F., 1900?-79, American; nonfiction CON
FARNHAM, Thomas Javery, 1938- , American; nonfiction CON
FARNIE, Douglas Antony, 1926- , British; nonfiction CON
FARNSWORTH, Dana Lyda, 1905- , American; nonfiction CON
'FARNSWORTH, James' see POHLE, Robert W., Jr.
FARNSWORTH, Robert M.,

1929- , American; nonfiction CON
'FARNUM, K. T.' see RIPS, Ervine M.
FARNWORTH, Warren, 1935- , British; juveniles, nonfiction CON
FARNY, Michael Holt, 1934- , American; nonfiction CON
FARQUHAR, Francis Peloubet, 1887-1975, American; nonfiction CON
FARQUHAR, George, 1677?-1707, Anglo-Irish; plays, poetry, fiction BRI BU DA HO MAG MCG PO VD
FARQUHAR, Margaret Cutting, 1905- , American; juveniles CO CON
FARR, Dorothy Mary, 1905- , British; nonfiction CON
FARR, Finis King, 1904-82, American; juveniles CO
'FARR, John' see WEBB, Jack
FARR, Kenneth Raymond, 1942- , American; nonfiction CON
'FARRA, Mme. E.' see FAWCETT, Frank D.
FARRAR, Frederick William, 1831-1903, English; nonfiction, juveniles BU DA
FARRAR, John Chipman ('John Prosper'), 1896-1974, American; fiction, nonfiction, poetry, plays CON
FARRAR, Lancelot Leighton, Jr., 1932- , American; nonfiction CON
FARRAR, Richard Bartlett, Jr., 1939- , American; nonfiction CON
FARRAR, Susan Clement, 1917- , American; juveniles CON
FARRAR-HOCKLEY, Anthony Heritage, 1924- , British; nonfiction CON
'FARRELL, Ben' see CEBULASH, Mel
FARRELL, Bryan Henry, 1923- , New Zealander; nonfiction CON
FARRELL, Cliff, 1899- , American; fiction CON
FARRELL, James Gordon, 1935-79, English; fiction CON HO VCN
FARRELL, James Thomas, 1904-79, American; fiction, nonfiction, poetry AM BR BU MAG

PO RO SEY VCN VN
FARRELL, John Philip, 1939- ,
American; nonfiction CON
FARRELL, Matthew Charles,
1921- , American; nonfiction
CON
FARRELL, Michael, 1899-1962,
Irish; fiction HO
FARRELL, Michael, 1944- ,
British; nonfiction CON
FARRELL, Robert Thomas, 1938- ,
American; nonfiction CON
'FARREN, David' see McFERRAN,
Douglass D.
FARREN, Mick, 1943- , Eng-
lish; fiction NI
FARRER, Claire Rafferty, 1936- ,
American; nonfiction CON
FARRER, Katharine Dorothy New-
ton, 1911- , British; fiction,
translations REI
'FARRERE, Claude' (Charles Bar-
gonne), 1876-1957, French;
fiction BU NI
FARRIMOND, John, 1913- ,
British; fiction, radio CON
FARRINGTON, Benjamin, 1891-
1974, American; nonfiction
CO CON
FARRINGTON, Brent, 1891-1974,
Irish; nonfiction CON
FARRINGTON, Conor, 1928- ,
Irish; plays HO
FARRINGTON, Selwyn Kip, Jr.,
1904- , American; juveniles,
nonfiction CO CON
FARRIS, John, American; fiction,
plays, film CON
FARROKHI, Abu'l-Hasan Ali
(Farrukhi), -1037/38, Per-
sian; poetry BU PRU
'FARROW, J.' see FONAROW,
Jerry
'FARROW, James S.' see TUBB,
Edwin C.
FARRUKHZAD, Furugh, 1935-67,
Persian; poetry BU PRU
FARSON, Daniel Negley ('Matilda
Excellent'), 1927- , British;
journalism, nonfiction, juven-
iles CON
FARSON, Negley, 1890-1960,
American; journalism, fiction
CON
FARWELL, George Michell,
1911-76, British-Australian;
nonfiction CON
FARZAD, Mas'ud, 1906- , Per-

sian; poetry, translations BU
PRU
FARZAN, Massud, 1936- , Amer-
ican; translations, poetry CON
FASI, Allal, 1910- , Moroccan;
journalism, nonfiction, poetry
PRU
FASSBINDER, Rainer Werner,
1946-82, German-American;
plays, film, tv CON
FASSETT, James, 1904- , Amer-
ican; nonfiction CON
FASSLER, Joan Grace, 1931- ,
American; juveniles CO CON
FAST, Howard ('E. V. Cunning-
ham'; 'Walter Ericson'),
1914- , American; fiction,
plays, nonfiction BR CO NI
PO REI VCN
FAST, Jonathan David, 1948- ,
American; fiction, film CON
'FASTLIFE' see GROGAN, Emmett
FASTOUL, Baude, 13th century,
French; poetry BU
FATCHEN, Max, 1920- , Aus-
tralian; juveniles, poetry CO
KI
FATEMI, Nasrollah Saifpour,
1901- , Iranian-American;
journalism, nonfiction CON
FATIGATI, Frances Evelyn,
1948- , American; fiction
CO CON
FATIO, Louise, Swiss-American;
juveniles CO KI
FAUCETTE, John Matthew, Jr.,
1943- , American; fiction
NI
FAUCHER, Claire see 'MARTIN,
Claire'
FAUCHER, Real, 1940- , Amer-
ican; poetry CON
FAUCHER, W. Thomas, 1945- ,
American; nonfiction CON
FAUCHET, Claude, 1530-1602,
French; nonfiction BU
FAUCHOIS, René, 1882-1962,
French; plays MCG
FAULHABER, Charles Bailey,
1941- , American; nonfiction
CON
FAULHABER, Martha, 1926- ,
American; juveniles CO
FAULK, John Henry, 1913- ,
American; nonfiction CON
FAULKNER, Anne Irvin ('Nancy
Faulkner'), 1906- , American;
juveniles CO DEM

FAULKNER, Elsie, 1905- , American; juveniles CON
FAULKNER, Harold Underwood, 1890-1968, American; nonfiction CON
FAULKNER, John Wesley Thompson III, 1901-63, American; fiction BA
FAULKNER, Joseph E., 1928- , American; nonfiction CON
'FAULKNER, Nancy' see FAULKNER, Anne I.
FAULKNER, Trader, 1930- , Australian; translations, radio CON
FAULKNER, Virginia Louise, 1913- , American; nonfiction CON
FAULKNER, Waldron, 1898-1979, American; nonfiction CON
FAULKNER, William, 1897-1962, American; fiction, poetry AM BA BR BU CON MAG PO REI SEY ST VN
FAULKNOR, Chauncey Clifford Vernon, 1913- , Canadian; juveniles KI
FAURE, Elie, 1873-1937, French; nonfiction BU CL
FAURE, Lucie, 1908-77, French; nonfiction, fiction CON
FAUROT, Albert, 1914- , American; nonfiction CON
FAUROT, Ruth Marie, 1916- , American; nonfiction CON
FAUSET, Arthur Huff, 1899- , American; fiction, nonfiction SH
FAUSET, Jessie Redmon, 1886-1961, American; fiction BA
FAUSSET, Hugh l'Anson, 1895-1965, British; poetry, nonfiction CON
FAUST, Albert Bernhard, 1870-1951, German-American; poetry, nonfiction, plays BU
FAUST, Clarence Henry, 1901-75, American; nonfiction CON
FAUST, Frederick see 'BRAND, Max'
FAUST, Irvin, 1924- , American; fiction HE VCN
FAUST, Naomi Flowe, American; poetry, nonfiction CON
FAUSTI, Remo Philip, 1917- , American; nonfiction CON
FAUTSKO, Timothy Frank ('Employee X'), 1945- , Amer-

ican; nonfiction CON
FAUX, Marian, 1945- , American; nonfiction CON
FAVA, Guido (Faba), early 13th century, Italian; nonfiction BU
FAVART, Charles Simon, 1710-92, French; plays BU
FAVERTY, Frederic Everett, 1902-81, American; nonfiction CON
FAVETTI, Carlo, 1819-92, Raeto-Romansch; poetry BU
FAVILLE, David Ernest, 1899-1970, American; nonfiction CON
FAVORINUS, 80-150, Greek; nonfiction GR LA
FAVRETTI, Rudy John, 1932- , American; nonfiction CON
FAWCETT, Brian, 1906- , Irish; nonfiction CON
FAWCETT, Claude Weldon, 1911- , American; nonfiction CON
FAWCETT, Edward Douglas, British; fiction NI
FAWCETT, Frank Dubrez ('Henri Dupres'; 'Ben Sarto'; 'Griff'; 'Eugene Glen'; 'Coolidge McCann'; 'Elmer Eliot Saks'; 'Mme. E. Farra'), 1891-1968, English; fiction NI
FAWCETT, James Edmund Sanford, 1913- , British; nonfiction CON
FAWCETT, Roger Knowlton, 1909-79, American; nonfiction CON
FAWKES, Richard Brian, 1944- , British; tv, radio, nonfiction, film CON
FAX, Elton Clay, 1909- , American; nonfiction, juveniles CO SH
FAXON, Alicia Craig, 1931- , American; nonfiction CON
FAXON, Arba D., 1895-1975, American; nonfiction CON
FAY, András, 1786-1864, Hungarian; fiction, nonfiction BU
FAY, Gordon Shaw, 1912- , American; nonfiction CON
FAY, John, 1921- , English; nonfiction CON
FAY, Peter Ward, 1924- , American; nonfiction CON
FAY, Samuel Prescott, Jr., 1926- , American; journalism CON
'FAY, Stanley' see STANLEY,

Fay G.
FAY, Thomas Arthur, 1927- ,
American; nonfiction CON
FAYE, Jean Pierre, 1925- ,
French; fiction, poetry, non-
fiction CL CON
FAYKO, Aleksey, 1893- , Rus-
sian; plays CL TH
FAYNZILBERG, Arnoldovich see
'IL'F'
FAYTURI, Muhammad Miftah,
1930- , Egyptian; poetry,
plays PRU
FAZAKAS, Ray, 1932- , Cana-
dian; nonfiction CON
FAZEKAS, Mihály, 1766-1828,
Hungarian; poetry TH
FAZIL, Maulana Muhammad, 19th
century, Baluchi; nonfiction
PRU
FAZIL HÜSNII DAGLARCA,
1914- , Turkish; poetry BU
FAZIO degli UBERTI, 1305-67,
Italian; poetry BO
FEAGANS, Raymond John, 1953- ,
American; nonfiction CON
FEAGLES, Anita MacRae ('Travis
MacRae'), 1926- , Amer-
ican; juveniles CO DEM
FEAGUE, Mildred H., 1915- ,
American; juveniles CO
FEAR, David E., 1941- , Amer-
ican; nonfiction CON
FEARING, Kenneth ('Donald F.
Bedford'), 1902-61, American;
poetry, fiction, journalism
BR CON NI PO REI SEY ST
VP
FEARN, John Russell, 1908-60,
British; fiction AS NI
FEARS, Gerald, American; non-
fiction CON
FEATHER, Leonard Geoffrey,
1914- , Anglo-American;
nonfiction CON
FEATHER, Norman Thomas,
1930- , Australian; nonfic-
tion CON
'FEATHERSTONE, D.' see
WARREN, David
FEATHERSTONE, Helen, 1944- ,
American; nonfiction CON
FEAVER, William Andrew,
1942- , British; nonfiction
CON
FECHER, Charles Adam, 1917- ,
American; nonfiction CON
FECHER, Constance ('Constance

Heaven'), 1911- , English;
fiction, juveniles CO CON
WAR
FECK, Luke, 1935- , American;
nonfiction CON
FEDER, Jane, 1940- , American;
juveniles CON
FEDER, Lillian, American; nonfic-
tion CON
FEDERER, Heinrich, 1866-1928,
Swiss; fiction BU
FEDERICO, Ronald Charles,
1941- , American; nonfiction
CON
FEDEROFF, Alex, 1927?-79,
American; fiction CON
FEDERSPIEL, Jürg, 1931- ,
Swiss; fiction, poetry CL
FEDIN, Konstantin Alexandrovich,
1892-1977, Russian; fiction
BU CL CON TH WA
FEDLER, Fred, 1940- , Ameri-
can; journalism, nonfiction
CON
FEDYSHYN, Oleh Sylvester,
1928- , Russian-American;
nonfiction CON
FEEGEL, John Richard, 1932- ,
American; nonfiction, fiction
CON
FEELEY, Patricia Falk, 1941- ,
American; fiction, nonfiction
CON
FEELINGS, Muriel Grey, 1938- ,
American; juveniles CO CON
DEM SH
FEELINGS, Tom, 1933- , Amer-
ican; nonfiction, juveniles CO
CON DE SH
FEENBERG, Eugene, 1906-77,
American; nonfiction CON
FEENEY, John, 1948- , Irish;
journalism, fiction HO
FEENEY, Leonard, 1897-1978,
American; nonfiction CON
FEERICK, John David, 1936- ,
American; nonfiction CON
FEFFER, Itzik, 1900-48/52, Yid-
dish; poetry BU TH
FEGELY, Thomas David, 1941- ,
American; juveniles, nonfiction
CON
FEHRS, Johann Hinrich, 1838-1916,
German; fiction BU
FEIBES, Walter, 1928- , Ameri-
can; nonfiction CON
FEIBLEMAN, Peter Steinam,
1930- , American; fiction BA

FEIERMAN, Steven, 1940- ,
American; nonfiction CON
FEIFEL, Herman, 1915- ,
American; nonfiction CON
FEIFFER, Jules, 1929- , Amer-
ican; plays, fiction, nonfic-
tion CO MCG MCN VCD
WAK
FEIGERT, Frank Brook, 1937- ,
American; nonfiction CON
FEIJOO y MONTENEGRO, Benito,
1676-1764, Spanish; nonfiction
BU TH
'FEIKEMA, Feike' see MANFRED,
Frederich F.
FEIL, Hila, 1942- , American;
juveniles CO
FEILDING, Dorothy see 'FIELD-
ING, A.'
FEILE, Reshad, 1934- , Anglo-
American; nonfiction CON
'FEILEN, John' see MAY, Julian
FEILER, Seymour, 1919- ,
American; translations, non-
fiction CON
FEIN, Irving Ashley, 1911- ,
American; nonfiction CON
FEIN, Leah Gold, Russian-
American; nonfiction CON
FEIN, Richard Jacob, 1929- ,
American; nonfiction CON
FEINBERG, Bea ('Cynthia Free-
man'), American; fiction
CON
FEINBERG, Hilda, American;
nonfiction CON
FEINBERG, Lawrence Bernard,
1940- , American; nonfiction
CON
FEINBERG, Mortimer Robert,
1922- , American; nonfiction
CON
FEINBERG, Walter, 1937- ,
American; nonfiction CON
FEINBLOOM, Deborah Heller,
1940- , American; nonfiction
CON
FEINGOLD, Benjamin Franklin,
1900- , American; nonfiction
CON
FEINGOLD, Michael, 1945- ,
American; plays, translations
CON
FEININGER, Andreas, 1906- ,
German; nonfiction CON
FEINMAN, Jeffrey, 1943- ,
American; nonfiction CON
FEINSTEIN, Elaine, 1930- ,

British; poetry, fiction, non-
fiction, translations, tv CON
VCP
FEINSTEIN, George Williamson,
1913- , American; nonfiction
CON
FEINSTEIN, Sherman C., 1923- ,
American; nonfiction CON
FEIRBERG, Mordechai Zeeb, 1874-
99, Hebrew; fiction, nonfiction
BU TH
FEIRSTEIN, Frederick, 1940- ,
American; plays, fiction CON
FEIS, Herbert, 1893-1972, Amer-
ican; nonfiction WA
FEIST, Aubrey Noel, 1903- ,
English; plays, juveniles, fic-
tion CON
FEITAMA, Sybrand, 1694-1758,
Dutch; translations, plays BU
FEITEL, Donald G., 1925?-76,
American; journalism, nonfic-
tion CON
FEITH, Rhijnois, 1753-1824, Dutch;
poetry, fiction BU
FEKRAT, M. Ali, 1937- , Amer-
ican; nonfiction CON
FELBER, Stanley B., 1932- ,
American; nonfiction CON
FELDENKRAIS, Moshe Pinchas,
1904- , Polish-Israeli; nonfic-
tion CON
FELDER, Eleanor, American;
juveniles WAR
'FELDER, Paul' see WELLEN,
Edward P.
FELDERMAN, Eric, 1944- ,
American; poetry, fiction
CON
FELDKAMP, Phyllis, American;
journalism, nonfiction CON
FELDMAN, Abraham Jehile, 1893-
1977, Ukrainian-American;
nonfiction CON
FELDMAN, Alan, 1945- , Amer-
ican; poetry, fiction CON
FELDMAN, Anne Rodgers, 1939- ,
American; juveniles CO CON
FELDMAN, Annette Gerber,
1913- , American; nonfiction
CON
FELDMAN, Ellet Bette ('Amanda
Russell'; 'Elizabeth Villars'),
1941- , American; fiction
CON
FELDMAN, Irving Mordecai,
1928- , American; poetry
BR VCP WAK

FELDMAN, Leon Aryeh, 1921- ,
German-American; nonfiction
CON
FELDMAN, Leonard ('Daniel El-
liot'), 1927- , American;
nonfiction CON
FELDMAN, Louis Harry, 1926- ,
American; nonfiction CON
FELDMAN, Maurice Philip,
1933- , English; nonfiction
CON
FELDMAN, Sandor S., 1891?-
1973, Hungarian; nonfiction
CON
FELDMAN, Saul Daniell, 1943- ,
American; nonfiction CON
FELDMAN, Silvia Dash, 1928- ,
American; nonfiction CON
FELDMEIR, Daryle Matthew,
1923- , American; journal-
ism CON
FELDON, Leah, 1944- , Amer-
ican; journalism, nonfiction
CON
FELDSTEIN, Martin Stuart,
1939- , American; nonfiction
CON
FELDSTEIN, Paul Joseph, 1933- ,
American; nonfiction CON
FELDT, Allan Gunnar, 1932- ,
American; nonfiction CON
FELICES, Jorge, 1917- , Puerto
Rican; journalism, fiction
HIL
FELICIANO MENDOZA, Ester,
1917- , Puerto Rican; poetry,
fiction HIL
FELINSKI, Alojzy, 1771-1820,
Polish; poetry, plays BU TH
'FELIPE, León' (León Felipe
Camino Galicia), 1884-1968,
Spanish; poetry CL
FELIU y CODINA, José, 1847-97,
Spanish; plays BU
FELIX, David, 1921- , American;
nonfiction CON
FELKENES, George Theodore,
1930- , American; nonfiction
CON
FELKER, Clay Schuette, 1925- ,
American; journalism, non-
fiction CON
FELKER, Evelyn H., 1933- ,
American; nonfiction CON
FELL, John Louis, 1927- ,
American; nonfiction CON
FELLINI, Federico, 1920- ,
Italian; film CON

FELLMAN, Gordon, 1934- ,
American; nonfiction CON
FELLMAN, Michael Dinion,
1943- , Canadian; nonfiction
CON
FELLMETH, Robert Charles,
1945- , American; nonfiction
CON
FELLOWS, Donald Keith, 1920- ,
American; nonfiction CON
FELLOWS, Jay, 1940- , American;
fiction, nonfiction CON
FELLOWS, Lawrence Perry,
1924- , American; nonfiction
CON
FELLOWS, Muriel H., American;
juveniles CO CON
FELLTHAM, Owen, 1602?-68,
English; poetry BU
FELSTEIN, Ivor ('Frank Steen'),
1933- , Scots; nonfiction
FELSTINER, L. John, Jr.,
1936- , American; nonfiction,
translations CON
FELTON, Bruce, 1946- , Amer-
ican; nonfiction CON SH
FELTON, Cornelius Conway, 1807-
62, American; nonfiction MY
FELTON, John Richard, 1917- ,
American; nonfiction CON
FELTON, Ronald Oliver ('Ronald
Welch'), 1909- , Welsh;
juveniles CO KI
FELTRE, Vittorino da see RAM-
BALDONI, Vittorino de
'LA Femme du Postillon' see
'GUEVREMONT, Germaine'
FENADY, Andrew, 1928- , Amer-
ican; nonfiction, film CON
FENBERG, Matilda, 1888?-1977,
Polish-American; nonfiction
CON
FENDELL, Bob ('Dell Roberts'),
1925- , American; nonfiction
CON
FENDELMAN, Helaine Woll,
1942- , American; nonfiction
CON
FENELON, Fania, 1918- , Amer-
ican; nonfiction CON
FENELON, Francois de Salignac,
1651-1715, French; nonfiction
BU TH
FENELON, Kevin Gerard, 1898- ,
British; nonfiction CON
FENEON, Félix, 1861-1944,
French; nonfiction CL

American; nonfiction CON
FERGUSON, Blanche E., 1906- ,
American; nonfiction SH
FERGUSON, Charles Albert,
1921- , American; nonfiction
CON
FERGUSON, Christopher William,
1944- , American; nonfiction,
fiction, poetry CON
FERGUSON, David L., 1930- ,
American; nonfiction CON
FERGUSON, Elmer James,
1917- , American; nonfiction
CON
FERGUSON, Franklin Cole,
1934- , American; nonfiction
CON
FERGUSON, Harry, 1903-80,
American; journalism CON
'FERGUSON, Helen' see 'KAVAN,
Anna'
FERGUSON, John Halcro, 1920-
68, American; journalism,
nonfiction CON
FERGUSON, Mary Anne, 1918- ,
American; nonfiction CON
FERGUSON, Milton Carr, 1931- ,
American; nonfiction CON
FERGUSON, Pamela, 1943- ,
American; journalism, fiction
CON
FERGUSON, Robert Bruce,
1927- , American; juveniles,
nonfiction CO CON
FERGUSON, Robert William,
1940- , American; nonfiction
CON
FERGUSON, Rowena, 1904- ,
American; nonfiction CON
FERGUSON, Sir Samuel, 1810-86,
Irish; poetry, nonfiction
BU DA HO VP
FERGUSON, Suzanne, 1939- ,
American; nonfiction CON
FERGUSON, Ted, 1936- , Cana-
dian; plays CON
FERGUSON, William Rotch,
1943- , American; poetry
CON
FERGUSSON, Erna, 1888-1964,
American; juveniles CO
FERGUSSON, Francis, 1904- ,
American; nonfiction, poetry,
plays BOR
FERGUSSON, Robert, 1750-74,
Scots; poetry BU DA PO VP
FERICANO, Paul Francis, 1951- ,
American; poetry CON

FERIENCIK, Mikuláš Stefan, 1825-
81, Slovak; fiction BU
FERLIN, Nils, 1898-1961, Swedish;
poetry BU TH
FERLINGHETTI, Lawrence, 1919/
20- , American; poetry, fic-
tion, plays BR BU MAL PO
SEY VCD VCP WA
FERM, Vergilius, 1896-1974,
American; nonfiction CON
FERMAN, Edward Lewis, 1937- ,
American; fiction AS NI
FERMAN, Joseph Wolfe, 1906-74,
American; editor, anthology
NI
FERMI, Laura, 1907- , Italian-
American; juveniles CO
FERMOR, Patrick Michael Leigh,
1915- , Anglo-Irish; nonfic-
tion, fiction CON WA
FERN, Eugene A., 1919- , Amer-
ican; juveniles CO
FERNANDEZ, Benedict J., III,
1936- , American; nonfiction
CON
FERNANDEZ, Celestino, 1949- ,
American; nonfiction MAR
FERNANDEZ, John Peter, 1941- ,
American; nonfiction CON
FERNANDEZ, Julio A., 1936- ,
American; nonfiction MAR
FERNANDEZ, Lucas, 1474?-1542,
Spanish; plays BU MCG TH
FERNANDEZ, Macedonio, 1874-
1952, Argentinian; fiction, po-
etry BR
FERNANDEZ, Pablo Armando,
1930- , Cuban; poetry BR
FERNANDEZ ALMAGRO, Melchor,
1893-1966, Spanish; nonfiction
CL
FERNANDEZ ARDAVIN, Luis,
1892- , Spanish; poetry, plays
MCG
FERNANDEZ de HEREDIA, Juan,
1310-96, Spanish; translations,
nonfiction BU
FERNANDEZ de JERENA, Garcí,
late 14th century, Spanish; po-
etry BU TH
FERNANDEZ de la REGUERA,
Ricardo, 1916- , Spanish;
fiction CL
FERNANDEZ de LIZARDI, José
Joaquín (El Pendador Mexi-
cano), 1776-1827, Mexican;
fiction, journalism BR BU
MAG

FERNANDEZ de MORATIN,
Leandro, 1760-1828, Spanish;
plays BU MCG
FERNANDEZ de MORATIN,
Nicolás, 1737-80, Spanish;
poetry, plays BU MCG
FERNANDEZ de OVIEDO, Gon-
zalo (Hernnadez), 1478-1557,
Spanish; nonfiction HIL
FERNANDEZ de VELASCO y
PIMENTEL, Bernardino,
1783-1851, Spanish; poetry
BU
FERNANDEZ FLOREZ, Wenceslao,
1885-1964, Spanish; fiction,
nonfiction BU CL
FERNANDEZ JUNCOS, Manuel,
1846-1928, Austrian-Puerto
Rican; journalism, poetry,
nonfiction HIL
FERNANDEZ-MARINA, Ramon,
1909- , Puerto Rican; non-
fiction, poetry, fiction CON
FERNANDEZ MENDEZ, Eugenio,
1924- , Puerto Rican; journalism, nonfiction HIL
FERNANDEZ MORENO, Baldo-
mero, 1885-1950, Argentinian;
poetry BR
FERNANDEZ RETAMAR, Roberto,
1930- , Cuban; poetry BR
FERNANDEZ SANTOS, Jesús,
1926- , Spanish; fiction,
journalism CL
FERNANDEZ VANGA, Epifanio,
1880-1961, Puerto Rican; non-
fiction, poetry, journalism
HIL
FERNANDEZ y GONZALEZ,
Manuel, 1821-88, Spanish;
fiction BU
FERNANDO, Lloyd, 1926- ,
British; nonfiction CON
FERNETT, Gene, 1924- , Amer-
ican; nonfiction CON
FERNSWORTH, Lawrence, 1893?-
1977, American; journalism,
nonfiction CON
'FERRANTE, Don' see GERBI,
Antonello
FERRANTE, Joan Marguerite,
1936- , American; nonfiction
CON
FERRARA, Antonio da see BEC-
CARI, Antonio
FERRARI, Paolo, 1822-89, Italian;
plays BO MCG
FERRARO, Gary Paul, 1940- ,

American; nonfiction CON
'FERRARS, Elixabeth X.' (Morna
Doris Brown; 'E. X. Ferrars'),
1907- , English; fiction REI
ST
FERRATER MORA, José, 1912- ,
Spanish; nonfiction CL
FERREIRA, Antonio, 1528-69,
Portuguese; poetry, plays BU
MAG TH
FERREIRA, Antonio Baticā,
1938?- , Guinean; poetry
HER
FERREIRA, José da Silva Maia,
1825?-50?, Angolan; poetry
HER
FERREIRA, José Gomes, 1900- ,
Portuguese; poetry, fiction,
nonfiction CL
FERREIRA, Vergílio, 1916- ,
Portuguese; fiction, nonfiction
CL
FERREIRA de CASTRO, José
María, 1898-1974, Portuguese;
fiction, journalism, nonfiction
CON SEY TH
FERREOL, Marcel Auguste see
'ACHARD, Marcel'
FERRER CANALES, José, 1913- ,
Puerto Rican; nonfiction HIL
FERRER del RIO, Antonio, 1814-
72, Spanish; nonfiction BU
FERRER HERNANDEZ, Gabriel,
1847-1900, Puerto Rican; po-
etry, plays, nonfiction HIL
FERRER OTERO, Rafael, 1885-
1951, Puerto Rican; nonfiction
HIL
FERRERO, Leo, 1903-33, Italian;
plays MCG
FERRES, Antonio, 1925- , Span-
ish; fiction CL
FERRERS, George, 1500?-78/79,
English; poetry, plays BU
FERRES, John Howard, 1932- ,
Australian-American; nonfiction
CON
FERRIER, Susan Edmonstone,
1782-1854, Scots; fiction BU
PO VN
FERRIL, Thomas Hornsby, 1896- ,
American; poetry, plays, non-
fiction CON VCP
FERRIS, Helen Josephine, 1890-
1969, American; juveniles, non-
fiction CO CON
FERRIS, Norman Bernard, 1931- ,
American; nonfiction CON

FERRIS, Timothy, 1944- , American; nonfiction CON
'FERRIS, Tom' see WALKER, Peter N.
FERRITOR, Daniel Edward, 1939- , American; nonfiction CON
FERRO, Marc, 1924- , French; nonfiction CON
FERRON, Jacques, 1921- , Canadian; plays, fiction CR
FERRY, Charles, 1927- , American; juveniles CON
FERRY, William Hawkins, 1914- , American; nonfiction CON
FERSI, Mustafa, 1931- , Tunisian; poetry, plays PRU
FERSTER, Charles Bohris, 1922- , American; nonfiction CON
FESHBACH, Norma Deitch, 1926- , American; nonfiction CON
FESSENDEN, Katherine, 1896?- 1974, American; juveniles CON
FEST, Joachim C., 1926- , American; nonfiction CON
FESTUS, Sextus Pompeius, fl. 200, Roman; nonfiction BU
FET, Afanasy Afanayevich, 1820- 92, Russian; poetry BU TH
FETHERLINE, Dale, 1941- , American; nonfiction CON
FETHERLING, Doug, 1947- , Canadian; poetry VCP
FETHRIDGE, William Harrison, 1906- , American; nonfiction CON
FETROS, John G., 1932- , American; nonfiction CON
FETSCHER, Iring, 1922- , German; nonfiction CON
'FETTAMEN, Ann' see HOFF- MAN, Anita
FETTER, Elizabeth Head, 1904- 73, American; nonfiction CON
FETTER, Richard Leland, 1943- , American; nonfiction CON
FETTERMAN, Elsie, 1927- , American; nonfiction CON
FETTERMAN, John, 1920-75, American; journalism, non- fiction CON
FETTIG, Arthur John, 1929- , American; fiction, nonfiction, poetry CON

FETZER, John Francis, 1931- , American; nonfiction CON
FEUCHT, Oscar Emil, 1895- , American; nonfiction CON
FEUCHTWANGER, Edgar Joseph, 1924- , German-British; non- fiction CON
FEUCHTWANGER, Lion, 1884-1958, German; fiction, plays, poetry, nonfiction BU CL MAG MCG TH
'FEUR, D. Cy' see STAHL, Fred A.
FEUERBACH, Ludwig Andreas, 1804-72, German; nonfiction TH
FEUERSTEIN, Emil see 'HAM- EIRI, Avigdor'
FEUILLET, Octave, 1821-90, French; fiction, plays BU TH
FEVAL, Paul Henri Corentin, 1817- 87, French; fiction BU
FEYDEAU, Ernest Aimé, 1821-73, French; fiction BU TH
FEYDEAU, Georges, 1862-1921, French; plays BU CL MCG TH WA
FEYDY, Anne Lindbergh, American; juveniles WAR
FEYLBRIEF, Jan K. see 'OUDS- HOORN, J. van'
FEZANDIE, Clement, American; plays NI
ffolliott, Rosemary, 1934- , Irish; nonfiction CON
ffFRENCH-BEYTAGH, Gonville Aubie, 1912- , British; non- fiction CON
ffRENCH BLAKE, Neil St. John, 1940- , British; nonfiction CON
FfRENCH-BLAKE, Robert Lifford Valentine, 1913- , English; nonfiction CON
'FIACC, Padraic' (Patrick Joseph O'Connor), 1924- , Irish; poetry CON HO
FIALKO, Nathan, 1881- , Rus- sian; fiction NI
FIALKOWSKI, Barbara, 1946- , American; poetry CON
FIAMMENGHI, Gioia, 1929- , American; juveniles CO
FIANDT, Mary K., 1914- , American; fiction CON
FIAROTTA, Noel, 1944- , Amer- ican; juveniles, nonfiction CO CON

FIAROTTA, Phyllis, 1942- , American; juveniles, nonfiction CO CON

FIAWOO, F. Kwasi, 1891- , Ghanaian; plays JA

FICHMAN, Yaakov, 1881-1958, Hebrew; nonfiction, poetry BU TH

FICHTE, Hubert, 1935- , German; fiction BU CL

FICHTE, Johann Gottlieb, 1762-1814, German; nonfiction TH

FICHTELIUS, Karl-Erik, 1924- , Swedish; nonfiction CON

FICHTER, George S. ('Matt Warner'), 1922- , American; juveniles CO WAR

FICINO, Marsilio, 1433-99, Italian; nonfiction, translations BO BU

FICKE, Arthur Davison, 1883-1945, American; poetry, nonfiction PAL

FICKEN, Frederick Arthur, 1910-78, American; nonfiction CON

FIDLER, Kathleen Annie, 1899- , British; juveniles, plays CO KI

FIE, Jacquelyn Joyce, 1937- , American; nonfiction CON

FIEDEL, Roslyn, American; juveniles WAR

FIELDER, Jean, American; juveniles CO

FIEDLER, Leslie, 1917- , American; nonfiction, fiction BOR BR BU SEY VCN WA

FIELD, Andrew, 1938- , American; translations, nonfiction CON

FIELD, Daniel, 1938- , American; nonfiction CON

FIELD, David Dudley, 1918- , American; nonfiction CON

FIELD, Dawn Stewart, 1940- , American; fiction CON

FIELD, Dick, 1912- , English; nonfiction CON

FIELD, Edward, 1924- , American; poetry, translations CO VCP WAK

FIELD, Eugene, 1850-95, American; poetry, journalism BR BU CO MAL VP

FIELD, Frances Fox (Frances Margaret Fox), 1913?-77,

American; juveniles CON

FIELD, Frank McCoy, 1887-1978, American; nonfiction CON

FIELD, George Brooks, 1929- , American; nonfiction CON

FIELD, Henry, 1902- , American; nonfiction CON

'FIELD, Michael' (Katherine Harris Bradley, 1846-1914; Edith Emma Cooper, 1862-1913), English; poetry, plays DA

FIELD, Nathaniel, 1587?-1620, English; plays BU DA PO RU VD

FIELD, Rachel Lyman, 1894-1942, American; juveniles, poetry, fiction CO KI

FIELD, Walter Sherman, 1899- , American; nonfiction CON

FIELDEN, Charlotte, Canadian; fiction, plays CON

'FIELDING, A.' (Dorothy Feilding; 'A. E. Fielding'), 1884- , British; fiction REI

'FIELDING, Gabriel' (Alan Gabriel Barnsley), 1916- , English; fiction, poetry VCN WA

FIELDING, Gordon J., 1934- , New Zealand-American; nonfiction CON

FIELDING, Henry, 1707-54, English; plays, fiction BRI BU DA MAG MCG PO VD VN

FIELDING, Joy, 1945- , Canadian-American; fiction CON

FIELDING, Sarah, 1710-68, English; fiction, juveniles, translations BU DA VN

FIELDING, Waldo L., 1921- , American; nonfiction CON

FIELDS, Arthur C., 1926?-74, American; fiction CON

FIELDS, Beverly, 1917- , American; nonfiction CON

FIELDS, Dorothy, 1905-74, American; plays CON

FIELDS, Howard Kenneth, 1938- , American; nonfiction CON

FIELDS, James Thomas, 1817-81, American; poetry MY

FIELDS, Joseph, 1895-1966, American; plays MCG

FIELDS, Julia, 1938- , American; poetry BA CON SH

FIELDS, Nora, American; nonfiction CON

FIELDS, Rick, 1942- , American; poetry, fiction CON

FIELDS, Rona Marcia, 1934- ,
American; nonfiction CON
FIELER, Frank Bernard,
1935- , American; nonfiction
CON
FIENE, Donald Mark, 1930- ,
American; nonfiction, trans-
lations CON
FIENNES, Ranulph, 1944- ,
English; nonfiction CON
FIESER, Louis Frederick, 1899-
1977, American; nonfiction
CON
FIESTER, Mark Lafayette, 1907- ,
American; nonfiction CON
FIFE, Austin Edwin, 1909- ,
American; nonfiction CON
FIFE, Dale Odile, 1910- ,
American; juveniles, fiction
CO CON DEM WAR
FIGES, Eva, 1932- , British;
fiction, juveniles, translations
CON VCN
FIGGINS, Ross, 1936- , Amer-
ican; nonfiction CON
FIGGIS, Darrell Edmund, 1882-
1925, Irish; nonfiction, fic-
tion HO
'A FIGHTER PILOT' see JOHN-
STON, Hugh A. S.
FIGUEIREDO, Fidelino de Sousa,
1888-1967, Portuguese; non-
fiction CL
FIGUEIREDO, Manuel de, 1725-
1801, Portuguese; plays BU
FIGUEIREDO, Tomaz de, 1920- ,
Portuguese; fiction CL
FIGUEROA, Edwin, 1925- ,
Puerto Rican; nonfiction, fic-
tion HIL
FIGUEROA, Francesco de, 1536?-
1617?, Spanish; poetry TH
FIGUEROA, Francisco de, 1600?-
20, Spanish; poetry BU
FIGUEROA, Gómez S. de see
'GARCILASO de la VEGA'
FIGUEROA, John Joseph, 1920- ,
Jamaican; poetry, nonfiction
VCP
FIGUEROA, John Lewis, 1936- ,
American; juveniles, fiction,
plays CON
FIGUEROA, Pablo, 1938- ,
Puerto Rican; juveniles, plays
CO CON
FIGUEROA, Richard A., 1941- ,
American; nonfiction MAR
FIGUEROA, Sotero, 1863-1923,

Cuban; journalism, plays, non-
fiction HIL
FIGUEROA-CHAPEL, Ramon,
1935- , Puerto Rican; poetry,
nonfiction CON
FIGUEROA de CIFREDO, Patria,
Puerto Rican; nonfiction HIL
FIGUEROA-MERCADO, Loida,
1917- , Puerto Rican; poetry,
fiction, nonfiction CON
FIGUEROA y CORDOBA, Diego,
1629-?, Spanish; plays BU
FIGUEROA y CORDOBA, Jose,
1625-?, Spanish; plays BU
FIGULI, Margita, 1909- , Slovak;
fiction BU
FIJAN, Carol, 1918- , American;
nonfiction CO CON
FIKRET, Tevfik, 1867-1915, Turk-
ish; poetry BU PRU
FILANGIERI, Gaetano, 1752-88,
Italian; nonfiction BO
FILELFO, Francesco, 1398-1481,
Italian; nonfiction BU
FILEP, Robert Thomas, 1931- ,
American; nonfiction CON
FILIATRAULT, Jean, 1919- ,
Canadian; fiction, plays CR
FILICAIA, Vincenzo da, 1642-1707,
Italian; poetry BU TH
FILICCHIA, Ralph ('Ralph Michaels'),
1935- , American; nonfiction,
fiction CON
FILIMON, Nicolae, 1819-65, Ru-
manian; fiction BU
FILIPPO, Eduardo de, 1900- ,
Italian; plays, poetry, film, tv
WAK
FILLMORE, Parker Haysted, 1878-
1944, American; juveniles
COM
FILOSA, Gary Fairmont R.,
1931- , American; nonfiction
CON
FILSON, Floyd Vivian, 1896- ,
American; nonfiction CON
FINBERG, Herbert Patrick Regi-
nald, 1900-74, American; non-
fiction CON
FINCH, Anne see WINCHILSEA,
Countess of
FINCH, Donald George, 1937- ,
American; poetry CON
FINCH, Henry Leroy, 1918- ,
American; nonfiction CON
FINCH, Robert Duer, 1900- ,
Canadian; poetry, plays, non-
fiction BU CON VCP

FINCHER, Cameron Lane, 1926- ,
American; nonfiction CON
FINCHER, Ernest Barksdale,
1910- , American; nonfiction
CON
FINCKE, Gary William, 1945- ,
American; poetry, nonfiction,
fiction CON
'FINDER, Martin' see SALZ-
MANN, Siegmund
FINDLATER, Richard see BAIN,
Kenneth B.
FINDLAY, James Franklin, Jr.,
1930- , American; nonfiction
CON
FINDLAY, Robert R. , 1932- ,
American; nonfiction CON
FINE, Benjamin, 1905-75, Amer-
ican; nonfiction CON
FINE, Elsa Honig, 1930- ,
American; nonfiction CON
FINE, Estelle see JELINEK,
Estele C.
FINE, Nathan, 1893?-1979, Amer-
ican; nonfiction CON
FINEMAN, Morton, American;
juveniles WAR
FINER, Samuel Edward, 1915- ,
English; nonfiction CON
FINESTONE, Harry, 1920- ,
American; nonfiction CON
FINGARETTE, Herbert, 1921- ,
American; nonfiction CON
FINK, Edith, 1918- , American;
nonfiction, translations CON
FINK, Eli E. , 1908?-79, Amer-
ican; poetry CON
FINK, Gary M. , 1936- , Amer-
ican; nonfiction CON
FINK, Joseph, 1915- , Amer-
ican; nonfiction CON
FINK, Lawrence Alfred, 1930- ,
American; nonfiction CON
FINK, Paul Jay, 1933- , Amer-
ican; nonfiction CON
FINK, Stevanne see AUERBACH,
Stevanne
FINK, William Bertrand, 1916- ,
American; juveniles, non-
fiction CO CON
FINKE, Blythe Foote, 1922- ,
American; juveniles CON
FINKE, Jack A. , 1918?-79,
American; journalism CON
FINKEL, Donald, 1929- ,
American; poetry VCP WAK
FINKEL, George Irvine ('E. M.
Pennage'), 1909-75, English;

juveniles CO KI
FINKELSTEIN, Bonnie Blumenthal,
1946- , American; nonfiction
CON
FINKELSTEIN, Jacob Joel, 1922-
74, American; nonfiction CON
FINKELSTEIN, Milton, 1920- ,
American; juveniles, nonfiction
CON
FINKELSTEIN, Sidney, 1910?-74,
American; nonfiction CON
FINKLEHOFFE, Fred F. , 1910-77,
American; plays, film CON
FINLATOR, John Haywood,
1911- , American; nonfiction
CON
FINLAY, Ian Hamilton, 1925- ,
Scots; poetry, fiction, plays
CON VCP WA
FINLAY, Virgil, 1914-71, Ameri-
can; illustrations AS
'FINLAY, William' see MACKAY,
James A.
FINLAY, Winifred Lindsay,
1910- , British; juveniles,
plays CO KI
FINLAYSON, Ann, 1925- , Amer-
ican; juveniles CO
FINLAYSON, Roderick David,
1904- , New Zealander; fic-
tion, nonfiction, juveniles
CON VCN VN
FINLER, Joel Waldo, 1938- ,
British; nonfiction CON
FINLETTER, Thomas Knight, 1893-
1980, American; nonfiction
CON
FINLEY, James, 1943- , Ameri-
can; nonfiction CON
FINLEY, Joseph Edwin, 1919- ,
American; nonfiction, fiction
CON
FINLEY, Lewis Merren, 1929- ,
American; nonfiction CON
FINN, David, 1921- , American;
nonfiction CON
FINN, Ralph Leslie, 1912- ,
British; fiction, journalism
NI
'FINNEGAN, Robert' (Paul William
Ryan; 'Mike Quin'), 1906-47,
American; fiction, nonfiction
REI
FINNERTY, Adam Daniel ('A. Dan-
iel McKenna'), 1944- , Amer-
ican; nonfiction CON
FINNEY, Ben Rudolph, 1933- ,
American; nonfiction CON

FINNEY, Charles Grandison,
1905- , American; journal-
ism, fiction NI
FINNEY, Humphrey S. ('Nothing
Venture'), 1902- , Anglo-
American; nonfiction CON
'FINNEY, Jack' (Walter Braden
Finney), 1911- , American;
fiction, journalism, plays
AS COW NI REI
FINNEY, Patricia, 1958- , Irish;
fiction, plays CON HO
FINNEY, Paul Burnham, 1929- ,
American; nonfiction CON
FINNEY, Theodore Mitchell,
1902- , American; nonfiction
CON
FINNEY, Walter B. see 'FINNEY,
Jack'
FINNIGAN, Joan, 1923- , Cana-
dian; poetry, plays VCP
FINZGAR, Franc Saleski, 1871-
1962, Slovene; fiction, plays
BU
FIORE, Edith, 1930- , American;
nonfiction CON
FIORE, Michael V. , 1934- ,
American; nonfiction CON
FIORE, Robert Louis, 1935- ,
American; nonfiction CON
FIORI, Pamela A. , 1944- ,
American; journalism CON
FIORINA, Morris Paul, Jr. ,
1946- , American; nonfiction
CON
FIORIO, Franco Emilio, 1912-75,
Italian; nonfiction CON
'FIRAQ, Gorakhpuri' (Raghupati
Sahay), 1896- , Urdu; poetry
PRU
FIRBANK, Ronald, 1886-1926,
English; fiction BU DA PO
SEY VN
FIRDAWSI, Mansûr, Abu'l-Qâsim,
935?-1020?, Persian; poetry
BU LA
FIRENZUOLA, Agnolo, 1493-
1543, Italian; poetry, plays
BO BU TH
FIRESTONE, Otto John, 1913- ,
Austrian-Canadian; nonfiction
CON
'FIRESTONE, Tom' see NEW-
COMB, Duane G.
FIRMICUS MATERNUS, Julius,
fl. 350, Latin; nonfiction
BU GR
FIRMIN, Peter, 1928- , English;

juveniles CO CON
FIRSOFF, Valdemar Axel, 1910- ,
British; translations, nonfiction
CON
FIRST, Ruth, South African; nonfic-
tion CON
FIRTH, Anthony, 1937- , English;
fiction MCC
FIRTH, Grace Ushler, 1922- ,
American; nonfiction CON
FIRTH, Raymond William, 1901- ,
New Zealander; nonfiction
CON
FIRTH, Robert E. , 1921- , Amer-
ican; nonfiction CON
FIRTH, Tony, 1937?-80, British;
fiction CON
FISCH, Edith L. , 1923- , Amer-
ican; nonfiction CON
FISCHART, Johann (Mentzer),
1546-89/90, German; fiction
BU TH
FISCHBACH, Julius, 1894- ,
American; juveniles CO
FISCHEL, Walter Joseph, 1902-73,
German-American; nonfiction
CON
FISCHER, Alfred George, 1920- ,
German-American; nonfiction
CON
FISHER, Bruno ('Russell Gray'),
1908- , German-American;
fiction CON REI
FISCHER, Donald Edward, 1935- ,
American; nonfiction CON
FISCHER, Fritz, 1908- , German;
nonfiction CON
FISCHER, George, 1923- , Ger-
man-American; nonfiction CON
FISCHER, Joel, 1939- , American;
nonfiction CON
FISCHER, John, 1910-78, Ameri-
can; nonfiction CON
FISCHER, Leonard, American?;
fiction NI
FISCHER, Otokar, 1883-1938,
Czech; nonfiction, translations,
poetry, plays BU CL
FISCHER, Otto Peter Leck, 1904-
56, Danish; fiction, plays BU
TH
FISCHER, Robert James, 1943- ,
American; nonfiction CON
FISCHER-DIESKAU, Dietrich,
1925- , German; nonfiction
CON
FISCHETTI, John, 1916-80, Amer-
ican; cartoons CON

FISCHTROM, Harvey see 'ZE-
MACH, Harve'
FISH, Byron, 1908- , American;
nonfiction CON
FISH, Peter Graham, 1937- ,
American; nonfiction CON
FISH, Robert L. ('Robert L.
Pike'; 'Lawrence Roberts'),
1912-81, American; fiction,
nonfiction CON REI ST
FISHBEIN, Meyer Harry, 1916- ,
American; nonfiction CON
FISHBEIN, Morris, 1889-1976,
American; nonfiction CON
FISHBURN, Peter Clingerman,
1936- , American; nonfiction
CON
FISHEL, Elizabeth, 1950- ,
American; nonfiction CON
FISHEL, Wesley Robert, 1919-
77, American; nonfiction CON
FISHER, Aileen Lucia, 1906- ,
American; juveniles, plays,
poetry CO KI
FISHER, Alan Washburn, 1939- ,
American; nonfiction CON
FISHER, Allen J., 1907?-80,
American; nonfiction CON
FISHER, Arthur Stanley ('Michael
Scarrott'), 1906- , British;
nonfiction CON
FISHER, Bart Steven, 1943- ,
American; nonfiction CON
FISHER, Clavin Cargill, 1912- ,
American; juveniles CO CON
'FISHER, Clay' see ALLEN,
Henry W.
'FISHER, Cyrus T.' see TEILHET,
Darwin L.
FISHER, David Elimelech,
1932- , American; fiction
CON
FISHER, Dorothy (Canfield), 1879-
1958, American; plays, juven-
iles, fiction, nonfiction COM
KI WAR
FISHER, Douglas, 1934- ,
American; nonfiction CON
FISHER, Douglas Mason, 1919- ,
Canadian; journalism, nonfic-
tion CON
FISHER, Esther Oshiver, 1910- ,
American; nonfiction CON
FISHER, Gary, 1938- , Ameri-
can; nonfiction CON
FISHER, Gene H., 1922- ,
American; nonfiction CON
FISHER, Gene Louis ('Gene Lan-

cour'), 1947- , American;
fiction CON NI
FISHER, Glenn William, 1924- ,
American; nonfiction CON
FISHER, Harold H., 1890-1975,
American; nonfiction CON
FISHER, Harvey Irvin, 1916- ,
American; nonfiction CON
FISHER, James Maxwell, 1912-70,
British; nonfiction CON
FISHER, James P., American;
fiction NI
FISHER, James Raymond, Jr.,
1937- , American; nonfiction
CON
FISHER, Joe, 1947- , British;
journalism, fiction, nonfiction
CON
FISHER, Johanna, 1922- , Amer-
ican; nonfiction CON
FISHER, John, 1459?-1535, Eng-
lish; nonfiction BU
FISHER, John Charles, 1927- ,
American; nonfiction CON
FISHER, John Oswald ('Roger
Piper'), 1909- , English;
juveniles, nonfiction CO CON
FISHER, John Robert, 1943- ,
English; nonfiction CON
FISHER, Laura Harrison, 1934- ,
American; juveniles CO
FISHER, Leonard Everett, 1924- ,
American; juveniles CO DE
FISHER, Margery Turner, 1913- ,
English; juveniles, nonfiction
CO CON
'FISHER, Margot' see PAINE,
Lauran B.
FISHER, Mary Frances Kennedy
('Mary Frances Parrish'),
1908- , American; nonfiction
CON
FISHER, Nigel, 1913- , British;
nonfiction CON
FISHER, Peter Jack, 1930- ,
Australian; nonfiction CON
FISHER, Philip Arthur, 1907- ,
American; nonfiction CON
FISHER, Ralph Talcott, Jr.,
1920- , American; nonfiction
CON
FISHER, Rhoda Lee, 1924- ,
American; nonfiction CON
FISHER, Richard Bernard, 1919- ,
American; nonfiction CON
FISHER, Robert Charles, 1930- ,
American; nonfiction CON
FISHER, Robert Jay, 1924- ,

American; nonfiction CON
FISHER, Robert Percival, 1935- ,
British; nonfiction CON
FISHER, Roy, 1930- , British;
poetry CON VCP
FISHER, Sterling Wesley, 1899?-
1978, American; nonfiction
CON
FISHER, Steve ('Stephen Gould';
'Grant Lane'), 1912- , Amer-
ican; fiction, plays, film
REI ST
FISHER, Vardis, 1895-1968,
American; fiction, poetry,
nonfiction BR MAG NI VN
FISHER, Welthy Honsinger, 1879-
1980, American; nonfiction
CON
FISHER, William Bayne, 1916- ,
English; nonfiction CON
FISHLER, Mary Shiverick,
1920- , American; juveniles
WAR
FISHMAN, Burton John, 1942- ,
American; nonfiction CON
FISHMAN, Charles, 1942- ,
American; poetry CON
FISHMAN, Joshua Aaron, 1926- ,
American; nonfiction CON
FISHMAN, Lew, 1939- , Amer-
ican; nonfiction CON
FISHMAN, Sterling, 1932- ,
American; nonfiction CON
FISHTA, Gjergi, 1871-1940,
Albanian; poetry CL
FISK, Nicholas, 1923- , British;
juveniles, nonfiction CO CON
KI
FISK, Samuel, 1907- , American;
nonfiction CON
FISKE, Edward B., 1937- ,
American; journalism, non-
fiction CON
FISKE, John, 1842-1901, Amer-
ican; nonfiction BR
FISKE, Marjorie see LOWENTHAL,
Marjorie
FISZMAN, Joseph R., 1921- ,
Polish-American; nonfiction
CON
FITCH, Alger Morton, Jr.,
1919- , American; nonfiction
CON
'FITCH, Clark' see SINCLAIR,
Upton
FITCH, Clyde, 1865-1909, Amer-
ican; plays BR MCG MCN
VD

FITCH, George Ashmore, 1883-
1979, American; nonfiction
CON
FITCH, Geraldine Townsend,
1892?-1976, American; nonfic-
tion CON
FITCH, James Marston, 1909- ,
American; nonfiction CON
'FITCH, John IV' see CORMIER,
Robert E.
FITCH, Kenneth Leonard, 1929- ,
American; nonfiction CON
FITCH, Willis Stetson, 1896?-
1978, American; nonfiction
CON
FITRAT, Abdurrauf, 1884-1947?,
Tajik; plays PRU
FITSCHEN, Dale, 1937- , Amer-
ican; juveniles, nonfiction
CO CON
'FITT, Mary' (Kathleen Freeman;
'Stuart Mary Wick'), 1897-1959,
British; fiction, nonfiction,
juveniles, translations REI
FITTER, Richard Sidney Richmond,
1913- , English; nonfiction
CON
FITTING, Greer A., 1943- ,
American; journalism, nonfic-
tion CON
FITTING, James E., 1939- ,
American; nonfiction CON
FITTS, Dudley, 1903-68, American;
poetry, translations BR CON
'FITZALAN, Roger' see TREVOR,
Elleston
FITZBALL, Edward, 1793-1873,
English; plays, fiction, poetry
VD
FITZ-GEFFRY, Charles, 1581-
1636/37, English; poetry BU
FITZ-GERALD, Carolyn, 1932- ,
American; nonfiction CON
FITZGERALD, Edmund Valpy Knox,
1947- , British; nonfiction
CON
FITZGERALD, Edward (Purcell),
1809-83, English; poetry,
translations, nonfiction BU
DA MAG PO VP
FITZGERALD, Edward Earl,
1919- , American; juveniles,
nonfiction CO CON
FITZGERALD, Frances, 1940- ,
American; nonfiction CON
FITZGERALD, Francis Anthony,
1940- , American; juveniles
CO

FITZGERALD, Francis Scott Key,
1896-1940, American; fiction
AM BR BU MAG PO RO SEY
ST VN
FITZGERALD, George R. , 1932- ,
American; nonfiction CON
'FITZGERALD, Gerald' see
MacGEARAILT, Gearóid
FITZ GERALD, Gregory, 1923- ,
American; nonfiction, fiction,
poetry CON
FITZGERALD, Hiram Earl,
1940- , American; nonfiction
CON
'FITZGERALD, Captain Hugh' see
BAUM, Lyman F.
FITZGERALD, James V. , 1889?-
1976, American; journalism
CON
FITZGERALD, John Dennis,
1907- , American; juveniles,
nonfiction CO CON WAR
'FITZGERALD, Julia' see WAT-
SON, Julia
FITZGERALD, Michael Garrett,
1950- , American; nonfiction
CON
FITZGERALD, Nancy, 1951- ,
American; fiction CON
FITZGERALD, Nigel, 1906- ,
Irish; fiction REI
FITZGERALD, Penelope, 1916- ,
British; nonfiction, fiction
CON
FITZGERALD, Richard Ambrose,
1938- , American; nonfiction
CON
FITZ GERALD, Robert David,
1902- , Australian; poetry
BU DA VCP VP WA
FITZGERALD, Robert Stuart,
1910- , American; poetry,
translations, journalism BR
VCP
FITZGERALD, Stephen Arthur,
1938- , Australian; nonfiction
CON
FITZGERALD, Tamsin, 1950- ,
American; fiction CON
FITZGERALD, Zelda Sayre,
American; fiction RO
FITZ GIBBON, Constantine,
1919- , American-Irish;
fiction, nonfiction HO NI WA
FITZ-GIBBON, Ralph Edgerton,
1904?- , American; fiction,
journalism NI
FITZGIBBON, Russell Humke,

1902- , American; nonfiction
CON
FITZHARDINGE, Joan M. see
'PHIPSON, Joan'
FITZHUGH, George, 1806-81,
American; nonfiction BA
FITZHUGH, Louise, 1928-74,
American; juveniles CO CON
DE KI
FITZHUGH, William, 1651-1701,
American; nonfiction BA
FITZLYON, Kyril, 1910- , Rus-
sian-British; nonfiction CON
FITZMAURICE, George, 1875-
1963, Irish; plays BU CON
HO MCG VD
FITZPATRICK, Daniel Robert,
1891-1969, American; cartoons
CON
FITZPATRICK, James Kevin,
1942- , American; nonfiction
CON
FITZPATRICK, Sir James Percy,
1862-1931, South African;
nonfiction DA
FITZPATRICK, William John, 1830-
95, Irish; nonfiction HO
FITZ-RANDOLPH, Jane Currens,
1915- , American; nonfiction
CON
FITZSIMON, Ellen O'Connell, 1805-
83, Irish; poetry HO
FITZSIMONS, Louise, 1932- ,
American; nonfiction CON
FITZSIMONS, Ruth Marie Mangan,
American; nonfiction CON
'FITZWILLIAM, Michael' see
LYONS, J. B.
FIX, Philippe, French; juveniles
WAR
FIX, William R. , 1941- , Amer-
ican; nonfiction CON
FIXX, James Fuller, 1932- ,
American; journalism, nonfic-
tion CON
FIZER, John, 1925- , American;
nonfiction CON
FLACH, Frederic Francis, 1927- ,
American; nonfiction CON
FLACIUS ILLYRICUS, Matthias,
1520-75, German; nonfiction
BU
FLACK, Dora Dutson, 1919- ,
American; nonfiction CON
FLACK, Marjorie, 1897-1958,
American; juveniles, poetry
COM KI
FLACKS, Richard, 1938- , Amer-

ican; nonfiction CON
FLADELAND, Betty, 1919- ,
American; nonfiction CON
FLADER, Susan L., 1941- ,
American; nonfiction CON
'FLAGG, Francis' (George Henry
Weiss), 1898?-1946, Amer-
ican; fiction AS NI
'FLAGG, Kenneth' see AYVAZIAN,
L. Fred
FLAHERTY, Daniel Leo, 1929- ,
American; nonfiction CON
FLAHERTY, Gloria, 1938- ,
American; nonfiction CON
FLAHERTY, Robert Joseph,
1884-1951, Canadian; juveniles
WAR
FLAHERTY, Robert Joseph,
1933- , American; journal-
ism CON
FLAHERTY, Vincent X., 1908?-
77, American; journalism,
film CON
'FLAKE, Otto' (Leo F. Kotta),
1880-1963, German; fiction
CL
FLAMHOLTZ, Eric, 1943- ,
American; nonfiction CON
FLAMINIO, Marcantonio, 1498-
1550, Italian; poetry BO
FLAMM, Gerald Robert, 1916- ,
American; nonfiction CON
FLAMMARION, Camille, 1842-
1925, French; fiction NI
FLAMMER, Philip Meynard,
1928- , American; nonfiction
CON
FLANAGAN, Geraldine Lux,
American; juveniles WAR
FLANAGAN, Thomas, 1923- ,
American; fiction ST
FLANAGAN, William George,
1940- , American; nonfiction
CON
FLANDERS, James Prescott,
1942- , American; nonfiction
CON
'FLANDERS, John' see 'RAY,
Jean'
FLANDERS, Michael Henry,
1922-75, British; nonfiction
CON
FLANERY, Edward Boyd, 1932- ,
American; nonfiction CON
FLANNER, Janet ('Genêt'), 1892-
1978, American; journalism,
fiction, nonfiction CON RO
WA

FLANNERY, Harry W., 1900-75,
American; nonfiction CON
FLATH, Arnold William J.,
1929- , American; nonfiction
CON
FLATMAN, Thomas, 1635-88, Eng-
lish; poetry BU
FLATTAU, Edward, 1937- ,
American; nonfiction CON
FLAUBERT, Gustave, 1821-80,
French; fiction, nonfiction
BU MAG TH
FLAVELL, Carol Willsey (Bell),
1939- , American; nonfiction
CON
FLAVIN, Martin, 1883-1967,
American; plays, fiction MCG
FLECHIER, Esprit, 1632-1710,
French; nonfiction TH
'FLECK, Betty' see PAINE, Lauran
B.
FLECK, Henrietta, 1903- , Amer-
ican; nonfiction CON
FLECK, Konrad, fl. 1220, German;
poetry BU
FLECK, Richard Francis, 1937- ,
American; nonfiction, poetry,
fiction CON
FLECKER, James Elroy, 1884-
1915, English; poetry, trans-
lations, play BU DA MCG
PO VP
FLECKNOE, Richard, -1678?,
English; nonfiction, plays BU
DA
FLEEGE, Urban Herman, 1908- ,
American; nonfiction CON
FLEESON, Doris, 1901-70, Amer-
ican; journalism CON
FLEETWOOD, Frances (Frank),
1902- , English; fiction, trans-
lations, poetry CON
FLEISCHHAUER-HARDT, Helga,
1936- , German; nonfiction
CON
FLEISCHMAN, Albert Sidney,
1920- , American; juveniles,
fiction, plays CO DE KI
FLEISCHMANN, Glen Harvey,
1909- , American; juveniles
WAR
FLEISHER, Belton Mendel, 1935- ,
American; nonfiction CON
FLEISHER, Martin, 1925- , Amer-
ican; nonfiction CON
FLEISHER, Wilfried, 1897?-1976,
American; journalism, nonfic-
tion CON

'FLEISSER, Marieluise' see
HAINDL, Marieluise
FLEMER, William III, 1922- ,
American; nonfiction CON
FLEMING, Alice Mulcahey,
1928- , American; juveniles
CO
FLEMING, David Arnold, 1939- ,
American; nonfiction CON
FLEMING, George James,
1904- , American; nonfiction
SH
FLEMING, Gerald, 1921- ,
American; nonfiction CON
'FLEMING, Guy' see MASUR,
Harold Q.
FLEMING, Ian Lancaster ('Atti-
cus'), 1908-64, English;
fiction, nonfiction, juveniles
CO DA MCC NI REI ST VN
WA
FLEMING, Irene, 1923?-79,
American; journalism CON
FLEMING, Jennifer Baker,
1943- , American; nonfic-
tion CON
FLEMING, Joan Margaret, 1908-
80, British; fiction, juveniles
CON REI
FLEMING, Macklin, 1911- ,
American; nonfiction CON
FLEMING, Paul, 1609-40, Ger-
man; poetry BU TH
FLEMING, Robert Peter, 1907-
71, British; nonfiction, fic-
tion DA NI
FLEMING, Susan, 1932- ,
American; journalism, juven-
iles CON
FLEMING, Theodore Bowman,
Jr., 1917- , American;
nonfiction CON
FLEMING, Thomas James
('Christopher Cain'; 'T. F.
James'; 'J. F. Thomas'),
1927- , American; juveniles
CO WAR
FLEMMING, Nicholas Coit
('Stanton James'), 1936- ,
British; nonfiction CON
FLEMMYNG, Robert, -1483,
English; poetry BU
FLENDER, Harold, 1924- ,
American; fiction, nonfiction
CON WAR
'FLERS, Robert de' (Marie Joseph
Pellevé de la Motte-Ango),
1872-1927, French; plays

BU CL MCG
FLESCHER, Joachim, 1906?-76,
Polish-American; nonfiction
CON
FLETCHER, Alan Mark, 1928- ,
American; juveniles, nonfiction
CON WAR
FLETCHER, Andrew, 1655-1716,
Scots; nonfiction DA
FLETCHER, Anthony John, 1941- ,
Welsh; nonfiction CON
FLETCHER, Basil Alais, 1900- ,
English; nonfiction CON
FLETCHER, Charlie May Hogue
('Charlie May Simon'), 1897- ,
American; juveniles CO
'FLETCHER, David' see BARBER,
Dulan F.
FLETCHER, Geoffrey Scowcroft,
1923- , British; juveniles,
nonfiction CON
FLETCHER, Giles the Elder, 1546-
1610/11, English; poetry BU
DA RU VP
FLETCHER, Giles the Younger,
1585/86-1623, English; poetry
BU DA PO RU VP
FLETCHER, Harris Francis, 1892-
1979, American; nonfiction
CON
FLETCHER, Helen Jill ('Carol
Lee'; 'Charles Morey'),
1911- , American; juveniles
CO
FLETCHER, Henry L. A. see
'WADE, Henry'
FLETCHER, Ian, 1920- , British;
nonfiction VCP
FLETCHER, Inglis, 1879-1969,
American; fiction BA
FLETCHER, John, 1579-1625,
English; plays BRI DA MAG
MCG PO RU VD
FLETCHER, John Gould, 1886-
1950, American; poetry, trans-
lations, nonfiction BA BR
BU RO VP
FLETCHER, John Walter James,
1937- , British; nonfiction
CON
FLETCHER, Joseph Smith, 1863-
1935, British; fiction, plays,
poetry, nonfiction REI ST
FLETCHER, Leon, 1921- , Amer-
ican; nonfiction CON
FLETCHER, Lucille, 1912- ,
American; fiction, plays, film
REI

FLETCHER, Phineas, 1582-1650,
English; poetry, plays BU
DA PO RU VP
FLETCHER, William Isaac, 1844-
1917, American; nonfiction
ENG
FLETCHER, William Whigham,
1918- , Scots; nonfiction
CON
FLETCHER-COOKE, John, 1911- ,
British; nonfiction CON
FLEXNER, Eleanor, 1908- ,
American; nonfiction CON
FLEXNER, James Thomas,
1908- , American; nonfic-
tion, juveniles CO WAK
FLEXNER, Jennie Maas, 1882-
1944, American; nonfiction
ENG
FLICK, Carlos Thomas, 1927- ,
American; nonfiction CON
FLIEGEL, Frederick Christian,
1925- , Canadian-American;
nonfiction CON
FLIEGEL, Hellmuth see 'HEYM,
Stefan'
FLIN(D)T, Homer Eon, 1892?-
1924, American; fiction AS
NI
FLINT, Cort Ray, 1915- ,
American; nonfiction CON
FLINT, Frank Stewart, 1885-
1960, English; poetry, trans-
lations DA PO
FLIPPO, Chet, 1943- , Amer-
ican; journalism, nonfiction
CON
FLITNER, David Perkins, 1949- ,
American; juveniles, nonfic-
tion CO CON
FLODOARD of RHEIMS (Frodo-
ard), 893/94-66, French;
poetry, nonfiction TH
FLOETHE, Louise Lee, 1913- ,
American; juveniles CO
FLOETHE, Richard, 1901- ,
American; juveniles CO
FLOHERTY, John Joseph, 1882-
1964, American; juveniles
CO
FLOOD, Charles Bracelen,
1929- , American; nonfic-
tion, fiction CON
FLOOD, Edward Thadeus, 1932- ,
American; nonfiction, trans-
lations CON
'FLOOD, Flash' see ROBINSON,
Jan M.

FLORA, Fletcher, 1914-68, Amer-
ican; fiction, nonfiction REI
FLORA, James Royer, 1914- ,
American; juveniles, plays
DE KI WAR
'FLORA del VALLE' see ROQUE
de DUPREY, Ana
FLORENCE of WORCESTER,
-1118, English; nonfiction
BU DA
FLORENTIN, Eddy, 1923- ,
French; nonfiction CON
FLORES, Albert W., 1946- ,
American; nonfiction MAR
FLORES, Angel, 1900- , Puerto
Rican; nonfiction, translations
CON
FLORES, Anton, 1818-65, Spanish;
journalism, fiction BU
FLORES, Ernest Y., 1928- ,
American; nonfiction MAR
FLORES, Gloria Amalia, 1949- ,
American; nonfiction MAR
FLORES, Janis, 1946- , Amer-
ican; fiction CON
FLORES, John, 1943- , Amer-
ican; nonfiction CON
FLORES, Joseph Alfonso, 1941- ,
American; nonfiction MAR
FLORES, Juan de, late 15th cen-
tury, Spanish; fiction BU
FLORESCU, Radu R., 1925- ,
Rumanian-American; nonfiction
CON
'FLORETE' see ABRIL, Mariano
FLOREZ de SETIEN y HUIDOBRO,
Enrique, 1702-73, Spanish;
nonfiction BU
FLORIAN, Douglas, 1950- ,
American; juveniles CO
FLORIAN, Jean Pierre Claris de,
1755-94, French; fiction, plays,
poetry BU
FLORIAN, Tibor, 1908- , Hun-
garian-American; poetry, non-
fiction CON
'FLORIN, Theo H.' (Teodor Her-
kel), 1908- , Slovak; poetry
BU
FLORIO, Giovanni (John), 1553?-
1625, English; translations,
nonfiction BU DA RU
FLORIOT, Rene, 1902-75, French;
nonfiction CON
FLORIT, Eugenio, 1903- , Cuban;
poetry BR
FLORMAN, Samuel Charles,
1925- , American; nonfiction

CON
FLORUS, Annaeus (Lucius), fl.
140, Roman; poetry, nonfic-
tion BU GR LA
FLORY, Charles David, 1902- ,
American; nonfiction CON
FLORY, Harry R., 1899-1976,
American; journalism CON
FLORY, Jane Trescott, 1917- ,
American; juveniles CO
WAR
FLOUD, Roderick, 1942- ,
American; nonfiction CON
FLOWER, Elizabeth Farquhar,
1914- , American; nonfic-
tion CON
FLOWER, Margaret Camerion,
American; nonfiction CON
FLOWER, Patricia M. B., 1914-
78, British; fiction, plays,
poetry REI
FLOWER, Robin, 1881-1946,
Irish; translations, poetry
HO
FLOWERDEW, Phyllis, British;
nonfiction CON
FLOWERS, Betty Sue, 1947- ,
American; nonfiction CON
FLOWERS, Charles Ely, Jr.,
1920- , American; nonfiction
CON
FLOYD, Harriet, 1925- , Amer-
ican; nonfiction CON
FLOYD, Lois Gray, 1910?-78,
American; nonfiction CON
FLUCHERE, Henri, 1914- ,
Franco-American; nonfiction
CON
FLUSSER, Martin, 1947- ,
American; journalism, non-
fiction CON
FLY, Claude Lee, 1905- , Amer-
ican; nonfiction CON
'FLYING OFFICER X' see
BATES, Herbert E.
FLYNN, Barbara, 1928- , Amer-
ican; juveniles CO
FLYNN, Charles Frederick,
1949- , American; nonfiction
CON
FLYNN, George L., 1931- ,
American; nonfiction CON
FLYNN, Gerard Cox, 1924- ,
American; nonfiction, fiction
CON
'FLYNN, Jackson' see SHIR-
REFFS, Gordon D.
FLYNN, James Joseph, 1911- ,

American; juveniles WAR
FLYNN, John Thomas, 1882-1964,
American; journalism, nonfic-
tion CON
FLYNT, Candace, 1947- , Amer-
ican; fiction CON
'FLYNT, Josiah' (Josiah Flynt Wil-
lard), 1869-1907, American;
fiction ST
FLYTHE, Starkey Sharp, Jr.,
1935- , American; journalism
CON
FO, Dario, 1926- , Italian; plays
BO
FOCILLON, Henri, 1881-1943,
French; nonfiction CL
'FOCK, Gorch' (Johann Kinau),
1880-1916, German; fiction,
plays BU
FOCQUENBORCH, Willem God-
schalk, 1635-75, Dutch; poetry,
plays BU
FODASKI-BLACK, Martha, 1929- ,
American; nonfiction CON
FODEBA, Keita, 1921- , Guinean;
poetry, songs, plays HER JA
LA
FODOR, M. W., 1890?-1977,
Hungarian-American; journalism
CON
FODOR, Ronald Victor, 1944- ,
American; juveniles CO CON
FOELL, Earl William, 1929- ,
American; journalism CON
FOERSTER, Leona Mitchell,
1930- , American; nonfiction
CON
FOERSTER, Lotte Brand ('Lotte
Brand Philip'), 1910- , Ger-
man-American; nonfiction
CON
FOERSTER, Norman, 1887- ,
American; nonfiction BR
FOFANOV, Konstantin Mikhailovich,
1862-1911, Russian; poetry
BU
FOGARTY, Robert Stephen, 1938- ,
American; nonfiction CON
FOGAZZARO, Antonio, 1842-1911,
Italian; fiction, poetry, plays
BO BU CL MAG MCG TH
'FOGEL, Daniel' see KAHN-
FOGEL, Daniel M.
FOGEL, David, 1891-1944, Hebrew;
poetry, fiction BU
FOGEL, Robert William, 1926- ,
American; nonfiction CON
FOGELQUIST, Donald Frederick,

1906- , American; nonfiction
CON
FOGLIO, Frank, 1921- , Amer-
ican; nonfiction CON
FOIGNY, Gabriel de see 'SADEUR,
Jacques'
FOIN, Theodore Chin, 1940- ,
American; nonfiction CON
FOIX, Josep Vincenc, 1894- ,
Catalan; poetry BU CL
FOKKE SIMONSZ, Arend, 1755-
1812, Dutch; poetry BU
FOLADARE, Joseph, 1909- ,
American; nonfiction CON
FOLB, Edith Arlene, 1938- ,
American; nonfiction CON
FOLCH-RIBAS, Jacques, 1928- ,
Spanish-Canadian; fiction
CON
FOLDS, Thomas M., American;
juveniles, nonfiction CON
FOLENGO, Teofilo, 1496-1544,
Italian; poetry BO BU TH
FOLEY, Allen Richard, 1898-
1978, American; nonfiction
CON
FOLEY, Cedric John ('John Saw-
yer'; 'Ian Sinclair'), 1917-74,
British; fiction, nonfiction
CON
FOLEY, Dave see 'HATCH,
Gerald'
FOLEY, Doug, 1942- , Amer-
ican; nonfiction CON
FOLEY, Duncan Karl, 1942- ,
American; nonfiction CON
FOLEY, Gerald Patrick, 1936- ,
British; nonfiction CON
FOLEY, Leonard, 1913- ,
American; nonfiction CON
FOLEY, Martha, 1897?-1977,
American; nonfiction CON
FOLEY, Mary Louise Munro,
1933- , Canadian; tv, radio,
juveniles WAR
FOLEY, Mary Mix, 1918- ,
American; nonfiction CON
'FOLEY, Rae' see DENNISTON,
Elinore
FOLEY, Richard N., 1910?-80,
American; nonfiction CON
'FOLEY, Scott' see DAREFF,
Hal
FOLEY, Vincent D., 1933- ,
American; nonfiction CON
FOLEY, Winifred, 1914- , Brit-
ish; nonfiction CON
FOLGORE de SAN GIMIGNANO,

1270-1330, Italian; poetry
BO BU
FOLKERS, George Fulton, 1929- ,
American; translations, non-
fiction CON
FOLKERTS, George William,
1938- , American; nonfiction
CON
FOLKERTSMA, Eeltsje Boates,
1893-1968, Frisian; nonfiction
BU
FOLLAIN, Jean René, 1903-71,
French; poetry, nonfiction CL
WAK
FOLLAND, Harold Freeze, 1906- ,
American; nonfiction CON
FOLLEN, Eliza Lee Cabot, 1787-
1860, American; juveniles,
nonfiction MY
FOLLETT, James, 1939- , Eng-
lish; fiction NI
FOLLETT, Kenneth ('Symon
Myles'), 1949- , English; fic-
tion, film CON MCC
FOLLEY, Vern LeRoy, 1936- ,
American; nonfiction CON
FOLLIARD, Edward Thomas, 1899-
1976, American; journalism
CON
FOLQUET de MARSEILLE, 1160-
1231, Provencal; poetry BU
TH
FOLSOM, Franklin Brewster
('Benjamin Brewster'; 'Samuel
Cutler'; 'Michael Gorham';
'Lyman Hopkins'; 'Troy Nes-
bit'), 1907- , American;
juveniles CO
FOLSOM, John Bentley, 1931- ,
American; nonfiction CON
FOLSOM, Marvin Hugh, 1929- ,
Canadian; nonfiction CON
FOLSOM, Robert Slade, 1915- ,
American; nonfiction CON
FOLZ, Hans, fl. 1479-1515, Ger-
man; nonfiction BU TH
FOMON, Samuel Joseph, 1923- ,
American; nonfiction CON
FONAROW, Jerry ('J. Farrow'),
1935- , American; fiction,
nonfiction CON
FONER, Jack Donald, 1910- ,
American; nonfiction CON
FONER, Nancy, 1945- , American;
nonfiction CON
FONFRIAS, Ernesto Juan, 1909- ,
Puerto Rican; poetry, journal-
ism, nonfiction HIL

FONG, Wen Chih, 1930- ,
Chinese-American; nonfiction
CON
FONG-TORRES, Ben, 1945- ,
American; nonfiction CON
FONSECA, Antonio José Bran-
quinho da, 1905- , Portu-
guese; fiction, plays, poetry
CL
FONSECA, Aguinaldo, 1922- ,
Cape Verde Islander; poetry
HER JA LA
FONSECA, Cristobal de, 1550?-
1621, Spanish; nonfiction BU
FONSECA, Manuel da, 1911- ,
Portuguese; poetry, fiction
CL
FONSECA, Mário Alberto, 1939- ,
Cape Verde Islander; poetry,
journalism HER
FONTAINAS, André, 1865-1948,
French; poetry BU
FONTAINE, Andre, 1910- ,
American; nonfiction CON
FONTAINE, Joan, 1917- , Amer-
ican; nonfiction CON
FONTANA, Dorothy C., American;
fiction, tv NI
FONTANA, Gian, 1897-1935,
Raeto-Romansch; poetry, fic-
tion BU
FONTANE, Theodor, 1819-98,
German; fiction, poetry, non-
fiction BU CL MAG TH
FONTANELLA, Girolamo, 1612?-
44?, Italian; poetry TH
FONTANES, Louis Marquis de,
1757-1821, French; poetry
BU TH
FONTENAY, Charles Louis,
1917- , American; fiction,
journalism NI
FONTENELLE, Bernard Le Bovier
de, 1657-1757, French; poetry,
plays BU TH
FONTES, Amando, 1899-1967,
Brazilian; fiction BU
FONVIZIN, Denis Ivanovich,
1745-92, Russian; plays
BU MCG TH
FONZI, Bruno, 1913?-76, Italian;
nonfiction, fiction, translations
CON
FOONER, Michael, American;
juveniles, journalism, nonfic-
tion, film CO CON WAR
FOOT, Philippa Ruth, 1901- ,
American; nonfiction CON

FOOTE, Avon Edward, 1937- ,
American; tv, nonfiction CON
FOOTE, Darby Mozelle, 1942- ,
American; fiction CON
FOOTE, Horton, 1916- , Amer-
ican; plays, fiction, film, tv
CON WA
FOOTE, Samuel, 1720-77, English;
plays, nonfiction BU DA MCG
PO VD
FOOTE, Shelby, 1916- , Amer-
ican; fiction, plays, nonfiction
BA HE VCN
FOOTE, Timothy Gilson, 1926- ,
British; journalism, nonfiction
CON
FOOTE, Wilder, 1905-75, Amer-
ican; journalism, nonfiction
CON
FOOTE-SMITH, Elizabeth, 1913- ,
American; fiction, poetry CON
FOOTMAN, David John, 1895- ,
British; fiction, nonfiction
CON
FOOTNER, William Hulbert, 1879-
1944, Canadian-American; fic-
tion, plays, nonfiction REI ST
FORBERG, Ati Gropius, 1925- ,
German; juveniles CO DEM
FORBES, Bryan, 1926- , British;
fiction, film CON
FORBES, Carob Lowell ('Christ-
opher Martin Smith'), 1943- ,
American; fiction CON
FORBES, Calvin, 1945- , Amer-
ican; poetry CON
FORBES, Clarence Allen, 1901- ,
American; nonfiction CON
'FORBES, Colin' see SAWKINS,
Raymond H.
'FORBES, D. F.' see 'FORBES,
Stanton'
'FORBES, Daniel' see KENYON,
Michael
'FORBES, Dee' see 'FORBES,
Stanton'
FORBES, DeLoris S. see
'FORBES, Stanton'
FORBES, Eric Gray, 1933- ,
Scots; nonfiction, translations
CON
FORBES, Esther, 1894?-1967,
American; fiction, juveniles
KI MAG
FORBES, John Douglas, 1910- ,
American; nonfiction CON
'FORBES, Kathryn' see McLEAN,
Kathryn A.

FORBES, Malcolm Stevenson, 1919- , American; nonfiction, journalism CON

'FORBES, Stanton' (DeLoris Stanton Forbes; 'Dee Forbes'; 'Forbes Rydell'; 'Tobias Wells'; 'D. F. Forbes'), 1923- , American; fiction REI ST

FORBES, Thomas Rogers, 1911- , American; nonfiction CON

FORBES-DENNIS, Phyllis see 'BOTTOME, Phyllis'

FORBIS, Judith, 1934- , American; nonfiction CON

FORCE, Roland Wynfield, 1924- , American; nonfiction CON

FORCHHEIMER, Paul, 1913- , American; nonfiction CON

FORD, Arthur Lewis, 1937- , American; nonfiction CON

FORD, Brian John, 1939- , English; nonfiction CON

FORD, Charles Henri, 1913- , American; poetry, plays, fiction, translations RO VCP

FORD, Colin John, 1934- , British; nonfiction CON

'FORD, David' see HARKNETT, Terry

FORD, Donald Herbert, 1926- , American; nonfiction CON

FORD, Douglas William Cleverly, 1914- , English; nonfiction CON

FORD, Edmund Brisco, 1901- , British; nonfiction CON

FORD, Elaine, 1938- , American; fiction CON

'FORD, Elbur' see HIBBERT, Eleanor

'FORD, Elizabeth' see BIDWELL, Marjory E. S.

FORD, Ford Madox (Hueffer), 1873-1939, English; fiction, poetry, nonfiction BU DA MAG NI PO SEY VN

FORD, Frank Bernard, 1932- , plays CON

FORD, George Barry, 1885-1978, American; nonfiction CON

FORD, George D., 1880?-1974, American; nonfiction CON

FORD, Harvey Seabury, 1905?-78, American; journalism CON

'FORD, Hilary' see 'CHRISTOPHER, John'

'FORD, Hildegarde' see MORRISON, Velma F.

FORD, Jesse Hill, 1928- , American; fiction, plays BA KIB VCN

FORD, John, 1586-1639/40, English; poetry, plays BRI BU DA MAG MCG PO RU VD

FORD, Josephine Massyngherde, Anglo-American; nonfiction CON

'FORD, Kirk' see SPENCE, William J. D.

'FORD, Leslie' (Zenith Jones Brown; 'David Frome'; 'Brenda Conrad'), 1898- , American; fiction REI ST

'FORD, Lewis' see PATTEN, Lewis B.

'FORD, Marcia' see RADFORD, Ruby L.

FORD, Murray John Stanley, 1923- , Canadian; nonfiction CON

'FORD, Norrey' see DILCOCK, Noreen

FORD, Richard, 1944- , American; fiction, film, nonfiction CON

FORD, Robert Arthur Douglass, 1915- , Canadian; poetry CON VCP

FORD, Stephen, 1949- , Canadian-American; journalism CON

FORD, Thomas Robert, 1923- , American; nonfiction CON

FORD, Whitey, 1928- , American; nonfiction CON

FORD, William Clayton, Jr., 1946- , American; nonfiction CON

FORDE, Gerhard Olaf, 1927- , American; nonfiction CON

FORDIN, Hugh, 1935- , American; nonfiction CON

FORDUN, John of, -1384, Scots; nonfiction BU DA

'FOREESTER, Pauwels' see ALBERDINGK, Thijn J. A.

FOREMAN, Carl, 1914- , American; nonfiction, film CON

FOREMAN, Clark Howell, 1902-77, American; nonfiction CON

FOREMAN, Gene, 1934- , American; journalism CON

FOREMAN, Michael, 1938- , British; juveniles KI

FOREMAN, Richard, 1937- ,

American; plays CON VCD
FOREMAN, Russell, 1921- ,
Australian; nonfiction CON
FORER, Mort, 1922- , Amer-
ican; fiction, plays CON
FOREST, Antonia, British; juven-
iles CON KI
FORESTER, Cecil Scott, 1899-
1966, English; fiction, non-
fiction, plays CO CON MAG
PO ST VN
'FORESTER, Frank' see HER-
BERT, Henry W.
FORGIE, George Barnard, 1941- ,
American; nonfiction CON
FORGUS, Ronald Henry, 1928- ,
South African-American; non-
fiction CON
FORKOSCH, Morris David, 1908- ,
American; nonfiction CON
FORM, William H., 1917- ,
American; nonfiction CON
FORMA, Warren, 1923- , Amer-
ican; nonfiction, fiction CON
FORMAN, Brenda, 1936- ,
American; juveniles CO
FORMAN, Celia Adler, 1890?-
1979, American; nonfiction
CON
FORMAN, Harrison, 1904-78,
American; nonfiction, jour-
nalism CON
FORMAN, James, 1932- , Amer-
ican; juveniles CO DE
FORMAN, Joan ('Pamela Greene'),
British; nonfiction, plays CON
FORMAN, Marc Allan, 1935- ,
American; nonfiction CON
FORMHALS, Robert Willard,
1919- , American; nonfiction
CON
FORNARI, Harry David, 1919- ,
Italian-American; nonfiction
CON
FORNELL, Earl Wesley, 1915-
69, American; nonfiction CON
FORNER, Juan Bautista Pablo,
1756-97, Spanish; nonfiction
BU TH
FORNES, María Irene, 1930- ,
Cuban-American; plays MCN
VCD
FORREST, Alfred Clinton, 1916-
78, American; nonfiction
CON
'FORREST, David' see FORREST-
WEBB, Robert
FORREST, Derek William, 1926- ,

British; nonfiction CON
FORREST, Earle Robert, 1883-
1969, American; journalism,
nonfiction CON
FORREST, Leon, 1937- , Amer-
ican; fiction, plays, poetry
CON
'FORREST, Norman' see MORLAND,
Nigel
FORREST, Richard Stockton,
1932- , American; fiction,
plays CON
'FORREST, Sybil' see MARKUN,
Patricia M.
FORREST, Wilbur S., 1887-1977,
American; journalism, nonfic-
tion CON
FORREST, William, fl. 1581,
English; nonfiction BU
FORRESTAL, Dan Joseph, Jr.,
1912- , American; journalism,
nonfiction CON
'FORRESTER, Helen' see BHATIA,
Jamunadevi
FORRESTER, Jay Wright, 1918- ,
American; nonfiction CON
FORRESTER, Leland S., 1905?-78,
American; journalism CON
'FORRESTER, Mary' see HUMPH-
RIES, Mary
FORRESTER, Rex Desmond,
1928- , New Zealander; non-
fiction CON
FORREST-WEBB, Robert ('David
Forrest'; 'Jonathan Tremayne';
'Forrest Webb'; 'Robert For-
rest Webb'), 1929- , English;
fiction CON
FORRISTAL, Desmond, 1930- ,
Irish; plays HO
FORSBERG, Charles Gerald,
1912- , Canadian; nonfiction,
poetry CON
FORSEE, Frances Aylesa, Amer-
ican; juveniles WAR
FORSH, Olga Dmitrievna, 1873-
1961, Russian; fiction BU CL
FORSNÄS, V. A. see 'KOSKEN-
NIEMI, Veikko A.'
FORSSELL, Lars Hans Carl,
1928- , Swedish; poetry,
plays, journalism BU CL
MCG TH WAK
FORSTER, Edward Morgan, 1879-
1970, English; fiction, nonfic-
tion, plays BOR BU DA MAG
NI PO SEY VN
'FORSTER, Friedrich' (Waldfried

Burggraf), 1895-1958, German; fiction, plays MCG
FORSTER, Johann George, 1754-94, German; nonfiction BU
FORSTER, John, 1812-76, English; journalism, nonfiction BU DA
FORSTER, Merlin Henry, 1928- , American; nonfiction CON
FORSTER, Robert, 1926- , American; nonfiction CON
FORSYTH, David James, 1940- , Scots; nonfiction CON
FORSYTH, Frederick, 1938- , English; fiction, journalism, nonfiction, juveniles CON MCC REI
FORSYTH, James Low, 1913- , British; plays CON VCD
FORSYTHE, Elizabeth, 1927- , British; nonfiction CON
FORSYTHE, Irene see HANSON, Irene
'FORSYTHE, Robert' see CRICHTON, Kyle S.
FORSYTHE, Sidney A., 1920- , American; nonfiction CON
FORT, Charles Hoy, 1874-1932, American; journalism AS NI
FORT, John, 1942- , American; nonfiction CON
FORT, Paul, 1872-1960, French; poetry BU CL TH WA
FORTE, Allen, 1926- , American; nonfiction CON
FORTE, Dan ('Donato Fortebraccia'), 1935- , American; nonfiction CON
FORTE, David F., 1941- , American; nonfiction CON
FORTESCUE, Sir John, 1394-1476, English; nonfiction BU
FORTIER, Alcée, 1856-1914, American; nonfiction BA
'FORTINI, Franco' (Franco Lattes), 1917- , Italian; poetry, nonfiction BO CL
FORTNUM, Peggy, English; juveniles DEM
FORTUNATUS, Venantus Honorius, 540-600, Latin; nonfiction BU TH
FORTY, George, 1927- , British; nonfiction CON
FORWARD, Robert Lull, 1932- , American; fiction CON
FORZANO, Giovacchino, 1884-

1970, Italian; plays CL
FOSBURGH, Hugh Whitney, 1916-76, American; fiction, nonfiction CON
FOSBURGH, Lacey, 1942- , American; fiction, nonfiction CON
FOSBURGH, Pieter Whitney, 1914?-78, American; nonfiction CON
FOSCOLO, Ugo, 1778-1827, Italian; poetry, plays BO BU MCG TH
FOSCUE, Edwin Jay, 1899-1972, American; nonfiction CON
FOSHEE, John Hugh, 1931- , American; nonfiction CON
FOSKETT, Daphne, 1911- , British; nonfiction CON
FOSS, Christopher Frank, 1946- , British; nonfiction CON
FOSSE, Giovanni P. delle see 'VALERIANO, Pierio'
FOSTER, Alan Dean, 1946- , American; fiction, nonfiction CON NI
FOSTER, C. E., 1919- , American; fiction NI
FOSTER, Carno Augustus, 1916- , American; nonfiction CON
FOSTER, Catharine Osgood, 1907- , American; nonfiction CON
FOSTER, Cedric, 1900-75, American; nonfiction CON
FOSTER, Charles William, 1939- , American; nonfiction CON
FOSTER, Craig Curtis, 1947- , American; nonfiction SH
FOSTER, David, 1908- , British; nonfiction CON
FOSTER, David Manning, 1944- , Australian; fiction, poetry CON VCN
FOSTER, Donald Le Roy, 1928- , American; nonfiction CON
FOSTER, Doris Van Liew, 1899- , American; juveniles CO CON
FOSTER, Dorothy, 1936- , American; nonfiction CON
FOSTER, Earl Masters, 1940- , American; nonfiction CON
FOSTER, Edward Halsey, 1942- , American; nonfiction CON
FOSTER, Eli, 1902- , American; fiction CON
FOSTER, Elizabeth, 1905-63, American; juveniles CO
FOSTER, Elizabeth Connell,

1902- , American; nonfiction,
fiction, juveniles CO CON
WAR
FOSTER, Elizabeth Vincent,
1902- , American; juveniles
CO
FOSTER, F. Blanche, 1919- ,
American; juveniles, nonfiction
CO CON
'FOSTER, Frederick' see GOD-
WIN, John F.
FOSTER, Genevieve Stump, 1893-
1979, American; juveniles
CO CON
FOSTER, Genevieve Wakeman,
1902- , American; nonfiction
CON
'FOSTER, George' see HASWELL,
Chetwynd J. D.
FOSTER, George Cecil, English;
fiction NI
FOSTER, Hannah Webster, 1759-
1840, American; fiction VN
FOSTER, Herbert Lawrence,
1928- , American; nonfiction
CON
FOSTER, Herbert W., 1920?-79,
American; journalism CON
'FOSTER, Iris' see POSNER,
Richard
FOSTER, James Caldwell, 1943- ,
American; nonfiction CON
FOSTER, Joanna, 1928- , Amer-
ican; juveniles WAR
FOSTER, John Lawrence, 1930- ,
American; nonfiction CON
FOSTER, John Thomas, 1925- ,
American; juveniles CO WAR
FOSTER, Joseph O'Kane ('O'Kane
Foster'), 1898- , American;
film, nonfiction, fiction CON
FOSTER, Kenneth Neill, 1935- ,
American; nonfiction CON
FOSTER, Laura Louise James,
1918- , American; juveniles
CO WAR
FOSTER, Lee, 1923?-77, Amer-
ican; journalism, nonfiction
CON
FOSTER, Margaret Lesser, 1899?-
1979, American; juveniles,
journalism CO CON
FOSTER, Marian Curtis ('Mari-
ana'), 1909-78, American;
juveniles CO CON DE
FOSTER, Michael Anthony,
1939- , American; fiction
CON NI

'FOSTER, O'Kane' see FOSTER,
Joseph O'K.
FOSTER, Paul, 1931- , American;
plays, fiction VCD
FOSTER, Philip John, 1927- ,
British; nonfiction CON
'FOSTER, Richard' see CROSSEN,
Kendell F.
FOSTER, Richard James, 1942- ,
American; nonfiction CON
FOSTER, Robert Alfred, 1949- ,
American; nonfiction CON
FOSTER, Stephen Collins, 1826-64,
American; poetry, songs VP
FOSTER, Walter Bertram, 1869- ,
American; fiction NI
FOSTER, William Eaton, 1851-
1930, American; nonfiction
ENG
FOUCAULT, Michel, 1926- ,
French; nonfiction CL WAK
FOUHY, Edward Michael, 1934- ,
American; nonfiction CON
FOULDS, Elfrida (Vipont; 'Charles
Vipont'), 1902- , English;
juveniles CON KI
'FOULIS, Hugh' see MUNRO, Neil
FOULKE, Adrienne, 1915- ,
American; translations, nonfic-
tion CON
FOULKE, Robert Dana, 1930- ,
American; nonfiction CON
FOULON, Roger, 1923- , Belgian;
poetry CL
FOUQUE, Freidrich Freiherr de la
Motte, 1777-1843, German;
fiction, plays BU TH
FOURIER, Francois Marie Charles,
1772-1837, French; nonfiction
BU
FOURNIER, Alain see ALAIN-
FOURNIER
FOURNIER, Claude, 1931- , Cana-
dian; poetry CR
FOURNIER, Pierre see 'GASCAR,
Pierre'
'THE FOURTH BROTHER' see
AUNG, Maung H.
FOUST, Paul John, 1920- , Amer-
ican; nonfiction CON
FOUT, John Calvin, 1937- ,
American; nonfiction CON
FOWKE, Edith Margaret, 1913- ,
Canadian; juveniles CO
FOWLER, Charles Bruner, 1931- ,
American; nonfiction CON
FOWLER, Douglas, 1940- , Amer-
ican; nonfiction CON

FOWLER, Elaine Wootten, 1914- ,
American; nonfiction CON
FOWLER, Elizabeth Millspaugh,
1921- , American; journal-
ism, nonfiction CON
FOWLER, Eugene Devlan, 1890-
1960, American; journalism
CON
FOWLER, Gene, 1931- , Amer-
ican; poetry, fiction CON
VCP
FOWLER, George Palmer, 1909- ,
American; nonfiction CON
FOWLER, Harry Jr., 1934- ,
American; nonfiction CON
FOWLER, Henry Watson, 1858-
1933, English; nonfiction
DA
FOWLER, John Major, 1926- ,
American; nonfiction CON
FOWLER, Mark, 1949- , Amer-
ican; nonfiction CON
FOWLER, Raymond Eveleth,
1933- , American; nonfic-
tion CON
FOWLER, Robert Howard,
1926- , American; fiction,
nonfiction CON
FOWLER, Roger, 1938- ,
English; nonfiction CON
'FOWLER, Sydney' (Sydney Fowler
Wright; 'Alan Seymour'),
1874-1965, British; fiction,
poetry, nonfiction, translations
AS NI REI
FOWLER, William Morgan, Jr.,
1944- , American; nonfiction
CON
FOWLER, Wilton Bonham, 1936- ,
American; nonfiction CON
FOWLES, Jib, 1940- , Amer-
ican; nonfiction CON
FOWLES, John, 1926- , Eng-
lish; fiction, juveniles, trans-
lations, nonfiction CO PO
VCN WA WAR
FOX, Allan Mark, 1948- , Amer-
ican; nonfiction CON
FOX, Charles James, 1749-1806,
English; nonfiction BU
FOX, Charles Philip, 1913- ,
American; juveniles CO
FOX, Dorothea M., American;
juveniles WAR
FOX, Dorothea Warren, 1914- ,
American; juveniles CON
FOX, Douglas Allan, 1927- ,
Australian-American; non-

fiction CON
'FOX, Eleanor' see ST. JOHN,
Wylly F.
FOX, Fontaine Talbot, Jr., 1884-
1964, American; cartoons CO
CON
FOX, Frances M. see FIELD,
Frances F.
FOX, Frederic Ewing, 1917-81,
American; nonfiction CON
'FOX, Freeman' see HAMILTON,
Charles H. S.
FOX, Gail, 1942- , American;
poetry CON
FOX, Gardiner, Francis, 1911- ,
American; fiction NI
FOX, Gilbert Theodore ('Gill Fox';
'Ted Fox'), 1915- , American;
cartoons CON
FOX, Helen Morgenthau, 1885?-
1974, American; nonfiction
CON
FOX, Henry Benjamin, 1910- ,
American; nonfiction CON
FOX, James M. ('Grant Holmes'),
Dutch-American; fiction, film
CON
FOX, John William, Jr., 1863?-
1919, American; fiction BA
FOX, Larry, American; juveniles
WAR
FOX, Levi, 1914- , British; non-
fiction CON
FOX, Logan Jordan, 1922- ,
American; nonfiction CON
FOX, Lorraine, American; juven-
iles CO
'FOX, Lucia U. de' see LOCKART,
Lucia A. F.
FOX, Michael Allen, 1940- ,
American; nonfiction CON
FOX, Michael Wilson, 1937- ,
Anglo-American; juveniles,
nonfiction CO CON WAR
FOX, Paula, 1923- , American;
juveniles, fiction CO CON
DEM KI WAR
FOX, Ralph Hartzler, 1913-73,
American; nonfiction CON
FOX, Ray Errol, 1941- , Amer-
ican; nonfiction, plays CON
FOX, Renee Claire, 1928- ,
American; nonfiction CON
FOX, Richard Gabriel, 1939- ,
American; nonfiction CON
FOX, Richard Wightman, 1945- ,
American; nonfiction CON
FOX, Robert, 1943- , American;

fiction CON
FOX, Robert J., 1927- , American; nonfiction CON
FOX, Ruth, 1895- , American; nonfiction CON
FOX, Samuel J., 1919- , American; nonfiction CON
FOX, Sharon Elizabeth, 1938- , American; nonfiction CON
FOX, Siv Cedering, 1939- , Swedish-American; nonfiction, poetry, translations CON
FOX, Sonny, 1925- , American; nonfiction, juveniles CON WAR
'FOX, Ted' see FOX, Gilbert T.
'FOX, Col. Victor' see WINSTON, Robert A.
FOX, William Price, Jr., 1926- , American; fiction, tv, film BA HE
FOXE, John, 1517-87, English; nonfiction BU DA PO RU
FOXELL, Nigel, 1931- , British; poetry, nonfiction CON
FOX-GENOVESE, Elizabeth, 1941- , American; nonfiction CON
FOXLEY, William McLachlan, 1926-78, American; nonfiction CON
FOX-MARTIN, Milton, 1914?-77, American?; nonfiction CON
FOXON, David Fairweather, 1923- , British; nonfiction CON
FOX-SCHEINWOLD, Patricia (Scheinwold), American; nonfiction, juveniles CON
'FOXX, Jack' see PRONZINI, Bill
FOXX, Redd, 1922- , American; nonfiction CON
FOXX, Richard Michael, 1944- , American; nonfiction CON
FOY, Nancy, 1934- , American; nonfiction CON
FOZDAR, Jamshed Khodadad, 1926- , American; nonfiction CON
FRACASTORO, Girolamo, 1478-1553, Italian; poetry BO BU
FRACCHIA, Charles Anthony, 1937- , American; nonfiction CON
FRACCHIA, Umberto, 1889-1930, Italian; fiction, journalism BU

FRACKMAN, Nathaline ('Nata Lee'), 1903?-77, American; nonfiction CON
FRADIN, Dennis Brindell, 1945- , American; juveniles CON
FRAENKEL, Michael, 1896-1957, Lithuanian-American; poetry RO
FRAET, Frans, -1558, Dutch; printer BU
FRAGER, Robert, 1940- , American; nonfiction CON
FRAIBERG, Selma, 1918-81, American; nonfiction CON
FRAME, Janet, 1924- , New Zealander; fiction, poetry BU DA VCN VCP VN WA
FRAMO, James Lawrence, 1922- , American; nonfiction CON
FRANC, Helen M., 1908- , American; nonfiction CON
FRANCA, Celia, 1921- , British; nonfiction CON
FRANCA, Jose Augusto, 1922- , Portuguese; fiction, nonfiction CON
'FRANCE, Anatole' (Jacques Anatole Thibault), 1844-1924, French; fiction, poetry, nonfiction BU CL MAG NI SEY TH
FRANCE, Anna Kay, 1940- , American; nonfiction CON
FRANCE, Harold Leroy, 1930- , American; poetry CON
FRANCE, Richard, 1938- , American; juveniles, plays, nonfiction CON MCN
FRANCES, Immanuel, 1618-1710, Italian; poetry BU
FRANCES, Stephen, American; fiction NI
'FRANCESCA, Rosina' see BROOKMAN, Rosina F.
FRANCESCO da BARBERINO, 1264-1348, Italian; poetry BU
FRANCHERE, Ruth, 1906- , American; juveniles, nonfiction CO CON DEM
'FRANCHI, Eda' see VICKERS, Antoinette L.
'FRANCIS, Anne' see BIRD, Florence B.
FRANCIS, Arlene, 1912- , American; nonfiction CON
'FRANCIS, C. D. E.' see HOWARTH, Patrick J.
'FRANCIS, Charles' see HOLME,

Bryan
FRANCIS, Clare, 1946- , British;
nonfiction CON
FRANCIS, Convers, 1795-1863,
American; nonfiction MY
FRANCIS, Dennis S., 1943?-80,
American; nonfiction CON
FRANCIS, Devon, 1901- ,
American; nonfiction CON
FRANCIS, Dick, 1920- , British;
fiction, journalism REI ST
VCN WAK
FRANCIS, Dorothy Brenner,
1926- , American; juveniles
CO
FRANCIS, Frank Chalton, 1901- ,
English; nonfiction CON
FRANCIS, Michael Jackson,
1938- , American; nonfiction
CON
FRANCIS, Pamela Mary, 1926- ,
English; juveniles CO
FRANCIS, Sir Philip, 1740-1818,
British; nonfiction BU
FRANCIS, Richard H., 1945- ,
British; fiction CON
FRANCIS, Robert Churchill,
1901- , American; poetry,
fiction, nonfiction VCP
FRANCIS, Wayne Louis, 1935- ,
American; nonfiction CON
FRANCIS of ASSISI, St. (Fran-
cesco d'Assisi), 1182-1226,
Italian; poetry BO BU TH
FRANCK, Phyllis, 1928- , Amer-
ican; nonfiction CON
'FRANCK, Sebastian' see
JACOBY, Henry
FRANCK, Sebastian, 1499-1542,
German; nonfiction BU TH
FRANCKE, Donald Eugene, 1910-
78, American; nonfiction
CON
FRANCKE, Kuno, 1855-1930,
German-American; nonfiction,
poetry BU
FRANCKE, Linda Bird, 1939- ,
American; nonfiction CON
FRANCO, Johan Henri, 1908- ,
Dutch-American; nonfiction
CON
FRANCO, Niccolo, 1515-70,
Italian; poetry BU
FRANCO, Veronica, 1546-91,
Italian; poetry BU
FRANCO OPPENHEIMER, Felix,
1912- , Puerto Rican; jour-
nalism, nonfiction, poetry

HIL
FRANCOEUR, Anna Kotlarchyk,
1940- , American; nonfiction
CON
FRANCOIS, André, 1915- ,
Rumanian-French; juveniles
CO CON DE
FRANCOIS, Marie Louise von,
1817-93, German; fiction BU
FRANCOIS de SALES, St., 1567-
1622, French; nonfiction BU
TH
'FRANCOISE' see SEIGNOBOSC,
Francoise
FRANCOIS-PONCET, Andre, 1887-
1978, French; journalism, non-
fiction CON
FRANCO-MENDES, David, 1713-92,
Hebrew; plays BU
FRANDSEN, Julius, 1907-76, Amer-
ican; journalism CON
FRANEY, Pierre, 1921- , Franco-
American; nonfiction CON
FRANK, Bruno, 1887-1945, Ger-
man; poetry, fiction, plays
CL MCG
FRANK, Florence Kiper, 1885?-
1976, American; poetry, plays
CON
FRANK, Hans Eric, 1921- ,
American; nonfiction CON
FRANK, Harry Thomas, 1933-80,
American; nonfiction CON
'FRANK, Janet' see DUNLEAVY,
Janet E.
FRANK, John G., 1896-1978,
American; nonfiction CON
FRANK, Joseph, 1916- , Amer-
ican; nonfiction WA
FRANK, Joseph Nathaniel, 1918- ,
American; nonfiction CON
FRANK, Josette, 1893- , Amer-
ican; juveniles CO
FRANK, Lawrence Kelso, 1890-
1968, American; nonfiction
CON
FRANK, Leonahard, 1882-1961,
German; fiction, plays CL
MCG TH
FRANK, Morton, 1912- , Amer-
ican; journalism CON
FRANK, Murray, 1908-77, Amer-
ican; journalism, nonfiction
CON
'FRANK, Pat' (Harry Hart),
1907- , American; fiction
AS NI
FRANK, Peter Solomon, 1950- ,

American; poetry CON
'FRANK, R., Jr.' see ROSS,
Frank X., Jr.
FRANK, Reuven, 1920- , Amer-
ican; journalism CON
FRANK, Robert Joseph, 1939- ,
American; nonfiction CON
FRANK, Sheldon, 1943- , Amer-
ican; nonfiction CON
FRANK, Stanley B., 1908-79,
American; nonfiction CON
FRANK, Waldo David ('Search-
light'), 1889-1967, American;
fiction, plays, nonfiction
BR CON VN
FRANKAU, Gilbert, 1884-1952,
British; fiction NI ST
FRANKAU, Mary Evelyn Atkinson
(M. E. Atkinson), 1899- ,
English; plays, juveniles CO
FRANKAU, Pamela ('Eliot Naylor'),
1908- , English; fiction,
journalism DA
FRANKE, Christopher,
1941- , American; poetry
CON
FRANKE, David, 1938- ,
American; nonfiction
CON
FRANKE, Herbert W., 1927- ,
Austrian-German; fiction AS
NI
FRANKE, Holly Lambro, 1943- ,
American; nonfiction CON
FRANKEL, Arthur Steven, 1942- ,
American; nonfiction CON
FRANKEL, Bernice, American;
juveniles CON
FRANKEL, Charles, 1917-79,
American; nonfiction CON
FRANKEL, Edward, 1910- ,
American; nonfiction CON
FRANKEL, Eliot, 1922- , Amer-
ican; journalism CON
FRANKEL, Hans Hermann,
1916- , German-American;
nonfiction CON
FRANKEL, Haskel, 1926- ,
American; journalism, non-
fiction CON
FRANKEL, Hermann F., 1899?-
77, American; nonfiction
CON
FRANKEL, Max, 1930- , Ger-
man-American; journalism
CON
FRANKEL, Zygmunt, 1929- ,
Polish-American; fiction CON

FRANKENBERG, Lloyd, 1907-75,
American; poetry, nonfiction
CON
FRANKENBERG, Robert, 1911- ,
American; juveniles CO
FRANKENTHAL, Kate, 1889-1976,
German-American; nonfiction
CON
FRANKFORTER, Albertus Daniel
III, 1939- , American; non-
fiction CON
FRANKFURT, Harry Gordon,
1929- , American; nonfiction
CON
FRANKFURTER, Philip, fl. 1400,
Austrian; poetry BU
FRANKL, Viktor Emil, 1905- ,
Austrian; nonfiction CON
FRANKLAND, Anthony Noble,
1922- , English; nonfiction
CON
FRANKLAND, Mark, 1934- ,
British; nonfiction CON
FRANKLE, Bernice, American;
juveniles CO
FRANKLIN, Adele, 1887?-1977,
American; nonfiction CON
FRANKLIN, Alfred White, 1905- ,
English; nonfiction CON
FRANKLIN, Benjamin, 1706-90,
American; nonfiction AM BR
BU ENG MAG PO
FRANKLIN, Benjamin A., 1927- ,
American; journalism CON
FRANKLIN, Colin, 1923- , Brit-
ish; nonfiction CON
'FRANKLIN, Edgar' (Edgar Frank-
lin Stearns), 1879-?, Amer-
ican?; fiction NI
FRANKLIN, Harold, 1920- ,
American; juveniles CO
FRANKLIN, Harold Leroy ('Chijuyo
Alimayo'), 1934- , American;
nonfiction CON
FRANKLIN, Howard Bruce, 1934- ,
American; nonfiction AS NI
FRANKLIN, Jennie Elizabeth,
1937- , American; nonfiction,
plays CON
FRANKLIN, Jerome Lee, 1943- ,
American; nonfiction CON
FRANKLIN, John Hope, 1915- ,
American; nonfiction SH
FRANKLIN, Marshall, 1929- ,
American; nonfiction CON
'FRANKLIN, Max' see DEMING,
Richard
FRANKLIN, Miles see 'BRENT

of BIN BIN'
FRANKLIN, Olga, 1912- , British; nonfiction, translations CON
FRANKLIN, Sidney, 1903-76, American; nonfiction CON
'FRANKLIN, Steve' see STEVENS, Franklin
FRANKLYN, Robert Alan, 1918- , American; nonfiction CON
FRANKO, Ivan, 1856-1916, Ukrainian; nonfiction BU CL TH
FRANKS, Charles Edwin Selwyn, 1936- , Canadian; nonfiction CON
FRANKS, Lucinda, 1946- , American; nonfiction CON
FRANQUIZ, José A., 1906- , Puerto Rican; nonfiction, poetry HIL
FRANTZ, Ralph Jules, 1902-79, American; journalism CON RO
FRANZBLAU, Rose Nadler, 1905-79, Austrian-American; journalism, nonfiction CON
FRANZEN, Franz Michael, 1772-1847, Swedish; poetry BU
FRANZEN, Gosta Knut, 1906- , Swedish-American; nonfiction CON
FRANZEN, Lavern Gerhardt, 1926- , American; nonfiction CON
FRANZEN, Nils-Olof, 1916- , Swedish; juveniles CO
FRARY, Michael, 1918- , American; nonfiction CON
FRASCA, John Anthony, 1916-79, American; nonfiction CON
FRASCONI, Antonio, 1919- , Italian-American; juveniles CO DE
FRASE, Larry E., 1945- , American; nonfiction CON
FRASER, Allan, 1900- , Scots; nonfiction, fiction CON
FRASER, Amy Stewart, 1892- , Scots; nonfiction CON
FRASER, Anthea ('Vanessa Graham'), English; fiction CON
FRASER, Lady Antonia, 1932- , English; fiction, juveniles, nonfiction CON REI WAK
FRASER, Arthur Ronald ('Arthur

Ronald'), 1888-1974, British; fiction, nonfiction CON
FRASER, B. Kay, 1941- , American; nonfiction CON
FRASER, Dorothy May ('Maxwell Fraser'), 1903?-80, British; nonfiction CON
FRASER, Douglas ('David Hope'), 1910- , Scots; poetry CON
FRASER, George MacDonald ('Dand MacNeill'), 1925- , English; nonfiction, film, fiction, journalism CON WAK
FRASER, George Sutherland, 1915-80, Scots; poetry, nonfiction, translations BOR BU CON DA VCP WA
'FRASER, James' see WHITE, Alan
'FRASER, Jane' see 'PILCHER, Rosamunde'
FRASER, John D. see FRAZER, John D.
FRASER, Julius Thomas, 1923- , Hungarian-American; nonfiction CON
'FRASER, Maxwell' see FRANSER, Dorothy M.
FRASER, Morris, 1941- , Scots; nonfiction CON
FRASER, Sir Ronald Arthur, 1888- , English; fiction NI
FRASER, Sylvia, 1935- , Canadian; nonfiction CON
FRASER, William Dean, 1916- , American; nonfiction CON
FRASER, William Hamish, 1941- , Scots; nonfiction CON
FRASER DARLING, Frank, 1903-79, Scots; nonfiction CON
FRASSANITO, William Allen, 1946- , American; nonfiction CON
FRATI, Carlo, 1863-1930, Italian; nonfiction ENG
FRATTI, Mario, 1927- , American; plays, translation, poetry CL CON VCD
FRAUENLOB, Heinrich von Meissen, -1318, German; poetry BU
FRAUNCE, Abraham, 1558/60-1633/34, English; poetry, nonfiction BU
'FRAY, Justo' see MATOS BERNIER, Felix
FRAYDAS, Stan, 1918- , Belgian-American; nonfiction, juveniles

CON
FRAYN, Michael, 1933- , English; fiction, journalism, plays NI VCD VCN WA
FRAYNE, June (Callwood), 1924- , Canadian; journalism, nonfiction CON
'FRAZER, Andrew' see 'MARLOWE, Stephen'
FRAZER, Sir James George, 1854-1941, Scots; nonfiction BU DA MAG PO
FRAZIER, John De Jean (Fraser), 1810?-50?, Irish; poetry HO
FRAZIER, Carl, American; juveniles WAR
FRAZIER, George, 1911-74, American; nonfiction, fiction CON
FRAZIER, Kendrick Crosby, 1942- , American; journalism, nonfiction CON
FRAZIER, Neta Lohnes, American; juveniles CO
FRAZIER, Rosalie, American; juveniles WAR
'FRAZIER, Sarah' see WIRT, Winola W.
FRAZIER, Shervert Hughes, 1921- , American; nonfiction CON
FRAZIER, Walter ('Clyde Cool'), 1945- , American; nonfiction CON
FREAS, Frank Kelly, 1922- , American; nonfiction AS CON
FRECH, Frances, 1923- , American; journalism, nonfiction CON
FRECHETTE, Louis Honoré, 1839-1908, Canadian; poetry BU
FREDE, Richard, 1934- , American; fiction, poetry CON
FREDERIC, Harold, 1856-98, American; journalism, fiction AM BR BU MAG PO VN
FREDERICK II, Emperor, 1194-1250, German-Norman; poetry, nonfiction BO BU
FREDERICK II, King of Prussia, 1712-86, German; nonfiction BU
FREDERICK, Carl Louis, 1942- , American; nonfiction CON
'FREDERICK, John' see 'BRAND,

Max'
'FREDERICK, Lee' see NUSSBAUM, Albert F.
FREDERICK, Pauline, 1908- , American; nonfiction CON
FREDERICK, Robert Allen, 1928- , American; nonfiction CON
FREDERICKS, Carlton, 1910- , American; nonfiction CON
FREDERIKSEN, Martin W., 1930-80, British; nonfiction CON
FREDERIKSON, Edna, 1904- , American; fiction CON
FREDMAN, Alice Green, 1924- , American; nonfiction CON
FREDRICKSON, Olive Alta, 1901- , American; fiction CON
FREDRO, Aleksander, 1793-1876, Polish; poetry, plays BU MCG TH
FREDRO, Andrzej Maksymilian, 1620-79, Polish; nonfiction BU
FREE, James Stillman, 1908- , American; journalism, nonfiction CON
FREE, John (Phreas), -1465, English; nonfiction, translations BU
FREEBORN, Brian James, 1939- , English; plays, fiction CON
FREED, Alvyn M., 1913- , American; juveniles, nonfiction CO CON
FREED, Donald, 1932- , American; nonfiction, plays CON
FREED, Margaret (De Haan), 1917- , American; nonfiction CON
FREEDEMAN, Charles Eldon, 1926- , American; nonfiction CON
FREEDGOOD, Morton see 'GODEY, John'
FREEDLAND, Michael Rooney, 1934- , English; nonfiction CON
FREEDLAND, Nathaniel ('Paul Kenyon'), 1936- , American; nonfiction CON
FREEDMAN, Alfred Mordecai, 1917- , American; nonfiction CON
FREEDMAN, Arthur Merton, 1916- , American; nonfiction CON

FREEDMAN, Benedict, 1919- ,
American; fiction CON
FREEDMAN, Daniel X., 1921- ,
American; nonfiction CON
FREEDMAN, Hy, 1914- , Amer-
ican; nonfiction CON
FREEDMAN, Maurice, 1920-75,
British; nonfiction CON
FREEDMAN, Morris David,
1938- , Canadian-American;
nonfiction CON
FREEDMAN, Nancy, 1920- ,
American; fiction CON NI
FREEDMAN, Richard, 1932- ,
American; nonfiction CON
FREEDMAN, Russell Bruce,
1929- , American; juveniles
CO
FREEHOF, Solomon Ennett,
1892- , British-American;
nonfiction CON
'FREELAND, Jay' see McLEOD,
John F.
FREELAND, Richard M., 1941- ,
American; nonfiction CON
FREELAND, Stephen L., 1911?-
77, American; journalism,
nonfiction CON
FREELING, Nicolas ('F. R. E.
Nicholas'), 1927- , British;
fiction, nonfiction CON REI
ST VCN WA
FREELY, Maureen, 1952- ,
American; nonfiction, fiction
CON
FREEMAN, A. Myrick III,
1936- , American; nonfic-
tion CON
'FREEMAN, Arthur' see LIEB-
ERMANN, Aharon S.
FREEMAN, Barbara Constance,
1906- , British; juveniles
CON KI
FREEMAN, Charles K., 1900-80,
British; journalism CON
'FREEMAN, Cynthia' see
FEINBERG, Bea
FREEMAN, David, 1922- , Brit-
ish; plays, film CON
FREEMAN, David, 1945- ,
Canadian; plays VCD
FREEMAN, Don, 1908-78, Amer-
ican; juveniles CO CON KI
FREEMAN, Donald Cary,
1938- , American; nonfiction
CON
FREEMAN, Douglas Southall,
1886-1953, American; nonfic-

tion MAG
FREEMAN, Edward Augustus,
1823-92, English; nonfiction
BU DA
FREEMAN, Eugene, 1906- ,
American; nonfiction CON
FREEMAN, Gary, 1945- , Amer-
ican; nonfiction CON
FREEMAN, Gillian, 1929- ,
British; fiction, plays, juven-
iles, nonfiction VCN
FREEMAN, Harry, 1906-78, Amer-
ican; journalism CON
FREEMAN, Ira Maximilian,
1905- , American; juveniles,
nonfiction CO CON
FREEMAN, James Montague,
1936- , American; nonfiction
CON
FREEMAN, Jo, 1945- , American;
nonfiction CON
FREEMAN, John, 1880-1929, Eng-
lish; poetry, nonfiction DA
FREEMAN, Joseph, 1897-1965,
Russian-American; poetry,
journalism, nonfiction CON
FREEMAN, Kathleen see 'FITT,
Mary'
FREEMAN, Lea David, 1887?-
1976, American; plays, film
CON
FREEMAN, Linton Clarke, 1927- ,
American; nonfiction CON
FREEMAN, Lucy Greenbaum,
1916- , American; juveniles
CO
FREEMAN, Mae Blacker, 1907- ,
American; nonfiction CO CON
FREEMAN, Margaret B., 1900?-
80, American; nonfiction CON
FREEMAN, Margaret Cooper,
1913- , American; nonfiction
CON
FREEMAN, Mary Eleanor Wilkins,
1852-1930, American; fiction
BR BU VN
FREEMAN, Paul, 1929?-80, Amer-
ican; nonfiction CON
FREEMAN, R. Austin see 'ASH-
DOWN, Clifford'
FREEMAN, Richard Barry,
1944- , American; nonfiction
CON
FREEMAN, Roger Anthony W.,
1928- , English; nonfiction
CON
FREEMAN, Roger Louis, 1928- ,
American; nonfiction CON

FREEMAN 364

FREEMAN, Ruth Benson, 1906- , American; nonfiction CON
FREEMAN, Susan Tax, 1938- , American; nonfiction CON
FREEMAN, Thomas, 1919- , Scots; nonfiction CON
FREEMANTLE, Brian Harry ('John Maxwell'), 1936- , English; fiction CON MCC REI
FREEMON, Frank Reed, 1938- , American; nonfiction CON
FREESE, Arthur S., 1917- , American; nonfiction CON
FREGAULT, Guy, 1918-77, Canadian; nonfiction CON
FREGLY, Bert, 1922- , American; nonfiction CON
FREGOSI, Claudia, 1946- , American; juveniles CO CON WAR
FREIDANK, fl. 1215-30, German; poetry BU
FREIDES, Thelma Katz, 1930- , American; nonfiction CON
FREILICH, Joan Sherman, 1941- , American; nonfiction CON
FREILIGRATH, Hermann Ferdinand, 1810-76, German; poetry BU TH
FREIRE, Albuquerque, 1935?- , Mozambican; poetry HER
FREITAS, Margarete Elisabeth, 1927- , German-American; nonfiction CON
FREIVALDS, John, 1944- , Latvian-American; nonfiction CON
FREMLIN, Celia, 1914- , British; fiction, nonfiction REI
'FREMONT, W. B.' see BOWERS, Warner F.
FRENAUD, André, 1907- , French; poetry CL WA
FRENCH, Alfred, 1916- , British; nonfiction CON
FRENCH, Allen, 1870-1946, American; juveniles, nonfiction COM
'FRENCH, Ashley' see ROBINS, Denise
FRENCH, Bevan Meredith, 1937- , American; nonfiction CON
FRENCH, Brandon, 1944- , American; poetry, nonfiction, film CON

FRENCH, Calvin Leonard, 1934- , American; nonfiction CON
FRENCH, Charles Ezra, 1923- , American; nonfiction CON
FRENCH, David, 1939- , Canadian; plays CON VCD
'FRENCH, Doris' see SHACKLETON, Doris C.
FRENCH, Dorothy Kayser, 1926- , American; juveniles CO
FRENCH, Fiona, 1944- , English; juveniles CO KI
FRENCH, Herbert Eliot, 1912- , American; nonfiction CON
FRENCH, Maida Parlow, 1901- , Canadian; fiction, nonfiction CR
FRENCH, Marilyn ('Mara Solwoska'), 1929- , American; fiction, nonfiction CON
FRENCH, Michael, 1944- , American; fiction, juveniles CON
'FRENCH, Paul' see ASIMOV, Isaac
FRENCH, Peter Andrew, 1942- , American; nonfiction CON
FRENCH, Philip Neville, 1933- , British; nonfiction CON
FRENCH, Richard De Land, 1947- , Canadian; nonfiction CON
FRENCH, Scott Robert, 1948- , American; nonfiction CON
FRENCH, Will, 1890?-1979, American; nonfiction CON
FRENCH, William Harold, 1926- , Canadian; nonfiction CON
FRENCH, William Percy, 1854-1920, Irish; fiction, poetry IIO
FRENEAU, Philip Morin, 1752-1832, American; poetry, journalism BR BU MAG PO VP
FRENKEL, Jacob Aharon, 1943- , American; nonfiction CON
FRERE, Emile George, 1917- , American; nonfiction CON
FRERE, John Hookham ('Whistlecraft'), 1769-1846, English; poetry, nonfiction, translations BU DA PO VP
FRERE, Maud, 1923- , Belgian; fiction CL
FRERON, Elie Catherine, 1718-76, French; journalism, nonfiction TH
FRESCHET, Berniece Louise

Speck, 1927- , American;
juveniles DEM WAR
FRESCOBALDI, Dino, 1270-1316,
Italian; poetry BO BU
FRESCOBALDI, Leonardo, 14-15th
centuries, Italian; nonfiction
BU
FRESCOBALDI, Matteo, 1297?-
1348, Italian; poetry BU
FRESE, Jacob, 1690-1729, Swed-
ish; poetry BU
FRETWELL, Stephen DeWitt,
1942- , American; nonfiction
CON
FREUCHEN, Lorentz Peter El-
fred, 1886-1957, Danish; fic-
tion, journalism BU TH
FREUD, Clement Raphael, 1924- ,
British; translations, nonfic-
tion, juveniles CON
FREUD, Sigmund, 1856-1939,
Austrian; nonfiction BU
MAG SEY TH
FREUDENHEIM, Leslie Ann
Mandelson, 1941- , Amer-
ican; nonfiction CON
'FREUGON, Ruby' see ASHBY,
Rubie C.
FREUND, Gisele, 1912- ,
Franco-American; nonfiction
CON
FREUNDLICH, August L.,
1924- , American; nonfiction
CON
FREVERT, Peter, 1938- ,
American; nonfiction CON
FREW, David Richard, 1943- ,
American; nonfiction CON
FREWER, Glyn, 1931- , Eng-
lish; juveniles CO
FREWIN, Anthony, 1947- ,
British; fiction NI
FREY, Erich A., 1931- , Ger-
man-American; nonfiction
CON
FREY, Frederick Ward, 1929- ,
American; nonfiction CON
FREY, Jakob, 1520?-62?,
German; plays BU
FREY, John Andrew, 1929- ,
American; nonfiction CON
FREY, Richard L., 1905- ,
American; nonfiction CON
FREYBE, Heidi H. see 'AL-
BRAND, Martha'
'FREYER, Frederic' see BALL-
INGER, Bill S.
FREYRE, Gilberto de Melo,

1900- , Brazilian; nonfiction,
fiction BR BU WA
FREYTAG, Gustav, 1816-95, Ger-
man; plays, fiction, nonfiction
BU MAG MCG TH
FREZZI, Federico, 1346?-1416,
Italian; poetry BU
FRIAR, Kimon, 1911- , American;
poetry, translations, nonfiction
CON WA
FRIAS, Heriberto, 1870-1928,
Mexican; fiction BR
FRICHE, Vladimir Maximovich
(Fritsche), 1870-1929, Russian;
nonfiction BU
'FRICK, C. H.' see IRWIN, Con-
stance F.
FRICK, Constance see IRWIN,
Constance
FRICK, Ford Christopher, 1894-
1978, American; nonfiction,
journalism CON
FRICKX, Robert see 'MONTAL,
Robert'
FRIDA, Emil see 'VRCHLICKY,
Jaroslav'
FRIDAY, Nancy, 1937- , Amer-
ican; nonfiction CON
'FRIDAY, Peter' see HARRIS,
Herbert
FRIDEGARD, Jan, 1897-1968,
Swedish; fiction BU CL TH
FRIDERIKS, Christiane von B.
see 'CHRISTEN, Ada'
FRIDMAN, Grigory Y. see
'BAKLANOV, Grigory Y.'
FRIEBERT, Stuart Alyn, 1931- ,
American; poetry CON
FRIED, Barbara, 1924- , Amer-
ican; nonfiction CON
FRIED, Emanuel ('Edward Mann'),
1913- , American; plays
CON
FRIED, Erich, 1921- , Austrian;
poetry, translations, fiction
CL TH WA
FRIED, Frederick, 1908- , Amer-
ican; nonfiction CON
FRIED, Marc Allen, 1922- ,
American; nonfiction CON
FRIED, Marc Bernard, 1944- ,
American; nonfiction CON
FRIED, Mary McKenzie Hill,
1914- , American; nonfiction
CON
FRIED, Richard Mayer, 1941- ,
American; nonfiction CON
FRIED, William, 1945- , Amer-

ican; nonfiction CON
FRIEDAN, Betty Naomi, 1921- ,
American; nonfiction CON
FRIEDBERG, Gertrude, American;
plays, fiction NI
FRIEDE, Eleanor Kask, 1920- ,
American; nonfiction CON
FRIEDELL, Egon, 1878-1938,
Austrian; fiction NI
FRIEDENBERG, Edgar Zodiag,
1921- , Canadian; nonfiction
CON
FRIEDENBERG, Walter Drew,
1928- , American; journal-
ism CON
FRIEDENTHAL, Richard, 1896-
1979, German; nonfiction
CON
FRIEDGUT, Theodore H. ,
1931- , American; nonfic-
tion CON
FRIEDL, John, 1945- , Amer-
ican; nonfiction CON
FRIEDLAND, Ronald Lloyd,
1937-75, American; nonfic-
tion CON
FRIEDLANDER, Joanne Kohn,
1930- , American; juveniles,
journalism, nonfiction CO
CON WAR
FRIEDMAN, Alice R. , 1900- ,
Austrian-American; nonfiction
CON
FRIEDMAN, Arnold Phineas,
1909- , American; nonfiction
CON
FRIEDMAN, Avner, 1932- ,
American; nonfiction CON
FRIEDMAN, Bruce Jay, 1930- ,
American; fiction, plays
BR HE MCG VCD VCN WA
FRIEDMAN, David, 1945- ,
American; nonfiction CON
FRIEDMAN, Elizabeth, 1893?-
1980, American; nonfiction
CON
FRIEDMAN, Estelle Ehrenwald,
1920- , American; juven-
iles CO
FRIEDMAN, Harold (Hal), 1942- ,
American; nonfiction CON
FRIEDMAN, Ina Rosen, 1926- ,
American; juveniles CON
WAR
FRIEDMAN, Irving Sigmund,
1915- , American; nonfiction
CON
FRIEDMAN, Isaiah, 1921- ,

Polish-American; nonfiction
CON
FRIEDMAN, Josephine Troth
(Joy), 1928- , American;
juveniles CON
FRIEDMAN, Judi, 1935- , Amer-
ican; nonfiction CON
FRIEDMAN, Kenneth Scott, Amer-
ican; nonfiction CON
FRIEDMAN, Lawrence J. , 1940- ,
American; nonfiction CON
FRIEDMAN, Lenemaja, 1924- ,
German-American; nonfiction
CON
FRIEDMAN, Leon, 1933- , Amer-
ican; nonfiction CON
FRIEDMAN, Marcia, 1925- ,
American; nonfiction CON
FRIEDMAN, Michael Henry,
1945- , American; nonfiction
CON
FRIEDMAN, Murray, 1926- ,
American; nonfiction CON
FRIEDMAN, Myles Ivan, 1924- ,
American; nonfiction CON
FRIEDMAN, Ralph, 1916- ,
American; nonfiction, journal-
ism CON
FRIEDMAN, Rose Director, Polish-
American; nonfiction CON
FRIEDMAN, Sanford, 1928- ,
American; fiction, plays CON
FRIEDMAN, Sara Ann, 1935- ,
American; nonfiction CON
FRIEDMAN, Saul S. , 1937- ,
American; nonfiction CON
FRIEDMAN, Warner George,
1934- , American; nonfiction
CON
FRIEDMAN, Winifred, 1923?-75,
American; nonfiction CON
FRIEDMANN, Arnold, 1925- ,
German-American; nonfiction
CON
FRIEDMANN, John, 1926- ,
Austrian-American; nonfiction
CON
FRIEDRICH, Carl Joachim, 1901- ,
German-American; nonfiction
CON
FRIEDRICH, Richard, 1936- ,
American; nonfiction, plays,
poetry CON
FRIEDRICH von HAUSEN, fl.
1170-90, Rhenish; poetry
BU TH
FRIEDRICH von SONNENBURG,
late 12th century, German;

poetry TH
FRIEDRICHS, Christopher Richard,
1947- , American; nonfiction
CON
FRIEDRICHS, Robert Winslow,
1923- , American; nonfiction
CON
FRIEL, Brian, 1929- , Irish;
plays, fiction HO MCG VCD
WA
FRIEND, Krebs, 1895?-1967?,
American; nonfiction RO
FRIEND, Oscar J., 1897-1963,
American; fiction AS NI
FRIENDLICH, Richard J.,
1909- , American; juveniles
CO
FRIENDLY, Alfred, 1911- ,
American; journalism, non-
fiction CON
FRIENDLY, Henry Jacob, 1903- ,
American; nonfiction CON
FRIERMOOD, Elisabeth Hamilton,
1903- , American; juveniles
CO
FRIES, James Franklin, 1938- ,
American; nonfiction CON
FRIESS, Horace Leland, 1900-
75, American; nonfiction
CON
FRIGGENS, Arthur Henry,
1920- , British; fiction CON
FRIIS, Erik Johan, 1913- ,
Norwegian-American; nonfic-
tion CON
FRIIS, Harald Trap, 1893-1976,
Danish-American; nonfiction
CON
FRIIS-BAASTAD, Babbis Ellinor
('Baastad'; 'Eleanor Babbis';
'Babbis Friis'), 1921-70,
Norwegian; juveniles CO DE
WAR
FRIIS MOLLER, Kai, 1888-1960,
Danish; poetry, nonfiction
BU TH
FRIJLING-SCHREUDER, Elisa-
beth C. M., 1908- , Dutch;
nonfiction CON
FRIK, 1230/40-1310, Armenian;
poetry PRU
'FRIMBO, E. M.' see WHITAK-
ER, Rogers E. M.
FRIMMER, Steven, 1928- ,
American; juveniles WAR
FRINGS, Ketti, 1915-81, Amer-
ican; plays, film, fiction
CON MCG

FRIPP, Patricia, 1945- , British;
nonfiction CON
FRISBIE, Louise Kelley, 1913- ,
American; nonfiction CON
FRISBY, Terence Peter M.,
1932- , English; plays CON
VCD
FRISCH, Karl von, 1886- ,
Austrian; nonfiction CON
FRISCH, Max Rudolf, 1911- ,
Swiss; plays, fiction BU CL
CON MCG SEY TH WA
FRISCH, Paul Z., 1926?-77, Amer-
ican; nonfiction CON
FRISCH, Rose E., American;
juveniles WAR
FRISCHLIN, Philipp Nicodemus,
1547-90, German; plays BU
TH
FRISHMAN, David, 1862-1922,
Hebrew; nonfiction, translations
BU TH
FRISKEY, Margaret Richards
('Elizabeth Sherman'), 1901- ,
American; juveniles CO
FRISON, George Carr, 1924- ,
American; nonfiction CON
FRITCH, Charles E., American;
fiction NI
FRITH, Harold James, 1921- ,
Australian; nonfiction CON
FRITH, Nigel Andrew, 1941- ,
British; poetry CON
FRITSCH, Albert Joseph, 1933- ,
American; nonfiction CON
FRITSCH, Bruno, 1926- , Czech;
nonfiction CON
FRITZ, Jean, 1915- , American;
juveniles DE KI
FRITZ, Leah, 1931- , American;
nonfiction CON
FRITZE, Julius Arnold, 1918- ,
American; nonfiction CON
FROBISH, Nestle John, 1930- ,
American; nonfiction CON
FRÖDING, Gustaf, 1860-1911,
Swedish; poetry, journalism
BU CL TH
FROELICH, Robert E., 1929- ,
American; nonfiction CON
FROHLICH, Norman, 1941- ,
Canadian; nonfiction CON
FROHOCK, Wilbur Merrill,
1908- , American; nonfiction
CON
FROISSART, Jean, 1337?-1405?,
French; nonfiction, poetry
BU MAG TH

FROLOV, Vadim, 1913- ,
Russian; juveniles WAR
FROMAN, Elizabeth Hull, 1920-
75, American; juveniles CO
CON
FROMAN, Robert Winslow,
1917- , American; juveniles
CO DEM
'FROME, David' see 'FORD,
Leslie'
FROMENTIN, Eugène, 1820-
75/76, French; nonfiction,
fiction BU MAG TH
FROMKIN, Victoria Alexandria,
1923- , American; nonfic-
tion CON
FROMM, Erich, 1900-80, Ger-
man-American; nonfiction BR
CON SEY
FROMM, Herbert, 1905- ,
German-American; nonfiction
CON
FROMM, Lilo, 1928- , German;
nonfiction CON
FROMMER, Harvey, 1937- ,
American; nonfiction CON
FRONCEK, Thomas Walter,
American; nonfiction CON
FRONDIZI, Risieri, 1910- ,
Argentinian-American; non-
fiction, translations CON
FRONTINUS, Sextus Julius,
30-104, Roman; nonfiction
BU LA
FRONTO, Marcus Cornelius,
100-166, Roman; nonfiction
BU LA
FROOKS, Dorothy, 1899- ,
American; nonfiction CON
FROSCH, Thomas Richard,
1943- , American; nonfic-
tion CON
FROST, Arthur Burdett, 1851-
1928, American; juveniles CO
FROST, C. Vernon see 'CHILD,
Charles B.'
FROST, Carol, 1948- , Amer-
ican; poetry CON
FROST, David Paradine, 1939- ,
British; nonfiction CON
'FROST, Erica' see SUPRANER,
Robyn
FROST, Everett Lloyd, 1942- ,
American; nonfiction CON
FROST, Frank Jasper, 1929- ,
American; nonfiction CON
'FROST, Frederick' see 'BRAND,
Max'

FROST, Gavin, 1930- , Anglo-
American; nonfiction CON
'FROST, Joni' see PAINE, Lauran
B.
FROST, Lawrence August, 1907- ,
American; nonfiction CON
FROST, Lesley, 1899- , Ameri-
can; juveniles CO
FROST, Robert Carlton, 1926- ,
American; nonfiction CON
FROST, Robert Lee, 1875-1963,
American; poetry AM BR
BU CO CON MAG PO SEY VP
FROST, Stanley Brice, 1913- ,
Anglo-Canadian; nonfiction
CON
FROST, William, 1917- , Amer-
ican; nonfiction CON
FROSTERUS, Theodor O. see
'PAKKULA, Teuvo'
FROTHINGHAM, Octavius Brooks,
1822-95, American; nonfiction
MY
FROUDE, James Anthony, 1818-94,
English; nonfiction BU DA PO
FROUMUND of TEGERNSEE, 960-
1008, German; poetry BU
FRUCHT, Phyllis, 1936- , Amer-
ican; nonfiction CON
FRUCHTENBAUM, Arnold Geneko-
vich, 1943- , Russian-Amer-
ican; nonfiction CON
FRUCHTER, Norman D., American;
fiction CON
FRUG, Simon Samuel, 1860-1916,
Yiddish; poetry TH
FRUGONI, Carlo Innocenzo, 1692-
1768, Italian; poetry BU TH
FRUGONI, Cesare, 1881-1978,
Italian; nonfiction CON
FRUGONI, Francesco Fulvio,
1620?-86?, Italian; poetry
BO
FRUHAN, William Edward, Jr.,
1943- , American; nonfiction
CON
FRUM, Barbara, 1937- , Amer-
ican; journalism, nonfiction
CON
FRUTON, Joseph Stewart, 1912- ,
Polish-American; nonfiction
CON
FRUYTIERS, Jan, -1580, Dutch;
poetry BU
FRY, Alan, 1931- , Canadian;
fiction CON
FRY, Carli, 1897-1956, Raeto-
Romansch; poetry, plays,

fiction BU
FRY, Christopher, 1907- ,
English; plays, translations
BU DA MAG MCG PO VCD
VCP VD
FRY, Earl Howard, 1947- ,
American; nonfiction CON
FRY, Edwin Maxwell, 1899- ,
English; nonfiction CON
FRY, John, 1930- , Canadian-
American; juveniles, non-
fiction CON
FRY, Michael Graham, 1934- ,
British; nonfiction CON
FRY, Ronald William, 1949- ,
American; nonfiction CON
FRY, Rosalie Kingsmill, 1911- ,
Canadian; juveniles CO DE
KI
FRYATT, Norma R., American;
juveniles CON
FRYD, Mitsuo, 1902?-76, Japan-
ese; nonfiction CON
FRYE, Ellen, 1940- , American;
nonfiction, translations CON
FRYE, Herman Northrop, 1912- ,
Canadian; nonfiction BOR BR
BU DA WA
FRYE, John, 1910- , American;
nonfiction CON
FRYE, Keith, 1935- , American;
nonfiction CON
FRYE, William Ruggles, 1918- ,
American; nonfiction CON
FRYER, Donald S. see SIDNEY-
FRYER, Donald
FRYER, Jonathan, 1950- , Brit-
ish; journalism, nonfiction
CON
FRYER, Judith, 1939- , Amer-
ican; juveniles, nonfiction
CON
FRYER, Mary Beacock, 1929- ,
Canadian; nonfiction CON
FRYER, William T., 1900?-80,
American; nonfiction CON
FRYSCAK, Milan, 1932- ,
Czech-American; nonfiction
CON
FUAT, Memet, 1926- , Turk-
ish; nonfiction PRU
FUCHS, Abraham Moses, 1890- ,
Yiddish; fiction BU
FUCHS, Daniel, 1909- , Amer-
ican; fiction, film, plays
BR CON PO SEY VCN WAK
FUCHS, Erich, 1916- , German;
juveniles CO DEM

FUCHS, Estelle, American; nonfic-
tion CON
FUCHS, Jerome Herbert, 1922- ,
American; nonfiction CON
FUCHS, Lucy, 1935- , American;
fiction CON
FUCHS, Roland John, 1933- ,
American; nonfiction CON
FUCHS, Summer see 'LISKY, I.
A.'
FUCHSHUBER, Annegert, German;
juveniles WAR
FUCIK, Julius, 1903-43, Czech;
nonfiction, journalism BU TH
FUCILLA, Joseph Guerin, 1897- ,
American; nonfiction, transla-
tions CON
FUCINI, Renato, 1843-1921, Ital-
ian; nonfiction, poetry BO BU
CL TH
'FÜM, Men' see RAUCH, Men
FUENTES, Carlos, 1928/29- ,
Mexican; fiction, plays, non-
fiction BR BU CON MAG
SEY WA
FUENTES, Dagoberto, 1940- ,
American; nonfiction MAR
FUENTES, Martha Ayers ('Scat
Lorimer'), 1923- , American;
plays CON
FUENTES, Roberto, 1934- ,
American; fiction CON
FUENTES MOHR, Alberto, 1928?-
79, Guatemalan; nonfiction
CON
FUERMANN, George Melvin,
1918- , American; nonfiction
CON
FÜSSLI, Johann Heinrich, 1741-
1825, Swiss; poetry BU
FÜST, Milán, 1888-1967, Hungari-
an; poetry, plays, fiction BU
CL TH
FÜETRER, Ulrich, fl. 1450-1500,
German; poetry BU
FÜZULI, Mehmed bin Süleyman,
-1556/80, Turkish; poetry
PRU
'FUFUKA, Karama' see MORGAN,
Sharon A.
FUGARD, Athol, 1932/33- ,
South African; plays BU CON
SEY VCD VD WAK
FUHRMAN, Lee, 1903?-77, Amer-
ican; plays, journalism CON
FUHRMANN, Joseph Teodore,
1940- , American; nonfiction
CON

FUJA

FUJA, Abayomi, Nigerian;
juveniles WAR
FUJIKAWA, Gyo, American;
juveniles DEM
FUJIOKA SAKUTARO, 1870-1910,
Japanese; nonfiction HI
FUJITA, Tamao, 1905- ,
Japanese; juveniles HI
FUJIWARA, Michiko ('Michiko
Saito'), 1946- , Japanese;
juveniles CO CON WAR
FUJIWARA no AKISUE, 1055-
1123, Japanese; poetry HI
FUJIWARA no AKISUKE, 1090-
1155, Japanese; poetry HI
FUJIWARA no IETAKA, 1158-
1237, Japanese; poetry HI
FUJIWARA no KINTO, 966-1041,
Japanese; poetry, nonfiction
BU HI
FUJIWARA no KIYOSUKE, 1104-
77, Japanese; poetry, non-
fiction HI
FUJIWARA no MICHITOSHI,
1047-99, Japanese; poetry
HI
FUJIWARA no MOTOTOSHI,
-1142, Japanese; poetry, non-
fiction HI
FUJIWARA no SHUNZEI (Toshi-
mari), 1114-1204, Japanese;
poetry, nonfiction BU HI
FUJIWARA no TAMEIE, 1198-
1275, Japanese; poetry HI
FUJIWARA no TAMEKANE, 1254-
1333, Japanese; poetry HI
FUJIWARA no TAMEUJI, 1222-
86, Japanese; poetry HI
FUJIWARA no TAMEYO, 1251-
1338, Japanese; poetry HI
FUJIWARA no TEIKA (Sadaie),
1162-1241, Japanese; poetry,
nonfiction BU HI
FUJIWARA SEIKA, 1561-1619,
Japanese; nonfiction, poetry
HI
FUKS, Ladislav, 1923- , Czech;
fiction CL
FUKUDA, Tsutomu, 1905- ,
Japanese; nonfiction CON
FUKUYAMA, Yoshio, 1921- ,
American; nonfiction CON
FUKUZAWA YUKICHI, 1835-1901,
Japanese; nonfiction PRU
FULA, Arthur Nuthall, 1908-66,
Afrikaans; fiction, poetry
HER JA
FULBERT of CHARTRES, 975-1029,

French; nonfiction, poetry BU
TH
FULCHER of CHARTRES, 1058-
1127, French; nonfiction TH
FULCO, William James, 1936- ,
American; nonfiction CON
FULDA, Ludwig, 1862-1932, Ger-
man; plays, translations CL
FULDAUER, Ivan, 1927- , Amer-
ican; nonfiction CON
FULDHEIM, Dorothy Snell, 1893- ,
American; nonfiction CON
FULFORD, Robert ('Marshall De-
laney'), 1932- , American;
journalism, nonfiction CON
FULFORD, Roger Thomas, 1902- ,
English; nonfiction CON
FULGENTIUS, Fabius Planciades,
fl. 500, Latin; nonfiction BU
TH
FULKS, Bryan, 1897- , American;
juveniles, nonfiction CON WAR
FULLER, Alvarado M., American;
fiction NI
FULLER, Beverley ('Beverley
Bozeman'), 1927- , American;
nonfiction CON
FULLER, Catherine Leuthold,
1916- , American; juveniles
CO
FULLER, David Otis, 1903- ,
American; nonfiction CON
FULLER, Dorothy Mason ('Sterling
Thorne'), 1898- , American;
nonfiction CON
FULLER, Edmund Maybank ('Amicus
Curiae'), 1914- , American;
juveniles, fiction, nonfiction
CO CON VCN WA
FULLER, Edward C., 1907- ,
American; nonfiction CON
FULLER, Edwin Wiley, 1847-76,
American; poetry, fiction BA
FULLER, Harold, 1940- , Amer-
ican; nonfiction CON
FULLER, Henry Blake, 1857-1929,
American; fiction, journalism,
plays BR BU PO VN
FULLER, Hoyt William ('William
Barrows'), 1927/28-81, Amer-
ican; nonfiction, fiction CON
SH
FULLER, Iola see McCOY, Iola
FULLER, John Frederick Charles,
1878-1966, English; nonfiction
WA
FULLER, John Leopold, 1937- ,
British; poetry, plays, nonfiction

VCP WAK
FULLER, Lois Hamilton, 1915- ,
American; juveniles CO WAR
FULLER, Lon Luvois, 1902-78,
American; nonfiction CON
FULLER, Margaret, 1810-50,
American; nonfiction, transla-
tions, juveniles BR CO MY
PO
FULLER, Paul Eugene, 1932- ,
American; nonfiction CON
FULLER, Peter Michael, 1947- ,
British; nonfiction CON
FULLER, Richard Buckminster,
1895- , American; nonfic-
tion, poetry BR WAK
FULLER, Roy, 1912- , Eng-
lish; poetry, fiction, nonfic-
tion, juveniles BU DA KI
PO REI SEY VCN VCP VP
FULLER, Sarah Margaret, 1810-
50, American; translations,
nonfiction BU
FULLER, Samuel Michael,
1911- , American; fiction,
film, tv REI
FULLER, Thomas, 1608-61,
English; nonfiction, poetry
BU DA MAG PO RU
FULLER, William Albert, 1924- ,
Canadian; nonfiction CON
FULMER, Robert Marion, 1939- ,
American; nonfiction CON
FULTON, Gere Burke, 1939- ,
American; nonfiction CON
FULTON, Len, 1934- , Amer-
ican; fiction, nonfiction CON
FULTON, Robin, 1937- , Scots;
poetry, nonfiction, transla-
tions VCP
FULTS, John Lee, 1932- ,
American; nonfiction CON
FULWEILER, Howard Wells,
1932- , American; nonfic-
tion CON
FULWELL, Ulpian,   -1585,
English; poetry BU
FUNAHASHI SEIICHI, 1904-76,
Japanese; fiction, plays
CON HI
FUNDABURK, Emma Lila,
1922- , American; nonfiction
CON
FUNDERBURK, Guy Bernard,
1902- , American; nonfic-
tion CON
FUNIGIELLO, Philip J., 1939- ,
American; nonfiction CON

FUNK, Thompson, 1911- , Amer-
ican; juveniles CO CON
FUNK, Wilfred John, 1883-1965,
American; nonfiction, poetry
CON
FUNKE, Lewis, 1912- , American;
nonfiction, juveniles CO CON
FUNT, Julian, 1907?-80, American;
tv, plays CON
FUNT, Marilyn, 1937- , American;
nonfiction CON
FUNYA no YASUHIDE, 9th century,
Japanese; poetry HI
FUOSS, Robert Martin, 1912-80,
American; journalism CON
FURBEE, Leonard J., 1896?-1975,
American; nonfiction CON
FURETIERE, Antoine, 1619-88,
French; poetry, fiction BU
'FUREY, Michael' see 'ROHMER,
Sax'
FURGURSON, Ernest Baker, Jr.
('Pat Furgurson'), 1929- ,
American; nonfiction, journal-
ism CON
FURLONG, Alice, 1875?- , Irish;
poetry HO
FURLONG, Thomas, 1794-1827,
Irish; poetry HO
FURMANOV, Dmitry Andreyevich,
1891-1926, Russian; fiction
BU CL
FURNAS, Joseph Chamberlain,
1905- , American; nonfiction,
journalism, fiction CON WA
FURNESS, William Henry, 1802-
96, American; nonfiction MY
FURNISS, Warren Todd, 1921- ,
American; nonfiction CON
FURPHY, Joseph ('Tom Collins'),
1843-1912, Australian; fiction,
poetry BU DA VN
FURQAT, Zokirjon, 1858-1909,
Uzbek; poetry PRU
FURRER, Juerg, 1939- , Swiss;
juveniles CON
FURST, Alan, 1941- , American;
fiction CON
FURST, Lilian Renee, 1931- ,
Austrian-American; nonfiction
CON
FURTH, George, 1932- , Amer-
ican; plays CON
FURTH, Hans G., 1920- , Aus-
trian-American; nonfiction
CON
FURUKAWA MOKUAMI see
'MOKUAMI'

FURUKAWA, Toshi (Toshiko Kanzawa), 1924- , Japanese; juveniles CO CON

FUSCO, Margie, 1949- , American; poetry, nonfiction CON

FUSERO, Clemente, 1913-75, Italian; nonfiction CON

FUSFELD, Daniel Roland, 1922- , American; nonfiction CON

FUSHIMI TENNO, 1265-1317, Japanese; poetry HI

FUSON, Robert Henderson, 1927- , American; nonfiction CON

FUSSELL, Edwin, 1922- , American; nonfiction, fiction, poetry CON

FUSSENEGGER, Gertrud, 1912- , Austrian; fiction TH

FUTABATEI, Shimei (Hasegawa Tatsunosuke), 1864-1909, Japanese; fiction, translations, nonfiction BU HI LA PRU

FUTRELLE, Jacques, 1875-1912, American?; fiction, journalism NI REI ST

FUZE, Magema ka Magwaza, 1845?-1922?, Zulu; fiction HER

'FUZULI' (Mehmed, son of Suleyman), 1494-1556, Turkish; poetry BU

FYFE, Horace Bowne, 1918- , American; fiction AS NI

FYLEMAN, Rose Amy, 1877-1957, English; juveniles, plays, poetry, translations CO KI

FYLER, John, 1943- , American; nonfiction CON

FYSON, Jenny Grace, 1904- , British; juveniles, plays KI

G

GAAN, Margaret, 1914- , American; nonfiction CON

GAATHON, Aryeh Ludwig ('Ludwig Gruenbaum'), 1898- , Israeli; nonfiction CON

GABASHVILI, Besarion see 'BESIKI'

GABE, Dora, 1886- , Bulgarian; poetry BU

GABEL, Joseh ('Kalman Geroely'; 'Zoltan Gombossy'; 'Lucien Martin'), 1912- , Hungarian; nonfiction CON

GABEL, Medard, 1946- , American; nonfiction CON

GABIROL, Solomon ben Judah (Ibn Gabirol), 1020-57, Spanish; nonfiction, poetry BU TH

GABLE, Tom, 1944- , American; fiction CON

GABO, Naum, 1890-1977, Russian-American; nonfiction CON

GABOR, Mark, 1939- , American; nonfiction CON

GABORIAU, Emile, 1835-73, French; fiction BU MAG REI ST TH

GABOURY, Antonio, Canadian-American; nonfiction CON

GABRA, Egzi'abeher, 1860?-1914?, Ambaric; poetry HER

GABRE-MEDHIN, Tsegaye see TSEGAYE, Gabre-Medhin

GABRIEL, Henry, 1922- , Scots; plays CON

GABRIEL, Joyce, 1949- , American; journalism, fiction CON

GABRIEL, Jueri Evald, 1940- , Estonian-British; translations, nonfiction CON

GABRIEL, Luci, 1597-1663, Raeto-Romansch; nonfiction BU

GABRIEL, Mabel McAfee, 1884?-1976, British; nonfiction CON

GABRIEL, Philip Louis, 1918- , American; nonfiction, fiction CON

GABRIEL, Stefan, 1565-1638, Raeto-Romansch; poetry BU

GABRIEL-ROBINET, Louis, 1909-75, French; nonfiction CON

GABRIEL y GALAN, José María, 1870-1905, Spanish; poetry BU CL TH

GABRIELSON, Frank, 1911?-80, American; tv CON

GABRIELSON, Ira Noel, 1889-1977, American; nonfiction CON

'GABRYELLA' see ZMICHOWSKA, Narcyza

GACE BRULE, -1212?, French; poetry BU TH

GACH, Gary, 1947- , American; poetry, translations, nonfiction CON

GACHENBACH, Dick, American; juveniles WAR

GADAMER, Hans-Georg, 1900- , German; nonfiction CON

GADD, David, 1912- , English; nonfiction CON

GADDA, Carlo Emilio, 1893-1973,

Italian; fiction, nonfiction BO
BU CL CON SEY TH WA
GADDIS, J. Wilson, 1910?-75,
American; nonfiction CON
GADDIS, John Lewis, 1941- ,
American; nonfiction CON
GADDIS, William, 1922- , Amer-
ican; fiction BR HE VCN
VN WA
GADDY, Curtis Welton, 1941- ,
American; nonfiction CON
GADEAU, Germain Coffi, 1913- ,
Ivory Coaster; plays JA
GADGIL, Gangadhur Gopal,
1923- , Marathi; fiction
PRU
GADKARI, Ram Ganes, 1885-1919,
Marathi; plays PRU
GADLER, Steve J., 1905- ,
American; nonfiction CON
GADNEY, Reg, 1941- , Amer-
ican; fiction, nonfiction
CON REI
GADO, Frank, 1936- , American;
nonfiction CON
GADOLA, Gugielm, 1902-61,
Raeto-Romansch; fiction BU
GADPAILE, Warren Joseph,
1924- , American; nonfiction
CON
GADSDEN, Christopher, 1724-
1805, American; nonfiction
BA
GAEDDERT, Lou Ann Bigge,
1931- , American; juveniles
CO CON
GAEDEKE, Ralph Mortimer,
1941- , German-American;
nonfiction CON
GAEDIATY, Taomaq, 1882-1931,
Ossetian; poetry, journalism,
nonfiction PRU
GAFF, Jerry Gene, 1936- ,
American; nonfiction CON
GAFFNEY, James, 1931- ,
American; nonfiction CON
GAFFNEY, Merrill Mason,
1923- , American; nonfiction
CON
GAG, Flavia, 1907-79, American;
juveniles CO
GAG, Wanda Hazel, 1893-1946,
American; juveniles COM
KI
GAGARIN, Michael, 1942- ,
American; nonfiction CON
GAGE, Edwin, 1943- , American;
fiction CON

GAGE, Nathaniel Lees, 1917- ,
American; nonfiction CON
'GAGE, Nicholas' see NGAGO-
YEANES, Nicholas
'GAGE, Wilson' see STEELE,
Mary Q.
GAGER, Nancy Land, 1932?-80,
American; nonfiction CON
GAGER, William, 1555-1622, Eng-
lish; plays BU
GAGLIANO, Frank, 1931- , Amer-
ican; plays CON VCD
GAGLAIRDO, Ruth Garver, 1895?-
1980, American; juveniles CO
GAGNIER, Ed, 1936- , American;
nonfiction CON
GAHERTY, Sherry, 1951- , Amer-
ican; nonfiction CON
GAIL, Marzieh, American; transla-
tions, nonfiction CON
GAIL, Otto Willi, 1896-1956, Ger-
man; fiction NI
GAILEY, Harry Alfred, 1926- ,
American; nonfiction CON
GAIMAR, Geoffrey, fl. 1140, Anglo-
Norman; nonfiction BU
GAINES, Ernest J., 1933- ,
American; fiction BA HE SH
VCN WAK WAR
GAINES, Jacob (Jack), 1918- ,
American; nonfiction CON
GAINES, Richard L., 1925- ,
American; nonfiction CON
'GAINHAM, Sarah' (Sarah Stainer;
Rachel Ames), 1922- , Eng-
lish; fiction CON MCC REI
GAINSBRUGH, Martin Reuben, 1907-
77, American; nonfiction CON
GAINZA PAZ, Alberto, 1899-1977,
Argentinian; journalism CON
GAIO, Maestro see RIETI, Moses
di
GAISER, Gerd, 1908-76, German;
fiction, poetry, nonfiction
BU CL TH WA
GAITHER, Frances, 1889-1955,
American; juveniles, plays,
fiction BA
GAIUS, fl. 130-80, Roman; nonfic-
tion GR
GAJ, Ljudevit, 1809-72, Croatian;
nonfiction BU TH
GAJCY, Tadeusz, 1922-44, Polish;
poetry BU
GAJDUSEK, Robert Elemer (Robin),
1925- , American; nonfiction
CON
GAL, Allon, 1934- , Israeli;

nonfiction CON
GALA, Antonio, 1936- , Spanish;
plays, poetry, fiction, non-
fiction CL
GALAAL see MUSA, Hajji I. G.
'GALACTION, Gala' (Grigore Pis-
culescu), 1879-1961, Ruman-
ian; fiction BU CL
GALAMBOS, Louis Paul, 1931- ,
American; nonfiction CON
GALAND, Rene, 1923- , Franco-
American; nonfiction CON
GALANOY, Terry, 1927- , Amer-
ican; nonfiction, fiction CON
GALANTAY, Ervin Yvan, 1930- ,
Hungarian; journalism, nonfic-
tion CON
GALARZA, Ernesto, 1905- ,
American; nonfiction, fiction
MAR
GALASSI, Jonathan White, 1949- ,
American; nonfiction CON
'IL GALATEO' see DE FERRARIIS,
Antonio
'GALAXAN, Sol' see 'COPPEL,
Alfred'
GALBRAITH, Georgie Starbuck
('G. S. Page'; 'Ann Patrice';
'Penny Pennington'; 'Stuart
Pennington'), 1909-80, Amer-
ican; poetry, nonfiction CON
GALBRAITH, John Kenneth,
1908- , American; nonfiction
WA
GALBRAITH, Vivian Hunter,
1889-1976, British; nonfiction
CON
GALBREATH, Robert Carroll,
1938- , American; nonfiction
CON
GALCZYNSKI, Konstanty Ildefons,
1905-53, Polish; poetry BU
CL TH
GALDONE, Paul, 1914- , Amer-
ican; juveniles CO CON DE
GALE, Vi, American; poetry
VCP
GALE, William, 1925- , Amer-
ican; nonfiction CON
GALE, Zona, 1874-1938, Amer-
ican; fiction, poetry, plays
BR MCG VN
GALECKI, Tadeusz see 'STRUG,
Andrzej'
GALELLA, Ron, 1931- , Amer-
ican; nonfiction CON
GALEN, 129-99, Greek; nonfiction
BU GR LA

'GALENDO, P. ' see HINOJASA-
SMITH, Rolando R.
GALEWITZ, Herb, 1928- , Amer-
ican; nonfiction CON
GALIANI, Ferdinando, 1728-87,
Italian; nonfiction, plays BO
BU MCG
'GÂLIB DEDE, Seyh' (Mehmed
Esad), 1757/58-99, Turkish;
poetry BU PRU
'GALICH, Aleksandr Arkadyevich'
(Aleksandr Ginzburg), 1919-77,
Russian; poetry, plays CL
CON
GALICIA, León F. C. see
'FELIPE, Léon'
GALILEI, Galileo, 1564-1642, Ital-
ian; nonfiction BO BU TH
GALINSKY, Ellen, 1942- , Amer-
ican; juveniles, nonfiction CO
CON
GALL, Meredith Damien, 1942- ,
American; nonfiction CON
GALL, Morris, 1907- , American;
nonfiction CON
GALLACHER, Tom, 1934- , Brit-
ish; plays VCD
GALLAGHER, Buell Gordon,
1904- , American; nonfiction
CON
GALLAGHER, Charles Augustus,
1927- , American; nonfiction
CON
GALLAGHER, David P. , 1944- ,
English; nonfiction CON
GALLAGHER, Dorothy, 1935- ,
American; nonfiction CON
GALLAGHER, Edward J. , 1892?-
1978, American; journalism
CON
GALLAGHER, Frank ('David
Hogan'), 1893-1962, Irish;
journalism, fiction, nonfiction
HO
GALLAGHER, James Roswell,
1903- , American; nonfiction
CON
GALLAGHER, Mary, 1947- ,
American; plays, fiction CON
GALLAGHER, Patricia, American;
fiction CON
GALLAGHER, Patrick Francis,
1930- , American; nonfiction
CON
GALLAGHER, Rachel ('Kimbal
Drake'), American; nonfiction
CON
'GALLAGHER, Richard' see

'JORDAN, Leonard'
GALLAGHER, William M. , 1923-
75, American; journalism
CON
GALLAHER, Lee, 1935?- ,
Irish; plays HO
GALLAHUE, David Lee, 1943- ,
American; nonfiction CON
GALLANT, Mavis, 1922- ,
Canadian; fiction CON VCN
WA
GALLANT, Roy Arthur, 1924- ,
American; juveniles CO
GALLARDO, Edgar Joseph,
1939- , American; nonfic-
tion MAR
GALLARDO y BLANCO, Bartolomé
José, 1776-1852, Spanish; non-
fiction BU
GALLE, Frederick Charles,
1919- , American; nonfiction
CON
GALLE, William, 1938- , Amer-
ican; journalism CON
GALLEGO, Juan Nicasio, 1777-
1853, Spanish; poetry BU TH
GALLEGO, Laura, 1924- ,
Puerto Rican; poetry HIL
GALLEGOS, Phil, Jr. , 1948- ,
American; nonfiction MAR
GALLEGOS, Rómulo, 1884-
1968/69, Venezuelan; fiction
BR BU MAG
GALLER, Meyer, 1914- , Polish-
American; nonfiction, fiction
CON
'THE GALLERITE' see BASON,
Frederick T.
GALLERY, Daniel V. , 1901-77,
American; nonfiction CON
GALLICO, Paul William, 1897-
1976, American; journalism,
fiction, nonfiction, plays,
juveniles CO CON NI VCN
WAR
GALLIE, Walter Bryce, 1912- ,
Scots; nonfiction CON
GALLIMORE, Ronald, 1938- ,
American; nonfiction CON
GALLINA, Giacinto, 1852-97,
Italian; plays BO BU
GALLIVAN, Gerald P. , 1920- ,
Irish; plays HO
GALLMAN, Waldemar John,
1899-1980, American; non-
fiction CON
GALLNER, Sheldon Mark, 1949- ,
American; nonfiction CON

GALLO, Max, 1932- , French;
fiction, nonfiction CON
GALLO, Paulino L. A. el see
ASCASUBI, Hilario
GALLOB, Edward, American;
juveniles WAR
GALLOIS, Claire, 1938- , French;
fiction CON
GALLON, Arthur James, 1915- ,
American; nonfiction CON
GALLOP, David, 1928- , Ameri-
can; translations, nonfiction
CON
GALLOWAY, George Barnes, 1898-
1967, American; nonfiction
CON
GALLOWAY, Jonathan Fuller,
1939- , American; nonfiction
CON
GALLOWAY, Joseph Lee, 1941- ,
American; journalism CON
GALLU, Samuel, American; plays
CON
GALLUCCI, Robert Lovis, 1946- ,
American; nonfiction CON
GALLUN, Raymond Zinke ('John
Callahan'; 'Dow Elstar'; 'E. V.
Raymond'), 1911- , American;
fiction AS CON NI
GALLUS, Gaius Asinius,   -33
A. D. , Roman; nonfiction LA
GALLUS, Gaius Cornelius, 69-26
B. C. , Roman; poetry BU GR
LA
GALLUS, Marcus Fadius, fl. 45
B. C. , Roman; nonfiction LA
GALLWEY, W. Timothy, 1938- ,
American; nonfiction CON
GALOUYE, Daniel Francis, 1920-
76, American; fiction, journal-
ism AS NI
GALSTON, Arthur William, 1920- ,
American; nonfiction CON
GALSWORTHY, John, 1867-1933,
English; fiction, plays, poetry
BU DA MAG MCG PO SEY
VD VN
GALT, John, 1779-1839, Scots;
fiction, poetry, nonfiction,
plays BU DA MAG PO VN
GALT, Thomas Franklin, Jr. ,
1908- , American; juveniles
CO
GALTON, Lawrence, 1913- ,
American; nonfiction CON
GALUB, Jack ('Chuck Gant'),
1915- , American; nonfiction
CON

GALVAN, Manuel de Jesus, 1834-
1910, Spanish; fiction BR BU
GALVAN, Roberto, 1923- ,
American; nonfiction MAR
GALVAO, Antonio, 1490-1557,
Portuguese; nonfiction BU
'GALVAO, Duarte' see LEMOS,
Virgílio
GALVEZ, Manuel, 1882-1962,
Argentinian; fiction, nonfiction
BR BU
GALVEZ de MONTALVO, Luis,
1549?-91?, Spanish; fiction,
poetry BU
GALVIN, Brendan, 1938- , Amer-
ican; poetry CON
GALVIN, Patrick, 1927?- ,
Irish; plays, poetry CON HO
'GALWAY, Robert C.' see Mc-
CUTCHAN, Donald P.
GAM, Rita Elenore, 1927- ,
American; nonfiction CON
GAMA, José Basilio da, 1741?-
95, Brazilian; poetry BR BU
GAMBARA, Veronica, 1485-1550,
Italian; poetry BU
GAMBINO, Thomas Dominic,
1942- , American; poetry,
nonfiction CON
GAMBLE, Andrew Michael,
1947- , British; nonfiction
CON
GAMBLE, Quo Vadis Gex, 1950- ,
American; nonfiction SH
GAMBOA, Federico, 1864-1939,
Mexican; fiction BR BU
GAMBOA, Manuel ('Manazar'),
1934- , American; poetry
MAR
GAMBOA, Reymundo, 1948- ,
American; poetry MAR
GAMBRILL, Eileen, 1934- ,
American; nonfiction CON
GAMER, Robert Emanuel, 1938- ,
American; nonfiction CON
GAMERMAN, Martha, 1941- ,
American; juveniles CO CON
GAMEZ, Juan, American; non-
fiction MAR
'GAMEZ, Tana de' see ALBA
de GAMEZ, Cielo C.
GAMM, David Bernard, 1948- ,
American; nonfiction, juven-
iles CON
GAMMAGE, William Leonard,
1942- , American; nonfiction
CON
GAMMELL, Susana Valentine

(Mitchell), 1897?-1979, Amer-
ican; poetry, fiction CON
GAMMON, Roland, 1820-81, Amer-
ican; nonfiction CON
GAMMOND, Peter, 1925- , Brit-
ish; nonfiction CON
GAMOW, George, 1904-68, Russian;
nonfiction CON NI
GAMSAKHURDIA, Konstantine,
1891- , Georgian; fiction LA
PRU
GANDARA, Albert, 1948- , Amer-
ican; journalism, nonfiction
MAR
GANDHI, Mohandas Karamchand,
1869-1948, Indian; nonfiction
BU LA
GANDLEY, Kenneth Royce see
'ROYCE, Kenneth'
GANGESA, 13th century, Indian;
nonfiction PRU
GANGWERE, Robert Jay, 1936- ,
American; nonfiction CON
GANGOPADHYAY, Narayan (Ganguli),
1918-70, Bengali; nonfiction
PRU
GANIVET, Angel, 1865-98, Spanish;
nonfiction, fiction BU CL
GANN, Ernest Kellogg, 1910- ,
American; fiction, nonfiction
WA
GANNETT, Lewis Stiles, 1891-
1966, American; journalism,
nonfiction CON
GANNETT, Ruth Stiles, 1923- ,
American; juveniles CO DEM
KI
GANNON, Robert Haines, 1931- ,
American; juveniles CO
GANNON, Robert Ignatius, 1893-
1978, American; nonfiction
CON
'GANPAT' (Martin Louis Alan Gom-
pertz), 1886-1951, American;
fiction, nonfiction NI
GANS, Bruce Michael, 1951- ,
American; journalism, nonfic-
tion, fiction CON
GANS, Roma, 1894- , American;
nonfiction, juveniles CON WAR
GANSBERG, Judith M., 1947- ,
American; nonfiction CON
GANSFORT, Wessel, 1419-89,
Dutch; nonfiction BU
GANS-RUEDIN, Erwin, 1915- ,
Swiss; nonfiction CON
GANSS, George Edward, 1905- ,
American; translations, non-

fiction CON
'GANT, Chuck' see GALUB, Jack
GANT, Elizabeth, American; juven-
   iles WAR
GANT, Katherine, American;
   juveniles WAR
GANT, Lisbeth, 1948- , Amer-
   ican; nonfiction SH
GANT, Phyllis, 1922- , Amer-
   ican; fiction, nonfiction CON
GANTILLON, Simon, 1887-1961,
   French; plays, film MCG
GANTOS, John Bryan, Jr.,
   1951- , American; juveniles,
   fiction CO CON WAR
GANTRY, Susan (Nadler), 1947- ,
   American; nonfiction CON
GANTT, William Andrew Horsley,
   1893-1980, American; nonfic-
   tion CON
GANTZ, Charlotte Orr, 1909- ,
   American; nonfiction CON
GANTZ, Kenneth Franklin,
   1905- , American; fiction
   NI
GANTZER, Hugh ('Arvind and
   Shanta Kale'; 'Shyam Dave'),
   1931- , American; fiction
   CON
GANZ, Arthur Frederick, 1928- ,
   American; nonfiction CON
GANZ, Margaret, 1927- ,
   Belgian-American; nonfiction
   CON
GANZO, Robert, 1898- , French;
   poetry WA
GAOS, Vicente, 1919- , Spanish;
   poetry, nonfiction CL TH
GARA, Larry, 1922- , American;
   nonfiction CON
GARAB, Arra M., 1930- , Amer-
   ican; nonfiction CON
GARARD, Ira Dufresne, 1888- ,
   American; nonfiction CON
GARAUDY, Roger, 1913- ,
   French; nonfiction CL
GARAY, János, 1812-53, Hun-
   garian; poetry, plays, jour-
   nalism BU
GARBARINO, Joseph W., 1919- ,
   American; nonfiction CON
GARBARINO, Merwyn Stephens,
   American; nonfiction CON
GARBE, Robert, 1878-1927,
   German; poetry BU
GARBER, Eugene K., 1932- ,
   American; nonfiction CON
GARBER, Frederick, 1929- ,

American; nonfiction CON
GARBO, Norman, 1919- , Amer-
   ican; fiction NI
GARBORG, Arne (Aadne), 1851-
   1924, Norwegian; fiction, po-
   etry, plays, nonfiction BU CL
   TH
GARBY, Mrs. Lee Hawkins, Amer-
   ican; fiction NI
GARCAO, Pedro Antonio, 1724-
   72/73, Portuguese; poetry BU
   TH
GARCIA, Alejandro, 1940- ,
   American; nonfiction MAR
GARCIA, Anita Huerta, 1928- ,
   American; nonfiction MAR
GARCIA, Anthony M., 1938- ,
   American; nonfiction MAR
GARCIA, Augustine, 1939- ,
   American; nonfiction MAR
GARCIA, Chris F., 1940- ,
   American; nonfiction MAR
GARCIA, Daniel Peter, 1947- ,
   American; nonfiction MAR
GARCIA, Eugene E., 1946- ,
   American; nonfiction MAR
GARCIA, Flaviano Chris, 1940- ,
   American; nonfiction CON
GARCIA, Jesus, 1941- , Amer-
   ican; nonfiction CON
GARCIA, John, 1917- , American;
   nonfiction MAR
GARCIA, Jorge, 1943- , Ameri-
   can; nonfiction MAR
GARCIA, Jose Zebedeo, 1945- ,
   American; nonfiction MAR
GARCIA, Joseph O., 1944- ,
   American; nonfiction MAR
GARCIA, Mario Ramon, 1947- ,
   Cuban-American; nonfiction
   CON
GARCIA, Mario T., 1944- ,
   American; nonfiction MAR
GARCIA, Maryellen, 1947- ,
   American; nonfiction MAR
GARCIA, Nasario, 1936- , Amer-
   ican; nonfiction MAR
GARCIA, Peter A., 1931- , Amer-
   ican; nonfiction MAR
GARCIA CALDERON, Francesco,
   1883-1953, Peruvian; nonfiction
   BR BU
GARCIA CALDERON, Ventura,
   1886-1959, Peruvian; fiction,
   nonfiction BR BU
GARCIA-CAMARILLO, Cecilio,
   1943- , American; nonfiction,
   poetry MAR

GARCIA CASTANEDA, Salvador, 1932- , Spanish-American; nonfiction CON

GARCIA de la HUERTO, Vicente, 1734-87, Spanish; plays BU MCG TH

GARCIA-GIRON, Edmundo, 1916- , American; nonfiction MAR

GARCIA GOMEZ, Emilio, 1905- , Spanish; translations TH

GARCIA GUTIERREZ, Antonio, 1813-84, Spanish; plays, poetry BU MCG TH

GARCIA HORTELANO, Juan, 1928- , Spanish; fiction CL

GARCIA LORCA, Federico, 1898-1936, Spanish; poetry, plays BU CL MAG MCG SEY TH

GARCIA MARQUEZ, Gabriel, 1928- , Colombian; fiction, journalism BR BU SEY WA

GARCIA NIETO, José, 1914- , Spanish; nonfiction, poetry CL

GARCIA PAVON, Francisco, 1919- , Spanish; nonfiction, fiction CL

GARCIA SERRANO, Rafael, 1917- , Spanish; fiction, nonfiction, journalism CL

GARCIA TASARA, Gabriel, 1817-75, Spanish; poetry BU TH

GARCIA TERRES, Jaime, 1924- , Mexican; poetry, nonfiction BR

GARCILASO de la VEGA, 1503-36, Spanish; poetry BU TH

'GARCILASO de la VEGA' ('El Inca'; Gómez Suárez de Figueroa), 1539-1616, Peruvian; nonfiction BR BU

'GARD, Joyce' (Joyce Reeves), 1911- , British; juveniles, translations CO CON KI

GARD, Robert Edward, 1910- , American; juveniles CO CON

GARDAM, Jane Pearson, 1928- , English; juveniles, fiction CON KI WAR

GARDEN, Alexander, 1730-91, American; nonfiction BA

'GARDEN, Bruce' see MACKAY, James A.

GARDEN, Nancy, 1938- , American; juveniles CO WAR

GARDEN, Robert Hal, 1937- , American; nonfiction CON

GARDINER, Charles Wrey, 1901-81, British; poetry CON

GARDINER, Dorothy, 1894-1979, American; nonfiction, fiction CON REI

GARDINER, Muriel, 1901- , American; nonfiction CON

GARDINER, Robert Worthington, 1932- , American; nonfiction CON

GARDINER, Samuel Rawson, 1829-1902, English; nonfiction BU

GARDINER, Stephen, 1925- , British; nonfiction CON

GARDIOL, Rita Mazzetti, American; nonfiction CON

GARDIZI, Abu Sa'id, 11th century, Persian; nonfiction BU

GARDNER, Alice Lucille, 1913- , American; poetry, nonfiction CON

'GARDNER, Anne' see SHULTZ, Gladys D.

GARDNER, David Bruce, 1924- , American; nonfiction CON

GARDNER, Eldon John, 1909- , American; nonfiction CON

GARDNER, Erle Stanley ('A. A. Fair'; 'Carleton Kendrake'; 'Charles J. Kenny'), 1889-1970, American; fiction, nonfiction BR REI ST VN

GARDNER, Dame Helen Louise, 1908- , English; nonfiction BOR CON WA

GARDNER, Howard, 1943- , American; nonfiction CON

GARDNER, Hy, 1908- , American; journalism, nonfiction CON

GARDNER, Isabella Stewart, 1915-81, American; poetry CON MAL VCP WA

GARDNER, Jack Irving, 1934- , American; nonfiction CON

GARDNER, Jeanne Le Monnier, American; juveniles CO

GARDNER, John, 1927- , English; fiction MCC

GARDNER, John Champlin, 1933-82, American; fiction, nonfiction, juveniles, translations CON HE NI VCN WAK WAR

GARDNER, John Edmund, 1926- , British; fiction, nonfiction REI

GARDNER, Lewis, 1943- , American; plays, nonfiction, poetry CON

GARDNER, Marilyn, American;

journalism CON
GARDNER, Martin, 1914- ,
American; journalism, juven-
iles CO CON NI WAR
GARDNER, Paul, American; non-
fiction, film CON
GARDNER, Richard ('John Car-
ver'; 'Richard Cummings';
'Richard Orth'; 'Clifford
Anderson'), 1931- , Amer-
ican; juveniles CO WAR
GARDNER, Richard Kent, 1928- ,
American; nonfiction CON
GARDNER, Richard Newton,
1927- , American; nonfiction
CON
GARDNER, Robert, 1911- ,
American; nonfiction CON
GARDNER, Robert, 1929- ,
American; juveniles WAR
GARDNER, Thomas Samuel,
1908-63, American; fiction
NI
GARDNER, Wanda Kirby, 1914- ,
American; fiction CON
GARDNER, Wayland Downig,
1928- , American; nonfiction
CON
GARDNER, Wynelle B., 1918- ,
American; fiction CON
GARDON, Margarita, Puerto
Rican; nonfiction HIL
GARDONYI, Géza, 1863-1922,
Hungarian; fiction, plays BU
CL TH
GAREAU, Etienne, 1915- ,
Canadian; nonfiction CON
GARELICK, May ('Garel Clark'),
1910- , Russian-American;
juveniles, nonfiction CO
CON
GARFIAS, Robert, 1932- ,
American; nonfiction MAR
GARFIELD, Brian ('Bennett Gar-
land'; 'Alex Hawk'; 'Drew
Mallory'; 'Frank O'Brian';
'Brian Wynne'; 'Frank Wynne';
'Jonas Ward'), 1939- ,
American; fiction MCC REI
GARFIELD, Evelyn Picon,
1940- , American; nonfic-
tion CON
GARFIELD, James B., 1881-?,
American; juveniles CO
GARFIELD, Leon, 1921- , Brit-
ish; juveniles DEM KI WAR
GARFIELD, Patricia Lee, 1934- ,
American; nonfiction CON

GARIBALDI, Giuseppe, 1807-82,
Italian; nonfiction BO
GARIEPY, Henry, 1930- , Amer-
ican; nonfiction CON
'GARIN, N. G.' (Nikolay Grigorye-
vich Mikhaylovsky), 1852-1906,
Russian; fiction BU
'GARIOCH, Robert' (R. G. Suther-
land), 1908-81, Scots; poetry
BU CON VCP
GARIS, Howard Roger ('Marion
Davidson'), 1873-1962, Amer-
ican; juveniles, fiction CO
CON NI
'GARLAND, Bennett' see GAR-
FIELD, Brian
GARLAND, Charles Talbot, 1910?-
76, American; nonfiction CON
GARLAND, Hamlin, 1860-1940,
American; fiction, nonfiction,
poetry, plays BR BU MAG
PO VN
GARLAND, John (de Garlandia),
1180-1258, English; nonfiction,
poetry BU
GARLAND, Mary, 1922- , Ger-
man-American; nonfiction CON
GARLAND, Phyllis T., 1935- ,
American; nonfiction CON SH
GARLICK, Peter Cyril, 1923- ,
American; nonfiction CON
GARLICK, Raymond Ernest,
1926- , Welsh; poetry, non-
fiction CON VCP
GARLINGTON, Phil, 1943- ,
American; journalism CON
GARNEAU, Francois Xavier, 1809-
66, Canadian; nonfiction BU
GARNEAU, Hector de Saint Denys,
1912-43, French-Canadian;
poetry BU CR WAK
GARNER, Alan, 1934/35- , Eng-
lish; juveniles, fiction, plays
BU CO CON DE KI NI
GARNER, Hessle Filmore,
1926- , American; nonfiction
CON
GARNER, Hugh ('Jarvis Warwick'),
1913- , Canadian; fiction,
nonfiction, plays BU CON CR
VCN
GARNER, Roberta ('Roberta Ash'),
1943- , American; nonfiction
CON
GARNET, Eldon, 1946- , Cana-
dian; poetry CON
GARNETT, Christopher Browne,
1906-75, American; nonfiction

CON
GARNETT, Constance Black,
1861-1946, English; transla-
tions DA
GARNETT, David ('Leda Burke'),
1892-1981, English; fiction,
nonfiction, translations BU
CON DA MAG NI VCN VN
GARNETT, David S., 1947- ,
English; fiction NI
GARNETT, Edward, 1868-1937,
English; nonfiction, plays BU
GARNETT, Emmeline, English;
juveniles WAR
GARNETT, Eve C. R., English;
juveniles CO KI
GARNETT, Richard, 1835-1906,
English; poetry, translation,
nonfiction BU DA ENG NI
'GARNETT, Roger' see MORLAND,
Nigel
GARNETT, Tay, 1894?-1977,
American; film CON
GARNETT, William John, 1941- ,
American; translations, film,
poetry, fiction CON
GARNIER, Robert, 1554-90,
French; plays, poetry BU
MCG TH
GAROFALO, Robert L. ('Reebee
Garofalo'), 1944- , Amer-
ican; nonfiction CON
GAROOGIAN, Rhoda, 1933- ,
American; nonfiction CON
GARRAD, Larch Sylvia, 1936- ,
English; nonfiction CON
GARRARD, Jeanne Sue ('Gene
Garrard'), American; jour-
nalism, nonfiction CON
GARRATY, John A., 1920- ,
American; juveniles CO
GARREAU, Joel, 1948- , Amer-
ican; journalism, nonfiction
CON
GARRETSON, Lucy Reed, 1936- ,
American; nonfiction CON
GARRETT, Almeida, 1799-1854,
Portuguese; plays, poetry,
fiction TH
GARRETT, Charles, 1925-77,
American; nonfiction CON
GARRETT, Clarke, 1935- ,
American; nonfiction CON
GARRETT, Franklin Miller,
1906- , American; nonfiction
CON
GARRETT, George Palmer,
1929- , American; poetry,

fiction, plays, nonfiction
BA HE MAG VCN VCP WA
GARRETT, Gerald R., 1940- ,
American; nonfiction CON
GARRETT, Gerard, 1928- , Brit-
ish; nonfiction CON
GARRETT, Helen, 1895- , Amer-
ican; juveniles CO
GARRETT, Howard, 1931- ,
American; nonfiction CON
GARRETT, João Baptista de Silva,
1799-1854, Portuguese; poetry,
fiction, plays BU
GARRETT, Randall ('Gordon Ag-
hill'; 'Mark Phillips'; 'Robert
Randall'), 1927- , American;
fiction AS NI
GARRETT, Richard, 1920- , Brit-
ish; journalism, nonfiction,
juveniles CON
GARRICK, David, 1717-79, Eng-
lish; nonfiction, plays BU DA
MCG VD
GARRIGUE, Jean, 1914-72, Amer-
ican; poetry, fiction BR VCP
GARRIGUE, Sheila, 1931- , Amer-
ican; juveniles CO CON WAR
GARRISON, Barbara, 1931- ,
Anglo-American; juveniles CO
GARRISON, Christian Bascom,
1942- , American; plays,
juveniles CON
'GARRISON, Frederick' see SIN-
CLAIR, Upton
GARRISON, James Dale, 1943- ,
American; nonfiction CON
GARRISON, Webb Black ('Gary
Webster'), 1919- , American;
juveniles CO
GARRISON, William Lloyd, 1805-
79, American; journalism MY
GARRITY, Devin Adair, 1906-81,
American; nonfiction CON
GARRITY, Joan Terry ('J'; 'Terry
Garrity'), 1940- , American;
nonfiction CON
GARRITY, Richard George, 1903- ,
American; nonfiction CON
GARROW, David Jeffries, 1953- ,
American; nonfiction CON
GARRY, Charles R., 1909- ,
American; nonfiction CON
GARSHIN, Vsevolod Mikhaylovich,
1855-88, Russian; fiction BU
TH
'GARSKOF, Michele H.' see
HOFFNUNG, Michele
'GARSON, Clee,' Ziff-Davis house

name NI
GARSON, Eugenia, American;
 juveniles WAR
GARSON, George David, 1943- ,
 American; nonfiction CON
GARSON, Paul, 1946- , Amer-
 ican; fiction CON NI
GARST, John Fredric, 1932- ,
 American; nonfiction CON
GARST, Robert Edward, 1900-80,
 American; journalism CON
GART, Murray Joseph, 1924- ,
 American; journalism CON
GART, Thiebold, 16th century,
 German; plays BU
GARTENBERG, Egon, 1911- ,
 Austrian-American; nonfiction
 CON
GARTH, Sir Samuel, 1661-1718/
 19, English; poetry BU DA
 PO VP
'GARTH, Will, ' house name NI
GARTHWAITE, Marion Hook,
 1893- , American; juveniles
 CO
GARTNER, Michael Gay, 1938- ,
 American; journalism CON
GARTON, Charles, 1926- ,
 Anglo-American; nonfiction
 CON
GARTON, Malinda Dean, -1976,
 American; nonfiction CON
'GARVE, Andrew' (Paul Winterton;
 'Roger Bax'; 'Paul Sommers'),
 1908- , British; fiction
 REI ST WA
GARVEY, Edward B., 1914- ,
 American; nonfiction CON
GARVEY, John, 1944- , Amer-
 ican; nonfiction CON
GARVEY, Terence Wilcocks,
 1915- , Irish; nonfiction
 CON
GARVIE, Alexander Femister,
 1934- , Scots; nonfiction
 CON
GARVIN, Charles D., 1929- ,
 American; nonfiction CON
GARVIN, Lawrence, 1945- ,
 American; plays CON
GARVIN, Philip, 1947- , Amer-
 ican; nonfiction CON
GARVIN, Richard McClellan,
 1934- , American; fiction
 CON NI
GARY, Madeleine Sophie, American;
 nonfiction SH
'GARY, Romain' (Romain Racew),

1914-80, French; fiction BU
 CL CON NI WA
GARZA, Roberto Jesus, 1934- ,
 American; plays, nonfiction
 MAR
GARZA, Rudolph O. de la, 1942- ,
 American; nonfiction MAR
GARZILLI, Enrico, 1937- , Amer-
 ican; nonfiction CON
'GASCAR, Pierre' (Pierre Fourni-
 er), 1916- , French; fiction
 CL CON WA
GASCOIGNE, George, 1539?-77,
 English; poetry, plays, trans-
 lations, fiction BU DA MAG
 MCG PO RU VP
GASCOYNE, David Emery, 1916- ,
 English; poetry, translations,
 fiction, plays, nonfiction CON
 DA PO SEY VCP VP WA
'GASH, Jonathan' see GRANT, John
'GASKE, Marina' see NJAU,
 Rebecca
GASKELL, Elizabeth Cleghorn
 Stevenson, 1810-65, English;
 fiction, nonfiction BU DA
 MAG PO VN
'GASKELL, Jane' (Jane Gaskell
 Lynch), 1941- , English; fic-
 tion NI
GASKILL, Harold V., 1905-75,
 American; nonfiction CON
GASKIN, Catherine, 1929- , Irish;
 fiction CON REI
GASKIN, David Edward, 1939- ,
 British; nonfiction CON
'GASPAR, Molendo' see ZENO
 GANDIA, Manuel
GASPARINI, Graziano, 1926- ,
 Italian; nonfiction CON
GASPE, Philippe-Joseph Aubert de,
 1786-1871, Canadian; fiction
 BU
GASQUE, Woodrow Ward, 1939- ,
 Canadian; nonfiction CON
GASS, William H., 1924- , Amer-
 ican; fiction, nonfiction BR
 HE MAG VCN WA
GASSAN, Arnold, 1930- , Amer-
 ican; nonfiction CON
GASSENDI, Pierre (Gassend), 1592-
 1655, French; nonfiction BU
GASSIER, Pierre, 1915- , French;
 nonfiction CON
'GAST, Kelly P., ' American; fiction
 CON
GASTER, Theodor Herzl, 1906- ,
 British; nonfiction CON

GASTEV, Alexey Kapitonovich,
1882- , Russian; poetry BU
GASTMANN, Albert Lodewijk,
1921- , Dutch-American; non-
fiction CON
GASTON, Jerry Collins, 1940- ,
American; nonfiction CON
GASTON PHOEBUS, Count of
Foix, 1331-91, French; non-
fiction BU
GATANYU, James, 1945- , Ken-
yan; plays HER
GATCH, Tom, Jr., 1926- ,
American; fiction NI
GATENBY, Greg, 1950- , Cana-
dian; nonfiction, poetry,
translations CON
GATER, Hubert, 1913?-80, Amer-
ican; nonfiction CON
GATES, David Murray, 1921- ,
American; nonfiction CON
GATES, Doris, 1901- , Amer-
ican; juveniles KI
GATES, Frieda, 1933- , Amer-
ican; juveniles CON
GATES, Jeannette McPherson,
1924- , American; nonfiction,
poetry CON
GATES, John D., 1939- , Amer-
ican; journalism, nonfiction
CON
GATES, Norman Timmins,
1914- , American; nonfiction
CON
GATES, William Byram, 1917-75,
American; nonfiction CON
GATHERU, Reuel John Mugo,
1925- , Kenyan; nonfiction
HER JA
GATHORNE-HARDY, Jonathan,
1933- , British; juveniles,
fiction KI
GATLEY, Richard Harry, 1936- ,
Canadian; nonfiction CON
GATLIN, Lila Lee, 1928- ,
American; nonfiction CON
'GATO, J. A.' see KELLER,
John E.
GATSOS, Nikos, 1911/14- ,
Greek; poetry, translations
SEY WAK
GATTI, Armand, 1924- ,
French; plays, journalism
BU CL MCG TH
GATTI, Arthur Gerard ('Andrew
Gerard'; 'Basho Katz';
'Charles Lane'), 1942- ,
American; nonfiction, poetry

CON
GATTI, Daniel Jon, 1946- ,
American; nonfiction CON
GATTI, Enzo, 1942- , Italian;
nonfiction CON
GATTI, Richard de Y., 1947- ,
American; nonfiction CON
GATTMANN, Eric, 1925- ,
German-American; nonfiction
CON
GATTO, Alfonso, 1909-76, Italian;
poetry, journalism BO CL
TH WAK
GATTY, Juliana H. see EWING,
Julian H.
GATTY, Ronald, 1929- , Amer-
ican; nonfiction CON
GAUCELM FAIDIT, 1185?-1220,
Provencal; poetry BU
GAUCH, Patricia Lee, 1934- ,
American; juveniles CON
GAUCHAT, Dorothy, 1921- ,
American; nonfiction CON
GAUDET, Frederick Joseph, 1902-
77, Canadian; nonfiction CON
GAUDIOSE, Dorothy Marie, 1920- ,
American; nonfiction CON
GAULDIE, Enid, 1928- , British;
nonfiction CON
GAULT, Clare, 1925- , Ameri-
can; juveniles CON
GAULT, Frank, 1926- , Ameri-
can; juveniles CON
GAULT, William Campbell ('Will
Duke'), 1910- , American;
fiction, juveniles CO CON
REI ST
GAUMNITZ, Walter Herbert, 1891-
1979, American; nonfiction
CON
'GAUNT, Michael' see ROBERT-
SHAW, James D.
GAUNT, William, 1900-80, British;
nonfiction CON
GAUQUELIN, Michel Roland,
1928- , French; nonfiction
CON
GAUTIER, Théophile, 1811-72,
French; fiction, nonfiction,
plays, poetry BU MAG TH
GAUTIER BENITEZ, José ('Gus-
tavo'), 1848/51-80, Puerto
Rican; journalism, poetry
HIL
GAUTIER d'ARRAS, 1135-98,
French; poetry BU
GAUTIER de COINCI, -1236,
French; poetry BU

GAUTIER de DARGIES, fl. 1200,
French; poetry BU
GAUTIER d'EPINAL, fl. 1220,
French; poetry BU
GAUTIER le LEU, 13th century,
French; poetry BU
GAVER, Jack, 1906?-74, American; nonfiction CON
GAVER, Jessyca Russell, 1915- ,
American; nonfiction, fiction
CON
GAVER, Rebecca, 1952- , American; juveniles CO
GAVIN, Eileen A., 1931- ,
American; nonfiction CON
GAVIN, Thomas, 1941- , American; fiction CON
GAVRONSKY, Serge, 1932- ,
Franco-American; nonfiction
CON
GAWAIN, Shakti, 1948- , American; nonfiction CON
GAWAIN POET, late 14th century, English; poetry DA
PO VP
GAWRON, Jean Mark, 1953- ,
American; fiction CON NI
'GAWSWORTH, John' see BATES,
Herbert E.
GAWTHROP, Louis C., 1930- ,
American; nonfiction CON
'GAY, Amelia' see HOGARTH,
Grace
GAY, Carlo Teofilo, 1913- ,
Italian-American; nonfiction
CON
'GAY, Francis' see GEE, Herbert L.
GAY, John, 1685-1732, English;
poetry, plays, songs BRI
BU DA MAG MCG PO VD
VP
GAY, John Edward, 1942- ,
American; nonfiction CON
GAY, Kathlyn McGarrahan,
1930- , American; juveniles
CO WAR
GAY, Zhenya, 1906-78, American; juveniles CO CON
GAYANGOS y ARCE, Pascual,
1809-97, Spanish; nonfiction,
translations BU
GAYA-NUNO, Juan Antonio, 1913-
75, Spanish; nonfiction CON
GAYARRE, Charles, 1805-95,
American; fiction, nonfiction
BA
GAY-CROSIER, Raymond,

1937- , Swiss; nonfiction
CON
GAYDOS, Michael J., 1940- ,
American; nonfiction CON
'GAYE, Carol' see SHANN, Renee
GAY-KELLY, Doreen, 1952- ,
American; juveniles CON
GAYLE, Addison, Jr., 1932- ,
American; nonfiction SH
'GAYLE, Henry K.' (Harold Gayle),
1910- , Canadian; fiction
NI
GAYLES, Anne Richardson,
1923- , American; nonfiction
CON
GAYLORD, Edward King, 1873-
1974, American; journalism
CON
GAYLORD, William, 1945- ,
American; nonfiction CON
GAYTON, Bertram, British; fiction
NI
GAZDA, George Michael, 1931- ,
American; nonfiction CON
GAZELL, James Albert, 1942- ,
American; nonfiction CON
GAZI, Stephen, 1914-78, Yugoslav-
American; nonfiction CON
GAZIS, Denos Constantinos,
1930- , Greek-American;
nonfiction CON
GAZLEY, John Gerow, 1895- ,
American; nonfiction CON
GAZZO, Michael, 1923- , American; plays MCG
GBADAMOSI, Bakare A., 1930- ,
Nigerian; fiction, poetry HER
'GDANSKI, Marek' see THEE,
Marek
GEACH, Peter Thomas, 1916- ,
British; nonfiction CON
GEAR, C. William, 1935- ,
English; nonfiction CON
GEARE, Mildred Mahler, 1888?-
1977, American; journalism
CON
GEARHART, Sally Miller, 1931- ,
American; nonfiction CON
GEARING, Catherine, 1916- ,
American; nonfiction CON
GEARNEY, John, 1926- , Canadian; nonfiction CON
GEASLAND, John Buchanan, Jr.,
1944- , American; fiction
CON
GEBHARD, Bruno Frederic,
1901- , German-American;
nonfiction CON

GEBHART, Benjamin, 1923- ,
American; nonfiction CON
GECK, Francis Joseph, 1900- ,
American; nonfiction CON
GECKLE, George L., 1939- ,
American; nonfiction CON
GEDDA, George, 1941- , Amer-
ican; journalism CON
GEDDES, Charles Lynn, 1928- ,
American; nonfiction CON
GEDDES, Joan Bel, 1916- ,
American; nonfiction CON
GEDDES, Virgil, 1897- ,
American; poetry, journalism
RO
GEDDIE, John ('M. Shannon'),
1937- , American; journal-
ism, nonfiction CON
'GEDEÃO, Antonio' (Rómulo de
Carvalho), 1906- , Portu-
guese; poetry CL
GEDYE, George Eric Rowe,
1890-1970, British; journal-
ism CON
GEE, Herbert Leslie ('Francis
Gay'), 1901-77, British;
journalism, nonfiction CON
GEE, Maurice Gaugh, 1931- ,
New Zealander; tv, fiction
CON VCN
GEE, Maurine H., American;
poetry WAR
GEEL, Jacob, 1789-1862, Dutch;
nonfiction BU TH
GEEMIS, Joseph Stephen, 1935- ,
American; nonfiction CON
GEER, Stephen DuBois, 1930- ,
American; journalism CON
GEER, Ursina C. see 'GIRUN,
Gian'
GEERTZ, Hildred, 1927- ,
American; nonfiction CON
GEESLIN, Campbell, 1925- ,
American; fiction CON
GEEFEN, Maxwell Myles, 1896-
1980, American; nonfiction
CON
GEFVERT, Constance Joanna,
1941- , American; nonfiction
CON
GEGA, Peter Christopher,
1924- , American; nonfic-
tion CON
GEHERIN, David John, 1943- ,
American; nonfiction CON
GEHLEN, Reinhard, 1902-79,
German; nonfiction CON
GEHRELS, Franz, 1922- ,

German-American; nonfiction
CON
GEHRIS, Paul, 1934- , American;
nonfiction CON
GEIBEL, Emanuel, 1815-84, Ger-
man; poetry BU TH
GEIER, Chester S., 1921- ,
American; fiction NI
GEIGEL POLANCO, Vicente, 1904-
79, Puerto Rican; journalism,
poetry, nonfiction CON HIL
GEIGER, Carl Ignaz, 1756-91,
German; fiction NI
GEIGLEY, Vance Acton, 1907- ,
American; fiction NI
GEIJER, Erik Gustaf, 1783-1847,
Swedish; nonfiction, poetry
BU TH
GEIJERSTAM, Gustaf af, 1858-
1909, Swedish; fiction BU
GEILER von KAISERSBERG,
Johann, 1445-1510, German;
nonfiction BU
GEIPEL, John, 1937- , British;
nonfiction, cartoons CON
GEIS, Darlene Stern ('Ralph Kelly';
'Jane Landon'; 'Peter Stevens'),
American; juveniles CO
GEIS, Florence Lindauer, 1933- ,
American; nonfiction CON
GEIS, Richard Erwin ('Frederick
Colson'; 'Albina Jackson';
'Sheela Kunzur'; 'Bob Owen';
'Robert N. Owen'; 'Ann Rad-
wa'; 'Peggy Swann'; 'Peggy
Swenson'), 1927- , American;
fiction, nonfiction AS CON
GEISEL, Theodore see 'SEUSS,
Dr.'
GEISER, Robert Lee ('Steven
Peters'), 1931- , American;
nonfiction CON
GEISMAR, Maxwell David, 1909-79,
American; nonfiction BOR
GEISSMAN, Erwin William, 1920-
80, American; nonfiction CON
GEIST, Kenneth Lee, 1936- ,
American; nonfiction CON
GEIST, Robert John, 1912- ,
American; nonfiction CON
GEIST, Roland C., 1896- , Amer-
ican; nonfiction CON
GEIST, Valerius, 1938- , Russian-
Canadian; nonfiction CON
GEITGEY, Doris A., 1920- ,
American; nonfiction CON
GEKIERE, Madeleine, 1919- ,
American; juveniles DE

GELB, Joyce, 1940- , American; nonfiction CON
GELB, Leslie Howard, 1937- , American; nonfiction CON
GELBART, Larry Simon, 1923- , American; tv, film, plays CON
GELBER, Jack, 1932- , American; plays, fiction BR BU MCG MCN PO VCD WA
GELBER, Steven Michael, 1943- , American; nonfiction CON
GELDARD, Frank Arthur, 1904- , American; nonfiction CON
GELDART, William, 1936- , English; juveniles CO
GELDENHAUER, Gerardus, 1482-1542, Dutch; nonfiction BU
GELEGBALSANG, 1846-1923, Mongolian; poetry PRU
GELFAND, Morris Arthur, 1908- , American; nonfiction CON
GELFMAN, Judith Schlein ('Judy Starr'), 1937- , American; nonfiction CON
GELFOND, Rhoda, 1946- , American; poetry CON
GELINAS, Gratien, 1909- , French-Canadian; plays BU MCG
GELINAS, Paul J., 1911- , American; juveniles, nonfiction CO CON
'GELL, Frank' see KOWET, Don
GELLER, Bruce, 1930-78, American; tv CON
GELLER, Uri, 1946- , Israeli; nonfiction CON
GELLERT, Christian Furchtegott, 1715-69, German; poetry, fiction, plays BU TH
'GELLERT, Lew' see WELLEN, Edward P.
GELLES, Richard J., 1946- , American; nonfiction CON
GELLHORN, Martha Ellis, 1908- , American; journalism, fiction, nonfiction CON VCN
GELLI, Giambattista, 1498-1563, Italian; fiction BO BU TH
GELLINEK, Janis Little see SOLOMON, Janis L.
GELLIUS, Aulus, 123?-165, Roman; nonfiction BU GR LA
GELLIUS, Gnaeus, fl. 150 B.C., Roman; nonfiction LA
GELLMAN, Estelle Sheila,

1941- , American; nonfiction CON
GELLMAN, Irwin Frederick, 1942- , American; nonfiction CON
GELMAN, David Graham, 1926- , American; journalism CON
GELMAN, Rita Golden, 1937- , American; journalism, juveniles CON
GELMAN, Steve, 1934- , American; juveniles CO WAR
GELMIS, Joseph Stephan, 1935- , American; nonfiction CON
GELSTED, Einar Otto, 1888-1968, Danish; poetry, nonfiction BU CL
'GEMIER, Firmin' (Firmin Tonnerre), 1869-1933, French; theater CL
GEMME, Leila Boyle, 1942- , American; nonfiction CON
GEMMILL, Paul F., 1890?-1976, American; nonfiction CON
GEMMING, Elizabeth, 1932- , American; juveniles, translations CO CON
GENDRON, George M., 1949- , American; journalism CON
GENESIUS, Joseph, mid 10th century, Byzantine; nonfiction LA
GENESTET, Petrus Augustus de, 1829-61, Dutch; poetry BU
'GENÊT' see FLANNER, Janet
GENET, Jean, 1910- , French; plays, fiction, poetry BU CL MCG SEY TH WA
GENETTE, Gérard, 1930- , French; nonfiction CL
GENEVOIX, Maurice, 1890-1980, French; fiction, nonfiction BU CL CON
GENG, Veronica, American; juveniles WAR
GENGENBACH, Pamphilus, 1480-1524/25, Swiss; poetry, plays BU
'GENN, Calder' see GILLIE, Christopher
GENNARO, Joseph Francis, Jr., 1924- , American; nonfiction CON
GENNEP, Jaspar von, 1515-80, German; printer, plays BU
GENOVESE, Eugene Dominick, 1930- , American; nonfiction CON WAK
GENSER, Cynthia ('Chinas Comidas'),

1950- , American; poetry
CON
GENSZLER, George William II,
1915- , American; nonfiction
CON
GENT, Peter, 1942- , American;
fiction, film CON
GENTIL, Richard, 1917- , Amer-
ican; nonfiction CON
GENTILE, Giovanni, 1875-1944,
Italian; nonfiction BO BU CL
GENTLEMAN, David William,
1930- , English; juveniles
CO
GENTRY, Curt, 1931- , Amer-
ican; fiction NI
'GENTRY, Peter' see NEWCOMB,
Kerry; SCHAEFER, Frank
GENTZLER, Jennings Mason,
1930- , American; nonfiction
CON
'GEOFFREY, Theodate' see
WAYMAN, Dorothy G.
GEOFFREY of MONMOUTH, 1100-
55, English; nonfiction BU
DA
GEOFFREY of VINSAUF, fl.
1210, English; nonfiction BU
GEOGHEGAN, Arthur Gerald,
1810?-89, Irish; poetry HO
GEORGAKAS, Dan, 1938- ,
American; nonfiction, poetry
CON
GEORGE, Collins Crusor, 1909- ,
American; journalism CON
'GEORGE, David' see VOGENITZ,
David G.
GEORGE, Edgar Madison, 1907-
75, American; nonfiction
CON
GEORGE, Emery Edward, 1933- ,
Hungarian-American; nonfic-
tion CON
GEORGE, Henry, 1839-97, Amer-
ican; nonfiction BR BU PO
GEORGE, Jean Craighead,
1919- , American; juveniles,
plays KI
GEORGE, John Edwin, 1936- ,
American; nonfiction CON
'GEORGE, Jonathan' see BURKE,
John F.
GEORGE, Malcom Farris, 1930- ,
American; nonfiction CON
GEORGE, Peter ('Peter Bryant'),
1924-66, Welsh; fiction AS
NI
GEORGE, Sara, 1947- , English;

fiction CON
GEORGE, Sidney Charles, 1898- ,
English; juveniles, nonfiction,
fiction CO CON
GEORGE, Stefan, 1868-1933, Ger-
man; poetry BU CL MAG SEY
TH
GEORGE, Susan Akers, 1934- ,
American; nonfiction CON
GEORGE, William Lloyd, 1900?-
75, American; juveniles CON
GEORGE, William Richard Philip,
1912- , Welsh; poetry CON
GEORGE ACROPOLITES, 1217-82,
Byzantine; nonfiction BU
GEORGE CEDRENUS, late 11th
century, Byzantine; nonfiction
BU
GEORGE CODINUS CUROPALATES,
14th century, Byzantine; non-
fiction BU
GEORGE GEMISTUS PLETHON,
1355-1452, Byzantine; nonfic-
tion BU
GEORGE MONACHUS (Hamartolus),
9th century, Byzantine; nonfic-
tion BU
GEORGE of PISIDIA, early 7th cen-
tury, Byzantine; poetry LA
GEORGE of TREBIZOND, 1395-
1484, Greek; nonfiction BU
GEORGE PACHYMERES, 1242-
1310, Byzantine; nonfiction
BU
GEORGE PHRANTZES (Sphrantzes),
1401- , Byzantine; nonfiction
BU
GEORGE PISIDES, 7th century,
Byzantine; poetry BU GR
GEORGE SCHOLARIUS (Gennadius),
-1468, Byzantine; nonfiction
BU
GEORGE SYNCELLUS, -810/14,
Byzantine; nonfiction LA
GEORGE the MONK (Archimandrite;
Hamartolus), fl. 842-67,
Greek; nonfiction GR LA
GEORGE the SYNCELLUS, fl. 750-
810, Byzantine; nonfiction BU
'GEORGES, Georges Martin' see
SIMENON, Georges
GEORGIEV, Mihalaki, 1854-1916,
Bulgarian; fiction BU
GEORGIOU, Constantine, 1927- ,
American; juveniles CO
GEORGIOU, Steven Demetre ('Cat
Stevens'), 1948- , British;
nonfiction CON

GEORGOPOULOS, Basil Spyros,
1926- , Greek-American;
nonfiction CON
GEPHART, William Jay, 1928- ,
American; nonfiction CON
GERACI, Philip C., 1929- ,
American; journalism, non-
fiction CON
'GERALDY, Paul' (Paul Lefèvre-
Géraldy), 1885- , French;
poetry, plays BU MCG
GERARD, Alexander, 1728-95,
Scots; nonfiction DA
'GERARD, Andrew' see GATTI,
Arthur G.
GERARD, David, 1909- , Amer-
ican; nonfiction CON
GERARD, David, 1923- , Scots;
nonfiction CON
GERARD, Ralph Waldo, 1900-74,
American; nonfiction CON
GERAS, Adele Daphne, 1944- ,
American; juveniles CO
CON
GERAS, Norman Myron, 1943- ,
American; nonfiction CON
GERASIMOV, Gennadi Ivanovitch,
1930- , Russian-American;
nonfiction CON
GERASSI, John, 1931- , Amer-
ican; juveniles WAR
GERAUD, Andre ('Pertinax'),
1882-1974, French; journal-
ism, nonfiction CON
GERBER, David Allison, 1944- ,
American; nonfiction CON
GERBER, Israel Joshua ('Ben
Mordechai'), 1918- , Amer-
ican; nonfiction CON
GERBER, John, 1907?-81, Amer-
ican; nonfiction CON
GERBER, Sanford Edwin, 1933- ,
American; nonfiction CON
GERBERS, Teresa, 1933- ,
American; fiction CON
GERBERT, 950-1003, Latin; non-
fiction GR
GERBERT of AURILLAC, 940?-
1003, French?; nonfiction
TH
GERBERT de MONTREUIL, 13th
century, French; poetry BU
GERBI, Antonello ('Don Ferrante'),
1904-76, Italian; nonfiction
CON
GERBNER, George, 1919- ,
Hungarian-American; nonfiction
CON

GERCHUNOFF, Alberto, 1883-1950,
Argentinian; journalism, fiction
BR
GERENA BRAS, Gaspar, 1909- ,
Puerto Rican; journalism,
poetry HIL
GERGELY, Tibor, 1900-78, Hun-
garian-American; juveniles
CO
GERHARD, Happy, 1920- , Amer-
ican; nonfiction CON
GERHARD von MINDEN, German;
fiction BU
GERHARDIE, William Alexander,
1895-1977, English; fiction,
plays, nonfiction CON NI VCN
VN
GERHARDT, Lydia Ann, 1934- ,
American; nonfiction CON
GERHARDT, Paul, 1607-76, Ger-
man; poetry BU TH
GERHART, Gail M., 1943- ,
American; nonfiction CON
GERHART, Genevra, 1930- ,
American; nonfiction CON
GERIG, Reginald Roth, 1919- ,
American; nonfiction CON
GERIN-LAJOIE, Antoine, 1824-82,
Canadian; poetry, fiction BU
GERLACH, John, 1941- , Amer-
ican; nonfiction CON
GERLACH, Luther Paul, 1930- ,
American; nonfiction CON
GERLACH, Russel Lee, 1939- ,
American; nonfiction CON
GERLACH, Vernon Samuel,
1922- , American; nonfiction
CON
GERLER, William Robert, 1917- ,
American; nonfiction, juveniles
CON WAR
GERMACAW, Takla Hawaryat,
1915- , Amharic; plays, fic-
tion HER
GERMAIN, Edward B., 1937- ,
American; nonfiction CON
GERMAN, Daniel see 'GRANIN,
Daniel'
GERMAN, Donald Robert, 1931- ,
American; nonfiction CON
GERMAN, Gene Arlin, 1933- ,
American; nonfiction CON
GERMAN, Joan Wolfe, 1933- ,
American; nonfiction, poetry
CON
GERMAN, Tony, 1924- , Canadian;
juveniles CON
GERMAN, Yury Pavlovich (Herman),

1910- , Russian; fiction BU
GERMANI, Gino, 1911- , Italian-
Argentinian; nonfiction CON
GERMANICUS (Nero Claudius
Germanicus), 15 B. C. -19
A. D., Latin; poetry GR LA
GERMANUS see BACHUR, Elijah
GERMANY, Vera Josephine, Eng-
lish; fiction CON
GERMINO, Dante Lee, 1931- ,
American; nonfiction CON
GERNSBACK, Hugo, 1884-1967,
American; fiction AS CON
COW NI
'GEROELY, Kalman' see GABEL,
Joseph
GEROLD, Karl, 1906-73, German;
journalism CON
GEROSA, Guido ('Sergio Guado'),
1933- , Italian; nonfiction,
film CON
GEROV, Nayden, 1823-1900, Bul-
garian; poetry BU
GEROW, Edwin, 1931- , Amer-
ican; nonfiction CON
GEROW, Joshua R., 1941- ,
American; nonfiction CON
GERRETSON, Frederik C. see
'GOSSAERT, Geerten'
GERRIETTS, John, 1912- ,
American; nonfiction CON
GERROLD, David, 1944- , Amer-
ican; fiction AS CON COW
NI
GERSCHENKRON, Alexander Pav-
lovich, 1904- , Russian-
American; nonfiction CON
GERSHATOR, Phillis, 1942- ,
American; nonfiction, poetry,
juveniles CON
GERSHENZON, Mikhail Osipovich,
1869-1925, Russian; nonfiction
BU
GERSHOM ben JUDAH (Me'or
Hagolah'), 960-1028, German;
poetry BU
GERSHON, Karen see TRIPP,
Karen
GERSHOY, Leo, 1897-1975,
Russian-American; nonfiction
CON
GERSHWIN, George, 1898-1937,
American; composer MCG
GERSON, Corinne, 1927- ,
American; fiction CON
GERSON, Jean (Jean Le Charlier),
1363-1428, French; nonfiction
BU

GERSON, Noel Bertram ('Anne
Marie Burgess'; 'Michael Bur-
gess'; 'Samuel Edwards'; 'Paul
Lewis'; 'Leon Phillips'; 'Carter
A. Vaughan'), 1914- , Amer-
ican; juveniles, nonfiction, fic-
tion CO CON
GERSON, Walter Max, 1935- ,
American; nonfiction CON
GERSONI, Diane (Gersoni-Stavn),
1947- , American; nonfiction
CON
GERSONIDES, Levi ben Gerson
('Ralbag'), 1288-1344, Hebrew;
nonfiction BU TH
GERSTAD, John Leif, 1924-81,
American; plays CON
GERSTER, Patrick George, 1942- ,
American; nonfiction CON
GERTH, Hans Heinrich, 1908-78,
German; poetry, nonfiction,
translations CON
GERULAITIS, Leonardas Vytautas,
1928- , Lithuanian-American;
nonfiction CON
GERVAIS, Charles Henry (Marty),
1946- , Canadian; journalism,
poetry, juveniles, nonfiction
CON
GERZON, Mark, American; nonfic-
tion CON
GESCHWENDER, James Arthur,
1933- , American; nonfiction
CON
GESSNER, Lynne ('Merle Clark'),
1919- , American; juveniles
CO
GERSTÄCKER, Friedrich, 1816-72,
German; fiction BU
GERSTENBERG, Heinrich Wilhelm
von, 1737-1823, German; plays,
poetry, nonfiction BU MCG
TH
GERSTLE, Kurt Herman, 1923- ,
German-American; nonfiction
CON
GERTEIS, Louis Saxton, 1942- ,
American; nonfiction CON
GERTH, Donald Rogers, 1928- ,
American; nonfiction CON
GERVASE of TILBURY, 1140-1220,
English; nonfiction BU
GERVASI, Frank Henry, 1908- ,
American; juveniles, journalism
WAR
GERVINUS, Georg Gottfried, 1805-
71, German; nonfiction TH
GESSNER, Salomon, 1730-88,

Swiss; nonfiction, poetry BU
TH
GESTON, Mark Symington, 1946- ,
American; fiction AS CON
COW NI
GETHERS, Peter, 1953- , Amer-
ican; fiction CON
GETHING, Thomas Wilson, 1939- ,
American; nonfiction CON
GETTENS, Rutherford John, 1900?-
74, American; nonfiction CON
GETTINGS, Eunice J., 1901?-78,
American; nonfiction CON
'GETTLEMAN, Susan' see BRAI-
MAN, Susan
GETTY, Gerald Winkler, 1913- ,
American; nonfiction CON
GETTY, Hilda F., 1938- , Ar-
gentinian-American; nonfiction
CON
GETTY, Jean Paul, 1892-1976,
American; nonfiction CON
GETZ, Malcolm, 1945- , Amer-
ican; nonfiction CON
GETZELS, Jacob Warren, 1912- ,
Polish-American; nonfiction
CON
GETZOFF, Carole, 1943- ,
American; nonfiction CON
GEUDER, Patricia Ann, 1931- ,
American; nonfiction MAR
GEVERS, Marie, 1883-1975,
Belgian; poetry, fiction BU
CL
GEWEHR, Wolf Max, 1939- ,
German; nonfiction CON
GEWIRTZ, Jacob Leon, 1924- ,
American; nonfiction CON
GEYL, Pieter Catharinus ('A. v.
d. Merwe'), 1887-1966, Dutch;
nonfiction, translations CON
WA
GEZELLE, Guido, 1830-99, Flem-
ish; poetry BU TH
GHADIMI, Hossein, 1922- ,
Iranian-American; nonfiction
CON
GHALIB, Mirza Asadullah Khan,
1797-1869, Urdu; poetry
BU LA PRU
GHAVVASI, 17th century, Urdu;
poetry PRU
GHAZALI, Abu Hamid, 1058/59-
1111, Islamic; nonfiction BU
LA PRU
GHAZAROS PHARPETSI, late 5th
century, Armenian; nonfiction
PRU

GHAZARYAN see 'SEVAK, Paruir'
GHEDDO, Piero, 1929- , Italian;
journalism, nonfiction CON
GHELARDI, Robert Anthony,
1939- , American; nonfiction
CON
'GHELDERODE, Michel de' (Adolphe
Adhémar Martens), 1898-1962,
Belgian; plays BU CL CON
MCG SEY TH WA
GHEON, Henri (Henri Vangeon),
1875-1944, French; plays BU
CL MCG TH
GHERARDI, Gherardo, 1891-1949,
Italian; journalism, plays
MCG
GHERARDI, Giovanni (Giovanni da
Prato), 1367-1442/46, Italian;
poetry BU
GHERARDI del TESTA, Tommaso,
1818-81, Italian; fiction, plays
BU
GHICA, Ion, 1816-97, Rumanian;
nonfiction BU
GHIGNA, Charles, 1946- , Amer-
ican; poetry CON
GHIL, René, 1862-1925, French;
poetry BU CL
GHIOTTO, Renato, 1923- , Italian;
fiction CON
GHISELIN, Brewster, 1903- ,
American; poetry, nonfiction
VCP
GHISELIN, Michael Tenant, 1939- ,
American; nonfiction CON
GHISTELE, Cornelis van, 1520-
70?, Dutch; poetry BU
GHNASSIA, Maurice Jean ('J. H.
Morriss'), 1920- , American;
fiction, plays CON
GHOSE, Aurobindo (Sri Aurobindo),
1872-1950, Indian; poetry, non-
fiction BU DA WAK
GHOSE, Manmohan, 1869-1924,
Indian; poetry VP
GHOSE, Sri Chinmoy Kumar ('Chin-
moy'), 1931- , Indian; nonfic-
tion CON
GHOSE, Sudhin N., 1889/99- ,
Indian; fiction BU DA
GHOSE, Zulfikar, 1935- , British;
fiction, poetry, nonfiction
CON NI VCN VCP
GHOSH, Jyotis Chandra, 1904?-75,
American; nonfiction CON
GHOSH, Tapan, 1928- , Indian;
fiction CON
GHOUGASSIAN, Joseph Peter,

1944- , Egyptian-American;
nonfiction CON
GHULAM FARID, 1845-1901, Pun-
jabi; poetry PRU
GHULOM, Ghafur, 1903-66, Uzbek;
poetry, nonfiction, fiction
PRU
GIACOMETTI, Paolo, 1816-82,
Italian; plays MCG
GIACOMINO da VERONA, mid 13th
century, Italian; poetry BU
GIACOMINO PUGLIESE, fl. 1200-
50, Italian; poetry BO BU
GIACOMO da LENTINI, early
13th century, Italian; poetry
BU
GIACOSA, Giuseppe, 1847-1906,
Italian; poetry, plays, jour-
nalism BO BU MCG TH
GIACUMAKIS, George, Jr., 1937- ,
American; nonfiction CON
GIALLOMBARDO, Rose Mary,
1925- , American; nonfiction
CON
GIAMATTI, Angelo Bartlett,
1938- , American; nonfiction
CON
GIAMBONI del VECCHIO, late
13th century, Florentine;
translations BU
GIAMBULLARI, Pier Francesco,
1495-1555, Italian; nonfiction
BU
GIANCARLI, Gigio Artemio, fl.
1500-50, Italian; plays MCG
GIANNARIS, George B., 1936- ,
Greek-American; nonfiction,
poetry CON
GIANNI degli ALFANI, 1271?-
1283?, Italian; poetry BO
GIANNI dei RICEVUTI, Lapo,
1270-1330, Italian; poetry BU
GIANNONE, Pietro, 1676-1748,
Italian; nonfiction BO BU
GIANNONI, Carlo Borromeo,
1939- , American; nonfiction
CON
GIANNOTTI, Donato, 1492-1573,
Italian; nonfiction, plays BO
BU MCG
GIBALDI, Joseph, 1942- ,
American; nonfiction CON
'GIBB, Lee' see WATERHOUSE,
Keith S.
GIBBARD, Graham Stewart,
1942- , American; nonfiction
CON
GIBBON, Edward, 1737-94, Eng-

lish; nonfiction BRI BU DA
PO MAG VN
GIBBON, John Murray, 1875-1952,
Canadian; poetry, nonfiction,
fiction CR
'GIBBON, Lewis Grassic' (James
Leslie Mitchell), 1901-35,
Scots; fiction, nonfiction BU
DA NI PO VN
GIBBON, Perceval, 1879-1926,
South African; poetry, fiction
BU
GIBBON, Vivian, 1917- , British;
nonfiction, juveniles CON
GIBBON, William Monk, 1896- ,
Irish; poetry, nonfiction BU
CON HO VCP
GIBBONS, Barbara Halloran,
1934- , American; nonfiction
CON
GIBBONS, Euell Theophilus, 1911-
75, American; nonfiction CON
GIBBONS, Floyd Phillip, 1886-
1939, American; fiction NI
GIBBONS, Gail, 1944- , American;
juveniles CO CON
GIBBONS, Maurice, 1931- , Cana-
dian; fiction, nonfiction, poetry
CON
GIBBONS, Reginald, 1947- ,
American; nonfiction, transla-
tions, poetry CON
GIBBONS, Stella Dorothea, 1902- ,
British; fiction, juveniles,
poetry DA MAG VCN
GIBBS, Alonzo Lawrence, 1915- ,
American; juveniles CO
GIBBS, C. Earl, 1935- , Ameri-
can; nonfiction CON
GIBBS, Cecilia May, 1877-1969,
Australian; juveniles, poetry
KI
GIBBS, Esther, 1904- , American;
nonfiction CON
'GIBBS, Henry' see 'HARVESTER,
Simon'
GIBBS, Henry St. J. C. Rumbold-
see 'HARVESTER, Simon'
GIBBS, James Atwood, 1922- ,
American; nonfiction CON
GIBBS, Joanifer, 1947- , Ameri-
can; nonfiction CON
GIBBS, John Gamble, 1930- ,
American; nonfiction CON
'GIBBS, Lewis' (Joseph Walter
Cove), 1891- , British;
fiction NI
'GIBBS, Mary Ann' see BIDWELL,

Marjory E. S.
GIBBS, Philip H., 1877-1962,
English; fiction, journalism,
nonfiction CON MCC
GIBBS, Wolcott, Jr. ('Tony
Gibbs'), 1935- , American;
nonfiction CON
GIBLIN, Charles Homer, 1928- ,
American; nonfiction CON
GIBNEY, Frank Bray, 1924- ,
American; journalism, non-
fiction CON
GIBRAN, Jean, 1933- , Amer-
ican; nonfiction CON
GIBRAN, Kahlil (Jibran), 1883-
1931, Syrian-American; fic-
tion, poetry, nonfiction BU
PRU
GIBSON, Alexander Dunnett, 1901-
78, American; nonfiction CON
GIBSON, Althea see DARBEN,
Althea G.
GIBSON, Arrell Morgan, 1921- ,
American; nonfiction CON
GIBSON, Charline, 1937- ,
American; nonfiction CON SH
GIBSON, Colin, New Zealander;
fiction NI
GIBSON, D. Parke, 1930-79,
American; nonfiction CON
GIBSON, Edward Lawrence,
1935- , American; fiction,
plays CON
GIBSON, Elsie Edith, 1907- ,
American; nonfiction
GIBSON, Gifford Guy, 1943- ,
American; nonfiction CON
GIBSON, Guadalupe, American;
nonfiction MAR
GIBSON, Hamilton Bertie, 1914- ,
British; nonfiction CON
GIBSON, James Jerome, 1904- ,
American; nonfiction CON
GIBSON, James William, 1932- ,
American; nonfiction CON
GIBSON, Janice Thorne, 1934- ,
American; nonfiction CON
'GIBSON, Josephine' see HINE,
Al; JOSLIN, Sesyle
GIBSON, Margaret, 1944- ,
American; nonfiction CON
GIBSON, Margaret, 1948- ,
Canadian; nonfiction CON
GIBSON, Miles, 1947- , British;
poetry CON
GIBSON, Nevin Herman, 1915- ,
American; nonfiction CON
GIBSON, Richard Thomas, 1931- ,

American; fiction, nonfiction
CON
GIBSON, Robert Donald D., 1927- ,
English; nonfiction CON
'GIBSON, Rosemary' see NEWELL,
Rosemary
GIBSON, Shirley, 1927- , Cana-
dian; nonfiction CON
GIBSON, Walter B. ('Ishi Black';
'Douglas Brown'; 'Maxwell
Grant'; 'Maborushi Kineji'),
1897- , American; fiction,
nonfiction REI ST
GIBSON, Walter Samuel, 1932- ,
American; nonfiction CON
GIBSON, Wilfred Wilson, 1878-
1962, English; poetry DA PO
GIBSON, William, 1914- , Amer-
ican; plays, poetry, fiction,
nonfiction BR MCG MCN VCD
WA
'GICARU, Muga' (John Mwangi),
1920- , Kenyan; fiction, non-
fiction HER JA LA
GICHON, Mordechai, 1922- ,
German-Israeli; nonfiction
CON
GIDAL, Peter, 1946- , British;
nonfiction, film CON
GIDDINS, Gary, 1948- , American;
journalism CON
GIDE, André, 1869-1951, French;
fiction, plays, poetry, nonfic-
tion BU CL MAG SEY TH
GIDLEY, Gustavus Mick, 1941- ,
British; nonfiction CON
GIDLOW, Elsa, 1898- , Anglo-
American; poetry, nonfiction
CON
GIDNEY, James B., 1914- ,
American; translations, non-
fiction CON
GIEGLING, John Allan, 1935- ,
American; juveniles CO
GIELGUD, Gwen see DUBOV, Gwen
GIELGUD, Val Henry, 1900- ,
British; fiction, plays, radio
REI ST
GIERE, Ronald Nelson, 1938- ,
American; nonfiction CON
GIEROW, Karl Ragnar, 1904- ,
Swedish; poetry, nonfiction,
plays BU
GIESBRECHT, Martin Gerhard,
1933- , American; nonfiction
CON
GIESSLER, Phillip Bruce, 1938- ,
American; nonfiction CON

GIESY, John Ulrich, 1877-1948,
American; fiction NI
GIFF, Patricia Reilly, 1935- ,
American; juveniles CON
GIFFARD, Hardinge G. see
HALSBURY, Earl of
GIFFIN, Frederick Charles,
1938- , American; nonfiction
CON
GIFFIN, Sidney F. , 1907-77,
American; nonfiction CON
GIFFORD, Barry, 1946- , Amer-
ican; poetry, nonfiction CON
GIFFORD, Denis, 1927- , Brit-
ish; nonfiction, fiction CON
GIFFORD, Don Creighton, 1919- ,
American; nonfiction, poetry
CON
GIFFORD, James Fergus, Jr. ,
1940- , American; nonfiction
CON
GIFFORD, Prosser, 1929- ,
American; nonfiction CON
GIFFORD, Thomas Eugene,
1937- , American; fiction
CON REI
GIFFORD, William, 1756-1826,
English; nonfiction, poetry
BU PO
GIGANTE, Arturo, 1890- ,
Puerto Rican; fiction, jour-
nalism HIL
GIGGAL, Kenneth see 'ROSS,
Angus'
GIGLI, Girolamo, 1660-1722,
Italian; plays BU
GIGUERE, Diane, 1937- , Cana-
dian; fiction CR
GIGUERE, Roland, 1929- ,
Canadian; poetry BU
'GIJSEN, Marnix' (J. A. Goris),
1899- , Flemish; poetry,
fiction, nonfiction BU CL
TH
GIL, Carlos B. , 1937- , Amer-
ican; nonfiction MAR
GIL, Ildefonso Manuel, 1912- ,
Spanish; poetry, fiction, non-
fiction CL
GIL de BIEDMA, Jaime, 1929- ,
Spanish; poetry, nonfiction
CL
GIL GILBERT, Enrique, 1919- ,
Ecuadorian; fiction BR
GIL y CARRASCO, Enrique, 1815-
46, Spanish; fiction, poetry
BU TH
GIL y ZARATE, Antonio, 1793-

1861, Spanish; plays, poetry
BU MCG
GIL-ALBERT, Juan, 1906- ,
Spanish; poetry CL
GILBERT, Agnes Joan S. , 1931- ,
American; juveniles CO
GILBERT, Amy Margaret, 1895- ,
American; nonfiction CON
GILBERT, Anne, 1927- , Amer-
ican; nonfiction CON
'GILBERT, Anthony' see MALLE-
SON, Lucy B.
GILBERT, Arlene Elsie, 1934- ,
American; nonfiction CON
GILBERT, Ben William, 1918- ,
American; nonfiction CON
GILBERT, Charles, 1913- , Eng-
lish; nonfiction CON
GILBERT, Christine Bell, 1909- ,
American; nonfiction CON
GILBERT, Douglas, 1942- ,
American; nonfiction CON
GILBERT, Edmund William, 1900-
73, English; nonfiction CON
GILBERT, Edwin, 1907?-76,
German-American; fiction,
plays, film CON
GILBERT, Florence Ruth, 1917- ,
New Zealander; poetry VCP
GILBERT, Gabriel, 1610-80,
French; plays, poetry BU
GILBERT, George ('Gil Jordan';
'Pam Stevens'), 1922- ,
American; nonfiction CON
GILBERT, Gordon Allan, 1942- ,
Scots-American; nonfiction
CON
GILBERT, Gustave M. , 1911-77,
American; nonfiction CON
GILBERT, Harriett, 1948- , Eng-
lish; fiction, nonfiction CON
GILBERT, Sir Humfrey, 1539?-83,
English; nonfiction BU
GILBERT, Jack, 1925- , Ameri-
can; poetry BR
GILBERT, Sir John Thomas, 1829-
98, Irish; nonfiction HO
GILBERT, Julie Goldsmith, 1949- ,
American; plays CON
GILBERT, Lerman Zack, 1925- ,
American; plays, poetry CON
GILBERT, Michael Francis,
1912- , English; fiction, plays
REI ST WA
GILBERT, Milton, 1909?-79,
American; nonfiction CON
GILBERT, Neil, 1940- , American;
nonfiction CON

GILBERT, Nicolas Joseph Laurent, 1751-80, French; poetry BU TH

GILBERT, Robert Emile, 1939- , American; nonfiction CON

GILBERT, Lady Rosa Mulholland, 1841-1921, Irish; fiction, poetry HO

GILBERT, Russell Wieder, 1905- , American; nonfiction CON

GILBERT, Sandra Mortola, 1936- , American; nonfiction, fiction CON

GILBERT, Sara Dulaney, 1943- , American; juveniles, nonfiction CO CON WAR

GILBERT, Stephen, 1912- , British; fiction HO NI

GILBERT, Stuart Reid, 1948- , Canadian; plays CON

GILBERT, Sir William Schwenck, 1836-1911, English; plays, poetry, juveniles BU DA MAG MCG PO VD WAR

GILBERT, Willie ('Oscar Bensol'; 'Glenville Mareth'), 1916- , American; plays, tv, film CON

GILBOA, Amir (Mir), 1917- , Hebrew; poetry BU WA

GILBORN, Alice, 1936- , American; nonfiction CON

GILBREATH, Alice, 1921- , American; juveniles CO

GILBREATH, Larry Kent, 1945- , American; nonfiction CON

GILCHRIST, Agnes Addison, 1907-76, American; nonfiction CON

GILDAS, 500-70, Roman; nonfiction BU DA

GILDAY, Robert M. , 1925?-80, American; nonfiction CON

GILDER, Eric, 1911- , British; plays, nonfiction CON

GILDER, Richard Watson, 1844-1909, American; journalism, poetry BR

GILDNER, Judith, 1943- , American; nonfiction CON

GILDON, Charles, 1665?-1724, English; plays, nonfiction, poetry BU

GILDRIE, Richard Peter, 1945- , American; nonfiction CON

GILDZEN, Alex, 1943- , American; poetry CON

GILES, Frederick John, 1928- ,

Canadian; nonfiction CON

GILES, James Richard, 1937- , American; nonfiction, fiction CON

GILES, Kenneth see 'McGIRR, Edmund'

'GILES, Norman' (Norman Robert McKeown), 1879-1947, South African; fiction BU

GILFILLAN, Edward Smith, Jr. , 1906- , American; nonfiction CON

GILFORD, Madeline Lee, 1923- , American; nonfiction CON

GILGE, Jeanette, 1924- , American; juveniles, fiction CO

GILGOFF, Alice, 1946- , American; nonfiction CON

GILHOOLEY, John, 1940- , American; plays CON

GILIOMEE, Hermann Buhr, 1938- , South African; nonfiction CON

GILISON, Jerome Martin, 1935- , American; nonfiction CON

GILKIN, Iwan, 1858-1924, Belgian; poetry, plays BU CL

'GILL, Alan' see GILLESPIE, Alfred

GILL, Brendan, 1914- , American; fiction, nonfiction, poetry BR CON VCN

GILL, Charles Ignace Adélard, 1871-1918, Canadian; poetry CR

GILL, David Lawrence, 1934- , British; poetry VCP

GILL, Derek Lewis, 1919- , American; nonfiction, juveniles CO CON

GILL, Inayat Khera, 1924- , German; nonfiction CON

GILL, Margery, 1925- , Scots; juveniles CO DEM

GILL, Peter, 1939- , British; plays CON VCD

GILL, Richard, 1922- , American; nonfiction CON

GILL, Ronald Crispin, 1916- , British; nonfiction CON

GILLAN, Garth J. , 1939- , American; nonfiction CON

GILLAN, Patricia Wagstaff, 1936- , British; nonfiction CON

GILLEN, Mollie, 1908- , Australian; nonfiction CON

GILLES, Albert Simeon, Sr. ('Oklahoma Peddler'), 1888- ,

American; nonfiction, poetry
CON
GILLES, Daniel, 1917- , Belgian;
fiction CL CON
GILLES de PARIS, fl. 1200, Latin;
poetry BU
GILLES le VINIER, -1252,
French; poetry BU
GILLESPIE, A. Lincoln, Jr.,
1895-1950, American; nonfic-
tion RO
GILLESPIE, Alfred ('Alan Gill'),
1924- , American; fiction
CON
GILLESPIE, Bruce, 1947- ,
Australian; fiction NI
GILLESPIE, Iris Sylvia ('Iris
Andreski'), 1923- , English;
nonfiction CON
GILLESPIE, James Ernest, Jr.,
1940- , American; nonfiction
CON
GILLESPIE, John Thomas, 1928- ,
Canadian-American; nonfiction
CON
GILLESPIE, Marcia Ann, 1944- ,
American; nonfiction SH
GILLET, Lev, 1892?-1980, Brit-
ish; nonfiction CON
GILLETT, John David, 1913- ,
English; nonfiction CON
GILLETT, Mary Bledsoe, Amer-
ican; juveniles CO
GILLETTE, Henry Sampson,
1915- , American; juveniles
CO
GILLETTE, Paul, 1938- , Amer-
ican; nonfiction, fiction, trans-
lations CON
GILLETTE, Virginia Mary ('J.
Sloan McLean'), 1920- ,
American; fiction CON
GILLETTE, William Hooker, 1853/
55-1937, American; plays,
fiction MCG VD
GILLIAM, Dorothy Butler,
1936- , American; nonfiction
CON
GILLIAM, Florence, American;
journalism RO
GILLIAMS, Maurice, 1900- ,
Flemish; fiction, poetry BU
'GILLIAN, Kay' see SMITH, Kay
N.
GILLIARD, Edmond, 1875-1969,
Swiss; nonfiction, poetry BU
GILLIATT, Penelope, 1932- ,
British; fiction, plays, non-

fiction NI VCN WAK
GILLIE, Christopher ('Calder
Genn'), 1914- , British; non-
fiction CON
GILLIE, Oliver John, 1937- ,
English; nonfiction CON
GILLIES, John, 1925- , American;
nonfiction, plays CON
GILLIGAN, Edmund, 1898-1973,
American; journalism, fiction
CON
GILLIGAN, Sonja Carl, 1936- ,
American; nonfiction CON
GILLILAND, Cleburne Hap, 1918- ,
American; nonfiction CON
GILLIN, Caroline Julia, 1932- ,
American; nonfiction CON
GILLIN, John Philip, 1907-73,
American; nonfiction CON
GILLINGHAM, John Bennett,
1940- , British; translations,
nonfiction CON
GILLINGS, Richard John, 1902- ,
British; nonfiction CON
GILLINGS, Walter, 1912- , Eng-
lish; journalism, fiction AS
NI
GILLION, Kenneth Lowell, 1929- ,
New Zealander; nonfiction CON
GILLIS, Everett Alden, 1914- ,
American; poetry CON
GILLIS, James Louis, 1857-1917,
American; nonfiction ENG
GILLMER, Thomas Charles,
1911- , American; nonfiction
CON
GILLMOR, Charles Stewart, 1938- ,
American; nonfiction CON
GILLMOR, Daniel S., 1917?-75,
American; nonfiction CON
GILLMOR, Donald Miles, 1926- ,
Canadian; nonfiction CON
GILLON, Diana Pleasance, 1915- ,
?; fiction NI
GILLON, Meir Selig, 1907- ,
English; fiction, journalism
NI
GILLOTT, Jacky, 1939-80, British;
journalism, fiction, nonfiction
CON
GILLULY, James, 1896-1980,
American; nonfiction CON
GILLUM, Helen Louise, 1909- ,
American; juveniles, film CON
GILMAN, Caroline Howard, 1794-
1888, American; fiction, poetry
BA MYE
GILMAN, Dorothy see BUTTERS,

Dorothy
GILMAN, Esther, 1925- , American; juveniles CO
'GILMAN, George G.' see HARK-NETT, Terry
'GILMAN, J. D.' see ORGILL, Douglas
'GILMAN, James' see GILMORE, Joseph
GILMAN, Richard, 1925- , American; nonfiction CON
'GILMAN, Robert C.' see 'COP-PEL, Alfred'
GILMAN, Sander Lawrence, 1944- , American; nonfiction CON
GILMAN, William Henry, 1911-76, American; nonfiction CON
'GILMER, Ann' see ROSS, William E. D.
GILMER, Francis Walker, 1790-1826, American; nonfiction BA
GILMORE, Alec, 1928- , British; nonfiction CON
GILMORE, Al-Tony, 1946- , American; nonfiction CON
'GILMORE, Anthony' (Harry Bales; Desmond W. Hall), ?; fiction NI
GILMORE, Christopher Cook ('C. C. Pary'), 1940- , American; fiction CON
GILMORE, Daniel Francis, 1922- , American; journalism CON
GILMORE, Harold Lawrence, 1931- , American; nonfiction CON
GILMORE, Haydn, 1928- , American; nonfiction CON
GILMORE, Iris, 1900- , American; juveniles CO CON
GILMORE, Joseph Lee ('Daniel Bennett'; 'James Gilman'), 1929- , American; fiction, nonfiction CON
GILMORE, Mary Jean, 1865-1962, Australian; poetry BU VP
GILMORE, Thomas Barry, Jr., 1932- , American; nonfiction CON
GILMOUR, H. B., 1939- , American; fiction CON
GILMOUR, Robert Scott, 1940- , American; nonfiction CON
GILNER, Elias, 1888?-1976,

Russian-American; plays, fiction CON
GILORE, Maeve, British; nonfiction CON
GILPIN, Alec Richard, 1920- , American; nonfiction CON
GILPIN, William, 1724-1804, English; nonfiction BU PO
GILROY, Frank Daniel, 1925- , American; plays, fiction, juveniles CON MCG MCN VCD
GILROY, Thomas Laurence, 1951- , American; juveniles, nonfiction CON
GILSON, Charles James Louis ('Barbara Gilson'), 1878-1943, English; juveniles COM
GILSON, Etienne, 1884-1978, French; nonfiction CL CON
GIMENEZ ARNAU y GRAN, José Antonio, 1912- , Spanish; fiction, plays MCG
GIMENEZ CABALLERO, Ernesto, 1899- , Spanish; journalism BU
GIMFERRER, Pere, 1945- , Spanish; poetry, nonfiction CL
GIMMESTAD, Victor Edward, 1912- , American; nonfiction CON
GIMPEL, Jean, 1918- , French; nonfiction CON
GINANDES, Shepard, 1928- , American; nonfiction CON
GINDER, Richard ('Christopher Mc-Glynn'; 'Michael Monday'), 1914- , American; nonfiction CON
GINER de los RIOS, Francisco, 1839-1915, Spanish; nonfiction BU CL
GINGER, Ann Fagan, 1925- , American; nonfiction CON
GINGERICH, Owen Jay, 1930- , American; nonfiction, translations CON
GINGERICH, Willard, 1945- , American; nonfiction MAR
GINGRICH, Arnold, 1903-76, American; journalism, nonfiction CON
GINNES, Judith S. ('Paige Mitchell'), American; fiction CON
GINNINGS, Harriett W. see 'HARRIETT'
GINNS, Patsy Lee Moore, 1937- , American; nonfiction, poetry CON

GINOTT, Haim G. , 1922-73,
Israeli-American; nonfiction
CON
GINSBERG, Allen, 1926- ,
American; poetry BR BU
MAL PO SEY VCP VP WA
GINSBURG, Herbert Paul, 1939- ,
American; nonfiction CON
GINSBURG, Louis, 1895-1976,
American; poetry CON
GINSBURG, Mirra, Russian-
American; fiction, translations
CO NI WAR
GINSBURG, Ruth Bader, 1933- ,
American; nonfiction CON
GINSBURGS, George, 1932- ,
American; nonfiction CON
GINTIS, Herbert, 1940- , Amer-
ican; nonfiction CON
GINZBERG, Asher see 'AHAD
HA-AM'
GINZBERG, Yevgeniya, 1906?-77,
Russian; nonfiction CON
GINZBURG, Alekandr see 'GALICH,
Aleksandr A. '
GINZBURG, Natalia Levi ('Ales-
sandra Tournimparte'), 1916- ,
Italian; fiction, plays BO
BU CL CON WA
GINZBURG, Simeon, 1890-1944,
Hebrew; poetry BU
GIOBERTI, Vincenzo, 1801-52,
Italian; nonfiction BO BU TH
GION NANKAI, 1677?-1751,
Japanese; poetry, nonfiction
HI
GIONO, Jean, 1895-1970, French;
fiction, plays, nonfiction BU
CL CON MAG MCG SEY TH
GIORDAN, Alma Roberts, 1917- ,
American; poetry, fiction,
nonfiction CON
GIORDANI, Pietro, 1774-1848,
Italian; nonfiction BU
GIORDANO da PISA (da Rivalto),
1260-1311, Italian; nonfiction
BU
GIOSEFFI, Daniela, 1941- ,
American; plays, fiction,
poetry CON
GIOVACCHINI, Peter Louis,
1922- , American; nonfiction
CON
GIOVANINETTI, Silvio, 1901-59,
Italian; plays MCG
GIOVANNI, Nikki, 1943- , Amer-
ican; poetry, juveniles, non-
fiction BA CO KI MAL SH

VCP WAK WAR
GIOVANNI FIORENTINO, 14th cen-
tury, Florentine; nonfiction,
fiction BO BU
GIOVANOPOULOS, Paul Arthur,
1939- , Greek-American;
juveniles CO DEM
GIOVENE, Andrea, 1904- , Italian;
nonfiction, fiction CON
GIOVIO, Paolo, 1483-1552, Italian;
nonfiction BO BU
GIPE, George, 1933- , American;
fiction, nonfiction CON
GIPPIUS, Zinaida Nikolayevna
(Hippius), 1869-1945, Russian;
nonfiction, poetry BU CL SEY
TH WAK
GIPSON, Frederick Benjamin, 1908-
73, American; juveniles, fic-
tion, film, nonfiction CO CON
DE KI
GIPSON, John Durwood, 1932- ,
American; nonfiction CON
GIPSON, Lawrence Henry, 1880-
1971, American; nonfiction
WA
GIRAGOSIAN, Newman H. , 1922- ,
American; nonfiction CON
GIRALDI, Giambattista ('Il Cinzio'),
1504-73, Italian; nonfiction,
poetry, fiction, plays BO BU
MCG TH
GIRALDI, Giglio Gregorio (Lilius
Gregorius Gyraldus), 1479-1552,
Italian; poetry BU
GIRALDUS CAMBRENSIS (Gerald of
Barry), 1145/47-1223?, Nor-
man-Welsh; nonfiction BU DA
GIRARD, Antoine see SAINT-
AMANT, Marc A. de G.
GIRARD, Henri see 'ARNAUD,
Georges'
GIRARD, James Preston, 1944- ,
American; fiction CON
GIRARD, Joe, 1928- , American;
nonfiction CON
GIRARD, Pierre, 1892-1956, Swiss;
poetry, fiction BU
GIRARD, Robert Colby, 1932- ,
American; nonfiction CON
GIRARD d'AMIENS, 13th century,
French; poetry BU
'GIRAUD, Albert' (Albert Kayen-
bergh), 1860-1929, Belgian;
poetry, nonfiction BU CL
GIRAUD, Giovanni, 1776-1834,
Italian; poetry, plays MCG
GIRAUD, Marcel, 1900- , French;

nonfiction CON
GIRAUDOUX, Jean, 1882-1944,
French; nonfiction, fiction,
plays BU CL MAG MCG
SEY TH
GIRDLESTONE, Cuthbert Morton,
1895-1975, British; nonfiction
CON
GIRHORI, Makhdum Abdu'r-rahim,
1739-78, Sindhi; poetry PRU
GIRION, Barbara, 1937- , Amer-
ican; juveniles CON
GIRLEANU, Emil, 1878-1914,
Rumanian; nonfiction BU
GIROD, Gerald Ralph, 1939- ,
American; nonfiction CON
GIRODO, Michel, 1945- , French-
Canadian; nonfiction CON
GIRONELLA, José María, 1917- ,
Spanish; fiction CL CON
MAG
GIROUD, Francoise, 1916- ,
Swiss; nonfiction CON
GIROUX, André, 1916- , Cana-
dian; fiction CR
GIROUX, Joan, 1922- , Canadian;
nonfiction CON
GIRRI, Alberto, 1919- , Ar-
gentinian; poetry BR
'GIRUN, Gian' (Ursina Clavuot-
Geer), 1898- , Raeto-
Romansch; fiction BU
GIRVAN, Helen Masterman,
1891- , American; nonfiction,
juveniles CON
GIRZAITIS, Loretta, 1920- ,
American; nonfiction CON
'GISANDER' see SCHNABEL,
Johann G.
GISHFORD, Anthony Joseph,
1908-75, British; nonfiction,
translations CON
GISSING, George Robert, 1857-
1903, English; fiction, non-
fiction BU DA MAG PO VN
GITCHOFF, George Thomas
(Tom), 1938- , American;
nonfiction CON
GITIN, David Daniel, 1941- ,
American; poetry CON
GITIN, Maria Kathleen, 1946- ,
American; poetry CON
GITLOW, Benjamin, 1891-1965,
American; nonfiction CON
GITTER, A. George, 1926- ,
Polish-American; nonfiction
CON
GITTINGER, James Price, Amer-

ican; nonfiction CON
GITTINGS, Jo Grenville ('Jo Man-
ton'), 1919- , English; juven-
iles CO
GITTINGS, Robert William, 1911- ,
British; poetry, plays, nonfic-
tion, juveniles CO VCP WAK
GITTLEMAN, Sol, 1934- , Amer-
ican; nonfiction CON
GIUDEO, Manoello see IMMANUEL
ben SOLOMON
GIUDICI, Ann Couper ('Ann Tuck-
er'), 1929- , American; non-
fiction, film CON
GIUDICI, Giovanni, 1924- , Italian;
poetry CL
GIURLANI, Aldo see 'PALAZ-
ZESCHI, Aldo'
GIUSTI, Giuseppe, 1809-50, Italian;
nonfiction, poetry BO BU TH
GIUSTI, Vincenzo, 1532-1619, Ital-
ian; plays MCG
GIUSTINIAN, Leonardo, 1388-1446,
Italian; poetry BU
GIVENS, Johns, 1943- , American;
nonfiction CON
GIVNER, Abraham, 1944- , Amer-
ican; nonfiction CON
'GJALLANDI, Thorgils' (Jón Stefáns-
son), 1851-1915, Icelander; fic-
tion BU
GJELLERUP, Karl Adolph, 1857-
1919, Danish; fiction BU CL
TH
GJÖRWELL, Carl Christoffer, 1731-
1811, Swedish; nonfiction BU
GLAD, Paul Wilbur, 1926- , Amer-
ican; nonfiction CON
GLADDEN, Vivianne Cervantes,
1927- , American; nonfiction
CON
GLADE, William Patton, Jr.,
1929- , American; nonfiction
CON
GLADILIN, Anatoly Tikhonovich,
1935- , Russian; nonfiction
CL CON
GLADISH, David Francis, 1928- ,
American; poetry CON
GLADKOV, Fëdor Vasileyevich,
1883-1958, Russian; fiction
BU CL
GLADSTONE, Arthur M. ('Maggie
Gladstone'; 'Lisabet Norcross';
'Margaret Sebastian'; 'Cilla
Whitmore'), 1921- , American;
fiction CON
GLADSTONE, Gary, 1935- ,

American; juveniles CO
GLADSTONE, Meredith, 1939- ,
American; nonfiction CON
GLADSTONE, Myron J. , 1923- ,
American; nonfiction CON
GLADSTONE, William Ewart,
1809-98, English; nonfiction
BU
GLANVILL, Joseph, 1636-80,
English; nonfiction BU DA
GLANVILLE, Bartholomew de
see BARTHOLOMAEUS
ANGLICUS
GLANVILLE, Brian, 1931- ,
English; fiction, juveniles,
nonfiction VCN WA WAR
GLANVILLE, Ernest, 1856-1925,
South African; fiction BU
GLANVILLE, Maxwell, 1918- ,
British; plays, poetry CON
'GLANZ, Aaron' see 'LEYELES,
A. '
GLANZ, Rudolf, 1892- , Austrian-
American; nonfiction CON
GLAPTHORNE, Henry, 1610-43,
English; plays, poetry BU
DA PO VD
GLASER, Daniel, 1918- , Amer-
ican; nonfiction CON
GLASER, Dianne Elizabeth,
1937- , American; juveniles
CON
GLASER, Isabel Joshlin, 1929- ,
American; poetry, nonfiction,
fiction CON
GLASER, Milton ('Max Catz'),
1929- , American; juveniles
CO DEM
GLASGOW, Ellen Anderson, 1874-
1945, American; fiction, poetry,
nonfiction AM BA BR BU
MAG PO VN
GLASGOW, Eric, 1924- , British;
nonfiction CON
GLASHEEN, Adaline, 1920- ,
American; nonfiction CON
GLASKIN, Gerald Marcus ('Neville
Jackson'), 1923- , American;
fiction, nonfiction, plays
CON NI
GLASPELL, Susan, 1882-1948,
American; fiction, plays,
juveniles COM MCG MCN
PAL VD
GLASRUD, Bruce Alden, 1940- ,
American; nonfiction CON
GLASS, Andrew James, 1935- ,
Polish-American; nonfiction
CON

GLASS, Bill, 1935- , American;
nonfiction CON
GLASS, David Victor, 1911-78,
British; nonfiction CON
GLASS, Ian Cameron, 1926- ,
American; journalism CON
GLASS, Joanna McClelland,
1936- , Canadian; fiction,
plays CON
GLASS, John Franklin, 1936- ,
German-American; nonfiction
CON
'GLASS, Sandra' see SHEA, Robert
J.
GLASSCO, John Stinson ('Miles
Underwood'), 1909-81, Cana-
dian; poetry, translations,
fiction BU CON VCN VCP
GLASSER, Stephen Andrew, 1943- ,
American; nonfiction CON
GLASSER, William, 1925- ,
American; nonfiction CON
GLASSGOLD, Peter, 1939- ,
American; nonfiction CON
GLASSMAN, Jon David, 1944- ,
American; nonfiction CON
GLASSNER, Martin Ira, 1932- ,
American; nonfiction CON
GLASSTONE, Victor, 1924- ,
English; nonfiction CON
GLATSTEIN, Jacob, 1896-1971,
Yiddish; poetry, nonfiction BU
GLATZER, Hal, 1946- , Ameri-
can; fiction CON
GLAUBER, Uta Heil, 1936- ,
German; juveniles CO
GLAVIN, John Patrick, 1933- ,
American; nonfiction CON
GLAZAROVA, Jarmila Podivinská,
1901- , Czech; fiction BU TH
GLAZE, Eleanor, 1930- , Amer-
ican; fiction CON
GLAZEBROOK, George Parkin de,
1899- , Canadian; nonfiction
CON
GLAZER, Tom, 1914- , American;
juveniles, nonfiction CO CON
WAR
GLEADOW, Rupert Seeley ('Justin
Case'), 1909-74, British; non-
fiction CON
GLEASNER, Diana Cottle, 1936- ,
American; nonfiction, juveniles
CON
GLEASON, Judith, 1929- , Amer-
ican; nonfiction CO CON
GLEASON, Ralph Joseph, 1917-75,
American; nonfiction CON

GLEASON, Robert James, 1906- ,
American; nonfiction CON
GLEASON, Sarel Everett, 1905-
74, American; nonfiction CON
GLEAVES, Robert Milnor,
1938- , American; nonfic-
tion CON
GLEIM, Johann Wilhelm Ludwig,
1719-1803, German; poetry
BU TH
GLEIMAN, Lubomir, 1923- ,
American; nonfiction CON
GLEMSER, Bernard see 'CRANE,
Robert'
GLEN, Duncan, 1933- , Scots;
poetry, nonfiction VCP
'GLEN, Eugene' see FAWCETT,
Frank D.
GLENDAY, Alice, 1920- , Cana-
dian-American; fiction CON
'GLENDENNING, Donn' see
PAINE, Lauran B.
GLENDINNING, Richard, 1917- ,
American; juveniles CO
GLENDINNING, Sara Wilson
('Sally Glendinning'), 1913- ,
American; juveniles CO CON
GLENDON, Mary Ann, 1938- ,
American; nonfiction CON
GLENN, Jacob B., 1905-74,
American; nonfiction CON
'GLENN, James' see PAINE,
Lauran B.
GLENN, Jerry Hesmer, Jr.,
1938- , American; nonfiction
CON
GLENN, Lois Ruth, 1941- ,
American; nonfiction CON
GLENN, Morton Bernard, 1922- ,
American; nonfiction CON
GLENNY, Michael Valentine,
1927- , British; translations,
nonfiction CON
GEES, Margaret Breitmaier,
1940- , American; juveniles,
nonfiction CO CON
GLESS, Darryl James, 1945- ,
American; nonfiction CON
GLICK, Carl Cannon ('Captain
Frank Cunningham'; 'Peter
Holbrook'), 1890-1971, Amer-
ican; juveniles, plays CO
CON PAL
GLICK, Ruth Burtnick, 1942- ,
American; nonfiction CON
GLICK, Virginia (Kirkus), 1893-
1980, American; journalism,
juveniles CO CON

GLICKMAN, Albert Seymour,
1923- , American; nonfiction
CON
GLICKMAN, Arthur P., 1940- ,
American; nonfiction CON
GLICKMAN, Beatrice Marden,
1919- , American; nonfiction
CON
GLIDDEN, Frederick Dilley ('Luke
Short'), -1975, American;
fiction CON
GLIEWE, Unada Grace ('Unada'),
1927- , American; juveniles
CO
GLIKBERG, Alexander M. see
'CHORNY, Sasha'
GLIMCHER, Arnold B., 1938- ,
American; nonfiction CON
GLINES, Carroll Vane, Jr.,
1920- , American; juveniles
CO
GLINKA, Fëdor Nikolayevich, 1786-
1880, Russian; poetry BU
GLIOZCO, Charles, 1932- , Amer-
ican; nonfiction CON
GLISIC, Milovan, 1847-1908, Ser-
bian; fiction, plays BU TH
GLOAG, John Edwards, 1896-1981,
English; nonfiction, fiction
CON NI
GLOAG, Julian, 1930- , British;
fiction CON VCN
GLOB, Peter Vilhelm, 1911- ,
Danish; nonfiction CON
GLOCK, Charles Young, 1919- ,
American; nonfiction CON
GLOGAU, Arthur H., 1922- ,
American; nonfiction CON
GLOGAU, Lillian Flatow Fleischer,
1925- , American; nonfiction
CON
GLORFELD, Louis Earl, 1916- ,
American; nonfiction CON
GLOSTER, Hugh Morris, 1911- ,
American; nonfiction SH
GLOVACH, Linda, 1947- , Amer-
ican; juveniles CO WAR
GLOVER, Albert Gould, 1942- ,
American; nonfiction CON
GLOVER, Denis James Matthews
('Peter Kettle'), 1912-80, New
Zealander; poetry, plays, non-
fiction BU CON DA VCP VP
GLOVER, Harry, 1912- , British;
nonfiction CON
GLOWACKI, Aleksander see 'PRUS,
Boleslaw'
GLUBOK, Shirley Astor, 1933- ,

American; juveniles CO DE
GLUCK, Felix, 1923-81, German; nonfiction CO CON
GLUCK, Herb, 1925- , American; nonfiction CON
GLUCKMAN, Max, 1911-75, South African; nonfiction CON
GLÜCK, Louise Elisabeth, 1943- , American; poetry MAL VCP WAK
GLUECK, Sheldon, 1896-1980, Polish-American; nonfiction CON
GLUECKEL von HAMELN, 1645-1724, Jewish; nonfiction TH
GLYCAS, Michael (Michael Sikidites), mid 12th century, Byzantine; nonfiction, poetry LA
GLYN, Anthony, 1922- , American; fiction CON NI
GLYN, Richard Hamilton, 1907-80, British; nonfiction CON
GLYNN, James A., 1941- , American; nonfiction CON
GLYNN, Thomas Peter, 1935- , Canadian-American; fiction CON
GLYNNE-JONES, William, 1907- , Welsh; juveniles CO
GMELCH, George, 1944- , American; nonfiction CON
GMELCH, Sharon Bohn, 1947- , American; nonfiction CON
GNAEDINGER, Mary, 1898-1976, American; editor NI
GNAEGY, Charles ('Chris Grange'; 'Chuck Gregory'), 1938- , American; nonfiction, juveniles CON
GNAGEY, Thomas David, 1938- , American; nonfiction CON
GNAGY, Michael Jacques ('John Gnagy'), 1907?-81, American; nonfiction CON
GNAPHEUS, Guilhelmus (Willem de Volder), 1493-1568, Dutch; nonfiction BU
GNAROWSKI, Michael, 1934- , Canadian; poetry, nonfiction CON VCP
GNEDICH, Nikolay Ivanovich, 1784-1833, Russian; poetry, translations BU
GNESSIN, Uri-Nissan, 1879-1913, Polish; fiction BU
GNOLI, Count Domenico ('Giulio Orsini'), 1838-1915, Italian;

nonfiction, poetry BU
'GNOSTICUS' see WESCHECKE, Carl L.
GOACHER, Denis, 1925- , British; poetry, nonfiction VCP
'GOAMAN, Muriel' see COX, Edith M.
GOBAR, Ash, 1930- , American; nonfiction CON
GOBETTI, Piero, 1901-26, Italian; nonfiction CL
GOBHAI, Mehlli, Indian; juveniles WAR
GOBINEAU, Joseph Arthur de, 1816-82, French; fiction, nonfiction, poetry BU TH
GOBLE, Dorothy, English; juveniles CON WAR
GOBLE, Neil, American; fiction NI
GOBLE, Paul, 1933- , American; juveniles CO CON DEM WAR
GOCEK, Matilda Arkenbout, 1923- , American; nonfiction CON
GODAIGO TENNO, 1288-1339, Japanese; poetry HI
GODARD, Jean Luc ('Hans Lucas'), 1930- , French; film CON
GODBER, Noël, 1881- , British; fiction NI
GODBOUT, Jacques, 1933- , Canadian; fiction, poetry BU CR
'GODDARD, Alfred' see HARPER, Carol E.
GODDARD, Gladys Benjamin, 1881?-1976, American; poetry, fiction, nonfiction CON
GODDARD, Nettye George, 1923- , American; nonfiction SH
GODDEN, Geoffrey, 1929- , British; nonfiction CON
GODDEN, Jon, 1906- , English; fiction CON WA
GODDEN, Rumer, 1907- , British; fiction, nonfiction, juveniles, translations CO KI VCN
GODE von AESCH, Alexander ('Alex Gode'), 1906-70, German-American; juveniles CO
GODECHOT, Jacques Leon, 1907- , French; nonfiction CON
GODEFROI de LEIGNI, fl. 1170, French; poetry BU
GODEFROY, Vincent, 1912- , British; plays, nonfiction CON
GODESCALC, 805-69, Latin; non-

fiction, poetry BU
GODET, Philippe, 1850-1922,
Swiss; nonfiction, journalism,
poetry BU
'GODEY, John' (Morton Freed-
good; 'Stanley Morton'), 1912- ,
American; fiction REI ST
GODFREY, Dave, 1938- , Cana-
dian; fiction VCN
GODFREY, Eleanor Smith, 1914- ,
American; nonfiction CON
GODFREY, Hollis, 1874-1936,
American; fiction NI
'GODFREY, Jane' see BOWDEN,
Joan C.
GODFREY, Lionel Robert ('Elliot
Kennedy'; 'Scott Mitchell'),
1932- , British; nonfiction,
fiction CON
GODFREY, Michael A., 1940- ,
American; nonfiction CON
GODFREY, Thomas, 1736-63,
American; poetry, plays BR
BU
GODFREY, Vincent H., 1895?-
1975, American; nonfiction
CON
GODFREY, Vivian ('Melita Den-
ning'), 1921- , English; non-
fiction CON
GODFREY, William Dave, 1938- ,
Canadian; fiction CON
GODFREY of VITERBO, 1120-91,
Latin; poetry, nonfiction
BU
GODIN, Gabriel, 1929- , Cana-
dian; translations, nonfiction
CON
GODINE, David Richard, 1944- ,
American; nonfiction CON
GODINEZ, Felipe, 1588-1637?,
Spanish; plays BU
GODLEY, Alfred Denis, 1856-
1925, English; poetry DA
'GODLY, J. P.' see PLAWIN,
Paul
GODOLPHIN, Francis R. B.,
1903-74, American; nonfiction
CON
GODOLPHIN, Sidney, 1610-43,
English; poetry, plays BU
VP
GODOWN, Marian Bailey, Amer-
ican; journalism, nonfiction
CON
GODSHALK, William Leigh,
1937- , American; nonfiction
CON

GODSON, John, 1937- , Australian;
nonfiction CON
GODWIN, Francis, 1562?-1633,
English; nonfiction, fiction BU
NI
GODWIN, Gail, 1937- , American;
fiction KIB
GODWIN, Gaylord, 1906?-79,
American; journalism CON
GODWIN, John Frederick ('Fred-
erick Foster'), 1922- , Brit-
ish; nonfiction CON
GODWIN, Joscelyn Roland, 1945- ,
British; nonfiction CON
GODWIN, Mary Wollstonecraft,
1759-97, Irish; nonfiction BU
DA
GODWIN, Parke, 1816-1904,
American; journalism, nonfic-
tion MYE
GODWIN, Tom, 1915- , American;
fiction AS NI
GODWIN, William, 1756-1836,
English; journalism, nonfiction,
juveniles, fiction BU DA MAG
PO REI ST VN
GOEBEL, Dorothy Burne, 1898-
1976, American; nonfiction
CON
GOEBEL, Julius, 1857-1931,
German-American; nonfiction
BU
GOEBEL, Julius, Jr., 1893?-
1973, American; nonfiction
CON
GOEDICKE, Hans, 1926- ,
Austrian-American; nonfiction
CON
GOEDICKE, Patricia, 1931- ,
American; poetry VCP
GÖKALP, Mehmed (Ziya), 1875-
1924, Turkish; poetry, nonfic-
tion BU PRU
'GÖKCELI, Yasa K.' see 'KEMAL,
Yashar'
GOEL, Madan Lal, 1936- , Indian-
American; nonfiction CON
GOENS, Rijklof Michaël van (Le
Philosophe Sans Fard), 1748-
1810, Dutch; nonfiction, trans-
lations BU
GOERDT, Arthur Linus, 1912- ,
American; nonfiction CON
GOERGEN, Donald, 1943- ,
American; nonfiction CON
'GOERING, Helga' see WALLMANN,
Jeffrey M.
GOERING, Reinhard, 1887-1936,

German; plays, fiction,
poetry CL MCG
GOERNER, Edward Alfred, 1929- ,
American; nonfiction CON
GÖRRES, Joseph von, 1776-1849,
German; nonfiction BU
GOERTZ, Donald Charles, 1939- ,
American; translations, non-
fiction CON
GOERTZEL, Ted George, 1942- ,
American; nonfiction CON
GOES, Albrecht, 1908- , Ger-
man; poetry, fiction BU
TH
GOES, Johannes Antonides van
der, 1647-84, Dutch; poetry
BU
GOETEL, Ferdynand, 1890-1960,
Polish; fiction, plays BU
CL TH
GOETHE, Johann Wolfgang von,
1749-1832, German; poetry,
fiction, plays BU MAG
MCG TH
GOETTEL, Elinor, 1930- , Amer-
ican; juveniles CO
GOETZ, Curt, 1888-1960, Ger-
man; fiction, plays MCG
GOETZ, Delia, 1898- , Amer-
ican; translations, nonfiction,
juveniles CO CON
'GOETZ, George' see CALVERTON,
Victor F.
GÖTZ, Johann Nikolaus, 1721-81,
German; poetry TH
GOEVERNEUR, Jan Jacob Anthony,
('Jan de Rijmer'), 1809-89,
Dutch; poetry, juveniles,
translations BU
GOFFE, Thomas, 1591-1629, Eng-
lish; poetry BU
GOFFIN, Raymond C., 1890?-
1976, British; nonfiction CON
GOFFIN, Robert, 1898- , Belgian;
poetry, fiction, nonfiction
CL
GOFFSTEIN, Marilyn Brooke,
1940- , American; juveniles
CO DEM WAR
GOFMAN, John William, 1918- ,
American; nonfiction CON
GOFMAN, Modest Lyudvigovich
(Hofman), 1887- , Russian;
nonfiction BU
GOFMAN, Victor Vicotrovich
(Hofman), 1884-1911, Russian;
poetry BU
GOGA, Octavian, 1881-1938,

Rumanian; poetry BU CL
GOGARTY, Oliver St. John, 1878-
1957, Irish; poetry, fiction
BU DA HO PO VP
GOGGAN, John P. see 'PATRICK,
John'
GOGGIN, Terrence Patrick,
1941- , American; nonfiction
CON
GOGOL, Nikolay, 1809-52, Russian;
fiction, plays BU MAG MCG
TH
GOH, Cheng-Teik, 1943- , Malay-
sian; nonfiction CON
GOIS, Damião de, 1502-74, Portu-
guese; nonfiction BU
GOTTEIN, Shelomo Dov, 1900- ,
German-American; nonfiction
CON
GOJ, Ervín see 'LYSOHORSKY,
Ondra'
GOJAWICZYNSKA, Pola (Apolonia),
1896-1963, Polish; fiction,
plays BU CL
GOKAK, Vinayak Krishna, 1909- ,
Indian; nonfiction CON
GOKHALE, Aravind Visnu, 1919- ,
Marathi; fiction PRU
GOLAN, Matti, 1936- , Israeli;
plays, nonfiction, fiction CON
GOLANN, Cecil Paige, 1921- ,
American; juveniles CO
GOLANN, Stuart Eugene, 1936- ,
American; nonfiction CON
GOLANT, William, 1937- , Amer-
ican; nonfiction CON
GOLBIN, Andrée, 1923- , German-
American; juveniles CO
GOLD, Aaron, 1937- , American;
journalism CON
GOLD, Alan Robert ('David Sim-
mons'), 1948- , American;
nonfiction CON
GOLD, Don, 1931- , American;
nonfiction CON
GOLD, Herbert, 1924- , American;
fiction, nonfiction, juveniles
BR HE VCN WA
GOLD, Horace ('Clyde Crane Camp-
bell'; 'Leigh Keith'), 1914- ,
American; fiction AS NI WA
GOLD, Ivan D., 1932- , American;
fiction VCN
GOLD, Michael (Irving Granich),
1894-1967, American; fiction,
juveniles, nonfiction, plays
BR CON PO VN
'GOLD, Phyllis' see GOLDBERG,

Phyllis
GOLD, Robert Stanley, 1924- ,
American; nonfiction CON
GOLD, Seymour Murray, 1933- ,
American; nonfiction CON
GOLD, Sharlya, American; juven-
iles CO CON
GOLD, Victor Roland, 1924- ,
American; nonfiction CON
GOLD, William Emil, 1912- ,
American; journalism CON
GOLDBARTH, Albert, 1948- ,
American; poetry CON
GOLDBECK, David M., 1942- ,
American; nonfiction CON
GOLDBECK, Frederick Ernest,
1902- , Dutch; nonfiction
CON
GOLDBECK, Nikki, 1947- ,
American; nonfiction CON
GOLDBECK, Willis, 1899?-1979,
American; film CON
GOLDBERG, Alvin Arnold,
1931- , American; nonfiction
CON
GOLDBERG, Arnold Irving,
1929- , American; nonfiction
CON
GOLDBERG, Arthur Joseph,
1908- , American; nonfiction
CON
GOLDBERG, Carl, 1938- ,
American; nonfiction CON
GOLDBERG, Dick, 1947- ,
American; plays CON MCN
GOLDBERG, Dorothy Kurgans,
American; nonfiction CON
GOLDBERG, Edward Morris,
1931- , American; nonfiction
CON
GOLDBERG, Elliott Marshall,
1930- , American; fiction,
nonfiction CON
GOLDBERG, George, 1935- ,
American; nonfiction CON
GOLDBERG, Gerald Jay, 1929- ,
American; fiction, nonfiction
CON
GOLDBERG, Harvey E., 1939- ,
American; nonfiction CON
GOLDBERG, Herb, 1937- ,
American; nonfiction CON
GOLDBERG, Herbert S.,
1926- , American; juveniles
CO
GOLDBERG, Jan see CURRAN,
Jan
GOLDBERG, Leah, 1911-70,

Hebrew; poetry, nonfiction BU
'GOLDBERG, Louis' see GRANT,
Louis T.
GOLDBERG, Lucianne Cummings,
1935- , American; nonfiction,
fiction CON
GOLDBERG, Maxwell Henry,
1907- , American; nonfiction
CON
GOLDBERG, Melvyn Hirsh, 1942- ,
American; nonfiction CON
GOLDBERG, Miriam Levin, 1914- ,
American; nonfiction CON
GOLDBERG, Moses Haym, 1940- ,
American; plays CON
GOLDBERG, Nathan, 1903?-79,
Polish-American; nonfiction
CON
GOLDBERG, Norman Lewis,
1906- , American; nonfiction
CON
GOLDBERG, Philip, 1944- , Amer-
ican; nonfiction CON
GOLDBERG, Phyllis ('Phyllis
Gold'), 1941- , American;
nonfiction, juveniles CO CON
GOLDBERG, Ray Allen, 1926- ,
American; nonfiction CON
GOLDBERG, Sidney, 1931- ,
American; nonfiction CON
GOLDBERG, Stan J., 1939- ,
American; juveniles CON
GOLDBERG, Steven, 1941- ,
American; nonfiction CON
GOLDE, Roger Alan, 1934- ,
American; nonfiction CON
GOLDEMBERG, Isaac, 1945- ,
American; poetry CON
GOLDEMBERG, Rose Leiman
('Rose Leiman Schiller';
'Beatrice Traven'), American;
plays, nonfiction CON
GOLDEN, Harry Lewis, 1902-81,
American; nonfiction, journal-
ism BR WA
GOLDEN, Robert Edward, 1945- ,
American; nonfiction CON
GOLDENBERG, Edie N., 1945- ,
American; nonfiction CON
GOLDENBERG, Herbert, 1926- ,
American; nonfiction CON
GOLDENSOHN, Barry, 1937- ,
American; nonfiction, poetry
CON
GOLDFADEN, Abraham Haim
Lipke, 1840-1908, Yiddish;
poetry, plays MCG TH
GOLDFEDER, Anne Cheryl ('Zan

Paz'; 'Pahz'), 1949- , American; juveniles CO CON
GOLDFEDER, Kenneth James (Jim; Pahz; 'A. Paz'), 1943- , American; juveniles CO CON
GOLDFRANK, Esther Schiff, 1896- , American; nonfiction CON
GOLDFRANK, Helen Colodny ('Helen Kay'), 1912- , American; juveniles CO
GOLDGAR, Bertrand Alvin, 1927- , American; nonfiction CON
GOLDHABER, Gerald Martin, 1944- , American; nonfiction CON
GOLDHAMER, Herbert, 1907- , Canadian-American; nonfiction CON
GOLDHURST, Richard, 1927- , American; nonfiction CON
GOLDIN, Augusta, 1906- , American; juveniles CO
GOLDIN, Ezra, 1867-1915, Hebrew; nonfiction, fiction TH
GOLDIN, Milton, 1927- , American; nonfiction CON
GOLDIN, Stephen ('Charles Stephens'), 1947- , American; fiction CON NI
GOLDING, Arthur, 1536-1606, English; translations BU DA PO
GOLDING, Lawrence Arthur, 1926- , American; nonfiction CON
GOLDING, Louis, 1895-1958, English; fiction NI
GOLDING, Martin Philip, 1930- , American; nonfiction CON
GOLDING, Peter, 1947- , British; nonfiction CON
GOLDING, William Gerald, 1911- , English; fiction, plays, poetry BU DA MAG NI PO SEY VCN VN WA
GOLDKNOPF, David, 1918- , American; fiction CON
GOLDMAN, Alan Harris, 1945- , American; nonfiction CON
GOLDMAN, Alexander J., 1917- , Polish-American; nonfiction CON
GOLDMAN, Alvin L., 1938- , American; nonfiction CON

GOLDMAN, Andrew E. O., 1947- , American; plays, fiction CON
GOLDMAN, Bernard, 1922- , Canadian; nonfiction CON
GOLDMAN, Bruce Eliot, 1942- , American; nonfiction CON
GOLDMAN, Carl Alexander, 1942- , American; nonfiction CON
GOLDMAN, Charles Remington, 1930- , American; nonfiction CON
GOLDMAN, Frederick, 1921- , American; nonfiction CON
GOLDMAN, Jacquelin Roberta, 1934- , American; nonfiction CON
GOLDMAN, James, 1927- , American; plays, fiction CON MCG VCD
GOLDMAN, Leo, 1920- , American; nonfiction CON
GOLDMAN, Marcus Selden, 1894- , American; nonfiction CON
GOLDMAN, Martin Raymond, 1920- , American; nonfiction CON
GOLDMAN, Ralph Morris, 1920- , American; nonfiction CON
GOLDMAN, Richard Franko, 1910-80, American; translations, nonfiction CON
GOLDMAN, Susan, 1939- , American; juveniles CON
GOLDMAN, William, 1931- , American; fiction, plays, juveniles BR PO VCN WAK
GOLDMANN, Lucien, 1913-70, French; nonfiction CL
GOLDMARK, Peter Carl, 1906-77, Hungarian-American; nonfiction CON
GOLDNER, Nancy, 1943- , American; nonfiction CON
GOLDNER, Orville Charles, 1906- , American; nonfiction CON
GOLDONI, Carlo, 1707-93, Italian; plays, poetry BO BU MAG MCG TH
GOLDOVSKY, Boris, 1908- , Russian-American; nonfiction CON
GOLDRING, Douglas, 1887-1960, British; fiction, nonfiction CON
GOLDSBOROUGH, June, 1923- ,

American; juveniles CO
GOLDSCHMIDT, Meïr Aron, 1819-87, Danish; fiction BU TH
'GOLDSMITH' see MILLER, Lynne E.
GOLDSMITH, Arnold Louis, 1928- , American; nonfiction CON
GOLDSMITH, Barbara, 1931- , American; fiction, nonfiction CON
GOLDSMITH, Cele, 1933- , American; editor NI
GOLDSMITH, Donald, 1943- , American; nonfiction CON
GOLDSMITH, Howard ('Ward Smith'), 1943- , American; juveniles CO CON
GOLDSMITH, Jack, 1931- , American; nonfiction CON
GOLDSMITH, Oliver, 1728/30-74, Irish; poetry, plays, fiction, nonfiction BRI BU DA HO MAG MCG PO VD VN VP
GOLDSMITH, Robert Hillis, 1911- , American; nonfiction CON
GOLDSMITH, Sharon Sweeney, 1948- , American; nonfiction CON
GOLDSTEIN, Arthur David ('Albert Ross'), 1937- , American; fiction CON REI
GOLDSTEIN, Bernard R., 1938- , American; nonfiction, translations CON
GOLDSTEIN, Howard, 1922- , Canadian-American; nonfiction CON
GOLDSTEIN, Irwin L., 1937- , American; nonfiction CON
GOLDSTEIN, Israel, 1896- , American; nonfiction CON
GOLDSTEIN, Jack, 1930- , American; nonfiction CON
GOLDSTEIN, Jeffrey Haskell, 1942- , American; nonfiction CON
GOLDSTEIN, Jerome, 1931- , American; nonfiction CON
GOLDSTEIN, Laurence, 1943- , American; nonfiction CON
GOLDSTEIN, Leon J., 1927- , American; nonfiction CON
GOLDSTEIN, Malcolm, 1925- , American; nonfiction CON
GOLDSTEIN, Martin Eugene, 1939- , American; nonfiction CON

GOLDSTEIN, Michael Joseph, 1930- , American; nonfiction CON
GOLDSTEIN, Milton, 1915- , American; nonfiction CON
GOLDSTEIN, Nathan, 1927- , American; nonfiction CON
GOLDSTEIN, Philip, 1910- , American; juveniles, nonfiction CO CON WAR
GOLDSTEIN, Rhoda Lois, 1926- , American; nonfiction CON
GOLDSTEIN, Ruth Tessler, 1924- , American; fiction CON
GOLDSTEIN, Stanley, 1922- , American; nonfiction CON
GOLDSTEIN, Stephen Robert, 1938- , American; nonfiction CON
GOLDSTEIN, Stewart, 1941- , American; nonfiction CON
GOLDSTON, Robert Conroy ('James Stark'), 1927- , American; juveniles CO DEM WAR
GOLDSTONE, Aline Lewis, 1878?-1976, American; poetry CON
GOLDSTONE, Harmon Hendricks, 1911- , American; nonfiction CON
GOLDSTONE, Herbert, 1921- , American; nonfiction CON
GOLDTHORPE, John Ernest, 1921- , English; nonfiction CON
GOLDWATER, Barry Morris, 1909- , American; nonfiction CON
GOLDWATER, Eleanor Lowenstein, 1909?-80, American; nonfiction CON
GOLDWIN, Robert Allen, 1922- , American; nonfiction CON
GOLENBOCK, Peter, 1946- , American; nonfiction CON
GOLENISHCHEV-KUTUZOV, Arseny Arkadyevich, 1848-1912, Russian; poetry BU
'GOLL, Yvan' (Isaac Lang; 'Iwan Lassang'; 'Iwan'; 'Tristan Thor'; 'Tristan Torsi'; 'Johannes Thor'), 1891-1950, French-German; poetry, plays, fiction BU CL SEY TH WA
GOLLEDGE, Reginald George, 1937- , Australian; nonfiction CON
GOLOB, Zvonimir, 1927- ,

Croatian; poetry BU
GOLOGO, Mamadou, 1924- ,
Malian; fiction JA
GOLOGOR, Ethan, 1940- , American; nonfiction CON
GOLOMB, Claire, 1928- , German-American; nonfiction CON
GOLOMB, Louis, 1943- , American; nonfiction CON
GOLOMBEK, Harry, 1911- , British; journalism, nonfiction, translations CON
GOLSON, G. Barry, 1944- , American; nonfiction CON
GOLSSENAU, Arnold F. V. von see 'RENN, Ludwig'
GOLUBIEW, Antoni, 1907-79, Polish; nonfiction CL
GOMBAULD, Jean Ogier de, 1590-1666, French; nonfiction BU
GOMBERG, V. see 'LIDIN, Vladimir G.'
GOMBERVILLE, Marin Le Roy, 1600-74, French; fiction BU
'GOMBOSSY, Zoltan' see GABEL, Joseph
GOMBRICH, Sir Ernest Hans Josef, 1909- , Austrian-British; nonfiction CON WA
GOMBROWICZ, Witold, 1904-69, Polish; fiction, plays, diary BU CL MCG SEY TH WA
GOMERSALL, Robert, 1602?-44, English; plays BU
GOMERY, Robert see MONTGOMERY, Robert
GOMES LEAL, Antonio Duarte, 1848-1921, Portuguese; poetry BU
GOMEZ, David Federico, 1940- , American; nonfiction CON MAR
GOMEZ, Fernando, 1947- , American; nonfiction, fiction MAR
GOMEZ, Jose, 1925- , Cuban-American; nonfiction CON
GOMEZ, Rudolph, 1930- , American; nonfiction CON MAR
GOMEZ COSTA, Arturo, 1895- , Puerto Rican; poetry, nonfiction HIL
GOMEZ de AVELLANEDA, Gertrudis, 1814-73, Cuban; poetry, plays BU TH
GOMEZ de la SERNA, Ramón,

1888-1963, Spanish; nonfiction, fiction BU CL TH
GOMEZ-GIL, Alfredo, 1936- , Spanish; poetry, nonfiction CON
GOMEZ-QUIÑONES, Juan, American; nonfiction MAR
GOMEZ TEJERA, Carmen, 1890- , Puerto Rican; nonfiction HIL
GOMPERTS, Henri Albert, 1915- , Dutch; poetry, nonfiction BU
GOMPERTZ, Martin L. A. see 'GANPAT'
GOMPERTZ, Rolf, 1927- , German-American; nonfiction CON
GOMRINGER, Eugen, 1925- , Swiss; poetry BU
GOMULICKI, Wiktor (Fantazy), 1848-1919, Polish; poetry, fiction BU
GOMURAKAMI TENNO, 1328-68, Japanese; poetry HI
GONÇALVES, Antonio Aurélio, 1920?- , Cape Verde Islander; fiction, nonfiction CL HER JA
GONCALVES DIAS, Antonio, 1823-64, Brazilian; poetry BR
GONCHAROV, Ivan Alexandrovich, 1812-91, Russian; fiction, nonfiction BU MAG TH
GONCOURT, Edmond Louis Antoine, 1822-96, French; fiction, nonfiction BU MAG TH
GONCOURT, Jules Alfred Huot de, 1830-70, French; fiction, nonfiction BU MAG TH
GONG, Alfred, 1920- , German-American; poetry BU
GONGORA y ARGOTE, Luis de, 1561-1627, Spanish; poetry BU TH
GONSALVES, Jacome, 18th century, Indian; nonfiction PRU
GONZAGA, Tomás Antonio, 1744-1810, Brazilian; poetry BR BU TH
GONZALES, Jesus J., 1940- , American; nonfiction MAR
'GONZALES, John' see TERRALL, Robert
GONZALES, Rodolfo, 1928- , American; nonfiction MAR
GONZALES, Sylvia Alicia, 1943- , American; nonfiction CON MAR
GONZALEZ, Alfonso, 1927- , American; nonfiction CON

GONZALEZ, Alfredo M. , American; nonfiction MAR
GONZALEZ, Angel, 1925- , Spanish; poetry CL CON TH
GONZALEZ, Arturo, 1928- , American; nonfiction CON
GONZALEZ, Carlos, 1936- , American; nonfiction MAR
GONZALEZ, Diego Tadeo, 1732-94, Spanish; poetry BU TH
GONZALEZ, Gloria, 1940- , American; plays CO CON
GONZALEZ, Gustavo, 1942- , American; nonfiction MAR
GONZALEZ, Joaquín V. , 1863-1923, Argentinian; nonfiction BR
GONZALEZ, Joe R. , American; nonfiction MAR
GONZALEZ, José Emilio, 1918- , Puerto Rican; poetry, nonfiction, journalism, fiction HIL
GONZALEZ, Jose Gamaliel, American; nonfiction MAR
GONZALEZ, Jose Luis, 1926- , Dominican; fiction HIL
GONZALEZ, Nancie Loudon, 1929- , American; nonfiction CON
GONZALEZ, Nestor Vicente Madali, 1915- , Filipino; poetry PRU
GONZALEZ, Rafael Jesus, 1935- , American; nonfiction, poetry MAR
GONZALEZ-ALLER, Faustino, 1922- , Spanish; plays, fiction, film CON
GONZALEZ de CLAVIJO, Ruy, -1412, Spanish; nonfiction BU
GONZALEZ de ESLAVA, Fernán, 1534?-1601?, Spanish; plays BR BU
GONZALEZ del CASTILLO, Juan Ignacio, 1763-1800, Spanish; plays BU
GONZALEZ GARCIA, Matias, 1866-1938, Puerto Rican; journalism, fiction HIL
GONZALEZ-GERTH, Miguel, 1926- , Mexican; poetry CON
GONZALEZ LOPEZ, Emilio, 1903- , Spanish-American; nonfiction CON
GONZALEZ MARTINEZ, Enrique, 1871-1952, Mexican; poetry

BR BU WA
GONZALEZ-MENA LOCOCO, Veronica, 1934- , American; nonfiction MAR
GONZALEZ-PAZ, Elsie F. , 1913- , Puerto Rican; nonfiction CON
GONZALEZ PRADA, Manuel, 1848-1918, Peruvian; nonfiction, poetry BR BU
GONZALEZ VERA, José Santos, 1897-1970, Chilean; nonfiction BR
GONZMART, Caesar, Jr. , American; nonfiction MAR
GOOCH, Bryan Neil Shirley, 1937- , Canadian; nonfiction CON
GOOCH, Robert Miletus, 1919- , American; nonfiction CON
GOOCH, Stanley Alfred, 1932- , British; nonfiction CON
GOOCH, Steve, 1945- , British; plays, translations CON VCD
GOOD, Harry Gehman, 1880-1971, American; nonfiction CON
GOOD, Paul, 1929- , American; nonfiction CON
GOOD, Robert Crocker, 1924- , American; nonfiction CON
GOOD, Thomas Lindall, 1943- , American; nonfiction CON
GOODACRE, Elizabeth Jane, 1929- , Australian; nonfiction CON
GOODALL, Jane see van LAWICK-GOODALL, Jane
GOODALL, John Strickland, 1908- , English; juveniles CO DEM
GOODALL, Leonard E. , 1937- , American; nonfiction CON
'GOODALL, Melanie' see DRACHMAN, Julian M.
GOODALL, Walter, 1706?-66, Scots; nonfiction DA
GOODCHILD, George, 1885-1969, British; fiction, plays NI
GOODE, Diane, 1949- , American; juveniles CO
GOODE, Erich, 1938- , American; nonfiction CON
GOODE, James M. , 1939- , American; nonfiction CON
GOODE, John, 1927- , British; nonfiction CON
GOODE, Kenneth G. , 1932- , American; nonfiction CON SH

GOODE, Ruth ('Ruth Seinfel'; 'Julia Rainer'), 1905- , American; fiction, juveniles CON
GOODE, Stephen Hogue, 1924- , American; nonfiction CON
GOODE, Stephen Ray, 1943- , American; nonfiction CON
GOODE, William Josiah, 1917- , American; nonfiction CON
GOODELL, Charles Ellsworth, 1926- , American; nonfiction CON
GOODELL, Donald James, 1938- , American; nonfiction CON
GOODELL, John S., 1939- , American; nonfiction CON
GOODELL, Rae, 1944- , American; journalism, nonfiction CON
GOODERS, John, 1937- , English; nonfiction, juveniles CON
GOODHART, Arthur Lehman, 1891-1978, American; nonfiction CON
GOODHART, Robert Stanley, 1909- , American; nonfiction CON
GOODING, Judson, 1926- , American; nonfiction CON
GOODMAN, Adolph Winkler, 1915- , American; nonfiction CON
GOODMAN, Alvin Harold, 1924- , American; nonfiction CON
GOODMAN, Elaine, 1930- , American; juveniles CO WAR
GOODMAN, Elizabeth B., 1912- , American; juveniles WAR
GOODMAN, Emily Jane, 1940- , American; nonfiction CON
GOODMAN, Felicitas Daniels, 1914- , Hungarian-American; nonfiction CON
GOODMAN, Grant Kohn, 1924- , American; nonfiction CON
GOODMAN, Henry Nelson, 1906- , American; nonfiction CON
GOODMAN, Joseph Irving, 1908- , American; nonfiction CON
GOODMAN, Jules Eckert, 1876-1962, American; plays MCG
GOODMAN, Len Evan, 1944- , American; nonfiction, translations CON
GOODMAN, Leonard Henry, 1941- , American; nonfiction CON

GOODMAN, Linda, 1925- , American; nonfiction CON
GOODMAN, Norman, 1934- , American; nonfiction CON
GOODMAN, Paul, 1911-72, American; fiction, plays, poetry, nonfiction BOR BR VCN VN
GOODMAN, Rebecca (Gruver), 1931- , American; nonfiction CON
GOODMAN, Richard Merle, 1932- , American; nonfiction CON
GOODMAN, Ronald A., 1938- , American; nonfiction CON
GOODMAN, Rubin Robert, 1913-78, American; nonfiction CON
GOODMAN, Saul, 1919- , American; nonfiction CON
GOODMAN, Seymour S., 1931- , American; nonfiction CON
'GOODMAN, Sonya' see ARCONE, Sonya
GOODMAN, Walter, 1927- , American; juveniles CO WAR
GOODPASTER, Kenneth Edwin, 1944- , American; nonfiction CON
GOODRICH, David Lloyd, 1930- , American; nonfiction, fiction CON
GOODRICH, Frances, 1891?- , American; plays MCG
GOODRICH, Leland Matthew, 1899- , American; nonfiction CON
GOODRICH, Lloyd, 1897- , American; nonfiction CON
GOODRICH, Norma Lorre, 1917- , American; fiction, nonfiction CON
GOODRICH, Samuel Griswold ('Peter Parley'), 1793-1860, American; juveniles CO MY
GOODRICH, William Lloyd, 1910?-75, American; nonfiction CON
GOODSELL, Charles True, 1932- , American; nonfiction CON
GOODSELL, Fred Field, 1880-1976, American; nonfiction CON
GOODSON, Felix Emmett, 1922- , American; nonfiction CON
GOODSPEED, Edgar Johnson, 1871-1962, American; translations, nonfiction CON
GOODSTEIN, Reuben Louis, 1912- , English; nonfiction CON
GOODWIN, Derek, 1920- , British; nonfiction CON

GOODWIN, Donald William, 1931-   , American; nonfiction CON
'GOODWIN, Eugene D.' see KAYE, Marvin N.
GOODWIN, Harold Leland ('John Blaine'; 'Hal Goodwin'; 'Hal Gordon'; 'Blake Savage'), 1914/19-   , American; juveniles CO CON
GOODWIN, John Robert, 1929-   , American; nonfiction CON
GOODWIN, Leonard, 1929-   , American; nonfiction CON
GOODWIN, Stephen, 1943-   , American; fiction CON
GOODWIN, Suzanne ('Suzanne Ebel'; 'Cecily Shelbourne'), British; fiction, nonfiction CON
GOOGE, Barnabe, 1540-94, English; poetry, translations BU RU VP
GOOL, Reshard ('Ved Devajee'), 1931-   , British; nonfiction CON
GOOLAGONG, Evonne, 1951-   , Australian; nonfiction CON
'GOOSSEN, Agnes' see EPP, Margaret A.
GORAN, Abdullah, 1904-62, Kurdish; poetry PRU
GORAN, Lester, 1928-   , American; fiction CON
GORBANEVSKAYA, Natalya, 1936-   , Russian; poetry, translations CL WAK
GORBATOV, Boris Leontyevich, 1898-1954, Russian; fiction BU
GORBUNOV, Ivan Fëdorovich, 1831-95, Russian; fiction BU
GORDEN, Raymond Lowell, 1919-   , American; nonfiction CON
GORDIMER, Nadine, 1923-   , South African; fiction BU DA SEY VCN VN WA
GORDIN, Jacob ('Yan'), 1853-1909, Russian; plays MCG
GORDIN, Richard Davis, 1928-   , American; nonfiction CON
GORDON, Adam Lindsay, 1833-70, Australian; poetry BU DA
GORDON, Aharon David, 1856-1922, Hebrew; nonfiction BU
GORDON, Alan F., 1947-   , American; nonfiction CON
'GORDON, Angela' see PAINE, Lauran B.

GORDON, Antoinette K., 1892?-1975, American; nonfiction CON
GORDON, Barbara, 1913-   , American; nonfiction CON
GORDON, Barry Lewis John, 1934-   , Australian; nonfiction CON
GORDON, Bernard K., 1932-   , American; nonfiction CON
GORDON, Bertram Martin, 1943-   , American; nonfiction CON
GORDON, Beverly, 1948-   , American; nonfiction CON
GORDON, Caroline, 1895-1981, American; fiction, nonfiction AM BA BR BU CON MAG RO VCN VN
GORDON, Charles W. see 'CONNOR, Ralph'
GORDON, Cyrus Herzl, 1908-   , American; juveniles WAR
GORDON, Diana Russell, 1938-   , American; nonfiction CON
'GORDON, Doreen' see CHARD, Judy
GORDON, Dorothy, 1893-1970, Russian-American; juveniles, nonfiction CO CON
GORDON, Edmund Wyatt, 1921-   , American; nonfiction SH
GORDON, Esther Saranga, 1935-   , American; juveniles CO CON
GORDON, Ethel Edison, 1915-   , American; fiction CON
GORDON, Felice, 1939-   , British; nonfiction CON
'GORDON, Gary' see EDMONDS, Ivy G.
'GORDON, George' see HASFORD, Jerry G.
GORDON, Gerald, 1909-   , South African; fiction BU
GORDON, Gilbert James, 1918-   , Scots; nonfiction CON
GORDON, Giles Alexander ('Boswell'), 1940-   , Scots; poetry, fiction, nonfiction, juveniles CON VCP
GORDON, Gordon, 1912-   , American; juveniles, fiction REI ST WAR
'GORDON, Col. H. R.' see ELLIS, Edward S.
'GORDON, Hal' see GOODWIN, Harold L.
GORDON, Henry Alfred (Harry),

1925- , Australian; fiction,
nonfiction CON
GORDON, Ian Robert Fraser,
1939- , British; nonfiction
CON
GORDON, Ira Jay, 1923- , American; nonfiction CON
GORDON, Irene Linda, 1940- ,
American; nonfiction CON
'GORDON, Jane' see LEE, Elsie
'GORDON, Janet' see WOODHAM-
SMITH, Cecil B.
'GORDON, Jean' see WICKHAM,
Jean
GORDON, John, 1925- , British;
juveniles CO KI
GORDON, John Steele, 1944- ,
American; nonfiction CON
GORDON, John William, 1925- ,
British; juveniles CON
GORDON, Kermit, 1916-76,
American; nonfiction CON
'GORDON, Kurtz' see KURTZ,
Clarence G.
GORDON, Leland James, 1897- ,
American; nonfiction CON
GORDON, Leonard, 1935- ,
American; nonfiction CON
'GORDON, Lesley' see ELLIOTT,
Lesley
'GORDON, Lew' see BALDWIN,
Gordon C.
GORDON, Lou, 1917?-77, American; journalism CON
GORDON, Margaret Ann Taber,
1939- , American; juveniles,
nonfiction CO CON
GORDON, Mary Catherine,
1949- , American; nonfiction,
fiction CON KIB
GORDON, Michael, 1940- ,
American; nonfiction CON
GORDON, Mildred Nixon, 1912-79,
American; juveniles, fiction
CO CON REI ST WAR
GORDON, Nancy see HEINL,
Nancy
GORDON, Patricia ('Joan Howard'),
1904- , Canadian; juveniles
WAR
GORDON, Percival Hector,
1884- , Canadian; nonfiction
CON
'GORDON, Rex' see HOUGH,
Stanley B.
GORDON, Richard see 'GORDON,
Stuart'
GORDON, Robert Aaron, 1908-78,

American; nonfiction CON
GORDON, Ruth Jones, 1896- ,
American; nonfiction, plays,
film CON
GORDON, Selma see LANES,
Selma
GORDON, Shirley, 1921- , American; journalism, juveniles,
film CON
GORDON, Sol, 1923- , American;
juveniles, nonfiction CO CON
WAR
'GORDON, Stewart' see SHIRREFFS,
Gordon D.
'GORDON, Stuart' (Richard Gordon;
'Alex R. Stuart'), 1947- ,
Scots; fiction NI
GORDON, Suzanne, 1945- , American; nonfiction CON
GORDON, Walter Lockhart, 1906- ,
Canadian; nonfiction CON
GORDON, Yehuda Leib ('Y. L.
G. '), 1830-92, Hebrew; poetry,
fiction, nonfiction BU TH
GORDONE, Charles, 1925- ,
American; plays CON MCG
MCN SH VCD
The GORDONS see GORDON, Gordon; GORDON, Mildred N.
GORDY, Berry, Sr. , 1888-1978,
American; nonfiction CON
GORE, Catherine Grace Moody,
1799-1861, English; fiction,
plays, poetry, nonfiction VN
GORE, Robert Hayes, 1886-1972,
American; nonfiction CON
GOREAU, Angeline, 1951- ,
American; nonfiction CON
GORE-BOOTH, Eva Selena, 1870-
1926, Irish; poetry, plays
HO
GORECKI, Jan, 1926- , Polish-
American; nonfiction CON
GORELICK, Molly C. , 1920- ,
American; juveniles CO
GOREN, Charles Henry, 1901- ,
American; nonfiction CON
GOREN, Judith, 1933- , American;
poetry CON
GORENKO, Anna A. see 'AKH-
MATOVA, Anna'
GORENSTEIN, Shirley, 1928- ,
American; nonfiction CON
GORER, Geoffrey Edgar, 1905- ,
British; fiction, nonfiction
CON NI
GORES, Joseph N. , 1931- ,
American; fiction, plays REI

GOREY, Edward, 1925- , American; juveniles DEM
GOREY, Hays, American; nonfiction CON
GORGANI, Fakhroddin, 11th century, Persian; poetry PRU
GORGIAS, 485-380 B. C. , Greek; nonfiction BU GR
GORHAM, Charles Orson, 1911-75, American; fiction CON
GORHAM, Jeanne Urich, 1920- , American; nonfiction CON
'GORHAM, Michael' see FOLSOM, Franklin B.
GORION, Micha J. B. see BERDICHEWSKI, M. J.
GORIS, J. A. see 'GIJSEN, Marnix'
'GORKY, Maxim' (Alexey Maximovich Peshkov), 1868-1936, Russian; fiction, plays BU CL MAG MCG SEY TH
'GORMAN, Beth' see PAINE, Lauran B.
GORMAN, John Andrew, 1938- , American; nonfiction, translations CON
GORMLEY, Gerard Joseph, 1931- , American; fiction CON
GORMLEY, Mike, 1945- , Canadian; journalism CON
GORN, Janice Leonora, 1915- , American; nonfiction CON
GORNEY, Roderic, 1924- , American; nonfiction CON
GORNEY, Sondra, 1918- , American; nonfiction CON
GORNFELD, Arkady Georgievich, 1867-1944, Russian; nonfiction BU
GORNICK, Vivian, 1935- , American; nonfiction CON
GORNICKI, Lukasz (Góra), 1527-1603, Polish; nonfiction BU
GORODETSKY, Gabriel, 1945- , Israeli; nonfiction CON
GORODETSKY, Sergey Mitrofanovich, 1885-1967, Russian; poetry BU CL
GORODETZKY, Charles W. , American; juveniles WAR
GOROSTIZA, José, 1901- , Mexican; nonfiction, poetry BR BU
'GORRI, Tobias' see BOITO, Arrigo
GORSLINE, Douglas Warner, 1913- , American; juveniles,

nonfiction CO CON
GORTER, Herman, 1864-1927, Dutch; poetry, nonfiction BU CL TH WA
GORTER, Simon, 1838-71, Dutch; nonfiction BU
GORTON, Richard A. , 1932- , American; nonfiction CON
'GORYAN, Sirak' see SAROYAN, William
GOSDEN, Peter Henry John, 1927- , British; nonfiction CON
GOSETT, Philip, 1941- , American; translations, nonfiction CON
GOSHIRAKAWA TENNO, 1127-92, Japanese; poetry HI
GOSHORN, Elizabeth, 1953- , American; juveniles CON
GOSLICKI, Wawrzyniec G. , 1530-1607, Polish; nonfiction BU
GOSLING, Justin Cyril Bertrand, 1930- , British; nonfiction CON
GOSNELL, Harold Foote, 1896- , American; nonfiction CON
GOSS, Clay, 1946- , American; plays, juveniles CON
'GOSSAERT, Geerten' (Frederik Carel Gerretson), 1884-1958, Dutch; poetry, nonfiction BU
GOSSE, Sir Edmund William, 1849-1928, English; nonfiction BU DA PO
GOSSON, Stephen, 1555-1624, English; plays, nonfiction BU DA RU
GOSSOUIN de METZ, 13th century, poetry BU
GOSTELOW, Mary, 1943- , American; nonfiction CON
GOSVAMI, Hemcandra, 1872-1928, Assamese; nonfiction PRU
GOSZCZYNSKI, Seweryn, 1801-76, Polish; poetry BU
GOTESKY, Rubin, 1906- , Polish-American; nonfiction CON
GOTLIEB, Phyllis, 1926- , Canadian; poetry, fiction, plays NI VCP
GOTOBA JOKO, 1180-1239, Japanese; poetry HI
GOTOVAC, Vlado, 1930- , Croatian; poetry, nonfiction BU
GOTS, Ronald Eric, 1943- , American; nonfiction CON
GOTSCHALK, Felix C. , 1929- ,

American; fiction NI
GOTT, Kenneth Davidson ('Sebastian Hogbotel'), 1923- ,
Australian; nonfiction CON
GOTT, Richard Willoughby,
1938- , British; nonfiction
CON
GOTTA, Salvatore, 1887- ,
Italian; fiction, plays BU
GOTTER, Friedrich Wilhelm,
1746-97, German; plays BU
'GOTTESMAN, S. D.' house name
NI
GOTTFRIED von NEIFEN, fl. 1234-
55, Swabian; poetry BU TH
GOTTFRIED von STRASSBURG,
fl. 1210, German; poetry BU
MAG TH
'GOTTHELF, Jeremias' (Albert
Bitzius), 1797-1854, German-
Swiss; fiction BU TH
GOTTIFREDI, Bartolomeo, 16th
century, Italian; poetry BU
GOTTLIEB, Beatrice M., 1889?-
1979, American; plays CON
GOTTLIEB, Darcy, 1922- ,
American; poetry CON
GOTTLIEB, Elaine (Elaine G.
Hemley), American; translations, fiction, nonfiction
CON
GOTTLIEB, Gerald, 1923- ,
American; juveniles CO
GOTTLIEB, Hinko, 1886- , Yugoslav; fiction NI
GOTTLIEB, Naomi Ruth, 1925- ,
American; nonfiction CON
GOTTLIEB, Paul, 1936- ,
Hungarian-Canadian; fiction,
film CON
GOTTLIEB, William Paul, 1917- ,
American; nonfiction, juveniles
CO CON
GOTTLOBER, Abraham Baer
('Abag'; 'Mahalel'), 1811-99,
Hebrew; poetry, fiction, plays
BU MCG
GOTTMAN, John Mordechai,
1942- , American; nonfiction,
film CON
GOTTSCHALK (Fulgentius Godescalchus), 805/10-67/70, Latin;
poetry GR TH
GOTTSCHALK, Elin Toona,
1937- , Estonian-American;
fiction CON
GOTTSCHALK, Louis August,
1916- , American; nonfiction

CON
GOTTSCHALK, Louis Reichenthal,
1899-1975, American; nonfiction CON
GOTTSCHALK, Paul A., 1939- ,
American; nonfiction CON
GOTTSCHALK, Shimon S., 1929- ,
German-American; nonfiction
CON
GOTTSCHALK, Stephen, 1940- ,
American; nonfiction CON
GOTTSCHED, Johann Christoph,
1700-66, German; nonfiction,
plays BU MCG TH
GOTTSCHED, Luise Adelgunde
Kulmus, 1713-62, German;
plays BU
GOTTSEGEN, Gloria Benar, 1930- ,
American; nonfiction CON
GOTZSCHE, Anne-Lise, 1939- ,
Danish-British; nonfiction CON
GOUD, Anne ('Anne-Mariel';
'Karina'), 1917- , Franco-
American; fiction CON
GOUDEKET, Maurice, 1889-1977,
French; nonfiction CON
GOUDEY, Alice E., 1898- ,
American; juveniles CO CON
DE
GOUDGE, Elizabeth de Beauchamp,
1900- , British; juveniles, fiction, poetry, plays, nonfiction
DE KI
GOUDIE, Andrew Shaw, 1945- ,
English; nonfiction CON
GOUDSMIT, Samuel Abraham, 1902-
78, Dutch; nonfiction CON
GOUGH, Barry Morton, 1938- ,
Canadian; nonfiction CON
GOUGH, Catherine ('Catherine
Mulgan'), 1931- , British;
juveniles CO
GOUGH, Richard, 1735-1809, English; nonfiction, translations
BU
GOUGOV, Nikola Delchev ('Pavel
Vezhínov'), 1914- , Bulgarian;
fiction CON
GOUL, Roman Borisovich (Gul),
1896- , Russian; fiction, nonfiction CL
GOULART, Frances Sheridan ('C.
F. Johnson'), 1938- , American; nonfiction CON
GOULART, Ronald Joseph ('Josephine
Kains'; 'Howard Lee'; 'Kenneth
R. Robeson'; 'Frank S. Shawn';
'Con Steffanson'), 1933- ,

American; fiction, nonfiction
AS CO NI REI
'GOULD, Alan' see CANNING,
Victor
GOULD, Bruce Grant, 1942- ,
American; nonfiction CON
GOULD, Carol C., 1946- ,
American; nonfiction CON
GOULD, Chester, 1900- , Amer-
ican; journalism, cartoons
CON ST
GOULD, Edwin Orrin, 1936- ,
Canadian; journalism, fiction,
film CON
GOULD, George, American; juven-
iles WAR
GOULD, Jay Reid, 1906- ,
Canadian-American; nonfiction,
plays CON
GOULD, Jean Rosalind, 1919- ,
American; juveniles CO
GOULD, John Allen, 1944- ,
American; nonfiction CON
GOULD, John Thomas, 1908- ,
American; nonfiction CON
GOULD, Josiah Bancroft, 1928- ,
American; nonfiction, trans-
lations CON
GOULD, Leroy C., 1937- ,
American; nonfiction CON
GOULD, Lewis Ludlow, 1939- ,
American; nonfiction CON
GOULD, Lilian, 1920- , Amer-
ican; juveniles CO CON
GOULD, Lois, 1938?- , Amer-
ican; journalism, fiction CON
GOULD, Marilyn, 1928- , Amer-
ican; juveniles CO WAR
'GOULD, Michael' see AYRTON,
Michael
GOULD, Milton Samuel, 1909- ,
American; nonfiction CON
GOULD, Randall, 1898?-1979,
American; nonfiction, journal-
ism CON
GOULD, Richard, 1660?-1709,
English; plays, poetry BU
GOULD, Richard Allan, 1939- ,
American; nonfiction CON
GOULD, Ronald, 1904- , British;
nonfiction CON
GOULD, Shirley Goldman, Amer-
ican; nonfiction CON
'GOULD, Stephen' see FISHER,
Steve
GOULD, Stephen Jay, 1941- ,
American; nonfiction CON
GOULD, Toni S., American;

juveniles WAR
GOULDE, Leslie, 1902-77, Ameri-
can; journalism CON
GOULDEN, Mark, 1896?-1980,
British; journalism CON
GOULDING, Brian, 1933- , Brit-
ish; nonfiction CON
GOULDING, Dorothy Jane, 1923- ,
Canadian; nonfiction, juveniles
CON
GOULDING, Francis Robert, 1810-
81, American; juveniles, fiction
BA
GOULDING, Raymond Walter,
1922- , American; nonfiction
CON
GOULDNER, Alvin Ward, 1920-80,
American; nonfiction CON
GOULED, Vivian Gloria ('Marcia
Peters'), 1911- , American;
juveniles, poetry CON
GOULET, Denis A., 1931- ,
American; nonfiction CON
GOULET, John, 1942- , American;
fiction CON
GOULIANOS, Joan Rodman,
1939- , American; nonfiction
CON
GOULYASHKI, Andreai, 1914- ,
Bulgarian; fiction CON
GOURI, Haim, 1923- , Israeli;
journalism, nonfiction, fiction
CON
GOURLEY, Jay, 1947- , Ameri-
can; nonfiction CON
GOURMONT, Remy de, 1858-1915,
French; fiction, plays, poetry,
nonfiction BU CL MAG
GOVAN, Christine Noble ('Mary
Allerton'; 'J. N. Darby'),
1898- , American; juveniles
CO
GOVAN, Thomas Payne, 1907- ,
American; nonfiction CON
GOVE, Phillip Babcock, 1902- ,
American; fiction NI
GOVER, Robert, 1929- , Ameri-
can; fiction BR SEY VCN WA
GOVERN, Elaine, 1939- , Ameri-
can; juveniles CON
GOVIER, Katherine, 1948- ,
American; fiction CON
GOVONI, Albert P., 1914- ,
American; nonfiction CON
GOVONI, Corrado, 1884-1965,
Italian; poetry, plays, fiction
BO BU SEY TH
GOW, Donald, 1920- , Canadian;

nonfiction CON
GOW, Ronald, 1897- , British;
plays VCD
GOWAN, Donald Elmer, 1929- ,
American; nonfiction CON
GOWAN, Elsie Park Young,
1905- , Canadian; plays
CR
GOWER, John, 1330-1408, Eng-
lish; poetry BRI BU DA PO
VP
GOWERS, Sir Ernest Arthur,
1880-1966, English; nonfiction
CON WA
GOWING, Margaret, 1921- ,
British; nonfiction CON
GOWING, Peter Gordon, 1930- ,
American; nonfiction CON
GOWLAND, John Stafford, 1898- ,
British; fiction NI
GOY, Philip, 1941- , French;
fiction NI
GOYDER, Margot see 'NEVILLE,
Margot'
GOYEN, Charles William,
1915- , American; fiction,
plays BA BR HE VCN WA
GOYER, Robert Stanton, 1923- ,
American; nonfiction CON
GOYTISOLO, Juan, 1931- ,
Spanish; fiction BU CL CON
WA
GOYTISOLO, Luis, 1937- ,
Spanish; fiction CL
GOZZANO, Guido, 1883-1916,
Italian; poetry BO BU CL
SEY TH
GOZZI, Carlo, 1720-1806, Italian;
poetry, plays BO BU MCG
TH
GOZZI, Gasparo, 1713-86, Italian;
journalism, poetry, transla-
tions BO BU TH
GQOBA, William Wellington, 1840-
88, South African; nonfiction,
poetry, journalism HER JA
'GRAAF, Peter' see 'CHRISTO-
PHER, John'
GRABBE, Christian Dietrich, 1801-
36, German; plays, poetry
BU MCG TH
GRABBE, Paul, 1902- , Russian-
American; journalism CON
GRABER, Alexander see 'CORDELL,
Alexander'
GRABER, Gerry Samuel, 1928- ,
British; nonfiction CON
GRABER, Richard Fredrick,

1927- , American; journalism,
juveniles CON
GRABIANSKI, Janusz, 1929- ,
American?; juveniles CON DE
GRABNER-HAIDER, Anton, 1940- ,
Austrian; nonfiction CON
GRABOSKY, Peter Nils, 1945- ,
American; nonfiction CON
GRABURN, Nelson Hayes, 1936- ,
American; nonfiction CON
GRACA, José M. V. da see
'VIEIRA, José L.'
GRACCHUS, Sidney Joseph, 1930- ,
American; nonfiction CON
GRACE, Gerald Rupert, 1936- ,
English; nonfiction CON
GRACE, Helen Kennedy, 1935- ,
American; nonfiction CON
GRACE, Joan Carroll, 1921- ,
American; nonfiction CON
GRACEY, Harry Lewis, 1933- ,
American; nonfiction CON
GRACIAN y MORALES, Baltasar,
1601-58, Spanish; fiction BU
TH
'GRACQ, Julien' (Lucien Poirier),
1910- , French; fiction, non-
fiction BU CL TH
GRADE, Chaim, 1910- , American;
fiction, poetry BU CON
GRADNIK, Alojz, 1882-1967,
Slovene; poetry, translations
BU CL
GRADO, Louis M. , 1924- ,
American; nonfiction MAR
GRADON, Pamela Olive Elizabeth,
1915- , British; nonfiction
CON
GRADY, Henry Woodfin, 1850-89,
American; nonfiction BA
GRADY, James Thomas, 1949- ,
American; fiction MCC
GRADY, Ronan Calistus, Jr. ('John
Murphy'), 1921- , American;
nonfiction CON
'GRADY, Tex' see WEBB, Jack
GRAE, Ida ('Ida Dean'), 1918- ,
American; nonfiction CON
GRAEBNER, Alan, 1938- ,
American; nonfiction CON
GRAEDON, Joe David, 1945- ,
American; nonfiction CON
'GRAEME, Bruce' (Graham Monague
Jeffries; 'Peter Bourne'; 'Davis
Graeme'), 1900- , British;
fiction, nonfiction CON MAC
REI ST
'GRAEME, Roderic' see 'JEFFRIES,

Roderic'
GRAF, Arturo, 1848-1913, Italian;
nonfiction, poetry BU
GRAF, Le Roy Philip, 1915- ,
American; nonfiction CON
GRAF, Oskar Maria, 1894-1967,
German; fiction CL TH
'GRAFF, Polly A.' see COLVER,
Anne
GRAFF, S. Stewart, 1908- ,
American; nonfiction, juveniles
CO CON
GRAFFE, Richard de see ST.
CLAIR, Leonard
'GRAFTON, Ann' see OWENS,
Thelma
GRAFTON, Carl, 1942- , Amer-
ican; nonfiction CON
'GRAFTON, Garth' see COTES,
Sara J. D.
GRAFTON, Richard, -1572,
English; printer, nonfiction
BU
GRAGLIA, Lino Anthony, 1930- ,
American; nonfiction CON
GRAHAM, Ada, 1931- , Amer-
ican; juveniles CO
GRAHAM, Alistair Dundas,
1938- , Kenyan; nonfiction
CON
GRAHAM, Andrew Guillemard,
1913-81, American; nonfiction
CON
GRAHAM, Brenda Knight, 1942- ,
American; nonfiction, juven-
iles CON
'GRAHAM, Carlotta' see WALL-
MANN, Jeffrey M.
'GRAHAM, Charles S.' see
TUBB, Edwin C.
'GRAHAM, Charlotte' see BOWDIN,
Joan C.
GRAHAM, David Duane, 1927- ,
American; nonfiction CON
GRAHAM, Desmond, 1940- ,
British; nonfiction CON
GRAHAM, Don, 1940- , Amer-
ican; nonfiction CON
GRAHAM, Dougal, 1724-79,
Scots; nonfiction, poetry DA
GRAHAM, Eleanor, 1896- ,
English; juveniles, nonfiction
CO CON KI
'GRAHAM, Elizabeth' see ED-
MONDS, Arthur D.
'GRAHAM, Ennis' see MOLES-
WORTH, Mary L.
GRAHAM, Frank, Jr., 1925- ,

American; juveniles CO
GRAHAM, Gene Swann, 1924- ,
American; nonfiction CON
GRAHAM, George Jackson, Jr.,
1938- , American; nonfiction
CON
GRAHAM, George Kenneth, 1936- ,
Scots; nonfiction CON
GRAHAM, Gerald Sandford, 1903- ,
Canadian; nonfiction CON
GRAHAM, Gwethalyn, 1913-65,
Canadian; fiction, nonfiction,
translations CR
GRAHAM, Henry, 1930- , British;
poetry CON VCP
GRAHAM, Ian James, 1923- ,
Anglo-American; nonfiction
CON
GRAHAM, Ilse, 1914- , German-
English; nonfiction CON
GRAHAM, J. W., 1925- , Cana-
dian; nonfiction CON
'GRAHAM, James' see 'MARLOWE,
Hugh'
GRAHAM, James, 1612-50, English;
poetry DA
GRAHAM, John, 1926- , American;
juveniles CO
GRAHAM, John Thomas, 1928- ,
American; nonfiction CON
'GRAHAM, Kennon' see HARRISON,
David L.
GRAHAM, Lawrence Sherman,
1936- , American; nonfiction
CON
GRAHAM, Le, American; nonfiction
SH
GRAHAM, Lee E., 1913?-77,
American; nonfiction CON
GRAHAM, Lorenz, 1902- , Amer-
ican; nonfiction, juveniles DE
KI SH WAR
GRAHAM, Lloyd M. ('Krypton'),
1889- , Canadian-American;
nonfiction CON
GRAHAM, Malcolm, 1923- ,
American; nonfiction CON
GRAHAM, Margaret Bloy, 1920- ,
Canadian; juveniles CO CON
GRAHAM, Milton Duke, 1916- ,
American; nonfiction CON
'GRAHAM, Neill' see DUNCAN,
William M.
GRAHAM, Peter Anderson, -1925,
English; fiction NI
GRAHAM, Philip Leslie, 1915-63,
American; journalism CON
'GRAHAM, Robert' see HALDEMAN,

Joe W.

GRAHAM, Robert Bontine, 1852-
1936, Scots; nonfiction, fiction DA VN

GRAHAM, Robin Lee, 1949- ,
American; nonfiction, juveniles
CO CON

GRAHAM, Roger P. see 'PHIL-
LIPS, Rog'

'GRAHAM, Ruth' see EVANS, Jean

GRAHAM, Shirley see DU BOIS,
Shirley

GRAHAM, Stephen, 1884-1975,
British; nonfiction CON

'GRAHAM, Vanessa' see FRASER,
Anthea

GRAHAM, Victor Ernest, 1920- ,
Canadian; nonfiction CON

'GRAHAM, Virginia' see GUTTEN-
BERG, Virginia

GRAHAM, William Sidney, 1918- ,
Scots; poetry, nonfiction BU
CON VCP WA

GRAHAM, Winston Mawdsley,
1910- , British; fiction CON
REI VCN

GRAHAM-WHITE, Anthony, 1940- ,
Anglo-American; nonfiction
CON

GRAHAME, James, 1765-1811,
Scots; poetry BU

GRAHAME, Kenneth, 1859-1932,
Scots; nonfiction, juveniles,
fiction BU COM DA KI
MAG VN

GRAHAME-WHITE, Claude, British; fiction NI

GRAINDOR de BRIE, 1189?- ,
French; poetry BU

GRAINDOR de DOUAI, fl. 1200,
French; poetry BU

GRAINGER, Francis E. see
'HILL, Headon'

GRAINGER, James, 1721?-66,
Scots; poetry VP

GRAINGER, John Herbert, 1917- ,
British; nonfiction CON

GRAM, Miltke Stefanus, 1928- ,
American; nonfiction CON

GRAMATKY, Hardie, 1907-79,
American; juveniles CO
CON KI

GRAMS, Armin, 1924- , American; nonfiction CON

GRAMSBERGEN, Matthijs, 17th
century, Dutch; plays BU

GRAMSCI, Antonio, 1891-1937,
Italian; nonfiction BO BU CL

GRANADA, Luis de, 1504?-88,
Spanish; nonfiction BU TH

'GRANADOS, Paul' see KENT,
Arthur W. C.

GRANBECK, Marilyn ('Nick Carter';
'Ben Grant'; 'Adam Hamilton';
'Clayton Moore'; 'Van Saxon'),
1927- , American; fiction
CON

GRANBERRY, Edwin, 1897- ,
American; plays, fiction, translations BA

'GRANBY, Milton' see WALLMANN,
Jeffrey M.

GRANDBOIS, Alain, 1900- , Canadian; poetry, fiction, translations BU CR DA

GRANDE, Félix, 1937- , Spanish;
fiction, poetry, nonfiction CL

GRANDFIELD, Raymond Joseph,
1931- , American; nonfiction
CON

'GRANDOWER, Elissa' see WAUGH,
Hillary

GRANDY, Richard Edward, 1942- ,
American; nonfiction CON

'GRANGE, Chris' see GNAEGY,
Charles

GRANGE, John, fl. 1577, English;
poetry BU

'GRANGE, Peter' see NICOLE,
Christopher R.

GRANGER, Peg, American; juveniles, fiction WAR

GRANICH, Irving see 'GOLD,
Michael'

GRANICK, Harry ('Harry Taylor'),
1898- , Russian-American;
plays, juveniles CON

GRANIK, Theodore, 1906-70,
American; tv CON

'GRANIN, Daniel' (Daniel German),
1918- , Russian; fiction CL
WAK

GRANOVETTER, Mark S. , 1943- ,
American; nonfiction CON

GRANOVSKY, Anatoli, 1922-74,
Russian; nonfiction CON

GRANOVSKY, Timofey Nikolayevich,
1813-55, Russian; nonfiction
BU

GRANSDEN, Antonia, 1928- ,
British; nonfiction CON

GRANSON, Oton de, 1345?-97,
French; poetry BU

GRANSTAFF, Bill, 1925- , American; juveniles CO

GRANT, Alexander Thomas Kingdom,

1906- , English; nonfiction
CON
'GRANT, Ambrose' see 'CHASE,
James Hadley'
GRANT, Barbara Moll, 1932- ,
American; nonfiction CON
'GRANT, Ben' see GRANBECK,
Marilyn
GRANT, Brian, 1939- , Amer-
ican; nonfiction CON
GRANT, Bruce, 1893-1977, Amer-
ican; journalism, fiction, juven-
iles, nonfiction CO CON
GRANT, Charles L. , 1942- ,
American; fiction, nonfiction
CON NI
GRANT, Donald Metcalf, 1927- ,
American; publisher NI
GRANT, Ellsworth Strong, 1917- ,
American; nonfiction CON
GRANT, Eva, 1907- , American;
juveniles, poetry CO CON
WAR
GRANT, Frederick Clifton, 1891-
1974, American; nonfiction
CON
GRANT, Gerald, 1938- , Amer-
ican; journalism, nonfiction
CON
GRANT, Gordon, 1875-1962,
American; juveniles CO CON
GRANT, H. Roger, 1943- ,
American; nonfiction CON
'GRANT, Hilda K. ' see HILLIARD,
Jan
GRANT, James G. , 1926?-79,
American; journalism CON
GRANT, James Russell, 1924- ,
Scots; poetry CON
'GRANT, Jane' see LEADER,
Evelyn B.
GRANT, John ('Jonathan Gash'),
1933- , British; fiction,
plays CON
GRANT, John Barnard, 1940- ,
American; nonfiction CON
GRANT, John Ernest, 1925- ,
American; nonfiction CON
GRANT, John J. , 1932- ,
American; nonfiction CON
'GRANT, Kay' see HILLIARD,
Jan
'GRANT, Landon' see GRIBBLE,
Leonard R.
GRANT, Leigh, 1947- , Amer-
ican; juveniles CO
GRANT, Louis Theodore ('Louis
Goldberg'; 'Joseph Magister'),

1943- , American; nonfiction
CON
GRANT, Madeleine Parker, 1895- ,
American; nonfiction CON
GRANT, Mary Kathryn, 1941- ,
American; nonfiction CON
GRANT, Matthew, British; fiction
NI
'GRANT, Matthew G. ' see MAY,
Julian
'GRANT, Maxwell' see 'COLLINS,
Michael'; GIBSON, Walter B.
GRANT, Myrna Lois, 1934- ,
Canadian-American; juveniles,
nonfiction, film CO CON
GRANT, Neil ('David Mountfield'),
1938- , English; juveniles
CO
GRANT, Robert, 1852-1940, Amer-
ican; fiction NI
GRANT, Robert Bruce, 1933- ,
American; nonfiction CON
GRANT, Robert McQueen, 1917- ,
American; nonfiction CON
'GRANT, Venzo' see STANSBERG-
ER, Richard
GRANT, Verne Edwin, 1917- ,
American; nonfiction CON
GRANT, Wilson Wayne, 1941- ,
American; nonfiction CON
GRANT, Zalin Belton, 1941- ,
American; nonfiction CON
GRANTON, Ester Fannie, 1914?-80,
American; journalism CON
GRANVILLE, Austyn, 19th century,
American; fiction NI
GRANVILLE, George, 1667-1734/35,
English; poetry, plays BU
GRANVILLE, Joseph Ensign,
1923- , American; poetry,
nonfiction CON
GRANVILLE-BARKER, Harley,
1877-1946, English; plays, non-
fiction BU DA MAG MCG PO
SEY VD
GRAS, Félix, 1844-1901, Provencal;
poetry, fiction CL
GRASS, Günter, 1927- , German-
Polish; fiction, poetry, plays
BU CL MAG MCG SEY TH WA
GRASSI, Joseph Augustus, 1922- ,
American; nonfiction CON
GRASSO, Domenico, 1917- , Italian;
nonfiction CON
GRATACAP, Louis Pope, 1851-
1917, American; fiction NI
GRATHWOHL, Larry David,
1947- , American; nonfiction

CON
GRATTAN, Clinton Hartley, 1902-
80, American; nonfiction
CON
GRATTAN, Henry, 1746-1820,
Irish; nonfiction HO
GRATTANS-GUINNESS, I. , 1941- ,
British; nonfiction CON
GRATTIUS, fl. 8 A. D. , Roman;
poetry BU
GRATUS, Jack, 1935- , South
African; fiction, nonfiction
CON
GRAU, Jacinto, 1877-1958, Span-
ish; plays BU CL MCG TH
GRAU, Joseph August, 1927- ,
American; nonfiction CON
GRAU, Shirley Ann, 1929- ,
American; fiction BA BR
CON HE VCN WA
GRAUBARD, Paul S. , 1932- ,
American; nonfiction CON
GRAUER, Benjamin Franklin,
1908-77, American; journal-
ism, nonfiction CON
GRAUPE, Daniel, 1934- , Amer-
ican; nonfiction CON
GRAUPERA, Carlos Manuel,
1915- , American; nonfiction
CON
GRAVA, Sigurd, 1934- , Latvian-
American; nonfiction CON
'GRAVEL, Fern' see HALL,
James N.
GRAVEL, Mike, 1930- , Amer-
ican; nonfiction CON
GRAVELY, William Bernard,
1939- , American; nonfiction
CON
GRAVES, Alfred Perceval, 1846-
1931, Irish; poetry HO
GRAVES, Barbara Farris, 1938- ,
American; nonfiction CON
GRAVES, Charles Parlin ('John
Parlin'), 1911-72, American;
juveniles CO
GRAVES, Eleanor MacKenzie,
1926- , American; nonfiction
CON
GRAVES, Nora Calhoun, 1914- ,
American; nonfiction CON
GRAVES, Richard, 1715-1804,
English; fiction, plays, poetry,
translations, nonfiction BU
PO VN
GRAVES, Richard Latshaw, 1928- ,
American; fiction CON
GRAVES, Richard Layton, 1931- ,

American; nonfiction CON
GRAVES, Richard Perceval,
1945- , English; nonfiction
CON
GRAVES, Robert Ranke ('Barbara
Rich'), 1895- , English; fic-
tion, plays, poetry BOR BU
DA MAG NI SEY PO VCN VN
VP
GRAVES, Susan Bernard ('Marley
Bernard'), 1933- , American;
nonfiction CON
GRAVES, William, American;
juveniles WAR
GRAVINA, Gian Vincenzo, 1664-
1718, Italian; nonfiction, plays
BO BU
GRAVLUND, Thorkild Thastum,
1879-1939, Danish; fiction BU
GRAY, Sir Alexander, 1882-1968,
Scots; poetry BU
'GRAY, Angela' see DANIELS,
Dorothy
GRAY, Anne, 1931- , English;
nonfiction CON
GRAY, Asa, 1810-88, American;
nonfiction MY
GRAY, Barry, 1916- , American;
nonfiction CON
'GRAY, Berkeley' (Edwy Searles
Brooks; 'Robert W. Comrade';
'Victor Gunn'; 'Carlton Ross'),
1889-1965, British; fiction,
juveniles REI ST
GRAY, Bettyanne, 1934- , Amer-
ican; nonfiction CON
GRAY, Bradford Hitch, 1942- ,
American; nonfiction CON
GRAY, Curme, American?; fiction
NI
GRAY, Darrell, 1945- , American;
poetry, fiction CON
GRAY, Dorothy Kamer, 1936- ,
American; nonfiction CON
GRAY, Dorothy Kate, 1918- ,
American; fiction CON
'GRAY, Dulcie' (Dulcie Winifred
Catherine Denison), 1920- ,
British; fiction, plays, nonfic-
tion REI
GRAY, Eden, 1907- , American;
nonfiction CON
GRAY, Edwyn A. , 1927- , Eng-
lish; nonfiction CON
GRAY, Elizabeth Janet see VINING,
Elizabeth Gray
GRAY, Farnum, 1940- , American;
nonfiction CON

GRAY, Francine du Plessix, 1930- , Franco-American; nonfiction, fiction CON
GRAY, Genevieve S. ('Jenny Gray'), 1920- , American; juveniles CO
'GRAY, Harriet' see ROBINS, Denise
GRAY, Jack, 1927- , American; journalism, plays, tv CON
GRAY, James Henry, 1906- , Canadian; nonfiction CON
GRAY, James Martin, 1930- , English; nonfiction CON
'GRAY, Jenny' see GRAY, Genevieve
GRAY, Jesse Glen, 1913-77, American; translations, nonfiction CON
GRAY, John, 1927- , Canadian; plays, fiction CR VCD
GRAY, John Edmund, 1922- , American; nonfiction CON
GRAY, John Morgan, 1907- , Canadian; nonfiction CON
GRAY, John Stephens, 1910- , American; nonfiction CON
GRAY, Juanita Ruth, 1918- , American; nonfiction CON
GRAY, Lee Learner, 1924- , American; nonfiction, juveniles CON WAR
GRAY, Lucy Noel C., English; nonfiction CON
'GRAY, Marian' see PIERCE, Edith G.
GRAY, Martin, Polish-American; nonfiction CON
GRAY, Michael Haslam, 1946- , Australian-American; nonfiction CON
GRAY, Nicholas Stuart, 1922-81, Scots; juveniles, plays CO CON KI WAR
GRAY, Nicolete Mary, 1911- , British; nonfiction CON
GRAY, Nigel, 1941- , Irish; fiction, plays, juveniles CON
GRAY, Patricia Clark ('Patsey Gray'; 'Virginia Clark'), American; juveniles CO
GRAY, Peter, 1908- , Anglo-American; nonfiction CON
'GRAY, Philip' see PERLMAN, Jess
GRAY, Robert, American; juveniles WAR
'GRAY, Russell' see FISCHER, Bruno

GRAY, Simon, 1936- , British; fiction, plays VCD VCN VD
GRAY, Stephen E., 1925- , American; nonfiction CON
GRAY, Thomas, 1716-71, English; poetry BRI BU DA MAG PO VP
'GRAY, Walter' see MATTHAEI, Clara
GRAY, Wellington Burbank, 1919-77, American; nonfiction CON
GRAY, William Ralph, 1946- , American; nonfiction CON
GRAY, Wood, 1905?-77, American; nonfiction CON
GRAY of HETON, Sir Thomas (Grey), -1369?, English; nonfiction BU
GRAYBAR, Lloyd Joseph, 1938- , American; nonfiction CON
GRAYBILL, Florence Curtis, 1898- , American; journalism, nonfiction CON
GRAYEFF, Felix, 1906- , German-British; nonfiction CON
GRAYLAND, Valerie Merle ('Lee Belvedere'; 'V. Merle Grayland'; 'Valerie Subond'), New Zealander; juveniles CO
GRAYMONT, Barbara, American; nonfiction CON
GRAYSON, Albert Kirk, 1935- , Canadian; nonfiction CON
GRAYSON, Benson Lee, 1932- , American; nonfiction CON
GRAYSON, Charles, 1905-73, American; fiction, film CON
GRAYSON, Ethel Vaughan Kirk, 1890- , Canadian; poetry, fiction, nonfiction CR
GRAYSON, Henry Wesley, 1910- , Canadian-American; nonfiction CON
GRAYSON, Janet, 1934- , American; nonfiction CON
GRAYSON, Linda Mary, 1947- , Canadian; nonfiction CON
GRAYSON, Marion F., 1906-76, American; juveniles CON
GRAYSON, Melvin Jay, 1924- , American; nonfiction CON
GRAYSON, Richard, 1951- , American; nonfiction CON
GRAYSON, Ruth King, 1926- , British; fiction CON
GRAYSON, William John, 1788-1863, American; poetry, nonfiction

BA MYE
GRAZIANO, Anthony Michael,
1932- , American; nonfiction
CON
GRAZIER, James, American; fiction NI
GRAZZINI, Anton Francesco (Il
Lasca), 1503-84, Italian;
plays, fiction, poetry BO
BU MCG TH
GREACEN, Robert, 1920- , Irish;
poetry HO
GREALEY, Thomas Louis ('Louis
Southworth'), 1916- , British;
fiction CON
GREALIS, Walter, 1929- , Canadian; nonfiction CON
GREALY, Desmond, 1923?-79,
Irish; journalism CON
'THE GREAT COMTE' see
HAWKESWORTH, Eric
GREATOREX, Wilfred, 1910- ,
British; nonfiction, tv CON
GREAVES, John, 1898- , British;
nonfiction CON
GREAVES, Margaret, 1914- ,
British; juveniles, nonfiction
CO KI WAR
GREAVES, Percy Laurie, Jr.,
1906- , American; nonfiction
CON
GREBAN, Arnoul, 1420-71,
French; plays BU
GREBAN, Simon, -1473, French;
plays, poetry BU
GREBENSHCHIKOV, Grigory
Dmitirevich, 1882- , Russian; fiction BU
GRECH, Nikolay Ivanovich, 1787-
1867, Russian; fiction BU
GRECO, Jose, 1918- , Italian-
American; nonfiction CON
GREDY, Jean Pierre, 1920- ,
French; film, plays MCG
GREE, Alain, 1936- , French;
juveniles CON
GREELEY, Horace, 1811-72,
American; nonfiction, journalism BU MYE
GREEN, Abel, 1900-73, American;
journalism CON
GREEN, Alan Baer ('Jack Alan';
'Glen Burne'; 'Roger Denbie'),
1906-75, American; fiction,
nonfiction CON
GREEN, Alan Singer, 1907- ,
American; nonfiction CON
GREEN, Andrew Malcolm, 1927- ,

British; fiction, nonfiction
CON
GREEN, Anita Jane ('Anita Bryant'),
1940- , American; nonfiction
CON
GREEN, Anna Katharine, 1846-
1935, American; fiction, poetry,
plays REI ST
GREEN, Barbara, American; juveniles WAR
GREEN, Celia Elizabeth, 1935- ,
English; nonfiction CON
GREEN, Constance McLaughlin,
1897-1975, American; nonfiction
CON
'GREEN, D.' see CASEWIT, Curtis
GREEN, David, 1942- , American;
nonfiction CON
GREEN, David Marvin, 1932- ,
American; nonfiction CON
GREEN, Donald Edward, 1936- ,
American; nonfiction CON
GREEN, Edith Pinero, 1929- ,
American; fiction CON
GREEN, Elmer Ellsworth, 1917- ,
American; nonfiction CON
GREEN, Fitzhugh, 1917- , American; nonfiction CON
GREEN, Frederick Charles, 1891-
1964, Scots; nonfiction CON
WA
GREEN, Frederick Laurence, 1902-
53, English; fiction HO
GREEN, Frederick Pratt, 1903- ,
American; poetry, nonfiction
CON
GREEN, Galen, 1949- , American;
poetry, fiction CON
GREEN, George MacEwan, 1931- ,
Scots; plays CON
GREEN, George Sherman, 1930- ,
American; nonfiction CON
GREEN, Georgia M., 1944- ,
American; nonfiction CON
GREEN, Gerald, 1922- , American; fiction, tv WA
GREEN, Gilbert, 1906- , American; nonfiction CON
GREEN, Hannah see GREENBERG,
Joanne
'GREEN, Henry' (Henry Vincent
Yorke), 1905-73/74, English;
fiction BU CON DA MAG PO
SEY VCN VN
GREEN, Hollis Lynn, 1933- ,
American; nonfiction CON
GREEN, I. G., American; fiction
NI

GREEN, Jane, 1937- , American;
juveniles, nonfiction CO CON
WAR
GREEN, Jane Nugent, 1918- ,
American; nonfiction CON
GREEN, John Lafayette, 1929- ,
American; nonfiction CON
GREEN, John Richard, 1837-83,
English; nonfiction, journalism
BU DA
GREEN, Jonathan William, 1939- ,
American; nonfiction CON
GREEN, Joseph Lee, 1931- ,
American; fiction, journalism
AS NI
GREEN, Julien, 1900- , Amer-
ican-French; fiction, plays,
diary, nonfiction BU CL
MAG MCG RO SEY TH
GREEN, Kathleen, Irish; juveniles
WAR
GREEN, Landis Knight, 1940- ,
American; nonfiction CON
GREEN, Lawrence Winter, 1940- ,
American; nonfiction CON
GREEN, Louis, 1929- , French-
Australian; nonfiction CON
GREEN, Mark Joseph, 1945- ,
American; nonfiction CON
GREEN, Martyn, 1899-1975,
American; nonfiction CON
GREEN, Mary Moore, 1906- ,
American; juveniles CO
GREEN, Matthew, 1696-1737,
English; poetry BU DA PO
VP
GREEN, Maureen Patricia, 1933- ,
British; nonfiction CON
GREEN, Maurice Berkeley,
1920- , British; nonfiction
CON
GREEN, Michael Frederick,
1927- , British; journalism,
nonfiction, fiction, plays
CON
GREEN, Milton Douglas, 1903- ,
American; nonfiction CON
GREEN, Morton, 1937- , Amer-
ican; fiction, poetry, plays,
nonfiction CO CON
GREEN, Norma Berger, 1925- ,
American; juveniles CON
WAR
GREEN, Paul Edgar, 1927- ,
American; nonfiction CON
GREEN, Paul Eliot, 1894-1981,
American; plays, fiction, non-
fiction, poetry BA BR CON

MCG MCN PO VCD VD
'GREEN, Peter' see BULMER,
Kenneth
GREEN, Peter, 1924- , British;
fiction, nonfiction, translations
VCN
GREEN, Phyllis, 1932- , Amer-
ican; juveniles CO CON
'GREEN, Robert' see SMITH, Rich-
ard R.
GREEN, Robert, British?; fiction
NI
GREEN, Robert David, 1942- ,
American; journalism CON
GREEN, Robert Lee, 1933- ,
American; nonfiction CON SH
GREEN, Roger Curtis, 1932- ,
American; nonfiction CON
GREEN, Roger Lancelyn, 1918- ,
British; juveniles, fiction, po-
etry, nonfiction DE KI NI
GREEN, Roland James, 1944- ,
American; fiction CON
GREEN, Ronald Michael, 1942- ,
American; nonfiction CON
GREEN, Rose Basile, 1914- ,
American; poetry, nonfiction
CON
GREEN, Samuel, 1948- , Ameri-
can; poetry CON
GREEN, Samuel Swett, 1837-1918,
American; nonfiction ENG
GREEN, Sheila Ellen ('Sheila Green-
wald'), 1934- , American;
juveniles CO
GREEN, Susan, 1941- , American;
nonfiction CON
GREEN, Thomas F., 1927- ,
American; nonfiction CON
GREEN, Thomas Hill, 1836-82,
English; nonfiction BU DA
GREEN, Timothy Seton, 1936- ,
English; nonfiction CON
GREEN, William, 1926- , Ameri-
can; nonfiction CON
GREEN, William A., Jr., 1935- ,
American; nonfiction CON
GREEN, William Mark ('William
Iden'), 1929- , American; fic-
tion, film CON
GREENAWAY, Gladys ('Julia Man-
ners'), 1901- , British; fiction
CON
GREENAWAY, Kate, 1846-1901,
English; juveniles COM
GREENBANK, Anthony Hunt, 1933- ,
American; nonfiction CON
GREENBERG, Barbara Levenson,

1932- , American; poetry,
nonfiction CON
GREENBERG, Bernard, 1922- ,
American; nonfiction CON
GREENBERG, Bernard Louis,
1917- , American; nonfiction
CON
GREENBERG, Edward Seymour,
1942- , American; nonfiction
CON
GREENBERG, Eliezer, 1897?-
1977, Russian-American; po-
etry, nonfiction BU CON
GREENBERG, Harvey R. , 1935- ,
American; juveniles CO
GREENBERG, Ira Arthur, 1924- ,
American; nonfiction CON
GREENBERG, Ivan see 'RAHV,
Philip'
GREENBERG, Joanne ('Hannah
Green'), 1932- , American;
juveniles, fiction CO CON
GREENBERG, Joseph Harold,
1915- , American; nonfiction
CON
GREENBERG, Judith Anne, 1938- ,
American; poetry CON
GREENBERG, Kenneth Ray,
1930- , American; nonfiction
CON
GREENBERG, Martin, 1918- ,
American; anthology AS NI
GREENBERG, Martin Harry,
1941- , American; anthology,
nonfiction CON NI
GREENBERG, Paul, 1937- ,
American; journalism CON
GREENBERG, Pearl, 1927- ,
American; nonfiction CON
GREENBERG, Polly, 1932- ,
American; juveniles, nonfiction
CON WAR
GREENBERG, Samuel, 1843-1917,
American; poetry BR
GREENBERG, Selig, 1904- ,
Russian-American; nonfiction
CON
GREENBERG, Simon, 1901- ,
Russian-American; nonfiction
CON
GREENBERG, Stanley Bernard,
1945- , American; nonfiction
CON
GREENBERG, Uri Zvi ('Tur-
Malka'), 1891/98-1981, Yid-
dish; poetry BU CON LA TH
WAK
GREENBERGER, Allen Jay,

1937- , American; nonfiction
CON
GREENBERGER, Howard, 1924- ,
American; plays, nonfiction
CON
GREENBERGER, Martin, 1931- ,
American; nonfiction CON
GREENBIE, Marjorie Barstow,
1889?-1976, American; nonfic-
tion CON
GREENBLATT, Augusta, 1912- ,
American; nonfiction CON
GREENBLATT, Edwin, 1920- ,
American; nonfiction CON
GREENBLATT Stephen Jay,
1943- , American; nonfiction
CON
GREENE, Bert, 1923- , American;
nonfiction CON
GREENE, Bette, 1934- , Ameri-
can; juveniles CO CON KI
WAR
GREENE, Constance Clarke,
1924- , American; juveniles
CO CON DEM KI WAR
GREENE, Ellin, 1927- , American;
juveniles, fiction, nonfiction
CO CON WAR
GREENE, Ernestine Leverne,
1939- , American; nonfiction
CON
'GREENE, Fred' see CADET, John
GREENE, Graham, 1904- , Eng-
lish; fiction, plays, juveniles
BU CO DA KI MAG MCC MCG
PO REI SEY ST VCD VCN VN
WAR
GREENE, Harry Joseph, 1906- ,
American; nonfiction CON
GREENE, Howard R. , 1937- ,
American; nonfiction CON
GREENE, Hugh Carleton, 1910- ,
British; journalism, nonfiction
CON
GREENE, John Colton, 1917- ,
American; nonfiction CON
GREENE, John William, Jr. ,
1946- , American; journalism,
nonfiction CON
GREENE, Jonathan Edward, 1943- ,
American; poetry, translations
VCP
GREENE, Lorenzo J. , 1899- ,
American; nonfiction SH
GREENE, Mabel see BEAN, Mabel
GREEN, Naomi, 1942- , American;
nonfiction CON
'GREENE, Pamela' see FORMAN,

Joan
GREENE, Robert, 1558-92, English; fiction, nonfiction, plays, poetry, translations BU DA MAG MCG PO RU VN
GREENE, Ruth Altman, 1896- , American; nonfiction CON
GREENE, Stephanie, 1953- , American; nonfiction CON
GREENE, Stephen, 1914-79, American; nonfiction CON
GREENE, Wade, 1933- , American; juveniles CO WAR
GREENEBAUM, Louise Guggenheim, 1919- , American; juveniles, nonfiction CON
GREENFELD, Howard, American; translations, juveniles CO CON WAR
GREENFIELD, Eloise, 1929- , American; juveniles, nonfiction CO CON SH
GREENFIELD, Irving A., 1928- , American; fiction NI
GREENFIELD, James Lloyd, 1924- , American; journalism CON
GREENFIELD, Norman Samuel, 1923- , American; nonfiction CON
'GREENGROIN, Artie' see BROWN, Harry P. M.
GREENHALGH, Peter Andrew Livsey, 1945- , English; nonfiction CON
GREENHOUGH, Terry ('Andrew Lester'), 1944- , English; fiction NI
GREENHOUSE, Linda, 1947- , American; journalism CON
GREENIDGE, Edwin, 1929- , American; nonfiction, juveniles SH WAR
'GREENING, Hamilton' see HAMILTON, Charles H. S.
GREENLAND, Francis Laffan, 1924- , English; fiction MCC
GREENLAW, Jean-Pierre, 1910- , French; nonfiction CON
GREENLEAF, Barbara Kaye, 1942- , American; juveniles CO
GREENLEAF, Margery, American; juveniles WAR
GREENLEAF, Peter, 1910- , American; nonfiction CON
GREENLEAF, Stephen Howell,

1942- , American; fiction CON
GREENLEE, Douglas, 1935-79, American; nonfiction CON
GREENLEE, James Wallace, 1933- , American; nonfiction CON
GREENLEE, Sam, 1930- , American; fiction, nonfiction, poetry CON NI SH
GREENLICK, Merwyn Ronald, 1935- , American; nonfiction CON
GREENOUGH, Horatio, 1805-52, American; nonfiction MY
GREENSPAN, Bud, 1927- , American; nonfiction, tv CON
GREENSPAN, Sophie, 1906- , Canadian; nonfiction CON
GREENSPUN, Roger Austin, 1929- , American; nonfiction CON
GREENSTEIN, Fred Irwin, 1930- , American; nonfiction CON
GREENWALD, Jerry, 1923- , American; nonfiction CON
'GREENWALD, Sheila' see GREEN, Sheila E.
GREENWAY, Hugh Davids Scott, 1935- , American; journalism CON
GREENWAY, Roger Selles, 1934- , American; nonfiction CON
GREENWOOD, David Charles, 1927- , Anglo-American; nonfiction CON
GREENWOOD, Kathryn Moore, 1922- , American; nonfiction CON
GREENWOOD, Ted, 1930- , Australian; juveniles DEM KI
GREENWOOD, Thomas, 1851-1908, British; nonfiction ENG
GREENWOOD, Val David, 1937- , American; nonfiction CON
GREENWOOD, Walter, 1903-74, British; fiction, plays, fiction, nonfiction CON DA
GREER, Ann Lennarson, 1944- , American; nonfiction CON
GREER, Arthur Ellis, Jr., 1929- , American; nonfiction CON
GREER, Ben, 1948- , American; fiction CON KIB
GREER, Georgeanna Herrmann, 1922- , American; nonfiction CON
GREER, Germaine, 1939- , Aus-

tralian; nonfiction CON
GREER, Rebecca Ellen, 1935- ,
  American; nonfiction, jour-
  nalism CON
'GREER, Richard' Ziff-Davis
  house name NI
GREER, Rita, 1942- , American;
  nonfiction CON
GREER, Scott Allen, 1922- ,
  American; nonfiction CON
GREER, Tom, American?; fiction
  NI
GREFFLINGER, Georg, 1620-77,
  German; poetry BU
GREG, Percy, 1836-89, English;
  poetry, fiction, nonfiction NI
GREG, Sir Walter Wilson, 1875-
  1959, English; nonfiction DA
GREGG, Charles Thornton, 1927- ,
  American; nonfiction CON
GREGG, Hubert, 1916- , British;
  fiction, plays CON
GREGG, Jess, 1926- , American;
  plays, nonfiction CON
GREGG, John Edwin, 1925- ,
  American; nonfiction CON
GREGG, Walter Harold, 1919- ,
  American; juveniles, nonfic-
  tion CO CON
GREGOR, Anthony James, 1929- ,
  American; nonfiction CON
GREGOR, Arthur, 1923- , Amer-
  ican; poetry, plays, juveniles
  VCP
GREGORAS, Nicephorus, 1290-
  1360, Byzantine; nonfiction
  LA
GREGORCIC, Simon, 1844-1906,
  Slovene; poetry BU
GREGORI, Leon, 1919- , Rus-
  sian-American; juveniles CO
GREGOROVIUS, Ferdinand Adolf,
  1821-91, German; poetry,
  nonfiction BU
GREGOROWSKI, Christopher,
  1940- , South African; juven-
  iles CON
GREGOR-TAJOVSKY, Jozef, 1874-
  1940, Slovak; fiction, plays
  BU
GREGORY, Bettina, 1946- ,
  American; journalism CON
'GREGORY, Chuck' see GNAEGY,
  Charles
GREGORY, Diana Jean, 1933- ,
  Canadian; nonfiction CON
GREGORY, Dick, 1932- , Amer-
  ican; nonfiction CON SH

GREGORY, Freida, 1938- , Amer-
  ican; nonfiction CON
GREGORY, Hollingsworth Franklin,
  1906- , American; nonfiction
  CON
GREGORY, Horace Victor, 1898-1982,
  American; poetry, nonfiction,
  translations BR VCP VP
GREGORY, Dame Isabella Augusta
  Persse, 1852-1932, Irish;
  plays, fiction, translations
  BU HO MAG MCG PO VD
GREGORY, James, 1912- , Brit-
  ish; nonfiction CON
GREGORY, Kenneth Malcolm,
  1921- , British; nonfiction
  CON
'GREGORY, Lisa' see CAMP, Can-
  dace P.
'GREGORY, Mark' see BURCH,
  Monte G.
GREGORY, Owen, British; fiction
  NI
GREGORY, Paul Rogerick, 1941- ,
  American; nonfiction CON
GREGORY, Peter, 1924- , Amer-
  ican; nonfiction CON
GREGORY, Richard Langton,
  1923- , English; nonfiction
  CON
GREGORY, Robert Granville,
  1924- , American; nonfiction
  CON
GREGORY, Ruth Wilhelmine,
  1910- , American; nonfiction
  CON
'GREGORY, Stephen' see PENDLE-
  TON, Donald E.; PENZLER,
  Otto
GREGORY, Thomas Bernard,
  1940- , American; nonfiction
  CON
GREGORY, Vahan, 1927- , Amer-
  ican; plays, fiction CON
GREGORY, Violet Lefler, 1907- ,
  Canadian-American; poetry
  CON
GREGORY, Yvonne, 1919?-79,
  American; poetry, nonfiction
  CON
GREGORY ACINDYNUS, 14th cen-
  tury, Byzantine; poetry, non-
  fiction BU
GREGORY of CYPRUS, 1241?-89?,
  Byzantine; nonfiction LA
GREGORY of NAREK, 950-1010,
  Armenian; poetry BU
GREGORY of NAZIANZUS, St.,

329-89, Greek; nonfiction
BU GR LA
GREGORY of NYSSA, St.,, 335-94,
Greek; nonfiction BU GR LA
GREGORY of TOURS, Georgius
Florentius, 538/39-94, Roman;
nonfiction BU GR TH
GREGORY PALAMAS, 14th cen-
tury, Byzantine; nonfiction
BU
GREGORY the GREAT, St., 540-
604, Latin; nonfiction BU GR
TH
GREGSTON, Gene, 1925- , Amer-
ican; nonfiction CON
GREIF, Martin, 1938- , Amer-
ican; nonfiction CON
GREIFEENBERG, Catharina Regina
von, 1638-94, German; poetry
BU
GREIG, Maysie ('Jennifer Ames';
'Ann Barclay'; 'Mary Douglas
Warren'), 1902- , Australian;
fiction CON
GREINER, Donald James, 1940- ,
American; nonfiction CON
GREINKE, Lawrence Eric,
1948- , American; poetry
CON
GREISMAN, Joan Ruth, 1937- ,
American; nonfiction CON
GREK, Maxim (Maxim the Greek),
1480-1556, Greek; nonfiction
BU
GRELE, Ronald John, 1934- ,
American; nonfiction CON
GREMILLION, Joseph, 1919- ,
American; nonfiction CON
GREMMELS, Marion Chapman,
American; juveniles WAR
GRENANDER, Mary Elizabeth,
1918- , American; nonfiction
CON
GRENDLER, Paul Frederick,
1936- , American; nonfiction
CON
'GRENDON, Stephen' see DER-
LETH, August
GRENELLE, Lisa, 1900- ,
American; nonfiction CON
GRENFELL, Joyce Irene, 1910-
79, British; nonfiction CON
GRENFELL, Julian, 1888-1915,
English; poetry DA
GRENIER, Judson Achille, 1930- ,
American; nonfiction CON
GRENNAN, Margaret Rose, Amer-
ican; nonfiction CON

'GRENVILLE, Pelham' see WODE-
HOUSE, P. G.
GRESHAM, Elizabeth Fenner ('Robin
Grey'), 1904- , American;
fiction, nonfiction, plays CON
GRESHAM, Perry Epler, 1907- ,
American; nonfiction CON
GRESHOFF, Jan, 1888- , Dutch;
poetry, nonfiction BU
GRESSET, Jean Baptiste Louis,
1709-77, French; poetry, plays
BU MCG TH
GRETSER, Jakob, 1562-1625, Ger-
man; plays BU
GRETZ, Susanna, 1937- , Amer-
ican; juveniles CO
GRETZER, John, American; juven-
iles CO
GREULACH, Victor August, 1906- ,
American; nonfiction CON
GREVE, Félix P. see 'GROVE,
Frederick P.'
GREVILLE, Charles Canvendich
Fulke, 1794-1865, English;
diary BU
GREVILLE, Fulke (Lord Brooke),
1554-1628, English; nonfiction,
poetry, plays BU DA PO RU
VP
GREVIN, Jacques, 1538-70, French;
plays, poetry BU TH
GREW, James Hooper, 1906- ,
American; nonfiction CON
'GREX, Leo' see GRIBBLE, Leonard
R.
GREY, Anthony, 1938- , English;
fiction MCC
'GREY, Charles' see TUBB, Edwin
C.
GREY, David Lennox, 1935- ,
American; nonfiction CON
GREY, Jerry, 1926- , American;
nonfiction, juveniles CO CON
'GREY, Louis' see GRIBBLE,
Leonard R.
GREY, Robert Waters, 1943- ,
American; poetry CON
'GREY, Robin' see GRESHAM,
Elizabeth F.
GREY, Zane, 1872-1939, American;
fiction, nonfiction BR PO VN
'GREY OWL' (Archibald Stansfeld
Belaney), 1888-1938, Canadian;
juveniles, fiction, nonfiction
CO CR KI
'GRI' see DENNEY, Diana
GRIBACHËV, Nikolai Matveyevich,
1910- , Russian; poetry BU

'GRIBBAN, Volsted' house name
NI
GRIBBEN, William James, 1943- ,
American; nonfiction CON
GRIBBLE, Charles Edward,
1936- , American; nonfiction
CON
GRIBBLE, Harry Wagstaff Graham,
1891?-1981, British; plays,
film CON
GRIBBLE, Leonard Reginald
('Sterry Browning'; 'Landon
Grant'; 'Leo Grex'; 'Louis
Grey'; 'Dexter Muir'), 1908- ,
British; fiction, plays, non-
fiction CON REI ST
GRIBBON, William L. see
'MUNDY, Talbot'
GRIBOYEDOV, Alexander Sergeye-
vich, 1795-1829, Russian;
plays BU MCG TH
GRICE, Frederick, 1910- ,
British; juveniles, poetry,
nonfiction CO KI
GRICE, Julia Haughey, 1940- ,
American; fiction, nonfiction
CON
'GRIDBAN, Volsted' see TUBBS,
Edwin C.
GRIDLEY, Marion Eleanor, 1906-
74, American; juveniles CON
WAR
GRIEB, Lyndal, 1940- , Amer-
ican; nonfiction CON
GRIECK, Claude de, 1625-70,
Flemish; plays BU
GRIEDER, Josephine, 1939- ,
American; nonfiction CON
GRIEDER, Theodore, 1926- ,
American; poetry, nonfiction
CON
GRIEDER, Walter, 1924- ,
Swiss; nonfiction, translations
CO CON
GRIEG, John Nordahl Brun, 1902-
43, Norwegian; poetry, fiction,
plays BU CL MCG SEY TH
GRIER, William H., American;
nonfiction SH
GRIERSON, Edward Dobbyn ('Brian
Crowther'; 'John P. Steven-
son'), 1914-75, British; fic-
tion, plays, nonfiction REI
GRIERSON, Sir Herbert John
Clifford, 1866-1960, Scots;
nonfiction BU CON DA
GRIERSON, John, 1909-77, British;
nonfiction CON

GRIES, Tom, 1923?-70, American;
film CON
GRIESE, Arnold Alfred, 1921- ,
American; juveniles CO CON
GRIESON, Ronald Edward, 1943- ,
American; nonfiction CON
GRIESSMAN, Benjamin Eugene,
1934- , American; nonfiction
CON
GRIEST, Guinevere Lindley, 1924- ,
American; nonfiction CON
GRIEVE, Christopher Murray ('Iso-
bel Guthrie'; 'A. K. Laidlaw';
'Hugh MacDiarmid'; 'James
MacLaren'; 'Pteleon'), 1892-
1978, Scots; poetry, nonfiction,
translations BU CON DA PO
SEY VCP VP
GRIEVES, Forest Leslie, 1938- ,
American; nonfiction CON
GRIFALCONI, Ann, 1929- , Amer-
ican; juveniles DE
'GRIFF' house name NI
'GRIFF, Alan' see SUDDABY, Wil-
liam D.
'GRIFF, Ben S.' see FAWCETT,
Frank D.
GRIFFEN, Elizabeth, American;
juveniles WAR
GRIFFIN, Arthur Gwyn, 1922?-67,
British; fiction CON WA
GRIFFIN, Arthur J. ('Lee Frank'),
1921- , American; fiction
CON
GRIFFIN, Barbara Cook, 1945- ,
American; nonfiction, fiction
CON
GRIFFIN, Charles Carroll, 1902-76,
American; nonfiction CON
GRIFFIN, Charles William, 1925- ,
American; nonfiction CON
GRIFFIN, David Ray, 1939- ,
American; nonfiction CON
GRIFFIN, Edward Michael, 1937- ,
American; nonfiction CON
GRIFFIN, Emilie Russell Dietrich,
1936- , American; nonfiction
CON
GRIFFIN, Gerald, 1803-40, Irish;
fiction, plays, poetry BU HO
MAG VN
GRIFFIN, Gerald Gehrig, 1933- ,
American; nonfiction CON
GRIFFIN, Gwyn, 1922?-67, ?;
fiction CON
GRIFFIN, Henry William, 1935- ,
American; nonfiction CON
GRIFFIN, John Howard, 1902-80,

American; fiction, nonfiction
BA BR CON SEY WA
GRIFFIN, John Quealy, 1948- ,
American; nonfiction CON
GRIFFIN, Judith Berry, American;
juveniles WAR
GRIFFIN, Keith Broadwell, 1938- ,
American; nonfiction CON
GRIFFIN, Mary, 1916- , Amer-
ican; nonfiction CON
GRIFFIN, Robert, 1936- , Amer-
ican; nonfiction CON
GRIFFIN, Susan, 1943- , Amer-
ican; poetry CON
GRIFFIN, Walter, 1937- , Amer-
ican; poetry CON
GRIFFITH, Arthur, 1872-1922,
Irish; journalism HO
GRIFFITH, Corinne, 1898?-1979,
American; nonfiction CON
GRIFFITH, Field, American;
juveniles WAR
'GRIFFITH, George' (George
Chetwynd Griffith-Jones), 1857-
1906, English; fiction AS NI
GRIFFITH, Jerry, 1932- , Amer-
ican; nonfiction CON
GRIFFITH, Kathryn, 1923- ,
American; nonfiction CON
GRIFFITH, Kenneth, 1921- ,
Welsh; film CON
GRIFFITH, Mary, 1800?-77,
American; nonfiction, fiction
NI
GRIFFITH, Patricia Browning,
1935- , American; journalism,
fiction CON
GRIFFITH, Robert, 1940- ,
American; nonfiction CON
GRIFFITH, Thomas Gwynfor
('Gwynfor Cilffriw'), 1926- ,
Welsh; nonfiction CON
GRIFFITH, William Edgar, 1920- ,
American; nonfiction CON
GRIFFITHS, Ann Thomas, 1776-
1805, Welsh; hymns BU
GRIFFITHS, Bryn lyn David,
1933- , Welsh; poetry, plays,
nonfiction CON VCP
GRIFFITHS, Gordon Douglas,
1910-73, English; juveniles
CO KI
GRIFFITHS, Helen, 1939- ,
British; juveniles, fiction
CO DEM KI WAR
'GRIFFITHS, Jeannette' see EYER-
LEY, Jeanette H.
GRIFFITHS, Naomi, 1934- ,

British; nonfiction CON
GRIFFITHS, Percival Joseph,
1899- , British; nonfiction
CON
GRIFFITHS, Thomas Melvin,
1910- , American; nonfiction
CON
GRIFFITHS, Trevor, 1935- ,
British; plays, juveniles CON
VCD
GRIFFOLINI, Francesco see AC-
COLTI, Francesco
GRIGGS, Earl Leslie, 1899- ,
American; nonfiction CON
GRIGGS, Lee, 1928- , American;
journalism CON
GRIGGS, Tamar, 1941- , Amer-
ican; nonfiction CON
GRIGNON, Claude Henri ('Valdom-
bre'), 1894- , Canadian; fic-
tion, radio BU
GRIGOR, Narekatsi, 945/49-1003/
11, Armenian; poetry PRU
GRIGORIS AGHTHAMARTSI, late
15th century, Armenian; poetry
PRU
GRIGOROVICH, Dmitry Vasilyevich,
1882-99, Russian; nonfiction,
fiction BU TH
GRIGORYEV, Apollon Alexandrovich,
1822-64, Russian; poetry, non-
fiction BU TH
GRIGSBY, Gordon, 1927- , Amer-
ican; poetry, fiction, nonfiction,
translations CON
GRIGSON, Geoffrey Edward, 1905- ,
English; poetry, nonfiction DA
SEY VCP
GRIGSON, Jane, 1928- , English;
translations, nonfiction CON
GRILL, Nannette L. ('Louise Chris-
tian'), 1935- , American;
juveniles, fiction CON
GRILLO, John, 1942- , British;
plays VCD
GRILLO, Ralph David, 1940- ,
English; nonfiction CON
GRILLO, Virgil, 1938- , American;
nonfiction CON
GRILLPARZER, Franz, 1791-1872,
Austrian; plays, poetry BU
MAG MCG TH
GRIMALD, Nicholas, 1519?-62?,
English; poetry, plays BU
GRIMES, Johnnie Marie, American;
nonfiction CON
GRIMES, Lee ('Fremont Dodge'),
1920- , American; fiction

CON
GRIMES, Nikki, 1950- , American;
poetry, juveniles, nonfiction
CON
GRIMES, Paul, 1924- , American;
journalism, nonfiction CON
GRIMES, Ronald L., 1943- ,
American; nonfiction CON
GRIMM, August Heinrich, 1873-
44, German; fiction BU
GRIMM, Cherry Barbar ('Cherry
Wilder'), 1930- , New Zea-
lander; fiction, nonfiction
CON NI
GRIMM, Friedrich Melchior, 1723-
1807, German; journalism,
nonfiction BU TH
GRIMM, Hans, 1875-1959, Ger-
man; fiction, nonfiction CL
GRIMM, Jacob Ludwig, 1785-
1863, German; juveniles, non-
fiction BU CO TH
GRIMM, Reinhold, 1931- ,
German-American; nonfiction
CON
GRIMM, Wilhelm Karkl, 1786-
1859, German; nonfiction,
juveniles BU CO TH
GRIMM, William Carey, 1907- ,
American; nonfiction CO
CON
GRIMME, Friedrich Wilhelm,
1827-87, German; fiction BU
GRIMMELSHAUSEN, Johann Jakob
Christopher von, 1622-76,
German; fiction BU MAG TH
GRIMSHAW, Allen Day, 1929- ,
American; nonfiction CON
GRIMSHAW, Nigel Gilroy, 1925- ,
British; nonfiction CO CON
GRIMSLEY, Linda, 1940- ,
American; fiction, nonfiction
CON
GRIMSTED, Patricia Kennedy,
1935- , American; nonfiction
CON
'GRIN, Alex' (Alexander Stepano-
vich Grinevsky), 1880-1932,
Russian; fiction BU CL
GRINDAL, Bruce T., 1940- ,
American; nonfiction CON
GRINDEL, Carl William, 1905- ,
American; nonfiction CON
GRINDEL, Eugene see 'ELUARD,
Paul'
GRINDEL, John Anthony, 1937- ,
American; nonfiction CON
GRINDER, Michael, 1942- ,

American; poetry CON
'GRINDLE, Carleton' see PAGE,
Gerald W.
GRINGHUIS, Richard H. (Dirk),
1918-74, American; juveniles
CO
GRINGOIRE, Pierre, 1475?-1538?,
French; poetry, plays BU
MCG
GRINNELL, George Bird, 1849-
1938, American; juveniles CO
GRINSPOON, Lester, 1928- ,
American; nonfiction CON
GRIPE, Maria K., 1923- , Amer-
ican; juveniles DE WAR
GRISE, Jeannette see THOMAS,
Jeannette
GRISHASHVILI, Joseb (Mamulaish-
vili), 1889-1965, Georgian;
poetry PRU
GRISWOLD, Rufus Wilmot, 1815-57,
American; anthology BR BU
MYE
GRISWOLD del CASTILLO, Richard
Allan, 1942- , American; non-
fiction CON MAR
GROCH, Judith Goldstein, 1929- ,
American; juveniles CO
GROCHOWIAK, Stanislaw, 1934-76,
Polish; poetry, plays, fiction
BU CL
GRÖLOH, Jan H. F. see 'NESCIO'
GROEN van PRINSTERER, Guil-
laume, 1801-76, Dutch; jour-
nalism BU
GROENBJERG, Kirsten Andersen,
1946- , Danish-American;
nonfiction CON
GRÖNDAL, Benedikt Sveinbjarnar-
son, 1826-1907, Icelander;
fiction, poetry BU
GROENE, Bertram Hawthorne,
1923- , American; nonfiction
CON
GROENHOFF, Edwin L., 1924- ,
American; nonfiction, fiction
CON
GROENINGEN, August Pieter ('Wil-
lem van Oevere'), 1865-94,
Dutch; fiction BU
GROENNINGS, Sven O., 1934- ,
American; nonfiction CON
GROENOSET, Dagfinn, 1920- ,
Norwegian; journalism, fiction
CON
GROF, Stanislav, 1931- , Czech-
American; nonfiction CON
GROFF, Patrick John, 1924- ,

American; nonfiction CON

GROFF, Warren Frederick, 1924- , American; nonfiction CON

GROGAN, Emmett ('Fastlife'; 'Kenny Wisdom'), 1942- , American; nonfiction CON

GROH, Edwin Charles, 1910- , American; nonfiction CON

GROH, George W., 1922- , American; journalism, nonfiction CON

GROHSKOPF, Bernice Appelbaum, 1921- , American; juveniles CO WAR

GROIA, Philip, 1941- , American; nonfiction CON

GROL, Lini Richarda, 1913- , Dutch-Canadian; nonfiction, fiction, poetry, juveniles CO CON

GROLLMAN, Earl A., 1925- , American; juveniles CO

GROLLMAN, Sharon Hya, 1954- , American; nonfiction CON

GROMACKI, Robert Glenn, 1933- , American; nonfiction CON

GROMADA, Thaddeus Vladimir, 1929- , American; nonfiction CON

GROMBACH, John Valentin, 1901- , American; nonfiction CON

GRONDONA, Leo St. Clare, 1890- , Australian; nonfiction CON

GROOCOCK, John Michael, 1929- , English; nonfiction CON

GROOM, Arthur John Pelham, British; fiction NI

GROOM, Arthur William ('Graham Adamson'; 'George Anderson'; 'Daphne du Blane'; 'Gordon Grimsley'; 'Bill Pembury'; 'John Stanstead'; 'Maurice Templar'; 'Martin Toonder'), 1898-1964, English; juveniles CO

GROOM, Winston, 1943- , American; fiction CON

GROOME, Francis Hindes, 1851-1902, English; nonfiction, fiction BU

GROOT, Hugo de (Grotius), 1583-1645, Dutch; nonfiction, poetry, plays BU MAG

GROOT, Pieter de, 1615-78, Dutch; nonfiction, poetry BU

GROOTE, Geert, 1340-84, Dutch; nonfiction BU

GROPMAN, Donald Sheldon, 1936- , American; nonfiction CON

GROPPER, William, 1897-1977, American; cartoons, juveniles CON

'GROS, J. H. de' see VILLIARD, Paul

GROSE, Burl Donald, 1943- , American; nonfiction CON

GROSJEAN, Jean, 1912- , French; poetry, translations CL

GROSMAN, Brian Allen, 1935- , Canadian; nonfiction CON

GROSMAN, Ladislav, 1921- , Czech; nonfiction CON

GROSS, Alan, 1947- , American; juveniles, plays CON

GROSS, Beatrice, 1935- , American; juveniles, plays CON

GROSS, Ben, 1891-1979, American; journalism, nonfiction CON

GROSS, Daniel Russell, 1942- , American; nonfiction CON

GROSS, David Charles, 1923- , Belgian-American; journalism, translations, film CON

GROSS, Hanns, 1928- , Austrian-American; nonfiction CON

GROSS, James A., 1933- , American; nonfiction CON

GROSS, Mary Anne, 1943- , American; nonfiction CON

GROSS, Michael, 1891?-1979, American; nonfiction CON

GROSS, Michael Robert ('Robert Alexander'), 1952- , American; fiction, nonfiction CON

GROSS, Milton, 1912?-73, American; journalism CON

GROSS, Phyllis Pennebaker, 1915- , American; nonfiction CON

GROSS, Ruth Belov, American; juveniles WAR

GROSS, Samuel Harry, 1933- , American; nonfiction CON

GROSS, Sarah Chokla, 1906-76, American; juveniles, translations, nonfiction CO CON

GROSS, Sheldon Harvey (Shelly), 1921- , American; fiction CON

GROSS, Stuart D., 1914- , American; nonfiction CON

GROSS, Terence ('Tristan Costinesu'), 1947- , American; fiction CON
GROSS, Theodore Lawrence, 1930- , American; nonfiction CON
GROSSACK, Irvin Millman, 1927- , American; nonfiction CON
GROSSEN, Neal E., 1943- , American; nonfiction CON
GROSSER, Alfred, 1925- , German; nonfiction CON
GROSSER, Morton, 1931- , American; nonfiction CON
GROSSETESTE, Robert, 1170-1253, English; nonfiction, poetry BU DA
GROSSI, Tommaso, 1790-1853, Italian; poetry, fiction BO BU TH
GROSSINGER, Richard Selig, 1944- , American; nonfiction CON
GROSSINGER, Tania, 1937- , American; nonfiction CON
GROSSKOPF, Johannes Friedrich Wilhelm, 1885-1948, Afrikaans; plays, journalism BU
GROSSMAN, Alfred, 1927- , American; fiction BR VCN
GROSSMAN, Edith Howitt Searle, 1863-1931, New Zealander; fiction, nonfiction VN
GROSSMAN, Frances Kaplan, 1939- , American; nonfiction CON
GROSSMAN, Gary Howard, 1948- , American; nonfiction CON
GROSSMAN, Josephine J. see 'MERRIL, Judith'
GROSSMAN, Julian, 1931- , American; nonfiction CON
GROSSMAN, Lawrence, 1945- , American; nonfiction CON
GROSSMAN, Lee, 1931- , American; nonfiction CON
GROSSMAN, Leonid Petrovich, 1888- , Russian; nonfiction BU
GROSSMAN, Martin A., 1951- , American; journalism CON
GROSSMAN, Martin Allen, 1943- , American; poetry CON
GROSSMAN, Mary Louise, 1930- , American; film, juveniles CON

GROSSMAN, Richard Lee, 1921- , American; nonfiction CON
GROSSMAN, Robert, 1940- , American; juveniles CO
GROSSMAN, Samuel, 1897- , American; nonfiction CON
GROSSMAN, Shelly, 1928?-75, American; nonfiction CON
GROSSMAN, Vasily Siměonovich, 1905-64, Russian; fiction BU CL
GROSSMAN, William Leonard, 1906-80, American; nonfiction, translations CON
GROSSMITH, George, 1847-1912, English; fiction, plays BU DA VN
GROSSMITH, Weedon, 1854-1919, English; fiction DA
GROSSO, Alfonso, 1928- , Spanish; fiction CL
GROSSU, Sergiu, 1920- , Rumanian-French; nonfiction CON
GROSVENOR, Gilbert Hovey, 1875-1966, British; journalism CON
GROSVENOR, Kali Diana, 1960- , American; poetry CON SH
GROSVENOR, Melville Bell, 1901- , American; nonfiction CON
GROSVENOR, Verta Mae, 1938- , American; nonfiction, poetry CON SH
GROTE, George, 1794-1871, English; nonfiction DA
GROTE, William, American; fiction, film, juveniles WAR
GROTH, Alexander Jacob, 1932- , Polish-American; nonfiction CON
GROTH, John, 1908- , American; juveniles, journalism, nonfiction CO CON
GROTH, Klaus, 1819-99, German; poetry BU
GROTIUS, Hugo see GROOT, Hugo de
GROTJAHN, Martin, 1904- , German-American; nonfiction CON
GROTO, Luigi, 1541-85, Italian; poetry, plays MCG
GROULING, Thomas Edward, 1940- , American; fiction NI
GROULX, Lionel-Adolphe, 1878-1967, French-Canadian; nonfiction BU
GROUNDS, Roger Ransford, 1938- , British; nonfiction CON

GROUSSAC, Paul, 1848-1929,
Argentinian; nonfiction, fiction
BR BU
GROUT, Donald Jay, 1902- ,
American; nonfiction CON
GROUT, Jack, 1910- , American;
nonfiction CON
'GROVE, Frederick Philip' (Félix
Paul Greve), 1879-1948,
German-Canadian; fiction,
poetry, nonfiction, translations
BU CR DA NI VN
GROVE, Pearce Seymour, 1930- ,
American; nonfiction CON
GROVER, David Steele, 1939- ,
British; nonfiction CON
GROVER, John Wagner, 1927- ,
American; nonfiction, film
CON
GROVES, Colin Peter, 1942- ,
English; nonfiction CON
'GROVES, Georgina' see SY-
MONDS, Geraldine
GROVES, Jay Voelker, 1922- ,
American; fiction NI
GROVES, John William, 1910- ,
British; fiction NI
GROVES, Paul, 1930- , British;
juveniles CON
GROW, Lawrence, 1939- ,
American; nonfiction CON
GRUBB, Davis Alexander, 1919-
80, American; fiction CON
KIB
GRUBB, Frederick, 1930- ,
British; poetry, nonfiction
CON VCP
GRUBB, Kenneth George, 1900-
80, British; nonfiction CON
GRUBBS, Donald H., 1936- ,
American; nonfiction CON
GRUBER, Frank ('Stephen Acre';
'Charles K. Boston'; 'John
K. Vedder'), 1904-69, Amer-
ican; fiction, plays REI ST
GRUBER, Frederick Charles,
1903- , American; nonfiction
CON
GRUBER, Gary R., 1940- ,
American; nonfiction CON
GRUBER, Helmut, 1928- ,
Austrian-American; nonfiction
CON
GRUBER, Ludwig see 'ANZEN-
GRUBER, Ludwig'
GRUBER Martin Jay, 1937- ,
American; nonfiction CON
GRUBER, Terry deRoy, 1953- ,

American; nonfiction CON
GRUBINSKI, Waclaw, 1883-1973,
Polish; fiction BU CL
'GRÜN, Anastasius' (Anton Alex-
ander Graf von Auersperg),
1806-76, Austrian; poetry BU
TH
GRÜN, Max von der, 1926- ,
German; plays CL
GRUEN, Victor David, 1903-80,
Austrian; nonfiction CON
GRUENBAUM, Ludwig see
GAATHON, Aryeh L.
GRUENBERG, Sidonie Matsner,
1881-1974, American; nonfiction
CON
GRUENING, Ernest Henry, 1887-
1974, American; nonfiction
CON
GRUENSTEIN, Peter, 1947- ,
American; nonfiction CON
GRUFFYDD, Peter, 1935- , Brit-
ish; poetry, plays VCP
GRUFFYDD, William John, 1881-
1954, Welsh; poetry, nonfiction
BU DA
GRULIOW, Leo, 1913- , Ameri-
can; nonfiction, translations
CON
GRUMET, Robert Steven, 1949- ,
American; nonfiction CON
GRUND, Josef Carl, 1920- ,
German; nonfiction, juveniles
CON
GRUNDBERG, John Andrew, 1947- ,
American; nonfiction CON
GRUNDT, Leonard, 1936- , Amer-
ican; nonfiction CON
GRUNDTVIG, Nicolai Frederik
Severin, 1783-1872, Danish;
poetry, nonfiction BU TH
GRUNDTVIG, Svend Hersleb, 1824-
83, Danish; nonfiction, transla-
tions BU
GRUNDY, Kenneth William,
1936- , American; nonfiction
CON
GRUNDY, Sydney, 1848-1914,
British; plays MCG
GRUNFELD, Frederic V., 1929- ,
German-American; nonfiction
CON
GRUNLAN, Stephen Arthur,
1942- , American; nonfiction
CON
GRUPP, Stanley Eugene, 1927- ,
American; nonfiction CON
GRUSON, Edward S., 1929- ,

American; nonfiction CON
GRUSS, Edmond Charles, 1933- ,
American; nonfiction CON
GRUTZ, Mariellen (Procopio),
1946- , American; nonfiction
CON
GRUVER, Rebecca see GOODMAN,
Rebecca
GRUVER, William R., II, 1929- ,
American; nonfiction CON
GRYLLS, David Stanway, 1947- ,
British; nonfiction CON
GRYLLS, Rosalie Glynn, English;
nonfiction CON
GRYPHIUS, Andreas, 1616-64,
German; poetry, plays BU
MCG TH
'GUADALOUPE, Brother Jose de'
see MOJICA, Jose
'GUADO, Sergio' see GEROSA,
Guido
GUAIFERIUS of SALERNO, fl.
1050, Lombard; poetry BU
'GUAMANI' see TAPIA y RIV-
ERA, Alejandro
GUARD, David, 1934- , Amer-
ican; nonfiction CON
GUARDATI, Tommaso see
MASUCCIO, Salernitano
GUARDO, Carol Joan, 1939- ,
American; nonfiction CON
GUARE, John Edward, 1938- ,
American; plays CON MCN
VCD WAK
GUARESCHI, Giovanni, 1908-68,
Italian; journalism, fiction
CL
GUARINI, Battista, 1537/38-1612,
Italian; poetry, plays BO BU
MCG RU TH
GUARINI, Guarino (Guarina da
Verona), 1374-1460, Italian;
nonfiction DU
GUARINO, Battista, 1434-1503,
Italian; nonfiction BU
GUARINO, Martin Vincent, 1939- ,
American; film, nonfiction
CON
GUAZZO, Stefano, 1530-93, Ital-
ian; nonfiction, poetry BO
GUBERN, Santiago G., 1933- ,
Spanish-Canadian; nonfiction,
translations CON
GUBRIUM, Jaber Fandy y,
1943- , Canadian-American;
nonfiction CON
GUCK, Dorothy, 1913- , Amer-
ican; nonfiction CON

GUDIOL i RICART, Josep, 1904- ,
Spanish; nonfiction CON
GUDJONSSON, Halldor Kiljan
('Halldor Laxness'), 1902- ,
Icelander; journalism CON
GUDZENKO, Semën Petrovich,
1922-53, Russian; poetry BU
GUDZY, Nikolai Kalinnikovich,
1887- , Russian; nonfiction
BU
GUEHENNO, Marcel (Jean), 1890-
1978, French; nonfiction BU
CL WAK
GÜIRALDES, Ricardo, 1886-1927,
Argentinian; fiction, poetry,
nonfiction BR BU MAG WA
GUELBENZU, José María, 1944- ,
Spanish; fiction, poetry, non-
fiction CL
GUELICH, Robert Allison, 1939- ,
American; translations, non-
fiction CON
GUEMPLE, Lee, 1930- , Ameri-
can; nonfiction CON
GÜNTEKIN, Reshad Nuri, 1892-
1956, Turkish; fiction, plays,
journalism LA PRU
'GUENTER, Erich' see 'EICH,
Günter'
GÜNTHER, Gotthard, German; non-
fiction, fiction NI
GÜNTHER, Johann Christian, 1695-
1723, German; poetry BU TH
GUENTHER, Johannes von, 1886- ,
German; journalism, poetry,
nonfiction, translations, plays
MCG
GUENTHER, Robert Wallace,
1929- , American; journalism
CON
GUERARD, Albert Joseph, 1914- ,
American; fiction, nonfiction
NI VCN
'GUERAU de LIOST' (Jaume Bofill
i Mates), 1877-1933, Catalan;
poetry BU
GUERIN, Charles, 1873-1907,
French; poetry BU
GUERIN, Maurice de, 1810-39,
French; nonfiction, poetry
BU TH
GUERNEY, Bernard Guilbert, 1894-
1979, American; translations,
nonfiction CON
GUERNSEY, Otis Love, Jr.,
1918- , American; journalism,
nonfiction, film CON
GÜRPINAR, Hüseyin Rahmi, 1864-

1944, Turkish; fiction PRU
GUERRA, Emilio Louis, 1909-80,
American; nonfiction CON
GUERRA, Henrique, 1937- ,
Angolan; fiction JA
GUERRA MONDRAGON, Miguel,
1880-1947, Puerto Rican;
journalism, nonfiction HIL
GUERRAZZI, Francesco Dominico,
1804-73, Italian; fiction, non-
fiction BO BU TH
GUERRERO, Manuel P., 1935- ,
American; nonfiction MAR
GUERRERO, Mario, American;
nonfiction MAR
GUERRERO, Wilfrido M., 1917- ,
Filipino; plays PRU
GUERRETTE, Richard Hector,
1930- , American; nonfiction
CON
GUERRINI, Olindo see 'STEC-
CHETTI, Lorenzo'
GUERS-VILLATE, Yvonne, 1924- ,
Franco-American; nonfiction
CON
GUESS, Edward Preston ('Edward
Preston'), 1925- , American;
journalism, nonfiction CON
GUEST, Barbara, 1920- , Amer-
ican; poetry, plays, nonfiction
VCP
GUEST, Lady Charlotte Elizabeth,
1812-75, Welsh; nonfiction
DA
GUEST, Edgar Albert, 1881-1959,
American; journalism, poetry
BR
GUEST, Henry Bayly (Harry),
1932- , Welsh; poetry, non-
fiction, translations, plays
CON VCP
GUEST, Judith, 1936- , Amer-
ican; fiction CON
'GÜTERSLOH, Albert Paris von'
(Albert Conrad Kiehtreiber),
1887- , Austrian; fiction
BU
GUETT, Dieter, 1924- , Czech-
American; nonfiction CON
GUEVARA, Antonio de, 1480?-
1545/46, Spanish; nonfiction,
letters BU RU TH
GUEVARA, Juan, 1944- , Amer-
ican; poetry MAR
GUEVARA, Miguel de, 1585?-
1646?, Mexican; poetry BR
GUEVARA CASTAÑEIRA, Josefina,
Puerto Rican; nonfiction,

journalism, poetry HIL
GUEVREMONT, Germaine ('La
Femme du Postillon'; 'Alice
Ber'), 1896/1900-68, Canadian;
fiction BU CR
GUEYE, Lamine, 1891- , Sene-
galese; nonfiction JA
GUEYE, Youssouf, 1928- ,
Mauritanian; poetry HER
GUGAS, Chris, 1921- , American;
nonfiction CON
GUGGENHEIM, Harry Frank, 1890-
1971, American; journalism
CON
GUGGENHEIM, Kurt, 1896- ,
Swiss; fiction BU
GUGGENHEIMER, Richard, 1906-77,
American; nonfiction CON
GUGGENMOS, Josef, 1922- ,
German; juveniles CON
GUGGISBERG, Charles Albert Walt-
er, 1913- , Swiss; nonfiction,
translations CON
GUGLIELMINETTI, Amalia, 1885-
1941, Italian; poetry, fiction,
plays CL
GUGLIOTTA, Bobette, 1918- ,
American; nonfiction, juveniles
CO CON
GUHIN, Michael Alan, 1940- ,
American; nonfiction CON
GUI, Châtelain de Coucy, -1203,
French; poetry TH
GUI de CAMBRAI, 12th century,
French; poetry BU
GUIART, Guillaume, 1280?-1316?,
French; nonfiction BU
GUIBERT de NOGENT, 1053-1124,
French; nonfiction BU TH
GUICCIARDINI, Francesco, 1483-
1540, Italian; nonfiction BO
BU TH
GUICE, John David Wynne, 1931- ,
American; nonfiction CON
GUICHARNAUD, June, 1922- ,
American; translations, nonfic-
tion CON
GUIDI, Alessandro, 1650-1712,
Italian; poetry BU TH
GUIDICCIONI, Giovanni, 1500-41,
Italian; poetry BU
GUIDO, Cecily Margaret ('C. M.
Piggot'), 1912- , English;
nonfiction CON
GUIDO da PISA, 14th century, ?;
nonfiction BU
GUIDO delle COLONNE, 1210?-87?,
Italian; poetry BO

GUIDON, Jon, 1892-1966, Raeto-
Romansch; poetry BU
GUILD, Nicholas M., 1944- ,
American; fiction CON
GUILDS, John Caldwell, Jr.,
1934- , American; nonfiction
CON
GUILHADE, João Garcia de, fl.
1250, Portuguese; poetry BU
GUILHEM IX, Duke of Aquitaine,
1071-1126, Provencal; poetry
BU
GUILHEM ADEMAR, 1165-1217,
Provencal; poetry BU
GUILHEM de BERGUEDAN, Vicomte,
fl. 1170-1200, Provencal;
poetry BU
GUILHEM de CABESTANH, late
12th century, Provencal;
poetry BU
GUILHEM de POITOU, 1071-1127,
French; poetry TH
GUILHEM FIGUEIRA, 1215-50,
Provencal; poetry BU
GUILHEM MONTANHAGOL, fl.
1233-58, Provencal; poetry
BU TH
GUILLAUME, Jeanette G., 1899- ,
American; juveniles CO
GUILLAUME de DEGUILLEVILLE,
1295-1358, French; poetry
BU
GUILLAUME de FERRIERES, fl.
1202- , French; poetry BU
GUILLAUME de LORRIS, 1215?-
40?, French; poetry BU
MAG
GUILLAUME de MACHAUT
(Machault), 1300-77, French;
poetry TH
GUILLAUME le BRETON, fl.
1225, French; poetry BU
GUILLAUME le CLERC, fl.
1200- , French; poetry BU
GUILLAUME le VINIER,   -1245,
French; poetry BU
GUILLE, Frances Vernor, 1908-
75, American; nonfiction
CON
GUILLEMIN, Henri, 1903- ,
French; nonfiction CON
GUILLEN, Jorge, 1893- ,
Spanish; poetry, nonfiction,
translations BU CL CON
SEY TH WA
GUILLEN, Nicolás, 1902- ,
Cuban; poetry BR BU WA
GUILLEN de SEGOVIA, 1413-74,

Spanish; poetry BU
GUILLET, Jacques, 1910- ,
French; nonfiction CON
GUILLEVIC, Eugene ('Serpieres'),
1907- , French; nonfiction,
poetry CL CON WAK
GUILLOT, Rene, 1900-69, French;
nonfiction, fiction, juveniles
CO CON
GUILLOUX, Louis, 1899-1980,
French; fiction BU CL
GUILMARTIN, John Francis, Jr.,
1940- , American; nonfiction
CON
GUILPIN, Everard, fl. 1588-1601,
English; poetry BU
GUIMARÃES, Afonso Henriquez da
Costa (Alphonsus de Guimaraens),
1870-1921, Brazilian; poetry
BR
GUIMARÃES, Bernardo, 1825-84,
Brazilian; fiction BR
GUIMARAES ROSA, João, 1908-67,
Brazilian; fiction BR BU SEY
GUIMARY, Donald Lee, 1932- ,
American; nonfiction CON
GUIMERA, Angel, 1847-1924, Cata-
lan; plays, poetry BU CL
MCG
GUIN, Wyman Woods ('Norman
Menasco'), 1915- , American;
fiction CON NI
GUINAN, John, 1874-1945, Irish;
plays HO
GUINDON, Arthur, 1864-1923,
Canadian; poetry CR
GUINEY, Louise Imogene, 1861-
1920, American; poetry, non-
fiction, juveniles VP
GUINEY, Mortimer, 1930- ,
American; nonfiction CON
GUINIZELLI, Guido, 1235?-76?,
Italian; poetry TH
GUINNESS, Bryan Walter, 1905- ,
British; poetry, fiction, juven-
iles, plays CON HO
GUINNESS, Ian Oswald, 1941- ,
English; nonfiction CON
GUINTHER, John, 1927- , Amer-
ican; nonfiction CON
GUIOT de DIJON, fl. 1220, French;
poetry BU
GUIOT de PROVINS, 12-13th cen-
turies, French; poetry BU
GUIRAUT de BORNELH (Borneil),
1165-1220, Provencal; poetry
BU TH
GUIRAUT, Riquier, 1230/35-92?,

French; poetry BU TH
GUIRDHAM, Arthur ('Francis
Eaglesfield'), 1905- , British;
nonfiction, fiction CON
'GUISA, Giano de' see PRAZ,
Mario
GUISINGER, Stephen Edward,
1941- , American; nonfiction
CON
GUITRY, Sacha, 1885-1957,
French; plays BU CL MCG
TH
GUITTONE d'AREZZO, 1230/35-
94?, Italian; poetry BO BU
TH
GUIZIZELLI, Guido, 1230/40-76,
Italian; poetry BO BU
GUL, Roman B. see GOUL,
Roman B.
GULA, Robert John, 1941- ,
American; nonfiction CON
GULIA, Drmit, 1874-1960,
Abkhazian; poetry, journalism,
plays PRU
GULKER, Virgil G., 1947- ,
American; nonfiction CON
GULLACE, Gino, 1925- ,
Italian-American; journalism,
nonfiction CON
GULLANS, Charles Bennett,
1929- , American; poetry,
nonfiction, translations VCP
GULLBERG, Hjalmar Robert,
1898-1961, Swedish; poetry
BU CL TH WAK
GULLICK, Etta, 1916- , British;
nonfiction CON
GULLIVER, Harold S., 1935- ,
American; nonfiction CON
'GULLIVER, Lemuel' see HAST-
INGS, Macdonald
GULUBOV, Konstantin, 1892- ,
Bulgarian; fiction BU
GULYASHKI, Andrei, Bulgarian;
fiction MCC
GUMA, Enoch Silinga, 1896/
1901- , South African; fiction
HER JA
GUMA, Samson Mbizo, 1923?- ,
Sotho; poetry, fiction HER
GUMILĔV, Nikolay Stephanovich,
1886-1921, Russian; poetry
BU CL SEY TH
GUMMERE, Richard Mott, Jr.,
1912- , American; nonfiction
CON
GUMPERTZ, Robert, 1925- ,
American; nonfiction, juveniles

CON WAR
GUNADHYA, Indian; nonfiction
PRU
GUNDERSHEIMER, Werner L.,
1937- , American; nonfiction
CON
GUNDREY, Elizabeth, 1924- ,
British; juveniles CO
GUNDULIC, Ivan, 1589-1638, Ragu-
san; poetry BU
GUNDY, Henry Pearson, 1905- ,
American; nonfiction CON
GUNN, Drewey Wayne, 1939- ,
American; nonfiction CON
GUNN, Elizabeth, 1926- , British;
fiction, poetry CON
GUNN, Giles Buckingham, 1938- ,
American; nonfiction CON
GUNN, James Edwin, 1923- ,
American; fiction AS COW NI
GUNN, John Charles, 1937- ,
English; nonfiction CON
GUNN, Neil Miller, 1891-1973,
Scots; fiction, plays, nonfiction
BU DA NI VN
GUNN, Thomson William, 1929- ,
English; poetry, nonfiction
BU DA PO SEY VCP VP WA
'GUNN, Victor' see 'GRAY, Berke-
ley'
GUNNARSSON, Gunnar, 1889-1973/
75, Icelander; fiction, plays,
poetry BU CL CON MAG
GUNNELL, Bryn, 1933- , British;
nonfiction CON
GUNNEWEG, Antonius H. J.,
1922- , Dutch; nonfiction CON
GUNNING, Monica Olwen, 1930- ,
American; juveniles CON
GUNNING, Robert, 1908-80, Amer-
ican; journalism CON
GUNSTON, William Tudor, 1927- ,
English; nonfiction, juveniles
CO CON WAR
GUNTHER, fl. 1180, Latin; poetry
BU
GUNTHER, Bernard, 1929- ,
American; nonfiction CON
GUNTHER, John, 1901-70, Amer-
ican; journalism, nonfiction
BR
GUNTHER, Richard Paul, 1946- ,
American; nonfiction CON
GUNTON, Sharon Rose, 1952- ,
American; nonfiction CON
GUNZBERG, Nicholas de, 1904-81,
American; journalism CON
GUOMUNDSSON, Kristmann Borgfjörd,

1901/02- , Icelander; fiction
BU CL
GUOMUNDSSON, Tómas, 1901- ,
Icelander; poetry BU CL
GUPTA, Brijen Kishore, 1929- ,
Indian-American; nonfiction
CON
GUPTA, Maithilisaran, 1886-1964,
Hindi; poetry PRU
GUPTA, Marie Jacqueline, 1946- ,
American; nonfiction CON
GUPTA, Sushil Kumar ('Morris
N. Placere'), 1927- , Indian-
American; nonfiction CON
GUPTA, Shiv Kumar, 1930- ,
Indian-American; nonfiction
CON
GUPTARA, Prabhu Siddhartha,
1949- , Indian; poetry, non-
fiction CON
GUPTILL, Nathanael Mann,
1917- , American; nonfiction
CON
GURAMISHVILI, Davit, 1705-92,
Georgian; poetry PRU
GURDAS BHALLA, Bhai, -1637,
Panjabi; poetry PRU
GURI, Chaim, 1923- , Israeli;
poetry BU
GURKO, Leo, 1914- , Polish-
American; juveniles CO DE
GURKO, Miriam, American;
juveniles CO DE
GURMAN, Alan Stephen, 1945- ,
American; nonfiction CON
GURNEE, Jeanne, 1926- ,
American; nonfiction CON
GURNEY, A. R., Jr., 1930- ,
American; plays, fiction
VCD
GURNEY, Albert Ramsdell, Jr.
('Peter Gurney'), 1930- ,
American; fiction, plays, film
CON
GURNEY, Nancy Jack, 1915?-73,
American; juveniles CON
GURO, Elena, 1877-1913, Russian;
poetry, plays BU CL
GURR, Ted Robert, 1936- ,
American; nonfiction CON
GURREY, Percival, 1890-1980,
British; nonfiction CON
GURULUGOMI, fl. 1200, Sinhalese;
nonfiction PRU
GURWITSCH, Aron, 1901-73,
Russian-American; nonfiction
CON
GUSEV-ORENBURGSKY, Sergey

Ivanovich, 1867-1963, Russian;
fiction BU
GUSFIELD, Joseph R., 1923- ,
American; nonfiction CON
GUSTAF-JANSON, Gösta, 1902- ,
Swedish; fiction BU
GUSTAFSON, Alrik, 1903-70,
American; nonfiction, transla-
tions CON
GUSTAFSON, Marjorie, American;
juveniles WAR
GUSTAFSON, Ralph Barker, 1909- ,
Canadian; poetry, fiction BU
VCP VP
GUSTAFSON, William Eric,
1933- , American; nonfiction
CON
GUSTAFSSON, Lars, 1936- ,
Swedish; fiction, plays, nonfic-
tion CL CON
GUSTAV III, King of Sweden; 1746-
92, Swedish; plays BU
'GUSTAVO' see GAUTIER BENITEZ,
José
GUSTIN, Lawrence Robert, 1937- ,
American; nonfiction CON
GUSTKEY, Earl, 1940- , American;
juveniles, nonfiction CON WAR
'GUT, Gom' see SIMENON, Georges
GUTCHEON, Beth (Richardson),
1945- , American; nonfiction
CON
GUTEK, Gerald Lee, 1935- ,
American; nonfiction CON
GUTERMAN, Simeon Leonard,
1907- , American; nonfiction
CON
GUTHAM, William Harold, 1924- ,
American; nonfiction CON
GUTHKE, Karl Siegfried, 1933- ,
German-American; nonfiction
CON
GUTHRIE, Alfred Bertram, Jr.,
1901- , American; fiction,
juveniles, nonfiction CON KIB
MAG VCN
GUTHRIE, Hunter, 1901-74, Amer-
ican; nonfiction CON
'GUTHRIE, Isobel' see GRIEVE,
Christopher M.
GUTHRIE, James W., 1936- ,
American; nonfiction CON
GUTHRIE, Ramon, 1896-1973,
American; poetry, fiction,
translations, nonfiction CON
RO VCP VP WAK
GUTHRIE, Robert Val, 1930- ,
American; nonfiction CON

GUTHRIE, Thomas Anstey see
  'ANSTEY, F.'
GUTHRIE, William Keith C.,
  1906-81, English; nonfiction
  CON
GUTHRIE, Woody, 1912-67, Amer-
  ican; nonfiction CON
GUTHRIE-SMITH, William Her-
  bert, 1861-1940, New Zea-
  lander; nonfiction BU
GUTIERREZ, Arturo Luis,
  1934- , American; nonfiction
  MAR
GUTIERREZ, Ezequiel, Jr.,
  1946- , American; nonfiction
  MAR
GUTIERREZ, G. G., American;
  nonfiction MAR
GUTIERREZ, Jose Angel, 1944- ,
  American; poetry, nonfiction
  MAR
GUTIERREZ, Juan María, 1809-78,
  Argentinian; poetry, nonfiction,
  fiction BR BU
GUTIERREZ del ARROYO, Isabel,
  1907- , Puerto Rican; non-
  fiction HIL
GUTIERREZ GONZALEZ, Gregorio,
  1826-72, Colombian; poetry
  BR BU
GUTIERREZ NAJERA, Manuel,
  1859-95, Mexican; poetry, fic-
  tion BR BU
GUTIERREZ-VEGA, Zenaida,
  1930- , Cuban-American;
  nonfiction CON
GUTKIN, Harry, 1915- , Cana-
  dian; nonfiction CON
GUTKIND, Lee, 1943- , Amer-
  ican; nonfiction CON
GUTMAN, Bill, American; juven-
  iles WAR
GUTMAN, Herbert George,
  1928- , American; nonfiction
  CON
GUTMAN, Naham, 1899?-1981,
  American; juveniles CO
GUTMAN, Richard Jay Stephen,
  1949- , American; nonfiction
  CON
GUTMAN, Robert, 1926- ,
  American; nonfiction CON
GUTMANN, Joseph, 1923- ,
  German-American; nonfiction
  CON
GUTMANN, Simcha A. see 'Ben-
  ZION, Sh.'
GUTNIK, Martin Jerome, 1942- ,

American; nonfiction CON
GUTO'R GLYN, fl. 1440-93, Welsh;
  poetry BU
GUTTENBERG, Barnett, American;
  nonfiction CON
GUTTENBERG, Virginia ('Virginia
  Graham'), 1914- , American;
  nonfiction CON
GUTTENTAG, Marcia, 1932- ,
  American; nonfiction, transla-
  tions CON
GUTTERIDGE, Donald George,
  1937- , Canadian; poetry, non-
  fiction, fiction CON VCP
GUTTERIDGE, Lindsay, 1923- ,
  English; fiction CON NI
GUTTING, Gary Michael, 1942- ,
  American; nonfiction CON
GUTTMACHER, Alan F., 1898-1974,
  American; nonfiction CON
GUTTRIDGE, Leonard Francis,
  1918- , American; nonfiction
  CON
GUTZKOW, Karl Ferdinand, 1811-
  78, German; journalism, plays,
  fiction BU MCG TH
GUY, Rosa Cuthbert, 1928- ,
  American; juveniles, plays CO
  KI
GUY of BAZOCHES, 1140?-1203,
  French; letters, poetry BU TH
GUYON, Jean see 'CESBRON,
  Gilbert'
GUYOT, James Franklin, 1932- ,
  American; nonfiction CON
GUYOTAT, Pierre, 1940- ,
  French; fiction CL
GUZMAN, Martín Luis, 1887- ,
  Mexican; fiction, nonfiction,
  film BR BU MAG
GUZMAN, Ralph, 1924- , Amer-
  ican; nonfiction MAR
GVADANYI, József, 1725-1801,
  Hungarian; poetry BU
GWAITNEY, John Langston, 1928- ,
  American; nonfiction SH
GWALTNEY, John Langston,
  1928- , American; nonfiction
  CON
GWINUP, Thomas, 1932- , Amer-
  ican; nonfiction CON
GWYN, Julian, 1937- , Anglo-
  Canadian; nonfiction CON
GWYNN, Stephen Lucius, 1864-1950,
  Irish; nonfiction, poetry, fiction
  HO
GWYNNE, Erskine, 1898-1948,
  American; nonfiction RO

GWYNNE, Peter, 1941- , Anglo-
American; journalism, non-
fiction CON
GYLLEMBOURG-EHRENSVÄRD,
Thomasine Christine Buntzen,
1773-1856, Danish; fiction
BU
GYLLENBORG, Carl, 1679-1746,
Swedish; plays BU
GYLLENBORG, Gustav Fredrik,
1731-1808, Swedish; poetry
BU
GYLLENHAMMAR, Pehr Gustaf,
1935- , Swedish; nonfiction,
juveniles CON
GYLLENSTEN, Lars, 1921- ,
Swedish; fiction, poetry BU
CL TH
GYOKURAN see KAJIKO
GYONGYOSI, István, 1629?-1704,
Hungarian; poetry BU
GYORGYEV, Clara, 1936- ,
Hungarian-American; nonfic-
tion, translations CON
GYRALDUS, Lilius G. see
GIRALDI, Giglio G.
GYSBERS, Norman Charles,
1932- , American; nonfiction
CON
GYULAI, Pál, 1826-1909, Hun-
garian; fiction, nonfiction,
poetry BU

H

'H. D.' see DOOLITTLE, Hilda
HAACK, Susan, 1945- , Amer-
ican; nonfiction CON
HAAF, Beverly Terhune, 1936- ,
American; fiction, nonfiction
CON
HAAFNER, Jacob Godfried (Haff-
ner), 1755-1809, Dutch; non-
fiction BU
HAAK, Theodore Dietrich, 1605-
90, German; nonfiction BU
HAAN, Jacob Israël de, 1881-
1924, Dutch; poetry, nonfic-
tion BU
HAANPÄÄ, Pentti, 1905-55, Fin-
nish; fiction BU TH
HAAR, Bernard ter, 1806-80,
Dutch; poetry, nonfiction BU
HAAR, Francis, 1908- , Amer-
ican; nonfiction CON
HAAR, Jaap ter, 1922- , Dutch;
juveniles DEM

HAAS, Benjamin Leopold ('John
Benteen'; 'Thorne Douglas';
'Richard Meade'), 1926- ,
American; fiction CON
HAAS, Carolyn Buhai, 1926- ,
American; nonfiction, juveniles
CON
HAAS, Charlie, 1952- , American;
film CON
HAAS, Ernst Bernard, 1924- ,
German-American; nonfiction
CON
HAAS, Irene, 1929- , American;
juveniles CO CON DE
HAAS, Irvin, 1916- , American;
nonfiction CON
HAAS, James Edward, 1943- ,
American; juveniles, nonfiction
CON
HAAS, John Eugene, 1926- ,
American; nonfiction CON
HAAS, Kenneth Brooks, Sr.,
1898- , American; nonfiction
CON
HAAS, Kurt, American; nonfiction
CON
HAAS, La Verne, 1942- , Amer-
ican; nonfiction CON
HAAS, Lynne, 1939- , American;
nonfiction CON
HAAS, Michael, 1938- , American;
nonfiction CON
HAAS, Robert Lewis, 1936- ,
American; juveniles CON
HAASSE, Hilla Serafia, 1918- ,
Dutch; fiction BU
HAAVIKKO, Paavo, 1931- , Fin-
nish; poetry, plays, nonfiction
BU TH
HAAVIO, Marlti see 'MUSTAPÄÄ,
P.'
'HABBEMA, Koos' see HEIJER-
MANS, Herman
'HABE, Hans' (Jean Bekessy), 1911-
77, Hungarian-American; fiction,
nonfiction CON
HABENSTREIT, Barbara Ziegler,
1937- , American; juveniles
CO WAR
HABER, Heinz, 1913- , German-
American; nonfiction CON
HABER, Jack, 1939- , American;
nonfiction CON
HABER, Joyce, 1932- , American;
journalism CON
HABER, Louis, 1910- , American;
juveniles CO
HABERER, Joseph, 1929- ,

German-American; nonfiction
CON
HABERLER, Gottfried, 1900- ,
Austrian-American; nonfiction
CON
HABERLY, Loyd, 1896-1981,
American; nonfiction, fiction,
poetry CON PAL
HABERMAN, Martin, 1932- ,
American; nonfiction CON
HABERMAN, Shelby Joel, 1947- ,
American; nonfiction CON
HABERMANN, Helen Margaret,
1927- , American; nonfiction
CON
HABERNIG, Christine see
'LAVANT, Christine'
HABERSTROH, Chadwick John,
1927- , American; nonfiction
CON
HABIB of ISFAHAN, Mirza,
-1897, Persian; poetry, trans-
lations BU
HABIBI, Abdhulhay, 1910- ,
Afghan; nonfiction PRU
HABINGTON, William, 1605-54,
English; poetry, nonfiction
BU PO VP
HACHIMONJIYA JISHO, 1666-1745,
Japanese; fiction HI
HACI HALIFA, Katib, 1609-57,
Turkish; nonfiction PRU
HACKER, Marilyn, 1942- , Amer-
ican; poetry CON
HACKER, Shyrle, 1910- , Amer-
ican; nonfiction CON
HACKES, Peter Sidney, 1924- ,
American; nonfiction CON
HACKETT, Blanche Ann, 1924- ,
American; plays CON
HACKETT, Charles Joseph, 1915- ,
American; fiction, poetry CON
HACKETT, Francis, 1883-1962,
Irish; nonfiction, fiction CON
HO
HACKETT, John Winthrop, 1910- ,
Australian; nonfiction CON
HACKETT, Patrick see HAICEAD,
Pádraigén
HACKETT, Philip, 1941- , Amer-
ican; poetry CON
HACKETT, Roger Fleming, 1922- ,
American; nonfiction CON
HACKFORTH-JONES, Gilbert,
1900- , English; fiction
MCC
HACKING, Ian, 1936- , Canadian;
nonfiction CON

HACKMAN, John Richard, 1940- ,
American; nonfiction CON
HACKNEY, Sheldon, 1933- ,
American; nonfiction CON
HACKS, Peter, 1928- , German;
plays, poetry BU CL MCG TH
HACOHEN, Shalom, 1772-1845,
Hebrew; poetry, plays TH
HADAMAR von LABER, fl. 1335-40,
Bavarian; fiction BU
HADAS, Moses, 1900-66, American;
nonfiction BR WA
HADAS, Pamela White, 1946- ,
American; nonfiction CON
HADDAD, Malek, 1927- , Algerian;
poetry PRU
HADDAD, Robert Mitchell, 1930- ,
American; nonfiction CON
HADDIX-KONTOS, Cecille P.
('Cecille Haddix'; 'Cecille Kon-
tos'), 1937- , American; non-
fiction, film CON
HADDOX, John Herbert, 1929- ,
American; nonfiction CON
HADER, Berta Hoerner, 1890-1976,
American; juveniles, poetry
CO CON KI
HADER, Elmer Stanley, 1889-1973,
American; juveniles CO CON
KI
HADEWIJCH, mid 13th century,
Dutch; poetry BU TH
HADINGHAM, Evan, 1951- , Brit-
ish; nonfiction CON
HADLAUB, Johannes, fl. 1300- ,
Swiss; poetry BU TH
HADLEY, Arthur Twining, 1924- ,
American; journalism, fiction
CON NI
'HADLEY, Franklin' see WINTER-
BOTHAM, Russell R.
HADLEY, Lee ('Hadley Irwin'),
1934- , American; fiction
CON
HADLEY, Leila Burton, 1926- ,
American; juveniles CON WAR
HADLEY, Morris, 1894-1979, Amer-
ican; juveniles, nonfiction CON
HADRIAN (Publius Aelius Hadrianus),
76-138, Latin; poetry BU GR
LA
HAECHT, Willem Van, 1530-85?,
Dutch; poetry BU
'HAEDREYI, Abgad' see DRUYANOV,
Alter
'HAEDRICH, Marcel,' 1913- ,
French; nonfiction, fiction CON
HAEKKERUP, Per, 1915-79, Danish;

nonfiction CON
HAENTZSCHEL, Adolph Theodore,
1881-1971, American; nonfiction CON
HÄRING, Georg W. see 'ALEXIS, Willibald'
HÄRTLING, Peter, 1933- , German; poetry, fiction, nonfiction BU CL CON
HÄTZLERIN, Clara, fl. 1452-76, German; poetry BU
HAFEN, Le Roy Reuben, 1893- , American; nonfiction CON
HAFFENDEN, Philip Spencer, 1926- , English; poetry, nonfiction CON
HAFFNER, Jacob G. see HAAF-NER, Jacob G.
HÂFIZ, Shams al-Dîn Muhammad, 1326?-90, Persian; poetry BU LA MAG PRU
HAFIZ IBRAHAM, Muhammad, 1871-1932, Egyptian; poetry BU
HAFNER, Marylin, 1925- , American; juveniles CO
HAFNER, Philip, 1731-64, Austrian; plays BU
HAFSTEIN, Hannes, 1861-1922, Icelander; poetry BU
HAGA YAICHI, 1867-1927, Japanese; nonfiction HI
HAGALIN, Gudmundur Gíslason, 1898- , Icelander; fiction, poetry, plays BU CL
HAGAN, Kenneth James, 1936- , American; nonfiction CON
HAGAN, Patricia see HOWELL, Patricia
HAGBERG, Carl August, 1810-64, Swedish; translations BU
'HAGE, J. van den' see OLT-MANS, Jan F.
HAGEDORN, Friedrich von, 1708-54, German; poetry BU TH
HAGEDORN, Robert Bruce, 1925- , American; nonfiction CON
HAGEE, John Charles, 1940- , American; nonfiction CON
HAGELSTANGE, Rudolf, 1912- , German; poetry, nonfiction BU CON TH
HAGEN, John Milton ('Sterling Sherwin'), 1902- , American; plays, nonfiction CON
HAGEN, John William, 1940- , American; nonfiction CON

HAGEN, Richard Lionel, 1935- , American; nonfiction CON
HAGEN, Uta, 1919- , German-American; nonfiction CON
HAGER, Alice Rogers, 1894-1969, American; nonfiction CON
HAGER, Jean ('Marlaine Kyle'; 'Amanda McAllister'; 'Sara North'; 'Jeanne Stephens'), 1932- , American; fiction CON
HAGER, Robert M., 1938- , American; nonfiction CON
HAGERTY, James Campbell, 1909-81, American; journalism, nonfiction CON
HAGG, G. Eric, 1908?-79, American; nonfiction CON
HAGGAI, Thomas Stephens, 1931- , American; nonfiction CON
HAGGARD, Sir Henry Rider, 1856-1925, English; fiction, nonfiction CO DA MAG NI VN
HAGGARD, J. Harvey, 1913- , American; fiction NI
'HAGGARD, William' (Richard Clayton), 1907- , British; fiction MCC NI REI ST VCN
HAGGERSON, Nelson L., 1927- , American; nonfiction CON
HAGGERTY, James Joseph, 1920- , American; juveniles, nonfiction CO CON
HAGGETT, Peter, 1933- , British; nonfiction CON
HAGGIN, Bernard H., 1900- , American; nonfiction CON
HAGIWARA, Michio Peter, 1932- , Japanese-American; nonfiction CON
HAGIWARA, Sakutaro, 1886-1942, Japanese; poetry HI SEY WA
HAGMAN, Bette, 1922- , American; fiction CON
'HAGON, Priscilla' see ALLAN, Mabel E.
HAGOPIAN, John V., 1923- , American; nonfiction, fiction, poetry CON
HAGOPIAN, Mark N., 1940- , American; nonfiction, translations CON
HAGUE, Douglas Chalmers, 1926- , British; nonfiction CON
HAGUE, William Edward, Jr., 1919- , American; nonfiction

CON
HAGY, Ruth see BROD, Ruth
HAHN, Emily, 1905- , American;
juveniles, nonfiction CO
HAHN, Fred, 1906- , Czech-
American; nonfiction CON
HAHN, Hannelore, 1926- , Ger-
man; juveniles, translations
CO
HAHN, James Sage, 1947- ,
American; juveniles, fiction
CO CON
HAHN, Mona Lynn, 1949- ,
American; juveniles CO CON
HAHN, Robert Oscar, 1916- ,
American; nonfiction, film
CON
HAI GAON (Hai Ben Sherira),
939-1038, Iraqi; poetry BU
HAIBLUM, Isidore, 1935- ,
American; nonfiction, fiction
CON NI
HAICEAD, Pádraigén (Patrick
Hackett), 1606-54, Irish;
poetry DA
HAIDAR, Qurratu'l-'ain, 1927- ,
Urdu; fiction, translations
PRU
HAIG-BROWN, Roderick Lang-
mere, 1908-76, Canadian;
juveniles, fiction, nonfiction
BU CO CON CR KI
HAIGHT, Amanda, 1939- ,
American; nonfiction CON
HAIGHT, Anne Lyon, 1895-1977,
American; nonfiction CON
HAIK, Vahe (Tinchian), 1896- ,
Armenian; nonfiction, fiction,
translations PRU
HAILE, Harry Gerald, 1931- ,
American; nonfiction CON
HAILES, Sir David Dalrymple,
1726-92, Scots; nonfiction
BU
HAILEY, Arthur, 1920- , Cana-
dian; fiction, tv NI VCN
WAK
HAILEY, Elizabeth Forsythe,
1938- , American; fiction
CON
HAILEY, Oliver, 1932- , Amer-
ican; plays CON VCD
HAILEY, Sheila, 1927- , British;
juveniles, tv CON
HAILPERIN, Herman, 1899-1973,
American; nonfiction CON
HAILSTONES, Thomas John,
1919- , Scots-American;

nonfiction CON
HAIMES, Norma, American; non-
fiction CON
HAIMOWITZ, Natalie Reader,
1923- , American; nonfiction
CON
HAINAUX, Rene, 1918- , French;
nonfiction CON
HAINDL, Marieluise ('Marieluise
Fleisser'), 1901-74, German;
fiction, plays CON
HAINE, Edgar A., 1908- , Amer-
ican; nonfiction CON
HAINES, Charles, 1928- , Amer-
ican; juveniles, nonfiction
CON WAR
HAINES, Charles Grove, 1906-76,
American; nonfiction CON
HAINES, Francis D., Jr., 1923- ,
American; nonfiction CON
HAINES, Gail Kay Beckman,
1943- , American; juveniles
CO WAR
HAINES, Helen Elizabeth, 1872-
1961, American; nonfiction
ENG
HAINES, John Meade, 1924- ,
American; poetry, translations
VCP
HAINES, Max, 1931- , Canadian;
journalism, nonfiction CON
HAINES, William Wister, 1908- ,
American; film, fiction PAL
HAINING, Peter, 1940- , British;
fiction, nonfiction, juveniles
AS CO CON NI
HAIRE, Wilson John, 1932- ,
British; plays CON VCD
HAIRSTON, Loyle, 1926- , Amer-
ican; nonfiction SH
HAISLIP, Harvey Shadle, 1889-
1978, American; film, nonfic-
tion CON
HAJEK Z LIBOCAN, Václav,
1553- , Czech; nonfiction
BU
'HÂJJI KHALFA' (Mustafa ibn Ab-
dullâh Kâtib Chelebi), 1609-57,
Ottoman; nonfiction LA
HAKIM, Seymour, 1933- , Amer-
ican; poetry CON
HAKIM, Tawfiq, 1898/1902- ,
Egyptian; fiction, plays BU
PRU
HAKLUYT, Richard, 1553?-1616,
English; nonfiction, translations
BU DA MAG PO RU
HAKOBIAN, Hakob, 1866-1937,

Armenian; poetry PRU
HAKUTANI, Yoshinobu, 1935- ,
Japanese-American; nonfiction
CON
HALA, 2nd century, Indian;
anthology PRU
HALACY, Daniel Stephen, Jr.,
1919- , American; journal-
ism NI
HALAS, Celia Mary, 1922- ,
American; nonfiction CON
HALAS, František, 1901-49,
Czech; poetry BU CL TH
HALBACH, Edward Christian,
Jr., 1931- , American; non-
fiction CON
HALBE, Max, 1865-1944, Ger-
man; plays, fiction CL MAG
TH
HALBERSTADT, John, 1941- ,
American; poetry, fiction
CON
HALBERSTAM, David, 1934- ,
American; journalism, fiction,
nonfiction CON WAK
HALBERSTAM, Michael Joseph,
1932-80, American; nonfic-
tion, fiction CON
HALBERTSMA, Eeltsje, 1797-
1858, Frisian; nonfiction BU
HALBERTSMA, Joast, 1789-1869,
Frisian; nonfiction, fiction
BU
HALBERTSMA, Tsjalling, 1792-
1852, Frisian; nonfiction, fic-
tion BU
HALCOMB, Ruth, 1936- , Amer-
ican; nonfiction CON
HALDANE, John Burdon Sander-
son, 1892-1964, British; non-
fiction, fiction CON KI NI
HALDANE, Robert Aylmer,
1907- , British; nonfiction
CON
HALDANE, Roger John, 1945- ,
Australian; juveniles CO
HALDANE-STEVENSON, James
Patrick ('J. P. Stevenson'),
1910- , Welsh; nonfiction
CON
HALDEMAN, Harry Robbins,
1926- , American; nonfiction
CON
HALDEMAN, Joe William ('Robert
Graham'), 1943- , American;
fiction CON COW NI
HALDEMAN, Linda Wilson,
1935- , American; fiction,

nonfiction CON
HALE, Agnes Burke, 1890-1981,
American; fiction, journalism
CON
HALE, Clarence Benjamin, 1905- ,
American; nonfiction CON
HALE, David George, 1938- ,
American; nonfiction CON
HALE, Edward Everett ('Col.
Frederic Ingham'), 1822-1909,
American; nonfiction, fiction
BR CO MAG MY NI
HALE, Francis Joseph, 1922- ,
American; nonfiction CON
HALE, Frank W., Jr., 1927- ,
American; nonfiction CON SH
'HALE, Helen' see MULCAHY,
Lucille B.
HALE, J. Russell, 1918- , Amer-
ican; nonfiction CON
HALE, Janet Campbell, 1947- ,
American; juveniles, poetry
CON WAR
HALE, John Barry, 1926- , Brit-
ish; plays, fiction CON VCD
HALE, John Rigby, 1923- , Brit-
ish; fiction, nonfiction CON
HALE, Judson Drake, 1933- ,
American; nonfiction CON
HALE, Julian Anthony Stuart,
1940- , Welsh; nonfiction
CON
HALE, Katherine ('Amelia Beers
Warnock'), 1878-1956, Canadian;
poetry, nonfiction CR
HALE, Kathleen, 1898- , Scots;
juveniles CO CON KI
HALE, Linda Howe, 1929- ,
American; juveniles CO
HALE, Loyde Wesley, 1933- ,
American; nonfiction CON
HALE, Lucretia Peabody, 1820-
1900, American; juveniles, fic-
tion, nonfiction KI
'HALE, Margaret' see HIGONNET,
Margaret R.
HALE, Sir Matthew, 1609-76, Eng-
lish; nonfiction BU
HALE, Nancy, 1908- , American;
fiction, plays VCN
HALE, Nathan Cabot, 1925- ,
American; nonfiction CON
HALE, Patricia Whitaker, 1922- ,
American; nonfiction CON
HALE, Richard Walden, 1909-76,
American; nonfiction CON
HALE, Sarah Josepha Buell, 1788-
1879, American; poetry, fiction

MY
HALE, William Harlan, 1910-74,
American; journalism, non-
fiction CON
HALEK, Vitézslav, 1835-74,
Czech; poetry, fiction, plays
BU
HALES, Edward Elton Young,
1908- , British; nonfiction
CON
HALES, John, 1584-1656, Eng-
lish; nonfiction BU
HALEVY, Daniel, 1872-1962,
French; nonfiction CL
HALEVY, Ludovic, 1834-1908,
French; plays, fiction BU
MAG MCG
HALEY, Alexander, 1921- ,
American; nonfiction, fiction
BA CON SH
HALEY, Gail Einhart, 1939- ,
American; juveniles DE KI
HALEY, James Lewis, 1951- ,
American; nonfiction CON
HALEY, Neale, American; non-
fiction, juveniles CON
HALI, Khvaja Altaf Husain,
1837-1914, Urdu; poetry,
nonfiction PRU
HALIBURTON, Thomas Chandler,
1796-1865, Canadian; nonfic-
tion, fiction BU DA VN
HALIDE EDIB ADIVAR, 1884-1964,
Turkish; fiction BU CL
HALID ZIYA USASLIGIL, 1866-
1945, Turkish; fiction BU
HALIFAX, George Savile, 1633-
95, English; nonfiction DA PO
HALIFAX, Joan Squire, 1942- ,
American; nonfiction CON
'HALIKARNAS BALIKCISI' (Cevat
Sakir Kabaagacli), 1886-1973,
Turkish; fiction BU CL
HALKETT, John George, 1933- ,
American; nonfiction CON
HALKIN, Shimon, 1899- , Is-
raeli; nonfiction, fiction,
poetry, translations BU CON
HALKIN, Shmuel, 1899-1960's,
Yiddish; poetry, plays BU
'HALL, Adam' see TREVOR,
Elleston
HALL, Adele, 1910- , American;
juveniles CO
HALL, Alice Clay, 1900- , Amer-
ican; poetry CON
'HALL, Ann' see DUKERT, Mary
HALL, Anna Gertrude, 1882-1967,

American; juveniles CO
HALL, Anna Maria Fielding, 1800-
81, Irish; fiction HO
HALL, Anthony Stewart, 1945- ,
British; nonfiction CON
HALL, Ariel Perry, 1906- ,
American; nonfiction CON
HALL, Austin, 1886?-1933, Amer-
ican; fiction AS NI
'HALL, Aylmer' see HALL, Norah
E. L.
HALL, Baxter Clarence, 1936- ,
American; nonfiction, fiction
CON
HALL, Brian Patrick, 1935- ,
English; nonfiction CON
HALL, Cameron Parker, 1898- ,
American; nonfiction CON
HALL, Carolyn Vosburg, 1927- ,
American; juveniles, nonfiction
CON WAR
HALL, Challis Alva, Jr., 1917-68,
American; nonfiction CON
HALL, Constance Margaret,
1937- , Anglo-American; non-
fiction CON
HALL, Daniel George Edward,
1891-1979, British; nonfiction
CON
HALL, Desmond W. ('Anthony Gil-
more'; 'H. G. Winter'), Amer-
ican; fiction NI
HALL, Donald Andrew, 1928- ,
American; poetry, nonfiction,
juveniles BR CO MAG VCP WA
HALL, Douglas John, 1928- ,
Canadian; nonfiction CON
HALL, Edward, 1498/99-1547, Eng-
lish; nonfiction BU DA
HALL, Edward Twitchell, Jr.,
1914- , American; nonfiction
CON
HALL, Elizabeth, 1929- , Amer-
ican; juveniles, nonfiction
CON WAR
HALL, Elvajean, American; juven-
iles CO
HALL, Eric John, 1933- , Anglo-
American; nonfiction CON
HALL, F. H., 1926- , American;
nonfiction CON
HALL, Fernau, Canadian; nonfiction
CON
HALL, Fréderic Sauser see
'CENDRARS, Blaise'
HALL, Frederick Leonard, 1899- ,
American; nonfiction CON
HALL, Gene Erwin, 1941- ,

American; nonfiction CON
HALL, George, 1941- , American; nonfiction CON
HALL, George Fridolph, 1908- , American; nonfiction CON
HALL, Georgette Brockman, 1915- , American; nonfiction CON
HALL, Gladys, 1891?-1977, American; nonfiction CON
HALL, Gwendolyn Midlo, 1929- , American; nonfiction CON
HALL, Halbert Weldon, 1941- , American; nonfiction CON NI
HALL, Haywood ('Harry Haywood'), 1898- , American; nonfiction CON
HALL, Hessel Duncan, 1891-1976, Australian; nonfiction CON
'HALL, J. de P.' see McKELWAY, St. Clair
HALL, Jacquelyn Dowd, 1943- , American; nonfiction CON
HALL, James, 1793-1868, American; journalism BR
HALL, James, 1918- , British; nonfiction CON
HALL, James Byron, 1918- , American; fiction VCN
HALL, James C., Jr., 1932- , American; nonfiction SH
HALL, James Curtis, 1926- , American; nonfiction CON
HALL, James Herrick, Jr., 1933- , American; nonfiction CON
HALL, James Norman ('Fern Gravel'), 1887-1951, American; juveniles, nonfiction CO MAG PAL
HALL, James W., 1937- , American; nonfiction CON
'HALL, Jay C.' see HALL, John C.
'HALL, Jesse' see BOESEN, Victor
HALL, John, 1627-56, English; poetry BU
HALL, John, 1937- , American; journalism CON
HALL, John C. ('Jay C. Hall'), 1915- , American; nonfiction CON
HALL, John Clive, 1920- , British; poetry, nonfiction CON VCP
HALL, Josef Washington ('Upton

Close'), 1894-1960, American; nonfiction CON
HALL, Joseph, 1574-1656, English; fiction, poetry, nonfiction BU DA PO RU VP
HALL, Joseph Sargent, 1906- , American; nonfiction CON
HALL, Katherine Murphy, American; nonfiction CON
'HALL, Kendall' see HEATH, Harry E., Jr.
HALL, Kermit Lance, 1944- , American; nonfiction CON
HALL, Laurence James, 1940- , American; nonfiction CON
HALL, Luella Jemima, 1890-1973, American; nonfiction CON
HALL, Lynn, 1937- , American; juveniles WAR
HALL, Malcolm, 1945- , American; juveniles CO CON WAR
HALL, Manly Palmer, 1901- , Canadian-American; nonfiction CON
HALL, Marjory see YEAKLEY, Marjory
HALL, Maurits Cornelis van ('Frank Floreszoon van Arkel'), 1768-1858, Dutch; fiction, nonfiction, poetry BU
HALL, Nancy Lee, 1923- , American; nonfiction, plays CON
HALL, Nathaniel B., 1916- , American; nonfiction SH
HALL, Norah E. L. ('Aylmer Hall'), 1914- , British; nonfiction, juveniles CON KI
HALL, Norman John, 1933- , American; nonfiction CON
HALL, Phil, 1953- , American; poetry CON
HALL, Richard Hammond, 1934- , American; nonfiction CON
HALL, Robert Benjamin, 1918- , American; nonfiction CON
HALL, Robert Cargill, 1937- , American; nonfiction CON
HALL, Robert Lee, 1941- , American; fiction CON NI
HALL, Rodney, 1935- , Australian; poetry, fiction, nonfiction VCP
HALL, Rosalys Haskell, 1914- , American; juveniles CO
HALL, Ross Hume, 1926- , Canadian-American; nonfiction CON
HALL, Steven Leonard, 1960- , American; poetry CON

HALL, Susan, 1940- , American; nonfiction CON
HALL, Tom T., 1936- , American; nonfiction CON
HALL, Van Beck, 1934- , American; nonfiction CON
HALL, William Norman, 1915-74, American; juveniles CON
HALL, Willis, 1929- , British; plays, juveniles CON VCD
HALL, Wilson Dudley, 1922- , American; nonfiction CON
HALLA, Robert Christian ('Ezra Billings'), 1949- , American; poetry CON
HALLAJ, Husain Ibn Mansur, 858-922, Muslim; nonfiction BU
HALLAM, Henry, 1777-1859, English; nonfiction BU DA
'HALLARD, Peter' see CATHERALL, Arthur
'HALLAS, Richard' see KNIGHT, Eric M.
HALLBERG, Peter, 1916- , Swedish; nonfiction CON
HALLE, Jean-Claude, 1939- , French; journalism, nonfiction CON
HALLE, Louis Joseph, 1910- , American; fiction NI
HALLECK, Fitz-Greene, 1790-1867, American; poetry, nonfiction BR BU MYE VP
HALLER, Albrecht von, 1708-77, Swiss; poetry BU TH
HALLER, Archibald Orben, Jr., 1926- , American; nonfiction CON
HALLER, Ellis Metcalf, 1915-81, American; nonfiction CON
HALLER, John Samuel, Jr., 1940- , American; nonfiction CON
HALLER, Robin Meredith, 1944- , American; nonfiction CON
HALLER, William, 1885-1974, American; nonfiction CON
HALLETT, Garth Lie, 1927- , American; nonfiction CON
HALLETT, Kathryn Josephine, 1937- , American; nonfiction CON
HALLETT, Robin, 1926- , British; nonfiction CON
HALLGARTEN, George Wolfgang, 1901-75, German-American; nonfiction CON
HALLGARTEN, Peter Alexander,

1931- , German-British; nonfiction CON
HALLGRIMSSON, Jónas, 1807-45, Icelander; poetry BU
HALLGRIMUR, Petursson, 1614?-74, Icelander; poetry TH
HALLIBURTON, Rudia, Jr., 1929- , American; nonfiction CON
HALLIBURTON, Warren J., 1924- , American; juveniles, nonfiction CO SH
'HALLIDAY, Brett' see DRESSER, Davis; TERRALL, Robert
HALLIDAY, Fred, 1937- , American; fiction CON
HALLIDAY, Jerry, 1949- , American; plays, nonfiction CON
HALLIDAY, Jon, 1939- , Irish; nonfiction CON
'HALLIDAY, Michael' see CREASEY, John
HALLIDAY, Richard, 1905-73, American; fiction, nonfiction CON
HALLIDAY, William Ross, 1926- , American; nonfiction CON
HALLIER, Amedee, 1913- , French; nonfiction CON
HALLIN, Emily Watson, 1919- , American; juveniles CO
HALLINAN, Patrick Kenneth, 1944- , American; juveniles CON
HALLION, Richard Paul, Jr., 1948- , American; nonfiction CON
HALLIWELL, David William ('Johnson Arms'), 1936- , English; plays CON VCD
HALLIWELL, Leslie, 1929- , English; nonfiction CON
HALLMAN, George Victor III, 1930- , American; nonfiction CON
HALLMAN, Ruth, 1929- , American; juveniles CON
HALLOWAY, Vance ('Alphaes van Woeart'), 1916- , Anglo-American; fiction, plays, poetry CON
HALLOWELL, Alfred Irving, 1892-1974, American; nonfiction CON
HALLOWELL, Christopher L., 1945- , American; nonfiction CON
HALLPIKE, C. R., 1938- ,

English; nonfiction CON
HALL-QUEST, Olga Wilbourne,
1899- , American; juveniles
CO
HALLS, Geraldine Mary ('Char-
lotte Jay'; 'G. S. Jay'),
1919- , Australian; fiction
CON REI
HALLSTEAD, William Finn III,
1924- , American; juveniles
CO WAR
HALLSTRÖM, Per, 1866-1960,
Swedish; fiction, poetry, plays,
nonfiction BU
HALLUMS, James R., British;
fiction NI
'HALLUS, Tak' see ROBINETT,
Stephen A.
HALLWARD, Michael, 1889- ,
English; juveniles, nonfiction
CO CON
'HALM, Friedrich' (Eligius Franz
Joseph, Freiherr von Münch-
Bellinghausen), 1806-71, Aus-
trian; plays BU
HALMAEL, Hendrik van, 1654-
1718, Dutch; plays BU
HALMAN, Talat Sait, 1931- ,
Turkish-American; nonfiction,
translations CON
HALPER, Thomas, 1942- ,
American; nonfiction CON
HALPERIN, Don Akiba, 1925- ,
American; nonfiction CON
HALPERIN, John, 1941- ,
American; nonfiction CON
HALPERIN, Mark Warren,
1940- , American; poetry
CON
HALPERIN, Maurice, 1906- ,
American; nonfiction CON
HALPERIN, Samuel William,
1905-79, Lithuanian-American;
nonfiction CON
'HALPERIN, Uriel' see RATOSH,
Yonathan
HALPERN, Howard Marvin,
1929- , American; nonfiction
CON
HALPERN, Moishe Leib, 1886-
1932, Yiddish; poetry BU
HALPERN, Oscar Saul ('Oscar
Saul'), 1912- , American;
fiction, plays, film CON
HALPERN, Paul G., 1937- ,
American; nonfiction CON
HALPERN, Paul Joseph, 1942- ,
American; nonfiction CON

HALPERN, Stephen Mark, 1940- ,
American; nonfiction CON
HALPINE, Charles Graham, 1829-
68, Irish; journalism, fiction
HO
HALPRIN, Anna Schuman, 1920- ,
American; nonfiction CON
HALPRIN, Lawrence, 1916- ,
American; nonfiction CON
HALSBURY, Earl of (Hardinge
Goulburn Giffard), 1880-1943,
English; fiction NI
HALSELL, Grace, 1923- , Amer-
ican; juveniles CO
HALSEY, Elizabeth Tower, 1903?-
76, American; nonfiction CON
HALSEY, George Dawson, 1889-
1970, American; nonfiction
CON
HALSEY, Margaret Frances,
1910- , American; nonfiction
CON
HALSMAN, Philippe, 1906-79,
American; nonfiction CON
HALSTED, Anna Roosevelt, 1906-
75, American; journalism, non-
fiction CON
HALTER, Jon Charles, 1941- ,
American; juveniles CO CON
WAR
HALTON, David, 1940- , British;
journalism CON
HALVERSON, Alton C. O., 1922- ,
American; nonfiction CON
HALWARD, Leslie G., 1904?-76,
British; nonfiction CON
HAMA, Boubou, 1909- , Nigerian;
nonfiction JA
HAMADA, Hirosuke, 1893- ,
Japanese; juveniles CON
HAMADHANI, Ahmad ibn al-Husain,
967-1007, Arab; nonfiction, fic-
tion BU LA
HAMALAINEN, Pekka Kalevi,
1938- , Finnish-American;
nonfiction CON
HAMANN, Bente, Danish; juveniles
WAR
HAMANN, Johan Georg, 1730-88,
German; nonfiction BU TH
HAMBERGER, John, 1934- ,
American; juveniles CO CON
'HAMBLETONIAN' see FAIRFAX-
BLAKEBOROUGH, John F.
HAMBLIN, Robert Lee, 1927- ,
American; nonfiction CON
HAMBLIN, W. K., 1928- , Amer-
ican; nonfiction CON

HAMBURGER, Ernest, 1891?-
1980, German; nonfiction CON
HAMBURGER, Michael, 1924- ,
English; poetry, nonfiction,
translations, plays VCP WA
HAMBURGER, Michael Jay,
1938- , American; nonfiction
CON
HAMBURGER, Robert, 1943- ,
American; nonfiction CON
HAMBURGH, Max, 1922- ,
German-American; nonfiction
CON
HAMDALLAH-I MUSTAUFI, 1281/
82- , Persian; nonfiction
BU LA
HAMDI, Mehmed Hamdüllah, 1449-
1503, Turkish; poetry PRU
HAMED bin MUHAMMED el
MURJEBI ('Tippu Tib'), 1830-
1905, Tanzanian; nonfiction
JA
'HAMEIRI, Avigdor' (Emil Feuer-
stein), 1886-1970, Hebrew;
poetry, translations, nonfiction
BU LA TH
HAMEL, Peter Michael, 1947- ,
German; nonfiction CON
HAMELINK, Jacques Marinus,
1939- , Dutch; poetry BU
HAMELMAN, Paul William,
1930- , American; nonfiction
CON
HAMER, David Allen, 1938- ,
New Zealander; nonfiction CON
HAMER, Martin J., 1931- ,
American; fiction SH
HAMEROW, Theodore Stephen,
1920- , Polish-American;
nonfiction CON
HAMERSTROM, Frances ('Claire
Windsor'), 1907- , American;
nonfiction, juveniles, poetry
CO CON
'HA-MEZAYER' see MANNE,
Mordecai Z.
HAMID KASHMIRI,   -1844, Kash-
miri; poetry PRU
HAMIDI, Mihdi, 1914- , Per-
sian; poetry BU
HAMIL, Thomas Arthur, 1928- ,
American; juveniles, nonfic-
tion CO CON
'HAMILTON, Adam' see GRAN-
BECK, Marilyn
HAMILTON, Alex John, 1939- ,
American; fiction, nonfiction
CON

HAMILTON, Alexander, 1712-56,
American; nonfiction BA
HAMILTON, Alexander, 1755-1804,
American; nonfiction MAG
HAMILTON, Alfred Starr, 1914- ,
American; poetry CON
HAMILTON, Anthony, 1646-1720,
Irish; nonfiction BU
HAMILTON, Bruce, 1900- , Eng-
lish; fiction ST
'HAMILTON, Buzz' see HEMMING,
Roy
HAMILTON, Carl, 1914- , Amer-
ican; nonfiction CON
HAMILTON, Carlos D., 1908- ,
Chilean-American; nonfiction
CON
HAMILTON, Charles, 1913- ,
American; juveniles WAR
HAMILTON, Charles Franklin,
1915- , American; nonfiction
CON
HAMILTON, Charles Granville,
1905- , American; nonfiction,
poetry CON
HAMILTON, Charles Harold St.
John ('Martin Clifford'; 'Harry
Clifton'; 'Clifford Clive'; 'Sir
Alan Cobham'; 'Owen Conquest';
'Gordon Conway'; 'Harry Dori-
an'; 'Frank Drake'; 'Freeman
Fox'; 'Hamilton Greening';
'Cecil Herbert'; 'Prosper
Howard'; 'Robert Jennings';
'Gillingham Jones'; 'T. Har-
court Llewelyn'; 'Clifford
Owen'; 'Ralph Redway'; 'Ridley
Redway'; 'Frank Richards';
'Hilda Richards'; 'Raleigh Rob-
bins'; 'Robert Rogers'; 'Eric
Stanhope'; 'Robert Stanley';
'Nigel Wallace'; 'Talbot Wyn-
yard'), 1875-1961, English;
juveniles CO CON KI
HAMILTON, Charles Nigel, 1944- ,
British; nonfiction CON
HAMILTON, Charles Vernon,
1929- , American; nonfiction
CON SH
'HAMILTON, Clare' see LAWLESS,
Bettyclare H.
'HAMILTON, Dave' see TROYER,
Byron L.
HAMILTON, Diane Brooks, Ameri-
can; juveniles WAR
HAMILTON, Donald Bengtsson,
1916- , American; fiction,
plays REI ST

HAMILTON, Dorothy, 1906- ,
American; juveniles CO
HAMILTON, Edith, 1867-1963,
American; juveniles, nonfic-
tion, translations CO CON
HAMILTON, Edmond Moore,
1904-77, American; fiction
AS COW NI
HAMILTON, Elizabeth, 1906- ,
Irish; juveniles CO
HAMILTON, Elizabeth, 1928- ,
Anglo-American; nonfiction
CON
'HAMILTON, Gail' see COR-
CORAN, Barbara
HAMILTON, George Rostrevor,
1888-1967, British; poetry,
nonfiction CON
HAMILTON, Holman, 1910-80,
American; journalism, non-
fiction CON
HAMILTON, James Robertson,
1921- , Scots; nonfiction
CON
HAMILTON, Joan Lesley ('Joan
Cline'), 1942- , American;
fiction CON
'HAMILTON, Julia' see WATSON,
Julia
'HAMILTON, Mollie' see KAYE,
Mary M.
HAMILTON, Neill Q., 1925- ,
American; nonfiction CON
HAMILTON, Patrick, 1904/95-62,
English; fiction, plays REI
SEY ST
'HAMILTON, Paul' see DENNIS-
JONES, Harold
HAMILTON, Peter Edward,
1947- , British; nonfiction
CON
HAMILTON, Robert, American;
poetry, film SH
HAMILTON, Robert Ian, 1938- ,
British; poetry, nonfiction
VCP WAK
HAMILTON, Russell George,
1934- , American; nonfiction
CON
HAMILTON, Virginia Esther,
1933/36- , American; juven-
iles CO DEM KI
HAMILTON, Wallace, 1919- ,
American; nonfiction, plays
CON
HAMILTON, William, 1939- ,
American; nonfiction CON
HAMILTON, William, Jr.,

1924- , American; nonfiction
CON
HAMILTON, William of Bangour,
1704-54, Scots; poetry BU DA
HAMILTON, William of Gilbert-
field, 1665?-1751, Scots; poetry
BU DA
HAMILTON, Sir William, 1788-
1856, Scots; nonfiction BU
HAMILTON, William Baillie,
1930- , Canadian; nonfiction
CON
HAMILTON-PATERSON, James,
English; juveniles, poetry
WAR
HAMIT, Abdülhak Tarhan, 1852-
1937, Turkish; poetry, plays
PRU
HAMLEY, Dennis, 1935- , Eng-
lish; juveniles, plays CON
HAMLIN, Charles Hughes, 1907- ,
American; nonfiction CON
HAMLIN, Wilfrid Gardiner,
1918- , American; nonfiction
CON
HAMLING, William Lawrence,
1921- , American; fiction NI
HAMM, Charles Edward, 1925- ,
American; nonfiction CON
HAMM, Glenn Bruce, 1936- ,
American; nonfiction CON
HAMM, Marie (Roberson), 1917- ,
American; nonfiction CON
HAMM, Michael Franklin, 1943- ,
American; nonfiction CON
HAMMACK, James W., Jr.,
1937- , American; nonfiction
CON
HAMMAN, Ray Tracy, 1945- ,
American; nonfiction CON
HAMMARSKOELD, Dag, 1905-61,
Swedish; nonfiction CON
HAMMARSKÖLD, Lars, 1785-1827,
Swedish; nonfiction BU
HAMMEN, Carl Schlee, 1923- ,
American; nonfiction CON
HAMMENHÖG, Waldemar, 1902- ,
Swedish; fiction BU
HAMMER, Carl, Jr., 1910- ,
American; nonfiction CON
HAMMER, David Harry, 1893?-
1978, American; nonfiction
CON
HAMMER, Jefferson Joseph,
1933- , American; nonfiction
CON
HAMMER, Kenneth M., 1918- ,
American; nonfiction CON

HAMMER, Richard, 1928- ,
American; juveniles CO
HAMMER, Signe, American; non-
fiction CON
HAMMERMAN, Gay Morenus,
1926- , American; juveniles
CO
HAMMERSTEIN, Oscar II, 1895-
1960, American; libretto
CON MCG
HAMMETT, Dashiell ('Peter Col-
linson'), 1894-1961, American;
fiction BR BU CON MAG PO
REI SEY ST VN
HAMMING, Richard W., 1915- ,
American; nonfiction CON
HAMMON, William Rogers, 1920- ,
American; nonfiction CON
HAMMOND, Albert Lanphier,
1892-1970, American; nonfic-
tion CON
HAMMOND, Dorothy, 1924- ,
American; nonfiction CON
HAMMOND, James Dillard,
1933- , American; nonfiction
CON
'HAMMOND, Jane' see POLAND,
Dorothy
HAMMOND, John,   -1663, Amer-
ican; nonfiction BA
HAMMOND, Lawrence, 1925- ,
British; nonfiction, fiction
CON
HAMMOND, Mason, 1903- ,
American; nonfiction CON
HAMMOND, Norman, 1944- ,
American; nonfiction CON
HAMMOND, Paul, 1947- , Eng-
lish; nonfiction, fiction,
translations CON
HAMMOND, Peter Boyd, 1928- ,
American; nonfiction CON
'HAMMOND, Ralph' see INNES,
Hammond
HAMMOND, Richard James,
1911- , Anglo-American;
nonfiction CON
HAMMOND, Winifred, American;
juveniles WAR
HAMMONDS, Michael Galen,
1942- , American; fiction
CON
HAMMONTREE, Marie Gertrude,
1913- , American; juveniles
CO
HAMNER, Earl Henry, Jr.,
1923- , American; fiction,
film, tv CON KIB

HAMOD, Sam, 1936- , American;
poetry, nonfiction CON
'HAMP, Pierre' (Henri Bourillon),
1876-1962, French; fiction
BU CL
HAMPSHIRE, Stuart Newton,
1914- , English; nonfiction
WA
HAMPSON, Richard Denman,
1929- , American; juveniles
CO
HAMPTON, Christopher, 1929- ,
British; poetry, juveniles, non-
fiction, translations CON
VCD VCP
HAMPTON, David Richard, 1933- ,
American; nonfiction CON
HAMRE, Leif, 1914- , Norwegian;
juveniles CO DEM
HAMSCHER, Albert Nelson,
1946- , American; nonfiction
CON
HAMSHER, J. Herbert, 1938- ,
American; nonfiction CON
HAMSHERE, Cyril Eric, 1912- ,
British; nonfiction, plays CON
HAMSUN, Knut, 1859-1952, Nor-
wegian; fiction, plays, poetry
BU CL MAG SEY TH
HAMZAH FANSURI (Hamzah of
Barus), fl. 1550-1600, Malayan;
poetry LA
HAMZATOV, Rasul, 1923- , Avar;
poetry PRU
HAN, Seung Soo, 1936- , Korean;
nonfiction CON
HAN, Sungjoo, 1940- , Korean-
American; nonfiction CON
HAN SOR-YA, 1900- , Korean;
nonfiction, journalism PRU
'HAN SUYIN' (Elizabeth Comber),
1917- , British; nonfiction,
fiction WA
HAN YONGUN, 1879-1944, Korean;
poetry BU PRU
HAN YÜ, 768-824, Chinese; nonfic-
tion, poetry BU LA PRU
HANAGAN, Eva Helen, 1923- ,
Scots; fiction CON
HANAGHAN, Jonathan, 1887-1967,
English; poetry CON
HANAMI, Tadashi Akamatsu,
1930- , Japanese; nonfiction
CON
HANAU, Laia, 1916- , American;
nonfiction CON
HANAWALT, Barbara Ann, 1941- ,
American; nonfiction CON

HANAZONO TENNO, 1297-1348,
Japanese; poetry, nonfiction
HI
HANBURY-TENISON, Airling
Robin, 1936- , English; non-
fiction CON
HANCE, Kenneth Gordon, 1903- ,
American; nonfiction CON
HANCHEV, Vesselin, 1919-66,
Bulgarian; poetry BU
HANCOCK, Carla, American; non-
fiction, juveniles CON
HANCOCK, Carol H. B. see
HANCOCK, Morgan
HANCOCK, Edward Leslie, 1930- ,
American; nonfiction CON
HANCOCK, Geoffrey, 1946- ,
Canadian; nonfiction CON
HANCOCK, Harold Bell, 1913- ,
American; nonfiction CON
HANCOCK, Lyn, 1938- , Aus-
tralian; nonfiction CON
HANCOCK, Maxine, 1942- ,
Canadian; nonfiction, fiction
CON
HANCOCK, Morgan (Carol Helen
Brooks Hancock), 1941- ,
American; nonfiction CON
HANCOCK, Neil Anderson, 1941- ,
American; fiction CON
HANCOCK, Roger Nelson, 1929- ,
American; nonfiction CON
HANCOCK, Sheila, 1942- ,
American; fiction CON
HANCOCK, Sibyl, 1940- , Amer-
ican; juveniles CO CON
HANCOCK, Taylor, 1920- ,
American; nonfiction CON
HAND, Andrus Jackson ('Fred
Carpenter'), 1913- , Amer-
ican; nonfiction CON
HAND, Joan Carole, 1943- ,
American; fiction, poetry
CON
HAND, Wayland Debs, 1907- ,
American; nonfiction CON
HANDELMAN, Howard, 1943- ,
American; nonfiction CON
HANDELMAN, John Robert,
1948- , American; nonfiction
CON
HANDELSMAN, Judith Florence,
1948- , American; nonfiction
CON
HANDKE, Peter, 1942- , Aus-
trian; plays, fiction BU CL
CON MCG WAK
HANDL, Irene, 1902- , British;

fiction CON
HANDLER, Jerome Sidney, 1933- ,
American; nonfiction CON
HANDLER, Meyer Srednick, 1905-
78, American; journalism
CON
HANDLER, Milton, 1903- , Amer-
ican; nonfiction CON
HANDLIN, Mary Flug, 1913-76,
American; nonfiction CON
HANDMAN, Herbert Ira, 1932- ,
American; nonfiction CON
HANDOVER, Phyllis Margaret,
1923?-74, British; journalism,
nonfiction CON
HANDY, Edward Smith, 1893?-
1980, American; nonfiction
CON
HANDY, Toni, 1930- , American;
fiction CON
HANDY, William J., 1918- ,
American; nonfiction CON
HANE, Mikiso, 1922- , American;
nonfiction CON
HANE, Roger, 1940-74, American;
juveniles CO
HANENKRAT, Frank Thomas,
1939- , American; nonfiction
CON
HANER, Frederick Theodore,
1929- , American; nonfiction
CON
HANES, Bailey Cass, 1915- ,
American; nonfiction CON
HANEY, David, 1938- , American;
nonfiction CON
HANEY, Erene Cheki, Russian-
American; juveniles WAR
HANEY, Lynn, 1941- , American;
fiction CO CON
HANEY, Thomas R., American;
nonfiction CON
HAN-FEI-TZU, -233 B.C.,
Chinese; nonfiction BU PRU
HANFF, Helene, American; juven-
iles CO
HANFORD, S.A., 1898-1978,
British; nonfiction, translations
CON
HANIFI, Mohammed Jamil, 1935- ,
Afghan-American; nonfiction
CON
HANING, James Robert, 1928- ,
American; fiction CON
HANKA, Václav, 1791-1861, Czech;
poetry BU TH
HANKE, Lewis Ulysses, 1905- ,
American; nonfiction CON

HANKEY, Cyril Patrick, 1886-
1973, British; nonfiction CON
'HANKEY, Rosalie A.' see
WAX, Rosalie H.
HANKIN, St. John Emile Claver-
ing, 1869-1909, English; jour-
nalism, plays MCG VD
'HANKINS, Clabe' see McDONALD,
E. L.
HANKINS, John Erskine, 1905- ,
American; nonfiction CON
HANKINS, Norman Elijah, 1935- ,
American; nonfiction CON
HANKS, Stedman Shumway, 1889-
1979, American; nonfiction
CON
HANLEY, Clifford ('Henry Cal-
vin'), 1922- , British; fic-
tion, plays VCN
HANLEY, Evelyn Alice, 1916-80,
American; nonfiction, poetry
CON
HANLEY, Gerald Anthony, 1916- ,
British; fiction, plays VCN
HANLEY, James ('Patric Shone'),
1901- , Irish; fiction, plays,
nonfiction CON DA SEY
VCD VCN VN
HANLEY, Michael F., IV, 1941- ,
American; nonfiction CON
HANLEY, William, 1931- ,
American; plays, fiction CON
VCD
HANLO, Jan Bernardus Maria,
1912-69, Dutch; poetry BU
HANLON, Emily, 1945- , Amer-
ican; juveniles CO CON
HANLON, John Joseph, 1912- ,
American; nonfiction CON
'HAN-MAC-TU' (Nguyen-trong-
Tri), 1912-40, Vietnamese;
poetry PRU
HANN, Jacquie, 1951- , Amer-
ican; juveniles CO CON
HANNA, Alfred Jackson, 1893- ,
American; nonfiction CON
HANNA, David, 1917- , Amer-
ican; nonfiction CON
HANNA, John Paul, 1932- ,
American; nonfiction CON
HANNA, Mary Carr, 1905- ,
American; nonfiction, fiction
CON
HANNA, Mary T. ('Mary Cole'),
1935- , American; journal-
ism, nonfiction CON
HANNA, Paul Robert, 1902- ,
American; nonfiction CO CON

HANNA, W. C., American; fiction
NI
HANNA, William John, 1931- ,
American; nonfiction CON
HANNAFORD, John, 1918- ,
American; nonfiction CON
HANNAH, Barbara, 1891- , Brit-
ish; nonfiction CON
HANNAH, Barry, 1942- , Amer-
ican; fiction KIB
HANNAM, Charles, 1925- , Eng-
lish; nonfiction CON
HANNAVY, John Michael, 1946- ,
Scots; nonfiction CON
HANNAWAY, Patricia Hinman
(Patti; 'L. P. Charnance'),
1929- , American; nonfiction
CON
HANNAY, James, 1827-73, Scots;
journalism, fiction BU
'HANNAY, Canon James O.' see
BIRMINGHAM, George A.
HANNAY, Patrick, -1629?,
Scots; poetry BU
'HANNIBAL' see ALEXANDER,
Stanley W.
HANNIFIN, Jerry Bernard, 1917- ,
American; journalism, nonfic-
tion CON
HANNING, Robert William, 1938- ,
American; nonfiction CON
HANNO, 5th century B.C., Carth-
aginian; nonfiction PRU
'HANNON, Ezra' see 'HUNTER,
Evan'
HANNUM, Alberta Pierson, 1906- ,
American; nonfiction CON
HANO, Arnold, 1922- , American;
juveniles CO
HANRAHAN, John David, 1938- ,
American; journalism CON
HANSBERRY, Lorraine, 1930-65,
American; plays BU MCG
MCN VD WA
HANSEN, Alvin Harry, 1887-1975,
American; nonfiction CON
HANSEN, Anton see 'TAMMSAARE,
A. H.'
HANSEN, Donald Andrew, 1933- ,
American; nonfiction, journal-
ism CON
HANSEN, Flemming, 1938- ,
Danish; nonfiction CON
HANSEN, Forest Warnyr, 1931- ,
American; nonfiction CON
HANSEN, Harry, 1884-1977, Amer-
ican; fiction, nonfiction CON
PAL

HANSEN, Joseph ('Rose Brock';
'James Colton'), 1923- ,
American; fiction, nonfiction
REI
HANSEN, Kenneth O., 1922- ,
American; nonfiction, poetry
CON
HANSEN, Martin Alfred, 1909-55,
Danish; fiction BU CL TH
HANSEN, Rodney Thor, 1940- ,
American; nonfiction CON
HANSEN, Ron, 1947- , American;
fiction CON
HANSEN, Thorkild, 1927- ,
Danish; journalism, nonfiction
BU CL
HANSEN, Vern, British; fiction
NI
HANSEN, William Freeman,
1941- , American; nonfiction
CON
HANSER, Richard Frederick,
1909-81, American; juveniles,
tv CO WAR
HANSFORD, Charles, 1685-1761,
American; poetry BA
HAN-SHAN, late 8th century,
Chinese; poetry PRU
HANSHEW, Thomas W. ('Char-
lotte Mary Kingsley'), 1857-
1914, American; fiction,
plays REI ST
'HANSI' see HIRSCHMANN, Maria
A.
HANSON, Albert Henry, 1913-71,
British; nonfiction CON
HANSON, Earl Dorchester,
1927- , American; nonfiction
CON
HANSON, Earl Parker, 1899- ,
American; nonfiction CON
HANSON, Fridolf Allan, 1939- ,
American; nonfiction CON
HANSON, Harvey, 1941- ,
American; fiction CON
HANSON, Howard Harold, 1896-
1981, American; nonfiction
CON
HANSON, Irene (Forsythe),
1898- , American; nonfiction
CON
HANSON, James Arthur, 1940- ,
American; nonfiction CON
HANSON, James Christian Mein-
ich, 1864-1943, American;
nonfiction ENG
HANSON, Jim, 1953- , Amer-
ican; poetry CON

HANSON, Joan, 1938- , American;
juveniles CO
HANSON, June Andrea, 1941- ,
American; juveniles CON
HANSON, Kenneth O., 1922- ,
American; poetry VCP
HANSON, Michael James, 1942- ,
English; nonfiction CON
HANSON, Paul David, 1939- ,
American; nonfiction CON
HANSON, Pauline, 1950- , Amer-
ican; poetry CON VCP
HANSON, Philip, 1936- , British;
nonfiction CON
HANSSON, Ola, 1860-1925, Swed-
ish; poetry, nonfiction BU TH
HANUSHEK, Eric Alan, 1943- ,
American; nonfiction CON
HANZLICEK, Charles George,
1942- , American; poetry
CON
HAO, Yen-ping, 1934- , American;
nonfiction CON
HAPGOOD, Fred, 1942- , Amer-
ican; nonfiction CON
HAPGOOD, Ruth Knott, 1920- ,
American; nonfiction CON
HAPPE, Peter, 1932- , American;
nonfiction CON
HAPPEL, Eberhard Werner, 1648-
90, German; nonfiction BU
HAPPOLD, Frederick Crossfield,
1892- , British; nonfiction
CON
HAQQGU, Abdu'l-hakim, 1912- ,
Baluchi; poetry, nonfiction
PRU
HAQQI, Yahya, 1905- , Egyptian;
fiction, nonfiction BU PRU
'HARALD, Eric' see BOESEN,
Victor
HARALDSSON, Erlendur, 1931- ,
Icelander; journalism, nonfic-
tion CON
HARAMBASIC, August, 1861-1911,
Croatian; poetry BU
HARAP, Louis, 1904- , American;
nonfiction CON
HARARI, Ehud, 1935- , Israeli;
nonfiction CON
HARASYMOWICZ, Jerzy, 1933- ,
Polish; poetry BU CL
HARAWAY, Donna Jeanne, 1944- ,
American; nonfiction CON
HARBAGE, Alfred Bennett, 1901-
76, American; nonfiction CON
HARBAUGH, Henry, 1817-67,
American; poetry BU

453 HARBAUGH

HARBAUGH, John Warvelle,
1926- , American; nonfiction
CON
HARBEN, William Nathaniel,
1858-1919, American; fiction
BA NI
HARBERT, Mary Ann, 1945- ,
American; nonfiction CON
HARBESON, Georgiana Brown,
1894?-1980, American; non-
fiction CON
HARBESON, John Willis, 1938- ,
American; nonfiction CON
HARBINSON, William Allen
('John Howarth'), 1941- ,
Irish; fiction, nonfiction CON
HARBISON, Frederick Harris,
1912-76, American; nonfiction
CON
HARBISON, Peter, 1939- ,
Irish; nonfiction CON
HARBISON, Robert, 1940- ,
American; nonfiction CON
HARBOTTLE, Philip James,
1941- , English; nonfiction
NI
HARBURG, Edgar Yipsel (Yip),
1896-1981, American; lyrics,
poetry CON
HARBURY, Colin Desmond,
1922- , British; nonfiction
CON
HARBY, Isaac, 1788-1828, Amer-
ican; plays, nonfiction BA
HARCOURT, Palma, British; fic-
tion CON
HARCOURT, Peter, 1931- ,
Canadian; nonfiction CON
HARD, Edward Wilhelm, Jr.
('T. W. Hard'), 1939- ,
American; fiction CON
HARD, Margaret Steel, 1888-1974,
American; nonfiction, fiction
CON
HARDALLO, 1860?-1919, Arab;
poetry HER
HARDAWAY, Francine, 1941- ,
American; nonfiction CON
HARDEN, John William, 1903- ,
American; journalism, non-
fiction CON
HARDENBERG, Friedrich L. von
see 'NOVALIS'
HARDER, Geraldine Gross, 1926- ,
American; nonfiction CON
HARDER, Raymond Wymbs, Jr.,
American; juveniles CON
HARDESTY, Nancy Ann, 1941- ,

American; nonfiction CON
HARDIN, Charles Meyer, 1908- ,
American; nonfiction CON
HARDIN, Richard Francis, 1937- ,
American; nonfiction CON
HARDIN, Robert, 1934- , Amer-
ican; fiction CON
HARDIN, Tim, 1941?-81, American;
songs CON
HARDING, Anthony Filmer, 1946- ,
British; nonfiction CON
HARDING, Barbara, 1926- ,
American; nonfiction CON
HARDING, Dennis William, 1940- ,
American; nonfiction CON
HARDING, Denys Clement Watt,
1906- , British; nonfiction,
translations BOR
HARDING, Donald Edward ('Donald
Day'; 'Donald Earl Edwards';
'Eugene Parrish'), 1916- ,
American; fiction, poetry CON
HARDING, Gunnar, 1940- , Swed-
ish; poetry, nonfiction, transla-
tions CL
HARDING, John, 1948- , British;
plays CON VCD
HARDING, Lee, 1937- , Austral-
ian; fiction NI
HARDING, Timothy D., 1948- ,
British; nonfiction CON
HARDING, Vincent, 1931- , Amer-
ican; nonfiction SH
HARDING, Virginia Hamlet, 1909- ,
American; fiction CON
HARDING, William Harry, 1945- ,
American; nonfiction CON
HARDMAN, John David, 1944- ,
English; nonfiction CON
HARDT, Ernst, 1876-1947, Ger-
man; plays MCG
HARDUYN, Justus de, 1582-1636,
Flemish; poetry BU
HARDWICK, Elizabeth, 1916- ,
American; fiction, nonfiction
BA KIB WA
'HARDWICK, Homer' see ROGERS,
Paul Patrick
HARDWICK, Michael ('John Drink-
row'), 1924- , English; non-
fiction CON
HARDWICK, Mollie ('Mary Atkin-
son'), English; nonfiction, fic-
tion CON
HARDWICK, Richard Holmes, Jr.,
1923- , American; juveniles
CO
HARDY, Alan, 1932- , British;

nonfiction CON
HARDY, Alexandre, 1575-1632?,
French; plays, poetry BU
MCG TH
HARDY, Alister Clavering, 1896- ,
American; nonfiction CON
HARDY, Arthur Sherburne, 1847-
1930, American; fiction ST
HARDY, Barbara Gladys, British;
nonfiction BOR CON
HARDY, C. Colburn ('Jonas
Blake'; 'Hart Munn'; 'Leonard
Peck'), 1910- , American;
nonfiction CON
HARDY, David Andrews, 1936- ,
English; juveniles, nonfiction
CO CON
HARDY, Eric, English; nonfiction
CON
'HARDY, Jason' see OXLEY,
William
HARDY, Melissa Arnold, 1952- ,
American; fiction CON
HARDY, Peter, 1931- , English;
nonfiction CON
'HARDY, Stuart' see SCHISGAL,
Oscar
HARDY, Thomas, 1840-1928,
English; fiction, poetry, plays,
nonfiction BU CO DA MAG
PO SEY VN VP
HARDY, William George, 1895- ,
Canadian; fiction, nonfiction
CR
HARDYNG, John, 1378-1465?,
English; poetry BU
HARE, Augustus John Cuthbert,
1834-1903, English; nonfiction
BU
'HARE, Cyril' (Alfred Alexander
Gordon Clark), 1900-58, Eng-
lish; fiction, plays, juveniles
REI ST
HARE, David, 1947- , British;
plays CON VCD
HARE, Douglas Robert, 1929- ,
Canadian-American; nonfiction
CON
HARE, Nathan, 1934- , Amer-
ican; nonfiction CON SH
HARE, Norma Quarles, 1924- ,
American; juveniles CON
HARE, Richard Mervyn, 1919- ,
American; nonfiction WAK
HARE, Ronald, 1899- , British;
nonfiction CON
HARE, William Moorman, 1934- ,
American; plays, film CON

HAREL, Isser, 1912- , Israeli;
fiction CON
HAREN, Jonkheer Onno Zweir van,
1713-79, Dutch; poetry BU
HAREN, Jonkher Willem van, 1710-
68, Dutch; poetry BU
HARFORD, David Kennedy, 1947- ,
American; fiction, poetry CON
HARGER, William Henderson, 1936- ,
American; poetry CON
HARGRODER, Charles Merlin, 1926- ,
American; nonfiction CON
HARGROVE, Nancy Duvall, 1941- ,
American; nonfiction CON
HARIAUDH, 1865-1941, Hindi; po-
etry PRU
HARINGTON, Sir John, 1561-1612,
English; nonfiction, poetry,
translations BU DA RU VP
HARIRI, Abu Muhammad al-Qasim,
1054-1122, Arab; nonfiction
BU LA PRU
HARISCANDRA, Bhartendu, 1850-
85, Hindi; poetry, plays, non-
fiction, journalism PRU
HARIZI, Judah Ben Solomon, 1165-
1235?, Spanish; poetry, trans-
lations BU
HARK, Mildred see McQUEEN,
Mildred
HARKABI, Yehoshafat, 1921- ,
Israeli; nonfiction CON
HARKER, Kenneth, 1927- , Eng-
lish; fiction CON NI
HARKER, Ronald, 1909- , Brit-
ish; journalism, nonfiction
CON
HARKEY, Ira Brown, Jr., 1918- ,
American; nonfiction CON
HARKINS, Arthur Martin, 1936- ,
American; nonfiction CON
HARKINS, Philip ('John Blaine'),
1912- , American; juveniles
CO
HARKNESS, Edward, 1947- ,
American; poetry CON
HARKNESS, Georgia Elma, 1891-
1974, American; nonfiction
CON
HARKNESS, Gladys Estelle Suiter,
1908?-73, American; nonfiction
CON
HARKNETT, Terry ('Frank Chand-
ler'; 'David Ford'; 'George G.
Gilman'; 'Jane Harman';
'Joseph Hedges'; 'Charles R.
Pike'; 'William Pine'; 'James
Russell'; 'Thomas H. Stone';

'William Terry'; 'William M. James'), 1936- , English; fiction, nonfiction CON
'HARLAN' see SHAW, William H.
'HARLAN, Glen' see CEBULASH, Mel
HARLAN, William Keith, 1938- , American; nonfiction CON
HARLAND, Henry, 1871-1905, American; fiction BR
HARLING, Robert, 1910- , British; fiction, nonfiction REI
'HARLING, Thomas' see EAST-HAM, Thomas
HARLOW, Enid, 1939- , American; fiction CON
HARLOW, Francis Harvey, 1928- , American; nonfiction CON
HARLOW, Harry Frederick, 1905- , American; nonfiction CON
HARLOW, Joan Hiatt, 1932- , American; juveniles CON
HARLOW, LeRoy Francis, 1913- , American; nonfiction CON
HARMAN, Gilbert Helms, 1938- , American; nonfiction CON
'HARMAN, Jane' see HARKNETT, Terry
HARMAN, Jeanne Perkins, 1919- , American; nonfiction CON
HARMAN, Nicholas, 1933- , British; journalism, fiction CON
HARMAN, Thomas, fl. 1567, English; nonfiction BU
HARMELINK, Barbara Mary, Anglo-American; juveniles CO CON
HARMIN, Merrill, 1928- , American; nonfiction CON
HARMON, Glynn, 1933- , American; nonfiction CON
'HARMON, H. H.' see WILLIAMS, Robert M.
HARMON, Jim, American; fiction NI
HARMON, Margaret, 1906- , American; juveniles, nonfiction, fiction CO CON
HARMON, Nolan Bailey, 1892- , American; nonfiction CON
HARMON, Susanne Marie, 1940- , American; nonfiction CON
HARMS, Ernest, 1895-1974, German-American; nonfiction CON

HARMS, Leroy Stanley, 1928- , American; nonfiction CON
HARMS, Valerie Sheehan, 1940- , American; nonfiction CON
HARMSEN, Dorothy B. Bahneman, American; nonfiction CON
'HARMSTON, Olivia' see WEBER, Nancy
HARMSWORTH, Esmond Cecil, Viscount Rothermere, 1898-1978, British; journalism CON
HARNACK, Adolf von, 1851-1930, German; nonfiction ENG
HARNACK, Curtis, 1927- , American; fiction PAL
HARNARN, Terry ('Eric Traviss Hull'), 1920- , American; juveniles, nonfiction CO CON
HARNDEN, Ruth Peabody, American; juveniles CON WAR
HARNESS, Charles Leonard, 1915- , American; fiction AS COW NI
HARNETT, Cynthia Mary, 1893- , British; juveniles CO DE KI
HARNIK, Bernard, 1910- , Austrian; nonfiction CON
HARNSBERGER, Caroline Thomas, 1902- , American; nonfiction CON
HARO, Roberto P., 1936- , American; nonfiction MAR
HARPER, Carol Ely ('Ilke Ben'; 'Alfred Goddard'), American; poetry, fiction CON
'HARPER, Daniel' see BROSSARD, Chandler
HARPER, Floyd Henry, 1899-1978, American; nonfiction CON
HARPER, Harold W., American; nonfiction CON
HARPER, Harry, British; juveniles, fiction NI
HARPER, James Edwin, 1927- , American; nonfiction CON
HARPER, Joan Marie, 1932- , American; nonfiction CON
HARPER, John Carsten, 1924- , American; nonfiction CON
HARPER, John Dickson, 1910- , American; nonfiction CON
HARPER, Katherine Erna, 1946- , American; nonfiction CON
HARPER, Marvin Henry, 1901- , American; nonfiction CON
HARPER, Michael, 1931- , American; nonfiction CON
HARPER, Michael Steven, 1938- ,

American; poetry, nonfiction
SH VCP
HARPER, Stephen Dennis, 1924- ,
American; fiction, nonfiction
CON
HARPER, Vincent, American;
fiction NI
HARPER, Wilhelmina, 1884- ,
American; juveniles CO
HARPER, William Arthur, 1944- ,
American; nonfiction CON
HARPESTRAENG, Henrik, -1244,
Danish; nonfiction BU
HARPSFIELD, Nicholas, 1519-75,
English; nonfiction BU
HARPUR, Charles, 1813-68, Aus-
tralian; poetry BU VP
HARR, Wilber C., 1908-71,
American; nonfiction CON
HARRAGAN, Betty Lehen, 1921- ,
American; nonfiction CON
HARRAH, David Fletcher, 1949- ,
American; nonfiction CON
'HARRIETT' (Harriett Wilcoxen
Ginnings), 1905- , American;
juveniles, nonfiction CON
HARRIGAN, Edward, 1845-1911,
American; plays, poetry, fic-
tion MCG VD
HARRIMAN, Sarah, 1942- ,
American; nonfiction CON
HARRINGTON, Alan, 1919- ,
American; fiction BR CON
HARRINGTON, Charles Christo-
pher, 1942- , American;
nonfiction CON
HARRINGTON, Curtis, 1928- ,
American; film CON
HARRINGTON, Denis James,
1932- , American; fiction
CON
HARRINGTON, Geri, American;
nonfiction CON
HARRINGTON, Jack, 1918- ,
American; nonfiction CON
HARRINGTON, James (Harington),
1611-77, English; nonfiction
BU DA
HARRINGTON, Jeremy, 1932- ,
American; nonfiction CON
HARRINGTON, Joseph James,
1903- , American; journal-
ism, fiction REI ST
HARRINGTON, Joseph Daniel,
1923- , American; nonfiction
CON
HARRINGTON, Joyce, 193?- ,
American; fiction REI

HARRINGTON, Lyn Evelyn, 1911- ,
Canadian; juveniles CO
HARRINGTON, Peter Tyrus,
1951- , American; nonfiction
CON
HARRIOTT, Thomas, 1560-1621,
English; nonfiction BA
HARRIS, Agnes Kuehner, American;
juveniles WAR
HARRIS, Alfred ('Gwen Addison';
'Harris Moore'), 1928- ,
American; nonfiction, fiction
CON
HARRIS, Aurand, 1915- , Amer-
ican; juveniles, plays CON
KI
HARRIS, Barbara Seger, 1927- ,
American; fiction CON
HARRIS, Benjamin Charles, 1907-
78, American; nonfiction CON
HARRIS, Bernice Kelly, 1892-1973,
American; fiction, poetry,
plays BA CON
HARRIS, Carl Vernon, 1937- ,
American; nonfiction CON
HARRIS, Charles, 1923- , Amer-
ican; nonfiction CON
HARRIS, Charles Burt, 1940- ,
American; nonfiction CON
HARRIS, Clare Winger, 1891- ,
American; fiction AS
HARRIS, Christie Lucy Irwin,
1907- , Canadian; juveniles
CO DEM KI WAR
'HARRIS, Colver' see COLVER,
Anne
HARRIS, Corra, 1869-1935, Amer-
ican; fiction BA
HARRIS, Curtis Clark, Jr.,
1930- , American; nonfiction
CON
HARRIS, Daniel Arthur, 1942- ,
American; nonfiction CON
HARRIS, David Victor, 1946- ,
American; nonfiction, poetry
CON
HARRIS, Delmer William, 1937- ,
American; nonfiction CON
HARRIS, Dorothy Joan, 1931- ,
Canadian; juveniles CO CON
HARRIS, Edward Arnold, 1910-76,
American; journalism, nonfic-
tion CON
HARRIS, Errol Eustace, 1908- ,
American; nonfiction CON
HARRIS, Frank, 1856-1931, Welsh;
fiction, journalism DA SEY
HARRIS, Fred Roy, 1930- ,

American; nonfiction CON
HARRIS, Frederick John, 1943- ,
American; nonfiction CON
HARRIS, George Washington,
1814-69, American; fiction,
journalism BA BR MYE PO
VN
HARRIS, Gertrude Margaret,
1916- , American; nonfiction
CON
HARRIS, Harold Arthur, 1902- ,
English; nonfiction CON
HARRIS, Helena Barbara, 1927- ,
English; nonfiction CON
HARRIS, Herbert ('Frank Bury';
'Peter Friday'; 'Michael
Moore'), 1911- , British;
fiction, nonfiction CON REI
ST
'HARRIS, Hyde' see HARRIS,
Timothy H.
HARRIS, Janet Urovsky, 1932-79,
American; juveniles, nonfiction
CO CON WAR
HARRIS, Janette Hoston, 1939- ,
American; nonfiction SH
HARRIS, Jay Stephen, 1938- ,
American; nonfiction CON
'HARRIS, Jed' see HOROWITZ,
Jacob
HARRIS, Joel Chandler, 1848-1908,
American; fiction, juveniles
BA BR BU COM KI MAG PO
VN
HARRIS, John, American; juveniles
WAR
HARRIS, John ('John Beynon'; 'Lucas
Parkes'; 'John Wyndham'),
1903-69, British; fiction AS
CON NI WA
HARRIS, John ('Mark Hebden';
'Max Hennessy'), 1916- ,
British; fiction CON
HARRIS, John Sterling, 1929- ,
American; nonfiction CON
HARRIS, Julie, 1925- , American;
juveniles, nonfiction CON
WAR
HARRIS, Karen Harriman, 1934- ,
American; nonfiction CON
HARRIS, Kathryn Beatrice Gibbs
('Wilson Hayes'), 1930- ,
American; nonfiction CON
'HARRIS, Larry Mark' see
'JANIFER, Laurence M. '
HARRIS, Leon A. , Jr. , 1926- ,
American; juveniles CO
HARRIS, Leonard, 1929- , Amer-

ican; fiction CON
HARRIS, Lloyd John, 1947- ,
American; nonfiction, poetry
CON
HARRIS, Lorle Kempe, 1912- ,
American; juveniles, nonfiction
CO CON
HARRIS, Mark, 1922- , American;
fiction HE VCN WAK
HARRIS, Mary Bierman, 1943- ,
American; nonfiction CON
HARRIS, Mary Imogene, American;
nonfiction CON
HARRIS, Mary Kathleen, 1905-66,
British; juveniles, fiction KI
HARRIS, Mary Law, 1892?-1980,
American; journalism CON
HARRIS, Michael Hope, 1941- ,
American; nonfiction CON
HARRIS, Middleton, 1908- ,
American; nonfiction SH
HARRIS, Patricia, American; non-
fiction CON
HARRIS, Ranso Baine, 1927- ,
American; nonfiction CON
HARRIS, Richard Colebrooke,
1936- , Canadian; nonfiction
CON
HARRIS, Richard H. , 1942- ,
American; nonfiction CON
HARRIS, Richard Nelson, 1942- ,
American; nonfiction CON
HARRIS, Ricky, 1922- , Amer-
ican; nonfiction CON
HARRIS, Robert Dalton, 1921- ,
American; nonfiction CON
HARRIS, Robert John C. , 1922- ,
English; nonfiction CON
HARRIS, Rodie, American; nonfic-
tion CON
HARRIS, Rosemary Jeanne, 1923- ,
British; juveniles, tv, fiction
CO DEM KI REI WAR
HARRIS, Roy J. , 1903?-80, Amer-
ican; journalism CON
HARRIS, Sara C. see STADELMAN,
Sara L.
HARRIS, Seymour Edwin, 1897-1974,
American; nonfiction CON
HARRIS, Sherwood, 1932- , Amer-
ican; journalism, nonfiction
CO CON
HARRIS, Sydney Justin, 1917- ,
Anglo-American; nonfiction
CON
HARRIS, T. George, 1924- ,
American; nonfiction CON
HARRIS, Theodore Wilson, 1921- ,

HARRITY, Richard, 1907-73,
American; plays CON
HARROD, Sir Roy Forbes, 1900-
78, English; nonfiction CON
WA
HARROLD, William Eugene,
1936- , American; poetry,
nonfiction CON
'HARROWE, Fiona' see HURD,
Florence
HARROWER, Elizabeth, 1928- ,
Australian; fiction, nonfiction
CON VCN
HARSA (Harsavardhana), Emperor
of Kanaiij, 606-47, Indian;
plays BU PRU
HARSANYI, Zsolt, 1887-1943,
Hungarian; fiction TH
HARSCH, Ernest, 1951- , Amer-
ican; nonfiction CON
HARSCH, Joseph Close, 1905- ,
American; nonfiction CON
HARSDÖRFFER, Georg Philip,
1607-58, German; poetry
BU TH
HARSENT, David, 1942- , Eng-
lish; poetry CON VCP
HARSH, George, 1908?-80,
Canadian; nonfiction CON
HARSHBARGER, David Dwight,
1938- , American; nonfic-
tion CON
HARSTON, Ruth, 1944- , Amer-
ican; nonfiction, juveniles,
plays CON
HART, Archibald Daniel, 1932- ,
South African-American; non-
fiction CON
'HART, Barry' see BLOOM,
Herman I.
HART, Carol, 1944- , American;
nonfiction CON
HART, Douglas C., 1950- ,
American; nonfiction CON
HART, Edward Jack, 1941- ,
American; nonfiction CON
HART, Ernest Huntley, 1910- ,
American; nonfiction CON
HART, Frances Newbold Noyes,
1890-1943, American; fiction,
plays, nonfiction REI ST
'HART, Francis' see PAINE,
Lauran B.
HART, George L., III, 1942- ,
American; nonfiction CON
'HART, Harry' see 'FRANK, Pat'
HART, Heinrich, 1855-1906, Ger-
man; nonfiction BU

HART, John, 1948- , American;
nonfiction CON
HART, John Lewis, 1931- , Amer-
ican; nonfiction CON
HART, Joseph, 1945- , American;
plays CON
HART, Julius, 1839-1930, German;
nonfiction, poetry BU
'HART, Kate' see KRAMER, Roberta
HART, Lorenz, 1895/96-1943,
American; lyrics MCG
HART, Mabel Marie, 1932- ,
American; nonfiction CON
HART, Marilyn McGuire, 1926- ,
American; nonfiction CON
HART, Moss, 1904-61, American;
plays BR BU CON MCG MCN
PO VD
HART, Patrick, 1925- , American;
nonfiction CON
HART, Stephanie, 1949- , Amer-
ican; juveniles CON
HART, Susanne, 1927- , Austrian;
juveniles CON
HART, Winston Scott, 1903?-79,
American; journalism CON
HART-DAVIS, Sir Rupert, 1907- ,
English; nonfiction WA
HARTE, Francis Brett, 1836-1902,
American; fiction BR BU MAG
PO VN
HARTE, Thomas Joseph, 1914-74,
American; nonfiction CON
HARTELIUS, Margaret A., Amer-
ican; juveniles WAR
HARTFORD, Margaret Elizabeth;
1917- , American; nonfiction
CON
HARTHAN, John Plant, 1916- ,
British; nonfiction CON
HARTHOORN, Antonie Marinus,
1923- , Dutch; nonfiction
CON
HARTING, Emilie Clothier, 1942- ,
American; nonfiction CON
HARTJEN, Clayton Alfred, 1943- ,
American; nonfiction CON
HARTLAUB, Geneoveva, 1915- ,
German; fiction TH
HARTLEBEN, Otto Erich, 1864-
1905, German; poetry, fiction,
plays BU
HARTLEY, David, 1705-57, Eng-
lish; nonfiction BU DA PO
HARTLEY, Ellen Rahael, 1915- ,
German-American; juveniles
CO
HARTLEY, Leslie Poles, 1895-

1972, English; fiction BU
CON DA NI PO SEY VCN VN
HARTLEY, Livingston, 1900- ,
American; nonfiction CON
HARTLEY, Margaret Lohlker,
1909- , American; nonfiction,
poetry CON
HARTLEY, Peter Roy, 1933- ,
British; nonfiction CON
HARTLEY, Robert Frank, 1927- ,
American; nonfiction CON
HARTLEY, Shirley Foster,
1928- , American; nonfiction
CON
HARTLEY, William Brown,
1913- , American; juveniles
CO
HARTLIB, Samuel, 1596/1600-62,
Polish; nonfiction, translations
BU NI
HARTLIEB, Johannes, fl. 1439-
63, German; translations BU
HARTMAN, Chester Warren,
1936- , American; nonfiction
CON
HARTMAN, Darlene see 'LANG,
Simon'
HARTMAN, Geoffrey, 1929- ,
German-American; nonfiction
BOR
HARTMAN, George Edward,
1926- , American; nonfiction
CON
HARTMAN, Jan, 1938- , Swedish-
American; plays, fiction
CON
HARTMAN, John Jacob, 1942- ,
American; nonfiction CON
HARTMAN, Louis Francis, 1901-
70, American; juveniles CO
HARTMAN, Mary Susan, 1941- ,
American; nonfiction CON
HARTMAN, Nancy Carol, 1942- ,
American; nonfiction CON
HARTMAN, Rhondda Evans,
1934- , Canadian; nonfiction
CON
HARTMAN, Robert Kintz, 1940- ,
American; nonfiction CON
HARTMAN, Robert S., 1910-73,
German-American; nonfiction
CON
HARTMAN, Shirley, 1929- ,
American; fiction CON
HARTMAN, William Ellis, 1919- ,
American; nonfiction CON
HARTMANN, Edward George,
1912- , American; nonfiction

CON
HARTMANN, Michael, 1944- ,
British; fiction, plays CON
HARTMANN, Moritz, 1821-72,
Austrian; nonfiction, journal-
ism, fiction BU
HARTMANN, Susan Marie, 1940- ,
American; nonfiction CON
HARTMANN, William Kenneth,
1939- , American; nonfiction
CON
HARTMANN von AUE, 1170-1215,
Swabian; poetry BU MAG TH
HARTNACK, Justus, 1912- ,
Danish-American; nonfiction
CON
HARTNETT, Michael, 1941- ,
Irish; poetry HO VCP
HARTNOLL, Phyllis, 1906- ,
British; poetry, nonfiction,
translations, plays CON
HARTOCOLLIS, Peter ('Loizos
Mandrepelias'; 'Pitsa Palli'),
1922- , Greek-American;
nonfiction CON
HARTOG, Jan de, 1914- , Dutch;
fiction, plays BU
HARTOG, Joseph, 1933- , Amer-
ican; nonfiction CON
HARTRIDGE, Jon, 1934- , Eng-
lish; fiction AS NI
HARTSHORN, Ruth M., 1928- ,
American; juveniles CO
HART-SMITH, William, 1911- ,
Australian; poetry VCP
HARTSUCH, Paul Jackson, 1902- ,
American; nonfiction CON
HARTUNG, Albert Edward, 1923- ,
American; nonfiction CON
HARTWELL, Dickson Jay, 1906-
81, American; nonfiction CON
HARTWIG see WESSELY, Naphtale
H.
HARTZENBUSCH, Juan Eugenio,
1806-80, Spanish; plays, poetry
BU MCG TH
HARTZLER, Daniel David, 1941- ,
American; nonfiction CON
HARVARD, Andrew Carson,
1949- , American; nonfiction
CON
HARVARD, Stephen, 1948- ,
American; nonfiction CON
'HARVESTER, Simon' (Henry St.
John Clair Rumbold-Gibbs;
'Henry Gibbs'), 1910-75, Brit-
ish; fiction, nonfiction MCC
REI

HARVEY, Christopher, 1597?-
1663, English; poetry BU
HARVEY, David Dow, 1931- ,
American; nonfiction CON
HARVEY, Donald Joseph, 1922- ,
American; nonfiction CON
HARVEY, Edward Burns, 1939- ,
Canadian; nonfiction CON
HARVEY, Frank, 1912-81, Amer-
ican; fiction NI
HARVEY, Gabriel, 1545-1630,
English; nonfiction BU DA
RU
HARVEY, Gina Paula, 1922- ,
Italian-American; nonfiction
CON
HARVEY, James Cardell, 1925- ,
American; nonfiction CON
HARVEY, Jean Charles, 1891-
1967, Canadian; nonfiction,
fiction, poetry BU
HARVEY, Joan Margaret, 1918- ,
British; nonfiction CON
HARVEY, John Robert, 1942- ,
British; nonfiction, fiction
CON
HARVEY, Jonathan, 1939- ,
English; nonfiction CON
HARVEY, Kenneth, 1919?-79,
American; tv CON
HARVEY, Maria Luisa Alvarez,
1938- , Mexican-American;
nonfiction CON
HARVEY, Marian, 1927- ,
American; nonfiction CON
HARVEY, Nancy Lenz, 1935- ,
American; nonfiction CON
HARVEY, Nigel ('Hugh Willough-
by'), 1916- , British; non-
fiction CON
'HARVEY, Paul' see AURANDT,
Paul H.
HARVEY, Richard Blake, 1930- ,
American; nonfiction CON
HARVEY, Ruth Charlotte, 1918-
80, British; nonfiction CON
HARVEY, Virginia Isham, 1917- ,
American; nonfiction CON
HARVEY, William Burnett,
1922- , American; nonfiction
CON
HARWARD, Donald W., 1939- ,
American; nonfiction CON
HARWELL, Ann Manning, 1936- ,
American; nonfiction CON
'HARWIN, Brian' see HENDERSON,
Le Grand
HARWOOD, Gwendoline Nessie,

1920- , Australian; poetry,
plays CON SEY VCP
HARWOOD, Jonathan, 1943- ,
American; nonfiction CON
HARWOOD, Lee, 1939- , British;
poetry, translations VCP
HARWOOD, Pearl Augusta Brag-
don, 1903- , American; juven-
iles CO WAR
HARY (Blind Harry; Henry the
Minstrel), 1440?-95?, English;
poetry BU DA VP
HASAM SAH, 1735?-1843, Panjabi;
poetry PRU
HASAN, Saiyid Zafar, 1930- ,
Indian-American; nonfiction
CON
HASAN ben ALÎ see 'NIZÂM al-
Mulk'
'HASAN DIHLAVI' (Amir Najmuddin
Hasan Sijzi), 1253-1328, Indo-
Persian; poetry PRU
HASBROUCK, Kenneth E., 1916- ,
American; nonfiction CON
HASDEU, Bogdan Petriceicu, 1838-
1907, Rumanian; nonfiction
BU
HASEBROEK, Johannes Petrus
('Jonathan'), 1812-96, Dutch;
poetry, nonfiction BU
HASEGAWA NYOZEKAN, 1875-
1969, Japanese; nonfiction HI
HASEK, Jaroslav, 1883-1923,
Czech; fiction, journalism BU
CL MAG SEY TH
HASEL, Gerhard Franz, 1935- ,
Austrian-American; nonfiction
CON
HASELER, Stephen Michael Alan,
1942- , American; nonfiction
CON
HASENCLEVER, Herbert Frederick,
1924-78, American; nonfiction
CON
HASENCLEVER, Walter, 1890-
1940, German; plays, fiction,
poetry BU CL MCG TH
HASFORD, Jerry Gustav ('George
Gordon'), 1947- , American;
fiction CON
HASHAM SHAH, 1735-1843, Pun-
jabi; poetry BU
HASHIM, Makhdum Mahammad,
1692-1761, Sindhi; nonfiction,
poetry PRU
HASHIMI, Zahur Muhammad Shah
Sa'id, 1926- , Baluchi; poetry
PRU

HASHMI, Alamgir, 1951- , Pakistani; poetry, nonfiction CON
HASIM, Ahmet, 1885-1933, Turkish; poetry PRU
HASKELL, Arnold Lionel, 1903-81, English; juveniles, nonfiction CO CON
HASKELL, Douglas, 1899-1979, American; nonfiction, journalism CON
HASKELL, Martin Roy, 1912- , American; nonfiction CON
HASKETT, Edythe Rance, American; nonfiction SH
HASKIN, Gretchen, 1936- , American; fiction CON
HASKINS, Barbara see STONE, Barbara
HASKINS, Ilma, 1919- , American; nonfiction CON
HASKINS, James, 1941- , American; juveniles, nonfiction CO SH WAR
HASKINS, Samuel Joseph, 1926- , South African; fiction, nonfiction CON
HASLERUD, George Martin, 1906- , American; nonfiction CON
HASPEL, Eleanor C., 1944- , American; nonfiction CON
HASRAT MOHANI, Sayyid Fazlu'l-hasan, 1850-1951, Urdu; poetry, nonfiction PRU
HASS, Eric, 1905?-80, American; nonfiction CON
HASSALL, Christopher Vernon, 1912-63, English; nonfiction, poetry, plays CON WA
HASSALL, Mark William Cory, 1940- , British; nonfiction CON
HASSAN, Ihab, 1925- , Egyptian-American; nonfiction BOR
HASSAN b. THABIT, 563-659/73, Arab; poetry BU PRU
HASSE, Henry L., American; fiction AS NI
'HASSE Z' see ZEUERSTRÖM, Hans H.
HASSEL, Sven, 1917- , Danish; fiction CON
HASSELBLATT, Dieter, 1936- , German; nonfiction NI
'HASSEN, Amy Van' see WILES, Domini
HASSLER, Donald M., II, 1937- , American; nonfiction CON

HASSLER, Jon Francis, 1933- , American; juveniles, fiction CO CON
HASSLER, Kenneth W., American?; fiction NI
HASSRICK, Peter Heyl, 1941- , American; nonfiction CON
'HASTINGS, Graham' see JEFFRIES, Roderic
HASTINGS, Ian, 1912- , New Zealand-American; juveniles CON
HASTINGS, Macdonald ('Lemuel Gulliver'), 1909- , English; fiction, juveniles, nonfiction CON REI ST
HASTINGS, Macdonald Max, 1945- , British; nonfiction CON
HASTINGS, Margaret, 1910- , American; nonfiction CON
'HASTINGS, March' see 'JORDAN, Leonard'
HASTINGS, Michael Gerald, 1938- , British; plays, fiction, poetry CON VCD
HASTINGS, Milo, 1884-1957, American; fiction NI
HASTINGS, Philip Kay, 1922- , American; nonfiction CON
HASTINGS, Robert Paul, 1933- , British; nonfiction CON
HASTORF, Albert Herman, 1920- , American; nonfiction CON
HASTY, Ronald W., 1941- , American; nonfiction CON
HASWELL, Chetwynd John Drake (Jock; 'George Foster'), 1919- , English; fiction, nonfiction CON
HASWELL, Harold Alanson, Jr., 1912- , American; nonfiction CON
HATAFIELD, Antoinette Kuzmanich, 1929- , American; nonfiction CON
HATCH, Alden, 1898-1975, American; nonfiction CON
HATCH, Elvin James, 1937- , American; nonfiction CON
HATCH, Eric Stowe, 1902?-73, American; fiction CON
'HATCH, Gerald' (Dave Foley), American; fiction NI
HATCH, James Vernon, 1928- , American; plays, poetry, nonfiction CON
HATCH, Robert McConnell,

1910- , American; nonfiction
CON
HATCHER, John Southall, 1940- ,
American; fiction, poetry
CON
HATCHER, Robert Anthony,
1937- , American; nonfiction
CON
HATEFI, Abdollah, 1440/50-1521,
Persian; poetry PRU
HATFIELD, Dorothy Blackmon,
1921- , American; nonfiction
CON
HATFIELD, Henry Caraway,
1912- , American; nonfiction
CON
HATFIELD, Mark Odom, 1922- ,
American; nonfiction CON
HATFIELD, Richard, 1853- ,
American; fiction NI
'HATHAWAY, Mavis' see AVERY,
Ira
HATHAWAY, Sibyl Collings, 1884-
1974, British; nonfiction
CON
HATHAWAY, William, 1944- ,
American; poetry CON
HATIF of ISFAHAN, Sayid Ahmad,
-1784, Persian; poetry BU
HATIM, Muhammad Abd al-Qadir,
1918- , Egyptian; nonfiction
CON
HATIM al-TA'I, fl. 600, Arab;
poetry BU
HATLO, Jimmy, 1898-1963,
American; cartoons CO CON
HATTA, Mohammed, 1902-80,
Indonesian; nonfiction CON
HATTAWAY, Herman Morell,
1938- , American; nonfiction
CON
HATTERAS, Owen III see Mc-
DAVID, Raven I., Jr.
HATTERSLEY, Ralph Marshall,
Jr., 1921- , American;
nonfiction CON
HATTERSLEY, Roy Sydney George,
1932- , British; nonfiction
CON
HATTORI NANKAKU, 1683-1759,
Japanese; nonfiction, poetry
HI
HATTORI RANSETSU, 1654-1707,
Japanese; poetry HI
HATTWICK, Richard Earl, 1938- ,
American; nonfiction CON
HATVARY, George Egon, Hun-
garian-American; nonfiction

CON
HATZFELD, Helmut Anthony, 1892-
1979, American; nonfiction
CON
HAUCH, Johannes Carsten, 1790-
1872, Danish; poetry, plays,
fiction BU TH
HAUCK, Paul Anthony, 1924- ,
German-American; nonfiction
CON
HAUCK, Richard Boyd, 1936- ,
American; nonfiction CON
HAUERWAS, Stanley Martin,
1940- , American; nonfiction
CON
HAUFF, Wilhelm, 1802-27, Ger-
man; fiction, poetry BU TH
HAUFRECHT, Herbert, American;
juveniles WAR
HAUGAARD, Erik Christian,
1923- , Danish; juveniles,
translations, plays, poetry
CO DE KI
HAUGE, Alfred, 1915- , Nor-
wegian; fiction CL
HAUGE, Olav, 1905- , Norwegian;
poetry CL
HAUGH, Richard, 1942- , Amer-
ican; nonfiction CON
HAUGH, Robert Fulton, 1910- ,
American; nonfiction CON
HAUGHEY, Betty Ellen, American;
fiction, juveniles WAR
HAUGHEY, John C., 1930- ,
American; nonfiction CON
HAUGHT, John Francis, 1942- ,
American; nonfiction CON
HAUGHTON, Claire Shaver, 1901- ,
American; nonfiction CON
HAUGHTON, Rosemary Luling,
1927- , English; juveniles
WAR
HAUGHTON, William, 1573-1605,
English; plays BU
HAUGLAND, Vernon Arnold,
1908- , American; nonfiction
CON
HAUN, Mildred Eunice, 1911-66,
American; fiction, nonfiction
BA
HAUPT, Zygmunt, 1907?-75,
Polish-American; nonfiction
CON
HAUPTMANN, Carl, 1858-1921,
German; plays, fiction BU CL
MCG
HAUPTMANN, Gerhart, 1862-1946,
German; plays, fiction, poetry,

nonfiction BU CL MAG MCG
SEY TH
HAURY, Emil Walter, 1904- ,
American; nonfiction CON
HAUSDORFF, Don, 1927- ,
American; nonfiction CON
HAUSER, Charles McCorkle,
1929- , American; journal-
ism CON
HAUSER, Hilary, 1944- , Amer-
ican; nonfiction CON
'HAUSER, Kaspar' see TUCHOL-
SKY, Kurt
HAUSER, Margaret Louise ('Gay
Head'), 1909- , American;
juveniles CO
HAUSER, Thomas, 1946- , Amer-
ican; nonfiction CON
HAUSER, William Barry, 1939- ,
American; nonfiction CON
HAUSHOFER, Albrecht, 1903-45,
German; poetry, plays CL
TH
HAUSMAN, Gerald, 1945- ,
American; poetry, juveniles
CO CON
HAUSRATH, Alfred Hartmann,
1901- , American; nonfiction
CON
HAUTZIG, Deborah, 1956- ,
American; juveniles CON
HAUTZIG, Esther (Rudomin),
1930- , Polish-American;
juveniles CO DE
HAVEL, Jean Eugene Martial,
1928- , French-Canadian;
nonfiction CON
HAVEL, Václav, 1936- , Czech;
plays, poetry BU CL WAK
HAVELOCK, Christine Mitchell,
1924- , Canadian-American;
nonfiction CON
HAVELOCK, Ronald Geoffrey,
1935- , Canadian; nonfiction
CON
HAVEMANN, Joel, 1943- ,
American; journalism, non-
fiction CON
'HAVENHAND, John' see COX,
John R.
HAVENS, Daniel Frederick,
1931- , American; nonfiction
CON
HAVENS, George Remington,
1890-1977, American; non-
fiction CON
HAVENS, Murray Clark, 1932- ,
American; nonfiction CON

HAVENS, Shirley Elise, 1952- ,
American; journalism CON
HAVENS, Thomas R. H., 1939- ,
American; nonfiction CON
HAVERSCHMIDT, Francois ('Piet
Paaltjens'), 1835-94, Dutch;
fiction BU
HAVERSTOCK, Mary Sayre,
1932- , American; juveniles,
nonfiction CON WAR
HAVERSTOCK, Nathan Alfred
('Richard Alfred'), 1931- ,
American; nonfiction CON
HAVIGHURST, Marion Boyd,
-1974, American; nonfiction,
poetry CON
HAVILAND, Virginia, 1911- ,
American; juveniles CO DEM
WAR
HAVLICEK BOROVSKY, Karel,
1821-56, Czech; journalism,
nonfiction BU TH
HAVLIK, John F., 1917- , Amer-
ican; nonfiction CON
HAVREHOLD, Finn, Norwegian;
juveniles, fiction, plays WAR
HAVRILESKY, Thomas Michael,
1939- , American; nonfiction
CON
HAWES, Grace M., 1926- ,
American; nonfiction CON
HAWES, Hampton, 1929?-77,
American; nonfiction CON
HAWES, Joseph Milton, 1938- ,
American; nonfiction CON
HAWES, Judy, 1913- , American;
juveniles CO
HAWES, Stephen, 1475?-1523?,
English; poetry BU DA PO
VP
HAWES, William Kenneth, 1931- ,
American; nonfiction CON
HAWI, Khalil, 1925- , Lebanese;
poetry PRU
'HAWK, Alex' see GARFIELD,
Brian
HAWKE, David Freeman, 1923- ,
American; nonfiction CON
HAWKE, Gary Richard, 1942- ,
New Zealander; nonfiction
CON
'HAWKE, Nancy' see NUGENT,
Nancy
HAWKER, Robert Stephen, 1803-
75, English; poetry BU PO
VP
HAWKES, Jacquetta Hopkins,
1910- , British; nonfiction,

plays, poetry CON NI
HAWKES, John, 1925- , American; fiction, plays BR BU HE MAG MCN PO SEY VCD VCN VN WA
HAWKESWORTH, Eric ('The Great Comte'), 1921- , English; juveniles CO WAR
HAWKESWORTH, John, 1715?-73, English; plays, nonfiction, translations BU
HAWKINS, Alec Desmond, 1908- , English; fiction, nonfiction CON
HAWKINS, Sir Anthony H. see 'HOPE, Anthony'
HAWKINS, Arthur, 1903- , American; juveniles CO
HAWKINS, Edward H., 1934- , American; fiction CON
HAWKINS, Gordon, 1919- , English; nonfiction CON
HAWKINS, Helen Ann Quail, 1907- , American; juveniles CO
HAWKINS, Henry, 1572?-1646, English; translations, poetry BU
HAWKINS, Jim, 1944- , American; journalism, nonfiction CON
HAWKINS, John Noel, 1944- , American; nonfiction CON
HAWKINS, Martin, English; fiction NI
HAWKINS, Odie, 1937- , American; nonfiction CON SH
HAWKINSON, John Samuel, 1912- , American; juveniles CO DEM
HAWKINSON, Lucy Ozone, 1924-71, American; juveniles CO CON
HAWKS, Howard Winchester, 1896-1977, American; film CON
HAWKSWORTH, Henry D., 1933- , American; nonfiction CON
HAWLEY, Donald Thomas, 1923- , American; nonfiction CON
HAWLEY, Florence M. see ELLIS, Florence H.
HAWLEY, Henrietta Ripperger, 1890?-1974, American; nonfiction, journalism CON
HAWLEY, Isabel Lockwood,

1935- , American; nonfiction CON
HAWLEY, Robert Coit, 1933- , American; nonfiction CON
HAWS, Duncan ('Pertinax'), 1921- , British; nonfiction CON
HAWTHORN, Jeremy, 1942- , British; nonfiction CON
HAWTHORNE, Julian, 1846-1934, American; poetry, fiction ST
HAWTHORNE, Nathaniel, 1804-64, American; fiction, juveniles, nonfiction AM BR BU COM MAG MY NI PO VN WAR
'HAWTHORNE, Captain R. M.' see ELLIS, Edward S.
HAWTON, Hector, 1901- , British; fiction NI
HAXTON, Josephine A. see 'DOUGLAS, Ellen'
HAY, David McKechnie, 1935- , American; nonfiction CON
HAY, George, 1922- , British; fiction AS NI
HAY, George Campbell, 1915- , Scots; poetry, translations BU DA
HAY, Gyula, 1900-75, Hungarian; plays CL TH WAK
HAY, Jacob, 1920- , American; fiction NI
HAY, James Gordon, 1936- , American; nonfiction CON
HAY, John, Australian; fiction NI
HAY, John, 1915- , American; juveniles, poetry, nonfiction CO CON
HAY, John Milton, 1838-1905, American; poetry, nonfiction, fiction BR BU VP
HAY, Robert Dean, 1921- , American; nonfiction CON
HAY, Thomas Robson, 1888-1974, American; nonfiction CON
'HAY, Timothy' see BROWN, Margaret W.
HAY, William Delisle, British; fiction NI
HAY, William Gosse, 1875-1945, Australian; fiction BU
HAYA de la TORRE, Victory Raul, 1895-1979, Peruvian; journalism CON
HAYAMI, Yujiro, 1932- , Japanese; nonfiction CON
HAYASHI FUMIKO, 1904-51, Japanese; fiction BU LA

HAYASHI RAZAN, 1583-1657,
Japanese; nonfiction HI
HAYCRAFT, Howard, 1905- ,
American; fiction, juveniles
CO ST
HAYCRAFT, Molly Costain,
1911- , Canadian-American;
juveniles CO
'HAYDEN, C. Gervin' see WICK-
ER, Randolfe H.
HAYDEN, Dolores, 1945- ,
American; nonfiction CON
'HAYDEN, Jay' see PAINE,
Lauran B.
HAYDEN, Jay G., 1884-1971,
American; journalism CON
HAYDEN, Martin Scholl, 1912- ,
American; journalism CON
HAYDEN, Naura, 1942- , Amer-
ican; nonfiction CON
HAYDEN, Robert Carter, Jr.,
1937- , American; nonfiction
CON
HAYDEN, Robert Earl, 1913-80,
American; poetry, juveniles
CO CON MAL SH VCP
VP WAK WAR
HAYDEN, Torey Lynn, 1951- ,
American; nonfiction CON
HAYDN, Hiram, 1907-73, Amer-
ican; nonfiction CON
HAYDON, Albert Eustace, 1880-
1975, Canadian; nonfiction
CON
HAYDON, Benjamin Robert, 1786-
1840, English; nonfiction,
diary BU MAG
HAYEK, Friedrich August von,
1899- , Austrian-British;
nonfiction CON
HAYES, Alden Cary, 1916- ,
American; nonfiction CON
HAYES, Bartlett Harding, Jr.,
1904- , American; nonfiction
CON
HAYES, Billy, American; nonfic-
tion CON
HAYES, Carlton J. H., 1882-
1964, American; juveniles
CO
HAYES, David, 1919- , Irish;
plays HO
HAYES, Dorsha, American; non-
fiction, fiction, poetry CON
HAYES, Edward C., 1937- ,
American; nonfiction CON
HAYES, Geoffrey, 1947- , Amer-
ican; juveniles CON

HAYES, Harold Thomas Pace,
1926- , American; nonfiction
CON
HAYES, John Francis, 1904- ,
Canadian; juveniles, nonfiction
CO CR KI
HAYES, John Haralson, 1934- ,
American; nonfiction CON
HAYES, John Philip, 1949- ,
American; nonfiction CON
HAYES, Joseph Arnold ('Joseph
H. Arnold'), 1918- , Amer-
ican; fiction, plays REI VCN
HAYES, Mary Rose, 1939- ,
British; fiction CON
HAYES, Paul James, 1922- ,
American; nonfiction CON
HAYES, Paul Martin, 1942- ,
British; nonfiction CON
HAYES, Will, American; juveniles
CO
HAYES, William Dimitt, 1913- ,
American; juveniles CO
'HAYES, Wilson' see HARRIS,
Kathryn B. G.
HAYES-BAUTISTA, David E.,
1945- , American; nonfiction
MAR
HAYFORD, Fred Kwesi, 1937- ,
Ghanaian; nonfiction CON
HAYKAL, Muhammad Husayn, 1888-
1956, Egyptian; journalism,
fiction, nonfiction PRU
HAYLEY, William, 1745-1820,
English; poetry, plays BU PO
HAYMAN, Carol Bessent, 1927- ,
American; poetry, nonfiction
CON
HAYMAN, LeRoy, 1916- , Amer-
ican; juveniles, nonfiction
CON WAR
HAYN, Annette, 1922- , German-
American; nonfiction, plays
CON
HAYNE, Paul Hamilton, 1830-86,
American; poetry, nonfiction
BA BR BU MYE VP
HAYNES, Betsy, 1937- , Amer-
ican; juveniles CON
HAYNES, Glynn Walker, 1936- ,
American; nonfiction CON
HAYNES, Nelma, American; juven-
iles WAR
HAYNES, Renee Oriana, 1906- ,
English; nonfiction CON
HAYNES, Richard Frederick,
1935- , American; nonfiction
CON

HAYNES, Robert Vaughn, 1929- ,
American; nonfiction CON
HAYNES, Sybille, 1926- ,
German-English; nonfiction
CON
HAYS, Helen Ireland, 1903- ,
American; poetry CON
HAYS, Hoffman Reynolds, 1904-80,
American; poetry, plays,
fiction, nonfiction, transla-
tions CON VCP
HAYS, Paul R., 1903-80, Amer-
ican; nonfiction CON
HAYS, R. Vernon, 1902- ,
American; nonfiction CON
HAYS, Robert Glenn, 1935- ,
American; nonfiction CON
HAYS, Samuel Pfrimmer, 1921- ,
American; nonfiction CON
HAYS, Terence Eugene, 1942- ,
American; nonfiction CON
HAYS, Wilma Pitchford, 1909- ,
American; juveniles DE
HAYSTEAD, Wesley, 1942- ,
American; nonfiction CON
HAYTER, Earl Wiley, 1901- ,
American; nonfiction CON
HAYTHORNTHWAITE, Philip John,
1951- , British; nonfiction
CON
HAYTON, Richard Neil ('Thomas
Starling'), 1916- , American;
nonfiction CON
HAYTOV, Nikolay, 1929- ,
Bulgarian; fiction BU
HAYWARD, Brooke, 1937- ,
American; nonfiction CON
HAYWARD, Jack, 1931- , Eng-
lish; nonfiction CON
HAYWARD, Max, 1925-79, Brit-
ish; translations, nonfiction
CON
HAYWARD, N. Richard, 1892-
1964, Irish; nonfiction HO
'HAYWARD, Richard' see KEN-
DRICK, Baynard H.
HAYWOOD, Carolyn, 1898- ,
American; juveniles KI
HAYWOOD, Eliza Fowler, 1693-
1756, English; fiction, poetry,
plays, translations BU DA
NI VN
'HAYWOOD, Harry' see HALL,
Haywood
HAYWOOD, Herbert Carlton,
1931- , American; nonfiction
CON
HAYWOOD, Richard Mansfield,

1905-77, American; nonfiction
CON
HAZARD, Paul, 1878-1944, French;
nonfiction CL
HAZAZ, Chaim, 1898- , Hebrew;
fiction BU
HAZELHURST, Cameron, 1941- ,
British; nonfiction CON
HAZELTINE, Mary Emogene, 1868-
1949, American; nonfiction
ENG
HAZELTON, Elizabeth Baldwin,
American; juveniles, tv WAR
'HAZHAR' (Sharafkandi Abdurrah-
man), 1920- , Kurdish; poetry
PRU
'HAZLIT, Joseph' see STRAGE,
Mark
HAZLITT, Henry, 1894- , Amer-
ican; journalism, fiction NI
HAZLITT, William, 1778-1830,
English; nonfiction BU DA
MAG PO VN
HAZO, Samuel John, 1928- ,
American; poetry VCP
HAZOUME, Paul, 1890- , Daho-
man; nonfiction, fiction HER
JA
HAZZARD, Lowell Brestel, 1898-
1978, American; nonfiction
CON
HAZZARD, Shirley, 1931- , Aus-
tralian; fiction VCN WAK
HEACOX, Cecil E., 1903- ,
American; film CON
HEAD, Bessie, 1937- , South
African; fiction HER JA VCN
'HEAD, Gay' see HAUSER, Mar-
garet L.
HEAD, Gwen, 1940- , American;
nonfiction CON
HEAD, Joanne Lee, 1931- ,
American; fiction CON
'HEAD, Matthew' (John Canaday),
1907- , American; nonfiction,
fiction REI ST WA
HEAD, Richard, 1637-87, English;
nonfiction, fiction BU
HEAD, Richard Glenn, 1938- ,
American; nonfiction CON
HEAD, Robert V., 1929- , Amer-
ican; nonfiction CON
HEAD, Sydney Warren, 1913- ,
Anglo-American; nonfiction
CON
HEADINGTON, Christopher, Eng-
lish; juveniles WAR
'HEADLEY, Elizabeth' see

CAVANNA, Betty
HEADSTROM, Richard, 1902- ,
American; juveniles, nonfiction
CO CON
HEADY, Eleanor Butler, 1917- ,
American; juveniles CO CON
WAR
HEADY, Harold Franklin, 1916- ,
American; nonfiction CON
HEAL, Edith (Edith Heal Berrien;
'Eileen Page'; 'Margaret Pow-
ers'), 1903- , American;
juveniles CO
HEALD, Charles Brehmer, 1882-
1974, American; nonfiction
CON
HEALD, Timothy Villiers, 1944- ,
English; nonfiction, fiction
CON MCC REI
HEALEY, Ben J. ('B. J. Healey';
'J. G. Jeffreys'; 'Jeremy
Sturrock'), 1908- , British;
fiction, nonfiction CON REI
'HEALEY, Brooks' see ALBERT,
Burton, Jr.
HEALEY, James, 1936- , Amer-
ican; nonfiction CON
HEALEY, James Stewart, 1931- ,
American; nonfiction CON
HEALEY, John, 1585/86-1609?,
English; translations BU
HEALEY, Larry, 1927- , Amer-
ican; nonfiction CON
HEALEY, Raymond J., 1907- ,
American; anthology AS
HEALEY, Robert Mathieu,
1921- , American; nonfiction
CON
HEALY, George William, Jr.,
1905- , American; nonfiction
CON
HEALY, Gerard, 1918-63, Irish;
plays HO
HEALY, John Delaware, 1921- ,
American; fiction CON
HEALY, Sr. Kathleen, American;
nonfiction CON
HEALY, Raymond J., 1907- ,
American; editor NI
HEALY, Timothy S., 1923- ,
American; nonfiction CON
HEANEY, Seamus Justin, 1939- ,
Irish; poetry CON HO VCP
VP WAK
HEAPS, Willard Allison, 1908- ,
American; nonfiction CON
HEARD, Henry Fitzgerald ('Gerald
Heard'), 1889-1971, English;

nonfiction, fiction AS NI REI
ST
HEARD, Nathan Cliff, 1936- ,
American; nonfiction, fiction
CON SH
HEARN, Charles Ralph, 1937- ,
American; nonfiction CON
HEARN, Janice W., 1938- ,
American; nonfiction CON
HEARN, John ('Martin Pentecost'),
1920- , British; poetry, non-
fiction, plays CON
HEARN, Lafcadio ('Koizumi Yaku-
mo), 1850-1904, American;
fiction, nonfiction, translations
BA BR BU DA HI MAG VN
HEARNDEN, Arthur George,
1931- , British; nonfiction
CON
HEARNE, John, 1926- , West
Indian; fiction, plays BU DA
VCN WA
HEARNE, Thomas, 1678-1735,
English; nonfiction BU DA
HEARNSHAW, Leslie Spencer,
1907- , British; nonfiction
CON
HEARST, George Randolph, 1904-
72, American; journalism CON
HEARST, James, 1900- , Amer-
ican; nonfiction, poetry CON
PAL
HEATER, Derek Benjamin, 1931- ,
English; nonfiction CON
HEATH, Catherine, 1924- , Brit-
ish; fiction CON
HEATH, Charles Chastain, 1921- ,
American; nonfiction CON
HEATH, Harry Eugene, Jr. ('Ken-
dall Hall'), 1919- , American;
nonfiction CON
HEATH, Peter Lauchlan, 1922- ,
American; nonfiction, transla-
tions, fiction CON NI
'HEATH, Sandra' see WILSON,
Sandra
HEATH, Terrence George, 1936- ,
Canadian; fiction, film CON
HEATH, Veronica see BLACKETT,
Veronica
HEATH-STUBBS, John Francis,
1918- , British; poetry, plays,
nonfiction, translations VCP
HEATON, Eric William, 1920- ,
English; nonfiction CON
HEATON, Herbert, 1890-1973,
Anglo-American; nonfiction
CON

HEATON, Rose Henniker, 1884-
1975, British; poetry CON
HEATON-WARD, William Alan,
1919- , British; nonfiction
CON
HEATTER, Gabriel, 1890-1972,
American; journalism CON
'HEAVEN, Constance' see FECHER,
Constance
HEAVILIN, Jay, American; juven-
iles WAR
HEAVYSEGE, Charles, 1816-76,
Canadian; poetry, fiction,
plays BU
HEBBEL, Christian Friedrich,
1813-63, German; plays,
poetry, fiction BU MAG
MCG TH
HEBBLETHWAITE, Peter ('Robert
Myddleton'), 1930- , British;
nonfiction CON
'HEBDEN, Mark' see HARRIS,
John
HEBEL, Johann Peter, 1760-1826,
German; poetry BU TH
HEBER, Reginald, 1783-1826,
English; poetry, hymns BU
DA
HEBERT, Anne, 1916- , Cana-
dian; poetry, fiction, plays
BU CON CR DA WA
HEBERT, Ernest, 1941- ,
American; fiction CON
HEBERT, Tom, 1938- , Amer-
ican; nonfiction CON
HECATAEUS, fl. 525 B.C.,
Greek; nonfiction BU GR LA
HECHINGER, Fred Michael,
1920- , German-American;
journalism, nonfiction CON
HECHT, Anthony, 1923- , Amer-
ican; poetry BR MAL SEY
VCP WA
HECHT, Ben, 1893-1964, Amer-
ican; fiction, plays, journalism
BR CON MCG MCN NI ST
VD
HECHT, George Joseph, 1895-
1980, American; juveniles,
journalism CO CON
HECHT, Henri Joseph ('Henri
Maik'), 1922- , French;
juveniles CO
HECHT, Warren Jay, 1946- ,
American; nonfiction CON
HECHTER, Michael, 1943- ,
American; nonfiction CON
HECHTKOPF, Henryk, 1910- ,

Polish-Israeli; juveniles CO
HECK, Frank Hopkins, 1904- ,
American; nonfiction CON
HECK, Harold Joseph, 1906- ,
American; nonfiction CON
HECK, Peter M., 1937- , Amer-
ican; nonfiction CON
HECK, Suzanne Wright, 1939- ,
American; nonfiction CON
HECKART, Beverly Anne, 1938- ,
American; nonfiction CON
HECKELMANN, Charles Newman
('Charles Lawton'), 1913- ,
American; fiction, nonfiction
CON
HECKER, Isaac Thomas, 1819-88,
American; nonfiction MY
HECKER, Willem, 1817-1909,
Dutch; poetry BU
HECKO, František, 1905-60, Slovak;
fiction BU TH
HEDAYAT, Sadeq, 1903-51, Iranian;
fiction PRU
HEDBERG, Frans, 1828-1908, Swed-
ish; nonfiction, translations,
poetry BU
HEDBERG, Olle, 1899- , Swedish;
fiction BU TH
HEDBERG, Tor, 1862-1931, Swed-
ish; fiction, plays, poetry BU
HEDBORN, Samuel, 1783-1849,
Swedish; poetry BU
HEDDEN, Walter Page, 1898?-
1976, American; nonfiction
CON
HEDENVIND-ERIKSSON, Gustav,
1880-1967, Swedish; nonfiction,
fiction BU TH
HEDGE, Frederic Henry, 1805-90,
American; translations, nonfic-
tion MY
HEDGES, Bob Atkinson, 1919- ,
American; nonfiction CON
HEDGES, David Paget, 1930- ,
English; nonfiction CON
HEDGES, Doris Ryde, 1900- ,
Canadian; poetry, fiction CR
HEDGES, Elaine Ryan, 1927- ,
American; nonfiction CON
'HEDGES, Joseph' see HARKNETT,
Terry
HEDIN, Mary, American; fiction,
poetry CON
HEDLEY, Gladys Olwen, 1912- ,
English; nonfiction CON
HEDRICK, Travis K., 1904?-77,
American; journalism CON
HEEMSKERK, Johan Van, 1597-

1656, Dutch; poetry BU
HEENEY, Brian, 1933- , Cana-
dian; nonfiction CON
HEERE, Lucas de, 1534-84,
Dutch; poetry BU
HEERESMA, Heere, 1932- ,
Dutch; fiction BU
HEEVER, Frans P. van den see
'VAN den HEEVER, Toon'
HEEZEN, Bruce Charles, 1924- ,
American; nonfiction CON
HEFFERN, Richard, 1950- ,
American; nonfiction CON
HEFFERNAN, Michael, 1942- ,
American; poetry CON
HEFFERNAN, Thomas Patrick,
1939- , American; poetry
CON
HEFFNER, Richard Douglas,
1925- , American; nonfiction
CON
HEFFRON, Dorris, 1944- ,
Canadian; fiction CON
'HEFLIN, Donald' see WALL-
MANN, Jeffrey M.
HEGARTY, Reginald Beaton,
1906-73, American; nonfiction,
juveniles CO CON
HEGARTY, Walter, 1922- ,
British; nonfiction CON
HEGEL, Georg Wilhelm Friedrich,
1770-1831, German; nonfiction
BU TH
HEGEL, Richard, 1927- , Amer-
ican; nonfiction CON
HEGEMAN, Elizabeth Blair,
1942- , American; nonfiction
CON
HEGGEN, Thomas O., 1919-49,
American; fiction, plays BR
MAG MCG
HEGIUS, Alexander, 1430-98,
German; nonfiction BU
HEGLAR, Mary Schnall, 1934- ,
American; fiction CON
HEGNER, William, 1928- ,
American; fiction CON
HEGSTAD, Roland Rex, 1926- ,
American; nonfiction CON
HEIBER, Helmut, 1924- ,
German; nonfiction CON
HEIBERG, Gunnar Edvard Rode,
1857-1929, Norwegian;
plays, nonfiction BU CL
MCG TH WA
HEIBERG, Johan Ludvig, 1791-
1860, Danish; nonfiction,
plays, poetry BU MCG TH

HEIBERG, Johanne Luise Pätges,
1812-90, Danish; plays BU
HEIBERG, Peter Andreas, 1758-
1841, Danish; poetry, plays
BU TH
HEICHBERGER, Robert Lee,
1930- , American; nonfiction
CON
HEIDE, Florence Parry ('Alex B.
Allen'; 'Jamie McDonald'),
1919- , American; juveniles,
fiction CON DEM WAR
HEIDE, Robert, 1939- , American;
nonfiction, plays CON
HEIDEGGER, Martin, 1889-1976,
German; nonfiction BU CL
CON
HEIDEMAN, Eugene P., 1929- ,
American; nonfiction CON
HEIDEN, Carol A., 1939- ,
American; nonfiction CON
HEIDENBERG, J. von see
'TRITHEIM, Johann von'
HEIDENSTAM, Verner von, 1859-
1940, Swedish; poetry, fiction
BU CL MAG TH
HEIDERSTADT, Dorothy, 1907- ,
American; juveniles CO
HEIDI, Gloria, American; nonfiction
CON
HEIDINGSFIELD, Myron S., 1914-
69, American; nonfiction CON
HEIDISHK, Marcy Moran, 1947- ,
American; fiction CON
HEIFERMAN, Ronald Ian, 1941- ,
American; nonfiction CON
HEIFETZ, Milton D., 1921- ,
American; nonfiction CON
HEIJERMANS, Herman ('Ivan
Jelakswitch'; 'Koos Habbema';
'Samuel Falkland'), 1864-1924,
Dutch; plays, fiction BU CL
MCG TH
HEILBRON, John Lewis, 1934- ,
American; nonfiction CON
HEILBRONER, Joan Knapp, 1922- ,
American; juveniles WAR
HEILBRUN, Carolyn Gold ('Amanda
Cross'), 1926- , American;
fiction, nonfiction CON REI
HEILMAN, Grant, 1919- , Amer-
ican; nonfiction CON
HEILMAN, Joan Rattner, American;
nonfiction CON
HEILMAN, Robert Bechtold,
1906- , American; nonfiction
BOR
HEILMAN, Samuel Chie, 1946- ,

471

HEIM

German-American; nonfiction
CON
HEIM, Bruno Bernard, 1911- ,
Swiss; nonfiction CON
HEIM, Ralph Daniel, 1895- ,
American; nonfiction CON
HEIMAN, Ernest Jean, 1930- ,
American; nonfiction CON
HEIMAN, Marcel, 1909-76,
Austrian-American; nonfiction
CON
HEIMBERG, Marilyn Markham
(Ross), 1939- , American;
nonfiction CON
HEIMDAHL, Ralph, 1909- ,
American; nonfiction CON
HEIMLICH, Henry Jay, 1920- ,
American; nonfiction CON
HEIN, Eleanor Charlotte, 1933- ,
American; nonfiction CON
HEIN, John, 1921- , German-
American; nonfiction CON
HEIN, Leonard William, 1916- ,
American; nonfiction CON
HEIN, Lucille Eleanor, 1915- ,
American; juveniles CO
WAR
HEIN, Norvin, 1914- , Amer-
ican; nonfiction CON
HEIN, Piet ('Kumbel'), 1905- ,
Danish; poetry BU CL CON
TH
HEINBERG, Paul, 1924- ,
American; nonfiction CON
HEINDEL, Richard Heathcote,
1912-79, American; nonfiction
CON
HEINE, Carl, 1936- , American;
nonfiction CON
HEINE, Heinrich, 1797-1856,
German; poetry, nonfiction
BU MAG TH
HEINE, Ralph William, 1914- ,
American; nonfiction CON
HEINE, William Colbourne,
1919- , Canadian; journalism,
fiction, nonfiction CON
HEINEMANN, Katherine ('Kaki'),
1918- , American; poetry
CON
HEINEN, Hubert Plummer,
1937- , American; nonfiction
CON
HEINESEN, Andreas William,
1900- , Danish; fiction,
poetry BU CL TH
HEINESEN, Jens Pauli, 1932- ,
Faroese; fiction BU

HEINKE, Clarence H., 1912- ,
American; nonfiction CON
HEINL, Nancy (Gordon), 1916- ,
British; nonfiction CON
HEINL, Robert Debs, Jr.,
1916-79, American; nonfiction CON
HEINLEIN, Robert Anson ('Anson
MacDonald'; 'Lyle Monroe';
'John Riverside'; 'Caleb Saund-
ers'), 1907- , American; fic-
tion AS BR CO COW KI NI
VCN
HEINRICH, Willi, 1920- , Ger-
man; fiction CON WA
HEINRICH der GLICKEZARE, fl.
1180-85, Alsatian; poetry BU
HEINRICH JULIUS, Duke of Bruns-
wick, 1564-1613, German;
plays BU
HEINRICH von dem TÜRLIN, fl.
1215-20, Austrian; poetry BU
HEINRICH von FREIBERG, fl. 1290,
German; poetry BU TH
HEINRICH von MEISSEN, -1318,
German; poetry TH
HEINRICH von MELK, fl. 1160,
Austrian; fiction, poetry BU
TH
HEINRICH von MORUNGEN, fl.
1200, German; poetry BU TH
HEINRICH von MÜGELN, 1320?-72,
German; poetry BU
HEINRICH von NEUSTADT, fl. 1312,
Austrian; fiction, poetry BU
HEINRICH von NÖRDLINGEN, fl.
1332, Swiss; translations BU
HEINRICH von VELDEKE, fl. 1170-
90, German; poetry BU
HEINRICH von WITTENWEILER,
early 15th century, Swiss;
poetry TH
HEINS, Ethel Leah, 1918- ,
American; nonfiction CON
HEINS, Marjorie, 1946- , Amer-
ican; nonfiction CON
HEINS, Paul, 1909- , American;
juveniles, nonfiction CO CON
HEINSE, Johann Jakob Wilhelm,
1749-1803, German; fiction,
poetry BU TH
HEINSIUS, Daniel, 1580-1655,
Dutch; nonfiction, poetry BU
TH
HEINSIUS, Nicholaes, Jr., 1656-
1718, Dutch; fiction BU
HEINTZ, Ann Christine, 1930- ,
American; nonfiction CON

HEINTZ, Bonnie Lee, 1924- ,
American; fiction, nonfiction
CON
HEINTZ, John, 1936- , Amer-
ican; nonfiction CON
HEINTZE, Carl, 1922- , Amer-
ican; nonfiction CON
HEINTZELMAN, Donald Shaffer,
1938- , American; nonfiction
CON
HEINZ, William Frederick,
1899- , New Zealander;
nonfiction CON
HEINZEN, Karl, 1809-80, Ger-
man-American; poetry BU
HEINZERLING, Larry Edward,
1945- , American; journal-
ism CON
HEINZLMAN, Kurt, 1947- ,
American; nonfiction CON
HEISE, David Reuben, 1937- ,
American; nonfiction CON
HEISE, Kenan, 1933- , Amer-
ican; nonfiction CON
HEISENBERG, Werner, 1901-76,
German; nonfiction CON
HEISER, Charles Bixler, Jr.,
1920- , American; nonfiction
CON
HEISERMAN, Arthur Ray, 1929-75,
American; nonfiction CON
HEISERMAN, David Lee, 1940- ,
American; nonfiction CON
HEISEY, Alan Milliken, 1928- ,
Canadian; nonfiction CON
HEISKELL, John Netherland,
1872-1972, American; jour-
nalism CON
HEISLER, Martin O., 1938- ,
Hungarian-American; nonfic-
tion CON
HEISSENBÜTTEL, Helmut,
1921- , German; poetry,
fiction, radio BU CL CON
TH WAK
HEIT, Robert, American; juven-
iles WAR
HEITMANN, Hans, 1904-70,
German; fiction, plays BU
HEITZMANN, William Ray ('Wil-
liam R. Vincent'), 1948- ,
American; nonfiction CON
HEIZER, Robert Fleming, 1915-
79, American; nonfiction CON
HEJAZI, Mohammad, 1900- ,
Iranian; fiction PRU
HEKKER, Terry, 1932- , Amer-
ican; nonfiction CON

HEKTOR, Enno, 1820-74, East
Frisian; plays BU
HEKTOROVIC, Petar, 1487-1572,
Dalmatian; poetry BU
HELALI, Badroddin (Hilali; Hiloli),
1470-1529, Persian; poetry
PRU
HELBIG, Alethea, 1928- , Amer-
ican; poetry, juveniles CON
HELBING, Terry, 1951- , Amer-
ican; journalism CON
HELBLING, Robert Eugene,
1923- , Swiss-American;
nonfiction CON
HELD, Jacqueline, 1936- , French;
poetry, juveniles CON
HELD, Joseph, 1930- , Hungarian-
American; nonfiction CON
HELD, Julius Samuel, 1905- ,
German-American; nonfiction
CON
'HELD, Peter' see VANCE, John
H.
HELD, Ray Eldred, 1918- ,
American; nonfiction CON
HELD, Richard, 1922- , American;
nonfiction CON
'HELDER, Dom' see CAMARA,
Helder P.
HELDER de OLIVEIRA, Herberto,
1930- , Portuguese; poetry,
fiction CL
HELFGOTT, Roy B., 1925- ,
American; nonfiction CON
HELFMAN, Elizabeth Seaver,
1911- , American; juveniles
CO
HELFMAN, Harry, 1910- , Amer-
ican; juveniles CO
'HELFORTH, John' see DOOLITTLE,
Hilda
HELFRITZ, Hans, 1902- , Ger-
man; nonfiction CON
HELGASON, Jón, 1899- , Ice-
lander; nonfiction, poetry BU
HELGESON, Poul, 1485-1535,
Danish; nonfiction BU
HELIADE-RADULESCU, Ion, 1802-
72, Rumanian; nonfiction BU
HELICZER, Piero, 1937- , Amer-
ican; poetry BR
HELINAND de FROIDMONT, 1160?-
1229?, French; poetry, nonfic-
tion TH
HELIODORUS, 3rd century, Greek;
fiction BU GR LA
HELLAAKOSKI, Aaro, 1893-1952,
Finnish; poetry, nonfiction

BU TH
HELLANICUS, 480?-06 B. C.,
Greek; nonfiction BU GR LA
HELLBERG, Hans-Eric, 1927- ,
Swedish; journalism, nonfic-
tion CON
HELLEGERS, Andre E. , 1926-79,
Dutch; nonfiction CON
HELLEN, John Anthony, 1935- ,
English; nonfiction, transla-
tions CON
'HELLENS, Franz' (Franz van
Ermengen), 1881-1972, Bel-
gian; poetry, fiction, nonfic-
tion BU CL
'HELLER' see IRANEK-OSMECKI,
Kazimierz
HELLER, Abraham M. , 1898-
1975, Lithuanian-American;
nonfiction CON
HELLER, Bernard, 1896-1976,
American; nonfiction CON
HELLER, Heinz Robert, 1940- ,
German-American; nonfiction
CON
HELLER, Jean, 1942- , Amer-
ican; journalism CON
HELLER, Joseph, 1923- , Amer-
ican; fiction, plays BR BU
HE MAG PO SEY VCD VCN
VN WA
HELLER, Mark, 1914- , Eng-
lish; nonfiction CON
HELLER, Michael, 1937- ,
American; poetry, nonfiction
CON
HELLER, Peter, 1920- ,
Austrian-American; nonfiction
CON
HELLER, Reinhold August,
1940- , German-American;
nonfiction CON
HELLER, Robert, 1899?-1973,
American; nonfiction CON
HELLER, Sipa, 1897?-1980,
Austrian-American; nonfiction
CON
HELLER, Yomtob Lipmann,
1579-1654, Hebrew; poetry
BU
HELLERMAN, Herbert, 1927- ,
American; nonfiction CON
HELLIE, Ann, 1925- , Amer-
ican; juveniles, fiction, non-
fiction CON
HELLINGER, Douglas Alan,
1948- , American; nonfiction
CON

HELLINGER, Stephen Henry,
1948- , American; nonfiction
CON
HELLISON, Donald Raymond,
1938- , American; nonfiction
CON
HELLMAN, Arthur David, 1942- ,
American; nonfiction CON
HELLMAN, Clarisse Doris, 1910-
73, American; nonfiction CON
HELLMAN, Geoffrey Theodore,
1907-77, American; nonfiction
CON
HELLMAN, Harold (Hal), 1927- ,
American; juveniles CO WAR
HELLMAN, Lillian, 1905- ,
American; plays, nonfiction
AM BA BR BU MAG MCG
MCN PO SEY VCD VD
HELLMANN, Donald Charles,
1933- , American; nonfiction
CON
HELLSTRÖM, Gustaf, 1882-1953,
Swedish; fiction, journalism
BU TH
HELLYER, Paul Theodore, 1923- ,
Canadian; nonfiction CON
HELM, Everett, 1913- , Ameri-
can; nonfiction CON
'HELMAN, Albert' (Lodewijk Al-
phonsus Maria Lichtveld),
1903- , Dutch; fiction, non-
fiction BU
HELMER, John, 1946- , Aus-
tralian-American; nonfiction
CON
HELMER, William Joseph ('Horace
Naismith'), 1936- , American;
nonfiction CON
HELMERING, Doris Wild, 1942- ,
American; nonfiction CON
HELMERS, George Dow, 1906- ,
American; nonfiction CON
HELMERS, Jan Frederik, 1767-
1813, Dutch; poetry BU
HELMOHOLZ, Richard Henry,
1940- , American; nonfiction
CON
HELMLINGER, Benita Trudy,
1943- , American; nonfiction
CON
HELM-PIRGO, Marian, 1897- ,
Polish-American; nonfiction,
fiction CON
HELMREICH, Paul Christian,
1933- , American; nonfiction
CON
HELMREICH, Robert Louis,

1937- , American; nonfiction
CON
HELMS, Randel, 1942- , American; nonfiction CON
HELMS, Roland Thomas, Jr.,
1940- , American; nonfiction
CON
'HELOISE' see REESE, Heloise B.
HELPER, Rose, Canadian-American; nonfiction CON
HELPERN, Milton, 1902-77,
American; nonfiction CON
HELPRIN, Mark, 1947- , American; fiction CON
HELPS, Racy, 1913-71, English;
juveniles CO WAR
HELTAI, Jenö, 1871-1957, Hungarian; poetry, plays BU TH
HELTERMAN, Jeffrey A., 1942- ,
American; nonfiction CON
HELVETIUS, Claude Adrien,
1715-71, French; nonfiction
BU TH
'HELVICK, James' see COCKBURN, Claud
HELWIG, David Gordon, 1938- ,
Canadian; poetry, plays, fiction VCP
HEMACANDRA (Hemacarya),
1089-1172, Indian; poetry
BU PRU
HEMANS, Felicia Dorothea
Browne, 1793-1835, English;
poetry, plays BU DA PO VP
HEMESATH, Caroline, 1899- ,
American; juveniles, nonfiction CON
HEMESATH, James Bartholomew
William, 1944- , American;
fiction NI
HEMING, John Winton, 1900-53,
Australian; fiction NI
HEMING, William (Hemminge),
1602-37/53, English; poetry,
plays BU
HEMINGWAY, Ernest Miller,
1898-1961, American; fiction, nonfiction AM BR
BU CON MAG PO RO SEY
VN
HEMINGWAY, Mary Welsh,
1908- , American; journalism, nonfiction CON
HEMINGWAY, Patricia Drake,
1926-78, American; nonfiction
CON
HEMLEY, Elaine G. see GOTTLIEB, Elaine

HEMMER, Jarl Robert, 1893-1944,
Finnish-Swedish; poetry, fiction BU
HEMMING, Roy ('Buzz Hamilton'),
1928- , American; nonfiction,
juveniles CO CON
HEMMINGS, Frederic William John,
1920- , British; nonfiction
CON
HEMMINGSEN, Niels, 1513-1600,
Dutch; nonfiction BU
HEMON, Louis, 1880-1913, French;
fiction BU CL MAG TH
HEMPHILL, Charles F., Jr.,
1917- , American; nonfiction
CON
HEMPHILL, John Knox, 1919- ,
American; nonfiction CON
HEMPHILL, Paul, 1936- , American; fiction, nonfiction CON
WAR
HEMSCHEMEYER, Judith, 1935- ,
American; juveniles CON WAR
HEMSTERHUIS, Francois, 1721-90,
Dutch; nonfiction BU
HEMYNG, Samuel Bracebridge,
1841-1901, English; fiction
ST
HENAGHAN, Jim ('Archie O'Neill'),
1919- , British; fiction CON
HENDEE, John Clare, 1938- ,
American; nonfiction CON
HENDERSHOT, Ralph, 1896?-1979,
American; nonfiction, journalism CON
HENDERSON, Archibald ('Erskine
Steele'), 1877-1963, American;
nonfiction CON
HENDERSON, Archibald, 1916- ,
American; translations, nonfiction, poetry CON
HENDERSON, Charles, Jr.,
1923- , American; nonfiction
CON
HENDERSON, Charles Packard,
Jr., 1941- , American; nonfiction CON
HENDERSON, Charles William,
1925- , American; nonfiction
CON
HENDERSON, Dwight F., 1937- ,
American; nonfiction CON
HENDERSON, George Leslie,
1925- , American; nonfiction
CON
HENDERSON, Hamish, 1919- ,
British; poetry VCP
HENDERSON, Harold Gould, 1889-

1974, American; nonfiction,
translations CON
HENDERSON, Jean Carolyn Glid-
den, 1916- , American;
nonfiction CON
HENDERSON, Laurance G. ,
1924?-77, American; nonfic-
tion CON
HENDERSON, Lawrence W. ,
1921- , American; nonfiction
CON
HENDERSON, Le Grand ('Brian
Harwin'; 'Le Grand'), 1901-65,
American; juveniles CO
HENDERSON, Lois Thompson,
1918- , American; nonfic-
tion, fiction CON
HENDERSON, Mary C. , 1928- ,
American; nonfiction CON
HENDERSON, Nancy, 1943- ,
American; nonfiction CON
HENDERSON, Nancy Wallace,
1916- , American; juveniles,
plays CO CON
HENDERSON, Richard Beveir,
1921- , American; nonfiction
CON
HENDERSON, Richard Ivan,
1926- , American; nonfiction
CON
'HENDERSON, Sylvia' see
ASHTON-WARNER, Sylvia
HENDERSON, Thomas Walter,
1949- , American; nonfiction
CON
HENDERSON, Vivian Wilson,
1923-76, American; nonfiction
CON
HENDERSON, Zenna Chlarson,
1917- , American; juveniles,
fiction AS CO COW NI
HENDIN, David Bruce, 1945- ,
American; nonfiction CON
HENDIN, Josephine, 1946- ,
American; nonfiction CON
HENDON, William Scott, 1933- ,
American; nonfiction CON
HENDRA, Tony, American; non-
fiction CON
HENDREN, Ron, 1945- , Amer-
ican; journalism CON
HENDRICK, Irving Guilford,
1936- , American; nonfiction
CON
HENDRICKS, Faye Neidhold,
1913- , American; nonfiction
CON
HENDRICKS, Gay, 1945- ,

American; nonfiction CON
HENDRICKS, Glenn Leonard,
1928- , American; nonfiction
CON
HENDRICKS, James Edwin, 1935- ,
American; nonfiction CON
HENDRICKS, Robert Joseph,
1944- , American; nonfiction
CON
HENDRICKS, Walter, 1892-1979,
American; nonfiction CON
HENDRICKS, William Lawrence,
1929- , American; nonfiction
CON
HENDRICKSON, Donald Eugene,
1941- , American; nonfiction
CON
HENDRICKSON, Robert, 1933- ,
American; nonfiction CON
HENDRICKSON, Walter Brookfield,
Jr. , 1936- , American; juven-
iles CO
HENDRIE, Donald Franz, Jr. ,
1942- , American; fiction
CON
HENDRIKS, Arthur Lemière,
1922- , Jamaican; poetry
CON VCP
HENDRY, Thomas, 1929- , Cana-
dian; nonfiction, plays, tv
CON VCD
HENDY, Philip Anstiss, 1900-80,
British; nonfiction CON
HENEGAN, Lucius Herbert, Jr. ,
1902?-79, American; journal-
ism, nonfiction CON
HENIG, Gerald Sheldon, 1942- ,
American; nonfiction CON
HENIG, Ruth Beatrice, 1943- ,
English; nonfiction CON
HENIG, Suzanne, 1936- , Ameri-
can; nonfiction CON
HENIGE, David, 1938- , American;
nonfiction CON
HENISCH, Heinz K. ('Benjamin
Spear'), 1922- , German-
American; nonfiction CON
HENISSART, Paul Henri, 1923- ,
American; fiction MCC
HENKE, Dan Ferdinand, 1924- ,
American; nonfiction CON
HENKELS, Robert MacAllister,
Jr. , 1939- , American; non-
fiction CON
HENKIN, Harmon, 1940?-80, Amer-
ican; film, fiction, nonfiction
CON
HENKLE, Henrietta ('Henrietta

Buckmaster'), 1909- , Amer-
ican; fiction, nonfiction,
juveniles CO CON WA
HENLE, Fritz, 1909- , German-
American; nonfiction CON
HENLE , Jane, 1913- , Amer-
ican; nonfiction CON
HENLEY, Gail, 1952- , Amer-
ican; fiction CON
HENLEY, Karyn, 1952- , Amer-
ican; juveniles, nonfiction
CON
HENLEY, Wallace Boynton,
1941- , American; nonfiction
CON
HENLEY, William Ballentine,
1905- , American; nonfiction
CON
HENLEY, William Ernest, 1849-
1903, English; poetry, plays,
nonfiction BU DA MAG PO
VP
HENN, Harry George, 1919- ,
American; nonfiction CON
'HENNEBERG, Charles' (Charles
Henneberg zu I. WASUNGEN,
1899-1959; Nathalie WASUNGEN,
1917-77), German-French;
fiction NI
HENNEDY, Hugh Louis, 1929- ,
American; nonfiction CON
HENNEMAN, John Bell, 1864-
1908, American; nonfiction
BA
HENNEMAN, John Bell, Jr.,
1935- , American; nonfiction
CON
'HENNESSEY, Caroline' see
von BLOCK, Sylvia
'HENNESSEY, Max' see HARRIS,
John
HENNIG, Margaret Marie,
1940- , American; nonfiction
CON
HENNING, Daniel Howard, 1931- ,
American; nonfiction CON
HENNINGS, Dorothy Grant,
1935- , American; nonfiction
CON
HENNINGSEN, Agnes Kathinka
Malling Andersen, 1868-1962,
Danish; fiction, plays BU
TH
HENNINGSEN, Poul, 1894-1967,
Danish; poetry, nonfiction
BU
HENNISSART, Martha ('R. B.
Dominic'; 'Emma Lathen'),

American; fiction CON REI
ST WAK
HENRI, Adrian Maurice, 1932- ,
British; poetry, plays, fiction
VCP
HENRI, Florette ('Marjorie Win-
ters'), 1908- , American;
fiction, nonfiction, plays CON
HENRI d'ANDELY, 13th century,
French; poetry BU
HENRI de MONDEVILLE, fl. 1300,
French; nonfiction BU
HENRICHSEN, Walter Arlie, Jr.,
1934- , American; nonfiction
CON
'HENRICKS, Kaw' see WOLFE,
Charles K.
HENRIES, A. Doris Banks, 1930?-
81, Liberian; poetry, nonfiction
CON HER
HENRIOD, Lorraine Stephens,
1925- , American; juveniles
CON WAR
HENRIQUES, Veronica, 1931- ,
British; nonfiction CON
HENRIQUEZ UREÑA, Pedro, 1884-
1946, Dominican; nonfiction
BR
HENRY VIII of England, 1491-
1547, English; poetry, nonfic-
tion BU
HENRY, Buck, 1930- , American;
film CON
'HENRY, Daniel' see KAHNWEILER,
Daniel H.
HENRY, Frances, 1931- , German-
Canadian; nonfiction CON
HENRY, Harriet see De STEUCH,
Harriet
HENRY, Dr. James, 1798-1876,
Irish; nonfiction HO
HENRY, James Shelburne, 1950- ,
American; nonfiction CON
HENRY, Joanne Landers, 1927- ,
American; juveniles CO
HENRY, Kenneth, 1920- , Amer-
ican; nonfiction CON
HENRY, Marguerite, American;
juveniles CO KI
'HENRY, Marion' see del RAY,
Lester
HENRY, Matthew, 1662-1714, Eng-
lish; nonfiction BU
'HENRY, Oliver' see PORTER,
William S.
HENRY, Robert Selph, 1889-1970,
American; nonfiction CON
HENRY, Will, American; juveniles

WAR
'HENRY, Will' see ALLEN, Henry W.
HENRY, William Claud, 1914- , American; nonfiction CON
HENRY, William Mellors, 1890-1970, American; journalism, nonfiction CON
HENRY of AVRANCHES, -1262, French; poetry BU
HENRY of HUNTINGDON, 1084?-1155, English; nonfiction BU
HENRY of SETTIMELLO, 12th century, Italian; poetry BU
HENRY the MINSTREL see HARY
HENRYSON, Robert, 1430?-1506?, Scots; poetry, fiction BU DA PO VP
HENSCHKE, Alfred see 'KLABUND'
HENSEY, Frederick Gerald (Fritz), 1931- , American; nonfiction CON
HENSHAW, James Ene, 1924- , Nigerian; plays CON HER JA VCD
HENSHAW, Richard, 1945- , American; nonfiction CON
HENSHAW, Tom, 1924- , American; journalism, nonfiction CON
HENSHEL, Richard Lee, 1939- , Canadian; nonfiction CON
HENSLEY, Charles Stanley, 1919- , American; nonfiction CON
HENSLEY, Joe Louis, 1926- , American; fiction AS NI
HENSLEY, Malcolm Stewart, 1914?-76, American; journalism CON
HENSLIN, James Marvin, 1937- , American; nonfiction CON
HENSLOWE, Philip, -1616, English; plays, diary DA PO RU
HENSON, Herbert Hensley, 1863-1947, English; nonfiction WA
HENSTRA, Friso, 1928- , Dutch; juveniles CO DEM
HENTHORN, William Ellsworth, 1928- , American; nonfiction CON
HENTOFF, Nathan Irving, 1925- , American; juveniles, fiction, nonfiction DE KI
HENTY, George Alfred, 1832-

1902, English; juveniles, fiction, nonfiction BU DA KI VN
HENTZ, Caroline Lee Whiting, 1800-56, American; fiction, poetry, plays BA MYE
HEPBURN, Andrew H., 1899?-1975, American; nonfiction CON
HEPBURN, James Gordon, 1922- , American; nonfiction, plays CON
HEPNER, James Orville, 1933- , American; nonfiction CON
HEPPENHEIMER, Thomas Adolph, 1947- , American; nonfiction
HEPPENSTALL, Rayner, 1911-81, English; fiction, poetry, nonfiction CON DA VCN VCP WA
HEPPLE, Peter, 1927- , British; nonfiction CON
HEPWORTH, James Michael, 1938- , British; nonfiction CON
HERACLIDES PONTICUS, 390-10 B.C., Greek; nonfiction BU GR LA
'HERACLITO' see NEGRON SAN-JURJO, José
HERACLITUS, 550 B.C. - , Greek; nonfiction GR LA
HERACLITUS of EPHESUS, fl. 500 B.C., Greek; nonfiction BU
HERALD, George William, 1911- , German-American; nonfiction CON
'HERALD, Kathleen' see PEYTON, Kathleen W.
HERAS, Ivonne, 1948- , American; nonfiction MAR
HERAUD, Brian Jeremy, 1934- , British; nonfiction CON
HERAUD, John Abraham, 1799-1887, English; poetry, plays BU
HERBEN, Jan, 1857-1936, Czech; fiction BU
HERBERG, Will, 1909-77, American; nonfiction CON
HERBERGER, Charles F., 1920- , American; nonfiction CON
HERBERT, Sir Alan Patrick, 1890-1971, English; poetry, plays, fiction CON DA
HERBERT, Alfred Francis Xavier, 1901- , Australian; fiction, nonfiction DA VN

HERBERT, Anthony Bernard,
1930- , American; nonfiction
CON
'HERBERT, Arthur' see SHAP-
PIRO, Herbert A.
HERBERT, Benson, 1912- ,
British; fiction NI
'HERBERT, Cecil' see HAMILTON,
Charles H. S.
HERBERT, David Thomas, 1935- ,
American; nonfiction CON
HERBERT, Edward, 1583-1648,
English; poetry RU
HERBERT, Edward Ivor, 1925- ,
South African; fiction, non-
fiction CON
HERBERT, Eugenia Warren,
1929- , American; nonfiction
CON
HERBERT, F. Hugh, 1897-1958,
American; fiction, plays
MCG
HERBERT, Frank Patrick,
1920- , American; fiction,
journalism AS CO CON
COW NI WAK
HERBERT, George, 1593-1633,
English; poetry, nonfiction
BRI BU DA MAG PO RU VP
HERBERT, Henry William ('Frank
Forester'), 1807-58, Amer-
ican; journalism, fiction MYE
HERBERT, James, 1943- ,
British; fiction CON
'HERBERT, John' (John Herbert
Brundge), 1926- , Canadian;
plays, nonfiction CON VCD
HERBERT, Marie, 1941- ,
Irish; nonfiction CON
HERBERT, Martin, 1933- , South
African; nonfiction CON
HERBERT, Mary (Countess of
Pembroke), 1561-1621, Eng-
lish; poetry, translations
BU
HERBERT, Miranda Carleton,
1950- , American; nonfiction
CON
HERBERT, Theodore Terence,
1942- , American; nonfiction
CON
HERBERT, Walter William (Wally),
1934- , British; nonfiction
CO CON
HERBERT, Xavier, 1901- ,
Australian; fiction BU CON
VCN
HERBERT, Zbigniew, 1924- ,

Polish; poetry, plays BU CL
CON SEY TH WA
HERBERT le DUC de DAMMARTIN,
fl. 1180-87, French; poetry
BU
HERBERT of CHERBURY, Lord
Edward, 1583-1648, English;
poetry, nonfiction BU DA PO
VP
HERBORT von FRITZLAR, fl. 1210-
17, Hessian; nonfiction BU
HERBRAND, Janice M., 1931- ,
American; nonfiction CON
HERBST, Josephine, 1897-1969,
American; fiction PAL PO
HERBST, Robert Leroy, 1935- ,
American; nonfiction CON
HERBURGER, Günter, 1932- ,
German; fiction, poetry CL
HERCULANO de CARVALHO e
ARAUJO, Alexandre, 1810-
66/77, Portuguese; fiction
BU TH
HERCULES, Frank, American;
nonfiction SH
HERCZEG, Ferenc, 1863-1954,
Hungarian; fiction, plays BU
CL TH
HERD, Dale, 1940- , American;
fiction, poetry CON
HERD, David, 1732-1810, English;
nonfiction DA
HERDAL, Herald, 1900- , Danish;
poetry, fiction BU TH
HERDECK, Donald E., 1924- ,
American; nonfiction CON
HERDER, Johann Gottfried, 1744-
1803, German; nonfiction BU
TH
HERDT, Sheryll Enette Patterson,
1941- , American; nonfiction
CON
HEREDIA, José María, 1803-39,
Cuban; poetry, plays, transla-
tion, nonfiction BR BU MAG
HEREDIA, José María de, 1842-
1903, French; poetry BU CL
TH
HERFINDAHL, Orris Clemens,
1918-72, American; nonfiction
CON
HERFORD, Oliver, 1863-1935,
English; plays, juveniles, poetry
WAR
'HERGE' see REMI, Georges
HERGESHEIMER, Joseph, 1880-
1954, American; fiction, nonfic-
tion BR BU MAG VN

'HERIAT, Philippe' (Raymond
Gérard Payelle), 1898-1971,
French; fiction, plays BU
HERITEAU, Jacqueline, 1925- ,
Franco-American; nonfiction
CON
HERITY, Michael, 1929- , Irish;
nonfiction CON
HERKEL, Teodor see 'FLORIN,
Theo H.'
HERKIMER, Lawrence Russell,
American; juveniles WAR
HERLIHY, David J., 1930- ,
American; nonfiction CON
HERLIHY, James Leo, 1927- ,
American; fiction, plays
MAG VCD VCN WA
HERLIN, Hans, 1925- , German;
journalism, nonfiction, fiction
CON
HERLING-GRUDZINSKI, Gustaw,
1919- , Polish; fiction, non-
fiction CL
HERMAGORAS, mid 2nd century
B. C., Greek; nonfiction GR
HERMAN, Arthur Ludwig, 1930- ,
American; nonfiction, trans-
lations CON
HERMAN, Charlotte, 1937- ,
American; juveniles CO CON
HERMAN, Donald L., 1928- ,
American; nonfiction CON
HERMAN, Esther, 1935- , Amer-
ican; nonfiction CON
HERMAN, George Edward, 1920- ,
American; journalism CON
HERMAN, Jan Jacob, 1942- ,
American; nonfiction CON
HERMAN, Judith, 1943- , Amer-
ican; nonfiction CON
HERMAN, Kenneth Neil, 1954- ,
American; journalism CON
HERMAN, Louis Jay, 1925- ,
American; nonfiction, trans-
lations CON
HERMAN, Marguerite Shalett,
1914- , American; nonfiction
CON
HERMAN, Masako, American;
nonfiction CON
HERMAN, Yury P. see GERMAN,
Yury P.
HERMAND, Jost, 1930- , Ger-
man-American; nonfiction
CON
HERMANN, Donald Harold, 1943- ,
American; nonfiction CON
HERMANN, John, 1917- , Amer-

ican; nonfiction CON
HERMANS, Willem Frederik,
1921- , Dutch; poetry, plays
BU CL TH WAK
HERMANSEN, John, 1918- ,
American; fiction CON
HERMANSON, Dennis Everett,
1947- , American; juveniles
CO
HERMANT, Abel, 1862-1950,
French; fiction, plays, nonfic-
tion CL
HERMEREN, Goeren A., 1938- ,
Swedish; nonfiction CON
HERMES, Johann Timotheus, 1738-
1821, German; fiction BU
'HERMLIN, Stephan' (Rudolf Leder),
1915- , German; poetry, fic-
tion BU TH
HERMOGENES, 161- , Greek;
nonfiction GR
HERNADI, Paul, 1936- , Hun-
garian; nonfiction CON
HERNAMAN-JOHNSON, Francis,
1879- , British; fiction NI
HERNANDEZ, Alfonso C., 1940- ,
American; plays MAR
HERNANDEZ, Amado V., 1903-70,
Filipino; poetry, fiction, plays
PRU
HERNANDEZ, Antonia, 1948- ,
American; nonfiction MAR
HERNANDEZ, Carrol A., 1947- ,
American; nonfiction MAR
HERNANDEZ, Deluvina, 1935- ,
American; nonfiction MAR
HERNANDEZ, Edward, Jr., 1944- ,
American; nonfiction MAR
HERNANDEZ, Frances, American;
nonfiction MAR
HERNANDEZ, Francisco, 1947- ,
American; nonfiction MAR
HERNANDEZ, Guillermo E.,
1940- , American; nonfiction,
poetry MAR
HERNANDEZ, José, 1834-86, Ar-
gentinian; poetry BR BU MAG
HERNANDEZ, Jose Amaro, 1930- ,
American; nonfiction MAR
HERNANDEZ, José P., 1892-1922,
Puerto Rican; poetry HIL
HERNANDEZ, Juan Donaldo, Amer-
ican; nonfiction MAR
HERNANDEZ, Juana Amelia,
Cuban-American; nonfiction
CON
HERNANDEZ, Leodoro, American;
nonfiction, poetry MAR

HERNANDEZ, Luis Felipe,
1923- , American; nonfiction
CON MAR
HERNANDEZ, Miguel, 1910-42,
Spanish; poetry, plays BU
CL TH WA
HERNANDEZ, Norma G., 1932- ,
American; nonfiction MAR
HERNANDEZ, Pedro Felix,
1925- , Mexican-American;
nonfiction CON MAR
HERNANDEZ, Ramón, 1935- ,
Spanish; fiction CL
HERNANDEZ AQUINO, Luis,
1907- , Puerto Rican; non-
fiction, fiction, journalism,
poetry HIL
HERNANDEZ-ARAICO, Susana,
1947- , American; nonfiction
MAR
HERNANDEZ CATA, Alfonso,
1885-1940, Cuban; fiction
BR BU
HERNANDEZ-CHAVEZ, Eduardo,
1932- , American; nonfiction
MAR
HERNANDEZ de ARAUJO, Carmen,
1832-77, Puerto Rican; poetry,
plays, fiction HIL
HERNANDEZ de OVIEDO y
VALDES, Gonzalo see FER-
NANDEZ de OVIEDO, Gonzalo
HERNANDEZ NIETO, Hector,
1929- , American; fiction,
nonfiction MAR
HERNANDEZ VARGAS, Francisco,
1914- , Puerto Rican; jour-
nalism, poetry HIL
HERNDON, James, 1926- , Amer-
ican; nonfiction CON
'HERNE, Huxley' see BROOKER,
Bertram R.
'HERNE, James A.' (James
Ahern), 1839-1901, American;
plays BU MCG VD
HERNES, Helga Maria, 1938- ,
German; nonfiction CON
HERNON, Peter, 1944- , Amer-
ican; nonfiction CON
HERNTON, Calvin C., 1933- ,
American; poetry, plays,
fiction, nonfiction SH VCP
HERO (Heron), 1st century,
Greek; nonfiction BU GR
HERODAS (Herondas; Herodes),
fl. 246-21 B.C., Greek;
poetry BU GR LA
HERODES ATTICUS, 101-177,

Greek; nonfiction LA
HERODIAN (Aelius Herodianus),
late 2nd century, Greek; non-
fiction BU GR LA
HERODIAN, 180-260, Greek; non-
fiction BU
HERODOTUS, 490/80-30/25 B.C.,
Greek; nonfiction BU GR LA
MAG
HERON, Laurence Tunstall,
1902- , American; nonfiction
CON
HERON-ALLEN, Edward see
'BLAYRE, Christopher'
HEROPHILUS, early 3rd century
B.C., Greek; nonfiction GR
HERP, Henricus, -1477, Dutch;
nonfiction BU
HERPEL, George Lloyd, 1921- ,
American; nonfiction CON
HERR, Michael, 1940?- , Amer-
ican; nonfiction, film CON
HERRAD von LANDSPERG, -1195,
German; nonfiction TH
HERRERA, Alfred John, 1934- ,
American; nonfiction MAR
HERRERA, Arnold E., 1949- ,
American; nonfiction MAR
HERRERA, Fernando de, 1534-97,
Spanish; poetry, nonfiction
BU TH
HERRERA, Gabriel Alonso de,
147?-1539?, Spanish; nonfic-
tion BU
HERRERA, Juan Felipe, 1948- ,
American; nonfiction, poetry
MAR
HERRERA y REISSIG, Julio, 1875-
1910, Uruguayan; poetry BR
BU
HERRERA y TORDESILLAS, An-
tonio de, 1559-1625, Spanish;
nonfiction BU
HERRICK, Jean M. see MELLIN,
Jeanne
HERRICK, Jo Field, 1930- ,
American; nonfiction CON
HERRICK, Neal Quentin, 1927- ,
American; nonfiction CON
HERRICK, Robert, 1591-1674, Eng-
lish; poetry BRI BU MAG PO
RU VN VP
HERRICK, Robert, 1868-1938,
American; fiction BR BU DA
PO
HERRICK, Robert Lee, 1930- ,
American; nonfiction CON
HERRICK, Sophia Bledsoe, 1837-

1919, American; nonfiction
BA
'HERRING, Geilles' see SOMER-
VILLE, Edith A.
HERRING, George C., Jr.,
1936- , American; nonfiction
CON
HERRINGTON, James Lawrence,
1928- , American; nonfiction,
journalism CON
'HERRIOT, James' see WIGHT,
James A.
HERRMANN, Ignát, 1854-1935,
Czech; fiction BU
HERRMANN, John, 1900-59,
American; nonfiction, fiction
RO
HERRMANN, Luke John, 1932- ,
German-British; journalism,
translations, nonfiction CON
HERRMANN, Nina, 1943- ,
American; nonfiction CON
HERRMANN, Robert Omer, 1932- ,
American; nonfiction CON
HERRMANN-NEISSE, Max, 1886-
1941, German; poetry TH
HERRMANNS, Ralph, 1933- ,
Swedish; juveniles CO WAR
HERRON, Edward Albert, 1912- ,
American; juveniles CO
HERRON, Shaun, 1912- , Cana-
dian; fiction REI
HERSCHENSOHN, Bruce, 1932- ,
American; film, fiction,
nonfiction CON
HERSEY, George Leonard,
1927- , American; nonfiction
CON
HERSEY, John, 1914- , Amer-
ican; fiction, nonfiction, jour-
nalism, juveniles BR BU
CO KIB MAG NI VCN
HERSH, Burton, 1933- , Amer-
ican; fiction, nonfiction CON
HERSH, Jacques, 1935- ,
French; nonfiction CON
HERSH, Seymour M., 1937- ,
American; nonfiction CON
HERSHATTER, Richard Lawrence,
1923- , American; fiction
CON
HERSHBERG, David, 1935- ,
American; nonfiction CON
HERSHENSON, David Bert,
1933- , American; nonfiction
CON
HERSHENSON, Maurice Eugene,
1933- , American; nonfiction

CON
HERSHER, Leonard, 1925- ,
American; nonfiction CON
HERSHEY, Daniel, 1931- ,
American; nonfiction CON
HERSHEY, Gerald L., 1931- ,
American; nonfiction CON
HERSHEY, Robert Delp, 1909- ,
American; nonfiction CON
HERSHFIELD, Harry, 1885-1974,
American; nonfiction CON
HERSHMAN, Morris ('Evelyn
Bond'; 'Arnold English';
'Lionel Webb'; 'Jess Wilcox'),
1920- , American; fiction,
plays CON
HERSKOWITZ, Mickey, American;
nonfiction, journalism CON
HERTEL, Francois ('Rudolphe
Dubé'), 1905- , Canadian;
poetry, nonfiction, fiction
BU CR
HERTLING, Gunter H., 1930- ,
American; nonfiction CON
HERTLING, James E., 1935- ,
American; nonfiction CON
HERTZ, Grete (Janus), 1915- ,
Danish; translations, journal-
ism, nonfiction CO CON
HERTZ, Henri, 1875-1966, French;
poetry, fiction, journalism,
nonfiction CL
'HERTZ, Henrik' (Henrik Heyman),
1797-1870, Danish; poetry,
plays BU MCG TH
HERTZ, Jackoline G., 1920- ,
American; juveniles, fiction
CON
HERTZ, Karl Herbert, 1917- ,
Canadian-American; nonfiction,
translations CON
HERTZBERG, Hazel Whitman,
1918- , American; nonfiction
CON
HERTZKA, Theodor, 1845-1924,
Austrian; fiction NI
HERTZLER, Joyce Oramel, 1895-
1975, American; nonfiction
CON
HERTZLER, Lois Shank, 1927- ,
American; nonfiction CON
HERUM, John Maurice, 1931- ,
American; nonfiction CON
HERUY, Sirek Walda Sellase,
1878-1938, Amharic; fiction,
nonfiction HER
HERVAS y COBO de la TORRE,
José ('Don Hugo Herrera de

Jaspedós'), -1742, Spanish; fiction BU
HERVAS y PANDURO, Lorenzo, 1735-1809, Spanish; nonfiction BU
'HERVE, Jean Luc' see HUM-BARACI, Demir Arslan
HERVE-BAZIN, Jean Pierre Marie see 'BAZIN, Herve'
HERVEY, James, 1714-58, English; nonfiction BU
HERVEY, John, 1696-1743, English; nonfiction BU DA
HERVIEU, Paul, 1857-1915, French; fiction, plays CL MCG
HERWEGH, Georg, 1817-75, German; poetry BU TH
HERWIG, Holger Heinrich, 1941- , German-Canadian; nonfiction CON
HERZ, Irene, 1948- , American; juveniles CON
HERZ, Jerome Spencer ('Spencer'), American; nonfiction, fiction CON
HERZ, John Hermann, 1908- , German-American; nonfiction CON
HERZ, Stephanie Margarette, 1900- , German-American; nonfiction CON
HERZBERG, Donald Gabriel, 1925-80, American; nonfiction CON
HERZBERG, Joseph Gabriel, 1907-76, American; journalism CON
HERZEN, Aleksandr Ivanovich, 1812-70, Russian; nonfiction BU TH
HERZOG, Arthur, 1928- , American; fiction NI
HERZOG, Chaim, 1918- , Irish; nonfiction CON
HERZOG, Emile see 'MAUROIS, André'
HERZOG, Werner, 1942- , American; film CON
HERZSTEIN, Robert Edwin, 1940- , American; nonfiction CON
HESELTINE, George Coulehan, 1895-1980, British; nonfiction CON
HESIOD, 735?- , Greek; poetry BU GR LA MAG
HESKES, Irene, 1928- , Amer-

ican; nonfiction CON
HESKY, Olga, -1974, British; fiction, film CON
HESLIN, Jo-Ann, 1946- , American; nonfiction CON
'HESPRO, Herbert' see ROBINSON, Herbert S.
HESS, Bartlett Leonard, 1910- , American; nonfiction CON
HESS, Beth Bowman, American; nonfiction CON
HESS, Eckhard Heinrich, 1916- , American; nonfiction CON
HESS, Hannah Spier, 1934- , German-American; nonfiction CON
HESS, Hans, 1908-75, British; nonfiction CON
HESS, John Loft, 1917- , American; nonfiction CON
HESS, Karl, 1923- , American; nonfiction CON
HESS, Lilo, 1916- , German-American; juveniles CO WAR
HESS, Margaret Johnston, 1915- , American; nonfiction CON
HESS, Thomas Baer, 1920-78, American; nonfiction CON
HESSE, Hermann, 1877-1962, German; fiction, poetry, nonfiction BU CL MAG NI SEY TH
HESSELBERG, Erik, Norwegian; juveniles WAR
HESSELGESSER, Debra, 1939- , American; poetry CON
HESSELGRAVE, David John, 1924- , American; nonfiction CON
'HESSING, Dennis' see DENNIS-JONES, Harold
HESSION, Roy, 1908- , British; nonfiction CON
HESSLER, Gene, 1928- , American; nonfiction CON
HESSUS KOCH(?), Helius Eobanus, 1485-1540, German; poetry, translations BU
HESTON, Alan Wiley, 1934- , American; nonfiction CON
HESTON, Leonard Lancaster, 1930- , American; nonfiction CON
HETHERINGTON, John Aikman, 1907-74, Australian; fiction, nonfiction CON
HETZELL, Margaret Carol, 1917-78, American; nonfiction CON

HEUER, John Michael, 1941- ,
American; juveniles, plays
CON
HEUMAN, William ('George Kram-
er'), 1912-71, American;
juveniles CO
HEUTERMAN, Thomas Henry,
1934- , American; journal-
ism, nonfiction CON
HEUVELMANS, Bernard Joseph,
1916- , French; translations,
nonfiction CON
HEUVELMANS, Martin, 1903- ,
Belgian-American; nonfiction
CON
HEUYER, Georges, 1884-1977,
French; nonfiction CON
HEVENER, John Watts, 1933- ,
American; nonfiction CON
HEWARD, Edmund Rawlings,
1912- , British; nonfiction
CON
HEWARD, William Lee, 1949- ,
American; nonfiction CON
HEWENS, Frank Edgar, 1912- ,
American; fiction CON
HEWES, Hayden, 1943- , Amer-
ican; nonfiction CON
HEWES, Jeremy Joan, 1944- ,
American; nonfiction CON
HEWES, Leslie, 1906- , Amer-
ican; nonfiction CON
HEWETT, Anita, 1918- , Eng-
lish; juveniles CO KI
HEWETT, Dorothy Coade, 1923- ,
Australian; plays, fiction,
poetry CON VCD
HEWINS, Caroline Maria, 1846-
1926, American; nonfiction
ENG
HEWISON, Robert, 1943- ,
British; nonfiction CON
HEWITT, Arthur Wentworth,
1883- , American; nonfiction,
poetry CON
HEWITT, Cecil Rolph ('R. H.
Cecil'; 'Oliver Milton'; 'C.
H. Rolph'), 1901- , British;
nonfiction CON
HEWITT, Emily Clark, 1944- ,
American; nonfiction CON
HEWITT, Geof, 1943- , Amer-
ican; poetry VCP
HEWITT, James, 1928- , Eng-
lish; nonfiction CON
HEWITT, Jean Daphne, 1925- ,
Anglo-American; nonfiction
CON

HEWITT, John Harold, 1907- ,
British; poetry, plays BU
CON HO VCP
HEWITT, John Paul, 1941- ,
American; nonfiction CON
HEWITT, Philip Nigel, 1945- ,
British; fiction, juveniles
CON
HEWLETT, Dorothy, -1979,
British; nonfiction CON
HEWLETT, Maurice, 1861-1923,
English; fiction, poetry DA
HEWLETT, Roger S., 1911?-77,
American; journalism CON
HEWLETT, Virginia B., 1912?-79,
American; nonfiction, journal-
ism CON
HEXNER, Ervin Paul, 1893-1968,
Czech-American; nonfiction
CON
'HEXT, Harrington' see PHILL-
POTTS, Eden
HEY, Nigel Stewart, 1936- ,
English; juveniles CO
HEYDENBURG, Harry E., 1891?-
1979, American; journalism
CON
HEYDON, Joseph Kentigern, Brit-
ish; fiction NI
HEYDUCK-HUTH, Hilde, 1929- ,
German; juveniles CO CON
HEYDUK, Adolf, 1835-1923, Czech;
poetry BU
HEYE, Jan Pieter, 1809-76, Dutch;
poetry BU
HEYER, Georgette ('Stella Martin'),
1902-74, English; fiction CON
REI ST
HEYLIGER, William ('Hawley Wil-
liams'), 1884-1955, American;
juveniles, fiction COM
HEYLYN, Peter, 1600-62, English;
nonfiction BU
HEYM, Georg, 1887-1912, German;
poetry, fiction BU CL SEY
TH
'HEYM, Stefan' (Hellmuth Fliegel),
1913- , German; fiction, jour-
nalism TH
HEYMAN, Abigail, 1942- , Amer-
ican; nonfiction CON
'HEYMAN, Henrik' see 'HERTZ,
Henrik'
HEYMANNS, Betty, 1932- , Amer-
ican; nonfiction CON
HEYNE, Paul, 1931- , American;
nonfiction CON
HEYNEN, Jim, 1940- , American;

translations, poetry, nonfiction
CON
HEYNS, Barbara, 1942- , American; nonfiction CON
HEYNS, Maria, 1621- , Dutch; poetry, fiction BU
HEYNS, Zacharias, 1566-1638?, Dutch; poetry, printer BU
HEYRICK, Thomas, 1650?-94, English; poetry BU
HEYSE, Paul, 1830-1914, German; fiction, nonfiction, translations BU CL TH
HEYWARD, Carter, 1945- , American; nonfiction CON
HEYWARD, Dorothy, 1890-1961, American; plays MCN
HEYWARD, Dubose, 1885-1940, American; fiction, poetry, plays BA BR CO MAG MCG MCN VN
HEYWOOD, Christopher, 1928- , British; nonfiction CON
HEYWOOD, Jasper, 1535-97/98, English; poetry, translations BU
HEYWOOD, John, 1497?-1580?, English; plays, poetry BU DA MCG PO RU VD
HEYWOOD, Lorimer D., 1899?-1977, American; journalism CON
HEYWOOD, Philip, 1938- , British; nonfiction CON
HEYWOOD, Rosalind, 1895- , American; translations, nonfiction CON
HEYWOOD, Thomas, 1573/74-1641, English; poetry, plays, nonfiction BU DA MAG MCG PO RU VD
HEYWORTH, Peter Lawrence, 1921- , American; nonfiction CON
HEYWORTH-DUNNE, James, -1974, American; nonfiction CON
HIBBARD, George Richard, 1915- , British; nonfiction CON
HIBBARD, Howard, 1928- , American; nonfiction CON
HIBBERD, Jack, 1940- , Australian; plays CON VCD
HIBBERT, Christopher, 1924- , English; juveniles, nonfiction CO
HIBBERT, Eleanor (Burford;

'Victoria Holt'; 'Jean Plaidy'; 'Ellalice Tate'; 'Elbur Ford'; 'Kathleen Kellow'), 1906- , English; fiction ST WA
HIBBS, Ben, 1901- , American; nonfiction CON
HIBBS, Douglas Albert, Jr., 1944- , American; nonfiction CON
HIBBS, John ('John Blyth'), 1925- , British; nonfiction CON
HICKEL, Walter Joseph, 1919- , American; nonfiction CON
HICKES, George, 1642-1715, English; nonfiction BU
HICKEY, Edward Shelby, 1928?-78, American; journalism CON
HICKEY, Joseph James, 1907- , American; nonfiction CON
HICKEY, Michael, 1929- , British; nonfiction CON
HICKEY, T. Earl, American; fiction NI
HICKEY, William, 1749-1830, English; journalism DA
HICKFORD, Jessie, 1911- , English; nonfiction, plays, juveniles CON
HICKIN, Norman Ernest, 1910- , British; nonfiction CON
HICKMAN, Charles Addison, 1916- , American; nonfiction CON
HICKMAN, Janet, 1940- , American; juveniles CO CON
HICKMAN, Martin Berkeley, 1925- , American; nonfiction CON
HICKMAN, Peggy, 1906- , British; nonfiction CON
HICKOK, Dorothy Jane, 1912- , American; nonfiction CON
HICKOK, Lorena A., 1892?-1968, American; juveniles, nonfiction CO CON
HICKOK, Robert Blair, 1927- , American; nonfiction CON
'HICKS, Eleanor B.' see COERR, Eleanor P.
HICKS, George Leon, 1935- , American; nonfiction CON
HICKS, Granville, 1901-82, American; fiction, nonfiction, poetry BOR BR VCN
HICKS, Jack, 1942- , American; nonfiction CON
HICKS, John Harland, 1919- , American; nonfiction CON

British; fiction AS CON NI
HIGH, Stanley Hoflund, 1895-
1961, American; nonfiction
CON
HIGHAM, Charles, 1931- ,
British; poetry, nonfiction
VCP
HIGHAM, Florence May Grier
('F. M. G. Evans'), 1896-
1980, British; nonfiction
CON
HIGHBERGER, Ruth, 1917- ,
American; nonfiction CON
HIGHET, Gilbert, 1906-78,
Scots-American; nonfiction
CON
'HIGHLAND, Dora' see AVAL-
LONE, Michael A., Jr.
HIGHSMITH, Patricia ('Claire
Morgan'), 1921- , American;
fiction, nonfiction, juveniles
REI SEY ST VCN WA
HIGHTOWER, Florence Cole,
1916-81, American; juveniles
CO CON DE KI
'HIGHTOWER, Paul' see COLLINS,
Thomas H.
HIGHWATER, Jamake ('J.
Marks'),
American; nonfiction CON
HIGMAN, Barry William,
1943- , American; nonfiction
CON
HIGNETT, Sean, 1934- , Eng-
lish; fiction, plays CON
HIGO, Aig, 1932- , Nigerian;
poetry HER JA
HIGONNET, Margaret Randolph
('Margaret Hale'), 1941- ,
American; nonfiction CON
HIGONNET, Patrice Louise,
1938- , French; nonfiction
CON
HIGSON, James Doran, 1925- ,
American; nonfiction CON
'HIGUCHI, Iciyo' (Higuchi Nat-
suko), 1872-96, Japanese; fic-
tion, poetry BU HI LA PRU
HIHETAH, Robert Kofi, 1935- ,
Ghanaian; fiction HER
'LA HIJA del CARIBE' see
PADILLA de SANZ, Trinidad
HIJAZI, Muhammad, 1899- ,
Persian; nonfiction BU
HIKMET RAN, Nazim, 1902-63,
Turkish; poetry, fiction, plays
CL CON LA PRU SEY WAK
HILARY, St. (Hilarius), 315-67,
Latin; nonfiction GR

HILARY, fl. 1125, English; poetry,
plays BU
HILARY, Christopher, 1927?-79,
American; journalism CON
HILBERT, Jaroslav, 1871-1936,
Czech; plays BU
HILDEBERT, 1056-1133, Latin;
poetry BU TH
'HILDEBRAND' see BEETS, Nico-
laas
HILDEBRAND, Grant, 1934- ,
American; nonfiction CON
HILDEGAERSBERCH, Willem van,
1350-1409?, Dutch; poetry
BU
HILDEGARD of BINGEN, 1098-1179,
German; nonfiction BU
HILDESHEIMER, Wolfgang, 1916- ,
German; fiction, radio, non-
fiction BU CL CON MCG TH
HILDICK, Edmund Wallace,
1925- , English; fiction,
juveniles DEM KI REI WAR
HILDRETH, Margaret Holbrook,
1927- , American; nonfiction
CON
HILDRETH, Richard, 1807-65,
American; fiction, nonfiction
MY
HILFER, Anthony Channell,
1936- , American; nonfiction
CON
HILGER, Sr. Mary Inez, 1891-
1977, American; nonfiction
CON
HILKEN, Glen A., 1936- , Amer-
ican; nonfiction CON
HILL, Aaron, 1685-1750, English;
translations, plays, poetry
BU VD
HILL, Adelaide Cromwell, Ameri-
can; nonfiction SH
HILL, Adrian Keith Graham, 1895-
1977, British; nonfiction CON
HILL, Archibald Anderson, 1902- ,
American; nonfiction CON
HILL, Carol Dechellis, 1942- ,
American; plays, fiction, non-
fiction CON VCN
HILL, Daniel G., Jr., 1896?-
1979, American; nonfiction
CON
HILL, Dilys Mary, 1935- , Eng-
lish; nonfiction CON
HILL, Donna Marie, American;
juveniles CO
HILL, Douglas Arthur ('Martin
Hillman'), 1935- , Canadian;

nonfiction, poetry CON
HILL, Elizabeth Starr, 1925- ,
American; juveniles CO WAR
HILL, Ellen Wise ('Nellie Hill'),
1942- , American; poetry
CON
HILL, Ernest, 1915- , British;
fiction CON NI
HILL, Errol Gaston, 1921- ,
West Indian; plays, nonfiction
BU CON VCD
'HILL, Fiona' see PALL, Ellen J.
HILL, Frank Ernest, 1888-1969,
American; nonfiction CON
HILL, Gene, 1928- , American;
nonfiction CON
HILL, Geoffrey, 1932- , British;
poetry CON VCP VP WAK
HILL, Grace Livingston ('Marcia
Macdonald'), 1865-1947,
American; fiction, juveniles
COM
'HILL, H. D. N.' see DISSTON,
Harry
HILL, Harold Everett, 1905- ,
American; nonfiction CON
'HILL, Headon' (Francis Edward
Grainger), 1857-1924, English;
fiction ST
HILL, Helen Morey, 1915- ,
American; nonfiction, poetry
CON
HILL, Herbert, 1924- , Amer-
ican; nonfiction CON
HILL, Isaac William, 1908- ,
American; nonfiction CON
'HILL, James' see JAMESON,
Margaret S.
HILL, Janet, English; juveniles
WAR
HILL, John Edward Christopher
('K. E. Holme'), 1912- ,
English; nonfiction WAK
HILL, John Wiley, 1890-1977,
American; nonfiction CON
HILL, Kathleen Louise (Kay),
1917- , Canadian; juveniles
CO
HILL, Larry Dean, 1935- ,
American; nonfiction CON
HILL, Lee Halsey, 1899-1974,
American; nonfiction CON
HILL, Leslie Pinckney, 1880-
1960, American; poetry,
plays, nonfiction BA
HILL, Lorna, 1902- , English;
juveniles CO
HILL, Marnesba D., 1913- ,

American; nonfiction CON
HILL, Marvin Sidney, 1928- ,
American; nonfiction CON
HILL, Mary A., 1939- , Amer-
ican; nonfiction CON
HILL, Mary Raymond ('Lee Ray-
mond'), 1923- , American;
nonfiction CON
HILL, Mary V., 1941- , Amer-
ican; nonfiction CON
'HILL, Monica' see WATSON,
Jane W.
'HILL, Nellie' see HILL, Ellen W.
HILL, Pamela, 1920- , English;
fiction CON
HILL, Pati, American; fiction,
poetry, nonfiction CON
HILL, R. Lance, 1943- , Cana-
dian; nonfiction CON
HILL, Reginald ('Dick Morland';
'Patrick Ruell'; 'Charles Under-
hill'), 1936- , British; fiction,
plays CON NI REI
HILL, Robert White, 1919- ,
American; juveniles CO
HILL, Ruth A. see VIGUERS,
Ruth H.
HILL, Ruth Beebe, 1913- , Amer-
ican; fiction CON
'HILL, Ruth L.' see MUNCE, Ruth
H.
HILL, Susan Elizabeth, 1942- ,
English; fiction, plays VCN
WAK
'HILL, W. M.' see DODD, Edward
H., Jr.
'HILL, Weldon' see SCOTT, William
R.
HILL, Wilhelmina, 1902- , Amer-
ican; nonfiction CON
HILL, William Speed, 1935- ,
American; nonfiction CON
HILLARD, James Milton, 1920- ,
American; nonfiction CON
HILLBRUNER, Anthony, 1914- ,
American; nonfiction CON
HILLCOURT, William, 1900- ,
Danish-American; nonfiction
CON
HILLE, Peter, 1854-1904, German;
poetry, fiction, plays BU
HILLEGAS, Mark R., 1926- ,
American; fiction AS NI
HILLENBRAND, Barry R., 1941- ,
American; journalism CON
HILLER, Carl E., American;
juveniles WAR
'HILLER, Doris' see NUSSBAUM,

Albert F.
'HILLER, Flora' see HURD,
Florence
HILLER, Kurt, 1885- , German;
nonfiction TH
HILLERMAN, Tony, 1925- ,
American; juveniles, fiction,
nonfiction CO REI
HILLERS, Delbert Roy, 1932- ,
American; nonfiction CON
HILLERS, Herman William ('Wil-
helm Hillus'), 1925- ,
American; nonfiction CON
HILLERT, Margaret, 1920- ,
American; juveniles, poetry
CO CON
HILLES, Frederick Whitley, 1900-
75, American; nonfiction
CON
HILLIARD, Jan ('Kay Grant';
Hilda Kay Grant), Canadian;
fiction, nonfiction CR
HILLIARD, Noel Harvey, 1929- ,
New Zealander; fiction, juven-
iles VCN
HILLIARD, Sam Bowers, 1930- ,
American; nonfiction CON
HILLIER, Caroline, American;
juveniles WAR
HILLINGER, Brad, 1952- ,
American; fiction CON
HILLIX, William Allen, 1927- ,
American; nonfiction CON
HILLMAN, Barry Leslie, 1942- ,
British; poetry, plays CON
HILLMAN, Howard, 1934- ,
American; nonfiction CON
HILLMAN, James, 1926- ,
American; nonfiction CON
'HILLMAN, Martin' see HILL,
Douglas A.
HILLMAN, Ruth Estelyn, 1925- ,
American; nonfiction CON
HILLOCKS, George, Jr., 1934- ,
American; nonfiction CON
HILLS, Dave, 1945- , American;
juveniles CON
HILLS, Denis Cecil, 1913- ,
English; nonfiction CON
HILLS, Lee, 1906- , American;
journalism, nonfiction CON
HILLS, Patricia Gorton Schulze,
1936- , American; nonfiction
CON
HILLSTROM, Tom, 1943- ,
American; fiction CON
'HILLUS, Wilhelm' see HILLERS,
Herman W.

HILLYER, Robert Silliman, 1895-
1961, American; poetry, fiction,
translations BR CON
HILSENRATH, Edgar, 1926- ,
German-American; fiction CON
HILT, Douglas Richard, 1932- ,
Anglo-American; nonfiction
CON
HILTEBEITAL, Alf, 1942- ,
American; translations, nonfic-
tion CON
HILTON, Conrad Nicholson, 1887-
1979, American; nonfiction
CON
HILTON, Della Marion, 1934- ,
Australian; nonfiction CON
HILTON, Irene Pothus, 1912- ,
English; juveniles CO
HILTON, James ('Glen Trevor'),
1900-54, English; fiction DA
MAG NI REI ST
HILTON, John Buxton ('Warwick
Stanley'), 1921- , English;
nonfiction, fiction, juveniles
CON REI
HILTON, Lewis B., 1920- ,
Canadian-American; nonfiction
CON
HILTON, Peter, 1913- , Ameri-
can; nonfiction CON
HILTON, Ralph, 1907- , Ameri-
can; juveniles CO
HILTON, Suzanne McLean, 1922- ,
American; juveniles CO WAR
HILTON, Walter, -1396, English;
nonfiction BU DA
HILTON SMITH, Robert Dennis,
-1974, Canadian; nonfiction
CON
HIMERIUS, 310-85, Greek; nonfic-
tion BU
HIMES, Chester, 1909- , Amer-
ican; fiction BA BR HE PO
REI SH VCN WA
HIMLER, Ann, 1946- , American;
juveniles CO CON
HIMLER, Ronald Norbert, 1937- ,
American; poetry, juveniles
CO CON
HIMMELFARB, Gertrude, 1922- ,
American; nonfiction CON
HIMMELFARB, Milton, 1918- ,
American; nonfiction CON
HINAWY, Sheikh Mbarak Ali,
1896- , Kenyan; nonfiction
HER
HINCHLIFF, Peter Bingham,
1929- , South African; nonfic-

tion CON
HINCHLIFFE, Arnold P., 1930- ,
American; poetry, nonfiction
CON
HINCKLE, Warren James III,
1938- , American; nonfiction
CON
HINCKLEY, Barbara, 1937- ,
American; nonfiction CON
HINCKLEY, Ted Charles, 1925- ,
American; nonfiction CON
HIND, Robert James, 1931- ,
English; nonfiction CON
'HINDE, Thomas' (Sir Thomas
Willes Chitty), 1926- , Eng-
lish; fiction VCN WA
HINDE, Wendy, 1919- , British;
journalism, nonfiction CON
HINDERER, Walter Hermann,
1934- , German-American;
nonfiction CON
HINDMAN, Josephine Long,
1910- , American; nonfiction
CON
HINE, Al ('Josephine Gibson';
'G. B. Kirtland'), 1915- ,
American; juveniles DE
HINE, Daryl, 1936- , Canadian;
poetry, plays, fiction VCP
HINE, James R., 1909- ,
American; nonfiction CON
HINE, Virginia Haglin, 1920- ,
American; nonfiction CON
HINER, Louis Chase, 1919- ,
American; journalism CON
HINES, Barry Melvin, 1939- ,
British; fiction, tv CON
HINES, Bede Francis, 1918- ,
American; nonfiction CON
HINES, Carl Wendell, Jr.,
1940- , American; poetry
BA
HINES, Thomas Spight, 1936- ,
American; nonfiction CON
HINES, William H., 1909?-76,
American; nonfiction CON
HINGLEY, Ronald Francis,
1920- , British; fiction NI
HINKEMEYER, Michael Thomas,
1940- , American; fiction,
nonfiction CON
HINKLE, Douglas Paddock,
1923- , American; nonfiction
CON
HINKLE, Gerald Hahn, 1931- ,
American; nonfiction CON
HINKSON, James, 1943- , Cana-
dian; nonfiction CON

HINMAN, Charlton Joseph, 1911-77,
American; nonfiction CON
HINMAN, George W., Jr., 1891-
1977, American; journalism
CON
HINNELLS, John Russell, 1941- ,
English; nonfiction CON
HINO ASHIHEI, 1907-60/61,
Japanese; fiction LA PRU
HINOJASA, David, American; non-
fiction MAR
HINOJASA, Jesus H., 1935- ,
American; nonfiction MAR
HINOJASA-SMITH, Rolando R.
('P. Galendo'), 1929- ,
American; fiction, nonfiction
MAR
'HINOJOSA, Agapito' see RODRI-
GUEZ CABRERO, Luis
HINRICHS, August, 1879-1956,
German; plays BU
HINRICHSEN, Ludwig, 1872-1957,
German; plays, fiction BU
HINSHAW, Randall Weston, 1915- ,
American; nonfiction CON
HINSHAW, Robert Eugene, 1933- ,
American; nonfiction CON
HINSON, Grady Maurice, 1930- ,
American; nonfiction CON
HINT, Aadu, 1910- , Estonian;
fiction, plays BU
HINTON, Charles Howard, 1853-
1907, British; fiction NI
HINTON, John, 1926- , English;
nonfiction CON
HINTON, Nigel, 1941- , American;
fiction, nonfiction, tv CON
'HINTON, Richard W.' see
ANGOFF, Charles
HINTON, Sam, 1917- , American;
nonfiction CON
HINTON, Susan Eloise, 1949/50- ,
American; juveniles CO CON
DEM KI WAR
HINTON, Ted C., 1904?-77, Amer-
ican; nonfiction CON
HINTZ, Joy, 1926- , American;
nonfiction MAR
HINTZ, Loren Martin, 1945- ,
American; nonfiction CON
HINTZE, Naomi A., 1909- ,
American; fiction, nonfiction
CON
HINZ, Evelyn J., 1938- , Cana-
dian; nonfiction CON
'HIPP, George' see ABRAMS,
George J.
HIPPARCHUS, 130 B.C., Greek;

nonfiction LA
HIPPARCHUS of NICAEA, late 2nd
century B. C. , Greek; nonfic-
tion BU
HIPPEL, Theodor Gottlieb von,
1741-96, German; fiction,
plays BU
HIPPIAS, 485-15 B. C. , Greek;
nonfiction BU GR
HIPPISLEY COXE, Antony Dacres
('Charles Lacy'), 1912- ,
British; nonfiction CON
HIPPIUS, Zinaida N. see GIP-
PIUS, Zinaida N.
HIPPLE, Theodore Wallace,
1935- , American; nonfiction
CON
HIPPLER, Arthur Edwin, 1935- ,
American; nonfiction CON
HIPPOCRATES of COS, 460?-380
B. C. , Greek; nonfiction BU
GR LA
HIPPONAX, 6th century B. C. ,
Greek; poetry BU GR LA
'HIPPOPOTAMUS, Eugene H.'
see KRAUS, Robert
HIPPS, Juanita (Redmond), 1913?-
79, American; nonfiction
CON
HIPSKIND, Judith, 1945- , Amer-
ican; nonfiction CON
HIRABAYASHI TAIKO, 1905- ,
Japanese; fiction HI
HIRAGA GENNAI, 1728-79,
Japanese; plays, fiction HI
HIRANO KUNIOMI, 1827-64,
Japanese; poetry HI
HIRAOKA, Kimitake see 'MISHIMA
YUKIO'
HIRAYAMA TOGO see 'IBARA
SAIKAKU'
HIRN, Yrjö, 1870-1952, Finnish-
Swedish; nonfiction BU
HIRO, Dilip, Pakistani; fiction,
plays, film CON
HIRSCH, Abby, 1946- , Amer-
ican; nonfiction CON
HIRSCH, Barbara B. , 1938- ,
American; nonfiction CON
HIRSCH, David H. , 1930- ,
American; nonfiction CON
HIRSCH, Eric Donald, Jr. ,
1928- , American; nonfiction
BOR
HIRSCH, Foster Lance, 1943- ,
American; nonfiction CON
HIRSCH, Fred, 1931-78, American-
British; nonfiction CON

HIRSCH, Herbert, 1941- , Amer-
ican; nonfiction CON
HIRSCH, Mark David, 1910- ,
American; nonfiction CON
HIRSCH, Monroe Jerome, 1917- ,
American; nonfiction CON
HIRSCH, Morris Isaac, 1915- ,
South African; nonfiction CON
HIRSCH, Phil ('Norman Lemon
Peel'; 'Bob Vlasic'), 1926- ,
American; nonfiction CON
HIRSCH, S. Carl, 1913- , Amer-
ican; juveniles DE WAR
HIRSCH, Thomas L. , 1931- ,
American; nonfiction CON
'HIRSCH, William Randolph' see
KITMAN, Marvin
HIRSCHBEIN, Peretz, 1880-1948,
Yiddish; plays, nonfiction
BU MCG
HIRSCHBERG, Cornelius, 1901- ,
American; fiction REI
HIRSCHFELD, Burt, American;
juveniles WAR
HIRSCHFELD, Georg, 1873-1942,
German; fiction, plays MCG
HIRSCHFIELD, Robert Sidney,
1928- , American; nonfiction
CON
HIRSCHHORN, Clive, 1940- ,
American; nonfiction CON
HIRSCHHORN, Howard Harvey,
1931- , American; nonfiction
CON
HIRSCHHORN, Richard Clark,
1933- , American; fiction,
nonfiction CON
HIRSCHI, Travis, 1935- , Amer-
ican; nonfiction CON
HIRSCHMAN, Jack, 1933- , Amer-
ican; poetry, translations
VCP
HIRSCHMANN, Maria Anne ('Han-
si'), American; nonfiction
CON
HIRSH, Marilyn, 1944- , Amer-
ican; juveniles CO CON WAR
HIRSHBERG, Albert S. , 1909-73,
American; journalism CON
HIRST, Paul Heywood, 1927- ,
English; nonfiction CON
HIRST, Stephen Michael, 1939- ,
American; nonfiction CON
HIRTIUS, Aulus,   -43 B. C. ,
Roman; nonfiction BU LA
HISAMATSU, Hoseki Shin'ichi,
1889- , Japanese; nonfiction
CON

HISCOCKS, Charles Richard,
1907- , English; nonfiction
CON
HISER, Iona Seibert, 1901- ,
American; juveniles CO
HISKETT, Mervyn, 1920- ,
English; nonfiction CON
HISS, Tony, 1941- , American;
nonfiction CON
HITCHCOCK, Alfred J. , 1899-
1980, American; films, juven-
iles CO CON
HITCHCOCK, George, 1914- ,
American; poetry, plays,
fiction VCP
HITCHCOCK, Hugh Wiley, 1923- ,
American; nonfiction CON
HITCHCOCK, Patricia, American;
juveniles WAR
HITCHCOCK, Raymond, 1922- ,
English; fiction CON NI
HITCHCOCK, Susan Tyler,
1950- , American; nonfiction
CON
HITCHENS, Dolores see 'OLSEN,
D. B. '
HITCHING, John Francis, 1933- ,
British; nonfiction CON
HITCHMAN, Janet, 1916-80,
British; nonfiction CON
HITE, James Cleveland, 1941- ,
American; nonfiction CON
HITE, Shere D. , 1942- ,
American; nonfiction CON
HITIRIS, Theodore, 1938- ,
Greek-English; nonfiction
CON
HITT, William Dee, 1929- ,
American; nonfiction CON
HITTE, Kathryn, 1919- , Amer-
ican; juveniles CO
HITTI, Philip Khuri, 1886-1978,
American; nonfiction CON
HITZ, Demi, 1942- , American;
juveniles CO CON
HIVELY, Peter Chester, 1934- ,
American; journalism CON
HIVNOR, Robert ('Jack Askew';
'Osbert Pismire'), 1916- ,
American; plays CON VCD
HIX, Charles Arthur, 1942- ,
American; nonfiction, jour-
nalism CON
HIXON, Don Lee, 1942- , Amer-
ican; nonfiction CON
HIXSON, Joseph Randolph, 1927- ,
American; nonfiction CON
HJÄRNE, Urban, 1641-1724,

Swedish; poetry BU
HJARTARSON, Snorri, 1906- ,
Icelander; fiction, poetry CL
HJORTO, Knud Anders, 1869-1931,
Danish; fiction BU
HJORTSBERG, William, 1941- ,
American; fiction NI
HLA, U, 1910- , Burmese; jour-
nalism, nonfiction, translations,
fiction PRU
HLAING, Princess of, 1833-75,
Burmese; plays PRU
HLASKO, Marek, 1934-69, Polish;
fiction BU CL TH WA
HLAVACEK, Karel, 1874-98,
Czech; poetry BU TH
'HLYBINNY, Vladimir' see
SEDURO, Vladimir
HMAIN, Thakhin Koujto, 1876-
1964, Burmese; poetry, plays,
nonfiction, journalism PRU
HO, Minfong, 1951- , Burmese;
juveniles, journalism CO CON
HO CH'I-FANG, 1911- , Chinese;
poetry, nonfiction BU PRU
HO CHING-CHIH, 1924- , Chinese;
poetry, plays PRU
HO KYUN, 1569-1618, Korean; fic-
tion PRU
HO XUAN HUONG, late 18th cen-
tury, Vietnamese; poetry LA
PRU
HOADLY, Benjamin, 1676-1761,
English; nonfiction BU
HOADLEY, Walter Evans, 1916- ,
American; nonfiction CON
HOAGLAND, Edward Morley,
1932- , American; nonfiction,
fiction KIB VCN WAK
HOAGLAND, Eric, American; non-
fiction SH
HOAGLAND, Jimmie Lee, 1940- ,
American; journalism CON
HOAGLAND, Mahlon Bush, 1921- ,
American; nonfiction CON
HOAR, Roger S. see 'FARLEY,
Ralph M. '
HOARE, Merval Hannah, 1914- ,
New Zealander; poetry, nonfic-
tion CON
HOARE, Wilber W. , Jr. , 1921-76,
American; nonfiction CON
HOBAN, Lillian, 1925- , Ameri-
can; juveniles CO CON DE
HOBAN, Russell Conwell, 1925- ,
American; juveniles, poetry,
fiction DE KI
HOBAN, Tana, American; juveniles

CO CON DEM WAR
HOBART, Billie, 1935- , Amer-
ican; nonfiction CON
HOBART, Lois Elaine, American;
juveniles CO
'HOBART, Robertson' see
'CORRIGAN, Mark'
HOBBES, Thomas, 1588-1679,
English; translations, nonfic-
tion BU DA MAG PO RU VN
HOBBING, Enno, 1920- ,
German-American; journalism,
nonfiction CON
HOBBS, Carl Fredric, 1931- ,
American; nonfiction CON
HOBBS, Peter Victor, 1936- ,
Anglo-American; nonfiction
CON
HOBBS, Williston C., 1925?-80,
American; nonfiction CON
HOBBY, Oveta Culp, 1905- ,
American; nonfiction CON
HOBBY, William P., 1932- ,
American; nonfiction CON
HOBDAY, Victor Carr, 1914- ,
American; nonfiction CON
'HOBEL, Phil' see FANTHORPE,
Robert L.
HOBERMAN, Mary Ann Freed-
man, 1930- , American;
juveniles CO CON WAR
HOBGOOD, Burnet M., 1922- ,
?; nonfiction CON
HOBHOUSE, Hermione, 1934- ,
English; nonfiction CON
HOBHOUSE, Janet, 1948- ,
American; nonfiction CON
HOBHOUSE, John Cam see
BROUGHTON, Baron
'HO-BIEU-CHANH' (Ho-van-
Trung), 1885-1958, Viet-
namese; fiction PRU
HOBSBAUM, Philip Dennis,
1932- , British; poetry, non-
fiction VCP
HOBSBAWM, Eric John Ernest
('Francis Newton'), 1917- ,
British; nonfiction WAK
HOBSON, Fred Colby, Jr.,
1943- , American; nonfiction
CON
HOBSON, Edmund Schobidd,
1931- , American; nonfiction
CON
HOBSON, George Carey, 1890-
1945, Afrikaans; nonfiction BU
HOBSON, Harold, 1904- , British;
journalism, nonfiction CON

HOBSON, Julius W., 1922?-77,
American; juveniles, nonfiction
CON SH WAR
HOBSON, Laura Zametkin, 1900- ,
American; fiction, juveniles
VCN
HOBSON, Samuel Bonnin, 1888-
1967, Afrikaans; nonfiction
BU
HOBSON, William, 1911- , Brit-
ish; nonfiction CON
HOBY, Sir Thomas, 1530-66, Eng-
lish; nonfiction, translations
BU DA RU
HOBZEK, Mildred Jane, 1919- ,
American; juveniles CON
HOCCLEVE, Thomas (Occleve),
1370-1426?, English; poetry
BU DA PO VP
HOCH, Edward Dentlinger ('Irwin
Booth'; 'Stephen Dentinger';
'Pat McMahon'; 'R. L.
Stevens'; 'Mr. X'), 1930- ,
American; fiction, nonfiction
MCC NI REI ST
HOCH, Paul Lawrence, 1942- ,
Anglo-American; nonfiction
CON
HOCHBAUM, Hans Albert, 1911- ,
American; nonfiction CON
HOCHHUTH, Rolf, 1931- , Ger-
man; plays BU CL MCG TH
WA
'HO-CHI-MINH' (Nguyen-tat-Thanh),
1890-1969, Vietnamese; nonfic-
tion PRU
HOCHMAN, Sandra, 1936- , Amer-
ican; poetry, fiction, plays,
journalism VCP WAK
HOCHMAN, Shel, 1944- , Amer-
ican; poetry, fiction, juveniles
CON
HOCHMAN, Shirley Dean, 1917- ,
American; nonfiction CON
HOCHMAN, Stanley Richard,
1928- , American; nonfiction
CON
HOCHSCHILD, Arlie Russell,
1940- , American; juveniles,
nonfiction CO CON
HOCHSCHILD, Harold K., 1892-
1981, American; nonfiction
CON
HOCHSTEIN, Rolaine, American;
nonfiction CON
HOCHWÄLDER, Fritz, 1911- ,
Austrian; plays BU MCG TH
WA

'HOCKABY, Stephen' see
  MITCHELL, Gladys M.
HOCKENBERRY, Hope see
  NEWELL, Hope
HOCKING, Anne ('Mona Messer'),
  1890's- , British; fiction
  REI
HOCKING, Anthony, 1938- ,
  British; nonfiction CON
HOCKING, Mary Eunice, 1921- ,
  British; fiction CON
HOCKS, Richard Allen, 1936- ,
  American; nonfiction CON
HODDER-WILLIAMS, Christopher,
  1926- , English; fiction
  AS NI
'HODDIS, Jakob van' (Hans
  Davidsohn), 1887-1942, Ger-
  man; poetry SEY TH
HODEIR, Andre, 1921- , French;
  nonfiction CON
'HODEMART, Peter' see AUDE-
  MARS, Pierre
HODES, Scott, 1937- , American;
  nonfiction CON
HODGE, Alan, 1915-79, British;
  journalism, nonfiction CON
HODGE, David Wayne, 1935- ,
  American; nonfiction CON
HODGE, Gene Meany, 1898- ,
  American; poetry CON
HODGE, James Lee, 1935- ,
  American; nonfiction CON
HODGE, Paul William, 1934- ,
  American; juveniles CO
'HODGE, T. Shirby' (Roger Sher-
  man Tracy), 1841-1926,
  American; fiction NI
HODGE, William Howard, 1932- ,
  American; nonfiction CON
HODGES, Carl G. , 1902-64,
  American; juveniles CO
HODGES, Cyril Walter, 1909- ,
  English; juveniles, nonfiction
  DE KI
HODGES, Donald Clark, 1923- ,
  American; nonfiction CON
HODGES, Herbert Arthur, 1905-
  76, British; nonfiction CON
HODGES, John Cunyus, 1892-67,
  American; nonfiction CON
HODGES, Louis W. , 1933- ,
  American; nonfiction CON
HODGES, Luther Hartwell, 1898-
  1974, American; nonfiction
  CON
HODGES, Margaret Moore, 1911- ,
  American; juveniles DEM

WAR
HODGES, Norman Edward, 1939- ,
  American; nonfiction SH
HODGES, Richard Edwin, 1928- ,
  American; nonfiction CON
HODGES, Zane Clark, 1932- ,
  American; nonfiction CON
HODGETTS, Alfred Birnie, 1911- ,
  Canadian; nonfiction CON
HODGETTS, Richard Michael,
  1942- , American; nonfiction
  CON
HODGINS, Eric, 1899-1971, Amer-
  ican; nonfiction WA
HODGINS, Jack, 1938- , Canadian;
  nonfiction CON
HODGKIN, Robert Allason (Robin),
  1916- , British; nonfiction
  CON
'HODGSON, David' see LEWIS,
  David
HODGSON, Margaret see BAL-
  LINGER, Violet M.
HODGSON, Martha Keeling,
  1906- , German-English; non-
  fiction CON
HODGSON, Pat, 1928- , English;
  nonfiction CON
HODGSON, Ralph, 1871-1962, Eng-
  lish; poetry CON DA MAG
  SEY VP
HODGSON, William Hope, 1877-
  1918, English; fiction AS NI
  REI ST
HODIN, Josef Paul, 1905- ,
  Czech-English; nonfiction CON
HODSDON, Nicholas Edward,
  1941- , American; fiction
  CON
HODZA, Michal Miloslav, 1811-70,
  Slovak; poetry BU
HOECK, Theobald, 1573-1618, Ger-
  man; poetry BU
HOECKER, Karla, 1901- , Ger-
  man; nonfiction CON
HÖFLER, Peter K. see 'THOOR,
  Jesse'
HOEHLING, Mary, 1914- , Amer-
  ican; nonfiction CON
HÖIJER, Benjamin, 1767-1812,
  Swedish; nonfiction BU
HOEL, Robert Floyd, 1942- ,
  American; nonfiction CON
HOEL, Sigurd, 1890-1960, Nor-
  wegian; fiction, plays, nonfic-
  tion BU CL TH
HÖLDERLIN, Johann Christian
  Friedrich, 1770-1843, German;

fiction, plays, poetry, trans-
lations BU MAG MCG TH
HÖLLERER, Walter, 1922- ,
German; poetry, nonfiction,
fiction, plays CL TH
HÖLTY, Ludwig Heinrich Chris-
toph, 1748-76, German;
poetry BU TH
HOELZEL, Alfred, 1934- ,
Austrian-American; nonfiction
CON
HOEN, Pieter T. ('A. Contra-
duc'; 'A. Produc'; 'Martinus
Scriblerus de Jonge'; 'J. A.
Schasz, M. D.'), 1744-1818,
Dutch; juveniles BU
HOENIG, Sidney Benjamin, 1907- ,
American; nonfiction CON
HOENIGER, Frederick David,
1921- , American; nonfiction
CON
HOEST, William, 1926- ,
American; nonfiction CON
HOEVELER, Diane Long, 1949- ,
American; nonfiction CON
HOEXTER, Corinne K., 1927- ,
American; juveniles, nonfiction
CO CON
HOEY, Frances Sarah Johnston,
1830-1908, Irish; fiction,
journalism HO
HOFDIJK, Willem Jakobszoon,
1816-88, Dutch; poetry BU
HOFF, Carol, 1900- , American;
juveniles CO
'HOFF, Gertrud' see MATTHAEI,
Clara
HOFF, Harry S. see 'COOPER,
William'
HOFF, Sydney, 1912- , American;
nonfiction, juveniles, plays
CO DE KI
HOFF EDDE, Curtis, 1906- ,
American; nonfiction CON
HOFFECKER, Carol Eleanor,
1938- , American; nonfiction
CON
HOFFECKER, John Savin, 1908- ,
American; juveniles WAR
HOFFENBERG, Jack, 1906-77,
American; fiction CON
HOFFER, Eric, 1902- , Amer-
ican; nonfiction WA
HOFFER, William, 1943- ,
American; nonfiction CON
HOFFHAM, Otto Christiaan Fred-
erik, 1744-99, Dutch; poetry,
plays BU

HOFFMAN, Alice, 1952- , Amer-
ican; fiction CON
HOFFMAN, Anita ('Ann Fettamen'),
1942- , American; fiction
CON
HOFFMAN, Bengt Runo, 1913- ,
Swedish; nonfiction CON
HOFFMAN, Bernard Gilbert,
1925- , American; nonfiction
CON
'HOFFMAN, Byrd' see WILSON,
Robert M.
HOFFMAN, Charles Fenno, 1806-
84, American; poetry, fiction,
nonfiction BR BU MYE VP
HOFFMAN, Daniel, 1923- , Amer-
ican; poetry, nonfiction VCP
WA
HOFFMAN, Donald Stone, 1936- ,
American; nonfiction CON
HOFFMAN, Edwin D., American;
nonfiction CON
HOFFMAN, Elizabeth Parkinson,
1921- , American; nonfiction
CON
HOFFMAN, Frederick John, 1909-
67, American; nonfiction WA
HOFFMAN, Harry G., 1911?-77,
American; journalism CON
HOFFMAN, Henry William,
1925- , American; fiction
BA
HOFFMAN, Jo Ann S., 1942- ,
American; journalism, juveniles
CON
HOFFMANN, Joseph Gilbert, 1909-
74, American; nonfiction CON
HOFFMAN, Lee, 1932- , Amer-
ican; fiction NI
HOFFMAN, Paul, 1934- , Amer-
ican; nonfiction CON
HOFFMAN, Phyllis M., 1944- ,
American; juveniles CO
HOFFMAN, Rosekrans, 1926- ,
American; juveniles CO CON
HOFFMAN, Ross John S., 1902- ,
American; nonfiction CON
HOFFMAN, Stanley, 1944- ,
American; fiction CON
HOFFMAN, Willa Matthews,
1914- , American; nonfiction
CON
HOFFMAN, William Moses,
1939- , American; plays,
poetry CON VCD
HOFFMANN, Dieter, 1934- ,
German; poetry CL
HOFFMANN, E. L. see 'LANG-

GASSER, Elisabeth'
HOFFMANN, Ernst Theodor Wil-
helm, 1776-1822, German;
nonfiction, fiction BU MAG
NI TH
HOFFMANN, Felix, 1911-75,
Swiss; juveniles CO CON DE
HOFFMANN, Kai Anton Carl
Nyholm, 1874-1949, Danish;
poetry BU TH
HOFFMANN, Leon Francois,
1932- , Franco-American;
nonfiction CON
HOFFMANN, Malcolm Arthur,
1912- , American; nonfiction
CON
HOFFMANN, Peter Conrad,
1930- , German-Canadian;
nonfiction CON
HOFFMANN, Stanley H., 1928- ,
Austrian-American; nonfiction
CON
HOFFMANN, Yoel, 1937- ,
Rumanian-Israeli; nonfiction
CON
HOFFMANN von FALLERSLEBEN,
August Heinrich, 1798-1874,
German; poetry, nonfiction
BU TH
HOFFMANOWA, Klementyna
Tánska, 1798-1845, Polish;
fiction BU
HOFFMEISTER, Adolf, 1902-73,
Czech; nonfiction, poetry,
plays CL TH
HOFFMEISTER, Donald Frederick,
1916- , American; nonfiction
CON
HOFFNUNG, Michele ('Michele
Hoffnung Garskof'), 1944- ,
American; nonfiction CON
HOFLING, Charles Kreimer,
1920- , American; nonfiction
CON
HOFMAN see also GOFMAN
HOFMANN, Adele Dellenbaugh,
1926- , American; nonfiction
CON
HOFMANN, Melita Cecelia,
-1976, American; nonfiction
CON
HOFMANN von HOFMANNSWAL- '
DAU, Christian, 1617-79,
German; poetry BU TH
HOFMANNSTHAL, Hugo von, 1874-
1929, Austrian; poetry, plays,
nonfiction BU CL MAG MCG
TH

HOFMO, Gunvor, 1921- , Nor-
wegian; poetry CL
HOFSHTEYN, David, 1889-1952,
Russian; poetry BU
HOFSINDE, Robert, 1902-73,
Danish-American; juveniles
CO CON DE
HOFSOMMER, Donovan Lowell,
1938- , American; nonfiction
CON
HOFSTADTER, Richard, 1916-70,
American; nonfiction BR WA
HOFSTEDE, Geert Hendrik,
1928- , American; nonfiction
CON
HOGAN, Bernice Harris, 1929- ,
American; juveniles CO
'HOGAN, David' see GALLAGHER,
Frank
HOGAN, Desmond, 1951- , Irish;
fiction, plays CON HO
HOGAN, James Patrick, 1941- ,
British; fiction CON
HOGAN, John D., 1927- ,
American; nonfiction CON
HOGAN, Judy, 1937- , American;
poetry, nonfiction CON
HOGAN, Michael, 1832-99, Irish;
poetry HO
HOGAN, Michael, 1943- , Amer-
ican; nonfiction CON
HOGAN, Paul, 1927- , American;
nonfiction CON
HOGAN, Robert Francis, 1927- ,
American; nonfiction CON
HOGAN, Thomas Eugene, Jr.,
1952- , American; nonfiction
CON
HOGAN, William T., 1919- ,
American; nonfiction CON
'HOGARTH, Jr.' see KENT, Rock-
well
HOGARTH, Burne, 1911- , Amer-
ican; nonfiction CON
HOGARTH, Grace ('Grace Allen';
'Amelia Gay'; 'Allen Weston'),
1905- , American; juveniles,
fiction CON KI
HOGARTH, Paul, 1917- , English;
nonfiction CON
'HOGAS, Calistrat' (Calistrat Dimit-
riu), 1847-1917, Rumanian;
nonfiction BU
HOGBEN, Lancelot, 1895-1975,
British; nonfiction CON
'HOGBOTEL, Sebastian' see
GOTT, Kenneth D.
HOGE, Dean Richard, 1937- ,

American; nonfiction CON
HOGE, James Otey, 1944- ,
American; nonfiction CON
HOGE, Warren McClamroch,
1941- , American; journalism
CON
HOGG, Helen Battles Sawyer,
1905- , American; nonfiction
CON
HOGG, James, 1770-1835, Scots;
poetry, fiction, nonfiction,
plays BU DA PO VN
HOGG, Oliver Frederick Gillilan,
1887-1979, British; nonfiction
CON
HOGG, Robert Lawrence, 1942- ,
American; poetry CON
HOGG, Thomas Jefferson, 1792-
1862, English; nonfiction
BU DA
HOGGART, Richard, 1918- ,
English; nonfiction WA
HOGHENDORP, Gijsbrecht van,
1589-1639, Dutch; plays BU
HOGINS, James Burl, 1936- ,
American; nonfiction CON
HOGNER, Dorothy Childs, Amer-
ican; juveniles CO
HOGNER, Nils, 1893-1970,
American; nonfiction, juveniles
CO CON
HOGROGIAN, Nonny, 1932- ,
American; juveniles CO CON
DE
HOGUE, Charles Billy, 1928- ,
American; nonfiction CON
HOGUE, Richard, 1946- ,
American; nonfiction CON
HOH, Israel Kafu, 1912- ,
Ghanaian; poetry, plays JA
HOHBERG, Wolfgang Helmhard
von, 1612-88, Austrian;
poetry BU
HOHENBERG, Dorothy Lannuier,
1905?-77, American; jour-
nalism CON
HOHENDAHL, Peter Euwe,
1936- , German-American;
nonfiction CON
HOHENHEIM, Theophrast B. von
see PARACELSUS, Philippus
A.
HOHENSTEIN, Henry John, 1931- ,
American; nonfiction CON
HOHIMER, Frank, 1928- ,
American; nonfiction CON
HOHLFELDER, Robert Lane,
1938- , American; nonfiction

CON
'HOHOFF, Tay' see TORREY,
Therese von H.
HOIJER, Harry, 1904-76, Amer-
ican; nonfiction CON
HOJEDA, Diego de, 1571-1615,
Spanish; poetry BR BU TH
HOJHOLT, Per, 1928- , Danish;
poetry, fiction CL
HOKE, Helen L. ('Helen Sterling'),
1903- , American; juveniles,
nonfiction CO CON
HOKE, John Lindsay, 1925- ,
American; juveniles CO CON
HOLAN, Vladimír, 1905- , Czech;
poetry, translations BU CL
SEY WA
HOLBACH, Paul Heinrich Dietrich,
1723-89, French; nonfiction
BU TH
'HOLBEACH, Henry' see RANDS,
William B.
HOLBERG, Ludvig, 1684-1754,
Danish; plays, nonfiction BU
MCG NI TH
HOLBROOK, Bill, 1921- , Amer-
ican; nonfiction CON
HOLBROOK, David Kenneth,
1923- , British; poetry, plays,
nonfiction VCP WA
HOLBROOK, Jennifer Kearns,
1931- , British; nonfiction
CON
'HOLBROOK, John' see VANCE,
John H.
'HOLBROOK, Peter' see GLICK,
Carl C.
HOLBROOK, Stewart, 1893-1964,
American; juveniles DE
HOLCOMB, Donald Frank, 1925- ,
American; nonfiction CON
HOLCOMB, George L., 1911- ,
American; nonfiction CON
HOLCOMBE, Arthur Norman, 1884-
1977, American; nonfiction
CON
HOLCROFT, Thomas, 1745-1809,
English; fiction, plays, journal-
ism BU PO VN
HOLDEN, Anthony Ivan, 1947- ,
British; journalism, transla-
tions, nonfiction CON
HOLDEN, David, 1931- , Ameri-
can; nonfiction CON
HOLDEN, David Shipley ('David
Shipley'), 1924-77, English;
nonfiction CON
HOLDEN, Inez, 1906-74, American;

journalism, fiction CON
HOLDEN, Jonathan, 1941- ,
American; poetry CON
HOLDEN, Matthew, Jr. , 1931- ,
American; nonfiction CON
HOLDEN, Molly, 1927- , Brit-
ish; poetry, fiction, juveniles
VCP
HOLDEN, Paul E. , 1894?-1976,
American; nonfiction CON
HOLDEN, Richard Cort, Amer-
ican; fiction NI
HOLDEN, Ursula, 1921- , Brit-
ish; fiction CON
HOLDEN, Willis Sprague, 1909-
73, American; journalism
CON
HOLDER, Glenn, 1906- , Amer-
ican; juveniles CON WAR
HOLDER, Ray, 1913- , Amer-
ican; nonfiction CON
HOLDER, William G. , 1937- ,
American; juveniles WAR
HOLDING, Elisabeth Sanxay,
1889-1955, American; fiction
REI ST
HOLDING, James ('Clark Car-
lisle'; 'Ellery Queen, Jr. '),
1907- , American; juveniles,
fiction CO REI
HOLDSTOCK, Robert P. , 1948- ,
British; fiction NI
HOLECEK, Josef, 1853-1929,
Czech; fiction, translations
BU CL
HOLENSTEIN, Elmar, 1937- ,
Swiss; nonfiction CON
HOLFORD, Ingrid, 1920- ,
British; nonfiction CON
'HOLIDAY, Homer' see De
BEAUBIEN, Philip F.
HOLINSHED, Raphael (Ralph;
Hollingshead), 1529?-80?,
English; nonfiction BU DA
PO RU
HOLISHER, Desider, 1901-72,
Hungarian-American; juveniles
CO
HOLL, Adelaide Hinkle, 1910- ,
American; juveniles CO
WAR
HOLL, Adolf, 1930- , Austrian;
nonfiction CON
HOLL, Jack M. , 1937- , Amer-
ican; nonfiction CON
HOLLADAY, Sylvia Agnes,
1936- , American; nonfiction
CON

HOLLADAY, William Lee, 1926- ,
American; nonfiction CON
HOLLAND, Barbara Adams,
1925- , American; poetry
CON
HOLLAND, Cecilia, 1943- ,
American; fiction NI
HOLLAND, Cecil Fletcher, 1907-
78, American; journalism, non-
fiction CON
HOLLAND, Deborah Katherine,
1947- , American; nonfiction
CON
HOLLAND, De Witt Talmage,
1923- , American; nonfiction
CON
HOLLAND, Hilda, 1901?-75,
American; nonfiction CON
HOLLAND, Isabelle, 1920- ,
American; juveniles, fiction
CO KI WAR
HOLLAND, Jack H. , 1922- ,
American; nonfiction CON
HOLLAND, Janice, 1913-62, Amer-
ican; juveniles CO CON
HOLLAND, John Lewis, 1919- ,
American; juveniles CO WAR
'HOLLAND, Katrin' see 'ALBRAND,
Martha'
'HOLLAND, Kel' see WHITTING-
TON, Harry
HOLLAND, Laurence Bedwell,
1920-80, American; nonfiction
CON
HOLLAND, Louise Adams, 1893- ,
American; nonfiction CON
HOLLAND, Lynwood M. , 1905- ,
American; nonfiction CON
HOLLAND, Marion, 1908- ,
American; juveniles CO CON
HOLLAND, Philemon, 1552-1637,
English; nonfiction BU
HOLLAND, Sir Richard ('Richard
de Holande'), fl. 1450, Scots;
poetry BU VP
HOLLAND, Sheila ('Charlotte
Lamb'; 'Sheila Lancaster'),
1937- , British; fiction CON
HOLLAND, Thomas Edward,
1934- , American; nonfiction
CON
HOLLAND, Tim, 1931- , Amer-
ican; nonfiction CON
HOLLAND, Viki, American; juven-
iles WAR
HOLLAND, Vyvyan Beresford,
1886-1967, British; nonfiction,
translations CON

HOLLANDER, Hans, 1899- ,
Austrian-British; nonfiction
CON
HOLLANDER, Herbert S. , 1904?-
76, American; journalism,
nonfiction CON
HOLLANDER, John, 1929- ,
American; poetry, nonfiction,
juveniles BR CO SEY VCP
WA
HOLLANDER, Phyllis, 1928- ,
American; nonfiction, juven-
iles CON WAR
HOLLANDER, Zander ('Alexander
Peters'), 1923- , American;
nonfiction, juveniles CON
WAR
HOLLAWAY, Otto, 1903- ,
American; nonfiction CON
HOLLEB, Arthur Irving, 1921- ,
American; nonfiction CON
HOLLENWEGER, Walter Jacob,
1927- , Belgian-English;
nonfiction CON
HOLLER, Frederick L. , 1921- ,
Austrian-American; nonfiction
CON
HOLLER, Ronald F. , 1938- ,
American; nonfiction CON
HOLLES, Everett R. , 1904?-78,
American; journalism, non-
fiction CON
HOLLICK, Ann Lorraine, 1941- ,
American; nonfiction CON
HOLLIDAY, Barbara Gregg,
1917- , American; journal-
ism CON
'HOLLIDAY, Don' see PLOTNICK,
Arthur
HOLLIDAY, Joseph ('Jack Bosco';
'Jack Dale'), 1910- , Brit-
ish; juveniles CO
HOLLINDALE, Peter, 1936- ,
British; nonfiction CON
HOLLING, Holling Clancy, 1900-
73, American; juveniles,
poetry CO KI
HOLLINGDALE, Reginald John,
1930- , British; nonfiction
CON
HOLLINGS, Michael, 1921- ,
British; nonfiction CON
HOLLINGSWORTH, Dorothy
Frances, 1916- , British;
nonfiction CON
HOLLINGSWORTH, Harold Marvin,
1932- , American; nonfiction
CON

HOLLINGSWORTH, Kent, 1929- ,
American; nonfiction CON
HOLLINGSWORTH, Lyman Burgess,
1919- , American; nonfiction
CON
HOLLINGSWORTH, Mary Head,
1910- , American; journalism,
fiction CON
HOLLIS, Christopher, 1902-77,
British; journalism, nonfiction
CON
'HOLLIS, H. H. ' (Ben N. Ramey),
1921-77, American; fiction
NI
HOLLIS, Harry Newcombe, Jr. ,
1938- , American; nonfiction
CON
HOLLIS, Helen Rice, 1908- ,
American; nonfiction CON
HOLLIS, James Russell, 1940- ,
American; nonfiction CON
HOLLISTER, Bernard Claiborne,
1938- , American; nonfiction
CON
HOLLO, Anselm Paul, 1934- ,
American; poetry, nonfiction,
translations VCP
HOLLONIUS, Ludwig (Holle), fl.
1605, German; plays BU
HOLLOWAY, James Young, 1927- ,
American; nonfiction CON
HOLLOWAY, John, 1920- , Eng-
lish; poetry, nonfiction BOR
VCP WA
HOLLOWAY, Joseph, 1861-1944,
Irish; diary HO
HOLLOWAY, Marcella Marie,
1913- , American; nonfiction,
plays CON
HOLLOWAY, Percival Geoffrey,
1918- , English; poetry CON
HOLLOWAY, Rufus Emory, 1885-
1977, American; nonfiction
CON
HOLLOWELL, John, 1945- ,
American; nonfiction CON
HOLLOWOOD, Albert Bernard,
1910-81, British; nonfiction
CON
HOLLY, Ján, 1785-1849, Slovak;
poetry BU
'HOLLY, Joan Hunter' (Joan Carol
Holly), 1932- , American;
fiction AS NI
HOLLYDAY, Frederic Blackmar,
1928- , American; nonfiction
CON
HOLM, Anne, 1922- , Danish;

juveniles DEM
HOLM, Sven, 1940- , Danish;
  fiction CL NI
HOLMAN, Clarence Hugh ('Clar-
  ence Hunt'), 1914- , Amer-
  ican; fiction, nonfiction REI
HOLMAN, Felice, 1919- , Amer-
  ican; juveniles, poetry CO
  DEM KI
HOLMAN, Lloyd Bruce, 1939- ,
  American; nonfiction CON
HOLMAN, Mary Alida, 1933- ,
  American; nonfiction CON
HOLMAN, William Roger, 1926- ,
  American; nonfiction CON
HOLMBERG, John Henri, 1949- ,
  Swedish; translations, non-
  fiction NI
HOLME, Bryan ('Charles Fran-
  cis'), 1913- , Anglo-American;
  nonfiction, juveniles CON
'HOLME, K. E.' see HILL,
  John E. C.
HOLME, Thea, 1903- , English;
  nonfiction, plays CON
HOLMES, Burnham, 1942- ,
  American; nonfiction CON
HOLMES, C. Raymond, 1929- ,
  American; nonfiction CON
HOLMES, Charles Shiveley,
  1916-76, American; nonfiction
  CON
HOLMES, Douglas, 1933- ,
  American; nonfiction CON
HOLMES, Efner Tudor, 1949- ,
  American; juveniles CON
HOLMES, Frederic Lawrence,
  1932- , American; nonfiction
  CON
HOLMES, George Frederick,
  1820-97, American; nonfiction
  BA
'HOLMES, Grant' see FOX,
  James M.
'HOLMES, H. H.' see 'BOUCHER,
  Anthony'
HOLMES, Jack David Lazarus,
  1930- , American; nonfiction
  CON
'HOLMES, John' see SOUSTER,
  Holmes R.
HOLMES, John Albert, 1904-62,
  American; poetry WA
HOLMES, John Clellon, 1926- ,
  American; fiction, nonfiction
  BR VCN
HOLMES, John Haynes, 1879-
  1964, American; nonfiction

CON
HOLMES, Martin Rivington,
  1905- , English; nonfiction,
  plays CON
HOLMES, Michael Stephan, 1942- ,
  American; nonfiction CON
HOLMES, Nancy, 1921- , Amer-
  ican; fiction CON
HOLMES, Oliver Wendell, 1809-94,
  American; nonfiction, poetry,
  fiction AM BR BU MAG MY
  PO VN VP
'HOLMES, Raymond' see SOUSTER,
  Holmes R.
HOLMES, Robert Alexander,
  1943- , American; nonfiction
  CON
HOLMES, Robert Lawrence,
  1935- , American; nonfiction
  CON
HOLMES, Robert Merrill, 1925- ,
  American; nonfiction CON
HOLMES, Tiffany, 1944- , Amer-
  ican; nonfiction CON
HOLMES, Tommy, 1903-75, Amer-
  ican; nonfiction CON
HOLMGREN, Helen Jean ('Sr.
  George'), 1930- , American;
  juveniles CON
HOLMGREN, Norah ('Nancy Walt-
  er'), 1939- , American; plays
  CON VCD
HOLMQUIST, Eve, 1921- , Amer-
  ican; juveniles CO CON
HOLMSTRÖM, Israel, 1660-1708,
  Swedish; poetry BU
HOLOGOUDOU, Emile see
  OLOGOUDOU, Emile
HOLQUIST, James Michael,
  1935- , American; nonfiction
  CON
HOLROYD, Michael, 1935- ,
  English; nonfiction, fiction
  CON WAK
HOLROYD, Stuart, 1933- , British;
  nonfiction CON
HOLSAERT, Eunice, -1974,
  American; juveniles CON
HOLSOPPLE, Barbara, 1943- ,
  American; journalism CON
HOLST, Lawrence Eberhardt,
  1929- , American; nonfiction
  CON
HOLSTEIN, Ludvig Detlef, 1864-
  1943, Danish; poetry BU CL
  TH
'HOLT, Andrew' see ANHALT,
  Edward

'HOLT, Conrad G.' see FEARN,
John Russell
HOLT, Edgar Crawshaw, 1900-
75, British; journalism,
nonfiction, fiction CON
'HOLT, Helen' see PAINE,
Lauran B.
HOLT, John Caldwell, 1923- ,
American; nonfiction CON
HOLT, Kare, 1917- , Norwegian;
fiction BU CL
HOLT, L. Emmett, Jr., 1895-
1974, American; nonfiction
CON
HOLT, Len, American; nonfiction
SH
HOLT, Margaret, 1937- , Amer-
ican; juveniles CO
HOLT, Michael Fitzgibbon,
1940- , American; nonfiction
CON
HOLT, Michael Paul, 1929- ,
American; juveniles CO
CON
HOLT, Robert Rutherford, 1917- ,
American; nonfiction CON
HOLT, Rochelle Lynn, 1946- ,
American; poetry, nonfiction
CON
'HOLT, Stephen' see THOMPSON,
Harlan H.
HOLT, Thomas Jung, 1928- ,
American; nonfiction CON
'HOLT, Victoria' see HIBBERT,
Eleanor B.
HOLT, William, 1897-1977,
British; nonfiction, fiction
CON
HOLTHUSEN, Hans Egon, 1913- ,
German-American; nonfiction,
poetry CON TH WA
HOLTJE, Herbert Franklin,
1931- , American; nonfiction
CON
HOLTON, Felicia Antonelli,
1921- , American; journal-
ism, nonfiction CON
'HOLTON, Leonard' see WIB-
BERLEY, Leonard
HOLTON, William Milne, 1931- ,
American; nonfiction CON
HOLTROP, William Frans,
1908- , American; nonfiction
CON
HOLTZMAN, Jerome, 1926- ,
American; nonfiction CON
HOLTZMAN, Will, 1951- ,
American; plays, nonfiction

CON
HOLUB, Miroslav, 1923- , Czech;
poetry, nonfiction BU SEY
WA
HOLWAY, John, 1929- , Amer-
ican; nonfiction CON
HOLYDAY, Barton (Holiday),
1593?-1661, English; transla-
tions, plays BU
HOLYER, Erna Maria, 1925- ,
German-American; juveniles
CO
HOLZ, Arno, 1863-1929, German;
poetry, plays BU CL TH
'HOLZ, Detlev' see BENJAMIN,
Walter
HOLZ, Loretta Marie, 1943- ,
American; juveniles CO CON
HOLZ, Robert Kenneth, 1930- ,
American; nonfiction CON
HOLZBERGER, William George,
1932- , American; poetry
CON
HOLZHAUSEN, Carl Johan,
1900- , Swedish; fiction NI
HOLZMAN, Franklyn Dunn,
1918- , American; nonfiction
CON
HOLZMAN, Robert Stuart, 1907- ,
American; juveniles WAR
HOLZMAN, William (Red), 1920- ,
American; nonfiction CON
HOLZNER, Burkart, 1931- ,
German-American; nonfiction
CON
HOME, Alexander see HUME,
Alexander
HOME, Alexander Frederick ('Alec
Douglas-Home'), 1903- ,
British; nonfiction CON
HOME, Henry (Lord Kames), 1696-
1782, Scots; nonfiction DA
HOME, John, 1722-1808, Scots;
nonfiction, plays BU DA VD
'HOME, Michael' see 'BUSH,
Christopher'
HOME, William Douglas, 1912- ,
British; plays, poetry, nonfic-
tion CON VCD VD WAK
HOMER, fl. 700 B.C., Greek;
poetry BU GR LA MAG NI
HOMER, Frederic Donald, 1939- ,
American; nonfiction CON
'HOMES, Geoffrey' (Daniel Main-
waring), 1901/02-78, American;
fiction, films REI ST
HOMGE, Alma C., 1932- ,
American; juveniles CO

HOMMIUS, Festus, 1567-1642, Dutch; nonfiction BU
HOMOLA, Samuel, 1929- , American; nonfiction CON
HOMRIGHAUSEN, Elmer George, 1900- , American; translations, nonfiction CON
HONAN, Park, 1928- , American; nonfiction CON
HONCE, Charles E., 1895-1975, American; nonfiction CON
HONCHAR, Oles, 1918- , Ukrainian; fiction CL TH
HONDIUS, Petrus, 1578-1621, Dutch; poetry BU
HONE, Joseph, 1937- , English; fiction, nonfiction CON
HONE, Joseph Maunsel, 1882-1959, Irish; nonfiction, translations HO
HONE, Josephine, 1937- , Irish; fiction MCC
HONE, William, 1780-1842, English; nonfiction BU
HONEN, 1133-1212, Japanese; nonfiction HI
HONEYCOMBE, Gordon, 1936- , British; plays, tv CON
HONEYCUTT, Benjamin Lawrence, 1938- , American; nonfiction CON
HONEYCUTT, Roy Lee, Jr., 1926- , American; nonfiction CON
'HONEYMAN, Brenda' see CLARKE, Brenda M. L.
HONG, Jane Fay ('Adora Sheridan'), 1954- , American; fiction CON
HONG, Yong Ki, 1929?-79, Korean-American; journalism CON
HONIG, Donald, 1931- , American; juveniles CO
HONIG, Edwin, 1919- , American; poetry, plays, nonfiction, translations VCP WA
HONIG, Louis, 1911-77, American; fiction CON
'HONIGFELD, Gilbert' see HOWARD, Gilbert
HONIGH, Cornelis, 1845-96, Dutch; poetry BU
HONNALGERE, Gopal, 1944- , Indian; poetry, nonfiction CON
HONORIUS AUGUSTODUNENSIS, 1090-1150, ?; nonfiction BU

HONORIUS of AUTUN, fl. 1120, German?; nonfiction TH
HONOUR, Hugh, 1927- , British; nonfiction CON
HONRI, Peter, 1929- , British; nonfiction CON
HONWANA, Luis Bernardo, 1942- , Mozambican; fiction, journalism HER JA
HOOBLER, Dorothy, American; nonfiction CON
HOOBLER, Thomas, American; nonfiction CON
HOOD, Graham, 1936- , British; nonfiction CON
HOOD, Hugh John Blagdon, 1928- , Canadian; fiction, nonfiction BU CON CR VCN
HOOD, Joseph F., 1925- , American; juveniles CO
HOOD, Robert E., 1926- , American; juveniles CO WAR
'HOOD, Sarah' see KILLOUGH, Lee
HOOD, Thomas, 1799-1845, English; poetry, fiction, journalism BU DA PO VP
HOOFT, Pieter Cornelisz, 1581-1647, Dutch; poetry BU TH
HOOFT, Willem Dircksz, 1594-1658, Dutch; plays BU
HOOGE, Romeyn de, 1645-1708, Dutch; nonfiction BU
HOOGENBOOM, Ari Arthur, 1927- , American; nonfiction CON
HOOGSTRATEN, David Fransz van, 1658-1724, Dutch; translations, poetry BU
HOOGSTRATEN, Frans van, 1632-96, Dutch; poetry BU
HOOGSTRATEN, Samuel van, 1627-78, Dutch; poetry BU
HOOGVLIET, Arnold, 1687-1763, Dutch; poetry BU
HOOK, Andrew, 1932- , Scots; nonfiction CON
HOOK, Diana ffarington, 1918- , Brazilian-English; nonfiction CON
HOOK, Donald Dwight, 1928- , American; nonfiction CON
HOOK, Theodore Edward, 1788-1841, English; fiction, plays, nonfiction BU VN
HOOKE, Nina Warner, 1907- , British; fiction, plays, nonfiction CON

HOOKER, Clifford Alan, 1942- ,
Canadian; nonfiction CON
HOOKER, Craig Michael, 1951- ,
American; nonfiction, poetry
CON
HOOKER, Jeremy, 1941- ,
British; poetry, nonfiction
CON VCP
HOOKER, Richard, 1553/54-1600,
English; nonfiction BRI BU
DA PO RU
HOOKER, Ruth, 1920- , Amer-
ican; juveniles CO CON WAR
HOOKER, Thomas, 1586-1647,
American; nonfiction BR
HOOKS, William Harris, 1921- ,
American; juveniles, nonfiction
CO CON
HOOLE, William Stanley, 1903- ,
American; nonfiction ENG
HOOP, Adriaan van der, 1802-41,
Dutch; poetry BU
'HOOPER, Byrd' see ST. CLAIR,
Byrd H.
HOOPER, David Vincent, 1915- ,
British; nonfiction CON
HOOPER, Johnson James, 1815-
62, American; fiction, jour-
nalism BA BR MYE PO VN
HOOPER, Paul Franklin, 1938- ,
American; nonfiction CON
HOOPES, Clement R., 1906-79,
American; nonfiction, tv,
fiction CON
HOOPES, James, 1944- , Amer-
ican; nonfiction CON
HOOPES, Ned Edward, 1932- ,
American; juveniles CO
HOOPES, Roy, 1922- , American;
juveniles CO WAR
HOOPES, Townsend Walter,
1922- , American; nonfiction
CON
HOOPLE, Cheryl G., American;
juveniles WAR
HOOPS, Richard Allen, 1933- ,
American; nonfiction CON
HOORNIK, Eduard Jozef Antonie
Marie, 1910-70, Dutch;
poetry, plays, nonfiction BU
HOOSON, Isaac Daniel, 1880-
1948, Welsh; poetry BU
HOOTEN, William Jarvis, 1900- ,
American; nonfiction CON
HOOVER, Calvin Bryce, 1897-
1974, American; nonfiction
CON
HOOVER, Dorothy Esheryne Mc-

Fadden, 1918- , American;
nonfiction CON SH
HOOVER, Francis Louis, 1913- ,
American; nonfiction CON
HOOVER, Helen Drusill ('Jennifer
Price'), 1910- , American;
juveniles CO
HOOVER, Herbert, 1874-1964,
American; nonfiction CON
PAL
HOOVER, John P., 1910- ,
American; nonfiction CON
HOOVER, Kenneth Harding,
1920- , American; nonfiction
CON
HOOVER, Marjorie Lawson,
1910- , American; nonfiction
CON
HOOVER, Mary Bidgood, 1917- ,
American; nonfiction CON
HOOVER, Thomas, 1941- , Amer-
ican; nonfiction CON
HOPE, Alec Derwent, 1907- ,
Australian; poetry, nonfiction
BU DA VCP VP WA
'HOPE, Amanda' see LEWIS,
Judith M.
'HOPE, Anthony' (Sir Anthony Hope
Hawkins), 1863-1933, English;
fiction DA MAG VN
HOPE, Bob, 1903- , American;
nonfiction CON
HOPE, Jack, 1940- , American;
nonfiction CON
HOPE, Karol, American; nonfiction
CON
HOPE SIMPSON, Jacynth, 1930- ,
English; juveniles CO KI
HOPE-WALLACE, Philip Adrian,
1911-79, British; nonfiction,
journalism CON
HOPF, Alice Lightner ('A. M.
Lightner'), 1904- , American;
juveniles CO NI WAR
'HOPKINS, A. T.' see TURNGREN,
Annette
HOPKINS, Antony, 1921- , British;
nonfiction CON
HOPKINS, Fred Wright, Jr.,
1935- , American; nonfiction
CON
HOPKINS, Gerary Manley, 1844-89,
English; poetry, nonfiction BU
DA MAG PO SEY VP
HOPKINS, J. L., 1938- , Amer-
ican; fiction CON
HOPKINS, John, 1570- , English;
nonfiction BU

HOPKINS, John Feely, 1922- ,
American; fiction CON
HOPKINS, John Richard, 1931- ,
British; plays CON VCD
HOPKINS, Joseph Gerard Ed-
ward, 1909- , American;
juveniles CO
HOPKINS, Joseph Martin, 1919- ,
American; nonfiction CON
HOPKINS, Lee Bennett, 1938- ,
American; juveniles CO
WAR
HOPKINS, Lee Wallace, 1934- ,
American; nonfiction CON
'HOPKINS, Lyman' see FOLSOM,
Franklin B.
HOPKINS, Marjorie, 1911- ,
American; juveniles CO WAR
HOPKINS, Nicholas Snowden,
1939- , American; nonfiction
CON
HOPKINS, Raymond Frederick,
1939- , American; nonfiction
CON
HOPKINS, Robert see 'ROSTAND,
Robert'
HOPKINS, Robert A., 1923- ,
American; nonfiction CON
HOPKINSON, Francis, 1737-91,
American; nonfiction, poetry,
fiction BR BU VP
HOPKINSON, Tom, 1905- ,
British; fiction, nonfiction
VCN
'HOPLEY, George' see WOOLRICH,
Cornel G. H.
HOPPE, Eleanor Sellers, 1933- ,
American; nonfiction CON
HOPPE, Joanne, 1932- , Amer-
ican; fiction CON
HOPPE, Ronald A., 1931- ,
American; nonfiction CON
HOPPER, Hedda, 1890-1966,
American; journalism CON
HOPPER, Robert, 1945- ,
American; nonfiction CON
HOPPER, Vincent Foster, 1906-
76, American; nonfiction,
translations CON
HOPPIN, Richard Hallowell,
1913- , American; nonfiction
CON
HOPSON, Janet Louise (Janet
Hopson Weinberg), 1950- ,
American; nonfiction CON
HOPWOOD, Avery, 1882-1928,
American; journalism, plays
MCG

HORA, Josef, 1891-1945, Czech;
poetry, fiction, journalism
BU CL SEY TH
HORACE (Quintus Horatius Flac-
cius), 65-8 B. C., Latin;
poetry BU GR LA MAG
HORAN, Francis Harding, 1900-78,
American; nonfiction CON
'HORATIO, Algernon,' American;
nonfiction CON
HORATIO-JONES, Edward Babatunde
Bankolé, 1930- , Nigerian;
poetry, plays HER JA
HORDON, Harris Eugene, 1942- ,
American; nonfiction CON
HORGAN, Denis E., 1941- ,
American; journalism CON
HORGAN, John Joseph, 1910- ,
American; nonfiction CON
HORGAN, Paul, 1903- , American;
fiction, plays, juveniles, non-
fiction CO VCN
HORI BAKUSUI, 1718-83, Japanese;
poetry HI
HORI TATSUO, 1904-53, Japanese;
fiction HI
HORIA, Vintila, 1915- , Ruman-
ian; fiction, poetry, nonfiction
WA
HORKHEIMER, Max, 1895-1973,
German-American; nonfiction
CON
HORLER, Sydney, 1888-1954,
English; fiction MCC REI ST
HORMAN, William, 1450-1535,
English; nonfiction BU
HORN, Edward Newman, 1903?-76,
American; fiction, poetry
CON
HORN, Francis Henry, 1908- ,
American; nonfiction CON
HORN, John see TOOKE, John
HORN, Linda Louise, 1947- ,
American; nonfiction CON
HORN, Maurice ('Franck Sauvage'),
1931- , Franco-American;
nonfiction, fiction CON
HORN, Pamela Lucy, 1936- ,
British; nonfiction CON
'HORN, Peter' house name NI
HORN, Peter Rudolf ('Roger Skel-
ton'), 1934- , Czech; poetry,
nonfiction CON
HORN, Stephen McCaffrey,
1931- , American; nonfiction
CON
HORNBAKER, Alice, 1927- ,
American; journalism, non-

HORTENSIUS (Quintus Horten-
sius Hortalus), 114-50 B. C. ,
Roman; nonfiction BU LA
HORTON, George Moses, 1797?-
1883?. , American; poetry
BA
HORTON, James Africanus Beale,
1832/35-83, Sierra Leonese;
nonfiction HER JA
HORTON, Louise, 1916- ,
American; nonfiction CON
HORTON, Lowell, 1936- ,
American; nonfiction CON
HORTON, Patricia Campbell,
1943- , American; fiction
CON
HORTON, Rod William, 1910- ,
American; nonfiction CON
HORTON, Russell M. , 1946- ,
American; nonfiction CON
HORTON, Stanley Monroe,
1916- , American; nonfiction
CON
HORVAT, Branko, 1928- ,
Yugoslav; nonfiction CON
HORVATH, Betty, 1927- , Amer-
ican; juveniles CO WAR
HORVATH, Janos, 1921- ,
Hungarian-American; nonfic-
tion CON
HORVATH, Joan, 1944- ,
Hungarian-American; nonfiction
CON
HORVATH, Ödön, 1901-38, Hun-
garian; plays, fiction BU
CL MCG
HORWICH, Frances Rappaport
('Miss Frances'), 1908- ,
American; juveniles CO WAR
HORWITZ, Elinor Lander, Amer-
ican; juveniles WAR
HORWITZ, Simi Louise, 1949- ,
American; nonfiction CON
HORWITZ, Sylvia Laibman,
1911- , American; nonfiction
CON
HOSEA, late 8th century B. C. ,
Israeli; nonfiction PRU
'HOSEYN Va'eze Kashefi' (Hoseyn
b. Ali Beyhaqi),   -1505,
Persian; poetry PRU
HOSFORD, Dorothy Grant, 1900-
52, American; juveniles CO
WAR
HOSFORD, Jessie, 1892- ,
American; nonfiction, juveniles
CO CON
HOSFORD, Philip Lewis, 1926- ,

American; nonfiction CON
HOSFORD, Ray E. , 1933- ,
American; nonfiction CON
HOSIER, Helen (Kooiman), 1928- ,
American; nonfiction CON
HOSKEN, Clifford J. W. see
'KEVERN, Richard'
HOSKEN, Franziska Porges,
1919- , Austrian-American;
nonfiction CON
HOSKIN, Cyril Henry ('Tuesday
Lobsang Rampa'), 1911?-81,
British; nonfiction CON
HOSKING, Eric John, 1909- ,
British; nonfiction CON
HOSKING, Geoffrey Alan, 1942- ,
Scots; nonfiction CON
HOSKINS, John, 1566-1638, Eng-
lish; poetry BU
HOSKINS, Katharine Bail, 1924- ,
American; nonfiction CON
HOSKINS, Katherine de Montalant,
1909- , American; poetry
VCP
HOSKINS, Robert, 1933- , Amer-
ican; fiction NI
HOSKYNS-ABRAHALL, Clare Con-
stance ('Clare Hoskyn Abrahall'),
English; juveniles CO
HOSMON, Robert Stahr, 1943- ,
American; nonfiction CON
HOSOKAWA YUSAI, 1534-1610,
Japanese; poetry, nonfiction
HI
HOSSENT, Harry, 1916- , English;
fiction MCC
HOSTETLER, Marian, 1932- ,
American; nonfiction CON
HOSTOS, Adolfo de, 1887- ,
Dominican; nonfiction HIL
HOSTOS, Bonilla Eugenio Maria de,
1839-1903, Puerto Rican; non-
fiction BR BU HIL
HOSTOVSKY, Egon, 1908-73,
Czech-American; fiction BU
CL CON TH WA
HOSTRUP, Jens Christian, 1818-92,
Danish; poetry, plays BU
HOTALING, Edward, 1937- ,
American; nonfiction CON
HOTCHNER, Aaron Edward,
1920- , American; nonfiction,
fiction, plays, film CON
HOTCHNER, Tracy, 1950- ,
American; nonfiction CON
'HOTSPUR' see CURLING, Bryan
W. R.
HOTTOIS, James W. , 1943- ,

American; nonfiction CON
HOTZ, Robert Bergmann, 1914-   ,
American; nonfiction, jour-
nalism CON
HOUBRAKEN, Arnold, 1660-1719,
Dutch; nonfiction BU
HOUCHIN, Thomas Douglas,
1925-   , American; nonfiction
CON
HOUCK, Carter, 1924-   , Amer-
ican; juveniles, nonfiction
CO CON
HOUDAR de la MOTTE, Antonie
(Lamotte-Houdar[t]), 1672-
1731, French; plays, poetry
BU TH
HOUEDARD, Pierre Sylvester,
1924-   , British; poetry,
translations CON VCP
HOUFE, Simon Richard, 1942-   ,
British; nonfiction CON
HOUGAN, James Richard, 1942-   ,
American; poetry, nonfiction
CON
HOUGH, Charlotte, 1924-   ,
British; juveniles, poetry
CO KI
HOUGH, Emerson, 1857-1923,
American; journalism, fiction
PAL
HOUGH, Graham Goulder, 1908-   ,
English; nonfiction, poetry
BOR CON WA
HOUGH, Hugh, 1924-   , Amer-
ican; journalism CON
HOUGH, Lindy Downer, 1944-   ,
American; poetry CON
HOUGH, Richard Alexander
('Bruce Carter'), 1922-   ,
English; juveniles CO KI
HOUGH, Stanley Bennett ('Rex
Gordon'; 'Bennett Stanley'),
1917-   , British; fiction,
nonfiction AS NI REI
HOUGHTON, Bernard, 1935-   ,
British; nonfiction CON
HOUGHTON, Charles Norris,
1909-   , American; nonfiction
CON
'HOUGHTON, Claude' (Claude
Houghton Oldfield), 1889-1961,
British; fiction NI
HOUGHTON, Eric, 1930-   ,
English; juveniles CO
HOUGHTON, Richard Monckton
Miles, 1809-85, English;
poetry BU
HOUGHTON, Samuel Gilbert, 1902-

75, American; nonfiction CON
HOUGHTON, William Stanley,
1881-1913, English; plays
MCG VD
HOUK, John L., 1920-   , Ameri-
can; nonfiction MAR
HOULDEN, James Leslie, 1929-   ,
British; nonfiction CON
HOULEHEN, Robert J., 1918-   ,
American; juveniles, nonfiction
CO CON
HOULGATE, Deke, 1930-   , Amer-
ican; nonfiction CON
HOULT, Norah, 1898-   , Irish;
fiction HO SEY
HOURANI, George Fadlo, 1913-   ,
Anglo-American; nonfiction
CON
HOURS, Madeleine (Hours-Miedan;
'Mageleine Hours-Miedan'),
1915-   , French; nonfiction
CON
HOUSE, Charles Albert, 1916-   ,
American; juveniles WAR
HOUSE, Ernest Robert, 1937-   ,
American; nonfiction CON
HOUSE, Humphrey, 1908-55, Eng-
lish; nonfiction WA
HOUSE, Robert J., 1932-   ,
American; nonfiction CON
HOUSE, Robert William, 1920-   ,
American; nonfiction CON
HOUSEHOLD, Geoffrey, 1900-   ,
English; fiction, juveniles CO
CON MCC REI ST VCN WAR
HOUSELANDER, Frances Caryll,
English; juveniles WAR
HOUSEMAN, Barton Leroy, 1933-   ,
American; nonfiction CON
HOUSER, Norman W., American;
juveniles WAR
HOUSMAN, Alfred Edward, 1859-
1936, English; poetry, nonfic-
tion BU DA MAG PO SEY VP
HOUSMAN, Laurence, 1865-1959,
English; plays, fiction, juven-
iles CO DA MCG NI VD
WAR
HOUSSAYES, Jean Baptiste Cotton
des, 1727-83, French; nonfic-
tion ENG
HOUSTON, Beverle Ann, 1936-   ,
American; film, nonfiction
CON
HOUSTON, James Archibald,
1921-   , Canadian; juveniles,
fiction, plays, nonfiction CO
CON DEM KI WAR

American; nonfiction CON
HOWARD, Michel S. , 1922-74,
British; nonfiction CON
'HOWARD, Nona' see LUXTON,
Leonora K.
HOWARD, Philip, 1933- , Eng-
lish; nonfiction CON
'HOWARD, Prosper' see HAMIL-
TON, Charles H. S.
HOWARD, Richard C. , 1929- ,
American; poetry, nonfiction,
translations CON MAL VCP
WA
HOWARD, Sir Robert, 1626-98,
English; plays, poetry, non-
fiction BU VD
HOWARD, Robert, 1926- ,
American; nonfiction CON
HOWARD, Robert Ervin, 1906-
36, American; fiction AS NI
HOWARD, Robert West ('Michael
Case'), 1908- , American;
juveniles CO
HOWARD, Roger, 1938- , British;
plays, fiction, poetry CON
VCD
HOWARD, Ronnalie Roper see
ROPER, Ronnalie R.
HOWARD, Roy Wilson, 1883-1964,
American; journalism CON
HOWARD, Sidney Coe, 1891-
1939, American; plays, film,
fiction BR BU MCG MCN
PO VD
HOWARD, Stanley E. , 1888?-
1980, American; nonfiction
CON
HOWARD, Theodore Korner,
1915- , American; nonfiction
CON
'HOWARD, Troy' see PAINE,
Lauran B.
HOWARD-HILL, Trevor Howard,
1933- , New Zealand-
American; nonfiction CON
HOWARTH, David, 1912- , Eng-
lish; juveniles CO
HOWARTH, Donald, 1931- ,
British; plays VCD
'HOWARTH, John' see HARBINSON,
William A.
HOWARTH, Pamela ('Pamela
Barrow'), 1954- , British;
fiction CON
HOWARTH, Patrick John ('C. D.
E. Francis'), 1916- , British;
nonfiction, fiction, poetry
CON

HOWARTH, William Driver,
1922- , English; nonfiction
CON
HOWAT, Gerald Malcolm David,
1928- , Scots; nonfiction
CON
HOWAT, John Keith, 1937- ,
American; nonfiction CON
HOWATCH, Joseph, 1935- ,
American; fiction CON
HOWATCH, Susan, 1940- ,
Anglo-American; fiction CON
HOWDEN, John of (Hoveden),
-1275, English; poetry BU
HOWDEN, Roger of (Hoveden),
-1201, English; nonfiction BU
HOWE, Charles Horace ('Carleton
Howard'), 1912- , American;
poetry, nonfiction CON
HOWE, Doris Kathleen ('Mary
Munro'; 'Kaye Stewart'; 'New-
lyn Nash'), English; fiction
CON
HOWE, Edgar Watson, 1853-1937,
American; journalism, fiction
BU MAG PO VN
HOWE, George Locke, 1898?-1977,
American; fiction, poetry
CON
HOWE, George Melvyn, 1920- ,
American; nonfiction CON
HOWE, Helen, 1905-75, American;
fiction, nonfiction CON
HOWE, Hubert Shattuck, Jr. ,
1942- , American; nonfiction
CON
HOWE, Irving, 1920- , American;
nonfiction BOR
HOWE, James Robinson, 1935- ,
American; nonfiction, poetry
CON
HOWE, Julia Ward, 1819-1910,
American; poetry, plays, non-
fiction BR MY
HOWE, Mark Anthony DeWolfe,
1864-1960, American; nonfic-
tion CON
HOWE, Quincy, 1900-77, American;
nonfiction CON
HOWE, Richard J. , 1937- ,
American; journalism CON
HOWE, Russell Warren, 1925- ,
English; fiction, nonfiction
CON
HOWE, William Hugh, 1928- ,
American; nonfiction CON
HOWELL, Anthony, 1945- , Brit-
ish; poetry VCP

HOWELL, Barbara, 1937- ,
American; fiction, nonfiction
CON
HOWELL, Benjamin Franklin,
1890-1976, American; non-
fiction CON
HOWELL, Helen Jane, 1934- ,
American; nonfiction CON
HOWELL, Joseph Toy III, 1942- ,
American; nonfiction CON
HOWELL, Pat, 1947- , Amer-
ican; juveniles CO
HOWELL, Patricia (Hagan),
1939- , American; fiction
CON
HOWELL, Richard Wesley,
1926- , American; nonfiction
CON
'HOWELL, S.' see STYLES,
Frank S.
HOWELL, Thomas, fl. 1567-81,
English; poetry BU
HOWELL, Thomas, 1944- ,
American; nonfiction CON
'HOWELL, Virginia Tier' see
ELLISON, Virginia H.
HOWELL, William Carl, 1932- ,
American; nonfiction CON
HOWELLS, James Harvey,
1912- , Scots; fiction, non-
fiction CON
HOWELLS, William Dean, 1837-
1920, American; fiction,
nonfiction, plays AM BR
BU MAG MCG NI PO VN
HOWER, Ralph Merle, 1903-73,
American; nonfiction CON
HOWES, Barbara, 1914- ,
American; poetry, nonfiction,
juveniles BR CO VCP WA
HOWES, Connie B., 1933- ,
American; nonfiction, journal-
ism CON
HOWES, Michael, 1904- , Eng-
lish; nonfiction CON
HOWES, Royce Bucknam, 1901-
73, American; journalism
CON
'HOWITH, Harry' (Marc Wyman),
1934- , Canadian; poetry,
plays VCP
HOWITT, Mary Bothan, 1799-
1888, English; poetry, trans-
lations, juveniles BU
HOWITT, William, 1792-1879,
English; juveniles, poetry
BU
HOWKINS, John, 1945- , English;

nonfiction CON
HOWLAND, Bette, 1937- , Amer-
ican; fiction CON
HOWLAND, Harold Edward, 1913-
80, American; nonfiction CON
HOWLETT, John, 1940- , Eng-
lish; fiction, film CON MCC
HOWSE, Ernest Marshall, 1902- ,
Canadian; nonfiction CON
HOXIE, Ralph Gordon, 1919- ,
American; nonfiction CON
HOY, James Franklin, 1939- ,
American; nonfiction CON
HOYEM, Andrew, 1935- , Amer-
ican; poetry VCP
HOYER, Mildred Naeher, Ameri-
can; poetry CON
HOYLE, Fred, 1915- , British;
fiction, nonfiction AS NI WA
HOYLE, Geoffrey, 1941/42- ,
English; juveniles, fiction
CO CON NI
HOYNE, Thomas Temple, 1875-
1946, American; fiction NI
HOYOS, Angela de, American;
poetry, translations MAR
HOYT, Clark, 1942- , American;
journalism CON
HOYT, Edwin Palmer, 1897-1979,
American; journalism CON
HOYT, Kenneth Boyd, 1924- ,
American; nonfiction CON
HOYT, Olga Gruhzit, 1922- ,
American; juveniles CO WAR
HOZ y MOTA, Juan Claudio de,
1622-1714?, Spanish; plays
BU MCG
HOZENY, Tony, 1946- , Ameri-
can; fiction CON
HOZUMI no MIKO, -715, Japan-
ese; poetry HI
HRABAL, Bohumil, 1914- ,
Czech; fiction, nonfiction BU
CL SEY TH
HRABANUS MAURUS, Magnentius,
780-856, Latin; nonfiction,
poetry GR TH
HRISTIC, Jovan, 1933- , Serbian;
poetry, plays BU
HRISTOV, Kiril, 1875-1944, Bul-
garian; poetry, plays, fiction
TH
HRONSKY, Jozef Ciger, 1896-1961,
Slovak; fiction BU
HROSWITHA (Hrotswitha; Hrosvitha;
Roswitha), 935?-1000?, Latin;
poetry, plays BU GR TH
HRUBIN, František, 1910-71,

Czech; poetry, plays BU
HRUSKA-CORTES, Elias, 1943- ,
American; nonfiction, poetry
CON
HRUSHEVS'KY, Mykhaylo, 1866-
1934, Ukrainian; nonfiction
BU
HRUZA, Zdenek, 1926- ,
Czech-American; nonfiction
CON
HSI-K'ANG, 223-63, Chinese;
nonfiction, poetry BU LA
HSIA, Adrian Rue Chun, 1938- ,
Chinese-Canadian; nonfiction
CON
'HSIA YEN' (Shên Tuan-hsien),
1900- , Chinese; plays BU
PRU
'HSIANG Yeh' see LIU, Sydney C.
HSIAO, Katharine Huei-Ying,
1923- , Chinese-American;
nonfiction CON
HSIAO CH'IEN, 1911- , Chinese;
journalism, fiction BU
'HSIAO CHUN' (T'ien Chün),
1908- , Chinese; fiction BU
HSIAO T'UNG, 501-31, Chinese;
anthology, nonfiction BU
PRU
HSIEH, T'iao, 464-99, Chinese;
poetry BU
HSIEH LING-YÜN, 385-433,
Chinese; poetry, translations
BU PRU
HSIEH PING-YING, 1908- ,
Chinese; nonfiction, fiction
BU
HSIN CH'I-CHI, 1140-1207,
Chinese; poetry BU PRU
'HSING CHING WENG' see
WENG, Wan-go
HSIUNG, Fu-hsi (Fo-hsi), 1900-
65, Chinese; plays BU
HSU, Benedict ('Chu Chung-yu),
1933- , Chinese-American;
journalism, nonfiction CON
HSÜ CHIH-MO, 1896-1931,
Chinese; poetry, nonfiction,
translations BU LA PRU
'HSÜ HSIA-K'O' (Hsü Hung-tsu),
1586-1641, Chinese; nonfiction
BU
HSÜ KUANG-CH'I, 1562-1633,
Chinese; nonfiction BU
HSÜ SHÊN, 1st century, Chinese;
nonfiction BU
HSÜ TI-SHAN, 1893-1941, Chinese;
nonfiction BU PRU

'HSÜAN-TSANG' (Ch'ên I), 600/02-
64, Chinese; nonfiction, trans-
lations BU PRU
HSUEH, Chun-tu, 1922- , Chinese-
American; nonfiction CON
HSÜEH FU-CH'ENG, 1838-94,
Chinese; nonfiction BU
HSÜN-TZU (Hsün K'uang), 300
B. C., Chinese; nonfiction BU
PRU
HTIN, Maun, 1909- , Burmese;
plays, journalism, translations
PRU
HU, Shu Ming ('Shi Ming Hu'),
1927- , Chinese-American;
nonfiction CON
HU, Sze-tsen, 1914- , American;
nonfiction CON
HU FENG (Chang Ku-fei), 1903- ,
Chinese; nonfiction, poetry
BU PRU
HU SHIH, 1891-1962, Chinese; non-
fiction BU PRU
HUANG, Parker Po fei, 1914- ,
Chinese-American; nonfiction,
poetry CON
HUANG, Ray Jen-yu, 1918- ,
Chinese-American; nonfiction
CON
HUANG, Stanley Shang Chien,
1923- , Chinese-American;
nonfiction CON
HUANG, T'ing-chien, 1045-1105,
Chinese; poetry, nonfiction
BU PRU
HUANG TSUN-HSIEN, 1848-1905,
Chinese; poetry, nonfiction
BU PRU
HUANG TSUNG-HSI, 1610-95,
Chinese; nonfiction BU
HUARTE de SAN JUAN, Juan,
1530?-91, Spanish; nonfiction
BU
HUBBARD, Andrew Ray, 1924- ,
American; nonfiction, fiction,
tv CON
HUBBARD, Barbara Marx, 1929- ,
American; nonfiction CON
HUBBARD, Frank T., 1921?-76,
American; nonfiction CON
HUBBARD, Lafayette Ronald
('René Lafayette'; 'Kurt Von
Rachen'), 1911- , American;
fiction AS CON NI
HUBBARD, Philip Maitland, 1910-
80, British; nonfiction, juven-
iles, plays CON REI
HUBBELL, Jay Broadus, 1885-

1979, American; nonfiction
BA
HUBBELL, John Gerard, 1927- ,
American; nonfiction CON
HUBBELL, Patricia, 1928- ,
American; juveniles CO
HUBBS, Carl Leavitt, 1894-1979,
American; nonfiction CON
HUBENKA, Lloyd John, 1931- ,
American; nonfiction CON
HUBENKO, Pavlo see 'VYSHNYA,
Ostap'
HUBER, Joan, 1925- , American;
nonfiction CON
HUBER, Leonard Victor, 1903- ,
American; nonfiction CON
HUBERT, Antonis de, 1583-1636,
Dutch; poetry BU
HUBERT, Sir Francis, 1568/69-
1629, English; poetry BU
HUBERT, James Lee, 1947- ,
American; poetry, nonfiction
CON
HUBERT, Renee Riese, 1916- ,
German-American; nonfiction,
poetry CON
HUBEY, Frederic Soler i see
'PITARRA, Serafi'
HUBIN, Allen J., 1936- , Amer-
ican; nonfiction ST
HUBLER, Herbert Clark, 1910- ,
American; nonfiction CON
HUBLEY, Faith Elliot, 1924- ,
American; film CON
HUBLEY, John, 1914-77, Amer-
ican; juveniles CO
HUC, Evariste Régis, 1813-60,
French; nonfiction BU
HUC, Philippe see 'DEREME,
Tristan'
HUCBALD, of ST. AMAND, 840?-
930, French; nonfiction TH
HUCH, Ricarda ('Richard Hugo'),
1864-1947, German; poetry,
fiction, nonfiction BU CL TH
HUCHEL, Peter, 1903- , Ger-
man; poetry, radio, transla-
tions BU CL CON TH WAK
HUCHOWN, 14th century, Scots;
poetry BU
HUCK, Charlotte S., American;
juveniles WAR
HUCKER, Charles Oscar, 1919- ,
American; nonfiction CON
HUCKLEBERRY, Evermont Rob-
bins, 1894- , American;
nonfiction CON
HUCKSHORN, Robert Jack,

1928- , American; nonfiction
CON
HUDDLE, David, 1942- , Ameri-
can; nonfiction, fiction, poetry
CON
HUDDLESTON, Eugene Lee,
1931- , American; nonfiction
CON
HUDSON, Darril, 1931- , Amer-
ican; nonfiction CON
HUDSON, Geoffrey Francis, 1903-
74, British; nonfiction CON
HUDSON, Gossie Harold, 1930- ,
American; nonfiction CON
HUDSON, Herman, 1923- , Amer-
ican; nonfiction CON
HUDSON, Hosea, American; non-
fiction SH
HUDSON, Jean Barlow, 1915- ,
American; fiction CON
'HUDSON, Jeffery' see CRICHTON,
Michael
'HUDSON, Meg' see KOEHLER,
Margaret H.
HUDSON, Richard McLain, Jr.,
1925- , American; nonfiction
CON
HUDSON, Theodore R., American;
nonfiction CON
HUDSON, William Henry, 1841-
1922, English; nonfiction, fic-
tion BU DA MAG NI PO VN
HUDSON, Wilson Mathis, 1907- ,
American; nonfiction CON
HUDSPETH, Robert N., 1936- ,
American; nonfiction CON
HUE de ROTELANDE, 12th century,
Anglo-Norman; poetry BU
HUEBEL, Harry Russell, 1943- ,
American; nonfiction CON
HUEBNER, Anna Ismelda, 1877-
1974, American; nonfiction
CON
HUEFFER, Ford Madox see
FORD, Ford M.
HÜLSMANN, Eva, 1928- ,
French; juveniles CO
HÜRLIMANN, Bettina, 1909- ,
German; juveniles DE
HUERTA, John Edmund, 1943- ,
American; nonfiction MAR
HUERTA, Jorge Alfonso, 1942- ,
American; nonfiction MAR
HÜSAIN, Mahti, 1909-65, Azerbai-
jan; plays, nonfiction, fiction
PRU
HÜSEYIN, Rahmi Gürpinar, 1864-
1944, Turkish; fiction BU

HUET, Conrad Busken ('Thrasy-
bublus'; 'Een Geabonneerde
op Het Bijblad'; 'Fantasio'),
1826-86, Dutch; nonfiction
BU TH
HUEY, Linda, 1947- , American;
nonfiction CON
HUFANA, Alejandrino G., 1926- ,
Filipino; poetry, plays, non-
fiction CON VCP
HUFF, Afton A. W., 1928- ,
Anglo-American; juveniles,
fiction CON
HUFF, Robert, 1924- , Amer-
ican; poetry VCP
HUFF, Roderick Remmele,
1920- , American; juveniles
WAR
HUFF, Tom E. ('Edwina Marlow';
'Beatrice Parker'; 'Katherine
St. Clair'; 'Jennifer Wilde'),
1938?- , American; fiction
CON
HUFFAKER, Sandy, 1943- ,
American; juveniles CO
HUFFMAN, Carolyn, 1928- ,
American; nonfiction CON
HUFFMAN, James Lamar, 1941- ,
American; nonfiction CON
HUFFMAN, Laurie, 1916- ,
American; fiction CON
HUFFORD, Susan, 1940- ,
American; fiction CON
HUFSCHMIDT, Maynard Michael,
1912- , American; nonfiction
CON
HUG, Bernal Dean, 1896- ,
American; nonfiction CON
HUGGETT, Richard, 1929- ,
English; nonfiction CON
HUGGETT, William Turner,
American; fiction CON
HUGGINS, Nathan Irvin, 1927- ,
American; nonfiction SH
HUGH of ST. VICTOR, 1096-
1141, Saxon; nonfiction BU
HUGH PRIMAS, fl. 1130, Latin;
poetry BU TH
HUGHES, Alan, 1935- , Aus-
tralian; nonfiction CON
HUGHES, Andrew, 1937- ,
Anglo-Canadian; nonfiction
CON
HUGHES, Arthur Montague D'Ur-
ban, 1873-1974, British; non-
fiction CON
HUGHES, Basil Perronet, 1903- ,
English; nonfiction CON

HUGHES, Catharine Rachel,
1935- , American; plays,
nonfiction CON
HUGHES, Charles Campbell,
1929- , American; nonfiction
CON
HUGHES, Daniel Thomas, 1930- ,
American; nonfiction CON
HUGHES, Denis, British?; fiction
NI
HUGHES, Dorothy Belle, 1904- ,
American; fiction, poetry,
nonfiction REI ST
HUGHES, Emmet John, 1920- ,
American; nonfiction CON
HUGHES, Everett Cherrington,
1897- , American; nonfiction
CON
HUGHES, Glyn, 1935- , British;
poetry VCP
HUGHES, Graham, 1928- ,
American; nonfiction CON
HUGHES, Gwilym Fielden, 1899- ,
British; fiction, journalism
CON
HUGHES, Irene Finger, American;
nonfiction CON
HUGHES, Isabelle Grace Bragg,
1912- , Canadian; fiction
CR
HUGHES, James Monroe, 1890-
1971, American; nonfiction
CON
HUGHES, James Wilfred, 1934- ,
American; juveniles CON
HUGHES, John, 1677-1720, English;
plays, nonfiction, translations
BU VD
HUGHES, John ('Ceiriog'), 1832-
87, Welsh; poetry BU DA
HUGHES, John Anthony, 1941- ,
English; nonfiction CON
HUGHES, John Jay, 1928- ,
American; nonfiction CON
HUGHES, John Lewis, 1938- ,
Welsh; fiction, plays CON
HUGHES, John Paul, 1920-74,
American; nonfiction CON
HUGHES, Johnson Donald, 1932- ,
American; nonfiction CON
HUGHES, Jonathan Roberts Tyson,
1928- , American; nonfiction
CON
HUGHES, Judy, 1943- , American;
nonfiction CON
HUGHES, Kathleen W., 1927?-77,
British; nonfiction CON
HUGHES, Langston, 1902-67,

American; poetry, nonfiction,
plays AM BA BR BU CO
DEM MAG MCG MCN PO
RO SEY VCP VP
HUGHES, Leo, 1908- , American;
nonfiction CON
HUGHES, Margaret Kelly, 1894?-
1980, American; nonfiction
CON
HUGHES, Marija Matich, Yugoslav-
American; nonfiction CON
HUGHES, Mary Gray, 1930- ,
American; fiction CON
HUGHES, Monica, 1925- , Eng-
lish; juveniles, nonfiction
CO CON
HUGHES, Patrick, 1939- , Eng-
lish; nonfiction CON
HUGHES, Peter, 1921- , Eng-
lish; juveniles WAR
HUGHES, Richard Arthur Warren,
1900-76, English; fiction,
poetry, plays, juveniles BU
CO CON DA KI MAG SEY
VCN VN
HUGHES, Riley, 1915?-81, Amer-
ican; fiction CON NI
'HUGHES, Sam' see WILKS, Brian
HUGHES, Shirley, 1929- ,
British; juveniles CO CON
KI
HUGHES, Stephen Ormsby,
1924- , English; nonfiction
CON
HUGHES, Ted, 1930- , English;
poetry, fiction, juveniles
BU DA KI NI PO SEY VCP
VP WA WAR
HUGHES, Terry A., 1933- ,
English; nonfiction CON
HUGHES, Thomas, fl. 1587, Eng-
lish; plays BU
HUGHES, Thomas, 1822-96,
English; fiction, nonfiction
BU DA MAG VN
HUGHES, Thomas Mears, 1927- ,
American; nonfiction CON
HUGHES, Thomas Rowland, 1903-
49, Welsh; fiction, poetry
BU
'HUGHES, Virginia' see CAMP-
BELL, Hope
HUGHES, Walter L. see
'WALTERS, Hugh'
'HUGHES, Zack' (Hugh Zachary),
American; fiction NI
HUGO, Herbert W., 1930?-79,
American; nonfiction CON

'HUGO, Richard' see HUCH,
Ricarda
HUGO, Richard Franklin, 1923-82,
American; poetry, nonfiction
CON VCP
HUGO, Victor Marie, 1802-85,
French; poetry, fiction, plays
BU MAG MCG ST TH
HUGO, Count of Montfort, 1357-
1423, German; poetry BU TH
HUGO von TRIMBERG, 1230-1313,
German; nonfiction BU TH
HUGUES de BERGE, 1150?-1219,
French; poetry BU
HUGUES d'OISY, 1150-90, French;
poetry BU
HUI-CHIAO, 497-554, Chinese;
nonfiction PRU
HUIDOBRO, Vicente, 1893-1948,
Chilean; poetry, fiction BR
BU SEY
HUIE, William Bradford, 1910- ,
American; fiction, nonfiction
VCN
HUISKEN, Ronald Herman, 1946- ,
Dutch-American; nonfiction
CON
HUITFELDT, Arild, 1546-1609,
Danish; nonfiction BU
HUIZINGA, Johan, 1872-1945,
Dutch; nonfiction BU MAG
HULBERT, James A., 1906- ,
American; nonfiction SH
HULET, Claude Lyle, 1920- ,
American; nonfiction CON
HULICKA, Karel, 1913- , Czech-
American; nonfiction CON
HULKE, Malcolm, 1924- , Brit-
ish; nonfiction, tv CON
HULL, David Lee, 1935- , Amer-
ican; nonfiction CON
HULL, Edna Mayne, -1975,
American; fiction AS
HULL, Eleanor Means, 1913- ,
American; juveniles CO
'HULL, Eric Traviss' see HAR-
NAN, Terry
HULL, George F., 1909?-74,
American; nonfiction CON
'HULL, H. Braxton' see JACOBS,
Helen H.
HULL, Katharine, 1921-77, British;
juveniles CO
'HULL, Richard' (Richard Henry
Sampson), 1896-1973, English;
fiction REI ST
HULL, Richard Francis Carring-
ton, 1913?-74, British; trans-

lations CON
HULL, Richard W. , 1940- ,
American; nonfiction CON
HULLEY, Clarence Charles,
1905- , Canadian-American;
nonfiction CON
HULME, Hilda Mary, 1914- ,
British; nonfiction CON
HULME, Thomas Ernest, 1883-
1917, English; nonfiction,
poetry DA PO SEY
HULME BEAMAN, Sydney George,
1886-1932, British; juveniles
KI
HULT, Ruby El, 1912- , Amer-
ican; nonfiction CON
HULTS, Dorothy Niebrugge,
1898- , American; juveniles
CO
HUMBARACI, Demir Arslan
('Omar Abdallah'; 'Jean Luc
Herve'), 1923- , British;
nonfiction CON
HUMBERT de MONTMORET,
-1525, French; poetry BU
HUMBLE, Richard, 1945- ,
English; nonfiction CON
HUMBOLDT, Alexander von,
1769-1859, German; nonfiction
BU TH
HUMBOLDT, Karl Wilhelm von,
1767-1835, German; nonfiction
BU TH
HUME, Alexander (Home), 1557?-
1609, Scots; poetry DA VP
HUME, David, 1711-76, Scots;
nonfiction BU DA MAG PO
HUME, Ferguson Wright, 1859-
1932, English; fiction, plays
REI ST
HUME, Kathryn, 1945- , Amer-
ican; nonfiction CON
HUME, Lotta Carswell, American;
juveniles CO
HUME, Paul Chandler, 1915- ,
American; journalism, non-
fiction CON
HUME, Ruth Fox, 1922-80,
American; juveniles, fiction,
nonfiction CO CON
HUMES, James C. , 1934- ,
American; nonfiction CON
HUMPHREY, David Churchill,
1937- , American; nonfiction
CON
HUMPHREY, Henry III, 1930- ,
American; juveniles CO CON
HUMPHREY, Hubert Horatio,

1911-78, American; nonfiction
CON
HUMPHREY, James Earl, 1939- ,
American; poetry CON
HUMPHREY, James Edward,
1918- , American; nonfiction
CON
HUMPHREY, James Harry,
1911- , American; nonfiction
CON
HUMPHREY, Robert L. , 1923- ,
American; nonfiction CON
HUMPHREY, William, 1924- ,
American; fiction, nonfiction
BA BR CON KIB VCN WA
HUMPHREYS, Emyr Owen, 1919- ,
British; fiction, plays, poetry
VCN WA
HUMPHREYS, Travers Christmas,
1901- , British; nonfiction
CON
HUMPHRIES, Mary ('Mary For-
rester'), 1905- , English;
nonfiction CON
HUMPHRIES, Sydney Vernon
('Michael Vane'), 1907- ,
South African; nonfiction CON
HUMPHRY, Derek, 1930- , Eng-
lish; nonfiction CON
HUMPSTONE, Charles Cheney,
1931- , American; nonfiction
CON
HUNDLEY, Daniel Robinson, 1832-
99, American; nonfiction BA
HUNDLEY, Joan Martin, 1921- ,
Australian; nonfiction CON
HUNEKER, James Gibbons, 1860-
1921, American; fiction, non-
fiction BR VN
HUNG SHÊN, 1893-1955, Chinese;
plays BU
HUNG SHÊNG, 1645?-1704, Chinese;
plays, poetry BU LA PRU
HUNGERFORD, Mary Jane,
1913- , American; nonfiction
CON
'HUNGERFORD, Pixie' see BRINS-
MEAD, Hesba F.
HUNKIN, Timothy Mark Trelawney,
1950- , British; juveniles
CON
HUNKINS, Francis Peter, 1938- ,
American; nonfiction CON
HUNNIS, William, -1597, Eng-
lish; poetry BU
HUNSBERGER, Warren Seabury,
1911- , American; nonfiction
CON

HUNSINGER, George, 1945- ,
American; nonfiction, trans-
lations CON
'HUNT, Clarence' see HOLMAN,
Clarence H.
HUNT, David Charles Hadden,
1926- , American; nonfiction
CON
HUNT, David Curtis, 1935- ,
American; nonfiction CON
HUNT, David Wathen, 1913- ,
British; nonfiction CON
HUNT, E. K., 1937- , Amer-
ican; nonfiction CON
HUNT, Earl B., 1933- , Amer-
ican; nonfiction CON
HUNT, Earl Wilbur, 1926- ,
American; juveniles CON
HUNT, Everette Howard ('John
Baxter'; 'Gordon Davis';
'Robert Dietrich'; 'David St.
John'), 1914/18- , American;
fiction CON MCC ST
HUNT, Frazier, 1885-1967,
American; journalism CON
HUNT, George Laird, 1918- ,
American; nonfiction CON
'HUNT, Gill' house name NI
'HUNT, Gill' see TUBB, Edwin C.
'HUNT, Harrison' see BALLARD,
Willis T.
HUNT, Herbert James, 1899-
1973, British; nonfiction
CON
HUNT, Irene, 1907- , American;
juveniles DE KI
HUNT, J. William, Jr., 1930- ,
American; nonfiction CON
HUNT, James Gerald, 1932- ,
American; nonfiction CON
HUNT, James Henry Leigh,
1784-1859, English; nonfic-
tion, poetry, journalism
BU DA MAG PO VN
'HUNT, John' see PAINE, Lauran
B.
HUNT, John Dixon, 1936- ,
British; nonfiction CON
HUNT, June, 1944- , American;
nonfiction CON
HUNT, Kari Eleanor B.,
1920- , American; nonfiction
CON
'HUNT, Kyle' see CREASEY,
John
HUNT, Leon Gibson, 1931- ,
American; nonfiction CON
HUNT, Mabel Leigh, 1892-1971,

American; juveniles KI
HUNT, Morton, 1920- , Ameri-
can; juveniles CO
HUNT, Nancy Ridgely, 1927- ,
American; nonfiction CON
HUNT, Noreen, 1931- , British;
nonfiction CON
HUNT, Patricia Joan, British;
juveniles CON
HUNT, Richard Paul, 1921- ,
American; journalism CON
HUNT, Sam, 1946- , New Zea-
lander; poetry, juveniles
VCP
HUNT, Violet, 1866-1942, English;
fiction DA
HUNT, Virginia Lloyd, 1888?-
1977, American; nonfiction
CON
HUNT, William, 1934- , Amer-
ican; poetry CON
HUNT, William Raymond, 1929- ,
American; nonfiction CON
HUNTER, Alan James Herbert,
1922- , English; poetry, fic-
tion REI ST
HUNTER, C. Bruce, 1917- ,
Canadian; nonfiction CON
'HUNTER, Dave' see DOWNIE,
Mary A.
HUNTER, Edward, 1902-78, Amer-
ican; journalism, nonfiction
CON
'HUNTER, Evan' (S. A. Lombino;
'Richard Marsten'; 'Hunt Col-
lins'; 'Ed McBain'; 'Curt Can-
non'; 'Ezra Hannon'), 1926- ,
American; fiction, plays,
juveniles BR CO NI REI SEY
ST VCN WA
HUNTER, Hilda, 1921- , English;
juveniles, nonfiction CO CON
WAR
HUNTER, Howard Eugene, 1929- ,
American; nonfiction CON
HUNTER, James Hogg, 1890- ,
Scots; journalism, nonfiction,
juveniles CON
HUNTER, Jim, 1939- , British;
fiction VCN
HUNTER, Kim ('Janet Cole'),
1922- , American; nonfiction
CON
HUNTER, Kristin, 1931- ,
American; fiction, juveniles,
plays CO DEM KI SH VCN
HUNTER, Louise Harris, American;
nonfiction CON

HUNTER, Marjorie, 1922- ,
American; journalism CON
HUNTER, Mel, 1927/29- ,
American; illustrations, juven-
iles AS CON
HUNTER, Mollie, 1922- , Scots;
juveniles, plays, nonfiction
DE KI
HUNTER, Norman Charles, 1908-
71, English; plays, fiction
VD
HUNTER, Norman George, 1899- ,
British; juveniles, nonfiction
CON KI NI
'HUNTER, Patrick' see SAMMIS,
John
'HUNTER, Paul' see WEAVER,
Bertrand
HUNTER, Robert Edwards,
1940- , American; nonfiction
CON
HUNTER, Robert Grams, 1927- ,
American; nonfiction CON
HUNTER, Stephen, 1946- ,
American; fiction CON
HUNTER, Tim, 1947- , Amer-
ican; fiction CON
HUNTER, William Bridges, Jr.,
1915- , American; nonfiction
CON
HUNTER BLAIR, Pauline Clarke
('Pauline Clarke'; 'Helen
Clare'), 1921- , English;
juveniles CO DE KI
HUNTING, Constance, 1925- ,
American; poetry, translations
CON
HUNTING, Gardner, 1872-1958,
American; fiction NI
HUNTINGTON, Henry S., Jr.,
1892-1981, American; nonfic-
tion CON
HUNTINGTON, Thomas Waterman,
1893-1973, American; nonfic-
tion CON
HUNTLEY, Chet, 1911-74, Amer-
ican; journalism, nonfiction
CON
HUNTLEY, James Lewis, 1914- ,
American; nonfiction CON
HUNTLEY, Timothy Wade,
1939- , American; nonfiction
CON
HUNTSBERRY, William Emery,
1916- , American; juveniles
CO
HUON de MERY, 13th century,
French; poetry BU

HUON le ROI de CAMBRAI, 13th
century, French; poetry BU
HUONDER, Gion Antoni, 1824-67,
Raeto-Romansch; poetry BU
HUPKA, Robert, 1919- , Aus-
trian-American; nonfiction
CON
HURBAN, Jozef Miloslav, 1817-88,
Slovak; fiction, poetry, nonfic-
tion BU
HURD, Douglas, 1930- , English;
fiction MCC
HURD, Florence ('Fiona Harrowe';
'Flora Hiller'), 1918- , Amer-
ican; fiction CON
HURD, Michael John, 1928- ,
English; nonfiction CON
HURD, Richard, 1720-1808, Eng-
lish; nonfiction DA PO
HURLEY, Alfred Francis, 1928- ,
American; nonfiction CON
HURLEY, Forrest Jack, 1940- ,
American; nonfiction CON
HURLEY, John J. see 'RAFFERTY,
S. S.'
HURLEY, Leslie John, 1911- ,
American; nonfiction CON
HURLEY, Mark Joseph, Jr.,
1919- , American; nonfiction
CON
HURLEY, Vic ('Jimm Duane';
'Duane Richards'), 1898-1978,
American; journalism, fiction
CON
HURLEY, Wilfred Geoffrey, 1895-
1973, American; nonfiction
CON
HURLOCK, Elizabeth B., 1898- ,
American; nonfiction CON
'HURMUZ' see 'URMUZ'
HURSCH, Carolyn Judge, American;
nonfiction CON
HURST, Charles G., Jr., Ameri-
can; nonfiction SH
HURST, George Cameron III,
1941- , American; transla-
tions, nonfiction CON
HURST, Norman, 1944- , Amer-
ican; nonfiction CON
HURST, Richard Maurice, 1938- ,
American; nonfiction CON
HURST, Virginia (Radcliffe), 1914?-
76, American; nonfiction CON
HURSTFIELD, Joel, 1911-80, Eng-
lish; nonfiction CON
HURSTON, Zora Neale, 1903-60,
American; fiction, plays BA
CON VN

HURT, Freda Mary Elizabeth, 1911- , American; fiction, juveniles, plays CON
HURT, James, 1934- , American; nonfiction CON
HURTADO, Juan, 1930- , American; nonfiction MAR
HURTADO de MENDOZA, Antonio, 1586-1644, Spanish; poetry, plays BU TH
HURTADO de MENDOZA, Diego, 1503-75, Spanish; poetry, nonfiction BU TH
HURTADO de TOLEDO, Luis, 1523-90, Spanish; plays, nonfiction BU
HURTGEN, Andre Oscar, 1932- , Belgian-American; nonfiction CON
HURWITZ, Johanna, 1937- , American; juveniles CO CON
HURWITZ, Stephen, 1901-81, Danish; nonfiction CON
HURWOOD, Bernardt J. ('Mallory T. Knight'; 'D. Gunther Wilde'; 'Father Xavier'), 1926- , American; juveniles CO
HUS, Jan, 1371?-1415, Czech; nonfiction BU TH
HUSAIN, Muhammad Kamil, 1901- , Egyptian; nonfiction, fiction BU
HUSAR, John, 1937- , American; journalism CON
HUSBAND, William Hollow, 1899?-1978, British; nonfiction CON
HUSSEIN, Taha, 1889-1973, Egyptian; nonfiction CON
HUSSERL, Edmund, 1859-1938, German; nonfiction WA
HUSSEY, David Edward, 1934- , English; nonfiction, juveniles CON
HUSSEY, John Adam, 1913- , American; nonfiction CON
HUSSON, Albert, 1912- , French; plays MCG
HUSSON, Jules see 'CHAMP-FLEURY'
HUSSOVIUS, Mikolaj (Hussowski), 1475/85-1533, Polish; poetry BU
HUSTE, Annemarie, 1943- , German; nonfiction CON
HUSTED, Darrell, 1931- , American; fiction CON

'HUSTON, Fran' see MILLER, R. S.
HUSTON, James Alvin, 1918- , American; nonfiction CON
HUSTON, John Marcellus, 1906- , American; film, plays CON
HUSTON, Mervyn James, 1912- , Canadian; nonfiction CON
HUTCHCROFT, Vera ('Vernon Richter'), 1923- , American; juveniles, nonfiction CON
HUTCHENS, John Kennedy, 1905- , American; nonfiction CON
HUTCHENS, Paul, 1902- , American; fiction, juveniles CON
HUTCHESON, Francis, 1694-1746, Irish; nonfiction BU DA
HUTCHINGS, Patrick Aelfred, 1929- , New Zealander; nonfiction CON
HUTCHINS, Carleen Maley, 1911- , American; juveniles CO
HUTCHINS, Frank Avery, 1851-1915, American; nonfiction ENG
HUTCHINS, Maude Phelps McVeigh, 1889?- , American; nonfiction, fiction, poetry CON VCN WA
HUTCHINS, Patricia, 1942- , English; juveniles CO CON DEM
HUTCHINS, Robert Maynard, 1899-1977, American; nonfiction CON
HUTCHINS, Ross Elliott, 1906- , American; juveniles CO DE
HUTCHINSON, Alfred, 1924-72, Nigerian; nonfiction, plays, fiction HER JA
HUTCHINSON, Arthur Stuart Menteth, 1879-1971, English; fiction, nonfiction MAG
HUTCHINSON, Eliot Dole, 1900- , American; nonfiction CON
HUTCHINSON, George, 1920-80, British; journalism, nonfiction CON
HUTCHINSON, John, 1921- , Anglo-American; nonfiction CON
HUTCHINSON, Lucy Apsley, 1619/20-76, English; nonfiction, translations BU
HUTCHINSON, Pearse, 1927- , Irish; poetry, translations CON HO VCP

HUTCHINSON, Peter, 1943- ,
English; nonfiction CON
HUTCHINSON, Ray Coryton, 1907-
75, British; fiction CON
VCN
HUTCHINSON, Richard Wyatt,
1894-1970, British; nonfiction
CON
HUTCHINSON, Thomas, 1711-80,
American; nonfiction BR
HUTCHINSON, Vernal, 1922- ,
American; nonfiction CON
HUTCHINSON, William Kenneth,
1945- , American; nonfiction
CON
HUTCHISON, Bruce, 1901- ,
Canadian; nonfiction CON
HUTCHISON, Dorothy Dwight,
1890?-1975, American; fic-
tion, nonfiction CON
HUTCHISON, John Alexander,
1912- , American; nonfiction
CON
HUTH, Angela, 1938- , British;
fiction, tv CON
HUTH, Mary Josephine, 1929- ,
American; nonfiction CON
HUTH, Tom, 1941- , American;
journalism, fiction CON
HUTHISON, Bruce, 1901- ,
Canadian; journalism, nonfic-
tion BU CR
HUTHMACHER, J. Joseph, 1929- ,
American; juveniles CO
HUTSCHNECKER, Arnold A.,
1898- , Austrian-American;
nonfiction CON
HUTSON, Anthony Brian Austen,
1934- , British; nonfiction
CON
HUTSON, James Howard, 1937- ,
American; nonfiction CON
HUTSON, Joan, 1929- , Ameri-
can; nonfiction CON
HUTT, Max L. , 1908- , Amer-
ican; nonfiction CON
HUTT, William Harold, 1899- ,
Anglo-American; nonfiction
CON
HUTTEN, Ulrich von, 1488-1523,
German; nonfiction BU TH
HUTTIG, Jack Wilfred, 1919- ,
American; nonfiction CON
HUTTO, Nelson Allen, 1904- ,
American; juveniles CO
HUTTON, Geoffrey, 1928- ,
English; nonfiction CON
'HUTTON, Ginger' see HUTTON,

Virginia
HUTTON, Harold, 1912- , Amer-
ican; nonfiction CON
HUTTON, James, 1902- , Scots;
nonfiction CON
HUTTON, Richard Holt, 1826-97,
English; nonfiction BU
HUTTON, Virginia Carol ('Ginger
Hutton'), 1940- , American;
journalism CON
HUTTON, Warwick, 1939- , Eng-
lish; juveniles, nonfiction
CO CON
HUVOS, Kornel, 1913- , Hun-
garian-American; translations,
nonfiction CON
HUWS, Daniel, 1932- , Welsh;
poetry, nonfiction CON VCP
HUXHOLD, Harry Norman,
1922- , American; nonfiction
CON
HUXLEY, Aldous Leonard, 1894-
1963, English; fiction, nonfic-
tion, poetry, plays AS BU
CON DA MAG NI PO SEY VN
HUXLEY, Elspeth, 1907- , Eng-
lish; fiction, nonfiction CON
REI ST WA
HUXLEY, Sir Julian ('Balbus'),
1887-1975, English; nonfiction,
poetry CON DA MAG
HUXLEY, Thomas Henry, 1825-95,
English; nonfiction BU DA
MAG PO
HUYCK, Dorothy Boyle, 1925?-79,
American; nonfiction, journal-
ism CON
HUYCK, Margaret Hellie, 1939- ,
American; nonfiction CON
HUYDECOPER, Balthazar, 1695-
1778, Dutch; nonfiction, poetry,
plays BU
HUYGEN, Wilibrord Joseph,
1922- , Dutch; nonfiction
CON
HUYGENS, Constantijn, 1596-1687,
Dutch; poetry, nonfiction BU
TH
HUYGHE, Rene, 1906- , French;
nonfiction CON
HUYKE, Juan B. , 1880-1961,
Puerto Rican; journalism HIL
HUYLER, Jean Wiley, 1935- ,
American; nonfiction CON
HUYSMAN, Roelof see AGRICOLA,
Rudolf
HUYSMANS, Joris Karl, 1848-1907,
French; fiction BU CL MAG

SEY TH
HUZAR, Eleanor Goltz, 1922- ,
American; nonfiction CON
'HVIEZDOSLAV' (Pavel Or száżgh),
1849-1921, Slovak; poetry,
plays BU TH
HWANG CHIN-I, 1516- , Korean;
poetry PRU
HYAM, Ronald, 1936- , British;
nonfiction CON
HYAMS, Edward Solomon, 1910-
75, English; fiction, nonfic-
tion, journalism, translations
CON NI WA
HYATT, Carole S. , 1935- ,
American; nonfiction CON
HYATT, Richard Herschel,
1944- , American; journal-
ism, nonfiction CON
HYBELS, Saundra, 1938- ,
American; nonfiction CON
HYDE, Dayton Ogden ('Hawk
Hyde'), American; juveniles
CO WAR
HYDE, Douglas (De hide, Dubh-
ghlas), 1860-1949, Irish;
poetry, nonfiction, transla-
tions BU DA HO
HYDE, Edward, Earl of Claren-
don, 1609-74, English; non-
fiction BU DA MAG PO RU
'HYDE, Eleanor' see COWEN,
Frances
'HYDE, Hawk' see HAWK, Dayton
O.
HYDE, Janet Shibley, 1948- ,
American; nonfiction CON
HYDE, Laurence Evelyn, 1914- ,
British; juveniles, fiction
KI
HYDE, Margaret O. , 1917- ,
American; juveniles DE
HYDE, Mary Morley Crapo,
1912- , American; nonfiction
CON
'HYDE, Robin' (Iris Guiver Wilkin-
son), 1906-39, New Zealander;
fiction, poetry SEY VN
HYDE, Stuart Wallace, 1923- ,
American; nonfiction CON
'HYDE, Tracy E. ' see VENNING,
Corey
HYDE, Wayne Frederick, 1922- ,
American; juveniles CO
HYDEN, Goeran, 1938- , Swedish;
nonfiction CON
HYECH'O, 8th century, Korean;
nonfiction PRU

HYER, James Edgar, 1923- ,
American; nonfiction, juveniles
CON
HYGENUS, Gaius Julius, 64 B. C. -
17 A. D. , Latin; nonfiction
BU GR LA
HYINK, Bernard Lynn, 1913- ,
American; nonfiction CON
HYLAND, Drew Alan, 1939- ,
American; nonfiction CON
HYLAND, Henry Stanley, 1914- ,
British; fiction, nonfiction
REI
HYLAND, Jean Scammon, 1926- ,
American; nonfiction CON
HYLANDER, Clarence John, 1897-
1964, American; juveniles
CO
HYMAN, Alan, 1910- , British;
journalism, nonfiction, film,
plays CON
HYMAN, Ann, 1936- , American;
fiction, nonfiction CON
HYMAN, David Neil, 1943- ,
American; nonfiction CON
HYMAN, Irwin Abraham, 1935- ,
American; nonfiction CON
HYMAN, Lawrence, 1919- ,
American; nonfiction CON
HYMAN, Linda, American; juven-
iles WAR
HYMAN, Paula, 1946- , American;
nonfiction CON
HYMAN, Richard Joseph, 1921- ,
American; nonfiction CON
HYMAN, Robin Philip, 1931- ,
English; nonfiction, juveniles
CO CON
HYMAN, Sidney, 1917- , Amer-
ican; nonfiction CON
HYMAN, Stanley Edgar, 1919-70,
American; nonfiction BOR BR
CON WA
HYMAN, Trina Schart, 1939- ,
American; juveniles CO CON
DEM
HYMANS, Jacques Louis, 1937- ,
Dutch-American; nonfiction
CON
HYMES, Lucia Manley, 1907- ,
American; juveniles CO
HYNAM, John C. see 'KIPPAX,
John'
HYND, Alan, 1904?-74, American;
nonfiction CON
HYNDMAN, Donald William,
1936- , Canadian-American;
nonfiction CON

HYNDMAN, Jane Andrews Lee
('Lee Wyndham'), 1912-78,
American; journalism, juven-
iles CO CON KI
HYNDMAN, Robert Utley ('Robert
Wyndham'), 1906?-73, Amer-
ican; juveniles, nonfiction
CO CON WAR
HYNDS, Frances Jane, 1929- ,
American; nonfiction CON
HYNE, Charles John Cutliffe,
1866-1944, English; fiction
NI ST
HYNEK, Josef Allen, 1910- ,
American; nonfiction CON
HYPERIDES, 389-23 B. C.,
Greek; nonfiction BU GR
LA
HYRY, Antti Kalevi, 1931- ,
Finniah; fiction TH
HYSLOP, Beatrice F., 1900?-73,
American; nonfiction CON
HYSLOP, Lois Boe, 1908- ,
American; nonfiction, trans-
lations CON

I

IACONE, Salvatore Joseph,
1945- , American; nonfiction
CON
IACUZZI, Alfred, 1896-1977,
Italian-American; nonfiction
CON
IAMBLICHUS, 250-325, Greek;
nonfiction BU GR LA
IAMBULUS, Greek; nonfiction LA
IAMS, Jack, 1910- , American;
fiction REI ST
IANNI, Francis Anthony, 1926- ,
American; nonfiction CON
IANNONE, Jeanne Koppel ('Gina
Bell'; 'Gina Bell-Zano'),
American; juveniles CO
IANNONE, Ronald Vincent, 1940- ,
American; nonfiction CON
IANNUZZI, John Nicholas, 1935- ,
American; fiction CON REI
IASHVILI, Paolo, 1894-1937,
Georgian; poetry PRU
'IBARA SAIKAKU' (Hirayama
Togo), 1642-93, Japanese;
poetry, fiction BU MAG
IBARBOUROU, Juana de, 1895- ,
Uruguayan; poetry BR BU
'IBARRA, Cristomo' see YABES,
Leopoldo

IBBOTSON, Eva, 1925- , Austrian-
American; juveniles CO CON
IBBOTSON, M. Christine, 1930- ,
English; juveniles CO
IBINGIRA, Grace Stuart Kate-
barirwe, 1932- , Ugandan;
nonfiction CON
IBN ABD RABBIHI, 860-940,
Arab; poetry BU PRU
IBN ABDUN, -1134, Arab; poetry
BU
IBN al-ARABI, Muhyi-al-Din, 1165-
1240, Arab; nonfiction BU
LA
IBN al-ATHIR, Izz al-Din, 1160-
1233, Arab; nonfiction BU
IBN al-FARID, Umar, 1181-1235,
Arab; poetry BU PRU
IBN al-MUQAFFA, 720-57, Arab;
translations, nonfiction BU
PRU
IBN al-MU'TAZZ, Abu'l-Abbas,
861-908, Arab; poetry, non-
fiction, anthology BU PRU
IBN al-NADIM, Abu al-Faraj,
-995/98, Arab; nonfiction BU
IBN al-RUMI, 836-90, Arab; poetry
BU
IBN BAJJA, Abu Bakr Muhammad,
-1138, Arab; nonfiction PRU
IBN BATTUTAH, Muhammad Ibn,
1304-68/77, Arab; nonfiction
BU LA PRU
IBN DA'UD, Abraham, 1110-80?,
Spanish; nonfiction, fiction
BU
IBN EZRA, Baraham Ben Meir,
1093-1167, Hebrew; poetry,
nonfiction BU LA TH
IBN EZRA, Moses, 1060-1139,
Hebrew; poetry, nonfiction
BU TH
IBN FARIS, Abu'l Husayn (Qazwani
ar-Razi), -1004?, Arab;
nonfiction PRU
IBN GABIROL see GABIROL, Solo-
mon ben J.
IBN HASDAI, Abraham, -1240,
Hebrew; poetry TH
IBN HAZM, Ali Ahmad, 994-1064,
Arab; poetry, nonfiction BU
LA PRU
IBN-i-YAMIN, Amir Mahmud,
1367- , Persian; poetry BU
IBN JUBAIR, Abu al-Hasan, 1145-
1217, Arab; nonfiction BU
IBN KHALDUN, Abd-al-Rahman,
1332-1406, Arab; nonfiction

BU LA PRU
IBN KHALLIKAN, Ahmad ibn
Muhammad, 1211-82, Arab;
nonfiction LA PRU
IBN QUTAIBAN, Abu Muhammad,
828-89, Arab; nonfiction
BU PRU
IBN QUZMAN,   -1160, Arab;
poetry BU
IBN RUSHD, Abu'l-Walid Muham-
mad, 1126-98, Arab; non-
fiction BU PRU
IBN SINA (Avicenna), 980-1037,
Muslim; nonfiction BU LA
PRU
IBN TAYMIYYA, Taqi al-Din
Ahmad, 1263-1328, Arab;
nonfiction PRU
IBN TUFAYL, Abu Bakr Muham-
mad, 1105-85, Arab; non-
fiction BU PRU
IBN ZAIDUN, 394-463, Arab;
poetry BU
IBRAHIM, Abdel-Sattar, 1939- ,
Egyptian-American; nonfiction
CON
IBRAHIM, Hafiz, 1870-1932,
Egyptian; poetry PRU
IBRAHIMI, Bashir, 1889-1965,
Algerian; nonfiction PRU
IBRAHIMOV, Mirzä, 1911- ,
Azerbaijan; plays, fiction
PRU
IBRAILEANU, Garabet, 1871-1936,
Rumanian; nonfiction BU CL
IBSEN, Henrik Johan, 1828-1906,
Norwegian; plays, poetry
BU CL MAG MCG TH
IBUKUN, Olu, 1945?- , Nigerian;
fiction HER
IBUKA, Masaru, 1908- ,
Japanese; nonfiction CON
IBUSE MASUJI, 1898- , Japanese;
fiction BU LA SEY
IBYCUS, late 6th century B. C. ,
Greek; poetry BU GR LA
ICAZA, Francisco A. de, 1863-
1925, Mexican; poetry BU
ICAZA, Jorge, 1906-79, Ecuador-
ean; fiction, plays BR BU
CON MAG
ICHIJO KANERA (Kaneyoshi),
1402-81, Japanese; poetry,
nonfiction HI
I-CHING (Chang Wên-ming), 635-
713, Chinese; translations,
nonfiction BU PRU
ICKS, Robert Joseph, 1900- ,

American; nonfiction, juveniles
CON WAR
ID, Muhammad Ali Khalifa,
1904- , Algerian; poetry
PRU
IDDON, Don, 1913?-79, British;
journalism CON
'IDEN, William' see GREEN, Wil-
liam M.
IDLEY, Peter, fl. 1450- , Eng-
lish; poetry BU
IDRIESS, Ion L. , 1891?-1979,
Australian; nonfiction CON
IDRIS, Yusuf, 1927- , Egyptian;
fiction, plays BU PRU
IDRISI, 1100-65, Arab; nonfiction
PRU
IDRUS, 1921- , Indonesian; po-
etry, journalism, fiction,
plays PRU
IESMANIASITA, Sulislyautami,
1933- , Javanese; poetry,
fiction PRU
'IEVAN GLAN GEIRIONYDD' (Evan
Evans), 1795-1855, Welsh;
poetry BU
IFETAYO, Femi Funni, American;
nonfiction SH
IFFLAND, August Wilhelm, 1759-
1814, German; plays BU MCG
TH
IFFT, James Brown, 1935- ,
American; nonfiction CON
IFKOVIC, Edward, 1943- , Amer-
ican; nonfiction CON
IGARASHI CHIKARA, 1874-1947,
Japanese; nonfiction HI
IGGULDEN, John, 1917- , Aus-
tralian; fiction NI
IGLAUER, Edith, American; non-
fiction CON
IGLESIAS, Mario, 1924- , Cuban-
American; nonfiction CON
IGLESIAS de la CASA, José, 1748-
91, Spanish; poetry BU TH
IGLESIES, Ignasi, 1871-1928,
Catalan; plays CL
IGLITZIN, Lynne, 1931- , Amer-
ican; nonfiction CON
IGNATIUS, St. ,   -107/10 A. D. ,
Greek; nonfiction GR
IGNATIUS the DEACON, early 9th
century, Byzantine; poetry,
nonfiction LA
IGNATOW, David, 1914- , Amer-
ican; poetry BR MAL VCP
WA
IGNJATOVIC, Jakob, 1824-88,

Serbian; fiction BU TH
'IGNOTUS' (Hugó Veigelsberg),
1869-1949, Hungarian; poetry
BU
IGNOTUS, Paul, 1901-78, Hungarian-British; journalism,
nonfiction CON
IHARA SAIHAKU, 1642-92/93,
Japanese; poetry, fiction
HI LA PRU
IHIMAERA, Witi, 1944- , New
Zealander; fiction, nonfiction
CON VCN
IIDA see 'SOGI'
IIDA DAKOTSU, 1885-1962,
Japanese; poetry HI
IINO, David Norimoto, 1910- ,
Japanese; nonfiction CON
'IJIMERE, Obotunde' (Ulli Beier),
German; plays, nonfiction
HER JA
IKASIA see CASIA
IKE, Vincent Chukwuemeka,
1931- , Nigerian; fiction
HER JA
IKEDA, Daisaku, 1928- , Japanese; nonfiction CON
IKELLE-MATIBA, Jean, 1936- ,
Cameroonian; fiction, non-
fiction, poetry HER JA
IKENBERRY, Oliver Samuel,
1908- , American; nonfiction
CON
IKETANI SHINZABURO, 1900-33,
Japanese; fiction, plays BU
IKIDDEH, Ime, 1938- , Nigerian;
plays, poetry, fiction HER
JA
IKKYU SOJUN, 1394-1481,
Japanese; nonfiction, poetry
HI
IKLE, Fred Charles, 1924- ,
American; nonfiction CON
IKO, Momoko, 1940- , American;
plays, film CON
IKROMI, Jalol, 1909- , Tajik;
plays, fiction PRU
IKUTA CHOKO, 1882-1936,
Japanese; nonfiction, fiction,
plays, translations HI
ILANKO, 2?-5?th centuries,
Tamil; poetry LA
ILANKOVATIKAL, 5-6th centuries,
Tamil; poetry PRU
ILARDO, Joseph Anthony, 1944- ,
American; nonfiction CON
ILARION, Metropolitan of Kiev,
fl. 1050, Russian; nonfiction

BU TH
ILDEFONSUS of TOLEDO, 1607-67,
Spanish; hymns TH
'ILES, Bert' see ROSS, Zola H.
'ILES, Francis' see 'BERKELEY,
Anthony'
'IL'F' (I. A. Fainzelberg; 'Yevgeniy Petrov'; 'Yevgeniy Petrovich Katayev'), 1897-1937/39,
Russian; fiction BU CL TH
ILGEN, Pedro Reinhold, 1869-
1926, German-American;
poetry BU
ILIC, Vojislaw, 1860-94, Serbian;
poetry BU TH
ILLAKOWICZOWNA, Kazimiera,
1892- , Polish; poetry BU
CL
ILLAN, Jose Manuel, 1924- ,
Cuban-American; nonfiction
CON
ILLES, Robert Enoch, 1914- ,
American; nonfiction CON
ILLIANO, Antonio, 1934- ,
Italian-American; nonfiction,
translations CON
ILLICH, Ivan D., 1926- , Austrian-Mexican; nonfiction CON
ILLINGWORTH, John, 1904-80,
British; nonfiction CON
ILLYES, Gyula, 1902- , Hungarian;
poetry, plays, fiction, nonfiction BU CL MCG TH WA
ILMI, Bownderi (Elmi), 1903?-
38?, Somali; poetry HER LA
ILSLEY, Velma Elizabeth, 1918- ,
Canadian-American; juveniles
CO
ILUMILKU, 14th century B.C.,
Ugarit; fiction PRU
'UN ILUSTRADO' see MORALES,
José P.
ILYIN, M. A. see 'OSORGIN,
Mikhail A. '
IMAGAWA RYOSHUN, 1326- ,
Japanese; poetry HI
IMAMURA, Shigeo, 1922- , American; nonfiction CON
IMBER, Gerald, 1941- , American;
nonfiction CON
IMBER, Naftali Hertz, 1856-1902,
Hebrew; poetry BU TH
IMBS, Bravig, 1904-46, American;
nonfiction, poetry, fiction
RO
IMFELD, Al, 1935- , Swiss; nonfiction CON
IMLAY, Gilbert, 1754?-1828?,

American; fiction BR
IMMANUEL ben SOLOMON (Mano-
ello Giudeo), 1268/72-1328?,
Italian; poetry BU
IMMERMAN, Leon Andrew,
1952- , American; nonfiction
CON
IMMERMANN, Karl Lebrecht,
1796-1840, German; plays,
fiction, poetry BU MCG TH
IMMERZEEL, Johannes, Jr.,
1776-1841, Dutch; nonfiction,
poetry BU
IMMOOS, Thomas, 1918- ,
Swiss; poetry, nonfiction
CON
IMPERIAL, Micer Francisco,
early 15th century, Spanish;
poetry BU TH
IMRU'U'L-QAIS (Amru'u'l-Qais,
ibn Hujr), -540?, Arab;
poetry BU LA PRU
INALCIK, Halil, 1916- , Turk-
ish-American; nonfiction CON
INAWASHIRO KENSAI, 1452-1510,
Japanese; poetry HI
INAYAT-KHAN, Pir Vilayat,
1916- , British; nonfiction
CON
INBER, Vera Mikhaylovna, 1890/
93-1972, Russian; poetry BU
CL TH
'EL INCA' see 'GARCILASO de
la VEGA'
INCE, Basil Andre, 1933- , West
Indian; nonfiction CON
INCHBALD, Elizabeth Simpson,
1753-1821, English; fiction,
plays, translations BU DA
VN
INCIARDI, James Anthony, 1939- ,
American; nonfiction CON
'INCOGNITUS' see MUÑOZ RIVERA,
Luis
INDELMAN-YINNON, Moshe,
1895?-1977, American; jour-
nalism, translations CON
INDERLIED, Mary Elizabeth
('Elizabeth Edwards'), 1945- ,
American; fiction CON
INFIELD, Glenn Berton ('George
Powers'; 'Frank Rodgers';
'Arthur Tolby'), 1920-81,
American; nonfiction, tv,
film CON
INGATE, Mary, 1912- , British;
fiction CON
INGBAR, Mary Lee, 1926- ,

American; nonfiction CON
INGE, William, 1913-73, Ameri-
can; plays BR MCG MCN
PO VD
INGELFINGER, Franz Joseph,
1910-80, German-American;
nonfiction CON
INGELGREN, Georg, 1782-1813,
Swedish; poetry BU
INGELOW, Jean, 1820-97, English;
fiction, poetry, juveniles BU
DA KI
INGEMANN, Bernhard Severin,
1789-1862, Danish; poetry,
fiction BU TH
'INGERSOL, Jared' see PAINE,
Lauran B.
INGERSOLL, David Edward,
1939- , American; nonfiction
CON
INGERSOLL, John H., 1925- ,
American; nonfiction CON
'INGHAM, Daniel' see LAMBOT,
Isobel
INGLÊS de SOUSA, Herculano Mar-
cos, 1853-1918, Brazilian; fic-
tion BR
INGLIN, Meinrad, 1893-1971,
Swiss; fiction BU CL
INGLIS, Ruth Langdon, 1927- ,
American; nonfiction CON
INGLIS, Stuart John, 1923- ,
American; nonfiction CON
INGOLD, Klara Schmid, 1913- ,
Swiss-American; nonfiction,
translations CON
'INGOLDSBY, Thomas' see BAR-
HAM, Richard H.
INGRAHAM, Joseph Holt, 1809-60,
American; fiction BA MYE
VN
INGRAHAM, Leonard William,
1913- , American; juveniles
CO
INGRAHAM, Mark Hoyt, 1896- ,
American; nonfiction CON
INGRAM, Anne Bower, 1937- ,
Australian; juveniles, nonfic-
tion CON
INGRAM, Collingwood, 1880-1981,
English; nonfiction CON
INGRAM, Forrest Leo ('Ignatius
van Rijn'), 1938- , American;
translations, nonfiction, fiction
CON
INGRAM, Gregory Keith, 1944- ,
American; nonfiction CON
INGRAM, John Keels, 1823-1907,

Irish; nonfiction, poetry
HO
INGRAM, Thomas Henry, 1924- ,
English; fiction, juveniles
CON
INGRAM, William, 1930- ,
American; nonfiction CON
INGRAMS, Doreen, 1906- ,
English; juveniles CO
INGRAMS, Richard Reid ('Philip
Reid'), 1937- , British;
nonfiction CON
INGRAO, Charles William,
1948- , American; nonfiction
CON
INGREY, Derek, British; fiction
NI
INGSTAD, Helge Marcus, 1899- ,
Norwegian; nonfiction CON
INGWERSEN, Faith, 1934- ,
American; nonfiction, trans-
lations CON
INGWERSEN, Niels, 1935- ,
Danish-American; nonfiction
CON
INJANASHI, 1837-92, Mongolian;
fiction, poetry, nonfiction
PRU
INKIOW, Dimiter ('Velko Verin'),
1932- , Bulgarian-American;
juveniles, fiction, plays
CON
'INMERITO' see JAVITCH, Daniel
G.
INNES, Cosmo, 1798-1874, Scots;
nonfiction BU
INNES, Frank C., 1934- ,
American; nonfiction CON
INNES, Hammond ('Ralph Ham-
mond'), 1913- , British;
fiction, juveniles, nonfiction
REI VCN WA
'INNES, Jean' see SAUNDERS,
Jean
INNES, John, 1863-1941, Canadian;
nonfiction CR
'INNES, Michael' see STEWART,
John I. M.
INNES, Thomas, 1662-1744,
Scots; nonfiction BU
INNIS, Donald Quayle, 1924- ,
Canadian-American; nonfiction
CON
INNIS, Mary Emma Quayle,
1899- , Canadian; nonfiction,
fiction CR
INSALL, Donald William, 1926- ,
English; nonfiction CON

INSHA, Sayyid Insha'llah Khan,
1757-1817, Urdu; poetry, non-
fiction PRU
'INSPECTOR F.' see 'WATERS'
INTRILIGATOR, Michael David,
1938- , American; nonfiction
CON
'INTRONATO, Stordito' see
PICCOLOMINI, Alessandro
INYART, Gene, 1927- , American;
juveniles CO
IOANE-ZOSIME,   -978?, Georgian;
nonfiction PRU
'IOLO MORGANWG' (Edward Wil-
liams), 1747-1826, Welsh;
poetry BU
ION, 480-22/21 B. C., Greek;
plays, nonfiction, poetry BU
IONESCO, Eugène, 1912- ,
French; plays BU CL CO
MAG MCG SEY TH WA
IONESCU, Ghita G., 1913- ,
Rumanian-British; nonfiction
CON
IOOR, William, 1780-1850, Amer-
ican; plays BA
IORGA, Nicolae, 1871-1940, Ru-
manian; nonfiction BU CL TH
IORIO, James, 1921- , Italian-
American; poetry CON
IORIO, John, 1925- , Italian-
American; nonfiction CON
IORISZO, Luciano John, 1930- ,
American; nonfiction CON
IOSIF, Stefan Octavian, 1875-
1913, Rumanian; poetry BU
IPCAR, Dahlov, 1917- , Ameri-
can; juveniles DE
IPUWAR, 13th century B. C.,
Egyptian; nonfiction PRU
IQBAL, Afzal, 1919- , Pakistani;
nonfiction CON
IQBAL, Sir Humammad, 1873-
1938, Urdu; nonfiction, poetry
BU LA BRU WAK
IRAIYANAR, 5-6th centuries,
Tamil; nonfiction PRU
IRAJ, Jalal al-Mamlik, 1874-1925,
Persian; poetry, fiction BU
PRU
IRAMALINKA PILLAI, Svami,
1823-74, Tamil; poetry PRU
IRANEK-OSMECKI, Kazimierz
('Antoni'; 'Heller'; 'Makary'),
1897- , Polish-English; non-
fiction, translations CON
IRAQI, Ibrahim,   -1289, Persian;
poetry BU

IRBY, Kenneth, 1936- , American; poetry CON VCP
IRELAND, David, 1927- , Australian; fiction, plays VCN
IRELAND, Joe C., 1936- , American; poetry CON
IRELAND, John of, 1435?-96, Scots; nonfiction BU
IRELAND, Kevin Mark, 1933- , New Zealander; poetry CON VCP
IRELAND, Robert Michael, 1937- , American; nonfiction CON
IRELAND, William Henry, 1777-1835, English; forger BU
IRELE, Abiola, 1936- , Nigerian; poetry JA
IREMONGER, Valentin, 1918- , Irish; poetry, plays, translations CON HO VCP
IRENAEUS, St., 130-200, Greek; nonfiction BU GR LA
IRGANG, Jacob, 1930- , American; nonfiction CON
IRIARTE, Tomás de, 1750-91, Spanish; poetry BU TH
IRION, Ruth Hershey, 1921- , American; juveniles CON
IRISH, Donald Paul, 1919- , American; nonfiction CON
IRISH, Richard K., 1932- , American; nonfiction CON
'IRISH, William' see WOOLRICH, Cornell G. H.
IROAGANACHI, J. O., 1940- , Nigerian; fiction HER
IRSFELD, John Henry, 1937- , American; fiction, poetry CON
IRVIN, Fred, 1914- , American; juveniles CO
IRVIN, Rea, 1881-1972, American; cartoons CON
IRVIN, Robert W., 1933-80, American; journalism CON
IRVINE, Betty Jo, 1943- , American; nonfiction CON
IRVINE, John, 1903-64, Irish; poetry HO
IRVINE, Robert Ralstone, 1936- , American; journalism, fiction CON
IRVING, Brian William, 1932- , American; nonfiction CON
IRVING, Clive, 1933- , British; nonfiction CON
'IRVING, Henry' see KANTER, Hal
IRVING, John, 1942- , American; fiction KIB
'IRVING, Robert' see ADLER, Irving
IRVING, Washington ('Fray Antonio Agapida'; 'Geoffrey Crayon'; 'Diedrich Knickerbocker'; 'Launcelot Langstaff'; 'Jonathan Oldstyle'), 1783-1859, American; juveniles, fiction, nonfiction AM BR BU COM MAG MYE PO VN
IRWIN, Annabelle Bowen ('Hadley Irwin'), 1915- , American; juveniles, plays CON
IRWIN, Constance Frick ('C. H. Frick'; Constance Frick), 1913- , American; juveniles CO
IRWIN, David, 1933- , English; nonfiction CON
IRWIN, George, 1910-71, New Zealander; nonfiction CON
'IRWIN, Hadley' see HADLEY, Lee; IRWIN, Annabelle B.
IRWIN, Inez Haynes, 1873-1970, American; journalism, fiction CON
IRWIN, James W., 1891?-1977, American; nonfiction CON
IRWIN, John Thomas ('John Bricuth'), 1940- , American; poetry, nonfiction CON
IRWIN, John Valeur, 1917- , American; nonfiction CON
IRWIN, Keith Gordon, 1885-1964, American; juveniles CO
IRWIN, Margaret, 1889-1967, British; fiction CON
'IRWIN, P. K.' see PAGE, Patricia K.
IRWIN, Raymond, 1902-76, British; nonfiction ENG
IRWIN, Theodore, 1907- , American; fiction, nonfiction CON
IRWIN, Thomas Caulfield, 1823-92, Irish; poetry, fiction HO
IRWIN, William Robert, 1915- , American; nonfiction CON
IRWIN-WILLIAMS, Cynthia, 1936- , American; nonfiction CON
IRYON, 1206-89, Korean; nonfiction PRU
IRZYKOWSKI, Karol, 1873-1944, Polish; fiction, nonfiction BU

CL TH
ISA dan USUMAN, 1818-81,
Hausan; translations, poetry
BU
ISAAC, Erich, 1928- , German-
American; nonfiction CON
ISAAC, Joanne, 1934- , Amer-
ican; juveniles CO
ISAAC ibn GAYYAT (Ghayyath;
Giat), 1038-89, Spanish;
poetry BU
ISAACS, Edith Somborn, 1884-
1978, American; plays, non-
fiction CON
'ISAACS, Jacob' see KRANZLER,
George G.
ISAACS, Jorge, 1837-95, Colom-
bian; fiction, poetry BR BU
ISAACS, Leonard, 1939- ,
American; nonfiction NI
ISAACS, Norman Ellis, 1908- ,
British; journalism, nonfic-
tion CON
ISAACS, Stephen David, 1937- ,
American; journalism, non-
fiction CON
ISAACS, Susan, 1943- , Amer-
ican; fiction CON
ISAAK, Robert Allen, 1945- ,
American; nonfiction CON
ISAEUS, 420?-350 B. C. , Greek;
nonfiction BU GR LA
ISAHAKIAN, Avetikh, 1875-1957,
Armenian; poetry PRU
ISAKOVIC, Antonije, 1923- ,
Serbian; fiction BU
ISAKOVSKY, Mikhail Vaselyevich,
1900-73, Russian; poetry,
journalism BU CON
ISAKSSON, Ulla Margareta Lund-
berg, 1916- , Swedish; fic-
tion BU CL
ISCHYRIUS, 16th century, Dutch;
poetry BU
ISE, 9-10th centuries, Japanese;
poetry HI
ISENHOUR, Thomas Lee, 1939- ,
American; nonfiction CON
ISER, Wolfgang, 1926- , German;
nonfiction CON
ISFAHANI, Abu'l-Faraj, 897-967,
Arab; nonfiction PRU
ISHAK, 13th century, Ethiopian;
fiction HER
ISHAK, Fayek Matta, 1922- ,
Egyptian; nonfiction CON
ISHAK bin HAJE Muhammad ('An-
war'), 1910- , Malayan;

fiction, journalism PRU
ISHAM, Charlotte Hickox, 1912- ,
American; juveniles, nonfiction
CO CON
ISHERWOOD, Christopher, 1904- ,
English; fiction, plays, nonfic-
tion, translations BU DA
MCG PO SEY VCD VCN VN
ISHIBASHI NINGETSU, 1865-1926,
Japanese; nonfiction, fiction
HI
ISHIDA, Tadeshi, 1923- , Japan-
ese; nonfiction CON
ISHIDA HAKYO, 1913-69, Japanese;
poetry HI
ISHIDANZANWANGJIL, 1854-1907,
Mongolian; poetry PRU
ISHIGO, Estelle, 1899- , Amer-
ican; nonfiction CON
ISHIKAWA MASAMOCHI, 1753-
1830, Japanese; nonfiction,
poetry HI
ISHIKAWA no IRATSUME, Japanese;
poetry HI
'ISHIKAWA TAKUBOKU' (Ishikawa
Hajime), 1885-1912, Japanese;
poetry, fiction, nonfiction
BU HI LA PRU
ISHIKAWA TATSUZO, 1905- ,
Japanese; fiction HI
ISHIKURE CHIMATA, 1869-1942,
Japanese; poetry HI
ISHIZAKA YOJIRO, 1900- ,
Japanese; fiction HI
ISH-KISHOR, Judith, 1892-1972,
American; juveniles, nonfiction,
journalism CO CON
ISH-KISHOR, Sulamith, 1896-1977,
English; juveniles, nonfiction
CO CON KI
ISHMOLE, Jack, 1924- , Amer-
ican; nonfiction CON
ISHQI, Muhammad-Reza, 1893-
1923, Persian; journalism,
poetry BU
ISHWARAN, Karigaudar, 1922- ,
Indian; nonfiction CON
ISICHEI, Elizabeth, 1939- , New
Zealander; nonfiction CON
ISIDORE of SEVILLE, St. (Isidorus
Hispalensis), 560-636, Latin;
nonfiction BU GR TH
ISKANDAR, Nur Sutan, 1893- ,
Indonesian; fiction PRU
ISKANDER, Fazil Abdulovich,
1929- , Persian-Russian;
poetry, fiction CL CON
ISLA, José Francisco de, 1703-81,

American; nonfiction CON
IVEY, Donald, 1918- , American;
nonfiction CON
'IVNËV, Ryurik' (Mikhail Alex-
androvich, Kovalëv), 1893- ,
Russian; fiction, poetry BU
IVRY, Alfred Lyon, 1935- ,
American; translations, non-
fiction CON
IWAMATSU, Jun Atsushi ('Taro
Yashima'), 1908- , Japanese-
American; juveniles CO CON
'IWAN' see 'GOLL, Yvan'
IWANO HŌMEI, 1873-1920,
Japanese; fiction, plays PRU
IWASZKIEWICZ, Jaroslaw ('Eleut-
er'), 1894-1980, Polish;
poetry, fiction BU CL CON
TH
IYENGAR, Bellur Krishnamachar
S., 1918- , Indian; nonfiction
CON
IYER, Baghavan Narashimhan,
1930- , Indian-American;
nonfiction CON
IZARD, Carroll Ellis, 1923- ,
American; nonfiction CON
IZBAN, Samuel, 1905- , Amer-
ican; nonfiction CON
IZENBERG, Jerry, American;
juveniles WAR
IZENOUR, George Charles,
1912- , American; nonfiction
CON
IZMAILOV, Alexander Efimovich,
1779-1831, Russian; fiction
BU
IZMIRLIEV, H. see 'SMIRNEN-
SKI, Hristo'
'IZUMI KYOKA' (Izumi Kyotaro),
1873-1939, Japanese; fiction
BU PRU
'IZUMI SHIKIBU' (Oe Shikibu),
974?-1030, Japanese; diary,
poetry BU HI
IZZET MOLLA KECECZADE,
1785-1829, Turkish; poetry
PRU
IZZO, Herbert John, 1928- ,
American; nonfiction CON

J

'J. P. M.' see MORALES, José
P.
JABAVU, Davidson Don Tengo,
1885-1959, South African;

nonfiction, poetry, journalism
HER JA LA
JABAVU, John Tengo, 1859-1921,
South African; journalism
HER JA
JABAVU, Noni Helen Nontando
('Alexandra N. Jababu'; Mrs.
Cadbury), 1919/21- , South
African; fiction, nonfiction
DA HER JA LA
JABBARLY, Jäfär, 1899-1934,
Azerbaijan; poetry, plays
PRU
JABBER, Fuad, 1943- , Ameri-
can; nonfiction CON
'JABEZ' see NICOL, Eric P.
JACCOTTET, Philippe, 1925- ,
Swiss-French; poetry BU
WAK
JACINTO, Antonio do Amaral Mar-
tins ('Orlando Tavora'),
1924- , Angolan; poetry, fic-
tion HER JA
JACK, Donald Lamont, 1924- ,
Canadian; plays, fiction CR
JACK, Homer Alexander, 1916- ,
American; nonfiction CON
JACK, Ian, 1923- , Scot; nonfic-
tion CON
JACK, Robert Ian, 1935- ,
American; nonfiction CON
JACKENDOFF, Ray S., 1945- ,
American; nonfiction CON
JACKINS, Harvey, 1916- , Amer-
ican; nonfiction CON
JACKLIN, Tony, 1944- , British;
nonfiction CON
JACKMAN, Stuart Brooke, 1922- ,
British; fiction, plays, nonfic-
tion CON REI
JACKMON, Marvin X. ('El Muha-
jir'), 1944- , American; non-
fiction, poetry, plays CON
'JACKS, Oliver' see 'ROYCE,
Kenneth'
JACKSON, Alan, 1938- , Scots;
poetry CON VCP
JACKSON, Albert, 1943- , British;
nonfiction CON
'JACKSON, Albina' see GEIS,
Richard E.
JACKSON, Allen, 1905?-76, Amer-
ican; journalism CON
JACKSON, Anna J. ('Anne Jackson'),
1926- , American; nonfiction
CON
JACKSON, Anthony, 1926- , Brit-
ish; nonfiction CON

JACKSON, Archibald Stewart,
    1922- , American; nonfiction
    CON
JACKSON, Barbara see WARD,
    Barbara
JACKSON, Basil, 1920- , Welsh-
    Canadian; fiction CON
JACKSON, Blyden, 1910- ,
    American; nonfiction CON
JACKSON, Brooks, 1941- ,
    American; journalism CON
JACKSON, Bruce, 1936- , Amer-
    ican; nonfiction CON
JACKSON, Caary Paul ('O. B.
    Jackson'; 'Colin Lochlons';
    'Jack Paulson'), 1902- ,
    American; juveniles CO
JACKSON, Charles R., 1903-68,
    American; fiction, nonfiction
    CON MAG
'JACKSON, Clarence J. -L.' see
    BULLIET, Richard W.
JACKSON, Clyde Owen, 1928- ,
    American; nonfiction SH
JACKSON, Dave, 1944- , Amer-
    ican; nonfiction CON
JACKSON, Derrick, 1939- ,
    British; nonfiction CON
JACKSON, Donald Dale, 1935- ,
    American; nonfiction CON
'JACKSON, E. F.' see TUBB,
    Edwin C.
JACKSON, Edgar Newman, 1910- ,
    American; nonfiction CON
'JACKSON, Everatt' see MUGGE-
    SON, Margaret E.
'JACKSON, Franklin J.' see
    WATKINS, Mel
JACKSON, Geoffrey Holt, 1915- ,
    English; juveniles, nonfiction
    CON
JACKSON, George D., 1929- ,
    American; nonfiction CON
JACKSON, George Stuyvesant,
    1906-76, American; nonfiction
    CON
JACKSON, Guida, 1930- , Amer-
    ican; fiction CON
JACKSON, Helen Hunt Fiske,
    1830-85, American; poetry,
    fiction, translations, nonfic-
    tion BU VN
JACKSON, Jacqueline Dougan,
    1928- , American; juveniles
    CON DEM WAR
JACKSON, James Pierre, 1925- ,
    French; nonfiction CON
JACKSON, Jesse, 1908- , Amer-

ican; juveniles, fiction KI SH
JACKSON, John Edgar, 1942- ,
    American; nonfiction CON
JACKSON, John Glover, 1907- ,
    American; nonfiction SH
JACKSON, John Howard, 1932- ,
    American; nonfiction CON
JACKSON, Jon Anthony, 1938- ,
    American; nonfiction, fiction
    CON
JACKSON, Karl Dion, 1942- ,
    American; nonfiction CON
JACKSON, Katherine Gauss, 1904-
    75, American; journalism,
    nonfiction CON
JACKSON, Laura see RIDING,
    Laura
JACKSON, Louise Allen, 1937- ,
    American; juveniles CON
JACKSON, Mae, 1946- , American;
    poetry, juveniles CON
JACKSON, Martin Alan, 1941- ,
    American; nonfiction CON
JACKSON, Mary, 1924- , Amer-
    ican; nonfiction CON
JACKSON, Miles Merrill, Jr.,
    1929- , American; poetry,
    fiction, nonfiction CON SH
JACKSON, Nell C., 1929- ,
    American; nonfiction SH
JACKSON, Neta, 1944- , Ameri-
    can; nonfiction, plays CON
'JACKSON, Neville' see GLASKIN,
    Gerald M.
'JACKSON, O. B.' see JACKSON,
    Caary P.
JACKSON, Robert Blake, 1926- ,
    American; juveniles CO
JACKSON, Robert Lowell, 1935- ,
    American; journalism CON
JACKSON, Ruth A., American;
    nonfiction CON
'JACKSON, Sally' see KELLOGG,
    Jean
'JACKSON, Sam' see TRUMBO,
    Dalton
JACKSON, Shirley, 1919-65, Amer-
    ican; fiction, nonfiction, juven-
    iles BR KIB NI REI VCN VN
JACKSON, Teague, 1938- , Amer-
    ican; nonfiction CON
JACKSON, Wes, 1936- , American;
    nonfiction CON
JACKSON, William Arthur Douglas,
    1923- , Canadian-American;
    nonfiction CON
JACKSON, William Keith, 1928- ,
    English; nonfiction CON

JACKSON, Wilma, 1931- ,
American; journalism, non-
fiction CON
JACOB, Francois, 1920- ,
French; nonfiction CON
JACOB, Helen Pierce, 1927- ,
American; juveniles CO CON
JACOB, Herbert, 1933- ,
German-American; nonfiction
CON
JACOB, Margaret Candee, 1943- ,
American; nonfiction CON
JACOB, Max, 1876-1944, French;
poetry, fiction, nonfiction
BU CL SEY TH WA
JACOB, Naomi Ellington, 1884-
1964, English; fiction DA
JACOB, Paul, 1940- , Indian;
poetry CON VCP
JACOB, Piers A. D. see
'ANTHONY, Piers'
JACOB, Philip Ernest, 1914- ,
American; nonfiction CON
JACOB, Violet, 1863-1946, Scots;
fiction, poetry BU DA
JACOB de BOINOD, Bernard
Louis, 1898-1977, British;
fiction, nonfiction CON
JACOB ben ASHER (Ba'al Ha
Turim; Ribah), 1269-1343,
Spanish; nonfiction BU
JACOBI, Carl, 1908- , Amer-
ican; fiction AS NI
JACOBI, Friedrich Heinrich, 1743-
1819, German; fiction BU
JACOBI, Johann Georg, 1740-
1814, German; poetry, jour-
nalism BU TH
JACOBS, Barry Douglas, 1932- ,
American; nonfiction CON
JACOBS, David Michael, 1942- ,
American; nonfiction CON
JACOBS, Diane, 1948- , Amer-
ican; nonfiction CON
JACOBS, Flora Gill, 1918- ,
American; juveniles CO
JACOBS, Francine, 1935- ,
American; juveniles CON
JACOBS, Genevieve Walker,
1948- , American; nonfiction
CON
JACOBS, Harold, 1941- , Amer-
ican; nonfiction CON
JACOBS, Harvey, 1930- , Amer-
ican; fiction NI
JACOBS, Helen Hull ('H. Braxton
Hull'), 1908- , American;
juveniles CO

JACOBS, Howard ('Bard of Avon-
dale'), 1908- , American;
nonfiction, poetry CON
JACOBS, James B., 1947- ,
American; nonfiction CON
JACOBS, Jerome L., 1931- ,
American; nonfiction CON
'JACOBS, Jill' see BHARTI, Satya
JACOBS, Jim, 1942- , American;
plays CON
JACOBS, Joseph, 1854-1916,
Australian-American; juveniles
CO
JACOBS, Laurence Wile, 1939- ,
American; nonfiction CON
JACOBS, Leland Blair, 1907- ,
American; juveniles CO CON
JACOBS, Lewis, 1906- , Amer-
ican; nonfiction CON
JACOBS, Linda C. ('Tom Austin';
'Claire Blackburn'), 1943- ,
American; juveniles CO
JACOBS, Lou, 1921- , American;
juveniles WAR
JACOBS, Melville, 1902-71, Amer-
ican; nonfiction CON
JACOBS, Norman Gabriel, 1924- ,
American; nonfiction CON
JACOBS, Paul, 1918-78, American;
journalism CON
JACOBS, Robert Durene, 1918- ,
American; nonfiction CON
JACOBS, Ruth Harriet ('Ruth Mill-
er'), 1924- , American; non-
fiction CON
'JACOBS, Susan' see QUINN, Susan
'JACOBS, T. C. H.' see PEN-
DOWER, Jacques
JACOBS, Vivian, 1916?-81, Amer-
ican; poetry CON
JACOBS, William Jay, 1933- ,
American; juveniles, nonfiction
CON
JACOBS, William Wymark, 1863-
1943, English; fiction, plays
BU DA ST VN
JACOBSEN, Hans J. see 'BRU,
Hedin'
JACOBSEN, Jens Peter, 1847-85,
Danish; fiction, poetry BU
CL MAG TH
JACOBSEN, Jorgen-Frantz, 1900-
38, Danish; fiction, nonfiction
BU TH
JACOBSEN, Josephine, 1908- ,
Canadian-American; nonfiction,
fiction VCP WAK
JACOBSEN, Lydik S., 1897?-1976,

Danish-American; nonfiction CON
JACOBSEN, Marion Leach, 1908- ,
American; nonfiction CON
JACOBSEN, Phebe Robinson,
1922- , American; nonfiction
CON
JACOBSEN, Rolf, 1907- , Nor-
wegian; poetry BU CL
JACOBSOHN, Gary J., 1946- ,
American; nonfiction CON
JACOBSON, Cliff, 1940- , Amer-
ican; nonfiction CON
JACOBSON, Dan, 1929- , South
African; fiction BU DA VCN
WA
JACOBSON, Daniel, 1923- ,
American; juveniles, nonfiction
CO CON WAR
JACOBSON, David Bernard,
1928- , American; nonfiction
CON
JACOBSON, Edith, 1897?-1978,
German-American; nonfiction
CON
JACOBSON, Frederick Lawrence,
1938- , American; nonfiction
CON
JACOBSON, Helen Saltz, 1921- ,
American; nonfiction, transla-
tions CON
JACOBSON, Jon, 1938- , Amer-
ican; nonfiction CON
JACOBSON, Julius, 1922- ,
American; nonfiction CON
JACOBSON, Michael F., 1943- ,
American; nonfiction CON
JACOBSON, Morris Karl, 1906- ,
German-American; juveniles
CO CON
JACOBSON, Robert, 1940- ,
American; journalism, nonfic-
tion CON
JACOBSON, Rodolfo, 1915- ,
German-American; nonfiction
CON
JACOBSON, Sibyl Chafer, 1942- ,
American; nonfiction CON
JACOBSON, Stephen A., 1934- ,
American; nonfiction CON
JACOBSTEIN, Joseph Myron,
1920- , American; nonfiction
CON
JACOBUS de VORAGINE (Jacopo
da Varazze), 1230?-98, Italian;
nonfiction BO BU TH
JACOBY, Henry ('Sebastian
Franck'; 'Andre Martin'),

1905- , German-American;
nonfiction CON
JACOBY, Joseph E., 1944- ,
American; nonfiction CON
JACOBY, Neil Herman, 1909-79,
Canadian; nonfiction CON
JACOBY, Russell, 1945- , Amer-
ican; nonfiction CON
JACOBY, Stephen Michael, 1940- ,
American; nonfiction, poetry
CON
JACOMB, Charles Ernest, 1888- ,
British; journalism NI
JACOPETTI, Alexandra, 1939- ,
American; juveniles CO CON
JACOPO da VARAZZE see
JACOBUS de VORAGINE
JACOPONE de TODI (de' Benedetti),
1230/40-1306, Italian; poetry,
plays BU MCG TH
JACQUEMART, Gelée, 13th cen-
tury, French; poetry BU
JACQUENEY, Mona Graubart,
American; nonfiction CON
JACQUENEY, Theodore, 1943?-79,
American; journalism CON
JACQUES, Robin, 1920- , Eng-
lish; juveniles DE
JACQUES de VITRY, 1180-1240,
?; nonfiction BU TH
'JADED OBSERVER' see ZOLF,
Larry
JAEGER, Frank, 1926-77, Danish;
poetry, nonfiction BU CL
JAEGER, Harry J., Jr., 1919?-
79, American; nonfiction CON
JÄGER, Johann see 'CROTUS
RUBEANUS'
JAEGER, Lorenz Cardinal, 1892-
1975, German; nonfiction
CON
JAEGER, Muriel, British; fiction
NI
JAEN, Didier T., 1933- , Amer-
ican; nonfiction MAR
JAENEN, Cornelius John, 1927- ,
American; nonfiction CON
JÄRNEFELT, Arvid, 1861-1932,
Finnish; fiction, plays BU TH
JAFFE, Dennis Theodore, 1946- ,
American; nonfiction CON
JAFFE, Irma Blumenthal, Amer-
ican; nonfiction CON
JAFFE, Rona, 1932- , American;
fiction CON
JAFFE, Sandra Sohn, 1943- ,
American; nonfiction CON
JAFFE, Sherril, 1945- , Amer-

ican; fiction CON
JAFFE, William, 1898- , American; nonfiction CON
JAFFEE, Dwight M., 1943- , American; nonfiction CON
JAFFEE, Mary L. see LINDSLEY, Mary F.
JAFFIN, David, 1937- , American; poetry CON VCP
JAGENDORF, Moritz Adolf, 1888-1981, Austrian; juveniles, plays, nonfiction CO CON
JAGER, Okke, 1928- , Dutch; nonfiction CON
JAGER, Ronald Albert, 1932- , American; nonfiction CON
JAGGER, Peter John, 1938- , British; nonfiction CON
JAGODA, Robert, 1923- , American; fiction CON
JAHAN, Rounaq, 1944- , Indian; nonfiction CON
JAHIER, Piero, 1884-1966, Italian; poetry, fiction, journalism BO BU SEY
JAHIZ, Abu Uthman Amr, 770/76-868, Arab; nonfiction BU LA PRU
JAHN, Ernst Adalbert, 1929- , German-American; nonfiction CON
JAHN, Joseph Michael (Mike), 1943- , American; nonfiction CON
JAHN, Moritz, 1884- , German; poetry BU
JAHNN, Hans Henry, 1894-1959, German; plays, nonfiction BU CL MCG TH
JAIMES FREYRE, Ricardo, 1868-1933, Bolivian; poetry BR BU
JAINENDRAKUMAR, 1905- , Hindi; fiction PRU
JAINI, Padmanabh S., 1923- , Indian-American; nonfiction CON
JAKEMES, 13th century, French; poetry BU
JAKES, John William ('Alan Payne'; 'Jay Scotland'), 1932- , American; fiction, plays, juveniles CON NI WAR
JAKOBER, Marie, 1941- , Canadian; fiction NI
JAKOBSON, Roman Osipovich, 1896- , Russian-American; nonfiction CON WAK

JAKOBSSON, Ejler, 1911- , American; editor NI
JAKOBSSON, Jökull, 1933- , Icelander; fiction, nonfiction, plays, poetry CL
JAKSIC, Djura, 1832-78, Serbian; poetry, plays, fiction BU TH
JAKUBAUSKAS, Edward Benedict, 1930- , American; nonfiction CON
JAKUBOWSKI, Maxim, 1944- , British; fiction, translations NI
JAKUBOWSKI, Patricia Ann, 1941- , American; nonfiction CON
JAKUREN, 1139?-1202, Japanese; poetry HI
JALĀL al-Dîn ('Rûmî), 1207-73, Persian; poetry LA PRU
JALIL, Musa, 1906-44, Tatar; poetry PRU
JALIL, Rahim, 1909- , Tajik; poetry, fiction, plays PRU
JALOUX, Edmond, 1878-1949, French; nonfiction, fiction, poetry CL
JAMALUDDIN, Afghan, 1838-97, Indian?; nonfiction PRU
JAMALZADEH, Sayyid Muhammad Ali, 1895/97- , Persian; nonfiction, fiction BU PRU
JAMES I, King of Catalonia and Aragon, 1208-76, Spanish; nonfiction BU
JAMES I of Scotland, 1394-1437, Scots; poetry BU DA VP
JAMES VI of Scotland (James I of England), 1566-1625, Scots; nonfiction, poetry BU DA
'JAMES, Andrew' see KIRKUP, James
'JAMES, C. B.' see COOVER, James B.
'JAMES, C. W.' see CUMES, James W.
JAMES, Charles Joseph, 1944- , American; nonfiction CON
JAMES, Charles L., 1934- , American; nonfiction SH
JAMES, Coy Hilton, 1915- , American; nonfiction CON
'JAMES, Cy' see WATTS, Peter C.
JAMES, Cyril Lionel Robert, 1901- , West Indian; nonfiction, journalism, fiction BU VCN

JAMES, David John, Welsh; fiction CON
'JAMES, Dynely' see MAYNE, William J.
'JAMES, Edward' see MASUR, Harold Q.
JAMES, Eleanor, 1912- , American; nonfiction CON
JAMES, George Payne Rainsford, 1799-1860, English; fiction, nonfiction BU PO
JAMES, Harry Clebourne, 1896- , Canadian-American; juveniles CO
JAMES, Heather ('Heather Jenner'), 1914- , English; fiction CON
JAMES, Henry, Sr., 1811-82, American; nonfiction BR
JAMES, Henry, 1843-1916, American; fiction, plays, nonfiction AM BR BU DA MAG MCG PO SEY VN
'JAMES, Josephine' see STERNE, Emma G.
'JAMES, Kristin' see CAMP, Candace P.
JAMES, Laurence, British; fiction NI
JAMES, Leonard Frank, 1904- , Anglo-American; nonfiction CON
JAMES, M. R. ('J. D. Danielson'), 1940- , American; nonfiction CON
JAMES, Marlise Ann ('Wabun'), 1945- , American; nonfiction CON
JAMES, Montague Rhodes, 1862-1936, English; fiction, nonfiction, translations, plays DA VN
JAMES, Muriel, American; nonfiction CON
JAMES, Naomi, 1949- , New Zealander; nonfiction CON
JAMES, Peter N., 1940- , American; nonfiction CON
'JAMES, Philip see CAWTHORN, James; del RAY, Lester
JAMES, Phyllis Dorothy, 1920- , English; fiction, nonfiction REI ST
JAMES, Preston Everett, 1899- , American; nonfiction CON
'JAMES, Stanton' see FLEMMING, Nicholas C.
'JAMES, T. F.' see FLEMING, Thomas J.

JAMES, Theodore Earle, 1913- , American; nonfiction CON
'JAMES, Thomas N.' see NEAL, James T.
'JAMES, Trevor' see CONSTABLE, Trevor J.
JAMES, Warren Edward, 1922- , American; nonfiction CON
'JAMES, Will' (Joseph Ernest Nephtali Dufault), 1892-1942, Canadian; juveniles, fiction KI
'JAMES, William' see CRADDOCK, William J.
JAMES, William, 1842-1910, American; nonfiction AM BR BU MAG PO SEY
'JAMES, William M.' see HARKNETT, Terry
JAMES, William Roderick, 1892-1942, American; juveniles CO
JAMESON, Cynthia, American; poetry, juveniles WAR
JAMESON, Johnette H., American; juveniles WAR
'JAMESON, Judith' see NEYLAND, James E.
JAMESON, Kenneth Ambrose, 1913- , British; nonfiction CON
JAMESON, Malcolm, 1891-1945, American; fiction NI
JAMESON, Margaret Storm ('James Hill'; 'William Lamb'), 1891- , British; fiction, nonfiction, tv CON
JAMESON, Samuel Haig, 1896- , American; nonfiction CON
JAMESON, Storm ('William Lamb'), 1891- , English; fiction, plays, nonfiction, translations DA NI VCN
JÂMÎ, Nûr al-Dîn 'Abd al-Rahmân, 1414-92, Persian; poetry, nonfiction BU LA PRU
JAMISON, Albert Leland, 1911- , American; nonfiction CON
JAMMES, Francis, 1868-1938, French; poetry, fiction BU CL SEY TH
JANAKIRAMAN, Ti, 1921- , Tamil; fiction, nonfiction, plays PRU
JANDL, Ernst, 1925- , Austrian; poetry, plays, nonfiction BU CL
JANDT, Fred Edmund, 1944- , American; nonfiction CON

JANDY, Edward Clarence, 1899-
1980, American; nonfiction
CON
JANE, Frederick Thomas, 1865-
1916, English; fiction NI
JANE, Mary Childs, 1909- ,
American; juveniles CO
JANE, Nancy, 1946- , American;
nonfiction CON
JANES, Edward C., 1908- ,
American; juveniles CO CON
JANEVSKI, Slavko, 1920- ,
Macedonian; poetry, fiction
CL
JANEWAY, Elizabeth Hall, 1913- ,
American; nonfiction, fiction,
juveniles CO CON
JANICIUS, Klemens (Janicki),
1516-43, Polish; poetry BU
JANIFER, Laurence M. ('Larry
Mark Harris'; 'Mark Phillips'),
1933- , American; fiction
AS NI
JANIK, Allan Stanley Peter,
1941- , American; nonfiction
CON
JANIK, Carolyn, 1940- , Amer-
ican; juveniles, nonfiction
CON
JANNSEN, Lydia E. F. see
'KOIDULA'
'JANOSCH' see ECKERT, Horst
JANOVY, John, Jr., 1937- ,
American; nonfiction CON
JANOWITZ, Phyllis, American;
poetry CON
JANOWSKI, Tadeus Marian,
1923- , American; nonfiction
CON
JANRUP, Ruth Birgit, 1931- ,
Swedish; juveniles CON
JANS, Adrien, 1905-73, Belgian;
poetry, nonfiction CL
'JANS, Zephyr' see ZEKOWSKI,
Arlene
JANSEN, Cornelius, 1585-1638,
French; nonfiction TH
JANSEN, Robert Bruce, 1922- ,
American; nonfiction CON
'JANSEVSKI, Jekabs' (Jekabs
Janovskis), 1865-1931, Lat-
vian; fiction, poetry, plays
BU
JANSON, Horst Woldemar,
1913-82, Russian-American;
juveniles CO
JANSSENS, Rev. Georges see
'DIALLO, Georges'

JANSSENS, Paul Mary, American;
nonfiction CON
JANSSON, Tove, 1914- , Finnish;
juveniles CO DE
JANSZ, Louris, late 16th century,
Dutch; poetry BU
JANTA, Alexander, 1908-74, Pol-
ish; poetry, journalism, trans-
lations, nonfiction CON
JANTSCH, Erich, 1929- , Aus-
trian; nonfiction CON
JANTZEN, Steven Lloyd, 1941- ,
American; nonfiction, juveniles
CON
'JANUS' see CLERY, Reginald V.
JANVIER, Thomas Allibone, 1849-
1913, American; journalism,
fiction NI
JANZEN, John Marvin, 1937- ,
American; nonfiction CON
JAPICX, Gysbert, 1603-66, West
Frisian; poetry BU
'JAPRISOT, Sebastien' (Jean Bap-
tiste Rossi), 1931- , French;
fiction REI
JAQUES, Faith, 1923- , English;
juveniles, nonfiction CO CON
JAQUES, Florence Page, 1890- ,
American; nonfiction, juveniles,
fiction, poetry CON
JARAMILLO, Heriberto J., 1936- ,
American; nonfiction MAR
JARAMILLO, Mari-Luci, American;
nonfiction MAR
JARAMILLO, Samuel, 1925- ,
Columbian; nonfiction CON
JARCHOW, Merrill Earl, 1910- ,
American; nonfiction CON
JARDIEL PONCELA, Enrique,
1901-52, Spanish; journalism,
fiction, plays CL MCG
JARDINE, Jack Owen see 'CORY,
Howard L.'; 'MADDOCK, Larry'
JARDINE, Julie A. see 'CORY,
Howard L.'
JARIR, 7-8th centuries, Arab;
poetry BU
JARMAN, Rosemary Hawley,
1935- , English; juveniles
CO CON
JARNES MILLAN, Benjamin, 1888-
1949, Spanish; fiction, nonfic-
tion BU CL
JARNOW, Jeannette, 1909- ,
American; nonfiction CON
JAROCH, Francis Anthony Randy,
1947- , American; poetry,
juveniles CON

JARRELL, John W., 1908?-78,
American; journalism CON
JARRELL, Mary Von Schrader,
1914- , American; nonfiction
CON
JARRELL, Randall, 1914-65,
American; poetry, nonfiction,
fiction AM BA BOR BR BU
CO DE KI MAG MAL PO
SEY VCP VP
JARRETT, Cora Hardy ('Faraday
Keene'), 1877-19?, American;
fiction, plays REI ST
JARRETT, James Louis, 1917- ,
American; nonfiction CON
JARRETT, John Derek, 1928- ,
English; nonfiction CON
JARROTT, Mattie L., 1881?-1973,
American; juveniles CON
JARRY, Alfred, 1873-1907,
French; poetry, fiction, plays
BU CL MCG NI SEY TH
JARVIE, Ian Charles, 1937- ,
American; nonfiction CON
JARVIS, Ana Cortesi, 1936- ,
Paraguayan-American; non-
fiction CON
'JARVIS, E. K.' see WILLIAMS,
Robert M.
'JARVIS, E. K.' house name NI
JARVIS, Rupert Charles, 1899- ,
British; nonfiction CON
JASADIPURA I. Raden Ngabehi,
1729-1803, Javanese; poetry,
nonfiction PRU
JASIK Rudolf, 1919-60, Slovak;
fiction BU
JASIMUDDIN, 1903- , Bengali;
poetry BU PRU
JASMIN, Claude, 1930- , Cana-
dian; fiction, plays BU
JASNORZEWSKA-PAWLIKOWSKA,
Maria, 1899-1945, Polish;
poetry, plays BU
'JASON' see STANNUS, James
G. D.
JASPAN, Norman, American;
nonfiction CON
'JASPEDOS, Don Hugh Herrera de'
see HERVAS y COBO de la
TORRE, Jose
JASPERS, Karl, 1883-1969, Ger-
man; nonfiction BU
JASPERSOHN, William, 1947- ,
American; juveniles CON
JASSIN, Hans Bagüe, 1917- ,
Indonesian; nonfiction PRU
JAST, Louis Stanley, 1868-1944,

British; nonfiction ENG
JASTAK, Joseph Florian, 1901-79,
Polish-American; nonfiction
CON
JASTRUN, Mieczyslaw, 1903- ,
Polish; poetry BU CL
JAUFRE RUDEL, Seigneur de
Blaya, mid 12th century, Pro-
vencal; poetry BU TH
JAUREGUI, Juan de, 1583-1641,
Spanish; poetry BU TH
JAURES, Jean, 1859-1914, French;
nonfiction CL
JAUSS, Anne Marie, 1907- ,
German-American; juveniles
CO DEM
JAUSSI, Laureen Richardson,
1934- , American; nonfiction
CON
JAVAKHISVILI, Mikhail, 1880-1937,
Georgian; fiction PRU
JAVITCH, Daniel Gilbert ('Inmer-
ito'), 1941- , French; nonfic-
tion CON
JAVOR, Frank A., American; fic-
tion NI
JAWAHIRI, Muhammad Mahdi,
1900- , Arab; poetry BU
PRU
JAWORSKA, Wladyslawa Jadwiga,
1910- , Polish; nonfiction
CON
JAWOSKYJ, Michael, 1921- ,
American; nonfiction CON
'JAXON, Milt' see KIMBRO, John
M.
'JAY, Charlotte' see 'HALLS,
Geraldine M.'
'JAY, Donald' see MEYER,
Charles R.
JAY, Douglas Patrick T., 1907- ,
English; nonfiction CON
JAY, James Monroe, 1927- ,
American; nonfiction CON
JAY, John, 1745-1829, American;
nonfiction MAG
JAY, Karla, 1947- , American;
nonfiction CON
JAY, Martin Evan, 1944- , Amer-
ican; nonfiction CON
'JAY, Mel' see FANTHORPE,
Robert L.
JAY, Peter A., 1940- , American;
nonfiction CON
JAY, Peter Anthony, 1945- ,
British; poetry, translations,
nonfiction CON VCP
JAY, Ruth Ingrid Johnson, 1920- ,

American; nonfiction CON
JAYADEVA, 12th century, Sanskrit;
poetry BU LA PRU
JAYAKANTAN, T., 1934- ,
Tamil; fiction PRU
JAYAWARDENA, Visakha Kumari,
1931- , Sri Lankan; nonfic-
tion CON
'JAYNE, Lt. R. H.' see ELLIS,
Edward S.
JAYNES, Julian, 1923- , Amer-
ican; nonfiction CON
JAYNES, Richard Andrus, 1935- ,
American; nonfiction CON
JAYNES, Roger W., 1946- ,
American; journalism CON
JEAN BODEL, 1165?-1210, French;
poetry TH
JEAN CHOPINEL (Clopinel) de
Meung, 1250?-1305?, French;
poetry BU MAG
JEAN d'ARRAS, 14th century,
French; nonfiction BU
JEAN de JANDUN, -1328,
French; nonfiction BU
JEAN de MEUNG see JEAN
CHOPINEL de Meung
JEAN de VIGNAI, 14th century,
French; nonfiction BU
JEAN le BEL, 1290?-1370,
French; nonfiction TH
JEAN LE COURT (Brisebarre),
-1340?, French; poetry BU
'JEAN PAUL' (Johann Paul
Friedrich Richter), 1763-1825,
German; fiction BU TH
JEAN RENART, 13th century,
French; poetry BU TH
JEANNIERE, Abel, 1921- ,
French; nonfiction CON
JEANS, Marylu Terral, 1914- ,
American; poetry, nonfiction
CON
JEBAVY, Václav I. see
'BREZINA, Otokar'
JEBODA, Joshua Ofuwafemi,
1930?- , Nigerian; fiction
HER
JEDAIAH ha-PENINI BEDERSI,
1270-1340, Provencal; poetry,
nonfiction BU
JEDREY, Christopher Michael,
1949- , American; nonfiction
CON
JEFFARES, Alexander Norman,
1920- , Irish; nonfiction
CON
JEFFER, Marsha, 1940- ,

American; nonfiction CON
JEFFERIES, Richard John, 1848-
87, English; fiction, nonfiction
BU CO DA NI PO VN
JEFFERIS, Barbara Tarlton,
1917- , British; journalism,
fiction, juveniles CON
JEFFERS, Harry Paul, 1934- ,
American; nonfiction CON
'JEFFERS, Jo' see JOHNSON,
Joan H.
JEFFERS, Lance, 1919- , Amer-
ican; poetry, fiction, nonfiction
CON SH
JEFFERS, Robinson, 1887-1962,
American; poetry, plays BR
BU CON MAG MCG PO SEY
VP
JEFFERS, Susan, 1942- , Amer-
ican; juveniles CO CON DEM
'JEFFERSON, Sarah' see FARJEON,
Eve A.
JEFFERSON, Thomas, 1743-1826,
American; nonfiction BA BR
BU MAG PO
JEFFERSON, Xavier Thomas
('Omar Xavier Jefferson'),
1952- , American; fiction,
plays CON
JEFFERY, William P., Jr.,
1919- , American; nonfiction
CON
JEFFERYS, Allane, American;
nonfiction CON
'JEFFREY, Christopher' see
LEACH, Michael
JEFFREY, David Lyle, 1941- ,
Canadian; nonfiction CON
JEFFREY, Lord Francis, 1773-
1850, Scots; nonfiction BU DA
PO
JEFFREY, Julie Roy, 1941- ,
American; nonfiction CON
JEFFREY, Richard Carl, 1926- ,
American; nonfiction CON
'JEFFREY, William' see PRONZINI,
Bill
JEFFREY, William, 1896-1946,
Scots; poetry DA
'JEFFREYS, J. G.' see HEALEY,
Ben J.
JEFFREYS-JONES, Rhodri, 1941- ,
Welsh; nonfiction CON
JEFFRIES, Derwin James, 1915- ,
American; nonfiction CON
JEFFRIES, Graham Montague see
'GRAEME, Bruce'
JEFFRIES, John Worthington,

1942- , American; nonfiction
CON
JEFFRIES, Lewis Ingles, 1942- ,
American; nonfiction CON
JEFFRIES, Ona Griffin, 1893?-
1973, American; nonfiction
CON
JEFFRIES, Roderic ('Peter Ald-
ing'; 'Jeffrey Ashford'; 'Hast-
ings Draper'; 'Roderic
Graeme'; 'Graham Hastings'),
1926- , British; fiction,
juveniles, nonfiction CO REI
ST
JEHLEN, Myra, 1940- , Franco-
American; nonfiction CON
'JELAKOWITCH, Ivan' see
HEIJERMANS, Herman
JELAVICH, Barbara, 1923- ,
American; nonfiction CON
JELENSKI, Constantin, 1922- ,
Polish-French; journalism
CON
JELINEK, Estele C. ('Estelle
Fine'), 1935- , American;
nonfiction CON
JELINEK, George, 1919- ,
Hungarian-American; nonfiction
CON
JELLEMA, Roderick, 1927- ,
American; nonfiction, poetry
CON
JELLICOE, Ann, 1927- , Brit-
ish; juveniles, plays, trans-
lations CON KI MCG VCD
WA
JELLINEK, Joseph Stephan,
1930- , German; nonfiction
CON
JELLY, George Oliver ('Alfred
Fosse'; 'Hilya Harsch'),
1909- , British; nonfiction,
fiction CON
JEMIE, Onwuchekwa, 1940- ,
Nigerian; nonfiction, poetry
CON
JENCKS, Charles, 1939- ,
American; nonfiction CON
JENCKS, Christopher, 1936- ,
American; nonfiction CON
JENKIN, Alfred Kenneth Hamil-
ton, 1900-80, British; non-
fiction CON
JENKINS, Alan, 1914- , English;
fiction, juveniles CON
JENKINS, Clarke, 1917- , Amer-
ican; nonfiction SH
JENKINS, David, 1928- , Amer-

ican; nonfiction CON
JENKINS, Ferrell, 1936- , Amer-
ican; nonfiction CON
JENKINS, Jerry Bruce, 1949- ,
American; nonfiction CON
JENKINS, John Holmes III, 1940- ,
American; nonfiction CON
JENKINS, John Robert, 1928- ,
Welsh-Canadian; nonfiction
CON
JENKINS, John Robin, 1912- ,
British; fiction VCN WA
JENKINS, Kenneth Vincent, 1930- ,
American; fiction, nonfiction
CON
JENKINS, Louis, 1942- , Amer-
ican; poetry CON
JENKINS, Margaret Elizabeth
Heald, 1905- , English; fic-
tion, nonfiction CON WA
JENKINS, Marie Magdalen ('Sr.
Mary Scholastica'; 'W. S.
Markins'), 1909- , American;
nonfiction, juveniles CO CON
WAR
JENKINS, Peter, 1951- , Amer-
ican; nonfiction CON
JENKINS, Raymond Leonard,
1935- , British; nonfiction,
plays CON
JENKINS, Reese Valmer, 1938- ,
American; nonfiction CON
JENKINS, Robert Thomas, 1881-
1969, Welsh; nonfiction, fiction
BU
JENKINS, Robin, 1912- , Scots;
fiction BU
JENKINS, Roy Harris, 1920- ,
Welsh; nonfiction, journalism
WA
JENKINS, Simon, 1943- , British;
journalism, nonfiction CON
JENKINS, William Atwell, 1922- ,
American; juveniles, nonfiction
CO CON
JENKINS, William Fitzgerald see
'LEINSTER, Murray'
JENKO, Simon, 1835-69, Slovene;
poetry, fiction BU
JENNER, Chrystie, 1950- ,
American; nonfiction CON
'JENNER, Heather' see JAMES,
Heather
JENNER, Philip Norman, 1921- ,
American; nonfiction CON
JENNINGS, Dana Close, 1923- ,
American; nonfiction CON
JENNINGS, Dean Southern, 1905-69,

American; journalism, non-
fiction CON
JENNINGS, Elizabeth Joan, 1926- ,
English; poetry, nonfiction
CON DA PO SEY VCP WA
JENNINGS, Gary Gayne, 1928- ,
American; juveniles CO
JENNINGS, Gordon, American;
juveniles WAR
JENNINGS, Jerry Edward, 1935- ,
American; nonfiction CON
JENNINGS, John E. ('Bates Bald-
win'; 'Joel Williams'), 1906-
73, American; fiction, nonfic-
tion CON
JENNINGS, Judson Toll, 1872-
1948, American; nonfiction
ENG
JENNINGS, Lane Eaton, 1944- ,
American; fiction, poetry
CON
JENNINGS, Michael ('Waco
Brazos'; 'Wyatt E. Kinkaid'),
1931- , American; fiction,
juveniles, journalism CON
WAR
'JENNINGS, Patrick' see MAYER,
Sydney L.
'JENNINGS, Robert' see HAMIL-
TON, Charles H. S.
JENNINGS, Robert Edward,
1931- , American; nonfiction
CON
'JENNINGS, S. M.' see MEYER,
Jerome S.
JENNINGS, Ted Charles, 1949- ,
American; fiction CON
JENNINGS, Vivien, American;
nonfiction CON
'JENNISON, C. S.' see STAR-
BIRD, Kaye
JENNISON, Christopher, 1938- ,
American; nonfiction CON
JENNISON, Keith Warren, 1911- ,
Canadian; juveniles, nonfic-
tion, fiction CO CON
JENNY, Hans Heinrich, 1922- ,
Swiss-American; nonfiction
CON
JENS, Walter, 1923- , German;
fiction, nonfiction CON TH
JENSEN, Alan Frederick, 1938- ,
American; nonfiction CON
JENSEN, Albert Christian,
1924- , American; nonfiction
CON
JENSEN, Andrew Frederick, Jr.,
1929- , American; nonfiction

CON
JENSEN, Axel, 1932- , Norwegian;
fiction BU NI
JENSEN, Dwight, 1934- , Amer-
ican; journalism, plays CON
JENSEN, Erik Aalbaek, 1923- ,
Danish; fiction BU
JENSEN, Frede, 1926- , Amer-
ican; nonfiction CON
JENSEN, Gwendolyn Evans,
1936- , American; nonfiction
CON
JENSEN, Irene Khin, 1925- ,
Burmese-American; nonfiction
CON
'JENSEN, Jared' see CEBULASH,
Mel
'JENSEN, Jo' see PELTON, Bever-
ly J.
JENSEN, Johannes Vilhelm, 1873-
1950, Danish; fiction, poetry,
nonfiction BU CL MAG NI TH
JENSEN, John Vernon, 1922- ,
American; nonfiction CON
JENSEN, Laura Linnea, 1948- ,
American; poetry CON
JENSEN, Lloyd, 1936- , Ameri-
can; nonfiction CON
JENSEN, Marlene, 1947- , Amer-
ican; nonfiction CON
JENSEN, Maxine (Dowd), 1919- ,
American; nonfiction CON
JENSEN, Merrill, 1905- , Amer-
ican; nonfiction CON
JENSEN, Michael Cole, 1939- ,
American; nonfiction CON
JENSEN, Niels, 1927- , Danish;
nonfiction CO CON
JENSEN, Paul Morris, 1944- ,
American; nonfiction CON
'JENSEN, Peter' see WALLMANN,
Jeffrey M.
JENSEN, Richard Carl, 1936- ,
American; nonfiction CON
JENSEN, Rosalie Seymour, 1938- ,
American; nonfiction CON
JENSEN, Thit Maria Kirstine
Dorothea, 1876-1957, Danish;
fiction BU
JENSEN, Virginia Allen, 1927- ,
American; juveniles, transla-
tions CO CON
JENSEN, Wilhelm, 1837-1911, Ger-
man; fiction BU
JENSENSKY, Janko, 1874-1945,
Slovak; poetry, fiction TH
'JENSI' Muganwa N.' see
SHORTER, Ayward

JENSON, William Robert, 1946- ,
American; nonfiction CON
JENYNS, Roger Soame, 1904-76,
British; nonfiction CON
JENYNS, Soame, 1704-87, English; poetry DA
JEPPSON, Janet O., 1926- ,
American; fiction CON
JESPEN, Hans Lyngby, 1920- ,
Danish; fiction BU
JEPSEN, Stanley Marius, 1912- ,
American; nonfiction CON
JEPSON, Selwyn, 1899- , English; fiction, plays REI ST
JEREMIAH, 7-6th centuries B. C.,
Israeli; nonfiction PRU
JEROME, St. (Eusebius Hieronymus), 340/48-420, Latin;
nonfiction BU GR LA
JEROME, Jerome Klapka, 1859-
1927, English; fiction, plays,
journalism BU DA MAG
MCG VN
JEROME, John, 1932- , American; nonfiction CON
JEROME, Judson, 1927- , American; poetry, plays, fiction,
nonfiction VCP
JEROME, Lawrence Edmund,
1944- , American; nonfiction
CON
JERROLD, Douglas William,
1803-57, English; plays,
journalism DA MCG VD
JERSILD, Per Christian, 1935- ,
Swedish; fiction CL
JERVELL, Jacob, 1925- , Norwegian; nonfiction CON
JESCHKE, Martin, 1929- ,
Canadian-American; nonfiction
CON
JESCHKE, Susan, 1942- , American; juveniles CON
JESENSKY, Janko, 1874-1945,
Slovak; poetry, fiction BU
CL
JESMER, Elaine, 1939- , American; fiction CON
JESPERSEN, James, 1934- ,
American; nonfiction CON
JESSE, Fryniwyd Tennyson, 1889-
1958, English; fiction, plays
REI ST
JESSEL, George Albert, 1898-
1981, American; nonfiction
CON
JESSEN, Carl A., 1887?-1978,
American; journalism, nonfiction CON
JESSNER, Lucie Ney, 1896-1979,
German-American; nonfiction
CON
JESSOR, Richard, 1924- , American; nonfiction CON
JESSUP, John Knox, 1907-79,
American; nonfiction CON
JESSUP, Philip Caryl, 1897- ,
American; nonfiction CON
JEURY, Michel, 1934- , French;
fiction NI
JEVONS, Frederic Raphael,
1929- , Austrian-Australian;
nonfiction CON
JEWELL, Edmund F., 1896?-1978,
American; journalism CON
JEWELL, Nancy, 1940- , American; juveniles CON
JEWETT, Ann Elizabeth, 1921- ,
American; nonfiction CON
JEWETT, Charles Coffin, 1816-68,
American; nonfiction ENG
JEWETT, Eleanore Myers, 1890-
1967, American; juveniles CO
JEWETT, Paul King, 1919- ,
American; nonfiction CON
JEWETT, Robert, 1933- , American; nonfiction CON
JEWETT, Sarah Orne, 1849-1909,
American; fiction, nonfiction,
juveniles AM BR BU CO
MAG PO VN
JEWSBURY, Geraldine Endsor,
1812-80, English; fiction, journalism DA
'JEZ, Teodor Tomasz' (Zygmunt
Fortunat Milkowski), 1824-1915,
Polish; fiction BU
JEZEWSKI, Bohdan Olgierd, 1900-
80, Polish-British; nonfiction
CON
JHABVALA, Ruth Prawer, 1927- ,
British; fiction, plays VCN
VN WA
JIBRAN, Khalil see GIBRAN, Kahlil
JIEN, 1155-1225, Japanese; poetry,
nonfiction III
'JIGAR MURADABADI' (Ali Sikandar), 1890-1960, Urdu; poetry
PRU
JILANI, Abd al-Qadir, 1077?-
1166?, Muslim; nonfiction BU
JILEMNICKY, Peter, 1901-49,
Slovak; fiction BU CL TH
JILES, Paulette, 1943- , American; poetry, film CON
JIMENEZ, Francisco, 1943- ,

American; nonfiction MAR
JIMENEZ, Janey Renee, 1953- ,
American; nonfiction CON
JIMENEZ, Juan Ramón, 1881-
1958, Spanish; poetry, fiction
BU CL MAY SEY TH WA
JIMENEZ de ENCISO, Diego,
1585-1634, Spanish; plays
BU
JIMENEZ de RADA, Rodrigo (El
Toledano), 1180?-1247,
Spanish; nonfiction BU
JIMENEZ de URREA, Pedro Man-
uel, 1486?-1528, Spanish;
poetry BU
JIMENEZ MALARET, Rene,
1903- , Puerto Rican; fic-
tion, plays, journalism, non-
fiction, poetry, translations
HIL
JIMENEZ MANTECON, Juan
Ramón see JIMENEZ, Juan
Ramón
JINKS, William Howard, Jr.,
1938- , American; nonfiction
CON
JIPPENSHA IKKU (Shigeta Sada-
kazu; Shigeta Ichijiro), 1765-
1831, Japanese; fiction, plays
BU HI LA MAG PRU
JIPSON, Wayne Ray, 1931- ,
American; nonfiction CON
JIRASEK, Alois, 1851-1930,
Czech; fiction, plays BU TH
JITO TENNO, -702, Japanese;
poetry HI
JNANESVAR, 1271-96?, Indian;
poetry BU LA PRU
JO, Yung-Hwan, 1932- , Korean-
American; nonfiction CON
JOACHIM, Paulin, 1931- , Daho-
man; poetry HER JA
JOACHIM of FIORE, 1145-1205,
Italian; nonfiction BU
JOAN, Polly, 1933- , American;
poetry, nonfiction CON
JOANS, Ted, 1928- , American;
nonfiction, poetry CON SH
JOAQUIN, Nick, 1917- , Filipino;
poetry, nonfiction, journalism
LA PRU
JOBB, Jamie ('Osh Kabibble'),
1945- , American; journal-
ism, nonfiction CON
JOBEN, -1356, Japanese; poetry
HI
JOBSON, Gary Alan, 1950- ,
American; nonfiction CON

JOBSON, Hamilton, 1914- ,
British; fiction CON REI
JOBSON, Sandra see DARROCH,
Sandra
JOCELIN of BRAKELOND, fl. 1170-
1200, English; nonfiction DA
JOCHNOWITZ, George, 1937- ,
American; nonfiction CON
JOCHUMSSON, Matthías, 1835-1920,
Icelander; poetry, plays BU
'JOCUNDUS, Father' see
MÜLLER, Wilhelm
JODELLE, Etienne, 1532-73,
French; plays, poetry BU
MCG TH
JOERS, Lawrence Eugene Claire,
1900- , American; nonfiction
CON
JOESTING, Edward Henry, 1925- ,
American; nonfiction CON
JOFEE, Joyce, 1940- , American;
nonfiction CON
JOGLAR CACHO, Manuel, 1898- ,
Puerto Rican; poetry HIL
JOHANN von NEUMARKT, 1310-80,
Bohemian; nonfiction BU
JOHANN von WÜRZBURG, fl. 1314,
German; fiction BU
'JOHANNES, R.' see MOSS, Rose
JOHANNES a LAPIDE (J. Heynlin),
1430-96, Swiss; nonfiction BU
JOHANNES de ALTA SILVA (Jean
de Hauteseille), fl. 1180-1200,
French; fiction BU TH
JOHANNES MAGNUS, 1488-1544,
Swedish; nonfiction BU
JOHANNES SCOTUS ERIGENA see
JOHN SCOTUS ERIGENA
JOHANNES SECUNDUS (Johann
Everts; Everaerts), 1511-36,
Dutch; nonfiction, poetry TH
JOHANNES von TEPL (Johannes
von Saaz), 1355?-1414?, Ger-
man; nonfiction BU TH
'JOHANNES úr KÖTLUM' (Johannes
B. Jónasson), 1899-1972, Ice-
lander; nonfiction, fiction, po-
etry BU CL
'JOHANNESSON, Olof' (Hannes Alf-
ven), 1908- , Swedish; non-
fiction, fiction NI
JOHANSON, Klara, 1875-1948,
Swedish; journalism, nonfiction
BU
JOHANSON, Stanley Morris,
1933- , American; nonfiction
CON
JOHANSSON, Lars (Lucidor), 1638-

74, Swedish; poetry BU
JOHANSSON, Thomas Hugo Bernard, 1943- , Swedish; nonfiction CON
JOHN VI CANTACUZENUS, 1292-1383, Byzantine; nonfiction BU
'JOHN, Dane' see MAJOR, Alan P.
JOHN, Errol, Trinidadian; plays VCD
JOHN, Eugenie see 'MARLITT, Eugenie'
JOHN, Helen James, 1930- , American; nonfiction CON
JOHN ARGYROPULOS, -1487, Byzantine; nonfiction LA
JOHN BECCUS, -1293, Byzantine; nonfiction BU
JOHN CHRYSOSTIM, 344/57-407, Greek; nonfiction BU GR
JOHN CINNAMUS, 1143?-95, Byzantine; nonfiction BU
JOHN CLIMAX, St. (Climacus), 550-649/70, Greek; nonfiction BU GR LA
JOHN CYPARISSIOTES, 14th century, Byzantine; nonfiction BU
JOHN DAMASCENE, St. (of Damascus), 675-749, Greek; nonfiction BU GR LA
JOHN DOXOPATRES the SICILIAN, early 11th century, Byzantine; nonfiction BU
JOHN GEOMETRES (Kyriotes), 10th century, Byzantine; poetry BU LA
JOHN ITALUS, late 11th century, Byzantine; nonfiction BU
JOHN MALALAS, 491?-578?, ?; nonfiction BU
JOHN MAUROPOUS of EUCHAITA, 11th century, Byzantine; nonfiction BU
JOHN MOSCHUS, -619, Greek; nonfiction BU GR LA
JOHN of ARDERNE, 1307-80, English; nonfiction BU
JOHN of DAMASCUS see JOHN DAMASCENE, St.
JOHN of HANVILLE (Hauteville), late 12th century, French; fiction TH
JOHN of HOWDEN (Hoveden), -1275, English; nonfiction, poetry DA
JOHN of SALISBURY, 1115/20-80, English; nonfiction BU DA

JOHN of the CROSS, St. (Juan de la Cruz), 1542-91, Spanish; poetry, nonfiction BU TH
JOHN of TREVISA, -1402?, English; nonfiction, translations DA
JOHN PAUL I, Pope (Albino Luciani), 1912-78, Italian; nonfiction CON
JOHN PECHAM, 1292- , English; nonfiction BU
JOHN PHILOPONUS, early 6th century, Greek; nonfiction BU
JOHN SCOTUS ERIGENA (Johannes), 810?-77?, Irish; nonfiction BU TH
JOHN SCYLITZES, late 11th century, Byzantine; nonfiction BU
JOHN the LYDIAN (John Laurentios Lydos), 490- , Byzantine; nonfiction BU
JOHN TZETZES, 1110-80, Byzantine; poetry, nonfiction BU LA
JOHN XIPHILINUS, 1010/13-75, Byzantine; nonfiction BU
JOHN ZONARAS, early 12th century, Byzantine; nonfiction BU
'JOHNN, David' see ENGLE, John D., Jr.
JOHNS, Albert Cameron, 1914- , American; nonfiction CON
JOHNS, Claude J., Jr., 1930- , American; nonfiction CON
JOHNS, Edward Alistair, 1936- , English; nonfiction CON
JOHNS, Glover S., Jr., 1911?-76, American; nonfiction CON
JOHNS, June, 1925- , English; nonfiction CON
'JOHNS, Kenneth' (Bulmer, Kenneth; Newman, John); fiction NI
'JOHNS, Marston' see FANTHORPE, Robert L.
JOHNS, Ray Earl, 1900- , American; nonfiction CON
JOHNS, Veronica Parker, 1907- , American; fiction ST
'JOHNS, Whitey' see WHITE, John I.
JOHNS, William Earle ('William Earle'), 1893-1968, British; journalism, juveniles, fiction, nonfiction CON KI
JOHNSGARD, Paul Austin, 1931- , American; nonfiction CON

'JOHNSON, A. E.' see JOHNSON,
Edgar R.
JOHNSON, Alicia L., 1944- ,
American; poetry SH
JOHNSON, Allen, American; non-
fiction CON
JOHNSON, Allison Heartz, 1910- ,
Canadian; nonfiction CON
JOHNSON, Amandus, 1877-1974,
Swedish-American; nonfiction
CON
JOHNSON, Andrew Nisseu, 1887- ,
American; nonfiction CON
JOHNSON, Annabell Jones, 1921- ,
American; juveniles DE KI
JOHNSON, Audrey Pike, 1915- ,
American; journalism, non-
fiction CON
JOHNSON, Barbara Ferry, 1923- ,
American; nonfiction, fiction
CON
JOHNSON, Barry Lee, 1943- ,
American; nonfiction CON
JOHNSON, Bea, -1976, Amer-
ican; journalism CON
JOHNSON, Ben Eugene, 1940- ,
American; nonfiction CON
'JOHNSON, Benjamin F., of
Boone' see RILEY, James W.
JOHNSON, Benton, 1928- ,
American; nonfiction CON
JOHNSON, Bernard H., Jr.,
1920- , American; nonfiction
SH
JOHNSON, Bertha French, 1906- ,
American; nonfiction CON
JOHNSON, Bradford, 1937- ,
American; poetry CON
JOHNSON, Bryan Stanley William
(Brian), 1933-73/74, English;
fiction, poetry, plays, film
CON VCP WAK
JOHNSON, Burges, 1877-1963,
American; nonfiction CON
'JOHNSON, C. F.' see GOULART,
Frances S.
JOHNSON, Carl Graves, 1915- ,
American; nonfiction CON
JOHNSON, Carroll Bernard,
1938- , American; nonfiction
CON
'JOHNSON, Charlene' see CRAW-
FORD, Char
JOHNSON, Charles Ellicott, 1920-
69, American; nonfiction CON
JOHNSON, Charles R. (Chuck),
1925- , American; juveniles,
nonfiction CO CON

JOHNSON, Claudia Alta (Lady
Bird), 1912- , American;
diary CON
JOHNSON, Corinne B., American;
juveniles WAR
'JOHNSON, Crockett' (David Johnson
Leisk), 1906-75, American;
juveniles CON DE KI
JOHNSON, Curtiss Sherman,
1899- , American; nonfiction
CON
JOHNSON, Dana William, 1945- ,
American; juveniles CO CON
JOHNSON, Dave William, 1931- ,
American; nonfiction CON
JOHNSON, David Bruce, 1942- ,
American; nonfiction CON
JOHNSON, Diane, 1934- , Amer-
ican; fiction CON
JOHNSON, Doris, 1922- , Amer-
ican; juveniles WAR
JOHNSON, Dorothy Biddle, 1887?-
1974, American; nonfiction
CON
JOHNSON, Dorothy Ethel, 1920- ,
American; nonfiction CON
JOHNSON, Dorothy Marie, 1905- ,
American; juveniles CO
JOHNSON, Douglas Wayne, 1934- ,
American; nonfiction CON
'JOHNSON, E. Ned' see JOHNSON,
Enid
JOHNSON, Earl, Jr., 1933- ,
American; nonfiction CON
JOHNSON, Edgar Raymond ('A. E.
Johnson'), 1912- , American;
juveniles DE KI
JOHNSON, Edward, 1598-1672,
American; nonfiction BR
JOHNSON, Elaine D., 1941- ,
American; nonfiction MAR
'JOHNSON, Eleanor' see SEYMOUR,
Dorothy J. Z.
JOHNSON, Elizabeth, 1911- ,
American; juveniles CO WAR
JOHNSON, Emil Richard, 1937- ,
American; fiction REI
JOHNSON, Enid ('E. Ned Johnson'),
1892- , American; juveniles
CON
JOHNSON, Eola, 1909- , Amer-
ican; nonfiction CON
JOHNSON, Eric Warner, 1918- ,
American; juveniles CO WAR
JOHNSON, Evelyne, 1932- ,
American; juveniles CO CON
JOHNSON, Eyvind Olof, 1900-76,
Swedish; fiction BU CL CON

TH WAK
JOHNSON, Ferd, 1905- , American; journalism, cartoons CON
JOHNSON, Frederick, 1932- , American; nonfiction CON
JOHNSON, Fridolf Lester, 1905- , American; nonfiction CON
JOHNSON, Gaylord, 1884- , American; juveniles CO
JOHNSON, George Clayton, American; fiction NI
JOHNSON, Georgia Douglas, 1886-1965, American; nonfiction, poetry BA
JOHNSON, Gerald White, 1890-1980, American; nonfiction, juveniles BA CO CON DE
JOHNSON, Gertrude Falk, 1929- , Polish-American; nonfiction CON
JOHNSON, Greer, 1920?-74, American; plays, nonfiction CON
JOHNSON, Harry Alleyn, 1920/21- , American; nonfiction CON SH
JOHNSON, Harry Gordon, 1923-77, Canadian; nonfiction CON
JOHNSON, Howard Albert, 1915-" 74, American; nonfiction CON
JOHNSON, Hugh, 1939- , British; journalism, nonfiction CON
JOHNSON, Humphrey Wynne, 1925-76, American; journalism, juveniles CON
JOHNSON, James Craig, 1944- , American; nonfiction CON
JOHNSON, James Edgar, 1927- , American; nonfiction CON
JOHNSON, James Pearce, 1937- , American; nonfiction CON
JOHNSON, James Turner, 1938- , American; nonfiction CON
JOHNSON, James Weldon, 1871-1938, American; poetry, nonfiction, juveniles BA BR BU DEM PO VP
JOHNSON, James William, 1927- , American; nonfiction CON
JOHNSON, Jane Maxine, 1914- , American; nonfiction, poetry CON
JOHNSON, Jerry Mack ('Jerry Mack'), 1927- , American; nonfiction CON

JOHNSON, Jesse J., 1914- , American; nonfiction SH
JOHNSON, Joan Helen ('Jo Jeffers'), 1931- , American; nonfiction CON
JOHNSON, Joe, 1940- , American; poetry, fiction SH
JOHNSON, Joe Donald, 1943- , American; poetry CON
JOHNSON, John Myrton, 1941- , American; nonfiction CON
JOHNSON, Joseph A., Jr., 1914?-79, American; nonfiction CON
JOHNSON, Joseph M., 1883-1973, American; nonfiction CON
JOHNSON, Josephine Winslow, 1910- , American; fiction, poetry, nonfiction VCN
JOHNSON, Karen, 1939- , American; plays CON
JOHNSON, Kendall, 1928- , American; nonfiction CON
JOHNSON, Kenneth Gardner, 1922- , American; nonfiction CON
JOHNSON, Kristi Planck, 1944- , American; translations CON
JOHNSON, L. P. V., British; fiction NI
JOHNSON, La Verne Bravo, 1925- , American; juveniles CO CON
JOHNSON, Lemuel, 1935?- , Nigerian; poetry, fiction HER
JOHNSON, Lemuel A., 1941- , American; nonfiction, translations CON
JOHNSON, Lincoln F., Jr., 1920- , American; nonfiction CON
JOHNSON, Lionel Pigot, 1867-1902, English; poetry, nonfiction BU DA PO
JOHNSON, Lois Smith, American; juveniles CO
JOHNSON, Lois Walfrid, 1936- , American; juveniles, poetry, fiction, nonfiction CO CON
JOHNSON, Louis, 1924- , New Zealander; poetry CON VCP
JOHNSON, Lyndon Baines, 1908-73, American; nonfiction CON
JOHNSON, M. Glen, 1936- , American; nonfiction CON
JOHNSON, Malcolm L., 1937- , American; journalism, nonfiction CON
JOHNSON, Malcolm Malone, 1904-

76, American; journalism,
nonfiction CON
JOHNSON, Manly, 1920- , Amer-
ican; nonfiction CON
JOHNSON, Marilue Carolyn ('Mari-
lue'), 1931- , American;
juveniles CON
JOHNSON, Marion Georgina
('Georgina Masson'), 1912-80,
British; nonfiction CON
JOHNSON, Mary Anne, 1943- ,
American; nonfiction CON
JOHNSON, Mauritz, Jr., 1922- ,
American; nonfiction CON
JOHNSON, Mendal William, 1928-
76, American; fiction CON
JOHNSON, Michael Lillard,
1943- , American; nonfiction
CON
JOHNSON, Niel Melvin, 1931- ,
American; nonfiction CON
JOHNSON, Nunnally, 1897-1977,
American; film CON
JOHNSON, Owen McMahon, 1878-
1952, American; fiction NI ST
JOHNSON, Pamela Hansford,
1912-81, British; fiction,
plays, poetry, nonfiction
LA PO VCN VN
JOHNSON, Paul Cornelius, 1904- ,
American; nonfiction CON
JOHNSON, Peter, 1930- , Eng-
lish; nonfiction CON
JOHNSON, Pierce, 1921- ,
American; nonfiction CON
JOHNSON, Ralph Whitney, 1923- ,
American; nonfiction CON
JOHNSON, Ray DeForest, 1926- ,
American; nonfiction CON
JOHNSON, Ray W., 1900- ,
American; fiction NI
'JOHNSON, Richard' see
RICHEY, David
JOHNSON, Richard, 1573-1659?,
English; poetry, fiction BU
JOHNSON, Richard Brigham,
1914- , American; nonfiction
CON
JOHNSON, Richard Tanner,
1938- , American; nonfiction
CON
JOHNSON, Robert A., 1921- ,
American; nonfiction CON
JOHNSON, Robert Ivar, 1933- ,
American; nonfiction CON
JOHNSON, Robert Sherlaw,
1932- , English; nonfiction
CON

JOHNSON, Roger Nylund, 1939- ,
American; nonfiction CON
JOHNSON, Ronald, 1935- , Amer-
ican; poetry, translations,
nonfiction VCP
JOHNSON, Ronald C., 1927- ,
American; nonfiction CON
JOHNSON, Ryerson, 1901- ,
American; juveniles WAR
JOHNSON, Sam Houston, 1914?-78,
American; nonfiction CON
JOHNSON, Samuel, 1709-84, Eng-
lish; nonfiction, poetry, fiction,
plays, translations BRI BU
DA MAG NI PO VN VP
JOHNSON, Samuel, 1822-82, Amer-
ican; nonfiction MY
JOHNSON, Sherman Elbridge,
1908- , American; nonfiction
CON
JOHNSON, Sherman Ellsworth,
1896-1978, American; nonfic-
tion CON
JOHNSON, Shirley King, 1927- ,
American; juveniles CO
JOHNSON, Siddie Joe, 1905-77,
American; juveniles CO
JOHNSON, Stanley J. F., 1920?-
78, American; journalism
CON
JOHNSON, Uwe, 1934- , German;
fiction BU CL MAG TH WA
JOHNSON, Vernon Edwin, 1920- ,
American; nonfiction CON
JOHNSON, Walter, 1915- , Amer-
ican; nonfiction CON
JOHNSON, Walter Ralph, 1933- ,
American; nonfiction CON
JOHNSON, Walter Ryerson,
1901- , American; juveniles
CO
JOHNSON, William see 'CORY,
William'
JOHNSON, William Clark, Jr.,
1945- , American; nonfiction
CON
JOHNSON, William Matthews,
1905- , American; journalism
SH
JOHNSON, William Weber, 1909- ,
American; juveniles CO
JOHNSTON, Alan William, 1942- ,
British; nonfiction CON
JOHNSTON, Albert H., 1914- ,
American; fiction, plays
CON
JOHNSTON, Anna I. see 'CAR-
BERY, Ethna' ·

JOHNSTON, Arthur, 1587-1641,
Scots; poetry BU
JOHNSTON, Basil H., 1929- ,
Canadian; nonfiction, poetry,
fiction CON
JOHNSTON, Brenda Arlivia,
1944- , American; juveniles,
nonfiction CON
JOHNSTON, Brian, 1932- ,
Anglo-American; nonfiction
CON
JOHNSTON, Bruce Foster, 1919- ,
American; nonfiction CON
JOHNSTON, Denis, 1901- , Irish;
fiction, plays BU MCG
JOHNSTON, Ellen Turlington,
1929- , American; poetry
CON
JOHNSTON, Francis E., 1931- ,
American; nonfiction CON
JOHNSTON, Frederick Charles,
1916- , English; juveniles
WAR
JOHNSTON, George, 1913- ,
Scots; nonfiction CON
JOHNSTON, George Benson,
1913- , Canadian; poetry,
translations CR VCP
JOHNSTON, Hugh Anthony Stephen
('A Fighter Pilot'; 'Hugh
Sturton'), 1913-67, English;
juveniles CO
JOHNSTON, Hugh Buckner,
1913- , American; nonfiction
CON
JOHNSTON, Hugh James Morton,
1939- , Canadian; nonfiction
CON
JOHNSTON, Jennifer Prudence,
1930- , Irish; fiction CON
HO
JOHNSTON, Jill ('F. J. Crowe'),
1929- , Anglo-American;
nonfiction CON
JOHNSTON, Johanna, American;
juveniles, nonfiction CO
CON DEM
JOHNSTON, John M., 1898?-
1979, American; journalism
CON
JOHNSTON, Mary, 1870-1936,
American; fiction, plays,
nonfiction BA MAG
JOHNSTON, Mireille, 1940- ,
Franco-American; nonfiction
CON
JOHNSTON, Norman, 1921- ,
American; nonfiction CON

'JOHNSTON, Portia' see TAKAK-
JIAN, Portia
JOHNSTON, Randolph W., 1904- ,
Canadian; nonfiction CON
JOHNSTON, Richard Malcolm,
1822-98, American; nonfiction,
fiction BA
JOHNSTON, Ronald John, 1941- ,
British; nonfiction CON
JOHNSTON, Thomas, Irish; juven-
iles WAR
JOHNSTON, Tony, 1942- , Amer-
ican; juveniles CO CON WAR
JOHNSTON, Velma B. ('Wild Horse
Annie'), 1912?-77, American;
nonfiction CON
JOHNSTON, William ('Susan Claud-
ia'; 'Heather Sinclair'),
1924- , American; nonfiction,
fiction, juveniles CON
JOHNSTON, William Arnold,
1942- , Scots-American;
plays CON
JOHNSTON, William Denis, 1901- ,
British; plays, nonfiction HO
VCD VD
JOHNSTON-SAINT, Peter, 1889-
1974, British; nonfiction CON
JOHNSTONE, Charles, 1719-1800,
Irish; fiction BU
JOHNSTONE, Keith, British; plays
VCD
JOHNSTONE, Lammy Olcott,
1946- , American; journalism
CON
JOHNSTONE, Parker Lochiel,
1903- , American; nonfiction
CON
JOHNSTONE, Robert Morton, Jr.,
1939- , American; nonfiction
CON
JOHNSTONE, Ted see 'McDANIEL,
David'
JOHNSTONE, William David Gordon,
1935- , American; nonfiction
CON
'JO-HSI, Chen' see TUANN, Lucy
JOINER, Charles Adrian, 1932- ,
American; nonfiction CON
JOINER, Edward Earl, 1924- ,
American; nonfiction CON
JOINVILLE, Jean, Sire de, 1225?-
1317, French; nonfiction BU
TH
JOJIN AZARI no HAHA, 10th cen-
tury, Japanese; poetry HI
JOKAI, Mór, 1825-1904, Hungarian;
fiction, plays, poetry

BU MAG NI TH
JOLAS, Eugene, 1894-1952, Amer-
ican; poetry, journalism RO
JOLIAT, Eugene, 1910- , Cana-
dian; nonfiction CON
JOLIN, Stephen Towne, 1941- ,
American; nonfiction, trans-
lations CON
'JOLKUNBAY' see QODIRIY,
Abdullo
JOLL, Dowrish Evelyn, 1925- ,
British; nonfiction CON
JOLLIFFE, Harold Richard, 1904-
78, Canadian; nonfiction,
translations CON
JOLLY, Alison, 1937- , Amer-
ican; nonfiction CON
JOLLY, Hugh R., 1918- ,
British; nonfiction CON
JOLLY, William Percy, 1922- ,
Anglo-American; nonfiction
CON
JOLOBE, James Ranisi, 1902- ,
Xhosan; fiction, poetry, plays
HER JA LA
JOLSON, Marvin Arnold, 1922- ,
American; nonfiction CON
JOMEI TENNO, 593/629-41,
Japanese; poetry HI
'JON úr VÖR' (Jón Jónsson),
1917- , Icelander; poetry
CL
JONAS, Carl, 1913-76, American;
fiction, journalism CON
JONAS, Doris Frances (Doris F.
Klein), 1916- , American;
nonfiction CON
JONAS, George, 1935- , Cana-
dian; poetry, plays VCP
JONAS, Gerald, 1935- , Amer-
ican; nonfiction CON
JONAS, Hans, 1903- , German-
American; nonfiction CON
JONAS, Paul, 1922- , Hungarian-
American; nonfiction CON
JONAS, Steven, 1936- , Amer-
ican; nonfiction CON
JONAS HALLGRIMSSON, 1807-
45, Icelander; poetry TH
JONASSEN, Christen Tonnes,
1912- , Norwegian-American;
nonfiction CON
JONASSON, Jóhannes see
'Jóhannes úr Kötlum'
'JONATHAN' see HASEBROEK,
Johannes P.
JONCKBLOET, Willem Jozef
Andries, 1817-85, Dutch;

nonfiction BU
JONCKHEERE, Karl, 1906- ,
Flemish; poetry, fiction, non-
fiction BU CL
JONCTIJS, Daniël Ewoutsz, 1611-
54, Dutch; poetry, nonfiction
BU
JONES, Adrienne ('Gregory Mason'),
1915- , American; juveniles,
fiction CO NI
JONES, Alan Griffith, 1943- ,
Welsh; nonfiction CON
JONES, Alan Moore, Jr., 1942- ,
American; nonfiction CON
JONES, Alexander, 1906-70, Brit-
ish; nonfiction CON
JONES, Andrew, 1921- , Amer-
ican; journalism, fiction CON
'JONES, Annabel' see BRAND,
Christianna M.
JONES, Arnold Hugh Martin, 1904-
70, British; nonfiction CON
JONES, Arthur Frederick, 1945- ,
American; nonfiction CON
JONES, Arthur L. see 'MACHEN,
Arthur'
JONES, Aubrey, 1910- , Welsh;
journalism, nonfiction CON
JONES, Audrey Christine, 1937- ,
Anglo-American; nonfiction,
juveniles CON
JONES, Barbara Mildred, 1917?-
78, British; nonfiction CON
JONES, Brian, 1938- , British;
poetry, plays VCP
JONES, Charles Colcock, Jr.,
1831-93, American; nonfiction
BA
JONES, Charles Edwin, 1932- ,
American; nonfiction CON
JONES, Christina Hendry, 1896- ,
Scots-American; nonfiction
CON
JONES, Craig, 1945- , American;
fiction CON
JONES, Dan Burne, 1908- ,
American; poetry, fiction CON
JONES, David, 1895-1974, Anglo-
Welsh; nonfiction BU CON DA
SEY
JONES, David Arthur, 1946- ,
American; nonfiction CON
JONES, David Gwenallt, 1899-1968,
Welsh; poetry BU
JONES, David Michael, 1895-1974,
English; poetry, nonfiction
VCP VP WA
JONES, David Rhodes, 1932- ,

American; journalism, non-
fiction CON
JONES, David Robert ('David
Bowie'), 1947- , British;
lyrics CON
JONES, Dennis Feltham, English;
fiction AS NI
JONES, Diana Wynne, 1934- ,
British; juveniles, plays,
fiction CO CON KI
JONES, Douglas Gordon, 1929- ,
Canadian; poetry, nonfiction
BU CR VCP
JONES, Ebenezer, 1820-60, Eng-
lish; poetry BU VP
JONES, Edgar Allen, Jr.,
1921- , American; nonfiction
CON
JONES, Eldred Duromisi, 1925- ,
Sierra Leonese; nonfiction,
fiction, poetry CON JA
JONES, Eli Stanley, 1884-1973,
American; nonfiction CON
JONES, Elizabeth Brown ('Betty
Brown'), 1907- , American;
nonfiction CON
JONES, Elizabeth Orton, 1910- ,
American; juveniles CO CON
JONES, Elwyn, 1923- , Welsh;
nonfiction CON
JONES, Enid Mary Huws, 1911- ,
English; nonfiction CON
JONES, Ernest, 1879-1958,
Welsh; nonfiction WA
JONES, Ernest Charles, 1819-68,
English; poetry, fiction BU
JONES, Evan, 1915- , American;
juveniles CO
JONES, Evan Lloyd, 1931- ,
Australian; poetry VCP
JONES, Ezra Earl, 1939- ,
American; nonfiction CON
JONES, Faustine Childress,
1927- , American; nonfiction
CON
JONES, Franklin Ross, 1921- ,
American; nonfiction CON
JONES, Gareth Elwyn, 1939- ,
Welsh; nonfiction CON
JONES, Garth Nelson, 1925- ,
American; nonfiction CON
JONES, Gayl, 1949- , American;
fiction CON
JONES, Gene Donald, 1931- ,
American; nonfiction CON
JONES, George Thaddeus, 1917- ,
American; nonfiction CON
'JONES, Gillingham' see

HAMILTON, Charles H. S.
JONES, Glyn, 1905- , Welsh;
fiction, plays, poetry, trans-
lations VCN VCP WA
JONES, Gonner, British; fiction
NI
JONES, Gordon Willis, 1915- ,
American; nonfiction CON
JONES, Gwilym Peredur, 1892-
1975, British; nonfiction CON
JONES, Gwyn, 1907- , Anglo-
Welsh; fiction, translations,
nonfiction BU VCN
JONES, Hardin Blair, 1914-78,
American; nonfiction CON
'JONES, Harold' see PAGE,
Gerald W.
JONES, Harold, 1904- , English;
juveniles, nonfiction CO CON
DE
'JONES, Harriet' see MARBLE,
Harriet C.
JONES, Helen L., 1904?-73,
American; juveniles CO
JONES, Henri ('Tristan Maxhim'),
1921- , French-Canadian;
nonfiction CON
JONES, Henry Albert, 1889-1981,
American; nonfiction CON
JONES, Henry Arthur, 1851-1929,
English; plays, nonfiction
BU DA MAG MCG PO VD
JONES, Hettie, 1934- , American;
poetry, nonfiction, fiction
CON WAR
JONES, Hortense P., 1918- ,
American; juveniles CO CON
JONES, Howard, 1940- , Amer-
ican; nonfiction CON
JONES, Howard Mumford, 1892-
1980, American; nonfiction
CON
JONES, Hugh, 1692-1760, American;
nonfiction BA
JONES, Inigo, 1573-1652, English;
designs RU
JONES, Iris Sanderson, 1932- ,
Canadian; nonfiction CON
JONES, Jack, 1884-1970, Anglo-
Welsh; fiction, plays BU WA
JONES, Jack ('Jay Edmond'),
1924- , American; journalism,
fiction CON
JONES, James, 1921-77, American;
fiction, nonfiction BR BU CON
HE MAG PO VCN VN
JONES, James Clinon, 1922- ,
American; journalism CON

JONES, James Henry, 1907?-77,
American; journalism, non-
fiction CON
JONES, Jeanne, 1937- , Amer-
ican; nonfiction CON
'JONES, Joanna' see BURKE,
John F.
JONES, John Gwilym, 1904- ,
Welsh; plays, fiction BU
JONES, John Paul, Jr., 1912- ,
American; nonfiction, fiction
CON
JONES, Joseph L., 1897-1980,
American; nonfiction CON
JONES, Kathleen, 1922- , Brit-
ish; nonfiction CON
JONES, Kathleen Eve ('Kathleen
Adler'), 1944- , South Af-
rican; nonfiction CON
JONES, Ken Duane, 1930- ,
American; nonfiction CON
JONES, Kenley, 1935- , Amer-
ican; journalism CON
JONES, Kenneth Effner, 1920- ,
American; nonfiction CON
JONES, Kenneth La Mar, 1931- ,
American; nonfiction CON
JONES, Kenneth Westcott ('Eric
Taunton'), 1921- , English;
nonfiction CON
JONES, Langdon, 1942- , Eng-
lish; fiction NI
JONES, Len, 1936- , American;
nonfiction CON
JONES, Leonidas Monroe, Sr.,
1923- , American; nonfiction
CON
JONES, Leroi (Imanu Amiri
Baraka), 1934- , American;
fiction, poetry, plays BR
BU MAL MCG MCN PO SEY
SH VCD VCN VCP VD WA
JONES, Lewis Pinckney, 1916- ,
American; nonfiction CON
JONES, Lyndon Hamer, 1927- ,
British; nonfiction CON
JONES, Madison Percy, 1925- ,
American; fiction, nonfiction
BA VCN
JONES, Major J., American;
nonfiction SH
JONES, Malcolm Vine, 1940- ,
British; nonfiction CON
JONES, Margaret, English; fic-
tion NI
JONES, Marvin, 1886-1976,
American; nonfiction CON
JONES, Mary Alice, American;

juveniles CO
JONES, Maynard Benedict (Nard
Jones), 1904-72, American;
journalism, fiction CON
JONES, Mervyn, 1922- , British;
fiction, translations, nonfiction
CON NI VCN
JONES, Michael Owen, 1942- ,
American; nonfiction CON
'JONES, Miriam' see SCHUCHMAN,
Joan
JONES, Neil Ronald, 1909- ,
American; fiction AS NI
JONES, Noel ('Patrick Aalben'),
1939- , Irish; radio CON
JONES, Paul Davis, 1940- ,
American; nonfiction CON
JONES, Paul J., 1897?-1974,
American; journalism, nonfic-
tion CON
JONES, Penelope, 1938- , Amer-
ican; juveniles CON
JONES, Peter, 1920- , British;
plays CON
JONES, Peter Austin, 1929- ,
English; poetry CON
JONES, Peter Gaylord, 1929- ,
American; nonfiction CON
JONES, Philip Howard, 1937- ,
American; journalism CON
JONES, Philip L., 1928?-79,
American; nonfiction, tv, fic-
tion CON
'JONES, Philippe' (Philippe Roberts-
Jones), 1924- , Belgian; po-
etry, nonfiction CL
JONES, Preston, 1936-79, Ameri-
can; plays CON MCN
JONES, Ray O., 1930- , Ameri-
can; nonfiction CON
JONES, Raymond F., 1915- ,
American; fiction, juveniles
AS NI
JONES, Reginald Lanier, 1931- ,
American; nonfiction CON SH
JONES, Reginald Victor, 1911- ,
British; nonfiction CON
JONES, Richard, 1926- , Welsh;
fiction CON
JONES, Richard Allan, 1943- ,
American; nonfiction CON
JONES, Richard Hutton, 1914- ,
American; nonfiction CON
JONES, Richard Matthew, 1925- ,
American; nonfiction CON
JONES, Robert A. see 'EMRYS ap
IWAN'
JONES, Robert Francis, 1934- ,

American; nonfiction CON
JONES, Robert Russell, 1927- ,
American; nonfiction CON
· JONES, Roger Winston, 1929- ,
British; fiction, nonfiction
CON
JONES, Rosie Lee Logan, 1924- ,
American; nonfiction SH
JONES, Royston Oscar, 1925-74,
British; nonfiction CON
JONES, Russell, 1918-79, Amer-
ican; journalism CON
JONES, Ruth Dorval, American;
nonfiction CON
JONES, Sally (Roberts), 1935- ,
British; poetry, nonfiction,
juveniles, plays CON
JONES, Sandy, 1943- , American;
nonfiction CON
JONES, Stephen Phillip ('Nelson
P. Falorp'; 'The Water Rat'),
1935- , American; fiction
CON
JONES, Thomas Gwynn, 1871-
1949, Welsh; poetry, fiction,
juveniles, nonfiction, trans-
lations BU DA
JONES, Thomas Warren ('Zulie
Butck'), 1947- , American;
poetry CON
JONES, Tom, 1928- , American;
plays CON
JONES, Tristan, 1924- , British;
nonfiction CON
JONES, Vernon, 1897- , Amer-
ican; nonfiction CON
JONES, Walton Glyn, 1928- ,
English; nonfiction CON
JONES, Weyman, 1928- ,
American; juveniles CO DEM
JONES, Sir William, 1746-94,
English; nonfiction, transla-
tions BU
JONES, William McKendrey,
1927- , American; nonfiction
CON
'JONES, Zelda' see SCHUCHMAN,
Joan
JONES-RYAN, Maureen, 1943- ,
American; nonfiction CON
JONG, Adrianius Michael de,
1888-1943, Dutch; fiction BU
JONG, Erica, 1942- , American;
poetry, fiction CON HE MAL
VCP WAK
'JONGE, Martinus S. de' see
HOEN, Pieter 'T
JONGEWARD, Dorothy, 1925- ,

American; nonfiction CON
JONK, Clarence, 1906- , Ameri-
can; juveniles CO
JONKER, Ingrid, 1933-65, Afri-
kaans; poetry SEY
'JONSOHN, Matthias' see THOMAS,
Johann
JONSON, Ben, 1573?-1637, Eng-
lish; plays BRU BU DA MAG
MCG PO RU VD VP
JONSSON, Hjálmar ('Bólu-Hjálmar),
1796-1875, Icelander; poetry
BU
JONSSON, Karl, -1212/13, Ice-
lander; fiction BU
JONSSON, Snaebjorn, 1888?-1978,
Icelander; poetry, translations
CON
JONSSON, Stefán, 1905-66, Ice-
lander; poetry, fiction CL
JONSSON, Thorsteinn see 'THOR-
STEIN fra HAMRI'
JONSSON, Thorsten Georg, 1910-50,
Swedish; fiction, nonfiction,
translations, journalism CL
JONSSON, Tor, 1916-51, Nor-
wegian; poetry, nonfiction CL
JOO, 1502-55, Japanese; poetry
HI
JOOST, Nicholas Teynac, 1916-80,
American; nonfiction CON
JOPP, Harold Dowling, Jr.,
1946- , American; nonfiction,
fiction CON
JORALEMON, Ira Beaman, 1884-
1975, American; nonfiction
CON
JORDAN, Archibald Campbell,
1906-68, Xhosan; fiction,
poetry HER JA LA
JORDAN, Borimir, 1933- ,
Bulgarian-American; nonfiction
CON
JORDAN, Dale Roderick, 1931- ,
American; nonfiction CON
JORDAN, David K., 1942- ,
American; nonfiction CON
JORDAN, David Paul, 1939- ,
American; nonfiction CON
JORDAN, David William, 1940- ,
American; nonfiction CON
JORDAN, Donald A., 1936- ,
American; nonfiction CON
'JORDAN, Gil' see GILBERT,
George
JORDAN, Gilbert John, 1902- ,
American; nonfiction CON
JORDAN, Hope Dahle, 1905- ,

American; juveniles, nonfiction CO CON
JORDAN, John, 1930- , Irish; nonfiction, fiction, poetry CON HO
JORDAN, June ('June Meyer'), 1936- , American; juveniles, poetry, nonfiction CO DEM KI SH WAR
'JORDAN, Leonard' ('Nicholas Brady'; 'Lee Chang'; 'Glen Chase'; 'Nelson De Mille'; 'Richard Gallagher'; 'March Hastings'; 'Robert Novak'; 'Philip Rawls'; 'Bruno Rossi'; 'Cynthia Wilkerson'), 1935- , American; fiction CON
JORDAN, Lois Breedlove, 1912- , American; nonfiction CON
JORDAN, Mildred, 1901- , American; juveniles CO
'JORDAN, Monica' see CARUBA, Alan
JORDAN, Neil, 1951- , Irish; fiction HO
JORDAN, Norman, 1938- , American; poetry SH
JORDAN, Robert F. see 'PLAYER, Robert'
JORDAN, Robert Smith, 1929- , American; nonfiction CON
JORDAN, Robin, 1947- , American; nonfiction, fiction CON
JORDAN, Ruth, 1926- , American; nonfiction CON
JORDAN, Wayne, 1903?-79, American; journalism CON
JORDAN, Wilbur Kitchener, 1902-80, American; nonfiction CON
JORDAN, Zbigniew Antoni, 1911-77, Polish-Canadian; nonfiction CON
JORDANES, 6th century, Latin; nonfiction BU GR TH
'JORGE PILL' see MORALEZ, Jose P.
JORGENS, Jack Johnstone, 1943- , American; nonfiction CON
'JORGENSEN, Ivar' (Jorgenson), house name NI
JORGENSEN, James Aleck, 1931- , American; nonfiction CON
JORGENSEN, James Dale, 1932- , American; nonfiction

CON
JORGENSEN, Jen Johannes, 1866-1956, Danish; poetry, nonfiction BU CL TH
JORGENSEN, Joseph Gilbert, 1934- , American; nonfiction CON
JORGENSEN, Neil, 1934- , American; nonfiction CON
'JORGENSON, Ivar' see SILVER-BERG, Robert
JORISZ, David, 1501-56, Dutch; poetry BU
JOSEFSBERG, Milt, 1911- , American; nonfiction CON
JOSEPH, Dov, 1899-1980, Canadian-Israeli; nonfiction CON
'JOSEPH, Franz' see SCHNAUBELT, Franz J.
JOSEPH, Joseph Maron, 1903-79, American; juveniles CO
JOSEPH, Marjory Lockwood, 1917- , American; nonfiction CON
JOSEPH, Michael Kennedy, 1914- , New Zealander; fiction, poetry NI VCN VCP
JOSEPH, Richard, 1910-76, American; nonfiction CON
JOSEPH, Stephen, 1921-67, British; nonfiction CON
JOSEPH GENESIUS, 10th century, Byzantine; nonfiction BU
JOSEPH of EXETER, -1210, English; poetry BU
JOSEPH of SICILY, 9th century, Byzantine; hymns BU
JOSEPH of VOLOKOLAMSK, 1440?-1515, Russian; nonfiction BU TH
'JOSEPHS, Stephens' see DOL-MATCH, Theodore
JOSEPHSON, Halsey D., 1906?-77, American; nonfiction CON
JOSEPHSON, Hannah, 1900-76, American; journalism, translations, nonfiction CON
JOSEPHSON, Harold, 1942- , American; nonfiction CON
JOSEPHSON, Matthew, 1899-1978, American; nonfiction, journalism BR CON RO
JOSEPHSON, Ragnar, 1891-1966, Swedish; nonfiction, fiction, plays BU
JOSEPHUS, Flavius, 37/38-100, Jewish; nonfiction BU GR LA

JOSEY, Elonnie Junius, 1924- ,
American; nonfiction SH
'JOSH MALIHABADI' (Shabir
Hasan Khan), 1894- , Urdu;
poetry PRU
JOSHI, Shivkumar, 1916- , In-
dian; plays, fiction, trans-
lations CON
JOSI, Ilacandra, 1902- , Hindi;
fiction PRU
JOSI, Umasankar, 1911- ,
Gujarati; poetry PRU
JOSIKA, Baron Miklós, 1794-
1865, Hungarian; fiction BU
TH
JOSKE, Anne N. see 'NEVILLE,
Margot'
JOSLIN, Sesyle ('Josephine Gib-
son'; 'G. B. Kirtland'),
1929- , American; juveniles
DE KI
JOSS, John, 1934- , Anglo-
American; nonfiction CON
JOSSELYN, John, fl. 1638-75,
American; nonfiction BR
JOTUNI, Maria Gustava Haggrén,
1880-1943, Finnish; fiction,
plays BU TH
JOUBERT, Andre J., 1924- ,
Canadian; nonfiction CON
JOUDRY, Patricia, 1921- ,
Canadian; plays CON
'JOUHANDEAU, Marcel' (Marcel
Provence), 1888-1979, French;
fiction, nonfiction BU CL
CON SEY TH WA
JOURARD, Sidney Marshall,
1926-74, Canadian-American;
nonfiction CON
JOURDAIN, Alice M., 1923- ,
Belgian-American; nonfiction
CON
JOURDAIN, Rose Leonora,
1932- , American; nonfiction,
fiction CON
JOURNET, Charles, 1891-1975,
Swiss; nonfiction CON
JOUVE, Pierre Jean, 1887-1976,
French; poetry, fiction, non-
fiction BU CL CON SEY TH
WA
JOUVENEL des URSINS, Jean,
1388-1473, French; nonfiction
BU
JOUVET, Louis, 1887-1951,
French; director CL
JOVELLANOS, Gaspar Melchor de,
1744-1811, Spanish; poetry,

plays BU TH
JOVINE, Francesco, 1902-50,
Italian; fiction BO BU TH
JOWETT, Benjamin, 1817-93, Eng-
lish; nonfiction, translations
BU
JOWETT, Garth Samuel, 1940- ,
South African; nonfiction CON
JOWETT, Margaret, 1921- ,
British; juveniles KI
JOWITT, Deborah ('Rachel Benson'),
1934- , American; transla-
tions, nonfiction CON
JOY, David Anthony Welton,
1942- , British; journalism,
nonfiction CON
JOY, Thomas Alfred, 1904- ,
British; nonfiction CON
JOYCE, James, 1882-1941, Irish;
fiction, plays, poetry BU CO
DA HO MAG MCG PO SEY VN
WAR
JOYCE, James Avery, 1902- ,
English; nonfiction CON
JOYCE, Jon Loyd ('Jay Dovlos'),
1937- , American; nonfiction
CON
JOYCE, P. W., 1827-1914, Irish;
nonfiction HO
JOYCE, Robert Dwyer, 1830-83,
Irish; poetry HO
JOYCE, Roger Bilbrough, 1924- ,
Australian; nonfiction CON
JOYCE, Trevor, 1947- , Irish;
poetry HO
JOYCE, William Walter, 1934- ,
American; nonfiction CON
JOYNSON, Robert Billington,
1922- , English; nonfiction
CON
JOZSEF, Attila, 1905-37, Hungar-
ian; poetry BU CL SEY TH
WA
JUAN CHI, 210-63, Chinese; poetry
BU PRU
'JUAN de la CASA' see ZENO
GANDIA, Manuel
JUAN de la CRUZ, San see JOHN
of the CROSS, ST.
'JUAN de MADRID' see BONAFOUX
y QUINTERO, Luis
JUAN MANUEL, Infante Don, 1282-
1348, Spanish; fiction BU TH
'JUAN SIN PATRIA' see MUÑOZ
RIVERA, José
JUAN TA-CH'ÊNG, 1587-1646,
Chinese; plays BU
'JUAN VICENTE RAFAEL' see

RIVERA VIERA, Juan
JUAREZ, Jose Roberto, 1934- ,
American; nonfiction MAR
JUAREZ, Leo Joseph, American;
nonfiction MAR
JUAREZ SANCHEZ, Armando,
1933- , American; nonfiction
MAR
JUCKERS, Sita, 1921- , Swiss;
juveniles CO
JUDAEUS, Leo see ABARBANEL,
Judah
JUDAH, Aaron, 1923- , British;
juveniles, fiction CON KI
JUDAH ben SAMUEL Ha-Levi,
1080-1145?, Spanish; poetry,
nonfiction BU TH
JUDAH ben SIMEON (Ha-Nasi),
130-92/219, Hebrew; nonfic-
tion BU
JUDAH the PIOUS of REGENS-
BURG, -1217, German;
nonfiction, poetry BU
'JUDD, Cyril' (Kornbluth, Cyril;
Merril, Judith), fiction NI
JUDD, Dennis R., 1943- ,
American; nonfiction CON
'JUDD, Harrison' see DANIELS,
Norman
JUDD, Howard Stanley, 1936- ,
American; nonfiction CON
JUDD, Larry R., 1937- ,
American; nonfiction CON
JUDD, Robert, 1939- , American;
nonfiction CON
JUDD, Sylvester, 1813-53, Amer-
ican; fiction BU MY
JUDGE, Michael, 1921- , Irish;
plays HO
JUDSON, David Malcolm, 1941- ,
British; nonfiction CON
JUDSON, Horace Freeland,
1931- , American; nonfiction
CON
JUDSON, Margaret Atwood,
1899- , American; nonfiction
CON
JUDSON, Sylvia Shaw, 1897- ,
American; nonfiction CON
JUDY, Stephen N., 1942- ,
American; nonfiction CON
JUENGER, Ernst, 1895- , Ger-
man; fiction, nonfiction BU
CL CON NI SEY TH
JÜNGER, Friedrich Georg, 1898- ,
German; poetry, nonfiction,
fiction TH
JUERGENSMEYER, Jane S. see

STUART, Jane
JUERGENSMEYER, John Eli,
1934- , American; nonfiction
CON
JUHASZ, Anne McCreary, 1922- ,
American; nonfiction CON
JUHASZ, Ferenc, 1928- , Hun-
garian; poetry CL SEY WA
JUHASZ, Gyula, 1883-1937, Hun-
garian; poetry, fiction, jour-
nalism BU CL
JUHASZ, Susanne, 1942- , Amer-
ican; nonfiction CON
JUKIC, Ilija, 1901-77, Yugoslav-
English; nonfiction CON
'JULIA MARIN, Ramon,' 1878-1917,
Puerto Rican; journalism, fic-
tion, poetry HIL
JULIAN the APOSTATE (Flavius
Claudius Julianus), 32/33-63,
Greek; nonfiction BU GR LA
JULIAN(A) of NORWICH, 1342-1416,
English; nonfiction BA DA
JULIANUS, Salvius, 100-69, Latin;
nonfiction GR
JULIARD, Pierre, 1939- , Belgian-
American; nonfiction CON
'JULIE (of Colorado Springs)' see
ROBBINS, June
JULIEN, Charles Andre ('Andre
Delorme'), 1891- , French;
nonfiction CON
'JULIUS' see CURLING, Bryan
W. S.
JULLIAN, Philippe, 1919-77,
French; fiction, nonfiction
CON
JULTY, Sam, 1927- , American;
nonfiction CON
JULY, Robert William, 1918- ,
American; nonfiction CON
'JUMPP, Hugo' see MacPEEK,
Walter G.
JUN, Jong Sup, 1936- , Korean-
American; nonfiction CON
JUNG, Carl Gustaf, 1875-1961,
Swiss; nonfiction BU MAG
SEY
JUNGK, Robert, 1913- , German-
American; journalism, nonfic-
tion CON
JUNGMANN, Josef, 1773-1847,
Czech; poetry, nonfiction,
translations BU TH
JUNG-STILLING, Johann Heinrich,
1740-1817, German; nonfiction,
fiction BU TH
JUNIPER, Dean Francis, 1929- ,

British; nonfiction CON
'JUNIUS,' fl. 1769-72, English;
letters DA
JUNIUS, Franciscus (Francois du
Jon), 1589-1677, Dutch; non-
fiction BU
JUNIUS, Hadrianus (Adriaen de
Jonghe), 1511-75, Dutch;
poetry, nonfiction BU
JUNQUEIRO, Abílio Manuel Guerra,
1850-1923, Portuguese; poetry
TH
JUNQUEIRA FREIRE, Luis José,
1832-55, Brazilian; poetry
BR
JUNTOKU-IN, 1197-1242, Japanese;
poetry HI
JUPO, Frank J., 1904- ,
German-American; juveniles
CO
JUPP, Kenneth, 1939- , English;
plays CON
'JUR, Jerzy' see LERSKI, George
JUR'AT, Shaikh Qalandar Bak-
hash, -1810, Urdu; poetry
PRU
JURCIC, Josip, 1844-81, Slovene;
fiction, plays BU
JUREK, Martin, 1942- , British;
journalism CON
JURGENS, William Anthony,
1928- , American; transla-
tions, nonfiction CON
JURIS, Hervey Asher, 1938- ,
American; nonfiction CON
JUSSIM, Estelle, 1927- , Amer-
ican; nonfiction CON
JUSTER, F. Thomas, 1926- ,
American; nonfiction CON
JUSTER, Norton, 1929- ,
American; juveniles CO DEM
KI
JUSTICE, Blair, 1927- , Amer-
ican; nonfiction CON
JUSTICE, Ronald Rodney, 1925- ,
American; poetry BA BR
VCP WA
JUSTICE, William Gross, Jr.,
1930- , American; nonfiction
CON
JUSTIN (Marcus Junianus Justinus),
Roman; nonfiction BU
JUSTIN MARTYR, 100-162/68,
Greek; nonfiction BU GR
'JUSTO, Fray' see MATOS
BERNIER, Felix
'JUSTO DERECHO' see MONGE,
José M.

JUTA, Jan ('Rene Juta'), 1895- ,
American; nonfiction CON
JUTSON, Mary Carolyn Hollers,
1930- , American; nonfiction
CON
JUVENAL, Decimus Junius Juvena-
tis, 50/70-127/40, Latin;
poetry BU GR LA MAG
JUVENCUS, Gaius Vettius Aquilinus,
4th century, Spanish; nonfiction
BU
JUVILER, Peter Henry, 1926- ,
Anglo-American; nonfiction
CON
JUVONEN, Helvi, 1919-59, Finnish;
poetry TH
'JUWAYNĒ' (Alâ al-Dîn Atâ Malik),
1226-83, Persian; nonfiction
LA

K

'K. R.' (Grand Duke Constantine
Romanov), 1858-1915, Russian;
translations, plays BU
KAALUND, Hans Vilhelm, 1818-85,
Danish; poetry BU
KA'B ibn ZUHAIR, late 7th century,
Arab; poetry BU
KABA, Lansine, 1941- , Guinean;
nonfiction CON
KABAAGACLI, Cevat S. see
'HALIKARNAS BALIKCISI'
KABAK, Abraham Abba, 1881-1944,
Hebrew; fiction, nonfiction
BU TH
KABBADA, Mika'el (Mikael Kebede),
1915- , Amharic; poetry,
plays HER
KABDEBO, Thomas (Tamas),
1934- , Hungarian-English;
juveniles, translations, fiction
CO CON
'KABIBBLE, Osh' see JOBB, Jamie
KABIR, 1440-1518, Indian; poetry,
nonfiction BU LA PRU
KACEW, Romani see 'GARY,
Romain'
KACHINGWE, Aubrey, 1926- ,
Malawian; fiction, journalism
HER JA
KACHRU, Braj Behari, 1932- ,
Indian-American; nonfiction
CON
KACIC-MEOSIC, Andrija, 1704-60,
Dalmatian; poetry BU TH
KACIYAPPA CIVACCARIYAR, 17th

century, Tamil; poetry PRU
KACYZNE, Alter, 1885-1941,
Yiddish; poetry, fiction, plays
BU
KADA no ARIMARO, 1706-51,
Japanese; nonfiction HI
KADA no AZUMAMARO, 1669-
1736, Japanese; nonfiction,
poetry HI
KADA no TAMIKO, 1722-86,
Japanese; poetry, nonfiction
HI
KADAR YAR, 1802-50?, Panjabi;
poetry PRU
KADEN-BANDROWSKI, Juliusz,
1885-1944, Polish; fiction
BU CL TH
KADESCH, Robert Rudstone,
1922- , American; nonfiction,
juveniles CON WAR
KADIMA-NZRIJI, Dieudonné,
1947- , Zairian; poetry JA
KADISH, Ferne, 1940- , Amer-
ican; nonfiction CON
'KADOSH, A.' see QUIÑONES,
Francisco M.
KADUBEK, Wincenty (Vincentius
Cadlubonis), 1150-1223,
Polish; nonfiction BU
KAEL, Pauline, 1919- , Amer-
ican; nonfiction, journalism
CON WAK
KAELIN, Eugene Francis, 1926- ,
American; nonfiction CON
'KAEMPFERT, Wade' see del
RAY, Lester
KAESE, Harold, 1909?-75, Amer-
ican; journalism, nonfiction
CON
KAESTLE, Carl Frederick,
1940- , American; nonfiction
CON
KAESTNER, Dorothy, 1920- ,
American; nonfiction CON
KÄSTNER, Erich ('Robert Neun-
er'), 1899-1974, German;
fiction, poetry, journalism
BU CL CO CON DE TH WA
KAFE, Joseph Kofi Thompson,
1933- , Ghanaian; nonfiction
CON
KAFFKA, Margit, 1880-1918,
Hungarian; poetry, fiction
BU CL TH
KAFKA, Franz, 1883-1924,
German; fiction, diary BU
CL MAG NI SEY TH
KAFKA, Vincent Winfield, 1924- ,

American; nonfiction CON
'KAGA no CHIYO' (Chujoni; Chiyojo;
Fukuzoya Chiyo), 1703-75,
Japanese; poetry BU HI
KAGAME, Abbé Alexis, 1912- ,
Rwandan; poetry, nonfiction
HER JA LA
KAGAMI SHIKO, 1665-1731,
Japanese; poetry HI
KAGAN, Norman, American; fiction
NI
KAGAN, Richard Clark, 1938- ,
American; nonfiction CON
KAGAN, Richard Lauren, 1943- ,
American; nonfiction CON
KAGAN-KANS, Eva, 1928- ,
American; nonfiction CON
KAGARA, Malam Abubakar Iman,
1910?- , Hausan; fiction,
journalism, nonfiction HER
KAGARA, Malam Muhammadu
Bello, 1905?- , Hausan;
nonfiction HER
KAGARLITSKI, Julius, 1926- ,
Russian; nonfiction NI
KAGAWA KAGEKI, 1768-1843,
Japanese; poetry, nonfiction
HI
KAHAN, Stuart, 1936- , American;
nonfiction CON
KAHANA-KARMON, Amaliah,
1920- , Israeli; fiction BU
KAHANE, Howard, 1928- , Amer-
ican; nonfiction CON
KAHANOVITCH, Pinchas P. see
'NISTOR, Der'
KAHHANA, 12th century, Sanskrit;
poetry PRU
KAHIGA, Samuel, 1940?- , Kenyan;
fiction HER
KAHIRAMDAS, late 16th century,
Bengali; poetry BU
KAHL, Virginia C., American;
juveniles, poetry CON KI
KAHLENBERG, Mary Hunt, 1940- ,
American; nonfiction CON
KAHLER, Hugh MacNair ('Murga-
troyd Elphinstone'), 1883-1969,
American; fiction CON
KAHM, Harold S. ('Henry Sacker-
man'), American; nonfiction,
fiction CON
KAHN, Albert E., 1912?-79,
American; nonfiction CON
KAHN, Alfred Edward, 1917- ,
American; nonfiction CON
KAHN, Arnold Dexter, 1939- ,
American; nonfiction CON

'KAHN, Balthazar' see CARLISLE, Thomas F.
KAHN, Ely Jacques, Jr., 1916- , American; nonfiction CON
KAHN, Gustave, 1859-1936, French; poetry, fiction, non-fiction BU CL TH
KAHN, Hannah, 1911- , American; poetry CON
KAHN, Herman, 1922- , American; nonfiction CON NI
KAHN, James M., 1903?-78, American; journalism CON
KAHN, Joan, 1914- , American; juveniles, fiction CON WAR
KAHN, Judd, 1940- , American; nonfiction CON
KAHN, Kathy, 1945- , American; nonfiction CON
KAHN, Lawrence Edwin, 1937- , American; nonfiction CON
KAHN, Ludwig Werner, 1910- , German-American; nonfiction CON
KAHN, Margaret, 1949- , American; nonfiction CON
KAHN, Richard Ferdinand, 1905- , British; nonfiction CON
KAHN, Sanders Arthur, 1919- , American; nonfiction CON
KAHN, Sholom Jacob, 1918- , American; nonfiction CON
KAHN-FOGEL, Daniel Mark ('Daniel Fogel'), 1948- , American; poetry, nonfiction CON
KAHNWEILER, Daniel Henry ('Daniel Henry'), 1884-1979, French; nonfiction CON
KAID, Lynda Lee, 1948- , American; nonfiction CON
KAIKAVUS ibn ISKANDAR, Unsur al-Ma'ali, 11th century, Persian; nonfiction BU
KAIKINI, Prabhakar Ramrao, 1912- , Indian; poetry CON
'KAILAS, Uuno' (Frans Uuno Salonen), 1901-33, Finnish; poetry TH
KAILASAM, 20th century, Indian; plays PRU
'KAIN, Malcolm' see OGLESBY, Joseph
'KAINS, Josephine' see GOULART, Ronald J.

KAIRYS, Anatolijus, 1914- , Russian-American; poetry, plays CON
KAISARI, Uri, 1899?-1979, Israeli; journalism CON
KAISER, Artur, 1943- , German; nonfiction CON
'KAISER, Bill' see SUMNER, David W. K.
KAISER, Edward John, 1935- , American; nonfiction CON
KAISER, Edwin George, 1893- , American; nonfiction, translations CON
KAISER, Ernest, 1915- , American; nonfiction CON SH
KAISER, Frances Elkan, 1922- , American; nonfiction, translations CON
KAISER, George, 1878-1945, German; plays BU CL MCG SEY TH
KAISER, Harvey H., 1936- , American; nonfiction CON
KAISER, Otto, 1924- , German; nonfiction CON
KAISER, Robert Greeley, 1943- , American; nonfiction CON
KAISER, Ward Louis, 1923- , Canadian-American; nonfiction CON
KAJAI, Abdul Rahim bin Salim, 1894-1943, Malayan; journalism, fiction PRU
KAJI NAZRUL ISLAM, 1899- , Bengali; poetry BU
KAJIKO, 18th century, Japanese; poetry HI
KAKAZA, Lillith, 1885?-1950?, Xhosa; fiction HER
'KAKI' see HEINEMANN, Katherine
KAKIMON-IN, 14th century, Japanese; poetry HI
KAKIMOTO, Kozo, 1915- , Japanese; juveniles CO
KAKINOMOTO no HITOMARO, 655-700/10, Japanese; poetry BU HI LA PRU
KAKONIS, Thomas E., 1930- , American; nonfiction CON
KAKUGAWA, Frances Hideko, 1936- , American; poetry CON
KALA, U, 1678?-1738?, Burmese; nonfiction PRU
KALASHNIKOFF, Nicholas, 1888-1961, Russian-American; juveniles, fiction CO CON

KALB, Jonah, 1926- , American;
juveniles CO CON WAR
KALBERER, Augustine, 1917- ,
American; nonfiction CON
KALCHEIM, Lee, 1938- , Amer-
ican; plays CON VCD
KALDOR, Mary, 1946- , British;
nonfiction CON
'KALE, Arvind and Shanta' see
GANTZER, Hugh
KALEB, Vjekoslav, 1905- ,
Croatian; fiction BU TH
KALECHOFSKY, Roberta, 1931- ,
American; nonfiction CON
KALEKO, Mascha, 1912- ,
German; poetry TH
KALENCIAK, Ján, 1822-71,
Slovak; fiction, poetry BU
KALENIK, Sandra, 1945- ,
American; nonfiction, plays
CON
KALER, James Otis ('James
Otis'), 1848-1912, American;
juveniles CO
KALFOV, Damyan, 1887- ,
Bulgarian; fiction BU
KALHANA, 13th century, Indian;
poetry BU
KALICH, Jacob, 1891-1975,
Polish-American; plays CON
KALICKI, Jan Henryk, 1948- ,
Anglo-American; nonfiction
CON
KALIDASA, 4th century, Sanskrit;
poetry, plays BU LA MAG
PRU
KALLJARVI, Thorsten Valentine,
1897-1980, American; nonfic-
tion CON
KALIM KASHANI, Abu Talib (of
Hamadan), -1651/52, Indo-
Persian; poetry BU PRU
KALIN, Martin Gregory, 1943- ,
American; nonfiction CON
KALIN, Robert, 1921- , Amer-
ican; nonfiction CON
KALIN, Rudolf, 1938- , Amer-
ican; nonfiction CON
KALINA, Sigmund, 1911- ,
American; juveniles, nonfic-
tion CON WAR
KALINSKY, George, 1936- ,
American; nonfiction CON
KALIR, Eleazer (Killir; Kiklir),
4-8th? centuries, Hebrew;
poetry BU
KALISH, Betty McKelvey, 1913- ,
American; nonfiction CON

KALIYANACUNTARAM, Mutaliyar
Tiruvarur, 1883-1953, Tamil;
nonfiction, journalism PRU
'KALKI' see KIRUSNAMURTTI, R.
'KALKUT' see 'BASU, Samarés'
KALLA, Makhdum see DONISH,
Ahmad
KALLAS, Aino, 1878-1956, Fin-
nish; fiction TH
KALLEN, Horace Meyer, 1882-
1974, American; nonfiction
CON
KALLEN, Laurence, 1944- ,
American; nonfiction CON
KALLEN, Lucille, American; fic-
tion, plays CON
KALLENBACH, Joseph Ernest,
1903- , American; nonfiction
CON
KALLESSER, Michael, 1886?-1975,
American; plays CON
KALLIFATIDES, Theodor, 1938- ,
Greek-Swedish; plays, fiction
CON
KALLIR, Otto, 1894-1978, Austrian-
American; nonfiction CON
KALLMAN, Chester Simon, 1921-
75, American; poetry, plays,
translations CON VCP
KALMA, Douwe, 1896-1953,
Frisian; translations, poetry,
nonfiction BU
KALMAN, Harold David, 1943- ,
Canadian; nonfiction CON
KALME, Egils, 1909- , Latvian-
American; fiction CON
KALNAY, Francis, 1899- , Amer-
ican; juveniles, nonfiction CO
CON
KALNOKY, Ingeborg Louise,
1909- , Hungarian-American;
nonfiction CON
KALONYMOS ben KALINYMOS,
1286-1322?, Hebrew; transla-
tions, nonfiction TH
KALONYMOS FAMILY, Hebrew;
nonfiction, poetry BU
KALPAKIAN, Laura Anne, 1945- ,
American; fiction CON
KALS, William Steven, 1910- ,
Austrian-American; nonfiction
CON
KALSTONE, Shirlee Ann, 1932- ,
American; nonfiction CON
KALT, Jeannette (Chappell), 1898?-
1970, American; poetry CON
KALTENBORN, Hans von, 1878-
1965, American; journalism

CON
KALTER, Joanmarie, 1951- ,
American; nonfiction CON
KALU, Ogbu Uke, 1944- ,
Nigerian; nonfiction CON
KALUGER, Meriem Fair, 1921- ,
American; nonfiction CON
'KALUNGANO' see DOS SANTOS,
Marcelino
KALVEN, Harry, Jr., 1914-74,
American; nonfiction CON
KALVOS, Andreas Ioannidas,
1792-1869, Greek; poetry
BU TH
KAMALESVAR, 1932- , Hindi;
tv, nonfiction, fiction PRU
KAMALODDIN ESMA'IL ESFA-
HANI, 1172/73-1237, Persian;
poetry PRU
KAMARCK, Lawrence, 1927- ,
American; fiction, journalism
CON
KAMATH, Madhav Vithal, 1921- ,
Indian; nonfiction CON
KAMBAN, Gudmundur Jónsson,
1888-1945, Icelander; plays,
fiction BU CL
KAMBARA ARIAKE, 1876-1952,
Japanese; poetry HI PRU
KAMEN, Gloria, 1923- , Amer-
ican; juveniles CO
KAMENEV, Gavrita Petrovich,
1772-1803, Russian; poetry
BU
KAMENOVA, Anna Majarova,
1894- , Bulgarian; fiction
BU
KAMENSKY, Vasily Vasilyevich,
1884-1961, Russian; fiction
BU CL
KAMERA, William, 1942- ,
Tanzanian; poetry JA
KAMERMAN, Sheila Brody, 1928- ,
American; nonfiction CON
KAMERSCHEN, David Roy, 1937- ,
American; nonfiction CON
KAMES, Henry Home, 1696-1782,
Scots; nonfiction BU
KAMIJIMA ONITSURA (Uejima),
1661-1738, Japanese; poetry
HI
KAMIL, Jill, 1930- , English;
nonfiction CON
KAMIN, Leon J., 1927- , Amer-
ican; nonfiction CON
'KAMIN, Nick' (Robert J. Anton-
ick), 1939- , American;
fiction NI

KAMINSKA, Ida, 1899-1980, Rus-
sian-American; nonfiction
CON
KAMINSKI, Margaret Joan,
1944- , American; poetry,
nonfiction CON
KAMINSKY, Marc, 1943- , Amer-
ican; nonfiction CON
KAMINSKY, Stuart Melvin, 1934- ,
American; nonfiction CON
KAMISAR, Yale, 1929- , Ameri-
can; nonfiction CON
KAMM, Herbert, 1917- , Ameri-
can; nonfiction CON
KAMM, Josephine Mary, 1905- ,
British; juveniles, fiction, non-
fiction CO KI
KAMMAN, Madeleine Marguerite,
1930- , Franco-American;
nonfiction CON
KAMMERER, Gladys M., 1909-70,
American; nonfiction CON
KAMO no CHOMEI (Kamo no
Nazaakira), 1153-1216, Japan-
ese; poetry BU HI LA PRU
KAMO no MABUCHI, 1697-1769,
Japanese; poetry, nonfiction
HI
KAMPAN, 1180-1250, Tamil; poetry
BU LA PRU
KAMPELMAN, Max M., 1920- ,
American; nonfiction CON
KAMPMANN, Christian, 1939- ,
Danish; fiction CL
KAMPOV, B. N. see 'POLEVOY,
Boris N.'
KAMSTRA, Leslie D., 1920- ,
American; nonfiction CON
KAN PAO, 4th century, Chinese;
nonfiction BU PRU
KANAGAKI ROBUN, 1829-94,
Japanese; poetry, nonfiction,
fiction PRU
KANAHELE, George Sanford,
1930- , American; nonfiction
CON
'KAN'AMI KIYOTSUGU' (Yusaki
Saburo Kiyatsugu), 1333-84,
Japanese; plays BU HI
KANDEL, Lenore, American; poetry
VCP
KANDINSKY, Nina, 1896?-1980,
Swiss; nonfiction CON
KANDO, Thomas M., 1941- ,
Hungarian-American; nonfiction
CON
KANDYBA, Oleksander see 'OLES,
Oleksander'

KANE, Basil Godfrey, 1931- ,
  Anglo-American; nonfiction,
  juveniles CON
KANE, Dennis Cornelius, 1918- ,
  American; nonfiction CON
'KANE, E. B.,' 1944- , Amer-
  ican; nonfiction, translations
  CON
KANE, Edward James, 1935- ,
  American; nonfiction CON
KANE, Frank ('Frank Boyd'),
  1912-68, American; plays,
  nonfiction REI
KANE, Frank R., 1925- , Amer-
  ican; journalism CON
KANE, George, 1916- , Amer-
  ican; nonfiction CON
KANE, Henry ('Anthony McCall'),
  1918- , American; fiction,
  nonfiction REI ST
KANE, Henry Bugbee, 1902-71,
  American; juveniles CO CON
KANE, J. Herbert, 1910- ,
  Canadian-American; nonfiction
  CON
'KANE, Julia' see ROBINS, Denise
KANE, Robert W., 1910- ,
  American; juveniles CO
KANE, Sheikh Hamidou, 1928- ,
  West African; fiction CL
  HER JA LA
KANE, William Everett, 1943- ,
  American; nonfiction CON
'KANE, Wilson' house name NI
KANEKO KUN'EN, 1876-1951,
  Japanese; poetry HI
KANELLOS, Nicolas C., 1945- ,
  American; nonfiction MAR
KANER, Hyman, British; fiction
  NI
KANFER, Frederick H., 1925- ,
  Austrian-American; nonfiction
  CON
KANFER, Stefan, 1933- , Amer-
  ican; journalism, nonfiction,
  fiction, plays CON
K'ANG YU-WEI, 1858-1927, Chi-
  nese; nonfiction BU PRU
KANGRO, Bernard, 1910- ,
  Estonian; poetry, fiction,
  nonfiction BU
KANI, Abu Bekir, 1712-92, Turk-
  ish; poetry PRU
KANIK, Orhan Veli, 1914-50,
  Turkish; poetry, translations
  CL PRU
KANIN, Garson, 1912- , Amer-
  ican; plays, fiction, nonfiction

  BR MCN VCD WA
KANIN, Michael, 1910- , Amer-
  ican; plays, film CON
KANITZ, Walter, 1910- , Austrian-
  Canadian; nonfiction CON
KANNER, Leo, 1894-1981,
  Austrian-American; nonfiction
  CON
KANSIL, Joli, 1943- , American;
  nonfiction CON
KANT, Hermann, 1926- , German;
  fiction BU
KANT, Immanuel, 1724-1804, Ger-
  man; nonfiction BU MAG TH
KANTAR, Edwin Bruce, 1932- ,
  American; nonfiction CON
KANTEMIR, Antioch Dmitrievich,
  1709-44, Russian; poetry BU
KANTER, Arnold, 1945- , Amer-
  ican; nonfiction CON
KANTER, Hal ('Henry Irving'),
  1918- , American; film, non-
  fiction CON
KANTER, Rosabeth Moss, 1943- ,
  American; nonfiction CON
KANTOR, Hal, 1924- , American;
  fiction CON
KANTOR, Herman I., 1909- ,
  American; nonfiction CON
KANTOR, Mackinley, 1904-77,
  American; fiction BR CON
  NI PAL ST VCN
KANTOR, Marvin, 1934- , Amer-
  ican; nonfiction CON
KANTOR, Seth, 1926- , American;
  nonfiction CON
KANTOR-BERG, Friedrich ('Fried-
  rich Torberg'), 1908-79, Aus-
  trian; poetry, fiction, transla-
  tions CON
KANTROWITZ, Arnie, 1940- ,
  American; nonfiction CON
KANTROWITZ, Joanne Spencer,
  1931- , American; nonfiction
  CON
KANWA, 11th century, Javanese;
  poetry, nonfiction PRU
KANZA, Thomas Rnsenga, 1933- ,
  Zairian; nonfiction, fiction
  CON JA
KANZAWA, Toshiko see FURUKA-
  WA, Toshi
'KANZEIN, Ko' see ISVGAI, Hiro-
  shi
KAO, Charles C. L., 1932- ,
  Chinese-American; nonfiction
  CON
KAO CH'I, 1336-74, Chinese;

ism, fiction, nonfiction CL
LA PRU
KARAPANOU, Margarita, 1946- ,
Greek-American; fiction
CON
'KARASEKZE LVOVIC, Jiří'
(Josef Jiří Antonín), 1871-
1951, Czech; poetry, fiction,
plays BU
KARASLAVOV, Georgi, 1904- ,
Bulgarian; fiction BU
KARAVAYEVA, Anna, 1893- ,
Russian; fiction BU
KARAVELOV, Lyuben, 1835-79,
Bulgarian; nonfiction, fiction
BU TH
KARDISH, Laurence, 1945- ,
Canadian-American; plays,
nonfiction CON
KAREL, Leonard, 1912- , Amer-
ican; nonfiction CON
KAREN, Robert Le Roy, 1925- ,
American; nonfiction CON
KAREN, Ruth, 1922- , German-
American; juveniles CO
KARGON, Robert Hugh, 1938- ,
American; nonfiction CON
KARIG, Walter, 1898- , Amer-
ican; journalism, fiction NI
KARIM, Ahmed Awad, 1890?- ,
Sudanese; poetry HER
'KARINA' see GOUD, Anne
KARINTHY, Frigyes, 1887-1938,
Hungarian; nonfiction, trans-
lations, fiction AS BU CL
NI TH
KARIOTAKIS, Kostas, 1896-1928,
Greek; poetry CL
KARIUKI, Joseph E., 1931- ,
Kenyan; poetry HER JA
KARIUKI, Josiah Mwangi, 1929- ,
Kenyan; nonfiction JA
KARIV, Abraham (Krivoruzhka),
1900- , Lithuanian; poetry,
nonfiction BU
KARK, Nina Mary M. see
'BAWDEN, Nina'
KARKOSCHKA, Erhard, 1923- ,
Czech; nonfiction CON
KARL, Barry Dean, 1927- ,
American; nonfiction CON
KARL, Jean, 1927- , American;
juveniles WAR
'KARL, Kashen' see KENNEDY,
Leo
KARLEE, Varfelli ('Charles Ed-
ward Cooper'), 1900?- ,
Liberian; fiction HER

KARLFELDT, Erik Axel, 1864-
1931, Swedish; poetry BU CL
TH
KARLIN, Eugene, 1918- , Amer-
ican; juveniles CO
KARLIN, Muriel Schoenbrun, Amer-
ican; nonfiction CON
KARLSDOTTIR, Helga M. see
'NOVAK, Helga'
'KARM, Dun' see PSAILA, Mon-
signor Carmelo
KARMAN, Mal ('Penelope Ashe'),
1944- , American; fiction
CON
KARMEL-WOLFE, Henia, 1923- ,
Polish-American; nonfiction,
fiction CON
KARMEN, Roman Lazarevich,
1906-78, Russian; journalism,
film CON
KARMI, Abdul Karim ('Abu Salma'),
1907?-80, Syrian-American;
poetry CON
KARMI, Hasan Said, 1908- ,
Arab; nonfiction CON
KARMIN, Monroe William, 1929- ,
American; journalism CON
KARNAD, Giris(h), 1937/38- ,
Kannadan; plays CON PRU
KARNES, Merle Briggs, 1916- ,
American; nonfiction CON
'KARNIEWSKI, Janusz' see WITT-
LIN, Thaddeus A.
KARNOW, Stanley, 1925- , Amer-
ican; nonfiction CON
KARO, Joseph (Caro), 1488-1575,
Spanish; nonfiction BU
'KAROL, Alex' see KENT, Arthur
W. C.
KARON, Bertram Paul, 1930- ,
American; nonfiction CON
'KARONIN' (Nikolay E. Petropav-
lovsky), 1857-92, Russian; fic-
tion BU
'KAROV, Rabbi' see LEVINSKI,
Elchaman L.
KARP, David, 1922- , American;
fiction, plays NI VCN
KARP, Laurence Edward, 1939- ,
American; nonfiction CON
KARP, Naomi J., 1926- , Amer-
ican; juveniles CO CON WAR
KARP, Walter, American; juveniles
WAR
KARPAT, Kemal Hasim, 1925- ,
Rumanian-American; nonfiction
CON
KARPATKIN, Marvin M., 1926-75,

American; nonfiction CON
'KARPAU, Uladzimir' see KAR-
POV, Vladimir
KARPEL, Craig S., 1944- ,
American; nonfiction CON
KARPINSKI, Franciszek, 1741-
1825, Polish; poetry, diary
BU TH
KARPMAN, Harold Lew, 1927- ,
American; nonfiction CON
KARPOV, Vladimir ('Uladzimir
Karpau'), 1912?-77, Bey-
lorussian; fiction CON
KARPOWICZ, Tymoteusz, 1921- ,
Polish; poetry, fiction, plays,
nonfiction BU CL
KARR, Jean Alphonse, 1808-90,
French; fiction, journalism
BU
KARR, Phyllis Ann, 1944- ,
American; fiction CON
KARRASS, Chester L., 1923- ,
American; nonfiction CON
KARRIS, Robert Joseph, 1938- ,
American; nonfiction, trans-
lations CON
KARSAVIN, Lev Platonovich,
1882- , Russian; nonfiction
BU
KARSAVINA, Jean Paterson,
1908- , American; juveniles
CON
KARSAVINA, Tamara, 1885-1978,
American-Russian; nonfiction
CON
KARSCH, Anna Luise Dürbach,
1722-91, German; poetry BU
KARSCH, Robert Frederick,
1909- , American; nonfiction
CON
KARSEN, Sonja Petra, 1919- ,
German-American; nonfiction,
translations CON
KARSH, Bernard, 1921- ,
American; nonfiction CON
KARTIGANER, Donald M., 1937- ,
American; nonfiction CON
KARU no HITSUGI-no-MIKO,
Japanese; poetry HI
KARU no OIRATSUME, 5th cen-
tury, Japanese; poetry HI
KARVE, Dinakar Dhondo, 1899-
1980, Indian; nonfiction
CON
KARYOTAKIS, Costas, 1896-1928,
Greek; poetry TH
KASA no IRATSUME, Japanese;
poetry HI

KASA no KANAMURA, 8th century,
Japanese; poetry HI
KASACK, Hermann, 1896-1966,
German; fiction, nonfiction,
poetry BU CL TH
KASAI ZENZO, 1887-1928, Japan-
ese; fiction PRU
KASARDA, John Dale, 1945- ,
American; nonfiction CON
KASCHNITZ, Marie Luise,
1901- , German; poetry,
fiction, radio BU CL TH
KASHIMA, Tetsuden, 1940- ,
American; nonfiction CON
KASHIWAGI, Isami, 1925- ,
American; juveniles CO
KASLOW, Florence Whiteman,
1930- , American; nonfiction
CON
KASPROWICZ, Jan, 1860-1926,
Polish; poetry, plays, transla-
tions BU CL TH
KASRA'I, Siyavush, 1925- ,
Persian; poetry BU
KASS, Jerome, 1937- , American;
plays CON
KASSABOV, Geo see MILEV, Geo
KASSAK, Lajos, 1887-1967, Hun-
garian; poetry, fiction BU
CL SEY TH
KASSALOW, Everett Malcolm,
1918- , American; nonfiction
CON
KASSAM, Amin, 1948- , Kenyan;
poetry JA
KASSNER, Rudolf, 1873-1959,
Austrian; nonfiction BU TH
KASSON, John Franklin, 1944- ,
American; nonfiction CON
KASTEELE, Pieter Leonard van de,
1748-1810, Dutch; poetry,
translations BU
'KASTEL, Warren' house name NI
KASTELAN, Jure, 1919- , Croat-
ian; poetry BU CL TH
KASTL, Albert Joseph, 1939- ,
American; nonfiction CON
KASTL, Lena, 1942- , American;
nonfiction CON
KASTLE, Herbert David, 1924- ,
American; fiction NI
KASTNER, Joseph, 1907- , Amer-
ican; nonfiction, journalism
CON
'KASZNAR, Kurt' see SERWICHER,
Kurt
KATAYEV, Evgeny see 'PETROV,
Evgeny P.'

KATAYEV, Valentin Petrovich, 1897- , Russian; fiction, plays, journalism BU CL MCG TH

KATAYEV, Yevgeniy P. see 'IL'F'

KATCHADOURIAN, Herant Aram, 1933- , Syrian-American; nonfiction CON

KATCHEN, Carole, 1944- , American; juveniles, nonfiction CO CON

KATE, Jan Jakob Lodewijk Ten ('Een Beunhaas in Bijschriften'), 1819-89, Dutch; poetry, translations BU

KATEB, Yacine, 1929- , Algerian; poetry, plays PRU

KATEBI TORSHIZI, -1434, Persian; poetry PRU

KATEN, Thomas Ellis, 1931- , American; nonfiction CON

KATENIN, Pavel Alexandrovich, 1792-1853, Russian; translations BU

'KATERLA, Józef' see ZEROM-SKI, Stefan

'KATHRYN' see SEARLE, Kathryn A.

KATI, Mahmud, 1468?-1570?, Arab; fiction HER

KÂTIB CELEBI, Mustafa (Hadji Khalifa), 1608-57, Turkish; nonfiction BU

KATKOV, Mikhayl Nikiforovich, 1818-87, Russian; journalism BU

KATO SHUSON, 1905- , Japanese; poetry HI

KATONA, Edita, 1913- , Austrian; nonfiction CON

KATONA, József, 1791-1830, Hungarian; plays BU MCG TH

KATONA, Robert, 1949- , American; juveniles CO

KATSAROS, Thomas, 1926- , American; nonfiction CON

KATTAN, Naim, 1928- , Iraqi-Canadian; journalism, nonfiction CON

KATTERJOHN, Arthur D., 1930?-80, American; nonfiction CON

KATYREV-ROSTOVSKY, Prince Ivan Mikhaylovich, -1640, Russian; nonfiction BU

KATZ, Abraham, 1926- , American; nonfiction CON

KATZ, Albert Michael, 1938- , American; nonfiction CON

KATZ, Alfred, 1938- , Polish-American; nonfiction CON

'KATZ, Basho' see GATTI, Arthur G.

KATZ, Bobbi, 1933- , American; juveniles CO

KATZ, Daniel, 1903- , American; nonfiction CON

KATZ, Eve, 1938- , Franco-American; nonfiction CON

KATZ, Fred Emil, 1927- , German-American; nonfiction CON

KATZ, Frederic Phillip, 1938- , American; juveniles, nonfiction CO CON

KATZ, Herbert Melvin, 1930- , American; nonfiction, fiction, juveniles CON WAR

KATZ, Jacqueline Hunt, English; juveniles WAR

KATZ, Jane Bresler, 1934- , American; nonfiction CON

KATZ, Jonathan, 1938- , American; plays, nonfiction CON

KATZ, Josef, 1918- , German-American; nonfiction CON

KATZ, Leon, 1919- , American; translations, nonfiction, plays CON

KATZ, Marjorie see WEISER, Marjorie

KATZ, Marjorie P., American; juveniles WAR

KATZ, Michael Ray, 1944- , American; nonfiction CON

KATZ, Mort, 1925- , American; nonfiction CON

KATZ, Myron Meyer (Mickey), 1909- , American; nonfiction CON

KATZ, William, 1940- , American; fiction, tv CON

KATZ, William Loren, 1927- , American; juveniles CO WAR

KATZENBACH, Maria, 1953- , American; fiction CON

KATZENBACH, William E., 1904-75, American; nonfiction CON

KATZENSTEIN, Mary Fainsod, 1945- , American; nonfiction CON

KATZENSTEIN, Peter Joachim, 1945- , German-American; nonfiction CON

KATZMAN, Anita, 1920- , Amer-
ican; fiction CON
KATZMAN, David Manners,
1941- , American; nonfiction
CON
KATZNELSON, Jehuda Loeb
('Bukki ben Yogli'), 1847-1917,
Hebrew; poetry, fiction TH
KATZNELSON-SHAZAR, Rachel,
1888-1975, Russian-Israeli;
nonfiction CON
KAUDZITE, Matiss, 1848-1926,
Latvian; fiction BU
KAUDZITE, Reinis, 1839-1920,
Latvian; fiction BU
KAUFELT, David Allan, 1939- ,
American; fiction CON
KAUFFELD, Carl F., 1911-74,
American; nonfiction CON
KAUFFMAN, James Milton,
1940- , American; nonfiction
CON
KAUFFMAN, Joseph Frank,
1921- , American; nonfiction
CON
KAUFFMAN, Milo Franklin,
1898- , American; nonfiction
CON
KAUFFMANN, Georg Friedrich,
1925- , German; nonfiction
CON
KAUFFMANN, Samuel Hay, 1898-
1971, American; nonfiction
CON
KAUFFMANN, Stanley Jules,
1916- , American; fiction,
plays BR WA
KAUFMAN, Barry Neil,
1942- , American; nonfic-
tion CON
KAUFMAN, Bob Garnell ('Bom-
kauf'), 1925- , American;
poetry BR CON SH
KAUFMAN, Daniel, 1949- ,
American; nonfiction
CON
KAUFMAN, David S. see
'SAMOYLOV, David S.'
KAUFMAN, Edmund George,
1891- , American; nonfic-
tion CON
KAUFMAN, George Simon, 1889-
1961, American; plays, jour-
nalism BR BU CON MCG
MCN PO VD
KAUFMAN, Harold Gerson, 1939- ,
American; nonfiction CON
KAUFMAN, Isadore ('William

Weer'), 1892-1978, Austrian-
American; journalism CON
KAUFMAN, Jacob Joseph, 1914- ,
American; nonfiction CON
KAUFMAN, Lloyd, 1927- ,
American; nonfiction CON
KAUFMAN, Mervyn D., 1932- ,
American; juveniles CO
KAUFMAN, Paul, 1886-1979,
American; nonfiction CON
KAUFMAN, Roger Alexander,
1932- , American; nonfiction
CON
KAUFMAN, Shirley, 1923- ,
American; poetry CON
KAUFMAN, Sue see BARONDESS
KAUFMAN, Angelika, 1935- ,
Austrian; juveniles CO
KAUFMANN, Harry, 1927- ,
American; nonfiction CON
KAUFMANN, Helen Loeb, 1887- ,
American; juveniles WAR
KAUFMANN, Henry William,
1913- , American; nonfiction
CON
KAUFMANN, John ('David Swift'),
1931- , American; juveniles
CO CON
KAUFMANN, Urlin Milo, 1934- ,
American; nonfiction CON
KAUFMANN, Walter, 1921-80,
German; nonfiction CON
KAUFMANN, Walter, 1933- ,
American; nonfiction CON
KAUFMANN, William John III,
1942- , American; nonfiction
CON
KAUL, Donald, 1934- , American;
plays, fiction CON
KAUL, Tedor, German; fiction
NI
KAULA, Edna Mason, 1906- ,
American; juveniles CO
KAUNDA, Kenneth, 1924- ,
Zambian; nonfiction JA
KAUPER, Paul Gerhardt, 1907-74,
American; nonfiction CON
KAUR, Sardarni Premka, 1943- ,
American; translations, nonfic-
tion CON
KAUTILYA (Canakya; Visnugupta),
4th century B. C., Sanskrit;
nonfiction BA LA PRU
KAUVAR, Gerald Bluestone,
1938- , American; nonfiction
CON
KAVAFIS, Konstantinos see
CAFAFY, Constantine P.

1932- , Russian; poetry CL
KAZANTZAKIS, Nikos, 1883-
1956/57, Greek; fiction, po-
etry, plays, translations,
journalism BU CL MAG
SEY TH
KAZARIAN, Edward Arshak,
1931- , American; nonfiction
CON
KAZICKAS, Jurate Catherine,
1943- , Lithuanian-American;
nonfiction CON
KAZIM KHAN KHATAK SHAYDA,
1725?-80?, Pashtun; poetry
PRU
KAZIN, Alfred, 1915- , Amer-
ican; nonfiction BOR BR BU
KAZIN, Vasily Vasilyevich,
1898- , Russian; poetry
BU
KAZINCZY, Ferenc, 1759-1831,
Hungarian; nonfiction BU TH
KAZMER, Daniel Raphael,
1947- , American; nonfiction
CON
KAZZIHA, Walid W., 1941- ,
Syrian; nonfiction CON
KEACH, Richard Leroy, 1919- ,
American; nonfiction CON
KEAN, Benjamin Harrison,
1912- , American; nonfiction
CON
KEAN, Edmund Stanley, 1915- ,
Austrian-American; nonfiction
CON
KEANE, Betty Winkler, 1914- ,
American; nonfiction CON
KEANE, Bil, 1922- , American;
juveniles CO
KEANE, John Brendan, 1928- ,
Irish; plays, fiction, poetry
HO VCD
KEANE, Patrick Joseph, 1939- ,
American; nonfiction CON
KEANEY, Marian, 1944- , Irish;
nonfiction CON
KEAREY, Charles, 1916- , South
African; fiction CON
KEARLEY, Floyd Furman,
1932- , American; nonfiction
CON
KEARNEY, Chalmers, 1881- ,
English; fiction NI
KEARNEY, Jean Nylander, 1923- ,
American; nonfiction CON
KEARNEY, Peadar, 1883-1942,
Irish; songs HO
KEARNEY, Robert Norman,

1930- , American; nonfiction
CON
KEARNS, Doris Helen, 1943- ,
American; nonfiction CON
KEARNS, Lionel John, 1937- ,
Canadian; poetry VCP
KEARNS, Martha, 1945- , Amer-
ican; nonfiction CON
KEARY, Annie, 1825-79, English;
juveniles, fiction BU
KEATING, Diane, 1940- , Amer-
ican; nonfiction, poetry CON
KEATING, Geoffrey see CEITINN,
Séathrún
KEATING, Henry Reymond Fitz-
walter, 1926- , English; fic-
tion, nonfiction, plays MCC
REI ST WAK
KEATING, John J., 1918?-75,
Canadian; nonfiction CON
KEATING, Lawrence A. ('John
Keith Bassett'; 'H. C.
Thomas'), 1903-66, American;
juveniles CO
KEATING, Leo Bernard (Bern),
1915- , Canadian-American;
juveniles CO
KEATING, Michael F., 1932- ,
Canadian-American; nonfiction
CON
KEATS, Ezra Jack, 1916- ,
American; juveniles CO CON
KI
KEATS, John, 1795-1821, English;
poetry BU DA MAG PO VP
KEATS, John C., 1920- , Amer-
ican; nonfiction, fiction CON
KEATS, Mark, 1905- , American;
juveniles, nonfiction CON
KEAVENEY, Sydney Starr, 1939- ,
American; nonfiction CON
KEAY, John Stanley M., 1941- ,
British; nonfiction CON
KEBEDE, Mikael see KABBADA,
Mika'el
KEBLE, John, 1792-1866, English;
poetry, nonfiction BU DA VP
PO
KEBSCHULL, Harvey Gustav,
1932- , American; nonfiction
CON
KEDGLEY, Susan Jane, 1948- ,
New Zealander-American; non-
fiction CON
KEDRIN, Dmitry, 1907-45, Russian;
poetry TH
KEE, Alistair, 1937- , Scots;
nonfiction CON

KEE, Robert, 1919- , English;
 fiction NI
KEEDY, Mervin Laverne, 1920- ,
 American; nonfiction CON
KEEFE, Carolyn, 1928- ,
 American; nonfiction CON
KEEFE, Michael, 1946- , Amer-
 ican; journalism, nonfiction
 CON
KEEFE, Robert, 1938- , Amer-
 ican; nonfiction CON
KEEGAN, Frank L., 1925- ,
 American; nonfiction CON
KEEGAN, John, 1809-49, Irish;
 poetry HO
KEEGAN, Marcia, 1943- ,
 American; nonfiction, juveniles
 CO CON
KEEGAN, Warren Joseph, 1936- ,
 American; nonfiction CON
KEELER, Harry Stephen, 1890-
 1967, American; fiction ST
KEELER, Mary Frear, 1904- ,
 American; nonfiction CON
KEELEY, Edmund Leroy, 1928- ,
 American; fiction, transla-
 tions, nonfiction WA
KEELEY, Steve, 1949- , Amer-
 ican; nonfiction CON
KEELY, Harry Harris, 1904- ,
 British; nonfiction CON
'KEEN, Geraldine' see NORMAN,
 Geraldine
KEEN, Martin L., 1913- ,
 American; juveniles CO WAR
KEENAN, Angela Elizabeth,
 1890- , American; nonfiction
 CON
KEENAN, Deborah Anne, 1950- ,
 American; nonfiction CON
KEENAN, Joseph Henry, 1900-77,
 American; nonfiction CON
KEENAN, Martha, 1927- ,
 American; juveniles CON
'KEENE, Burt' see BICKERS,
 Richard L. T.
'KEENE, Carolyn' (Edward L.
 Stratemeyer, 1862-1930,
 American; juveniles, fiction
 ST
KEENE, Day,   -1969?, Amer-
 ican; fiction NI REI
'KEENE, Faraday' see JARRETT,
 Cora H.
KEENEN, George, American;
 juveniles WAR
KEENER, Frederick Michael,
 1937- , American; nonfiction

CON
KEENEY, Ralph Lyons, 1944- ,
 American; nonfiction CON
KEENEY, William Echard, 1922- ,
 American; nonfiction CON
KEENLEYSIDE, Terence Ashley,
 1940- , American; nonfiction,
 fiction CON
KEEP, Carolyn, 1940- , English;
 nonfiction CON
KEEP, David John, 1936- , Eng-
 lish; nonfiction CON
KEEPING, Charles William James,
 1924- , British; juveniles,
 plays CO DE KI
KEES, Beverly Ann, 1941- ,
 American; nonfiction CON
KEES, Weldon, 1914-55, American;
 poetry BR MAL WA
KEEVER, Jack, 1938- , American;
 nonfiction CON
KEFFERSTAN, Jean see PEDRICK,
 Jean
KEGELS, Anne-Marie, 1912- ,
 Belgian; poetry CL
KEHOE, Patrick Emmett, 1941- ,
 American; nonfiction CON
KEICHU, 1640-1701, Japanese;
 nonfiction, poetry HI
KEIFETZ, Norman, 1932- ,
 American; nonfiction, fiction
 CON
KEIGHTLEY, David Noel ('Noel
 Keyes'), 1932- , American;
 fiction, nonfiction CON NI
KEIKAI, Japanese; fiction HI
KEIL, Harold Bill, 1926- ,
 American; nonfiction CON
KEIL, Sally Van Wagenen, 1946- ,
 American; nonfiction CON
'KEIMBERG, Allyn' see KIMBRO,
 John M.
KEINZLEY, Frances, 1922- ,
 Irish; fiction CON
'KEIR, Christine' see PULLEIN-
 THOMPSON, Christine
KEISER, Beatrice, 1931- , Amer-
 ican; nonfiction CON
KEITA FODEBA see 'FODEBA,
 Keita'
'KEITH, David' see STEEGMULLER,
 Francis
KEITH, Elmer Merrifield, 1899- ,
 American; nonfiction CON
KEITH, Eros, 1942- , American;
 juveniles DEM
KEITH, Harold Verne, 1903- ,
 American; juveniles KI

'KEITH, J. Kilmeny' see MALLE-
SON, Lucy B.
KEITH, Jean E., 1921-79, Amer-
ican; nonfiction CON
KEITH, Judith, 1923- , American;
nonfiction CON
KEITH, Larry Ficquette, 1947- ,
American; journalism, non-
fiction CON
'KEITH, Leigh' see GOLD, Horace
KEITH, Marian (Mary Esther
Miller MacGregor), 1874-
1961, Canadian; nonfiction,
fiction CR
KEITH, Noel L., 1903- , Amer-
ican; nonfiction CON
'KEITH, Robert' see APPLEBAUM,
Stan
KEITH, Sam, 1921- , American;
nonfiction CON
KEITHLEY, Erwin M., 1905- ,
American; nonfiction CON
KEITH-SPIEGEL, Patricia,
1939- , American; nonfiction
CON
KEIUN (Kyoun), 13th century,
Japanese; poetry HI
KEKES, John, 1936- , Hungarian-
American; nonfiction CON
KEKKONEN, Sylvi, 1900?-74,
Finnish; fiction, nonfiction
CON
KELCH, Ray Alden, 1923- ,
American; nonfiction CON
KELDYSH, Mstilav Vsevolodovich,
1911-78, Russian; nonfiction
CON
KELEMAN, Stanley, 1931- ,
American; nonfiction CON
KELEN, Emery, 1896-1978,
Hungarian-American; juveniles
CO CON WAR
KELF-COHEN, Reuben, 1895- ,
English; nonfiction CON
'KELL, Joseph' see 'BURGESS,
Anthony'
KELL, Richard Alexander, 1927- ,
British; poetry VCP
KELLAM, Sheppard Gordon,
1931- , American; nonfiction
CON
KELLAND, Clarence Budington,
1881-1964, American; fiction,
plays CON REI
KELLAR, Kenneth Chambers,
1906- , American; nonfiction
CON
KELLEAM, Joseph Everidge,

1913- , American; fiction
NI
KELLEHER, Stephen Joseph,
1915- , American; nonfiction
CON
KELLER, Beverly Lou Harwick,
American; juveniles, fiction,
nonfiction CO CON WAR
KELLER, Charles, 1942- ,
American; juveniles CO CON
WAR
KELLER, Clair Wayne, 1932- ,
American; nonfiction CON
KELLER, David Henry, 1880-
1966, American; fiction AS
NI
KELLER, Dean Howard, 1933- ,
American; nonfiction CON
KELLER, Edward Anthony, 1942- ,
American; nonfiction CON
KELLER, Frances Richardson,
1914- , American; nonfiction
CON
KELLER, Franklin J., 1887?-
1976, American; nonfiction
CON
KELLER, Fred Simmons, 1899- ,
American; nonfiction CON
KELLER, Gail F. see FAITHFULL,
Gail
KELLER, Gerard, 1829-99, Dutch;
journalism BU
KELLER, Gottfried, 1819-90,
Swiss; poetry, fiction BU
MAG TH
KELLER, Harry Stephen, 1890-
1967, American; fiction REI
KELLER, Helen Adams, 1880-
1968, American; nonfiction
CON
KELLER, Howard Hughes, 1941- ,
American; nonfiction CON
KELLER, James Gregory, 1900-77,
American; nonfiction CON
KELLER, John Esten ('J. A.
Gato'), 1917- , American;
nonfiction CON
KELLER, Karl, 1933- , American;
nonfiction CON
KELLER, Marti, 1948- , Ameri-
can; journalism CON
KELLER, Suzanne, 1930- , Aus-
trian-American; nonfiction
CON
KELLER, Walter David, 1900- ,
American; nonfiction CON
KELLERMANN, Bernhard, 1879-
1951, German; fiction NI

KELLETT, Arnold, 1926- ,
British; nonfiction CON
KELLEY, Albert Ben, 1936- ,
American; nonfiction CON
KELLEY, Alice van Buren,
1944- , American; nonfiction
CON
KELLEY, Dean Maurice, 1926- ,
American; nonfiction CON
KELLEY, H. N. , 1911- ,
American; nonfiction CON
KELLEY, Jane Holden, 1928- ,
American; nonfiction CON
KELLEY, John Charles, 1913- ,
American; nonfiction CON
KELLEY, Joseph John, Jr.,
1914- , American; nonfiction
CON
KELLEY, Kitty, 1942- , Amer-
ican; journalism, nonfiction
CON
KELLEY, Robert Emmett,
1938- , American; nonfiction
CON
KELLEY, William Melvin,
1937- , American; fiction,
nonfiction CON NI SH VCN
WA
KELLEY, Win, 1923- , Amer-
ican; plays, fiction CON
KELLGREN, Johan Henric, 1751-
95, Swedish; poetry BU
KELLIN, Sally Moffet, 1932- ,
American; juveniles CO
CON
KELLING, George Walton,
1944- , American; nonfiction
CON
KELLISON, Stephen G. , 1942- ,
American; nonfiction CON
KELLOGG, Alfred Latimer,
1915- , American; nonfiction
CON
KELLOGG, Charles Edwin, 1902-
80, American; nonfiction
CON
KELLOGG, James C. , III, 1915-
80, American; nonfiction
CON
KELLOGG, Jean ('Sally Jackson';
'Gene Kellogg'), 1916- ,
American; juveniles CO
KELLOGG, Marjorie, 1922- ,
American; fiction CON
KELLOGG, Mary Alice, 1948- ,
American; nonfiction CON
KELLOGG, Steven, 1941- ,
American; juveniles CO

CON DEM
KELLOUGH, Richard Dean,
1935- , American; nonfiction
CON
'KELLOW, Kathleen' see HIBBERT,
Eleanor
KELLUM, David Franklin, 1936- ,
American; nonfiction, fiction
CON
KELLY, Alfred H. , 1907-76,
American; nonfiction CON
KELLY, Charles Brian, 1935- ,
American; journalism, fiction
CON
KELLY, Clarence, 1941- , Amer-
ican; nonfiction CON
KELLEY, Emmett Leo, 1898-1979,
American; nonfiction CON
KELLY, Eric Philbrook, 1884-
1960, American; juveniles
CON COM KI
KELLY, Ernece Beverly, American;
nonfiction SH
KELLY, Frank K. , 1914- , Amer-
ican; fiction AS
KELLY, Frederic Joseph, 1922- ,
American; nonfiction CON
KELLY, Gail Paradise, 1940- ,
American; nonfiction CON
KELLY, Gary Frank, 1943- ,
American; nonfiction CON
KELLY, George Anthony, 1916- ,
American; juveniles WAR
KELLY, George E. , 1887-1974,
American; plays CON MCG
MCN VD
KELLY, George Vincent, 1919- ,
American; journalism, nonfic-
tion CON
KELLY, George W. , 1894- ,
American; nonfiction CON
KELLY, Hugh, 1739-77/78, Irish;
plays, journalism, fiction,
poetry HO VD
KELLY, James Burton, 1905- ,
American; fiction CON
KELLY, James Plunkett see
'PLUNKETT, James'
KELLY, John, 1921- , American;
nonfiction, fiction CON
KELLY, John Rivard, 1939- ,
American; nonfiction CON
KELLY, Karen ('Kay Lee'),
1935- , American; nonfiction
CON
KELLY, Kathleen Sheridan,
1945- , American; nonfiction
CON

KELLY, Laurence, 1933- ,
Belgian-British; nonfiction
CON
KELLY, Leo J., 1925- ,
American; nonfiction CON
KELLY, Linda, 1936- , British;
nonfiction CON
KELLY, Maeve, 1930- , Irish;
fiction HO
KELLY, Mahlon George, 1939- ,
American; nonfiction CON
KELLY, Marguerite Lelong,
1932- , American; nonfiction
CON
KELLY, Martha Rose (Marty),
1914- , American; poetry,
juveniles CON
KELLY, Mary Theresa, 1927- ,
British; fiction REI
KELLY, Maurice Anthony ('Spring-
field'), 1931- , English;
nonfiction CON
KELLY, Milton Terry, 1947- ,
American; fiction, poetry
CON
KELLY, Nora Hickson, 1910- ,
British; juveniles CON
KELLY, Pauline Agnes ('Raina
Barrett'), 1936- , American;
nonfiction CON
'KELLY, Ralph' see GEIS, Darlene
S.
'KELLY, Ray' see PAINE, Lauran
B.
KELLY, Regina Z., American;
juveniles CO
KELLY, Richard John, 1938- ,
American; nonfiction CON
KELLY, Rita Mae, 1939- ,
American; nonfiction CON
KELLY, Robert, 1935- , Amer-
ican; poetry, plays, fiction
BR MAL NI VCP
KELLY, Rosalie Ruth, American;
juveniles, fiction CON
KELLY, Walter Crawford, 1913-
73, American; juveniles, jour-
nalism CO CON
KELLY-GADOL, Joan, 1928- ,
American; nonfiction CON
KELMAN, Mark, 1951- , Amer-
ican; fiction, nonfiction CON
KELPIUS, Johann, 1673-1708,
German-American; nonfiction
BU
KELSEY, Robert John, 1927- ,
American; nonfiction CON
KELSON, Allen Howard, 1940- ,

American; nonfiction CON
KEMAL, Namik, 1840-88, Turkish;
poetry BU
'KEMAL, Orhan' (Mehmet R. K.
Öğütöü), 1914-70, Turkish;
journalism, film, fiction PRU
'KEMAL, Yashar' (Yasa Kemal
Gökceli), 1922/23- , Turkish;
fiction, journalism CL CON
PRU SEY WA
KEMAL TAHIR, 1910-73, Turkish;
fiction BU CL
KEMELMAN, Harry, 1908- ,
American; fiction REI ST
WAK
KEMENY, Peter, 1938-75, Ameri-
can; nonfiction CON
KEMENY, Baron Zsigmond, 1814-
75, Hungarian; fiction BU TH
KEMERER, Frank Robert, 1940- ,
American; nonfiction CON
KEMP, Abraham, 17th century,
Dutch; plays BU
KEMP, Arnold, American; nonfic-
tion SH
KEMP, Edward C., 1929- ,
American; nonfiction CON
KEMP, Gene, 1926- , British;
juveniles CO CON
KEMP, Jerrold Edwin, 1921- ,
American; nonfiction CON
KEMP, John Crocker, 1942- ,
American; nonfiction CON
KEMP, Lysander Schaffer, Jr.,
1920- , American; poetry,
translations CON
KEMP, Patrick Samuel, 1932- ,
American; nonfiction CON
KEMP, William, fl. 1600, English;
plays BU
KEMPE, Margery, 1373-1440, Eng-
lish; nonfiction BU DA
KEMPER, Rachel H., 1931- ,
American; nonfiction CON
KEMPFER, Lester Leroy, 1932- ,
American; nonfiction CON
KEMPNER, Mary Jean, 1913-69,
American; juveniles CO
KEMPNER, S. Marshal, 1898- ,
American; nonfiction CON
KEMPSTER, Norman, 1936- ,
American; journalism CON
KEMPTON, Jean Welch ('Jean
Louise Welch'), 1914- ,
American; juveniles, nonfiction
CO CON
KEMPTON, Murray, 1918- ,
American; journalism, nonfic-

tion CON WA
KEMSLEY, William George, Jr.,
1928- , American; nonfiction
CON
KEN(N), Thomas, 1637-1709/10,
English; nonfiction, hymns
BU
KENDALL, Carol Seeger, 1917- ,
American; juveniles, fiction
CO DE KI
KENDALL, Dorothy Steinbomer,
1912- , American; nonfiction
CON
KENDALL, Elizabeth Bemis,
1947- , American; nonfiction
CON
KENDALL, Henry Clarence, 1839-
82, Australian; poetry VP
'KENDALL, John' (Margaret Maud
Brash), 1880- , British;
fiction NI
KENDALL, Kenneth Everett,
1913- , American; nonfiction
CON
'KENDALL, Lace' see STOUTEN-
BERG, Adrien
KENDALL, Robert Tillman,
1935- , American; nonfiction
CON
KENDALL, Thomas Henry, 1839-
82, Australian; poetry BU
KENDALL, Thomas Robert,
1935- , American; nonfiction
CON
KENDLE, John Edward, 1937- ,
Anglo-Canadian; nonfiction
CON
'KENDRAKE, Carleton' see
GARDNER, Erle S.
KENDRICK, Baynard Hardwick
('Richard Hayward'), 1894-
1977, American; fiction, non-
fiction CON REI ST WA
KENDRICK, Frank Jenness,
1928- , American; nonfiction
CON
KENDRICK, Thomas Downing,
1895- , British; nonfiction
CON
KENEALLY, Thomas Michael,
1935- , Australian; fiction,
plays, juveniles BU CON
VCN VN WAK
KENEALY, James P., 1927- ,
American; nonfiction CON
KENKEL, William Francis,
1925- , American; nonfiction
CON

KENNA, Peter Joseph, 1930- ,
Australian; plays, nonfiction
CON VCD
KENNAN, George Frost, 1904- ,
American; nonfiction WA
'KENNAWAY, James' (James
Ewing Peebles), 1928-68,
Scots; fiction, film, plays
CON NI WA
KENNEBECK, Edwin, 1924- ,
American; nonfiction CON
KENNEBECK, Paul, 1943- ,
American; nonfiction CON
KENNEDY, Adrienne Lita, 1931- ,
American; plays, poetry, fic-
tion CON SH VCD WAK
KENNEDY, Andrew Karpati,
1931- , Hungarian-English;
nonfiction, poetry CON
KENNEDY, Bruce M., 1929- ,
American; nonfiction CON
KENNEDY, D. James, 1930- ,
American; nonfiction CON
KENNEDY, Don Henry, 1911- ,
American; nonfiction CON
KENNEDY, Eddie C., 1910- ,
American; nonfiction CON
'KENNEDY, Elliot' see GODFREY,
Lionel R.
KENNEDY, Florynce R., 1916- ,
American; nonfiction SH
KENNEDY, Gavin, 1940- , Amer-
ican; nonfiction CON
KENNEDY, George, 1899?-1977,
American; journalism CON
KENNEDY, Hubert Collings,
1931- , American; nonfiction
CON
KENNEDY, James Gettier, 1932- ,
American; nonfiction CON
KENNEDY, James Young, 1916- ,
American; nonfiction CON
KENNEDY, Jerome Richard,
1932- , American; nonfiction,
juveniles CO CON
KENNEDY, John Fitzgerald, 1917-
63, American; juveniles CO
KENNEDY, John Joseph, 1914- ,
American; nonfiction CON
KENNEDY, John Pendleton, 1795-
1870, American; fiction, non-
fiction BA BR BU MAG MYE
PO VN
'KENNEDY, Joseph' see KENNEDY,
X. J.
KENNEDY, Judith Mary, 1935- ,
Canadian; nonfiction CON
KENNEDY, Kathleen, 1947?-75,

American; nonfiction CON
KENNEDY, Kenneth Adrian Raine,
1930- , American; nonfiction
CON
KENNEDY, L. D., 1924- ,
American; nonfiction CON
KENNEDY, Lena see SMITH,
Lena
KENNEDY, Leo ('Leonard Bullen';
'Edgar Main'; 'Peter Quinn';
'Kashen Karl'), 1907- ,
Canadian; poetry CR
KENNEDY, Leonard Milton,
1925- , American; nonfiction
CON
KENNEDY, Ludovic Henry C.,
1919- , Scots; nonfiction
CON
KENNEDY, Margaret, 1896-1967,
American; fiction, plays
DA MCG
KENNEDY, Mary ('Mary Lee
Emerson'), American; jour-
nalism, plays, juveniles,
fiction CON
'KENNEDY, Milward' (Milward
Rodon Kennedy Burge; 'Evelyn
Elder'; 'Robert Milward Ken-
nedy'), 1894-1968, British;
fiction REI ST
KENNEDY, Paul Michael, 1945- ,
English; nonfiction CON
KENNEDY, R. A., English; fic-
tion NI
KENNEDY, Richard, 1910- ,
British; nonfiction CON
KENNEDY, Robert Lee, 1930- ,
American; nonfiction CON
'KENNEDY, Robert M.' see
'KENNEDY, Milward'
KENNEDY, Robert Woods, 1911- ,
American; nonfiction, fiction
CON
KENNEDY, Rose Fitzgerald,
1890- , American; nonfiction
CON
KENNEDY, Sighle Aileen, 1919- ,
American; nonfiction CON
KENNEDY, Susan Estabrook,
1942- , American; nonfiction
CON
KENNEDY, Thomas Fillans,
1921- , English; nonfiction
CON
KENNEDY, William, 1928- ,
American; fiction CON
'KENNEDY, X. J.' (Joseph
Charles Kennedy), 1929- ,

American; poetry, nonfiction
BR CO VCP WA
KENNEDY-MARTIN, Ian, 1936- ,
British; fiction, film CON
KENNEL, LeRoy Eldon, 1930- ,
American; nonfiction CON
KENNELL, Ruth Epperson, 1893-
1977, American; juveniles CO
KENNELLY, Timothy Brendan,
1936- , Irish; poetry, fiction
HO VCP
KENNER, William Hugh, 1923- ,
Canadian; nonfiction BOR WA
KENNERLY, David Hume, 1947- ,
American; journalism CON
KENNETT, Houn Jiyu, 1924- ,
American; nonfiction CON
KENNEY, Douglas, 1947?-80,
American; journalism, film
CON
KENNEY, Edwin James, Jr.,
1942- , American; nonfiction
CON
KENNY, Anthony John Patrick,
1931- , British; nonfiction
CON
'KENNY, Charles J.' see GARD-
NER, Erle S.
KENNY, Ellsworth Newcomb
('Ellsworth Newcomb'), 1909-
71, American; fiction, nonfic-
tion CON
KENNY, Herbert Andrew, 1912- ,
American; nonfiction, journal-
ism, poetry CO CON
KENNY, John Peter, 1916- ,
Australian; nonfiction CON
'KENNY, Kathryn' see BOWDEN,
Joan C.
KENNY, Nicholas Napoleon, 1895-
1975, American; journalism,
poetry CON
KENNY, Shirley Elise Strum,
1934- , American; nonfiction
CON
KENNY, Vincent, 1919- , Amer-
ican; nonfiction CON
KENOFER, Charles Louis, 1923- ,
American; nonfiction CON
KENREIMON-IN no UKYO-no-
DAIBU, 1157?- , Japanese;
poetry HI
KENRICK, Donald Simon, 1929- ,
American; nonfiction CON
KENRICK, Tony, 1935- , British;
fiction REI
KENSHALO, Daniel Ralph, 1922- ,
American; nonfiction CON

KENSHO, 1130?-1210?, Japanese;
poetry, nonfiction HI
'KENT, Arden' see MARION,
Frieda
KENT, Arthur William Charles,
('James Bradwell'; 'M. Du-
bois'; 'Paul Granados'; 'Alex-
ander Karol'; 'Alexander
Stamper'; 'Brett Vane'),
1925- , British; journalism,
fiction CON
KENT, Charles William, 1860-
1917, American; nonfiction
BA
KENT, Deborah Ann, 1948- ,
American; nonfiction CON
KENT, Edward Allen, 1935- ,
American; translations, non-
fiction CON
KENT, Frank Richardson, Jr.,
1907?-78, American; jour-
nalism CON
KENT, George Edward, 1920- ,
American; nonfiction SH
KENT, Harold Winfield, 1900- ,
American; nonfiction CON
KENT, John Wellington, 1920- ,
American; juveniles CO CON
'KENT, Katherine' see DIAL, Joan
'KENT, Kelvin' (BARNES, Arthur
K.; KUTTNER, Henry); fiction
NI
KENT, Leonard J., 1927- ,
American; nonfiction CON
KENT, Malcolm, 1932- , Amer-
ican; nonfiction CON
'KENT, Philip' see BULMER,
Kenneth
KENT, Rockwell ('Hogarth, Jr.'),
1882-1971, American; juveniles
CO
KENT, Sherman, 1903- , Amer-
ican; nonfiction, juveniles
CO CON
KENTFIELD, Calvin, 1924- ,
American; fiction, nonfiction
PAL
'KENTON, Maxwell' see SOUTHERN,
Terry
KENWARD, Michael, 1945- ,
British; nonfiction CON
KENWORTHY, Brian John, 1920- ,
British; nonfiction CON
KENWORTHY, Leonard S.,
1912- , American; juveniles
CO
'KENYATTA, Jomo' (Kamaua
Ngengi), 1893- , Kenyan;

nonfiction HER JA
KENYON, Ernest Monroe, 1920- ,
American; fiction CON
KENYON, Ley, 1913- , English;
juveniles CO
KENYON, Michael ('Daniel Forbes'),
1931- , British; fiction,
juveniles REI
'KENYON, Paul' see FREEDLAND,
Nathaniel
KEOGH, James, 1916- , Ameri-
can; journalism, nonfiction
CON
KEOHANE, Robert O., 1941- ,
American; nonfiction CON
KEPES, Gyorgy, 1906- , Hun-
garian-American; nonfiction
CON
KEPES, Juliet Appleby, 1919- ,
American; juveniles CO CON
DE
KEPHART, William M., 1921- ,
American; nonfiction CON
KEPLER, Johannes, 1571-1630,
German; nonfiction NI
KEPPEL-JONES, Arthur, South
African; fiction NI
KEPPLER, Herbert, 1925- ,
American; nonfiction CON
KER, William Paton, 1855-1923,
Scots; nonfiction DA
KER WILSON, Barbara, 1929- ,
English; juveniles CO DEM
KI
KERBABAYEV, Berdi, 1894- ,
Turmen; poetry, translations,
fiction PRU
KERBY, Joe Kent, 1933- , Amer-
ican; nonfiction CON
KERBY, Robert Lee, 1934- ,
American; nonfiction CON
'KERBY, Susan Alice' see BURTON,
Alice E.
KEREK, Andrew, 1936- , Hun-
garian-American; nonfiction
CON
KERENSKY, Vasil Michael, 1930- ,
American; nonfiction CON
KERES, Paul Petrovich, 1916-75,
Estonian; nonfiction CON
KEREWSKY-HALPERN, Barbara,
1931- , American; nonfiction
CON
KERIGAN, Florence ('Frances
Kerry'), 1896- , American;
juveniles CO
KERKVLIET, Benedict John,
1943- , American; nonfiction

CON
KERLINGER, Fred Nichols,
1910- , American; nonfiction
CON
KERMAN, Cynthia Earl, 1923- ,
American; nonfiction CON
KERMAN, Gertrude Lerner,
1909- , Canadian-American;
juveniles CO
KERMAN, Joseph Wilfred,
1924- , Anglo-American;
nonfiction CON
KERMAN, Judith Berna, 1945- ,
American; poetry, plays
CON
KERMAN, Sheppard, 1928- ,
American; tv, plays CON
KERMODE, John Frank, 1919- ,
English; nonfiction BOR WA
'KERN, Canyon' see RABORG,
Frederick A., Jr.
KERN, Gary, 1938- , American;
nonfiction, translations
CON
'KERN, Gregory' see TUBB,
Edwin C.
KERN, Jean Bordner, 1913- ,
American; nonfiction CON
KERN, Jerome David, 1885-1945,
American; composer MCG
KERN, Mary Margaret, 1906- ,
American; journalism, non-
fiction, fiction, juveniles
CON
KERN, Robert William, 1934- ,
American; nonfiction CON
KERN, Seymour, 1913- , Amer-
ican; nonfiction CON
KERN, Stephen, 1943- , Amer-
ican; nonfiction CON
KERNAN, Alvin Bernard, 1923- ,
American; nonfiction CON
KERNAN, Michael, 1927- ,
American; nonfiction, fiction
CON
KERNER, Justinus, 1786-1862,
German; poetry BU
KERNOCHAN, Sarah, 1947- ,
American; fiction CON
KERNODLE, George Riley, 1907- ,
American; nonfiction CON
KERNS, Frances Casey, 1937- ,
American; fiction CON
KERNS, Robert Louis, 1929- ,
American; journalism, non-
fiction CON
KEROUAC, Jack, 1922-69, Amer-
ican; fiction, poetry, non-

fiction BR BU HE PO SEY
VCN VN WA
KERR, Alexander McBride, 1921- ,
Australian; nonfiction CON
'KERR, Alfred' (A. Klemptner),
1868-1948, German; nonfiction
CL TH
KERR, Anne Judith, 1923- ,
British; juveniles CON KI
KERR, Barbara, 1913- , British;
nonfiction CON
'KERR, Carole' see CARR, Mar-
garet
KERR, Catherine, 1945- , Cana-
dian; nonfiction CON
KERR, Clark, 1911- , American;
nonfiction CON
KERR, Howard Hastings, 1931- ,
American; nonfiction CON
KERR, Hugh Thomson, 1909- ,
American; nonfiction CON
KERR, James Lennox ('Peter
Dawlish'), 1899-1963, Scots;
fiction, juveniles, nonfiction
CON KI
KERR, Jean Collins, 1923- ,
American; plays WA
KERR, Jessica Gordon, 1901- ,
Irish; juveniles CO WAR
KERR, Joan P., 1921- , Ameri-
can; nonfiction CON
KERR, Judith, 1923- , German-
English; juveniles CO WAR
KERR, Malcolm Hooper, 1931- ,
American; nonfiction CON
'KERR, M. E.' see MEAKER,
Marijane
'KERR, Robert,' 1899- , Scots;
fiction CON
KERR, Stanley E., 1894?-1976,
American; nonfiction CON
KERR, Walter, 1913- , American;
nonfiction, plays WA
KERRIGAN, Anthony, 1918- ,
American; translations, non-
fiction, poetry CON
KERRIGAN, William Joseph,
American; nonfiction CON
'KERRY, Frances' see KERIGAN,
Florence
KERSELL, John Edgar, 1930- ,
American; nonfiction CON
KERSH, Gerald, 1911-68, Russian-
British; fiction, plays, nonfic-
tion AS NI REI ST
KERSHAW, Gordon Ernest, 1928- ,
American; nonfiction CON
KERSHAW, John Hugh ('Hugh

D'Allenger'), 1931- , British;
nonfiction, tv CON
KERSHNER, Howard Eldred,
1891- , American; nonfiction
CON
KERSLAKE, Susan, 1943- ,
American; fiction CON
KERSNIK, Janko, 1852-97, Slovene;
fiction BU
KERSNOWSKI, Frank L., 1934- ,
American; poetry CON
KERTESZ, Andre, 1894- ,
American; nonfiction CON
KERTESZ, Louise, 1939- ,
American; journalism, non-
fiction CON
KERWOOD, John R., 1942- ,
American; nonfiction CON
KESA'I, Abu l-Hasan, 953-1002,
Persian; poetry PRU
KESAVA DEV, 1905- , Malay-
alan; plays, fiction PRU
'KESAVSUT' (Krsnaji Kesav
Damle), 1866-1905, Marathi;
poetry PRU
KESEY, Ken, 1935- , American;
fiction BR BU HE PO SEY
VCN WAK
KESHAV DAS, 1555-1617, Hindi;
poetry BU
KESHISHIAN, John M., 1923- ,
American; fiction NI
KESLER, Jay, 1935- , Amer-
ican; nonfiction CON
KESLER, William Jackson II,
1938- , American; nonfiction
CON
KESS, Joseph Francis, 1942- ,
American; nonfiction CON
KESSEL, Joseph Elie, 1898-1979,
French; fiction, journalism
BU CL CON WA
KESSEL, Maurice see 'DRUON,
Maurice'
KESSELL, John Lottridge,
1936- , American; nonfiction
CON
KESSELMAN, Judi Rosenthal
('Pauline Turkel'), 1934- ,
American; nonfiction CON
KESSLER, Diane Cooksey,
1947- , American; nonfiction
CON
KESSLER, Edward, 1927- ,
American; nonfiction, poetry
CON
KESSLER, Gail, 1937- , Amer-
ican; nonfiction CON

KESSLER, Henry Howard, 1896-
1978, American; nonfiction
CON
KESSLER, Leonard P., 1921- ,
American; juveniles CO CON
KESSLER, Milton, 1930- , Amer-
ican; poetry, plays VCP
KESSLER, Ronald, 1943- , Amer-
ican; nonfiction CON
KESSLER, Sheila, American; non-
fiction CON
KESSLER, Walter R., 1913-78,
American; nonfiction CON
KESSNER, Thomas, 1946- ,
German-American; nonfiction
CON
KESTELOOT, Lilyan ('Lilyan
Lagneau-Kesteloot'), 1931- ,
Belgian; nonfiction CON
KESTEN, Hermann, 1900- , Ger-
man; fiction, nonfiction, trans-
lations, plays CL SEY TH
KESTERSON, David Bert, 1938- ,
American; nonfiction CON
KESTERTON, Wilfred Harold,
1914- , Canadian; nonfiction
CON
'KESTEVEN, G. R.' see CROSHER,
Geoffrey R.
KESTNER, Joseph Aloysius,
1943- , American; nonfiction
CON
'KETCH, Jack' see TIBBETTS,
John C.
KETCHUM, Carlton Griswold,
1892- , American; nonfiction
CON
'KETCHUM, Jack' see PAINE,
Lauran B.
KETEL, Cornelis, 1548-1616,
Dutch; poetry BU
KETTE, Dragotin, 1876-99, Slo-
vene; poetry BU
KETTELKAMP, Larry, 1933- ,
American; juveniles COM
KETTERER, David, 1942- ,
British-Canadian; nonfiction
CON NI
KETTLE, Arnold Charles, 1916- ,
British; nonfiction BOR
KETTLE, Jocelyn Pamela,
1934- , British; fiction NI
'KETTLE, Peter' see GLOVER,
Denis J.
KETTLE, Thomas, 1880-1916,
Irish; nonfiction HO
KETTNER, James Harold, 1944- ,
American; nonfiction CON

KEUCHER, William F., 1918- ,
American; nonfiction CON
'KEVERN, Barbara' see SHEP-
HERD, Donald L.
'KEVERN, Richard' (Clifford
James Wheeler Hosken), 1882-
1950, British; fiction, nonfic-
tion REI
KEVLES, Bettyann, 1938- ,
American; fiction CO CON
KEVLES, Daniel Jerome, 1939- ,
American; nonfiction CON
KEW, Stephen, 1947- , British;
nonfiction CON
KEXEL, Olof, 1748-96, Swedish;
plays BU
KEY, Alexander Hill, 1904-79,
American; juveniles, fiction
CO CON
KEY, Ellen, 1849-1926, Swedish;
nonfiction BU
KEY, Eugene George, American;
fiction NI
KEY, Francis Scott, 1779-1843,
American; nonfiction, poetry
BA
KEY, Mary Ritchie, 1924- ,
American; nonfiction CON
KEY, William Henry, 1919- ,
American; nonfiction CON
KEY, Wilson Bryan, 1925- ,
American; nonfiction CON
KEYES, Daniel, 1927- , Amer-
ican; fiction AS NI
KEYES, Edward, 1927- , Amer-
ican; nonfiction CON
KEYES, Evelyn, 1919?- ,
American; fiction, nonfiction
CON
KEYES, Frances Parkinson,
1885-1970, American; fiction,
nonfiction, journalism BA
BR
KEYES, Margaret Frings, 1929- ,
American; nonfiction CON
'KEYES, Noel' see KEIGHTLEY,
David N.
KEYES, Ralph, 1945- , Amer-
ican; nonfiction CON
KEYES, Sidney Arthur, 1922-43,
English; poetry, plays BU
DA PO SEY VP WA
KEYISHIAN, Harry, 1932- ,
American; nonfiction, poetry
CON
KEYLOR, William Robert,
1944- , American; nonfiction
CON

KEYNES, Geoffrey Langdon,
1887- , American; nonfiction
CON
KEYNES, John Maynard, 1883-1946,
English; nonfiction PO
KEYS, Ancel, 1904- , American;
nonfiction CON
KEYS, Ivor Christopher Banfield,
1919- , British; nonfiction
CON
KEYSER, George Gustave, 1910- ,
American; poetry CON
KEYSER, William Russell, 1916- ,
American; nonfiction CON
KEYSERLING, Eduard, Graf von,
1855-1918, German; fiction,
plays CL
KEYSERLING, Hermann Alexander,
Graf, 1880-1946, German;
nonfiction TH
KEYSTERLING, Leon H., 1908- ,
American; nonfiction CON
KEZDI, Paul, 1914- , Hungarian-
American; nonfiction CON
KEZYS, Algimanas, 1928- ,
Lithuanian-American; nonfiction
CON
KGOSITSILE, Keorapetse William,
1938- , South African; poetry
CON HER JA VCP
KHADILKAR, Krsnaji Prabhakar,
1872-1948, Marathi; plays
PRU
KHADIM, Qiyamuddin, 1912- ,
Afghan; poetry, journalism
PRU
'KHAI-HUNG' (Tran-khanh-Du),
1896-1947, Vietnamese; fiction,
journalism PRU
KHAKETLA, Bennett Makalo,
1913- , Sotho; poetry, plays,
journalism HER JA
KHAKETLA, Caroline Ntseliseng,
1918?- , Sotho; fiction, poetry
HER
KHALATDARI, Adel-Sultan, 1901?-
77, Iranian; journalism, poetry
CON
KHALID, Khalid Muhammad,
1920- , Egyptian; nonfiction
BU
KHALIFA, Hadji see KÂTIB CELE-
BI, Mustafa
KHALILI, Khalilullah, 1907- ,
Afghan; poetry, nonfiction
PRU
KHAMISI, Abdarrahman, 1920- ,
Egyptian; poetry, journalism

PRU
KHAN, Lurey, 1927- , American;
nonfiction CON
KHAN, Shabir H. see 'JOSH
MALEHABADI'
KHANDEKAR, Visnu Sakharam,
1898- , Marathi; fiction
PRU
KHANI, Ahmade, 1650-1707,
Kurdish; poetry PRU
KHANLARI, Parviz Natel, 1914- ,
Persian; poetry BU
KHANSA, early 7th century,
Arab; poetry BU PRU
'KHANSHENDEL, Chiron' see
ROSE, Wendy
KHAQANI, Afzal-al-Din Ibrahim,
1126-98, Persian; poetry
BU PRU
KHARASCH, Robert Nelson,
1926- , American; nonfiction
CON
'KHARMS, Daniil Ivanovich'
(Daniil Yuvachov), 1905-42,
Russian; poetry, nonfiction,
plays, juveniles CL
KHATCHADOURIAN, Haig, 1925- ,
Palestinian; nonfiction CON
KHEDOURI, Franklin, 1944- ,
Iranian-American; nonfiction
CON
KHEMNITSER, Ivan Ivanovich
(Chemnitzer), 1745-84, Rus-
sian; fiction, poetry BU
KHER, Inder Nath, 1933- ,
Indian-Canadian; nonfiction
CON
KHERASKOV, Mikhail Matveyevich,
1733-1807, Russian; poetry,
fiction BU
KHERDIAN, David, 1931- ,
American; juveniles CO
KHETAEGKATY, Kosta, 1859-
1906, Ossetian; poetry PRU
KHETY see AKHTOY
KHIENGSIRI, Kanha see 'SURANG-
KHANANG, K.'
KHIN HNIN JU, 1925- , Bur-
mese; fiction PRU
KHLEBNIKOV, Velemir Vladi-
mirovich (Victor), 1885-
1922, Russian; poetry, non-
fiction BU CL SEY TH WA
KHODASEVICH, Vladislav Felit-
sianovich (Chodasiewicz),
1886-1939, Russian; poetry,
nonfiction BU CL WA
KHOMYAKOV, Aleksey Stepano-

vich, 1804-60, Russian; non-
fiction, poetry BU TH
KHRAIEF, al-Bashir, 1917- ,
Tunisian; fiction PRU
'KHRAKHUNI, Zareh' (Artho
Tchiumpiushian), 1926- ,
Armenian; poetry PRU
KHU'KRIT PRAMOJ, Mom Ratcha-
wong, 1912- , Thai; journal-
ism, fiction, plays, nonfiction
LA
KHUMALO, Philios Mtshane,
1925- , Rhodesian; fiction
JA
KHUSHHÂL KHÂN KHATTAK, 1613-
89, Persian; poetry BU PRU
KHUSRAU DIHLAVI, Abu'l Hasan,
1253-1325, Persian; poetry
BU
KHVAJUYE KERMANI, Kamaloddin,
1281-1352, Persian; poetry
PRU
'KHVYL'OVY' (Mykola Fitilov),
1893-1933, Ukrainian; fiction
CL TH
KHWAND MIR, Ghiyath-al-Din,
1475-1535/37, Persian; non-
fiction BU
KHWARIZMI, Abu-Abdullah, 8-
10?th centuries, Arab; nonfic-
tion BU PRU
KI no IRATSUME, 8th century,
Japanese; poetry HI
KI no KAION, 1663-1742, Japanese;
poetry, plays HI
KI no TOMONORI, late 9th century,
Japanese; poetry HI
KI no TSURAYUKI, 862?-946,
Japanese; poetry, diary BU
HI LA
KIANTO, Ilmari (Calamnius), 1874-
1970, Finnish; poetry, fiction
TH
KIBERA, Leonard, 1940?- ,
Kenyan; fiction, plays HER
KICKHAM, Charles J., 1828-82,
Irish; fiction HO
KICKNOSWAY, Faye, 1936- ,
American; poetry, nonfiction
CON
KIDD, Virginia, 1921- , Ameri-
can; nonfiction CON
KIDDE, Harald, 1878-1918, Danish;
fiction BU TH
KIDDELL, John, 1922- , Aus-
tralian; fiction, juveniles CO
KIDDER, Barbara Ann, 1933- ,
American; juveniles CON

KIDDER, Rushworth Moulton,
1944- , American; nonfiction
CON
KIDNER, Frank Derek, 1913- ,
English; nonfiction CON
KIDNEY, Walter Curtis, 1932- ,
American; nonfiction CON
KIDO, Koichi, 1890?-1977,
Japanese; diary CON
KIECKHEFER, Richard, 1946- ,
American; nonfiction CON
KIEFER, Christie Weber, 1937- ,
American; nonfiction CON
KIEFER, Irene, 1926- ,
American; juveniles, nonfic-
tion CO CON
KIEFER, Warren, 1929- ,
American; fiction, film CON
KIELLAND, Alexander Lange,
1849-1906, Norwegian; fic-
tion, plays BU CL TH
KIELTY, Bernardine see SCHER-
MAN, Bernardine
KIELY, Benedict, 1919- , Irish;
fiction, nonfiction, journalism
HO VCN WA
KIENZLE, William Xavier ('Mark
Boyle'), 1928- , American;
fiction CON
KIERAN, John F., 1892-1981,
American; juveniles, nonfic-
tion CON WAR
KIERAN, Sheila, 1930- , Cana-
dian; nonfiction CON
KIERKEGAARD, Soren Aabye,
1813-55, Danish; nonfiction
BU CL MAG TH
KIERLAND, Joseph Scott, 1937- ,
American; plays CON
KIERNAN, Walter, 1902-78,
American; journalism CON
KIESER, Rolf, 1936- , Swiss-
American; nonfiction CON
KIESLING, Herbert J., 1934- ,
American; nonfiction CON
KIESZAK, Kenneth, 1939- ,
American; nonfiction CON
KIGUNDU, Clement, 1928- ,
Ugandan; nonfiction JA
KIJOWSKI, Andrezej, 1928- ,
Polish; nonfiction, fiction
CL
'KIKAKU' (Takemoto Yasoya),
1661-1707, Japanese; poetry
BU
KIKER, Bill Frazier, 1937- ,
American; nonfiction CON
KIKER, Douglas, 1930- , Amer-

ican; fiction CON
KIKUCHI KAN (Kikuchi Hiroshi),
1888-1948, Japanese; fiction,
plays BU HI LA
KILBOURN, Jonathan, 1916?-76,
American; journalism CON
'KILBURN, Henry' see RIGG,
Henry K.
KILDAHL, John P., 1927- ,
American; nonfiction CON
KILEY, Jed, 1889-1962, American;
nonfiction RO
KILEY, Margaret Ann, American;
nonfiction CON
KILGALLEN, Dorothy, 1913-65,
American; journalism CON
'KILGORE, John' see PAINE,
Lauran B.
KILGORE, William Jackson,
1917- , American; nonfiction
CON
'KILIAN, Patricia' see TARNAW-
SKY, Patricia W.
KILLAM, Gordon Douglas, 1930- ,
Canadian; nonfiction CON
KILLEBROW, Carl, American;
nonfiction SH
KILLEEN, Jacqueline, 1931- ,
American; nonfiction CON
KILLENBERG, George Andrew,
1917- , American; journalism
CON
KILLENS, John Oliver, 1916- ,
American; nonfiction, film
BA CON SH VCN WAK
KILLIAN, Ida Faith, 1910- ,
American; nonfiction CON
KILLIAN, James R., Jr., 1904- ,
American; nonfiction CON
'KILLIAN, Larry' see WELLEN,
Edward P.
KILLIGREW, Henry, 1612/13-99/
1700, English; plays BU
KILLIGREW, Thomas the Elder,
1611/12-82/83, English; plays
BU VD
KILLIGREW, Sir William, 1606-
95, English; plays BU
KILLINGER, John, 1933- ,
American; nonfiction CON
KILLINGSWORTH, Frank R.,
1873?-1976, American; non-
fiction CON
KILLION, Ronald Gene, 1931- ,
American; nonfiction CON
KILLOUGH, Lee ('Sarah Hood';
'Kathy Leigh'), 1942- ,
American; fiction, nonfiction

CON
KILPATRICK, Carroll, 1913- ,
American; nonfiction CON
KILPATRICK, Terrence, 1920- ,
American; fiction, plays, tv
CON
KILPI, Volter, 1874-1939, Finish;
nonfiction, fiction TH
'KILREON, Beth' see WALKER,
Barbara K.
KILROY, Thomas, 1934- , Irish;
plays, fiction, nonfiction
CON HO
KILSON, Martin L., 1931- ,
American; nonfiction CON SH
KILVERT, B. Cory, Jr.,
1930- , American; nonfiction
CON
KILWORTH, Garry, 1941- ,
English; fiction NI
'KIM' see SIMENON, Georges
KIM, Hyung-chan, 1938- ,
American; nonfiction CON
KIM, Ilpyong John, 1931- ,
Korean-American; nonfiction
CON
KIM, Jung-Gun, 1933- , Korean-
American; nonfiction CON
KIM, Richard, 1932- , Korean-
American; fiction VCN
KIM, Se-jin, 1933- , Korean-
American; nonfiction CON
KIM, Yong Choon, 1935- ,
Korean-American; nonfiction
CON
KIM MAN-JUNG, 1637-92, Korean;
fiction PRU
KIM PU-SIK, 1075-1151, Korean;
nonfiction PRU
KIM SI-SUP, 1435-93, Korean;
fiction PRU
KIM SOWOL, 1903-34, Korean;
poetry PRU
KIM TON-IN, 1900-51, Korean;
fiction, nonfiction PRU
KIMATA OSAMU, 1906- ,
Japanese; poetry HI
KIMBALL, Arthur Gustaf, 1927- ,
American; nonfiction CON
KIMBALL, Dean, 1912- ,
American; nonfiction CON
WAR
KIMBALL, George, 1943- ,
American; fiction, nonfiction
CON
KIMBALL, John P., 1941- ,
American; nonfiction CON
KIMBALL, John Ward, 1931- ,

American; nonfiction CON
'KIMBALL, Nancy' see UPSON,
Norma
KIMBALL, Penn Townsend,
1915- , American; nonfiction
CON
KIMBALL, Richard Laurance,
1939- , American; nonfiction
CON
KIMBALL, Spencer Woolley,
1895- , American; nonfiction
CON
KIMBERLY, Gail, American; fic-
tion CON
KIMBLE, Daniel Porter, 1934- ,
American; nonfiction CON
KIMBRO, John M. ('Kym Allyson';
'Charlotte Bramwell'; 'Milt
Jaxon'; 'Allyn Keimberg';
'Katheryn Kimbrough'; 'Zoltan
Lambec'; 'Jack Milton'),
1929- , American; plays,
fiction CON
KIMBROUGH, Emily, 1899- ,
American; nonfiction, journal-
ism WA
'KIMBROUGH, Katheryn' see
KIMBRO, John M.
KIMBROUGH, Ralph Bradley,
1922- , American; nonfiction
CON
KIMBROUGH, Richard Benito,
1931- , American; juveniles,
fiction CON
KIMBROUGH, Sara Dodge, 1901- ,
American; nonfiction CON
KIMBUGWE, Henry S. see
'SERUMA, Eneiko'
KIMCHE, David, British; nonfiction
CON
KIMCHI, David (Kimhi; Qimhi;
Qamhi), 1160?-1235, Proven-
cal; poetry BU
KIMENYE, Barbara, 1940?- ,
Ugandan; fiction, journalism
CON HER JA KI
KIMMEL, Arthur Sandor, 1930- ,
American; nonfiction CON
KIMMEL, Douglas Charles,
1943- , American; nonfiction
CON
KIMMEL, Eric A., 1946- ,
American; juveniles CO CON
KIMMEL, Jo, 1931- , American;
nonfiction CON
KIMMICH, Christoph Martin,
1939- , German-American;
nonfiction CON

KIMPEL, Ben Drew, 1915- ,
American; nonfiction CON
KIMREY, Grace Saunders, 1910- ,
American; poetry, fiction,
juveniles CON
KIMURA, Jiro, 1949- , American;
nonfiction CON
KIMURA MASAKOTO, 1827-1913,
Japanese; nonfiction HI
KINAU, Johann see 'FOCK, Gorch'
KINAU, Rudolf, 1887- , German;
fiction BU
KINCAID, James Russell, 1937- ,
American; nonfiction CON
KINCH, Sam E., Jr., 1940- ,
American; nonfiction CON
KINCHELOE, Raymond McFarland,
1909- , American; nonfiction
CON
KINCK, Hans Ernst, 1865-1926,
Norwegian; fiction, plays, non-
fiction BU CL TH
KINDER, Marsha, 1940- , Amer-
ican; nonfiction CON
KINDI, Abu Yusuf Ya'qub, -870?,
Arab; nonfiction BU PRU
KINDLEBERGER, Charles Poor,
II, 1910- , American; nonfic-
tion CON
KINDRED, Leslie Withrow, 1905- ,
American; nonfiction CON
KINDRED, Wendy Good, 1937- ,
American; juveniles CO
'KINEJI, Maborushi' see GIBSON,
Walter B.
KINES, Pat Decker (Pat Decker
Tapio), 1937- , American;
juveniles CO CON
KING, Alan, 1927- , American;
nonfiction CON
'KING, Albert' see 'CONRAD, Paul'
KING, Algin Braddy, 1926- ,
American; nonfiction CON
'KING, Arthur' see CAIN, Arthur
H.; LAKE, Kenneth R.
KING, Ben Frank, 1937- ,
American; nonfiction CON
KING, Bert Thomas, 1927- ,
American; nonfiction CON
KING, Betty Alice, 1919- ,
British; fiction CON
KING, Billie Jean, 1943- ,
American; nonfiction, juveniles
CO CON
KING, Bruce A. ('Zolar'), 1933-
76, American; nonfiction CON
KING, Charles Daly, 1895-1963,
American; fiction, nonfiction

REI ST
KING, Charles Lester, 1922- ,
American; nonfiction CON
KING, Clarence, 1884?-1974,
American; nonfiction CON
KING, Clyde Richard, 1924- ,
American; nonfiction CON
KING, Coretta Scott, 1927- ,
American; nonfiction SH
KING, Cynthia, 1925- , American;
juveniles CO
KING, Daniel Patrick, 1942- ,
American; nonfiction CON
KING, David Clive, 1924- , Brit-
ish; juveniles, plays KI
KING, Edward, 1612-37, English;
poetry BU
KING, Edward L., 1928- , Amer-
ican; nonfiction, film CON
KING, Florence, 1936- , Ameri-
can; nonfiction CON
KING, Francis Edward, 1931- ,
American; nonfiction CON
KING, Francis Henry, 1923- ,
British; fiction, poetry, non-
fiction SEY VCN WA
KING, Frank O., 1883-1969, Amer-
ican; juveniles CO CON
KING, Franklin Alexander (Frank
A. King), 1923- , American;
nonfiction CON
KING, Fredrick Jerry, 1941- ,
Canadian; journalism CON
KING, Grace Elizabeth, 1852-1932,
American; fiction BA
KING, Harold, 1945- , American;
fiction CON
KING, Helen H., 1931- , Ameri-
can; nonfiction SH
KING, Henry, 1592-1669, English;
poetry, nonfiction BU DA PO
RU VP
KING, Irving Henry, 1935- ,
American; nonfiction CON
KING, Ivan Robert, 1927- , Amer-
ican; nonfiction CON
KING, James Cecil, 1924- ,
American; nonfiction CON
KING, James G., 1898?-1979,
American; nonfiction, poetry
CON
KING, Jerome Babcock, 1927- ,
American; nonfiction CON
KING, Joe, 1909?-79, American;
journalism CON
KING, John Edward, 1947- ,
British; nonfiction CON
KING, John Lafayette, 1917- ,

American; nonfiction CON

KING, John Robert, 1948- , English; fiction NI

KING, Marian, American; juveniles CO

KING, Mark, 1945- , American; nonfiction CON

'KING, Martin' see MARKS, Stanley

KING, Martin Luther, Jr., 1929-68, American; juveniles CO

'KING, Michael' see BUSE, Renee

KING, Morton Brandon, 1913- , American; nonfiction CON

KING, Philip, 1904- , British; plays CON

'KING, Reefe' see BARKER, Albert W.

KING, Richard H., 1942- , American; nonfiction CON

KING, Richard Louis, 1937- , American; nonfiction CON

KING, Robert Harlen, 1935- , American; nonfiction CON

KING, Robert L., 1950- , American; journalism CON

KING, Robert Ray, 1942- , American; nonfiction CON

KING, Rufus, 1893-1966, American; fiction, plays REI ST

KING, Ruth R. see MANLEY, Ruth R.

KING, Stella, British; nonfiction CON

KING, Stephen, 1947- , American; fiction CO CON NI

KING, Stephen William, 1947- , American; nonfiction CON

'KING, Teri,' 1940- , British; nonfiction CON

KING, Terry Johnson, 1929-78, American; journalism, nonfiction CON

KING, Thomas Mulvihill, 1929- , American; nonfiction CON

'KING, Vincent' see VINSON, Rex T.

KING, Willard I., 1893-1981, American; nonfiction CON

KING, William, 1663-1712, English; plays, nonfiction, poetry BU VP

KING, William Donald Aelian, 1910- , British; nonfiction CON

KING, Winston Lee, 1907- , American; nonfiction CON

KING, Woodie, Jr., 1937- ,

American; nonfiction, plays CON SH

KINGERY, Robert Ernest, 1913-78, American; nonfiction CON

KINGHORN, Alexander Manson ('James Sharp'), 1926- , British; nonfiction CON

KINGHORN, Kenneth Cain, 1930- , American; nonfiction CON

KINGLAKE, Alexander William, 1809-91, English; nonfiction BU DA PO

KINGMAN, Mary Lee, 1919- , American; juveniles KI

KINGMAN, Russ, 1917- , American; nonfiction CON

KINGO, Thomas Hansen, 1634-1703, Danish; poetry, hymns BU TH

KINGRY, Philip L., 1942- , American; nonfiction CON

KING-SCOTT, Peter see 'EDGAR, Peter'

KINGSLAND, Leslie William, 1912- , English; juveniles, translations CO CON

KINGSLEY, Charles ('Parson Lot'), 1819-75, English; fiction, poetry, juveniles, plays BU COM DA MAG PO VN

'KINGSLEY, Charlotte Mary' see HANSHEW, Thomas W.

KINGSLEY, Henry, 1830-76, English; fiction, journalism, juveniles BU DA MAG VN

KINGSLEY, Mary Henrietta, 1862-1900, English; nonfiction BU

KINGSLEY, Sidney, 1906- , American; plays BR CON MCG MCN PO VCD VD

KINGSLEY-SMITH, Terence, 1940- , American; fiction CON

'KINGSMILL, Hugh' (Hugh Kingsmill Lunn), 1889-1949, English; fiction NI

KINGSTON, Jeremy Henry Spencer, 1931- , British; plays, fiction, juveniles CON

KINGSTON, Maxine Hong, 1940- , American; nonfiction, fiction CON

KINGSTON, William Henry Giles, 1814-80, English; juveniles BU

KING-STOOPS, Joyce, 1923- , Anglo-American; nonfiction CON

KININMOUTH, Christopher ('Chris-

topher Brennan'), 1917- ,
American; nonfiction CON
'KINKAID, Wyatt E. ' see JEN-
NINGS, Michael
KINKER, Johannes, 1764-1845,
Dutch; nonfiction BU
KINLOCH, A. Murray, 1923- ,
Scots; nonfiction CON
KINNAIRD, Clark ('John Paul
Adams'; 'Edgar Poe Norris'),
1901- , American; nonfiction
CON
KINNAIRD, John William, 1924-
80, American; nonfiction CON
KINNAIRD, William McKee,
1928- , American; nonfiction
CON
KINNARD, Douglas Leo, 1921- ,
American; nonfiction CON
KINNEAVY, James Louis,
1920- , American; nonfiction
CON
KINNELL, Galway, 1927- ,
American; poetry, fiction,
translations BR MAL VCP
SEY WA
KINNEY, C. Cleland, 1915- ,
Canadian-American; juveniles
CO WAR
KINNEY, Harrison, 1921- ,
American; juveniles CO
KINNEY, James Roser, 1902?-78,
American; nonfiction CON
KINNEY, Jean Stout, 1912- ,
American; juveniles CO WAR
KINNEY, Peter, 1943- , Amer-
ican; nonfiction CON
KINNEY, Richard, 1924?-79,
American; poetry CON
KINNICUTT, Susan (Sibley; 'Susan
Shelby'), 1926- , American;
fiction, nonfiction CON
'KINOR, Jehuda' see ROTHMUL-
LER, Aron M.
KINOSHITA CHOSHOSHI, 1569-1649,
Japanese; poetry HI
KINOSHITA JUNJI, 1914- ,
Japanese; plays BU LA PRU
KINOSHITA RIGEN, 1886-1925,
Japanese; poetry HI
KINOSHITA TAKABUMI, 1779-1821,
Japanese; poetry HI
KINROSS, Patrick ('Patrick Bal-
four'), 1904-76, British; jour-
nalism, nonfiction CON
KINSEL, Paschal, 1895?-1976,
American; nonfiction CON
KINSELLA, Thomas, 1928/29- ,

Irish; poetry, translations BU
DA HO SEY VCP VP WA
KINSELLA, William Patrick,
1935- , Canadian; fiction
CON
KINSER, Charleen, American;
juveniles WAR
'KINSEY, Elizabeth' see CLYMER,
Eleanor
KINSLEY, Daniel Allen ('Allen Ed-
wardes'), 1939- , American;
nonfiction, fiction CON
KINTNER, Earl Wilson, 1912- ,
American; nonfiction CON
KINTNER, Robert Edmonds, 1909-
80, American; journalism,
nonfiction CON
KINTON, Jack Franklin, 1939- ,
American; nonfiction CON
KIN-WUN MIN-GYI U KAUNG, 1821-
1908, Burmese; poetry, letters,
diary LA
KINYANJUI, Peter, 1940?- ,
Kenyan; plays HER
KINZER, Donald Louis, 1914- ,
American; nonfiction CON
KINZER, Harless Mahlon, 1923?-
75, American; nonfiction CON
KIPLING, Rudyard, 1865-1936, Eng-
lish; poetry, fiction, juveniles,
nonfiction BU COM DA KI
MAG NI PO SEY VN VP
KIPLINGER, Austin Huntington,
1918- , American; nonfiction
CON
KIPLINGER, Willard Monroe, 1891-
1967, American; journalism,
nonfiction CON
KIPNIS, Claude, 1938-81, French;
nonfiction CON
KIPPAX, Janet, 1926- , English;
fiction CON
'KIPPAX, John' (John Charles
Hynam), 1915-74, English; fic-
tion NI
KIPPHARDT, Heinar, 1922- ,
German; plays, fiction BU CL
CON MCG
KIPPLEY, Sheila K. , 1939- ,
American; nonfiction CON
KIRACK, Alexander Gallo, 1935- ,
American; poetry MAR
KIRALY, Bela Kalman, 1912- ,
Hungarian-American; nonfiction
CON
KIRBY, David G. , 1942- , British;
nonfiction CON
KIRBY, David Kirk, 1944- , Amer-

ican; nonfiction, poetry CON
KIRBY, Frank Eugene, 1928- ,
  American; translations, non-
  fiction CON
KIRBY, George Blaik, 1928- ,
  Canadian; journalism CON
KIRBY, Gilbert Walter, 1914- ,
  British; nonfiction CON
'KIRBY, Jean' see McDONNELL,
  Virginia B.
KIRBY, William, 1817-1906, Cana-
  dian; poetry, fiction BU
KIRCHER, Athanasius, 1601-80,
  German; nonfiction NI
KIRCHHOFF, Theodor, 1828-99,
  German-American; nonfiction,
  poetry BU
KIRCHMAIR see NAOGEORGUS,
  Thomas
KIRCHNER, Audrey Burie, 1937- ,
  American; nonfiction CON
KIRCHWEY, Freda, 1893-1976,
  American; nonfiction CON
KIREYEVSKY, Ivan Vasilyevich
  (Kireevsky), 1806-56, Russian;
  nonfiction BU
KIREYEVSKY, Pyotr Vasilyevich,
  1808-56, Russian; nonfiction
  BU
KIRILINE, Louise de see LAW-
  RENCE, Louise
KIRILL of TUROV, 12th century,
  Russian; nonfiction TH
KIRK, Clara Marburg, 1898-1976,
  American; nonfiction CON
KIRK, Donald R., 1935- , Amer-
  ican; nonfiction CON
KIRK, Elizabeth Doan, 1937- ,
  American; nonfiction CON
KIRK, Hans Rudolf, 1898-1962,
  Danish; fiction, nonfiction,
  journalism BU CL TH
KIRK, Jerome Richard, 1937- ,
  American; nonfiction CON
KIRK, John Esben, 1905-75,
  American; nonfiction CON
KIRK, John Thomas, 1933- ,
  American; nonfiction CON
KIRK, Mary Wallace, 1889- ,
  American; nonfiction CON
'KIRK, Michael' see KNOX, Bill
KIRK, Rhina, American; juveniles
  WAR
KIRK, Robert Warner,   -1980,
  American; nonfiction CON
KIRK, Roger Edward, 1930- ,
  American; nonfiction CON
KIRK, Russell, 1918- , Amer-

ican; nonfiction, fiction WA
KIRK, Ruth Kratz, 1925- , Amer-
  ican; juveniles CO
KIRK, Samuel Alexander, 1904- ,
  American; nonfiction CON
'KIRK, Ted' see BANK, Theodore
  P.
KIRKCONNELL, Watson, 1895- ,
  Canadian; poetry, translations
  BU
KIRKENDALL, Donald M., 1923- ,
  American; nonfiction CON
KIRKENDALL, Richard Stewart,
  1928- , American; nonfiction
  CON
KIRK-GREEN, Anthony ('Nicholas
  Caverhill'), 1925- , English;
  nonfiction CON
KIRKHAM, George L., 1941- ,
  American; nonfiction CON
KIRKLAND, Caroline ('Mrs. Mary
  Clavers'), 1801-64, American;
  fiction MYE
KIRKLAND, Jack, 1901- , Amer-
  ican; plays MCG
KIRKLAND, Joseph, 1830-94, Amer-
  ican; fiction, plays, nonfiction
  BU VN
KIRKLAND, Wallace W., 1891?-
  1979, American; journalism
  CON
KIRKMAN, Francis, 1632?- ,
  English; translations BU
KIRKMAN, James Spedding,
  1906- , British; nonfiction
  CON
KIRKPATRICK, Diane, 1933- ,
  American; nonfiction CON
KIRKPATRICK, Donald Lee,
  1924- , American; nonfiction
  CON
KIRKPATRICK, Doris Upton,
  1902- , American; journalism,
  nonfiction CON
KIRKPATRICK, Evron Maurice,
  1911- , American; nonfiction
  CON
KIRKPATRICK, Jean, 1923- ,
  American; nonfiction CON
KIRKPATRICK, Jeane Duane Jordan,
  1926- , American; nonfiction
  CON
KIRKPATRICK, John, 1905- ,
  American; nonfiction CON
KIRKPATRICK, Oliver Austin,
  1911- , American; nonfiction,
  translations CON SH
KIRKPATRICK, Ralph, 1911- ,

American; nonfiction CON
KIRKPATRICK, Samuel Alexander
III, 1943- , American; non-
fiction CON
KIRKPATRICK, Smith, 1922- ,
American; nonfiction CON
KIRKUP, James, 1918- , British;
poetry, translations, plays
DA WA
KIRKUP, James ('James Falconer';
'Andrew James'), 1927- ,
English; juveniles, plays, fic-
tion, nonfiction, translations
CO VCP
KIRKWOOD, Gordon Macdonald,
1916- , Canadian-American;
nonfiction CON
KIRKWOOD, Jame, 1650-1708,
Scots; nonfiction ENG
KIRN, Ann Minette, 1910- ,
American; juveniles CON
KIRONDE, Erisa, 1940?- ,
Ugandan; plays HER
KIRSANOV, Semën Isaakovich,
1906-72, Russian; poetry BU
CL TH
KIRSCH, Anthony Thomas, 1930- ,
American; nonfiction CON
KIRSCH, Robert R. ('Robert Ban-
croft'; 'Robert Dundee'),
1922-80, American; journal-
ism, fiction CON
KIRSCHENBAUM, Howard, 1944- ,
American; nonfiction CON
'KIRSCHNER, Fritz' see BICKERS,
Richard L. T.
KIRSCHTEN, Ernest, 1902-74,
American; journalism, nonfic-
tion CON
KIRSHENBLATT-GIMBLETT, Bar-
bara, 1942- , Canadian; non-
fiction CON
KIRSHNER, Gloria Ifland, Amer-
ican; nonfiction CON
KIRSHON, Vladimir Mikhaylovich,
1902-38, Russian; plays BU
CL TH
KIRSNER, Douglas, 1947- ,
Australian; nonfiction CON
KIRST, Hans Hellmut, 1914- ,
German; fiction BU NI REI
WA
KIRST, Michael Weile, 1939- ,
American; nonfiction CON
'KIRTLAND, G. B.' see HINE,
Al; JOSLIN, Sesyle
KIRTLAND, Helen Johns, 1890?-
1979, American; journalism

CON
KIRTLAND, Kathleen, 1945- ,
American; nonfiction CON
KIRTTIVASA, 1385-?, Bengali;
translations BU
KIRUSNA PILLAI, Henry Alfred,
1827-1900, Tamil; poetry
PRU
KIRUSNAMURTTI, R. ('Kalki'),
1899-1954, Tamil; fiction,
journalism BU PRU
KIS, Danilo, 1935- , Serbian; fic-
tion BU
KISCH, Egon Erwin, 1885-1948,
German; fiction, journalism
TH
KISEN HOSHI, 9th century, Japan-
ese; poetry HI
KISFALUDY, Károly, 1788-1830,
Hungarian; plays, poetry, fic-
tion BU MCG TH
KISFALUDY, Sándor, 1772-1844,
Hungarian; poetry BU TH
KISH, Kathleen Vera, 1942- ,
American; nonfiction CON
KISHIDA, Eriko, 1929- , Japanese;
poetry, juveniles CO CON
KISHON, Ephraim, 1924- , Hun-
garian-Israeli; nonfiction,
translations, plays CON
KISIELEWSKI, Jan August, 1876-
1918, Polish; plays BU
KISINGER, Grace Gelvin Maze,
1913-65, American; juveniles
CO
KISOR, Henry Du Bois, 1940- ,
American; journalism CON
KISS, József, 1843-1921, Hungarian;
poetry TH
KISSAN, Edward, 1943- , Ameri-
can; nonfiction, translations,
poetry CON
KISSANE, John Michael, 1928- ,
American; nonfiction CON
KISSIN, Eva H., 1923- , Ameri-
can; juveniles CO
KIST, Willem, 1758-1841, Dutch;
fiction BU
KISTE, Robert Carl, 1936- ,
American; nonfiction CON
KISTLER, Mark Oliver, 1918- ,
American; nonfiction CON
KISTNER, Robert William, 1917- ,
American; nonfiction CON
KITA MORIO, 1927- , Japanese;
fiction PRU
KITABATAKE CHIKAFUSA, 1293-
1354, Japanese; poetry HI

KITAGAWA FUYUHIKO, 1900- ,
Japanese; poetry PRU
KITAHARA HAKUSHU, 1885-1942,
Japanese; poetry HI PRU
KITAMURA KIGIN, 1624-1705,
Japanese; nonfiction, poetry
HI
KITCHEN, Martin, 1936- ,
Anglo-Canadian; nonfiction
CON
KITCHIN, Clifford Henry Benn,
1895-1967, English; fiction,
poetry REI ST
KITERIZA, Aniceti, 1900?- ,
Kikerebe; fiction HER
KITMAN, Marvin ('William Ran-
dolph Hirsch'), 1929- ,
American; journalism, non-
fiction CON
KITOWICZ, Jedrzej, 1728-1804,
Polish; diary BU
KITT, Eartha Mae, 1928- ,
American; nonfiction CON SH
KITTO, Humphrey Davy Findley,
1897-1982, British; nonfiction,
translations BOR
KITTRIE, Nicholas Norbert,
1928- , Polish-American;
nonfiction CON
KITZBERG, August, 1855-1927,
Estonian; plays, fiction BU
'KIVI, Aleksis' (A. Stenvall),
1834-72, Finnish; fiction,
plays BU TH
KIVIMAA, Kaarlo Arvi, 1904- ,
Finnish; poetry, fiction, non-
fiction TH
KIVY, Peter Nathan, 1934- ,
American; nonfiction CON
KIYINGI, Wycliffe, 1932- ,
Ugandan; plays JA
KIZER, Carolyn Ashley, 1925- ,
American; poetry BR CON
MAL VCP WA
KI-ZERBO, Joseph, 1922- ,
Upper Voltan; nonfiction JA
KJAER, Nils, 1870-1924, Nor-
wegian; plays, nonfiction BU
KJELGAARD, James Arthur,
1910-59, American; juveniles
CO KI
KJELLGREN, Josef, 1907-48,
Swedish; fiction BU
'KLABUND' (Alfred Henschke),
1890-1928, German; nonfiction
CL TH
KLADSTRUP, Donald, 1943- ,
American; journalism CON

KLAIBER, Jeffrey L., 1943- ,
American; nonfiction CON
KLAICH, Dolores, 1936- , Amer-
ican; nonfiction CON
KLAITS, Barrie, 1944- , Amer-
ican; nonfiction, juveniles CON
KLAJ, Johann, 1616-56, German;
poetry BU TH
KLAMKIN, Charles, 1923- ,
American; nonfiction CON
KLAMKIN, Lynn, 1950- , Amer-
ican; fiction, poetry CON
KLAMKIN, Marian, 1926- ,
American; nonfiction CON
KLANN, Margaret L., 1911- ,
American; nonfiction CON
KLAPERMAN, Gilbert, 1921- ,
American; nonfiction CON
KLAPPER, Molly Roxana, 1937- ,
German-American; nonfiction
CON
KLAPPHOLZ, Kurt, 1913-75,
German-American; nonfiction
CON
KLARE, Hugh John, 1916- ,
Austrian-British; nonfiction
CON
KLAREN, Peter Flindell, 1938- ,
American; nonfiction CON
KLARSFELD, Beate, 1939- ,
German; nonfiction CON
KLASS, Allan Arnold, 1907- ,
Russian-Canadian; nonfiction
CON
KLASS, Morton, 1927- , Ameri-
can; juveniles CO WAR
KLASS, Philip see TENN, William
KLASSEN, Peter James, 1930- ,
Canadian-American; nonfiction
CON
KLASSEN, Randolph Jacob, 1933- ,
Canadian-American; nonfiction
CON
KLAUCK, Daniel L., 1947- ,
American; nonfiction CON
KLAUDER, Francis John, 1918- ,
American; nonfiction CON
KLAUSNER, Joseph, 1874-1958,
Hebrew; nonfiction BU
KLAUSNER, Margot, 1905-76?,
Israeli; plays, fiction, nonfic-
tion CON
KLDIASHVILI, Sergo, 1893- ,
Georgian; fiction, plays PRU
KLEBERGER, Ilse, 1921- , Ger-
man; juveniles, fiction CO
CON
KLEEBURG, Irene Cumming,

585 KLEENE

1932- , American; juveniles,
nonfiction CON WAR
KLEENE, Stephen Cole, 1909- ,
American; nonfiction CON
KLEILER, Frank Munro, 1914- ,
American; nonfiction CON
KLEIN, Aaron E., 1930- ,
American; juveniles WAR
KLEIN, Abraham Moses, 1909-72,
Canadian; poetry, plays, trans-
lations BU CON CR DA VP
KLEIN, Alan Fredric, 1911- ,
American; nonfiction CON
KLEIN, Charlotte, 1925- , Ger-
man; nonfiction CON
KLEIN, Daniel Martin, 1939- ,
American; nonfiction CON
KLEIN, Dave, 1940- , American;
nonfiction CON
KLEIN, David Ballin, 1897- ,
American; nonfiction CON
KLEIN, Edward, 1936- , Amer-
ican; fiction CON
KLEIN, Gerard ('Gilles d'Argyre'),
1937- , French; fiction, non-
fiction CON NI
KLEIN, H. Arthur, American;
juveniles, translations CO
KLEIN, Herbert Sanford, 1936- ,
American; nonfiction CON
KLEIN, Holger Michael, 1938- ,
German; nonfiction CON
KLEIN, Isaac, 1905- , Hungarian-
American; nonfiction CON
KLEIN, Jeffrey B., 1948- ,
American; fiction CON
KLEIN, Joseph, 1946- , Amer-
ican; journalism CON
'KLEIN, K. K.' see TURNER,
Robert H.
KLEIN, Leonore Glotzer, 1916- ,
American; juveniles CO
KLEIN, Marymae E., 1917- ,
American; nonfiction CON
KLEIN, Maxine, 1934- , Amer-
ican; nonfiction, plays CON
KLEIN, Milton Martin, 1917- ,
American; nonfiction CON
KLEIN, Mina Cooper, Anglo-
American; juveniles CO
KLEIN, Norma, 1938- , Amer-
ican; fiction, juveniles, poetry
CO CON KI WAR
KLEIN, Randolph Shipley, 1942- ,
American; nonfiction CON
KLEIN, Stanley, 1930- , Amer-
ican; juveniles CON
KLEIN, Stanley D., 1936- ,

American; nonfiction CON
KLEIN, Suzanne Marie, 1940- ,
American; juveniles CON
KLEIN, Thomas Decker, 1941- ,
American; nonfiction CON
KLEIN, Walter Julian, 1923- ,
American; nonfiction, film
CON
KLEINE, Glen, 1936- , American;
nonfiction CON
KLEINFELD, Gerald R., 1936- ,
American; nonfiction CON
KLEINFELD, Judith S., 1944- ,
American; nonfiction CON
KLEINFIELD, Sonny, 1950- ,
American; nonfiction CON
KLEINKE, Chris Lynn, 1944- ,
American; nonfiction CON
KLEIST, Ewald Christian von,
1715-59, German; poetry BU
TH
KLEIST, Heinrich von, 1777-1811,
German; plays, fiction, nonfic-
tion BU MAG MCG TH
KLEJMENT, Anne M., 1950- ,
American; nonfiction CON
KLEM, Kaye Wilson, 1941- ,
American; journalism, fiction
CON
KLEMAS, Antanas, 1924- ,
Lithuanian-American; nonfiction
CON
KLEMESRUD, Judy, American;
journalism CON
KLEMIN, Diana, American; jour-
nalism, nonfiction CON WAR
KLEMM, Edward G., Jr.,
1910- , American; nonfiction
CON
KLEMM, Roberta Kohnhorst,
1884- , American; poetry
CON
KLEMM, William Robert, 1934- ,
American; nonfiction CON
KLEMPNER, Irving Max, 1924- ,
Polish-American; nonfiction
CON
KLEMPTNER, A. see 'KERR, Al-
fred'
'KLENBORT, Charlotte' see
SEMPELL, Charlotte
KLERMAN, Lorraine Vogel,
1929- , American; nonfiction
CON
KLEUSER, Louise Caroline, 1889?-
1976, German; nonfiction CON
KLEVER, Anita, American; juven-
iles WAR

KLEYMAN, Paul Fred, 1945- ,
American; nonfiction CON
KLEYN, Johannes Petrus, 1760-
1805, Dutch; poetry BU
KLICPERA, Václav Kliment,
1792-1859, Czech; plays BU
KLIEWER, Evelyn, 1933- ,
American; nonfiction CON
KLIEWER, Warren, 1931- ,
American; nonfiction, plays,
poetry CON
KLIGERMAN, Jack, 1938- ,
American; nonfiction CON
KLIGMAN, Ruth, 1930- , Amer-
ican; nonfiction CON
KLIJN, Hendrik Harmsen, 1773-
1856, Dutch; poetry, plays
BU
'KLIKSPAAN' see KNEPPELHOUT,
Johannes
KLIMEK, David Ernest, 1941- ,
American; nonfiction CON
KLIMENKO, Michael, 1924- ,
American; nonfiction CON
KLIMENT of OHRID (Kliment
Ohridski; St. Clement of
Ochrida), 840-916, Bulgarian;
nonfiction BU
KLIMENTOV, Andrei P. see
'PLATONOV, Andrei'
KLIMO, Vernon ('Jake Klimo'),
1914- , American; nonfiction
CON
KLIMOWICZ, Barbara Tingley,
1927- , American; juveniles
CO WAR
KLIN, George, 1931- , Belgian-
American; nonfiction CON
KLINCK, Carl Frederick, 1908- ,
Canadian; nonfiction BU
KLINCK, George Alfred, 1903-73,
Canadian; nonfiction CON
KLINDT-JENSEN, Ole, 1918-80,
Danish; nonfiction CON
KLINE, Nancy Meadors, 1946- ,
American; nonfiction CON
KLINE, Nathan S., 1916- ,
American; nonfiction CON
KLINE, Otis Adelbert, 1891-1946,
American; fiction AS NI
KLINE, Thomas Jefferson, 1942- ,
American; nonfiction CON
KLINEBERG, Stephen Louis,
1940- , American; nonfiction
CON
KLINGER, Friedrich Maximilian
von, 1752-1836, German;
plays, fiction BU MCG TH

KLINGER, Henry, American; fiction
REI
KLINGHOFFER, Arthur Jay,
1941- , American; nonfiction
CON
'KLINGSOR, Tristan' (Léon Le-
clère), 1874-?, French; poetry
TH
KLINGSTEDT, Joe Lars, 1938- ,
American; nonfiction CON
KLINK, Johanna L., 1918- ,
Dutch; nonfiction CON
KLINKOWITZ, Jerome, 1943- ,
American; nonfiction CON
KLISE, Thomas S., 1928- ,
American; fiction CON
KLITGAARD, Mogens, 1906-45,
Danish; fiction BU TH
KLOBUCHAR, James John, 1928- ,
American; nonfiction CON
KLOEPFER, Marguerite Fonnes-
beck, 1916- , American; fic-
tion, nonfiction CON
KLONGLAN, Gerald Edward,
1936- , American; nonfiction
CON
'KLONIS, N. I.' see CLONES,
Nicholas J.
KLONOWIC, Sebastian Fabian,
1545-1602, Polish; poetry BU
TH
KLOOR, Mary Conway, American;
fiction NI
KLOOS, Peter, 1936- , Dutch;
nonfiction CON
KLOOS, Willem Johannes Theodorus,
1859-1938, Dutch; poetry, non-
fiction BU CL TH
KLOPF, Donald William, 1923- ,
American; nonfiction CON
KLOPFER, Peter Hubert, 1930- ,
American; nonfiction CON
KLOPFER, Walter George, 1923- ,
German-American; nonfiction
CON
'KLOPP, Vahrah von' see MAL-
VERN, Gladys
KLOPPENBURG, Boaventura,
1919- , German; nonfiction
CON
KLOPSTOCK, Friedrich Gottlieb,
1724-1803, German; poetry,
fiction, plays BU MCG TH
KLOR de ALVA, Jose Jorge,
1948- , American; nonfiction
MAR
KLOSE, Kevin, 1940- , American;
nonfiction CON

KLOSINSKI, Emil, 1922- , American; nonfiction CON
KLOSS, Robert James, 1935- , American; nonfiction CON
KLOSS, Robert Marsh, 1938- , American; nonfiction CON
KLOSSOWSKI, Pierre, 1903- , French; fiction, nonfiction CL
KLOTMAN, Phyllis Rauch, American; nonfiction CON
KLOTMAN, Robert Howard, 1918- , American; nonfiction CON
KLOTTER, James Christopher, 1947- , American; nonfiction CON
KLOTTER, John Charles, 1918- , American; nonfiction CON
KLUCKHOHN, Clyde, 1905-60, American; nonfiction PAL
KLUG, Eugene Frederick, 1917- , American; nonfiction CON
KLUGE, Alexander, 1932- , German; fiction CL CON
KLUGE, Eike-Henner W., 1942- , German-Canadian; nonfiction, translations CON
KLUGE, Paul Frederick, 1942- , American; fiction CON
KLUGH, Henry Elicker III, 1927- , American; nonfiction CON
'KLYCHKOV, Sergey' (Sergey Antonovich Leshenkov), 1889- , Russian; fiction BU
KLYUCHEVSKY, Vasily Osipovich, 1842-1911, Russian; nonfiction BU
KLYUSHNIKOV, Ivan Pavlovich, 1811-95, Russian; poetry BU
KLYUYEV, Nikolay Alexeyevich, 1887-1937, Russian; poetry BU CL TH
KMOCH, Hans, 1897?-1973, Austrian-American; nonfiction CON
KNAN, Zillur Rahman, 1938- , Indian; nonfiction CON
KNAPP, David Allan, 1938- , American; nonfiction CON
KNAPP, John Merrill, 1914- , American; nonfiction CON
KNAPP, Joseph George, 1924- , American; nonfiction CON
KNAPP, Mark Lane, 1938- , American; nonfiction CON
KNAPP, Robert Hampden, 1915-74, American; nonfiction CON

KNAPP, Ron, 1952- , American; nonfiction, juveniles CON
KNAUB, Richard K., 1928- , American; nonfiction CON
KNAUTH, Percy, 1914- , American; nonfiction, fiction CON
KNAUTH, Victor W., 1895?-1977, American; journalism, fiction CON
KNEALE, Thomas Nigel, 1922- , British; fiction AS NI
KNEBEL, Fletcher, 1911- , American; fiction NI VCN
KNECHTGES, David Richard, 1942- , American; nonfiction CON
KNEF, Hildegard (Neff), 1925- , German; nonfiction, fiction CON
KNELMAN, Fred H., 1919- , Canadian; nonfiction CON
KNELMAN, Martin, 1943- , Canadian; journalism, nonfiction CON
KNEPPELHOUT, Johannes ('Klikspaan'), 1814-85, Dutch; nonfiction BU
KNEVET, Ralph, 1600-71/72, English; poetry BU
KNIAZNIN, Franciszek Dionizy, 1750?-1807, Polish; poetry, plays BU TH
'KNICKERBOCKER, Diedrich' see IRVING, Washington
KNICKMEYER, Steve, 1944- , American; journalism, fiction CON
'KNIFESMITH' see CUTLER, Ivor
KNIGGE, Adolf Franz Friedrich, 1752-96, German; fiction BU
KNIGHT, Alanna, British; fiction, plays CON
KNIGHT, Alice Valle, 1922- , American; nonfiction, translations CON
KNIGHT, Arthur, 1916- , American; nonfiction CON
KNIGHT, Arthur Winfield, 1937- , American; nonfiction CON
KNIGHT, Bernard ('Bernard Picton'), 1931- , Welsh; nonfiction, fiction CON
KNIGHT, Bertram, 1904- , British; juveniles, nonfiction CON
KNIGHT, Charles, 1791-1873, English; nonfiction BU
KNIGHT, Damon Francis ('Donald Laverty'), 1922- , American;

fiction, juveniles AS CO
CON COW NI WA
'KNIGHT, David' see PRATHER,
Richard S.
KNIGHT, David Carpenter, 1925- ,
American; nonfiction, juveniles
CO CON
KNIGHT, David Marcus, 1936- ,
English; nonfiction CON
KNIGHT, Douglas E., 1925- ,
American; nonfiction CON
KNIGHT, Douglas Maitland,
1921- , American; nonfiction
CON
KNIGHT, Eric Mowbray ('Richard
Hallas'), 1897-1943, Anglo-
American; juveniles, fiction
CO DEM MAG
KNIGHT, Etheridge, 1931- ,
American; poetry, nonfiction
SH VCP
KNIGHT, Francis Edgar ('Frank
Knight'; 'Cedric Salter'),
1905- , English; juveniles,
nonfiction, fiction CO CON
KNIGHT, Frank, 1905- , British;
juveniles, fiction KI
KNIGHT, Franklin Willis, 1942- ,
American; nonfiction CON
KNIGHT, Frida, 1910- , Eng-
lish; nonfiction, translations
CON
'KNIGHT, Gareth' see WILBY,
Basil L.
KNIGHT, George Richard Wilson,
1897- , British; nonfiction,
poetry, plays BOR DA
KNIGHT, Glee, 1947- , American;
poetry CON
KNIGHT, Hilary, 1926- , Amer-
ican; juveniles CO CON DEM
KNIGHT, Janet Margaret, 1940- ,
American; nonfiction CON
KNIGHT, John Snively, 1894-1981,
American; journalism CON
'KNIGHT, Mallory T.' see HUR-
WOOD, Bernhardt J.
KNIGHT, Max ('Peter Fabrizius'),
1909- , Austrian-American;
nonfiction, translations, fic-
tion CON WAR
KNIGHT, Norman Louis, 1895- ,
American; fiction AS NI
KNIGHT, Robin, 1943- , British;
journalism CON
KNIGHT, Roderic Copley, 1942- ,
American; nonfiction, trans-
lations CON

KNIGHT, Ruth Adams, 1898-1974,
American; fiction, juveniles
CO CON
KNIGHT, Sarah Kemble, 1666-1727,
American; nonfiction BR
KNIGHT, Stephen, 1951- , British;
nonfiction, fiction CON
KNIGHT, Thomas Joseph, 1937- ,
American; nonfiction CON
KNIGHT, Vick Ralph, Jr. ('J. H.
Tweed'), 1928- , American;
nonfiction CON
KNIGHT, Wallace Edward, 1926- ,
American; fiction CON
KNIGHTS, John Keell, 1930-81,
British; journalism CON
KNIGHTS, Lionel Charles, 1906- ,
English; nonfiction BOR DA
KNIGHTS, Ward Arthur, Jr.,
1927- , American; nonfiction
CON
KNIGIN, Michael Jay, 1942- ,
American; nonfiction CON
KNIKER, Charles Robert, 1936- ,
American; nonfiction CON
KNIPE, Wayne Bishop III, 1946- ,
American; nonfiction CON
KNIST, Frances Emma ('Felicia
Fallere'), 1948- , American;
fiction, nonfiction CON
KNISTER, Raymond, 1899?-1932,
Canadian; fiction, plays CR
KNOBLER, Peter Stephen, 1946- ,
American; journalism CON
KNOCK, Warren, 1932- , English;
nonfiction CON
KNOEPFLE, John, 1923- , Amer-
ican; poetry, juveniles VCP
WAR
KNOERLE, Jeanne, 1928- , Amer-
ican; nonfiction CON
KNOKE, David Harmon, 1947- ,
American; nonfiction CON
KNOLL, Erwin, 1931- , Austrian-
American; journalism, nonfic-
tion CON
KNOLLENBERG, Bernhard, 1892-
1973, American; nonfiction
CON
KNOLLES, Richard, 1550?-1610,
English; nonfiction BU
KNOOP, Faith Yingling, 1896- ,
American; juveniles CON
KNOPF, Kenyon Alfred, 1921- ,
American; nonfiction CON
KNOPFLI, Rui, 1932- , Portu-
guese; poetry CL
KNOPP, Josephine Zadovsky,

1941- , American; nonfiction
CON
KNORR, Marian Lockwood ('Lori-
mer DeKalb'), 1910- ,
American; fiction, poetry
CON
KNORRING, Sophie Zelow, 1797-
1848, Swedish; fiction BU
KNORTZ, Karl, 1841-1918,
German-American; poetry
BU
KNOTT, Frederick M. P., 1918- ,
Anglo-American; plays ST
KNOTT, John Ray, Jr., 1937- ,
American; nonfiction CON
KNOTT, William Cecil, Jr. ('Bill
J. Carol'), 1927- , Amer-
ican; juveniles CO WAR
KNOTT, William Kilborn, 1940- ,
American; poetry MAL VCP
KNOTTS, Howard Clayton, Jr.,
1922- , American; juveniles
CO CON
KNOWLAND, William Fife, 1908-
74, American; journalism
CON
KNOWLER, John, 1933?-79, Brit-
ish; nonfiction CON
KNOWLES, Albert Sidney, Jr.,
1926- , American; nonfiction
CON
KNOWLES, Anne, 1933- , Brit-
ish; juveniles, fiction CON
KNOWLES, Clayton, 1908-78,
American; journalism CON
KNOWLES, David, 1896- , Eng-
lish; nonfiction WA
KNOWLES, Henry Paine, 1912- ,
American; nonfiction CON
KNOWLES, James Sheridan,
1784-1862, English; plays
BU HO MCG VD
KNOWLES, John, 1926-79, Amer-
ican; fiction, nonfiction BU
CO CON KIB VCN WA
KNOWLES, John Hilton, 1926-79,
American; nonfiction CON
KNOWLES, Mabel W. see
'LURGAN, Lester'
KNOWLES, Michael Clive David,
1896-1974, British; nonfiction
CON
KNOWLES, Yereth Kahn, 1920- ,
American; nonfiction CON
KNOWLTON, Derrick, 1921- ,
English; nonfiction CON
KNOWLTON, Edgar Colby, Jr.,
1921- , American; trans-

lations, nonfiction CON
KNOWLTON, Robert Almy, 1914-
68, American; journalism, non-
fiction, fiction CON
KNOX, Alexander, 1907- , Cana-
dian; fiction, plays, film,
journalism CON
KNOX, Bill ('Michael Kirk'; 'Robert
MacLeod'; 'Noah Webster'),
1928- , British; fiction, plays,
nonfiction REI
'KNOX, Calvin M.' see SILVER-
BERG, Robert
KNOX, Collie T., 1897?-1977,
British; journalism, nonfiction
CON
KNOX, David H., Jr., 1943- ,
American; nonfiction CON
KNOX, Donald Edward, 1936- ,
American; nonfiction CON
KNOX, Hugh Randolph ('H. R.
Kaye'), 1942- , American;
nonfiction, fiction CON
'KNOX, James' see BRITTAIN,
William
KNOX, John, 1513-72, Scots; non-
fiction BU DA
KNOX, Malcolm, 1900-80, British;
nonfiction, translations CON
KNOX, Monsignor Ronald Arbuth-
nott, 1888-1957, English; fic-
tion, poetry, nonfiction, trans-
lations, plays NI REI ST
KNOX, Vicesimus, 1752-1821, Eng-
lish; nonfiction BU
KNOX, Warren Barr, 1925- ,
American; poetry CON
KNUDSEN, Erik, 1922- , Danish;
poetry, plays BU CL TH
KNUDSEN, Jakob Christian Lind-
berg, 1858-1917, Danish; fic-
tion, poetry BU CL TH
KNUDSON, Danny Alan, 1940- ,
New Zealander; nonfiction
CON
KNUDSON, Rozanne ('R. R. Knud-
son'), 1932- , American;
juveniles CO
KNUEMANN, Carl Heinz, 1922- ,
American; nonfiction CON
KNUTH, Helen, 1912- , American;
nonfiction CON
KNUTSON, Jeanne Nickell, 1934- ,
American; nonfiction CON
KNUTSON, Kent Siguart, 1924-73,
American; nonfiction CON
KNYAZHNIN, Yakov Borisovich,
1742-91, Russian; plays BU

KO, Won, 1925- , Korean-
American; nonfiction, poetry,
translations CON
KO HUNG, 253-333?, Chinese;
nonfiction BU
KOBAL, John, 1943- , Canadian;
nonfiction CON
KOBAYASHI, Noritake, 1932- ,
Japanese; nonfiction CON
KOBAYASHI, Tetsuya, 1926- ,
Japanese; nonfiction CON
KOBAYASHI HIDEO, 1902- ,
Japanese; nonfiction HI
'KOBAYASHI ISSA' (Kobayashi
Nobuyuki), 1763-1827/28,
Japanese; poetry BU HI
KOBAYASHI TAKIJI, 1903-33,
Japanese; nonfiction, fiction
BU LA PRU
KOBER, Arthur, 1900-75, Uk-
rainian-American; journalism,
plays CON
KOBLER, Albert John, Jr.,
1910- , American; nonfiction
CON
KOBRE, Sidney, 1907- , Amer-
ican; nonfiction CON
KOBRIN, David, 1941- , Amer-
ican; nonfiction CON
KOBRIN, Janet, 1942- , Amer-
ican; juveniles CON
KOBRYN, Allen Paul, 1949- ,
American; poetry, fiction
CON
KOBYLYANSKA, Olha, 1863-1942,
Ukrainian; fiction TH
KOCBEK, Edvard, 1904- ,
Slovene; poetry, nonfiction,
fiction BU CL
KOCH, Charlotte ('Charles Ray-
mond'), American; juveniles
CON
KOCH, Christine Wüllner, 1869-
1951, German; poetry BU
KOCH, Dorothy Clarke, 1924- ,
American; juveniles CO
KOCH, Eric, 1919- , German;
fiction CON
KOCH, Hannsjoachim Wolfgang,
1933- , German-British;
nonfiction CON
KOCH, Howard, 1902- , Amer-
ican; nonfiction, plays, film
CON
KOCH, Joanne, 1940- , Amer-
ican; nonfiction CON
KOCH, Kenneth, 1925- , Amer-
ican; poetry, plays, nonfiction

BR MAL PO VCD VCP WA
KOCH, Lewis Z., 1935- , Amer-
ican; nonfiction CON
KOCH, Martin, 1882-1940, Swedish;
journalism, fiction BU TH
KOCH, Michael, 1916?-81, Amer-
ican; nonfiction CON
KOCH, Raymond ('Charles Ray-
mond'), American; juveniles
CON
KOCH, Stephen, 1941- , American;
fiction CON
KOCH, Thomas John, 1947- ,
American; nonfiction, juveniles
CON
KOCHAN, Miriam, 1929- , British;
nonfiction, translations CON
KOCHAN, Paul Cranston, 1906- ,
American; nonfiction CON
KOCHANOWSKI, Jan, 1530-84,
Polish; poetry, plays BU TH
KOCHANOWSKI, Piotr, 1566-1620,
Polish; poetry BU
KOCHENBURGER, Ralph J.,
1919- , American; nonfiction
CON
KOCHER, Eric, 1912- , American;
plays CON
KOCHER, Paul Harold, 1907- ,
American; nonfiction CON
KOCHETOV, Vsevolod Anisimovich,
1912-73, Russian; nonfiction
CON
KOCHISS, John Matthew, 1926- ,
American; nonfiction CON
KOCHKUROV, Nikolay I. see
'VESELEY, Artëm'
KOCHOWSKI, Wespazjan, 1633-
1700, Polish; poetry, nonfiction
BU TH
KOCIC, Petar, 1877-1916, Serbian;
fiction, plays BU TH
KOCK, Carl, American; juveniles
WAR
KOCK, Charles Paul de, 1793-1871,
French; fiction BU TH
'KOCSIS, J. C.' see PAUL, James
'KODA ROHAN' (Koda Shigeyuki),
1867-1947, Japanese; fiction,
nonfiction, poetry, plays BU
HI PRU
KOEHLER, Ludmila, 1917- ,
Russian-American; nonfiction
CON
KOEHLER, Margaret Hudson ('Meg
Hudson'; 'Russell Mead'),
American; nonfiction CON
KÖLCSEY, Ferenc, 1790-1838,

Hungarian; poetry, nonfiction
BU TH
KOEMAN, Jacob, 17th century,
Dutch; poetry BU
KÖNEMANN, von JERXHEIM,
-1316, German; poetry BU
KOENEN Hendrik Jacob, 1809-74,
Dutch; poetry BU
KOENERDINGH, Jan, 1632-1705,
Dutch; plays BU
KÖNIG, Barbara, 1925- , German;
fiction CL
KOENIG, Franz, 1905- , Aus-
trian; nonfiction CON
KOENIG, Fritz Hans, 1940- ,
German-American; nonfiction
CON
KÖNIG, Johann Ulrich, 1688-
1744, German; poetry BU
KOENIG, John Thomas, 1938- ,
American; nonfiction CON
KOENIG, Leo, 1889-1970, Yid-
dish; nonfiction BU
KOENIG, Rene, 1906- , German;
nonfiction CON
KOENNER, Alfred, 1921- ,
German; nonfiction, juveniles
CON
KOEPF, Michael, 1940- , Amer-
ican; fiction CON
KOEPKE, Wulf, 1928- , German-
American; nonfiction CON
KOEPPEL, Gary, 1938- , Amer-
ican; nonfiction CON
KOEPPEN, Wolfgang, 1906- ,
German; fiction, nonfiction
BU CL
KÖPRÜLU, Mehmed Fuad, 1890-
1966, Turkish; nonfiction BU
KÖRMENDI, Ferenc, 1900-72,
Hungarian-American; fiction,
plays WA
KÖRNER, Karl Theodor, 1791-
1831, German; poetry BU
KOERNER, William Henry David,
1878-1938, German-American;
juveniles CO
KOERTE, Mary Norbert, 1934- ,
American; poetry CON VCP
KOERTGE, Ronald, 1940- ,
American; nonfiction CON
KOESTLER, Arthur, 1905- ,
English; fiction, nonfiction,
plays BU DA MAG NI PO
SEY VCN VN
KOETHE, John Louis, 1945- ,
American; poetry CON
KOETSVELD, Cornelis Eliza van,

1807-93, Dutch; juveniles, non-
fiction BU
KOFF, Richard Myram, 1926- ,
American; nonfiction CON
KOFFI, Raphael Atta, 1935?- ,
Ivory Coaster; fiction, plays
HER
KOFOED, John C., 1894-1979,
American; journalism, nonfic-
tion CON
KOFSKY, Frank Joseph, 1935- ,
American; nonfiction CON
KOGALNICEANU, Mihail, 1817-91,
Russian; nonfiction BU
KOGAN, Herman, 1914- , Amer-
ican; juveniles WAR
KOGAN, Leonard Saul, 1919-76,
American; nonfiction CON
KOGAWA, Joy Nozomi, 1935- ,
Canadian; poetry CON
KOGON-IN, 1313-64, Japanese; po-
etry HI
KOGOS, Frederick, 1907-74,
Russian-American; nonfiction
CON
KOHAN, Rhea, American; fiction
CON
KOHL, Herbert, 1937- , Amer-
ican; nonfiction CON
KOHL, James Virgil, 1942- ,
American; nonfiction CON
KOHL, Marvin, 1932- , American;
nonfiction CON
KOHLER, Julilly House, 1908-76,
American; juveniles CO CON
KOHLER, Saul, 1928- , American;
journalism CON
KOHLMEIER, Louis Martin, Jr.,
1926- , American; nonfiction
CON
KOHLSTEDT, Sally Gregory,
1943- , American; nonfiction
CON
KOHN, Bernice Herstein, 1920- ,
American; juveniles CO
KOHN, Eugene, 1887-1977, Amer-
ican; nonfiction CON
KOHN, George Childs, 1940- ,
American; nonfiction CON
KOHN, Jacob, 1881-1968, Ameri-
can; nonfiction CON
KOHN, Melvin Lester, 1928- ,
American; nonfiction CON
KOHNER, Frederick, 1905- ,
Czech-American; juveniles CO
KOHOUT, Pavel, 1928- , Czech-
Swiss; poetry, plays CON
KOHR, Louise Hannah, 1903- ,

American; fiction, nonfiction
CON
KOHT, Halvdan, 1873-1965, Norwegian; nonfiction CON
KOHUT, Heinz, 1913-81, Austrian-American; nonfiction CON
KOHUT, Nester Clarence (Les), 1925- , Canadian; nonfiction CON
KOIDAHL, Ilona, 1924- , American; juveniles CON
'KOIDULA' (Lydia Emilie Florentine Jannsen), 1843-86, Estonian; poetry BU
KOILPILLAI, Charles (Das), Indian; nonfiction CON
KOINER, Richard B., 1929- , American; nonfiction SH
KOIZUMI YAKUMO see HEARN, Lafcadio
KOJECKY, Roger, 1943- , British; nonfiction CON
KOJIMA SHOZO (Kimima Hajime), 1928- , Japanese; juveniles, poetry, fiction, nonfiction, translations CON
'KOKHANOVSKAYA' (Nadezhda Stepanovna Sokhanskaya), 1825?-84, Russian; fiction BU
KOKOSCHKA, Oskar, 1886-1980, Austrian; poetry, plays CL CON MCG
KOLAKOWSKI, Leszek, 1927- , Polish; nonfiction, fiction CON WAK
KOLAR, Slavko, 1891-1963, Croatian; fiction BU TH
'KOLAS, Jakub' (Kanstancin Michajlavič Mickievič), 1882-1956, Byelorussian; fiction, plays, poetry BU
KOLATCH, Jonathan, 1943- , American; nonfiction, translations CON
KOLB, Carolyn, 1942- , American; nonfiction CON
KOLB, David Allen, 1939- , American; nonfiction CON
KOLB, John F., 1916?-74, American; nonfiction CON
KOLB, Philip, 1907- , American; nonfiction CON
KOLBA, Tamara ('St. Tamara'), Russian-American; juveniles CO CON
KOLBAS, Grace Holden, 1914- , American; nonfiction CON
KOLBENHEYER, Edwin Guido,

1878-1962, German; fiction, plays CL
KOLCHIN, Peter, 1943- , American; nonfiction CON
KOLDE, Endel Jakob, 1917- , American; nonfiction CON
KOLERS, Paul A., 1926- , Canadian; nonfiction CON
KOLEVZON, Edward R., 1913?-76, American; nonfiction CON
KOLHATKAR, Sripad Krsna, 1871-1934, Marathi; plays PRU
KOLINSKY, Martin, 1936- , Canadian; nonfiction CON
KOLKER, Zane, 1934- , American; fiction CON
KOLLAR, Jan, 1793-1852, Slovak; poetry BU TH
KOLLAT, David Truman, 1938- , American; nonfiction CON
KOLLATAJ, Hugo, 1750-1812, Polish; nonfiction BU
KOLLBRUNER, Oskar, 1895-1932, Swiss-American; fiction, poetry BU
KOLLER, Charles W., American; nonfiction CON
KOLLER, James, 1936- , American; nonfiction, poetry, fiction CON VCP
KOLLMAR, Richard Tompkins, 1910-71, American; producer CON
KOLMAN-CASSIUS, Jaroslav, 1883-1951, Czech; poetry BU
'KOLMAR, Gertrud' (G. Chodziesner), 1894-1943, German; poetry CL TH
KOLMODIN, Olof, 1690-1753, Swedish; poetry BU
KOLNAI, Aurel Thomas, 1900-73, Hungarian; nonfiction CON
KOLODIN, Irving, 1908- , American; nonfiction CON
KOLODNY, Annette, 1941- , American; nonfiction CON
KOLODZIEJ, Edward Albert, 1935- , American; nonfiction CON
'KOLON, Nita' see ONADIPE, Kola
KOLOSIMO, Peter, 1922- , American; nonfiction CON
KOL'TSOV, Alexey Vasilyevich, 1809-42, Russian; poetry BU
KOLTUN, Frances Lang, American; nonfiction CON
KOLYER, John McNaughton, 1933- , American; poetry CON

KOMAROV, Matvey (Kamarov), 18th century, Russian; fiction BU

KOMATSU, Sakyo, Japanese; fiction AS

KOMENSKY, Jan Amos (Johannes Amos Comenius), 1592-1670, Czech; nonfiction BU TH

KOMEY, Ellis Ayetey, 1927-72, Ghanaian; poetry, fiction HER JA

KOMISAR, Lucy, 1942- , American; juveniles CO WAR

KOMMERELL, Max, 1902-44, German; poetry, nonfiction CL

KOMODA, Beverly, 1939- , American; juveniles CO CON

KOMODA, Kiyo, 1937- , Japanese-American; juveniles CO

KOMPARU ZINCHIKU, 1405-68, Japanese; plays HI

KOMROFF, Manuel, 1890-1974, American; juveniles, nonfiction, fiction CO CON RO

KONADU, Samuel Asare ('Bediako'; 'Kwabena Asare'; 'Konadu Asare'), 1932- , Ghanaian; fiction HER JA

KONAKAMURA KIYONORI, 1821-95, Japanese; nonfiction HI

KONARSKI, Hieronim Stanislaw, 1700-73, Polish; poetry BU

KONDO YOSHIMI, 1913- , Japanese; poetry HI

KONDRASHOV, Stanislav Nikolaevich, 1928- , Russian; nonfiction CON

KONDRATOWICZ, Ludwik see 'SYROKOMLA, Wladyslav'

KONE, Maurice, 1932- , Ivory Coaster; poetry, fiction HER JA

KONECKY, Edith, 1922- , American; fiction CON

KONESKI, Blaze, 1921- , Macedonian; poetry, nonfiction BU CL

KONETSKY, Viktor Viktorovich, 1929- , Russian; fiction CL

'KONEVSKOY, Ivan Ivanovich' (Konevsky; I. D. Oraeus), 1877-1901, Russian; poetry BU

KONI, Anatoly Fedorovich, 1844-1927, Russian; nonfiction BU

KONIG, David Thomas, 1947- ,

American; nonfiction CON

KONIGH, Abraham de, 1587-1619, Dutch; poetry BU

KONINGSBERGER, Jans ('Hans Koning'), 1921- , Dutch-American; juveniles, fiction CO WA

KONIGSBURG, Elaine Lobl, 1930- , American; juveniles, plays CO DE KI

KONKLE, Janet Everest, 1917- , American; juveniles CO

KONNER, Linda, 1951- , American; juveniles, journalism CON

KONOPNICKA, Marie Wasilowska, 1842-1910, Polish; poetry, fiction, juveniles BU CL TH

KONRAD, (Pfaffe Konrad), mid 12th century, German; poetry, translations BU TH

KONRAD, Gyoergy (George), 1933- , Hungarian; fiction CON

KONRAD Von AMMENHAUSEN, fl. 1337, Swiss; nonfiction BU

KONRAD von FUSSESBRUNN, fl. 1180-1210, Austrian; poetry BU

KONRAD von HEIMESFURT, fl. 1225-30, German; nonfiction BU

KONRAD von MEGENBURG, 1309-74, German; nonfiction BU

KONRAD von WÜRZBURG, 1220/30-87, German; poetry BU TH

KONSTANTIN FILOZOF (Constantine the Philosopher), early 15th century, Serbian; nonfiction BU

KONSTANTINOV, Aleko, 1863-97, Bulgarian; fiction BU TH

KONSTANTINOV, Georgi, 1902-70, Bulgarian; nonfiction BU

KONSTANTINOV, Konstantin, 1890-1970, Bulgarian; fiction BU

KONSTANTINOVIC, Radomir, 1928- , Serbian; fiction BU TH

KONVITZ, Jeffrey, 1944- , American; fiction CON

KONWICKI, Tadeusz, 1926- , Polish; fiction, film, journalism CL CON

KOO, Anthony Ying Chang, 1918- , Chinese-American; nonfiction CON

KOO, Samuel, 1941- , Korean-

American; journalism CON
KOO, Vi Kyuin Wellington, 1888- ,
Chinese-American; nonfiction
CON
KOOB, Charles Albert, 1920- ,
American; nonfiction CON
KOOB, Theodora Johanna, 1918- ,
American; juveniles CO
KOOIMAN, Gladys, 1927- ,
American; nonfiction CON
KOOIMAN, Helen see HOSIER,
Helen
KOONTS, Jones Calvin, 1924- ,
American; poetry CON
KOONTZ, Dean Ray ('K. M. Dwyer';
'Brian Coffey'; 'David Axton'),
1945- , American; fiction
AS NI
KOONTZ, Harold, 1908- , Amer-
ican; nonfiction CON
KOOPMAN, LeRoy George, 1935- ,
American; nonfiction CON
KOPAL, Zdenek, 1914- , Czech-
British; nonfiction CON
KOPF, David, 1930- , American;
nonfiction CON
KOPIT, Arthur Lee, 1937- ,
American; plays BR BU
CON MCG MCN PO VCD VD
WA
KOPLINKA, Charlotte see
LUKAS, Charlotte
KOPMAN, Henri Marshall, 1918- ,
American; nonfiction CON
KOPP, Harriet Green, American;
nonfiction CON
KOPP, William La Marr, 1930- ,
American; nonfiction CON
KOPPEL, Ted, 1940?- , Anglo-
American; journalism, non-
fiction, fiction CON
KOPPER, Edward Anthony, Jr. ,
1937- , American; nonfiction
CON
KOPPER, Philip Dana, 1937- ,
American; nonfiction CON
KOPPERMAN, Paul Edward,
1945- , Colombian-American;
nonfiction CON
KOPS, Bernard, 1926- , British;
poetry, plays, fiction VCD
VCN VCP WA
KOPTA, Josef, 1894-1962, Czech;
fiction BU
KOPULOS, Stella, 1906- , Amer-
ican; nonfiction CON
KORACH, Mimi, 1922- , Amer-
ican; juveniles CO

KORAÏS, Adamantios, 1748-1833,
Greek; nonfiction BU TH
KORB, Lawrence Joseph, 1939- ,
American; nonfiction CON
KORBEL, Josef, 1909-77, Czech-
American; nonfiction CON
KOREN, Edward, 1935- , Amer-
ican; juveniles CO
KORENBAUM, Myrtle, 1915- ,
American; nonfiction, transla-
tions CON
KORINETZ, Yuri I. (Kurii Kori-
nets), 1923- , Russian; juven-
iles, nonfiction, poetry CO
CON
KORINFSKY, Apollon Apollonovich,
1868-1937, Russian; poetry
BU
KORIUN (Skantcheli), 5th century,
Armenian; nonfiction, transla-
tions PRU
KORMAN, A. Gerd, 1928- ,
American; nonfiction CON
KORMAN, Keith, 1956- , Amer-
ican; fiction CON
KORN, Alfons Ludwig, 1906- ,
American; nonfiction CON
KORN, Henry James, 1945- ,
American; fiction, nonfiction
CON
KORN, Noel, 1923- , American;
nonfiction CON
KORN, Peggy see LISS, Peggy
KORN, Walter, 1908- , Czech-
American; nonfiction CON
KORNAROS, Vitzentzos, early 17th
century, Cretan; poetry, plays
BU
KORNBLUM, Allan, 1949- , Amer-
ican; poetry CON
KORNBLUM, Cinda (Wormley),
1950- , American; poetry
CON
KORNBLUM, Sylvan, 1927- ,
Belgian-American; nonfiction
CON
KORNBLUTH, Cyril M. ('Cyril
Judd'; 'Scott Mariner'), 1923-
58, American; fiction AS COW
NI WA
KORNEICHUK, Nikolai I. see
'CHUKOVSKY, Kornei'
KORNFELD, Anita Clay, 1928- ,
American; fiction CON
KORNFELD, Paul, 1889-1942,
German; plays MCG
KORNHAUSER, David Henry,
1918- , American; nonfiction

CON
KORNILOV, Boris, 1907-39, Russian; poetry TH
KORNIYCHUK, Olexander, 1905-72, Ukrainian; plays BU CL TH
KOROLENKO, Vladimir Galaktionovich, 1853-1921, Russian; fiction BU CL TH
KOROTKIN, Judith, 1931- , American; fiction CON
KORS, Alan Charles, 1943- , American; nonfiction CON
KORTEN, David Craig, 1937- , American; nonfiction CON
KORTEPETER, Carl Max, 1928- , American; nonfiction CON
KORTUM, Karl Arnold, 1745-1824, German; nonfiction BU
KORTY, Carol, 1937- , American; juveniles CO CON
KORWIN-PIOTROWSKA, Gabriela see 'ZAPOLSKA, Gabriela'
KORY, Robert Bruce, 1950- , American; nonfiction CON
KORZENIOWSKI, Józef, 1797-1863, Polish; poetry, plays, fiction BU
'KORZHAVIN, Naum Moiseyevich' (Naum M. Mandel), 1925- , Russian; poetry, plays, nonfiction CL
KORZYBSKI, Alfred H. S., 1879-1950, Polish-American; fiction NI
KOS, Erih, 1913- , Serbian; fiction BU
KOSACH, Larysa see 'UKRAINKA, Lesya'
KOSHETZ, Herbert, 1907?-77, American; journalism CON
KOSINSKI, Jerzy ('George Novak'; 'Joseph Novak'), 1933- , Polish-American; fiction, nonfiction HE NI VCN VN WA
'KOSKENNIEMI, Veikko Anterö' (V. A. Forsnäs), 1885-1962, Finnish; poetry, fiction, translations, nonfiction BU TH
KOSKOFF, David Elihu, 1939- , American; nonfiction CON
KOSOF, Anna, 1945- , Hungarian-American; nonfiction CON
KOSOR, Josip, 1879-1961, Croatian; plays, fiction BU TH
KOSOVEL, Srečko, 1904-26, Slovene; poetry BU CL
KOSSAK-SZCZUCKA, Zofia, 1890-

1968, Polish; fiction BU CL
KOSSIN, Sandy (Sanford), 1926- , American; juveniles CO
KOSSOFF, David, 1919- , English; nonfiction, juveniles CON
KOSSUTH, Lajos, 1802-94, Hungarian; nonfiction TH
KOST, Mary Lu, 1924- , American; nonfiction CON
KOSTANDIN, Yerznkatsi, 1250/60-1336?, Armenian; poetry PRU
KOSTASH, Myrna, 1944- , American; nonfiction CON
KOSTE, Robert Francis ('Barry Cuff'), 1933- , American; fiction CON
KOSTELANETZ, Richard, 1940- , American; poetry, fiction, nonfiction VCP
KOSTER, Donald Nelson, 1910- , American; nonfiction CON
KOSTER, John Peter, Jr., 1945- , American; nonfiction CON
KOSTIC, Laza, 1841-1910, Serbian; poetry, plays BU TH
KOSTIS, Nicholas, American; nonfiction CON
KOSTIUK, Hryhory ('Boris Podoliak'), 1902- , American; nonfiction CON
KOSTOMAROV, Nikolai Ivanovich, 1817-85, Russian; nonfiction BU
KOSTOV, Stefan, 1879-1939, Bulgarian; plays BU
KOSTRA, Ján, 1910- , Slovak; poetry BU
KOSTROV, Efim Ivanovich, 1752-96, Russian; poetry, translations BU
KOSTROWITSKI, Wilhelm A. de see 'APOLLINAIRE, Guillaume'
KOSTRUBALA, Thaddeus, 1930- , American; nonfiction CON
KOSTYLEV, Valentin Ivanovich, 1888-1950, Russian; fiction BU
KOSTYU, Frank Alexander, 1919- , American; nonfiction CON
KOSYGIN, Alexei Nikolayevich, 1904-80, Russian; nonfiction CON
KOSZTOLANYI, Dezsö, 1885-1936, Hungarian; poetry BU CL TH
KOT, Stanislaw, 1886?-1976, Polish-American; nonfiction CON

KOTLYAREVSKY, Ivan, 1769-1838,
Ukrainian; plays, poetry BU
TH
KOTLYAREVSKY, Nestor Alex-
androvich, 1863-1925, Russian;
nonfiction BU
KOTOSHIKHIN, Grigory Karpovich,
1630-67, Russian; nonfiction
BU
KOTOWSKA, Monika, 1942- ,
Polish; poetry CON
KOTOWSKI, Joanne, 1930- ,
American; nonfiction CON
KOTRE, John Nicholas, 1940- ,
American; nonfiction CON
KOTSUJI, Abraham Setsuzau,
1899-1973, Japanese; nonfic-
tion CON
KOTSYUBYNSKY, Mykhaylo, 1864-
1913, Ukrainian; nonfiction,
fiction BU CL TH
KOTT, Jan, 1914- , Polish; non-
fiction, translations WA
KOTTA, Leo F. see 'FLAKE,
Otto'
KOTTLER, Dorothy, 1918- ,
American; juveniles CON
KOTZ, David Michael, 1943- ,
American; nonfiction CON
KOTZEBUE, August von, 1761-
1819, German; plays BU
MCG TH
KOTZWINKLE, William, 1938- ,
American; juveniles, nonfic-
tion, fiction CO CON NI
KOUADIO-TIACOH, Gabriel,
1920- , Ivory Coaster; fic-
tion HER
KOUBOURLIS, Demetrius John,
1938- , Greek-American;
nonfiction CON
KOUFAX, Sandy, 1935- , Amer-
ican; journalism CON
KOULACK, David, 1938- ,
American; nonfiction CON
KOUMOULIDES, John Thomas,
1938- , Greek-American;
nonfiction LA
KOUN (Nagachika), -1429,
Japanese; poetry, nonfiction
HI
KOUPERNIK, Cyrille, 1917- ,
Russian-French; nonfiction
CON
KOUROUMA, Ahmadou, 1940- ,
Ivory Coaster; fiction JA
KOUSSER, Joseph Morgan,
1943- , American; nonfiction

CON
'KOUTOUKAS, H. M.' see RIVOLI,
Mario
KOUTS, Anne, 1945- , American;
juveniles CO
KOUTS, Hertha Pretorius ('Hertha
Pretorius'), 1922-73, American;
fiction CON
KOUWENAAR, Gerrit, 1923- ,
Dutch; poetry BU
KOUYATE, Seydu see BADIAN,
Seydou K.
KOVAC, Mirko, 1938- , Serbian;
fiction BU
KOVACH, Bill, 1932- , American;
journalism CON
KOVACH, Francis Joseph, 1918- ,
Hungarian-American; nonfiction
CON
KOVACIC, Ante, 1854-89, Croatian;
fiction BU TH
KOVACIC, Goran Ivan, 1913-43,
Croatian; poetry BU TH
KOVACS, Alexander, 1930?-77,
Rumanian-American; journalism
CON
KOVACS, Imre, 1913-80, Hungarian-
American; journalism, nonfic-
tion CON
KOVALËV, Mikhail A. see 'IVNËV,
Ryurik'
KOVALEVSKAYA, Sofya Vaselyevna,
(Kovalevsky), 1850-91, Russian;
nonfiction BU
'KOVNER, B.' see ADLER, Jacob
KOWET, Don ('Frank Gell'),
1937- , American; juveniles,
nonfiction CON WAR
KOWNSLAR, Allan Owen, 1935- ,
American; nonfiction CON
KOYAMA, Kosuke, 1929- , New
Zealander; nonfiction CON
KOYI, Haji Kadyr, 1817-97, Kurd-
ish; poetry PRU
KOZAK, Jan Blahoslav, 1889?-1974,
Czech-American; nonfiction
CON
KOZAK, Juš, 1892-1964, Slovene;
fiction BU
KOZAKOV, Mikhail Emmanuilovich,
1897-1954, Russian; fiction
BU
KOZAR, Andrew Joseph, 1930- ,
American; nonfiction CON
KOZARAC, Josip, 1858-1906,
Croatian; fiction BU TH
KOZER, Jose, 1940- , Cuban-
American; nonfiction CON

KOZIEBRODZKI, Leopold Bolesta,
1906- , Polish-American;
nonfiction CON
KOZINTSEV, Grigori Mikhailovich,
1905-73, Russian; nonfiction,
film CON
KOZIOL, Urszula, 1931- ,
Polish; poetry, fiction CL
KOZLENKO, William, 1917- ,
American; nonfiction, plays
CON
KOZLOV, Ivan Ivanovich, 1779-
1840, Russian; poetry BU
KOZMA, Presbyter, 10th century,
Bulgarian; nonfiction BU
KOZMIAN, Kajetan, 1771-1856,
Polish; poetry BU
KOZNICKI, Henry, 1924- , Amer-
ican; nonfiction CON
KOZOL, Jonathan, 1936- ,
American; nonfiction CON
KRACHOLOV, P. see 'YAVOROV,
Peyu'
KRAEMER, Richard Howard,
1920- , American; nonfiction
CON
KRAENZEL, Carl Frederick,
1906- , American; nonfiction
CON
KRAF, Elaine, American; fiction
CON
KRAFFT, Maurice, 1946- ,
French; nonfiction CON
KRAFSUR, Richard Paul, 1940- ,
American; nonfiction CON
KRAFT, Barbara, 1939- , Amer-
ican; plays CON
KRAFT, Betsy Harvey, 1937- ,
American; juveniles CON
KRAFT, Charles Howard, 1932- ,
American; nonfiction CON
KRAFT, Charlotte, 1922- ,
American; nonfiction CON
KRAFT, Hyman Solomon, 1899-
1975, American; plays, film,
journalism, nonfiction CON
KRAFT, Leo, 1922- , American;
nonfiction CON
KRAG, Vilhelm Andreas Wexels,
1871-1933, Norwegian; fiction,
poetry, plays BU
'KRAGEN, Jinx' see MORGAN,
Judith A.
KRAHN, Fernando, 1935- ,
Chilean-American; juveniles
CON DEM
KRAIG, Bruce, 1939- , American;
nonfiction CON

KRAINES, Oscar, 1916- , Amer-
ican; nonfiction CON
KRAINES, Samuel Henry, 1906- ,
American; nonfiction CON
KRAINS, Hubert, 1862-1934, Bel-
gian; fiction, nonfiction CL
KRAJEWSKI, Frank R., 1938- ,
American; nonfiction CON
KRAJEWSKI, Robert Joseph,
1940- , American; nonfiction
CON
KRAKEL, Dean Fenton, 1923- ,
American; nonfiction CON
KRAKOWSKI, Lili, 1930- ,
German-American; translations,
fiction, nonfiction CON
KRAL, Frano, 1903-55, Slovak;
poetry, fiction BU
KRAL, Janko, 1822-76, Slovak;
poetry BU TH
KRAMER, Bernard Mordecai,
1923- , American; nonfiction
CON
KRAMER, Dale, 1911- , Ameri-
can; nonfiction PAL
KRAMER, Dale, 1936- , Ameri-
can; nonfiction CON
KRAMER, Daniel Caleb, 1934- ,
American; nonfiction CON
KRAMER, Gene, 1927- , Ameri-
can; journalism CON
'KRAMER, George' see HEUMAN,
William
KRAMER, Jack, 1923- , Ameri-
can; nonfiction LA
KRAMER, Jane, 1938- , American;
journalism, nonfiction CON
KRAMER, Joel Herbert, 1937- ,
American; nonfiction CON
KRAMER, Judith Rita, 1933-70,
American; nonfiction CON
KRAMER, Leonie Judith, 1924- ,
Australian; nonfiction CON
KRAMER, Mark William, 1944- ,
American; nonfiction CON
KRAMER, Nancy, 1942- , Amer-
ican; nonfiction CON
KRAMER, Paul Jackson, 1904- ,
American; nonfiction CON
KRAMER, Rita, 1929- , American;
nonfiction CON
KRAMER, Roberta ('Kate Hart'),
1935- , American; nonfiction
CON
KRAMER, Theodor, 1897-1958,
Austrian; poetry TH
KRAMER, Victor A., 1939- ,
American; nonfiction CON

American; nonfiction CON
KRAWITZ, Henry, 1947- ,
   Belgian-American; nonfiction
   CON
KRAWITZ, Herman Everett,
   1925- , American; nonfiction
KRAYBILL, Donald Brubaker,
   1945- , American; nonfiction
   CON
KRCMERY, Stefan, 1892-1955,
   Slovak; poetry, nonfiction BU
KRECH, David, 1909-77, Polish-
   American; nonfiction CON
KREDEL, Fritz, 1900-73, German-
   American; juveniles CO
KREDENSER, Gail, 1936- , Amer-
   ican; juveniles WAR
KREEFT, Peter, 1937- , Amer-
   ican; nonfiction CON
KREGEL, Jan Allen, 1944- ,
   American; nonfiction CON
KREH, Bernard, 1925- , Amer-
   ican; nonfiction CON
KREIDER, Barbara, 1942- ,
   American; nonfiction CON
KREIDL, John Francis, 1939- ,
   American; nonfiction CON
KREISEL, Henry, 1922- , Cana-
   dian; fiction, plays CON CR
KREISMAN, Marvin, 1933?-79,
   American; nonfiction CON
KREITLER, Hans, 1916- ,
   Austrian-Israeli; nonfiction
   CON
KREITLER, Shulamith, 1938- ,
   Israeli; nonfiction CON
KREJCI, Jaroslav, 1916- ,
   Czech-American; nonfiction
   CON
KREMEN, Bennett, 1936- , Amer-
   ican; nonfiction CON
KREMENLIEV, Boris Angeloff,
   1911- , Bulgarian-American;
   nonfiction CON
KREMENTZ, Jill, 1940- , Amer-
   ican; nonfiction, juveniles
   CO CON
KREMER, Laura Evelyn, 1921- ,
   American; nonfiction CON
KREMER, Raymond J. M. de
   see 'RAY, Jean'
KREMER, William F., 1919- ,
   Dutch-American; nonfiction
   CON
KREN, George M., 1926- ,
   Austrian-American; nonfiction
   CON

KRENEK, Ernst, 1900- , Austrian-
   American; nonfiction CON
KRENKEL, Roy G., American; il-
   lustrations AS
KRENSKY, Stephen Alan, 1953- ,
   American; juveniles CON
KRESKIN, 1935- , American; non-
   fiction CON
KRESS, Robert Lee, 1932- ,
   American; nonfiction, transla-
   tions CON
KRESSY, Michael, 1936- , Amer-
   ican; nonfiction, plays, poetry
   CON
KRESTOVSKY, Vsevolod Vladimiro-
   vich, 1840-95, Russian; fiction
   BU
KRETSCH, Robert W., 1913?-79,
   American; nonfiction CON
KRETZER, Max, 1854-1941, Ger-
   man; fiction CL
KRETZMANN, Norman, 1928- ,
   American; nonfiction, transla-
   tions CON
KREUGER, Miles, 1934- , Amer-
   ican; nonfiction CON
KREUSLER, Abraham Arthur,
   1897- , American; nonfiction,
   fiction CON
KREUTZWALD, Friedrich Reinhold,
   1903-82, Estonian; poetry, non-
   fiction, fiction BU
KREVE-MICKIEVICIUS, Vincas,
   1882-1954, Lithuanian; poetry,
   plays, fiction BU CL
KREVOLIN, Nathan, 1927- , Amer-
   ican; nonfiction CON
KREYMBORG, Alfred, 1883-1966,
   American; poetry, plays, jour-
   nalism RO
KREZ, Konrad, 1828-97, German-
   American; poetry BU
KRIEG, Saul, 1917- , American;
   nonfiction CON
KRIEGER, Murray, 1923- , Amer-
   ican; nonfiction BOR
KRIENSKY, Morris Edward,
   1917- , American; poetry
   CON
KRIER, James Edward, 1939- ,
   American; nonfiction CON
KRIGE, Uys, 1910- , South Afri-
   can; poetry, plays, fiction, non-
   fiction BU DA LA VCN
KRIKORIAN, Yervant Hovhannes,
   1892-1977, Turkish-American;
   nonfiction CON
KRING, Hilda Adam, 1921- ,

German-American; nonfiction
CON
KRIPPENDORFF, Klaus, 1932- ,
German-American; nonfiction
CON
KRIPPNER, Stanley Curtis, 1932- ,
American; nonfiction CON
KRISHER, Bernard, 1931- ,
German; journalism, nonfiction
CON
KRISHNA, Gopi, 1903- , Indian;
nonfiction CON
KRISHNAMURTI, Jiddu ('Alcyone'),
1895- , Indian-English; non-
fiction CON
KRISHNAMURTI, R. see KIRUS-
NAMURTTI, R.
KRISLOV, Joseph, 1927- , Amer-
ican; nonfiction CON
KRISS, Ronald Paul, 1934- ,
American; nonfiction CON
KRISTENSEN, Aage Tom, 1893-
1974, Danish; poetry, fiction,
nonfiction BU CL SEY TH
KRISTEVA, Julia, 1941- , French;
nonfiction CL
'KRISTIAN, Hans' see NEERSKOV,
Hans K.
KRISTMUNDSSON, Avalsteinn see
'STEINARR, Steinn'
KRISTOF, Jane, 1932- , American;
juveniles CO
KRISTOF, Ladis Kris Donabed,
1918- , Rumanian-American;
nonfiction CON
KRIZAY, John, 1926- , American;
nonfiction CON
KRKLEC, Gustav, 1899- , Croat-
ian; poetry BU TH
KRLEZA, Miroslav, 1893-1981,
Croatian; fiction, poetry, plays,
nonfiction BU CL CON TH WA
KRMPOTIC, Vesna, 1932- , Yugo-
slav; nonfiction CON
KROCH, Adolph A., 1882-1978,
Austrian-American; nonfiction
CON
KROCHMAK, Arnold, 1919- ,
American; nonfiction CON
KROCHMAL, Connie, 1949- ,
American; nonfiction CON
KROCHMAL, Nachman ('Renak'),
1785-1840, Galician; nonfiction
BU
KROCK, Arthur, 1887-1974, Amer-
ican; journalism CON
KRODEL, Gerhard, 1926- ,
American; nonfiction CON

KROEBER, Karl, 1926- , Amer-
ican; nonfiction CON
KROEBER, Theodora, 1897-1979,
American; nonfiction CON
KROEGER, Alice Bertha, 1864-
1909, German-American; non-
fiction ENG
'KROEPCKE, Karol' see KROLOW,
Karl
KROETSCH, Robert Paul, 1927- ,
Canadian; fiction VCN
KROETZ, Franz Xaver, 1946- ,
German; plays CL
KROG, Helge, 1889-1962, Norwegian;
plays, nonfiction BU CL MCG
TH
KROHN, Robert, 1937- , Ameri-
can; nonfiction CON
KROKANN, Inge, 1893-1962, Nor-
wegian; fiction CL
KROLL, Ernest, 1914- , American;
poetry CON
KROLL, Francis Lynde, 1904-73,
American; juveniles CO
KROLL, Harry Harrison, 1888-
1967, American; fiction BA
KROLL, Judith, 1943- , American;
poetry, nonfiction CON
KROLL, Morton, 1923- , American;
nonfiction CON
KROLL, Steven, 1941- , American;
juveniles CO CON WAR
KROLOW, Karl ('Karol Kroepcke'),
1915- , German; poetry, non-
fiction, translations BU CL
CON TH
KROMER, Helen, American; plays,
nonfiction CON
KRIMMINGA, John Henry, 1918- ,
American; nonfiction CON
KRONCHMAL, Nachman, 1785-1840,
Hebrew; nonfiction TH
KRONENBERGER, Louis, 1904-80,
American; nonfiction CON
'KRONKEL' see CARMIGGELT,
Simon J.
KRONSTDT, Henry Lippin, 1915- ,
Polish-American; fiction, jour-
nalism CON
KROOSS, Herman E., 1912-75,
American; nonfiction CON
KROPF, Linda Stoddart, 1947- ,
American; nonfiction CON
KROPF, Richard William B.,
1932- , American; nonfiction
CON
KROPOTKIN, Prince Peter Alexeye-
vich, 1842-1921, Russian; non-

fiction BU
KROSBY, Hans Peter, 1929- ,
Norwegian-Canadian; nonfiction
CON
KROTKI, Karol Jozef ('Jozef Krzy-
wan'), 1922- , Polish-Amer-
ican; nonfiction CON
KROTKOV, Yuri, 1917- , Russian-
American; nonfiction, fiction
CON
KROUT, John Allen, 1896-1979,
American; nonfiction CON
KRSNA PILLA, Cannampuza
('Changampuzha'), 1914-48,
Malayalam; poetry PRU
KRSNADEVARAYA, 16th century,
Telugu; poetry BU PRU
KRUCHKOW, Diane, 1947- ,
American; poetry, journalism
CON
KRUCHONYKH, Alexey Eliseye-
vich, 1886-1968, Russian;
poetry BU CL
KRUCZYKOWSKI, Leon, 1900-62,
Polish; poetry, fiction, plays,
nonfiction BU CL
KRUDY, Gyula, 1878-1933, Hun-
garian; fiction, poetry BU
CL TH
KRÜGER, Bartholomäus, 1540?-
80?, German; plays BU
KRÜGER, Ferdinand, 1843-1915,
German; fiction BU
KRUEGER, Hardy, 1928- , Ger-
man; nonfiction CON
KRUEGER, Ralph R., 1927- ,
Canadian; nonfiction CON
KRUEGER, Robert Blair, 1928- ,
American; nonfiction CON
KRUESS, James ('Markus Polder';
'Felix Ritter'), 1926- ,
German; nonfiction, juveniles
CO CON DE
KRUGER, Mollee, 1929- , Amer-
ican; poetry, tv CON
KRUGLAK, Haym, 1909- , Amer-
ican; nonfiction CON
KRUL, Jan H., 1602-46, Dutch;
poetry BU
KRULEWITCH, Melvin Levin,
1895-1978, American; nonfic-
tion CON
KRUMGOLD, Joseph Quincy, 1908-
80, American; juveniles, fic-
tion CO CON KI ST
KRUMPELMANN, John Theodore,
1892- , American; nonfiction,
translations CON

KRUPAT, Edward, 1945- , Amer-
ican; nonfiction CON
KRUSCHKE, Earl Roger, 1934- ,
American; nonfiction CON
KRUSE, Harry Dayton, 1900-77,
American; nonfiction CON
KRUSE, Hinrich, 1916- , German;
poetry, fiction, radio BU
KRUSENSTJERNA, Agnes von, 1894-
1940, Swedish; fiction BU TH
KRUSH, Beth, 1918- , American;
juveniles CO
KRUSH, Joe, 1918- , American;
juveniles CO
KRUSICH, Walter Steve, 1922- ,
American; nonfiction CON
KRUSTEV, Krustyu ('V. Mirolyu-
bov'), 1866-1919, Bulgarian;
nonfiction BU
KRUTCH, Joseph Wood, 1893-1970,
American; nonfiction BR
KRUWK, Hans, 1937- , Dutch;
nonfiction, translations CON
KRYLOV, Ivan Andreyevich, 1768-
1844, Russian; fiction BU TH
KRYMOW, Virginia Pauline,
1930- , American; nonfiction
CON
'KRYMOV, Yuriy Solomonovich'
(Yuriy Beklennishev), 1905-41,
Russian; fiction BU
'KRYPTON' see GRAHAM, Lloyd
M.
'KRZYWAN, Jozef' see KROTKI,
Karol J.
KU YEN-WU (Ku Chiang), 1613-82,
Chinese; nonfiction BU
KUAN HAN-CH'ING, 13th century,
Chinese; plays BU LA PRU
KUAN-TZU (Kuan Chung), 7th cen-
tury B.C., Chinese; nonfiction
BU
KUBAL, David Lawrence, 1936- ,
American; nonfiction CON
KUBIAK, Timothy James, 1942- ,
American; nonfiction CON
KUBILIUS, Walter, 1918- , Amer-
ican; fiction NI
KUBIN, Alfred, 1877-1959, Austri-
an; fiction BU CL
KUBINYI, Laszlo, 1937- , Amer-
ican; juveniles CO CON
KUBLIN, Hyman, 1919- , Amer-
ican; juveniles WAR
KUBO, Sakae, 1926- , American;
nonfiction CON
KUBOSE, Gyomay Masao, 1905- ,
American; nonfiction, transla-

tions CON
KUBOTA MANTARO, 1889-1963,
Japanese; poetry, plays PRU
KUBOTA UTSUBO, 1877-1967,
Japanese; poetry HI
KUBRICK, Stanley, 1928- , Amer-
ican; film AS CON
KUCHAREK, Casimir Anthony,
1928- , American; nonfiction
CON
KUCHARSKY, David Eugene,
1931- , American; nonfiction
CON
KUCZYNSKI, Pedro-Pablo, 1938- ,
Peruvian-American; nonfiction
CON
KUDIRKA, Vincas ('Vincas Kap-
sás'), 1858-99, Lithuanian;
poetry, fiction BU
KÜBLER, Arnold, 1890- , Swiss;
fiction BU
KÜCHELBECKER, Wilhelm Karlo-
vich (Kyukhelbeker), 1797-
1846, Russian; poetry BU
KÜHN, Christoffel H. see
'MIKRO'
KUEHNER, Louis C., American;
juveniles WAR
KUEI YU-KUANG, 1507-71,
Chinese; nonfiction BU
KUEMMERLY, Walter, 1903- ,
Swiss; nonfiction CON
KUENG, Hans, 1928- , Swiss;
nonfiction CON
KÜNSTLER, Morton ('Mutz'),
1927- , American; juveniles
CO
KÜRENBERG(ER), fl. 1150-70,
Austrian; poetry BU TH
KUESEL, Harry N., 1892?-1977,
American; nonfiction CON
KUESTER, David, 1938- , Amer-
ican; nonfiction CON
KUETHER, Edith Lyman ('Mar-
garet Malcolm'), 1915- ,
American; fiction CON
KUGELMAN, Richard, 1908- ,
American; nonfiction, trans-
lations CON
KUH, Frederick Robert, 1895-
1978, American; journalism
CON
KUHAR, Lovro see 'PREZIHOV,
Voranc'
KUHL, Ernest Peter, 1881- ,
American; nonfiction CON
KUHLKEN, Kenneth Wayne,
1945- , American; fiction

CON
KUHLMAN, James Allen, 1941- ,
American; nonfiction CON
KUHLMAN, Kathryn, 1910?-76,
American; nonfiction CON
KUHLMANN, Quirinus, 1651-89,
German; poetry BU TH
KUHLMANN, Susan, 1942- , Amer-
ican; nonfiction CON
KUHN, Doris Young, -1969,
American; juveniles WAR
KUHN, Edward, Jr., 1924?-79,
American; fiction CON
KUHN, Ferdinand, 1905-78, Amer-
ican; journalism, nonfiction
CON
KUHN, Harold Barnes, 1911- ,
American; nonfiction CON
KUHN, Karl Francis, 1939- ,
American; nonfiction CON
KUHN, Reinhard, 1930- , German-
American; nonfiction CON
KUHNE, Cecil, 1952- , American;
nonfiction CON
KUHNE, Marie Ahnighito (Peary),
1893-1978, American; juveniles
CON
KUIMBA, Giles, 1936- , Rhodesi-
an; fiction JA
KUIPER, Gerard Peter, 1905-73,
Dutch-American; nonfiction
CON
KUJOTH, Jean Spealman, 1935-76,
American; juveniles WAR
KUKAI, 774-835, Japanese; nonfic-
tion HI
KUKLA, Robert John, 1932- ,
American; nonfiction CON
KUKLICK, Bruce, 1941- , Amer-
ican; nonfiction CON
KUKOL'NIK, Nestor Vasileyevich,
1809-68, Russian; fiction, plays
BU
'KUKUCIN, Martin' (Matej Bencúr),
1860-1928, Slovak; fiction BU
CL TH
KULA, Elsa, American; juveniles
WAR
KULACHIKOV, Seraphim R. see
'ELLEY'
KULAKOVSKIY, Aleksey Yeleseye-
vich, 1877-1926, Yakut; poetry
PRU
KULENOVIC, Skender, 1910- ,
Serbian; poetry BU
KULESHOV, Arkady A., 1914-78,
Byelorussian; poetry, journalism
CON

KULISH, Mykola, 1892-1937/42,
Ukrainian; plays CL TH
KULISH, Panteleymon, 1819-97,
Ukrainian; translations, non-
fiction TH
KULKARNI, Hemant Balvantrao,
1916- , Indian-American;
nonfiction CON
KULLMAN, Harry, 1919- ,
Swedish; juveniles CON
KULMANN, Elisabeth, 1808-25,
Russian; translations, poetry
BU
KULTERMANN, Udo, 1927- ,
German-American; nonfiction
CON
KUMAGAI NAOYOSHI, 1782-
1862, Japanese; poetry HI
KUMALO, Peter E. ('Peter E.
Clarke), 1929- , South Afri-
can; fiction, poetry HER
KUMARADASA, 8th century,
Indian; poetry BU
KUMARAN ASAN, 1873-1924,
Malayalam; poetry PRU
KUMARANATUNGA (Kumaratunga),
1887-1944, Sinhalese; nonfic-
tion PRU
KUMARAVYASA, 15th century,
Kannadan; poetry PRU
'KUMBEL' see HEIN, Piet
KUMICIC, Evgenij, 1850-1904,
Croatian; fiction BU TH
KUMIN, Maxine Winokur, 1925- ,
American; poetry, fiction,
juveniles CO VCP WAK
KUNANBAYEV, Abay, 1845-1904,
Kazakhstan; poetry PRU
KUNCAN NAMPYAR, 18th cen-
tury, Malayalam; poetry PRU
KUNCE, Joseph Tyree, 1928- ,
American; nonfiction CON
KUNCEWICZOWA, Maria Szcze-
pánska, 1899- , Polish;
fiction BU CL TH
KUNCZ, Aladár, 1886-1931, Hun-
garian; fiction, journalism
BU
KUNDERA, Milan, 1929- ,
Czech; fiction, poetry, plays
BU CL CON TH WAK
KUNENE, Mazisi Raymond,
1930- , South African; po-
etry, plays HER
KUNER, Mildred Christophe,
1922- , American; nonfiction,
plays CON
KUNERT, Günter, 1929- , Ger-

man; poetry BU CL
KUNEV, Trifon, 1880-1954, Bul-
garian; poetry BU
K'UNG SHANG-JÊN, 1648-1718,
Chinese; plays BU PRU
KUNG TZU-CHÊN, 1792-1841,
Chinese; nonfiction, poetry BU
KUNHAPPA, Murkot, 1905- ,
Indian; fiction, juveniles, non-
fiction CON
KUNHARDT, Dorothy Meserve,
1901-79, American; juveniles
CO CON WAR
KUNHARDT, Philip Bradish, Jr.,
1928- , American; fiction,
nonfiction CON WAR
KUNHI KRISHNAN, Taramal Van-
meri, 1919- , Indian; nonfic-
tion CON
KUNICZAK, Wiselaw Stanislaw,
1930- , Polish-American;
journalism, fiction, nonfiction
CON
'KUNIKIDA DOPPO' (Kunikida Tet-
suo), 1871-1908, Japanese; fic-
tion, nonfiction, poetry BU
HI PRU
KUNIN, Madeleine May, 1933- ,
Swiss-American; journalism,
nonfiction CON
KUNITZ, Joshua, 1896?-1980,
American; journalism, nonfic-
tion CON
KUNITZ, Stanley Jasspon, 1905- ,
American; poetry, nonfiction,
translations BR CON PO SEY
VCP VP WA
KUNJUFU, Johari M. Amini ('Jo-
hari M. Amini'), 1935- ,
American; poetry CON
KUNKA GYANTSEN, 1182-1251,
Tibetan; nonfiction PRU
KUNKEL, Francis Leo, 1921- ,
American; nonfiction CON
KUNO, Susumu, 1933- , Japanese-
American; translations, nonfic-
tion CON
KUNST, David William, 1939- ,
American; fiction CON
KUNSTLER, James Howard,
1948- , American; fiction
CON
KUNTHOLM, Bruce Robellet,
1942- , American; nonfiction
CON
KUNTZLEMAN, Charles Thomas,
1940- , American; nonfiction
CON

KUNZ, Marji, 1939?-79, American; journalism CON
KUNZE, Reiner, 1933- , German; poetry, fiction, translations CON
KUNZLE, David Mark, 1936- , Anglo-American; nonfiction CON
'KUNZUR, Sheela' see GEIS, Richard E.
KUO, Ting-yee, 1904?-75, Chinese-American; nonfiction CON
KUO MO-JO, 1892-1978, Chinese; poetry, fiction, nonfiction BU CON PRU
KUOH MOUKOURI, Jacques, 1909- , Cameroonian; nonfiction JA
'KUPALA, Janka' (Janka Lucevič), 1882-1942, Byelorussian; poetry, plays BU
KUPER, Adam Jonathan, 1941- , South African; nonfiction CON
KUPERMAN, Yuri ('Yuri Kuper'), 1940- , Russian; fiction CON
KUPFERBERG, Herbert, 1918- , American; juveniles CO
KUPRIN, Alexander Ivanovich, 1870-1938, Russian; fiction BU CL NI TH
KURALT, Charles Bishop, 1934- , American; nonfiction, journalism CON
KURATOMI, Chizuko, 1939- , Japanese; juveniles CO
KURBSKY, Audrey Mikhaylovich, 1528-88, Russian; nonfiction BU TH
'KURDSEN, Stephen' see NOON, Brian
KUREK, Jalu, 1904- , Polish; poetry CL
KURELEK, William, 1927- , Canadian; juveniles CO CON WAR
KURLAND, Gerald, 1942- , American; nonfiction, juveniles CO CON
KURLAND, Michael ('Jennifer Plum'), 1938- , American; fiction CON NI
KURMAN, George, 1942- , American; nonfiction CON
KURNITZ, Harry see 'PAGE, Marco'
KUROCHKIN, Vasily Stepanovich,

1831-75, Russian; poetry, translations BU
KURODA, Yasumasa, 1931- , Japanese-American; nonfiction CON
KURPOAS, Myron Bohdon, 1932- , American; nonfiction CON
KUROSAWA, Akira, 1910- , Japanese; film CON
KURRIK, Maire Jaanus, 1940- , Estonian-American; nonfiction CON
KURTZ, Clarence Gordon ('Kurtz Gordon'), 1902- , American; fiction CON
KURTZ, David Lee, 1941- , American; nonfiction CON
KURTZ, Donna Carol, 1943- , American; nonfiction CON
KURTZ, Katherine, 1944- , American; fiction NI
KURTZ-PHELAN, James Lanham, 1946- , American; nonfiction CON
KURZ, Hermann, 1813-73, German; translations, fiction BU
KURZ, Ron, 1940- , American; fiction CON
KURZMAN, Dan, 1927- , American; journalism, nonfiction CON
KURZWEIL, Arthur, 1951- , American; nonfiction CON
KURZWEIL, Baruch, 1907- , Hebrew; nonfiction BU
KUSCHE, Lawrence David, 1940- , American; nonfiction CON
KUSHCHEVSKY, Ivan Afanasyevich, 1847-76, Russian; fiction, journalism BU
KUSHNER, Aleksandr Semyonovich, 1936- , Russian; poetry CL
KUSHNER, David Zakeri, 1935- , American; nonfiction CON
KUSHNER, Howard Irvin, 1943- , American; nonfiction CON
KUSHNER, Rose, 1929- , American; nonfiction CON
KUSKE, Martin, 1940- , Polish; nonfiction CON
KUSKIN, Karl ('Nicholas Charles'), 1932- , American; juveniles, poetry, plays DE KI
KUSLAN, Louis Isaac, 1922- , American; nonfiction CON
KUSMER, Kenneth Leslie, 1945- , American; nonfiction CON
KUSNICK, Barry A., 1910- ,

American; nonfiction CON
KUSNIEWICZ, Andrzej, 1904- ,
Polish; fiction, poetry CL
KUSPIT, Donald Burton, 1935- ,
American; nonfiction CON
KUSTERMEIR, Rudolf, 1893?-
1977, German; journalism
CON
KUTSCHER, Charles Lawrence,
1936- , American; nonfiction
CON
KUTTIKKRASNAN, P. C. ('Urub'),
1915- , Malayalam; fiction
PRU
KUTTNER, Henry see 'KENT,
Kelvin'
KUTTNER, Henry, 1914-58, Amer-
ican; fiction AS COW NI ST
KUTTNER, Paul, 1931- , German-
American; juveniles, fiction,
translations CO CON
KUVEMPU see PUTTAPU, K. V.
KUYKENDALL, Jack Lawrence,
1940- , American; nonfiction
CON
KUZMANY, Karol, 1806-66,
Slovak; poetry, fiction BU
KUZMIN, Mikhail Alexeyevich,
1875-1936, Russian; plays,
poetry BU CL TH
KUZNETSOV, Anatoly Vasilyevich
('A. Anatoli'), 1929-79, Rus-
sian; fiction CL CON
KUZNETSOV, Edward, 1939- ,
Russian-English; translations
CON
KVALE, Velma Ruth, 1898- ,
American; juveniles CO
KVAM, Wayne Eugene, 1938- ,
American; nonfiction CON
KVARAN, Einar Hjörleıfsson,
1859-1938, Icelander; fiction,
plays, poetry BU CL
KVASNICKA, Robert Michael,
1935- , American; nonfiction
CON
KVITKA-OSNOVYANENKO, Grigory
Fëdorovich, 1779-1843, Rus-
sian; fiction, plays BU
KVITKO, Leib, 1893-1952, Yid-
dish; poetry, juveniles BU
KWANTEN, Luc, 1944- ,
Belgian-American; nonfiction
CON
KWAVNICK, David, 1940- ,
Canadian; nonfiction CON
KWIATKOWSKA, Hanna Yaxa,
1907?-80, Polish-American;

nonfiction CON
KWITNY, Jonathan, 1941- , Amer-
ican; nonfiction CON
KYD, Thomas, 1558-94, English;
plays BRI BU DA MAG MCG
PO RU VD
'KYD, Thomas' (Alfred Bennett
Harbage), 1901-76, American;
fiction REI ST
'KYDD, Thomas (Tom) see MEYER,
Thomas
KYEI, Kojo Gyinaye, 1932- ,
Ghanaian; poetry HER JA
KYEMBA, Henry, 1939- , Ugan-
dan; nonfiction CON
KYES, Robert Lange, 1933- ,
American; nonfiction CON
KYGER, Joanne, 1934- , Ameri-
can; poetry CON VCP
KYI, U, 1838?-98?, Burmese; po-
etry PRU
KYIN, U U., 1773?-1838?, Bur-
mese; plays PRU
KYLE, David A., 1912?- , Amer-
ican; fiction NI
'KYLE, Duncan' see BROXHOLME,
John F.
'KYLE, Elisabeth' see DUNLOP,
Agnes M. R.
'KYLE, Marlaine' see HAGER,
Jean
'KYLE, Robert' see TERRALL,
Robert
'KYLE, Sefton' see VICKERS,
Roy C.
KYME, Ernest Hector, 1906- ,
British; nonfiction CON
KYOKUTEI BAKIN, 1767-1848,
Japanese; fiction LA
'KYORAI' (Mukai Kanetoki), 1651-
1704, Japanese; poetry BU
KYOUN see KEIUN
KYPER, Frank, 1940- , Ameri-
can; nonfiction CON
KYRKLUND, Paul Wilhelm
('Willy'), 1921- , Swedish;
fiction, plays CL
KYSAR, Robert Dean, 1934- ,
American; nonfiction CON
KYUKHELBEKER, Wilhelm K. see
KÜCHELBECKER, Wilhelm K.
KYUSEI, 1284-1378, Japanese;
poetry HI
KYVIG, David Edward, 1944- ,
American; nonfiction CON